PRINCIPLES OF CORPORATE
INSOLVENCY LAW

PRINCIPLES OF CORPORATE INSOLVENCY LAW

by

Roy Goode

SWEET & MAXWELL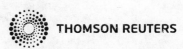

First edition 1990
Second edition 1997
Third edition 2005

Published in 2011 by Sweet & Maxwell, 100 Avenue Road, London NW3 3PF
part of Thomson Reuters (Professional) UK Limited
(Registered in England & Wales, Company No 1679046. Registered Office and
address for service: Aldgate House, 33 Aldgate High Street, London EC3N 1DL)

Typeset by LBJ Typesetting Ltd
Printed in the UK by CPI William Clowes Ltd, Beccles, NR34 7TL

For further information on our products and services, visit
www.sweetandmaxwell.co.uk
A CIP catalogue record for this book is available from the British Library

ISBN: 978-0-414-04787-7 (Paperback)
ISBN: 978-0-421-96610-9 (Hardback)

For Catherine to whom I owe so much

Preface

If reformers of our penal system were looking for new forms of non-custodial sentence they could do worse than introduce the penalty of six months' reading of UK insolvency legislation, enough to make the stoutest member of the criminal fraternity quail and repent of his evil ways. The phrase "United Kingdom" itself now needs some qualification in that we have a new concept, "British" (or, more shortly, "DisUK") insolvency law, following our adoption of the UNCITRAL Model Law on Cross-Border Insolvency. The Model Law is in many ways admirable. This cannot be said of our domestic legislation, which is badly drafted, bizarrely numbered—or rather, lettered—and organisationally incoherent. Perhaps Parliament and the Insolvency Rules Committee could be inspired by a verse from the Rubáiyát of Omar Khayyám:

> *Ah Love! could you and I with Him conspire*
> *To grasp this sorry Scheme of Things entire,*
>   *Would not we shatter it to bits-and then*
> *Re-mould it nearer to the Heart's Desire!*

But it would take five years' hard work to do it properly! The experience of wrestling with the mass of legislation, case law and literature on corporate insolvency that has appeared during the six years following the appearance of the third edition of this work has left me in no doubt that it is high time I took my bow and left the stage to younger and more vigorous scholars. My plan is to essay a work of fiction. The more unkind of my Oxford colleagues remarked that he thought that was what I had been writing for years!

Yet I cannot deny that the subject is one of endless fascination involving the most intricate analyses of the general law of contract, unjust enrichment and, above all, property. It is this interrelationship with non-insolvency law that makes corporate insolvency such an intensely interesting object of study.

My aim, as in previous editions, is not to try to cover every situation or every rule but rather to lay down the fundamental concepts and principles underpinning the subject and set them in the context of practical problems, so that the reader—whether scholar, student or practitioner—is enabled to see the wood for the trees and to apply what he or she reads to new situations. It is very easy to get lost in the tangle of legislative rules, EU instruments and case law. But good advocates, like good scholars, know that what courts look for is lucid thinking and clear presentation, and that is what I have striven to provide in this book, very imperfectly, over the past two decades.

The major developments since the appearance of the third edition have necessitated a substantial rewriting of the entire work. The opening chapter surveys the legislative scene, including (albeit briefly) the effects of the banking crisis and the new regimes governing bank insolvency under the Banking Act 2009. Two chapters have been split, so that there are now 16 chapters instead of 14. A complete chapter has been devoted to the anti-deprivation rule, on which the ruling of the Supreme Court is eagerly awaited.

A welcome development over the past 10 years has been the growth of empirical studies into corporate insolvency, enabling us to see how the law works in practice. From studies by leading insolvency scholars—Professors John Armour, Adrian Walters, Sandra Frisby and Audrey Hsu, to name but a few—we have learned the outcomes of different forms of insolvency proceeding and the success or failure of certain statutory regimes that had been thought to promote the rescue culture. Among other things, we now know that the small company moratorium appears to be a dead letter and that the assumption that a statutory moratorium is crucial to a successful restructuring or arrangement is far from axiomatic. I have drawn attention to several of these studies in different chapters. Prepack administrations ("pre-packs"), in which a prearranged sale of the insolvent company is concluded immediately after the appointment of an administrator, have also been the subject of empirical research and have given rise to intense debate and a measure of disquiet. The relevant aspects are examined in a revised chapter on administration. The chapter on restructuring and CVAs has been substantially expanded, as have the two chapters on the European Insolvency Regulation and international insolvency.

The enactment of the UNCITRAL Model Law has given rise to a good deal of litigation on the recognition and enforcement of foreign judgments, in decisions of the Privy Council and the House of Lords such as *HIH Casualty* and *Cambridge Gas* and of the Court of Appeal in *Rubin*, now on its way to the Supreme Court. Fascinating questions potentially arise as to what our courts should do when faced with conflicting decisions of, say, our own Supreme Court and New York courts if the latter were to seek recognition and enforcement of their decisions under the Model Law. Questions concerning the treatment of post-administration liabilities under pre-administration contracts have continued to exercise the courts and even now the textbook writers are not wholly agreed on the correct analysis. Pension liabilities, particularly those arising from contribution notices, have played an increasingly important role in corporate insolvency, as described in the chapter on administration, and the Court of Appeal is due to rule on this issue in the *Bloom* case. All these issues have been extensively addressed in this new edition.

I have incurred debts to many people in the writing of this book. They are identified in a separate page of acknowledgments. To all of them I express my deep appreciation.

Finally, I owe a deep debt of gratitude to my long-suffering wife, Catherine, who has heard on countless occasions, and with growing disbelief, of my complete retirement from law (at long last about to happen!) and has patiently and with good humour put up with the trials and tribulations of an author's spouse. I could not have written this, my final legal text, without her constant encouragement and support.

Roy Goode
Oxford
15 April 2011

Acknowledgments

AN EXPRESSION OF THANKS

Every author builds on the labours of his predecessors. Many other writers in this field, whether as scholars or as practising lawyers, have shed light on dark places. They are too numerous to mention individually here but throughout the book I have freely acknowledged my indebtedness to them.

Three Oxford colleagues, John Armour, Louise Gullifer and Jennifer Payne, have helped me in various ways, in particular through their own writings and by inviting me to have drafts of the different chapters distributed to the postgraduate students on the BLC/MJur corporate insolvency course and to participate in seminars in which questions and comments by the students helped me to sharpen my analysis of particular issues. Louise and Jennifer kindly gave me advance sight of their new book *Corporate Finance*, while Sandra Frisby did the same as regards her joint empirical research with Adrian Walters into the outcome of CVAs. Professor Jay Westbrook, of the University of Texas at Austin, from whose encyclopaedic knowledge of cross-border insolvency so many of us have learned so much, was kind enough to review what are now chapter 2, as regards the references to US literature, and chapter 16 on international insolvency, and to offer a number of helpful comments and criticisms. Other leading academics with whom I had fruitful exchanges were David Fox and Richard Nolan, both of Cambridge University. In addition I benefited from constructive criticisms made of the 3rd edition by Look Chan Ho of Freshfields Bruckhaus Deringer.

Anxious to ensure that I was up to date on practice and on the identification of key issues I had meetings with numerous practising corporate insolvency experts—lawyers, accountants, bankers and asset-based lenders—who gave me the benefit of their immense experience and were generous both with their time and with their expertise and the provision of specimen documents. The various meetings were kindly set up for me by Steven Brown, who himself has a considerable knowledge of insolvency affecting retailers and their leased premises.

The practising lawyers whom I consulted were: Jennifer Marshall of Allen & Overy; Adrian Cohen, Gabrielle Ruiz and Nicola Reader of Clifford Chance; Inga West of CMS Cameron McKenna; Nigel Barnett and Neil Griffiths of Denton Wilde Sapte; Andrew Watson of Hammonds LLP; Robert Elliott and Jo Windsor of Linklaters; and Sarah Paterson of Slaughter & May. To all of them I am indebted for their imvaluable comments on the state of the law and on current practice, particularly as regards concepts and strategies of financial and business restructuring, schemes of arrangement and the pros and cons of statutory moratoria.

Insolvency practitioners from leading accountancy firms with whom I had fruitful discussions were: Shay Bannon of BDO; Neville Kahn, Paul

Thompson and Marcus Rea of Deloittes; Alan Bloom, Ben Cairns and Steve Leinster of Ernst & Young; Richard Heis of KPMG; and Mike Jervis of PWC. With them I discussed, among other things, issues arising out of the move from relationship lending by banks to asset-based lending, debt fragmentation through distressed debt trading and bond issues; administration and CVAs, and the rise of the pre-pack. They too were generous with their time and knowledge and gave me fresh insights.

Members of both groups made thought-provoking comments on cross-border corporate insolvency, the impact of the EC Insolvency Regulation and the problems associated with identification and change of the debtor's centre of main interests.

Andrew McKnight of Salans was good enough to undertake the burdensome task of reading drafts of most of the chapters and making detailed comments which saved me from many errors, and I am very grateful to him. I have also derived great benefit from various discussions with Nick Segal, of Freshfields Bruckhaus Deringer, drawing on his long experience in corporate insolvency practice both in England and in New York.

The bankers whom I consulted were Kevin Booth and Malcolm Weir of Barclays Corporate and Duncan Parkes of Lloyds Banking Group. In very helpful discussions they told me about the approach of bankers to the handling of corporate insolvency problems, the focus on financial and management reconstruction with a view to maintaining relationships with their customers and the problems they encountered with the fragmentation of debt.

Finally, I had lively discussions with Steven Chait and Dennis Levine of Burdale, a leading player in the asset-based lending market in the UK and the US. They explained the move from receivables financing to comprehensive asset-based lending and the differences in philosophy between traditional bank lending and asset-based finance, the latter involving a much more intensive valuation of assets. As Dennis Levine explained, "banks lend on the probability of default, asset-based lenders on the probability of loss."

I am also grateful to the publishers, Sweet & Maxwell, for all their work on the production side. In particular I would like to thank the senior publishing editor, Suzanna Wong; the production controller, Kathryn Harrison; the House editor, Ed Meadows; the typesetter, Laurie Burgess of LBJ Typesetting; the copy-editor, Sophie Rosinke; the tabler, Jane Belford; and the indexer, Andrew Prideaux. All of them have put in a great deal of effort to bring this work to publication.

My biggest debt, however, is to Kristin van Zwieten, an Oxford DPhil student who, sadly for us, is about to leave Oxford to take up a law post at Trinity Hall, Cambridge. She undertook responsibility for researching the huge volume of legislation, case law and literature, selecting and summarising the most important cases and articles and, at a later stage, reading the manuscript and the proofs. Her grasp of complex issues, her ability to set these out succinctly and her meticulous proof-reading were of the highest order, and I do not know what I would have done without her help, for which I am truly grateful.

Preface to the Third Edition

Astonishingly, eight years have now passed since the publication of the second edition of this work, and encouraged by the cordial reception given to it by the practising profession I decided to defer performance of my vow to give up law to write one last edition. After that the mantle will pass to a younger and more energetic scholar who I hope will find the subject as absorbing as I have done over the past 25 years.

Part of the fascination of corporate insolvency lies in the fact that it is inseparable from the general law of property and obligations. Since the starting position of insolvency law is respect for pre-insolvency entitlements, the subject cannot be understood without a good grasp of the general law, particularly the law relating to property, trusts, equity and security interests; and in all of these fields the law is in a state of flux. Thus in insolvency cases the courts are periodically exercised by that most fundamental of questions: what is property?

This has been a period of intensive legislative and judicial activity. The Insolvency Act 2000 was swiftly followed by the Enterprise Act 2000, which largely abolished new administrative receiverships, replacing them with administration, in respect of which both the principal Insolvency Act and the Insolvency Rules were entirely recast. The Act also introduced provisions requiring a prescribed part of floating charge assets to be surrendered for the benefit of ordinary unsecured creditors. These provisions are not free from ambiguity and it remains to be seen how they will be interpreted. A new section 1A of the Insolvency Act enables directors of a small eligible company to obtain a moratorium, but the process, set out in a new Schedule A1 of some 45 paragraphs, is so tortuous that it is hard to see why insolvency practitioners would want to make use of it.

To read the amended Insolvency Act 1986 it no longer suffices to be a lawyer; it is necessary to become a physical geographer in order to find one's way around provisions which are randomly dispersed among the body of the Act, the bizarrely numbered Schedules A1 and B1 and the Insolvency Rules, with seemingly no logic in the distribution nor any conception that it might be useful if all the provisions dealing with the same subject were brought together in clearly stated requirements. So if one reads paragraph 23 of Schedule B1 dealing with restrictions on the power of directors or the company to appoint an administrator there is neither an explicit statement nor the slightest hint of any requirement that the company must be unable or likely to become unable to pay its debts. Indeed, there is no provision anywhere in the Act that says this is a condition of such an appointment. It comes in by inference as a matter to be included in the statutory declaration under paragraph 27(2). And those who enjoy finding their way round mazes might give Hampton Court a miss and try their hands at tracking down the meaning of "hire-purchase agreement" in paragraph 43(3). All that is required is perseverance and a passion for concentric circles.

Many other important legislative changes have taken place or are impending. They include the settlement finality Directive and the financial collateral Directive, providing significant immunities from insolvency law for market and exchange contracts; the EC Insolvency Regulation, replacing in almost identical form the ill-fated European Insolvency Convention, which had foundered on the twin rocks of John Major's refusal of cooperation with Europe because of the row over British beef and a desire not to prejudice the UK's sovereignty over Gibraltar; and the UNCITRAL Model Law on Cross-Border Insolvency, which it is planned to bring into force in the UK on April Fool's day 2006.

The courts, too, have been hard at work, with a cornucopia of cases covering everything from disclaimer of waste licences to voidable transactions, from wrongful trading and the disqualification of directors to the provision of assistance to foreign courts and the extent of jurisdiction over oversea companies, and from receivership and administration to a company voluntary arrangement for the Dean and Chapter of Bradford Cathedral—the first ecclesiastical feat of its kind and, sad to say, the last as a perceived loophole in the system was closed. The Insolvency Regulation has also attracted its fair share of case law, mainly focused on the identification of the debtor company's centre of main interests (COMI) but also addressing difficult issues relating to the time when proceedings are deemed to have been opened and the effect of a change of the COMI before the hearing of a winding-up petition.

As an indication of the speed of development, the decision of Peter Smith J. in *Krasner v McMath* on the insolvency super-priority of protective awards and claims for payment in lieu of notice was handed down on July 25, 2005 only to be overruled by the Court of Appeal in *Re Ferrotech* on August 9! Through the good offices of Ruth Pedley, of CMS Cameron McKenna, I was just in time to include a reference to both of these unreported cases.

All these developments, coupled with a range of new ideas, have necessitated a substantial amount of rewriting. The treatment of assets comprising the company's property has been substantially expanded; the chapter on administration has been completely rewritten and considerably enlarged; the analysis of vulnerable transactions has been refined in the light of major decisions of the House of Lords and lower courts. There is a new chapter on the Insolvency Regulation, which deals with the applicable law, jurisdiction, recognition and enforcement in relation to intra-Community insolvencies and raises complex issues as to determination of the applicable law and its relationship to the *lex concursus*. A number of these have not yet come before English courts but I have sought wherever possible to offer an analysis which combines reasonable textual interpretation with an approach that leads to a sensible outcome. The concluding chapter, on international insolvency, has been substantially rewritten to reflect modern theories of jurisdiction and to provide a treatment of the UNCITRAL Model Law.

   With all this legislative and judicial activity going on, I find myself increasingly in sympathy with Baron Bramwell who, on being told that the line he was proposing to take in a case was at complete variance with one of his own earlier decisions replied: "The matter does not appear to me now as it appears to have appeared to me then."

   In writing this, my final edition, I have received valuable assistance both from the writings of other scholars, here and abroad, and more directly from a number of people whom I consulted. They are identified in a separate page of acknowledgments. To all of them I am greatly indebted. I should like to say in conclusion, as so often in the past, that this new edition could not have been written without the constant support of my wife Catherine, who has shown extraordinary tolerance towards this obsessive author and made no protest when almost every living room in our small house was taken up with manuscript, proofs, books and other writing paraphernalia.

Roy Goode
Oxford
August 12, 2005.

Preface to the Second Edition

In the first edition of this book I sought to lay out the fundamental principles of corporate insolvency law and to demonstrate that it is not simply a collection of rules but possesses a structure and concepts a knowledge of which is essential to a true understanding of the subject. So much has happened over the past seven years, and so many new ideas have surfaced, that this new edition is almost a new book. I have rewritten and reorganised most of the original text, and substantially expanded both the general theoretical treatment and the analysis of particular issues and statutory provisions.

There are four entirely new chapters. The first, dealing with the philosophical foundations of corporate insolvency law, examines the different perceptions of the role of corporate insolvency law and the interests which it is designed to protect. There is a new chapter on the winding-up process which focuses on the principles governing entitlement to a winding-up order: *locus standi*, the existence of grounds for winding-up and a material interest in the order being made. The third new chapter briefly examines the complex but extremely important subject of set-off and netting. Decisions of the House of Lords and Court of Appeal have radically changed the perception of rights of set-off on insolvency. Also dealt with are arrangements for the pre-insolvency netting of obligations by novations, close-outs and payment netting. The fourth new chapter gives a brief treatment of some of the key issues arising in cross-border insolvency and the various steps taken by legislation, conventions and judicial cooperation to bring about orderly cross-border reorganisations and arrangements.

In preparing this new edition I owe a particular debt of gratitude to my friend and colleague Dan Prentice, with whom I share a postgraduate course on corporate insolvency law and whose meticulous reading of the typescript and detailed comments saved me from a number of errors. I am also indebted to my friend Nick Segal, of Allen & Overy, who performed a like service and who has been so generous in imparting the fruits of his long experience. The students themselves have provided a rich harvest of ideas which I have sought to capture before they were lost to an ever-fading memory. I should also like to express my thanks to the Society of Practitioners of Insolvency and its form President, Gordon Stewart, for kindly supplying me with copies of the Society's annual surveys and other material; to the Department of Trade and Industry for statistical information and copies of annual reports on companies; to Jane Whitfield, one of my postgraduate students at Oxford, for her very effective research assistance over the Long Vacation in searches in legal literature on insolvency; and to Sweet and Maxwell for piloting through this new edition so smoothly. Finally, a word of gratitude to that long line of corporate debtors without whom this book could never have been written.

This new edition is dedicated to my wife Catherine. For nearly 33 years, despite all the pressures of her own demanding work, she has given me unstinting encouragement and support and has borne with good humour and grace the rigours of marriage to an absent-minded academic who at certain critical points in the process of authorship has engulfed our small home with law reports, textbooks and manuscripts. My debt to her is immeasurable.

St. John's College,   Roy Goode
Oxford,
July 9, 1997.

Preface to the First Edition

Corporate insolvency law is a subject of peculiar fascination; one, indeed, of which universities in this country are in the course of acquiring practical experience! Part of its intellectual interest lies in its close relationship to company law and to law relating to security interests in personal property, which come together in that most brilliant of equity's creations, the floating charge. But for the scholar it possesses the additional attraction of encompassing a wide range of complex, not to say controversial, policy issues which are only now beginning to receive in this country the attention the deserve.

This book had its origins in my Commercial Law Lectures 1989, a set of five lectures on corporate insolvency law delivered at the Centre for Commercial Law Studies, Queen Mary College, in January and February 1989. In addition to substantially revising and expanding these I have added four more topics, resulting in a work of nine chapters and 219 pages of text.

My principal objective in this book, as in others in the same series, has been to concentrate on fundamentals: to stand back from the minutiae of the statutory provisions governing the insolvency of companies and to identify the concepts and principles of corporate insolvency law, showing how these both implement and modify the general law relating to property and obligations. This is an unusual approach but I make no apology for it, because I firmly believe that corporate insolvency law cannot be adequately comprehended without a grasp of the basic principles of property and contract law and of equitable obligation. Also central to corporate insolvency law is the principle of *pari passu* distribution, which can itself be understood only if one has a clear perception of the concept of *value* and of what constitutes an unjust enrichment of a particular creditor or other party at the expense of the general body of creditors. In concentrating on fundamental principles I have sought to provide for insolvency practitioners, academic lawyers and students in this country and in other parts of the Commonwealth a framework of the kind that Professor Thomas H. Jackson of Harvard University has furnished for American practitioners and scholars in his outstanding work *The Logic and Limits of Bankruptcy Law* published in 1986.

But this book is not concerned solely with general principle; it also examines the provisions of the Insolvency Act 1986 and related legislation and case law with what I hope is sufficient analytical rigour and detail to be of assistance in the resolution of everyday problems confronting the insolvency practitioner, and to provide a reliable guide to those intending to move into this field. Particular attention has been devoted to three topics: vulnerable transactions (transactions at an undervalue, preferences, etc.), which will continue to play a prominent role in corporate insolvency; receivership and the new administration order procedure; and improper trading, with particular reference to wrongful trading and the duties and liabilities of directors.

The current legislation is still very young, so that we are all feeling our way and it will be many years before certain key problems are fully worked out by the courts and by writers in the field.

I should like to express my particular indebtedness to John Gibson of Price Waterhouse for his invaluable assistance in providing information and in commenting in detail on the manuscript; to Nick Segal of Allen and Overy for a like service and for a number of helpful ideas; to Neil Cooper of Robson Rhodes for material supplied; to Mark Homan, also of Price Waterhouse, for supplying me with a copy of his admirable survey on the administration order procedure to which I have made numerous references in the text; and to my brother-in-law Philip Rueff, a member of the Bar, for bringing to my attention some cases in the criminal law which I would otherwise have overlooked. Finally, I should like to express once again my thanks to Sweet & Maxwell, for guiding this new creation safely to publication, replete with tables and index.

The law is stated on the basis of information available to me at November 24, 1989.

St. John's College   Roy Goode
Oxford,
January 1990.

Contents

Preface   vii
Acknowledgements   xi
Preface to Third Edition   xiii
Preface to Second Edition   xvii
Preface to First Edition   xix
Sources of Definitions   xxvii
Table of UK Statutes   xxxiii
Table of Foreign Legislation   xlvii
Table of Statutory Instruments   xlix
Table of European and International Treaties and Conventions   lv
Table of European Directives   lvii
Table of European Regulations   lix
Table of Uniform Rules   lxi
Table of UK Cases   lxiii
Table of Foreign Cases   ciii

                                                                                   PARA.

**Chapter 1 The History and Framework of Corporate
  Insolvency Law**   **1-01**

   1.   Introduction   1-01
   2.   History and Sources   1-10
   3.   The Institutional Setting   1-30
   4.   The Various Insolvency Regimes   1-31
   5.   Bank Failures and their Policy Implications   1-57
   6.   Exemptions from Rules of Insolvency Law   1-60

Chapter 2 The Foundations of Corporate Insolvency Law   **2-01**

   1.   Introduction   2-01
   2.   The Objectives of English Corporate Insolvency Law   2-02
   3.   The Instruments of Corporate Insolvency Law   2-07
   4.   The Philosophy of Corporate Insolvency Law   2-14

Chapter 3 The Principles of Insolvency Law   **3-01**

Chapter 4 The Concept of Corporate Insolvency   **4-01**

   1.   General Principles   4-01
   2.   The Cash Flow Test   4-15
   3.   The Balance Sheet Test: General Considerations   4-22
   4.   The Balance Sheet Test: Computation of Assets
       and Liabilities   4-32

Chapter 5 The Winding Up Process: An Outline   **5-01**

   1. The Liquidator and his Role   5-02
   2. Creditors' Voluntary Winding Up   5-07
   3. Compulsory Winding Up   5-10
   4. Winding Up through Administration   5-25

Chapter 6 Winding Up: Assets Available for Distribution   **6-01**

   1. Delineation of the Property of the Company   6-02
   2. Disclaimer of Onerous Property   6-27
   3. Swelling the Assets Available to Creditors   6-32
   4. Assets Belonging to Third Parties   6-41
   5. Effect of Dissolution of Company   6-47

Chapter 7 The Anti-Deprivation Rule   **7-01**

   1. Three Common Law Rules   7-01
   2. The Sphere of Application of the Anti-Deprivation Rule   7-04
   3. The *Perpetual Trustee* Case   7-13

**Chapter 8 The Proof, Valuation and Ranking of Claims in
Winding Up**   **8-01**

   1. The Pari Passu Principle of Distribution   8-02
   2. Impact of the Pari Passu Principle   8-07
   3. Exceptions to the Pari Passu Principle   8-15
   4. Liquidation Expenses   8-32
   5. Proof of Debt   8-40
   6. Ranking of Claims   8-49

Chapter 9 Set-Off and Netting   **9-01**

   1. The Nature and Purpose of Set-Off and Netting   9-01
   2. Types of Set-Off   9-02
   3. Contractual Set-Off, Netting and the Impact of Insolvency 9-08
   4. Insolvency Set-Off: General Principles   9-16
   5. Insolvency Set-Off in Special Situations   9-36
   6. Set-Off in Administration   9-48

Chapter 10 Administrative Receivership   **10-01**

   1. The Development of Administrative Receivership   10-01
   2. The Partial Abolition of Administrative Receivership   10-05
   3. The Legal Nature of Administrative Receivership   10-06
   4. Appointing the Receiver Out of Court   10-25
   5. Effect of the Appointment   10-36
   6. Powers of the Receiver   10-41
   7. Duties and Liabilities of the Receiver   10-48
   8. Impact of Winding Up on the Receivership   10-66

9. Order of Application of Realisations by Receiver   10-68
10. Termination of the Receivership   10-72
11. The Position of the Debenture Holder After
    Appointing a Receiver   10-75

Chapter 11   Administration   **11-01**

1. Genesis of the Administration Procedure   11-01
2. Principal Changes Introduced by the
   Enterprise Act 2002   11-05
3. Nature and Purposes of Administration   11-17
4. Administration Compared with other Insolvency
   Procedures   11-29
5. The Rise of the Pre-Pack   11-37
6. The Appointment Procedure in Outline   11-43
7. Effect of Administration   11-49
8. Powers and Agency of the Administrator   11-80
9. Duties and Liabilities of the Administrator   11-92
10. The Administrator's Proposals   11-109
11. Termination of the Appointment and the Administration   11-113
12. Exists from Administration   11-115
13. Administration followed by Liquidation and Vice Versa   11-116
14. Variation or Rescission of the Administration Order   11-117
15. The Effectiveness of Administration   11-118

Chapter 12   Restructuring and Arrangements   **12-01**

1. Restructurings   12-02
2. Schemes   12-12
3. Company Voluntary Arrangements   12-26

**Chapter 13   The Avoidance of Transactions on Winding Up or
Administration**   **13-01**

1. The Diverse Nature of the Avoidance Provisions   13-02
2. The Policies Underlying the Avoidance Provisions   13-03
3. The Minimum Conditions for Avoidance   13-05
4. Other Relevant Conditions   13-10
5. The Grounds for Avoidance: A Summary   13-11
6. Transactions at an Undervalue   13-12
7. Preferences   13-71
8. Extortionate Credit Transactions   13-108
9. Floating Charges for Past Value   13-111
10. Registrable but Unregistered Charges   13-123
11. Dispositions of Property after the Commencement
    of Compulsory Winding Up   13-127
12. Transactions Defrauding Creditors   13-136

13. Application of Recoveries 13-140
14. Exemptions for Market and Related Contracts 13-143
15. Critique of the Avoidance Provisions 13-144
16. Do Common Law Restitutionary Principles Apply? 13-145

**Chapter 14 Improper Trading and the Duties and Liabilities
    of Directors** **14-01**

1. The Duties of Directors: Some General Observations 14-03
2. The Duties of Directors under the Criminal Law 14-06
3. The Duties of Directors to the Company 14-07
4. Duties to Creditors at Common Law 14-20
5. Liability for Fraudulent Trading 14-21
6. Liability for Wrongful Trading 14-27
7. Civil Sanctions for Improper Trading 14-51
8. Disqualification of Directors: General Considerations 14-57
9. Disqualification for Unfitness of Director of Insolvent
   Company 14-67

Chapter 15 The European Insolvency Regime **15-01**

1. Introduction 15-01
2. Background to the Insolvency Regulation 15-02
3. An Overview of the Regulation 15-05
4. Scope of the Regulation 15-09
5. Jurisdiction Generally 15-20
6. The Principle of Recognition and Respect within the
   Community 15-28
7. The Opening of Main Proceedings and its Effect 15-39
8. Main Proceedings 15-45
9. Determination of Debtor's COMI 15-49
10. Powers of the Liquidator 15-59
11. Territorial Proceedings 15-60
12. Co-Ordination of Parallel Proceedings 15-69
13. The Applicable Law under Art.4 15-70
14. Exclusions from Art.4 15-73

Chapter 16 International Insolvency **16-01**

1. The Problems of International Insolvency 16-01
2. The Insolvency Jurisdiction of English Courts 16-11
3. Foreign Insolvencies and English Courts 16-57
4. Concurrent Insolvency Proceedings 16-63

Appendix 1 Council Regulation 1346/2000 **A3**
Appendix 2 Council Regulation 210/2010 **A28**

**Appendix 3 Cross-Border Insolvency Regulations 2006
  incorporating the UNCITRAL Model Law**   **A45**
Appendix 4 UK Insolvency Act 1986, section 426   **A117**
Appendix 5 UK Insolvency Act 2000, section 14   **A121**
**Appendix 6 Virgós-Schmit Report on the Convention on
  Insolvency Proceedings**   **A123**

Index   Index-1

Sources of Definitions

A finding aid to selected defined terms relating to corporate insolvency

Abbreviations

CA	= Companies Act 2006
CA 1989	= Companies Act 1989
CBIR	= Cross-Border Insolvency Regulations 2006
CCA	= Consumer Credit Act 1974
CCDA	= Company Directors Disqualification Act 1986
EC Reg	= EC Regulation on Insolvency Proceedings 2000
FCAR	= Financial Collateral Arrangements (No.2) Regulations 2003
FMIR 1996	= Financial Markets and Insolvency Regulations 1996
FMISFR	= Financial Markets and Insolvency (Settlement Finality) Regulations 1999
IA	= Insolvency Act 1986
IR	= Insolvency Rules 1986

Note: the sources listed below are confined to companies and to statutory provisions relating to England and Wales. They do not include sources of definitions relating to bankruptcy or to provisions confined to Scotland. The provisions relating to administration are those contained in Sch.B1 to the Insolvency Act 1986, which take effect under the revised s.8 of the Act and, with certain exceptions, replace the original Part II of the Act.

"Acquired property"	IA Sch.B1, para.70(3)
"Administration order"	IA Sch.B1, para.10
"Administrative receiver"	IA ss.29(2), 251, 388(4), Sch.11 para.1(2); CDDA s.22(3); CA 1989 s.190(1)
"Administrator"	IA Sch.B1, paras 1(1), 75(5), 111(1)
"Associate"	IA ss.249, 435, 436
"Business"	IA s.436
"Become insolvent"	CDDA ss.6(2), 7, 9(2), Sch.1.
"Beginning of the moratorium"	IA Sch.A1, paras 1, 8(1)
"British insolvency law"	CBIR Sch.1, art.2(a)

"British insolvency office-holder" CBIR Sch.1, art.2(b)

"Capital market arrangement" IA s.72B(2), Sch.2A, para.1

"Capital market investment" IA s.72B(2), Sch.2A, paras 2,3

"Cash" FCAR reg.3

"Centre of main interests" IA Sch.1, para.111(1B); IR, r.13.13(8); EC Regulation, Preamble, para.13;

"Chattel leasing agreement" IA s.251

"Close-out netting provision" FCAR rg.3

"Collateral security" IA Sch.A1, para.23(6); FMISFR reg.2(1)

"Collateral security charge" IA s.72F(c), Sch.A1, para.23(6); FMISFR, reg.2(1)

"Commencement of winding up" IA ss.86, 129

"Companies Act" IA s.436; IR r.0.2; CDDA ss.22(7), 22A(4), 22B(4)

"Companies Acts" CDDA s.22(7),(8); CA s.2(1)

"Company" CA s.1; IA ss.111(4)(a), 216(8), 217(6), 388(4), 435(11), Sch.B1, para.111(1A); CDDA s.22(2)

"Conditional sale agreement" IA s.436; CCA s.189(1)

"Connected with a company" IA s.249

"Control of a company" IA s.435(10)

"Creditor" IA Sch.B1, para.12(4); IR r.4.218(1)

"Creditors" IR rr.4.44, 11.1(2)(b)

"Creditors' voluntary winding up" IA s.90

"CVL" IR reg.4.1(5)

"Debt" IR r.13.12

"Debtor" IA s.423(5)

"Director" CA s.250; IA ss.214(7), 251; CDDA ss.6(3), 7, 22(4)

"EEA State" IA s.436; CBIR Sch.1, art.1(3)(b)

"EC Regulation" IA s.436

"EC Insolvency Regulation" CBIR Sch.1, art.2(d)

"Enters into a transaction with a person at an undervalue"	IA ss.238(4) 423
"Enters administration"	Sch.B1, paras 1(2)(b), 111(1)
"Establishment"	CBIR Sch.1, art.2(e)
"Extortionate" (credit transaction)	IA s.244(3)
"Expenses of the liquidation"	IR r.4.218(1)
"Expenses of the winding up"	IA s.176ZA(4)
"Fixed security"	IA s.71
"Financed project"	IA s.72E(2)(a)
"Financial collateral"	FCAR reg.3
"Financial collateral arrangement"	FCAR rg.3
"Financial instruments"	FCAR reg.3
"Floating charge"	IA ss.251, 176A(9); Sch.B1, para.111(1)
"Foreign main proceeding"	CBIR Sch.1, art.2(g)
"Foreign non-main proceeding"	CBIR Sch.1, para.2(h)
"Foreign proceeding"	CBIR Sch.1, art.2(i)
"Foreign representative"	CBIR Sch.1, art.2(j)
"Give a preference"	IA s.239(4)
"Goes into insolvent liquidation"	IA ss.214(6), 216(7)
"Goes into liquidation"	IA s.247(2), CDDA s.22(3)
"Hire-purchase agreement"	IA s.436; CCA s.189(1); IA Sch.B1, para.111(1) CCA s.189(1)
"Holder of a qualifying floating charge"	IA Sch.B1, paras 14(3), 111
"In administration"	IA Sch.B1, paras 1(2)(a), 111(1)
"Insolvency"	IA s.247(1); CDDA s.22(3)
"Insolvency winding up"	IR rr.4.151(a), 4.173(2)
"Involved in the management of a company"	IA s.217(4)
"Liability"	IA s.382(4); IR r.13.12(4)

"Main proceedings"	IR r.13.13(10)
"Market contract"	CA 1989 s.155
"Market charge"	IA s.72F(a); CA 1989 s.173(1),(4)
"Market value"	IA Sch.B1, para.111(1)
"Model Law"	CBIR Sch.2, para.1(1), Sch.3, para.1(1)
"Moratorium"	IA s.1A, Sch.A1, para.1
"Mutual dealings"	IR, r.2.85(2)
"Nominee"	IA ss.1(2), 253(2), Sch.A1, para.1
"Office holder"	IA ss.233(1), 234(1), 235(1), 238(1), 246(1); CDDA s.7(3)
"Onerous property"	IA s.178(3)
"Onset of insolvency"	IA ss.240(3), 245(5)
"Person connected with a company"	IA s.249
"Person with control"	IA s.435(10)
"Preference"	IA s.239(4)
"Preferential creditor"	IA ss.4(7), 258(7), 386(1)
"Preferential debt"	IA ss.4(7), 386, Sch.6
"Project company"	IA ss.72C(3), 72D(2)(d), Sch.2A, paras 7(1), (2)
"Proof", "proof of debt"	IR r.2.72(2); IR r. 4.73(3),(4)
"Property"	IA s.436; IR r.7.21(3)
"Property of the company"	IA s.42(2)(b)
"Prove"	IR r.4.73
"Public-private partnership project"	IA s.2C(2)
"Purpose of administration"	IA Sch.B1, para.111(1)
"Qualifying floating charge"	IA Sch.B1, para.14(2)
"Receiver"	IA s.251
"Relevant date"	IA s.387
"Relevant time"	IA ss.240, 245(3),(4)

"Retention of title agreement"	IA s.251
"Secured creditor"	IA s.248(a)
"Security"	IA ss.248(b), 454(4)
"Security interest"	FCAR reg.3
"Shadow director"	CA s.251; IA s.251; CDDA s.22(5)
"Small company"	CA ss.382, 383
"Solvent winding up"	IR rr.4.151(b), 4.173(2)
"Step-in rights"	IA ss.72C(3), 72D(2), Sch.2A, para.6
"System-charge"	IA s.72F(b); FMIR 1996, reg.2(1)
"Transaction"	IA s.436
"Transaction at an undervalue"	IA s.238(4)
"Unable to pay its debts"	IA ss.8, 123, 222, 223, 224; Sch. B1, para.111(1)
"Voluntary arrangement"	IA s.1(1)
"Winding-up proceedings"	IR r.13.13(14A); FCAR reg.3; EC Reg. art.2(c)
"Writing"	IA Sch.B1, para.111(2)

For more comprehensive tables of sources, see Sealy & Milman: Annotated Guide to the Insolvency Legislation (14th edition), Appendices I and II.

Table of Statutes

*Paragraph references in **bold** indicate where text of legislation is reproduced*

1542   Statute of Bankrupts (34 & 35 Hen. VIII c.4) 1–10, 2–27, 7–03

1571   Fraudulent Conveyances Act (13 Eliz. 1 c.5) 1–10

1705   Bankruptcy Act (4 & 5 Anne c.17) 1–10

1813   Lord Redesdale's Act (53 Geo. III c.102) 1–10

1828   Statute of Frauds Amendment Act (Lord Tenterden's Act) (9 Geo. 4 c.14)
     s.6 14–26

1844   Joint Stock Companies Act (7 & 8 Vict. c.110) 1–10, 3–12
     Joint Stock Companies Winding-Up Act (7 & 8 Vict. c.111) 1–10
     s.1 1–10

1848   Joint Stock Companies Winding-Up Act (11 & 12 Vict. c.45) 1–10

1849   Joint Stock Companies Winding-Up Act (12 & 13 Vict.) 1–10

1855   Limited Liability Act (18 & 19 Vict. c.133) 1–10, 3–12

1856   Joint Stock Companies Act (19 & 20 Vict. c.47) 1–10
     s.104 1–10
     Mercantile Law Amendment Act (19 & 20 Vict. c.97)
     s.5 13–35

1857   Joint Stock Companies Winding-Up (Amendment) Act (20 & 21 Vict. c.80) 1–10

1861   Bankruptcy Act (24 & 25 Vict. c.134)
     s.69 1–10

1862   Companies Act (25 & 26 Vict. c.89) 1–10
     s.80(4) 4–04

     s.110 1–10
     s.133(1) 1–10
     s.144 1–10
     s.159 1–55

1869   Bankruptcy Act (32 & 33 Vict. c.71)
     s.32 1–10
     s.39 .... 9–24, 9–28
     s.92 1–10

1870   Apportionment Act (33 & 34 Vict. c.35) 10–55
     Joint Stock Companies Act (33 & 34 Vict.) ... 12–12

1875   Supreme Court of Judicature Act (38 & 39 Vict. c.77)—
     s.10 .... 1–10, 9–28

1883   Companies Act (46 & 47 Vict. c.28)—
     ss.4–6 1–10
     s.6 1–10
     Bankruptcy Act (46 & 47 Vict. c.52) 1–10

1888   Preferential Payments in Bankruptcy Act (51 & 52 Vict. c.62) 1–10

1897   Preferential Payments in Bankruptcy Act (60 & 61 Vict. c.19) 1–10, 8–51
     s.2 8–51

1907   Companies Act (7 Edw. 7 c.50)—
     s.28 4–04

1908   Law of Distress Amendment Act (8 Edw. 7 c.53)—
     s.1 10–57
     s.6 10–57
     Companies (Consolidation) Act (8 Edw. 7 c.69) 1–10
     s.130(iv) 4–04

1914   Bankruptcy Act (4 & 5 Geo. 5 c.59) 1–10, 13–99
     s.6 4–23
     s.33(7) 1–19
     s.38 2–29
     s.42 13–142
     s.44 13–71

1925	Trustee Act (15 & 16 Geo. 5 c.19)—	
	s.33	7–05
	(3)	7–05
	s.44	13–54
	s.48	13–54
	Law of Property Act (15 & 16 Geo. 5 c.20)—	
	s.101	10–26
	(1)(iii)	1–38, 10–01
	s.109	10–01
	(2)	10–23
	s.146(7)	7–05
	(9)	7–05
	(10)	7–05
	s.172	13–136
1929	Companies Act (19 & 20 Geo. 5 c.23)	1–10
	s.143	10–32
	s.169	4–04
	Table A	10–32
1930	Third Parties (Rights against Insurers) Act (20 & 21 Geo. 5 c.25)	6–04, 6–24, 16–24
	s.1(1)	6–24
1948	Companies Act (11 & 12 Geo. 6 c.38)	1–10
	s.94(1)	10–61
	s.223(d)	4–04
	s.319	8–20
	s.320	13–71
	s.321	13–126
	s.322	13–111, 13–116, 13–122
1954	Landlord and Tenant Act (2 & 3 Eliz. 2 c.56)—	
	Pt II	11–27, 11–67, 11–78
1968	Theft Act (c.60)—	
	s.19	14–06
1972	European Communities Act (c.68)	1–17
1973	Powers of Criminal Courts Act (c.62)—	
	s.35	14–64
1974	Consumer Credit Act (c.39)	11–67
	s.90(2)	11–73
	s.138(1)	13–109
	s.139(1)	13–109
	ss.140A–140C	13–109
	s.171(7)	13–109
	s.173(3)	11–73
	s.185(5)	13–109
	s.189(1)	11–63
	Insurance Companies Act (c.49)—	
	s.50	5–21
1975	Evidence (Proceedings in Other Jurisdictions) Act (c.34)	16–58
1976	Insolvency Act (c.60)—	
	s.9	14–01
1977	Unfair Contract Terms Act (c.50)	10–51
1978	Employment Protection (Consolidation) Act (c.44)—	
	s.122	16–50
	Civil Liability (Contribution) Act (c.47)	6–37, 13–142
1979	Sale of Goods Act (c.54)	6–23
	s.16	6–23
	s.17	6–23
	s.20A	6–42
	s.28	6–23
	s.41	11–57
1980	Magistrates' Courts Act (c.43)—	
	s.87A	5–17, 11–48
1981	Senior Courts Act (c.54)—	
	s.37(1)	10–26
	Supreme Court Act. *See* Senior Courts Act	
1982	Civil Aviation Act (c.16)	11–67
	s.88	11–57
	Civil Jurisdiction and Judgments Act (c.27)	15–02
1985	Companies Act (c.6)	1–10, 1–11, 1–24, 4–04
	s.196	10–61
	(1)	10–60
	(2)	10–60
	s.300	14–01, 14–75
	s.395(1)	11–29
	s.425	1–46, 11–02, 11–85, 12–12, 12–41, 12–43, 16–51, 16–65
	s.518	4–04
	s.522	13–127
	s.612	1–19

s.614(2) 10–60
      (6) 10–60
s.617 . . . . 13–111, 13–112
s.727 . . . . 14–18, 14–51
s.735(1) 12–26
s.741(2) 14–05
Company Securities
  (Insider Dealing)
  Act (c.8) 14–63
Insolvency Act (c.65) 1–11,
              1–24, 1–35, 2–12,
              4–03, 4–04, 10–04,
              10–06, 10–23, 10–60,
              11–02, 11–03, 13–71,
              13–72, 13–96, 13–142
1986 Insolvency Act (c.45) 1–08,
              1–11, 1–12, 1–19,
              1–20, 2–03, 10–06,
              10–21, 16–11, 16–12
    Pt I 1–47, 1–52, 1–54,
              1–55, 2–25, 2–26,
              4–11, 6–38, 8–03,
              11–01, 11–03, 11–17,
              11–25, 11–85, 11–109,
              11–115, 12–01,
              12–26, 15–12
    Pts I–VII 14–63
    Pt II 10–04, 11–01, 11–19
    Pt III 10–05, 16–16,
              16–26, 16–54
    Pt V 16–49
    s.1 . . . . 1–43, 3–01, 12–26
      (1) 1–47, 12–26,
              12–28, 12–34,
              12–35
      (3) 11–17, 11–25,
              12–30, 12–35
        (b) 12–32, 12–33
      (4) 15–24, 16–55
    s.1A 11–51
    s.2(2) 12–38
      (3) 12–37
    s.3 12–40
    s.4 . . . . 11–30, 11–109
      (1) 12–40
      (3) 11–18, 11–20,
              12–40, 12–41,
              12–42, 12–44
      (4) 8–03, 11–20,
              11–21, 12–40,
              12–42, 12–44
        (a) 11–21
    s.4A 11–23, 11–34, 15–14

      (2)(b) 12–42
      (6) 12–42
    s.5(1) 11–23
      (2) 12–45
        (b) 1–54, 11–36,
              12–26, 12–41
    s.6 12–55
      (1) 12–54
      (2) 12–54
      (4) 12–54
    s.7(3) 12–51
      (4) 5–01
        (b) 5–17, 11–48,
              12–32, 12–33
    s.8 . . . . 11–12, 11–26
      (1)(a) 11–11
      (3) 11–25
      (4) 11–04
    s.9(3) 10–04, 10–19,
              11–04
    s.10 . . . . 11–51, 11–70
    s.11 11–51
      (3) 11–76
      (c) 11–64
    s.12 14–57
    s.14 10–04
    s.15(4) 1–29
    s.18(3) 11–85
    s.19 10–54
      (4) 11–16
    s.20 16–50
    s.28 16–54
    s.29 . . . . 10–14, 15–47
      (2) 1–38, 10–07,
              10–10, 10–18,
              10–20, 11–07, 11–68
        (a) 10–12, 10–14
        (b) 10–11, 10–12
    s.31 10–14
    s.33 . . . . 10–31, 10–35
      (1) 10–14
      (2) 10–12
    ss.33–38 10–14
    s.34 10–32
    s.35 10–38
    s.40 . . . . 2–05, 10–14,
              10–60, 10–61, 10–62
      (1) 8–51, 10–60
      (2) 10–60, 10–61
    s.41(1) 10–67
    s.42 2–07
      (1) 10–41, 10–43
      (2)(b) 10–41, 10–43

(3) 10–47
s.43 10–43
  (1) 10–46
  (2) 10–46
  (3) 10–46, 11–83
  (7) 10–46
s.44 . . . . **10–50**, 10–54,
               10–55, 10–56
  (1) 10–23, 10–666
    (a) 10–14, 10–24,
             10–44, 10–51,
       10–56, 13–20, 14–37
    (b) 10–51, 10–54,
             11–30, 11–99
    (c) 10–51, 10–56
  (2) 10–54, 10–55
    (b) 10–54
  (2A) 10–55
  (2C) 10–55
  (2D) 10–55
  (3) 10–56
s.45(1) 10–12, 10–23,
       10–24, 10–72, 10–73
  (2) 10–72, 10–74
  (4) 10–72
s.46(1) 10–14, 10–35
s.47 10–23
s.48 10–23
s.70(1) 2–23
s.72A 10–05, 10–14
  (4)(b) 10–05
ss.72A–72GA 10–05
ss.72B–72GA 10–14
s.73(2)(b) 11–109
s.74 . . . . 3–12, 10–41
  (2)(f) 8–27, 13–78
s.84(1)(b) 5–01, 5–07
  (2A) 5–07
s.86 5–08
s.89 . . . . 4–12, 5–01
  (1) 4–12
s.90 5–01
s.95 . . . . 5–01, 5–07
s.96 5–01
s.98 . . . . 9–09, 9–31, 9–34
  (1A) 5–07
s.99 5–07
s.100 . . . . 1–40, 5–07
s.103 5–08
s.107 . . . 1–04, 3–07, **6–03**, 8–02
s.110 . . . . 1–49, 1–50, 1–52,
              1–55, 12–01
s.111 1–55
s.112 5–08

s.114 5–07
  (2) 5–08
s.115 . . . . 8–32, 8–35
s.116 5–11
s.117(1) 16–50
  (7) 16–48
s.122 . . . . 4–02, 5–01,
             5–12, 16–50
  (1)(a)–(e) 5–11
    (b) 5–17
    (c) 5–17
    (f) 4–02, 4–09, 4–13,
              5–11, 5–15,
             5–16, 5–19
    (g) 4–08, 5–11,
        5–15, 5–18, 5–19
  (2) 5–19
s.123 . . . . 4–01, 4–09, 4–22,
      4–30, 4–37, 11–11,
     11–45, 11–47, 13–08,
   13–39, 13–74, 13–113
  (1) **4–03**, 4–08,
             5–15, 5–19
    (a) 4–03, 4–09,
           4–21, 5–16
    (b) 4–03
    (e) 4–03, 4–04, 4–08,
       4–09, 4–15, 4–17
  (2) **4–03**, 4–04, 4–08,
      4–17, 4–22, **4–23**,
     4–27, 4–29, 4–37
s.124 . . . 1–40, 5–17, 5–18, 5–19
  (1) 5–17
  (4) 5–17
  (4A) 5–17
s.124A 5–11, 5–17,
      5–22, 11–54, 15–11
s.124B 5–22, 11–54
s.125 . . . . 5–01, 11–48
  (1) 2–06, 5–02,
             5–10, 5–22
  (2) 5–21
s.126 . . . . 11–03, 11–32
s.127 . . . . 1–65, 3–03, 5–08,
    5–11, 5–23, 6–02, 6–25,
    6–26, 7–01, 7–18, 9–13,
    10–28, 11–06, 11–74,
    13–02, 13–03, 13–08,
  13–127, 13–128, 13–129,
  13–131, 13–132, 13–133,
  13–134, 13–135, 13–141,
  13–142, 13–144, 13–147,
  13–148, 13–151, 13–153,
               13–154

s.129 .... 5–23, 13–127, 15–41
  (2) 3–03
s.130(2) 5–08, 5–24,
            8–47, 11–32,
            12–35, 16–62
  (4) 5–19
s.131(1) 5–10
s.135 1–42
s.136(2) 1–40, 5–10, 5–24
  (4) 5–02, 5–10
s.137 5–02
  (1) 5–10
  (3) 5–10
s.139(3) 5–10
s.141(5) 5–04
s.144 5–24
s.145 .... 3–05, 5–24
  (1) 5–02
s.154 1–04
s.156 .... 8–33, 8–35, 8–37
s.165 .... 2–07, 5–07, 5–08
  (3) 5–04
ss.165–167 .... 1–52, 1–55,
               12–01
s.166(2) 5–07
s.167 .... 2–07, 5–08
  (1) 5–04
    (a) 5–02, 8–35
  (3) 13–18
s.168(5) 5–03, 6–28, 13–18
s.171(6) 5–09
s.173(2)(e) 5–09
s.175 .... 11–01, 11–29,
               11–85
  (2) 10–60
    (a) 8–32, 10–60
    (b) 5–01, 6–38,
           8–51, 10–60,
           10–62, 13–93
s.176ZA 3–03, 5–01,
       5–09, 8–32, 8–51,
       10–60, 11–29
  (1) 5–01
  (2)(a) 5–01
s.176A 2–05, 3–03, 6–38,
       6–40, 8–04, 8–50,
       11–85, 13–93
  (1)(d) 10–64
  (2) 8–03, 11–91
    (a) 11–109
    (b) 6–40
  (3) 6–38
  (3)–(5) 11–91
  (4) 6–38, 11–85

(5) 6–38
(6) 6–38
(9) 6–38, 8–50
s.178 .... 6–15, 9–43
  (3) 6–22, 6–29, 11–29
    (a) 8–08
  (4) 6–30, 6–31
  (5) 6–31
  (6) 6–30, 6–31
ss.178–182 6–28
s.181(2) 6–30
s.183(1) 8–48
  (2) 8–48
  (3) 8–48
s.186 .... 6–22, 9–43
  (1) 6–31
  (2) 6–31
s.187 13–21
s.189(2) 8–26
s.201 5–09
ss.201–205 1–41
s.202 2–13
s.205 2–13
  (2) 5–09
s.212 .... 2–10, 5–03, 5–06,
       6–35, 11–29, 11–93,
       13–01, 13–142, 14–07,
       14–14, 14–15, 14–17,
       14–18, 14–43, 14–47,
       14–48, 14–49, 14–50,
       16–59, 16–61
  (1) 13–18, 14–14, 14–15
    (b) 10–67
  (3) 14–14, 14–17
  (5) 14–49
s.213 ...... 4–02, 5–04, 6–37,
       8–27, 8–34, 11–29,
       13–127, 14–02, 14–21,
       14–22, 14–23, 14–24,
       14–25, 14–29, 14–53,
       14–54, 15–02, 15–34,
       16–50, 16–59, 16–61
  (2) 6–37, 14–51
s.214 .... 4–02, 4–27, 4–29,
       4–33, 5–04, 5–06, 6–37,
       8–27, 8–34, 11–29,
       13–142, 14–02, 14–16, 14–24,
       14–27, **14–28**, 14–29, 14–30,
       14–31, 14–32, 14–36, 14–40,
       14–42, 14–43, 14–45, 14–47,
       14–48, 14–49, 14–50, 14–51,
       14–52, 14–53, 14–54, 14–55,
       14–56, 14–64, 15–02, 15–34,
       16–50, 16–59, 16–61

(1) 6–37, 14–15, 14–51
(2) 14–30
　(a) 14–30
　(b) 14–41
(3) 14–43
(4) 14–11, 14–42,
　　　　　　　14–44, 14–45
(5) **14–44**
(6) 4–02, 4–13, 4–22,
　　　　4–27, 4–29, 4–38,
　　　　13–82, 14–30, 14–42
(7) 1–28, 14–15, 14–32
s.215 14–53
　(2)(a) 8–27, 14–51
　(2)–(4) 14–51
　(4) 8–27
s.216 14–06
　(7) 4–02, 13–82
s.217 .... 14–06, 14–51
s.220(1) 16–49
s.221 16–50
　(2) 16–49
　(4) 5–01, 15–13, 16–52
　(5) 16–50
　(a) 5–13
ss.222–224 .... 4–01, 4–08
s.225 16–50
s.230(2) 2–12, 10–25
s.232 .... 10–23, 10–25,
　　　　　　10–28, 10–32
s.233 8–39
　(1) 10–23
　(2) 11–90
　(a) 8–39
s.234 11–95
　(1) 10–23
　(3) 10–59
　(4) 10–59
　(a) 11–95
s.235 .... 11–87, 14–46
　(2) 11–29
s.236 .... 5–02, 11–37,
　　　　　　16–59, 16–61
　(3) 5–02
s.238 .... 1–11, 4–05, 4–22,
　　　　5–04, 7–01, 7–03, 7–18,
　　　　8–34, 11–116, 13–02,
　　　　13–03, 13–12, 13–14,
　　　　13–15, 13–19, 13–20,
　　　　13–21, 13–23, 13–24,
　　　　13–28, 13–34, 13–36,
　　　　13–40, 13–41, 13–44,
　　　　13–45, 13–47, 13–53,
　　　　13–54, 13–68, 13–69,

13–107, 13–113, 13–142,
13–143, 13–147, 13–148,
13–149, 13–150, 13–151,
13–152, 13–154, 15–34,
15–71, 16–30, 16–43,
16–59, 16–61
　(1) 13–73, 13–108,
　　　　　　13–113
　(2) 4–13, 13–36, 13–39
　(3) 13–45, 13–46,
　　　　　　13–47, 13–48,
　　　　　　13–61, 13–150
　(4) 13–13, 13–136
　　(a) 13–24, 13–25
　　(b) 13–24
　(5) 13–14, 13–15,
　　　　　　13–16, 13–22,
　　　　　　13–40, 13–150
　　(a) 13–41
ss.238–240 .... 10–26, 11–04,
　　　　　　　11–45
ss.238–245 ..... 11–29, 15–02
s.239 .... 1–11, 4–05, 4–22,
　　　　5–04, 5–06, 7–03, 8–34,
　　　　11–116, 13–02, 13–03,
　　　　13–12, 13–24, 13–74,
　　　　13–76, 13–78, 13–88,
　　　　13–89, 13–97, 13–102,
　　　　13–105, 13–107, 13–113,
　　　　13–122, 13–142, 13–143,
　　　　13–147, 13–148, 13–149,
　　　　13–150, 13–151, 13–152,
　　　　13–154, 14–48, 15–34,
　　　　15–71, 16–30, 16–43
　(1)–(3) 13–73
　(2) 4–13, 13–103
　(3) 13–105
　(4) 13–77
　　(a) 13–79
　　(b) 13–72, 13–82,
　　　　　　13–91
　(5) 13–96
　(6) ... 13–76, 13–78, 13–104
　(7) 13–82
s.240 ..... 4–13, 13–12, 13–73
　(1) 13–39, 13–104
　　(b) 13–103
　　(c) 13–127
　(2) 4–09, 4–33, 4–37,
　　　　　　13–16, 13–36,
　　　　　　13–39, 13–74
　(3) 4–01, 13–05,
　　　　　　13–39
　　(d) 11–116

s.241 . . . . . 1–11, 10–28, 13–02,
            13–12, 13–15, 13–24,
            13–48, 13–54, 13–73,
            13–88, 13–142
  (1) 13–46, 13–47,
            13–61, 13–68, 13–106
    (a) 13–02
    (c) 13–93
    (d) 13–24, 13–103,
            13–106
    (e) 13–106
    (f) 13–53
    (g) 13–47
  (2) 13–23, 13–44,
            13–47, 13–48,
            13–51, 13–62,
            13–68, 13–75,
            13–139, 13–149,
            13–150
    (b) 13–98, 13–106
  (2A) 13–16, 13–68,
            13–104
  (3) 13–15, 13–16
  (3A)–(3C) 13–68
s.242 . . . . 5–04, 8–34
ss.242–245 16–43
s.243 . . . . 5–04, 8–34
s.244 . . . . 13–02, 13–08,
            13–108, 13–109,
            13–110, 13–142, 13–147
  (1) 13–108
  (2) 4–09
  (3) 13–109
  (4) 13–110
  (5) 13–110
s.245 . . . . 4–02, 4–05, 4–13,
            4–22, 10–26, 10–28,
            11–04, 11–45, 13–02,
            13–08, 13–113, 13–114,
            13–116, 13–117, 13–118,
            13–120, 13–141, 13–142,
            13–147, 13–148
  (1) 13–113
  (2) 13–114
    (a) 13–118
    (b) 13–118
  (4) 4–09, 4–37, 13–113
  (5) 13–113
  (6) 13–117
s.246A 5–07, 11–118
s.246B 11–118
s.247(1) 4–01
  (2) 4–13
s.248(b) 11–08, 11–57

s.249 . . . . . . 1–28, 4–09, 13–10,
            13–39, 13–68, **13–104**
  (b) 13–78, 13–104
s.251 . . . . 1–28, 4–12, 8–51,
            10–17, 11–63, 11–82,
            13–112, 13–113, 14–04,
            14–05, 14–36, 16–42
s.252 11–67
s.260(2) 12–25, 12–26
s.268 4–03
s.284 13–127
s.306 6–14
  (1) 3–05, 5–02
s.323 1–29
s.339 13–20
  (3)(c) 13–33
s.387 . . . . 8–22, 10–61,
            11–30, 11–116
  (3) 11–116
    (a) 11–116
    (ba) 11–116
    (b) 11–116
    (c) 11–116
  (3A) 11–30
  (4)(a) 10–60
s.388(1) 1–30
s.389 10–72
  (1) 1–30
s.390 . . . . 10–28, 10–72
  (1) 10–25
  (3) 10–25, 11–113
  (4)–(5) 10–25
ss.390–392 . . . . . . 2–12, 10–25
s.392(2) 1–30
s.423 . . . . 5–04, 7–05, 8–34,
            13–01, 13–06, 13–08,
            13–20, 13–28, 13–38,
            13–136, 13–137, 13–138,
            13–139, 13–143, 13–147,
            13–149, 13–150, 13–151,
            13–152, 13–154, 15–02
s.424 13–138
s.425 . . . 13–139, 13–150, 16–61
  (1)(d) 13–150
  (2) 13–149, 13–150
s.426 . . . . . 8–31, 16–10, 16–13,
            16–15, 16–23, 16–44,
            16–53, 16–58, 16–59,
            16–60, 16–62, 16–65
  (4) **16–58**, 16–60
  (5) 16–25, 16–57,
            16–58, 16–59
  (10) 16–30, 16–59
  (11) 16–59

s.435 . . . . 1–28, 13–39,
              13–68, 13–104
(2)–(5) 13–104
(4) 13–104
(5) 13–104
(6) 13–104
(7) 13–78, 13–104
(8) 13–104
(9) 13–104
(10) 13–78
s.436 . . . . . . 6–03, 6–05, 6–08,
              6–09, 6–11, 11–61,
           11–63, 13–13, 13–34,
              15–24, 15–46
s.436A 15–46
s.436B 11–43
s.438 13–42
s.452(2) 13–104
Sch.A1 11–51
para.2(2) 12–35
(3) 12–35
paras 2–4 12–39
paras 2–5 12–35
para.3(4) 12–35
para.4(1) 12–39
(d) 12–51
para.4A 12–39
paras 4A–4C 12–35
para.7 12–35
para.8 12–51
para.39(3) 12–55
(5)(b) 5–01
Sch.B1 . . . . 1–35, 11–19
para.1(2) 11–48, 11–71,
              11–114
para.3 . . . . . . **11–25**, 11–28,
           11–47, 11–109
(1) 1–35, 11–26,
           11–27, 11–29,
           11–41, 11–109
(2) 11–06, 11–27,
              11–93
(4) 1–35
para.6 11–43
para.8 11–45
(1) 11–04, 11–13
para.11 . . . . . 11–09, 11–25,
              11–47
(a) 4–01, 4–02, 4–08,
           4–13, 4–22, 4–27,
           11–06, 11–11
(b) 4–02, 4–28
para.12(1) . . . 11–09, 11–44,
              11–48

(2) 10–27
(3) 11–48
(4) 11–48
(5) 11–48
para.13 11–72
(1) 11–48
(2) 11–48, 11–71
(3) 11–74
para.14 . . . . . 10–05, 11–06,
           11–07, 11–08, 11–09,
           11–10, 11–11, 11–43,
              11–47, 13–39
(1) 11–08
(2) 11–07, 11–43
(3) 11–08
para.15 11–44
(1) 11–44
(2) 11–44
para.16 11–09
para.17 . . . . . 11–09, 11–10,
              11–46
(b) 10–05, 10–27,
              11–20
para.18 11–44
(1) 11–10
para.19 11–44
para.22 . . . . . 11–10, 11–11,
           11–43, 11–54, 13–39
para.23 11–45
(1) 11–54
para.25 . . . . . 11–06, 11–44,
              11–46
(a) 11–45, 11–54
(b) 11–45
(c) 10–05, 10–13,
           10–27, 11–43, 11–45
para.26 . . . . . . 11–45, 11–70
(1) 11–43, 11–45
para.27 11–45
(2)(a) 11–11
para.28(1) . . . 11–43, 11–44,
              11–45
(2) 11–74
para.29(1) 11–10
para.35(1)(a) 11–06
(2) 4–02, 11–06,
           11–09, 11–11, 11–47
para.36 . . . . . 10–27, 11–06,
              11–10
para.37 . . . . . 11–06, 11–13,
              11–116
(2) 11–44
para.38 11–13
(2) 11–13

para.39 ..... 10–13, 10–19,
        10–26, 10–27, 11–45
    (1) 10–27, 11–04
    (2) 10–27
para.40(1) 5–22, 11–06
para.41(1) ... 10–13, 10–23,
        10–26, 10–27,
        11–50
    (2) 10–23, 11–50
    (3) 11–50
    (4) 11–50
para.42 .... 2–23, 5–22,
        11–44, 11–51,
        11–53, 11–71
    (1) 11–54
    (1)–(4) 11–54
    (2) 11–54, 11–116
    (4) 5–22
paras 42–44 11–71
para.43 ..... 2–23, 10–23,
        11–51, 11–53,
        11–58, 11–59,
    11–69, 11–71, 11–76,
    11–77, 12–44, 16–43
    (1) 11–63
    (2) 11–56, 11–58,
        11–63, 11–64,
        11–68
    (3) 1–29, 1–65,
        11–57, 11–62,
        11–64, 11–105
    (4) 11–57, 11–66,
        11–105
    (6) . 11–58, 11–66, 11–67
    (6A) 10–13, 10–23,
        10–26, 10–27, 11–53,
        11–55, 11–58, 11–68
    (7) 11–53
para.44 .... 5–22, 11–51
    (2) 11–44
    (4) 11–74
    (5) ... 1–65, 11–44, 11–71
    (6) 11–71
    (7) 11–06, 11–71
para.45(1) 11–94
    (2) 11–94
    (3) 11–94
para.49 11–23
    (3) 11–109, 11–115
    (4) 11–109
    (5) 11–109
para.51 ...... 11–06, 11–23
    (1) 11–109
    (2) 11–109

para.52 11–109
    (1)(b) 2–21, 11–118
    (2)(a) 2–21
para.53(1) 11–109,
        11–111
para.54 11–109
para.56 11–06
para.57 11–06
para.59 .... 2–07, 10–23
    (1) 11–81
    (3) 11–88
para.60 ...... 10–23, 11–81
para.61 11–81,
        11–89
para.62 11–81
para.63 ..... 11–81, 11–97
    (3) 11–97
para.64 11–87
    (1) 10–23
    (2) 11–89
para.65 ..... 11–80, 11–81,
        11–85, 11–90
    (1) 11–20
    (2) 10–60, 11–01,
        11–29, 11–85
    (3) 11–20, 11–85,
        11–115
para.66 ..... 11–85, 11–90,
        11–104
para.67 ...... 11–08, 11–95
para.68(1) 11–81
    (2) 11–81
para.69 11–89
para.70 11–18
    (1) 3–03, 11–82
    (2) 1–29, 11–82
    (3) 1–29, 11–82
paras 70–72 11–80
para.71 11–18
    (1) 3–03, 11–83
    (2) 11–83
para.73 ...... 11–20, 11–84
    (1) 11–18, 11–109
para.74 ..... 11–23, 11–41,
        11–93, 13–18
    (1)(b) 11–105
    (6)(c) 11–23
para.75 ..... 11–41, 11–93,
        14–14, 14–15
    (2) 11–29
para.76 .... 11–14, 11–113,
        12–30
    (1) 11–14
    (2) 11–113

para.77 11–14
para.78 11–113
  (1) 11–14
para.79 11–116
  (1) 11–97, 11–113
  (2) 11–97
  (3) 11–97
  (4)(d) 5–01, 5–25,
        11–115, 15–13
para.80 11–97
  (3) 11–113
para.81 11–41
  (1) 11–113
  (2) 11–113
  (3) 11–113, 15–13
para.82(3) 11–113
para.83 ..... 11–53, 11–54,
        11–115, 11–116,
               15–13
  (1) 11–116
  (3)–(7) 11–116
  (6) 5–01, 5–25,
        11–113, 15–13
para.84 ...... 2–13, 11–115
  (2) 11–115
  (4) 11–113
  (6) 1–41
para.87 11–113
para.88 ..... 11–06, 11–41,
               11–113
para.89(1) 11–113
para.92 11–06
para.96 11–113
para.97 11–113
para.99 ...... 1–29, 11–16,
               11–91
  (1) 10–72, 11–113
  (3) ... 1–29, 5–01, 11–91,
        11–98, 11–101
  (4) 1–29, 11–30,
        11–91, 11–94,
   11–96, 11–101, 11–104
  (5) 11–30, 11–91,
               11–106
  (6) 11–96
para.105 11–43
para.107 11–109
para.108 11–109
para.111 16–42
  (1) 11–47, 11–63,
               11–80
  (1A) 15–24, 16–53,
               16–55

Sch.1 .... 2–07, 10–04,
        10–14, 10–23,
     10–41, 10–43, 11–81
  para.13 ...... 11–85, 11–90
  para.21 ...... 5–01, 5–17
  item 8 10–41
  item 13 ..... 11–29, 11–85
  item 19 10–41
  item 21 10–37
Sch.2A 10–05
Sch.4 .... 10–12, 12–01
  Pt I 2–07
  Pt II 8–34
  para.2 .... 1–52, 1–55, 5–05
  para.3A 5–04, 8–34
  para.4 .... 3–10, 5–04, 5–08
  para.5 ... 1–39, 2–07, 5–02,
        5–08, 8–35,
     11–29, 12–33
  para.6 ... 5–06, 6–06, 14–55
  para.6A 5–05
Sch.6 ..... 8–19, 8–20, 8–21,
        8–22, 10–60, 11–116
  para.8 8–22
  para.9 8–22
  paras 9–10 8–23
  para.11 8–23
  para.23 8–22
  category 5 .. 11–05, 11–106
Company Directors
 Disqualification Act
 (c.46) 1–11, 1–24, 4–10,
        10–25, 14–57, 14–58,
     16–26, 16–30, 16–57
  s.1 14–59
  (1) 14–79, 14–81
  s.1A 14–72
  (2) 14–72
  s.2 .... 14–60, 14–70
  (1) 14–63
  s.3 .... 14–60, 14–70
  (1) 14–63
  (2) 14–63
  (3) 14–63
  (4A) 14–63
  s.4 .... 14–60, 14–70
  (1)(a) 14–51, 14–63
    (b) 14–63
  s.5 ...... 14–60, 14–63, 14–70
  s.6 .... 1–24, 4–05, 4–06, 4–27,
        11–87, 14–01, 14–57,
        14–60, 14–61, 14–65,
  14–67, 14–70, 14–73, 14–77

(1) 4–02, 14–69
  (a) 4–13
  (b) 14–73
(2) 4–01, 4–10, 4–22,
             4–27, 4–38,
            14–67, 14–70
(3) 14–73
(3C) 14–67
(4) 14–62, 14–80
s.7 14–69
  (1) 14–70
  (2A) 14–72
  (3) 10–23, 14–69
s.8 .... 14–60, 14–63
s.9 .... 11–87, 14–73
s.9A 14–57, 14–60, 14–65
s.10 .... 14–51, 14–60,
         14–63, 14–70
  (1) 14–64
s.11 14–66
s.12 14–66
s.13 14–82
s.15 .... 14–82, 15–02
  (3) 14–82
s.16(1) 14–70
s.17 ..... 14–06, 14–77, 14–78
s.18(1) 14–84
  (2) 14–84
s.21A 14–57
s.21B 14–57
s.21C 14–57
s.22(4) ... 14–04, 14–67, 14–73
  (5) 14–05, 14–67
  (7) 14–63
Sch.1 Pt I 14–73
  Pt II 14–73
  para.10(g) 11–87
Building Societies Act
  (c.53) 14–57
s.90E 14–57
s.119 .... 16–14, 16–56
Financial Services Act
  (c.60) 1–61
1989 Companies Act (c.40) 9–13
  Pt VII 1–12, 1–22, 1–60,
          9–15, 16–24, 16–57
  s.155 .... 1–61, 6–28
  (1) 6–28
  s.158 16–57
  s.159 .... 1–61, 16–57
  s.164(1) 6–28
  s.165 13–143
  s.173 1–62

s.175 1–61
  (1) 11–56
s.183(2) 16–57
1990 Contracts (Applicable
  Law) Act (c.36) 15–92
  Environmental Protection
  Act (c.43) 2–25, 4–11,
         6–11, 8–30
  s.26(1) 2–25
  s.78X(3) 8–30
  (4)(a) ... 8–30, 10–48, 10–65
  s.82(2) 2–25
  s.183(3) 4–11
  s.184 4–11
  s.189(2) 8–21
1992 Trade Union and Labour
  Relations (Consolidation)
  Act (c.52)—
  s.189 8–41
1993 Railways Act (c.43)—
  s.59 11–05
  Sch.6 11–05
  Pension Schemes Act (c.48)—
  s.127(3) 8–21
  Sch.4 8–22
1994 Insolvency Act (c.7) 10–54
  Coal Industry Act (c.21)—
  s.36 6–11
1995 Private International Law
  (Miscellaneous Provisions)
  Act (c.42)—
  Pt III 15–92
1996 Employment Rights Act
  (c.18) 4–06
  Pt XII 4–05
  Arbitration Act (c.23) ... 16–18
  Housing Grants, Construction
  and Regeneration Act
  (c.53) 5–13
  s.108 11–67
1998 Human Rights Act (c.42) . 1–25
  Sch.1 13–41
1999 Youth Justice and Criminal
  Evidence Act (c.23)—
  s.59 11–87
  Sch.3 para.7(3)(a) 11–87
  para.8(3)(a) 11–87
  Welfare Reform and
  Pensions Act (c.30)—
  s.11 6–09
2000 Financial Services and
  Markets Act (c.8) 1–13
  Pt XXIV 1–13, 1–22

s.31 1–13
s.367 11–54
　(1) 1–13
ss.376–379 1–61
s.400(1) 14–06
　(5) 14–06
Limited Liability Partnerships
　Act (c.12) 3–12
s.1(2) 3–12
Insolvency Act (c.39) 1–14,
　　　　　　　　　　　1–35
s.14 .... 1–20, 15–01
2002　　　　Proceeds of Crime Act
　(c.29) 3–09, 5–02,
　　　　　　　14–82, 16–30
s.84 3–09
s.426 3–09
Enterprise Act (c.40) 1–14,
　　　　　　1–15, 1–32, 1–38,
　　　　　　2–03, 2–20, 5–25,
　　　　　　　　11–01, 11–04,
　　　11–29, 11–113, 11–118
s.249 1–35
　(1) 11–05
s.251 ...... 1–10, 8–20, 10–60
2004　Pensions Act (c.35) 8–37
s.38 2–24
s.38A 2–24
s.43 8–37
　(2) 2–24
s.47 8–37
ss.52–53 .... 13–02, 13–11
s.75 .... 8–36, 11–103
　(4A) 11–103
　(8) 8–36, 11–103
s.100 8–37
s.120 11–107
s.127 .... 8–22, 11–115
s.162 11–115
s.173 8–22
s.257 2–24
s.258 2–24
Sch.7 11–115
2005　Mental Capacity Act
　(c.9) 10–25
Gambling Act (c.19) 11–67
2006　Fraud Act (c.35) 14–06
ss.1–10 14–06
s.11 14–06
s.12 14–06
Companies Act (c.46) ... 1–12,
　　　　　11–87, 12–22, 16–26,
　　　　　　　　16–49, 16–53

Pt 10 Ch.2 ..... 14–01, 14–07
Pt 16 Ch.10 2–15
Pt 17 Ch.10 13–01
Pt 25 .... 1–12, 11–63
Pt 26 ...... 1–12, 1–46, 1–49,
　　　　　1–51, 1–52, 1–53, 1–54,
　　　　　4–11, 6–38, 8–03, 11–01,
　　　11–03, 11–17, 11–18, 11–24,
　　　11–25, 11–32, 11–33, 11–85,
　　11–109, 11–115, 12–01, 12–12,
　　　12–14, 12–17, 15–14, 16–51
Pt 31 1–39
s.1 12–26
　(1) 15–24
s.2(1) 14–63
s.3 3–12
s.31(1) 13–01
s.170(5) 14–04, 14–09
s.171 14–09
s.172 14–09
　(1) 14–11, 14–20
　(3) 14–11, 14–20
s.173 14–09
s.174 .... 14–09, 14–11
　(2) 14–11
s.175 14–09
ss.175–177 14–12
s.176 14–09
s.177 14–09
s.178(1) 14–09
ss.238–242 4–02
s.245 13–112
s.247 13–21
s.250 14–04
s.251(1) 14–05
　(3) 14–05
s.281 5–07
s.283(1) 5–07
　(4) 5–07
　(5) 5–07
s.288 5–07
s.307(1) 5–07
　(2) 5–07
　(4) 5–07
　(5) 5–07
s.323 5–07
　(1) 5–07
s.382(3) 12–35, 12–39
s.393(1) 4–32
ss.403–408 1–28
s.425(6) 16–51
s.464 4–32
s.641 12–43

s.648 12–43
s.655 8–27
s.735 8–27
s.735A 16–51
s.754 .... 1–12, 2–05, 8–51,
              10–60, 10–61
  (1) 10–60
  (2) 10–60
s.830 14–14
s.860 ..... 6–46, 11–95, 13–02,
          13–123, 15–82, 15–94
  (7)(b) 6–46
s.870(1) 15–72
s.873 .... 10–26, 13–123
  (1) 13–125
  (2) 13–125
s.874 .... 10–28, 13–02, 13–08,
        13–123, 13–124, 13–141,
        13–142, 13–147. 13–148
s.895 .... 12–11, 12–28
  (2) 12–17
    (b) 16–55
s.896(1) 12–20
  (2) 12–20
s.899 .... 1–43, 1–46, 1–53,
          1–55, 2–21, 11–17,
        12–13, 12–15, 12–25,
        12–28, 12–43, 15–02,
        15–12, 16–14, 16–30,
        16–48, 16–55, 16–65
  (3) 12–24
s.900 12–43
  (2) 1–54
s.993 ...... 2–06, 4–02, 14–06,
              14–21
  (2) 14–21
  (3) 14–26
s.994 5–11
s.1012 6–47
s.1029 .... 1–39, 6–47
  (2) 1–41
s.1032(1) 1–41
s.1044 16–49
s.1079 13–127
s.1121(3) 14–06

s.1157 ... 14–18, 14–45, 14–51
s.1182 14–57
s.1184 14–57
2007 Serious Crime Act (c.27)—
  s.27 5–17
2008 Banking (Special Provisions)
      Act (c.2) 1–16
2009 Banking Act (c.1) 1–16,
        1–26, 1–35, 2–14, 14–57,
              16–11, 16–48
  Pt 2 1–59
  Pt 3 11–01
  s.1(2) 1–59
    (3) 1–59
    (4) 1–59
  s.11 1–35
  s.12 1–35
    (1) 1–35
  s.84 16–56
  s.91 .... 16–14, 16–56
    (3) 16–14, 16–56
  s.94(1) 5–02
    (2) 5–02
  s.96(1)(a) 4–02
    (2)–(4) 1–59
  s.97 1–59
  s.99 1–59
  s.103 Table 1–59
  s.113 1–59
  s.117 1–59
  s.118 1–59
  s.121 14–57
  s.137 1–35
  s.143(3) 4–02
  Corporation Tax Act (c.4)—
  s.10(1) 11–01
  s.626(3) 11–01
  Perpetuities and
    Accumulations Act
    (c.18) 7–09
2010 Corporation Tax (c.4)—
  s.37 11–01
  Third Parties (Rights against
    Insurers) Act (c.10) 6–24
  s.1(2) 6–04

Table of Foreign Legislation

Australia

2001   Corporations Act (Cth)
       s.95A 4–04, 4–16, 4–20
       s.180 10–49
       s.563A 8–27
       s.588FA(1)(b) 13–89
       (3) 13–88

Canada

Personal Property Security Act (NS)
       s.2 6–11
1992   Bankruptcy and Insolvency Act
       s.2 6–11
       s.244 10–30
       s.247 10–49

Germany

1965   Aktiengesetz (Stock
       Corporations Act) 16–10

Ireland

1963   Companies Act
       s.218 13–131
       s.220(2) 15–36, 15–41

New Zealand

1993   Receiverships Act
       s.18 10–49

1999   Personal Property
       Securities Act 13–124

United States of America

Bankruptcy Code 13–03
       Ch.11 ...... 2–01, 2–07, 6–22,
              7–14, 7–15, 7–19,
              11–11, 11–18,
              11–22, 11–23,
              11–37, 12–01,
              12–11, 15–15,
              16–30, 16–65
       Ch.15 .... 16–10, 16–22
       s.304 16–10
       s.362(a) 7–14, 7–22
       s.365(e)(1) 7–14
       s.510(c) 8–27
       s.541(c)(1) 7–05
       (B) 7–14, 7–22
       s.547(c)(4) 13–88
       s.1129(b)(2) 11–18
1933   Banking Act
       (Glass-Steagall Act) ... 2–14
2010   Dodd-Frank Wall Street
       Reform and Consumer
       Protection Act (Public
       Law 111–203) 2–14

Table of Statutory Instruments

1986 Insolvency Practitioners
    (Recognised Professional
    Bodies) Order (SI 1986/
    1764) 2–12, 10–25
    Insolvency Rules
    (SI 1986/1925) ... 1–21, 1–39
    Pt 1 1–55
      Ch.2 12–36
      Ch.3 12–36
      Ch.4 12–36
      Ch.5 12–36
      Ch.7 12–36
      Ch.8 12–36
      Ch.9 12–36
    Pt 2 11–19
      Ch.2 11–48
      Ch.4 11–45
      Ch.10 .... 8–18, 11–85
      Ch.12A 11–118
    rr.1.2—1.5 12–34
    r.1.3(1) 12–36
      (2) 12–36
        (r) 12–36
    r.1.4(1) 12–37
      (2) 12–36, 12–37
      (3) 12–37
    r.1.5 12–37
    r.1.6 12–37
      (1)(a) 12–26
      (3) 12–37
    r.1.7(2) 12–38
    r.1.17(1) 12–41, 12–47
      (3) 12–41
    r.1.17A(2) 12–41
      (3) 12–41, 12–47
      (4) 12–41
      (5) 12–41
      (6) 12–47
    r.1.19(1) 11–36, 12–42
      (3) 12–41, 12–42, 12–45
      (4) 11–36
    r.1.20(1) 12–42
    r.2.3(5) 11–25
    R.2.4(4) 15–22
    r.2.6(3) 10–27
    r.2.8(1) 10–27
      (5) 10–27
    r.2.12 11–48
    r.2.13(a) 11–13

r.2.15 11–44
r.2.16 11–44
  (6) 11–44
r.2.18 11–06
r.2.19 11–44
  (1) 11–44
  (3) 11–44
  (5) 11–44
r.2.33 11–109
  (2)(ka) 11–98
  (2A) 11–98
r.2.38(4) 11–112
r.2.40 .... 2–21, 11–112
r.2.43(1) 11–36
  (2) 11–36
r.2.67 .... 1–29, 11–98, 11–104
  (1) 1–29, 11–91, 11–96,
             11–98, 11–105
    (a) .. 1–29, 8–38, 11–104
    (f) 8–33, 11–98
    (h) 11–98
    (j) 11–01
  (2) 11–98, 11–105
  (3) 8–37, 11–98, 11–105
  (4) 11–96
r.2.67A 11–91, 11–98
r.2.69 .... 3–07, 8–02
r.2.85 ...... 3–05, 6–20, 9–07,
            9–16, 9–48,
          11–29, 12–30
  (1) 9–48
r.2.95 9–48
r.2.105 .... 8–09, 8–43
rr.2.119—2.121 11–113
r.3.1 10–35
r.3.2(e) 10–14
r.3.33 10–72
r.3.34 10–72
r.3.35 10–72
  (1) 10–72
r.4.7(7) 11–53, 11–54
rr.4.8—4.10 5–10
r.4.11 .... 5–10, 5–20
r.4.12(8) 15–22
r.4.19 5–13
r.4.51 5–07
r.4.58(4) 11–29
r.4.63A 11–118
r.4.67(1) 5–07

r.4.70 5–07
r.4.73 8–40
r.4.75(1)(e) 8–47
r.4.83 .... 5–08, 8–40, 9–23
r.4.86 ...... 2–26, 8–43, 9–23
  (1) 3–11, 9–21
r.4.88(1) 8–47
  (2) 8–47
r.4.90 ..... 3–05, 6–20, 9–07,
         9–16—9–23, 9–26,
         9–28, 9–41, 9–47,
       9–48, 11–29, 13–128,
         16–60, 16–61
  (1) 8–18, 9–20, 9–23
  (2) 9–22, 9–25,
         9–30—9–34
   (d) 9–20, 9–34, 9–45
  (3) 8–18, 9–18
  (4) 9–25
   (b) 9–22
  (6) 9–47
  (8) 8–18, 9–18, 9–38
r.4.91(1) 9–47
r.4.92 .... 8–09, 8–41
r.4.93 8–41
r.4.94 .... 3–11, 8–41, 8–43
r.4.95(1) 8–47
r.4.96 8–47
r.4.97(1) 8–47
r.4.101(2) 5–07
r.4.127 5–09
r.4.127A 5–09
r.4.180(1) 8–35
r.4.181 .... 1–19, 3–07
  (1) 6–03, 8–02
r.4.182(1) 8–40
  (2) 5–09, 8–40
  (3) 5–03, 8–40
r.4.184(2) 5–04
r.4.218 ..... 5–09, 8–33, 8–35,
        11–98, 11–105
  (2)(a) 8–34
  (3)(a) 8–38
   (m) 8–33, 8–37
   (o) 8–37
r.4.218A(1)(c) 8–34
  (2) 8–32
rr.4.218A—4.218E 3–10,
        5–01
r.4.218B 8–34
r.4.218E(3) 8–34
r.4.219 .... 5–09, 8–35
r.4.220(1) 8–33, 8–37
r.4.228 14–06

rr.4.228—4.230 14–06
r.6.5(4)(d) 13–109
r.7.47 .... **11–117**
r.7.51 11–117
r.7.62 .... 5–08, 15–13
  (8) 15–13
r.7.63 .... 5–08, 15–13
r.8.1(1) 5–07
r.8.7 5–07
r.11.6(1) 8–40
r.11.11(1) 8–08
r.11.13 .... 3–11, 8–43
  (2) 8–09, 9–37
r.12.2 8–35
r.12.3 1–29
  (1) 2–26, 3–11,
        8–41, 9–28
  (2) 8–41
  (2A) 8–27, 8–41
  (3) 8–41
r.12.9 10–27
r.12A.10(1) 11–35
r.12A.22 5–07
r.12A.38 11–35
r.13.12 ..... 2–26, 4–17, **4–24**,
        4–25, 12–18
  (1) 4–23, 4–27,
        8–36, 8–41
   (a) 8–37
  (2) 2–26, 4–24,
        8–41, 9–28
  (3) 4–23, 4–27, 8–41,
        9–18, 9–23, 9–28
  (4) 8–41
form 2.2B 11–25
form 2.5B 11–44
form 2.6B 11–44
Insolvency Proceedings
  (Monetary Limits) Order
  (SI 1986/1996)
  art.4 8–22
Co-operation of Insolvency
  Courts (Designation of
  Relevant Countries and
  Territories) Order
  (SI 1986/2123) 16–59
1987 Insolvent Companies
  (Disqualification of Unfit
  Directors) Proceedings
  Rules (SI 1987/2023) ... 14–70
1989 European Economic Interest
  Grouping Regulations
  (SI 1989/638) 3–12
  reg.3 3–12

1991 Financial Markets and
Insolvency Regulations
(SI 1991/880)
reg.8 1–62
1995 Financial Markets and
Insolvency (Money
Markets) Regulations
(SI 1995/2049) 1–61
1996 Co-operation of
Insolvency Courts
(Designation of
Relevant Countries)
Order (SI 1996/253) ... 16–59
Financial Markets and
Insolvency Regulations
(SI 1996/1469) 1–22
Pt II 1–60, 1–61
reg.3(2) 1–63
Insolvent Companies
(Reports on Conduct of
Directors) Rules
(SI 1996/1909) 14–69
1998 Co-operation of
Insolvency Courts
(Designation of Relevant
Country) Order
(SI 1998/2766) 16–59
Civil Procedure Rules
(SI 1998/3132) 11–117
r.25.13(2)(c) 10–52
r.35.4(1) 14–76
Pt 49 12–21
Pt 70 16–30
Pt 73 16–30
Sch.1 RSC Ord.41 r.6 ... 14–76
1999 Financial Markets and
Insolvency (Settlement
Finality) Regulations
(SI 1999/2979)
Pt 3 16–24
reg.2(1) 9–09
reg.16(1) 6–28
reg.19(1) 1–65, 11–56
(3) 1–65
2001 Financial Services and
Markets Act 2000
(Recognition Requirements
for Investment Exchanges
and Clearing Houses)
Regulations
(SI 2001/995) 1–61
Sch.1 para.11(2)(b) 1–61
para.12(2)(c) 1–61
para..25(2) 1–61

Financial Markets and
Services (Settlement
Finality) Regulations
(SI 2001/1349) 1–64
Insurers (Winding Up)
Rules (SI 2001/3635) ... 1–61
2003 Insolvency Act 1986
(Prescribed Part) Order
(SI 2003/2097) ... 3–03, 6–39
art.1 .... 6–38, 8–50
Financial Collateral
Arrangements
(No.2) Regulations
(SI 2003/3226) ... 1–22, 1–66
Pt 3 ...... 1–71, 16–24, 16–57
Pt 4 16–24
reg.3 .... 1–67, 9–12
reg.8 ..... 8–32, 11–56, 11–91
reg.9 .... 8–32, 11–91
reg.10 13–124
(4) 6–28
reg.11 .... 8–32, 11–91
reg.15A 16–57
2004 Insurers (Reorganisation and
Winding Up) Regulations
(SI 2004/353) 1–61
reg.52 11–10
Credit Institutions
(Reorganisation and
Winding Up) Regulations
(SI 2004/1045) ... 1–60, 1–72,
5–02
reg.3 .... 16–05, 16–48
reg.4 16–48
reg.34 9–09
2005 Insolvency Practitioners
Regulations
(SI 2005/524) 1–30
Proceeds of Crime Act
2002 (External Requests
and Orders) Order
(SI 2005/3181) 16–30
2006 Transfer of Undertakings
(Protection of Employment)
Regulations (SI 2006/
246) 2–24, 8–24,
11–23, 11–106
reg.4 15–98
reg.8(7) 8–24, 15–98
Cross-Border Insolvency
Regulations (SI 2006/
1030) 1–18, 1–20, 7–22,
16–15, 16–16,
16–21, 16–57

reg.2(2) 16–22
reg.3(2) 16–13
reg.7 16–13
Sch.1 UNCITRAL Model
Law ... 16–11, 16–21—16–47,
            16–57, 16–59,
            16–65
    Ch.IV 16–44
    art.1(1) 16–23
    (2) 16–23
    (4) 16–24
    (5) 16–24
    (6) 16–24
    art.2 .... 15–01, 15–12,
            16–25, 16–26
    (a) **16–25**
    (e) 16–29, 16–35
    (e)—(j) **16–25**
    (g) 16–28, 16–32
    (h) 16–32, 16–35
    (i) 16–30, 16–34,
            16–35
    (j) 16–39, 16–34
    (k) 16–42
    (n) 16–42
    (q) 16–25
    art.3 .... 15–01, 16–12
    art.4 .... 16–21, 16–34
    art.6 16–36
    art.7 .... 16–13, 16–58
    art.9 .... 16–32, 16–38
    art.10 16–38
    art.11 .... 16–21, 16–39
    arts 11—13 16–32
    art.13(1) 16–40
    (2) 16–40
    art.14 16–40
    (3)(c) 16–25
    art.15 16–32
    (1) 16–41
    (2) 16–34, 16–35,
            16–42
    (3) 16–42
    art.16(1) 16–35
    (3) 16–28
    art.17 .... 16–32, 16–35,
            16–36
    (1) 16–32, 16–34
    (2) 16–32, 16–34,
            16–35
    art.19 .... 16–13, 16–32,
            16–45
    (1) 16–43

    art.20 .... 16–42, 16–43,
            16–45
    (1) 16–43
    (2) 16–25, 16–42,
            16–43
    art.21 .... 5–02, 16–13,
            16–42, 16–43,
            16–45
    (1) 16–25, 16–43
    (2) 16–43
    (3) 16–25, 16–43
    art.22(1) 16–43, 16–45
    (2) 16–43
    (3) 16–45
    art.23 .... 16–21, 16–25,
            16–43
    art.24 ...... 16–25, 16–38
    art.25 16–42
    arts 25—27 16–23
    art.26 .... 16–21, 16–42
    art.27 .... 16–42, 16–44
    art.28 .... 16–25, 16–31,
            16–32, 16–42
    art.29 .... 16–13, 16–25,
            16–45
    art.30 16–23
    art.31 .... 16–35, 16–46
    art.32 16–47
    Sch.2 Pt 8 16–13
    Sch.3 Pt 2 16–13
2007 Cross-Border Insolvency
        Regulations (Northern
        Ireland) (SI 2007/
        115) 16–11
    Financial Services and
        Markets Act 2000
        (Markets in Financial
        Instruments) Regulations
        (SI 2007/126) 1–72
2008 Non-Domestic Rating
        (Unoccupied Property)
        (England) Regulations
        (SI 2008/386) 8–33,
            11–105
    Large and Medium-Sized
        Companies and Groups
        (Accounts and Reports)
        Regulations (SI 2008/410)
        Sch.1 Pt 2 para.11 4–35
    Accounting Standards
        (Prescribed Body)
        Regulations (SI 2008/651)
        reg.2 4–32

2009   Environmental Damage
          (Prevention and
          Remediation) Regulations
          (SI 2009/153) 8–30
       Company (Disqualification
          Orders) Regulations (SI
          2009/2471) 14–84

2011   Investment Bank Special
          Administration Regulations
          (SI 2011/245) 1–59

Table of European and International Treaties and Conventions

1950 European Convention on
Human Rights 11–87
Protocol No.1 art.1 13–41
1957 EC Treaty. *See* Treaty on
the Functioning of the
European Union
1968 Brussels Convention on
Jurisdiction and
Enforcement of
Judgments in Civil
and Commercial
Matters 15–02, 15–03,
15–34
art.1 15–02
1980 Convention on the Law
applicable to Contractual
Obligations (Rome
Convention)
art.1(2)(e) 15–02
art.2 .... 15–92, 15–98
art.6 15–98
art.7 15–98
1985 UNCITRAL Model Law on
International Commercial
Arbitration 16–18
1990 European Convention on
certain International
Aspects of
Bankruptcy 15–71
1997 UNCITRAL Model Law
on Cross-Border
Insolvency 1–18, 1–20,
7–22, 15–01, 15–20,
15–56, 15–61, 16–01,
16–07, 16–08, 16–10,
16–11, 16–17—16–47,
16–57, 16–63

art.2 .... 16–19, 16–31
(c) 16–07
art.8 16–22
art.13 16–19
art.14 16–19
art.21(1)(a)—(f) 16–19
(g) 16–19
art.27 16–65
art.28 .... 16–19, 16–21,
16–31
2001 Convention on International
Interests in Mobile
Equipment
Protocol on Aircraft
Equipment 15–01, 15–63
art.I(m) 15–63
art.XI 15–01
2002 Convention on the Law
applicable to certain
Rights in respect of
Securities Held with an
Intermediary
art.11(1) 16–36
2006 Convention on the Law
applicable to certain
Rights in respect of
Securities Held with an
Intermediary (Hague
XXXVI) 1–65
2007 Lisbon Treaty 15–04
2008 Treaty on the Functioning
of the European Union
art.61(c) EC (now art.67
TFEU) 15–04
art.67(1) EC
(repealed) 15–04
art.267 (ex 234 EC) 15–04

Table of EU Directives

1980   Dir.80/97 on insolvency
    [1980] OJ L282/23 8–25
    art.8 8–25

1998   Dir.98/26 on settlement
    finality [1998] OJ
    L166/45 .... 1–17, 1–64,
                 1–65, 1–67,
                 15–01, 15–93
    art.9(2) 1–65

2001   Dir.2001/17 on reorganisation
    and winding up of insurance
    undertakings [2001] OJ
    L110/28 .... 1–17, 1–61,
                 15–01
    art.2(c) 11–10
    Dir.2001/23 on acquired rights
    [2001] OJ L82/16   8–24, 15–98
    art.8(7) 15–98
    Dir.2001/24 on reorganisation
    and winding up of credit
    institutions [2001] OJ
    L125/15 ... 1–17, 1–60, 5–02,
                 15–01, 16–05

2002   Dir.2002/47 on financial
    collateral arrangements
    [2002] OJ L168/43 1–06,
       1–17, 1–64, 1–66—1–71,
       13–123, 15–01, 15–93

Preamble paras
  (9)—(10) 1–66, 1–69
  art.1(4)(a) 1–67
    (5) 1–66, 1–69
  art.2(1)(d) 1–67
    (e) 1–67
    (l) 1–70
    (n) 1–71
    (2) 1–67
    (3) 1–67
  art.3 .... **1–69**
    (1) 1–66, 1–69
    (2) 1–66, 1–69
  art.6 1–68
  art.7 1–71
  art.8 1–71

2004   Dir.2004/25 on takeover
    bids [2004] OJ
    L142/12 12–12
    Dir.2004/35 on environmental
    damage [2004] OJ
    L143/56 8–30

2006   Dir.2006/48 on capital
    requirements [2006]
    OJ L177/1 .... 1–17, 9–09
    Dir.2006/49 on capital
    adequacy [2006] OJ
    L177/201 .... 1–17, 9–09

Table of EU Regulations

1985   Reg.2137/85 on the
European Economic
Interest Grouping (EEIG)
[1985] OJ L199/1 3–12
    art.24(1) 3–12
2000   Reg.1346/2000 on insolvency
proceedings [2000] OJ
L160/1 .... 1–17, 1–27,
5–01, 5–08, 12–28,
15–04—15–98, 16–05,
16–07, 16–08, 16–10,
16–11, 16–12, 16–15,
16–19, 16–20, 16–22,
16–28, 16–29, 16–30,
16–31, 16–34, 16–35,
16–48, 16–58, 16–63
    Preamble 15–06
    recital (4) 15–47
    recital (9) 15–18
    recital (10) 15–13
    recital (11) 15–22
    recital (13) .. 15–49, 15–53,
16–28
    recital (14) 15–17
    recital (15) 15–24
    recital (16) 15–47
    recital (17) 15–47
    recital (18) 15–47
    recital (19) 15–47
    recital (22) 15–28
    recital (24) 15–71
    recital (25) 15–47
    art.1(1) 15–11, 15–15
    (2) 15–18
    art.2(a) 15–11
    (b) 5–17, 15–06, 15–13
    (c) 15–13
    (d) 15–13
    (f) 15–06, 15–39, 15–41
    (g) 15–49, 15–82,
15–83, 15–84, 15–85
    (h) 15–62
    art.3 .... 12–26, 15–13, 15–17,
15–24, 15–29
    (1) 5–17, 15–36,
15–47, 15–48,
15–49, 15–53
    (2) 15–62, 15–68, 16–07
    (3) 15–45, 15–59, 15–60

    (4) 15–23
    (b) 15–47
  art.4 .... 15–19, 15–45,
15–46, 15–70—15–98
    (1) 15–70, 15–90
    (2) 15–24, 15–70, **15–72**
    (a)–(m) 15–70
    (b) 15–75
    (d) 15–92
    (m) 15–45, 15–71,
15–75, 15–91,
15–92, 15–95,
15–97, 15–98
  art.5 .... 15–45, 15–46, 15–49,
15–71, **15–74**, 15–75,
15–79, 15–83, 15–86,
15–92, 15–94, 15–96,
15–97, 15–98
    (1) 15–80, 15–82,
15–86—15–92
    (2) 15–70, 15–76,
15–78—15–80
    (3) 15–76, 15–78, 15–81
    (4) 15–75, 15–91
  arts 5–15 ...... 15–19, 15–71,
15–72
  art.6 15–71
    (1) 15–72, 15–92
    (2) 15–92
  art.7 .... 15–45, 15–49,
15–71, 15–94
    (2) 15–95
  art.8 .... 15–96, 15–98
  arts 8–11 15–71
  art.9 .... 15–93, 15–98
    (1) 15–97
    (2) 15–97
  art.10 15–98
  art.11 15–98
  art.13 ... 15–71, 15–72, 15–75,
15–91, 15–97, 15–98
  art.14 .... 15–71, 15–98
  art.15 .... 15–71, 15–98
  art.16 .... 15–13, **15–28**,
15–31, 15–47
    (1) 15–29, 15–45
  art.17 .... **15–28**
    (1) 15–45, 15–68
    (2) 15–68

art.18 15–59
  (1) 15–45, 15–59
  (2) 15–59
  (3) 15–45, 15–59
art.20(2) 15–69
art.21(1) 15–59
art.22(1) 15–59
art.25 . . . . **15–28**, 15–34
  (1) 15–07, 15–09,
              15–34, 15–35
  (2) 15–02
art.26 . . . . **15–36**, 15–67
art.27 . . . . 15–13, 15–88
art.28 . . . . 15–68, 15–70
art.29 . . . . 15–13, 15–45,
              15–47, 15–59
  (3) 5–17
art.31 15–69
arts 31–35 15–21
art.32 . . . . 15–66, 15–69
art.33 15–59
art.34(1) 15–59
art.35 15–66
art.37 . . . . 15–21, 15–59
art.38 . . . . 15–06, 15–35,
       15–48, 15–70, 15–89
Annex A 15–04, 15–06,
             15–11, 15–12,
             15–13, 15–14

Annex B 15–04, 15–13,
                     15–60
Annex C 5–17, 15–04,
              15–06, 15–13,
                     15–14
2001 Reg.44/2001 on jurisdiction
     and judgments
     (Brussels I) [2001] OJ
     L12/1 . . . . 15–02, 15–05,
                 15–34, 15–38,
                 15–94, 16–48
     art.1(2)(b) 16–48
     art.22(2) 16–48
Reg.2157/2001 on the Statute for
     a European company
     [2001] OJ L294/1 5–22
2007 Reg.864/2007 on law
     applicable to non-
     contractual obligations
     (Rome II) [2007] OJ
     L199/40 15–92
2008 Reg.593/2008 on law
     applicable to non-
     contractual obligations
     (Rome I) [2008] OJ
     L177/6 15–92
2010 Reg.210/2010 codifying
     Annexes to Reg.1346/2000
     [2010] OJ L65/1 15–04

Table of Uniform Rules

2007 ICC Uniform Customs
      and Practice for
      Documentary Credits
      art.3 15–85

2010 ICC Uniform Rules for
      Demand Guarantees
      art.3 15–85
      art.15 13–102

Table of UK Cases

A Straume (UK) Ltd v Bradlor Developments Ltd [2000] B.C.C. 333; (2000) 2 T.C.L.R. 409, Ch D 11–67

A&C Supplies Ltd, Re [1998] B.C.C. 708; [1998] 1 B.C.L.C. 603; [1998] B.P.I.R. 303; (1997) 94(43) L.S.G. 29, Ch D 10–14

A&J Fabrications (Batley) Ltd v Grant Thornton (A Firm) (No.1) [1999] B.C.C. 807; [1998] 2 B.C.L.C. 227; [2000] Lloyd's Rep. P.N. 565, Ch D 5–03

AA Mutual International Insurance Co Ltd, Re [2004] EWHC 2430 (Ch); [2005] 2 B.C.L.C. 8 4–28

ABC Coupler and Engineering Co (No.3), Re [1970] 1 W.L.R. 702; [1970] 1 All E.R. 650; (1970) 114 S.J. 242, Ch D 3–11, 8–33, 8–38

AES Barry Ltd v TXU Europe Energy Trading (In Administration) [2004] EWHC 1757 (Ch); [2005] 2 B.C.L.C. 22; [2006] B.P.I.R. 1109 11–79

AG (Manchester) Ltd (formerly Accident Group Ltd) (In Liquidation), Re [2008] EWHC 64 (Ch); [2008] B.C.C. 497; [2008] 1 B.C.L.C. 321 14–75

AI Levy (Holdings) Ltd, Re [1964] Ch. 19; [1963] 2 W.L.R. 1464; [1963] 2 All E.R. 556; (1963) 107 S.J. 416, Ch D 13–135

Abbey National Building Society v Cann [1991] 1 A.C. 56; [1990] 2 W.L.R. 832; [1990] 1 All E.R. 1085; [1990] 2 F.L.R. 122; (1990) 22 H.L.R. 360; (1990) 60 P. & C.R. 278; (1990) 87(17) L.S.G. 32; (1990) 140 N.L.J. 477, HL 6–33

Abou-Rahmah v Abacha [2006] EWCA Civ 1492; [2007] Bus. L.R. 220; [2007] 1 All E.R. (Comm) 827; [2007] 1 Lloyd's Rep. 115; [2007] W.T.L.R. 1; (2006–07) 9 I.T.E.L.R. 401 14–24

Addlestone Linoleum Co, Re (1888) L.R. 37 Ch. D. 191, CA 8–27

Agip (Africa) Ltd v Jackson [1991] Ch. 547; [1991] 3 W.L.R. 116; [1992] 4 All E.R. 451; (1991) 135 S.J. 117, CA (Civ Div) 6–08

Agnew v IRC. See Brumark Investments Ltd, Re

Agricultural Mortgage Corp Plc v Woodward [1994] B.C.C. 688; [1995] 1 B.C.L.C. 1; [1996] 1 F.L.R. 226; [1996] 2 F.C.R. 796; (1995) 70 P. & C.R. 53; [1995] 1 E.G.L.R. 1; [1995] 04 E.G. 143; [1996] Fam. Law 149; [1994] E.G. 98 (C.S.), CA (Civ Div) 13–24, 13–27, **13–28**, 13–38, 13–137

Agriplant Services Ltd (In Liquidation), Re [1997] B.C.C. 842; [1997] 2 B.C.L.C. 598, Ch D 13–101

Ailyan v Smith [2010] EWHC 24 (Ch); [2010] B.P.I.R. 289 13–26

Aim Underwriting Agencies (Ireland) Ltd, Re [2004] EWHC 2114 (Ch); [2005] I.L.Pr. 22 15–56

Air Ecosse Ltd v Civil Aviation Authority, 1987 S.C. 285; 1987 S.L.T. 751; (1987) 3 B.C.C. 492, IH (2 Div) 11–67

Airbase Services (UK) Ltd, Re. See Thorniley v Revenue and Customs Commissioners

Airlines Airspares v Handley Page [1970] Ch. 193; [1970] 2 W.L.R. 163; [1970] 1 All E.R. 29, Ch D 10–53

Akers v Lomas [2002] 1 B.C.L.C. 655; [2002] B.P.I.R. 606, Ch D 16–61

Aktieselskabet Dansk Skibsfinansiering v Bros [2001] 2 B.C.L.C. 324 14–24

Albany Building Ltd, Re [2007] B.C.C. 591, Ch D 13–127

Alderson v Temple, 96 E.R. 384; (1768) 1 Wm. Bl. 660, KB 1–10

Alderson v Temple, 98 E.R. 165; (1768) 4 Burr. 2235, KB 13–71

Alexander Sheridan Ltd v Beaujersey Ltd [2004] EWHC 2072 (Ch) 5–13
Alipour v Ary [1997] 1 W.L.R. 534; [1997] B.C.C. 377; [1997] 1 B.C.L.C. 557,
    CA (Civ Div) 5–13
Allied Business & Financial Consultants Ltd, Re [2008] EWHC 1973 (Ch);
    [2009] B.C.C. 517; [2009] 1 B.C.L.C. 328 14–12
Allso v Secretary of State for Trade and Industry [2004] EWHC 862 (Ch);
    [2004] 1 W.L.R. 1566; [2004] 3 All E.R. 56; [2004] B.C.C. 631 ..... 5–11, 5–21
Alman v Approach Housing Ltd [2002] B.C.C. 723; [2001] 1 B.C.L.C. 530;
    [2001] B.P.I.R. 203, Ch D 12–51
Alpa Lighting Ltd, Re [1997] B.P.I.R. 341, CA (Civ Div) 12–26, 12–42
Aluminium Industrie Vaassen BV v Romalpa Aluminium [1976] 1 W.L.R.
    676; [1976] 2 All E.R. 552; [1976] 1 Lloyd's Rep. 443; (1976) 120 S.J.
    95, CA (Civ Div) 6–46
Ambrose Lake Tin & Copper Mining Co Ex p. Moss, Re (1880) L.R. 14 Ch.
    D. 390, CA 14–16
American Express International Banking Corp v Hurley [1985] 3 All E.R.
    564; (1986) 2 B.C.C. 98993; [1986] B.C.L.C. 52; [1985] F.L.R. 350;
    (1985) 135 N.L.J. 1034, QBD 10–75
Anchor Line (Henderson Bros) Ltd, Re [1937] Ch. 483; [1937] 2 All E.R.
    823, Ch D 3–02
Anderson v Hyde (t/a Hyde Property Services) [1996] N.I. 304; [1996]
    2 B.C.L.C. 144, CA (NI) 10–52
Andrabell, Re [1984] 3 All E.R. 407, Ch D 9–26
Andrew Rhodes Ltd v Rhodes [2005] EWHC 1005 (Ch) 14–56
Anglo American Insurance Co Ltd, Re [2001] 1 B.C.L.C. 755, Ch D 12–19,
                                                                    12–20
Anglo-Austrian Printing and Publishing Union (No.3), Re [1895] 2 Ch. 891,
    Ch D 14–16, 14–20
Anglo French Co-operative Society Ex p. Pelly, Re (1882) L.R. 21 Ch. D.
    492, CA 14–16
Appleyard Ltd v Ritecrown Ltd [2007] EWHC 3515 (Ch); [2009] B.P.I.R.
    235 12–55
Applied Database Ltd, Re [1995] 1 B.C.L.C. 272, Ch D 5–20
Applied Database Ltd v Secretary of State for Trade and Industry. *See*
    Applied Database Ltd, Re
Arbuthnot Leasing International Ltd v Havelet Leasing Ltd (No.2) [1990]
    B.C.C. 636, Ch D 13–137, 13–139
Arctic Engineering (No.2), Re [1986] 1 W.L.R. 686; [1986] 2 All E.R. 346;
    (1985) 1 B.C.C. 99563; [1986] P.C.C. 1; (1986) 83 L.S.G. 1895; (1985)
    130 S.J. 429, Ch D 14–63
Arena Corp Ltd, Re. *See* Customs and Excise Commissioners v Arena Corp
    Ltd (In Provisional Liquidation)
Aries Tanker Corp v Total Transport Ltd (The Aries) [1977] 1 W.L.R. 185;
    [1977] 1 All E.R. 398; [1977] 1 Lloyd's Rep. 334; (1977) 121 S.J.
    117, HL 9–04
Aries, The. *See* Aries Tanker Corp v Total Transport Ltd
Armour v Thyssen Edelstahlwerke AG [1991] 2 A.C. 339; [1990] 3 W.L.R.
    810; [1990] 3 All E.R. 481; [1991] 1 Lloyd's Rep. 95; 1990 S.L.T. 891;
    [1990] B.C.C. 925; [1991] B.C.L.C. 28; (1990) 134 S.J. 1337, HL 6–46
Ashton, Re [1920] 2 Ch. 481, Ch D 7–09
Asphaltic Wood Pavement Co, Re (1885) L.R. 30 Ch. D. 216, CA 9–28
Astor Chemical Ltd v Synthetic Technology Ltd [1990] B.C.C. 97; [1990]
    B.C.L.C. 1, Ch D 11–102

Atlantic Computer Systems Plc, Re [1992] Ch. 505; [1992] 2 W.L.R. 367; [1992] 1 All E.R. 476; [1990] B.C.C. 859; [1991] B.C.L.C. 606, CA (Civ Div) 8–33, 10–52, 11–64, **11–77**, 11–78, 11–91, 11–104, 11–105

Attorney General's Reference (No.2 of 1982), Re [1984] Q.B. 624; [1984] 2 W.L.R. 447; [1984] 2 All E.R. 216; (1984) 1 B.C.C. 98973; (1984) 78 Cr. App. R. 131; [1985] Crim. L.R. 241; (1984) 81 L.S.G. 279; (1984) 128 S.J. 221, CA (Crim Div) 14–19

Attorney General's Reference (No.7 of 2000), Re [2001] EWCA Crim 888; [2001] 1 W.L.R. 1879; [2001] 2 Cr. App. R. 19; [2001] H.R.L.R. 41; [2001] B.P.I.R. 953; [2001] Crim. L.R. 736; (2001) 98(22) L.S.G. 35; (2001) 145 S.J.L.B. 109 11–87

Augustus Barnett & Son Ltd, Re (1986) 2 B.C.C. 98904; [1986] P.C.C. 167, Ch D 14–23, 14–24

Auto Management Services Ltd v Oracle Fleet UK Ltd [2007] EWHC 392 (Ch); [2008] B.C.C. 761 .... 11–29, 11–47

Automatic Bottle Makers Ltd, Re [1926] Ch. 412, CA 10–12

Aveling Barford Ltd v Perion Ltd (1989) 5 B.C.C. 677; [1989] B.C.L.C. 626; [1989] P.C.C. 370, Ch D 13–01, 14–19

Ayala Holdings Ltd (No.2), Re [1996] 1 B.C.L.C. 467, Ch D 5–06

Ayerst (Inspector of Taxes) v C&K (Construction) Ltd [1976] A.C. 167; [1975] 3 W.L.R. 16; [1975] 2 All E.R. 537; [1975] S.T.C. 345; [1975] T.R. 117; (1975) 119 S.J. 424, HL 3–04, 3–09, 3–10

Azoff Don Commercial Bank, Re [1954] Ch. 315; [1954] 2 W.L.R. 654; [1954] 1 All E.R. 947; (1954) 98 S.J. 252, Ch D 16–50, 16–51

B Johnson & Co (Builders) Ltd, Re [1955] Ch. 634; [1955] 3 W.L.R. 269; [1955] 2 All E.R. 775; (1955) 99 S.J. 490, CA 10–53

B Mullan & Sons (Contractors) Ltd v Ross. *See* McLaughlin & Harvey Plc (In Liquidation), Re

BCPMS (Europe) Ltd v GMAC Commercial Financial Plc [2006] EWHC 3744 (Ch) 11–09

BHT (UK) Ltd, Re [2004] EWHC 201 (Ch); [2004] B.C.C. 301; [2004] 1 B.C.L.C. 569 10–63

BICC Plc v Burndy Corp [1985] Ch. 232; [1985] 2 W.L.R. 132; [1985] 1 All E.R. 417; [1985] R.P.C. 273; (1984) 81 L.S.G. 3011; (1984) 128 S.J. 750, CA (Civ Div) 9–04

BLV Realty Organization Ltd v Batten [2009] EWHC 2994 (Ch); [2010] B.P.I.R. 277 .... **11–25**, 11–93, 15–14

BNY Corporate Trustee Services Ltd v Eurosail–UK 2007–3BL Plc [2011] EWCA Civ 227 .... 4–06, 4–23, 4–34, 4–37

BRAC Rent-A-Car International Inc, Re [2003] EWHC 128 (Ch); [2003] 1 W.L.R. 1421; [2003] 2 All E.R. 201; [2003] B.C.C. 248; [2003] 1 B.C.L.C. 470; [2003] B.P.I.R. 531; (2003) 100(14) L.S.G. 28 15–17

BTR Plc, Re [1999] 2 B.C.L.C. 675, Ch D 12–19, 12–23

BTR Plc (Leave to Appeal), Re [2000] 1 B.C.L.C. 740, CA (Civ Div) 12–15

Bacal Contracting Ltd v Modern Engineering (Bristol) Ltd [1980] 2 All E.R. 655, QBD 10–52

Bailey v Finch (1871) L.R. 7 Q.B. 34 9–06

Ballast Plc (In Administration), Re [2004] EWHC 2356 (Ch); [2005] 1 W.L.R. 1928; [2005] 1 All E.R. 630; [2005] B.C.C. 96; [2005] 1 B.C.L.C. 446; (2004) 101(44) L.S.G. 33 .... 11–115, 11–116

Ballast Plc, Re [2006] EWHC 3189 (Ch); [2007] B.C.C. 620; [2007] B.P.I.R. 117; [2007] Lloyd's Rep. I.R. 742 6–30

Bamberski v Krombach (C–7/98) [2001] Q.B. 709; [2001] 3 W.L.R.
488; [2001] All E.R. (EC) 584; [2000] E.C.R. I–1935; [2001] I.L.Pr. 36,
ECJ 15–37
Banco Nacional de Cuba v Cosmos Trading Corp [2000] B.C.C. 910; [2000]
1 B.C.L.C. 813, CA (Civ Div) 16–50
Banco de Portugal v Waddell (1879–80) L.R. 5 App. Cas. 161, HL 16–63
Bang & Olufsen UK Ltd v Ton Système Ltd Unreported July 16, 1993, CA
(Civ Div) 5–06
Bangla Television Ltd (In Liquidation), Re [2009] EWHC 1632 (Ch); [2010]
B.C.C. 143 14–54
Bank of Baroda v Panessar [1987] Ch. 335; [1987] 2 W.L.R. 208; [1986] 3 All
E.R. 751; (1986) 2 B.C.C. 99288; [1987] P.C.C. 165; (1987) 84 L.S.G.
339; (1986) 136 N.L.J. 963; (1987) 131 S.J. 21, Ch D 10–30, 10–32
Bank of Credit and Commerce International SA, Re [1993] B.C.C. 787,
Ch D 16–59, 16–60, 16–61
Bank of Credit and Commerce International SA, Re. *See also* Morris v
Bank of India
Bank of Credit and Commerce International SA (In Liquidation) (No.2),
Re [1992] B.C.L.C. 579, CA (Civ Div) 16–51
Bank of Credit and Commerce International SA (In Liquidation) (No.3),
Re [1992] B.C.C. 715; [1993] B.C.L.C. 1490, CA (Civ Div) 1–28, 1–55, 16–65
Bank of Credit and Commerce International SA (In Liquidation) (No.8),
Re [1998] A.C. 214; [1997] 3 W.L.R. 909; [1997] 4 All E.R. 568; [1998]
Lloyd's Rep. Bank. 48; [1997] B.C.C. 965; [1998] 1 B.C.L.C. 68; [1998]
B.P.I.R. 211; (1997) 94(44) L.S.G. 35; (1997) 147 N.L.J. 1653;
(1997) 141 S.J.L.B. 229, HL 2–28, 3–07, 8–12, 9–40, 9–42, 14–51
Bank of Credit and Commerce International SA (In Liquidation) (No.9),
Re [1994] 1 W.L.R. 708; [1994] 3 All E.R. 764; [1994] 2 B.C.L.C. 664;
[1994] I.L.Pr. 300, CA (Civ Div) 16–02
Bank of Credit and Commerce International SA (In Liquidation) (No.11),
Re [1997] Ch. 213; [1997] 2 W.L.R. 172; [1996] 4 All E.R. 796; [1996]
B.C.C. 980; [1997] 1 B.C.L.C. 80, Ch D 16–09, 16–60, 16–61, 16–64
Bank of Credit and Commerce International SA (In Liquidation) v Al-Saud
[1997] 6 Bank. L.R. 121; [1997] B.C.C. 63; [1997] 1 B.C.L.C. 457;
(1996) 93(36) L.S.G. 35; (1996) 140 S.J.L.B. 209, CA (Civ Div) 9–24
Bank of Credit and Commerce International (Overseas) Ltd (In
Liquidation) v Habib Bank Ltd [1999] 1 W.L.R. 42; [1998] 4 All E.R.
753; [1998] 2 B.C.L.C. 459; [1999] B.P.I.R. 1, Ch D 9–23
Bank of Ethiopia v National Bank of Egypt and Liguori [1937] Ch. 513,
Ch D 16–57
Banque Belge pour l'Etranger v Hambrouck [1921] 1 K.B. 321, CA 6–08
Banque des Marchands de Moscou (Koupetschesky) v Kindersley [1951]
Ch. 112; [1950] 2 All E.R. 549; (1950) 66 T.L.R. (Pt 2) 654, CA 16–50
Barbados Trust Co Ltd (formerly CI Trustees (Asia Pacific) Ltd) v Bank of
Zambia [2007] EWCA Civ 148; [2007] 2 All E.R. (Comm) 445; [2007]
1 Lloyd's Rep. 495; [2007] 1 C.L.C. 434; (2006–07) 9 I.T.E.L.R. 689, CA
(Civ Div) 6–10
Barclay v Astley Industrial Trust [1970] 2 Q.B. 527; [1970] 2 W.L.R. 876;
[1970] 1 All E.R. 719, QBD 13–132
Barclays Bank Plc v Eustice [1995] 1 W.L.R. 1238; [1995] 4 All E.R. 511;
[1995] B.C.C. 978; [1995] 2 B.C.L.C. 630; (1995) 145 N.L.J. 1503;
(1995) 70 P. & C.R. D29, CA (Civ Div) 13–28
Barclays Bank Plc v HHY Luxembourg Sarl [2010] EWCA Civ 1248 12–04

Barclays Bank Plc v Homan [1992] B.C.C. 757; [1993] B.C.L.C. 680, CA
 (Civ Div) 16–62, 16–65
Barclays Bank Ltd v Quistclose Investments Ltd [1970] A.C. 567; [1968] 3
 W.L.R. 1097; [1968] 3 All E.R. 651; (1968) 112 S.J. 903, HL 6–42
Barclays Bank Ltd v TOSG Trust Fund Ltd [1984] A.C. 626; [1984] 2 W.L.R.
 650; [1984] 1 All E.R. 1060; (1984) 1 B.C.C. 99081; (1984) 81 L.S.G.
 1360; (1984) 134 N.L.J. 656; (1984) 128 S.J. 261, HL 8–14, 13–128
Barclays Mercantile Business Finance Ltd v Sibec Developments Ltd [1992]
 1 W.L.R. 1253; [1993] 2 All E.R. 195; [1993] B.C.C. 148; [1993]
 B.C.L.C. 1077, Ch D 11–53, 11–58, 11–108
Barings Plc (No.5), Re. *See* Secretary of State for Trade and Industry v
 Baker (No.6)
Barlow Clowes International Ltd (In Liquidation) v Eurotrust International
 Ltd [2005] UKPC 37; [2006] 1 W.L.R. 1476; [2006] 1 All E.R. 333;
 [2006] 1 All E.R. (Comm) 478; [2006] 1 Lloyd's Rep. 225; [2005]
 W.T.L.R. 1453; (2005–06) 8 I.T.E.L.R. 347; (2005) 102(44) L.S.G. 32;
 [2006] 1 P. & C.R. DG16 14–24
Barlow Clowes International Ltd (In Liquidation) v Vaughan [1992] 4 All
 E.R. 22; [1992] B.C.L.C. 910, CA (Civ Div) 3–03
Barn Crown Ltd, Re [1995] 1 W.L.R. 147; [1994] 4 All E.R. 42; [1994]
 B.C.C. 381; [1994] 2 B.C.L.C. 186, Ch D 13–128, 13–131
Barrow Borough Transport Ltd, Re [1990] Ch. 227; [1989] 3 W.L.R. 858;
 (1989) 5 B.C.C. 646; [1989] B.C.L.C. 653; (1989) 86(42) L.S.G. 39;
 (1989) 133 S.J. 1513, Ch D 11–67
Barrows v Chief Land Registrar, *The Times*, October 20, 1977 ...... 10–41, 10–66
Barter Ex p. *See* Walker Ex p. Black, Re
Barton Manufacturing Co Ltd, Re [1998] B.C.C. 827; [1999] 1 B.C.L.C 740,
 Ch D 13–40
Base Metal Trading Ltd v Shamurin [2004] EWCA Civ 1316; [2005]
 1 W.L.R. 1157; [2005] 1 All E.R. (Comm) 17; [2005] B.C.C. 325; [2005]
 2 B.C.L.C. 171; [2004] 2 C.L.C. 916; (2004) 148 S.J.L.B. 1281 15–02
Bastable Ex p. Trustee, Re [1901] 2 K.B. 518, CA 6–23
Bath Glass Ltd, Re (1988) 4 B.C.C. 130; [1988] B.C.L.C. 329, Ch D 14–73,
 14–75, 14–76
Bayoil SA, Re [1999] 1 W.L.R. 147; [1999] 1 All E.R. 374; [1999] 1 Lloyd's
 Rep. 211; [1998] B.C.C. 988; [1999] 1 B.C.L.C. 62; (1998) 142 S.J.L.B.
 251, CA (Civ Div) 5–13, 5–18
Beacon Leisure Ltd, Re [1991] B.C.C. 213; [1992] B.C.L.C. 565, Ch D 13–79
Beck Foods Ltd, Re. *See* Rees v Boston BC
Bell v Long [2008] EWHC 1273 (Ch); [2008] 2 B.C.L.C. 706; [2008] B.P.I.R.
 1211; [2008] 25 E.G. 172 (C.S.) 10–48, 10–49, 11–30
Bell Group Finance (Pty) Ltd (In Liquidation) v Bell Group (UK) Holdings
 Ltd [1996] B.C.C. 505; [1996] 1 B.C.L.C. 304, Ch D 2–06
Beloit Walmsley Ltd, Re [2008] EWHC 1888 (Ch); [2009] 1 B.C.L.C. 584;
 [2008] B.P.I.R. 1445 12–42
Benjamin Cope & Sons Ltd, Re [1914] 1 Ch. 800, Ch D 10–12
Bentinck v Fenn (1887) L.R. 12 App. Cas. 652, HL 14–14
Berkeley Applegate (Investment Consultants) Ltd (No.3), Re (1989) 5
 B.C.C. 803, Ch D 3–03
Berton v Alliance Economic Investment Co Ltd [1922] 1 K.B. 742, CA 13–91
Beverley Group Plc v McClue [1995] B.C.C. 751; [1995] 2 B.C.L.C. 407;
 [1996] B.P.I.R. 25, Ch D 12–41
Bibby Trade Finance Ltd v McKay [2006] EWHC 2836 (Ch) 11–96

Biosource Technologies Inc v Axis Genetics Plc (In Administration) [2000]
  B.C.C. 943; [2000] 1 B.C.L.C. 286; [2000] F.S.R. 448; (2000) 23(2)
  I.P.D. 23011; (1999) 96(45) L.S.G. 33; (1999) 143 S.J.L.B. 278 11–67
Bishopsgate Investment Management Ltd (In Provisional Liquidation) v
  Maxwell [1993] Ch. 1; [1992] 2 W.L.R. 991; [1992] 2 All E.R. 856;
  [1992] B.C.C. 222; (1992) 136 S.J.L.B. 69, CA (Civ Div) 11–87
Blackburne, Re (1892) 9 Morr. 249 8–44
Blackspur Group Plc (No.3), Re [2001] EWCA Civ 1595; [2004] B.C.C. 839;
  [2002] 2 B.C.L.C. 263 14–72
Bloom v Harms Offshore AHT Taurus GmbH & Co KG. *See* Harms
  Offshore AHT Taurus GmbH & Co KG v Bloom
Bloom v Pensions Regulator. *See* Nortel GmbH, Re
Bluebrook Ltd, Re [2009] EWHC 2114 (Ch); [2010] B.C.C. 209; [2010]
  1 B.C.L.C. 338 . . . . 1–46, 1–53, 2–21, 12–10, 12–23, 12–24
Booth v Hutchinson (1872–73) L.R. 15 Eq. 30, Ct of Chancery 9–28
Borland's Trustee v Steel Bros & Co Ltd [1901] 1 Ch. 279, Ch D 7–06, 7–08
Brabon, Re [2000] B.C.C. 1171; [2001] 1 B.C.L.C. 11; [2000] B.P.I.R. 537;
  [2000] E.G. 38 (C.S.); [2000] N.P.C. 21, Ch D 13–20, 13–26, 13–33
Bracey v Read [1963] Ch. 88; [1962] 3 W.L.R. 1194; [1962] 3 All E.R. 472;
  (1962) 106 S.J. 878, Ch D 11–66
Bradley-Hole (A Bankrupt), Re [1995] 1 W.L.R. 1097; [1995] 4 All E.R.
  865; [1995] B.C.C. 418; [1995] 2 B.C.L.C. 163; [1995] 2 F.L.R. 838;
  [1996] 2 F.C.R. 259; [1995] Fam. Law 673, Ch D 12–41
Brady v Brady [1989] A.C. 755; [1988] 2 W.L.R. 1308; [1988] 2 All E.R. 617;
  (1988) 4 B.C.C. 390; [1988] B.C.L.C. 579; [1988] P.C.C. 316; [1988]
  2 F.T.L.R. 181; (1988) 132 S.J. 820, HL 14–20
Brampton Manor (Leisure) Ltd, Re [2009] EWHC 1796 (Ch) 14–73
Brampton Manor (Leisure) Ltd v McLean [2006] EWHC 2983 (Ch); [2007]
  B.C.C. 640 10–26
Bristol Airport Plc v Powdrill [1990] Ch. 744; [1990] 2 W.L.R. 1362; [1990]
  2 All E.R. 493; [1990] B.C.C. 130; [1990] B.C.L.C. 585; (1990) 87(17)
  L.S.G. 28, CA (Civ Div) 6–03, **11–56**, 11–57, 11–58,
                                                                      11–59, 11–61, 11–67
Bristol & West Building Society v Mothew (t/a Stapley & Co) [1998] Ch. 1;
  [1997] 2 W.L.R. 436; [1996] 4 All E.R. 698; [1997] P.N.L.R. 11; (1998)
  75 P. & C.R. 241; [1996] E.G. 136 (C.S.); (1996) 146 N.L.J. 1273; (1996)
  140 S.J.L.B. 206; [1996] N.P.C. 126, CA (Civ Div) 10–48, 14–11
British Aviation Insurance Co Ltd, Re [2005] EWHC 1621 (Ch); [2006]
  B.C.C. 14; [2006] 1 B.C.L.C. 665; [2010] Lloyd's Rep. I.R. 254 . . 12–21, 12–23
British Eagle International Airlines Ltd v Compagnie Nationale Air France
  [1975] 1 W.L.R. 758; [1975] 2 All E.R. 390; [1975] 2 Lloyd's Rep. 43;
  (1975) 119 S.J. 368, HL 3–05, 6–17, 6–18, 7–03, 7–18,
                                                                8–08, 8–11, 8–12, 9–14, 9–15
British Equitable Bond and Mortgage Corp Ltd, Re [1910] 1 Ch. 574,
  Ch D 4–27
British & Commonwealth Holdings Plc (No.3), Re [1992] 1 W.L.R. 672;
  [1992] B.C.C. 58; [1992] B.C.L.C. 322, Ch D 12–22, 12–41
British & Commonwealth Holdings Plc v Barclays Bank Plc [1996] 1 W.L.R.
  1; [1996] 1 All E.R. 381; [1996] 5 Bank. L.R. 47; [1995] B.C.C. 1059;
  [1996] 1 B.C.L.C. 1; (1995) 139 S.J.L.B. 194, CA (Civ Div) 1–53
Brown v City of London Corp [1996] 1 W.L.R. 1070; [1996] B.C.C.
  351; [1996] 1 B.C.L.C. 446; [1996] 1 E.G.L.R. 139; [1996] 22 E.G.
  118; [1996] R.A. 93; [1995] E.G. 189 (C.S.); [1995] N.P.C. 180,
  Ch D 10–52, 10–58

Brumark Investments Ltd, Re [2001] UKPC 28; [2001] 2 A.C. 710; [2001] 3 W.L.R. 454; [2001] Lloyd's Rep. Bank. 251; [2001] B.C.C. 259; [2001] 2 B.C.L.C. 188 .... 1–15, 10–16
Bryanston Finance Ltd v De Vries (No.2) [1976] Ch. 63; [1976] 2 W.L.R. 41; [1976] 1 All E.R. 25; (1975) 119 S.J. 709, CA (Civ Div) 5–19
Bryant Investment Co, Re [1974] 1 W.L.R. 826; [1974] 2 All E.R. 683; (1974) 118 S.J. 441, Ch D 4–18
Buchler v Talbot [2004] UKHL 9; [2004] 2 A.C. 298; [2004] 2 W.L.R. 582; [2004] 1 All E.R. 1289; [2004] B.C.C. 214; [2004] 1 B.C.L.C. 281; (2004) 101(12) L.S.G. 35; (2004) 154 N.L.J. 381; (2004) 148 S.J.L.B. 299 .... 1–10, 3–07, 3–10, 5–01, 8–51, 10–60, 10–62
Buckingham International Plc (In Liquidation) (No.1), Re [1997] B.C.C. 71; [1997] 1 B.C.L.C. 673, Ch D 3–10
Buhr v Barclays Bank Plc [2001] EWCA Civ 1223; [2002] B.P.I.R. 25; [2001] 31 E.G. 103 (C.S.); (2001) 98(31) L.S.G. 38; [2001] N.P.C. 124; [2002] 1 P. & C.R. DG7 9–26
Bulawayo Market and Offices Co Ltd, Re [1907] 2 Ch. 458, Ch D 14–05
Bunting Electric Manufacturing Co Ltd, Re [2005] EWHC 3345 (Ch); [2006] 1 B.C.L.C. 550 14–73
Butlers Wharf Ltd, Re [1995] B.C.C. 717; [1995] 2 B.C.L.C. 43, Ch D 8–44, 9–18
Butters v BBC Worldwide Ltd. *See* Perpetual Trustee Co Ltd v BNY Corporate Trustee Services Ltd
Bwllfa and Merthyr Dare Steam Collieries (1891) Ltd v Pontypridd Waterworks Co [1903] A.C. 426, HL 13–32
Byblos Bank SAL v Al–Khudhairy (1986) 2 B.C.C. 99549, CA (Civ Div) 4–04, 4–14, 4–34, 10–26
Byers v Yacht Bull Corp [2010] EWHC 133 (Ch); [2010] B.C.C. 368; [2010] 2 B.C.L.C. 169; [2010] I.L.Pr. 24; [2010] B.P.I.R. 535 .... 15–02, 15–34
CKE Engineering Ltd (In Administration), Re [2007] B.C.C. 975, Ch D 6–46
CPBD (No.001889 of 1975), Re [1975] C.L.Y. 322 5–18
Calgary and Edmonton Land Co Ltd (In Liquidation), Re [1975] 1 W.L.R. 355; [1975] 1 All E.R. 1046; (1974) 119 S.J. 150, Ch D 1–46
Calgary and Edmonton Land Co Ltd v Dobinson [1974] Ch. 102; [1974] 2 W.L.R. 143; [1974] 1 All E.R. 484; (1973) 26 P. & C.R. 516; (1973) 118 S.J. 99, Ch D 3–10
Cambridge Gas Transport Corp v Official Committee of Unsecured Creditors of Navigator Holdings Plc [2006] UKPC 26; [2007] 1 A.C. 508; [2006] 3 W.L.R. 689; [2006] 3 All E.R. 829; [2006] 2 All E.R. (Comm) 695; [2006] B.C.C. 962; [2007] 2 B.C.L.C. 141 ..... 1–19, 3–02, 3–13, 16–08, 16–30, 16–57, 16–58
Camdex International Ltd v Bank of Zambia (No.1) [1998] Q.B. 22; [1996] 3 W.L.R. 759; [1996] 3 All E.R. 431; [1996] C.L.C. 1477, CA (Civ Div) 5–06
Campbell v Commercial Banking Co of Sydney (1879) 40 L.T. 137 10–30
Canadian Land Reclaiming & Colonizing Co, Re (1880) L.R. 14 Ch. D. 660, CA 14–04
Cancol Ltd, Re [1996] 1 All E.R. 37; [1995] B.C.C. 1133; [1996] 1 B.C.L.C. 101; [1996] B.P.I.R. 252; [1995] E.G. 146 (C.S.); [1995] N.P.C. 156, Ch D.. 12–18, 12–41
Capital Annuities Ltd, Re [1979] 1 W.L.R. 170; [1978] 3 All E.R. 704; (1978) 122 S.J. 315, Ch D 4–19, 5–21
Capital Prime Properties Plc v Worthgate Ltd (In Liquidation) [2000] B.C.C. 525; [2000] 1 B.C.L.C. 647; [1999] E.G. 112 (C.S.), Ch D 6–30

Carecraft Construction Co Ltd, Re [1994] 1 W.L.R. 172; [1993] 4 All E.R.
499; [1993] B.C.C. 336; [1993] B.C.L.C. 1259, Ch D 14–70, 14–72
Cargo Agency Ltd, Re [1992] B.C.C. 388; [1992] B.C.L.C. 686, Ch D 14–80
Carr v British International Helicopters Ltd [1993] B.C.C. 855; [1994]
2 B.C.L.C. 474; [1994] I.C.R. 18; [1994] I.R.L.R. 212, EAT 11–67
Carreras Rothmans Ltd v Freeman Mathews Treasure Ltd (In Liquidation)
[1985] Ch. 207; [1984] 3 W.L.R. 1016; [1985] 1 All E.R. 155; (1984) 1
B.C.C. 99210; [1985] P.C.C. 222; (1984) 81 L.S.G. 2375; (1984) 128 S.J.
614, Ch D 6–42
Celestial Aviation Trading 71 Ltd v Paramount Airways Private Ltd [2010]
EWHC 185 (Comm); [2011] 1 All E.R. (Comm) 259; [2011] 1 Lloyd's
Rep. 9; [2010] 1 C.L.C. 165 7–05
Celtic Extraction Ltd (In Liquidation), Re [2001] Ch. 475; [2000] 2 W.L.R.
991; [1999] 4 All E.R. 684; [2000] B.C.C. 487; [1999] 2 B.C.L.C. 555;
[2000] Env. L.R. 86; [1999] B.P.I.R. 986; [1999] 3 E.G.L.R. 21; [1999]
46 E.G. 187; (1999) 96(32) L.S.G. 33; [1999] N.P.C. 92 . . . . . 2–25, 6–03, 6–07,
6–11, 6–29, 8–30
Central Sugar Factories of Brazil, Re [1894] 1 Ch. 369, Ch D 16–62
Centre Reinsurance International Co v Curzon Insurance Ltd [2006]
UKHL 45; [2007] Bus. L.R. 284; [2006] 1 W.L.R. 2863; [2006] 4 All
E.R. 1153; [2006] 2 All E.R. (Comm) 943; [2006] B.C.C. 971; [2007]
1 B.C.L.C. 85; [2006] B.P.I.R. 1405; [2007] Lloyd's Rep. I.R. 32;
(2006) 103(41) L.S.G. 35; (2006) 156 N.L.J. 1613; (2006) 150 S.J.L.B.
1395 . . . . 11–17, 11–53, 11–98
Centrebind Ltd, Re [1967] 1 W.L.R. 377; [1966] 3 All E.R. 889, Ch D 5–07
Chantrey Martin & Co v Martin [1953] 2 Q.B. 286; [1953] 3 W.L.R. 459;
[1953] 2 All E.R. 691; 46 R. & I.T. 516; 38 A.L.R.2d 663; (1953) 97 S.J.
539, CA 10–41
Charge Card Services Ltd (No.2), Re [1989] Ch. 497; [1988] 3 W.L.R. 764;
[1988] 3 All E.R. 702; (1988) 4 B.C.C. 524; [1988] B.C.L.C. 711; [1988]
P.C.C. 390; [1988] Fin. L.R. 308; (1989) 8 Tr. L.R. 86; (1988) 85(42)
L.S.G. 46; (1988) 138 N.L.J. Rep. 201; (1988) 132 S.J. 1458 . . . . . . 6–18, 14–51
Charnley Davies Ltd (No.2), Re [1990] B.C.C. 605; [1990] B.C.L.C. 760,
Ch D 11–30
Charter Reinsurance Co Ltd (In Liquidation) v Fagan [1997] A.C. 313;
[1996] 2 W.L.R. 726; [1996] 3 All E.R. 46; [1996] 2 Lloyd's Rep. 113;
[1996] C.L.C. 977; [1996] 5 Re. L.R. 411; (1996) 140 S.J.L.B. 148,
HL 3–07
Chase Manhattan Bank NA v Israel-British Bank (London) Ltd [1981]
Ch. 105; [1980] 2 W.L.R. 202; [1979] 3 All E.R. 1025; (1980) 124 S.J. 99,
Ch D 6–42
Chattey v Farndale Holdings Inc (1998) 75 P. & C.R. 298; [1997] 1 E.G.L.R.
153; [1997] 06 E.G. 152; [1996] N.P.C. 136, CA (Civ Div) 13–153
Cherry v Boultbee, 41 E.R. 171; (1839) 4 My. & C. 442, Ch D 8–46, 9–23
Cheshire West and Chester BC, Petitioners [2010] CSOH 115; [2011]
B.C.C. 174; 2010 G.W.D. 33–684 . . . . 3–11, 11–78, 11–93, 11–105
Cheyne Finance Plc (In Receivership), Re [2007] EWHC 2402 (Ch); [2008]
Bus. L.R. 1562; [2008] 2 All E.R. 987; [2008] B.C.C. 182; [2008]
1 B.C.L.C. 741 . . . . 1–38, 4–16, 4–18
Chittenden v Pepper [2006] EWHC 1511 (Ch); [2007] B.C.C. 195; [2006]
B.P.I.R. 1230; [2006] 2 E.G.L.R. 7; [2006] 33 E.G. 100; [2006] 27 E.G.
234 (C.S.); [2006] N.P.C. 75 12–41
Chohan v Saggar [1992] B.C.C. 750; [1993] B.C.L.C. 661, Ch D 13–139

Christonette International, Re [1982] 1 W.L.R. 1245; [1982] 3 All E.R. 225;
(1982) 79 L.S.G. 1025; (1982) 126 S.J. 561, Ch D 10–60
Christopher Moran Holdings Ltd v Bairstow. *See* Park Air Services Plc, Re
Churchill Hotel (Plymouth) Ltd, Re (1988) 4 B.C.C. 112; [1988] B.C.L.C.
341; [1988] P.C.C. 220, Ch D 14–73, 14–75
Ci4Net.com.Inc, Re [2004] EWHC 1941 (Ch); [2005] B.C.C. 277 .... 15–17, 15–56
City Equitable Fire Insurance Co Ltd, Re [1925] Ch. 407; [1924] All E.R.
Rep. 485, CA 14–11
City of London Corp v Bown (1990) 22 H.L.R. 32; (1990) 60 P. & C.R. 42;
[1989] E.G. 136 (C.S.); (1990) 87(3) L.S.G. 33; (1990) 134 S.J. 82,
CA (Civ Div) 6–14
Clark v Finnerty. *See* St Georges Property Services (London) Ltd (In
Administration), Re
Claybridge Shipping Co SA, Re [1997] 1 B.C.L.C. 572; [1981] Com. L.R.
107, CA (Civ Div) 5–13, 5–18
Clayton's Case. *See* Devaynes v Noble
Clifton Place Garage, Re [1970] Ch. 477; [1970] 2 W.L.R. 243; [1970] 1 All
E.R. 353; (1969) 113 S.J. 895, CA (Civ Div) 13–135
Clough v Samuel [1904] 2 K.B. 769, CA 3–04
Clough Mill Ltd v Martin [1985] 1 W.L.R. 111; [1984] 3 All E.R. 982;
(1985) 82 L.S.G. 1075; (1985) 82 L.S.G. 116; (1984) 128 S.J. 850, CA
(Civ Div) 6–46
Clydesdale Financial Services Ltd v Smailes [2009] EWHC 1745 (Ch);
[2009] B.C.C. 810; [2010] B.P.I.R. 62 .... 11–41, 11–113, 13–138
Coca-Cola Financial Corp v Finsat International Ltd (The Ira) [1998] Q.B.
43; [1996] 3 W.L.R. 849; [1996] 2 Lloyd's Rep. 274; [1996] 2 B.C.L.C.
626; [1996] C.L.C. 1564, CA (Civ Div) 9–04
Cohen v Davis [2006] EWHC 768 (Ch); [2007] B.C.C. 95; [2007] 2 B.C.L.C.
274; [2006] P.N.L.R. 33, Ch D 6–35, 6–37, 13–142, 14–16
Collins, Re [1925] Ch. 556, Ch D 3–04, 6–33
Collins & Aikman Europe SA, Re [2006] EWHC 1343 (Ch); [2006] B.C.C.
861; [2007] 1 B.C.L.C. 182; [2007] I.L.Pr. 2 ..... 1–19, 5–02, 11–85, 15–67, 16–10
Colt Telecom Group Plc. *See* Highberry Ltd v Colt Telecom Group Plc
(No.1)
Colt Telecom Group Plc (No.2), Re. *See* Highberry Ltd v Colt Telecom
Group Plc (No.2)
Columbian Fireproofing Co Ltd, Re [1910] 1 Ch. 758, Ch D 13–116
Commercial Bank of South Australia, Re (1886) L.R. 33 Ch. D. 174,
Ch D 16–50
Compania Merabello San Nicholas SA, Re [1973] Ch. 75; [1972] 3 W.L.R.
471; [1972] 3 All E.R. 448; [1972] 2 Lloyd's Rep. 268; (1972) 116 S.J.
631, Ch D 6–04, 16–50
Company (No.1573 of 1983), Re (1983) 1 B.C.C. 98937; [1983] Com. L.R.
202, Ch D 4–27, 5–12, 5–19
Company (No.006794 of 1983), Re [1986] B.C.L.C. 261 4–20
Company (No.00175 of 1987), Re (1987) 3 B.C.C. 124, Ch D 10–27
Company (No.000359 of 1987), Re [1988] Ch. 210; [1987] 3 W.L.R. 339;
[1987] 3 All E.R. 137; (1987) 3 B.C.C. 160; [1987] B.C.L.C. 450; [1988]
P.C.C. 64; (1987) 84 L.S.G. 1811; (1987) 131 S.J. 938, Ch D 16–50, 16–51
Company (No.003028 of 1987), Re (1987) 3 B.C.C. 575; [1988] B.C.L.C.
282; [1988] P.C.C. 192, Ch D 4–08, 5–18, 5–19
Company (No.005009 of 1987) Ex p. Copp, Re (1988) 4 B.C.C. 424; [1989]
B.C.L.C. 13, Ch D 14–35

Company (No.001992 of 1988), Re [1989] B.C.L.C. 9 11–67
Company (No.008122 of 1989) Ex p. Trans Continental Insurance Services,
    Re [1990] B.C.L.C. 697 . . . . 5–16, 5–18
Company (No.008790 of 1990), Re [1992] B.C.C. 11; [1991] B.C.L.C. 561,
    Ch D 5–16
Company (No.001946 of 1991) Ex p. Fin Soft Holdings SA, Re [1991]
    B.C.L.C. 737 5–18
Company (No.012209 of 1991), Re [1992] 1 W.L.R. 351; [1992] 2 All E.R.
    797, Ch D 5–13, 5–18
Company (No.006273 of 1992), Re [1992] B.C.C. 794; [1993] B.C.L.C. 131,
    Ch D 4–21, 5–12
Company (No.0010382 of 1992) Ex p. Computer Partnership, Re [1993]
    B.C.L.C. 597, Ch D 5–19
Company (No.002180 of 1996), Re [1996] 2 B.C.L.C. 409, Ch D 5–18
Company (No.006685 of 1996), Re [1997] B.C.C. 830; [1997] 1 B.C.L.C.
    639, Ch D 5–13
Compaq Computer Ltd v Abercorn Group Ltd (t/a Osiris) [1991] B.C.C.
    484; [1993] B.C.L.C. 603, Ch D 6–46
Condon Ex p. James, Re (1873–74) L.R. 9 Ch. App. 609; [1874–80] All E.R.
    Rep. 388, CA in Chancery 1–19, 5–02
Conley, Re [1938] 2 All E.R. 127 . . . . 13–99, 13–106
Consolidated Entertainments Ltd v Taylor [1937] 4 All E.R. 432 10–57
Consumer & Industrial Press Ltd (No.2), Re (1988) 4 B.C.C. 72, Ch D 11–81
Contex Drouzhba Ltd v Wiseman [2007] EWCA Civ 1201; [2008] B.C.C.
    301; [2008] 1 B.C.L.C. 631; (2007) 157 N.L.J. 14–26
Continental Assurance Co of London Plc, Re. *See* Singer v Beckett
Contract Corp (Winding Up: Production of Documents), Re (1871–72)
    L.R. 7 Ch. App. 207, CA in Chancery 5–02
Corbett v Nysir UK Ltd [2008] EWHC 2670 (Ch) 11–48
Cornhill Insurance Plc v Cornhill Financial Services Ltd [1992] B.C.C. 818;
    [1993] B.C.L.C. 914, CA (Civ Div) 11–117
Cornhill Insurance Plc v Improvement Services Ltd [1986] 1 W.L.R. 114;
    (1986) 2 B.C.C. 98942; [1986] P.C.C. 204, Ch D 4–21
Cosslett (Contractors) Ltd, Re [1998] Ch. 495; [1998] 2 W.L.R. 131; [1997]
    4 All E.R. 115; [1997] B.C.C. 724; [1999] 1 B.C.L.C. 205; 85 B.L.R. 1,
    CA (Civ Div) 7–10, 11–57
Country Farm Inns Ltd, Re [1997] 1 B.C.L.C. 174 14–73
County Bookshops Ltd v Grove [2002] EWHC 1160 (Ch); [2003] 1 B.C.L.C.
    479; [2002] B.P.I.R. 772 4–26
Courts Plc (In Liquidation), Re [2008] EWHC 2339 (Ch); [2009] 1 W.L.R.
    1499; [2009] Bus. L.R. 741; [2009] 2 All E.R. 402; [2008] B.C.C. 917;
    [2009] 2 B.C.L.C. 363 . . . . 6–38, 8–03
Coutts & Co v Stock [2000] 1 W.L.R. 906; [2000] 2 All E.R. 56; [2000]
    Lloyd's Rep. Bank. 14; [2000] B.C.C. 247; [2000] 1 B.C.L.C. 183; [2000]
    B.P.I.R. 400; (1999) 96(48) L.S.G. 39; (2000) 144 S.J.L.B. 24, Ch D . . . 13–133
Coventry and Dixon's Case. *See* Canadian Land Reclaiming & Colonizing
    Co, Re
Coyne v DRC Distribution Ltd [2008] EWCA Civ 488; [2008] B.C.C. 612;
    [2008] B.P.I.R. 1247 11–41
Craven v Blackpool Greyhound Stadium Co [1936] 3 All E.R. 512 5–08
Craythorne v Swinburne, 33 E.R. 482; (1807) 14 Ves. Jr. 160, Ct of
    Chancery 13–35
Crigglestone Coal Co Ltd, Re [1906] 2 Ch. 327, CA 5–19

Croftbell Ltd, Re [1990] B.C.C. 781; [1990] B.C.L.C. 844, Ch D 10–19
Cryne v Barclays Bank [1987] B.C.L.C. 548, CA (Civ Div) 10–26
Cuckmere Brick Co v Mutual Finance [1971] Ch. 949; [1971] 2 W.L.R. 1207;
    [1971] 2 All E.R. 633; (1971) 22 P. & C.R. 624; (1971) 115 S.J. 288, CA
    (Civ Div) 10–34, 10–48, 10–49
Currie v Consolidated Kent Collieries Corp [1906] 1 K.B. 134, CA 5–08
Customs and Excise Commissioners v Arena Corp Ltd (In Provisional
    Liquidation) [2003] EWHC 3032 (Ch); [2004] B.P.I.R. 375 15–04
DFC Financial Services Ltd v Coffey [1991] B.C.C. 218, PC 10–31
DKG Contractors Ltd, Re [1990] B.C.C. 903, Ch D 14–48
DKLL Solicitors v Revenue and Customs Commissioners [2007] EWHC
    2067 (Ch); [2007] B.C.C. 908; [2008] 1 B.C.L.C. 112 .... 11–40, 11–41
D'Jan of London Ltd, Re [1993] B.C.C. 646; [1994] 1 B.C.L.C. 561, Ch D 14–11,
                                                                    14–14, 14–18
Dairy Farmers of Britain Ltd, Re [2009] EWHC 1389 (Ch); [2010] Ch. 63;
    [2010] 2 W.L.R. 311; [2009] Bus. L.R. 1627; [2009] 4 All E.R. 241;
    [2010] B.C.C. 637; [2010] 1 B.C.L.C. 637 10–05
Daisytek-ISA Ltd, Re [2003] B.C.C. 562; [2004] B.P.I.R. 30, Ch D ... **15–53**, 15–56
Dale and Plant Ltd, Re (1890) L.R. 43 Ch. D. 255, Ch D 8–27
Dallhold Estates (UK) Pty Ltd, Re [1992] B.C.C. 394; [1992] B.C.L.C. 621;
    [1992] E.G. 18 (C.S.), Ch D 16–53, 16–60, 16–61
Dane v Mortgage Insurance Corp Ltd [1894] 1 Q.B. 54, CA 12–25
David Lloyd & Co, Re (1877) L.R. 6 Ch. D. 339, CA 8–47
David Meek Plant Ltd, Re [1993] B.C.C. 175; [1994] 1 B.C.L.C. 680,
    Ch D 11–65
Dawson Print Group, Re (1987) 3 B.C.C. 322; [1987] B.C.L.C. 601, Ch D ... 14–75
Day v Haine [2008] EWCA Civ 626; [2008] B.C.C. 845; [2008] 2 B.C.L.C.
    517; [2008] I.C.R. 1102; [2008] I.R.L.R. 642; [2008] B.P.I.R. 1343 8–41
De Beers Consolidated Mines Ltd v British South Africa Co [1910]
    1 Ch. 354, Ch D 3–02
Dear v Reeves [2001] EWCA Civ 277; [2002] Ch. 1; [2001] 3 W.L.R. 662;
    [2001] 1 B.C.L.C. 643; [2001] B.P.I.R. 577; (2001) 98(18) L.S.G. 44 6–12
Dearle v Hall, 38 E.R. 475; (1828) 3 Russ. 1, Ch D 10–57
Debtor (No.82 of 1926), Re [1927] 1 Ch. 410, Ch D 9–29
Debtor (No.17 of 1966), Re [1967] Ch. 590; [1967] 2 W.L.R. 1528; [1967] 1
    All E.R. 668; (1967) 111 S.J. 130 4–23
Debtor (Order in Aid No.1 of 1979), Re [1981] Ch. 384; [1980] 3 W.L.R.
    758; [1980] 3 All E.R. 665; (1980) 124 S.J. 811, Ch D 16–61
Debtor (No.87 of 1993) (No.2), Re [1996] B.C.C. 80; [1996] 1 B.C.L.C. 63;
    [1996] B.P.I.R. 64, Ch D 14–04
Debtor (No.140 IO of 1995), Re [1996] 2 B.C.L.C. 429; [1997] B.P.I.R. 24,
    Ch D 12–38
Delaney v Chen [2010] EWCA Civ 1455; [2011] B.P.I.R. 39 13–29
Delberry Ltd, Re [2008] EWHC 925 (Ch); [2008] B.C.C. 653; [2008] B.P.I.R.
    1277 .... 5–02, 11–37
Delhi Electric Supply & Traction Co Ltd, Re. *See* India v Taylor
Demite Ltd v Protec Health Ltd [1998] B.C.C. 638, Ch D 13–20
Denney v John Hudson & Co Ltd. *See* SA&D Wright Ltd, Re
Derek Randall Enterprises Ltd, Re [1990] B.C.C. 749; [1991] B.C.L.C. 379,
    CA (Civ Div) 14–14
Destone Fabrics, Re [1941] Ch. 319, CA 13–118
Devaynes v Noble, Clayton's Case (1816) 1 Mer. 572 .... 3–03, 13–53,
                                                        13–121, 13–122, 13–131

Dewrun Ltd, Re. *See* Royal Bank of Scotland Plc v Bhardwaj

Deyes v Wood [1911] 1 K.B. 806, CA 10–23

Divine Solutions (UK) Ltd, Re [2003] EWHC 1931 (Ch); [2004] B.C.C. 325;
    [2004] 1 B.C.L.C. 373 11–67

Dollar Land Holdings Plc, Re [1993] B.C.C. 823; [1994] 1 B.C.L.C. 404,
    Ch D 4–27

Dolphin Quays Developments Ltd v Mills [2008] EWCA Civ 385; [2008] 1
    W.L.R. 1829; [2008] Bus. L.R. 1520; [2008] 4 All E.R. 58; [2008] C.P.
    Rep. 29; [2008] B.C.C. 471; [2008] 2 B.C.L.C. 774; [2008] 4 Costs L.R.
    599; [2008] B.P.I.R. 607; [2008] N.P.C. 48 .... 10–23, 10–52

Doltable Ltd v Lexi Holdings Plc [2005] EWHC 1804 (Ch); [2006] B.C.C.
    918; [2006] 1 B.C.L.C. 384 11–20

Don King Productions Inc v Warren (No.1) [2000] Ch. 291; [1999] 3 W.L.R.
    276; [1999] 2 All E.R. 218; [1999] 1 Lloyd's Rep. 588; [2000] 1 B.C.L.C.
    607; [1999] E.M.L.R. 402, CA (Civ Div) 6–10

Donoghue v Stevenson [1932] A.C. 562; 1932 S.C. (H.L.) 31; 1932 S.L.T.
    317; [1932] W.N. 139, HL 10–48

Doorbar v Alltime Securities Ltd (No.2) [1995] B.C.C. 728; [1995]
    2 B.C.L.C. 513; [1996] B.P.I.R. 128, Ch D 12–41

Dorchester Finance Co v Stebbing [1989] B.C.L.C. 498, Ch D 14–08

Douglas Ex p. Wilson, Re (1871–72) L.R. 7 Ch. App. 490, CA in Chancery 16–63

Douglas Construction Services Ltd, Re (1988) 4 B.C.C. 553; [1988] B.C.L.C.
    397, Ch D 14–75

Dovey v Cory [1901] A.C. 477, HL 14–11

Downer Enterprises, Re [1974] 1 W.L.R. 1460; [1974] 2 All E.R. 1074;
    (1974) 118 S.J. 829, Ch D 8–33, 8–38

Downsview Nominees Ltd v First City Corp Ltd [1993] A.C. 295; [1993] 2
    W.L.R. 86; [1993] 3 All E.R. 626; [1993] B.C.C. 46; [1994] 2 B.C.L.C.
    49; (1992) 89(45) L.S.G. 26; (1992) 136 S.J.L.B. 324 .... 10–12, 10–34,
                                                               10–48, 10–49

Drax Holdings Ltd, Re [2003] EWHC 2743 (Ch); [2004] 1 W.L.R. 1049;
    [2004] 1 All E.R. 903; [2004] B.C.C. 334; [2004] 1 B.C.L.C. 10 16–51

Drew & Co v Josolyne (1887) L.R. 18 Q.B.D. 590, CA 8–11

Duomatic Ltd, Re [1969] 2 Ch. 365; [1969] 2 W.L.R. 114; [1969] 1 All E.R.
    161; (1968) 112 S.J. 922, Ch D 14–19

Dynamics Corp of America (In Liquidation) (No.2), Re [1976] 1 W.L.R.
    757; [1976] 2 All E.R. 669; (1976) 120 S.J. 450, Ch D 3–07, 8–14

E Pfeiffer Weinkellerei-Weineinkauf GmbH & Co v Arbuthnot Factors Ltd
    [1988] 1 W.L.R. 150; (1987) 3 B.C.C. 608; [1987] B.C.L.C. 522, QBD 6–46

EVTR, Re (1987) 3 B.C.C. 389; [1987] B.C.L.C. 646; [1987] P.C.C. 425;
    [1987] 2 F.T.L.R. 309, CA (Civ Div) 6–42

Earl of Leicester v Wells-next-the-Sea UDC [1973] Ch. 110; [1972] 3 W.L.R.
    486; [1972] 3 All E.R. 77; (1972) 24 P. & C.R. 72; (1972) 116 S.J. 647,
    Ch D 13–91

Earl of Sefton v Tophams Ltd (No.2) [1967] 1 A.C. 50; [1966] 2 W.L.R. 814;
    [1966] 1 All E.R. 1039; (1966) 110 S.J. 271, HL 13–91

Eastern Capital Futures (In Liquidation), Re (1989) 5 B.C.C. 223; [1989]
    B.C.L.C. 371, Ch D 3–03

Eastgate Ex p. Ward, Re [1905] 1 K.B. 465, KBD 3–05, 6–17

Eberle's Hotels and Restaurant Co v Jonas (1887) L.R. 18 Q.B.D. 459, CA 9–27

Edwin Hill & Partners v First National Finance Corp [1989] 1 W.L.R. 225;
    [1988] 3 All E.R. 801; [1989] B.C.L.C. 89; [1988] 48 E.G. 83; [1988]
    E.G. 116 (C.S.); (1988) 85(32) L.S.G. 44; (1988) 138 N.L.J. Rep. 268;
    (1988) 122 S.J. 1389, CA (Civ Div) 10–53

Ellis v Emmanuel (1875–76) L.R. 1 Ex. D. 157, CA 8–44
Eloc Electro-Optieck and Communicatie BV, Re [1982] Ch. 43; [1981] 3
    W.L.R. 176; [1981] 2 All E.R. 1111; [1981] I.C.R. 732; (1981) 125 S.J.
    412, Ch D 16–50
Emmadart Ltd, Re [1979] Ch. 540; [1979] 2 W.L.R. 868; [1979] 1 All E.R.
    599; (1979) 123 S.J. 15, Ch D 10–37
4 Eng Ltd v Harper [2009] EWHC 2633 (Ch); [2010] B.C.C. 746; [2010] 1
    B.C.L.C. 176; [2010] B.P.I.R. 1; [2010] Bus. L.R. D58 ... 13–137, 13–139, 13–150
England v Smith [2001] Ch. 419; [2000] 2 W.L.R. 1141; [2000] B.C.C. 123;
    [2000] 2 B.C.L.C. 21; [2000] I.L.Pr. 730; [2000] B.P.I.R. 28; (1999)
    96(47) L.S.G. 29; (2000) 144 S.J.L.B. 8, CA (Civ Div) 16–59, 16–61
English & American Insurance Co Ltd, Re [1994] 1 B.C.L.C. 649, Ch D 6–42
English Scottish and Australian Chartered Bank, Re [1893] 3 Ch. 385, CA 16–57
Enron Europe Ltd (In Administration) v Revenue and Customs
    Commissioners [2006] EWHC 824 (Ch); [2006] S.T.C. 1339; [2006]
    B.C.C. 953; [2006] B.T.C. 5299; [2006] B.V.C. 368; [2006] S.T.I. 1353 9–10
Environment Agency v Hillridge Ltd [2003] EWHC 3023 (Ch); [2004]
    2 B.C.L.C. 358; [2004] Env. L.R. 32; [2004] J.P.L. 1258; [2003] N.P.C.
    155 .... 2–25, 6–30
Equitable Life Assurance Society (No.2), Re [2002] EWHC 140 (Ch);
    [2002] B.C.C. 319; [2002] 2 B.C.L.C. 510; 12–19
Equitable Life Assurance Society v Bowley [2003] EWHC 2263 (Comm);
    [2003] B.C.C. 829; [2004] 1 B.C.L.C. 180 .... 14–09, 14–18
Equiticorp International Plc, Re [1989] 1 W.L.R. 1010; (1989) 5 B.C.C. 599;
    [1989] B.C.L.C. 597; (1989) 86(41) L.S.G. 36; (1989) 133 S.J. 1405,
    Ch D 5–17
Etic Ltd, Re [1928] Ch. 861, Ch D 14–14
Euro Commercial Leasing Ltd v Cartwright & Lewis [1995] B.C.C. 830;
    [1995] 2 B.C.L.C. 618, Ch D 11–52, 11–58
Eurofood IFSC Ltd, Re (C–341/04) [2006] Ch. 508; [2006] 3 W.L.R. 309;
    [2006] All E.R. (EC) 1078; [2006] E.C.R. I–3813; [2006] B.C.C.
    397; [2007] 2 B.C.L.C. 151; [2006] I.L.Pr. 23; [2006] B.P.I.R. 661,
    ECJ .... 15–06, 15–07, 15–30, **15–36—15–37**,
                                       15–41, 15–52, 16–28, 16–36
European Directories (DH6) BV, Re [2010] EWHC 3472 (Ch) 15–08
European Life Assurance Society (No.1), Re (1869–70) L.R. 9 Eq. 122,
    Ct of Chancery 4–04, 4–23
Exchange Travel (Holdings) Ltd (No.3), Re [1996] B.C.C. 933; [1996]
    2 B.C.L.C. 524; [1997] B.P.I.R. 623, Ch D 9–45, 13–78, 13–94
Exchange Travel Agency Ltd v Triton Property Trust Plc [1991] B.C.C. 341;
    [1991] B.C.L.C. 396, Ch D 11–67
Exeter City Council v Bairstow [2007] EWHC 400 (Ch); [2007] Bus. L.R.
    813; [2007] 4 All E.R. 437; [2007] B.C.C. 236; [2007] 2 B.C.L.C. 455;
    [2007] 2 P. & C.R. 8; [2007] R.A. 109; [2007] N.P.C. 28 .... 3–11, 8–38,
                                          11–98, 11–105
Expro International Group Plc, Re [2008] EWHC 1543 (Ch); [2010]
    2 B.C.L.C. 514 .... 12–13, 12–23
F&E Stanton Ltd, Re [1929] 1 Ch. 180, Ch D 13–116
Facia Footwear Ltd (In Administration) v Hinchcliffe [1998] 1 B.C.L.C. 218,
    Ch D 14–20
Fairway Magazines Ltd, Re [1992] B.C.C. 924; [1993] B.C.L.C. 643,
    Ch D 13–97, 13–118
Fashoff (UK) Ltd (t/a Moschino) v Linton [2008] EWHC 537 (Ch); [2008]
    B.C.C. 542; [2008] 2 B.C.L.C. 362 11–64

Faulks v Faulks [1992] 1 E.G.L.R. 9; [1992] 15 E.G. 15 6–11
Faure Electric Accumulator Co, Re (1889) L.R. 40 Ch. D. 141, Ch D 14–11
Feakins v Department for the Environment, Food and Rural Affairs. *See* Secretary of State for the Environment, Food and Rural Affairs v Feakins
Fearns (t/a Autopaint International) v Anglo–Dutch Paint & Chemical Co Ltd [2010] EWHC 2366 (Ch); [2011] 1 W.L.R. 366; (2010) 154(37) S.J.L.B. 29 9–04
Feetum v Levy [2005] EWCA Civ 1601; [2006] Ch. 585; [2006] 3 W.L.R. 427; [2006] B.C.C. 340; [2006] 2 B.C.L.C. 102; [2006] B.P.I.R. 379; (2006) 103(5) L.S.G. 29 10–05
Felixstowe Dock & Railway Co v United States Lines Inc [1989] Q.B. 360; [1989] 2 W.L.R. 109; [1988] 2 All E.R. 77; [1987] 2 Lloyd's Rep. 76; [1987] 2 F.T.L.R. 75; (1989) 133 S.J. 82, QBD 16–09, 16–57, 16–62
Fender v IRC [2003] EWHC 3543 (Ch); [2003] B.P.I.R. 1304 12–18
Fenton Ex p. Fenton Textile Association Ltd (No.1), Re [1931] 1 Ch. 85, CA 9–23
Fidelity Investments International Plc v MyTravel Group Plc. *See* MyTravel Group Plc, Re
Financial Services Authority v Dobb White & Co [2003] EWHC 3146 (Ch); [2004] B.P.I.R. 479 15–18
First Independent Factors & Finance Ltd v Churchill [2006] EWCA Civ 1623; [2007] Bus. L.R. 676; [2007] B.C.C. 45; [2007] 1 B.C.L.C. 293; [2007] B.P.I.R. 14; (2006) 150 S.J.L.B. 1606 14–06
Fitness Centre (South East) Ltd, Re [1986] B.C.L.C. 518; (1986) 2 B.C.C. 99535, Ch D 5–19
Flack's Case. *See* Central Sugar Factories of Brazil, Re
Fleet Disposal Services Ltd, Re [1995] B.C.C. 605; [1995] 1 B.C.L.C. 345, Ch D 6–42
Fleetwood and District Electric Light and Power Syndicate, Re [1915] 1 Ch. 486, Ch D 8–41
Flint (A Bankrupt), Re [1993] Ch. 319; [1993] 2 W.L.R. 537; [1993] 1 F.L.R. 763; (1992) 136 S.J.L.B. 221, Ch D 13–127, 13–128, 13–129
Fliptex Ltd v Hogg [2004] EWHC 1280 (Ch); [2004] B.C.C. 870 11–44
Focus Insurance Co Ltd, Re [1996] B.C.C. 659; [1997] 1 B.C.L.C. 219, Ch D 16–60
Foley v Hill, 9 E.R. 1002; (1848) 2 H.L. Cas. 28, QB 13–131
Forbes v Jackson (1881–82) L.R. 19 Ch. D. 615, Ch D 13–35
Ford & Carter Ltd v Midland Bank Ltd (1979) 129 N.L.J. 543 . . . . . . 10–28, 10–30
Foskett v McKeown [2001] 1 A.C. 102; [2000] 2 W.L.R. 1299; [2000] 3 All E.R. 97; [2000] Lloyd's Rep. I.R. 627; [2000] W.T.L.R. 667; (1999–2000) 2 I.T.E.L.R. 711; (2000) 97(23) L.S.G. 44, HL 13–146
Foster Clark's Indenture Trust, Re [1966] 1 W.L.R. 125; [1966] 1 All E.R. 43; (1966) 110 S.J. 108, Ch D 10–36
Fraser v Oystertec Plc [2003] EWHC 2787 (Pat); [2004] B.C.C. 233; [2004] B.P.I.R. 486; [2004] F.S.R. 22 7–16
Freevale Ltd v Metrostore (Holdings) Ltd [1984] Ch. 199; [1984] 2 W.L.R. 496; [1984] 1 All E.R. 495; (1984) 47 P. & C.R. 481; (1984) 81 L.S.G. 516; (1984) 128 S.J. 116, Ch D 10–53
French's (Wine Bar) Ltd, Re (1987) 3 B.C.C. 173; [1987] B.C.L.C. 499, Ch D 13–127, 13–129, 13–148
Funding Corp Block Discounting Ltd v Lexi Holdings Plc (In Administration) [2008] EWHC 985 (Ch); [2008] 2 B.C.L.C. 596; [2008] N.P.C. 57 11–78

G Stanley & Co Ltd, Re [1925] Ch. 148, Ch D 13–106
GBI Investments Ltd, Re [2010] EWHC 37 (Ch); [2010] 2 B.C.L.C. 624;
    [2010] B.P.I.R. 356 5–14
GHE Realisations Ltd (formerly Gatehouse Estates Ltd), Re [2005] EWHC
    2400 (Ch); [2006] 1 W.L.R. 287; [2006] 1 All E.R. 357; [2006] B.C.C.
    139 .... 11–86, 11–115
GL Saunders Ltd (In Liquidation), Re [1986] 1 W.L.R. 215; (1986) 83
    L.S.G. 779; (1985) 130 S.J. 166, Ch D 10–60, 10–71
GP Stores Ltd, Re Unreported July 29, 2004 3–03
GT Whyte & Co Ltd, Re [1983] B.C.L.C. 311 13–117
Gallagher v Jones. *See* Threlfall v Jones (Inspector of Taxes)
Gallery Capital SA, Re Unreported April 21, 2010, Ch D 16–50
Gardiner v Secretary of State for Business, Enterprise and Regulatory
    Reform [2009] B.C.C. 742 14–72
Gardner v Parker [2004] EWCA Civ 781; [2005] B.C.C. 46; [2004] 2
    B.C.L.C. 554; (2004) 148 S.J.L.B. 792 14–20
Garner's Motors Ltd, Re [1937] Ch. 594, Ch D 12–25
Garrud Ex p. Newitt, Re (1880–81) L.R. 16 Ch. D. 522, CA 7–10
Geldof Metaalconstructie NV v Simon Carves Ltd [2010] EWCA Civ 667;
    [2010] 4 All E.R. 847; [2010] 1 C.L.C. 895; [2010] B.L.R. 401; [2010]
    T.C.L.R. 6; 130 Con. L.R. 37; [2010] C.I.L.L. 2880 9–04
Gemma Ltd (In Liquidation) v Davies [2008] EWHC 546 (Ch); [2008]
    B.C.C. 812; [2008] 2 B.C.L.C. 281; [2009] Bus. L.R. D4 14–04
Gerald Cooper Chemicals Ltd, Re [1978] Ch. 262; [1978] 2 W.L.R. 866;
    [1978] 2 All E.R. 49; (1977) 121 S.J. 848, Ch D 14–23, 14–24
German Graphics Graphische Maschinen GmbH v van der Schee
    (C–292/08) [2009] E.C.R. I–8421; [2010] C.E.C. 499; [2010] I.L.Pr. 1,
    ECJ 15–02, 15–34, 15–94
Gibraltar Residential Properties Ltd v Gibralcon 2004 SA [2010] EWHC
    2595 (TCC); [2011] B.L.R. 126 15–38
Gibson Davies Chemists Ltd, Re [1995] B.C.C. 11, Ch D 14–81
Giles v Rhind [2008] EWCA Civ 118; [2009] Ch. 191; [2008] 3 W.L.R. 1233;
    [2008] Bus. L.R. 1103; [2008] 3 All E.R. 697; [2009] B.C.C. 590; [2008]
    2 B.C.L.C. 1; [2008] B.P.I.R. 342 13–138
Gilford Motor Co Ltd v Horne [1933] Ch. 935, CA 3–12
GlaxoSmithKline Export Ltd v UK (Aid) Ltd [2003] EWHC 1090 (Ch);
    [2003] 2 B.C.L.C. 351; [2003] B.P.I.R. 1206; (2003) 100(27) L.S.G. 34 ... 5–13
Glen Express Ltd, Re [2000] B.P.I.R. 456, Ch D 9–23
Glenister v Rowe (Costs) [2000] Ch. 76; [1999] 3 W.L.R. 716; [1999] 3 All
    E.R. 452; [1999] B.P.I.R. 674; (1999) 96(20) L.S.G. 39; (1999) 149
    N.L.J. 858, CA (Civ Div) 4–26
Globe New Patent Iron & Steel Co, Re (1875) L.R. 20 Eq. 337, Ct of
    Chancery 4–21
Glyncorrwg Colliery Co Ltd, Re [1926] Ch. 951, Ch D 10–56, 10–60
Godwin Warren Controls Systems Plc, Re [1992] B.C.C. 557; [1993]
    B.C.L.C. 80, Ch D 14–80
Goldacre (Offices) Ltd v Nortel Networks UK Ltd (In Administration)
    [2009] EWHC 3389 (Ch); [2010] Ch. 455; [2010] 3 W.L.R. 171; [2010]
    Bus. L.R. 870; [2010] B.C.C. 299; [2010] 2 B.C.L.C. 248; [2010] 1
    E.G.L.R. 25; [2010] 9 E.G. 168 .... 3–11, 8–38,
                                                               11–105
Goldburg (No.2), Re [1912] 1 K.B. 606, KBD 10–28
Golden Key Ltd (In Receivership), Re [2009] EWCA Civ 636 8–03

Gomba Holdings (UK) Ltd v Homan [1986] 1 W.L.R. 1301; [1986] 3 All
    E.R. 94; (1986) 2 B.C.C. 99102; [1986] P.C.C. 449; (1987) 84 L.S.G. 36;
    (1986) 130 S.J. 821, Ch D 10–37, 10–40
Goodwin v Gray (1974) 22 W.R. 312 8–44
Gordon & Breach Science Publishers Ltd, Re [1995] B.C.C. 261; [1995] 2
    B.C.L.C. 189, Ch D 5–11
Gorne v Scales [2006] EWCA Civ 311 13–32
Gosling v Gaskell [1897] A.C. 575, HL 10–01, 10–41, 10–66
Gourdain v Nadler (133/78) [1979] E.C.R. 733; [1979] 3 C.M.L.R. 180,
    ECJ 15–02, 15–34
Gray v G-T-P Group Ltd [2010] EWHC 1772 (Ch) 1–06, 1–67
Grayan Building Services Ltd (In Liquidation), Re [1995] Ch. 241; [1995] 3
    W.L.R. 1; [1995] B.C.C. 554; [1995] 1 B.C.L.C. 276; (1995) 92(1) L.S.G.
    36; (1994) 138 S.J.L.B. 227, CA (Civ Div) 14–76, 14–77, 14–81
Gray's Inn Construction Co Ltd, Re [1980] 1 W.L.R. 711; [1980] 1 All E.R.
    814; (1980) 124 S.J. 463, CA (Civ Div) 13–127, 13–131, 13–132,
                                                              13–133, 13–135
Greene King Plc v Stanley [2001] EWCA Civ 1966; [2002] B.P.I.R. 491 12–25
Greenwich Millennium Exhibition Ltd v New Millennium Experience Ltd
    Co [2003] EWHC 1823 (Ch); [2004] 1 All E.R. 687; [2004] 1
    B.C.L.C. 19 4–12
Gresham International Ltd (In Liquidation) v Moonie [2009] EWHC 1093
    (Ch); [2010] Ch. 285; [2010] 2 W.L.R. 362; [2010] Bus. L.R. 67; [2009]
    2 B.C.L.C. 256; [2010] B.P.I.R. 122 .... 5–04, 8–34
Greystoke, Re. *See* Debtor (No.140 IO of 1995), Re
Griffin v Awoderu [2008] EWHC 349 (Ch); [2008] B.P.I.R. 877 13–139
Griffin Hotel Co Ltd, Re [1941] Ch. 129; [1940] 4 All E.R. 324, Ch D 10–60
Griffiths v Secretary of State for Social Services [1974] Q.B. 468; [1973] 3
    W.L.R. 831; [1973] 3 All E.R. 1184; (1973) 117 S.J. 873, QBD 10–36
Griffiths v Yorkshire Bank Plc [1994] 1 W.L.R. 1427; (1994) 91(36) L.S.G.
    36, Ch D 10–61
Grovewood Holdings Plc v James Capel & Co Ltd [1995] Ch. 80; [1995] 2
    W.L.R. 70; [1994] 4 All E.R. 417; [1995] B.C.C. 760; [1994] 2 B.C.L.C.
    782; [1994] E.G. 136 (C.S.); (1994) 144 N.L.J. 1405, Ch D 5–06
Grupo Torras SA v Al-Sabah (No.1) [1995] 1 Lloyd's Rep. 374, QBD 15–02
Guardian Assurance Co, Re [1917] 1 Ch. 431, CA 1–45
Guy v Churchill (1889) L.R. 40 Ch. D. 481, Ch D 5–06
H&K (Medway) Ltd, Re [1997] 1 W.L.R. 1422; [1997] 2 All E.R. 321; [1997]
    B.C.C. 853; [1997] 1 B.C.L.C. 545, Ch D 10–61
HHO Licensing Ltd (In Liquidation), Re [2007] EWHC 2953 (Ch); [2008]
    1 B.C.L.C. 223; [2007] B.P.I.R. 1363 .... 13–19, 13–107
HIH Casualty & General Insurance Ltd, Re [2008] UKHL 21; [2008] 1
    W.L.R. 852; [2008] Bus. L.R. 905; [2008] 3 All E.R. 869; [2008] B.C.C.
    349; [2008] B.P.I.R. 581; [2008] Lloyd's Rep. I.R. 756; (2008) 105(16)
    L.S.G. 26; (2008) 152(16) S.J.L.B. 30 .... 3–13, 8–16, 8–31, 16–08,
                                                      16–30, 16–58, 16–60, 16–61
HPJ UK Ltd (In Administration), Re [2007] B.C.C. 284, Ch D 8–03, 11–85
Hachette UK Ltd v Borders (UK) Ltd [2009] EWHC 3487 (Ch) 11–84, 11–108
Hague v Nam Tai Electronics [2008] UKPC 13; [2008] B.C.C. 295; [2008]
    B.P.I.R. 363; [2008] P.N.L.R. 27 5–03
Halcyon the Great, The (No.1) [1975] 1 W.L.R. 515; [1975] 1 All E.R. 882;
    [1975] 1 Lloyd's Rep. 518; [1975] 1 C.M.L.R. 267; (1974) 119 S.J. 10,
    QBD 9–06

Halliwells LLP, Re [2010] EWHC 2036 (Ch); [2011] B.C.C. 57; (2010)
    107(32) L.S.G. 14; (2010) 154(32) S.J.L.B. 28 11–40
Halson Packaging Ltd, Re [1997] B.C.C. 993; [1997] B.P.I.R. 194, Ch D 12–26
Halt Garage (1964) Ltd, Re [1982] 3 All E.R. 1016, Ch D 14–19
Hammonds (A Firm) v Pro-Fit USA Ltd [2007] EWHC 1998 (Ch); [2008]
    2 B.C.L.C. 159; (2007) 104(35) L.S.G. 38 . . . . 4–28, 11–47, 11–48
Hand v Blow [1901] 2 Ch. 721, CA 10–14, 10–57
Hans Brochier Holdings Ltd v Exner [2006] EWHC 2594 (Ch); [2007]
    B.C.C. 127 . . . . 15–49, 15–56
Hans Place Ltd, Re [1992] B.C.C. 737; [1993] B.C.L.C. 768; [1992] 44 E.G.
    143, Ch D 6–28
Harms Offshore AHT Taurus GmbH & Co KG v Bloom [2009] EWCA Civ
    632; [2010] Ch. 187; [2010] 2 W.L.R. 349; [2009] Bus. L.R. 1663; [2009]
    C.P. Rep. 43; [2010] B.C.C. 822; [2009] 2 B.C.L.C. 473 . . . . 3–09, 11–29, 11–67
Harrington Motor Co Ltd Ex p. Chaplin, Re [1928] Ch. 105; (1927–28) 29
    Ll. L. Rep. 102; 59 A.L.R. 1111, CA 3–07, 6–24
Harris Simons Construction Ltd, Re [1989] 1 W.L.R. 368; (1989) 5 B.C.C.
    11; [1989] B.C.L.C. 202; [1989] P.C.C. 229; (1989) 86(8) L.S.G. 43;
    (1989) 133 S.J. 122, Ch D 11–47
Harrison Ex p. Jay, Re (1880) L.R. 14 Ch. D. 19, CA 7–09, 7–10
Harrods (Buenos Aires) Ltd (No.2), Re [1992] Ch. 72; [1991] 3 W.L.R. 397;
    [1991] 4 All E.R. 348; [1991] B.C.C. 249; [1992] I.L.Pr. 453, CA
    (Civ Div) 16–51
Hawk Insurance Co Ltd, Re [2001] EWCA Civ 241; [2002] B.C.C. 300;
    [2001] 2 B.C.L.C. 480 . . . . 12–15, 12–19
Hawkes Hill Publishing Co Ltd (In Liquidation), Re [2007] B.C.C. 937;
    [2007] B.P.I.R. 1305; (2007) 151 S.J.L.B. 743, Ch D 13–100, 14–40, 14–44
Hay v Swedish & Norwegian Railway Co Ltd (1892) 8 T.L.R. 775 10–52
Hayward (Deceased), Re [1997] Ch. 45; [1996] 3 W.L.R. 674; [1997] 1 All
    E.R. 32; [1997] B.P.I.R. 456, Ch D 15–02, 15–34
Hellas Telecommunications (Luxembourg) II SCA, Re [2009] EWHC 3199
    (Ch); [2010] B.C.C. 295 . . . . 11–37, 11–39, 11–40, 15–08
Helstan Securities Ltd v Hertfordshire CC [1978] 3 All E.R. 262; 76 L.G.R.
    735, QBD 6–10
Hemming deceased, Re. *See* Raymond Saul & Co v Holden
Henderson v Merrett Syndicates Ltd (No.1) [1995] 2 A.C. 145; [1994] 3
    W.L.R. 761; [1994] 3 All E.R. 506; [1994] 2 Lloyd's Rep. 468; [1994]
    C.L.C. 918; (1994) 144 N.L.J. 1204, HL 10–48
Hendy Lennox (Industrial Engines) Ltd v Grahame Puttick Ltd [1984]
    1 W.L.R. 485; [1984] 2 All E.R. 152; [1984] 2 Lloyd's Rep. 422; (1984)
    81 L.S.G. 585; (1984) 128 S.J. 220, QBD 9–26
Henry v Hammond [1913] 2 K.B. 515, KBD 9–26
Hibernian Merchants, Re [1958] Ch. 76; [1957] 3 W.L.R. 486; [1957] 3 All
    E.R. 97; (1957) 101 S.J. 647, Ch D 16–50
Highberry Ltd v Colt Telecom Group Plc (No.1) [2002] EWHC 2503 (Ch);
    [2003] 1 B.C.L.C. 290; [2003] B.P.I.R. 311; (2003) 100(5) L.S.G. 32 11–47
Highberry Ltd v Colt Telecom Group Plc (No.2) [2002] EWHC 2815 (Ch);
    [2003] B.P.I.R. 324 . . . . 4–28, 5–18, 12–08
Hill v East & West India Dock Co (1883–84) L.R. 9 App. Cas. 448, HL 6–30
Hill v Haines [2007] EWCA Civ 1284; [2008] Ch. 412; [2008] 2 W.L.R. 1250;
    [2008] 2 All E.R. 901; [2008] 1 F.L.R. 1192; [2007] 3 F.C.R. 785; [2007]
    B.P.I.R. 1280; [2008] W.T.L.R. 447; [2008] Fam. Law 199; [2007] 50
    E.G. 109 (C.S.); (2007) 151 S.J.L.B. 1597; [2007] N.P.C. 132 . . . . 13–19, 13–24

Hill v Spread Trustee Co Ltd [2006] EWCA Civ 542; [2007] Bus. L.R. 1213;
  [2007] 1 W.L.R. 2404; [2007] 1 All E.R. 1106; [2006] B.C.C. 646; [2007]
  1 B.C.L.C. 450; [2006] B.P.I.R. 789; [2006] W.T.L.R. 1009 ...... 13–38, 13–138
Hindcastle Ltd v Barbara Attenborough Associates Ltd [1997] A.C. 70;
  [1996] 2 W.L.R. 262; [1996] 1 All E.R. 737; [1996] B.C.C. 636; [1996] 2
  B.C.L.C. 234; [1996] B.P.I.R. 595; [1996] 1 E.G.L.R. 94; [1996] 15 E.G.
  103; [1996] E.G. 32 (C.S.); (1996) 93(12) L.S.G. 29; (1996) 140 S.J.L.B.
  84; [1996] N.P.C. 28, HL 6–30
Hitco 2000 Ltd, Re [1995] B.C.C. 161; [1995] 2 B.C.L.C. 63, Ch D 14–80
Hollicourt (Contracts) Ltd (In Liquidation) v Bank of Ireland [2001]
  Ch. 555; [2001] 2 W.L.R. 290; [2001] 1 All E.R. 289; [2001] 1 All
  E.R. (Comm) 357; [2001] Lloyd's Rep. Bank. 6; [2000] B.C.C. 1210;
  [2001] 1 B.C.L.C. 233; [2001] B.P.I.R. 47; (2000) 97(45) L.S.G. 41, CA
  (Civ Div) 13–03, 13–134
Hollington v F Hewthorn & Co Ltd [1943] K.B. 587, CA 14–71
Hollinshead v Hazleton [1916] 1 A.C. 428, HL 6–03
Holloway v York (1877) 25 W.R. 627 6–23
Holmes v Godson, 44 E.R. 347; (1856) 8 De G.M. & G. 152, Ct of Chancery ... 7–09
Holroyd v Gwynne (1809) 2 Taunt. 176 7–11
Hong Kong and Shanghai Banking Corp v Kloeckner & Co AG [1990] 2
  Q.B. 514; [1990] 3 W.L.R. 634; [1989] 3 All E.R. 513; [1989] 2 Lloyd's
  Rep 323, QBD 9–03
 Horsley & Weight, Re [1982] Ch. 442; [1982] 3 W.L.R. 431; [1982] 3 All E.R. 1045;
  (1982) 79 L.S.G. 919, CA (Civ Div) 14–19
Houlder, Re [1929] 1 Ch. 205, Ch D 8–44
Houldsworth v Glasgow City Bank (1879–80) L.R. 5 App. Cas. 317, HL 8–27
Household Mortgage Corp Plc v Whitehead [2002] EWCA Civ 1657; [2003]
  1 W.L.R. 1173; [2003] 1 All E.R. 319; [2003] 1 All E.R. (Comm) 263;
  [2003] 2 F.C.R. 369; [2003] B.P.I.R. 1482; (2003) 100(4) L.S.G. 32;
  (2002) 146 S.J.L.B. 262; (2003) 147 S.J.L.B. 26; [2002] N.P.C. 141 12–26
Huddersfield Fine Worsteds Ltd, Re [2005] EWCA Civ 1072; [2005] 4 All
  E.R. 886; [2005] B.C.C. 915; [2006] 2 B.C.L.C. 160; [2006] I.C.R. 205;
  [2005] I.R.L.R. 995; (2005) 155 N.L.J. 1355 11–96
Hudson v Gambling Commission [2010] All E.R. (D) 59 11–67
Hughes v Hannover Ruckversicherungs AG [1997] B.C.C. 921; [1997]
  1 B.C.L.C. 497; [1999] B.P.I.R. 224; [1997] 6 Re. L.R. 96, CA (Civ
  Div) 16–59, 16–60, 16–61
Hydrodan (Corby) Ltd (In Liquidation), Re [1994] B.C.C. 161; [1994] 2
  B.C.L.C. 180, Ch D 14–04, 14–05,
                                                            14–32, 14–39
Hydroserve Ltd, Re [2007] EWHC 3026 (Ch); [2008] B.C.C. 175 ..... 6–38, 11–91
ICS Incorporation Ltd v Michael Wilson & Partners Ltd [2005] EWHC 404
  (Ch); [2005] B.P.I.R. 805 5–14
ILG Travel Ltd (In Administration), Re [1996] B.C.C. 21; [1995] 2 B.C.L.C.
  128, Ch D 9–24, 9–26
IMO Carwash. See Bluebrook Ltd, Re
Independent Trustee Services Ltd v Hope [2009] EWHC 2810 (Ch); [2010]
  I.C.R. 553; [2009] Pens. L.R. 379 8–25
India v Taylor [1954] Ch. 131; [1953] 3 W.L.R. 1085; [1953] 2 All E.R. 1452;
  46 R. & I.T. 817; (1953) 32 A.T.C. 413; [1953] T.R. 385; (1953) 97 S.J.
  861, CA 8–41
IRC v Adam & Partners Ltd [2002] B.C.C. 247; [2001] 1 B.C.L.C. 222;
  [2000] B.P.I.R. 986, CA (Civ Div) 1–44, 1–48

IRC v Goldblatt [1972] Ch. 498; [1972] 2 W.L.R. 953; [1972] 2 All E.R. 202; 47 T.C. 483; (1971) 116 S.J. 332, Ch D 10–60, 10–61, 10–63
IRC v Hashmi [2002] EWCA Civ 981; [2002] B.C.C. 943; [2002] 2 B.C.L.C. 489; [2002] B.P.I.R. 974; [2002] W.T.L.R. 1027 13–137
IRC v Richmond [2003] EWHC 999 (Ch); [2003] S.T.C. 1394; [2003] 2 B.C.L.C. 442; 75 T.C. 77; [2003] S.T.I. 1029; [2003] S.T.I. 1873 14–16
IRC v Wimbledon Football Club Ltd [2004] EWCA Civ 655; [2004] B.C.C. 638; [2005] 1 B.C.L.C. 66; [2004] B.P.I.R. 700; (2004) 148 S.J.L.B. 697; 8–19, 11–21, 12–42
Innovate Logistics Ltd v Sunberry Properties Ltd. *See* Sunberry Properties Ltd v Innovate Logistics Ltd (In Administration)
Instrumentation Electrical Services Ltd, Re (1988) 4 B.C.C. 301; [1988] B.C.L.C. 550; [1989] P.C.C. 101 5–17
International Bulk Commodities Ltd, Re [1993] Ch. 77; [1992] 3 W.L.R. 238; [1993] 1 All E.R. 361; [1992] B.C.C. 463; [1992] B.C.L.C. 1074, Ch D 16–54
International Championship Management Ltd, Re. *See* Cohen v Davis
International Sections Ltd (In Liquidation), Re [2009] EWHC 137 (Ch); [2009] B.C.C. 574; [2009] 1 B.C.L.C. 580; [2009] B.P.I.R. 297 6–38
International Tin Council, Re [1987] Ch. 419; [1987] 2 W.L.R. 1229; [1987] 1 All E.R. 890; (1987) 3 B.C.C. 103; [1987] B.C.L.C. 272; [1987] P.C.C. 283; [1987] 1 F.T.L.R. 305; (1987) 84 L.S.G. 1732; (1987) 131 S.J. 690 .... 5–02, 5–19
Invertec Ltd v De Mol Holding BV [2009] EWHC 2471 (Ch) 4–18
Ira, The. *See* Coca–Cola Financial Corp v Finsat International Ltd
Irish Reel Productions Ltd v Capitol Films Ltd [2010] EWHC 180 (Ch); [2010] Bus. L.R. 854; [2010] B.C.C. 588 11–98
Irwin (Administrator of Daniel Lynch Ltd) v Lynch [2010] EWCA Civ 1153; [2011] B.P.I.R. 158 14–14
J Leslie Engineers Co Ltd (In Liquidation), Re [1976] 1 W.L.R. 292; [1976] 2 All E.R. 85; (1976) 120 S.J. 146, Ch D 3–07, 13–133, 13–134
J Smiths Haulage Ltd, Re [2007] B.C.C. 135, Ch D 11–06
JN2 Ltd, Re [1978] 1 W.L.R. 183; [1977] 3 All E.R. 1104; (1977) 121 S.J. 46, Ch D 5–14
Jackson & Bassford Ltd, Re [1906] 2 Ch. 467, Ch D 13–78, 13–116
James Dolman & Co Ltd v Pedley [2003] EWCA Civ 1686; [2004] B.C.C. 504; [2004] B.P.I.R. 290; (2003) 147 S.J.L.B. 1121; [2003] N.P.C. 110; ... 5–12, 5–13
James Smith & Sons (Norwood) v Goodman [1936] Ch. 216, CA 5–03
Jartay Developments Ltd, Re (1983) 22 B.L.R. 134 6–44
Jeavons Ex p. Mackay, Re (1872–73) L.R. 8 Ch. App. 643, CA in Chancery 7–03, 7–09, 7–12, 8–06
Jerome v Kelly (Inspector of Taxes) [2004] UKHL 25; [2004] 1 W.L.R. 1409; [2004] 2 All E.R. 835; [2004] S.T.C. 887; 76 T.C. 147; [2004] B.T.C. 176; [2004] W.T.L.R. 681; [2004] S.T.I. 1201; [2004] 21 E.G. 151 (C.S.); (2004) 101(23) L.S.G. 33; [2004] N.P.C. 75 6–23
John Slack Ltd, Re [1995] B.C.C. 1116, Ch D 11–85
Johns, Re [1928] Ch. 737 .... 7–03, 7–12
Johnson v Davies [1999] Ch. 117; [1998] 3 W.L.R. 1299; [1998] 2 All E.R. 649; [1999] B.C.C. 275; [1998] 2 B.C.L.C. 252; [1998] B.P.I.R. 607; (2000) 79 P. & C.R. 14; [1998] L. & T.R. 69; [1998] 3 E.G.L.R. 72; [1998] 49 E.G. 153; (1998) 95(19) L.S.G. 23; (1998) 142 S.J.L.B. 141; [1998] N.P.C. 50, CA (Civ Div) 12–25, 12–26, 12–50, 12–53

Johnson v Gore Wood & Co (No.1) [2002] 2 A.C. 1; [2001] 2 W.L.R. 72;
    [2001] 1 All E.R. 481; [2001] C.P.L.R. 49; [2001] B.C.C. 820; [2001] 1
    B.C.L.C. 313; [2001] P.N.L.R. 18; (2001) 98(1) L.S.G. 24; (2001) 98(8)
    L.S.G. 46; (2000) 150 N.L.J. 1889; (2001) 145 S.J.L.B. 29, HL 14–20
Johnson Machine and Tool Co Ltd, Re [2010] EWHC 582 (Ch); [2010]
    B.C.C. 382; (2010) 160 N.L.J. 805 11–98
Joiner v George [2002] EWCA Civ 160; [2003] B.C.C. 298 4–35
Jones v Lipman [1962] 1 W.L.R. 832; [1962] 1 All E.R. 442; (1962) 106 S.J.
    531, Ch D 5–04
Jubilee International Inc v Farlin Timbers Pte Ltd [2005] EWHC 3331 (Ch);
    [2006] B.P.I.R. 765 5–13
Kappler v Secretary of State for Trade and Industry [2006] EWHC 3694
    (Ch); [2006] B.C.C. 845; [2008] 1 B.C.L.C. 120 14–68
Kaupthing Capital Partners II Master LP Inc, Re [2010] EWHC 836 (Ch) .. 15–56
Kaupthing Singer & Friedlander Ltd (In Administration), Re [2009]
    EWHC 740 (Ch); [2009] 2 Lloyd's Rep. 154; [2009] 2 B.C.L.C.
    137 .... 9–03, 9–04
Kaupthing Singer & Friedlander Ltd (In Administration), Re [2010]
    EWHC 316 (Ch) 8–08, 8–18, 11–01, 11–85
Kaupthing Singer & Friedlander Ltd (In Administration), Re [2010] EWCA
    Civ 518; [2010] Bus. L.R. 1500; [2010] B.P.I.R. 839; (2010) 107(21)
    L.S.G. 16 .... 9–38, 11–115
Kayford Ltd (In Liquidation), Re [1975] 1 W.L.R. 279; [1975] 1 All E.R.
    604; (1974) 118 S.J. 752, Ch D 6–42
Kayley Vending Ltd, Re [2009] EWHC 904 (Ch); [2009] B.C.C. 578 11–37,
                                                                    11–39, 11–40
Kaytech International Plc, Re [1999] B.C.C. 390; [1999] 2 B.C.L.C. 351, CA
    (Civ Div) 14–04, 14–05
Keever, Re [1967] Ch. 182; [1966] 3 W.L.R. 779; [1966] 3 All E.R. 631;
    [1966] 2 Lloyd's Rep. 475; (1966) 110 S.J. 847, Ch D 13–132
Kelly v Inflexion Fund 2 Ltd [2010] EWHC 2850 (Ch); [2011] B.C.C. 93 6–40
Kentish Homes, Re. *See* Powdrill & Lyle (Joint Liquidators of Kentish
    Homes Ltd) v Tower Hamlets LBC
Kernohan Estates v Boyd [1967] N.I. 27 10–53
Kilnoore Ltd, Re. *See* Unidare Plc v Cohen
King v Anthony [1998] 2 B.C.L.C. 517; [1999] B.P.I.R. 73, CA (Civ Div) 12–55
Klempka v Miller [2008] EWHC 3554 (Ch); [2010] B.C.C. 309; [2009]
    B.P.I.R. 549 .... 9–45, 13–91
Knights v Seymour Pierce Ellis Ltd (formerly Ellis & Partners Ltd) [2001] 2
    B.C.L.C. 176; [2002] B.P.I.R. 203, Ch D 13–19
Knowles v Scott [1891] 1 Ch. 717, Ch D 5–03
Krasner v Dennison [2001] Ch. 76; [2000] 3 W.L.R. 720; [2000] 3 All E.R.
    234; [2000] B.P.I.R. 410; [2000] O.P.L.R. 299; [2000] Pens. L.R. 213;
    (2000) 97(19) L.S.G. 42; (2000) 150 N.L.J. 543; (2000) 144 S.J.L.B. 205,
    CA (Civ Div) 6–09
Kyrris v Oldham [2003] EWCA Civ 1506; [2004] B.C.C. 111; [2004] 1
    B.C.L.C. 305; [2004] B.P.I.R. 165; [2004] P.N.L.R. 18; (2003) 100(48)
    L.S.G. 17; (2003) 147 S.J.L.B. 1306; [2003] N.P.C. 133 .... 5–03, 11–92, 14–17
LH Charles & Co Ltd, Re [1935] W.N. 15 13–125
La Seda De Barcelona SA, Re [2010] EWHC 1364 (Ch) 12–17
Lafayette Electronics Europe Ltd, Re [2006] EWHC 1006 (Ch); [2007]
    B.C.C. 890 5–18
Land Rover Group Ltd v UPF (UK) Ltd (In Administrative Receivership)
    [2002] EWHC 3183 (QB); [2003] 2 B.C.L.C. 222 10–53

Landau (A Bankrupt), Re [1998] Ch. 223; [1997] 3 W.L.R. 225; [1997] 3 All
    E.R. 322; [1997] 2 B.C.L.C. 515; [1997] 2 F.L.R. 660; [1997] B.P.I.R.
    229; [1996] O.P.L.R. 371; [1997] Pens. L.R. 25; [1998] Fam. Law 68;
    (1997) 94(4) L.S.G. 25; (1997) 141 S.J.L.B. 28, Ch D 6–09
Lathia v Dronsfield Bros [1987] B.C.L.C. 321, QBD 10–48, 10–53
Lazard Bros & Co v Midland Bank Ltd [1933] A.C. 289; (1932) 44 Ll. L.
    Rep. 159, HL 16–57
Leas Hotel Co, Re [1902] 1 Ch. 332, Ch D 6–04
Legends Surf Shops Plc (In Administrative Receivership) v Sun Life
    Assurance Society Plc [2005] EWHC 1438 (Ch); [2006] B.C.C. 204;
    [2005] B.P.I.R. 1145; [2005] 3 E.G.L.R. 43; [2005] 46 E.G. 178; [2005]
    N.P.C. 94; [2006] 1 P. & C.R. DG1 10–57
Lehman Brothers International (Europe) (In Administration), Re [2008]
    EWHC 2869 (Ch); [2009] B.C.C. 632; [2009] 1 B.C.L.C. 161; [2009]
    Bus. L.R. D28 11–93
Lehman Brothers International (Europe) (In Administration), Re [2009]
    EWCA Civ 1161; [2010] Bus. L.R. 489; [2010] B.C.C. 272; [2010] 1
    B.C.L.C. 496 .... 12–18, 13–80
Lehman Brothers International (Europe) (In Administration), Re [2010]
    EWHC 47 (Ch); [2010] 2 B.C.L.C. 301 .... 9–24, 9–26
Lehman Brothers International (Europe) (In Administration), Re [2010]
    EWHC 2914 (Ch) 15–01
Lehman Brothers International (Europe) (In Administration), Re [2010]
    EWCA Civ 917; [2011] Bus. L.R. 277; [2011] 1 C.M.L.R. 27 ...... 3–07, 6–42
Leigh Estates (UK) Ltd, Re [1994] B.C.C. 292; [1994] R.A. 57; [1993] E.G.
    212 (C.S.), Ch D 5–21
Lennox Holdings Plc, Re [2009] B.C.C. 155, Ch D 15–56
Leon v York-o-Matic Ltd [1966] 1 W.L.R. 1450; [1966] 3 All E.R. 277;
    (1966) 110 S.J. 685, Ch D 5–03
Levi & Co Ltd, Re [1919] 1 Ch. 416, Ch D 3–11
Levy McCallum Ltd v Allen [2007] NI Ch. 3 13–34
Lewis Merthyr Consolidated Collieries Ltd, Re (No.1) [1929] 1 Ch. 498,
    CA 10–60, 10–71
Lexi Holdings Plc (In Administration) v Luqman [2009] EWCA Civ 117;
    [2009] B.C.C. 716; [2009] 2 B.C.L.C. 1 .... 14–11, 14–19
Leyland DAF Ltd v Automotive Products Plc [1993] B.C.C. 389; [1994]
    1 B.C.L.C. 245; [1994] E.C.C. 289; (1993) 137 S.J.L.B. 133, CA (Civ
    Div) 10–55
Leyland Printing Co Ltd (In Administration), Re [2010] EWHC 2105
    (Ch) 11–29
Lind, Re [1915] 2 Ch. 345, CA 3–04
Linden Gardens Trust Ltd v Lenesta Sludge Disposal Ltd [1994] 1 A.C. 85;
    [1993] 3 W.L.R. 408; [1993] 3 All E.R. 417; 63 B.L.R. 1; 36 Con. L.R.
    1; [1993] E.G. 139 (C.S.); (1993) 143 N.L.J. 1152; (1993) 137 S.J.L.B.
    183, HL 6–10
Lindsay v O'Loughnane [2010] EWHC 529 (QB) 14–26
Lines Bros (In Liquidation), Re [1983] Ch. 1; [1982] 2 W.L.R. 1010;
    [1982] 2 All E.R. 183; [1982] Com. L.R. 81; (1982) 126 S.J. 197, CA
    (Civ Div) 5–12
Lipkin Gorman v Karpnale Ltd [1991] 2 A.C. 548; [1991] 3 W.L.R. 10;
    [1992] 4 All E.R. 512; (1991) 88(26) L.S.G. 31; (1991) 141 N.L.J. 815;
    (1991) 135 S.J.L.B. 36, HL 13–127
Liquidator of Marini Ltd v Dickenson [2003] EWHC 334 (Ch); [2004]
    B.C.C. 172 14–52

Liquidator of West Mercia Safetywear Ltd v Dodd (1988) 4 B.C.C. 30;
  [1988] B.C.L.C. 250; [1988] P.C.C. 212, CA (Civ Div) 14–14
Lister v Hooson [1908] 1 K.B. 174, CA 9–29
Living Images Ltd, Re [1996] B.C.C. 112; [1996] 1 B.C.L.C. 348, Ch D 14–74,
                                                                        14–80
Lloyd Generale Italiano, Re (1885) L.R. 29 Ch. D. 219, Ch D 16–50
Local London Residential Ltd (Liquidator's Costs), Re [2004] EWHC 114
  (Ch); [2004] 2 B.C.L.C. 72; [2004] B.P.I.R. 599 3–03
Lo-Line Electric Motors Ltd, Re [1988] Ch. 477; [1988] 3 W.L.R. 26; [1988]
  2 All E.R. 692; (1988) 4 B.C.C. 415; [1988] B.C.L.C. 698; [1988] P.C.C.
  236; [1988] 2 F.T.L.R. 107; (1988) 138 N.L.J. Rep. 119; (1988) 132 S.J.
  851, Ch D 14–04, 14–05, 14–67, 14–73, 14–74, 14–75, 14–81
Lomas v JFB Firth Rixson Inc [2010] EWHC 3372 (Ch) 7–03, 7–04, 7–19
Lomax Leisure Ltd, Re [2000] Ch. 502; [1999] 3 W.L.R. 652; [1999] 3 All
  E.R. 22; [2000] B.C.C. 352; [1999] 2 B.C.L.C. 126; [1999] L. & T.R. 519;
  [1999] 2 E.G.L.R. 37; [1999] 23 E.G. 143; [1999] E.G. 61 (C.S.); (1999)
  96(21) L.S.G. 38, Ch D 11–57
Lomax Leisure Ltd (In Liquidation) v Miller [2007] EWHC 2508 (Ch);
  [2008] 1 B.C.L.C. 262; [2007] B.P.I.R. 1615 .... 5–03, 8–40
No.1 London Ltd, Re [1991] B.C.C. 118, Ch D 6–30
London Chartered Bank of Australia, Re [1893] 3 Ch. 540, Ch D 12–25
London and Cheshire Insurance Co Ltd v Laplagrene Property Co Ltd
  [1971] Ch. 499; [1971] 2 W.L.R. 257; [1971] 1 All E.R. 766; (1971) 22 P.
  & C.R. 108; (1970) 114 S.J. 912, Ch D 13–123
London and Paris Banking Corp, Re (1874–75) L.R. 19 Eq. 444, Ct of
  Chancery 5–16
Lowerstoft Traffic Services Ltd, Re [1986] B.C.L.C. 81 5–21
Lundy Granite Co, Re (1870–71) L.R. 6 Ch. App. 462, CA in Chancery 3–11,
                               8–33, 8–38, 11–100, 11–104, 11–105
Lune Metal Products Ltd (In Administration), Re [2006] EWCA Civ 1720;
  [2007] Bus. L.R. 589; [2007] B.C.C. 217; [2007] 2 B.C.L.C. 746 11–85
Lyons, Re Ex p Barclays Bank Ltd v Trustee (1934) 152 L.T. 201 13–106
Lysaght v Edwards (1875–76) L.R. 2 Ch. D. 499, Ch D 6–23
MC Bacon Ltd (No.1), Re [1990] B.C.C. 78; [1990] B.C.L.C. 324,
  Ch D 13–27, 13–38, **13–96**
MC Bacon Ltd (No.2), Re [1991] Ch. 127; [1990] 3 W.L.R. 646; [1990]
  B.C.C. 430; [1990] B.C.L.C. 607, Ch D 13–142, 14–55
MDA Investment Management Ltd (No.1), Re [2003] EWHC 2277 (Ch);
  [2005] B.C.C. 783; [2004] 1 B.C.L.C. 217; [2004] B.P.I.R. 75 13–45
MFP Foundations & Piling Ltd v Shaw. *See* Shaw v MFP Foundations &
  Piling Ltd
MG Probud Gdynia sp z oo (C–444/07) [2010] B.C.C. 453, ECJ 15–32
MG Rover Beluxl SA/NV (In Administration), Re [2006] EWHC 1296
  (Ch); [2007] B.C.C. 446 .... **11–86**, 15–67
MS Fashions Ltd v Bank of Credit and Commerce International SA (In
  Liquidation) [1993] Ch. 425; [1993] 3 W.L.R. 220; [1993] 3 All E.R.
  769; [1993] B.C.C. 360; [1993] B.C.L.C. 1200; (1993) 137 S.J.L.B. 132,
  CA (Civ Div) 8–44, 9–23, 9–38, 9–40, 9–42
MTI Trading Systems Ltd (In Administration), Re [1998] B.C.C. 400, CA
  (Civ Div) 11.48
McCourt v Baron Meats Ltd [1997] B.P.I.R. 114, Ch D 8–42
Mace Builders (Glasgow) Ltd v Lunn [1986] Ch. 459; [1985] 3 W.L.R. 465;
  (1985) 1 B.C.C. 99438; [1986] P.C.C. 307; (1985) 82 L.S.G. 2331; (1985)
  129 S.J. 573, Ch D 13–126

Machu, Re (1882) L.R. 21 Ch. D. 838, Ch D 7–09
MacJordan Construction Ltd v Brookmount Erostin Ltd [1992] B.C.L.C.
    350; [1994] C.L.C. 581; 56 B.L.R. 1, CA (Civ Div) 6–44
Mack Trucks (Britain) Ltd, Re [1967] 1 W.L.R. 780; [1967] 1 All E.R. 977;
    (1967) 111 S.J. 435, Ch D 10–36
Mackay Ex p. *See* Jeavons Ex p. Mackay, Re
Maclaine Watson & Co Ltd v International Tin Council (No.1) [1989]
    Ch. 253; [1988] 3 W.L.R. 1169; [1988] 3 All E.R. 257; (1988) 4 B.C.C.
    659; (1988) 132 S.J. 1495, CA (Civ Div) 3–12
McLaughlin & Harvey Plc (In Liquidation), Re [1996] N.I. 618; 86 B.L.R.
    1; 54 Con. L.R. 163, CA (NI) 6–17
McMullen & Sons Ltd v Cerrone [1994] B.C.C. 25; [1994] 1 B.C.L.C. 152;
    (1993) 66 P. & C.R. 351; [1994] 19 E.G. 134; [1993] N.P.C. 93, Ch D . . . 11–67
McNulty's Interchange Ltd, Re (1988) 4 B.C.C. 533; [1989] B.C.L.C. 709,
    Ch D 14–75
MacPlant Services Ltd v Contract Lifting Services (Scotland) Ltd [2008]
    CSOH 158; 2009 S.C. 125; 2008 G.W.D. 38–577 . . . . 4–13, 4–16, 4–18,
                                                                4–20, 4–21
Macquarie Internationale Investments Ltd v Glencore UK Ltd [2010]
    EWCA Civ 697; [2010] 1 C.L.C. 1035 4–32
Magical Marking Ltd v Phillips [2008] EWHC 1640 (Pat); [2008] F.S.R. 36;
    (2008) 31(8) I.P.D. 31052 11–78
Majestic Recording Studios Ltd, Re (1988) 4 B.C.C. 519; [1989] B.C.L.C. 1,
    Ch D 14–11, 14–75, 14–81
Managa Properties Ltd v Brittain [2009] EWHC 157 (Ch); [2010] Bus. L.R.
    599; [2009] 1 B.C.L.C. 689; [2009] B.P.I.R. 306 8–40
Manifest Shipping Co Ltd v Uni-Polaris Insurance Co Ltd (The Star Sea)
    [2001] UKHL 1; [2003] 1 A.C. 469; [2001] 2 W.L.R. 170; [2001] 1 All
    E.R. 743; [2001] 1 All E.R. (Comm) 193; [2001] 1 Lloyd's Rep. 389;
    [2001] C.L.C. 608; [2001] Lloyd's Rep. I.R. 247 14–24
Mann v Goldstein [1968] 1 W.L.R. 1091; [1968] 2 All E.R. 769; (1968) 112
    S.J. 439, Ch D 4–21, 5–12, 5–14, 5–18
Manning v AIG Europe UK Ltd [2006] EWCA Civ 7; [2006] Ch. 610; [2006]
    2 W.L.R. 1369; [2006] B.C.C. 233; [2007] 1 B.C.L.C. 29; [2006] B.P.I.R.
    457; [2006] W.T.L.R. 705 . . . . 6–03, 6–25, 6–27, 6–29, 8–08, 8–46
Manson v Smith (Liquidator of Thomas Christy Ltd) [1997] 2 B.C.L.C. 161,
    CA (Civ Div) 9–26, 9–29, 14–16
Maple Environmental Services Ltd, Re [2000] B.C.C. 93; [2001] B.P.I.R.
    321, Ch D 12–30
Marann Brooks CSV Ltd, Re [2003] B.C.C. 239; [2003] B.P.I.R. 1159,
    Ch D 15–11
March Estates Plc v Gunmark Ltd [1996] 2 B.C.L.C. 1; [1996] B.P.I.R. 439;
    [1996] 2 E.G.L.R. 38; [1996] 32 E.G. 75; [1996] E.G. 49 (C.S.); [1996]
    N.P.C. 46, Ch D 12–27
Marconi Corp Plc, Re (Company: Scheme of Arrangement) [2003] EWHC
    1083 (Ch) 12–24
Marriage Neave & Co, Re [1896] 2 Ch. 663, CA 10–58
Maxwell Communications Corp Plc (No.2), Re. *See also* Barclays Bank Plc
    v Homan
Maxwell Communications Corp Plc (No.2), Re [1993] 1 W.L.R. 1402; [1994]
    1 All E.R. 737; [1993] B.C.C. 369; [1994] 1 B.C.L.C. 1, Ch D 8–08
Maxwell Fleet and Facilities Management Ltd (In Administration) (No.1),
    Re [2001] 1 W.L.R. 323; [2000] 1 All E.R. 464; [1999] 2 B.C.L.C. 721;
    [2000] B.P.I.R. 294, Ch D 11–29

Mayhew v King [2010] EWHC 1121 (Ch); [2010] 2 B.C.L.C. 440; [2010] B.P.I.R. 1155 7–05

Mea Corp, Re. *See* Secretary of State for Trade and Industry v Aviss

Meadrealm Ltd v Transcontinental Gulf Construction Ltd Unreported November 29, 1991 10–20

Measures Bros Ltd v Measures [1910] 2 Ch. 248, CA 5–24

Medforth v Blake [2000] Ch. 86; [1999] 3 W.L.R. 922; [1999] 3 All E.R. 97; [1999] B.C.C. 771; [1999] 2 B.C.L.C. 221; [1999] B.P.I.R. 712; [1999] Lloyd's Rep. P.N. 844; [1999] P.N.L.R. 920; [1999] 2 E.G.L.R. 75; [1999] 29 E.G. 119; [1999] E.G. 81 (C.S.); (1999) 96(24) L.S.G. 39; (1999) 149 N.L.J. 929, CA (Civ Div) 10–48, 10–49

Mejnertsen v Barsoe (C–148/08) [2008] OJ C142/08, removed from register ECJ 15–04

Menastar Finance Ltd (In Liquidation), Re [2002] EWHC 2610 (Ch); [2003] B.C.C. 404; [2003] 1 B.C.L.C. 338 13–82

Mercantile Investment & General Trust Co v International Co of Mexico [1893] 1 Ch. 484n 1–45

Mercury Solutions Ltd, Re. *See* Secretary of State for Trade and Industry v Hall

Mersey Steel & Iron Co Ltd v Naylor Benzon & Co (1883–84) L.R. 9 App. Cas. 434, HL 9–28

Merton v Hammond Suddards. *See* Mond v Hammond Suddards (No.1)

Mess v Duffus & Co (1901) 6 Com. Cas. 165 5–24

Metcalfe v Metcalfe (1890) L.R. 43 Ch. D. 633 7–09

Mid-Kent Fruit Factory, Re [1896] 1 Ch. 567, Ch D 9–24

Midland Coal Coke & Iron Co, Re [1895] 1 Ch. 267, CA 12–18

Miliangos v George Frank (Textiles) Ltd [1976] A.C. 443; [1975] 3 W.L.R. 758; [1975] 3 All E.R. 801; [1976] 1 Lloyd's Rep. 201; [1975] 2 C.M.L.R. 585; (1975) 119 S.J. 774, HL 9–06

Miller v Bain (Director's Breach of Duty) [2002] 1 B.C.L.C. 266, Ch D 14–20

Mills v HSBC Trustee (CI) Ltd [2009] EWHC 3377 (Ch); [2010] W.T.L.R. 235 .... 8–46, 9–23

Mills v Sportsdirect.com Retail Ltd (formerly Sports World International Ltd) [2010] EWHC 1072 (Ch); [2010] 2 B.C.L.C. 143; [2010] 2 P. & C.R. DG19 11–87

Mineral Resources Ltd, Re [1999] 1 All E.R. 746; [1999] B.C.C. 422; [1999] 2 B.C.L.C. 516; [1999] Env. L.R. 407; [1998] B.P.I.R. 576; [1998] 4 P.L.R. 56; [1998] E.G. 78 (C.S.); [1998] N.P.C. 78 .... 2–25, 6–11, 8–30

Mineral Resources Ltd, Re Environment Agency v Stout. *See* Mineral Resources Ltd, Re

Minna Craig Steamship Co v Chartered Mercantile Bank of India London and China [1897] 1 Q.B. 460, CA 16–62

Minrealm Ltd, Re [2007] EWHC 3078 (Ch); [2008] 2 B.C.L.C. 141 4–14

Modelboard Ltd v Outer Box Ltd (In Liquidation) [1992] B.C.C. 945; [1993] B.C.L.C. 623, Ch D 6–46

Modern Jet Support Centre Ltd, Re [2005] EWHC 1611 (Ch); [2005] 1 W.L.R. 3880; [2006] S.T.C. 808; [2006] B.C.C. 174; [2006] 1 B.C.L.C. 703; [2005] B.P.I.R. 1382; [2005] R.V.R. 379; [2006] B.T.C. 362 8–48

Mond v Hammond Suddards (No.1) [1996] 2 B.C.L.C. 470, Ch D 13–141

Money Markets International Stockbrokers Ltd (In Liquidation) v London Stock Exchange Ltd [2002] 1 W.L.R. 1150; [2001] 4 All E.R. 223; [2001] 2 All E.R. (Comm) 344; [2001] 2 B.C.L.C. 347; [2001] B.P.I.R. 1044, Ch D 6–09, 6–13, 7–04, 7–07, 7–09

Montgomery v Wanda Modes Ltd [2002] 1 B.C.L.C. 289; [2003] B.P.I.R.
    457, Ch D 5–13
Moon v Franklin [1996] B.P.I.R. 196, Ch D 13–137, 13–139
Moor v Anglo Italian Bank (1878–79) L.R. 10 Ch. D. 681, Ch D 5–18, 8–47
Moorgate Metals Ltd, Re [1995] B.C.C. 143; [1995] 1 B.C.L.C. 503,
    Ch D 14–04, 14–73, 14–80
Moriarty v Various Customers of BA Peters Plc [2008] EWCA Civ 1604;
    [2010] 1 B.C.L.C. 142; [2009] B.P.I.R. 248 6–44
Morphitis v Bernasconi [2003] EWCA Civ 289; [2003] Ch. 552; [2003] 2
    W.L.R. 1521; [2003] B.C.C. 540; [2003] 2 B.C.L.C. 53; [2003] B.P.I.R.
    973; (2003) 100(19) L.S.G. 30; (2003) 147 S.J.L.B. 300 . . . . 14–23, 14–24,
                                                              14–26, 14–53
Morris v Bank of India [2005] EWCA Civ 693; [2005] B.C.C. 739; [2005] 2
    B.C.L.C. 328; [2005] B.P.I.R. 1067 . . . . 14–22, 14–24
Morris v Kanssen [1946] A.C. 459, HL 10–32
Morris & Atkinson v 3i Plc and the Development Commission Unreported
    July 27, 1988 11–83
Moss Steamship Co Ltd v Whinney [1912] A.C. 254, HL 10–37
Mourant & Co Trustees Ltd v Sixty UK Ltd (In Administration) [2010]
    EWHC 1890 (Ch); [2010] B.C.C. 882; [2010] B.P.I.R. 1264; [2010] 2
    E.G.L.R. 125 . . . . 12–44, 12–54, 12–55
Multinational Gas & Petrochemical Co v Multinational Gas &
    Petrochemical Services Ltd [1983] Ch. 258; [1983] 3 W.L.R. 492; [1983]
    2 All E.R. 563; (1983) 127 S.J. 562, CA (Civ Div) 14–19
Murray-Watson Ltd, Re Unreported April 6, 1977 14–24
MyTravel Group Plc, Re [2004] EWCA Civ 1734; [2005] 2 B.C.L.C.
    123 . . . . 1–50, **12–15**, 12–22, 12–41, 12–43
N Joachimson (A Firm) v Swiss Bank Corp (Costs) [1921] 3 K.B. 110;
    (1921) 6 Ll. L. Rep. 435, CA 13–131
NT Gallagher & Son Ltd, Re [2002] EWCA Civ 404; [2002] 1 W.L.R. 2380;
    [2002] 3 All E.R. 474; [2002] B.C.C. 867; [2002] 2 B.C.L.C. 133; [2002]
    B.P.I.R. 565; (2002) 99(19) L.S.G. 29 . . . . 12–30, 12–44, 12–52
NW Robbie & Co Ltd v Witney Warehouse Co Ltd [1963] 1 W.L.R. 1324;
    [1963] 3 All E.R. 613; (1963) 107 S.J. 1038, CA 6–37
National Arms and Ammunition Co, Re (1885) L.R. 28 Ch. D. 474, CA 8–38
National Farmers Union Development Trusts, Re [1972] 1 W.L.R. 1548;
    [1973] 1 All E.R. 135; (1972) 116 S.J. 679 . . . . 1–44, 1–46
National Provincial Bank Ltd v Ainsworth [1965] A.C. 1175; [1965] 3
    W.L.R. 1; [1965] 2 All E.R. 472; (1965) 109 S.J. 415, HL 6–07, 6–11
National Provincial Bank Ltd v Hastings Car Mart. *See* National Provincial
    Bank Ltd v Ainsworth
National Westminster Bank Ltd v Halesowen Presswork and Assemblies
    Ltd [1972] A.C. 785; [1972] 2 W.L.R. 455; [1972] 1 All E.R. 641; [1972]
    1 Lloyd's Rep. 101; (1972) 116 S.J. 138, HL 8–08, 9–19, 9–24
National Westminster Bank Plc v Jones [2001] EWCA Civ 1541; [2002] 1
    B.C.L.C. 55; [2002] B.P.I.R. 361; (2001) 98(44) L.S.G. 35; (2001) 145
    S.J.L.B. 246; [2002] 1 P. & C.R. DG12 13–20
New Bullas Trading Ltd, Re [1994] B.C.C. 36; [1994] 1 B.C.L.C. 485, CA
    (Civ Div) 10–16
New Millennium Experience Co Ltd, Re. *See* Greenwich Millennium
    Exhibition Ltd v New Millennium Experience Co Ltd
New Oriental Bank Corp (No.2), Re [1895] 1 Ch. 753, Ch D 3–11
Newdigate Colliery Ltd, Re [1912] 1 Ch. 468, CA 10–52, 10–53

Newhart Developments Ltd v Cooperative Commercial Bank Ltd [1978]
Q.B. 814; [1978] 2 W.L.R. 636; [1978] 2 All E.R. 896; (1977) 121 S.J.
847, CA (Civ Div) 10–37, 10–38
Nokes v Doncaster Amalgamated Collieries Ltd [1940] A.C. 1014, HL 6–03
Norditrack (UK) Ltd, Re [2000] 1 W.L.R. 343; [2000] 1 All E.R. 369; [2000]
B.C.C. 441; [2000] 1 B.C.L.C. 467, Ch D 11–116
Norman Holding Co Ltd (In Liquidation), Re [1991] 1 W.L.R. 10; [1990] 3
All E.R. 757; [1991] B.C.C. 11; [1990] B.C.L.C. 1; (1991) 135 S.J. 84,
Ch D 9–23
Nortel Networks SA, Re [2009] EWHC 206 (Ch); [2009] B.C.C. 343; [2009]
I.L.Pr. 42; [2009] B.P.I.R. 316 15–69
Nortel Networks SA, Re [2009] EWHC 1482 (Ch); [2010] B.C.C. 21 . 15–66, 15–67
Nortel GmbH, Re [2010] EWHC 3010 (Ch); [2011] Pens. L.R. 37 ..... 2–24, 8–33,
8–36, 8–37, 11–103
Nortel Networks UK Ltd (In Administration), Re [2010] EWHC 826 (Ch);
[2010] B.C.C. 706; [2010] 2 B.C.L.C. 674; [2010] I.R.L.R. 1042; [2010]
B.P.I.R. 1003 .... 11–53, 11–79
Nottingham General Cemetery Co, Re [1955] Ch. 683; [1955] 3 W.L.R. 61;
[1955] 2 All E.R. 504; 53 L.G.R. 519; (1955) 99 S.J. 400 6–27
OBG Ltd v Allan [2007] UKHL 21; [2008] 1 A.C. 1; [2007] 2 W.L.R. 920;
[2007] Bus. L.R. 1600; [2007] 4 All E.R. 545; [2008] 1 All E.R. (Comm)
1; [2007] I.R.L.R. 608; [2007] E.M.L.R. 12; [2007] B.P.I.R. 746; (2007)
30(6) I.P.D. 30037; [2007] 19 E.G. 165 (C.S.); (2007) 151 S.J.L.B. 674;
[2007] N.P.C. 54 .... 6–04, 10–32, 10–59
OJSC Ank Yugraneft, Re [2008] EWHC 2614 (Ch); [2010] B.C.C. 475;
[2009] 1 B.C.L.C. 298; [2009] Bus. L.R. D33 16–51
OTG Ltd v Barke [2011] I.R.L.R. 272, EAT 8–24, 15–98
Oak Pits Colliery Co, Re (1882) L.R. 21 Ch. D. 322, CA 3–11, 8–38
Oakfame Construction Ltd, Re [1996] B.C.C. 67, Ch D 14–76
Oakland v Wellswood (Yorkshire) Ltd [2009] EWCA Civ 1094; [2010]
B.C.C. 263; [2010] I.C.R. 902; [2010] I.R.L.R. 82 .... 8–24, 15–98
Oakley v Ultra Vehicle Design Ltd (In Liquidation) [2005] EWHC 872
(Ch); [2006] B.C.C. 57; [2005] I.L.Pr. 55; [2006] B.P.I.R. 115 .... 15–23, 15–34
Oakley-Smith v Greenberg [2002] EWCA Civ 1217; [2004] B.C.C. 81;
[2005] 2 B.C.L.C. 74; [2003] B.P.I.R. 709 .... 11–29, 12–26, 12–45, 12–47,
12–48—12–49, 12–52
Oasis Merchandising Services Ltd (In Liquidation), Re [1998] Ch. 170;
[1997] 2 W.L.R. 764; [1996] 1 All E.R. 1009; [1997] B.C.C. 282; [1997]
1 B.C.L.C. 689; (1996) 146 N.L.J. 1513 .... 5–02, 5–06, 6–06, 6–37,
13–142, 14–47, 14–55
Oceanic Steam Navigation Co Ltd, Re [1939] Ch. 41; [1938] 3 All E.R. 740,
Ch D 12–22
O'Driscoll v Manchester Insurance Committee [1915] 3 K.B. 499, CA 4–17
Official Receiver v Dhaliwall [2006] 1 B.C.L.C. 285, CC 14–75
Official Receiver v Eichler [2007] B.P.I.R. 1636, Ch D 15–08
Official Receiver v Key [2009] B.C.C. 11; [2009] 1 B.C.L.C. 22, CC 14–68, 14–75
Offshore Ventilation Ltd, Re. *See* Rhodes v Allied Dunbar (Pension
Services) Ltd
Olympia & York Canary Wharf Ltd (No.1), Re [1993] B.C.C. 154; [1993]
B.C.L.C. 453, Ch D 11–58, 11–67
Olympia & York Canary Wharf Ltd (No.4), Re [1993] B.C.C. 866; [1994] 1
B.C.L.C. 702, Ch D 12–10
Oriental Bank Corp, Re (1886) L.R. 32 Ch. D. 366, Ch D 5–24

Oriental Bank Corp Ex p. The Crown, Re (1885) L.R. 28 Ch. D. 643,
Ch D 1–10
Oriental Inland Steam Co Ex p. Scinde Railway Co, Re (1873–74) L.R. 9
Ch. App. 557, CA in Chancery 16–62
Orleans Motor Co Ltd, Re [1911] 2 Ch. 41, Ch D 13–118
Osborn Ex p. Trustee, Re [1931]32] B. & C.R. 189 16–61
Osiris Insurance Ltd, Re [1999] 1 B.C.L.C. 182, Ch D 12–19
Overnight Ltd (In Liquidation), Re [2009] EWHC 601 (Ch); [2009] Bus.
L.R. 1141; [2010] B.C.C. 787 13–127
Overnight Ltd (In Liquidation), Re [2010] EWHC 613 (Ch); [2010] B.C.C.
796; [2010] 2 B.C.L.C. 186; [2011] Bus. L.R. D30 14–54
PFTZM Ltd, Re [1995] B.C.C. 280; [1995] 2 B.C.L.C. 354, Ch D 14–35
Pacific & General Insurance Co Ltd v Hazell [1997] L.R.L.R. 65; [1997]
B.C.C. 400; [1997] 6 Re. L.R. 157, QBD 1–42
Palk v Mortgage Services Funding Plc [1993] Ch. 330; [1993] 2 W.L.R. 415;
[1993] 2 All E.R. 481; (1993) 25 H.L.R. 56; (1993) 65 P. & C.R. 207;
[1992] N.P.C. 114, CA (Civ Div) 10–49
Palmer v Day & Sons [1895] 2 Q.B. 618, QBD 9–27
Pantmaenog Timber Co Ltd, Re [2003] UKHL 49; [2004] 1 A.C. 158; [2003]
3 W.L.R. 767; [2003] 4 All E.R. 18; [2003] B.C.C. 659; [2003] 2 B.C.L.C.
257; [2004] B.P.I.R. 139; (2003) 153 N.L.J. 1346; (2003) 147 S.J.L.B.
936 14–58
Papanicola v Fagan [2010] 2 P. & C.R. DG1 13–137
Paragon Finance Plc (formerly National Home Loans Corp) v Nash [2001]
EWCA Civ 1466; [2002] 1 W.L.R. 685; [2002] 2 All E.R. 248; [2001] 2
All E.R. (Comm) 1025; [2002] 2 P. & C.R. 20; (2001) 98(44) L.S.G. 36;
(2001) 145 S.J.L.B. 244; [2002] 1 P. & C.R. DG13 13–109
Paramount Airways Ltd, Re. *See* Bristol Airport Plc v Powdrill
Paramount Airways Ltd (No.2), Re [1993] Ch. 223; [1992] 3 W.L.R. 690;
[1992] 3 All E.R. 1; [1992] B.C.C. 416; [1992] B.C.L.C. 710;
(1992) 89(14) L.S.G. 31; (1992) 136 S.J.L.B. 97; [1992] N.P.C. 27, CA
(Civ Div) 13–45
Park Air Services Plc, Re [2000] 2 A.C. 172; [1999] 2 W.L.R. 396; [1999] 1
All E.R. 673; [1999] B.C.C. 135; [1999] 1 B.C.L.C. 155; [1999] B.P.I.R.
786; [1999] L. & T.R. 289; [1999] 1 E.G.L.R. 1; [1999] 14 E.G.
149; [1999] E.G. 17 (C.S.); (1999) 149 N.L.J. 195; [1999] N.P.C. 12,
HL 3–11, 6–31, 8–43, 9–16
Park Ward & Co Ltd, Re [1926] Ch. 828, Ch D 13–135
Parker-Tweedale v Dunbar Bank Plc (No.1) [1991] Ch. 12; [1990] 3 W.L.R.
767; [1990] 2 All E.R. 577; (1990) 60 P. & C.R. 83; (1990) 140 N.L.J.
169; (1990) 134 S.J. 886, CA (Civ Div) 10–48
Parkside International Ltd, Re. *See* Klempka v Miller
Parmalat Capital Finance Ltd v Food Holdings Ltd (In Liquidation) [2008]
UKPC 23; [2008] B.C.C. 371; [2009] 1 B.C.L.C. 274; [2008] B.P.I.R.
641 .... 5–13, 5–14, 5–18
Patrick and Lyon Ltd, Re [1933] Ch. 786, Ch D 14–24
Peachdart Ltd, Re [1984] Ch. 131; [1983] 3 W.L.R. 878; [1983] 3 All E.R.
204; (1983) 1 B.C.C. 98920; (1984) 81 L.S.G. 204; (1983) 127 S.J. 839,
Ch D 6–46
Pearce v Bastable [1901] 2 Ch. 122, Ch D 6–23
Pearce v Bastable's Trustee in Bankruptcy. *See* Pearce v Bastable
Pearl Maintenance Services Ltd, Re [1995] B.C.C. 657; [1995] 1 B.C.L.C.
449, Ch D 10–63

Penrose v Official Receiver [1996] 1 W.L.R. 482; [1996] 2 All E.R. 96; [1995]
B.C.C. 311; [1996] 1 B.C.L.C. 389, Ch D 14–06
Permacell Finesse Ltd (In Liquidation), Re [2007] EWHC 3233 (Ch);
[2008] B.C.C. 208 .... 6–40, 8–03
Perpetual Trustee Co Ltd v BNY Corporate Trustee Services Ltd [2009]
EWCA Civ 1160; [2010] Ch. 347; [2010] 3 W.L.R. 87; [2010] Bus.
L.R. 632; [2010] B.C.C. 59; [2010] 1 B.C.L.C. 747; [2010] B.P.I.R.
174 .... 3–05, 6–18, 6–26, 7–03, 7–05, 7–06, 7–07,
7–08, 7–10, **7–13—7–22**, 11–69, 12–08
Perry v Day [2004] EWHC 1398 (Ch); [2005] B.C.C. 375 14–20
Phillips (Liquidator of AJ Bekhor & Co) v Brewin Dolphin Bell Lawrie Ltd
(formerly Brewin Dolphin & Co Ltd) [2001] UKHL 2; [2001] 1
W.L.R. 143; [2001] 1 All E.R. 673; [2001] B.C.C. 864; [2001] 1 B.C.L.C.
145; [2001] B.P.I.R. 119; (2001) 98(12) L.S.G. 43; (2001) 145 S.J.L.B.
32 .... 4–35, 13–19, 13–20, 13–26,
13–31—13–32, 13–46, 13–67
Phoenix Bessemer Steel Co Ex p. Carnforth Haematite Iron Co, Re
(1876–77) L.R. 4 Ch. D. 108, CA 5–24
Pickard v FIM Advisers LLP [2010] EWHC 1299 (Ch) 5–02
Pinewood Joinery v Starelm Properties Ltd [1994] B.C.C. 569; [1994] 2
B.C.L.C. 412, Ch D 13–137, 13–139
Pitt v Mond [2001] B.P.I.R. 624, Ch D 12–55
Pleatfine Ltd, Re [1983] B.C.L.C. 102; (1983) 1 B.C.C. 98942, Ch D 5–19
Polly Peck International Plc (In Administration) (No.4), Re [1996] 2 All
E.R. 433; [1996] B.C.C. 486; [1996] 1 B.C.L.C. 428, Ch D 8–45, 12–18
Portbase Clothing Ltd, Re [1993] Ch. 388; [1993] 3 W.L.R. 14; [1993] 3 All
E.R. 829; [1993] B.C.C. 96; [1993] B.C.L.C. 796, Ch D 8–52
Portsmouth Borough (Kingston, Fratton & Southsea) Tramways Co, Re
[1892] 2 Ch. 362, Ch D 5–18
Portsmouth City Football Club (In Administration), Re [2010] EWHC 2013
(Ch); [2011] B.C.C. 149; [2010] B.P.I.R. 1123; (2010) 107(33) L.S.G.
14 12–54
Pott v Clegg. *See* Pott, Assignees of John Ryle, a Bankrupt v Clegg,
Executor of William Turner, Deceased
Pott, Assignees of John Ryle, a Bankrupt v Clegg, Executor of William
Turner, Deceased, 153 E.R. 1212; (1847) 16 M. & W. 321, Ct of Exch ... 9–23
Potters Oils Ltd, Re [1985] B.C.L.C. 203; (1985) 1 B.C.C. 99384; [1985]
P.C.C. 148, Ch D 6–29
Potters Oils, Re (No.2) [1986] 1 W.L.R. 201; [1986] 1 All E.R. 890; (1985) 1
B.C.C. 99593; [1986] P.C.C. 185; (1986) 83 L.S.G. 869; (1985) 130 S.J.
166, Ch D 10–28, 10–34, 10–66
Pound & Hutchins, Re (1889) L.R. 42 Ch. D. 402, CA 10–28
Powdrill v Watson [1995] 2 A.C. 394; [1995] 2 W.L.R. 312; [1995] 2 All E.R.
65; [1995] B.C.C. 319; [1994] 1 B.C.L.C. 386; [1995] I.C.R. 1100; [1995]
I.R.L.R. 269; (1995) 92(17) L.S.G. 47; (1995) 145 N.L.J. 449; (1995)
139 S.J.L.B. 110, HL 10–54, 10–55, 11–03
Powdrill & Lyle (Joint Liquidators of Kentish Homes Ltd) v Tower Hamlets
LBC [1993] B.C.C. 212; [1993] B.C.L.C. 1375; [1993] R.A. 39; (1993)
137 S.J.L.B. 45; [1992] N.P.C. 12, Ch D 8–33
Power v Sharp Investments Ltd [1993] B.C.C. 609; [1994] 1 B.C.L.C. 111,
CA (Civ Div) 13–116
Powerstore (Trading) Ltd, Re [1997] 1 W.L.R. 1280; [1998] 1 All E.R. 121;
[1998] B.C.C. 305; [1998] 1 B.C.L.C. 90; (1997) 94(24) L.S.G. 31;
(1997) 141 S.J.L.B. 137, Ch D 11–04

Practice Direction (Ch D: Validation Orders: Insolvency Act 1986 ss127 and 284) [2007] B.C.C. 91; [2007] B.P.I.R. 94, Ch D 13–135

Practice Direction (Companies: Directors Disqualification Proceedings) [1999] B.C.C. 717, Ch D 14–70

Practice Statement (Ch D: Schemes of Arrangements with Creditors) [2002] 1 W.L.R. 1345; [2002] 3 All E.R. 96; [2002] B.C.C. 355; (2002) 146 S.J.L.B. 99, Ch D 1–53, 12–19, 12–21

Prestige Grindings Ltd, Re [2005] EWHC 3076 (Ch); [2006] B.C.C. 421; [2006] 1 B.C.L.C. 440; [2006] B.P.I.R. 844 14–82

Pritchard (Inspector of Taxes) v MH Builders (Wilmslow), Ltd [1969] 1 W.L.R. 409; [1969] 2 All E.R. 670; 45 T.C. 360; [1968] T.R. 429; (1969) 113 S.J. 285, Ch D 3–09

Proceedings brought by Staubitz-Schreiber (C–1/04) [2006] E.C.R. I–701; [2006] B.C.C. 639; [2006] I.L.Pr. 30; [2006] B.P.I.R. 510, ECJ 15–06, 15–08, 15–47

Produce Marketing Consortium (In Liquidation) Ltd, Re (No.1) [1989] 1 W.L.R. 745; [1989] 3 All E.R. 1; (1989) 5 B.C.C. 399; [1989] B.C.L.C. 513; [1989] P.C.C. 290; (1989) 133 S.J. 945, Ch D 14–51

Produce Marketing Consortium (In Liquidation) Ltd, Re (No.2) (1989) 5 B.C.C. 569; [1989] B.C.L.C. 520, Ch D 14–44, 14–45, 14–53, 14–56

Prosser v Castle Sanderson Solicitors [2002] EWCA Civ 1140; [2003] B.C.C. 440; [2002] B.P.I.R. 1163; [2002] Lloyd's Rep. P.N. 584; [2002] N.P.C. 112 12–55

Prout v Gregory (1890) L.R. 24 Q.B.D. 281, QBD 3–10

Prudential Assurance Co Ltd v PRG Powerhouse Ltd [2007] EWHC 1002 (Ch); [2007] Bus. L.R. 1771; [2007] B.C.C. 500; [2008] 1 B.C.L.C. 289; [2007] B.P.I.R. 839; [2007] 3 E.G.L.R. 131; [2007] 19 E.G. 164 (C.S.); (2007) 104(20) L.S.G. 30 . . . . 12–28, 12–44, 12–50, 12–54

Pulsford v Devenish [1903] 2 Ch. 625, Ch D 5–03

Purewal Enterprises Ltd, Petitioner [2008] CSOH 127; 2008 G.W.D. 37–555 4–21

Purpoint Ltd, Re [1991] B.C.C. 121; [1991] B.C.L.C. 491, Ch D 14–47, 14–55

Pyle Works (No.1), Re (1890) L.R. 44 Ch. D. 534, CA 6–18, 6–45

Queen's Moat Houses Plc (No.2), Re. *See* Secretary of State for Trade and Industry v Bairstow

R. v Austen (Styliano Pierre) (1985) 1 B.C.C. 99528; (1985) 7 Cr. App. R. (S.) 214; (1985) 82 L.S.G. 2499, CA (Crim Div) 14–63

R. v Bott-Walters (John Anthony) [2005] EWCA Crim 243; [2005] 2 Cr. App. R. (S.) 70 14–80

R. v Corbin (Nigel Ian Henry) (1984) 6 Cr. App. R. (S.) 17; [1984] Crim. L.R. 302, CA (Crim Div) 14–63

R. v Georgiou (Christakis) (1988) 4 B.C.C. 322; (1988) 87 Cr. App. R. 207; (1988) 10 Cr. App. R. (S.) 137; [1988] Crim. L.R. 472, CA (Crim Div) 14–63

R. v Goodman (Ivor Michael) [1993] 2 All E.R. 789; [1992] B.C.C. 625; [1994] 1 B.C.L.C. 349; (1993) 97 Cr. App. R. 210; (1993) 14 Cr. App. R. (S.) 147; [1992] Crim. L.R. 676, CA (Crim Div) 14–60, 14–63

R. v Grantham (Paul Reginald) [1984] Q.B. 675; [1984] 2 W.L.R. 815; [1984] 3 All E.R. 166; (1984) 1 B.C.C. 99075; (1984) 79 Cr. App. R. 86; [1984] Crim. L.R. 492, CA (Crim Div) 14–24

R. v Holmes (David Leonard) [1991] B.C.C. 394; (1992) 13 Cr. App. R. (S.) 29; [1991] Crim. L.R. 790, CA (Crim Div) 14–64

R. v Kohn (David James) (1979) 69 Cr. App. R. 395; [1979] Crim. L.R. 675, CA (Crim Div) 13–133

R. v Seager (Mornington Stafford) [2009] EWCA Crim 1303; [2010] 1
    W.L.R. 815; [2010] 1 Cr. App. R. (S.) 60; [2009] Lloyd's Rep. F.C. 492;
    [2009] Crim. L.R. 816 14–82
R. v Tower Hamlets LBC Ex p. Chetnik Developments Ltd [1988] A.C. 858;
    [1988] 2 W.L.R. 654; [1988] 1 All E.R. 961; 86 L.G.R. 321; [1988] R.A.
    45; [1988] E.G. 36 (C.S.); (1988) 138 N.L.J. Rep. 89; (1988) 132 S.J.
    4621, HL 5–02
R. (on the application of SRM Global Master Fund LP) v Treasury
    Commissioner [2009] EWHC 227 (Admin); [2009] B.C.C. 251; [2009]
    U.K.H.R.R. 712; (2009) 159 N.L.J. 279 4–19
RA Cripps (Pharmaceutical) and Son Ltd v Wickenden [1973] 1 W.L.R.
    944; [1973] 2 All E.R. 606; (1972) 117 S.J. 446, Ch D 10–26, 10–30,
                                                                      10–31, 10–32
RA Securities Ltd v Mercantile Credit Co Ltd [1995] 3 All E.R. 581; [1994]
    B.C.C. 598; [1994] 2 B.C.L.C. 721; [1994] 44 E.G. 242; [1994] N.P.C. 76,
    Ch D 12–47, 12–53
Railtrack Plc (In Administration) (No.2), Re [2002] EWCA Civ 955; [2002]
    1 W.L.R. 3002; [2002] 4 All E.R. 435; [2002] 2 B.C.L.C. 755; [2003]
    B.P.I.R. 507; [2002] A.C.D. 103; (2002) 99(35) L.S.G. 37; (2002) 146
    S.J.L.B. 183 11–05
Ramlort v Reid. *See* Reid v Ramlort Ltd
Ramsey v Hartley [1977] 1 W.L.R. 686; [1977] 2 All E.R. 673; (1977) 121 S.J.
    319, CA (Civ Div) 5–06
Random House UK Ltd v Allason [2008] EWHC 2854 (Ch) 13–137
Ratford v Northavon DC [1987] Q.B. 357; [1986] 3 W.L.R. 770; [1986] 3 All
    E.R. 193; (1986) 2 B.C.C. 99242; [1986] P.C.C. 268; (1986) 150 J.P. 605;
    85 L.G.R. 443; [1986] R.A. 137; (1986) 83 L.S.G. 3253; (1986) 130 S.J.
    786, CA (Civ Div) 10–58
Rawnsley v Weatherall Green & Smith North Ltd [2009] EWHC 2482 (Ch);
    [2010] B.C.C. 406; [2010] 1 B.C.L.C. 658; [2010] B.P.I.R. 449; [2010]
    P.N.L.R. 6 5–06
Rayack Construction Ltd v Lampeter Meat Co Ltd (1979) 12 B.L.R. 30,
    Ch D 6–44
Raymond Saul & Co v Holden [2008] EWHC 2731 (Ch); [2009] Ch. 313;
    [2009] 2 W.L.R. 1257; [2009] B.P.I.R. 50; [2008] W.T.L.R. 1833; [2008]
    N.P.C. 122 .... 3–10, 6–05
Rayner v Preston (1880–81) L.R. 18 Ch. D. 1, CA 6–23
Real Estate Development Co, Re [1991] B.C.L.C. 210, Ch D 16–50
Real Meat Co Ltd (In Receivership), Re [1996] B.C.C. 254, Ch D 10–45
Rees v Boston BC [2001] EWCA Civ 1934; [2002] 1 W.L.R. 1304; [2002]
    B.C.C. 495; [2002] B.P.I.R. 665; [2002] R.A. 23; [2002] 2 E.G. 101
    (C.S.); (2002) 99(9) L.S.G. 31; [2002] N.P.C. 8 10–58
Reid v Explosives Co Ltd (1887) L.R. 19 Q.B.D. 264, CA 10–21
Reid v Ramlort Ltd (Preliminary Issue) [2002] EWHC 2416 (Ch); [2003] 1
    B.C.L.C. 499; [2003] B.P.I.R. 489; (2003) 100(4) L.S.G. 31 .... 4–35, 13–32
Reid v Ramlort Ltd [2004] EWCA Civ 800; [2005] 1 B.C.L.C. 331; [2004]
    B.P.I.R. 985; (2004) 148 S.J.L.B. 877 .... 13–19, 13–26, **13–32**,
                                                             13–45, 13–67
Reis, Re. *See* Clough v Samuel
Remblance v Octagon Assets Ltd [2009] EWCA Civ 581; [2010] Bus. L.R.
    119; [2010] 2 All E.R. 688; [2010] 1 B.C.L.C. 10; [2009] B.P.I.R. 1129;
    [2009] N.P.C. 79 5–13
Reprographic Exports (Euromat), Re (1978) 122 S.J. 400 10–37

Revenue and Customs Commissioners v Enron Europe Ltd. *See* Enron Europe Ltd (In Administration) v Revenue and Customs Commissioners

Revenue and Customs Commissioners v Holland [2010] UKSC 51; [2010] 1 W.L.R. 2793; [2011] Bus. L.R. 111; [2011] 1 All E.R. 430; [2011] S.T.C. 269; [2011] B.C.C. 1; [2011] B.P.I.R. 96; [2010] S.T.I. 3074 . . . . 14–04, 14–05, 14–15

Rhodes v Allied Dunbar (Pension Services) Ltd [1989] 1 W.L.R. 800; [1989] 1 All E.R. 1161; (1989) 5 B.C.C. 160; [1989] B.C.L.C. 318; (1989) 58 P. & C.R. 42; [1989] 19 E.G. 70; [1988] E.G. 152 (C.S.); (1989) 133 S.J. 1170, CA (Civ Div) 10–57

Rhondda Waste Disposal Ltd (In Administration), Re [2001] Ch. 57; [2000] 3 W.L.R. 1304; [2000] B.C.C. 653; [2000] Env. L.R. 600; [2000] 1 E.G.L.R. 113; [2000] E.G. 25 (C.S.); (2000) 150 N.L.J. 227, CA (Civ Div) 11–67

Rica Gold Washing Co Ltd, Re (1879) L.R. 11 Ch. D. 36, CA 5–19

Richbell Strategic Holdings Ltd (No.1), Re [1997] 2 B.C.L.C. 429, Ch D 5–13

Richborough Furniture Ltd, Re [1996] B.C.C. 155; [1996] 1 B.C.L.C. 507, Ch D 14–04, 14–32, 14–73

Ridge Securities Ltd v IRC [1964] 1 W.L.R. 479; [1964] 1 All E.R. 275; 44 T.C. 373; (1963) 42 A.T.C. 487; [1963] T.R. 449; (1964) 108 S.J. 377, Ch D 14–19

Ridgeway Motors (Isleworth) Ltd v ALTS Ltd [2005] EWCA Civ 92; [2005] 1 W.L.R. 2871; [2005] 2 All E.R. 304; [2005] C.P. Rep. 34; [2005] B.C.C. 496; [2005] 2 B.C.L.C. 61; [2005] B.P.I.R. 423; [2005] R.V.R. 173; [2005] N.P.C. 27 5–18

Robins v Secretary of State for Work and Pensions (C–278/05) [2007] All E.R. (EC) 648; [2007] E.C.R. I–1053; [2007] 2 C.M.L.R. 13; [2007] I.C.R. 779; [2007] I.R.L.R. 270; [2007] Pens. L.R. 55, ECJ 8–25

Rodencroft Ltd, Re. *See* Allso v Secretary of State for Trade and Industry

Rolled Steel Products (Holdings) Ltd v British Steel Corp [1986] Ch. 246; [1985] 2 W.L.R. 908; [1985] 3 All E.R. 52; (1984) 1 B.C.C. 99158, CA (Civ Div) 10–32, 14–19

Rolls Razor Ltd v Cox [1967] 1 Q.B. 552; [1967] 2 W.L.R. 241; [1967] 1 All E.R. 397; (1966) 110 S.J. 943, CA 9–27

Rose v AIB Group (UK) Plc [2003] EWHC 1737 (Ch); [2003] 1 W.L.R. 2791; [2004] B.C.C. 11; [2003] 2 B.C.L.C. 374; [2003] B.P.I.R. 1188; (2003) 100(30) L.S.G. 31 . . . . 13–132, 13–135, 13–148, 13–150

Rose v Hart (1818) 8 Taunt. 499 . . . . 9–26, 9–27

Rose v Watson, 11 E.R. 1187; (1864) 10 H.L. Cas. 672, HL 13–153

Rothschild v Bell (A Bankrupt) [2000] Q.B. 33; [1999] 2 W.L.R. 1237; [1999] 2 All E.R. 722; [1999] 1 F.L.R. 1246; [1999] B.P.I.R. 300; (2000) 32 H.L.R. 274; [1999] L. & T.R. 320; [1999] 1 E.G.L.R. 35; [1999] 16 E.G. 155; [1999] Fam. Law 385; [1999] E.G. 27 (C.S.); [1999] N.P.C. 23; (1999) 78 P. & C.R. D5, CA (Civ Div) 6–14

Rover Espana SA, Re [2006] EWHC 3426 (Ch); [2006] B.C.C. 599; [2005] B.P.I.R. 1162 11–85

Rowbotham Baxter Ltd, Re [1990] B.C.C. 113; [1990] B.C.L.C. 397, Ch D 11–26

Royal Bank of Scotland Plc v Bhardwaj [2002] B.C.C. 57, Ch D 13–135

Rubin v Eurofinance SA [2010] EWCA Civ 895; [2011] 2 W.L.R. 121; [2011] Bus. L.R. 84; [2011] 1 All E.R. (Comm) 287; [2011] C.P. Rep. 2; (2010) 160 N.L.J. 1192 . . . . 7–22, 13–03, **16–30**, 16–34, 16–43, 16–44

Rudd & Son Ltd, Re (1986) 2 B.C.C. 98955, CA (Civ Div) 10–67

Russian & English Bank, Re. *See* Russian & English Bank v Baring Bros &
  Co Ltd (No.2)
Russian & English Bank v Baring Bros & Co Ltd (No.2) [1932] 1 Ch. 663,
  Ch D 5–13
Ruttle Plant Hire Ltd v Secretary of State for the Environment, Food and
  Rural Affairs [2008] EWHC 238 (TCC); [2009] 1 All E.R. 448; [2008]
  B.P.I.R. 1395 5–06
SA&D Wright Ltd, Re [1992] B.C.C. 503; [1992] B.C.L.C. 901, CA (Civ
  Div) 13–135
SCT Industri AB (In Liquidation) v Alpenblume AB (C–111/08) [2010]
  Bus. L.R. 559; [2009] E.C.R. I–5655; [2010] C.E.C. 47; [2009] I.L.Pr.
  43, ECJ 15–02, 15–34
SSSL Realisations (2002) Ltd, Re. *See* Manning v AIG Europe UK Ltd
Sabre International Products Ltd, Re [1991] B.C.C. 694; [1991] B.C.L.C.
  470, Ch D 11–59
Said v Butt [1920] 3 K.B. 497, KBD 10–53, 10–59
St Georges Property Services (London) Ltd (In Administration), Re [2010]
  EWHC 2538 (Ch); [2010] Bus. L.R. 1747; [2011] B.C.C. 64 11–113
St Ives Windings, Re (1987) 3 B.C.C. 634, Ch D 11–85
Salmet International Ltd, Re. *See* Spring Valley Properties Ltd v Harris
Salomon v Salomon & Co Ltd [1897] A.C. 22, HL 3–12
Salvage Association, Re [2003] EWHC 1028 (Ch); [2004] 1 W.L.R. 174;
  [2003] 3 All E.R. 246; [2003] B.C.C. 504; [2003] 2 B.C.L.C. 333; [2003]
  B.P.I.R. 1181; (2003) 100(24) L.S.G. 36 .... 12–26, 15–14
Samsun Logix Corp v DEF [2009] EWHC 576 (Ch); [2009] B.P.I.R.
  1502 .... 16–42, 16–43
Sarflax Ltd, Re [1979] Ch. 592; [1979] 2 W.L.R. 202; [1979] 1 All E.R. 529;
  (1979) 123 S.J. 97, Ch D 8–02, 13–42, 14–24
Sass Ex p. National Provincial Bank of England Ltd, Re [1896] 2 Q.B. 12,
  QBD 5–19, 8–44, 8–45
Sass, Re. *See* Sass Ex p. National Provincial Bank of England Ltd, Re
Saunders v United Kingdom (19187/91) [1997] B.C.C. 872; [1998] 1
  B.C.L.C. 362; (1997) 23 E.H.R.R. 313; 2 B.H.R.C. 358, ECHR 11–87
Savoy Hotel Ltd, Re [1981] Ch. 351; [1981] 3 W.L.R. 441; [1981] 3 All E.R.
  646; (1981) 125 S.J. 585, Ch D 1–46, 12–16
Scheibler Ex p. Holthausen, Re (1873–74) L.R. 9 Ch. App. 722, CA in
  Chancery 3–02
Scientific Investment Pension Plan (No.2), Re [1999] Ch. 53; [1998] 3
  W.L.R. 1191; [1998] 3 All E.R. 154; [1998] 2 B.C.L.C. 360; [1998] 2
  F.L.R. 761; [1998] B.P.I.R. 410; [1998] O.P.L.R. 41; [1998] Pens. L.R.
  141; [1998] Fam. Law 582 .... 7–02, 7–05
Scottish Lion Insurance Co Ltd, Petitioner [2010] CSIH 6; 2010 S.C. 349;
  2010 S.L.T. 459; 2010 S.C.L.R. 167; [2010] B.C.C. 650; 2010 G.W.D.
  7–117 12–19
Scottish Widows Plc v Stewart [2005] EWHC 1831 (QB) 9–23
Seagon v Deko Marty Belgium NV (C–339/07) [2009] 1 W.L.R. 2168; [2009]
  Bus. L.R. 1151; [2009] E.C.R. I–767; [2009] B.C.C. 347; [2009] I.L.Pr.
  25, ECJ 15–22, 15–72
Secretary of State for Business, Enterprise and Regulatory Reform v Aaron
  [2008] EWCA Civ 1146; [2009] Bus. L.R. 809; [2009] C.P. Rep. 10;
  [2009] B.C.C. 375; [2009] 1 B.C.L.C. 55; [2009] Lloyd's Rep. F.C. 1 14–71,
                                                              14–78
Secretary of State for Business, Enterprise and Regulatory Reform v
  Poulter [2009] B.C.C. 608, Ch D 14–04, 14–73

Secretary of State for the Environment, Food and Rural Affairs v Feakins
  [2005] EWCA Civ 1513; [2007] B.C.C. 54; [2006] Env. L.R. 44; [2006]
  B.P.I.R. 895; (2006) 103(4) L.S.G. 28 .... 13–13, 13–19, 13–20,
                                                              13–38, **13–45**
Secretary of State for Trade and Industry v Arif [1996] B.C.C. 586; [1997] 1
  B.C.L.C. 34, Ch D 14–46, 14–79, 1–80
Secretary of State for Trade and Industry v Aviss [2006] EWHC 1846 (Ch);
  [2007] B.C.C. 288; [2007] 1 B.C.L.C. 618 .... 14–05, 14–67
Secretary of State for Trade and Industry v Bairstow [2004] EWHC 1730
  (Ch); [2005] 1 B.C.L.C. 136 14–75
Secretary of State for Trade and Industry v Baker (No.5) [2000] 1 W.L.R.
  634; [1999] 1 All E.R. 1017; [1999] B.C.C. 960; [1999] 1 B.C.L.C. 262;
  (1998) 95(45) L.S.G. 38; (1998) 148 N.L.J. 1474, Ch D 14–81
Secretary of State for Trade and Industry v Baker (No.6) [1999] 1 B.C.L.C
  433, Ch D 14–11
Secretary of State for Trade and Industry v Becker [2002] EWHC 2200
  (Ch); [2003] 1 B.C.L.C. 555 .... 14–04, 14–05
Secretary of State for Trade and Industry v Creegan [2001] EWCA Civ
  1742; [2004] B.C.C. 835; [2002] 1 B.C.L.C. 99 14–02
Secretary of State for Trade and Industry v Dawes [1997] B.C.C. 121,
  Ch D 14–76
Secretary of State for Trade and Industry v Deverell [2001] Ch. 340; [2000]
  2 W.L.R. 907; [2000] 2 All E.R. 365; [2000] B.C.C. 1057; [2000] 2
  B.C.L.C. 133; (2000) 97(3) L.S.G. 35; (2000) 144 S.J.L.B. 49, CA (Civ
  Div) **14–05**
Secretary of State for Trade and Industry v Frid [2004] UKHL 24; [2004] 2
  A.C. 506; [2004] 2 W.L.R. 1279; [2004] 2 All E.R. 1042; [2004] B.C.C.
  525; [2004] 2 B.C.L.C. 1; [2004] B.P.I.R. 841; (2004) 154 N.L.J. 770;
  (2004) 148 S.J.L.B. 631 .... 9–23, 9–24, 9–25
Secretary of State for Trade and Industry v Goldberg (No.2) [2003] EWHC
  2843 (Ch); [2004] 1 B.C.L.C. 597 14–68
Secretary of State for Trade and Industry v Green [2006] EWHC 1739
  (Ch) 14–73
Secretary of State for Trade and Industry v Griffiths. *See* Westmid Packing
  Services Ltd (No.2), Re
Secretary of State for Trade and Industry v Hall [2006] EWHC 1995 (Ch);
  [2009] B.C.C. 190 14–04
Secretary of State for Trade and Industry v Hickling [1996] B.C.C. 678,
  Ch D 14–04, 14–68, 14–73
Secretary of State for Trade and Industry v Hollier [2006] EWHC 1804
  (Ch); [2007] Bus. L.R. 352; [2007] B.C.C. 11 .... 14–04, 14–68
Secretary of State for Trade and Industry v Kaczer. *See* Kaytech
  International Plc, Re
Secretary of State for Trade and Industry v Langridge [1991] Ch. 402; [1991]
  2 W.L.R. 1343; [1991] 3 All E.R. 591; [1991] B.C.C. 148; [1991]
  B.C.L.C. 543, CA (Civ Div) 14–70, 14–74
Secretary of State for Trade and Industry v McTighe (No.2) [1997] B.C.C.
  224; [1996] 2 B.C.L.C. 477, CA (Civ Div) 14–80, 14–83
Secretary of State for Trade and Industry v Swan [2005] EWHC 603 (Ch);
  [2005] B.C.C. 596 14–68
Secretary of State for Trade and Industry v Swan (No.2) [2005] EWHC 2479
  (Ch) 14–81
Secretary of State for Trade and Industry v Taylor [1997] 1 W.L.R. 407;
  [1997] B.C.C. 172; [1997] 1 B.C.L.C. 341, Ch D 14–02, 14–46

Secretary of State for Trade and Industry v Tjolle [1998] B.C.C. 282; [1998]
   1 B.C.L.C. 333; (1997) 94(24) L.S.G. 31; (1997) 141 S.J.L.B. 119,
   Ch D 14–04
Sevenoaks Stationers (Retail) Ltd, Re [1991] Ch. 164; [1990] 3 W.L.R. 1165;
   [1991] 3 All E.R. 578; [1990] B.C.C. 765; [1991] B.C.L.C. 325; (1990)
   134 S.J. 1367, CA (Civ Div) 14–68, 14–75, 14–80, 14–83
Shaker v Al-Bedrawi [2002] EWCA Civ 1452; [2003] Ch. 350; [2003] 2
   W.L.R. 922; [2002] 4 All E.R. 835; [2003] B.C.C. 465; [2003] 1 B.C.L.C.
   157; [2003] W.T.L.R. 105; (2002–03) 5 I.T.E.L.R. 429 14–20
Shamji v Johnson Matthey Bankers [1991] B.C.L.C. 36, CA (Civ Div) 10–34
Sharafi v Woven Rugs Ltd. *See* Woven Rugs Ltd, Re
Sharp's Settlement Trusts, Re [1973] Ch. 331; [1972] 3 W.L.R. 765; [1972] 3
   All E.R. 151; (1972) 116 S.J. 666, Ch D 7–05
Shaw v Foster (1871–72) L.R. 5 H.L. 321, HL 6–23
Shaw v MFP Foundations & Piling Ltd [2010] EWHC 9 (Ch); [2010] 2
   B.C.L.C. 85; [2010] B.P.I.R. 397; [2010] 1 E.G.L.R. 1; [2010] 11 E.G.
   122; [2010] C.I.L.L. 2831; [2010] 3 E.G. 102 (C.S.) 5–13
Sheppard & Cooper Ltd v TSB Bank Plc (No.2) [1996] 2 All E.R. 654;
   [1996] B.C.C. 965, Ch D 10–30
Sherborne Associates Ltd, Re [1995] B.C.C. 40, QBD 14–41, 14–51
Shierson v Vlieland-Boddy [2005] EWCA Civ 974; [2005] 1 W.L.R. 3966;
   [2005] B.C.C. 949; [2006] 2 B.C.L.C. 9; [2006] I.L.Pr. 12; [2005] B.P.I.R.
   1170 . . . . 15–17, 15–41, 15–49
Shoe Lace Ltd, Re. *See* Power v Sharp Investments Ltd
Siebe Gorman & Co Ltd v Barclays Bank Ltd [1979] 2 Lloyd's Rep. 142,
   Ch D 10–16
Sigma Finance Corp (In Administration), Re [2009] UKSC 2; [2010] 1 All
   E.R. 571; [2010] B.C.C. 40; (2009) 159 N.L.J. 1550; (2009) 153(42)
   S.J.L.B. 29 8–03
Silven Properties Ltd v Royal Bank of Scotland Plc [2003] EWCA Civ 1409;
   [2004] 1 W.L.R. 997; [2004] 4 All E.R. 484; [2003] B.C.C. 1002; [2004]
   1 B.C.L.C. 359; [2003] B.P.I.R. 1429; [2003] 3 E.G.L.R. 49; [2003] 50
   E.G. 96; [2003] 44 E.G. 168 (C.S.); (2003) 100(44) L.S.G. 33; [2003]
   N.P.C. 121; [2004] 1 P. & C.R. DG6 . . . . 10–49, 11–30
Sinai Securities Ltd v Hooper [2003] EWHC 910 (Ch); [2004] B.C.C. 973;
   [2004] 2 B.C.L.C. 575 10–21
Sinclair v Wilson, 52 E.R. 627; (1855) 20 Beav. 324, Ct of Chancery 13–80
Singer v Beckett [2007] 2 B.C.L.C. 287; [2001] B.P.I.R. 733, Ch D . . . 14–14, 14–41,
                                                                     14–44, 14–52
Singla v Brown [2007] EWHC 405 (Ch); [2008] Ch. 357; [2008] 2 W.L.R.
   283; [2008] 2 F.L.R. 125; [2007] B.P.I.R. 424; [2009] W.T.L.R. 165;
   [2008] Fam. Law 413 . . . . 13–23, 13–45
Singla v Hedman [2009] EWHC 3510 (Ch); [2010] B.C.C. 674 14–44
Sisu Capital Fund Ltd v Tucker (Costs) [2005] EWHC 2321 (Ch); [2006] 1
   All E.R. 167; [2006] B.C.C. 463; [2006] 2 Costs L.R. 262; [2006] B.P.I.R.
   154; [2006] F.S.R. 21; (2005) 155 N.L.J. 1686 . . . . 11–113, 12–54, 12–55
Slavenburg's Bank NV v Intercontinental Natural Resources [1980] 1
   W.L.R. 1076; [1980] 1 All E.R. 955; (1980) 124 S.J. 374, QBD 13–126
Smallman Construction Ltd, Re (1988) 4 B.C.C. 784; [1989] B.C.L.C. 420;
   [1989] P.C.C. 433, Ch D 11–111
Smith (Administrator of Cosslett (Contractors) Ltd) v Bridgend CBC [2001]
   UKHL 58; [2002] 1 A.C. 336; [2001] 3 W.L.R. 1347; [2002] 1 All E.R.
   292; [2001] B.C.C. 740; [2002] 1 B.C.L.C. 77; [2002] B.L.R. 160; [2002]
   T.C.L.R. 7; 80 Con. L.R. 172; [2001] N.P.C. 161 . . . . . 9–26, 9–29, 11–95, 13–123

Smith Knight & Co Ex p. Ashbury, Re (1867–68) L.R. 5 Eq. 223, Ct of
  Chancery 8–02
Sneezum Ex p. Davis, Re (1876) L.R. 3 Ch. D. 463, CA 6–31
Sobam BV, Re. *See* Brown v City of London Corp
Soden v British & Commonwealth Holdings Plc (In Administration) [1998]
  A.C. 298; [1997] 3 W.L.R. 840; [1997] 4 All E.R. 353; [1997] B.C.C. 952;
  [1997] 2 B.C.L.C. 501; (1997) 94(41) L.S.G. 28; (1997) 147 N.L.J. 1546,
  HL 8–27
Somerfield Stores Ltd v Spring (Sutton Coldfield) Ltd (In Administration)
  [2010] EWHC 2084 (Ch); [2011] L. & T.R. 8; [2010] 47 E.G. 142; [2010]
  33 E.G. 71 (C.S.) 11–27, 11–67, 11–78
Sonatacus Ltd, Re [2007] EWCA Civ 31; [2007] B.C.C. 186; [2007] 2
  B.C.L.C. 627; [2007] B.P.I.R. 106; (2007) 104(6) L.S.G. 30; (2007) 151
  S.J.L.B. 162 .... **13–24**, 13–56
South Africa Co v De Beers Consolidated Mines Ltd. *See* De Beers
  Consolidated Mines Ltd v British South Africa Co
South African Supply and Cold Storage Co, Re [1904] 2 Ch. 268, Ch D 1–50
Sovereign Life Assurance Co (In Liquidation) v Dodd [1892] 2 Q.B. 573,
  CA 12–19
Sowman v Samuel (David) Trust Ltd (In Liquidation) [1978] 1 W.L.R. 22;
  [1978] 1 All E.R. 616; (1978) 36 P. & C.R. 123; (1977) 121 S.J. 757,
  Ch D 10–66, 13–129
Spectrum Plus Ltd (In Liquidation), Re [2005] UKHL 41; [2005] 2 A.C.
  680; [2005] 3 W.L.R. 58; [2005] 4 All E.R. 209; [2005] 2 Lloyd's
  Rep. 275; [2005] B.C.C. 694; [2005] 2 B.C.L.C. 269; (2005) 155 N.L.J.
  1045 .... 1–15, 10–16
Spence v Coleman [1901] 2 K.B. 199, CA 3–10, 5–03
Sports Betting Media Ltd (In Administration), Re [2007] EWHC 2085
  (Ch); [2008] B.C.C. 177; [2008] 2 B.C.L.C. 89 .... 11–91, 11–101
Spring Valley Properties Ltd v Harris [2001] B.C.C. 796; [2001] B.P.I.R. 709,
  Ch D 11–16, 11–91
Stacey v Hill [1901] 1 Q.B. 660, CA 6–30
Stack v Dowden [2007] UKHL 17; [2007] 2 A.C. 432; [2007] 2 W.L.R. 831;
  [2007] 2 All E.R. 929; [2007] 1 F.L.R. 1858; [2007] 2 F.C.R. 280; [2007]
  B.P.I.R. 913; [2008] 2 P. & C.R. 4; [2007] W.T.L.R. 1053; (2006–07) 9
  I.T.E.L.R. 815; [2007] Fam. Law 593; [2007] 18 E.G. 153 (C.S.); (2007)
  157 N.L.J. 634; (2007) 151 S.J.L.B. 575; [2007] N.P.C. 47; [2007] 2 P. &
  C.R. DG11 13–23
Stanford International Bank Ltd (In Receivership), Re [2010] EWCA Civ
  137; [2010] 3 W.L.R. 941; [2010] Bus. L.R. 1270; [2010] Lloyd's Rep.
  F.C. 357; [2010] B.P.I.R. 679 .... 3–09, 15–56, 16–22,
                                                          16–28, 16–30
Stanford Services, Re (1987) 3 B.C.C. 326; [1987] B.C.L.C. 607; [1987]
  P.C.C. 343, Ch D 14–75
Star Sea, The. *See* Manifest Shipping Co Ltd v Uni-Polaris Insurance Co
  Ltd (The Star Sea)
Staubitz-Schreiber. *See* Proceedings brought by Staubitz-Schreiber
  (C–1/04)
Stead Hazel & Co v Cooper [1933] 1 K.B. 840, KBD 6–31
Stein v Blake (No.1) [1996] A.C. 243; [1995] 2 W.L.R. 710; [1995] 2 All E.R.
  961; [1995] B.C.C. 543; [1995] 2 B.C.L.C. 94; (1995) 145 N.L.J. 760,
  HL 9–18, 9–20, 9–23, 9–25
Stocznia Gdanska SA v Latreefers Inc [2000] C.P.L.R. 65; [2001] B.C.C.
  174; [2001] 2 B.C.L.C. 116; [2001] C.L.C. 1267, CA (Civ Div) ... 16–50, 16–51

Stone & Rolls Ltd (In Liquidation) v Moore Stephens (A Firm) [2009]
UKHL 39; [2009] 1 A.C. 1391; [2009] 3 W.L.R. 455; [2009] Bus. L.R.
1356; [2009] 4 All E.R. 431; [2010] 1 All E.R. (Comm) 125; [2009] 2
Lloyd's Rep. 537; [2009] 2 B.C.L.C. 563; [2009] 2 C.L.C. 121; [2009]
Lloyd's Rep. F.C. 557; [2009] B.P.I.R. 1191; [2009] P.N.L.R. 36; (2009)
159 N.L.J. 1218; (2009) 153(31) S.J.L.B. 28 .... 3–05, 6–17, 14–14
Stonegate Securities Ltd v Gregory [1980] Ch. 576; [1980] 3 W.L.R. 168;
[1980] 1 All E.R. 241; (1980) 124 S.J. 495, CA (Civ Div) 4–26, 4–27, 5–13,
5–14, 5–18
Stooke v Taylor (1879–80) L.R. 5 Q.B.D. 569, QBD 4–17
Sunberry Properties Ltd v Innovate Logistics Ltd (In Administration)
[2008] EWCA Civ 1321; [2009] B.C.C. 164; [2009] 1 B.C.L.C. 145;
[2008] N.P.C. 129 11–78
Sutherland deceased, Re. *See* Winter v IRC
Sweatfield Ltd, Re [1997] B.C.C. 744; [1998] B.P.I.R. 276, Ch D 12–41
Swift v Dairywise Farms Ltd (No.1) [2000] 1 W.L.R. 1177; [2000] 1 All E.R.
320; [2000] B.C.C. 642; [2000] 1 B.C.L.C. 632; [1999] E.G. 137 (C.S.);
[1999] N.P.C. 142, Ch D 6–10, 6–11
SwissAir Schweizerische Luftverkehr-Aktiengesellschaft, Re [2009] EWHC
2099 (Ch); [2010] B.C.C. 667; [2009] B.P.I.R. 1505 .... 16–43, 16–61
Syska v Vivendi Universal SA [2009] EWCA Civ 677; [2009] Bus. L.R. 1494;
[2009] 2 All E.R. (Comm) 891; [2010] B.C.C. 348; [2010] 1 B.C.L.C.
467; [2009] 2 C.L.C. 10; [2009] B.P.I.R. 1304; [2009] 28 E.G. 84 (C.S.);
(2009) 159 N.L.J. 1033 15–98
3T Telecom Ltd, Re [2005] EWHC 275 (Ch); [2006] 2 B.C.L.C. 137 15–56
T&D Industries Plc, Re [2000] 1 W.L.R. 646; [2000] 1 All E.R. 333; [2000]
B.C.C. 956; [2000] 1 B.C.L.C. 471; (1999) 96(46) L.S.G. 37 11–81
T&D Services (Timber Preservation & Damp Proofing Contractors) Ltd,
Re [1990] B.C.C. 592, Ch D 14–80
T&N Ltd, Re [2004] EWHC 1680 (Ch); [2004] O.P.L.R. 343; [2004] Pens.
L.R. 351 1–19
T&N Ltd, Re [2005] EWHC 2870 (Ch); [2006] 1 W.L.R. 1728; [2006] 3 All
E.R. 697; [2006] 2 B.C.L.C. 374; [2006] B.P.I.R. 532 .... 2–26, 4–24,
12–18, 12–54
T&N Ltd, Re [2006] EWHC 1447 (Ch); [2007] Bus. L.R. 1411; [2007] 1 All
E.R. 851; [2007] 1 B.C.L.C. 563; [2006] B.P.I.R. 1283; [2006] Lloyd's
Rep. I.R. 817 .... 1–46, 12–18, 12–19, 12–24, 12–41
TBL Realisation Plc, Re. *See* Oakley-Smith v Greenberg
TH Knitwear (Wholesale) Ltd, Re [1988] Ch. 275; [1988] 2 W.L.R. 276;
[1988] 1 All E.R. 860; [1988] S.T.C. 79; (1988) 4 B.C.C. 102; [1987]
B.C.L.C. 195; [1988] P.C.C. 281; (1988) 85(4) L.S.G. 35; (1987) 131 S.J.
1696, CA (Civ Div) 1–19, 5–02
TM Kingdom Ltd (In Administration), Re [2007] EWHC 3272 (Ch); [2007]
B.C.C. 480 5–01
TT Industries Ltd, Re [2006] B.C.C. 372; [2006] B.P.I.R. 597, Ch D 11–14
TXU Europe German Finance BV, Re [2005] B.C.C. 90; [2005] B.P.I.R. 209,
Ch D 15–13
TXU UK Ltd (In Administration), Re [2002] EWHC 2784 (Ch); [2003] 2
B.C.L.C. 341; [2003] B.P.I.R. 1062 11–04
Tain Construction Ltd, Re. *See* Rose v AIB Group (UK) Plc
Tasbian Ltd (No.2), Re [1990] B.C.C. 322; [1991] B.C.L.C. 59, CA (Civ
Div) 11–117
Tasbian Ltd (No.3), Re [1992] B.C.C. 358; [1993] B.C.L.C. 297, CA (Civ
Div) 14–04, 14–34

Taurusbuild Ltd v Svenska Handelsbanken Unreported December 16, 1994,
CA (Civ Div) 1–46
Taylor's Industrial Flooring Ltd v M&H Plant Hire (Manchester)) [1990]
B.C.C. 44; [1990] B.C.L.C. 216, CA (Civ Div) 4–21, 5–16
Tea Corp, Re [1904] 1 Ch. 12, CA 1–53, 2–21, 12–22, 12–41
Telemetrix Plc v Modern Engineers of Bristol (Holdings) Plc (1985) 1
B.C.C. 99417; (1985) 82 L.S.G. 1561, Ch D 10–53
Television Trade Rentals Ltd, Re [2002] EWHC 211 (Ch); [2002] B.C.C.
807; [2002] B.P.I.R. 859 16–59
Telia AB v Hilcourt (Docklands) Ltd [2002] EWHC 2377 (Ch); [2003]
B.C.C. 856 15–62
Telomatic Ltd, Re [1993] B.C.C. 404; [1994] 1 B.C.L.C. 90, Ch D 13–125
Thoars deceased, Re. *See* Reid v Ramlort Ltd
Thomas v Ken Thomas Ltd [2006] EWCA Civ 1504; [2007] Bus. L.R. 429;
[2007] B.P.I.R. 959; [2007] L. & T.R. 21; [2007] 1 E.G.L.R. 31; [2007] 1
E.G. 94; [2006] 42 E.G. 244 (C.S.); (2006) 150 S.J.L.B. 1396 12–54
Thompson Ex p. Williams, Re (1877–78) L.R. 7 Ch. D. 138, CA 8–13
Thorniley v Revenue and Customs Commissioners [2008] EWHC 124 (Ch);
[2008] 1 W.L.R. 1516; [2008] Bus. L.R. 1076; [2008] B.C.C. 213; [2008]
1 B.C.L.C. 436 6–40
Three Rivers DC v Bank of England (Indemnity Costs) [2006] EWHC 816
(Comm); [2006] 5 Costs L.R. 714 15–01
Threlfall v Jones (Inspector of Taxes) [1994] Ch. 107; [1994] 2 W.L.R. 160;
[1993] S.T.C. 537; 66 T.C. 77; (1993) 90(32) L.S.G. 40; (1993) 137
S.J.L.B. 174, CA (Civ Div) 4–25
Thunderbird Industries LLC v Simoco Digital UK Ltd [2004] EWHC 209
(Ch); [2004] 1 B.C.L.C. 541, Ch D 11–48
Tilley v Bowman Ltd [1910] 1 K.B. 745, KBD 3–05, 6–17
Titan International Inc, Re [1998] 1 B.C.L.C. 102, CA (Civ Div) 16–50
Toshoku Finance UK Plc (In Liquidation), Re [2002] UKHL 6; [2002] 1
W.L.R. 671; [2002] 3 All E.R. 961; [2002] S.T.C. 368; [2002] B.C.C. 110;
[2002] 1 B.C.L.C. 598; [2002] B.P.I.R. 790; [2003] R.V.R. 106; [2002]
B.T.C. 69; [2002] S.T.I. 237; (2002) 99(12) L.S.G. 33; (2002) 146
S.J.L.B. 55 .... 8–33, 8–35, 8–38, 11–105
Tottenham Hotspur Plc v Edennote Plc [1994] B.C.C. 681; [1995] 1 B.C.L.C.
65, Ch D 4–24, 5–18
Tout and Finch Ltd, Re [1954] 1 W.L.R. 178; [1954] 1 All E.R. 127; 52
L.G.R. 70; (1954) 98 S.J. 62, Ch D 6–17, 8–11
Trading Partners Ltd, Re. *See* Akers v Lomas
Transag Haulage Ltd (IAR) v Leyland DAF Finance Plc [1994] B.C.C. 356;
[1994] 2 B.C.L.C. 88; (1994) 13 Tr. L.R. 361, Ch D 6–17, 7–05
Transbus International Ltd (In Liquidation), Re [2004] EWHC 932 (Ch);
[2004] 1 W.L.R. 2654; [2004] 2 All E.R. 911; [2004] B.C.C. 401; [2004]
2 B.C.L.C. 550 .... 2–03, 11–39, 11–81
Transworld Trading, Re [1999] B.P.I.R. 628, Ch D 13–76
Travel Mondial (UK) Ltd, Re [1991] B.C.C. 224; [1991] B.C.L.C. 120,
Ch D 14–80
Trendtex Trading Corp v Credit Suisse [1982] A.C. 679; [1981] 3 W.L.R.
766; [1981] 3 All E.R. 520; [1981] Com. L.R. 262; (1981) 125 S.J. 761,
HL 5–06
Trevor v Whitworth (1887) L.R. 12 App. Cas. 409, HL 13–01
Trident Fashions Plc, Re. *See* Exeter City Council v Bairstow
Trix, Re [1970] 1 W.L.R. 1421; [1970] 3 All E.R. 397; (1970) 114 S.J. 768,
Ch D 1–55, 12–01

Tudor Grange Holdings Ltd v Citibank NA [1992] Ch. 53; [1991] 3 W.L.R.
750; [1991] 4 All E.R. 1; [1991] B.C.L.C. 1009; (1991) 135 S.J.L.B. 3,
Ch D 10–38
Turcan, Re (1889) L.R. 40 Ch. D. 5, CA 6–10
Tweeds Garages, Re [1962] Ch. 406; [1962] 2 W.L.R. 38; [1962] 1 All E.R.
121; (1961) 105 S.J. 1085, Ch D 5–18
Twinsectra Ltd v Yardley [2002] UKHL 12; [2002] 2 A.C. 164; [2002] 2
W.L.R. 802; [2002] 2 All E.R. 377; [2002] P.N.L.R. 30; [2002] W.T.L.R.
423; [2002] 38 E.G. 204 (C.S.); (2002) 99(19) L.S.G. 32; (2002) 152
N.L.J. 469; (2002) 146 S.J.L.B. 84; [2002] N.P.C. 47 14–24
Twyne's Case (1602) 3 Co. Rep. 80b 2–27
UBS AG v Omni Holding AG (In Liquidation) [2000] 1 W.L.R. 916; [2000]
1 All E.R. (Comm) 42; [2000] B.C.C. 593; [2000] 2 B.C.L.C. 310; [2000]
I.L.Pr. 51, Ch D 15–02
UCT (UK) Ltd (In Administration), Re [2001] 1 W.L.R. 436; [2001] 2 All
E.R. 186; [2001] B.C.C. 734; [2001] 1 B.C.L.C. 443; [2002] B.P.I.R. 414,
Ch D 3–09, 11–04, 11–29
UK-Euro Group Plc, Re [2006] EWHC 2102 (Ch); [2007] 1 B.C.L.C. 812 5–11
Ultraframe Ltd, Re. *See* Ultraframe (UK) Ltd v Fielding
Ultraframe (UK) Ltd v Fielding [2005] EWHC 1638 (Ch); [2006] F.S.R. 17;
[2007] W.T.L.R. 835; (2005) 28(9) I.P.D. 28069 .... 10–37, 14–05, 14–09,
14–12, 14–35
Unidare Plc v Cohen [2005] EWHC 1410 (Ch); [2006] Ch. 489; [2006] 2
W.L.R. 974; [2005] 3 All E.R. 730; [2006] 2 B.C.L.C. 140; [2005]
B.P.I.R. 1472 13–104
Unit 2 Windows Ltd (In Liquidation), Re [1985] 1 W.L.R. 1383; [1985] 3 All
E.R. 647; (1985) 1 B.C.C. 99489; [1986] P.C.C. 194, Ch D 9–44
Various Customers of BA Peters Plc v Moriarty. *See* Moriarty v Various
Customers of BA Peters Plc
Verby Print for Advertising Ltd, Re [1998] B.C.C. 652; [1998] 2 B.C.L.C. 23,
Ch D 14–68, 14–75
Vimbos Ltd, Re [1900] 1 Ch. 470, Ch D 10–23
Vintage Hallmark Plc, Re [2006] EWHC 2761 (Ch); [2008] B.C.C. 150;
[2007] 1 B.C.L.C. 788 14–73
Vocalion (Foreign) Ltd, Re [1932] 2 Ch. 196, Ch D 16–62
WBSL Realisations 1992 Ltd, Re [1995] B.C.C. 1118; [1995] 2 B.C.L.C. 576,
Ch D 11–04, 11–29, 11–85
Walker Ex p. Black, Re (1884) L.R. 26 Ch. D. 510, CA 7–05
Walker v WA Personnel Ltd [2002] B.P.I.R. 621, Ch D 13–45
Wallace Smith & Co, Re [1992] B.C.L.C. 970 16–50
Wallach v Secretary of State for Trade and Industry [2006] EWHC 989 (Ch);
[2007] 1 B.C.L.C. 208 13–42
Warnford Investments Ltd v Duckworth [1979] Ch. 127; [1978] 2 W.L.R.
741; [1978] 2 All E.R. 517; (1978) 36 P. & C.R. 295; (1978) 122 S.J. 63,
Ch D 6–30
Washington Diamond Mining Co, Re [1893] 3 Ch. 95, CA 4–04
Watson Kipling & Co, Re (1883) L.R. 23 Ch. D. 500, Ch D 8–33
Watts v Midland Bank Plc (1986) 2 B.C.C. 98961; [1986] B.C.L.C. 15,
Ch D 10–39
Weisgard v Pilkington [1995] B.C.C. 1108, Ch D 13–46, 13–53, 13–154
Welsby v Brelec Installations Ltd (In Liquidation) [2001] B.C.C. 421; [2000]
2 B.C.L.C. 576; [2001] B.P.I.R. 210; (2000) 97(20) L.S.G. 43, Ch D 12–30
Welsh Brick Industries Ltd, Re [1946] 2 All E.R. 197 5–18

Welsh Development Agency v Export Finance Co Ltd [1992] B.C.C. 270;
   [1992] B.C.L.C. 148, CA (Civ Div) 10–53, 10–59
West End Networks Ltd, Secretary of State for Trade and Industry v Frid.
   See Secretary of State for Trade and Industry v Frid
Westdeutsche Landesbank Girozentrale v Islington LBC [1996] A.C. 669;
   [1996] 2 W.L.R. 802; [1996] 2 All E.R. 961; [1996] 5 Bank. L.R. 341;
   [1996] C.L.C. 990; 95 L.G.R. 1; (1996) 160 J.P. Rep. 1130; (1996) 146
   N.L.J. 877; (1996) 140 S.J.L.B. 136, HL 6–42, 13–127
Westmid Packing Services Ltd (No.2), Re [1998] 2 All E.R. 124; [1998]
   B.C.C. 836; [1998] 2 B.C.L.C. 646, CA (Civ Div) 14–11, 14–75
Westminster CC v Treby [1936] 2 All E.R. 21 10–63
Westminster Corp v Haste [1950] Ch. 442; [1950] 2 All E.R. 65; 66 T.L.R.
   (Pt. 1) 1083; (1950) 114 J.P. 340; 49 L.G.R. 67, Ch D 10–63
Whistlejacket Capital Ltd (In Receivership), Re [2008] EWCA Civ
   575; [2008] B.C.C. 826; [2008] 2 B.C.L.C. 683; (2008) 105(22) L.S.G.
   24 .... 1–38, 8–03
Whitaker (No.1), Re [1901] 1 Ch. 9, CA 1–10
White v Davenham Trust Ltd [2010] EWHC 2748 (Ch); [2011] B.C.C. 77;
   [2011] B.P.I.R. 280 13–109
White & Carter (Councils) Ltd v McGregor [1962] A.C. 413; [1962] 2
   W.L.R. 17; [1961] 3 All E.R. 1178; 1962 S.C. (H.L.) 1; 1962 S.L.T. 9;
   (1961) 105 S.J. 1104, HL 6–31
White & Osmond (Parkstone) Ltd, Re Unreported 1960, referred to in
   R. v Grantham (Paul Reginald)
Whitmore v Mason, 70 E.R. 1031; (1861) 2 John. & H. 204, KB 7–05, 7–16
Wigzell Ex p. Hart, Re [1921] 2 K.B. 835, CA 1–19
Wilkinson Ex p. Fowler, Re [1905] 2 K.B. 713, KBD 6–17, 8–11
Wilkinson Ex p. Stubbins, Re (1881) L.R. 17 Ch. D. 58, CA 13–80
William Hockley Ltd, Re [1962] 1 W.L.R. 555; [1962] 2 All E.R. 111; (1962)
   106 S.J. 308, Ch D 4–26
Williams v Natural Life Health Foods Ltd [1998] 1 W.L.R. 830; [1998] 2 All
   E.R. 577; [1998] B.C.C. 428; [1998] 1 B.C.L.C. 689; (1998) 17 Tr. L.R.
   152; (1998) 95(21) L.S.G. 37; (1998) 148 N.L.J. 657; (1998) 142 S.J.L.B.
   166, HL 14–08, 14–09
Willmott v London Celluloid Co (1887) L.R. 34 Ch. D. 147, CA 13–142
Wilmot v Alton [1897] 1 Q.B. 17, CA 6–33
Wilson v Masters International Ltd [2009] EWHC 1753 (Ch); [2010] B.C.C.
   834; [2009] 2 B.C.L.C. 485; [2010] B.P.I.R. 608 .... 13–88, 13–101
Wiltshire Iron Co, Re (1867–68) L.R. 3 Ch. App. 443, CA in Chancery 13–135
Windsor Refrigerator Co v Branch Nominees [1961] Ch. 375; [1961] 2
   W.L.R. 196; [1961] 1 All E.R. 277; (1961) 105 S.J. 205, CA 10–31
Winkworth v Edward Baron Development Co Ltd [1986] 1 W.L.R. 1512;
   [1987] 1 All E.R. 114; (1987) 3 B.C.C. 4; [1987] B.C.L.C. 193; [1987] 1
   F.L.R. 525; [1987] 1 F.T.L.R. 176; (1987) 53 P. & C.R. 378; [1987] Fam.
   Law 166; (1987) 84 L.S.G. 340; (1986) 130 S.J. 954, HL 14–20
Winsor v Bloom Winsor v Special Railway Administrators of Railtrack Plc.
   See Railtrack Plc (In Administration) (No.2), Re
Winter v IRC [1963] A.C. 235; [1961] 3 W.L.R. 1062; [1961] 3 All E.R. 855;
   (1961) 40 A.T.C. 361; [1961] T.R. 349; (1961) 105 S.J. 929, HL 4–26
Woodroffes (Musical Instruments) Ltd, Re [1986] Ch. 366; [1985] 3 W.L.R.
   543; [1985] 2 All E.R. 908; [1985] P.C.C. 318; (1985) 82 L.S.G. 3170;
   (1985) 129 S.J. 589, Ch D 8–52
Woods v Winskill [1913] 2 Ch. 303, Ch D 10–63

Woven Rugs Ltd, Re [2008] B.C.C. 903, Ch D 5–11
Wyvern Developments, Re [1974] 1 W.L.R. 1097; [1974] 2 All E.R. 535;
    (1974) 118 S.J. 531, Ch D 5–02
Yagerphone Ltd, Re [1935] Ch. 392, Ch D 6–37, 13–142
Yeovil Glove Co, Re [1965] Ch. 148; [1964] 3 W.L.R. 406; [1964] 2 All E.R.
    849; (1964) 108 S.J. 499, CA 13–122
Yorkshire Bank Plc v Hall [1999] 1 W.L.R. 1713; [1999] 1 All E.R. 879;
    (1999) 78 P. & C.R. 136, CA (Civ Div) 10–48
Zirceram Ltd (In Liquidation), Re [2000] B.C.C. 1048; [2000] 1 B.C.L.C.
    751, Ch D 5–11

Table of Foreign Cases

Australia

AWA Ltd v Daniels (1992) 7 A.C.S.R. 759 14–09
Airservices Australia v Ferrier (1996) 185 C.L.R. 483, HCA 13–88
Australian Kitchen Industries Pty Ltd v Albarran (2005) 51 A.C.S.R. 604,
    Sup Ct (NSW) 13–19
Bank of Australasia v Hall (1907) 4 C.L.R. 1514 4–16
Bayley v National Australia Bank (1995) 16 A.C.S.R. 38 13–141
Bell Group Ltd v Westpac Banking Group Corp (No.9) (2008) 70
    A.C.S.R. 1 .... 4–04, 4–13, 4–16
Brinds Ltd v Offshore Oil NL (1986) 2 B.C.C. 98916, PC 5–13
Brolrik Pty Ltd v Sambah Holdings Pty Ltd (2002) 40 A.C.S.R. 361 4–19
Bunbury Foods Pty Ltd v National Bank of Australasia Ltd (1984) 51
    A.L.R. 609 10–30
Caboche v Ramsay (1993) 119 A.L.R. 215, FCA 7–09
Campbell v Michael Mount PSB (1995) 16 A.C.S.R. 296 13–141
Capt'n Snooze Management Pty Ltd v McLellan [2002] V.S.C. 432 8–23
Commissioner of Stamp Duties (Queensland) v Livingston [1965] A.C. 694;
    [1964] 3 W.L.R. 963; [1964] 3 All E.R. 692; (1964) 43 A.T.C. 325; [1964]
    T.R. 351; (1964) 108 S.J. 820, PC 3–10
Commissioner of Taxation v Linter Textiles Australia Ltd (2005) 215
    A.L.R. 1 3–09
Daniels v Anderson (1995) 16 A.C.S.R. 607 14–09
Diesels & Components Pty Ltd, Re (1985) 9 A.C.L.R. 2825 10–53
Emanuel (No.14) Pty Ltd, Re, Macks v Blacklaw & Shadforth Pty Ltd
    (1997) 1 A.L.R. 281 13–19
Expo International Ltd v Chant [1979] N.S.W.L.R. 820 4–16
Ferrier v Civil Aviation Authority (1995) 127 A.L.R. 472 13–88
French Caledonia Travel Service Pty Ltd, Re (2003) 204 A.L.R. 353, Sup Ct
    (NSW) 3–03
Fresjac Pty Ltd, Re (1995) 65 S.A.S.R. 334 13–141
G&M Aldridge Pty Ltd v Walsh (2001) 203 C.L.R. 662, HCA 13–89
Global Television Pty Ltd v Sportsvision Australia Pty Ltd (2000) 35
    A.C.S.R. 1314, Sup Ct (NSW) 6–29
Gye v McIntyre (1991) 171 C.L.R. 609, CA 9–24
Hall v Poolman (2007) 65 A.C.S.R. 123 4–20
Harris & Lewine Pty Ltd (In Liquidation) v Harris & Lewin (Agents)
    (1975) A.C.L.C. 28 10–28
Horne v Chester & Fein Property Development Pty Ltd (1987) 11 A.C.L.R.
    485 8–08
International Air Transport Association v Ansett Australia Holdings Ltd
    (2008) 234 C.L.R. 151; [2008] B.P.I.R. 57, HC 9–14
Iso Lilodw' Aliphumeleli Pty Ltd v Commissioner of Taxation (2002) 42
    A.C.S.R. 561 .... 4–16, 4–19
Kinsela & Am v Russell Kinsela Pty Ltd (1986) 10 A.C.L.R. 395 14–19
Kratzmann Pty Ltd (In Liquidation) v Tucker (No.2) (1968) 123 C.L.R. 295,
    HCA 13–142
Leeholme Stud Pty Ltd, Re [1965] N.S.W.R. 1649 9–24
Lewis v Doran (2005) 219 A.L.R. 555, CA (NSW) 4–13, 4–16

Loteka Pty Ltd, Re (1989) 7 A.C.L.C. 998 .... 13–131, 13–134
M&R Jones Shopfitting Co Pty Ltd v National Bank of Australasia Ltd
    (1983) 7 A.C.L.R. 445 13–88
Mal Bower's Macquarie Electrical Centre Pty Ltd, Re [1974] 1 N.S.W.L.R.
    254 .... 13–128, 13–134
Margart Pty Ltd, Re (1984) 9 A.C.L.R. 269; [1985] B.C.L.C. 314, Sup Ct
    (NSW) 13–129
Media World Communications Ltd, Crosbie v Nadoo, Re [2005] F.C.A. 51 ... 8–27
National Australia Bank v KDS Construction Services Pty Ltd (1987) 163
    C.L.R. 668 .... 13–93, 13–129, 13–132
New Cap Reinsurance Corp v Grant (2008) 68 A.C.S.R. 176 .... 4–16, 4–18,
                                                                 4–26, 4–27
New Zealand Loan & Mercantile Agency Co Ltd v Morrison [1898] A.C.
    349, PC 12–24
Permanent Building Society v Wheeler (1994) 14 A.C.S.R. 109 14–11
Quick v Stotland Pty Ltd (1998) 29 A.C.S.R. 130, FCA 4–16
Robertson v Grigg (1932) 47 C.L.R. 257 13–84
Row Dal Construction Pty Ltd, Re [1966] V.R. 249 13–126
Sandell v Porter (1966) 115 C.L.R. 666 4–16
Sheahan Carrier Pty Ltd v Air Conditioning Pty Ltd (1997) 189 C.L.R. 407,
    HCA 13–89
Sons of Gwalia Ltd v Margaretic (2007) 232 A.L.R. 232, HCA 8–27
Somerset Marine Inc v New Cap Reinsurance Group [2003] NSWCA 38 ... 13–19
Southern British National Trust Ltd v Pither (1937) 57 C.L.R. 89 8–27
Southern Cross Interiors Pty Ltd v Deputy Commissioner of Taxation
    (2001) 39 A.C.S.R. 305, Sup Ct (NSW) 4–19
Stein v Saywell [1969] A.L.R. 481 10–60
Sutherland v Eurolinx Pty Ltd (2001) 37 A.C.S.R. 477 4–19
Sycotex Pty Ltd v Baseter (1993) 13 A.C.S.R. 766 4–19
Tasmanian Primary Distributors Pty Ltd v RC&MB Steinhardt Pty Ltd
    (1994) 13 A.C.S.R. 92 13–134
Timbatec Pty Ltd, Re (1974) 24 F.L.R. 30 4–20
Transmetro Corp Ltd v Real Investments Pty Ltd (1999) 17 A.C.L.C. 1314,
    Sup Ct (Qd) 6–29
Walker v Wimborne (1976) 50 A.L.J.R. 446 14–19
Water v Widows [1984] V.R. 503 8–52
Webb Distributors (Aust) Pty Ltd v State of Victoria (1993) 179 C.L.R. 15 ... 8–27
Weiss, Re [1970] A.L.R. 654 13–88
Westpac Banking Group Corp (No.9), Re. *See* Bell Group Ltd v Westpac
    Banking Group Corp (No.9)

Bahamas

Space Investments Ltd v Canadian Imperial Bank of Commerce Trust
    Co (Bahamas) Ltd [1986] 1 W.L.R. 1072; [1986] 3 All E.R. 75;
    (1986) 2 B.C.C. 99302; (1986) 83 L.S.G. 2567; (1986) 130 S.J. 612,
    PC 6–43

Brunei

Royal Brunei Airlines Sdn Bhd v Tan [1995] 2 A.C. 378; [1995] 3 W.L.R.
    64; [1995] 3 All E.R. 97; [1995] B.C.C. 899; (1995) 92(27) L.S.G.
    33; (1995) 145 N.L.J. 888; [1995] 139 S.J.L.B. 146; (1995) 70 P. & C.R.
    D12, PC 14–24

Canada

Canada Deposit Insurance Corp v Canadian Commercial Bank (No.3)
(1993) 97 D.L.R. (4th) 385, Sup Ct 8–27
Parsons v Sovereign Bank of Canada [1913] A.C. 160, PC 10–21
Peoples Department Stores Inc v Wise (2004) 244 D.L.R. (4th) 564 14–20
Ronald Elwyn Lister Ltd v Dunlop Canada Ltd (1982) 135 D.L.R. (3d) 1 ... 10–30
Saulnier v Royal Bank of Canada [2008] 3 S.C.R. 166, Sup Ct 6–11
Waldron v Royal Bank of Canada [1991] 4 W.W.R. 289, CA (BC) 10–30

Cayman Islands

Cleaver v Delta American Reinsurance Co (In Liquidation) [2001] UKPC
6; [2001] 2 A.C. 328; [2001] 2 W.L.R. 1202; [2001] 1 B.C.L.C.
482; [2001] B.P.I.R. 438; [2002] Lloyd's Rep. I.R. 167; (2001) 145
S.J.L.B. 85 .... 8–14, 16–63
Wight v Eckhardt Marine GmbH [2003] UKPC 37; [2004] 1 A.C. 147;
[2003] 3 W.L.R. 414; [2003] B.C.C. 702; [2004] 2 B.C.L.C. 539 .... 2–08, 3–07,
8–14, 9–18

France

Daisy-Tek. *See* Klempka v ISA Daisytek SA
Klempka v ISA Daisytek SA [2003] B.C.C. 984; [2004] I.L.Pr. 6, Cour
d'Appel (Versailles) 15–54
Klempka v ISA Daisytek SA [2006] B.C.C. 841, Cour de Cassation 15–29,
15–54, 16–10
MPOTEC GmbH [2006] B.C.C. 681, Tr de Gde Instance (Nanterre) 15–56
Public Prosecutor v Segard (Administrator of Rover France SAS) [2006]
I.L.Pr. 32, Cour d'Appel (Versailles) 15–67

Hong Kong

Attorney General of Hong Kong v Nai-Keung (Daniel Chan) [1987] 1
W.L.R. 1339; (1987) 3 B.C.C. 403; (1988) 86 Cr. App. R. 174; [1988]
Crim. L.R. 125; (1987) 131 S.J. 1185, PC 6–05, 6–07, 6–11
CA Pacific Finance Ltd (In Liquidation), Re [2000] 1 B.C.L.C. 494, CFI 6–42
China and South Seas Bank Ltd v Tan [1990] 1 A.C. 536; [1990] 2 W.L.R.
56; [1989] 3 All E.R. 839; [1990] 1 Lloyd's Rep. 113; (1989) 86(46)
L.S.G. 37; (1989) 139 N.L.J. 1669; (1990) 134 S.J. 165, PC 10–48, 10–49
Concorde Construction Co Ltd v Colgan Co Ltd (1984) 29 B.L.R. 120, HC 6–44
Industrial Equity (Pacific) Ltd, Re [1991] 2 H.K.L.R. 614 12–23
UDL Holdings Ltd, Re [2002] 1 H.K.C. 172 12–19

India

Bombay Official Assignee v Shroff (1932) 48 T.L.R. 443 .... 6–09, 7–07

Ireland

Baife v Blake (1850) 1 I.R. Ch. Rep. 365 10–57
Eurofood IFSC Ltd (No.1), Re [2004] IESC 47; [2005] B.C.C. 999; [2005]
Eu. L.R. 148; [2005] I.L.Pr. 2 .... 15–08, **15–36—15–37**,
15–41, 15–56, 15–57
Glow Heating Ltd v Eastern Health Board [1988] I.R. 110; (1992) 8 Const.
L.J. 56, HC 6–17

Industrial Services Co (Dublin) Ltd, Re [2001] 2 I.R. 118 13–131
King's Trust, Re (1892) 29 L.R. Ir. 401 7–05
Minister for the Environment and Local Government v Irish ISPAT Ltd
    Unreported July 29, 2004, HC 8–30
Pat Ruth Ltd, Re [1981] I.R.L.M. 51 13–131

New Zealand

Attorney General v McMillan & Lockwood Ltd [1991] 1 N.Z.L.R. 53,
    CA 6–17, 8–11
Clyde Properties Ltd v Tasker [1970] N.Z.L.R. 754 10–30
Jaffe v Premier Motors Ltd [1970] N.Z.L.R. 146 10–30
Nicholson v Permakraft (NZ) Ltd [1985] 1 N.Z.L.R. 242 14–19
Orion Sound Ltd, Re (1979) 2 N.Z.L.R. 574 8–08
R Jaffe Ltd (in liquidation) v Jaffe (No.2) [1932] N.Z.L.R. 195 10–28
Vujnovich v Vujnovich (1989) 5 B.C.C. 740; [1990] B.C.L.C. 227, PC 5–21

Singapore

Hitachi Plant Engineering & Construction Ltd v Eltraco International Pte
    Ltd [2003] 4 S.L.R. 384, CA 6–17
Libra Industries Pte Ltd, Re [1999] S.L.R. (R) 105 13–88
Liquidators of Progen Engineering Pte Ltd v Progen Holdings Ltd [2010]
    SGCA 31 .... 13–88, 14–20
Pacific Rim Investments Pte Ltd v Lam Seng Tiong [1995] 3 S.L.R. 1 9–04

United States of America

Lehman Brothers Holdings Inc v BNY Corporate Trustee Services Ltd, 25
    January 2010 (US Bankruptcy Court for the Southern District of New
    York, Case 08–1355) 7–22
Maxwell Communication Corp, Re, 93 F.3d 1036 (1966), US Ct of Appeals 7–22
Mobil Steel Co, Re, 563 F.2d 692 (5th Cir. 1977) 8–27
NLRB v Bildisco & Bildisco, 465 US 513 (1984) 2–17

Chapter 1

The History and Framework of Corporate Insolvency Law

1. INTRODUCTION

Nature of the subject

This book is devoted to the subject of corporate insolvency law: the law relating to the insolvency of companies. Historically, this developed separately from the law relating to the insolvency of individuals.[1] In consequence, whereas in American law the term "bankruptcy" in the sense of a legally declared state of insolvency applies alike to individuals and corporations, English insolvency law possesses no such generic term. Individuals become bankrupt, or go into bankruptcy; companies go into liquidation, or winding up (the terms are synonymous).

1–01

When a company becomes insolvent, many questions may arise. Is it capable of being rehabilitated or at least got into better shape before liquidation? If it does go into liquidation, what assets in its possession are to be considered available for distribution among its creditors, who are to be treated as creditors and how are the various classes of claim to be ranked? In what circumstances will transactions entered into by a company before winding up be rendered void or liable to be set aside, and how should recoveries be dealt with? What duties are owed by the directors of an insolvent company to the company itself and its creditors, and what sanctions may be imposed for breaches of those duties? What are the qualifications for acting as an insolvency practitioner and what duties and liabilities are imposed upon those who so act? Finally, what rules govern cross-border insolvencies, particularly on matters such as the applicable law, jurisdiction, the recognition and enforcement of judgments and inter-jurisdiction co-operation? All

---

[1] See below, paras 1–10 et seq.

these issues, and others besides, fall within the province of corporate insolvency law and will be examined in the ensuing pages.

There are special rules governing bank failures[2] and these have objectives somewhat different from those of ordinary corporates.[3]

This book is primarily concerned with corporate insolvency law and policy as these currently exist (albeit with critical comment at appropriate places) rather than with normative theories of corporate insolvency law which have over recent years engaged the interest of scholars.[4] There has been a wealth of valuable literature from American scholars in particular,[5] and more recently from academics in England and elsewhere, who have sought to identify from a law and economics perspective the rational goals of a modern insolvency law. These call for a different kind of book.[6] An outline of some of these theories, and the extent to which the objectives they identify are reflected in English corporate insolvency law, will be given in the next chapter.

The role of credit

1–02 Insolvency is the inability to pay one's debts. It therefore necessarily arises from the extension of credit, for without credit there can be no debt. A world without credit is impossible to imagine. Credit—that is, contractual deferment of debt—has existed from the earliest times, well before the advent of banking institutions. A huge amount of credit is extended every year by suppliers, banks and other financial institutions and by investors in the financial markets. Credit facilitates the smooth running and expansion of business and, in good trading conditions, gives a company leverage to increase its profits by undertaking more business than would be possible if it were restricted to using its own funds. The higher the degree of leverage (or "gearing")—i.e. the ratio of borrowed funds to shareholders' funds—the greater the profits, so long as trading income exceeds the cost of servicing the borrowings. The converse, of course, is that where the volume of trading declines or trading otherwise becomes unprofitable the obligation to continue servicing the debts accentuates the losses and may precipitate the

---

[2] See below, para.1–59.

[3] See below, paras 1–57 et seq., 2–14.

[4] One American scholar has classified bankruptcy scholarship as observational (objectively describing existing law and policy), normative (the values that courts and legislatures should seek to achieve in bankruptcy), standard reform (how the law can best achieve its existing objectives) and critical reform (what purposes the law should seek to achieve and how best it could achieve them). See Donald R. Korobkin, "The Role of Normative Theory in Bankruptcy Debates" 82 Iowa L. Rev. 75 (1986).

[5] See paras 2–15 et seq.

[6] See, e.g. Rizwaan Jameel Mokal, *Corporate Insolvency Law: Theory and Application* (Oxford: Oxford University Press, 2005); and Vanessa Finch, *Corporate Insolvency Law: Perspectives and Principles*, 2nd edn (Cambridge: Cambridge University Press, 2009).

collapse of the company. A major factor contributing to the collapse of so many large companies in recent years has been massive over-leveraging. On the other hand, the refusal of ordinary credit to a sound business can be very damaging, as witness failures of good business because of the refusal of banks to continue funding companies with an overdraft when they had never previously gone into default.

The cost of credit depends on the creditworthiness of the borrower, which itself is linked to the soundness of its business and the realisable value of its assets. With major organisations, a crucial role is played by credit rating agencies—notably Moody's, Standard & Poor's and Fitch—for upon the rating they give an organisation depends the cost of the credit they obtain.

Forms of credit

Credit takes three distinct forms: the purchase of debt instruments (bonds, **1–03** notes, etc.) issued on a market; loan credit, in which money is advanced on terms of repayment; and sale credit, in which goods, services or other things are supplied on the basis of payment at a later date, whether in a single sum or by instalments.[7] Sale credit does not in law constitute the lending of money: it is simply the contractual deferment of a price obligation. It enables a company to obtain goods or services in advance of payment, but does not, of course, give it the free funds it needs to conduct its business. For that purpose the company must look to other sources, in particular, share capital (equity) contributed by its members and borrowings from lenders (debt) whether in the form of bank lending or through the issue of bonds and other debt instruments on the capital market.

There are three basic types of lending: "relationship lending", normally bank lending, which is primarily against the borrower's credit standing and which, even if secured on assets, is not based on their valuation; asset-based financing, which is based on the value of specific tangible or intangible assets such as receivables, stock in trade, equipment and property; and project finance, a form of limited recourse financing which, although secured on all the contracts and other assets of the project, is intended to be repaid out of the cash flows from the project, with no personal liability on the part of the borrower.[8]

---

[7] From an economic perspective, finance leasing is equated with conditional sale, and assets subject to a finance lease are required to be shown as an asset in the books of the lessee, not the lessor. See Statements of Accounting Practice, SSAP 21: Accounting for Leases and Hire Purchase Contracts; and *Goode on Commercial Law*, edited by Ewan McKendrick, 4th edn (2009), pp.767–768. SSAP 21 is due to be superseded as the result of a project being undertaken jointly by the International Accounting Standards Board and the US Financial Accounting Standards Board, which issued an exposure draft of the new proposals on August 17, 2010.

[8] See Philip Wood, *Project Finance, Securitisations and Subordinated Debt*, 2nd edn (London: Sweet & Maxwell, 2007); and Andrew McKnight, *Law of International Finance* (Oxford: Oxford University Press, 2008), Ch.13.

Equity and debt[9]

1–04   For the purpose of insolvency law there is a vitally important difference between equity and debt. Shareholders are not creditors. Unlike creditors they have no claim to payment from the company except when a dividend is declared or there is a surplus of assets over liabilities on the winding up of the company. In general, creditors are entitled to be paid ahead of shareholders in the event of a company going into liquidation; only when creditors have been paid in full (which is rarely the case) do shareholders come in to participate in the surplus remaining.[10] Neither group is homogeneous. Frequently debt is multi-tiered, with one or more layers of senior debt at the top, several layers of junior debt underneath and at the bottom mezzanine debt, a form of hybrid which typically consists of either preferential shares carrying an entitlement to a fixed dividend ahead of ordinary shareholders or convertible warrants, which carry an interest coupon and a right to convert into shares. Only shareholders rank below mezzanine creditors.

Other forms of hybrid security, which combine debt and equity, are: convertible bonds or notes; payment in kind (PIK) loans, in which an amount equal to the interest is paid in stock in the borrower company or interest is rolled into the capital at maturity and which carry a detachable warrant; and income security, a mixture of debt and equity in which the debt part pays interest and the equity part dividends. The ranking of creditors among themselves may be influenced by the grant of security, which vis-à-vis the debtor[11] may leave a junior creditor in a better position than an unsecured senior creditor, or by subordination techniques, which may be contractual or structural,[12] shares may be ordinary, preferred or deferred, depending on the terms of issue; and insolvency law itself distinguishes between different categories of creditor in the priority stakes.

A more recent form of financing is second lien financing, in which agreement is reached between the first lien lender and the second lien lender as to rights of enforcement and the allocation of proceeds of realisation of collateral. Second lien financing differs from contractual subordination in that there is no formal subordination of the second lien to the first. Instead, there

---

[9] See generally Louise Gullifer and Jennifer Payne, *Corporate Finance Law: Principles and Policy* (Oxford: Hart Publishing, 2011), Chs 2 and 3.

[10] Insolvency Act 1986 ss.107, 154.

[11] But not normally vis-à-vis the senior creditor, because the subordination agreement will usually control the junior creditor's freedom of action with regard to collection and the application of proceeds of his debt.

[12] Structural subordination results from lending to a holding company rather than the operating company. If the operating company becomes insolvent, its creditors will be paid ahead of the holding company, which is not a creditor but a shareholder, so that creditors of the holding company have to look primarily to dividends received in the winding up of the holding company. See further below, para.8–08, as to subordination.

is an allocation of specific rights and duties designed to give the first lien lender control without a contractual subordination as such. Agreements commonly include restrictions on enforcement of the security by the second lien lender and allocation of the whole or most of the proceeds of realisation to repayment of the debt due to the first lien lender, coupled with a waiver by the second lien lender of any right it might otherwise have to challenge the first lien lender's security. Second lien lending has been widely used to overcome legal restrictions on investment in contractually subordinated debt.

Security and quasi-security

A financially strong company will often be able to obtain credit simply on the strength of its undertaking to pay without providing any security. But banks and other lenders frequently feel the need to buttress this undertaking with security in order to ensure that if by mischance the borrower company does become insolvent, they will be able to jump ahead of other creditors. Security may be real or personal. Real security is security in an asset or pool of assets and typically takes the form of a mortgage or charge covering specific assets or a class of existing and future assets.[13] Personal security consists of the reinforcement of the debtor company's undertaking by that of a third party, usually in the form of a guarantee of the debt, or by a stronger undertaking by the debtor himself, for example, in a negotiable instrument, claims on which are less easily resisted than those based on the underlying transaction.

1–05

Nature of security

Real security in the true sense involves the grant of rights by the debtor company in an asset which it owns or in which it has an interest. Consensual security takes four forms: mortgage, fixed or floating charge, pledge and contractual lien.[14] The trust, if created for the purpose of securing an obligation, is not an independent security device, but a form of equitable mortgage or charge, which may be effected either by the debtor declaring itself to be trustee of the asset or by transfer of the asset by the debtor to a trustee to hold on trust for the creditor (which could be the trustee itself)[15] as security for payment.[16] But there are other types of transaction which fulfil the

1–06

---

[13] See *Goode on Legal Problems of Credit and Security*, edited by Louise Gullifer, 4th edn (2008), Ch.1.

[14] See *Goode on Legal Problems*, paras 1–42 et seq. As to the distinction between a fixed and a floating charge see below, para.10–16.

[15] See *Re Gray v G-T-P Group Ltd, F2G Realisations Ltd* [2010] EWHC 1772 (Ch). For a discussion of this case in the context of perfection under the Financial Collateral Directive, see below, para.1–67.

[16] *Goode on Legal Problems*, 2008, para.1–53.

function of security but do not involve the grant of such rights. Notable among these is the supply of goods on terms that ownership is not to pass to the buyer until payment. Just as a sale on credit is not in law a loan, so also the retention of title under a sale contract does not constitute a security interest in law, for the debtor is not granting rights over its own asset, but merely agreeing that it will not acquire ownership until payment of the price. This reflects English law's formal, rather than functional, approach to the characterisation of agreements. The courts look to the legal rather than the economic substance of the agreement. This approach is to be contrasted with that adopted throughout the United States, Canada, New Zealand and, more recently, Australia, whose personal property security laws look to the economic function of title reservation and treat this, and certain forms of leasing also, as security interests, on the basis that while the creditor may be the legal owner it is the debtor who is the economic owner and is therefore to be treated as a person granting a security interest in his own asset.[17] Other quasi-security devices include sale and repurchase, finance leasing, contractual set-off and the imposition of conditions on the right to withdraw a deposit.[18] In addition, outright sales of receivables are governed, in the above jurisdictions, by the registration and priority rules concerning security interests, but are not treated as security interests for the purpose of the default provisions and the treatment of surplus on repossession and sale, reflecting the fact that the factor or invoice discounter is an outright buyer and thus solely entitled to what it has purchased.

In addition to the consensual security and quasi-security devices, there are various forms of security created not by agreement, but by operation of law. These include various forms of lien and statutory charges as well as procedural security.[19]

Functions and effects of security

1–07   Security and quasi-security play a crucial part in expanding the availability of credit,[20] and sophisticated arguments have been advanced to demonstrate the efficiency of secured credit.[21]

But in insolvency security interests also have implications for the general body of creditors, for their effect is to reduce the pool of assets available for

---

[17] See *Goode on Legal Problems*, 2008, para.1–04.
[18] See *Goode on Commercial Law*, edited by Ewan McKendrick, 4th edn (London: Penguin Books and LexisNexis, 2009), pp.626–627 and 645–660.
[19] See *Goode on Commercial Law*, 2009, pp.660–664.
[20] See further paras 2–18 and 2–29.
[21] One of the earliest was the extensively cited article by Thomas H. Jackson and Anthony Kronman, "Secured Financing and Priorities Among Creditors" 88 Yale L.J. 1143 (1979). See below, para.2–29.

the general body of creditors, since secured creditors normally have priority over unsecured creditors.[22] This is a point to which we shall return later when considering the extent to which corporate insolvency law has a redistributive role.[23]

However, it would be a mistake to assume that the sole purpose of security is to give the secured creditor priority in a winding up. Security fulfils a number of other functions which are of considerable importance. One of these, particularly in the case of global security under a combined fixed and floating charge, is to provide the secured creditor with a significant degree of control both in relation to the company's conduct and in relation to that of unsecured creditors, who have little incentive to pursue individual enforcement measures when control of most of the assets is vested in a single lender.[24] When insolvency intervenes and the company is going to go into administration, a dominant, secured creditor, or a dominant group of secured creditors acting collectively, becomes an even more influential player. First, although a dominant, secured creditor, for reputational reasons, does not usually appoint an administrator itself, it undoubtedly influences the appointment, and usually there will have been an established working relationship between, say, a bank and an administrator appointed by the directors with the bank's approval. Secondly, if the creditor is under-secured, it has every incentive to ensure that the administrator does his best to maximise returns and keep down the costs of the administration, including the administrator's fees.[25] By contrast, an adequately secured or over-secured creditor has little interest in the administration except for the purpose of ensuring that its rights are preserved. Another function of security is to enhance the secured creditor's risk-weighted capital for capital adequacy purposes.[26]

The collective nature of the corporate insolvency regime

When a debtor, whether a private individual, a sole trader, a partnership firm or a company, fails to pay a debt on its due date, the creditor is entitled to avail himself of all the rights and remedies given to him by his contract and by law. Such rights and remedies are of two kinds. First, there are those exercisable by self-help. They include, in given conditions, the creditor's right to

1–08

---

[22] But this priority is qualified in the case of the holder of a floating charge. See below, paras 8–49 et seq.

[23] See below, paras 2–15 et seq.

[24] This is borne out by a study by Julian R. Franks and Oren Sussman, "Financial Distress and Bank Restructuring of Small-to-Medium Size UK Companies" (2005) 9 *Review of Finance* 65. See further para.2–20. But see below, para.1–15, as to the impact of fragmentation of security interests consequent upon the shift from bank relationship lending to asset-based finance by specialist financiers.

[25] See Office of Fair Trading, "The Market for Corporate Insolvency Practitioners" (June 2010), paras 4.29 et seq.

[26] See generally *Goode on Legal Problems*, 2008, paras 1–01–1–02.

accelerate the debtor's liability, to withhold his own performance under the contract or to terminate the contract by reason of the default; the right to enforce—by possession, sale, the appointment of a receiver or otherwise—a security interest, reservation of title or other real right in an asset held by the debtor; the right to forfeit a lease or to distrain against the debtor's goods for rent; and the right to set off the debt against a countervailing money obligation owed by the creditor to the debtor. Secondly, there are judicial (or curial) rights and remedies, including the institution of proceedings against the debtor for payment, delivery, possession, foreclosure or sale, and the enforcement of an ensuing judgment by one or more processes of judicial execution against the debtor's income or assets or enforcement of an order for specific delivery or possession of an asset belonging to the creditor himself.

A creditor who holds a security interest or other real right in an asset owned or possessed by the debtor may proceed to realise that right and to take what is due to him from the proceeds in priority to all other creditors except for those having a stronger claim than he to the asset. A creditor having no right *in rem* in any asset held by the debtor may nevertheless exercise any other form of self-help open to him, such as acceleration of the debt and/or set-off. Failing this, the only remaining method open to him of exacting payment, short of a threat of insolvency proceedings, is to obtain and enforce a judgment against the debtor. But other creditors may be pursuing the same course, in which case he will find himself in competition, with the race going to the swiftest. The individual debtor faces the bleak prospect of having all his assets seized, except for the modest value of items exempt from execution, and of having all his income diverted to his creditors to the extent that this exceeds what the court considers it necessary for him to live on. The corporate debtor is in even worse case, for none of its property or income is exempt from execution.

The primary purpose of insolvency law[27] is to replace the free-for-all attendant upon the pursuit of individual claims by different creditors with a statutory regime in which creditors' rights and remedies are suspended, wholly or in part, and a mechanism is provided for the orderly collection and realisation of assets and the distribution of the net realisations of the assets among creditors in accordance with the statutory scheme of distribution.[28] English insolvency law distinguishes individual debtors (including sole traders and

---

[27] This term is used in a broad sense to cover both collective procedures initiated by the debtor or creditors following the debtor's default (in particular, administration, bankruptcy and winding up) and administrative receivership resulting from the steps taken by an individual secured creditor holding a floating charge embracing (with any fixed security) substantially the whole of the debtor company's assets. For a more detailed summary of the objectives of *corporate* insolvency law, see below, and for the particular purposes and principles of administrative receivership, see Ch.10.

[28] This is the theme of Ch.2.

partnerships) from corporate debtors. Although there is no longer a separate statute for bankruptcy, and what is now the Insolvency Act 1986 reduces the differences between the rules and procedures governing the insolvency of individuals from those applicable to the insolvency of companies, the regimes remain distinct.[29]

As stated earlier, this book is confined to the principles of insolvency law relating to companies, a subject of peculiar fascination because it involves an examination not only of complex statutory provisions, but also of fundamental questions concerning the distinction between real and personal rights and the extent to which creditors have a legally protectable interest in the proper application of a company's assets. It is impossible to understand corporate insolvency law without a true perception of the principles of the general law of property and obligations and the interrelationship of these and the insolvency legislation.

The causes of insolvency

There are many reasons why companies become insolvent. They include **1–09** under-capitalisation, over-trading, over-leveraging, failure to keep pace with changing markets, lack of adequate management and financial controls, failure to take remedial measures in due time and, in the case of banks, sub-prime lending (i.e. lending to high-risk borrowers, often against property that is or becomes insufficient in value to constitute adequate security), and engaging in increasingly complex trading in derivative instruments they do not truly understand. Sometimes a business fails through no fault on the part of the management, for example, because a product unexpectedly becomes valueless through a new discovery by a competitor or because of the unexpected withdrawal by a bank of working capital normally available to the borrower with no history of default. Occasionally, an enterprise fails because of fraud.

2. HISTORY AND SOURCES

The early history of insolvency law[30]

The law governing the insolvency of individuals has its roots in the earliest **1–10** days of the common law, when there was no collective procedure for the

---

[29] For some of the major differences between bankruptcy and winding up, see below, para.1–41.
[30] V. Markham Lester, *Victorian Insolvency* (Oxford: Clarendon Press, 1995); the Cork Report (below, n.50), Ch.2; Ian F. Fletcher, *The Law of Insolvency*, 4th edn (London: Sweet & Maxwell, 2009), paras 1–015 et seq.; and Andrew R. Keay, *McPherson's Law of Company Liquidation*, 2nd edn (London: Sweet & Maxwell, 2009), paras 1.015 et seq.

administration of an insolvent's estate and a disappointed creditor could seize the effects of his debtor and, at a later date, his person also.[31] Although the mediaeval law merchant recognised the institution of bankruptcy,[32] borrowed from the *cessio bonorum* of Roman law, bankruptcy law in the modern sense of an official procedure for the collection and realisation of a debtor's estate for distribution among his creditors generally was first introduced in 1542 by a statute of Henry VIII,[33] which, after a thunderous preamble denouncing debtors acting in fraud of their creditors, directed that the bodies of the offenders and all of their assets be taken by the requisite authorities and the assets sold to pay their creditors "a portion, rate and rate alike, according to the quantity of their debts". Thus was introduced the principle of *pari passu* distribution, which is still the central principle of distribution of an insolvent's free estate, although in practice there are usually few assets left for ordinary unsecured creditors to which it can be applied. Numerous bankruptcy statutes followed. But in contrast to modern bankruptcy law, their aim was penal rather than rehabilitative. The Fraudulent Conveyances Act 1571 outlawed transfers made with intent to delay or defraud creditors. This Elizabethan statute was later held by Lord Mansfield effective to avoid not only fraudulent conveyances, but also fraudulent preferences,[34] which defeated the law by usurping the function of the authorities and defeated the equality intended by the law.[35] As the list of bankruptcy offences grew, so did the severity of the laws increase.[36] Not until 1705 was legislation introduced for the relief of bankrupts through the concept of discharge from debts for those who co-operated with their creditors.[37] For centuries the bankruptcy legislation was confined to traders, on the theory that while traders might become insolvent through accident or misfortune, such as loss of a ship, the insolvency of a private individual was almost invariably due to his profligacy. So there were two systems in place: bankruptcy for traders and "insolvency" for non-traders. Insolvents who were not traders continued to suffer the rigours of individual action under the common law—most notably, imprisonment for a debt and all too often death through disease or starvation—although statutes were enacted for the

---

[31] Edward Cooke, *An Inquiry into the State of the Law of Debtor and Creditor in England* (London: Butterworth, 1829).

[32] Indeed, the word "bankrupt" itself is said to be derived from the practice at mediaeval fairs of breaking the bench (*banca*) of an insolvent merchant found to have acted dishonestly, thus signifying that he was no longer considered worthy to participate as a member of the mercantile community.

[33] Statute of Bankrupts, 34 & 35 Hen. VIII, c.4.

[34] That is, preferences of one creditor over others made voluntarily rather than under compulsion of proceedings or threats. The precursor of the modern legislation specifically rendering eve of bankruptcy preferences voidable was the Bankruptcy Act 1869 s.92. For the current law relating to voidable preferences, see paras 13–71 et seq.

[35] *Alderson v Temple* (1768) 96 E.R. 384.

[36] See *Goode on Commercial Law*, 2009, p.903.

[37] Bankruptcy Act 1705, 4 & 5 Anne, c.17.

relief of debtors and Lord Redesdale's Act of 1813[38] established a Court for the Relief of Insolvent Debtors.[39]

It was only with the enactment of the Bankruptcy Act 1861 that the distinction between traders and non-traders was abolished.[40] That Act was later replaced by a series of bankruptcy statutes culminating in the Bankruptcy Act 1914, which codified bankruptcy law and remained in force until 1986, when it was repealed by the Insolvency Act 1985. Mr Markham Lester has recorded the huge importance attached to insolvency law in Victorian England, with numerous reports of royal commissions and parliamentary select committees, the introduction of nearly 100 bills between 1831 and 1914, and a government bureaucracy and budget which dwarfed those of the Home Office.[41] Noteworthy was the Bankruptcy Act 1869, which in s.32 established the first general statutory regime for preferential debts in bankruptcy, covering within defined limits local rates, taxes and wages or salary of clerks, servants, labourers or workers in the employ of the bankrupt,[42] a regime carried over with additions and variations to subsequent bankruptcy legislation.

The Bankruptcy Acts never applied to companies. The birth of corporate insolvency law goes back no further than 1844, when Parliament enacted the Joint Stock Companies Act 1844, the first general Act to provide for the incorporation of a company as a distinct legal entity, albeit with unlimited liability for its members.[43] This was followed by the Joint Stock Companies Winding-Up Act 1844, which enabled a company to be made bankrupt in the same way as an individual,[44] and the Joint Stock Companies Winding-Up Acts 1848 and 1849, conferring general winding up jurisdiction on the Court of Chancery, a jurisdiction overlapping that of the Bankruptcy Court until the passing of the Joint Stock Companies Act 1856 and the Joint Stock Companies Winding Up (Amendment) Act 1857, which left the Court of Chancery with exclusive jurisdiction and thus formally separated bankruptcy and winding up procedure.[45]

But corporate insolvency law initially piggy-backed on bankruptcy law and did not assume a truly distinctive status until the advent of limited liability

---

[38] 53 Geo III, c.102.

[39] See Lester, *Victorian Insolvency*, 1995, Ch.3.

[40] Bankruptcy Act 1861 s.69.

[41] Markham Lester, *Victorian Insolvency*, 1995, pp.2 and 4–5.

[42] As regards taxes payable to the Crown, these in any event had priority under the Crown prerogative. Earlier statutes had empowered the court or, under some statutes, the bankruptcy commissioners to allow certain payments to employees and apprentices, but this was a matter of discretion, not of right.

[43] Prior to the Joint Stock Companies Winding-Up Act 1844, a company could be incorporated only by charter from the Crown or by special Act of Parliament, which might or might not leave the members of the company liable for its debts.

[44] s.1.

[45] See L.C.B. Gower, *Principles of Modern Company Law*, 6th edn (London: Sweet & Maxwell, 1997), Ch.2 and literature there cited (much of the historical treatment has been omitted from subsequent editions); and Lester, *Victorian Insolvency*, 1995, Ch.6.

for members of a company with the enactment of the Limited Liability Act 1855; and the first modern company law statute was the Companies Act 1862, which contained detailed winding up provisions, including a provision for *pari passu* distribution.[46] Section 10 of the Judicature Act 1875 was designed, amongst other things, to align rules as to proof of debt in company liquidations with those applicable to bankruptcies, but its scope was a matter of controversy and it was not until 1901 that it was finally established by the Court of Appeal that the bankruptcy priority rules were carried over into winding up.[47] By then, legislation had expressly established categories of preferential debt for winding up as well as bankruptcy,[48] and from that time until 1986 corporate insolvency law was to remain governed primarily by successive Companies Acts[49]—which incorporated by reference the provisions of the various Bankruptcy Acts relating to provable debts and fraudulent preferences—the last of these being the Companies Act 1985.

The Insolvency Acts 1985 and 1986 and the Company Directors Disqualification Act 1986

1-11 Following the recommendations of the Insolvency Law Review Committee under the chairmanship of Sir Kenneth Cork,[50] the Insolvency Act 1985 made substantial changes to insolvency provisions of the Companies Act 1985. On the very day the Insolvency Act 1985 came into force,[51] it was replaced by the Insolvency Act 1986, a consolidating enactment which repealed and re-enacted the Insolvency Act 1985 and the insolvency provisions of the Companies Act 1985 other than those relating to the disqualification of directors and a few other provisions noted below. The Insolvency

---

[46] Companies Act 1862 s.133(1), which, however, was confined to voluntary winding up. It appears to have been assumed that the court would exercise its powers to produce a similar result. From the outset of the companies legislation, the expenses of the winding up, including the liquidator's remuneration, were made payable in priority to the claims of other creditors (see the Joint Stock Companies Act 1856 s.104, which again was confined to voluntary winding up, and the Companies Acts 1862 ss.110 and 144 and Companies Act 1883 s.6, which were not so confined), a rule which pertains to this day.

[47] *Re Whitaker, Whitaker v Palmer* [1901] 1 Ch. 9, a decision about a deceased person's insolvent estate, but the section applied equally to winding up of a company. However, the provisions of the Bankruptcy Act 1883 abrogating the Crown's right to priority were held inapplicable to a company liquidation (*Re Oriental Bank Corp* (1884) 28 Ch.D. 643) and the right was not fully abolished until 2003 (Enterprise Act 2002 s.251).

[48] Companies Act 1883 ss.4–6; Preferential Payments in Bankruptcy Acts 1888 (which applied both to bankruptcy and to winding up) and 1897. The last of these also provided that claims secured by a floating charge were subordinated to preferential debts. The provision to this effect in the 1897 Act was considered by the House of Lords in *Buchler v Talbot* [2004] 2 A.C. 298 to be of crucial relevance to the understanding of the modern law.

[49] The principal enactments being the Acts of 1908, 1929, 1948 and 1985.

[50] *Insolvency Law and Practice*, Report of the Review Committee (Cmnd. 8558, 1982) (the "Cork Report")..

[51] December 29, 1986.

Act 1986 was later amended by the Insolvency Act 1994 in order to resolve problems relating to the personal liability of administrators and administrative receivers,[52] and further amended by the Insolvency (No.2) Act 1994 to remove uncertainty concerning the impact of orders under ss.238, 239 and 241 of the 1986 Act[53] on *bona fide* purchasers. The disqualification provisions of the Companies Act and the Insolvency Act 1985 were themselves repealed and re-enacted in a separate consolidation, the Company Directors Disqualification Act 1986.

The Companies Acts 1989 and 2006

Part VII of the Companies Act 1989, which was not repealed by the **1–12** Companies Act 2006, contains a set of provisions to modify the general law of insolvency so as to exempt contracts and arrangements in the financial markets from various rules of insolvency law and substitute for these the rules of the relevant exchange or clearing house. Several statutory instruments have been made pursuant to Part VII.[54] The purpose is to ensure the stability of the financial markets which might otherwise be threatened if market contracts and arrangements were to be invalidated on the insolvency of a major player. Apart from these provisions, most of the legislation governing companies has been consolidated in the Companies Act 2006. Provisions on insolvency which were at one time in the Companies Acts were long ago transferred to what is now the Insolvency Act 1986. However, there remain certain provisions which are relevant in an insolvency situation, notably s.754, dealing with priorities where debentures are secured by a floating charge,[55] those contained in Pt 25, relating to the registration of company charges,[56] and Pt 26, relating to arrangements and reconstructions.[57]

The Financial Services and Markets Act 2000

Part XXIV of the Financial Services and Markets Act 2000 empowers **1–13** the Financial Services Authority (FSA), which oversees the financial markets, to petition for the winding up of authorised firms and unauthorised firms that have been carrying on regulated activities in breach of the

---

[52] See below paras 10–50 et seq. and 11–99 et seq.
[53] Involving the reversal of the effect of transactions at an undervalue and preferences. See below.
[54] See below, paras 1–60 et seq.
[55] See below, paras 8–51 and 10–70.
[56] See below, para.13–123.
[57] See below, paras 12–12 et seq.

general prohibition[58] and to participate in proceedings relating to voluntary arrangements, receivership and voluntary and compulsory winding up of a company that is an authorised person under s.31 of the Act. Amendments introduced by s.7 of the Financial Services Act 2010 provide for the FSA to make rules as to recovery and resolution plans for dealing with likely business failures.

The Insolvency Act 2000 and the Enterprise Act 2002

The move from administrative receivership to administration

1–14   The Insolvency Act 1986 was further amended by the Insolvency Act 2000, which introduced into the 1986 Act new provisions on voluntary arrangements and moratoria and amended the provisions of the Company Directors Disqualification Act 1986 on the disqualification of directors. Of much greater import, however, were the insolvency provisions of the Enterprise Act 2002, of which the most significant were those that, with certain exceptions, abolished the long-established institution of administrative receivership. This is not a collective insolvency procedure, rather a debt enforcement remedy available to a creditor holding a floating charge which, with any fixed charges, covers the whole or substantially the whole of the debtor company's property.[59] The remedy is a powerful one, enabling the creditor to appoint an administrative receiver to take control of the company and its assets, largely displacing the directors, and to continue trading as deemed agent of the company, sell off the business or individual assets or hive them down to a new, debt-free company which can then be sold off. There had long been disquiet over the power held by such a creditor, the making of what were sometimes seen to be precipitate appointments at almost no notice and, where the creditor was over-secured (as was not uncommon) the lack of incentive to ensure that the costs of the receivership were kept down and the assets realised at the best price. Moreover, the receiver's primary duty (apart from discharging preferential debts from floating charge assets) was to its appointing creditor, not to the general body of creditors. A further cause for concern was the ability of the creditor to block an administration—a collective procedure designed for the benefit of the creditors generally—by appointing an administrative receiver before the making of an administration order; and although in many cases the creditor was content to allow an administration, this was not always the case and its ability to block it was perceived as inimical to the rescue culture which had begun to be promoted

---

[58] s.367(1). See *Blackstone's Guide to the Financial Services and Markets Act 2000*, edited by Michael Blair, 2nd edn (Oxford: Oxford University Press, 2009) at [26.21].
[59] See para.1–38 and Ch.10.

during the 1990s.[60] The Insolvency Act 1986 had introduced a system of company voluntary arrangements, but it proved to be a rather ineffective mechanism for corporate rescue, largely because it did not in itself trigger a moratorium, which could only be brought about through administration.

Following a series of studies[61] and a flurry of government papers,[62] the decision was taken that in principle all insolvency proceedings should be collective in character. To that end, the Enterprise Act 2002 introduced into the Insolvency Act 1986 a provision prohibiting, with certain exceptions, the appointment of an administrative receiver by the holder of a floating charge created on or after September 15, 2003. Instead, the chargee may appoint an administrator, but the making of distributions to the chargee is not a legitimate objective if it is reasonably practicable to achieve either of the two prior-ranking objectives (rescue of the company as a going concern and achieving a better result for creditors as a whole than on an immediate winding up). The Act also provided that in an insolvency proceeding a prescribed part of the assets subject to a floating charge should be made available for the satisfaction of unsecured debts. The effect is to reduce the advantages of a floating charge. The Act also abolished Crown preference.

The fragmentation of debt

The overall effect of the changes introduced by the Enterprise Act is to strengthen the position of ordinary unsecured creditors and to transfer management control of the insolvent company's business and assets from the secured creditor and its administrative receiver to the insolvency administrator, a trend observable in other jurisdictions that have moved away from the practice of piecemeal realisation of assets to reorganisation of the company and its business.[63] However, a study conducted some years after the enactment of the Enterprise Act indicated that while there was an

1–15

---

[60] See Vanessa Finch, *Corporate Insolvency Law*, 2009, Chs 6, 7 and 9; and Louise Gullifer, "The Reforms of the Enterprise Act 2000 and the Floating Charge as a Security Device" in Wolf-Georg Ringe, Louise Gullifer and Philippe Théry (eds), *Current Issues in European Financial and Insolvency Law: Perspectives from France and the UK* (Oxford: Hart Publishing, 2009), Ch.2. For further discussion of the rescue culture, see paras 1–32 and 2–23.

[61] See, e.g. P. Aghion, O. Hart and J. Moore, "A Proposal for Bankruptcy Reform in the UK" (1993) 9 I.L. & P. 103; and "Insolvency Reform in the UK: A Revised Proposal" (1995) 11 I.L. & P. 67.

[62] DTI, *Productivity and Enterprise—Insolvency: A Second Chance* (Cmnd. 5234, 2001); DTI/Treasury, "A Review of Company Rescue and Business Reconstruction Mechanisms: Report by the Review Group" (2000); DTI Insolvency Service, *Company Voluntary Arrangements and Administration Orders: A Consultative Document* (1993); and *Revised Proposals for a New Company Voluntary Arrangement Procedure* (1995).

[63] For a perceptive analysis of this trend, with references to the shift in the UK approach, see Jay Lawrence Westbrook, "The Control of Wealth in Bankruptcy" 82 Texas L. Rev. 795, 805 (2004).

increase in recoveries, this was offset by increased costs, due to greater professional regulation and also to the fragmentation of financing, making it more difficult to co-ordinate creditors in a rescue plan since many of them, unlike the banks, had no particular interest in seeking rescue solutions, but simply wished to enforce their rights and terminate their involvement in the administration process.[64] This fragmentation is to a limited extent due to a marked shift away from relationship lending by banks, based on the debtor's credit and business prospects and secured against the debtor's assets generally without specific identification and valuation, to finance by specialist companies against specific assets (receivables, inventory, plant and machinery, property) on the basis of careful valuation. This shift was partly influenced by the decisions of the House of Lords in *Brumark*[65] and *Spectrum*,[66] which largely put paid to the ability of banks to obtain a fixed charge over receivables. But the main reason for the move from relationship lending to asset-based finance has been the decision of the banks to shore up their share capital and restrict lending, driving companies seeking finance to approach specialist, asset-based financiers and the banks themselves to set up subsidiaries for asset-based lending, which being secured carries a lower risk and reduces capital adequacy requirements. Asset-based finance takes various forms: asset-based lending, factoring and invoice discounting,[67] conditional sale, hire-purchase and leasing.[68] It is also not uncommon for factors and invoice discounters to take and register a charge over assets other than the receivables they are purchasing.

Although the move to asset-based financing is an element in the diffusion of debt, the more dominant causes of fragmentation are capital market debt issuances, the multi-tiering of debt, syndicated financing, sales and resales of credit default swaps[69] and the slicing of distressed debt through sales of participations. A consequence of this is to complicate restructurings because

---

[64] Sandra Frisby, "Report on Insolvency Outcomes", a report to the Insolvency Service in 2006, pp.33 et seq., later amplified by her "Interim Report to the Insolvency Service on Returns to Creditors from Pre- and Post-Enterprise Act Insolvency Procedures" (2007); and John Armour, Audrey Hsu and Adrian Walters, "The Impact of the Enterprise Act 2002 on Realisations and Costs in Corporate Rescue Proceedings" (2006), a report prepared for the Insolvency Service.

[65] *Re Brumark Investments Ltd, sub. nom. Agnew v IRC* [2001] 2 A.C. 710.

[66] *Re Spectrum Plus Ltd* [2005] 2 A.C. 680. For the ramifications of this case, see Joshua Getzler and Jennifer Payne (eds), *Company Charges: Spectrum and Beyond* (Oxford: Oxford University Press, 2006).

[67] Usually this consists of the sale of receivables, the credit coming from arrangements to prepay the price in advance of maturity of the receivables.

[68] See John Armour, "Should We Redistribute in Insolvency?" in J. Getzler and J. Payne (eds), *Company Charges: Spectrum and Beyond* (Oxford: Oxford University Press, 2006), pp.189–226; and Vanessa Finch, "Corporate Rescue in a World of Debt" (2008) J.B.L. 756.

[69] Some of which are held as "naked" CDSs, that is, without ownership of the underlying security, so that the purchaser is either buying to resell or speculating on the likelihood of default and consequent right to collect payment from the protection seller. In theory, this latter variety of CDSs provides a perverse incentive to holders of the CDSs to force a bankruptcy. Whether this happens in practice is another matter.

the composition of the creditors is constantly changing, with major creditors being unwilling to reveal themselves, participate in creditors' meetings and receive information on account of the constraints which rules on insider trading impose on their ability to trade their debt holdings. Bondholders in particular can be a source of difficulty in that unless a representative is appointed, there is usually no way of knowing who the current bondholders are.

As stated above, the move to asset-based financing has created a distinct problem for rescue operations in that whilst banks engaged in relationship lending tend to value the preservation of the business and will make efforts to bring this about, the general approach of asset-based financiers is to exercise their default remedies against the assets and then pull out, without too much regard to the impact on the company.[70]

The Insolvency Service has recently issued a consultation paper containing proposals to improve the corporate rescue regime through a combination of a debtor-in-possession approach[71] and a court-ordered, three-month moratorium for companies that are seeking a contractual compromise, a company voluntary arrangement (CVA) or a scheme of arrangement and are in need of restructuring, have a viable business and are not already insolvent.[72]

The Banking Act 2009

This Act, which replaced the emergency Banking (Special Provisions) Act 2008, is designed to provide a more efficient and effective system of regulation for bank failures, consequent upon the collapses of Northern Rock and Lehman Brothers.[73]   **1–16**

The European dimension

Though the European Community has not yet assumed general competence in the field of substantive insolvency law, there are several Community instruments which affect English insolvency law, jurisdiction and procedure and which, so far as not directly applicable, have been implemented in the United Kingdom by subordinate legislation under the European Communities Act 1972. Some of these are specific to particular types of   **1–17**

---

[70] This was already noted some years ago by Frisby, "Report on Insolvency Outcomes", 2006, pp. 35 and 39, and appears to be the same today.
[71] Or DIP. See below, para.2–07.
[72] "Proposals for a Restructuring Moratorium: A Consultation" (July 2010). This followed an earlier consultation paper, "Encouraging Company Rescue" (June 2009). See further para.11–32.
[73] See below, paras 1–57 et seq.

organisation. For example, the Capital Requirements Directive[74] contains provisions resulting from the Basel II Accord requiring the authorisation of banks and other credit institutions and capital adequacy requirements for such institutions and for investment banks in order to ensure their solvency,[75] while the reorganisation and winding up of credit institutions is governed by the Credit Institutions Reorganisation and Winding Up Directive.[76] Similarly, there has been a series of directives on insurance, followed by the 2001 Insurance Winding Up Directive.[77] Special protection against rules of insolvency law has been given to the financial markets by the Settlement Finality Directive and the Financial Collateral Directive.[78] But what affects insolvent companies generally in an EU insolvency is the 2000 EC Insolvency Regulation,[79] containing detailed provisions on jurisdiction to open main and territorial insolvency proceedings in a Member State, the right of a liquidator in the main proceedings to request the opening of and to participate in secondary proceedings, the applicable law and rules of recognition of foreign insolvency proceedings.[80]

International insolvency

1–18   There has also been much activity in relation to cross-border insolvency at the international level. The United Nations Commission on International Trade Law (UNCITRAL) has been particularly prominent in this field. A growing number of countries, including the United Kingdom,[81] have adopted the 1997 UNCITRAL Model Law on cross-border insolvency, which is discussed in Chapter 16. In addition, the *UNCITRAL Legislative Guide on Insolvency Law*, a major work, was published in 2004, while in 2010 Part III, the

---

[74] This consists of two Directives: Directive 2006/48/EC of the European Parliament and the Council of June 14, 2006 relating to the taking up and pursuit of the business of credit institutions (recast), [2006] OJ L177/1; and Directive 2006/49/EC of the European Parliament and the Council on the capital adequacy of investment firms and credit institutions (recast), [2006] OJ L177/201.

[75] In the light of major bank failures, the European Commission is now consulting on changes to the two Directives. See below, paras 1–57 et seq.

[76] European Parliament and Council Directive 2001/24/EC of April 4, 2001 on the reorganisation and winding up of credit institutions, [2001] OJ L125/15. Again, the Commission is consulting on changes to this Directive.

[77] Council Directive 2001/17/EC of March 19, 2001 on the reorganisation and winding up of insurance undertakings, [2001] OJ L110/28. See Michael Blair, George Walker and Robert Purves, *Financial Services Law*, 2nd edn (Oxford: Oxford University Press, 2009), paras [14.160]–[14.170]; and Gabriel Moss and Bob Wessels (eds), *EU Banking and Insurance Insolvency* (Oxford: Oxford University Press, 2006).

[78] See below, paras 1–60 et seq.

[79] Council Regulation 1346/2000/EC of 29 May 2000 on insolvency proceedings, [2000] OJ L160/1.

[80] See Ch.15. The Insolvency Regulation does not apply to credit institutions or insurance undertakings.

[81] Cross-Border Insolvency Regulations 2006, SI 2006/1030.

work of UNCITRAL's Working Group V, was issued dealing with enterprise groups in insolvency both at the domestic and at the international levels.[82]

The sources of corporate insolvency law

(1) The common law

Although the greater part of corporate insolvency law is statutory,[83] there are certain regimes governed wholly or partly by common law principles and by the inherent jurisdiction of the court. Until the passing of what is now the Insolvency Act 1986, the law relating to the receivership of companies was almost entirely based on contract and on rules developed by the courts, and although the powers and principal obligations of administrative receivers[84] are now codified in the Insolvency Act 1986, much of receivership law continues to be based on common law principles. Arrangements and compromises concluded between a company and its creditors by contract without any insolvency proceeding remain wholly outside the purview of legislation except so far as they involve dispositions and other dealings which would be void or voidable under the Insolvency Act if the company were subsequently to go into winding up or administration. By contrast, winding up is almost exclusively governed by the Act and subordinate legislation. Yet even winding up is influenced by the creative power of the courts. The principle of *pari passu* distribution of assets among ordinary, unsecured creditors, which under the Bankruptcy Act 1914 was encapsulated in precisely 11 words[85] and in the case of compulsory winding up is now relegated to subordinate legislation,[86] has been developed by the courts into a fundamental concept of insolvency law having the most profound repercussions on the validity of pre-liquidation contracts and dispositions entered into between the company and its creditors and between creditors *inter se*.[87] Moreover, the statutory provisions delimiting the assets available for distribution predicate

1–19

---

[82] See below, para.16–10 and n.43.

[83] There are several good compilations of the insolvency legislation, of which the most comprehensive is that by Len Sealy and David Milman, *Sealy & Milman: Annotated Guide to the Insolvency Legislation 2010*, 13th edn (London: Sweet & Maxwell, 2010).

[84] See below, paras 10–41 et seq.

[85] Bankruptcy Act 1914 s.33(7), incorporated into companies winding up by the Companies Act 1985 s.612 (later repealed).

[86] Insolvency Rules 1986 r.4.181.

[87] In this connection it should be appreciated that what the courts are at bottom concerned with is to invalidate contractual provisions designed to bypass the collective distribution machinery laid down by the Insolvency Act, to the detriment of the general body of creditors. That would be the concern whatever the insolvency distribution rules might be. But since the rule for ordinary creditors is that of *pari passu* distribution, such provisions are commonly attacked as undermining the principle of such distribution, by which is meant the collective machinery leading to *pari passu* distribution. See below, paras 3–07 and 8–02.

that unless otherwise provided, the attachment, perfection and priority of security interests and other real rights are to be determined by the general law applicable to transactions outside winding up,[88] the bulk of which is non-statutory.

The court's inherent jurisdiction over its own officers enables it to deny to a liquidator appointed by the court[89] rights and remedies to which he or she is on the face of it entitled by law where the exercise of those rights or remedies would in the opinion of the court be unfair or inequitable.[90] But the rule is rarely invoked successfully and is generally considered the last resort for a party who has no other reasonable grounds for challenging a liquidator's decision. For this reason it is confined to the exceptional case involving dishonourable behaviour or the threat of dishonourable behaviour or to enable the court to allow the liquidator to fulfil a promise even if not legally binding.[91]

Finally, at common law, which posits that ideally bankruptcy proceedings should have universal application, the court, in the absence of statutory jurisdiction, has power to assist a foreign court dealing with the bankruptcy of a company over which that court had jurisdiction. Bankruptcy proceedings are neither *in rem* nor *in personam*, since their function is not to determine rights, but to provide a mechanism of collective execution against the debtor's assets in favour of the creditors. Accordingly, conflict of laws rules governing claims *in rem* or *in personam* have no application and the judgment of a foreign bankruptcy court of competent jurisdiction suffices to enable the court to give assistance at common law.[92]

(2) Primary and subordinate legislation

1–20   There are six principal sets of primary and subordinate legislation dealing with the insolvency of companies at large and a seventh specifically directed to the insolvency of banks.

---

[88] See below, para.6–01.

[89] A liquidator in a creditors' voluntary winding up is not an officer of the court and is not bound by the rule in *ex p. James*, nor can he be treated by analogy in the same way as an officer of the court (*Re T. & H. Knitwear Ltd* [1988] Ch. 275).

[90] This is commonly known as the rule in *Ex p. James*, having been formulated (although not for the first time) in the Court of Appeal decision in *Re Condon Ex p. James* (1874) L.R. 9 Ch. 609.

[91] *Re T. & N. Ltd* [2004] O.P.L.R. 343, *per* David Richards J., citing the judgment of Salter J. in *Re Wigzell, ex p. Hart* [1921] 2 K.B. 835; and *Re Collins & Aikman Europe SA* [2006] B.C.C. 861.

[92] *Cambridge Gas Transportation Corp. v Official Committee of Unsecured Creditors of Navigator Holdings plc* [2007] 1 A.C. 508, in which the Privy Council upheld the decision of the Manx Court of Appeal that it had a broad discretion to give assistance to the New York Federal Bankruptcy Court.

INSOLVENCY ACT 1986

The Insolvency Act 1986, as amended by the Insolvency Act 1994, the Insolvency (No.2) Act 1994, the Insolvency Act 2000 and the Enterprise Act 2002, is the main enactment dealing with corporate insolvency. It also covers personal bankruptcy. There are also a few free-standing provisions in the amending legislation, for example, s.14 of the Insolvency Act 2000 empowering the Secretary of State to make regulations implementing the UNCITRAL Model Law on Cross-Border Insolvency.[93]

INSOLVENCY RULES 1986

The Insolvency Rules 1986[94] provide the procedural underpinning of the Insolvency Act, although as will be seen the division between Act and Rules is not clear-cut, the Act itself containing various procedural requirements, while the Rules embody a few substantive provisions.[95]   **1–21**

FINANCIAL MARKETS LEGISLATION AFFECTING CORPORATE INSOLVENCY

Reference has already been made to the powers of intervention in insolvency conferred on the Financial Services Authority by Part XXIV of the Financial Services and Markets Act 2000.[96] Major dispensations from the rules of insolvency law, mostly implementing Community legislation, have been given by and under the Companies Act 1989[97] in respect of market charges and market contracts[98] and systems-charges taken by settlement banks to secure obligations arising from dealings in uncertificated securities[99] and financial collateral arrangements.[100]   **1–22**

EMPLOYMENT AND PENSIONS LEGISLATION

There are also provisions under both employment legislation and pensions legislation for the protection of employees on the insolvency of their   **1–23**

---

[93] See the Cross-Border Insolvency Regulations 2006, SI 2006/1030.
[94] SI 1986/1925 as amended, the most recent amendments being made in 2010. For details of the various amending instruments and the dates on which these became operative, see the general note to the Insolvency Rules 1986, in *Sealy & Milman: Annotated Guide to the Insolvency Legislation*, 13th edn (2010), Vol.1, p.664, and the separate introductory note at p.683.
[95] See below, para.1–29.
[96] See above, para.1–13.
[97] As amended by the Financial Markets and Insolvency Regulations 2009, SI 2009/853, which provide further protection for the actions of recognised investment exchanges and recognised clearing houses in the event of default by any of their members.
[98] Companies Act 1989 Pt VII, as amended; Financial Markets and Insolvency Regulations 1991 (SI 1991/880), as amended by the Financial Markets and Insolvency Regulations 2009.
[99] Financial Markets and Insolvency Regulations 1996 (SI 1996/1469).
[100] Financial Collateral Arrangements (No.2) Regulations 2003 (SI 2003/3226). See further paras 1–60 et seq. as to these exemptions under Pt VII of the Companies Act 1989.

employer or on transfer of the employer's undertaking.[101] Pension liabilities have become an increasingly important feature of corporate insolvency in recent years.

DISQUALIFICATION OF DIRECTORS

1–24   The Company Directors Disqualification Act 1986,[102] to which reference has been made earlier, gathers together the statutory provisions on disqualification of directors previously dispersed over the Companies Act 1985 and the Insolvency Act 1985. However, although s.6 of the Company Directors Disqualification Act imposes on the court a duty to disqualify directors of an insolvent company who it is satisfied are unfit to be concerned in the management of a company, the Act is directed primarily at improper conduct on the part of directors rather than on insolvency as such. It is therefore considered only briefly in Chapter 14.

HUMAN RIGHTS LEGISLATION

1–25   Certain provisions of the insolvency legislation may possibly attract the application of the Human Rights Act 1998. It is beyond the scope of this work to address human rights issues.[103]

BANK AND BUILDING SOCIETY INSOLVENCY

1–26   The Banking Act 2009 creates a special insolvency regime for failing banks and building societies.[104]

(3) European Community legislation

1–27   The various EC directives mentioned earlier have been implemented by statutory instrument. By contrast, the 2000 EC Insolvency Regulation[105] has direct effect, and implementing legislation is neither required nor permissible.

---

[101] See below, para.2–24.
[102] As amended by the Companies Act 1989, the Insolvency Act 2000, the Financial Services and Markets Act 2000 (Consequential Amendments and Repeals) Order 2001 (SI 2001/3649), the Enterprise Act 2002 and sundry other legislation peripheral to insolvency.
[103] See E. Bailey and H. Groves, *Corporate Insolvency: Law and Practice*, 3rd edn (LexisNexis Butterworths, 2007), Ch.20.
[104] See below, para.1–59.
[105] Examined in detail in Ch.15.

Business, entity or group enterprise?

The subject of insolvency proceedings has always been, and continues to be, **1–28** the particular corporate entity that has become insolvent, and this focus is accentuated by the reluctance of English law to pierce the corporate veil.[106] What insolvency law here and overseas has so far singularly failed to accommodate is the management of enterprise groups[107] where one or more, or possibly all, members of the group have become insolvent. Whereas the preparation and filing of group accounts has long been required,[108] when it comes to insolvency the distinct legal personality of each individual company within the group is respected, with separate proceedings for each company,[109] yet the insolvency of one member of a group may threaten the viability of previously solvent members and where the group activity is integrated a co-ordination of the management of the group as a whole may be highly desirable. This is particularly the case as regards multinational groups of enterprises, where the complexity is exacerbated by the variety of corporate structures and the possibility of concurrent proceedings in different jurisdictions governed by different laws, and we return to the subject in Chapter 16. Much attention has been devoted in recent years to ways in which it might be possible to treat a group as a single economic enterprise for insolvency purposes.[110] This is not easy to achieve even for procedural consolidation, which would treat the member of the group as one for the purpose of administration, while keeping the assets and liabilities separate.[111] It is harder still, in policy terms, to effect substantive consolidation, involving the pooling of assets and liabilities, for this interferes with the existing rights of creditors, in particular creditors of a group member having substantial assets who can legitimately argue that they dealt with that member and should not have their position impaired by consolidation of

---

[106] See below, para.3–12.

[107] Defined by UNCITRAL Working Group V (Insolvency Law) as "two or more legal entities (group members) that are linked together by some form of control (whether direct or indirect) or ownership" (A/CN.9WG.V/WP.92,2010, para.2).

[108] See now Companies Act 2006 ss.403–408.

[109] Although there are rules governing associates, as defined by s.435 of the Insolvency Act 1986 (see, e.g. s.249 and, below, para.13–104) and shadow directors, as defined by s.251, under which a parent company is in certain circumstances capable of being held responsible as a shadow director of its subsidiary, e.g. for the purpose of the provisions on wrongful trading (s.214(7)).

[110] See, e.g. Irit Mevorach, *Insolvency within Multinational Enterprises* (Oxford: Oxford University Press, 2009); Vanessa Finch, *Corporate Insolvency Law*, 2009, pp.581 et seq.; Harry Rajak, "Corporate Groups and Cross-Border Bankruptcy" 44 Texas International L.J. 521 (2009); Eike Thomas Bicker, "Creditor Protection in the Corporate Group", *http://ssrn.com/abstract=920472* [Accessed February 14, 2011]; and papers produced by UNCITRAL's Working Group V on the treatment of enterprise groups in insolvency (A/CN.9/WG.V/WP.92 and A/CN.9/WG.V/WP.92 Add. 1). UNCITRAL has now published Part III of its "Guide on Insolvency Legislation" devoted to the treatment of corporate groups. See below, para.16–10.

[111] Problems arise as regards those members of the group that are solvent.

assets and liabilities with less well-placed members of the group.[112] In principle, a parent company is not liable for the debts of its subsidiary. If it is only infrequently that English courts will be willing to pierce the corporate veil,[113] it is rarer still to consolidate assets and liabilities; indeed, the only case where this is likely to happen is where the assets and liabilities of the different companies within the group are so intermingled that it is impracticable to separate them.[114]

So UK corporate insolvency law, like that of many other jurisdictions, does not readily accommodate group structures. This can cause problems where the lines of management of a group do not match the line of management of an individual company within the group, as where financial management is centralised, so that management control does not lie with the boards of the individual companies. This allows cash and other assets to be readily moved from one member of the group to another as circumstances require. But if directors of a company within the group that has a surplus are asked to transfer funds to another group member that has a deficiency of assets, they may need to seek assurance from senior management that in giving this support for the group their own company will not suffer. Otherwise, they may run a risk of being held liable for breach of their statutory duty to exercise independent judgment and reasonable care, skill and diligence[115] and one or more other members of the group may be susceptible to a contribution notice or financial support directions from the Pensions Regulator.[116]

Defects in the legislative structure and arrangement

1–29   It has to be said that the structure of English insolvency legislation does not display a particularly rational structure or organisation.[117] One might, for

---

[112] There may be indirect partial consolidation of liabilities because of the existence of intra-group cross-guarantees and intra-group liabilities. Many years ago the author was involved in some aspects of the winding up of members of the Gorringe group of companies. One of the companies that was solvent owed money to another member of the group, which on receipt of partial payment was thereby enabled to pay a dividend to a third group member to whom it owed money, this in turn allowing that group member to pay a dividend itself to yet another member, with the ultimate result that dividends went round in a circle, returning to the solvent company, and the whole process would begin again. The Official Receiver pointed out that technically each distribution attracted a statutory insolvency fee, and this would solve all problems as there would be no money left to distribute!

[113] See below, para.3–12. However, pensions legislation allows the Determinations Panel of the Pension Regulator to issue contribution notices and financial support directions. See para.2–24.

[114] See, e.g. *Re Bank of Credit and Commerce International SA (No.3)* [1993] B.C.L.C. 1490, affirming the decision at first instance of Sir Donald Nicholls V-C [1993] B.C.L.C. 106, who had approved a scheme by the liquidators for the pooling of the assets and liabilities of two companies within the BCCI group.

[115] See below, para.14–09.

[116] See below, para.2–24.

[117] What is criticised here is the drafting, not the Parliamentary draftsmen, who faced an immense task and frequently had to work under the extreme pressures of the Parliamentary timetable.

example, have expected a relatively simple division between the Insolvency Act and the Insolvency Rules, in which the former was directed to substantive rights and the latter to procedural requirements. Instead, we find a number of provisions of the Insolvency Act that are given over to procedural matters, such as the summoning of meetings and the contents of reports, whilst important substantive rights, such as what debts are provable, set-off in winding up[118] and the priority rules for the payment of liquidation expenses are relegated to the Insolvency Rules.

The ordering of subjects within the Rules themselves is also mildly eccentric. For example, Ch.9 in Pt 4 deals with proof of debts, but we have to trawl through to Pt 12, "Miscellaneous and General", to discover the answer to the vital question of what debts are provable.[119] Overall, the Insolvency Act and the Insolvency Rules have become a legislative morass through which even the experienced practitioner cannot pick his way without difficulty. Even the numbering of the schedules to the Act is eccentric, with Sch.1 being bizarrely preceded by Schs A1 and B1.[120] Definitions are dispersed through the Act, the same term is sometimes defined in different ways, several definitions refer to definitions in other legislation[121] and language that was perfectly comprehensible in earlier legislation has been perversely displaced by language that involves the provision of a definition quite at odds with the normal meaning of the term defined.[122] On even the simplest questions the reader is likely to find himself having to shuttle constantly between the body of the Act, Sch.B1 and the Insolvency Rules. A good example is provided by the treatment of the expenses of an administration, which may involve reference both to para.99 of Sch.B1 and to para.2.67 of the Rules. Moreover, what constitutes an expense of the administration and whether it is payable as a matter of right or of discretion are issues continuing to

---

[118] But not in bankruptcy, where it is dealt with in the Act itself (s.323), a further illustration of the lack of coherence in the statutory framework.

[119] Insolvency Rules 1986 r.12.3.

[120] It has to be conceded that this is not without precedent. The late Desmond Heap once wrote a book on betterment levy in which Ch.1 was preceded by Ch.1A. His explanation was simple: Ch.1A contained matters normally to be found in a preface, but in his experience most people did not read the preface!

[121] For an extreme case of definitional complexity, see para.11–63, n.312, describing the path that has to be followed to determine the meaning of "hire-purchase agreement" in Sch.B1, para.43(3).

[122] e.g. s.15(4), dealing with the effect of disposal by the administrator of property subject to a floating charge, provided that the charge should have the same priority in respect of any property of the company directly or indirectly representing the property disposed of as he would have had in respect of the property subject to the charge—in other words, the priority in the original property carries through to its product or proceeds. In Sch.B1 para.70(2), the reference is to "the same priority in respect of after-acquired property", which does not convey the same idea at all, since after-acquired property may have no connection with what was originally disposed of, and it takes a definition in para.70(3) to get us back on track.

attract litigation, while the distinction drawn in r.2.67 between "expenses properly incurred by the administrator in performing his functions in the administration of the company" (r.2.67(1)(a)) and "any necessary disbursements by the administrator in the course of the administration" seems to serve little purpose other than to provoke fruitless discussion as to its meaning. Finally, instead of following the golden rule that wherever possible all provisions dealing with the same issue should be dealt with in the same place, the draftsman has adopted the pervasive practice of appearing to do this and then catching the reader out by additional and related provisions elsewhere.[123] A complete rearrangement of the Act and Rules, with substantive rules in the Act, procedural provisions in the Rules, the avoidance of duplication of numbering, a better organisation of the definitions and substantive provisions, greater clarity and the avoidance of over-refined distinctions is long overdue.[124]

3. THE INSTITUTIONAL SETTING

1–30   The institutional framework within which corporate insolvency law operates is as follows. The Secretary of State for Business, Innovation and Skills is given extensive powers to make orders and regulations under the Insolvency Act, and is also given a *locus standi* in certain cases to apply for the winding up of a company. Ministerial responsibility for policy matters relating to corporate insolvency falls within the province of the Department for Business, Innovation and Skills (BIS). Responsibility for the development and implementation of policy and securing compliance with the insolvency legislation has been delegated to the Insolvency Service, an executive agency of BIS. This operates under the direction of the Inspector General and Agency Chief Executive. The Insolvency Service[125] is organised into:

- a network of 42 official receiver (OR) offices throughout England and Wales;

- Enforcement and Investigations Directorates in London, Birmingham, Manchester and Edinburgh;

---

[123] e.g. para.99(3) and (4) of Sch.B1 deals with the priority of the administrator's remuneration and expenses vis-à-vis other claims, but to find the order of priority of the expenses themselves it is necessary to turn to r.2.67(1) of the Insolvency Rules.

[124] Mr Francis Bennion QC, a former Parliamentary draftsman who was famous for his original thinking and techniques in relation to legislative drafting, was a keen advocate of a process of restatement of statutes after they had completed the Parliamentary process. But if this is to work then it is necessary to avoid undoing it with fresh legislation in the old style, a fact which appears to have eluded successive administrations in relation to the simplification of tax law.

[125] The details given below are taken from the Insolvency Service's website.

- Estate Accounts Services (EAS) in Birmingham;

- Redundancy Payments Offices (RPOs) in Edinburgh, Birmingham and Watford;

- Companies Investigation Branch (CIB) in London and Manchester; and

- Corporate and Business Services and policy functions in London, Birmingham and Leeds.

In relation to companies, the service fulfils a variety of functions. In particular, its staff:

- administer and investigate the affairs of companies wound-up by the court and establish why they became insolvent;

- act as liquidator where no private-sector insolvency practitioner (IP) is appointed;

- act on reports of directors' misconduct;

- deal with the disqualification of unfit directors in all corporate failures;

- authorise and regulate the insolvency profession;

- assess and pay statutory entitlement to redundancy payments when an employer cannot or will not pay its employees;

- provide estate accounting and investment services for liquidation estate funds;

- conduct confidential, fact-finding investigations into companies where it is in the public interest to do so;

- advise BIS Ministers and other government departments and agencies on insolvency, redundancy and other related issues; and

- provide information to the public on insolvency, redundancy and investigation matters via the Service's website, leaflets, Insolvency Enquiry Line and Redundancy Payments Helpline;

- conduct confidential fact-finding investigations into companies where it is in the public interest to do so. These enquiries are carried out by Companies investigation Branch.

The Insolvency Rules Committee is an advisory, non-departmental, public body which advises the Lord Chancellor on proposed amendments to the Insolvency Rules. The Insolvency Practices Council examines ethical and professional standards in the insolvency profession and puts proposals to the professional bodies. It works in close co-operation with the Joint

Insolvency Committee, a major forum for discussion of insolvency issues and professional ethics and standards which has representatives from the Insolvency Service and the professional bodies. The Association of Business Recovery Professionals,[126] operating under the brand name "R3", prepares Statements of Insolvency Practice for the Joint Insolvency Committee, and if they are approved they are then adopted by each of the seven Recognised Professional Bodies. The advent of turnaround specialists engaged in devising and implementing restructurings and other recovery strategies led to the establishment of the Society of Turnaround Professionals, since renamed the Institute for Turnaround.

The organisation of corporate insolvency and insolvency procedures is the task of the insolvency practitioner, who is usually either an accountant or a solicitor.[127] A person acts as an insolvency practitioner in relation to a company by acting as its liquidator, administrator, administrative receiver or supervisor under a voluntary arrangement.[128] It is an offence to act as an insolvency practitioner without being qualified to do so[129] by authorisation from a recognised professional body[130] of which he is a member or from "the competent authority", i.e. the Secretary of State or a person or body designated by the Secretary of State.[131] Authorisation will only be given to those who are renewing an existing authorisation or have passed the qualifying Joint Insolvency Examination set by the Joint Insolvency Examination Board. An appeal against refusal or withdrawal of authorisation by the competent authority lies to the Insolvency Practitioners Tribunal. But the tribunal has no jurisdiction to entertain appeals against decisions by the recognised professional bodies, which have established their own internal appeal procedures. Monitoring includes regular visits to offices. Also relevant in this context are the rules of the different Recognised Professional Bodies regulating the conduct of practice in general and of insolvency practitioners in particular. Each of these has its own monitoring unit.

Prominent at the international level is the International Federation of Insolvency Professionals (INSOL International), a worldwide federation of national associations of insolvency professionals, which amongst other things assists in the development of cross-border insolvency policies, participates in government, NGO and intergovernmental advisory groups and implements research into international insolvency issues. It has an international academic group which meets annually. Widely used by practitioners

---

[126] Formerly the Society for Practitioners in Insolvency (SPI).
[127] By far the greatest number of insolvency practitioners are accountants.
[128] Insolvency Act 1986 s.388(1).
[129] Insolvency Act 1986 s.389(1).
[130] i.e. the accountants' and solicitors' professional bodies and the Insolvency Practitioners Association.
[131] Insolvency Act 1986 s.392(2). See the Insolvency Practitioners Regulations 2005, SI 2005/524.

is its set of principles for multi-creditor workouts for debtors in financial difficulties.[132]

4. THE VARIOUS INSOLVENCY REGIMES

It will facilitate an understanding of the purposes of corporate insolvency law, and the methods by which these purposes are sought to be achieved, if we first outline the different types of insolvency proceeding. Each of these will be examined in more detail in later chapters. There are five distinct legal regimes for handling the insolvency of a company, namely:

1–31

(1) administration;

(2) administrative receivership;

(3) winding up (liquidation);

(4) statutory compromises, compositions and arrangements with creditors; and

(5) restructurings ("workouts") which are arranged contractually outside the framework of corporate insolvency law, although they may include provision for a particular insolvency proceeding.

Each of these has its own distinctive purposes and principles. But the usual outcome, sooner or later, is winding up and subsequent dissolution of the company. In the case of a company in administration, winding up ensues because the administrator's efforts to restore the company to profitable trading or to bring about a voluntary arrangement involving all of the creditors have failed and distribution in the administration has not been adopted as a liquidation-substitute. In the case of a company in administrative receivership (now available only in a limited number of cases), the administrative receiver either disposes of the company's assets on a break-up basis, where he or she sees no prospect of restoring it to profitability prior to sale, or manages the company to the point where it can be sold off as a going concern and then effects the sale, typically through hive-down of the business to a specially formed subsidiary which is then sold as a company with assets but no liabilities. The purchase price is channelled back to the debtor company and utilised in discharge of the receiver's remuneration and expenses and payment of preferential debts and sums due to the receiver's debenture holder. In most cases, the company remains insolvent and a voluntary or compulsory winding up ensues.

---

[132] Statement of Principles for a Global Approach to Multi-Creditor Workouts (October 2000). See below, para.12–3.

Corporate Insolvencies in England and Wales: 2004–2009

Type of insolvency	2004	2005	2006	2007	2008	2009	(Third quarterly release 2010)
Liquidations							
Total	12,192	12,893	13,137	12,507	15,535	19,077	(12,171)
Compulsory liquidations	4,584	5,233	5,418	5,165	5,494	5,643	(3,597)
Creditors' voluntary liquidations	7,608	7,660	7,719	7,342	10,041	13,434	(8,574)
Creditors' voluntary liquidations following administration[1]	165	681	914	1,095	993	1469	(1,201)
Proceedings related to insolvency							
Receiverships[2]	864	590	588	337[3]	867	1,468	(1,007)
Administrator appointments	1	4	0	3	2	0	(4)
Voluntary arrangements	597	604	534	418	587	726	(595)
In administration (Enterprise Act 2002)	1,601	2,257	3,560[4]	2,509	4,820[5]	4,161	(2,189)

1. These are additional to those reported under "Creditors Voluntary Liquidations". There are no data available on the number of administrations followed by a compulsory liquidation, or a CVA [see Editor's Notes on the statistics *http://www. insolvency.gov.uk/otherinformation/statistics/201008/index.htm* [Accessed February 14, 2011] at para.8].

2. Includes receiverships other than administrative receiverships (such as Law of Property Act receiverships).

3. The 2007 receivership data was affected by a counting error resulting from an IT upgrade.

4. Includes 844 companies created and managed by "Safe Solutions Accountancy Ltd", for which a single administrator was appointed.

5. Includes 729 managed service companies, for which a single administrator was appointed.

Source: author compilation of the Insolvency Service's "Insolvency Statistics".

The relative use of these four insolvency procedures is shown in the table above, subject to the caveat that some companies may have been involved in more than one procedure, so that the table needs to be read in the light of the notes at the end. The figures for administrator appointments relate to court-appointed administrators (the only method of appointment prior to September 15, 2003) and the drop in administrator appointments to zero in 2009 reflects the changes made by the Enterprise Act 2002 in providing for out-of-court appointments, which will be the normal method and are shown under the label "In Administration (Enterprise Act 2002)' ", of which there were 4,161 in 2009. What is striking is the rise in the number of liquidations, no doubt due in large measure to the credit crunch.

The rescue culture

Although winding up is the fate of most insolvent companies, it is not every insolvency that leads to liquidation. Indeed, with the introduction of the company voluntary arrangement (almost always within the administration procedure) and the use of non-statutory, bank-led workouts, facilitated by the London Approach[133] and the INSOL International Statement of Principles for a Global Approach to Multi-Creditor Workouts,[134] it had been expected that there would be greater scope for business rescues through restructuring and reorganisation where the enterprise was fundamentally sound and has good prospects of being restored to profitability. Prior to the changes effected by the Insolvency Act 2000 and the Enterprise Act 2002, it had been increasingly recognised that:

1–32

> ". . . the corporate rescue and reorganization procedures in England are inadequate and, as a consequence, many companies which are capable of being saved are forced into liquidation with loss to creditors. The goal of promoting rehabilitation and rescue is not being adequately served by the existing procedures."[135]

The combination of the CVA and the enhanced administration procedure resulting from the Enterprise Act were seen as the drivers of the rescue

---

[133] Initiated by the Bank of England, originally under the label The London Rules, an exercise in moral suasion designed to secure the co-operation of the banking community in taking a positive approach to the continuance of financial support for distressed companies pending a reorganisation.

[134] See below, para.12–3.

[135] Nick Segal, "An Overview of Recent Developments and Future Prospects in the United Kingdom" in Jacob S. Ziegel (ed.), *Current Developments in International and Comparative Corporate Insolvency Law* (Oxford: Clarendon Press, 1994), p.12. For a valuable comparative UK-US study of the political and social dynamics of corporate insolvency law, see Bruce G. Carruthers and Terence C. Halliday, *Rescuing Business* (Oxford: Oxford University Press, 1998). For recent proposals for a restructuring moratorium, see above, n.72 and below para.12–11.

process. The view of the Cork Committee was that the rescue culture was concerned with the preservation of the business, not that of the company itself. This remains the case in practice. Experience has shown that while there is now much greater focus on rescue than formerly, the impact of the Enterprise Act 2002 has been more limited than its progenitors had hoped. Although administration has largely replaced administrative receivership, the holder of a qualifying floating charge continues to influence the appointment of the administrator and in some cases the conduct of the administration. In general, efforts are focused on sale of the company's business (typically through a pre-packaged administration, or "pre-pack") rather than on the company's reorganisation, with a view to its continuance as a going concern. This is because most corporate insolvencies are trading insolvencies in which the business itself is not viable, rather than financial insolvencies, where the business is sound and the difficulties arise from excessive debt or a substantial decrease in the value of assets, which can sometimes be dealt with by strategies involving sometimes complex inter-creditor agreements for debt restructuring, debt for equity swaps, the injection of new money by way of loan participations with a view to conversion to equity ("loan to own") and the like. There is also a substantial amount of trading in distressed debt, in which hedge funds and private equity groups, which have become competitors to banks in the provision of finance for companies in difficulty, play a major role. Where there is a reorganisation of a major company or group, this is generally effected by an informal restructuring without any formal insolvency proceeding where agreement can be reached, or by a scheme of arrangement where it cannot.[136] Though one might have expected of the free-standing CVA to be less frequent because of the lack of a moratorium except for small companies, research has shown that the great majority of CVAs for the sampled companies were arranged outside framework of administration and that almost no use has been made of the small companies moratorium, a point to which we return in Chapter 11.

Remedial measures

1–33   There are various steps that can be taken to turn a failing company around. These include the injection of additional funds, the disposal of surplus assets, the reduction of costs (which is likely to involve the redundancy of at least some employees), a change in the strategic direction of the company and, in the case of large companies, restructuring of the company, as by conversion of debt to equity, elimination of mezzanine debt, transfer of the business and assets to a new company and the like. The more tiers of creditor there are, the greater the complexity and expense. The conclusion of standstill agreements (in effect, contractual or informal moratoria) and inter-creditor

---

[136] For a detailed discussion, see Finch, *Corporate Insolvency Law*, 2009, Pt III.

agreements covering the adjustment of rights are crucial elements, since cross-default clauses in agreements will usually have the effect that default in payment of one creditor triggers an automatic default under its agreement with other creditors, giving them the right to call for immediate repayment and to close out and net mutual transactions.

Rescue finance

The rescue of a company depends crucially on the availability of funding to enable the company to continue trading. The company will need working capital to enable it to pay its trade suppliers, without whom it will be unable to continue in business and who will require payment for new supplies and not uncommonly for supplies already made. There is usually no great difficulty in securing additional funding from existing lenders already holding security who can add new advances to the secured obligations and thereby preserve their existing priority. If the company is in administration, new advances will constitute expenses of the administration and as such rank ahead of the claims of ordinary unsecured creditors and the holders of a floating charge.[137] The amount of new funds required may be quite small in relation to the income the company is thereby able to generate.

1–34

Administration[138]

Nature and purposes of administration

Administration, unlike administrative receivership,[139] is a collective insolvency procedure designed to promote the rescue culture by placing the company's affairs in the hands of an administrator entrusted with the task of promoting the interests of the general body of creditors, primarily by rescuing the company as a going concern or, if that is not practicable, by achieving a better result for its creditors than would be achieved on an immediate liquidation.[140] The administration procedure was first introduced by the Insolvency Act 1985, following a recommendation of the Cork Committee.[141] The Insolvency Act 2000 introduced a limited moratorium for company voluntary arrangements relating to small companies. Of much greater significance was the Enterprise Act 2002, which greatly enhanced the administration procedure: first, by enabling companies to go into administration without

1–35

---

[137] See below, para.11–96.
[138] See Ch.11.
[139] See below, para.1–38.
[140] Insolvency Act 1986 Sch.B1 para.3(1).
[141] "Insolvency Law and Practice" (Cmnd. 8558, 1982), Ch.9.

a court order; secondly, by abolishing administrative receivership (with certain important exceptions), thereby removing a debenture holder's power to block an administration with its attendant freeze on the exercise of remedies; and, thirdly, by precluding an administrator from having as his objective distribution to secured or preferential creditors except where he thinks it is not reasonably practicable to achieve either of the higher-ranking objectives specified in the legislation, namely rescuing the company as a going concern or achieving a better result than would be achieved on putting it into liquidation without first being in administration.[142] However, administration is not usually used for major corporate restructurings, most of which are conducted, at least initially, outside formal insolvency proceedings.[143]

There are special administration regimes for water and sewerage undertakers, protected railway companies, air traffic service companies, public-private partnership companies and building societies. These are excluded from the regime embodied in Sch.B1 to the Insolvency Act 1986.[144] The Banking Act 2009 prescribes a special regime for bank administrations, which does not displace Sch.B1, but modifies that schedule and other provisions of the Insolvency Act in important respects. Amongst other things, the objectives set out in para.3(1)(a) and (b) of Sch.B1[145] are subordinated to the overriding objective of providing support for a commercial purchaser or bridge bank buying all or part of the business of the failed bank as the first and second of the three available stabilisation options,[146] while the objective in para.3(1)(c) of Sch.B1 (realising property to make a distribution to one or more secured or preferential creditors) does not feature at all as an objective in bank administrations.[147]

Pre-packaged administration

1–36 A particular form of administration that has gained prominence in recent years is the pre-packaged administration ("pre-pack"), in which a company in financial difficulty, with the approval of its dominant creditors and the involvement of an insolvency practitioner as prospective administrator, reaches an agreement for the sale of its business or all of its assets shortly prior to going into administration. The agreement is placed in escrow pending the appointment of the administration and the sale takes effect immediately on such appointment. A survey undertaken by R3 indicates that

---

[142] Insolvency Act 1986 Sch.B1 para.3(4). See Ch.11, which is devoted to administration.
[143] See below, Ch.12.
[144] Enterprise Act 2002 s.249.
[145] See below.
[146] Banking Act 2009 ss. 11, 12 and 137. A bridge bank is a company wholly owned by the Bank of England (s.12(1)).
[147] See further below, para.1–59.

in the majority of cases the previous business owner continued in charge.[148] Pre-packs are not new, featuring in the now largely abolished administrative receivership, but they have become more highly developed.[149]

Administration as liquidation substitute

There is some evidence that administration is being used as a liquidation **1-37** substitute and enables court procedures for liquidation to be by-passed. Whether this has proved detrimental remains to be seen.[150]

Administrative receivership[151]

The nature of receivership

Although the Enterprise Act 2002 largely abolished the institution of admin- **1-38** istrative receivership, this continues to be available under charges made before September 15, 2003, and also under charges made after that date in respect of a number of categories of charge exempted from the statutory provisions. Nevertheless, it is nowadays of limited importance and has been largely replaced by administration.

There are broadly three categories of receiver. Arranged in ascending order of powers they are: receivers appointed under statutory powers, in particular s.101(1)(iii) of the Law of Property Act 1925; receivers appointed under the terms of a security agreement; and administrative receivers. The function of the Law of Property Act receiver is very limited. His task is to collect in income and apply it to keep down outgoings and mortgage interest. He has no statutory or implied power to gather or dispose of the charged assets for the purpose of satisfying the debt, his security is specific, not global, and he has no management powers. Hence this form of receivership does not impact on creditors generally in the way that other forms of receivership do: it is merely a method by which a secured creditor enforces his security. In practice, the appointment of a receiver who is not an administrative receiver is made not under the Law of Property Act, but under the provisions of the charge instrument or security trust deed, which typically confers much wider powers. So the security agreement or security trust deed will usually empower the receiver not merely to collect in income, but to

---

[148] "Pre-Packaged Sales ('Pre-Packs'): A Survey of R3 Members" (May 2009).
[149] See below, para.11–37.
[150] See Frisby, *Report on Insolvency Outcomes*, 2006, pp.74 et seq.; and Alan Katz and Michael Mumford, "Study of Administration Cases", a report to the Insolvency Service (2006), pp.22 et seq.
[151] See Ch.10.

manage the assets comprised in the security, to pay debts in a particular order of priority and to realise assets for the purpose of making the payments.[152] The term "administrative receiver" is that used by the Insolvency Act 1986 to describe one whose previous formal appellation was receiver and manager, usually abbreviated to "receiver". An administrative receiver is a receiver appointed under a debenture secured by a floating charge covering (with any fixed security that may have been taken by the debenture holder) the whole or substantially the whole of the company's assets.[153] The primary function of the administrative receiver is to take control of the company's assets and effect such dispositions as will result in payment of the amount due under the debenture, after allowing for the administrative receiver's remuneration and expenses and any sums payable to preferential creditors. The global nature of the debenture holder's security is made an essential ingredient of the statutory definition because without this the administrative receiver would be unable effectively to exercise the management powers conferred upon him. In contrast to the administrator, who must act in the interests of all of the creditors, the administrative receiver is concerned primarily to protect the interests of his debenture holder. Accordingly, administrative receivership is not a true collective insolvency proceeding. Nevertheless, its very breadth means that it has a profound impact on the general body of creditors.

Winding up[154]

Nature of winding up

1–39   Winding up, or liquidation, is a collective insolvency process leading to the end of the company's existence (dissolution). The principal role of the liquidator is to collect in and realise the assets, ascertain claims, investigate the causes of failure and, after covering the expenses of the liquidation, distribute the net proceeds by way of dividend to creditors in the order of priority laid down by the Insolvency Act and the Insolvency Rules. When all of this has been done, investigations concluded and reports made, the company is dissolved pursuant to the provisions of the Companies Act[155] and its legal life comes to an end.[156] In contrast to an administrative receiver or administrator, a liquidator has no power to carry on the business of the

---

[152] See, e.g. *Re Whistlejacket Capital Ltd* [2008] B.C.C. 826; and *Re Cheyne Finance plc* [2008] B.C.C. 182.

[153] Insolvency Act 1986 s.29(2) and see below, para.10–08.

[154] See Ch.5.

[155] Companies Act 2006, Pt 31.

[156] Subject to the power of the court to restore it on application under s.1029 of the Companies Act 2006. See n.165 below.

purpose except so far as may be necessary for its beneficial winding up.[157] The jurisdiction of the English courts in winding up is not confined to UK registered companies: it also applies to foreign companies.[158]

Modes of winding up

There are now two main methods of winding up of an insolvent company under the Insolvency Act 1986,[159] namely a creditors' voluntary winding up and a compulsory winding up. These sub-divide into a total of five forms of winding up according to whether they involve the normal winding up process, an exit from administration or a conversion from a CVA.[160] At this point we need concern ourselves only with the normal winding up process. A creditors' voluntary winding up is not, as one might think, a winding up effected by the creditors themselves, but results from a resolution of the members to put the company into voluntary winding up by reason of insolvency. This form of liquidation is termed a creditors' winding up because the control of the liquidation is primarily in the hands of the creditors rather than the court. Both the company and the creditors have a right to nominate the liquidator, but in the case of a difference the creditors' nomination prevails unless the court otherwise orders.[161] A compulsory winding up is a winding up by order of the court made upon a winding up petition presented, in the case of insolvency, by the company, the directors or one or more creditors.[162] A compulsory winding up is more formal and more closely controlled by the court, and the official receiver becomes the liquidator unless and until an outside liquidator is appointed.[163] A company which is in voluntary liquidation may be put into compulsory winding up on a petition presented for that purpose, and if an order is made the winding up thereafter continues as a compulsory winding up.

1–40

Winding up and bankruptcy

Winding up has much in common with bankruptcy. Under both regimes an insolvency practitioner is appointed—a liquidator of a company, a trustee of

1–41

---

[157] Insolvency Act 1986 Sch.4 para.5.
[158] See below, para.16–50.
[159] Formerly there was a third, namely winding up under the supervision of the court (i.e. a creditors' voluntary winding up continued under the court's supervision), but this was abolished by the Insolvency Act 1985 s.88.
[160] See below, para.5–01.
[161] Insolvency Act 1986 s.100.
[162] Insolvency Act 1986 s.124. Most petitions are presented by creditors. As to the legitimacy of using a winding up petition as a debt collection device, see para.5–12.
[163] Insolvency Act 1986 s.136(2).

a bankrupt—to collect in and realise the insolvent's estate and to distribute dividends according to a statutory order of priority. The two regimes have common underlying principles as to proof and priority of debts and the avoidance of transactions as preferences and transactions at a undervalue.[164] But whereas the ultimate objective of the bankruptcy process is the discharge of the bankrupt from his liabilities, so that he can begin again with a clean slate, free from the burden of his debts, and thus rehabilitate himself into the community, the ultimate fate of a company in winding up is not discharge, but legal death through statutory dissolution.[165]

Provisional liquidation

1–42   Instead of moving directly to a winding up order, the court may appoint a provisional liquidator at any time after presentation of a winding up petition and before the making of a winding up order.[166] The primary role of a provisional liquidator is to preserve the assets pending the hearing of the winding up petition, and his appointment also gives him an early opportunity to conduct investigations into the affairs of the company. Appointment of the provisional liquidator terminates the authority of agents appointed to act by or under the authority of the directors except so far as that authority is coupled with an interest, in which case it is irrevocable.[167]

Compositions, compromises and arrangements with creditors; moratoria[168]

1–43   A company unable to pay its debts as they are due may be able to reach an agreement with its creditors for the satisfaction of their claims otherwise than by payment in full. Such an agreement may be made either within or outside of a statutory framework.[169] There are many different forms of

---

[164] The word "avoidance" is here used in a loose sense. Technically the transactions remain valid, but the court is given power to reverse their effect and restore the position to what it would have been if they had not been entered into. See below, para.13–02.

[165] Insolvency Act 1986 ss.201–205 and Sch.B1 para.84(6) (which enables a company in administration and without assets to move directly to dissolution without first being put into winding up). However, the court may revive the corpse by restoring the company to the register on application by a person listed in s.1029(2) of the Companies Act 2006.The usual ground for exercising this power is that fresh assets have been discovered (e.g. insurance policies) which the company needs to be able to collect and distribute. The effect of an order for restoration of the company to the register is that it is deemed to have continued in existence as if it had not been dissolved or struck off the register (s.1032(1)).

[166] Insolvency Act 1986 s. 135.

[167] *Pacific and General Insurance Co. Ltd v Hazell* [1997] B.C.C. 400.

[168] See Ch.12.

[169] For an early instructive and practical analysis, see J.R. Lingard, *Corporate Rescues and Insolvencies*, 2nd edn (1989), Ch.5. Non-statutory workouts are discussed below.

agreement and these possess a bewildering variety of names: composition, compounding, compromise, arrangement, scheme of arrangement, voluntary arrangement, moratorium, reorganisation, reconstruction and restructuring (or workout).[170] In statutory provisions these tend to be used in pairs, but without consistency of terminology. Thus, s.899 of the Companies Act 2006 refers to "compromise or arrangement", while s.1 of the Insolvency Act 1986 speaks of "composition in satisfaction of its debts or a scheme of arrangement of its affairs", both of these being then brought under the single rubric "voluntary arrangement".

Composition; compounding

A composition is an agreement by which creditors accept, in a single sum or by instalments, an amount less than that which is due to them. It involves no transfer of assets or change of any kind in the structure of the company or the rights of its members *inter se* or *vis-à-vis* creditors. Debts which become the subject of a composition are said to be compounded, so that composition and compounding are synonymous. An arrangement cannot be a composition if no payment will be received by preferential and unsecured creditors,[171] but this does not prevent it from being a voluntary arrangement so long as such creditors retain rights after the end of any moratorium and accordingly do not suffer a confiscation or appropriation.[172]

1–44

Compromise

A compromise is an agreement in settlement of a claim which is in doubt, dispute or difficulty of enforcement.[173] The term would seem to cover agreements between a company and its creditors which cannot be enforced in full[174] because of the company's insolvency. In the context of insolvency, "compromise" generally appears in the statutory provisions as part of the phrase "compromise or arrangement.". The word "arrangement" is the wider term, covering both compromises in the sense of settlement of a dispute or

1–45

---

[170] And in the case of an individual insolvent, an assignment (to trustees) for the benefit of his creditors.

[171] See below.

[172] *IRC v Adam & Partners Ltd* [2001] 1 B.C.L.C. 222, distinguishing *Re NFU Development Trust Ltd* [1973] 1 All E.R. 135.

[173] *Mercantile Investment & General Trust Co v International Co. of Mexico* [1893] 1 Ch. 484n, at 491n, cited in *Re Guardian Assurance Co* [1917] 1 Ch. 431, *per* Younger J. at 443, whose decision was reversed by the Court of Appeal on a different point. See further para.1–52.

[174] In the words of Younger J. (*Guardian Assurance*), "to the uttermost farthing of the rights of the claimant".

difficulty and arrangements in which there is an agreement to modify rights with no dispute at all.[175]

Arrangement; scheme of arrangement

1–46   "Arrangement" (which is the statutory shorthand for what is usually referred to as "scheme of arrangement") is a compromise or arrangement submitted to the court for approval under Pt 26 of the Companies Act 2006. The term "arrangement" has a very wide meaning,[176] embracing such diverse schemes as conversion of debt into equity, subordination of secured or unsecured debt, conversion of secured into unsecured claims and vice versa, increase or reduction of share capital and other forms of reconstruction and amalgamation.[177] Though typically it involves agreement with a number of creditors, it has been held that even an agreement with a single creditor may constitute an arrangement.[178] It is not a necessary element of an arrangement for the purpose of Pt 26 of the Companies Act that it should alter the rights existing between the company and creditors or members with whom it is made.[179] But both "compromise" and "arrangement" imply an element of give and take and do not cover a situation in which rights are surrendered or extinguished with no countervailing benefit.[180] This does not, of course, mean that creditors who collectively agree to accept less than what is due to them are not concluding a compromise or arrangement, for each creditor benefits from the partial surrender of rights by the others.

---

[175] *Re Guardian Assurance Co* [1917] 1 Ch. 431; and see below, para.1–46.
[176] *Re Savoy Hotel Ltd* [1981] Ch. 351, *per* Nourse L.J. at 359; and *Re Calgary & Edmonton Land Co Ltd* [1975] 1 All E.R. 1046 at 1054.
[177] For the meaning of "reconstruction", see below, para.1–50.
[178] *Taurusbuild Ltd v Svenska Handelsbanken*, unreported, December 16, 1994, CA.
[179] *Re T. & N. Ltd (No.4)* [2007] Bus. L.R. 1411, *per* David Richards J. at [53]. In that case employees and former employees of T. & N. Ltd and associated companies had or might have in the future claims against the companies arising from exposure to asbestos, which the companies asserted were covered by insurance, although this was disputed by the insurers. A term of the proposed scheme of arrangement was that the scheme companies and actual or potential claimants would not assert claims against the insurers. David Richards J. rejected the argument that because the scheme did not alter rights as between claimants and the companies but was only an arrangement with the insurers it fell outside s.425 of the Companies Act 1985 (now s.899 of the Companies Act 2006). It was necessary that the scheme be proposed with creditors or members in their capacity as such, but it sufficed that it affected their rights against a third party, even though the rights against the company remained unchanged.
[180] *Re NFU Development Trust Ltd* [1973] 1 All E.R. 135 at 140, *per* Brightman J.; and *Re Savoy Hotel Ltd,* above, n. 176, at 652. See also *Re Bluebrook Ltd* [2010] B.C.L.C. 338, where Mann J. rejected the applicability of the principle enunciated in those cases the facts of the case before him.

Voluntary arrangement

"Voluntary arrangement" is the phrase used in s.1(1) of the Insolvency Act to cover both compositions and schemes of arrangement to which Pt I of the Act applies.[181]

1–47

Moratorium

A moratorium is a freeze on the exercise of creditors' rights agreed among the creditors (in which case it may also constitute a voluntary arrangement[182]) or imposed by the Insolvency Act as the result of proceedings for administration. A moratorium arranged by agreement differs from other forms of agreement with creditors in that it does not by itself operate to reduce the debts, merely to defer payment or postpone collection.

1–48

Reorganisation

"Reorganisation" is not a term of art, but generally denotes any method by which the capital structure of a company is modified, and thus encompasses amalgamations, demergers, changes in capital through rights issues and bonus issues, reconstructions under s.110 of the Insolvency Act 1986, and any form of restructuring, whether contractual or under Pt 26 of the Companies Act 1986 or within a CVA.

1–49

Reconstruction

A reconstruction is a form of reorganisation by which the business of a company is transferred to a new company in consideration of the issue of shares in the new company to the members of the old company in exchange for their shares in the latter. A scheme is not a reconstruction unless the business carried on by the new company is substantially the same as that carried on by the old company and the corporators of the old and new company are substantially the same.[183] Section 110 of the Insolvency Act 1986 applies to reconstructions by a company proposed to be, or being, wound up voluntarily. It rarely has anything to do with insolvency, because creditors have to be paid in full and almost invariably the winding up is a members' voluntary winding up.

1–50

---

[181] The heading of Pt I of the Act refers to "Company Voluntary Arrangements", commonly abbreviated to CVA. Only arrangements within Pt I of the Act are CVAs.

[182] *IRC v Adam & Partners Ltd.* [2001] 1 B.C.L.C. 222, above n.172.

[183] *Re Mytravel Group plc* [2004] All E.R. (D) 385 (this point was not considered on appeal, [2005] 2 B.C.L.C. 123); and *Re South African Supply & Cold Storage Co* [1904] 2 Ch. 268.

Restructuring (workout)

1–51 A restructuring, or workout, is a reorganisation which is effected by agreement among creditors rather than as an arrangement under the Insolvency Act or the Companies Act, although the terms of the workout may provide for an insolvency proceeding such as administration or winding up or for the distribution of assets to follow the rules of distribution in winding up, and if there is a dissenting minority it may be necessary to apply to the court to sanction a scheme of arrangement under Pt 26 of the Companies Act.

Modes of compromise and arrangement

1–52 Compromises and arrangements may be concluded in one of five ways:

(1) as a compromise or arrangement (scheme of arrangement) under Pt 26 of the Companies Act;

(2) as a CVA under Pt I of the Insolvency Act;

(3) as an arrangement by way of reconstruction pursuant to s.110 of the Insolvency Act;

(4) as a compromise or arrangement by a liquidator under the Insolvency Act ss.165–167 and Sch.4 para.2; or

(5) as a non-statutory arrangement or compromise concluded by contract or informal arrangement ("restructuring" or "workout").

Schemes of arrangement

1–53 Part 26 of the Companies Act, which can be invoked whether or not the company is in liquidation, involves obtaining the sanction of the court to a scheme approved by the requisite majority of creditors of each class at separately convened meetings ordered by the court. A scheme of arrangement requires a majority in number representing 75 per cent in value of each class of creditors and each class of members present and voting either in person or by proxy.[184] It can therefore be blocked by a voting dissenting minority of more than 25 per cent in value. However, members and creditors with no economic interest in the company, in the sense that value breaks above them, need not be consulted or involved in separate meetings,[185] nor need creditors who have no interest in the sense that they are not

---

[184] Companies Act 2006 s.899.
[185] *Re Tea Corp Ltd* [1904] 1 Ch. 12.

participants in the scheme and are not bound by it, so that their legal rights remain unaffected.[186]

The scheme process is both cumbersome and expensive, involving the presentation of a scheme proposal by the board on behalf of the company, the approval of the court to the convening of a meeting of the various classes of creditor and member involved so far as they have an economic interest and, if the scheme is adopted by the requisite majority, the court's approval. The classes have to be correctly identified, otherwise the whole process is vitiated, and at one time the court did not rule on this until the final stage, so that meetings might be held and proposals approved which the court then found itself unable to sanction. That process has been improved by the movement of the approval of the classes to the second stage.[187] Further, an application for the court's sanction of a scheme of arrangement does not attract a moratorium. Despite these disadvantages, there has been a resurgence in the use of schemes to effect a restructuring of large companies where there is a dissenting minority, since once the scheme has been approved by the requisite majority and received the sanction of the court, all creditors are bound.[188] Moreover, the absence of a moratorium has in some cases been overcome by filing a winding up petition and obtaining an order for provisional liquidation first, the court being informed that it is intended to present a scheme for approval. There has now been a government proposal for a court-ordered, three-month moratorium to facilitate schemes of arrangement, CVAs and contractual restructuring in appropriate cases.[189]

CVAs

For smaller companies, most things that can be done under Pt 26 can be more simply and expeditiously achieved by a CVA under Pt I of the Insolvency Act, particularly since this can (and almost always will) be effected in the course of administration of the company, where the administrator has the benefit of a statutory freeze on the enforcement of creditors' rights. However, in contrast to a scheme of arrangement, a CVA binds only those creditors who in accordance with the rules were entitled to vote at the meeting approving the arrangement or would have been so entitled if they had had notice of the meeting.[190] Where the compromise or arrangement has been proposed for the purposes of or in connection with a scheme for reconstruction of any

1–54

---

[186] *Re Bluebrook Ltd* [2010] B.C.C. 209.
[187] See Practice Statement (Companies: Schemes of Arrangement) [2002] 1 W.L.R. 1345; and L.C.B. Gower and P.L. Davies, *Principles of Modern Company Law*, edited by P.L. Davies, 8th edn (2008), paras 29-4–29-6.
[188] *British & Commonwealth Holdings plc v Barclays Bank plc* [1995] B.C.C. 19, affirmed [1995] B.C.C. 1059.
[189] See above, n.72.
[190] Insolvency Act 1986 s.5(2)(b).

company or companies or any amalgamation, the court is given specific powers when sanctioning the compromise or arrangement.[191]

Compromises or arrangements by liquidator

1–55   Section 110 deals with a specific form of arrangement by which the liquidator in a voluntary winding up may, with the sanction of the court or the liquidation committee, dispose of the company's business to another company in exchange for shares, policies or other like interests in the transferee company. Reconstructions under s.111 need no further mention because they arise in solvent companies about to go into a members' voluntary winding up. Sections 165–167 and Sch.4 to the Insolvency Act deal with the liquidator's power to make compromises or arrangements with creditors, subject to his or her obtaining the requisite sanction. It has been held that this procedure is not appropriate as a means of distributing assets otherwise than in accordance with creditors' strict legal rights, since the procedure lacks the safeguards for prospective dissentient creditors provided by s.899.[192] Compromises and arrangements under ss.165–167 and Sch.4 are quite distinct from CVAs, which are governed by Pt I of the Insolvency Act 1986 and Pt I of the Insolvency Rules 1986 and may be made even if the company is not in liquidation or administration. By contrast, arrangements under ss.165–167 and para.2 of Sch.4 are confined to companies in liquidation and may be sanctioned either by the liquidation committee or by the court. The provisions relating to such arrangements are of long standing.[193] They are particularly useful in cases where it is impracticable to convene meetings of creditors.[194]

Restructuring[195]

1–56   Finally, if the creditors are willing, a restructuring, or workout, can be effected outside the statutory provisions altogether, by a combination of informal and contractual arrangements. The final agreement is typically complex and may involve a substantial period of negotiation.[196] The workout has several advantages; it avoids the formality, expense and delay of the statutory modes of arrangement, is much more flexible and generally leaves a greater degree of control with the management. In addition, it may enable

---

[191] Companies Act 2006 s.900(2). As to what constitutes reconstruction, see above, para.1–50.
[192] *Re Trix Ltd* [1970] 3 All E.R. 397.
[193] They go back to s.159 of the Companies Act 1862.
[194] See, e.g. *Re Bank of Credit and Commerce International SA (No.3)* [1993] B.C.L.C. 1490.
[195] See Chris Howard and Bob Hedger, *Restructuring Law and Practice*, 2nd edn (London: LexisNexis, 2008).
[196] See below, paras 12–6, 12–9.; and Finch, *Corporate Insolvency Law*, 2009, Ch.7.

the company to avoid an event of default under its loan agreements, and the fact that it is being supported by its major creditors helps to reduce in some measure the effect of the damage to its reputation of becoming insolvent.[197]

5. BANK FAILURES AND THEIR POLICY IMPLICATIONS

The rise of bank failures

In recent years we have witnessed the failure or near-collapse of several large **1–57** financial institutions both in this country and overseas. Prominent in the United Kingdom were the collapse of Northern Rock in September 2007, leading to a run on the bank, the ill-fated merger of Lloyds TSB and HBOS in 2008 and the near-failure of the Royal Bank of Scotland in the same year, leading to all three banks coming under State control at an estimated bail-out cost of a staggering £650 billion. Failures on a comparable scale were reported in the United States, where statistics issued by the Federal Deposit Insurance Corporation showed that in two-and-a-half years there were no fewer than 248 bank failures, with total assets of over $615 billion. Notable among these was the investment bank Lehman Brothers. Also in crisis were Fannie Mae and Freddie Mac, the two US government agencies involved in the secondary market for mortgage-backed securities, which in effect became nationalised. Huge sums had to be injected into the banking sector by the US Treasury, with bail-outs for such giants as Bears Stearns and American International Group, although Lehman Brothers, controversially, was allowed to go into insolvency, partly because of a decision by the then US Treasury Secretary Henry Paulson, partly because of the impossibility of securing the approval of the UK regulators for a takeover by Barclays Bank within the short time available, if at all. The principal causes on both sides of the Atlantic were the making of sub-prime loans on real estate on a massive scale, a collapse in the property market leading to widespread default and a loss of confidence among prospective lenders and purchasers of some of the banks in question. Continental Europe also did not go unscathed, with the collapse of Kaupthing, Fortis and Dexia, amongst others.

In general, it can be said that the insolvency of a company does not represent a failure of capitalism, but is a necessary concomitant of entrepreneurial activity. The only way of avoiding risk is by not doing business. It is therefore not the role of regulators to eliminate financial risk so as to prevent business failures.[198] But the failure of a large bank raises distinct considerations

---

[197] See Ch.12 and Totty and Moss, *Insolvency*, Ch.H19.
[198] "Financial System Inquiry: Final Report" ("the Wallis Report", March 1997, which examined the financial system in Australia), p.19; Roy Goode, *Commercial Law in the Next Millennium* (The Hamlyn Lectures, 1997), pp.45–47.

because of its potential impact on a country's macroeconomic health, and the problems are exacerbated where the failure is of a multinational banking group.[199]

Too big to fail?

1–58   Though the failure of particular companies is inevitable in a capitalist society, systemic risk is another matter. No government can view with equanimity the failure of a large bank, with the prospect of a domino effect leading to the collapse of the entire banking market. Governments are particularly sensitive to bank failures. First, there is the impact on depositors. The sight of ordinary members of the public being seen on television queuing to withdraw their deposits is itself a spur to rescue operations, as was graphically demonstrated in the case of Northern Rock. Equally alarming, however, is the potential effect on other banks, which may have a substantial exposure because of high volumes of inter-bank lending. So governments face a dilemma. On the one hand, there is the problem of moral hazard, the inducement to banks and their depositors to rely on the government's implicit guarantee of support to take unnecessary risks in the knowledge that if things go wrong they will be bailed out; on the other, there is the potentially huge loss of confidence in the system if a major bank is allowed to fail, with depositors having only limited protection which may take considerable time to crystallise, and the likely domino effect on the market as a whole. Lehman Brothers was allowed to fail, and the result was catastrophic, with a near-meltdown of the financial markets. But the cost of bail-outs by the State may be so huge as to place severe stress on its economy. Hence the opposing questions: "Too big to fail?" and "Too big to save?"[200] Or in the words of the former Chairman of the Federal Reserve, Mr Alan Greenspan: "If they're too big to fail, they're too big.[201]

The legislative response of the UK Government

1–59   The UK Government responded to the crisis in legislative terms by introducing what became the Banking Act 2009.[202] This is an enactment of some 265

---

[199] See the Consultative Document "Report and Recommendations of the Cross-Border Bank Resolution Group" issued by the Basel Committee on Banking Supervision (September 2009).

[200] For a fascinating account of the development of the financial crisis, based on interviews with more than 200 major players in the drama, see Andrew Ross Sorkin, *Too Big to Fail* (2009).

[201] In an address to the Council of Foreign Relations, October 16, 2009.

[202] See Roman Tomasic, "Creating a Template for Banking Insolvency Law after the Collapse of Northern Rock" (2009) 22 Ins. Int. 65; and Emilios Avgouleas, "Banking Supervision and the Special Resolution Regime of the Banking Act 2009: The Unfinished Reform" (2009) Capital Markets L.J. 201.

sections but (amazingly for modern legislation) not a single schedule, and it is characterised by a remarkable succinctness and clarity of drafting. The Act[203] established a special resolution regime (SRR) for UK banks[204] that are in or approaching financial difficulty. The SRR consists of a threefold regime: the three stabilisation options, the bank insolvency procedure and the bank administration procedure.[205] The bank stabilisation options are transfer to a private sector purchaser, transfer to a bridge bank and transfer to temporary public ownership.[206] Each of these options is to be achieved through the exercise of one or more stabilisation powers, namely share transfer powers and property transfer powers.[207] Part 2 of the Act is devoted to bank insolvency and prescribes a special procedure for the winding up of an insolvent bank through a bank insolvency order, which may be applied for only by the Bank of England, the Financial Services Authority or the Secretary of State[208] and only on one of the grounds specified in s.97. The bank liquidator is required to pursue two objectives according to the priorities set out in s.99, the first of which is to see that an eligible depositor either has his account transferred to another financial institution or receives payment from or on behalf of the Financial Services Compensation Scheme. The bank liquidator may propose a company voluntary arrangement.[209] Section 127 of the Insolvency Act[210] is disapplied,[211] and actions done in connection with the exercise of a stabilisation power do not constitute a transaction at an undervalue or a preference.[212] The Act does not preclude the presentation of an ordinary winding up or administration petition, but the court may instead make a bank insolvency order on the application of the FSA with the consent of the Bank of England or on the application of the Bank of England,[213] while a resolution for voluntary winding up has no effect without the prior approval of the court.[214]

So far no bank has yet been made subject to the regime, although it has been invoked in the case of the Dunfermline Building Society. A similar scheme for investment banks is now in force.[215]

---

[203] As amended by the Financial Services Act 2010 ss.20–21 and supplemented by several statutory instruments.
[204] Separate definitions of "bank" are given in ss.2 and 91. "Bank" does not include a building society, but under s.84 the SSR may be applied, with modifications, to building societies.
[205] Banking Act 2009 s.1(2).
[206] Banking Act 2009 s.1(3).
[207] Banking Act 2009 s.1(4).
[208] Banking Act 2009 s.96(2)–(4).
[209] Banking Act 2009 s. 113.
[210] See below, para.13–127.
[211] Banking Act 2009 s.103, Table.
[212] Banking Act 2009 s.103, Table.
[213] Banking Act 2009 s.117.
[214] Banking Act 2009 s.118.
[215] Investment Bank Special Administration Regulations. SI 2011/245. See HM Treasury, Establishing Resolution Arrangements for Investment Banks (December 2009).

6. EXEMPTIONS FROM RULES OF INSOLVENCY LAW

1–60   In order to safeguard the securities markets against the invalidation of dealings in securities, netting arrangements and rules of recognised exchanges
and clearing houses governing these matters, under rules of insolvency law
which could adversely affect the efficient functioning of the market and
thereby produce systemic risk, wide-ranging provisions have been introduced
both by Pt VII of the Companies Act 1989, supplemented by subordinate
legislation, and by EC Directives designed to insulate such transactions from
such insolvency law rules and, in the case of transactions covered by Pt VII,
to replace them with the approved rules of the exchange or clearing house
in question. Under Pt VII, these exemptions apply to market contracts,
market charges and, with limitations, system charges.[216] The Directives are
concerned with securing settlement finality and the protection of dealings
in financial collateral and related close-out arrangements by requiring
Member States to ensure that dealings and arrangements of the kind specified in the directives are not invalidated by rules of insolvency law. There are
also special rules governing the winding up of credit institutions, including
EEA credit institutions,[217] and insurance companies.[218] These modify the
general rules of corporate insolvency law in a number of important respects.
They are not dealt with in the present work.

Market contracts

1–61   A market contract is a contract connected with a recognised investment
exchange or recognised clearing house and entered into by a member or
designated non-member of the exchange on or otherwise subject to its rules,
or by the exchange itself with a member or with a recognised clearing house
or another recognised investment exchange for the purpose of enabling the
settlement of liabilities or the provision of central counterparty clearing services.[219] Market contracts and the settlement rules of a recognised investment
exchange or a recognised clearing house relating to the settlement of market

---

[216] Financial Markets and Insolvency Regulations 1996 (SI 1996/1469), Pt II, as amended by the
Enterprise Act 2002 (Insolvency) Order 2003 (SI 2003/2096), Sch. paras 62–64.

[217] Credit Institutions (Reorganisation and Winding up) Regulations 2004 (SI 2004/1045),
implementing the EC directive on the reorganisation and winding up of credit institutions
(2001/24/EC dated April 4, 2001), [2001] OJ L125/15.

[218] Financial Services and Markets Act 2000 ss.376–379; Insurers (Reorganisation and Winding
Up) Regulations 2004 (SI 2004/353); and Insurers (Winding Up) Rules 2001 (SI 2001/3635).
These implement the EC directive on the reorganisation and winding up of insurance under-
takings (2001/17/EC dated March 19, 2001), [2001] OJ L110/28.

[219] Companies Act 1989 s.155, as amended by the Financial Markets and Insolvency
Regulations 1998, SI 1998/1748 and the Financial Markets and Insolvency Regulations 2009,
SI 2009/853, the latter of which substantially expanded the definition of market contracts.

contracts are not to be regarded as invalid at law on the ground of inconsistency with the law relating to the distribution of the assets of a person on winding up or administration,[220] and more limited provisions apply to market charges[221] and system charges.[222] The proceedings of the exchange or clearing house are to take precedence over insolvency procedures.[223] The broad effect is to substitute the approved rules of the exchange or clearing house for the insolvency distribution rules, thus in effect creating a self-contained, mini-insolvency distribution system for such contracts and charges. The requirements for recognition of an investment exchange or clearing house under the Financial Services Act 1986 include those set out in the Financial Services and Markets Act 2000 (Recognition Requirements for Investment Exchanges and Clearing Houses) Regulations 2001,[224] which oblige UK investment exchanges and UK clearing houses to have rules enabling action to be taken in the event of a member's default. The rules must provide for the rights and liabilities of a defaulter,[225] and in particular must provide for sums payable by or to the defaulter in respect of different contracts to be aggregated or set off so as to produce a net sum,[226] and, in the case of a clearing house, for that sum, if payable by the defaulter to the clearing house, to be set off against any property provided by the defaulter as cover for margin, and if payable by the clearing house to the defaulter to be aggregated with any property provided by the defaulter as cover for margin.[227]

Market charges

A market charge means a charge, whether fixed or floating, granted in favour **1–62** of (*inter alios*) a recognised investment exchange for the purpose of securing debts or liabilities arising in connection with the settlement of market contracts or in favour of a recognised clearing house for the purpose of securing

---

[220] Companies Act 1989 s.159, as amended, most recently by SI 2009/853.

[221] Companies Act 1989 s.175. See below, para.1–62.

[222] Financial Markets and Insolvency Regulations 1996, SI 1996/1469, Pt II. In addition, the Financial Markets and Insolvency (Money Markets) Regulations 1995, SI 1995/2049 had provided exemptions with regard to money market contracts and money market charges, but the regulations were revoked by the Financial Services and Markets Act 2000 (Consequential Amendments and Repeals) Order 2001, SI 2001/3649, art.513 as spent, consequent on regulations implementing the Settlement Finality Directive. See below, paras.1–65 et seq. as to the Settlement Finality Directive.

[223] Companies Act 1989 s.159.

[224] SI 2001/995, as amended by SI 2006/3386, replacing Companies Act 1989 s.56 and Sch.1, repealed by the Financial Services and Markets Act 2000 (Consequential Amendments and Repeals) Order 2001 (SI 2001/3649), art.75.

[225] These include, in the case of a clearing house, rights and liabilities arising in respect of the effecting by the clearing house of offsetting contracts ("corresponding contracts"), a form of close-out mentioned below, para.9–12. See SI 2001/995 (above, n. 224), Sch.1, para.25(2).

[226] ibid., Sch.1, para.11(2)(b).

[227] ibid., Sch.1, para.12(2)(c).

debts or liabilities arising in connection with their ensuring the performance of market contracts.[228]

System charges

1–63   A system charge is a charge granted in favour of a settlement bank for the purpose of securing debts or liabilities arising from various types of transfer or transfer agreement relating to uncertificated securities by means of a relevant system.[229]

Settlement finality in dealings in financial collateral

1–64   Two EC Directives have been issued designed to remove from attack under insolvency law netting and close-out arrangements under the rules of designated systems[230] and, more broadly, contractual arrangements to similar effect relating to financial collateral.[231] The European Community has long been concerned to limit systemic risk[232] to ensure both the efficiency and stability of dealings among participants in recognised clearing and settlement systems: hence, the two Directives in question, the 1998 Settlement Finality Directive[233] and the 2002 Directive on financial collateral arrangements.[234] The latter in particular is designed to override rules of national law that impair the legal efficacy of financial collateral arrangements and provision within or outside insolvency.

(1) The Settlement Finality Directive

1–65   The effect of the Directive and implementing regulations is largely to remove from attack under general insolvency law the rules of a designated

---

[228] Companies Act 1989, s.173. Charges on land are excluded (Financial Markets and Insolvency Regulations 1991 (SI 1991/880), reg.8).

[229] Financial Markets and Insolvency Regulations 1996, SI 1996/1469, reg.3(2).

[230] Directive on settlement finality in payment and securities systems, 98/26/EC dated May 19, 1998, implemented in the UK by what are now the Financial Markets and Insolvency (Settlement Finality) Regulations 2001, SI 2001/1349. But see below, n.231.

[231] Directive on financial collateral arrangements, 2002/47/EC, implemented in the UK by the Financial Collateral Arrangements (No.2) Regulations 2003, SI 2003/3226. The two Directives have been amended by Directive 2009/44/EC of May 6, 2009 ([2009] OJ L146/37), implemented by the Financial Markets and Insolvency (Settlement Finality and Financial Collateral Arrangements (Amendment) Regulations 2010, SI 2010/2993.

[232] The risk that the failure of one major participant will have a domino effect on the system as a whole.

[233] See above, n.230. The regulations were amended by SI 2001/997, but for technical reasons revoked immediately on the date of entry into force by SI 2001/1349.

[234] See above, n.231.

settlement system and transactions (including the realisation of collateral security) effected in connection with participation in such a system. Thus, system rules governing default arrangements, in particular, arrangements for netting and the closing-out of open positions[235] and the application or transfer of collateral security,[236] are to be respected notwithstanding any rules of insolvency law which might otherwise invalidate them. So the restrictions imposed by paras 43(2) and 44(5) of Sch.B1 to the Insolvency Act 1986 on the enforcement of security while an administration is current or pending or the order is in force do not apply in relation to a collateral security charge,[237] and s.127 of the Act (which invalidates dispositions made after the commencement of a winding up unless approved by the court) does not apply to a disposition of property as the result of which it becomes subject to a collateral security charge.[238] Of some importance also is the conflict of laws rule embodied in Art.9(2) of the Directive,[239] which provides that where securities are provided as collateral to a (system) participant and/or central bank of a Member State and their right with respect to the securities is legally recorded in a register, account or centralised deposit system located in a Member State, the rights of holders of the collateral are to be determined by the law of that Member State. One effect of this is that rights in relation to securities held through an account with a securities intermediary in a Member State are governed by the PRIMA law.[240] A modified PRIMA approach was adopted by the Hague Convention on indirectly held securities.[241]

(2) The Directive on financial collateral arrangements

The 2002 Directive on financial collateral arrangements is altogether broader and more ambitious in scope. Its purpose is to facilitate the provision of financial collateral under bilateral transactions, and thereby promote not only the

1–66

---

[235] See paras 9–08 et seq.

[236] Including security provided under a charge or repurchase or similar agreement for the purpose of securing rights and obligations potentially arising in connection with the system.

[237] Financial Markets and Insolvency (Settlement Finality) Regulations 1999, SI 1999/2979, reg.19(1).

[238] Financial Markets and Insolvency (Settlement Finality) Regulations 1999, reg.19(3).

[239] Implemented in the UK by reg.23 of the Financial Markets and Insolvency (Settlement Finality) Regulations 1999. It is likely that art.9(2) will be modified in the light of the 2006 Hague Convention on the law applicable to certain rights held with an intermediary.

[240] The place of the intermediary approach.

[241] Convention on the Law Applicable to Certain Rights in respect of Securities Held with an Intermediary, July 5, 2006. The Convention was in fact concluded in December 2002, but under the procedures of the Hague Conference on Private International Law then prevailing texts were treated as drafts until the first signature. For a detailed analysis, see Roy Goode, Hideki Kanda and Karl Kreuzer, assisted by Christophe Bernasconi, *Hague Securities Convention: Explanatory Report* (The Hague: Hague Conference on Private International Law, 2005). So far the EU has declined to adopt the Convention.

stability of the market, but also its efficiency, by requiring Member States to disapply rules of law and statutory provisions that would otherwise invalidate financial collateral arrangements and provision, whether before insolvency (as by rendering void transactions not carried out or perfected in conformity with prescribed formalities) or on insolvency. The Directive covers both directly held and indirectly held securities. Regrettably, an understanding of the Directive is somewhat impeded by technical defects, linguistic problems in the English text and the practice of placing in the Preamble substantive rules of interpretation which should be in the text,[242] coupled with a measure of duplication of provisions[243] and inconsistency of terminology.[244] Nevertheless, the Directive is to be warmly welcomed as a great step forward in ensuring the legal stability of financial collateral arrangements and provision. We shall note only those provisions relevant to insolvency.

(A) SCOPE OF THE DIRECTIVE

1–67   The Directive covers financial collateral in the form of cash or financial instruments.[245] It distinguishes between arrangements for the provision of collateral and its actual provision. The Directive applies only when the collateral has actually been provided and only where the provision is evidenced in writing[246] and the collateral arrangement (i.e. agreement) is evidenced in writing or in a legally equivalent manner.[247] Moreover, collateral is to be considered "provided" only where it is delivered, transferred, held, registered or otherwise designated so as to be in the possession or under the control of the collateral taker or of a person acting on his behalf.[248] In short, the security interest must be not only created, but perfected by possession or

---

[242] e.g. art.3(1) can be fully understood only by reference to paras (9) and (10) of the Preamble. See below, para.1–69.

[243] e.g. art.3(2) repeats the substance of art.1(5).

[244] e.g. in relation to the expression of formal requirements. See below. Some of these defects have been corrected in Directive 2009/44/EC or overcome in the Financial Collateral Arrangements (No.2) Regulations 2003 (SI 2003/3226) which implement the Directive.

[245] See art.1(4)(a). "Financial instruments" are defined in art.2(1)(e) and cover virtually all forms of instrument issued on a market. See SI 2003/3226, reg.3. "Cash" means "money credited to an account in any currency, or similar claims for the repayment of money, such as money market deposits" (art.2(1)(d)).

[246] This requires that the financial collateral be identifiable, which in the case of book-entry securities or cash is satisfied by crediting to an account.

[247] The Directive uses the phrase "can be evidenced in writing", which is a somewhat unusual way of saying that it *is* evidenced in writing. This does not mean that the agreement must be *in* writing, merely that if it is made orally or inferred from conduct there must be written evidence of it. It is not clear why the phrase "or in a legally equivalent manner" appears in reference to arrangements for the provision of collateral, but not in relation to the provision itself, nor what the phrase adds, given that by art.2(3) "writing" includes "recording by electronic means and any other durable medium".

[248] See art.2(2). The same paragraph (reflected in SI 2003/3226, reg.3) makes it clear that this requirement is not to exclude techniques for the substitution of collateral or withdrawal of excess collateral by the collateral provider. See further below.

control. Until then, the Directive has no application and the efficacy of the security interest is left to national law. So it has been held that an uncrystallised floating charge is not within the scope of the Directive.[249] However, recent amendments to this and the Settlement Finality Directive provide that possession of financial collateral in the form of cash or financial instruments includes the case where financial collateral in the form of cash or financial instruments has been credited to an account in the name of the collateral-taker.[250] All of the methods of possession or control referred to represent methods of perfection available under existing English law.

(B) CATEGORIES OF FINANCIAL COLLATERAL ARRANGEMENT

Financial collateral arrangements are divided into two categories: title transfer financial collateral arrangements and security financial collateral arrangements, whether in the case of securities the collateral is held directly or through a securities intermediary ("book-entry securities"). The former are arrangements, including repurchase agreements, under which full ownership is transferred to the collateral taker.[251] This reflects the securities industry's usage in treating title transfer as a form of collateral even though in English law an outright transfer does not constitute a security interest.[252]   **1–68**

In the case of direct holdings, outright title transfer is by entry on the share register; in the case of indirect, or book-entry, holdings, title transfer presumably includes not only transfer by novation, that is, transfer to the collateral taker's account, but also assignment. As stated above, title transfer arrangements do not include mortgages, which transfer only security ownership, not full ownership, but do include outright sale and repurchase agreements which are intended to fulfil a security function even if not, under English law, constituting security agreements.[253] Security financial collateral arrangements are, in English law terms, arrangements which create charges or, in the case of bearer securities, pledges. Mortgages, which on a literal

---

[249] *Re Gray v G-T-P Group Ltd, F2G Realisations* [2010] EWHC 1772 (Ch), citing the analysis in Beale et al., *Law of Personal Property Security* (Oxford: Oxford University Press, 2007), paras 10.24 et seq. The case involved moneys held in a bank account in the name of the creditor on which the debtor was free to draw.

[250] Directive 2009/44/EC of May 6, 2009 ([2009] OJ L146/37), art.2, amending Directive 98/26/EC on settlement finality in payment and securities settlement systems and Directive 2002/47/EC on financial collateral arrangements as regards linked systems and credit claims. These amendments have been implemented by the Financial Markets and Insolvency (Settlement Finality and Financial Collateral Arrangements) (Amendment) Regulations 2010, SI 2010/2993, which came into force on April 6, 2011.

[251] Some countries do not recognise the grant of security by title transfer. Article 6 requires Member States to ensure that a title transfer financial collateral arrangement can take effect in accordance with its terms.

[252] See *Goode on Legal Problems of Credit and Security*, 2008, paras 1–37 and 6–38. The 2009 amending Directive corrected an error in art.3 of the original Directive which on a literal construction would have not have extended to English law mortgages.

[253] *Goode on Legal Problems of Credit and Security*, 2008, para.6–38.

construction fell outside the definition of the Directive as originally issued, but were obviously intended to be covered, are now expressly included as the result of the 2009 amending Directive.[254] The position of floating charges has already been discussed.[255] Crystallised floating charges have always been within the scope of the UK regulations.[256]

(C) REDUCTION OF FORMALITIES

1–69   One of the main purposes of the Directive is to reduce the requirements for attachment and perfection of a security interest in financial collateral to a minimum. Article 3, of which the first paragraph is expressed in very wide terms, provides as follows:

> "1. Member States shall not require that the creation, validity, perfection, enforceability or admissibility in evidence of a financial collateral arrangement or the provision of financial collateral under a financial collateral arrangement be dependent on the performance of any formal act.
>
> 2. Paragraph 1 is without prejudice to the application of this Directive to financial collateral only once it has been provided and if that provision can be evidenced in writing and where the financial collateral arrangement can be evidenced in writing or in a legally equivalent manner."

Article 3(1) states the basic principle that no formal act is necessary for the creation, validity, etc. of a financial collateral arrangement or the provision of financial collateral. This, however, is subject to Art.3(2), which would have been clearer if it had said simply that Art.3(1) takes effect subject to the provisions of Art.1(5). These, as stated above, make the application of the Directive dependent on the provision of collateral. What Art.3(2) fails to state is that in order for the collateral to be considered as "provided", the collateral taker's interest must be perfected by some form of "dispossession" of the debtor if the Directive is to apply. The effect would seem to be that, notwithstanding Art.3(1), national law continues to apply to the creation and validity of security interests, but that once perfected by possession or control by the collateral taker, the provision of financial collateral must be recognised even if not created in the manner prescribed by national law. For interests not so perfected, it remains open to the collateral taker to perfect by any other means available under national law, for example, registration, and to national law to prescribe such means.

---

[254] Above, n.250.
[255] Above, para.1–67.
[256] See also *Goode on Legal Problems of Credit and Security*, 2008, para.6–38, suggesting that the rights of withdrawal and substitution imply that at least some floating charges may be covered by the Directive.

Article 3(1) must also be read in conjunction with the Preamble, which in effect states[257] that Member States may continue to require the creation or transfer of a security interest in financial collateral to be effected by acts such as endorsement of instruments to order[258] and registration of transfers of directly held securities, which for the purposes of the Directive are not formal acts, but that there should be no formalities for the attachment or perfection of transfers of or security interests in indirectly held (book-entry) securities. As to these, it will no longer be open to a Member State to require that a document be executed in any particular form or in a particular manner, that the date of its execution or the amount of the relevant financial obligations be evidenced in any manner or that perfection of a security interest be dependent on registration in a public register, filing with or notification to a public officer, or advertisement. In fact, there are currently no formal requirements under English law for the *attachment* of a security interest in registered securities, and formal perfection requirements in the shape of registration in the Companies Registry apply only to floating charges, charges on book debts and charges to secure any issue of debentures. Floating charges are largely outside the scope of the Directive,[259] but in any event these requirements were abolished when the United Kingdom implemented the Directive, thereby eliminating, for registration purposes, the risk of recharacterisation of a purported fixed security as a floating charge or of a sale and repurchase as a registrable security transaction.

(D) Enforcement

Member States are required to ensure that on the occurrence of an enforcement event[260] the collateral taker has available to it a range of enforcement measures, subject to the parties' agreement.

1–70

(E) Protection from insolvency avoidance

Articles 7 and 8 are designed to protect the provision of financial collateral against avoidance for insolvency. Article 7 requires Member States to ensure

1–71

---

[257] See paras (9) and (10).

[258] It is not clear how the requirement that the provision of collateral (as opposed to arrangements for such provision) be evidenced in writing is to be applied in the case of bearer securities, which by nature are transferred by delivery.

[259] See above, para.1–67.

[260] Defined by art.2(1)(l) as an event of default or any similar event agreed between the parties on the occurrence of which, under the terms of a collateral financial arrangement or by operation of law, the collateral taker is entitled to realise or appropriate financial collateral or a close-out netting comes into force. Again, the drafting is a little strange, for read literally it does not cover a right of realisation given by law unless the relevant event is one agreed between the parties! This comes from the misplacing of the phrase "or by operation of law", which should have been inserted after "parties". It is thought that art.2(1)(l) is to be interpreted as if drafted in this way.

that a close-out netting provision can take effect in accordance with its terms notwithstanding the commencement or continuation of winding up proceedings or reorganisation measures and other specified events. One effect of this provision is to preserve the validity of close-out netting provisions[261] expressed to be triggered by the commencement of a winding up. Article 8 of the Directive requires Member States to ensure that financial collateral arrangements are protected from avoidance under various rules of insolvency law. In particular, Art.8 precludes avoidance on the sole basis that the financial collateral arrangement has come into existence, or the financial collateral has been provided, within a prescribed period prior to, and defined by reference to, the commencement of winding up proceedings. Another precludes avoidance of transactions involving the provision of top-up collateral solely on the ground that the top-up was provided on the day of commencement of the winding up proceedings or after the relevant financial obligations had been incurred. Part 3 of the financial collateral regulations implements all of these provisions.

EEA credit institutions

1-72   There are special rules restricting the institution of winding up proceedings or the undertaking of reorganisational measures against an European Economic Area (EEA) credit institution.[262]

---

[261] "Close-out netting provision" is defined in art.2(1)(n) of the Financial Collateral Directive and art.3 of the implementing regulations, above, n.231. See further below, para.9–12.

[262] Credit Institutions (Reorganisation and Winding Up) Regulations 2004 (SI 2004/1045, as amended by the Financial Services (EEA State) Regulations 2007), SI 2007/108; the Financial Services and Markets Act 2000 (Markets in Financial Instruments) Regulations 2007, SI 2007/126; and the Credit Institutions (Reorganisation and Winding Up) (Amendment) Regulations 2007, SI 2007/830. The current text of the regulations, incorporating amendments made by the above statutory instruments, is reproduced in *Sealy and Milman: Annotated Guide to the Insolvency Legislation*, Vol.2, p.1025. See further below, para.15–01.

Chapter 2

The Foundations of Corporate Insolvency Law

1. INTRODUCTION

It is often assumed that the task of public regulation is to prevent business failures and that the insolvency of a company denotes that the regulatory regime is in some way at fault. This is a misconception. It is not the function of regulation to eliminate risk. That would create moral hazard in that lenders and investors would have no incentive to exercise prudence in their dealings with the company. The risk of business failure is an essential concomitant of entrepreneurial activity. Risk can only be eliminated by not doing business at all.[1] What has to be controlled is systemic risk, the risk of collapse of an entire market through the domino effect of failure of a major player, particularly a large bank. This may necessitate government intervention through the provision of support finance or the nationalisation of a failing bank.[2] Hence measures both in the public law and the private law domain to reduce systemic risk: public law, by increased capital requirements for banks and tighter regulation; and private law, by immunising contracts for netting, close-outs and the like from the ordinary effects of insolvency law.[3]

---

[1] See Roy Goode, *Commercial Law in the Next Millennium* (Hamlyn Lectures 1998) (London: Sweet & Maxwell, 1998), pp.45–46, citing *Financial System Inquiry: Final Report* (the Wallis Report) (Canberra: Australian Government Publishing Service, 1997), p.19.

[2] See above, para.1–57.

[3] Financial Collateral Arrangements (No.2) Regulations 2003, SI 2003/3226, implementing Directive 2002/47/EC on financial collateral arrangements. The view has been expressed that similar protection against systemic risk given by the US Bankruptcy Code through the provision of safe harbours for swaps, repos, netting, set-off and the like has led to creditor counterparties rushing to enforce their rights and seize and sell margin collateral, leading to the dismemberment of the failing institutions. See Edward R. Morrison, "Is the Bankruptcy Code an Adequate Mechanism for Resolving the Distress of Systemically Important Institutions" 82 Temple L. Rev. 449 (2009). Informal discussions by the author with English insolvency practitioners have not indicated the existence of a similar problem in the United Kingdom.

But systemic risk aside, the role of regulation is not to prevent corporate failure, but to ensure that when it occurs rules of insolvency law come into play which will produce the best possible outcome for those with an economic stake in the enterprise.

2–01   Corporate insolvency law has three overriding objectives: to maximise the return to creditors; to establish a fair and equitable system for the ranking of claims and the distribution of assets among creditors,[4] involving a limited redistribution of rights; and to provide a mechanism by which the causes of failure can be identified and those guilty of mismanagement brought to book and, where appropriate, deprived of the right to be involved in the management of other companies.[5] To facilitate achievement of these objectives insolvency law provides a battery of legal and administrative instruments and institutional structures.

The instruments by which the above objectives are achieved include the placement of the company and its assets under the control of an external manager,[6] with wide powers of investigation and management, including: disposal or closing down of the business; the suspension of rights of individual pursuit of claims and their replacement by a collective debt collection process, followed by distribution of net realisations according to a statutory system of priorities; the avoidance of transactions entered into by the company which are improper or which it would otherwise be unfair to allow to stand, and the recovery of misapplied assets; the imposition of civil and criminal sanctions, including disqualification, for improper conduct on the part of the directors; and qualification requirements for insolvency practitioners designed to ensure their integrity and competence. Insolvency law also provides for the ultimate death of a company in winding up by a procedure for dissolution.

Despite this battery of instruments, an insolvent company has essentially only three options: to trade out of its difficulties, usually after a process of reorganisation which typically involves adjustments of creditors' rights, whether by reduction or even extinguishment of certain claims, debt deferral, conversion of debt into equity or otherwise; to dispose of its business or assets without or prior to liquidation; and to go into immediate liquidation. Administration is usually an interim procedure which may be a route to any of these processes, although it is now possible for a company to move directly from administration to dissolution without first being reorganised or going into winding up.[7]

---

[4] The phrase "distribution among creditors" is here used as a shorthand to denote the distribution of realisations of assets. On the winding up of an insolvent company, assets are rarely distributed in specie; they are sold and the net proceeds used to pay cash dividends to creditors.

[5] Discussed in more detail below, paras 14–57 et seq. See also the Report of the Insolvency Law Review Committee, *Insolvency Law and Practice*, Cmnd. 8558 (London: HMSO, 1982), paras 191–199.

[6] Alternatively, continuance of the existing management under the supervision of the court and creditors, as in the case of a reorganisation under Ch.11 of the American Bankruptcy Code, where the debtor-in-possession has the powers of a bankruptcy trustee. See paras 2–07 and 11–18.

[7] See below, para.11–115.

The philosophy underpinning English corporate insolvency law is much harder to state since it has rarely been clearly articulated. Questions such as the legitimate province of corporate insolvency law and the social and economic policy basis for its ordering of entitlements, which have long been the subject of debate and controversy in the United States, for long lay dormant in this country, and only recently have they begun to attract the attention of scholars. One writer has drawn attention to what he perceives to be the deliberate ambiguity about the respective merits of reorganisation and liquidation, serving to obscure, or gloss over, difficult policy choices between potentially competing goals.[8] For ease of exposition I shall begin with the particular—the objectives and instruments of corporate insolvency law—before going on to discuss the broader issues of policy which inform, or should inform, legislative and judicial decisions in this field.

2. THE OBJECTIVES OF ENGLISH CORPORATE INSOLVENCY LAW

The principles of English corporate insolvency law will be examined in the next chapter. At this stage we would simply note certain basic features of corporate insolvency law and establish what it is trying to do.

2–02

As with other insolvency laws, English insolvency law addresses two central questions: priority and control. These questions need to be kept separate. Priority is concerned with the order of distribution of assets as a matter of substantive law. Control is essentially procedural and is designed to safeguard the assets by placing them in the hands of a manager acting for the benefit of the creditors at large, individual actions and enforcement measures being stayed. Such control would be necessary whatever the priority rules.

The priority of claims is largely based on pre-insolvency entitlements, but our insolvency law does possess limited redistributional aspects, particularly in relation to floating charges.[9] Before the abolition (with some exceptions) of administrative receivership, it could fairly be said that English law adopted a contractual approach to control, allowing the holders of global security through fixed and floating charges to displace the management of the debtor company by appointing an administrator receiver, whose control of all the assets largely inhibited action by other creditors and left a liquidator waiting on the sidelines until completion of the receivership. That has now changed and our insolvency law has moved away from contractualism to neutral management through an administrator or liquidator, whose appointment imposes an automatic stay on the enforcement of individual claims.

---

[8] Gerard McCormack, "Apples and Oranges? Corporate Rescue and Functional Convergence in the US and UK" (2009) 18 Int. Insol. Rev. 109.

[9] See paras 8–49 et seq.

As in other jurisdictions, English law offers two alternative routes for an insolvent company: on the one hand, reorganisation, and on the other, disposal of the company's business as a going concern or sale of its assets and, in either case, distribution of proceeds. Administration is an interim procedure which is a prelude to one or other of these or, if they are not achievable, to realisation for the benefit of a secured creditor having a fixed and floating charge over all or substantially all of the company's property.

With these preliminary remarks we can turn to the particular objectives of corporate insolvency law.

Restoring the company to profitable trading

2–03   This objective is realised in only a small percentage of cases, usually as the result of a CVA (whether as part of or without an administration), the appointment of an administrator or a contractually agreed reorganisation ("workout") which may take a variety of forms, including conversion of debt into equity, so that the loans to the company are extinguished and the quondam lenders become shareholders.[10] Sometimes an administrator is able to restore the company to profitable trading and hand back control to the directors. But while this is specified by the Insolvency Act 1986 as the first objective to be considered by an administrator, that is not how it has worked out in practice. The general experience has been that the Enterprise Act 2002 has had little effect in restoring insolvent businesses to profitable trading. The most common outcome of insolvency proceedings, of whatever kind, is cessation or disposal of the company's business and the winding up of the company. The primary concern of administrators and administrative receivers is to safeguard the business and its assets for the benefit of creditors rather than to keep the company in being as a viable trading entity.[11] In most cases, this is achieved by getting the business into a position where it can be sold on a going concern basis, after which the company usually ends up in liquidation. The majority of large corporate insolvencies are dealt with by informal workouts, or restructurings, without any formal insolvency proceeding, although an increasingly dominant form of workout is the pre-packaged administration ("pre-pack") by which, after independent valuation or market testing, a buyer is found willing to take over the business under a sale agreement that is held in escrow until the appointment of an administrator, upon which the sale is completed.[12]

---

[10] See further below, paras 12–10 and 12–43.

[11] See below, paras 10–05 and 11–23.

[12] An administrator has power to sell without either court approval or the laying of proposals before creditors (*Re Transbus International Ltd* [2004] 1 W.L.R. 2654), and this facilitates a rapid sale where time is of the essence. See further below, para.11–39.

Maximising returns to creditors

This objective has three distinct aspects. First, it necessitates a rule to ensure that the company's assets are not removed from the reach of creditors on the onset of insolvency. Hence the "anti-deprivation" rule which is designed to strike down arrangements that would have the effect of reducing on insolvency the assets available for the general body of creditors. This rule is distinct from the rule of *pari passu* distribution. The former is concerned to ensure that the size of the pie available for division is not improperly reduced, the latter with the appropriate division of the pie. Both rules are examined in detail in Chapters 7 and 8. Secondly, the objective of maximising returns to creditors reflects the fundamental assumption underlying insolvency law that the interests of individual creditors, and in particular their rights to collect in the debts due to them by one or other of the methods of enforcing payment of judgment debts, must give way to the collective interest of the general body of creditors. The free-for-all in which the race goes to the swiftest and individual assets of the company are picked off one by one in the process of execution is seen as inimical to the efficient organisation of the company's affairs for the benefit of creditors as a whole. This is considered best achieved through a collective debt collection procedure involving the ascertainment of the company's liabilities, the collection and realisation of its assets and the distribution of the proceeds by way of dividend among creditors in the statutory order of priority. Whether in any given case a particular creditor does better by pursuing an individual remedy or seeking a collective proceeding through winding up or administration will, of course, depend on the action taken by other creditors, and in particular on the order in which executions against assets of the company are effected and whether the execution process will be frustrated before completion by the company's being put into winding-up, administration or administrative receivership. The various perceptions of the individual creditors as to the possible outcomes of individual versus collective action provide a typical example of the prisoner's dilemma in game theory.[13] Thirdly, the interests of creditors are in principle to be given precedence over all other interests. So in a winding up only a very a limited measure of statutory support is given to employees,[14] whilst in an administration the interests of shareholders, employees and the wider community come low down on the priority list of most administrators.

2–04

---

[13] Where the question of whether a prisoner is released or serves a term of imprisonment and, if so, the length of that term, is made to depend on whether both prisoners confess, one only confesses or both refuse to confess, and neither prisoner knows the intentions of the other. See Thomas H. Jackson, "Bankruptcy, Non-Bankruptcy Entitlements, and the Creditors' Bargain" 91 Yale L.J. 857 (1982).

[14] See below, para.2–24 and paras 8–20 et seq.

Providing a fair and equitable system for the ranking of claims

2–05   Equally important in any statutory insolvency regime are the rules governing the ranking of creditors' claims and the distribution of dividends. Since the ranking of claims has no significance for the general body of creditors except in the context of an entitlement to dividend, and since dividends are distributed only in a winding up or administration, it follows that the statutory rules of priority are in general confined to winding up and administration and have no function in other insolvency proceedings. To this rule there are two exceptions. The holder of a debenture secured by a floating charge is postponed to preferential creditors as regards any property comprised in the charge of which he takes possession[15] or which comes into the hands of a receiver he appoints;[16] and the provisions relating to the prescribed part[17] apply not only in liquidation or administration, but also where there is a provisional liquidator or a receiver.[18] As will be seen, English corporate insolvency law adopts the general principle that pre-liquidation rights are to be respected, but also plays a limited redistributive role through rules of subordination and avoidance.[19]

Identifying the causes of the company's failure and imposing sanctions for culpable management by its directors and officers

2–06   The insolvency of a company causes loss to its creditors and hardship to its employees, many of whom are likely to lose their jobs. Moreover, the government has a particular interest in the insolvency of a company for it is very often a creditor for unpaid taxes, in addition to which the National Insurance Fund will be exposed to wage-related and redundancy claims by dismissed employees. Accordingly, insolvency legislation provides for the investigation by the liquidator into the causes of failure, the imposition of criminal and/or civil liability on anyone concerned in the management of the company who has been guilty of culpable acts or omissions causing loss to creditors[20] and the disqualification for a specified period of those considered unfit to be directors from participating in the future management of a company.

    In theory, therefore, there is adequate machinery to deal with delinquent directors. Unhappily, in practice, the position is rather different. The task of bringing an offender to book is expensive, time-consuming and uncertain in

---

[15] Companies Act 2006 s.754.
[16] Insolvency Act 1986 s.40.
[17] See below, paras 6–38 et seq.
[18] Insolvency Act 1986 s.176A.
[19] See below, para.3–02.
[20] See Ch.14 as to civil sanctions imposed by the Insolvency Act 1986 for fraudulent and wrongful trading. Criminal penalties for fraudulent trading are prescribed by s.993 of the Companies Act 2006.

result. In criminal proceedings for fraudulent trading, the prosecution has a heavy burden of proof, the trial is by jury, which has to be taken through often complicated accounts, records and evidence going back over a substantial period, the recollections of witnesses tend to become blurred with the usually lengthy passage of time before the case comes to trial and the defendant has every chance of being acquitted. In the result, no more than a handful of prosecutions for fraudulent trading are brought every year. Wrongful trading is much easier to establish, since the proceedings are civil, not criminal, so that the standard of proof is somewhat less onerous, and in any event it is open to the defendant to show that he took every reasonable step to avoid loss to creditors.[21] But civil proceedings also involve substantial expense and creditors are extremely reluctant to throw good money after bad unless they can be satisfied that there is a strong case and that the defendant is worth powder and shot. So while the pursuit of wrongdoers is in theory a central plank of insolvency law policy, in practice investigations are likely to be limited, and matters taken no further than a report by the office holder, unless there is compelling prima facie evidence of wrongdoing causing substantial loss and of the defendant's ability to meet any order made against him for contribution to the company's assets.

There is, however, an encouraging increase in the numbers of proceedings leading to disqualification, following a decision by the Insolvency Service to pursue a more aggressive policy in having unfit directors disqualified.[22] For this purpose, winding up orders can be made, and have been sought, even where the company has no assets.[23] The great majority of disqualifications are achieved by undertakings to the Secretary of State not to act in the management of a company, etc., rather than by disqualification orders.[24]

3. THE INSTRUMENTS OF CORPORATE INSOLVENCY LAW

Placement of the company and its assets under external management

Although directors of a company which is subject to an insolvent proceeding retain vestigial powers, they are for the most part displaced by the administrator, administrative receiver (in those cases where an administrative receiver can still be appointed) or liquidator. English corporate insolvency law is firmly attached to the notion that if a company fails it is necessary to bring in outside

2–07

---

[21] See below, paras 14–43 et seq.
[22] For data on this, see John Armour and Adrian Walters, "Funding Liquidation: A Functional View" (2006) 122 L.Q.R. 295 at 312–313.
[23] Insolvency Act 1986 s.125(1); and *Bell Group Finance (Pty) Ltd (in liquidation) v Bell Group (UK) Holdings Ltd* [1996] B.C.C. 505.
[24] See below, para.14–72.

management in the form of an individual who is now required to be a qualified insolvency practitioner. The concept of the debtor in possession which is embodied in Ch.11 of the American Bankruptcy Code[25] and under which the existing management is left in office, subject to the superintendence of the court and the creditors, is a feature of company voluntary arrangements, but not of administration. As regards administration, individual directors may be retained to assist the insolvency practitioner, with whom they have a statutory duty to co-operate, but it is he who performs the management functions previously undertaken by the board. The debtor-in-possession concept could become more widely adopted under the proposals for a restructuring moratorium put out by the Insolvency Service.[26]

Administrators and administrative receivers (where the latter can still be validly appointed) are given the widest possible powers of management by the Insolvency Act 1986.[27] These include the power to collect in the company's assets, dispose of assets, carry on or close down the business,[28] establish subsidiaries and transfer the whole or any part of the business and property to subsidiaries, bring proceedings and make arrangements and compromises on behalf of the company and petition for the winding up of the company.

The powers of liquidators are somewhat more restricted, reflecting the fact that the aim of liquidation is not rehabilitation, but disposal of the business and assets and distribution of the net realisations. Thus, a liquidator may carry on the company's business only so far as may be necessary for the beneficial winding up of the company and then only with the sanction of the court in the case of a compulsory winding up.[29] Some of the other powers are exercisable only with the sanction of the court or the liquidation committee.[30]

Substitution of collective action for individual rights of pursuit

2–08   Inherent in the winding up process, and also a crucial element in the administration procedure, is the freeze on the pursuit of individual debt enforcement remedies against the company in favour of collective action by the creditors as a whole through the medium of the liquidator in a winding-up or the administrator in an administration. If individual creditors were left free to pursue their rights and to enforce judgments by execution against the company's, assets these would quickly disappear, destroying the business enterprise and frustrating the purpose of the particular insolvency proceeding. Hence the legislative provisions by which the rights of individual pursuit

---

[25] See below, para.11–18.
[26] "Proposals for a Restructuring Moratorium—A Consultation" (July 2010).
[27] Sch.B1 para.59, s.42 and Sch.1.
[28] In cases of urgency an administrator can do this without the approval of the creditors, typically under a pre-packaged administration. See below, para.11–39.
[29] Insolvency Act 1986 Sch.4 Pt II para.5.
[30] Insolvency Act 1986 ss.165 and 167 and Sch.4 Pt I.

are suspended and the liquidator in a winding up is made responsible for determining the existence and quantum of the company's liabilities and distributing the net proceeds of realisations of assets among creditors in the form of dividends proportionate to their admitted claims,[31] while the role of the administrator in an administration is to lay proposals before the creditors for the achievement of the purpose for which the administration order was made. These proposals may include the distribution of assets among creditors in the administration, under a CVA or in a voluntary winding up.

However, not all types of insolvency proceeding involve the suspension of rights and remedies, and those that do are not applicable to all forms of right or remedy. Thus, winding up, while not changing creditors' rights into something juridically different as would be the case where a judgment was obtained,[32] converts unsecured creditors' rights of enforcement by legal proceedings into rights of proof in competition with other creditors, but does not affect the enforcement of security interests or other real rights. By contrast, administration[33] freezes the enforcement of both real rights and judicial remedies, including winding up, but does not bar other forms of self-help such as equitable or contractual set-off. Neither of these two proceedings interferes with any contractual right to accelerate the debtor company's liability or to terminate a contract for default in payment. Administrative receivership, where available, does not in theory affect the enforcement of the rights of individual creditors at all, but in practice it contributes powerfully to the orderly management of the company's affairs since all the assets are subject to the debenture holder's security and are taken into the possession or control of the administrative receiver, so that any judgment taken by an unsecured creditor is likely to prove a *brutum fulmen*, and his only effective weapon is to put the company into liquidation.

Statutory distribution scheme

Although winding up is no longer the only insolvency regime which is concerned with distributions among the general body of creditors, it remains the paradigm case, although increasingly administration is being used as a liquidation substitute. Whichever of the two processes is used, the Insolvency Act and Insolvency Rules lay down a detailed system of priorities for dealing with claims. These fall into four groups. Arranged in descending order of priority they are: the expenses of the liquidation, which are paid, not proved, and which now have priority over claims secured by floating charge assets; preferential debts, which rank at the head of provable debts; ordinary unsecured debts; and deferred debts, which come at the end of the line of

2–09

---

[31] Known technically as proofs of debt.
[32] *Wight v Eckhart Marine GmbH* [2004] 1 A.C. 147, *per* Lord Hoffmann at [26]–[27].
[33] And to a somewhat less extent, initiation of the administration process.

creditors. Shareholders receive nothing unless there is a surplus after all creditors' claims have been paid. The expenses of the liquidation have to be met in the prescribed order of priority. By contrast, creditors in each of the remaining three categories are not prioritised and rank *pari passu* among themselves. Secured creditors and the holders of other real rights (for example, suppliers of goods under reservation of title) are not affected by the priority rules, and can resort to the assets in which the security or other rights subsist in disregard of other creditors, except that a charge which as created was a floating charge is subordinate to the claims of preferential creditors and surrender of the prescribed part.[34] The policy underlying the statutory distribution scheme is discussed below.[35]

Avoidance of transactions and recovery of misapplied assets

2–10   A major instrument of corporate insolvency law is the set of statutory provisions under which transactions entered into by the company that are improper or unfair to the general body of creditors or that it would otherwise be unfair to allow to stand are made void or their effect is liable to be reversed on an application to the court by the office-holder. In principle, the assets of a company available to the general body of creditors upon a liquidation or for the purposes of an administration order are those owned by the company when it goes into winding up or administration. But those assets may have been depleted by dispositions and transactions which run contrary to the policy of insolvency law, whilst there may be other transfers or transactions which, although not affecting the net asset value of the company, unfairly favour one creditor at the expense of the general body of creditors, as by giving him a preference or other benefit at a time when the company was unable to pay its debts. Then again, the company may have given charges over its assets which were not registered in conformity with statutory requirements, thus potentially misleading creditors into believing that the company was still the owner of the assets transferred by it under the disposition.

In some cases, the transaction is made totally void; in other cases, although the transaction remains valid, its effect may be reversed so as to restore the status quo.[36] There is also a summary remedy against delinquent officers for the recovery of assets misappropriated or otherwise acquired by misfeasance.[37] It does not always follow that recoveries of assets by the liquidator under these statutory provisions will enure for the benefit of the general

---

[34] That is, a percentage of the assets subject to a floating charge which must be surrendered for the benefit of ordinary unsecured creditors, excluding the holder of the floating charge. See below, para.6–38.

[35] See below, paras 2–15, 2–18 and 2–23.

[36] See below, para.6–36 and Ch.13.

[37] Insolvency Act 1986 s.212. See below, para.14–14.

body of creditors; in certain cases they will be treated as part of the company's general assets so as to be picked up by a prior assignment or charge or by an after-acquired property clause in a debenture.[38]

Sanctioning of delinquent directors

Directors of an insolvent company are also exposed to criminal proceedings if guilty of fraudulent trading and can be required to contribute to the assets of the company in civil proceedings for fraudulent or wrongful trading.[39] They may also, in appropriate cases, be disqualified from acting as directors or being otherwise concerned in the management of companies for a specified period.[40]

2–11

Statutory authorisation of insolvency practitioners

Prior to the Insolvency Act 1985 any individual who was not an undischarged bankrupt could practise as an insolvency practitioner, without being required to have either a professional qualification or prior experience. The Cork Committee considered that one of the aims of a good modern insolvency law was "to ensure that the processes of realisation and distribution are administered in an honest and competent manner"[41] and recommended that insolvency practitioners be required to have a professional qualification and to have been in general practice for five years before acting as an insolvency practitioner.[42] That recommendation has been implemented in modified form by requiring insolvency practitioners to be qualified by authorisation from a recognised professional body, the Secretary of State or a competent authority designated by the Secretary of State.[43] There are also rules imposing statutory obligations on insolvency practitioners in the handling of money they receive and in relation to their functions as office-holders.

2–12

Dissolution of a company in winding up

Sooner or later, most insolvent companies end up in liquidation, voluntary or compulsory. The final act in the drama is to terminate the company's existence by having it dissolved and struck off the register of companies. Dissolution after winding up may occur in one of two ways. The first is where

2–13

---

[38] See below, paras 13–140 et seq.
[39] See below, paras 14–26 and 14–51.
[40] See below, paras 14–57 et seq.
[41] Above, n. 5,, para.198(g).
[42] ibid., para.758.
[43] Insolvency Act 1986 ss.230(2) and 390–392; and Insolvency Practitioners (Recognised Professional Bodies) Order 1986 (SI 1986/1764).

the carrying out of the winding up would serve no useful purpose because the realisable assets are insufficient to cover the costs of winding up and the affairs of the company do not require further investigations. In such a case, the official receiver, if he is the liquidator of the company, may apply for its early dissolution.[44] The second occurs where the winding up has been completed and the liquidator has vacated office.[45] In addition, there is now provision for dissolution of a company in administration where the administrator thinks that the company has no property which might permit a distribution to its creditors and sends notice to that effect to the registrar of companies.[46]

4. THE PHILOSOPHY OF CORPORATE INSOLVENCY LAW

2–14   The failure of a corporate enterprise potentially affects a wide range of interests. Those most immediately concerned are, of course, creditors, management, other employees and shareholders. But the failure may have wider repercussions. It may force customers and suppliers into insolvency; it may, in causing job losses, tear the heart out of the local community; in the case of a major bank or industrial company it may even affect the national economy, for example by undermining confidence or by removing a key player from the export market. The community at large may also have an interest in the continued performance of the company's obligations in public law, for example, in the clean-up of environmental pollution caused by the company's activities. So when a company becomes insolvent there are stark choices to be faced: should the sole or primary concern be to maximise returns to creditors? Or should it be to preserve the company and/or its business, even if this can only be done at some expense to creditors' rights? Is the primary concern the protection of private rights or of public interests?

The collapse of a major bank raises distinctive issues because of the central role played by banks in retail and wholesale financing and the risk of systemic failure resulting from the domino effect of the insolvency of a large bank. Hence the traditional view that some banks may be "too big to fail" and, if on the point of collapse, must be taken over or otherwise supported by the State or merged with or taken over by other banks willing to do so.[47] One way of

---

[44] Insolvency Act 1986 s.202.

[45] Insolvency Act 1986 s.205.

[46] Insolvency Act 1986 Sch.B1 para.84. As to revival of a dissolved company, see above, para.1–41, n.165.

[47] A striking exception to this approach was the decision of the US Federal Reserve Board to allow the parent company of the Lehman Brothers group to enter insolvency. It seems that the near-meltdown produced by this decision was not foreseen and that if it had been a different approach would have been adopted. See further above, para.1–57.

reducing the risk of such major failures is to ensure that a bank is not allowed to grow too large. Governments are also particularly sensitive to the adverse publicity resulting from potential loss to ordinary depositors, and since a good part of the losses stems from the high-risk investment activities of major banks, a perceived solution is to return to the rule embodied in the US Banking Act 1933[48] prohibiting commercial banks from engaging in investment banking. However, the US Government has adopted a different approach, enacting legislation to restrict the ability of banks to engage in proprietary trading, i.e. trading on their own account, or to acquire or retain any equity, partnership or other ownership interest in or sponsor a hedge fund or private equity fund.[49] Moreover, this would not have addressed the problems arising from the failure of Lehman Brothers, an investment bank. In the United Kingdom, as elsewhere, rules on capital adequacy are being tightened, and in addition the United Kingdom has enacted the Banking Act 2009, which introduced a special resolution regime for banks in difficulties, consisting of three stabilisation options, a special bank insolvency procedure and a special bank administration procedure.[50] But the debate on the "Too Big to Fail?" question continues to rage, since it raises acute issues as to the balance to be maintained between ensuring financial stability and avoiding moral hazard.[51]

It will be apparent, therefore, that there are serious questions to be addressed as to the legitimate province of corporate insolvency law and as to its philosophical foundations. Given the pragmatic way in which English law in general has developed, it is perhaps unsurprising, but nevertheless disconcerting, to discover the lack of a clearly articulated philosophy of law in this field. Scholars in North America have long been interested in the bankruptcy process,[52] and have devoted much time and effort to policy issues and theoretical constructs, as well as to empirical research, which has always been at a much greater level than in other jurisdictions and is beginning to become prominent.[53] More recently, academics and insolvency practitioners in the United Kingdom have begun not merely to identify the need for more information about insolvency and the impact of insolvency law—on which there is a serious dearth of hard data—and to explore policy issues and undertake or

---

[48] Commonly known as the Glass-Steagall Act after its legislative sponsors. The Act was repealed in 1999.

[49] Dodd-Frank Wall Street Reform and Consumer Protection Act, Public Law 111-203, July 21, 2010.

[50] See above, para.1–59. See also the special regime now in force for investment banks, above, ch.1, n.215.

[51] The danger that if investors and depositors are made immune from risk because of express or implicit government guarantees they will have no incentive to take prudent steps for their own protection, but on the contrary will seek high-yielding, and thus high-risk, investments and accounts.

[52] In this context, "bankruptcy" includes the liquidation of companies.

[53] See below, paras 2–15 and 2–18.

commission empirical research designed to cast light on the effectiveness of the legal regime governing individual and corporate insolvency, but also to concern themselves with normative theories of insolvency law.[54] Space does not permit more than a brief examination of these issues, on which there is now an enormous amount of literature, particularly in North America. But it is worth reminding the reader that normative theories of bankruptcy law are concerned not simply with the existing state of the law and its current objectives, but with the question of what those objectives should be and how best they may be achieved.[55]

The province of corporate insolvency law

To what extent should bankruptcy affect pre-bankruptcy entitlements?

2–15   How should we mark out the territory that should be occupied by corporate insolvency law? What is its legitimate province? These questions have been much debated among scholars in the United States. They divide into broadly two camps: the proceduralists, whose position is that the primary function of bankruptcy law is to respect pre-bankruptcy entitlements and to organise a collective procedure to that end; and the traditionalists, whose position, reflecting existing bankruptcy policy, is that bankruptcy law has a wider role to play and a wider range of interests to accommodate.[56]

Professors Baird, Jackson and Scott are leading proponents of the view that it is not for insolvency law to concern itself with employment protection or with wider community interests, or to re-order substantive rights acquired under pre-bankruptcy law. Their thesis is that whatever rights and privileges may be conferred in other areas of law, insolvency law has one overriding goal: to allocate the common pool of assets in such a way as to maximise benefits for creditors as a whole.[57] The attainment of this goal is threatened whenever individual creditors take unilateral action to fish in the common pool of assets without regard to the interests of other fishers. Therefore,

---

[54] See, e.g. Rizwaan Jameel Mokal, *Corporate Insolvency Law: Theory and Application* (2005); and Vanessa Finch, *Corporate Insolvency Law: Perspectives and Principles*, 2nd edn (2009).

[55] There are scholars who distrust the value of normative theories, arguing that what matters is the reality of bankruptcy law and policy. For a discussion of the issue, see Donald R. Korobkin, "The Role of Normative Theory in Bankruptcy Debates" 82 Iowa L. Rev. 75 (1996). See below, para.2–15.

[56] For an overview by an English scholar of some of the principal theories advanced, see Finch, *Corporate Insolvency Law*, 2009, Ch.2.

[57] See Thomas H. Jackson, "Bankruptcy, Nonbankruptcy and the Creditors' Bargain" 91 Yale L.J. 857 (1982); Jackson, *The Logic and Limits of Bankruptcy Law* (Cambridge, MA: Harvard University Press,1986); D.G. Baird and T.H. Jackson, "Corporate Reorganizations and the Treatment of Diverse Ownership Interests: A Comment on Adequate Protection of Secured Creditors" 51 Univ. of Chicago Law Rev. 97 (1984); and T. Jackson and R. Scott, "On the Nature of Bankruptcy: an Essay on Bankruptcy Sharing and the Creditors' Bargain" 75 Virginia Law Rev. 155 (1989).

insolvency law must impose a collective procedure for the taking of fish. One other principle, which relates to substantive rights, must be strictly observed if the aim of collective asset maximisation is to be fulfilled, namely that insolvency law must respect the pre-bankruptcy ordering of entitlements. A particular aspect of this principle is that there must be rigid adherence to the absolute priority rule, i.e. that shareholders receive nothing until creditors have been paid in full.[58] This is a rule not only of insolvency law, but also of pre-insolvency law in that, under rules designed for the protection of creditors, a company may not reduce its share capital except in accordance with Ch.10 of Pt 16 of the Companies Act 2006.[59]

The thesis, then, is that it is the function of insolvency law to translate pre-bankruptcy assets and liabilities into the bankruptcy forum with minimal dislocation.[60] Among the reasons advanced for this view are that: (i) the redistribution of rights on insolvency would create a perverse incentive for a particular creditor who would be advantaged by the change to go for an insolvency proceeding even if this would not be in the general interest of the creditors; and (ii) insolvency law should distribute assets according to a scheme for which creditors lacking prior knowledge of how they would fare in relation to other creditors in the event of the debtor's insolvency could have been expected to bargain ex ante in order to maximise the collective value of the proceedings, and that they would have seen this as best achieved, as regards unsecured creditors, by an offer of *pari passu* distribution and, as regards secured creditors, by an assurance that their priority would be maintained and their participation in the collective process compensated so as not to affect the net value of their pre-bankruptcy entitlements, i.e. there would be no transfer of net value from them to unsecured creditors. It follows that rehabilitation of the debtor's business is not a legitimate objective of bankruptcy law, except to the extent that it is designed to maximise recoveries for existing entitlement holders.

These basic propositions, which have been developed into very elegant and sophisticated theories of bankruptcy law based on the concept of the creditors' bargain, have not passed unchallenged. Powerful attacks have been launched both on the notion that the sole purpose of insolvency proceedings is to maximise returns to creditors and on the assertion that it is not the function of bankruptcy law to alter relative pre-bankruptcy entitlements.[61] Professor Elizabeth Warren has argued convincingly that there are

---

[58] See Baird and Jackson, "Bargaining after the Fall and the Contours of the Absolute Priority Rule" 55 Univ. of Chicago Law Rev. 738 (1988).

[59] It is, however, entitled to make distributions out of profits available for the purpose. See generally P.L. Davies (ed.), *Gower and Davies: Principles of Modern Company Law*, 8th edn (London: Sweet & Maxwell, 2008), Chs 12 and 13.

[60] T.H. Jackson, "Translating Assets and Liabilities to the Bankruptcy Forum" 14 *Journal of Legal Studies* 73 (1985).

[61] See Elizabeth Warren, "Bankruptcy Policy" 54 Univ. of Chicago Law Rev. 775 (1987).

other interests to consider apart from those of creditors, and that to concentrate so exclusively on maximising returns to creditors is a dangerous oversimplification of the nature and purpose of the bankruptcy process.[62] She has also joined with Professor Jay Westbrook in a trenchant criticism of the use of theoretical constructs to reach policy conclusions without any attempt being made to verify by empirical evidence the premises upon which they are based.[63] However, it is fair to say that in recent years much valuable empirical work has been undertaken in both the United States and the United Kingdom.

2–16   The elegance and conceptual clarity of the theories advanced by Jackson and his colleagues have greatly illumined our understanding of the functions of corporate insolvency law. But there is force too in the criticisms that have been made. In postulating that insolvency law should respect the bargain that actual creditors in their own best interests would have reached ex ante as to how the debtor's assets should be distributed in the event of its insolvency, the creditors' bargain theory and similar contractarian theories[64] based on a hypothetical agreement among creditors take it as axiomatic that only those with consensual claims against the debtor's assets at the time of opening of the insolvency proceedings (compendiously described as "owners") qualify for consideration as parties to the hypothetical bargain. These include shareholders of the insolvent company. The holders of non-consensual interests, such as tort creditors, employees with regard to job preservation claims, local suppliers as regards the impact on their business of the insolvent company's failure and the local community at large when a major employer ceases trading, might deserve distributions of the assets in bankruptcy, but this would be conceptually different in character from distributions based on the *ex ante* bargain.[65] Thus, bankruptcy law is essentially procedural in character; its role is not to affect pre-bankruptcy the substance of entitlements, but rather to organise a collective regime designed to ensure the preservation of those entitlements to the maximum extent

---

[62] Warren, "Bankruptcy Policy", 1987, pp.800 et seq.

[63] Elizabeth Warren and Jay Lawrence Westbrook, "Contracting Out of Bankruptcy: An Empirical Intervention" 118 Harv. L. Rev. 1197 (2005). This article led to vigorous exchanges with Professor Robert K. Rasmussen, "Empirically Bankrupt" Col. Bus. L. Rev. 179 (2007), arguing that the empirical study was fundamentally flawed, and a response, "The Dialogue Between Theoretical and Empirical Scholarship", U. of Texas Law and Econ. Research Paper No.88, Harvard Public Law Working Paper No.137.

[64] Not to be confused with contractualism, which is concerned with control of the bankruptcy process rather than the ordering of priorities. See below, para.2–20.

[65] Jackson and Scott, "On the Nature of Bankruptcy", 1989, p.177, disclaiming any intent to assess the normative value of distributions to non-consensual interests. For a criticism of the exclusion of non-consensual creditors from representation in the hypothetical creditors' bargain, see Donald R. Korobkin, "Contractarianism and the Normative Foundations of Bankruptcy Law" 71 Tex. L. Rev. 541, 554–555 (1993).

possible.[66] Only to this extent is the rehabilitation of an insolvent business a legitimate function of bankruptcy law.[67]

But there are values to be protected that go beyond the interests of those with accrued rights at the commencement of the insolvency process. One of these is the investigation of the directors' conduct of the directors with a view to sanctions for improper trading and disqualification so as to protect the public against future misconduct, a course of action available in England through the winding up process even where the company has no assets at all.[68] Another is the interest of the workforce in preserving its investment of labour, expertise and loyalty to the enterprise, and a third is that of the community at large, for example, in the continuance of the business[69] or the payment of clean-up costs of pollution.[70] To focus so exclusively on maximising returns to creditors is to ignore the fact that there may be different ways of protecting creditors, some of which will also benefit other interests, such as those of employees, shareholders and the local community, and in so doing may even advance creditors' interests.

The answer Professors Baird and Jackson give to all this is that if interests other than those of common pool creditors are to be protected, this should be done outside bankruptcy law and the protection should not be exclusive to bankruptcy, but should be slotted into the scheme of relative non-bankruptcy entitlements. So if it is desired to give special rights to employees or tort claimants, that should be done through labour law or tort law and in the latter case should be a protection equally available against closure of a business outside bankruptcy. It is then for bankruptcy law to respect the special non-bankruptcy entitlement given by labour law or tort law,[71] rather than itself to create a new entitlement in the bankruptcy.

The argument is neat, but ultimately unpersuasive, for it overlooks the fact **2–17** that certain problems confronting claimants outside the common pool creditors arise specifically due to the company's insolvency and for no other reason. For example, in England, labour law already gives rights and remedies to employees who are wrongfully or unfairly dismissed or are made

---

[66] For a developed treatment of the procedural theory of bankruptcy law, see Charles W. Mooney, Jr, "A Normative Theory of Bankruptcy Law: Bankruptcy As (Is) Civil Procedure" 61 Wash. & Lee L. Rev. 931 (2004). See also Douglas G. Baird, "Bankruptcy's Uncontested Axioms" 108 Yale L.J. 573 (1998).

[67] Thus, stopping an insolvent company from closing a plant which it would be entitled to close outside bankruptcy is not legitimate: Mooney, "A Normative Theory of Bankruptcy Law", 2004, pp.957–959.

[68] See above, para.2–06.

[69] For a discussion of this communitarian approach, see Karen Gross, "Taking Community Interests into Account in Bankruptcy" 72 Wash. Univ. L.Q. 1031 (1994). The communitarian approach has been criticised for its indeterminacy and the wide range of interests that would have to be considered.

[70] See below, para.2–25.

[71] See Jackson, *The Logic and Limits of Bankruptcy Law*, 1986, pp.31–32; and D. Baird, "Loss Distribution, Forum Shopping and Bankruptcy: a Reply to Warren" 54 Univ. of Chicago Law Rev. 815 (1987).

redundant. But in the pursuit of these remedies against a solvent company, the former employees are not competing with other creditors, for there are by definition enough assets to meet all claims. It is only on insolvency that the ranking of unsecured claims arises. There is therefore no scope for the *general law* to prescribe priority for employees or tort claimants. Such a priority rule would make no sense except in the context of bankruptcy, when there is not enough to go round. Moreover, to treat bankruptcy law as confined to creditors confronting the common pool problem is surely to pre-judge the very question in issue. It is also wholly inconsistent with insolvency laws around the world, all of which include provisions for claimants outside the common pool creditors.[72] Again, the event most likely to attract the need for investigation of a company's affairs and disqualification of its directors is the company's insolvency; and it is exclusively in the context of insolvency that the need arises to provide for the making of orders against directors guilty of fraudulent or wrongful trading, requiring them to contribute to the shortfall of net assets.

If it is conceived to be beneficial to bring all creditors within a collective proceeding for the common benefit of creditors, rather than allow each cred-itor to pursue his own self-serving interests, why should it not be equally ben-eficial to require creditors as a class to co-operate as part of a wider class of beneficiaries that would include employees and shareholders as regards interests and expectations beyond their pre-bankruptcy entitlements? There was a time in England when the receiver and manager (now termed the administrative receiver) appointed by a debenture holder would see his task as being to move in, sell up and get out. If the business could be sold on a break-up basis to produce enough to cover the debt due to the debenture holder, why invest effort in keeping the business going? Nowadays, receivers (in those limited cases where administrative receivership is still available) take an altogether broader view of their role. If there are alternative courses of action, one of which will benefit creditors only, while another, with a little delay, will confer benefits on employees and shareholders without significant detriment to the creditors, then why should it not be a legitimate function of insolvency law to have regard to those wider interests? They may be subor-dinate to those of creditors, but that is not a ground for denying that they have their own place in the scheme of things. This theme has been repeated again and again in statements of national policy concerning the role of insolvency law.

"We believe that the aims of a good modern insolvency law are . . .

(i)   to recognise that the effects of insolvency are not limited to the private interests of the insolvent

---

[72] For the current position under English law, see below, paras.2–22, 2–24.

and his creditors, but that other interests of society or other groups in society are vitally affected by the insolvency and its outcome, and to ensure that these public interests are recognised and safeguarded;

(j) to provide means for the preservation of viable commercial enterprises capable of making a useful contribution to the economic life of the country . . ."[73]

"The fundamental purpose of reorganization is to prevent a debtor from going into liquidation, with an attendant loss of jobs and possible misuse of economic resources."[74]

It is also quite clear that insolvency law has at least some redistributional role **2–18** to play, for every legal system has developed rules under which some categories of unsecured claim (for example, government taxes[75] and unpaid wages) are accorded preferential status, and may even trump certain forms of security interest,[76] while other categories are ranked below the general body of creditors.[77] Moreover, the concept of the creditors' bargain is fraught with difficulty. Although the creditors' bargain is based on the concept of what real-world parties will do, the parties presented are not in truth real-world parties at all—for example, those examined in a major market survey—but imaginary characters invested with the qualities that the scholars would attribute to real persons. But what is the source of identification of these qualities and how do we know that they have any relationship with the qualities of actual creditors? Since in practice creditors do not act collectively in taking credit decisions, we have no idea how they would proceed, or what range of factors they would take into consideration, if they were to come together before taking their credit decisions. Secondly, the models that have been constructed postulate that each creditor would be in a position to gauge with reasonable accuracy the relative risks and benefits of individual versus collective action and would thus be guided to a rational outcome. But since no creditor can be sure, in the absence of agreement, what other

---

[73] *Insolvency Law and Practice*, Report of the (Cork) Review Committee (Cmnd. 8558, 1982), para.198. See also paras 235–240 making the same point in relation to individual bankruptcy.

[74] *NLRB v Bildisco & Bildisco*, 465 US 513, 528 (1984), citing views expressed by Congress, HR Rep. No.95–595, p.220 (1977). See further G.D. Pont and L. Griggs, "A Principled Justification for Business Rescue Laws: A Comparative Perspective (Part I)" (1995) 4 I.I.R. 189.

[75] Which were at one time preferential debts in the United Kingdom, but ceased to be so several years ago. See below, para.8–20.

[76] e.g. in England charges which as created were floating charges are subordinate to the claims of preferential creditors (see para.8–21), in addition to which a percentage of net assets subject to a floating charge has to be surrendered to form a fund for unsecured creditors (see para.6–38).

[77] For an argument that large creditors, who are better able to withstand the impact of the debtor's insolvency than small creditors, should suffer some diminution in their distributional rights in favour of small creditors, see Karen Gross, *Failure and Forgiveness: Rebalancing the Bankruptcy System* (New Haven: Yale University Press, 1997), Ch.10.

creditors will do, such a risk assessment is impossible and any creditors' bargain reached on the basis of it cannot in reality be more than a gamble for each creditor—possibly an inspired gamble, in some cases, but a gamble all the same. It is hard to see how such a notional bargain could form the basis of a rational system of insolvency law. Moreover, if one could imagine a situation in which all creditors, secured and unsecured, *were* to come together to decide what was to happen in the event of disaster, would it not be likely that unsecured trade suppliers, on having had brought home to them as a group the relative vulnerability of their position, would insist on a slice of the corporate cake as a condition of their co-operation?

This, indeed, was for a long time the central problem of law and economics theories of insolvency, that they began with untested hypotheses of creditor behaviour which, by the end of the argument, had become imperceptibly converted into findings of fact and are thus made the basis for firm conclusions and policy recommendations. A simple example will suffice. It is assumed as an article of faith that a creditor taking security will charge a lower rate of interest than one who lends on an unsecured basis.

> "Secured creditors, for example, would have paid for their priority position by accepting a lower rate of return and should therefore be allowed to retain the benefits of their initial bargain by receiving an equivalent value for their collateral in bankruptcy. Unsecured creditors, on the other hand, would have obtained a higher interest rate by foregoing security and, in so doing, would have assumed a greater risk that their claims would not be fully satisfied upon default and subsequent bankruptcy. The participants in the bankruptcy bargain could thus be expected to honor this relationship by maintaining the secured creditors' nonbankruptcy entitlements and by preventing redistribution in bankruptcy from secured creditors to unsecured creditors and the debtor."[78]

At the time this statement was made, there appears to have been little or no empirical evidence that it was true.[79] It was essentially a postulate of the rational man and it assumed a situation in which a bank or other lender was prepared to offer and quote for the alternatives of a secured or unsecured loan to the same borrower. But there are many cases in which this is simply not how lending works. Banks charge what they consider the market will bear. In many cases, a bank does not quote a lower rate of interest *because* it is secured; it takes

---

[78] Jackson and Scott, "On the Nature of Bankruptcy", 1989, p.161.

[79] More has been done since. See the valuable article by John Armour, "The Law and Economics Debate About Secured Lending: Lessons for European Lawmaking?" (2008) *European Company and Financial Law Review* (Special Volume: *The Future of Secured Lending in Europe*) 3 at 10–11. However, the empirical evidence, such as it is, seems at best equivocal (see text and n.80, below). Professor Armour points out (at p.13) that "the theoretical claims about interest rate reductions are made *ceteris paribus*—that is, all other things being equal", but goes on to add: "Of course, in the real world, all other things are seldom equal."

security because of a perceived risk of non-payment and may charge a *higher* rate because of the risk.[80] Similarly, the mere fact that a loan is unsecured does not necessarily mean that the bank will charge a higher rate. Indeed, as regards blue-chip borrowers, one could stand the argument on its head and note that with the intense competition for their business among banks, at least in periods when finance is more readily available than at present, they would be well placed to refuse to give security at all, and this same bargaining power would enable them to negotiate the most favourable lending rate.

A strict adherence to the absolute priority rule would not only disadvan- **2–19** tage those generally considered in need of some protection, such as employ- ees, but could also deprive creditors themselves of the co-operation from shareholders which in some reorganisations has been shown to be essential to the success of the plan. If shareholders are to be persuaded not to obstruct a reorganisation considered desirable by creditors, they too will expect a slice of the pie, although experience has shown that their ability to negotiate this is extremely limited in the case of failure of a large public corporation where management decides to co-operate with the creditors and abandon the shareholders.[81] Indeed, it is not only shareholders who may be left with noth- ing. In a complex restructuring, mezzanine creditors[82] are likely to be squeezed out altogether by senior creditors or given only a modest solatium, for example, through the issue of shares to them in a company higher up in the chain than the operating company—a form of structural subordination.[83] With a view to meeting considerations of this kind, the creditors' bargain the- ory was reconstructed to hypothesise that creditors would not necessarily bargain for total priority and that what should be predicated is an ex ante bargain based on an assumed willingness by all creditors to bear in some degree the risk of an exogenous, or externally imposed, disaster, as opposed to one caused by internal management.[84] Dr Rizwaan Mokal, who is also critical of the creditors' bargain model on a number of counts, has advanced an alternative theory which he terms the authentic consent model.[85] This model, which extends participation to parties other than creditors, for exam- ple, shareholders and employees, builds on the work of John Rawls and is based on the concept of "dramatic ignorance", in which the parties to the creditors' bargain are ignorant not only of insolvency outcomes and of how

---

[80] See the studies cited by Ephraim Benmelech and Nittai Bergman, "Collateral Pricing" (2007, http://papers.ssrn.com/sol3/papers.cfm?abstract_id=960787),, who, however, suggest that, at least in the case of aircraft financing, the ability to pledge collateral lowers the cost of external financing.
[81] I am indebted to Professor Jay Westbrook for this insight.
[82] See below, para.12–04.
[83] See above, para.1–04.
[84] See Robert E. Scott, "A Relational Theory of Secured Financing" (1986) 86 Col. L. Rev. 901; and Jackson and Scott, "On the Nature of Bankruptcy", 1989.
[85] Rizwaan Jameel Mokal, "The Authentic Consent Model: Contractarianism, Creditors' Bargain, and Corporate Liquidation" (2001) 21 *Legal Studies* 400; and see now Mokal, *Corporate Insolvency Law*, 2005.

other creditors would behave, but also of their own attributes, such as whether they are voluntary or involuntary creditors, and whether they are in a dominant or subordinate position. The assumption to be made is that all parties are free and equal and enter into a bargain that is fair and just.[86]

The problem confronting those who have to consider to what extent the different variants of the creditors' bargain theory should influence bankruptcy policy is that most of them assume an original position in which the various players act in an economically rational manner according to a single set of criteria. This may be an elegant model, but has no necessary connection with fact. Human beings and even corporations are usually actuated by wider considerations than pure economic rationality. Moreover, the factors that enter into a rational decision are often much more diverse than those on which economic reasoning is based, so diverse indeed that it is hard to see how any single set of *ex ante* assumptions can be expected to match the complex realities of business life or to accommodate the many categories of decision-maker and the variety of circumstances in which their decisions may have to be made. Finally, in the real world, the relevant players, even if influenced by the widest range of considerations, do not and cannot act rationally all the time. All of this is not to decry the value of normative theories, simply to note the danger of equating models with fact in reaching policy conclusions.

A leading international insolvency specialist has also attacked the creditors' bargain theory as based on a central assumption of a common pool of assets to which creditors would *ex ante* wish to have recourse.

"This central assumption is not in accord with basic economic facts and legal structures. There is no common pool of assets to which creditors wish to have and could have a claim before bankruptcy. Credit, unless it is secured by specific pieces of property, is normally extended with the expectation that not only payment of interest but also repayment of capital will come from the debtor's income, not from a sale of fixed assets. The debtor's income is normally produced not by the assets themselves, but rather by the activities of the debtor which only partly consist in using the assets. This means that, if the debtor is (or has) an enterprise, income is produced by the organizational set-up consisting of owners, managers, employees, and a functioning network of relations with the outside world, particularly with customers, suppliers, and, under modern conditions, with various government agencies; and it is the expected stream of income

---

[86] For a not unsympathetic critique of Mokal's book (*Corporate Insolvency Law*), see Anthony Duggan, "Contractarianism and the Law of Corporate Insolvency" (2005) 42 Can. Bus. L.J. 463 and the response by R.J. Mokal, "Contractarianism, Contractualism and the Law of Corporate Insolvency" [2007] Sing. J. of Legal Studies 51.

produced by the ongoing enterprise that allows for the normally peaceful coexistence of creditors with claims of different maturities."[87]

Who should control the bankruptcy?

Leading American scholars have pointed out that earlier debates on the theory of bankruptcy concentrated heavily on priority issues and tended to neglect the central question of control of the bankruptcy assets.[88] Only recently has attention focused on the relevance of the distinction between cases where there is a dominant security interest and those where security interests are diffused among a number of creditors, none of whom is dominant.[89] This is a crucial consideration in considering whether as a matter of policy insolvency proceedings should fall within the public domain or whether on the other hand the State should permit parties to contract out of bankruptcy rules and adopt their own arrangements, leaving public control as the default situation where no relevant contracts are in place. In America, contractualism has secured powerful support[90] and equally powerful opposition.[91] One of the major problems is that in any given case there are likely to be numerous contracts made at different times, on different terms and in different circumstances, and even if there were statutory provision for public notice of agreements, that would not, in relation to any one agreement, assist those who became creditors prior to that agreement. Professor Jay Westbrook has effectively demonstrated that contractualism cannot function effectively unless there is a creditor holding a dominant security interest, without which "the contractualist proposals are crippled by intractable problems".[92] But control of the bankruptcy process by a dominant secured creditor is incompatible with the concept of neutral management and can lead to a failure to realise full value for the assets for the benefit of other creditors. Indeed, as Professor Westbrook points out, it was just such a consideration that led the

2–20

---

[87] Axel Flessner, "Philosophies of Business Bankruptcy Law: An International Overview" in Jacob S. Ziegel (ed.), *Current Developments in International and Comparative Corporate Insolvency Law* (Oxford: Oxford University Press, 1994), pp.25–26.

[88] Jay Lawrence Westbrook, "The Control of Wealth in Bankruptcy" 82 Texas L. Rev. 795 (2004); Douglas G. Baird and Robert K. Rasmussen, "Control Rights, Priority Rights, and the Conceptual Foundations of Corporate Reorganizations" 87 Virginia L. Rev. 921 (2001); Ronald J. Mann, "Strategy and Force in the Liquidation of Secured Debts" 96 Mich. L. Rev. 159 (1997); and Robert K. Rasmussen, "Debtor's Choice: A Menu Approach to Corporate Insolvency" 71 Texas L. Rev. 51 (1992).

[89] Westbrook, "The Control of Wealth in Bankruptcy", 2004.

[90] Alan Schwartz, "A Normative Theory of Business Bankruptcy" 91 Va. L. Rev. 1199 (2005); Alan Schwartz, "A Contract Theory Approach to Business Bankruptcy" 107 Yale L.J. 1807 (1998); and Ramussen, "Debtor's Choice", 1992.

[91] Lynn M. LoPucki, "The Case for Cooperative Territoriality in International Bankruptcy" 98 Mich. L. Rev. 2216 (2000); Lynn M. LoPucki, "Contract Bankruptcy: A Reply to Alan Schwartz" 109 Yale L.J. 317 (1999); and Westbrook, "The Control of Wealth in Bankruptcy", 2004.

[92] Westbrook, "The Control of Wealth in Bankruptcy", 2004, p.831.

United Kingdom largely to abandon the institution of administrative receivership, which did indeed operate in large degree as a privately contracted ordering of the business and assets of an insolvent company.[93] The problem is less acute in the case of a secured creditor whose claim exceeds the value of the collateral he holds.[94]

A novel approach, which certainly has the merit of giving advance notice of the applicable rules while avoiding the problem of multiplicity of contracts and contract choices, is the so-called "menu" approach advocated by Professor Robert Rasmussen, which would allow an enterprise, upon its formation, to select from a statutory menu of options the particular bankruptcy regime that would apply in the event of its becoming insolvent.[95] This certainly solves the notice problem, but it commits the enterprise and other interested parties to a pre-determined bankruptcy regime which may in the event turn out to be quite unsuited to the maximisation of returns to creditors.[96]

Even before the debtor's default, the creditor is in a position to monitor the debtor's business activities and performance and to indicate what corrective measures are required if the creditor is not to withdraw its support.[97] After default, a creditor whose security interest covers the whole or substantially the whole of the debtor's assets will be in a position to play the lead role in any out-of-court restructuring.[98] Moreover, such a creditor is in a position to divest the directors of their management powers by making an out-of-court appointment of an administrator.[99] At one time the creditor's position was even stronger in that it could appoint an administrative receiver, whose role was to take control of the company's business and assets and deal with them for the benefit of the creditor who appointed him. But the Enterprise Act 2002 introduced a marked shift away from dominant secured party control in insolvency towards a more neutral concept of management for the benefit of all creditors, and an abandonment of the position taken by the

---

[93] This is because by definition an administrative receiver was one appointed by the holder of a floating charge which, with other charges, covered the whole or substantially the whole of the debtor company's assets. The result was that there were few, if any, free assets available to unsecured creditors outside liquidation or to the liquidator himself prior to discharge of the receivership by collection of sums sufficient to pay off the appointing creditor's claims and, from the proceeds of assets subject to a floating charge, preferential debts. Thus, if receivership was followed by liquidation, the liquidator had to remain on the sidelines while the receiver was in office, and the appointment of a receiver was usually a bar to the making of an administration order. See below, paras 10–36 and 10–67 et seq.

[94] See below.

[95] Robert K. Rasmussen, "Debtor's Choice: A Menu Approach to Corporate Bankruptcy" 71 Texas L. Rev. 51 (1992).

[96] See to the same effect Jay Westbrook, "The Control of Wealth in Bankruptcy" 22 Texas L. Rev. 795, 832 (2004); and, more recently, E. Warren and J. Westbrook, "Contracting Out of Bankruptcy: An Empirical Intervention" 118 Harv. L. Rev. 1197 (2005).

[97] However, the creditor should refrain from too much interference in the conduct of the business, which in the event of liquidation or administration may expose it to liability as a shadow director. See below, paras 14–35 et seq.

[98] See below, para.12–10.

[99] See Chapter 11.

Cork Committee that the rescue culture should be concerned only with the restoration of the business, not the preservation of the company owning the business,[100] although in practice it is the preservation of the business that is the prime concern. With limited exceptions,[101] administrative receivership has been abolished and replaced by administration, and the function of the administrator is to have regard to the interests of creditors generally, not merely the secured party appointing. Even so, a major secured creditor is in a strong position of influence when it comes to both the choice of administrator and the approval of proposals he puts forward. Further, a creditor who is under-secured has a strong incentive to monitor performance by the administrator and to ensure that the business or assets are disposed of to best advantage and that the costs of the administration, including the administrator's fees, are kept within reasonable bounds.

Even without control of the enterprise, a secured creditor has control over the assets the subject of the security interest, and in the case of liquidation (but not administration) the secured creditor remains entitled to realise the collateral without the consent of the liquidator or the court.[102]

Economic interest and the right to participate

In some degree English insolvency law limits participation in the insolvency process to those who have an economic interest in the outcome. For this reason, secured creditors are not allowed to vote or participate in distributions unless they surrender their security or limit their claims to the excess of the valuation they place on their security,[103] while unsecured creditors who have no hope of receiving any return are not entitled to be consulted on a scheme of arrangement under s.899 of the Companies Act 2006[104] and an administrator is not obliged to call an initial creditors' meeting if the company has insufficient property to enable a distribution to be made to unsecured creditors except out of the prescribed part.[105] The hapless position of unsecured

2–21

---

[100] "In the case of an insolvent company, society has no interest in the preservation or rehabilitation of the company as such, though it may have a legitimate concern in the preservation of the commercial enterprise" (Report of the Insolvency Law Review Committee, "Insolvency Law and Practice", para.193). See also Robert Stevens, "Security After the Enterprise Act" in Joshua Getzler and Jennifer Payne (eds), *Company Charges: Spectrum and Beyond* (Oxford: Oxford University Press, 2006), p.153.

[101] See below, paras 10–05 et seq.; and John Armour, Audrey Hsu and Adrian Walters, "Corporate Insolvency in the United Kingdom: The Impact of the Enterprise Act 2002" (2008) 5 *European Company and Financial Law Review* 148.

[102] See below, para.8–47.

[103] Insolvency Rules 1986 r.2.40. See below, para.8–47.

[104] *Re Bluebrook Ltd* [2010] B.C.C. 209; and *Re Tea Corp Ltd* [1904] 1 Ch. 12.

[105] Insolvency Act 1986 Sch.B1 para.52(1)(b). It is, of course, possible that the company's assets will subsequently be enhanced by recoveries under the provisions for the avoidance of transactions, as to which see Ch.13.

creditors in most cases no doubt explains their apathy in the insolvency process, with most unsecured creditors not exercising their right to attend creditors' meetings.[106] But the policy of permitting exclusion of creditors with no economic interest in the outcome of insolvency proceedings is not uniform. For example, an administrator can be required to summon an initial creditors' meeting if requested to do so by creditors whose debts amount to at least 10 per cent of the debts of the company[107] even if they have no prospect of receiving any return. Similarly, there is nothing to prevent an unsecured creditor from presenting a winding up petition even if it is clear that there will be nothing for unsecured creditors. Of course, there are some aspects of insolvency in which creditors have an interest going beyond a material return, for example, in having delinquent directors brought to book.

Social and economic policy

2–22   What is clear from any comparative survey is that the role of corporate insolvency law cannot be constructed in the abstract, and that the extent to which the law of a particular country adheres to or deviates from the principle of collective maximisation of returns for creditors in an insolvency is directly related to its pre-insolvency social and economic policy.[108] Civil law jurisdictions tend to be more debtor-oriented than common law jurisdictions and to place greater emphasis on workers' rights and the importance of preserving the enterprise. This is particularly true of France,[109] which has a long tradition of government paternalism, coupled with strong judicial control over debt collection activity. English law traditionally stood at the opposite end of the spectrum, with an extremely liberal attitude towards creditors' rights, self-help and the use of contractual remedies, coupled with a steady erosion of workers' rights and immunities. However, the changes made by the Enterprise Act 2002 undoubtedly affected the enforcement of creditors' rights. American law is significantly more pro-debtor than English law, imposing greater restrictions than English law on enforcement both within

---

[106] Insolvency Service, "Enterprise Act 2002—Corporate Insolvency Provisions: Evaluation Report" (January 2008), *http://www.insolvency.gov.uk/insolvencyprofessionandlegislation/legislation/EA02CorporateInsolvencyReport.pdf* [Accessed February 15, 2011], p.115, referring to research by Dr Sandra Frisby; and Office of Fair Trading, "The Market for Corporate Insolvency Practitioners" (June 2010), *http://www.oft.gov.uk/shared_oft/reports/Insolvency/oft1245* [Accessed February 15, 2011], paras 4.47 and 4.56. In para.7.43 of the last report, the OFT urged regulators to consider making changes to address difficulties faced by unsecured creditors in the insolvency process.

[107] Insolvency Act 1986 Sch.B1 para.52(2)(a).

[108] See in particular José M. Garrido, "The Distributional Question in Insolvency: Comparative Aspects" (1995) 4 I.I.R. 25.

[109] See Axel Flessner, "Philosophies of Business Bankruptcy Law: An International Overview" in Jacob S. Ziegel (ed.), *Current Developments in International and Comparative Corporate Insolvency Law* (Oxford: Oxford University Press, 1994), p.22.

and outside bankruptcy. There is no doubt that English corporate insolvency law places a heavy emphasis on creditors' rights and adopts as a general principle respect for the pre-liquidation ordering of entitlements. Moreover, English law, like other legal systems, does recognise certain types of claim as justifying a priority in bankruptcy that they would not otherwise enjoy. Thus, within defined limits the claims of employees rank ahead of other unsecured creditors, reflecting the fact that they lack the opportunities open to other creditors to limit their risk and typically have no source of income other than their wages. The same was true of government taxes, but persistent criticism of Crown preference led to its abolition.[110]

One has to be careful not to overstate the distinction between the civil law and the common law, because whether a particular bankruptcy rule, such as an automatic stay, is considered to favour a creditor may depend on whether the creditor is secured, in which case he might be happier without an automatic stay, or unsecured, where an automatic stay might be welcome. Moreover, there are significant variations within the same legal family, whether it is common law or civil law.[111] Finally, there has been a general move within Europe towards a greater concern for the debtor.[112]

The implications of the rescue culture

Reference has already been made to the growth of the rescue culture and the increasing attention paid to the rehabilitation of the business. The corporate reorganisation which this typically entails cannot readily be achieved without some interference with pre-existing entitlements. So far as possible, the UK legislation seeks to avoid a significant diminution in a creditor's substantive rights. Rather, it aims to restrict their enforcement, as by imposing a temporary freeze on remedial measures or by requiring the creditor to accept a monetary equivalent rather than enforcement *in specie*. So rights to non-monetary performance of a contract which the liquidator declines to have performed by the company are converted into a right to prove for damages for the loss suffered through non-performance; the initiation of administration, in or out of court, imposes a freeze on most forms of enforcement, a freeze which continues during the currency of the administration;[113] and the

2–23

---

[110] See below, para.8–20.
[111] John Armour, Gerard Hertig and Hideki Kanda, "Transactions with Creditors" in Reinier Kraakman et al (eds), *The Anatomy of Corporate Law*, 2nd edn (Oxford: Oxford University Press,2009), p.147. See also John Armour et al, "How do Legal Rules Evolve? Evidence from a Cross-Country Comparison of Shareholder, Creditor and Worker Protection" (2009) 57 Am. Jnl of Comp. Law 579.
[112] Régis Blazy et al, "How do the Courts Choose between Different Bankruptcy Outcomes? The Results of a French Survey" in W.-G. Ringe, L. Gullifer and P. Théry (eds), *Current Issues in European Financial and Insolvency Law* (Oxford, Hart Publishing, 2009), Ch.12.
[113] Insolvency Act 1986 Sch.B1 paras 42 and 43. See below, paras 11–53 et seq.

administrator of a company is in certain conditions given power to dispose of charged assets free from the security interest.[114] But in certain cases there is a positive disturbance of the relative entitlements that existed before bankruptcy. For example, even a crystallised floating charge is subordinate to the claims of unsecured preferential creditors.[115] A still more significant interference with pre-bankruptcy entitlements is the obligatory surrender of a percentage of assets subject to a floating charge ("the prescribed part") so as to make this available to unsecured creditors.[116]

So the redistribution of pre-liquidation rights does feature, albeit in a limited way, in corporate insolvency law. On the other hand, its primary concern has to be with the disposal or closing down of the company's business and the collection and distribution of net realisations. It is not equipped, except in a very small degree, to address wider economic or social problems, such as the maintenance of employment or the protection of the environment. These can only be tackled by measures outside the purview of insolvency law, for example, employment legislation and environmental regulation, to which reference will be made shortly. Moreover, it may be found necessary not merely to leave these larger issues to be dealt with outside corporate insolvency law, but positively to subordinate insolvency law to economic interests that are considered to require a higher priority. Striking in this respect is the almost total exclusion from rules of insolvency law of market contracts, market charges and financial collateral,[117] an exclusion dictated by the desire not to jeopardise the dominance of the City of London as a financial centre by exposing normal market operations and dealings in uncertificated securities to a challenge under insolvency law.

Insolvency law and employment

2–24   There is an almost inevitable tension between creditors' rights on insolvency and those of the company's employees. Where the business is viable and the failure is due to short-term problems or mismanagement, the insolvency practitioner will usually wish to maintain a substantial part of the workforce,[118] and if the business is sold off or hived down to a newly formed subsidiary, the employees may be able to treat their contracts of employment as transferred to the new owner of the business under the Transfer of Undertakings

---

[114] Insolvency Act 1986 s.70(1). See below, paras 11–82 and 11–84.
[115] See below, para.8–51.
[116] See below, para.6–38.
[117] See above, paras 1–60 et seq.
[118] The importance attached by insolvency practitioners to turnaround and job preservation is shown by the change of name of the leading association of insolvency professionals from SPI (Society of Insolvency Practitioners) to R3 (the Association of Business Recovery Professionals) and the creation of the Society of Turnaround Practitioners (now the Institute for Turnaround).

(Protection of Employment) Regulations 2006,[119] which apply not only to the transfers of businesses, but also to a change of service provider. But whether with or without such a transfer or change of service provision, employees of an insolvent company face the prospect of redundancy, particularly where the insolvency practitioner considers that the company is substantially over-staffed or where the business is disposed of and merged with that of another company which sees the opportunity to make efficiency savings. Whilst employees clearly have a legitimate interest in the outcome of their employer's insolvency, it would obviously be unrealistic to impose on the insolvency practitioner a duty to protect that interest by keeping them in employment where this would damage the company's economic prospects. Quite apart from the duties he owes to existing creditors, the insolvency practitioner will be guilty of fraudulent trading if he allows the company to incur new debts when there is no real prospect that these will be paid when due or reasonably soon thereafter,[120] and may incur a liability for wrongful trading if the company goes into insolvent liquidation and he has failed to take proper steps to minimise loss to creditors.[121]

So other ways have to be found of giving help to employees of an insolvent company. These are provided partly by employment law, partly by insolvency law and partly by the law governing occupational pensions. Employment law gives a measure of protection through statutory provisions as to the transfer of undertakings,[122] and entitlements to arrears of pay, redundancy payments and compensation for unfair dismissal, all backed by the National Insurance Fund.[123] Under the Insolvency Act 1986, a claim for arrears of pay is preferential, within defined limits.[124] Broadly speaking, these measures do no more than protect in insolvency, and then only to a limited degree, rights the employee would have had against the employer outside winding up. Under ss.257 and 258 of the Pensions Act 2004, the transferee is required to ensure that transferred employees who were active members of the transferor's occupational pension scheme, or who were eligible to be, or would have been if they had been employed by the transferor for a longer time, are, or are eligible to be, active members of the transferee's occupational pension scheme. The same Act establishes a Pension Protection Fund (PPF) to provide compensation to employees of an insolvent employer where a pension scheme provided by the employer is under-funded and certain other conditions are fulfilled. Alternatively, the PPF Board may be asked to assume responsibility for taking over the scheme. The Pensions Regulator also has power to issue a contribution notice requiring an employer or a person connected

---

[119] SI 2006/246. See Finch, *Corporate Insolvency Law*, 2009, Ch.17, as to TUPE and other legislation relating to the impact of insolvency on employees.

[120] See below, para.14–23.

[121] See below, paras 14–30 et seq.

[122] See above.

[123] See generally Peter Totty, Gabriel Moss and Nick Segal, *Insolvency* (London: Sweet & Maxwell, looseleaf), Ch.H-15.

[124] See below, para.8–22.

with, or an associate of, the employer to make good a shortfall where that person took steps to avoid or limit pension fund liabilities[125] or the Regulator is of the opinion that the relevant act or failure has detrimentally affected in a material way the likelihood of accrued scheme benefits being received.[126]

In addition, the Pensions Regulator may issue financial support directions requiring an associate or connected person to secure and maintain the provision of financial support for the pension scheme where the employer is under-resourced and it is reasonable to require the person concerned to make a financial contribution,[127] as where funds have been channelled away from the employer company to another member of the group,[128] and to issue a contribution notice if financial support directions are not complied with.[129]

Insolvency law and the environment

2–25   We have noted instances where English corporate insolvency law departs from the general principle that relative entitlements acquired before winding up should be respected. These departures are all concerned with the adjustment of private rights. Altogether more dramatic, although in a restricted area, is the potential impact of public law, and in particular the prospect that an insolvency practitioner might be obliged, under pain of criminal sanctions against the company, to utilise the debtor company's assets to meet the cost of remedying environmental pollution caused by the company's activities, pursuant to a clean-up order under the Environmental Protection Act 1990.[130] This could completely wipe out the assets that would otherwise have been available to meet creditors' claims. The issue has been litigated in several North American cases and has featured in England in relation to a liquidator's right to disclaim a waste management licence as onerous property, thereby bringing an end to the company's duties as licensee.[131] It is not without interest that in *Re Mineral Resources*

---

[125] See s.38 of the Act and *Bloom v Pensions Regulator* [2010] EWHC 3010 (Ch). The first contribution notice, for just over £5 million, was issued to Michel Van De Wiele NV on May 14, 2010 in relation to the Bonas Group pension scheme. As to the ranking of the liability in the employer's insolvency, see paras 8–36, 8–37 and 11–103.

[126] s.38A, inserted by the Pensions Act 2008 Sch.9 para.2.

[127] Pensions Act 2004 s.43(2).

[128] On July 8, 2010 the Pensions Fund Regulator issued financial support directions to 25 companies in the Nortel Group. A major factor was the conclusion of the Determinations Panel that the group had increasingly been operating as a single entity, the distinction between the separate corporate entities of the individual members of the group being largely ignored. This was the second FSD to be issued, the first having been issued to Sea Containers in June 2007.

[129] Such liabilities are provable debts if the financial services directions are issued before the insolvency event, but are payable as expenses of the liquidation if issued on or after the insolvency event. See below, paras 8–36, 8–37 and 11–103.

[130] ss. 26(1) and 82(2). See Totty, Moss and Segal, *Insolvency*, Ch.H1, and below, paras 8–30 et seq.

[131] In *Re Celtic Extraction Ltd* [2001] Ch. 475; and *Environment Agency v Hillridge* [2004] 2 B.C.L.C. 358. See below, para.8–30.

Ltd,[132] another case concerning disclaimer of a waste management licence, Neuberger J. held that the interests of the community in a healthy environment should prevail over the fair and orderly winding up of companies, so that the principle of "polluter pays" in the Environmental Protection Act 1990 took precedence over the distribution rules in the Insolvency Act 1986, with the result that although the waste management licence was property, it was not property of a kind that could be disclaimed; and he reached this conclusion in full agreement with counsel that the effect would be to make clean-up costs an expense of the liquidation payable in priority to the claims of unsecured creditors. This aspect of the judge's decision was later overruled by the Court of Appeal in *Re Celtic Extraction Ltd*,[133] on the ground that an important aspect of implementation of the oft-repeated public policy requirement that the property of unsecured insolvents should be divided equally amongst unsecured creditors was the power of disclaimer, without which the available assets would be appropriated to the claims of future or prospective creditors, so that such a power should not be regarded as overridden unless statute so provided. Nevertheless, the *Mineral Resources* case and the discussion of it in *Celtic Extraction* provide a vivid illustration of the way in which the interests of the community may come into consideration as of a higher order than those of unsecured creditors.

The recognition and ordering of creditors' rights

Who are to be considered creditors?

It would be possible to take a very restricted view of creditor status and to confine creditors for insolvency purposes to those whose claims were in existence and had already matured at the time of winding up. Indeed, one could go further and exclude the holders of non-consensual claims, such as claims in tort, from the insolvency process. Such an approach, however, would be grossly unfair both to unsecured creditors holding unmatured claims and to tort creditors. In relation to the former, it would discriminate against long-term lenders and make them bear the primary loss burden despite their contribution to the company, which arguably is even more important than that of short-term suppliers of credit. In consequence, it would discourage long-term loan capital and be likely to precipitate contractual debt acceleration in the event of default. Holders of existing but unmatured debts thus qualify for inclusion in the distribution stakes.[134] So too do contingent creditors,[135] so long as their claims are not so shadowy as to be incapable of valuation.

2–26

---

[132] *Re Mineral Resources Ltd, Environment Agency v Stout*, [1999] 1 All E.R. 746.
[133] [2001] Ch. 475.
[134] See further below, para.8–41.
[135] Insolvency Rules 1986 rr.4.86 and 12.3(1).

Similarly, to exclude tort claimants would be to debar those who are sharing with contract creditors in a common disaster. Claims for unliquidated damages in contract have always been allowed; similar claims in tort were at one time not provable unless reduced to liquidated sums by judgment or agreement, supposedly because of the much greater difficulty of valuing them than unliquidated claims in contract, but the distinction, criticised by the Cork Committee, has been abandoned.[136] Indeed, under a change in the insolvency rules a claim in tort is now a provable debt if by the date the company goes into liquidation the cause of action has accrued or would have accrued but for the fact that no actionable damage had by then occurred.[137] This change was made in the light of the decision in *Re T & N Ltd*,[138] where a company in administration was potentially faced with a massive number of asbestos claims and the administrators sought directions as to whether future asbestos claimants were "creditors" capable of being bound by a scheme of arrangement and also whether they would be able to prove as creditors in a winding up. The evidence showed that a long period, commonly more than 20 years, might elapse between exposure to asbestos and the onset of any recognisable medical consequences. The judge held that while asbestos claimants who had not at the time of liquidation been found to have detectable medical consequences of exposure were nevertheless creditors for the purpose of a scheme or CVA, since for that purpose "creditors" was not limited to persons with provable debts, their claims were not provable in the liquidation under r.13.12(2) of the Insolvency Rules, because the occurrence of loss or damage was an essential ingredient of the relevant tort: negligence. Such claimants would now be entitled to prove in the liquidation as creditors.

So in deciding who qualifies for admission to the insolvency process no distinction is made between voluntary (consensual) and involuntary (non-consensual) claimants. The objection to the admissibility of unliquidated tort claims was on the ground of the perceived difficulty of valuation, not their involuntary character. Indeed, some would argue that involuntary creditors should enjoy a higher status in the priority ranking than voluntary creditors, because they did not intend to assume a risk, but had it thrust upon them. A similar argument could be made for Crown preference in relation to taxes and duties. But English insolvency law has not followed this path; on the contrary, Crown preference was initially restricted under the Insolvency Act 1986[139] and subsequently abolished by the Enterprise Act 2002,[140] while tort claimants rank with other unsecured creditors. The distinction between voluntary and involuntary creditors is in any event less clear than might be supposed. Many debtors delay payment and take credit which was never

---

[136] Insolvency Rules 1986 rr.12.3(1) and 13.12.
[137] Insolvency Rules 1986 r.13.12(2).
[138] [2006] 1 W.L.R. 1728.
[139] See below, para.8–20.
[140] Enterprise Act 2002 s.251, amending Sch.6 to the Insolvency Act 1986.

offered, and many creditors, faced with competition in the market, have little choice but to allow credit to be taken, with or without their prior agreement. So the distinction is not so much between voluntary and involuntary credit as between having and not having a real choice whether to allow the debt to be incurred in the first place.

Priority entitlements and their impact on the insolvency regime

It is a fundamental principle of insolvency law, and one which has many aspects,[141] that the debtor's assets are to be distributed *pari passu*. In the language of the Act of 1542, the proceeds of realisations were to be distributed among creditors "rate and rate alike, according to the quantity of their debts". However, we have already remarked that the expenses of the liquidation have to be deducted in computing the net realisations available for distribution and that no dividends can be paid to ordinary unsecured creditors until the preferential debts have been paid in full. Moreover, with some exceptions it is only those assets in which the company has a beneficial interest that are available to its creditors. So property held by the company as bailee or trustee does not form part of the common pool, nor do goods in the possession of the company under a contract of sale reserving title until payment, if payment has not been completed. Again, property beneficially owned by the company but over which it has given security rights constitutes an asset only to the extent of the company's equity of redemption, measured by the difference between the value of the asset and the amount of the secured indebtedness. Similarly, the liquidator takes control of the company's assets subject to equities, such as rights of set-off and rescission of contracts. All these illustrations of the rule that only assets of the company are available for distribution are manifestations of the broader principle, previously discussed, that corporate insolvency law respects pre-liquidation rights, and in particular property rights and equities.

When bankruptcy was first introduced, property and trust law were much less developed than they are today. Trusts were largely confined to land, debts were not considered assignable, the common law drew a clear distinction between transfers of property and uncompleted agreements for transfer, and non-possessory security over goods was almost invariably considered fraudulent.[142] But since the sixteenth century there has been an explosive growth in the concept of ownership and other real rights (rights *in rem*). The maxim that equity treats as done that which ought to be done, so that an agreement for a mortgage is treated in equity as a completed mortgage, is now so taken for granted that we no longer realise what an enormous step

2–27

---

[141] See below, paras 8–07 et seq.
[142] *Twyne's Case* (1602) 3 Co. Rep. 80b.

this was, one which largely obliterated the distinction between a *ius in re* and a *ius ad rem*, between a right *in* an asset and a personal right *to* an asset.[143] Thus evolved the concept, remarkable to the eyes of civilians, of an informal security able to be created by pure agreement without any act of conveyance and, in the case of goods, without even the requirement of writing.

2–28   Nor was this all. Recognition of the non-possessory security interest in existing personal property was rapidly followed by its extension in equity to future property and, in the case of companies, to global security capable of covering all classes of asset, present and future, to secure all forms of existing and future obligation. The peak of sophistication was reached with the development of the floating charge, a security in a shifting fund of assets from time to time held by the company and given under an agreement which left the company free to dispose of the assets in the ordinary course of business, but in certain eventualities, including those specified by contract between the parties, became converted into a full-blooded specific security.

Even now we have not exhausted the range of real rights and rights having comparable effect which are available to the creditor. A profusion of quasi-security devices developed. The retention of title under contracts of sale and hire-purchase agreements, blessed by the courts as falling outside the legal regime governing usury and bills of sale, grew in popularity and became extended to cover products and proceeds and to secure not only the price of the particular goods, but all current-account indebtedness. Netting arrangements between parties engaged in mutual dealings became ever more sophisticated.[144] The so-called "flawed asset" was conjured up by ingenious practitioners.[145] It has even been held, by-passing theoretical objections, that a bank can take a charge over its own customer's credit balance.[146] Meanwhile, equity lawyers had developed the resulting trust, where money paid or property transferred for a purpose which had failed was held to be impressed with a trust in favour of the payer or transferor; and more recently the constructive trust has been forged into a restitutionary proprietary weapon of enormous power which shows few signs of abating.

The result of all of these developments has been disastrous for the ordinary unsecured creditor. Every new property right, every added security interest, every proprietary restitutionary remedy, every equity, has eroded his stake in the insolvency process. Add to this the categories of debt still enjoying preferential status[147] and it can readily be seen that the lot of the general body of creditors is a very unhappy one, with the result that they

---

[143] See R.M. Goode, "Ownership and Obligation in Commercial Transactions" (1987) 103 L.Q.R. 433.

[144] See below, Ch.9.

[145] *Re Goode on Commercial Law*, edited by Ewan McKendrick, 4th edn (London: Penguin Books and LexisNexis, 2009,), pp.652–653.

[146] *Re Bank of Credit and Commerce International S.A. (No.8)* [1998] A.C. 214.

[147] See *Goode on Commercial Law*, 2009, pp.914–915; and below, para.8–20.

display understandable apathy when it comes to participation in the insolvency process. The *pari passu* rule remains the guiding principle of distribution in English winding up, but the free assets available to meet ordinary unsecured claims are in the typical case so small that there is little on which the principle can bite.[148] Thus, in those cases where the insolvency estate is swollen by recoveries in respect of void or voidable transactions, it is likely to be the preferential creditors who are the main beneficiaries.

The justification for protecting ownership and security rights

It is now far too late to turn back the clock and unwind equitable security interests, equities and resulting and constructive trusts, although not too late to change our insolvency law and bring the more extended forms of constructive trust into the ambit of our rules on preferences and transactions at an undervalue or subject them to the exercise of judicial discretion which would take account of the existing or potential interests of unsecured creditors.[149] But if we leave on one side the more doubtful (in policy terms) extensions of equitable proprietary rights, we can see that the protection of ownership and security interests rests on sound principles. Rights of ownership should in principle be respected, for if they are not upheld on insolvency the distinction between property and obligation becomes largely meaningless.[150] The same is true of security interests. To deny recognition of the secured creditor's real rights upon the debtor's insolvency would be to use the very event against which the security interest was designed to give protection as the ground for its destruction. The economic justification for upholding security rights was well put by Professors Jackson and Kronman in a much-cited article published 26 years ago:

2–29

"... if the law denied debtors the power to prefer some creditors over others through a system of security agreements, a similar network of priority relationships could be expected to emerge by consensual arrangement between creditors. Permitting debtors to encumber their assets achieves the same result, but in a simpler and more economical fashion. If a debtor has more than two or three creditors, free-rider and holdout difficulties are likely to plague any attempt on the part of creditors to work

---

[148] See below, paras 3–07 and 8–04.
[149] See Roy Goode, "Property and Unjust Enrichment" in *Essays on the Law of Restitution*, edited by Andrew Burrows (Oxford: Clarendon Press, 1991), Ch.9.
[150] However, ownership has not always been fully protected in English bankruptcy law. Section 38 of the Bankruptcy Act 1914 embodied a concept of reputed ownership by which goods in the possession of the bankrupt under such circumstances as to make him the reputed owner were brought within the bankrupt's estate. The concept was not formally abolished until the repeal of the Act by the Insolvency Act 1985, by which time it had become largely a dead letter anyway.

out a set of priority relationships among themselves. These transaction costs can be avoided by allowing the debtor himself to prefer one creditor over another. The rule permitting debtors to encumber their assets by private agreement is therefore justifiable as a cost-saving device that makes it easier and cheaper for the debtor's creditors to do what they would do in any case."[151]

In policy terms, the secured creditor is accorded priority because he bargained for it; other creditors who chose to lend unsecured cannot complain of their subordinated position.[152] If I may be allowed the indulgence of quoting from an earlier paper of my own on the subject:

"The bargain element is widely accepted as a proper ground for giving the secured creditor priority so long as the grant of security does not involve an unfair preference and other creditors have notice of the security interest, so that they are not misled into thinking that the assets comprising the security are the unincumbered property of the debtor. The battle rages over three crucial questions: in what circumstances should new value be required as a condition of making a security interest effective against other creditors? where it is to be required, what should suffice to constitute new value? and what classes of creditor should be entitled to complain of want of value or absence of notice?"[153]

I shall explore these issues later in relation to the avoidance of transactions on winding up or administration.[154]

---

[151] "Secured Financing and Priorities Among Creditors" 88 Yale L.J. 1143, 1157 (1979).
[152] See R. M. Goode, "Is the Law Too Favourable to Secured Creditors?" (1983–84) 8 Can. Bus. L.J. 53, 57.
[153] Goode, "Is the Law Too Favourable to Secured Creditors?", 1983–84, pp.57–58.
[154] See below, Ch.13.

Chapter 3

The Principles of Corporate Insolvency Law

Although the Insolvency Act 1986, with its 587 sections and 20 schedules, obviously embodies the heart of corporate insolvency law, so that there is a natural temptation to commence any study of the subject by plunging straight into s.1 of the Act and working through the various statutory provisions in sequence, the Act itself is not the best starting point. One cannot understand corporate insolvency law without a thorough grasp of the fundamental principles underpinning the legislation. These are not brought together in the Act, nor, indeed, are they readily extracted from it. This is because corporate insolvency law for the most part recognises and adopts rights conferred by the general law and by contract. If, for example, we want to know the rights of a secured creditor when the debtor company goes into liquidation, we must first ascertain what rights he acquired before the winding up. Only then can we assess, in the light of the statutory provisions, the legal impact of winding up on the continued existence and enforceability of those rights. So also with rights under a contract. First, we must determine their scope under the general law; then we have to consider how far those rights are affected by the winding up. An examination of the statutory provisions is thus the last part of the analysis, not the first; and it is the interplay between the general law and the particular principles and rules of insolvency legislation that should engage our special attention. This interplay is reflected in a number of basic principles of corporate insolvency law, and it is to these that I now turn. For convenience of exposition, I shall take winding up as the paradigm, though for the most part the principles apply equally to administration.

3–01

First principle: corporate insolvency law recognises rights accrued under the general law prior to liquidation

This principle is of cardinal importance. Its effect is that relative entitlements created before liquidation are preserved, so that insolvency law will in

3–02

general respect the priority of proprietary over personal claims (and thus of secured over unsecured claims), the subjection of the company's proprietary or contractual rights to countervailing equities, such as rights of rescission,[1] the priority or subordination attached to securities by the terms of their issue and agreements between creditors for the subordination of secured or unsecured debt. In line with this principle, the general rule is that liquidation does not of itself terminate contracts or extinguish rights, though it does inhibit the pursuit of remedies.

> "The important point is that bankruptcy, whether personal or corporate, is a collective proceeding to enforce rights and not to establish them."[2]

So the starting position of insolvency law is that rights accrued prior to the insolvency proceeding[3] will be respected. To this principle there are important exceptions, and it is these which give the transactional side of corporate insolvency law its distinctive character. Most of the remaining principles are particular aspects of this first principle.

Second principle: only the assets of the debtor company are available for its creditors

3–03   This principle follows from the first. It is not the function of corporate insolvency to confiscate for the benefit of creditors assets in the company's possession or control which belong to others. Only that which is the property of the company at the time of liquidation or comes into its hands thereafter is available for its creditors. So assets held by the company on trust do not form part of its estate, nor do goods supplied to it under reservation of title. Similarly, assets over which the company has given security are not available

---

[1] In English insolvency proceedings, what constitutes an equity is governed by English law even if the asset in question is situated abroad or the transaction is otherwise governed by foreign law, and that equity will be enforced by an English court even if not recognised by the *lex rei sitae*. In *Re Scheibler, ex p. Holthausen* (1874) 9 Ch. App. 722, a firm of merchants, following negotiations for a line of credit with the appellants which were opened when the parties were in Prussia, deposited by way of security the title deeds to a house in Shanghai to cover their liabilities on bills of exchange and then became bankrupt. The Court of Appeal held that the contract was governed by English law under which the deposit created a valid security interest binding on the trustee, but that even if it had been governed by German law the contract was personally binding on those who signed the agreement to deposit the title deeds, and who signed it as a personal contract, and was therefore binding on the trustee. A similar decision was given by Luxmoore J. in *Anchor Line (Henderson Bros) Ltd* [1937] Ch. 483, citing *British South Africa Co v De Beers Consolidated Mines Ltd* [1910] 1 Ch. 354, *per* Swinfen Eady J. at 387. In this respect, English insolvency law may have the unusual effect of expanding pre-insolvency entitlements under the applicable foreign law.

[2] *Cambridge Gas Transportation Corp v Official Committee of Unsecured Creditors of Navigator Holdings plc* [2007] 1 A.C. 508, *per* Lord Hoffmann at [15].

[3] But not contractual provisions under which liquidation or administration is the trigger for removal of an asset from the company, contrary to the anti-deprivation rule discussed in Ch.7.

to the creditors except to the extent of the company's equity of redemption. Again, there are exceptions to the principle. The assets available for creditors may be swelled by the statutory avoidance or reversal of pre-liquidation transfers and transactions, for example, as transactions at an undervalue, preferences and floating charges which are void for want of registration or because they were given by an insolvent company for past consideration.[4] Transfers made after the commencement of the winding up are also void unless sanctioned by the court,[5] and since the winding up of a company not already in voluntary liquidation is deemed to relate back to the presentation of the petition,[6] assets of which the company had ceased to be the owner by the time of the winding up order may be brought back into its estate. In addition, a percentage in value of assets subject to a floating charge has to be surrendered to form a fund available to unsecured creditors[7] and liquidation expenses have priority over claims secured by a floating charge.[8]

As a corollary of the rule that only the company's assets are available for its creditors, the liquidator has no power *as liquidator* to sell assets not beneficially owned by the company or subject to a security interest,[9] although if the company is a trustee with management powers under an active trust the liquidator may, with the consent of the beneficiaries or under an order of the court, manage the trust property on behalf of the beneficiaries and realise trust assets as part of that management. Where the liquidator does so, his remuneration and expenses for so doing cannot be treated as expenses of the liquidation, being for the benefit of the trust beneficiaries rather than the company, and must be borne by the trust assets.[10] Conversely, any portion of the liquidator's work and expenses not attributable to the trust property ought in principle to be borne by the general creditors out of the company's free assets.[11] Nevertheless, the courts have in some cases been prepared to allow these to be taken, wholly or in part, from the trust assets,[12] although it is

---

[4] See below, Ch.13.

[5] Insolvency Act 1986 s.127; and below, paras 13–127 et seq.

[6] Insolvency Act 1986 s.129(2). See below, para.5–23.

[7] Insolvency Act 1986 s.176A; Insolvency Act 1986 (Prescribed Part) Order 2003, SI 2003/2097. See below, para.6–38.

[8] Insolvency Act 1986 s.176ZA.

[9] The position of an administrator is somewhat different as he may sell property subject to a floating charge as if it were not subject to the charge and may dispose of property subject to any other form of security by order of the court (Insolvency Act 1986 Sch.B1 paras 70(1) and 71(1)). See below, paras 11–82 and 11–83.

[10] *Re Berkeley Applegate (Investment Consultants) Ltd (No.3)* (1989) 5 B.C.C. 803, *per* Peter Gibson J. at 805; and *Re French Caledonia Travel Service Pty Ltd* (2003) 204 A.L.R. 353 (NSW Supreme Court). Despite this, in *Re G.P. Stores Ltd,* unreported July 29, 2004, HH Judge Weeks QC ordered costs of the liquidator attributable in part to charged assets to be paid in the first instance out of the free assets of the company. See Claire Sharp (2005) 18 *Insolvency Intelligence* 8.

[11] *Re French Caledonia Travel Service* Pty. Ltd above, n. 10.

[12] See, e.g. *Re London Local Residential Ltd* [2004] 2 B.C.L.C. 72. The basis of this decision by Evans-Lombe J. is unclear, since his conclusion seems inconsistent with his earlier reasoning rejecting the deductibility of all of the liquidator's heads of expense not attributable to the administration of property allegedly held on trust.

thought that this should be done only in exceptional cases, as where the trust assets form part of a commingled fund and it is difficult to distinguish between trust assets and assets beneficially owned by the company. In cases involving a commingled fund where the task of establishing each individual's beneficial entitlement would be complex and expensive, the courts have generally refused to apply the rule in *Clayton's Case*[13] and have directed that the fund, so far as comprising trust assets, be distributed among the beneficiaries *pro rata*.[14] Where the assets consisted partly of trust assets and partly of the company's own assets, Morritt J. ordered that the trust moneys be notionally aggregated with the company's assets and that there should be paid from the trust assets the proportion of the liquidator's total remuneration which the trust assets bore to the aggregate fund.[15]

Third principle: security interests and other real rights created prior to the insolvency proceeding are unaffected by the winding up

3–04   This principle follows from the first two. In general, a creditor holding a security interest or other real right is unaffected by winding up and may proceed to realise his security or assert other rights of property as if the company were not in liquidation. So firmly is this principle applied that where the instrument of charge provides for security in after-acquired property, the secured creditor can assert rights even over moneys or other assets falling in after the commencement of the winding up,[16] provided that the consideration for these was already executed before that time, as opposed to being furnished by the liquidator himself, for example, by performance of a contract entered into by the company.[17] The position is the same in administration except that the administrator can dispose of assets subject to a floating charge as if they were not so subject and the floating charge then ranks for priority in relation to the proceeds of sale.[18]

---

[13] *Devaynes v Noble, Clayton's Case* (1816) 1 Mer. 572, under which payments in a current account are allocated on the basis of first in, first out.

[14] *Barlow Clowes International Ltd v Vaughan* [1992] B.C.L.C. 910; *Re Eastern Capital Futures Ltd* [1989] B.C.L.C. 371; and *French Caledonia Travel Service*, cited above n.10.

[15] *Eastern Capital Futures*, cited above n.14.

[16] *Re Reis* [1904] 2 K.B. 769; and *Re Lind* [1915] 2 Ch. 345. See *Goode on Legal Problems of Credit and Security*, edited by Louise Gullifer, 4th edn (London: Sweet & Maxwell, 2008), paras 2–13 and 2–14.

[17] *Re Collins* [1925] Ch. 556. Where moneys come into the hands of the liquidator as the result of his procuring performance of the company's contract, these do not fall within the after-acquired property clause because they are at no time money of which the company is beneficial owner, but on the contrary from the moment of their receipt become subject to the so-called statutory trust for creditors upon which a company in liquidation is considered to hold its free assets. See *Ayerst (Inspector of Taxes) v C. & K. Construction Ltd* [1976] A.C. 167, and cases there cited, which embody the eighth principle referred to below. The trust is a trust for purposes, not for persons. See below, para.3–09.

[18] See above, n.9.

Fourth principle: the liquidator takes the assets subject to all limitations and defences

In asserting rights in the name of the company,[19] the liquidator stands in no better position than the company itself; he takes them as they stand, warts and all.[20] So where the company is a party to a contract, the other party remains entitled to raise any defences that could have been raised prior to the winding up and to exercise any rights of termination given by the contract.[21] The same is true of equities. In general, an equity, that is, a person's right to impeach or qualify a transaction by which another party acquires an interest in an asset, survives the other party's liquidation. An equity is not in itself an interest in property, nor on the other hand is it a mere right *in personam*; rather, it is an inherent limitation of the interest that has been acquired. A typical equity is a right to rescind a contract by reason of some external vitiating factor such as fraud, misrepresentation or undue influence. This right of defeasance constitutes an inherent qualification of the contract rights. So where a party is induced by the company's fraud or misrepresentation to enter into a contract for the sale of goods or the transfer of other property to the company, he does not lose his right to rescind merely by reason of the winding up.[22] The right of rescission can be a very useful remedy for an unpaid seller who was induced to sell by fraud or misrepresentation (for example, the furnishing of a cheque which the buyer company knew would be dishonoured), since ownership in the asset transferred revests in him upon rescission, whereas if he had asserted his right to the price under the contract of sale, he would have had to prove in competition with other creditors. Other

3–05

---

[19] Unlike a trustee in bankruptcy, in whom the bankrupt's estate vests immediately on his appointment taking effect (Insolvency Act 1986 s.306(1)), a liquidator does not acquire title to the assets of the company in liquidation unless this is vested in him by order of the court under s.145 of the Insolvency Act, a procedure rarely found necessary. What the liquidator acquires is control of the assets and the right to collect them in.

[20] For a recent example, see *Perpetual Trustee Co Ltd v BNY Corporate Trustee Services Ltd* [2010] Ch. 347, discussed below, paras 7–13–7–22. But the liquidator may by statute be able to assert *defences* which the company itself could not have raised prior to liquidation, e.g. that a security interest asserted by a creditor is void for want of registration or that a transaction relied on in proceedings against the company should be set aside as a transaction at an undervalue or a preference. Such defences will be discussed in detail in Ch.13.

[21] Thus, in *Stone & Rolls Ltd v Moore Stephens* [2009] 1 A.C. 1391, the House of Lords held that where a person who was the sole directing mind and will of the company obtained funds from banks for sham transactions, so that the company was to be treated as the perpetrator of the crime, not a victim, auditors sued by the liquidator for negligence were entitled to plead *ex turpi causa non oritur actio* as a defence to the claim. As to contractual provisions for the termination of a contract or a limited interest, see Ch.7.

[22] *Re Eastgate* [1905] 1 K.B. 465; and *Tilley v Bowman Ltd* [1910] 1 K.B. 745. See also *Perpetual Trustee Co Ltd v BNY Corporate Trustee Services Ltd* [2010] 3 W.L.R. 87, where the Court of Appeal upheld a provision for a change in priority upon (inter alia) an insolvency proceeding, on the ground that the "flip" provision under which the priority changed was an inherent qualification of the priority right. The case is discussed in detail in Ch.7.

types of equity are the right to apply for rectification of the contract or to have it set aside for mistake or breach of fiduciary duty; and the right of the holder of a crystallised floating charge to assert priority over a subsequent incumbrancer who took his security interest while the prior charge was still floating, but with notice of a negative pledge clause in the charge.[23]

These equities likewise survive the liquidation of the company against whom they are asserted. The pre-liquidation right of set-off is also an equity, but by exception to the general rule it is not exercisable against a party which has gone into liquidation, being displaced by the insolvency rules of set-off.[24]

A case which is difficult to reconcile with the principle that the liquidator takes subject to equities is the majority decision of the House of Lords in *British Eagle*,[25] a controversial decision discussed later.[26]

Fifth principle: a contractual provision for the removal of an asset from the estate of an insolvent company upon winding up is void as contrary to public policy

3–06   While under the previous principle corporate insolvency law treats a liquidator as taking the assets subject to defences and equities existing prior to the winding up, it is another matter altogether where the advent of liquidation is itself the trigger for a contractual provision divesting the company of an asset it previously held. Such a provision contravenes the anti-deprivation rule in that its effect is to remove from the reach of the general body of creditors an asset held by the company at the time of liquidation.[27] This principle is distinct from that of *pari passu* distribution, which is concerned to ensure rateable distribution among creditors and to avoid transactions which, although not reducing the net asset value of the company, unfairly benefit one creditor at the expense of others, while the anti-deprivation rule is aimed at transactions which improperly reduce the value of the company's assets, to the detriment of all unsecured creditors.[28]

---

[23] See *Goode on Legal Problems of Credit and Security*, 2008, para.5–40.

[24] *Goode on Legal Problems of Credit and Security*, 2008, paras 7–76 et seq.; and Philip Wood, *English and International Set-Off* (London: Sweet & Maxwell, 1989), Ch.7. The insolvency rule of set-off applicable to a company in liquidation is embodied in the Insolvency Rules 1986 r.4.90. The equivalent rule for administration is r.2.85, applicable where the administrator proposes to make a distribution.

[25] *British Eagle International Air Lines Ltd v Compagnie Nationale Air France* [1975] 2 All E.R. 390.

[26] See below, para.9–14. See also para.6–17.

[27] See Ch.7.

[28] See para.7–03.

Sixth principle: unsecured creditors rank *pari passu*

As mentioned earlier,[29] the *pari passu* principle is one of the most fundamen-   **3–07**
tal principles of corporate insolvency law.[30] All unsecured creditors are
required to share and share alike in a common pool of assets and realisations.
This principle, formerly confined to winding up, now applies also to administrations in which a distribution is made.[31] Agreements and transfers designed
to favour a particular creditor by removing from the pool upon liquidation
assets which would otherwise be available to the general body of creditors are
in principle null and void.[32] As stated above, this rule is distinct from the anti-
deprivation rule. The *pari passu* rule is designed to ensure that one creditor
does not get more than his fair slice of the pie, whereas the anti-deprivation
rule seeks to secure that the size of the pie is not reduced by withdrawal of an
asset from the company in favour of one who is not a creditor.

Although the *pari passu* rule is statutory, it has been left to the common law
to develop the rule's impact on the validity of pre-liquidation agreements.
The rule is buttressed by statutory provisions invalidating as a preference
transactions made by an insolvent company in the run-up to liquidation[33] that
unfairly benefit one creditor at the expense of others. The principle has
many facets which I shall discuss in detail, together with the exceptions to the
principle, in a later chapter.[34]

It has been objected with some vigour that the *pari passu* principle is not a
central principle of insolvency law at all.[35] Two grounds have been advanced
for this contention. First, unsecured creditors usually receive little, if
anything, by way of dividend. This is true, but the reason is not the lack of cen-
trality of the *pari passu* principle, which has been adopted in every substantive
insolvency enactment since the time of Henry VIII, but the fact that by its
nature it applies only to the free assets of the company, and with the development of a huge range of security interests, trusts, reservation of title and other
real rights, as well as various equities,[36] the amount of free assets in relation
to unsecured claims is usually relatively small.[37] Moreover, it would be a mistake to measure the impact of the rule by reference to the amount distributed

---

[29] Above, para.2–27.
[30] Insolvency Act 1986 s.107 (voluntary winding up); and Insolvency Rules 1986 r.4.181 (compulsory winding up). For a detailed discussion, see Michael Bridge, "Collectivity, Management of
Estates and the *Pari Passu* Rule in Winding up" in John Armour and Howard Bennett (eds),
Vulnerable Transactions in Corporate Insolvency (Oxford: Hart Publishing, 2003), Ch.1.
[31] Insolvency Rules 1986 r.2.69.
[32] For recent statements of the rule, see the judgment of Arden L.J. in *Re Lehman Brothers
International (Europe) Ltd*, [2010] EWCA Civ 917 at [76].
[33] The run-up period varies from six months to three years, depending on the circumstances.
[34] See below, paras 8–01 et seq.
[35] Rizwaan Jameel Mokal, "Priority as Pathology: The *Pari Passu* Myth" [2001] C.L.J. 581.
[36] See below, para.8–04.
[37] See to similar effect Richard Calnan, *Proprietary Interests and Insolvency* (Oxford: Oxford
University Press, 2010), para.1.147.

to the general body of creditors in a winding up. The fact is that the rule has been applied in a wide diversity of situations to invalidate many hundreds of transactions and its mere existence may have discouraged as many again. It is true that the benefits of invalidation go in the first instance to swell the assets available for the expenses of the liquidation and the payment of preferential claims, and there are no doubt many cases in which unsecured creditors derive no benefit. Nevertheless, the rule may improve the prospects of a payment to unsecured creditors and, even where it does not, its effect is to preclude creditors who would benefit from the absence of the rule from diluting the assets available for distribution.

Secondly, it is argued that what the law disallows is not evasion of the *pari passu* principle as such, but rather attempts to by-pass the collective mechanism which an insolvency proceeding is designed to produce. If one takes references to the *pari passu* principle literally, there is force in this criticism in that evasion of the principle of collectivity, which is essentially procedural in character, would be outlawed whatever the order of distribution of assets under substantive insolvency law. In other words, what the courts are concerned to do is to bar devices that would by-pass the collective regime, with its restraints on individual enforcement, and allow an individual creditor to evade the statutory order of distribution, whatever that might be. Yet the fact that *pari passu* distribution is the general principle and the importance of its observance have been stressed in countless decisions by eminent judges[38] as well as by innumerable writers, including scholars from overseas describing their own insolvency laws. Is it, then, the case that all of these have been guilty of a "misunderstanding of the nature of the liquidation regime"?[39] Clearly not; they have simply invoked the *pari passu* rule as a form of shorthand to describe what is in fact the general statutory rule of distribution, and it is in that sense that it is referred to in the analysis of the rule which follows later.[40]

Seventh principle: the pursuit of personal rights against the company is converted into a right to prove for a dividend in the liquidation

3–08   It is upon liquidation that the distinction between real and personal rights against a company becomes of crucial importance. So long as the company is solvent, it matters little in financial terms whether the claimant has a mere personal right to payment of a debt or damages or a proprietary interest in

---

[38] See, e.g. *Buchler v Talbot* [2004] 2 A.C. 298, *per* Lord Nicholls at [32]; *Wight v Eckhardt Marine GmbH* [2004] 1 A.C. 147, *per* Lord Hoffmann at [28]–[32]; *Re Bank of Credit and Commerce International SA (No.8)* [1998] A.C. 214, *per* Lord Hoffmann at [5] and [9]; *Re Charter Reinsurance Co v Fagan* [1997] A.C. 313, *per* Mance J. at 351; *Re J. Leslie Engineers Co Ltd* [1976] 2 All E.R. 85, *per* Oliver J. at 95; *Re Dynamics Corp of America* [1976] 2 All E.R. 669, *per* Oliver J. at 675; and *Re Harrington Motor Co, ex p. Chaplin* [1928] Ch. 105, *per* Atkin L.J. at 122.

[39] Mokal, "Priority as Pathology: The *Pari Passu* Myth" (above, n. 35), p.591.

[40] See Ch.8.

an asset from which he can obtain satisfaction of what is owed to him, for he can obtain a judgment on his personal claim and enforce it against any or all of the debtor company's assets or income so far as not subject to a prior interest in favour of a third party. But when the company becomes insolvent, so that there are insufficient assets to go round, the creditor with real rights in an asset (for example, a seller of goods under reservation of title, a mortgagee or chargee of property) can remove it from the maw of the general creditors, whereas the creditor with a purely personal right, although not deprived of the right itself, loses the ability to engage in individual pursuit of satisfaction and is required to lodge his claim with the liquidator in what is called a proof of debt and participate with other unsecured creditors in such *pari passu* distributions of dividend as the liquidator is able to make from realisation of the company's assets after allowing for the expenses of the liquidation and the claims of preferential creditors.

Eighth principle: on liquidation the company ceases to be the beneficial owner of its assets

Although winding up does not of itself divest the company of legal title to its **3–09** assets, it ceases to be the beneficial owner and holds the assets on trust to apply them in discharge of the company's liabilities in accordance with the statutory scheme of distribution. The key decision on this point is that of the House of Lords in *Ayerst (Inspector of Taxes) v C. & K. (Construction) Ltd*,[41] where it was held that on winding up a company ceased to be entitled to use its assets for its own benefit, so that on the sale of its business after the commencement of its winding up its trade ceased to belong to the company beneficially and the purchaser could therefore not offset the company's unrelieved tax losses against its own tax assessment.[42] So the fact that the company loses beneficial ownership on winding up may have important tax consequences. A different approach was taken by the High Court of Australia in *Commissioner of Taxation v Linter Textiles Australia Ltd*,[43] Kirby J. dissenting. In the majority view it is not correct to say that the company's beneficial ownership ceases on its going into liquidation. Rather, the position is that the company holds its property beneficially, but subject to the statutory scheme of liquidation under which the liquidator is to pay creditors and distribute any surplus among members.[44] In a strong dissenting judgment, Kirby J. pointed out that the English decisions to the effect that the company lost beneficial ownership were not an

---

[41] [1976] A.C. 167. As to the special nature of the trust, see the eighth principle below.
[42] See also *Harms Offshore AHT Taurus GmbH v Bloom* [2010] Ch. 187, in which Stanley Burnton L.J. considered (at [24]) that the *Ayerst* principle applied equally in administration; and *Pritchard v M H. Builders (Wilmslow) Ltd* [1969] 2 All E.R. 670.
[43] (2005) 215 A.L.R. 1.
[44] Approving a passage from H.A.J. Ford and R.O. Austin (eds.), *Ford and Austin's Principles of Corporations Law*, 7th edn (Sydney: Butterworths, 1995), p.1013.

attempt to import all of the features of trust law into the defined statutory relationships following a company liquidation. Rather, they were drawing an analogy to explain the construction and operation of the relevant statute. Noting that the decision in *Ayerst* was consistent with the approach taken by courts of New Zealand, Ireland and Hong Kong, Kirby J. said:

"I can see no reason of legal authority, principle or policy to justify this Court's taking a different course from that adopted by the unanimous opinion of the House of Lords on a precisely identical point of revenue law . . . There is no reason why we should take such a course. There are many reasons why we should not."[45]

The trust concept features in a number of other winding up situations. Sums recovered by the liquidator in respect of wrongful trading, transactions at an undervalue and preferences are not considered to be assets of the company, but are held by the liquidator for the benefit of creditors in accordance with the statutory order of priority.[46] They are therefore not susceptible to capture by a secured creditor under an after-acquired property clause.[47] Sums paid and property transferred to the supervisor under a company voluntary arrangement are held on trust for the company voluntary arrangement (CVA) creditor, a trust which survives any subsequent winding up of the company unless the CVA itself otherwise provides.[48] Such trust may also arise at an earlier stage if the terms of the proposal or the CVA itself indicate an intention to create a trust.[49]

In *Re UCT (UK) Ltd,*[50] Arden J. acceded to an application by administrators to release them while at the same time authorising them to retain in a designated trust account sums to meet the claims of creditors who would be preferential creditors in a compulsory winding up in order to facilitate a voluntary winding up and thereby avoid the additional costs of a compulsory liquidation.

There are, however, limits to the application of the *Ayerst* principle. In the first place, the statutory trust applies only in relation to property beneficially owned by the company. Therefore, it does not extend to property in the company's possession but belonging to another, for example, goods supplied under reservation of title, nor does it apply to assets given in security except to the extent of the company's equity of redemption.[51] Secondly, the liquidator is not for all purposes treated as distinct from the company itself. In

---

[45] At [245].
[46] See below, paras 6–37 and 13–140 et seq.
[47] See below, para.13–142.
[48] See below, para.12–52.
[49] See below, para.12–52.
[50] [2001] B.C.C. 734.
[51] See below, paras 6–45 and 6–46.

Re Stanford International Bank Ltd,[52] a bank alleged to have been involved in a fraudulent "Ponzi" scheme was wound-up in Antigua, with the result that under Antiguan law its movable assets became vested in the liquidator. Upon an application by the UK Serious Fraud Office, on behalf of the US Department of Justice, a restraint order had been made under the Proceeds of Crime Act 2002 and subordinate legislation made thereunder freezing the company's assets as being allegedly the proceeds of a fraud on investors pending an application for a confiscation order.[53] The Antiguan liquidators contended that their status was not that of the company itself, but of a third party holding the assets for the benefit of creditors in the winding up and that a restraint order ought therefore not to be made. The Court of Appeal held that the liquidators were not third parties, but stood in the shoes of the company itself and that while the original restraint order should be discharged on the ground that it was obtained by misrepresentation and non-disclosure, a new restraint order should be granted. However, Arden L.J. considered that it was reasonably arguable that the unsecured creditors had an interest in the assets under the *Ayerst* principle and that a restraint order should not be made until the parties had had an opportunity to argue the position of unsecured creditors. The difficulty with this approach, which was doubted by other members of the court and had not been raised by any party to the proceedings, is that if it were correct, the underlying principle by which a restraint order made before liquidation or other insolvency proceeding has priority over the insolvency could never have effect. Moreover, s.84 of the Proceeds of Crime Act provides that references to property held by a person include references to property held by its liquidator. The only right of unsecured creditors in a winding up is to have the assets realised, and the proceeds distributed, by the liquidator in accordance with the statutory regime. But those assets are susceptible to all restraints imposed by law.

Ninth principle: no creditor has any interest *in specie* in the company's assets or realisations

The statutory trust upon which the company in winding up holds the assets   **3–10**
and realisations is not of a kind which confers on the creditors beneficial

---

[52] [2010] 3 W.L.R. 941. For other aspects of this case see below, para.16–30.
[53] The Proceeds of Crime Act does not create a proprietary right over the assets of the insolvent company: it simply requires that the value of the tainted property be paid out of the company's assets (see *Re Stanford International Bank Ltd,* [2010] 3 W.L.R. 941, *per* Hughes L.J. at [162]). A restraint order cannot be made against a company which has already gone into liquidation (Proceeds of Crime Act 2002 s.426), and the same would appear to apply to a post-liquidation confiscation order in the absence of a pre-liquidation restraint order, although on this point there was a division of opinion between Hughes L.J. and Mary Arden L.J., the former taking the view that a confiscation order could be made even after the commencement of a winding up. This, however, runs contrary to the statement in para.568 of the Explanatory Notes to the legislation and would seem to be incorrect.

co-ownership or, indeed, a proprietary interest of any kind in the assets or realisations until completion of the liquidation.[54] Their rights are limited to invoking the protection of the court to ensure that the liquidator fulfils his statutory duties.[55] Their position is analogous to that of residuary legatees in an unadministered estate.[56] They have a right to compel performance of the executor's duties but no interest in the assets comprising the estate until completion of the administration, pending which beneficial ownership of the assets is in suspense, and to have the residue paid to them when the administration is completed.[57] The company thus holds the assets for statutory purposes, not for persons. Even the declaration of a dividend confers no right on the creditors to sue for the dividend; all they can do is to make an application to the court for an order requiring the liquidator to perform his duties.[58] These principles apply to preferential and ordinary creditors alike. So while preferential creditors can apply to the court to restrain a distribution which ignores their statutory priority, they have no proprietary interest in the assets or realisations as such. Moreover, until recently the liquidator's power to engage in litigation on behalf of the company without sanction in a voluntary winding up[59] and treat the costs incurred as an expense of the liquidation ranking in priority to the claims of the holder of a floating charge and preferential creditors meant that they had no absolute right to prevent the liquidator from incurring expenditure in the pursuit of legal proceedings for the benefit of creditors generally, even if there were sufficient assets to pay the preferential creditors and the holder of a floating charge without any recoveries from the proceedings, so that these would be of no benefit to those creditors. However, some protection is now provided by the Insolvency Rules, the effect of which is that where the litigation expenses are likely to exceed £5,000 and to reduce the payment that would otherwise be made to preferential creditors or the holder of a floating charge, such expenses will not have priority over their claims unless their approval has been obtained for the litigation expenses.[60]

---

[54] *Ayerst*, cited above n.41; *Buchler v Talbot* [2004] 2 A.C. 298, *per* Lord Hoffmann at [28]; and *Re Buckingham International plc* [1997] B.C.L.C. 673, *per* Millett L.J. at 683–684.

[55] *Buchler v Talbot*, cited above n.54; *Calgary and Edmonton Land Co Ltd v Dobinson* [1974] Ch. 102.

[56] *ibid*.

[57] *Commissioner of Stamp Duties v Livingston* [1965] A.C. 694; and *Re Hemming deceased* [2009] Ch. 313.

[58] *Prout v Gregory* (1889) 24 Q.B.D. 281; *Spence v Coleman* [1901] 2 K.B. 199.

[59] Insolvency Act 1986 Sch.4 para.4.

[60] This is a very brief summary of the effect of the rather complex provisions contained in rr.4.218A–4.218E.

Tenth principle: liquidation accelerates creditors' rights to payment

When a company goes into liquidation, its liability for payment of unmatured **3–11** debts becomes notionally accelerated[61] to the extent that it has already been earned by performance. This results from the fact that a creditor has an immediate right of proof not only for debts already due to him, but for those payable in the future or on a contingency.[62] Debts payable in the future are provable in full, but if not due at the date of a dividend distribution are discounted for the purpose of computing the dividend,[63] while contingent debts are valued.[64] However, a claim qualifies as a debt for this purpose only to the extent that it has been earned, in the sense that the consideration for it is executed. For example, the principle of acceleration applies to a loan made before winding up but maturing three years later, and to the future instalments payable at the time of winding up in respect of the price of goods already delivered, for in both cases the consideration furnished by the creditor is executed. By contrast, a lessor cannot claim to accelerate the future rentals payable under a lease upon the winding up of the lessee because these have not yet been earned; his remedy, if the liquidator retains possession for the benefit of the winding up, is to recover each amount of rent as it falls due as an expense of the liquidation,[65] or if possession is not so retained, then to prove for each amount of rent as it falls due,[66] or alternatively, if the lease comes to an end through forfeiture by the lessor or disclaimer by the liquidator, to prove for the loss of the future rentals as unliquidated damages.[67]

Eleventh principle: members of a company are not as such liable for its debts

It is a well-established principle of English company law, particularly relevant **3–12** to insolvency, that where a body is created with corporate personality,

---

[61] It may also, of course, become contractually accelerated. For the effect of acceleration clauses in a winding up, see below, para.8–09.

[62] Insolvency Rules 1986 rr.4.94 and 12.3(1).

[63] Insolvency Rules 1986 r.11.13.

[64] Insolvency Rules 1986 r.4.86(1).

[65] *Christopher Moran Holdings Ltd v Bairstow* [2000] 2 A.C. 172 (on appeal from *Re Park Air Services plc* [1997] 1 W.L.R. 1376), *per* Lord Millett at 187; *Re ABC Coupler & Engineering Ltd (No.3)* [1970] 1 W.L.R. 702; *Re Oak Pits Colliery Co* (1882) 21 Ch. D. 322; *Re New Oriental Bank Corp (No.2)* [1895] 1 Ch. 753; and *Re Lundy Granite Co* (1871) LR 6 Ch. 462, *per* Sir W.M. James L.J. at 466. The principle was extended to dilapidations in *Re Levi & Co* [1919] 1 Ch. 416 (see further below, para.8–43) and has recently been held to apply in an administration (*Goldacre (Offices) Ltd v Nortel Networks UK Ltd* [2010] 3 W.L.R. 171, approved by Lord Menzies in the Scottish case *Cheshire West and Chester BC v In the administration of Springfield Retail Ltd* [2010] C.S.O.H. 115. On the contrary, see *Exeter CC v Bairstow* [2007] B.C.C. 1236. See further para.11–104.

[66] See paras. 6–22, 8–41. This is not an exception to the rule that post-liquidation debts are not provable; the rent accruing due after the time of commencement of the winding up is already a future debt at that time.

[67] See below, para.8–43.

contracts entered into in the name of that body are its contracts, not those of its members, and liabilities incurred under such contracts are the liabilities of the body corporate, for which the members do not have even a secondary liability unless otherwise provided by statute. In contrast to the position in Continental law and Scots law, a partnership firm is not considered by English law to have separate legal personality; the partnership is merely a business association of individual partners, who are jointly and severally liable for debts incurred in the name of the firm.[68] Under English law, the separation of the body corporate from its members and their insulation from liability are a necessary concomitant of corporate personality. This principle was reaffirmed by the Court of Appeal in its rulings in the International Tin Council litigation[69] and applies also to limited liability partnerships.[70] There was a brief period in the history of English law in which creditors had a direct right of action against members of a defaulting company, but such a right has been unknown to English law since 1855.[71] The principle applies as much to the one-man company as to others[72]; and in the celebrated decision in *Salomon v Salomon & Co*[73] the House of Lords saw nothing objectionable in the sole shareholder holding a debenture over the company's assets to secure payment to him of the price of the business he had sold to the company, thus enabling him as a secured creditor to obtain priority over unsecured creditors when the company became insolvent.

The principle that members of a company are not liable for its debts applies not only to companies controlled by individual members, but to wholly owned subsidiaries of other companies. So, in general, a parent company is not liable for the debts of its wholly owned subsidiary, nor does it incur a liability merely because it exercises overall control of the subsidiary through a group structure and group management and financial control, although if it interferes in day-to-day management it could be held to be a shadow director.[74]

---

[68] However, partnerships may now be formed with limited liability under the Limited Liability Partnerships Act 2000.

[69] *Maclaine Watson & Co Ltd v Department of Trade and Industry* [1988] 3 All E.R. 257.

[70] Limited Liability Partnerships Act 2000 s.1(2). Such partnerships are not discussed further in the present work.

[71] As explained earlier (above, para.1–10), the first general statute providing for incorporation was the Joint Stock Companies Act 1844, under which the company had legal personality, but its members remained liable for its debts. That was changed by the Limited Liability Act 1855. Since that time, members of a company have never been *directly* liable as such to creditors. However, upon winding up, members of a limited liability company are liable to contribute to the assets of the company to the amount unpaid on their shares or, in the case of a company incorporated by guarantee, the amount they undertook to contribute to the assets of the company in the event of its being wound-up, and members of an unlimited company are liable to contribute to the assets without limitation in whatever amount is needed to cover the company's debts and the expenses of winding up. See Companies Act 2006 s.3 and Insolvency Act 1986 s.74.

[72] *Salomon v Salomon & Co* [1897] A.C. 22.

[73] [1897] A.C. 22.

[74] See below, para.14–05.

Members of a company will, of course, incur a liability where the company is registered, or re-registered, as an unlimited company, and may also do so where the company acts as their agent or where they undertake a collateral liability, for example, under a guarantee or other contract. Moreover, there are special situations in which the court is willing to pierce the corporate veil, as where the company has been created and used as an engine of fraud[75]; but such cases are exceptional, and it is extremely difficult to persuade an English court to look behind the veil of incorporation. Finally, although a European Economic Interest Grouping created under EEC regulations[76] and registered in this country has legal personality,[77] its members are jointly and severally liable for its debts without limit of liability.[78]

Twelfth principle: in cross-border insolvencies, a principle of modified universalism applies

In general, where a main insolvency proceeding has been opened in a foreign jurisdiction, English courts should co-operate to ensure that all the insolvent company's assets are distributed to its creditors under a single system of distribution,[79] so that the role of the English courts is to aid the foreign insolvency. Allied to this is the principle that in English insolvency proceedings there should be no discrimination against foreign creditors.[80]   **3–13**

---

[75] *Gilford Motor Co v Horne* [1933] Ch. 935. See generally L.C.B. Gower, *Principles of Modern Company Law*, 8th edn (London: Sweet & Maxwell, 2008), Ch.8.

[76] Council Regulation 2137/85 of July 25, 1985 on the European Economic Interest Grouping (EEIG). The regulation has direct effect under Community law, but various matters were left to national law and are provided for by the European Economic Interest Grouping Regulations 1989 (SI 1989/638).

[77] European Economic Interest Grouping Regulations 1989 (SI 1989/638) reg.3.

[78] Council Regulation 2137/85 art.24(1).

[79] *Re HIH Casualty and General Insurance Ltd* [2008] 1 W.L.R. 852, *per* Lord Hoffmann at [6]; and *Cambridge Gas Transportation Corp v Official Committee of Unsecured Creditors of Navigator Holdings plc* [2007] 1 A.C. 508, *per* Lord Hoffmann at [16].

[80] See generally Ch.16.

Chapter 4

The Concept of Corporate Insolvency

1. GENERAL PRINCIPLES

The legal significance of insolvency

A company is insolvent when it is unable to pay its debts. The concept is sim- **4–01**
ple enough, but as we shall see there is more than one test of inability to pay
debts and in marginal cases it may be far from easy to determine whether the
test is satisfied as at the relevant time. Insolvency as such is not a condition to
which legal consequences attach. These occur only after there has been some
formal proceeding, such as winding up or the appointment of an administrator or administrative receiver.[1] Thus it is neither a criminal offence nor a civil
wrong for a company to become insolvent or even to trade while insolvent.[2] It
is only if the company becomes subject to a formal insolvency proceeding and
improper trading is established that the question of civil or criminal liability
can arise.[3] Again, insolvency does not per se prevent creditors from taking
steps to enforce payment; indeed, the strong support given by English law to
individual initiative means that almost always the race goes to the swiftest.
Further, payments and transfers of property made by an insolvent company
are not on that account alone rendered void or voidable, even if the fact that
the company is insolvent is known to the payee or transferee; a formal insolvency proceeding is necessary. But the advent of insolvency proceedings may
affect transactions previously concluded.[4]

Insolvency legislation confines the terms "insolvency" and "insolvent" to a
formal insolvency proceeding.[5] When referring to a *state of insolvency*, it does

---

[1] See below Chs 5, 10 and 11.
[2] Indeed, the premature cessation of trading may be wrongful. See below, para.14–46.
[3] See Ch.14.
[4] See below and Ch.12.
[5] See, e.g. the Insolvency Act 1986, ss.240(3), 247(1); Company Directors Disqualification Act
1986, s.6(2).

not use this term, but embodies the concept in the phrase "unable to pay its debts".[6] What is a debt for this purpose[7] depends on the particular test of insolvency that is being applied. As we shall see, in determining whether a company can pay its debts as they fall due, the word "debt" is strictly confined.[8] By contrast, the balance sheet test of insolvency, where this is applicable, requires assets to be measured not against debts, but against "liabilities", an altogether wider expression.[9]

The relevance of a company's inability to pay its debts

4–02   It is with the advent of a formal insolvency proceeding that the company's inability to pay its debts becomes material. This is true not only where the state of insolvency exists at the time of the proceedings in question but where it existed at some earlier time. Thus a winding up or administration gives retroactive legal significance to an earlier state of insolvency which at the time it first arose had no impact in law. Inability to pay debts is the fundamental concept on which all insolvency law is based.

(i)   Inability to pay debts is a ground for winding up.[10]

(ii)   A bank insolvency order may be made against a bank that is unable, or likely to become unable, to pay its debts.[11]

(iii)   A bank administration order may be made against a bank that is unable to pay its debts or is likely to become unable to pay its debts as a result of the property transfer which the Bank of England intends to make.[12]

(iv)   If a company goes into insolvent liquidation,[13] directors engaged in fraudulent trading[14] or wrongful trading[15] will in certain circumstances incur a liability to contribute to the company's assets.[16]

---

[6] See, e.g. the Insolvency Act 1986 ss.123, 222–224 and Sch.B1 para.11(a).
[7] As to the various meanings of "debt" for the purposes of admissibility of claims to proof, see below, paras 8–41 et seq.
[8] See below, para.4–18.
[9] See below, paras 4–23 and 4–24.
[10] Insolvency Act 1986 s.122(l)(f). Section 122 sets out eight other grounds on which a company may be wound-up.
[11] Banking Act 2009 s.96(1)(a). See generally above, para.1–57, as to bank insolvency.
[12] Banking Act 2009 s.143(3).
[13] Defined by the Insolvency Act 1986 ss.214(6) and 216(7) in terms embodying one of the two principal tests of insolvency, namely insufficiency of assets to meet liabilities.
[14] Insolvency Act 1986 s.213.
[15] Insolvency Act 1986 s.214.
[16] Fraudulent trading is also a criminal offence, whether or not the company has been, or is in the course of being, wound-up (Companies Act 2006 s.993).

(v)   Transfers at an undervalue and preferences may be set aside if made when the company is unable to pay its debts and it subsequently goes into administration or liquidation.[17]

(vi)   A floating charge given otherwise than for a specified form of new value by a company unable to pay its debts may be void if the company subsequently goes into liquidation or administration.[18]

(vii)   An administration order can be made against a company only if it is or is likely to become unable to pay its debts,[19] except where the application for administration is made by the holder of a qualifying floating charge.[20]

(viii) A person who is or has been a director of a company which has at any time become insolvent may have a disqualification order made against him where the conditions of s.6(1) of the Company Directors Disqualification Act 1986 are satisfied.

The tests of inability to pay debts

The Insolvency Act 1986 and related legislation prescribe a bewildering variety of tests for determining whether a company is to be deemed insolvent for the purpose of the relevant statutory provisions. The reasons for selecting different tests for different provisions have never been clearly articulated. In some cases, these differences would seem to have resulted from the piecemeal development of corporate insolvency law prior to the Insolvency Act 1985, although for the most part they are not too difficult to justify.[21] These various tests are set out in s.123(1) and (2) of the Insolvency Act 1986:   **4–03**

"123(1) **Inability to pay debts** A company is deemed unable to pay its debts—

(a)   if a creditor (by assignment or otherwise) to whom the company is indebted in a sum exceeding £750 then due has served on the company, by leaving it at the company's

---

[17] Companies Act 2006 ss.238–242. See paras 13–12 et seq. For a detailed discussion of the concept of insolvency in this context from the perspective of Australian law, see Andrew R. Keay, "The Insolvency Factor in the Avoidance of Antecedent Transactions in Corporate Liquidations" (1995) 21 Monash Univ. L. Rev. 305.

[18] Insolvency Act 1986 s.245. See para.13–112.

[19] *ibid.*, Sch.B1, para.11(a). It also necessary to show that the administration order is likely to achieve the purpose of the administration (para.11(b)).

[20] Insolvency Act 1986 Sch.B1 para.35(2)(a). Moreover, a company or its directors cannot put the company into administration unless it is or is likely to become unable to pay its debts. See below, para.11–11.

[21] See generally below, paras 4–07 et seq.

registered office, a written demand (in the prescribed form) requiring the company to pay the sum so due and the company has for 3 weeks thereafter neglected to pay the sum or to secure or compound for it to the reasonable satisfaction of the creditor, or

(b)   if, in England and Wales, execution or other process issued on a judgment, decree or order of any court in favour of a creditor of the company is returned unsatisfied in whole or in part, or

(c)   *[provision for Scotland]*, or

(d)   *[provision for Northern Ireland]*, or

(e)   if it is proved to the satisfaction of the court that the company is unable to pay its debts as they fall due.

(2)   **Proof that assets less than liabilities** A company is also deemed unable to pay its debts if it is proved to the satisfaction of the court that the value of the company's assets is less than the amount of its liabilities, taking into account its contingent and prospective liabilities."

These various tests fall broadly into two groups. The first group, embodied in paragraphs (a) and (b) of s.123(1) of the Insolvency Act 1986, consists of two very specific and readily ascertainable facts deemed to establish inability to pay debts, namely failure to meet a statutory demand for payment of a debt in excess of £750 within three weeks and the return of an execution unsatisfied in whole or in part. The second group, contained in s.123(1)(e) and (2), consists of more general criteria of inability to pay debts and divides into the two primary tests described below.[22]

The two primary tests

4–04   The two primary tests of inability to pay debts are the cash flow test (inability to pay debts as they fall due) and the balance sheet test (shortfall of assets in relation to liabilities).[23] The cash flow test, where it applies, is always that formulated by s.123(1)(e) of the Insolvency Act. By contrast, the formulation of the balance sheet test varies from one statutory provision to another, but the effect in all cases appears to be the same.[24] For most purposes, it is the present inability to pay debts that is the crucial factor. However, a company

---

[22] There are no comparable provisions in relation to bankruptcy, where inability to pay is established by the specific tests laid down in s.268 of the Insolvency Act.

[23] Insolvency Act 1986 ss.123(1)(e) and 123(2).

[24] See below, paras 4–24 and 4–29.

is permitted to go into a members' voluntary winding up if the directors make a declaration that in their view the company will be able to pay its debts in full, with interest, within a period not exceeding 12 months.[25]

The statutory expression of the distinction between the cash flow test and the balance sheet test is of quite recent origin. Section 80(4) of the Companies Act 1862 embodied a single, general formulation, namely that a company was to be deemed insolvent "whenever it is proved to the satisfaction of the court that the company is unable to pay its debts". This formulation, which contrasted sharply with that applicable to bankruptcy,[26] was held to exclude contingent and prospective liabilities when applying the balance sheet test,[27] a deficiency remedied by the Companies Act 1907 s.28, which required the court to take account of contingent and prospective liabilities. This was carried over into successive Companies Acts up to and including the 1985 Act.[28] The present division into inability to pay debts as they fall due and insufficiency of assets in relation to liabilities was first introduced by the short-lived Insolvency Act 1985 in its amendment of s.518 of the Companies Act 1985, replaced by the present s.123(l)(e) and (2). These changes in the statutory formulations since the Act of 1862 need to be borne in mind when referring to earlier case law on the meaning of inability to pay debts. There is in fact a remarkable dearth of English authority on the meaning and content of the two primary tests.[29] This stands in striking contrast to Australian corporate insolvency law, which throughout the present century has built up a substantial doctrine of case law on the cash flow test[30] to which appropriate references will be made in the ensuing passages.

---

[25] See below, para.4–12.

[26] The Bankruptcy Acts never used a general test of insolvency as a basis for making a debtor bankrupt; this could be done only by proof that the debtor had committed one or more acts of bankruptcy. But payments and transfers by the debtor could be set aside as fraudulent preferences if made within a designated period prior to the petition on which the adjudication order was made by a debtor "unable to pay his debts as they become due from his own money", and prior to the Insolvency Act 1985 bankruptcy rules of preference were applicable in the winding up of companies. See, e.g. *Re Washington Diamond Mining Co* [1893] 3 Ch. 95.

[27] *Re European Life Assurance Society (No.1)* (1869) L.R. 9 Eq. 122. Consideration of such liabilities does not, in principle, arise in relation to the cash flow test, where the question is whether the company is able to pay its debts as they fall due. See, however, para.4–18 below.

[28] Companies (Consolidation) Act 1908 s.130(iv); Companies Act 1929 s.169; Companies Act 1948 s.223(d); and Companies Act 1985 s.518.

[29] As was noted by Nicholls L.J. in *Byblos Bank SAL v Al-Khudhairy* (1986) 2 B.C.C. 99, 549 at 99, 563, where he observed that only three decisions had been found relevant to the point he had to decide.

[30] The Australian provision on insolvency, namely s.95A of the Corporations Act 2001 (Cth), adopts only a cash flow test. However, the balance sheet may be relevant in the context of application of the cash flow test (*Bell Group Ltd v Westpac Banking Group Corp (No.9)* (2008) 70 A.C.S.R. 1 at [1073]–[1075]). For a detailed survey which considers both the Australian and the English cases, see Andrew R. Keay, *McPherson's Law of Company Liquidation*, 2nd edn (London: Sweet & Maxwell, 2009), paras 3.19–3.20; and Andrew R. Keay, "The Insolvency Factor in the Avoidance of Antecedent Transactions in Corporate Liquidations" (1995) 21 Monash Univ. L. Rev. 305.

(1) Cash flow

4–05   Under the cash flow, or commercial insolvency, test, which will be examined in more detail later in this chapter,[31] a company is insolvent when it is unable to pay its debts as they fall due. For this purpose, the fact that its assets exceed its liabilities is irrelevant; if it cannot pay its way in the conduct of its business it is insolvent, for there is no reason why creditors should be expected to wait while the company realises assets, some of which may not be held in readily liquidated form.

Despite a number of theoretical problems which have not been fully resolved in English insolvency law,[32] the cash flow test is relatively easy to apply in practice, for the court looks at what the company is actually doing; if it is not in fact paying its debts as they fall due (ignoring cases where there is a bona fide dispute as to the indebtedness), it is assumed to be insolvent.[33] A company which cannot meet its debts as they fall due is considered insolvent for the purpose of grounding a winding up order or administration order or vitiating a transaction under s.238, 239 or 245 of the Act.[34] But the cash flow test has no relevance to the determination of insolvency for the purposes of the wrongful trading provisions of the Insolvency Act[35] or for the purposes of s.6 of the Company Directors Disqualification Act 1986[36] or Pt XII of the Employment Rights Act 1996.[37]

(2) Balance sheet

4–06   The alternative primary test of insolvency is the balance sheet (or asset) test—i.e. the company's assets are insufficient to discharge its liabilities. The idea underlying this test, which is discussed in greater detail later, is that it is not sufficient for the company to be able to meet its current obligations if its total liabilities can ultimately be met only by the realisation of its assets and these are insufficient for the purpose. If the cash flow test were the only relevant test, then current and short-term creditors would in effect be paid at the expense of creditors to whom liabilities were incurred after the company had reached the point of no return because of an incurable deficiency in its assets.[38]

---

[31] Below, paras 4–15–4–21.
[32] See below, para.4–15.
[33] See below, para.4–21.
[34] Relating respectively to transactions at an undervalue, preferences and floating charges given otherwise than for specified forms of new value.
[35] See below, para.4–29.
[36] See below, para.4–10.
[37] See below, para.4–11.
[38] See *BNY Corporate Trustee Services Ltd v Eurosail-UK* [2011] EWCA Civ 227, in which the above passage was approved, and below, paras 4–22 to 4–31.

In the typical case, there is no real doubt as to the inadequacy of the company's assets. But in marginal situations it may be very difficult to decide whether the balance sheet test of insolvency is satisfied. This is because the valuation of assets (and, where these are required to be taken into account, of contingent liabilities) is not an exact science, but to a considerable extent a matter of judgment as to the amount a willing buyer would pay in the market when dealing with a willing seller. One has only to see the sometimes huge disparity between the estimate put on a work of art by a leading auction house and the actual sale price at auction to realise how difficult it is to give an accurate valuation of assets not having an established market price. Moreover, there is a close link between cash flow insolvency and balance sheet insolvency, in that where a company is a going concern and its business can be sold as such with its assets in use in the business, those assets will usually have a substantially higher value than if disposed of on a break-up basis, divorced from their previous business activity. So a company which is commercially solvent has a much greater chance of satisfying the balance sheet test of solvency than one which is unable to pay its debts as they fall due.

The balance sheet test is one of the tests prescribed for the purpose of grounds for winding up, administration or the avoidance of transactions at an undervalue,[39] preferences[40] and floating charges given otherwise than for a prescribed form of new value,[41] and the disqualification of directors under s.6 of the Company Directors Disqualification Act 1986,[42] and is the sole test for the purpose of identifying an insolvent liquidation under the provisions relating to wrongful trading.[43] It does not, however, feature in the insolvency provisions of the Employment Rights Act 1996.[44] The reason for the exclusive use of the balance sheet test in the wrongful trading provisions is that there is no reason to impose liability of the delinquent directors to contribute to the assets of the company except where the assets are insufficient to meet the liabilities and expenses of winding up.

Other tests of inability to pay debts

Both the cash flow test and the balance sheet test suffer the disadvantage that they require evidence and an analysis of the debtor company's position, which may take time to organise and may be the subject of dispute. There are various situations in which the legislature perceived a need to establish insolvency by reference to some irrefutable and easily established external fact or event, either as an alternative to the other two tests or in replacement of them.

4–07

---

[39] See below, para.13–12.
[40] See below, para.13–71.
[41] See below, para.13–111.
[42] See below, para.14–57.
[43] See below, para.14–30.
[44] See below, para.4–11.

(1) Under the Insolvency Act 1986

4–08 It will be recalled that, in addition to the cash flow and balance sheet tests in s.123(1)(e) and (2) of the Insolvency Act, s.123(1) prescribes two very specific means of showing a company's inability to pay its debts, namely if:

(a) it neglects to pay, secure or compound to the reasonable satisfaction of the creditor a debt exceeding £750 within three weeks of a written demand in the prescribed form[45]; or

(b) execution or other process on a judgment against the company is returned unsatisfied, wholly or in part.[46]

The same rules apply for the purpose of grounding an administration order, except that the court may also make an administration order if the company, although currently able to pay its debts, is likely to become unable to do so,[47] for example, where it is likely to begin or to continue trading at a loss without recovery prospects.[48]

A separate ground for a winding up order is that it is just and equitable that the company be wound-up.[49] This ground is also available to actual and prospective creditors.[50]

4–09 Although s.123 is primarily designed to complement the provisions of s.122(l)(f) making inability to pay debts a ground for winding up by the court, the tests of insolvency laid down in s.123 have a much wider application. In determining whether a company was insolvent at a particular time for the purpose of the provisions relating to transactions at an undervalue,[51] preferences[52] and floating charges given for past value,[53] the company is to be deemed insolvent if at the relevant time it was unable to pay its debts within the meaning of s.123 of the Insolvency Act (i.e. within any of the tests for winding up purposes as set out above) or became unable to do so in consequence of the transaction at an undervalue or preference or (in the case of the floating charge) the transaction under which it was created.[54]

---

[45] See further below, paras 4–09 and 5–16.
[46] Separate and more limited provisions are contained in ss.222–224 in relation to unregistered companies.
[47] Insolvency Act 1986 Sch.B1 para.11(a).
[48] See further para.11–47.
[49] Insolvency Act 1986 s.122(l)(g).
[50] *Re A Company (No.003028 of 1987)* (1987) 3 B.C.C. 575.
[51] See para.13–12.
[52] See para.13–71.
[53] See para.13–111.
[54] Insolvency Act 1986 ss.240(2) and 245(4). Inability to pay debts is presumed, unless the contrary is shown, in relation to any transaction at an undervalue which is entered into by the company with a person who is connected with the company (s.240(2)), i.e. is a director or shadow director of the company, an associate of such a director or shadow director or an associate of the company (s.249).

It is not hard to see why it was felt that there was a need for alternative and more specific tests of insolvency for the purpose of a winding up or administration order. To establish that a company is insolvent, and was already insolvent at an earlier point in time, is much easier for a person already in the saddle as liquidator, administrator or administrative receiver than it is for a party seeking a winding up or administration order, who at that stage has no access to the company's records and no right to interrogate its officers. This lack of information could deprive unpaid creditors of speedy recourse to winding up or administration and in so doing inhibit efforts to protect the company's business and assets through the expeditious appointment of a liquidator or administrator. Hence, to facilitate the proof of insolvency for the purpose of winding up or administration proceedings, the Insolvency Act (continuing, as regards winding up, the rules originally prescribed by the Companies Acts) permits alternative methods of satisfying the court that a company is unable to pay its debts and ought to be placed in liquidation or administration. Despite this, the statutory notice procedure under s. 123(1)(a) is not the preferred option for creditors, who in the case of an undisputed debt will either institute proceedings to obtain a quick judgment,[55] in the hope that if the debtor does not pay, execution against its assets will produce payment without bringing the house down,[56] or present a winding up petition immediately based on s.123(1)(e) because they do not wish to be constrained by the three-week period allowed to the debtor company and hope that the threat of winding up will induce payment.[57]

Somewhat different considerations apply to the avoidance of transactions. These can be invoked only where the company is already in liquidation or administration, so that there is not the same need for speedy determination as there is in the case of a petition for winding up or administration. But the alternative tests of insolvency—failure to meet a statutory demand and an unsatisfied execution against the company—avoid the necessity for expensive and time-consuming investigations by the liquidator or administrator into the company's state of solvency at the time of transactions, which may have taken place up to three years[58] before the winding up or administration order.

---

[55] In particular, a default judgment or a judgment by way of summary judgment on the ground that the defendant has no arguable defence.

[56] The success of this does, of course, depend on the extent to which other creditors are ahead in the execution stakes.

[57] It is established law that in the case of a debt which cannot reasonably be disputed, the presentation of a winding up petition with the object of collecting payment rather than having the company wound-up is perfectly legitimate. See para.4–21.

[58] In the case of the provisions relating to the re-opening of extortionate credit transactions (Insolvency Act 1986 s.244(2)). In other cases the relevant periods are shorter except for transactions defrauding creditors, where there is no time limit.

(2) Under the Company Directors Disqualification Act 1986

4–10 For the purpose of the provisions relating to the disqualification of a director, a company becomes insolvent if it goes into liquidation at a time when its assets are insufficient for the payment of its debts and other liabilities and the expenses of winding up, or an administration order is made or an administrative receiver appointed.[59] Although the occurrence of either of the last two of these events does not necessarily indicate insolvency, the fact that it proved necessary to place the company under external management is a sufficient justification for deeming a state of insolvency to have existed.

(3) Under the Employment Rights Act 1996

4–11 Finally, for the purpose of the provisions of the Employment Rights Act 1996 entitling an employee to payments from the National Insurance Fund[60] upon the employer's insolvency and termination of the employment, an employer is considered to have become insolvent when: (i) a winding up order or an administration order has been made, or a resolution for voluntary winding up has been passed,[61] with respect to the company; (ii) a receiver or manager of the company's undertaking has been duly appointed, or possession has been taken by or on behalf of the holders of any debentures secured by a floating charge, of any property of the company comprised in or subject to the charge; or (iii) a voluntary arrangement proposed in the case of the company for the purposes of Pt I of the Insolvency Act 1986 has been approved under that Part of the Act.[62] It will be seen that in this case neither the cash flow test nor the balance sheet test comes into consideration. Presumably this reflects a concern to ensure that claims on the National Insurance Fund are triggered only by a readily ascertainable external event not involving questions of judgment or valuation.

Declaration of solvency for members' voluntary winding up

4–12 A somewhat different approach to the concept of insolvency is adopted by s.89 of the Insolvency Act relating to members' voluntary winding up. This

---

[59] Company Directors Disqualification Act 1986 s.6(2). See Adrian Walters and Malcolm Davis-White, *Directors' Disqualification and Insolvency Restrictions*, 3rd edn (London: Sweet & Maxwell, 2009), para.3–98.

[60] For arrears of pay, holiday pay, compensation for unfair dismissal and the like (see s.184 of the Act).

[61] This is not confined to insolvent liquidation, but applies equally to a members' voluntary winding up.

[62] Employment Rights Act 1996 s.183(3). However, a compromise or arrangement under Pt 26 of the Companies Act 2006 is not specified as an event by which the employer is deemed to be insolvent.

requires the directors to make and file a statutory declaration of solvency, but in contrast to the requirement set by the cash flow test it is not necessary for the declaration to state that the company is currently able to pay its existing debts or that its assets are sufficient to cover its liabilities. It suffices for the declaration to state that the directors have formed the opinion that the company will be able to pay its debts in full, together with interest at the official rate (as defined in s.251) within such period, not exceeding 12 months from the commencement of the winding up, as may be specified in the declaration.[63] It is thus technically possible for the directors properly to file a declaration of solvency and put the company into a members' voluntary winding up even though it is unable to pay its debts both on a cash flow and on a balance sheet basis. In practice, it is highly unlikely that a declaration could properly be made in the case of a company with both a deficiency of assets and an inability to pay its debts as they fell due, for a reasonable forecast of an ability to pay debts in full in 12 months would almost invariably enable the company to obtain temporary accommodation to pay its current debts as they fell due.

The time at which inability to pay debts is relevant

At what time must the company be unable to pay its debts in order to attract the statutory provisions? This varies with the provision in question. The relevant time is: **4–13**

(i)   for the purpose of the provisions relating to the making of a winding up or administration order, on the hearing of the petition on which the order is to be made[64];

(ii) for the purpose of the provisions relating to wrongful trading, when the company goes into liquidation[65];

(iii) for the purpose of the provisions relating to avoidance of transactions at an undervalue and preferences, when the transaction is made or the preference given[66];

(iv) for the purpose of the provisions relating to avoidance of a floating charge given for past value, when the charge is created[67];

---

[63] Insolvency Act 1986 s.89(1). Deficiencies in a statement of assets and liabilities do not deprive it of the quality of a statement of assets and liabilities (*Re New Millennium Experience Co Ltd* [2004] 1 All E.R. 687).

[64] Insolvency Act 1986 s.122(1)(f) and Sch.B1 para.11(a); and *MacPlant Services Ltd v Contract Lifting Services (Scotland) Ltd* [2009] S.C. 125.

[65] Insolvency Act 1986 s.214(6). As to when this is, see s.247(2).

[66] Insolvency Act 1986 ss.238(2) and 239(2), as qualified by s.240.

[67] Insolvency Act 1986 s.245.

(v) for the purpose of the provisions relating to the disqualification of a director, any time while he was a director or any subsequent time[68]; and

(vi) for the purpose of considering whether, at a time when the company was insolvent, a transaction entered into by the company or its directors breached a duty to consider the interests of creditors, the time of entry into the transaction.[69]

It will thus be seen that the question of a company's insolvency may arise prospectively or retrospectively. In assessing a company's financial position for the purpose of the avoidance of antecedent transactions, the court has "the inestimable benefit of the wisdom of hindsight".[70] But the use of hindsight is not legitimate in every case. It can properly be used to determine whether the evaluation of the situation at the relevant time was correct. For example, a relevant factor in determining solvency is whether at the relevant time the company has the capacity to borrow, and its subsequent success in borrowing is indicative of its capacity to do so at the relevant time.[71] On the other hand, hindsight cannot be used to take account of events occurring or data acquired after the relevant time that have no bearing on the evaluation made at the relevant time, for example, an unexpected rise in the valuation of shares held by the company in a drugs company because of the discovery of a new drug with great curative properties. The distinction drawn by the accountancy profession between adjusting and non-adjusting events is as helpful in the context of the cash flow test as it is in relation to the balance sheet test.[72]

Where the question is whether a winding up order should be made on the ground of the company's inability to pay its debts as they fall due, such inability must be determined not only as at the date of the hearing of the petition by reference to debts then payable, but also as at some near future time by reference to those which will be payable at that time.[73] Hence, although the time as at which the company's inability to pay its debts must be tested is very precisely identified, this does not mean that the court is required to treat the company's business as frozen at that very time. On the contrary, both of the primary tests involve an element of projection, the cash flow test, because the court looks to see not merely whether at the time of the enquiry the company is unable to pay debts then, but whether its position as seen at that time is such that it will be unable to pay its debts becoming due in the near future at the time those fall due,[74] and the

---

[68] Company Directors Disqualification Act 1986 s.6(1)(a).

[69] See, e.g. *Lewis v Doran* (2004) 208 A.L.R. 385; and below, para.14–20, as to the duty to have regard to creditors rather than shareholders when the company is insolvent or is approaching insolvency.

[70] *Lewis v Doran* (2004) 208 A.L.R. 385, per Palmer, J. at [108]. The decision was affirmed by the New South Wales Court of Appeal (2005) 219 A.L.R. 555.

[71] The example given by Owen J. in the Western Australian decision in *Bell Group Ltd v Westpac Banking Group Corp (No.9)* (2008) 70 A.C.S.R. 1 at [1111].

[72] See below, para.4–35.

[73] *Lewis v Doran*, per Palmer J. at [107]; and see below, para.4–16.

[74] See below, para.4–16.

balance sheet test because in most cases the court is required to take into account prospective and contingent liabilities.[75]

Inability to pay debts is not the sole criterion for the exercise of the court's powers

In the discussion that follows, it should be borne in mind that a conclusion **4–14** that the relevant test of inability to pay debts is satisfied merely establishes the statutory ground for the requisite order; it does not necessarily entitle the petitioner to ask for the order as of right. In the first place, a creditor must show a tangible interest in the making of the order.[76] It is not enough that the company is technically insolvent, as many are when starting to trade with the aid of a bank loan repayable on demand. Secondly, the making of an administration or winding up order is within the discretion of the court, as also is an order setting aside a vulnerable transaction or directing a contribution to the assets of the company by reason of wrongful trading and an order for disqualification of a director. Accordingly, factors which do not as a matter of law enter into the determination of a state of insolvency—for example, the prospect of additional finance for a company with a deficiency of assets—may nevertheless be relevant when the judge comes to consider whether to exercise his discretion.[77] However, the discretion must be exercised in accordance with settled principles and there is a presumption that a creditor in respect of an undisputed debt is entitled to a winding up order *ex debito justitiae*.[78]

With these preliminary observations, I turn to consider in more detail the various statutory formulations of the cash flow and balance sheet tests of insolvency and to explore some of the more intricate problems awaiting judicial decision.

2. THE CASH FLOW TEST[79]

The test restated

The root statutory provision, from which all of the other provisions adopting **4–15** the cash flow test are derived, is s.123(1)(e) of the Insolvency Act, by which a company is deemed unable to pay its debts:

---

[75] See below, paras 4–26 et seq.
[76] See below, paras 5–18 and 5–19.
[77] *Byblos Bank SAL v Al-Khudhairy* (1986) 2 B.C.C. 99, 549, per Nicholls L.J. at 99 and 562; and *Re Minrealm Ltd* [2008] 2 B.C.L.C. 141, where the winding up petition was adjourned pending a prospective court order against a director to make a payment due to the company which would result in the company being solvent under the cash flow test.
[78] See below, para.5–12.
[79] See also Andrew R. Keay, *McPherson's Law of Company Liquidation*, 2nd edn (London: Sweet & Maxwell, 2009), paras 3.019–3.020 for a detailed examination of the English and Australian authorities.

"... if it is proved to the satisfaction of the court that the company is unable to pay its debts as they fall due."

This formulation is deceptive in its simplicity. It raises a number of questions which have not been fully explored in English cases. What is the meaning of "debts"? To what extent, if at all, may or should the court look at debts becoming payable in the future? Are debts to be included which, although legally due, are not the subject of any current demand for payment? Is ability to pay to be determined exclusively by reference to the company's own money or can the prospect of raising funds through borrowing or the disposal of assets be taken into account? Must it be shown that the company is able to pay its debts exactly on the due date, or is some margin of tolerance to be allowed?

The element of futurity

4–16   In answering these questions, the court looks at the company's financial position taken as a whole. In *Quick v Stoland Pty Ltd*,[80] Emmett J., discussing the comparable concept of insolvency under s.95A of the Australian Corporations Law (now the Corporations Act 2001 (Cth)), put the matter in the following way:

"In order to determine whether the company was solvent at a given time, it would be relevant to consider the following matters:

– All of the company's debts as at that time in order to determine when those debts were due and payable.
– All of the assets of the company as at that time in order to determine the extent to which those assets were liquid or were realisable within a timeframe that would allow each of the debts to be paid as and when it became payable.
– The company's business as at that time in order to determine its expected net cash flow from the business by deducting from projected future sales the cash expenses which would be necessary to generate those sales.
– Arrangements between the company and prospective lenders, such as its bankers and shareholders, in order to determine whether any shortfall in liquid and realisable assets and cash flow could be made up by borrowings which would be repayable at a time later than the debts."

---

[80] (1998) 29 A.C.S.R. 130 at 138 (Federal Court of Australia).

Moreover, the court adopts a commercial, rather than a technical, view of insolvency.[81] So while the phrase "is unable" might at first sight be thought to refer to the inability at the relevant time[82] to pay debts which have then fallen due, its conjunction with the phrase "as they fall due" indicates a continuous succession of debts rather than a calculation of debts existing on any particular day.[83] The essential question is whether the company's financial position is such that it can continue in business and still pay its way.[84] The court therefore has to consider whether any liquidity problem the company may have is purely temporary and can be cured in the reasonably near future.

"The conclusion of insolvency ought to be clear from a consideration of the debtor's financial position in its entirety and generally speaking ought not to be drawn simply from evidence of a temporary lack of liquidity. It is the debtor's inability, utilizing such cash resources as he has or can command through the use of his assets, to meet his debts as they fall due which indicates insolvency."[85]

For this purpose the court will have regard not only to debts due and payable at the date for assessment, "due and payable" being construed in a commercial rather than a legal sense,[86] but also to claims falling due in the near future,[87] and to the likely availability of funds to meet such future claims and the company's existing debts.[88] In determining this question, regard must be had to the company's total financial position.

"Insolvency is to be judged by a proper consideration of the company's financial position, in its entirety, based on commercial reality. It is not to be found or inferred simply from evidence of a temporary lack of liquidity. Nor should it be assessed as if the company had to keep cash reserves sufficient to meet all outstanding indebtedness, however distant the date of payment might be in the fullness of time. But nor can directors rely on some faint

---

[81] *Sandell v Porter* (1966) 115 C.L.R. 666; *Iso Lilodw' Aliphumeleli Pty Ltd v Commissioner of Taxation* (2002) 42 A.C.S.R. 561; and *Re Cheyne Finance Plc* [2008] B.C.C. 182.

[82] As to which see above, para.4–13.

[83] *Bank of Australasia v Hall* (1907) 4 C.L.R. 1514 at 1528, discussing the meaning of the comparable phrase "as they become due" in the Australian legislation. See Keay, *McPherson's Law of Company Liquidation*, 2009, para.3.019.

[84] This was accepted as an accurate summary by Lord Hodge in *Macplant Services v Contract Lifting Services* (2009) S.C. 125 at [67].

[85] *Sandell v Porter* (1966) 115 C.L.R. 666, per Barwick C.J. at 670–671.

[86] See below, para.4–19.

[87] In *Re Cheyne Finance Plc* [2008] B.C.C. 182, Briggs J., in following the Australian jurisprudence, considered that it was not necessarily limited to consideration of the near future, but in most cases the court is likely to be reluctant to look beyond the immediate future. See, e.g. *New Cap Reinsurance Corp v Grant* (2008) 68 A.C.S.R. 176, per White J. at [44]; and *Bell Group Ltd v Westpac Banking Group Corp (No.9)* (2008) 70 A.S.C.R. 1 at [1128].

[88] *Sandell v Porter*, cited above n.85; *Expo International Ltd v Chant* [1979] 2 N.S.W.L.R. 820; and *Lewis v Doran*, cited above n.69, at [107].

hope that help is at hand and that all will be well. The word 'reality' in the phrase 'commercial reality' has a bite. Commercial reality dictates that the assessment of available funds is not confined to the company's cash resources. It is legitimate to take into account funds the company can, on a real and reasoned view, realise by sale of assets, borrowing against the security of its assets, or by other reasonable means. It is a question of fact to be determined in accordance with the evidence."[89]

We shall now examine these questions in more detail.

Only debts are to be taken into account

4–17   A debt is a liquidated claim, that is, a claim for an amount which is ascertained or can be readily and without difficulty ascertained,[90] as by mere calculation or the taking of an account.[91] It is to be distinguished from an unliquidated claim, for example, for damages for breach of contract or tort, which involves questions of liability and assessment. So if B Ltd buys goods from S and the price has become payable, that constitutes a debt which is to be taken into account in deciding whether B Ltd is able to pay its debts as they fall due. But if the price is payable only after delivery and B wrongfully refuses to accept the goods, S's claim is for unliquidated damages for breach of contract and cannot be taken into account under s.123(1)(e), for it involves questions of evidence and valuation.[92]

Only due debts are to be taken into account

4–18   The word "due" is capable of being used in both a narrow sense and a broad sense. In its narrow sense, it denotes a debt which is both existing and immediately payable; in its broad sense, it embraces *debitum in praesenti, solvendum in futuro,* that is, an existing indebtedness which has not yet matured. For the purpose of the cash flow test, only those liabilities which viewed at the relevant time constitute existing debts presently payable may be considered. In principle, existing debts payable in the future,[93] prospective debts,

---

[89] *Bell Group Ltd v Westpac Banking Group Corp (No.9)* (2008) 70 A.C.S.R. 1, per Owen J. at [1090].
[90] *Stooke v Taylor* (1880) 5 Q.B.D. 569 at 575, per Cockburn L.J.
[91] See *O'Driscoll v Manchester Insurance Committee* [1915] 3 K.B. 499.
[92] It follows that the wide definition of "debt" in r.13.12 of the Insolvency Rules 1986 is not applicable for the purpose of the cash flow test in s.123(1)(e), although it is for the purpose of the balance sheet test in s.123(2) (see para.4–24). See further below.
[93] *Re Bryant Investment Co Ltd* [1974] 2 All E.R. 683.

contingent liabilities,[94] and prospective liabilities[95] must all be ignored. However, it is important to bear in mind the point made earlier, that in looking at the state of the company's affairs the court does not confine itself to the way matters stand on the date of assessment, but looks at what is likely to happen in the near future. So although debts payable in the future and contingent debts have to be excluded in determining whether, *at the date of the hearing*, the company is able to discharge debts then due and payable, the court also has to consider whether, in relation to debts which will become due and payable in the near future, the company will be able to pay those debts at the time when payment has to be made.[96] In other words, the date of the hearing is not the only temporal point. Where the court is satisfied that debts which at the date of the hearing have not then become payable or are only contingent will at a later point in the not too distant future become existing debts presently payable and that at that point the company will be unable to pay them, the cash flow test of insolvency is satisfied. The point was neatly expressed by Briggs J. in *Re Cheyne Finance plc*:[97]

> "In my judgement, the effect of the alterations to the insolvency test made in 1985 and now found in s.123 of the 1986 Act was to replace in the commercial solvency test now in s.123(1)(e), one futurity requirement, namely to include contingent and prospective liabilities, with another more flexible and fact-sensitive requirement encapsulated in the new phrase 'as they fall due'."

Two examples will suffice.

Example 1

The hearing of a winding up petition takes place on May 1. The company's liability to its bank for repayment of a loan matures on May 20. In deciding whether on May 1, the company is able to pay its debts as they fall due the court will consider, amongst other things, whether the company will be in a position to repay the loan on May 20.

Example 2

A payment by the company to one of its creditors is being attacked as a preference, and the question for decision is whether at the time of the payment the company was unable to pay its debts as they fell due. At that time the company had a contingent liability as surety under a guarantee.

---

[94] See below, para.4–26.
[95] See below, para.4–27.
[96] *Re Cheyne Finance Plc* [2008] B.C.C. 182; *Macplant Services v Contract Letting Services* [2009] S.C. 125; *Invertec Ltd v De Mol Holding BV* [2009] EWHC 2471 (Ch); and *New Cap Reinsurance Corp Ltd v Grant* (2008) 68 A.C.S.R. 176.
[97] [2008] B.C.C. 182 at [56].

Payment was due from the principal debtor four weeks later and the principal debtor had already convened a meeting to pass a resolution for voluntary winding up by reason of its insolvency. It would have been clear at the time of the alleged preference that the contingent liability would shortly mature into an existing liability. The court can therefore properly take that liability into account in considering whether at the time of the payment in question the company was able to pay its debts as they fell due.

Only debts of which current repayment is required are to be considered

4–19   In deciding whether a company is able to pay debts becoming payable in the future, the court will take a commercial view of when payment is required, and will have regard to the fact that it is quite normal for debtors to make, and for creditors to accept, late payment.[98] So even if payment cannot be made on the exact date due, it suffices that it can be made within the period that a creditor would consider acceptable, for which purpose the court will have regard to any indulgence customarily granted by that creditor.[99] By the same token, even debts which are technically due are to be ignored where there is no current indication that the creditors concerned are requiring repayment.[100] If the position were otherwise, most banks would be insolvent, for banks operate on the basis that only a relatively small proportion of their depositors will demand repayment at any one time. Where a company arranges an overdraft facility with its bank this is likely, whether as an express or an implied term of the banker-customer contract, to be repayable on demand. But neither party contemplates that such demand will be made so long as the company is continuing to operate as a going concern and the bank is content to allow the relationship to continue. In most cases, the overdraft facility will be renewed from year to year and continue indefinitely. Accordingly, unless the bank has either demanded immediate repayment or is likely to do so in the immediate future, the overdraft should be ignored in deciding whether the company is able to pay its debts as they fall due. That is no doubt why, in *R.(on the application of SRM Global Master Fund LP) v Commissioners of HM Treasury*,[101] it was said that, in the context of banking, insolvency refers to balance sheet insolvency, so that a bank may be solvent even if it is unable to pay debts as they fall due, although if the lack of liquidity were sufficiently serious this would mean that the bank was insolvent.[102]

---

[98] *Iso Lilodw' Aliphumeleli Pty Ltd v Commissioner of Taxation* (2002) 42 A.C.S.R. 561.
[99] See below.
[100] *Re Capital Annuities Ltd* [1978] 3 All E.R. 704, per Slade J. at 718. This case is notable for the fact that the company went into winding up on its own petition and was anxious for the court to declare it insolvent, a declaration the court found unable to make on the available evidence!
[101] [2009] B.C.C. 251.
[102] ibid. at [17].

The same applies to debts due to trade creditors who, by way of indulgence and without contractual commitment to do so, customarily allow a period of trade credit as regards the debts in question.[103]

Again, where a winding up order was made against a company and creditors of the company in respect of debts payable on demand were related entities of the company and were controlled by the same person controlling the company, and that person had intimated his concern to save the company from liquidation, the court directed that the winding up should be terminated if each of the creditors gave a written undertaking not to make demand for payment and the controller gave a written undertaking not to procure or permit a breach of the creditors' undertakings.[104]

Insufficiency of liquid assets does not necessarily indicate inability to pay

A company is not necessarily insolvent on the cash flow test simply because
it does not have sufficient ready cash to meet its debts as they fall due. It suffices that it can raise the funds needed within the required time, for example by borrowing them[105] or by disposing of liquid assets. But in considering the prospect of borrowing, the court will consider whether the company had a history of borrowing or whether its ability to do so is purely speculative. There must be a significant probability of borrowed funds being available in time to meet the debts.[106] Moreover, if the borrowing is to be short term and it is clear that it will be unable to be repaid when due, allowing for any indulgence the company can reasonably expect from the lender, then all the company is doing is substituting a prospective creditor who will not be paid for an existing creditor, and the existence of the borrowing ability will not affect its insolvent status. Further, the borrowing must not affect the solvency of the lender, as could happen if the lender is an associated company. In the words of Palmer J. in the Australian case *Hall v Poolman*[107]:

4–20

---

[103] *Sycotex Pty Ltd v Baseter* (1993) 13 A.C.S.R. 766, per Gummow J. at 775, applied in *Sutherland v Eurolinx Pty Ltd* (2001) 37 A.C.S.R. 477. In *Southern Cross Interiors Pty Ltd v Deputy Commissioner of Taxation* (2001) 39 A.C.S.R. 305, the New South Wales Supreme Court held that the court will assume that a debt is payable at the time stipulated in the contract unless this presumption is displaced by proof of an express or implied agreement between the parties, a course of conduct sufficient to ground an estoppel or a well-established course of conduct in the industry as to payment other than as stipulated in the contract.

[104] *Brolrik Pty Ltd v Sambah Holdings Pty Ltd* (2002) 40 A.C.S.R. 361.

[105] *Re A Company (No.006794 of 1983)* [1986] B.C.L.C. 261, where the evidence was that the company kept itself going by borrowing from associated companies and other sources. The Australian cases generally disregarded unsecured borrowing as a resource, but that was because the Australian legislation required companies to be able to make payment from their own moneys. This is no longer the case. See the Corporations Act 2001 s.95A. There has never been such a requirement in English corporate insolvency law.

[106] *MacPlant Services Ltd v Contract Lifting Services (Scotland) Ltd* [2009] S.C. 125, per Lord Hodge at [76].

[107] (2007) 65 A.C.S.R. 123 at [64].

"If one member of a group of companies has, as a matter of commercial reality, ready recourse to the assets of another member of the group for payment of the first company's debts as they fall due, and that recourse will not result in the insolvency of the second company or in merely delaying the insolvency of the first, then the court may have regard to that fact in assessing whether the first company is able to pay its debts as they fall due."

Again, the prospective proceeds of an asset cannot be taken into account if the asset that is to be disposed of to pay the current debts cannot realistically be turned into cash in time to meet those debts[108] or is an asset which is essential to the continuance of the company's business as a going concern.[109]

Default in payment is sufficient evidence of inability to pay

4–21   Where a company defaults in payment of an undisputed debt after demand has been made, that is sufficient evidence that it is unable to pay its debts as they fall due,[110] and if it persists in its failure to pay it will be taken to be unable to pay its debts even if in fact it appears to be solvent.[111] This salutary rule, which applies on the failure to pay even a single debt,[112] reflects the view that a company which is able to pay an undisputed debt and chooses not to do so has only itself to blame if the inference is drawn that it is unable to pay. The decision of Harman J. in *Cornhill Insurance Plc v Improvement Services Ltd*[113] provides a graphic illustration. In that case, the defendants made a claim on the plaintiffs under an insurance policy covering damage by fire, and agreement was reached between the defendants' solicitors and the plaintiffs' loss adjusters for payment of a total of £1,154. Despite repeated demands by the defendants' solicitors, the agreed sum was not paid and eventually the defendants' solicitors threatened to present a winding up petition. The plaintiffs, a large and prosperous insurance company, applied for an injunction to restrain the presentation of the petition on the ground that it was a public company carrying on a substantial business with huge assets and there was absolutely no evidence that it was insolvent, so that the presentation of a petition would be an abuse of the process of the court. An ex parte injunction was granted, but Harman J. refused to continue it on the substantive hearing, holding that in the circumstances the defendants were entitled to present a petition.

---

[108] *Hall v Poolman* (2007) 65 A.C.S.R. 123 at [187].
[109] *Re Timbatec Pty Ltd* (1974) 24 F.L.R. 30.
[110] *Re Globe New Patent Iron & Steel Co* (1875) L.R. 20 Eq. 337; *Mann v Goldstein* [1968] 2 All E.R. 769, per Ungoed-Thomas J. at 773; and *Cornhill Insurance Plc v Improvement Services Ltd* [1986] 1 W.L.R. 114.
[111] *Mann v Goldstein*, cited above n.110; *Cornhill Insurance*, cited above n.110; and *Re A Company (No.006273 of 1992)* [1993] B.C.L.C. 131.
[112] *Cornhill Insurance*, cited above n.110.
[113] Above, n.110.

"This is a case of a rich company which could pay an undoubted debt and has chosen—I think I must use that word—not to do so from June 12, to today. In my view in such circumstances the creditor was entitled to (a) threaten to and (b) in fact if it chooses present a winding up petition . . ."[114]

In *Cornhill*, the debt was undisputed. What if there is a bona fide dispute as to the debt in that the alleged debtor honestly believes that it is not liable? This is not a sufficient answer to the petition; it is necessary for the respondent to go further and show substantial grounds for disputing liability. Thus, in *Taylors Industrial Flooring Ltd v M. & H. Plant Hire (Manchester) Ltd*,[115] the Court of Appeal held that in the absence of evidence of grounds for dispute of the debt a creditor was perfectly entitled to proceed with the presentation of a winding up petition on the ground of presumed insolvency without the need to serve a statutory demand under s.123(1)(a). Only if there was a bona fide dispute on substantial grounds would the presentation of a petition be an abuse of the process of the court.[116] A mere honest belief by the debtor that it was not liable would not be sufficient if there was no substantial ground of defence. Accordingly, the only course open to a solvent debtor against whom a winding up petition is presented is to pay the debt before the hearing, although it would then be open to any supporting creditors to apply to be substituted for the petitioner.[117] The presentation of a winding up petition is thus a perfectly legitimate debt collection device; it is not an objection that the creditor's motive is to obtain payment of the debt rather than a winding up order.

Failure to pay a debt which cannot reasonably be disputed may enable the court to infer insolvency even if there has been no demand.[118] On the other hand, non-payment of an undisputed debt does not necessarily raise the inference that the debtor company is insolvent; the petitioner must prove the circumstances from which that inference can be drawn.[119] In *Cornhill*, there were repeated demands for payment which were ignored; in *Purewal*, there were moves towards tender of payment if certain conditions were agreed, so that non-payment did not raise the inference of inability to pay.

3. THE BALANCE SHEET TEST: GENERAL CONSIDERATIONS

The basic test

Under the balance sheet test, a company is insolvent if its assets are insufficient to meet its liabilities. However, the insolvency legislation adopts two

4–22

---

[114] Above, n.110, at 118. The debt was later paid.
[115] [1990] B.C.L.C. 216.
[116] See para.5–13.
[117] See para.5–18.
[118] *MacPlant Services Ltd v Contract Lifting Services (Scotland) Ltd* [2009] S.C. 125.
[119] *Purewal Enterprises Ltd, Petitioner* [2008] C.S.O.H. 127.

different formulations of the test, although their effect would seem to be the same. Section 123(2) specifically requires account to be taken of contingent and prospective liabilities.[120] This definition therefore provides an applicable test of insolvency for the purposes of winding up and of all other provisions applying s.123, namely those relating to administration[121] and the avoidance of transactions.[122] Section 214(6), in defining insolvent liquidation, speaks of "debts and other liabilities and the expenses of winding up". This formulation is adopted verbatim in s.6(2) of the Company Directors Disqualification Act 1986. We shall begin with the test laid down in s.123(2) and then go on to consider whether s.214(6) is different in substance.

The balance sheet test in s.123(2)

4–23   Section 123(2) provides as follows:

> "A company is also deemed unable to pay its debts if it is proved to the satisfaction of the court that the value of the company's assets is less than the amount of its liabilities, taking into account its contingent and prospective liabilities."

The fundamental purpose of s.123(2) should not be overlooked. The mere excess of liabilities over assets is not in itself determinative. What has to be shown is that by the reason of the deficiency of its assets the company has reached the point of no return.[123] In contrast to the cash flow basis, which is concerned with the payment of debts as they fall due,[124] the balance sheet basis embodied in s.123(2) requires account to be taken of liabilities, including contingent and prospective liabilities. "Liabilities" is a much broader term than "debts".[125] It embraces all forms of liability, whether liquidated or unliquidated and whether arising in contract or in tort or by way of restitution or for damages for breach of statutory duty. It would also seem to encompass contingent and prospective liabilities,[126] but to put the matter beyond doubt s.123(2) expressly covers these.

---

[120] For the history of this formulation, see above, para.4–04.
[121] Insolvency Act 1986 Sch.B1 para.11(a).
[122] Insolvency Act 1986 ss.238, 239 and 245.
[123] *BNY Corporate Trustee Services Ltd v Eurosail-UK* [2011] EWCA Civ 227. See above, para.4–06.
[124] But these words do import consideration of debts falling due in the near future. See above, para.4–16.
[125] See, e.g. *Re A Debtor (No.17 of 1966)* [1967] Ch. 590, where Goff J., applying the decision in *Re European Life Assurance Co* (1869) L.R. 9 Eq. 122, held that for the purpose of s.6 of the Bankruptcy Act 1914, which referred only to the debtor's inability to pay his "debts", future liabilities could not be taken into account, and dismissed the bankruptcy petition. However, r.13.12(1) of the Insolvency Rules 1986 defines debt in terms which include a future liability. See below.
[126] Indeed, r.13.12(3) of the Insolvency Rules expressly so provides.

"Debt" and "liability"

Rule 13.12 is of some importance in the application of the above definition **4–24** for the purposes of the balance sheet test of insolvency in winding up.

"13.12 'Debt', 'liability' (winding up)

(1) 'Debt', in relation to the winding up of a company, means (subject to the next paragraph) any of the following—

    (a) any debt or liability to which the company is subject—

        (i) in the case of a winding up which was not immediately preceded by an administration, at the date on which the company went into liquidation;

        (ii) in the case of a winding up which was immediately preceded by an administration, at the date on which the company entered administration;

    (b) any debt or liability to which the company may become subject after that date by reason of any obligation incurred before that date; and

    (c) any interest provable as mentioned in Rule 4.93(1).

(2) For the purposes of any provision of the Act or the Rules about winding up, any liability in tort is a debt provable in the winding up, if either—

    (a) the cause of action has accrued—

        (i) in the case of a winding up which was not immediately preceded by an administration, at the date on which the company went into liquidation;

        (ii) in the case of a winding up which was immediately preceded by an administration, at the date on which the company entered administration;

    (b) all the elements necessary to establish the cause of action exist at that date except for actionable damage.

(3) For the purposes of references in any provision of the Act or the Rules about winding up to a debt or liability, it is immaterial whether the debt or liability is present or future, whether it is certain or contingent, or whether its amount is fixed or liquidated, or is capable of being ascertained by fixed rules or as a matter of opinion; and references in any such provision to owing a debt are to be read accordingly.

(4) In any provision of the Act or the Rules about winding up, except in so far as the context otherwise requires, 'liability' means (subject to paragraph (3) above) a liability to pay money or money's worth, including

any liability under an enactment, any liability for breach of trust, any liability in contract, tort or bailment, and any liability arising out of an obligation to make restitution.

(5) This Rule shall apply where a company is in administration and shall be read as if:

   (a) references to winding up were references to administration,
   (b) references to administration were references to winding up,
   (c) references to going into liquidation were references to going into administration, and
   (d) references to entering administration were references to going into liquidation."

Except in relation to the cash flow test, for which purpose "debt" has a narrower meaning,[127] these definitions are relevant to all statutory provisions relating to winding up and proof of debt, and they have been successfully invoked as showing that a creditor has a locus standi to present a winding up petition even if the amount of the relevant debt is unascertained, as where it is a liability for untaxed costs.[128] However, they do not exhaustively convey the concept of a liability, particularly with regard to executory contracts and loss and expenditure not arising from a purely legal obligation, nor do they deal with what constitutes an asset. Accordingly, these concepts must now be examined. We may note in passing that while r.13.12(2) is confined to debts arising from liability in tort, it is a general principle that only debts in existence at the time of commencement of the winding up are provable, although it is not necessary that they shall have become payable by that time.[129] By way of exception, a claim in tort that would have been established but for the fact that the actionable loss or damage had not occurred by the time of liquidation is now a provable debt.[130]

Legal form and economic substance

4–25   The question of what constitutes an asset is discussed in Chapter 6. At this point we should note that there is a difference between the legal and accounting conceptions of assets and liabilities. Both law and accountancy distinguish between capital transactions, in which an asset is acquired for a price, and revenue transactions, in which rent is paid for the use of another's assets, or some other revenue expenditure is incurred. But while the general

---

[127] See above para.4–17.
[128] *Tottenham Hotspur Plc v Edennote Plc* [1995] 1 B.C.L.C. 65.
[129] See below, para.8–41.
[130] Insolvency Rules 1986 r.13.12(2), introduced in consequence of the decision in *Re T & N Ltd* [2006] 2 B.C.L.C. 374 that a claim in tort in respect of which loss or damage had not yet occurred was not provable. The word "or" should have been inserted after the end of sub-paragraph (a) but the sense is clear.

law and tax law concentrate on the location of title,[131] accounting standards[132] focus on economic substance. For example, in law, ownership of an asset held by a company as buyer under a contract reserving title to the seller until payment remains with the seller until payment has been completed, while for accounting purposes it is treated as the asset of the buyer. Similarly, the law does not distinguish finance leases from operating leases; both are contracts of hire and in neither case is the lessee treated as owner. But modern accounting rules distinguish a finance lease from an operating lease.[133] A finance lease is one that transfers substantially all of the risks and rewards of ownership of an asset to the lessee; an operating lease is one in which such risks and rewards are retained by the lessor.[134] For accounting purposes, a finance lease is treated very much as if it were a purchase financed by a loan. The lessee's balance sheet will show the leased item as an asset (which will be depreciated annually) capitalised as the present value of the minimum rentals, while the capital element of the total future rentals outstanding at year-end will be shown as a liability.[135] Accordingly, for the purpose of the balance sheet test, both entries are relevant in computing the relationship between the debtor company's assets and liabilities. In contrast, an item comprised in an operating lease will not feature as an asset in the lessee's balance sheet, and payments due under the lease after the end of the accounting period will not appear as liabilities.[136]

That is how matters stand at the moment in relation to accounting for leases. However, there has been much criticism of the finance lease/operating lease dichotomy as failing to meet the needs of users of financial statements, and the International Accounting Standards Board has issued an exposure draft containing proposals that would require recognition of both types of lease in the balance sheet.[137] Again, while the definition of "debt or liability"

---

[131] However, in tax law this point has become blurred by the practice of HM Revenue & Customs, upheld in *Gallagher v Jones* [1994] Ch. 107, in requiring that rentals should be spread not as provided by the lease, but in accordance with generally accepted principles of commercial accounting, and in particular those embodied in SSAP 21.

[132] For the UK accountancy profession, International Financial Reporting Standards (IFRSs) issued by the International Accounting Standards Board and replacing Statements of Standard Accounting Practice (SSAPs).

[133] See SSAP 21 and *Goode on Commercial Law*, edited by Ewan McKendrick, 4th edn (London: Penguin Books and LexisNexis, 2009), p.768, n.7. Although SSAP 21 is primarily concerned with equipment leasing (and it is in this context that the terms "finance lease" and "operating lease" are normally used), it is equally applicable to leases of buildings. See, e.g. para.SSAP 21, para. 56.

[134] See SSAP 21, paras 6–8, 15 and 17; and IAS 17, para.8.

[135] In the lessor's balance sheet the asset that will be recorded is not the item itself, but the net investment value, represented in the first year by the difference between its cost and the capital element of lease payments attributable to that year and in each subsequent year by the previous year's net investment value less the capital element of lease payments attributable to the subsequent year in question.

[136] This analysis is also relevant to the question of whether liability for future rent under a lease is a provable debt. See below, para.8–43.

[137] Exposure Draft ED/2010/9, *Leases* (August 2010).

in r.13.12 of the Insolvency Rules 1986 is broad, covering contingent liabilities and unliquidated claims, the accounting concept of a liability is broader still and includes projected losses and expenditure which are not obligatory in law, but are commercially unavoidable.

These differences between the legal and accounting concepts of what constitutes an asset and what constitutes a liability do not normally matter for the purpose of the balance sheet test of insolvency, so long as the company is able to maintain the payments needed to preserve its right to retain assets which in law do not belong to it. In such a situation, the crucial factor in applying the balance sheet test is not the status of an individual balance sheet item, but the net asset or net liability position. For this purpose, it is usually immaterial whether an item for which future payments have to be made by the company is shown as an asset, and the future payments as a capitalised liability, in the company's balance sheet or is treated as still the property of the other party, in which case the company's balance sheet will record neither an asset nor a liability in respect of the transaction. The net effect will in many cases be broadly the same. However, if the company is not in a position to keep up its payments under a conditional sale or hire-purchase agreement or finance lease, then it faces the prospect of loss of the equipment without a corresponding reduction in its liability, for the other party will have a claim for damages based on the discounted value of the lost value rentals. In that situation, it is the legal rather than the accounting treatment that will give a better picture of the company's net asset position.

In most cases, therefore, the court is likely to follow generally accepted accounting principles in deciding what constitutes a balance sheet asset or liability, but may decline to do so where for any reason it considers that this would be inappropriate. The discussion which follows should be read with this caveat in mind.

Contingent and prospective liabilities

(1) Contingent liabilities

4–26   A contingent event is one which may or may not occur. But to say that a contingent liability is a liability which may or may not be incurred is to spread the net far too wide, for the number of contingencies as thus defined is infinite. Is it to be said, for example, that because I may decide at some future date to buy goods and incur a liability for the price I have a contingent liability? Clearly not. No one can tell what transactions I may decide to enter into in the future or on what terms. To give the phrase "contingent liability" any meaning we must restrict it to a liability or other loss which arises out of an existing legal obligation or state of affairs, but which is dependent on the happening of an event that may or may not occur. Many of the cases have stressed the need for the liability to arise out of an existing obligation.[138] Examples are: the liability of a surety, which is created by the guarantee, but arises only on default by the principal debtor; of a drawer or indorser of a bill of exchange, which is created by signature of the bill, but comes into existence only if the acceptor as the party primarily liable fails to pay; of an insurer under a policy of indemnity insurance, which is created by issue of the policy, but depends on the occurrence of the event against which cover is given; and of a defendant or prospective defendant in a claim for negligence which may or may not succeed. However, it is not every contingent liability that springs from an existing legal obligation. In *Re Sutherland deceased*[139] a majority of the House of Lords considered that to require an existing legal obligation was to take too narrow a view of what constitutes a contingent liability. It is true that this was a tax case, not a decision on insolvency legislation, but what it does show is that in considering whether there is a contingent liability the court has regard to the existing commercial situation, not merely an existing legal obligation. In this regard, assistance can be derived from Financial Reporting Standard 12, which defines a contingent liability in the following terms:

(a) "A possible obligation that arises from past events and whose existence will be confirmed only by the occurrence or non-occurrence of one or more uncertain future events not wholly within the entity's control; or

(b) a present obligation that arises from past events but is not recognised because:

  (i) it is not probable that a transfer of economic benefits will be required to settle the obligation; or

  (ii) the amount of the obligation cannot be measured with sufficient reliability."[140]

It will be seen that in this definition the reference is to "past events" rather than legal obligations. Of course, accounting definitions do not necessarily correspond to legal definitions. But as has rightly been pointed out, the term "contingent liabilities" is ultimately not a term of art and its precise meaning

---

[138] See *New Cap Reinsurance Ltd v Grant* (2008) 68 A.C.S.R. 176; *Winter v I.R.C.* [1961] 3 All E.R. 855, per Lord Hodson at 864; *Re William Hockley Ltd* [1962] 2 All E.R. 111, per Pennycuick J. at 113; and *Stonegate Securities Ltd v Gregory* [1980] 1 Ch. 576, per Buckley L.J. at 579 ("a creditor in respect of a debt which only becomes due in an event which may or may not occur").

[139] *Re Sutherland deceased, Winter v I.R.C.* [1963] A.C. 235.

[140] FRS 12, Provisions, Contingent Liabilities and Contingent Assets (replacing SSAP 18, Accounting for Contingencies). Contingencies are distinguished from provisions, that is, liabilities which are bound to arise in the nature, but where the timing and amount are uncertain. See also below, para.4–32, as to accounting standards. For a detailed discussion of contingent and prospective creditors, see Lee Beng Tat, "Claiming a Pound of Flesh as a Contingent or Prospective Creditor under the [Singapore] Companies Act" [1993] Singapore Journal of Legal Studies 144.

will depend on its context.[141] The court is thus entitled to have regard to commercial realities. In *Re Sutherland* the factual situation was the near-certainty that ships would be sold, producing balancing charges for tax purposes. An example in terms of an existing commercial situation is the projected expenditure to be incurred if a product has to be recalled in order to remedy as a matter of goodwill defects for which the company has no legal liability, past experience having shown that such a recall is likely to be needed at least once during the course of a year. By contrast, the potential liability of a litigant to have an order for costs made against him is too uncertain and too much in the discretion of the court to rank as a contingent liability.[142]

(2) Prospective liabilities

4–27 The phrase "prospective liability" is neither a legal nor an accounting term of art. It has been judicially defined as:

> ". . . a debt which will certainly become due in the future, either on some date which has already been determined or on some date determinable by reference to future events."[143]

In two other cases it has been described in argument as an unmatured liability which will inevitably ripen into a debt with the passage of time.[144] Such a definition encompasses all forms of *debitum in praesenti, solvendum in futuro*,[145] including an indisputable claim for unliquidated damages which remains only to be quantified and will result in a debt for more than a nominal amount.[146] "Prospective liability" thus embraces both future debts, in the sense of liquidated sums due, and unliquidated claims. Examples are liability on an unmatured bill of exchange,[147] a liability payment for work in progress

---

[141] *County Bookshops Ltd v Grove* [2003] 1 B.C.L.C. 479.

[142] *Glenister v Rowe* [2000] Ch. 76.

[143] *Stonegate Securities*, cited above n.137, per Buckley L.J. at 579; and *New Cap Reinsurance Corp Ltd v Grant* (2008) 68 A.C.S.R. 176, per White J. at [75].

[144] See, e.g. the arguments of counsel in *Re British Equitable Bond and Mortgage Corp Ltd* [1910] 1 Ch. 574 at 576; and *Re A Company (No.001573 of 1983)* (1983) 1 B.C.C. 98,937 at 98,939.

[145] Although it is not relevant to the present discussion, we may note at this point that other parts of the insolvency legislation speak not of "prospective" debts, but of "future" debts. For example, r.13.12(3) of the Insolvency Rules 1986, which provides that for the purposes of references in any provision of the Act or Rules about winding up to a debt or liability it is immaterial whether the debtor or liability is present or future, certain or contingent. Given that "debt" is defined in r.13.12(1) as a debt or liability to which the company is subject at the date on which it goes into liquidation or any debt or liability to which it may become subject by reason of any obligation incurred before that date, it is evident that in the phrase "present or future" the word "present" denotes an existing debt that has become payable, while the word "future" means an existing debt that has not yet become payable, in other words, a class of prospective debt, the other class being an unliquidated claim.

[146] *Re Dollar Land Holdings Ltd* [1994] B.C.L.C. 404.

[147] *Re A Company (No.001573 of 1983)*, cited above n.143.

that has been carried out but not yet quantified, and the prospective liability of a building owner under a completed building contract where the sum payable depends not only on completion of the contract works, but on adjustments to be made in respect of prime cost sums, provisions, variations and the like. Also included is the capital value of the future rentals payable by a lessee under a finance lease.[148] Where it is necessary to establish inability to pay debts for the purpose of winding up, the projected expenses of winding up must, it is thought, be taken into account as a prospective liability, for it is inevitable that such expenses will be incurred. It is curious, however, that while specific reference is made to the expenses of winding up in the definition of insolvent liquidation in s.214 relating to wrongful trading[149] and of an insolvent company in s.6 of the Company Directors Disqualification Act 1986,[150] there is no mention of it in s.123(2), perhaps because it was thought otiose in view of the reference to contingent and prospective liabilities. Similarly, where for the purpose of obtaining an administration order[151] it is necessary to show that the company is or is likely to become unable to pay its debts,[152] the projected costs of the administration should be included as prospective liabilities.

The balance sheet test as a ground for an administration order

An administrator can now be appointed out of court, in which event it is not necessary that the company be insolvent, or even likely to become insolvent, except where the appointment is made by the company or the directors.[153] But where the company or its directors apply for an administration order, the court has to be satisfied either that the company is unable to pay its debts—the test here being the same as for a winding up order—or that it is likely to become unable to do so.[154] Where the cash flow test is relied on—i.e. where the contention is that the company is likely to be unable to pay its debts as they fall due—it would seem that this is not confined to the prospect of the company being unable at a future time to pay debts existing at the date of the administration order, but extends to the likelihood of its inability to pay future debts. If this is right, the test is satisfied by showing that the company, although currently paying its own way, is likely to trade at a loss in the future

4–28

---

[148] See below, para.8–43.
[149] Insolvency Act 1986 s.214(6).
[150] Company Directors Disqualification Act 1986 s.6(2).
[151] As opposed to an out-of-court administration.
[152] Insolvency Act 1986 Sch.B1 para.11(a).
[153] See below, para.11–11.
[154] See below, para.11–11.

and to be unable to pay its future debts as these arise. In this context, "likely" means "more probable than not".[155]

The balance sheet test as a ground for a contribution order for wrongful trading

4–29   As previously stated, in determining whether a company has gone into insolvent liquidation for the purposes of an order under s.214 of the Insolvency Act requiring a director involved in wrongful trading to contribute to the assets of the company, the test is that the assets are insufficient for the payment of its debts and other liabilities and the expenses of winding up. Although s.214(6), in contrast to s.123(2), does not expressly refer to contingent or prospective liabilities, the word "liabilities" on its own would seem sufficient to cover these.[156]

The balance sheet test as a ground of avoidance of transactions

4–30   For the purpose of the provisions of the Insolvency Act 1986 relating to transactions at an undervalue made, preferences given and floating charges created by an insolvent company, the test is whether the company was unable to pay its debts within the meaning of s.123 of the Act or became unable to do so in consequence of the transaction or preference sought to be avoided.

The balance sheet test as a ground of disqualification of directors

4–31   For a company that has not gone into administration or administrative receivership, the balance sheet test is applied in the same terms as for wrongful trading.

4. THE BALANCE SHEET TEST: COMPUTATION OF ASSETS AND LIABILITIES

Problems of valuation

4–32   As previously stated, the valuation of assets is not an exact science, and the same is true of the estimation of contingent liabilities. The purpose of

---

[155] *Hammonds v Pro-Fit USA Ltd* [2008] 2 B.C.L.C. 159; and *Re AA Mutual Insurance Co Ltd* [2005] 2 B.C.L.C. 8, following *Re COLT Telecom Group Plc* [2003] B.P.I.R. 324. For the somewhat different meaning of "reasonably likely" in Sch.B1 para.11(b), see below, para.11–47.
[156] See above, para.4–24.

accounts is to furnish a true and fair view of a company's financial position and of profit or loss for the accounting period; indeed, the directors of a company must not approve accounts unless they are satisfied that they give a true and fair view of the company's assets, liabilities, financial position and profit or loss.[157] Accounts must be prepared in conformity with legislation, and subject to this they are also expected either to conform to guidelines laid down by the accountancy professional bodies or to disclose and explain significant departures from such guidelines. Numerous Statements of Standard Accounting Practice (SSAPs) were issued by the Accounting Standards Committee covering such diverse matters as stock and work in progress,[158] accounting for depreciation,[159] accounting for post-balance sheet events,[160] accounting for contingencies,[161] foreign currency translation,[162] accounting for leases and hire-purchase contracts[163] and accounting for goodwill.[164] The Committee's successor, the Accounting Standards Board (ASB), has adopted many of the SSAPs, while amending or withdrawing others, and has issued its own standards, Financial Reporting Standards (FRSs). These include cash flow statements,[165] accounting for subsidiary undertakings,[166] tangible fixed assets,[167] goodwill and intangible assets,[168] and provisions, contingent liabilities and contingent assets.[169] The adopted SSAPs and the FRSs together constitute the statements of standard accounting practice and these are recognised for the purposes of the Companies Act 2006.[170]

Compliance with published professional standards is strong evidence that accounts do reflect a true and fair view.[171] However, the accounting standards are not intended to be rigid rules; they may and should be departed from where this is necessary in order to give a true and fair view of a company's financial affairs. There are a number of issues of accounting practice which are regarded as unsettled, even controversial, and the published standards themselves recognise that there are areas of particular difficulty in which valuation is very much a matter of informed judgment. Much of the problem centres on the extent to which accounts for the period under consideration should reflect costs incurred or to be incurred and revenue received or to be

---

[157] Companies Act 2006 s.393(1).
[158] SSAP 9.
[159] SSAP 12, prospectively replaced by FRS 15.
[160] FRS 21.
[161] SSAP 18, since replaced by FRS 12.
[162] SSAP 20.
[163] SSAP 21, which is expected to be superseded shortly.
[164] FRS 10, replacing SSAP 22.
[165] FRS 1.
[166] FRS 2.
[167] FRS 15.
[168] FRS 10.
[169] FRS 12.
[170] Companies Act 2006 s.464. The ASB has been prescribed as the issuing body by the Accounting Standards (Prescribed Body) Regulations 2008, SI 2008/651, reg.2.
[171] *Macquarie Internationale Investments Ltd v Glencore UK Ltd* [2010] EWCA Civ 697 at [52].

received in the previous or subsequent accounting period. Particularly difficult is the valuation of stock and work in progress, on which there are widely differing approaches. The crux of the problem was succinctly stated in a written opinion of counsel obtained by the Accounting Standards Committee on the meaning of "true and fair", with particular reference to accounting standards[172]:

> "... it is first necessary to examine the nature of the 'true and fair view' concept as used in the Companies Act. It is an abstraction or philosophical concept expressed in simple English. The law uses many similar concepts, of which 'reasonable care' is perhaps the most familiar example. It is a common feature of such concepts that there is seldom any difficulty in understanding what they mean but frequent controversy over their application to particular facts. One reason for this phenomenon is that because such concepts represent a very high level of abstraction which has to be applied to an infinite number of concrete facts, there can never be a sharply defined line between, for example, what is reasonable care and what is not. There will always be a penumbral area in which views may differ ... The issue of an SSAP has the effect ... of creating a *prima facie* presumption that accounts which do not comply are not true and fair. This presumption is then strengthened or weakened by the extent to which the SSAP is actually accepted and applied."

In most cases there is little or no doubt as to a company's insolvency, but in marginal situations the basis of valuation and the assessment of values upon that basis can be crucial. Here lie the seeds of a potentially difficult problem. For the purposes of insolvency legislation, the court has to be able to decide whether on a balance of probabilities a particular company is or was at a particular time unable to pay its debts. Different accountants may have different views on the proper approach to a particular valuation; and in relation to the valuation of particular assets professional valuers may place widely differing values on the same asset. Audited accounts are the accounts of the company, not of the auditors.[173] It is not for the company's auditors to force their own views on the company; where there are different and equally legitimate approaches to a particular valuation of an asset or estimation of a liability, the company is free to select whichever of these it regards as the most appropriate to its business, the overriding requirement being that the

---

[172] This extract is taken from one of two joint Opinions given by Leonard Hoffmann Q.C. (now Lord Hoffman) and Mary Arden in 1983 and 1984 and was subsequently updated by Mary Arden Q.C. (now Arden L.J.) in an Opinion given in 1993, which does not, however, affect the substance of the quoted extract. The continued influence of this Opinion is reflected in the decision of the Court of Appeal in *Macquarie Internationale Investments*, cited above 171, at [51].

[173] A fact which directors of companies in financial difficulties conveniently forget when suing their auditors for negligence!

accounts must give a true and fair view. Moreover, as stated earlier, balance sheets are historical documents and values stated in them are not necessarily those current at the time that the valuation has to be made and may be valuations at historic cost rather than current value anyway.

It is thus perfectly possible to envisage a situation in which the application **4–33** of the balance sheet test shows on one reasonable view that the company is solvent and on another, equally reasonable, view that it is insolvent. Given such a conflict, how should the court deal with the matter? In general, it is for the party asserting a state of insolvency to prove it, not for the other party to refute it. It is thus for the applicant to show that on the balance of probabilities the company was insolvent at the relevant time.[174] In many cases, this will become apparent with the benefit of hindsight. For example, it is unlikely that a liquidator will institute proceedings for wrongful trading, or apply to set aside voidable transactions, until the liquidation is sufficiently advanced for him to have a reasonable knowledge of the relevant facts, by which time the actual amounts realised on disposal of assets will furnish an additional guide to their value at the relevant date. But this is not, of course, the case where proof of insolvency is the threshold which has to be passed at the outset, as where a creditor petitions for winding up on the ground of insolvency. Here, the court has to do the best it can on the evidence available at the time and must weigh conflicting valuations and decide on the balance of probabilities whether the company is able to pay its debts.

Moreover, great care must be taken not to rely too heavily on hindsight. The crucial question is the value of assets and liabilities at the relevant date, not their value at a later date. The latter may be a guide to the former, but this is not necessarily the case. Assets may rise or fall in value because of events occurring after the relevant date. It is necessary to be particularly cautious in applying hindsight to cases involving personal liability, for example, for wrongful trading, or the setting aside of a transaction, for example, as a transaction at an undervalue or preference. Business life is neither static nor certain. Information has constantly to be updated, predictions made about a range of uncertain events, snap judgments formed, rapid decisions taken and adaptations continually made in the light of shifts in customer demand, tax changes, industrial action, political events, international relations and the like. Just as it is all too easy for historians to pick their way leisurely across the battlefields of Waterloo identifying Napoleon's errors in the tranquillity of academic research, unhindered by all of the confusions engendered by blazing guns, cavalry charges, mud, darkness, uncertainty as to the current arrivals or dispositions of troops and ignorance of the enemy's intentions, so too a professional acquainted with subsequent events in a company's life is

---

[174] However, where a company enters into a transaction at an undervalue with a person connected with the company, its inability to pay its debts at that time is presumed unless the contrary is shown (Insolvency Act 1986 s.240(2)).

all too readily beguiled into the view that he would have done things differently, that what is now apparent was obvious from the start.

It is submitted that where the question is whether a director of a company ought to have concluded that there was no reasonable prospect of the company avoiding insolvent liquidation,[175] the director's reliance on a reasonable accounting view that if the company did go into liquidation its assets would be sufficient in value to cover its liabilities and the expenses of winding up should suffice to render him immune from liability, even if in the event the assets realise a much lower figure than estimated, with the result that at the time of liquidation the company in fact has an asset deficiency.

Assets that can be taken into account

4–34   In principle, only the assets of the company at the relevant time[176] can be included; contingent or prospective assets, such as the prospect of receiving further injections of cash or other assets, cannot be taken into account.[177] These are in general what are referred to in accounting standards as contingent assets.[178] However, it is necessary to distinguish prospective assets unconnected with future or contingent liabilities from prospective assets that will arise from the incurring of future or contingent liabilities and thus go to the estimation of the latter.[179] For example, in estimating the contingent liability of a surety it must, it is thought, be legitimate to set against this the value of any security held by the creditor to whose rights the surety would be subrogated on paying off the debt. This is not to bring speculative new assets into account, but rather to set a net figure on the contingent liability after taking into account countervailing assets that the discharge of the liability can reasonably be expected to produce.

Valuation of assets: break-up basis or going concern basis?

4–35   Whether assets should be valued on a break-up basis or a going concern basis depends on the circumstances. In principle, this should turn on whether, as seen at the relevant time,[180] the business will be continued as a going concern. If so, the assets should be valued on a going concern basis, which is

---

[175] A question which arises in proceedings for wrongful trading under s.214 of the Insolvency Act 1986.

[176] As to the relevant time, see above, para.4–13.

[177] *Byblos Bank SAL v Al-Khudhairy* (1986) 2 B.C.C. 99, 549, applied in *BNY Corporate Trustee Services Ltd v Eurosail-UK* [2011] EWCA Civ 227.

[178] That is, a possible asset arising from past events and whose existence will be confirmed only on the occurrence of one or more uncertain future events not wholly within the entity's control (FRS 12, para.2).

[179] See *BNY Corporate Trustee Services*, cited above n.177.

[180] i.e. the time as at which the company's solvency falls to be tested.

likely to give them a substantially higher value than on a break-up basis. One of the accounting principles laid down in accounting regulations is that a company is presumed to be carrying on business as a going concern.[181] The only accounting standard relevant to the going concern basis is FRS 18, para.21 of which provides as follows:

"Going concern

21 An entity should prepare its financial statements on a going concern basis, unless

(a) the entity is being liquidated or has ceased trading, or

(b) the directors have no realistic alternative but to liquidate the entity or cease trading, in which circumstances the entity may, if appropriate, prepare its financial statements on a basis other than that of a going concern."

This is explained in the next paragraph in the following terms:

"22 The information provided by financial statements is usually most relevant if prepared on the hypothesis that the entity is to continue in operational existence for the foreseeable future. This hypothesis is commonly referred to as the going concern assumption. Financial statements are usually prepared on the basis that the reporting entity is a going concern because measures based on break-up values tend not to be relevant to users seeking to assess the entity's cash-generation ability and financial adaptability."

There is a separate auditing standard which deals exclusively with the auditor's responsibilities in the audit of financial statements relating to management's use of the going concern assumption in the preparation of the financial statements.[182]

Suppose that in the event the business cannot be sold on a going concern basis. Should this affect the relevant date for the valuation of the assets? In answering this question, it is helpful to apply by analogy the guidance given by FRS 21, Events After the Balance Sheet Date.[183] FRS 21, like its predecessor SSAP 17, distinguishes "adjusting events" from "non-adjusting events". Adjusting events are defined by para.3(a) as "those that provide evidence of conditions that existed at the balance sheet date", and under

---

[181] Large and Medium-Sized Companies and Groups (Accounts and Reports) Regulations 2008, SI 2008/410, Sch.1 Pt 2 para.11.

[182] ISA 570, "Going Concern", revised December 2009.

[183] This FRS, which embodies International Accounting Standard 10 (revised 2003), replaced SSAP 17, Accounting for Post Balance Sheet Events. Events after the balance sheet date are defined as "those events, favourable or unfavourable, that occur between the balance sheet date and the date when the financial statements are authorised for issue" (para.3).

para.8 they require adjustment of amounts recognised in the entity's financial statements. Among the examples given in para.9 are: the settlement after the balance sheet date of a court case that confirms that the entity had a present obligation at the balance sheet date; the receipt of information after the balance sheet date indicating that an asset was impaired at the balance sheet date; the bankruptcy of a customer after the balance sheet date; the sale of inventories after the balance sheet date which gives evidence of their net realisable value at the balance sheet date; and the discovery of fraud or errors that show that the financial statements are incorrect. Of particular relevance also is the direction in para.14 not to prepare financial statements on a going concern basis if management determines after the balance sheet date that it intends to liquidate the entity or to cease trading or that it has no realistic alternative but to do so. In effect, therefore, such a determination by the management is an adjusting event. Although the concept of adjusting events has not so far featured expressly in any reported case, it is reflected in two decisions to the effect that in considering whether there has been a transaction at an undervalue the court may have regard to post-transaction events in order to determine the value as at the time of the transaction.[184]

By contrast, non-adjusting events are defined by para.3(b) as those that are indicative of conditions that arose after the balance sheet date and therefore do not allow of changes in amounts in financial statements.[185] An example given is a decline in the value of market investments between the balance sheet date and the date on which the financial statements are authorised for issue.[186] Again, one of the decisions referred to above, although not referring in terms to non-adjusting events, offers further examples that would fall within this category, namely the sale of a lottery ticket which subsequently produces a large win, the sale or purchase of quoted shares before the disclosure of market sensitive information, the sale of land with hope value which is subsequently realised or the sale of residential property the value of which goes up in line with the market.[187] In all of these cases, the subsequent event is no evidence at all of the value of what was sold at the time of the transaction: it is an unconnected post-transaction condition.[188]

The same criteria can be applied to determine whether an event occurring after the relevant date for determining inability to pay debts should affect a valuation made as at that date. On this basis, an actual or impending cessation of trading after the relevant date could normally be expected to result in a retrospective revaluation of the assets as at the relevant date for the purpose of the balance sheet test of insolvency.

---

[184] *Phillips v Brewin Dolphin Bell Lawrie Ltd* [2001] 1 W.L.R. 143; and *Re Thoars deceased, Reid v Ramlort Ltd* [2003] 1 B.C.L.C. 499.

[185] FRS 21, para.10.

[186] FRS 21, para.11. However, material non-adjusting events may require disclosure (para.21).

[187] *Re Thoars deceased*, cited above n.184.

[188] See also *Joiner v George* [2003] B.C.C. 298 (in valuing shares it was not legitimate to trade results after the valuation date for those actually known before the valuation date).

Liabilities to be taken into account

As previously stated, the liabilities to be taken into account in applying   **4–36**
the balance sheet test vary with the applicable statutory provision. The
legislation employs two distinct formulations:

(1) All liabilities, taking into account contingent and prospective liabilities

This is the formulation used in the provisions relating to winding up,[189]   **4–37**
administration[190] and the avoidance of vulnerable transactions.[191] It would
also appear to include the expenses of a winding up in determining inability
to pay debts for the purpose of a winding up order or the disqualification of
a director and the expenses of an administration for the purpose of showing
jurisdiction to make an administration order.[192] "Taking into account" contingent and prospective liabilities" does not mean simply adding their face
value to the value of existing liabilities. In the first place, the present value of
future liabilities is obviously less than the value of liabilities that have already
become payable. Secondly, the accrual of contingent and prospective liabilities may be so far ahead, and subject to so many assumptions and uncertainties, that no account should be taken of them at all at the stage where the
balance sheet test has to be applied.[193]

(2) Debts and other liabilities and the expenses of winding up

This formulation is adopted in the provisions relating to wrongful trading[194]   **4–38**
and the disqualification of directors.[195] It appears to include contingent or
prospective liabilities[196] and thus to have the same meaning as in (1) above,
except, of course, that the former will not cover liquidation expenses where
no liquidation is involved.

Estimation of liabilities

Just as problems may arise in the valuation of assets, so also there may be   **4–39**
difficulties in the estimation of liabilities. This is particularly likely to be the

---

[189] Insolvency Act 1986 s.123(2).
[190] Insolvency Act 1986 s.123(2).
[191] Insolvency Act 1986 ss.240(2) and 245(4), applying s.123.
[192] See above, para.4–27.
[193] *Corporate Trustee Services Ltd v Euro-Sail UK* [2011] EWCA Civ 227.
[194] Insolvency Act 1986 s.214(6).
[195] Company Directors Disqualification Act 1986 s.6(2).
[196] Company Directors Disqualification Act 1986 s.6(2).

case as regards unqualified existing liabilities, contingent liabilities and the expenses of liquidation. In the case of existing liabilities which are as yet unquantified, the uncertainty is merely as to the amount, not as to the existence of the liability. A good example is liability incurred to a supplier of services for the value of work in progress, which is as difficult to estimate for the purpose of quantifying liability as it is to value as an asset and will in many cases depend on whether the work is ultimately completed. Another example is the expenses of liquidation. Who can predict what these will be? They depend on a whole variety of factors, for example, whether and to what extent the liquidator will have to take professional advice, whether he will be involved in litigation, or how long and complex his investigation into the company's affairs will be. These are matters which are incapable of estimation in any real sense, but the legislation requires the attempt to be made.

In the case of a contingent liability the difficulty is greater still, since the prospects of the contingency occurring may range from almost zero to a near-certainty. Accountancy standards are of limited value in this context, because contingent liabilities are not "recognised" (i.e. included as an item in the accounts), but are merely required to be disclosed by a note to the accounts unless the possibility of a transfer of economic benefits to settle the obligation is remote,[197] while the crucial question of measurement of a contingent liability remains largely unaddressed.

Where a contingent liability is capable of valuation, it should presumably be valued on the same basis as if it were being admitted to proof by the liquidator as a claim by the creditor. This does not carry us much further, since the amount for which contingent claims are admitted to proof in a winding up is usually settled by negotiation. The assessment of contingent claims and liabilities is, of course, the particular province of the actuary, but again actuarial practice is of limited relevance, because actuaries base their assessments not on individual cases, but on the total of the relevant population, whereas the question with which we are concerned is the valuation of a particular contingent liability incurred by a particular company.

There is no great difficulty in valuing many contingent liabilities. For example, if at the relevant date the company is drawer or indorser of a bill of exchange, or a surety under a guarantee, and the party primarily liable has convened a meeting for the purpose of going into insolvent voluntary winding up with no prospect of paying a dividend, the contingent liability will be little less than the face value of the bill or debt. At the other end of the scale, where the party primarily liable is financially strong or the creditor already holds massive security from the debtor, the contingent liability can be treated as so remote that it need not be given any value. The problem case is the contingency which is not so remote that it can be ignored nor so imminent that it is almost bound to happen. Different approaches are possible. One is to

---

[197] FRS 12, paras 27–28.

say that if there is a more than even chance of the contingency occurring, the liability should be taken as the present value of the contingent liability, for example, the amount of a guaranteed debt discounted to take account of its futurity. On this approach, a contingent liability with an 80 per cent chance of accrual, although discounted for futurity would not be discounted for the 20 per cent chance that it would not accrue, whilst a liability with a 50 per cent chance of accrual would be disregarded altogether. An alternative approach is to value the contingent liability at the percentage of likelihood of its occurrence, so that if the likelihood were 80 per cent the liability would be taken in at the present value of 80 per cent of the full liability, whilst a contingent liability with a 10 per cent chance of accrual would be estimated at the present value of 10 per cent of the full liability. Neither of these approaches seems fully satisfactory. The first seems to set the threshold of likelihood too high, while the second is contrary to prevailing practice, which is to value the contingency in full (less any discount for futurity) if it will probably occur and is capable of valuation and disregard it altogether in other cases. It is thought that the question to be asked is whether there is a real prospect that the contingency will occur, in which case it should be brought in at its present value without further discount for the possibility that it may not accrue.

Chapter 5

The Winding Up Process: An Outline

We have seen earlier[1] that the winding up of a company is a prelude to its ultimate demise. Leaving aside the special case of bank insolvency, there are two kinds of winding up in insolvency: a creditors' voluntary winding up and a compulsory winding up by the court. But each of these divides into sub-groups, depending on whether the winding up is brought about in the ordinary way or in the form of exit from administration. This sub-division produces four kinds of insolvency winding up: a creditors' voluntary winding up by resolution of the members[2]; a compulsory winding up by court order on a petition[3]; a creditors' voluntary winding up as an exit from administration by registration of an administrator's notice[4]; and a compulsory winding up as an exit from administration by court order.[5] An unregistered company,[6] including a company incorporated outside the United Kingdom, may be wound-up if there is a sufficient connection with the United Kingdom,[7] but an overseas company may not be put into a creditors' voluntary winding up except in accordance with the EC Insolvency Regulation.[8] The exception allows a company incorporated in another EU Member State but having its centre of main interests in England to be wound-up in England through a creditors' voluntary winding up, whether this is effected by conversion from a

5–01

---

[1] See above, para.1–39.

[2] Insolvency Act 1986 s.84(1)(b). Under s.90 the winding up will be a creditors' voluntary winding up, as opposed to a members' voluntary winding up, if the directors do not make a declaration of solvency under s.89. A creditors' voluntary winding up can also result from a resolution passed at a meeting convened by the liquidator in a members' voluntary winding up who is of the opinion that the company will be unable to pay its debts in full with interest within the period specified in the directors' declaration of solvency (ss.95 and 96).

[3] Insolvency Act 1986 s.125. Compulsory winding up may also be an exit from a CVA or administrative receivership, but there is no special procedure for this; the supervisor of the CVA simply exercises his power under s.7(4) of the Act (duplicated in para.39(5)(b) of Sch.A1) to apply to the court for the winding up of the company under s.122, while a similar power is vested in an administrative receiver under Sch.1 para.21.

[4] Insolvency Act 1986 Sch.B1 para.83(6)(b).

[5] Insolvency Act 1986 Sch.B1 para.79(4)(d).

[6] See below, para.16–49.

[7] See below, paras 16–50–16–51.

[8] Insolvency Act 1986 s.221(4).

members' voluntary winding up under ss.95 and 96 of the Insolvency Act, by special resolution under s.84(1)(b) of the Act[9] or by registration of an administrator's notice under para.83(6)(b) of Sch.B1 to the Insolvency Act.

Insolvency practitioners tend to favour a creditors' voluntary winding up in order to avoid the need to utilise the Insolvency Services Account, which is obligatory in compulsory winding up and has the disadvantage that while the rate of interest it pays has moved nearer towards market rates, a substantial *ad valorem* fee is charged in connection with the operation of the account.[10] From the perspective of the insolvency practitioner, both forms of winding up at one time suffered a disadvantage by comparison with administration following the controversial ruling of the House of Lords in *Buchler v Talbot*[11] that the expenses of the winding up ranked after the claims of a creditor secured by a floating charge instead of having priority over such claims, as had previously been thought to be the case, whereas the expenses of administration ranked, and continue to rank, ahead of floating charge claims.[12] This left liquidators in the difficult position of having almost no assets with which to conduct the liquidation. In consequence, a new provision was inserted into the Insolvency Act 1986 to the effect that the expenses of winding up have priority over any claims to property the subject of a floating charge to the extent that the assets of the company available for payment of general creditors[13] are insufficient.[14]

The purpose of the present chapter is to depict the winding up process in outline and to focus on a few key issues that arise in connection with the initiation and effect of that process, with particular emphasis on compulsory winding up.

1. THE LIQUIDATOR AND HIS ROLE

Duties and powers

5–02   The liquidator is an authorised insolvency practitioner whose primary function is to collect in the assets, realise them and distribute the net realisations

---

[9] That is, a special resolution without a statutory declaration of solvency, so that the winding up is a creditors' voluntary winding up (s.90).

[10] It was for this reason that in *Re T M Kingdom Ltd* [2007] B.C.C. 480, HH Judge Norris QC acceded to an application by the administrators to move to a creditors' voluntary liquidation rather than a compulsory liquidation.

[11] [2004] 2 A.C. 298. See below, para.8–32. The decision split academics. Supporters include John Armour and Adrian Walters, "Funding Liquidation: A Functional View" (2006) 122 L.Q.R. 295; for a criticism of the decision, see Riz Mokal, "What Liquidation Does for Secured Creditors, and What it Does for You" (2008) 71 M.L.R. 699.

[12] Insolvency Act 1986 s.175(2)(b) as applied by Sch.B1 para.99(3).

[13] Excluding the prescribed part (s.176ZA(2)(a)), as to which see below, para.6–38.

[14] Insolvency Act 1986 s.176ZA, inserted by the Companies Act 2006 s.1282 (the numbering of sections of the Insolvency Act is becoming increasingly bizarre!). However, the operation of s.176ZA(1) is limited by rr.4.218A–218E of the Insolvency Rules 1986, which require the liquidator to obtain the approval of preferential creditors and floating charge holders before paying litigation expenses out of property subject to the floating charge.

according to a statutory order of priority, paying any surplus to the person entitled.[15] He may carry on the company's business, but only so far as may be necessary for its beneficial winding up.[16] Part of the liquidator's job is also to investigate the causes of failure and to take appropriate steps to bring to book any delinquent directors. For this purpose, the liquidator can apply to the court for an order summoning to appear before it an officer of the company, any person known or suspected to have in his possession any property of the company or supposed to be indebted to the company and any person whom the court thinks capable of giving information concerning the promotion, business dealings, affairs or property of the company.[17] Such officer or other person may also be required to produce any relevant books, papers or other records in his possession.[18] This provision has been successfully invoked to enable a liquidator to obtain an order for production of documents relating to the remuneration paid to the former administrative receivers and the conduct of the company's affairs while in receivership.[19]

The liquidator may be appointed by the creditors, the company, the court or, on the application of the official receiver when acting as liquidator and desiring a private liquidator to be appointed in his place, the Secretary of State.[20] Separate provision is made by the Banking Act 2009 for a bank insolvency order appointing a qualified insolvency practitioner to act as the bank liquidator of a bank.[21] There is also an EC Directive governing the reorganisation and winding up of banks.[22] In a compulsory winding up, the liquidator is an officer of the court.[23] As such, he is required to act with scrupulous fairness and impartiality,[24] avoiding "dirty tricks" that might be open to an

---

[15] The liquidator may not, however, exercise his powers where prior to the winding up a confiscation or restraint order has been made under the Proceeds of Crime Act 2002. See above, para.3–09, n.53.

[16] Insolvency Act 1986,, Sch.4 Pt II para.5. Where the company is in compulsory winding up, this power may be exercised only with the sanction of the court or liquidation committee (s.167(1)(a)).

[17] Insolvency Act 1986 s. 236.

[18] Insolvency Act 1986 s.236(3). See *Pickard v FIM Advisers LLP* [2010] EWHC 1299 (Ch), where Kitchen J. set out the principles on which the court will exercise its power under s.236 and the Cross-Border Insolvency Regulations (SI 2006/1030), Sch. 1, art.21.

[19] *Re Delberry Ltd* [2008] B.C.C. 653.

[20] Insolvency Act 1986 s.137. The usual practice, however, is to convene a meeting of creditors and contributories to choose another liquidator under s.136(4) of the Insolvency Act.

[21] Banking Act 2009 s.94(1) and (2). The provisions of the Banking Act relating to winding up are not discussed further.

[22] Council Directive (EC) 2001/24/EC on the reorganisation and winding up of credit institutions, implemented in the United Kingdom by the Credit Institutions (Reorganisation and Winding Up) Regulations 2004, SI 2004/1045.

[23] *Re Oasis Merchandising Ltd* [1998] Ch. 170, per Peter Gibson L.J. at 186; *Re T.H. Knitwear (Wholesale) Ltd* [1988] Ch. 275, per Slade L.J. at 288; and *Re International Tin Council* [1987] Ch. 419, per Millett J. at 446. This is not true of a liquidator in a voluntary winding up (*T.H. Knitwear*).

[24] *Re Contract Corp, Gooch's Case* (1872) L.R. 7 Ch. App. 207, per Sir W.M. James L.J. at 213; and *Ex p. James, re Condon* (1873–74) L.R. 9 Ch. App. 609.

ordinary person,[25] and his status as an officer of the court is relevant to the propriety of contracts into which he enters.[26] While the liquidator is responsible for taking custody of the company's assets, they do not automatically vest in him or her,[27] although where the company is in compulsory winding up the liquidator can apply to the court for a vesting order.[28] The court cannot refuse to make a winding up order on the ground that the company's assets are fully mortgaged or that it has no assets,[29] but where the company is in administration or administrative receivership, so that all of its assets are under the control of the administrator or administrative receiver, the liquidator must perforce wait on the sidelines as regards his distribution role until completion of the administration or receivership, after which he will take over whatever assets, if any, remain.

Liability

5–03   The liquidator is not a trustee for individual creditors but rather an agent for the company in much the same position as a director and with statutory duties which may be enforced by application to the court.[30] His duty is owed to the company and to the creditors as a class, but he does not in general owe any duty to an individual creditor.[31] Accordingly, it is not normally open to an individual creditor to institute proceedings against a liquidator outside the winding up. His remedy for a breach of duty causing loss to the company is to institute misfeasance proceedings under s.212 of the Insolvency Act for an order compelling the liquidator to contribute to the company's assets.[32] There are, however, exceptions to the rule that an individual creditor cannot pursue a remedy in his own right. The liquidator may incur a liability to an individual creditor for loss caused by fraud or other personal misconduct,[33] such as breach of fiduciary duty or misfeasance,[34] or for breach of

---

[25] *R. v Tower Hamlets LBC, ex p. Chetnik Ltd* [1988] A.C. 858, per Lord Bridge at 874–875, invoking the rule laid down long ago in *Ex p. James* (1874) L.R. 9 Ch. App. 609 in relation to trustees in bankruptcy. See to similar effect: *Re Wyvern Developments Ltd* [1974] 1 W.L.R. 1097; and *Re Collins & Aikman Europe SA* [2006] B.C.C. 861.

[26] *Oasis Merchandising*, cited above n.23 (in which the liquidator entered into an agreement held to be champertous).

[27] In this respect, a liquidator differs from a trustee in bankruptcy, in whom the bankrupt's estate vests immediately on the trustee's appointment without the need for any conveyance, assignment or transfer (Insolvency Act 1986 s.306(1)).

[28] Insolvency Act 1986 s.145(1).

[29] Insolvency Act 1986 s.125(1).

[30] *Knowles v Scott* [1891] 1 Ch. 717; and *Leon v York-O-Matic Ltd* [1966] 1 W.L.R. 1450.

[31] *Hague v Nam Tai Electronics Inc* [2008] B.C.C. 295, citing *Kyrris v Oldham* [2004] 1 B.C.L.C. 305, a decision on the duties of an administrator, but the principles are the same.

[32] ibid. Alternatively, the creditor can apply to the court under s.168(5) of the Act as a person aggrieved by the liquidator's act or decision.

[33] *Knowles v Scott*, cited above n.30.

[34] *Knowles v Scott*, above, n. 30; *Kyrris v Oldham*, above, n. 31.

contract,[35] or for negligently distributing the company's assets without taking account of a debt which has been or should have been admitted to proof,[36] but in this last case only where the company has been dissolved, and consequently is no longer in course of winding up, so that the creditor is deprived of his ordinary remedy of application to the court.[37] Where the company has not been dissolved, the liquidator cannot be sued for a dividend even if this has been declared[38]; the creditor's remedy is to apply to the court in the winding up for an order under what is now r.4.182(3) of the Insolvency Rules 1986 directing the liquidator to pay out of the moneys in his hands or, if he has already paid away the moneys he had held, a claim for payment by the liquidator personally in misfeasance proceedings under s.212.[39] In *Lomax Leisure Ltd v Miller*,[40] in which there was thought to be a surplus of assets allowing a member's voluntary winding up as the exit route from administration, a creditor whose proof had been rejected by the liquidators successfully appealed. However, by that time the liquidators, who had been unaware of the creditor's application to reverse the decision to reject its proof, had issued cheques to the creditors whose proofs they had accepted. Consequent upon the appeal, they stopped the cheques. The effect of the appeal was that the surplus was turned into a deficit, with the result that the liquidation became a creditors' voluntary winding up and a new liquidator was appointed. The first liquidators were then sued by one creditor on the stopped cheque. It was held that r.4.182(3) precluded such a claim and that the creditor's only remedy was an application for an order for payment under r.4.182(3) (applicable by analogy in a members' voluntary winding up) if the liquidator was still in funds or, if not, a misfeasance claim under s.212. It followed that the liquidators were not liable on the cheque, which had been given without consideration, there being no antecedent debt or liability.

Proceedings by liquidator

On behalf of the creditors, the liquidator can bring proceedings in the name of the company in respect of causes of action vested in the company but he has no locus standi to pursue claims vested in persons *qua* creditors. So if a company establishes a subsidiary to carry on the business of deposit-taking and the parent runs the subsidiary as its *alter ego*, effectively depriving the subsidiary's directors of any management function and using the subsidiary as a façade through which deposited funds are transferred to the parent,

5–04

---

[35] The firm employing the individual liquidator may also be liable as a contracting party where it undertakes to appoint one of its employees as liquidator and procure him to do a proper job (*A & J Fabrications (Batley) Ltd v Grant Thornton* [1999] B.C.C. 807).

[36] *James Smith & Sons (Norwood) Ltd v Goodman* [1936] Ch. 216; and *Pulsford v Devenish* [1903] 2 Ch. 625.

[37] *Kyrris v Oldham*, cited above nn. 31, 34; *Spence v Coleman* [1901] 2 K.B. 199.

[38] Insolvency Rules 1986 r.4.182(3).

[39] *Kyrris v Oldham*, cited above n.31.

[40] [2008] 1 B.C.L.C. 262.

then if in consequence the subsidiary is driven into insolvent liquidation, the liquidator may be able to pursue a claim in the name of the subsidiary against its parent, but has no standing to assert claims on behalf of the subsidiary's depositors, who must pursue their own proceedings.[41]

In a compulsory winding up, the liquidator must obtain the sanction of the court or liquidation committee before commencing proceedings in the name and on behalf of the company.[42] In the case of a voluntary winding up no sanction is required[43] except for proceedings under ss.213, 214, 238, 239, 242, 243 or 423.[44] His failure to obtain the requisite sanction does not nullify the proceedings, but would preclude the liquidator from recovering his expenses unless the court or the liquidation committee exercises its statutory power to ratify what the liquidator has done, which cannot ordinarily be done unless the committee or the court is satisfied that the liquidator has acted in a case of urgency and has sought ratification without undue delay.[45] However, the court has a residual discretion to dispense with these conditions, which in most cases it will do if the liquidator's failure was inadvertent.[46]

Liquidator's powers of compromise

5–05   The liquidator has power, with the sanction of the court or the committee of inspection, to make any compromise or arrangement with creditors or persons claiming to be creditors or having or alleging themselves to have any claim against the company[47] and also has power, exercisable without sanction, to compromise all calls and other claims subsisting between the company and a contributory[48] and all questions relating to or affecting the assets or the winding up of the company.[49]

---

[41] This may be one of those exceptional cases where the court will be willing to pierce the corporate veil and hold the parent company liable to the depositors. See, e.g. *Jones v Lipman* [1962] 1 W.L.R. 832.

[42] Insolvency Act 1986 s.167(1). Where for the time being there is no liquidation committee (by which is meant a committee that is quorate) and the liquidator is a person other than the official receiver, the functions of such committee are vested in the Secretary of State except to the extent that the rules otherwise provide (s.141(5)).

[43] Insolvency Act 1986 s.165(3); and Sch.4 para.4.

[44] In these cases the power given by Sch.4 para.4 is not exercisable because the proceedings are brought in the name of the liquidator, not in the name and on behalf of the company, and under para.3A their exercise requires the sanction of the liquidator or the liquidation committee. The sections in question relate to proceedings for fraudulent trading, wrongful trading and recovery under the various provisions for avoidance of transactions

[45] Insolvency Rules 1986 r.4.184(2).

[46] *Gresham International Ltd v Moonie* [2009] 2 B.C.L.C. 256, in which Peter Smith J. was not persuaded that there was a mere matter of inadvertence and declined to give retrospective sanction, granting a sanction only for future expenses.

[47] Insolvency Act 1986, Sch.4 para.2.

[48] Insolvency Act 1986, Sch.4, para.6A.

[49] Insolvency Act 1986, Sch.4, para.6A But this last power is given subject to para.2, so that if the question to be compromised concerns a creditor, the sanction of the court or the liquidation committee must be obtained.

Liquidator's powers of sale

The liquidator has power, exercisable without sanction, to sell any of the company's property by public auction or private contract.[50] In general, the availability of this power does not give rise to any difficulty. However, problems have arisen in a number of cases involving the assignment of a cause of action, either for an agreed price or in consideration of a share of the fruits of the action, or an assignment of the fruits of the action themselves. Here the authorities establish the following:

5–06

(i) Although under the general law the assignment of a bare cause of action unconnected to any legitimate interest of the assignee[51] savours of maintenance[52] and champerty[53] and is unenforceable as being contrary to public policy,[54] the assignment by a liquidator of a bare cause of action vested in the company is allowed as an exception to the rule because a right of action is an asset of the company and the liquidator has a statutory power to sell the company's assets, and thus to sell a bare cause of action. Moreover he can validly agree to do so in consideration of payment to the company of part of the fruits of the action.[55] But the exemption from maintenance or champerty in respect of sale of a cause of action by a liquidator does not extend to an agreement to finance the litigation.[56]

(ii) A sale of the fruits of the action is lawful even under the general law, so long as it does not involve the conferment on the assignee of a right to control or influence the course of the proceedings.[57] But the funding of the action by the assignee does not by itself appear to render the assignment objectionable.[58]

(iii) The liquidator is not entitled to sell causes of action vested not in the company but in him as liquidator, for example, a claim for wrongful trading under s.214 of the Insolvency Act 1986, or a claim to set aside a

---

[50] Insolvency Act 1986 Sch.4 para.6.

[51] As opposed, e.g. to a sale of a debt (whether or not disputed) with a right of action related to the debt, which is perfectly legitimate (*Camdex International Ltd v Bank of Zambia* [1998] Q.B. 22 at 32–33).

[52] The giving of assistance to a litigant by a person having no interest in the litigation or other legitimate reason for supporting it.

[53] The provision of maintenance in consideration of a share of the fruits of the litigation.

[54] *Trendtex Trading Corp v Credit Suisse* [1981] 3 All E.R. 520.

[55] *Ramsey v Hartley* [1977] 1 W.L.R. 686, applying *Guy v Churchill* (1889) L.R. 40 Ch.D. 481; and *Grovewood Holdings Plc v James Capel & Co Ltd* [1995] Ch. 80. All these cases were cited with approval in *Re Oasis Merchandising Services Ltd* [1998] Ch. 170.

[56] *Grovewood*, cited above n.55; and *Camdex International*, cited above n.51, at 36.

[57] *Oasis Merchandising*, cited above n.55; and *Bang & Olufsen UK Ltd v Ton Système Ltd*, unreported, July 16, 1993, CA (transcript no.834 of 1993), referred to in *Oasis Merchandising* at 179.

[58] See *Ruttle Plant Ltd v Secretary of State for Environment, Food and Rural Affairs (No.3)* [2008] EWHC 328 (TCC), per Ramsey J. at [52]–[56], doubting a passage to contrary effect in the judgment of Lightman J. in *Grovewood Holdings*, cited above n.55, at 87.

transaction as a preference under s.239, because such causes of action do not relate to the company's property, but are statutory rights conferred on the liquidator and thus fall outside the scope of Sch.4 para.6.[59] Moreover, they have a public or penal element in them as regards which the court is entitled to have the assistance of the liquidator, so that it is contrary to public policy for the liquidator to pass control of those causes of action to another.[60] The position is otherwise as regards misfeasance proceedings under s.212, since these relate to a right of action vested in the company prior to the winding up.[61]

2. CREDITORS' VOLUNTARY WINDING UP[62]

The procedure

5–07   As mentioned before, a creditors' voluntary winding up (other than as an exit from administration) is effected by a resolution of the *members*, not the creditors, but once in place operates under the control of the creditors. It is necessary to convene a meeting to pass a special resolution to wind-up the company.[63] Not less than 14 days' notice must be given[64] and a resolution passed at a meeting on a show of hands must be passed by a majority of not less than 75 per cent of: (i) the members who, being entitled to do so, vote in person on the resolution; and (ii) the persons who vote on the resolution as duly appointed proxies of members entitled to vote on it.[65] In the case of a private company, the resolution may be passed without a meeting or prior notice by resolution in writing of all of the members who would be entitled to attend and vote at such a meeting.[66] The company is required to convene a meeting of creditors for a day no later than the 14th day after that fixed for the company

---

[59] *Oasis Merchandising*, above, n.55, approving the decision of Robert Walker J. [1995] 2 B.C.L.C. 493; and *Re Ayala Holdings Ltd (No.2)* [1996] B.C.L.C. 467, per Knox J. at 480.

[60] *Ruttle Plant Ltd v Secretary of State for Environment, Food and Rural Affairs (No.2)* [2009] 1 All E.R. 448; and *Rawnsley v Weatherall Green & Smith North Ltd* [2010] B.C.C. 406.

[61] *Oasis Merchanding*, cited above n.55.

[62] See Peter Loose and Michael Griffiths, *Loose on Liquidators*, 6th edn (Bristol: Jordans, 2010), Ch.2.

[63] Insolvency Act 1986 s.84(1)(b). A members' voluntary winding up must be converted into a creditors' voluntary winding up where the liquidator forms the opinion that the company will be unable to pay its debts in full together with interest within the period specified in the declaration of solvency (s.95). Winding up through administration is a distinctive procedure discussed in para.11–116.

[64] Companies Act 2006 s.307(1) and (2). But the meeting may be called upon short notice if so agreed by the requisite majority (s.307(4) and (5)).

[65] *ibid.*, s.283(1),(4). A similar majority is required to pass a resolution on a poll (s. 283(5)). As to remote attendance at meetings, see the Insolvency Act 1986, s. 246A and the Insolvency Rules 1986, r. 12A.22.

[66] Companies Act 2006 ss.281 and 288.

meeting, at least seven days' notice being given and advertised.[67] In practice, the creditors' meeting is usually held after and on the same day as the company meeting. It is presided over by a director of the company appointed for that purpose by the directors, who must lay a statement of affairs before the creditors' meeting showing particulars of the company's assets, debts and liabilities, the names and addresses of the company's creditors and any securities held by them.[68] The creditors and the company may (and almost invariably do) nominate a liquidator at their respective meetings,[69] the creditors' nomination (if any) prevailing unless the court orders otherwise.[70] A liquidator nominated by the company before the holding of a meeting of creditors may not exercise the powers conferred by s.165 of the Insolvency Act until that meeting.[71]

The notice convening a meeting of creditors must specify the date by which creditors must lodge any proxies necessary to entitle them to vote at the meeting.[72] If the proxy is not lodged in due time, the proxy-holder cannot vote. However, it is often overlooked that a company need not act by proxy, but can appear and vote by its duly authorised representative.[73] The difference between a proxy-holder and a representative is that the former is "another person" authorised to speak and vote as the company's representative,[74] whereas a representative is treated as the personification of the company itself. The representative must be authorised by resolution of the directors,[75] a sealed or certified copy of which must be produced to the chairman of the creditors' meeting,[76] but need not be lodged before the meeting. At any meeting a creditor can vote only if, in addition to any necessary proxy, it has also duly lodged a proof of debt which has been admitted by the chairman under r.4.70 of the Insolvency Rules.[77] The chairman is likely to reject a proof where the creditor has not obtained judgment and the debt is

---

[67] Insolvency Act 1986 s.98(1A). At least five business days' written notice must also be given to the holder of any qualifying floating charge (s.84(2A)). As to what constitutes a qualifying floating charge, see below, para.11–07.

[68] Insolvency Act 1986 s.99.

[69] If the company defers the appointment of a liquidator, the directors are disabled from continuing to exercise their powers except on an order of the court or to comply with the obligation to convene a creditors' meeting or to dispose of perishable goods or protect the company's assets (Insolvency Act 1986 s.114).

[70] Insolvency Act 1986 s.100.

[71] Insolvency Act 1986 s.166(2), a provision designed to overcome the effect of the decision in *Re Centrebind Ltd* [1967] 1 W.L.R. 377, by which a company that deferred calling a meeting of creditors (albeit in breach of the statutory requirements) could get its liquidator in place exercising his statutory powers before the creditors had had an opportunity to make their own nomination.

[72] Insolvency Rules 1986 r.4.51.

[73] Companies Act 2006 s.323.

[74] Insolvency Rules 1986 r.8.1(1).

[75] Companies Act 2006 s.323(1).

[76] Insolvency Rules 1986 r.8.7.

[77] Insolvency Rules 1986 r.4.67(1). The chairman may allow a creditor to vote, notwithstanding his failure to comply with this requirement, if satisfied that the failure was due to circumstances beyond the creditor's control (r.4.68).

genuinely disputed by the company, and in that event the creditor cannot vote at the meeting. The chairman must certify the liquidator's appointment, but may only do so when the person appointed has provided him with a written statement that he is an insolvency practitioner duly qualified under the Insolvency Act to be the liquidator and that he consents to act.[78]

Creditors' voluntary winding up distinguished from compulsory winding up

5–08   The effect of a creditors' voluntary winding up differs in a number of respects from that of a compulsory winding up. Whereas in a compulsory winding up the winding up order operates to terminate the director's powers and dismiss them from office,[79] on a voluntary liquidation the powers of the directors come to an end only on the appointment of the liquidator,[80] although between the time of passing of the resolution for voluntary winding up and the appointment of the liquidator these powers are severely restricted.[81] The liquidation is primarily under the control of the creditors rather than the court and the liquidator can exercise without sanction certain powers which in a compulsory winding up would require the sanction of the court or the liquidation committee.[82] There is no equivalent to the retrospective effect of a winding up order[83]; the winding up commences on the passing of the resolution to wind-up.[84] In consequence, there is also no equivalent of s.127 of the Act, which invalidates dispositions of the company's property between winding up petition and order unless sanctioned by the court.[85] Whereas a winding up order automatically stays all proceedings against the company except by leave of the court,[86] there is no automatic stay in the case of a voluntary winding up. It is for the liquidator to apply for a stay,[87] which will normally be granted as a matter of course if the claimant's claim is admitted, but not if it is disputed and the creditor has not submitted a proof.[88] The position is otherwise where the creditor has submitted a proof and the liquidator has not

---

[78] Insolvency Rules 1986 r.4.101(2).
[79] See below para.5–24.
[80] Insolvency Act 1986 s.103, which, however, allows the liquidation committee or, if none, the creditors to sanction their continuance.
[81] Insolvency Act 1986 s.114(2). See n.69 above.
[82] That is, the power to bring or defend proceedings in the name and on behalf of the company and to carry on the business of the company so far as may be necessary for its beneficial winding up (Insolvency Act 1986 ss.165 and 167 and Sch.4 paras 4 and 5).
[83] See below, para.5–23.
[84] Insolvency Act 1986 s.86. There is now a procedure by which the court can be asked to confirm the winding up (Insolvency Rules 1986 rr.7.62, 7.63), but this is purely to bring the proceedings within the ambit of the European Insolvency Regulation. See below, para.15–13.
[85] See below, para.13–127.
[86] Insolvency Act 1986 s.130(2).
[87] Under s.112 of the Act. The application is made in the action sought to be stayed, not in the liquidation.
[88] *Currie v Consolidated Kent Collieries Corp Ltd* [1906] 1 K.B. 134.

been dilatory in dealing with it, for by lodging a proof the creditor has elected to have his claim dealt with in the liquidation in the ordinary way and if the proof is rejected the creditor can appeal to the court against the rejection in the winding up proceedings.[89]

Procedural similarities

Although there are procedural differences between a creditors' voluntary winding up and a compulsory winding up, much of the procedure is common to both forms. The liquidator in a voluntary winding up, as in a compulsory winding up, will admit or reject proofs of debt,[90] convene meetings of creditors as necessary, report on the conduct of the liquidation from time to time, collect in and realise the assets and make interim and final distributions of dividend to creditors whose proofs have been lodged and accepted. A creditor who fails to lodge a proof prior to a dividend distribution cannot disturb that distribution, but upon lodging his proof and having it accepted is entitled to payment of the dividend he would have received ahead of other creditors before any subsequent distribution is made.[91] When the winding up is completed, the liquidator convenes final meetings of the company and creditors, and subsequently gives notice to the registrar of companies that the meetings have been held and of the decisions (if any) taken at them, upon which he is released.[92] The company is dissolved automatically three months after registration of the liquidator's notice.[93]

    The liquidator is entitled to remuneration, fixed either: (i) as a percentage of the value of the assets realised or distributed or of the one value and the other in combination; (ii) by reference to the time properly given; or (iii) as a set amount, the remuneration and any percentage being fixed either by the liquidation committee or, if there is none, by a resolution of a meeting of creditors.[94] The liquidator's remuneration and expenses together constitute expenses of the liquidation payable ahead of the claims of creditors[95] and ranking towards the end of the list of priorities for payment of liquidation expenses.[96]

5–09

---

[89] *Craven v Blackpool Greyhound Stadium Co* [1936] 3 All E.R. 512. Appeals against rejection of proofs are dealt with by r.4.83 of the Insolvency Rules 1986.

[90] As to proofs of debt generally, see below, paras 8–40–8–48.

[91] Insolvency Rules 1986 r.4.182(2).

[92] Insolvency Act 1986 ss.171(6) and 173(2)(e)(ii).

[93] Insolvency Act 1986 ss.201 and 205(2).

[94] Insolvency Rules 1986 rr.4.127 and 4.127A.

[95] Insolvency Act 1986 s.176ZA. As to the treatment of liquidation expenses, see para.8–32.

[96] Insolvency Rules 1986 rr.4.218 and 4.219.

3. *COMPULSORY WINDING UP*[97]

Procedural outline

5–10   Proceedings for compulsory winding up are initiated by petition issued by a creditor or other person having an appropriate locus standi.[98] The petition must be served on the company and other parties specified in the Insolvency Rules[99] and must be advertised as prescribed by the Rules.[100] Various other procedural requirements must be fulfilled prior to the hearing. These too are set out in the Rules. On the hearing, the court may in its discretion make a number of different orders.[101] If the court makes a winding up order, the official receiver becomes liquidator automatically unless and until another liquidator is appointed.[102] Any such liquidator must be an authorised insolvency practitioner. The official receiver may summon meetings of the creditors and contributories for the purpose of choosing another person as liquidator.[103] At such meetings, the nomination (if any) of the creditors prevails unless the court orders otherwise.[104] In practice, an outside liquidator will not accept an appointment unless he or she is satisfied that there are at least enough assets to cover the costs and expenses of winding up, including the liquidator's remuneration. In such cases, the official receiver will continue in office as liquidator.[105]

The official receiver will normally require the company to furnish a statement of affairs in the prescribed form,[106] showing the company's assets, debts and liabilities, names and addresses of its creditors and details of any securities they hold. The official receiver will convene a first meeting of creditors, notice being given to each creditor and contributory as well as being advertised. If an outside liquidator is to be appointed, it is usually at this meeting that the requisite resolution will be passed.

The various stages in the administration of the liquidation broadly follow the same pattern as for a creditors' voluntary winding up, although there are numerous differences, some of the more important of which have been set out above.

---

[97] See Derek French, *Applications to Wind Up Companies*, 2nd edn (Oxford: Oxford University Press, 2008); and Loose and Griffiths, *Loose on Liquidators*, 2010, Ch.4.

[98] See below, para.5–18.

[99] Insolvency Rules 1986 rr.4.8–4.10.

[100] Insolvency Rules 1986 r.4.11.

[101] See below, para.5–22.

[102] Insolvency Act 1986 s.136(2).

[103] Insolvency Act 1986 s.136(4). Alternatively, the official receiver may apply to the Secretary of State to appoint a liquidator in his place, although the Secretary of State may decline to do so (s.137(1) and (3)).

[104] Insolvency Act 1986 s.139(3).

[105] The fact that all of the assets are mortgaged up to the hilt or that there are no assets at all is not a ground for refusing a winding up order (Insolvency Act 1986 s.125(1)); there may well be matters to be investigated.

[106] Insolvency Act 1986 s.131(1).

With these preliminary remarks, we can go on to consider certain features of compulsory winding up deserving particular attention.

Grounds for compulsory winding up of insolvent company

The primary ground for the compulsory winding up of an insolvent company[107] is that it is unable to pay its debts.[108] Winding up petitions commonly add as a separate ground that it is just and equitable that the company be wound-up.[109] A winding up order may be made even where the company is already in voluntary winding up.[110] The principles governing the exercise of the court's discretion are well set out in the judgment of Lawrence Collins J. in *Re Zirceram Ltd*.[111] The usual ground of application is that the voluntary winding up is not being properly conducted or that, even if it is, the circumstances call for the more rigorous investigation of the company's affairs afforded by a compulsory winding up and one which is not only independent, but seen to be independent. The general principle that a creditor has a prima facie right to a winding up order also applies here, but the court will have regard not only to the quantity and quality of the petitioning creditor's claim, but also to the wishes of a majority of creditors; if they desire the voluntary winding up to continue, that will be an important factor in the court's decision.[112]

5–11

---

[107] Insolvency is only one ground of compulsory winding up. Others are set out in the Insolvency Act 1986 s.122(1)(a)–(e). In addition, a winding up petition may be presented by the Secretary of State on the grounds of public interest (Insolvency Act 1986 s.124A). Sometimes such petitions are insolvency-related, as in *Re UK-Euro Group Plc* [2007] 1 B.C.L.C. 812 and *Re Rodencroft Ltd* [2004] B.C.C. 631, where the ground of the application by the Secretary of State for a winding up order was that the companies in question were being used as vehicles for fraud. A winding up order may also be sought by a member of a company as an alternative to an order for relief under s.994 of the Companies Act 2006 (unfairly prejudicial conduct of company's affairs), but this should not be done as a matter of course, only if that is the remedy preferred by the petitioner or it is thought to be the only remedy to which the petitioner is entitled, and the petitioner must state whether he consents or objects to an order under s.127, which validates post-petition dispositions (Practice Direction—Order under s.127 of the Insolvency Act 1986 [2007] B.C.C. 91, L. Sealy and D. Milman, *Sealy & Milman: Annotated Guide to the Insolvency Legislation*, 13th edn (London: Sweet & Maxwell, 2010), Vol.2, App.V). See also *Sharafi v Woven Rugs Ltd* [2008] B.C.C. 903, where the judge upheld the decision of the registrar dismissing an application to wind-up the company on the just and equitable ground, having concluded that the petitioners' allegations amounted in substance to allegations of unfair prejudice, for which the appropriate remedy was an application under s.994 of the Companies Act 2006.

[108] Insolvency Act 1986 s.122(1)(f). See above, Ch.4.

[109] Insolvency Act 1986 s.122(1)(g).

[110] Insolvency Act 1986 s.116.

[111] [2000] 1 B.C.L.C. 751 at [24] et seq.

[112] *Re Gordon & Breach Science Publishers Ltd* [1995] 2 B.C.L.C. 189.

What must be shown

5–12   To obtain a winding up order on the grounds of insolvency, a petitioner must show that:

(i)   grounds exist for the making of the order under s.122 of the Insolvency Act, the usual grounds being that the company is unable to pay its debts and that it is just and equitable for it to be wound-up;

(ii)   he has a statutory locus standi to present the petition; and

(iii)   he has a legitimate interest in the making of a winding up order.

If these requirements are satisfied, prima facie the petitioner is entitled to a winding up order *ex debito justitiae* and the onus is then on those who oppose the petition to show why a winding up order should not be made. Admittedly, it has been said on more than one occasion that the winding up procedure in the Companies Court cannot properly be used for the purpose of debt collection:

> ". . . it is trite law that the Companies Court is not, and should not be used as (despite the methods in fact often adopted) a debt-collecting court. The proper remedy for debt collecting is an execution upon a judgment, a distress, a garnishee order, or some such procedure."[113]

However, if this statement means that it is somehow improper for a creditor to resort to winding up instead of execution in the hope of inducing the company to pay the debt, then it undoubtedly goes too far. Very often this is precisely the reason why the petition is launched, and the courts have emphasised that a petition presented in order to bring pressure on a company to pay a debt which is indisputably due is perfectly proper, even where other proceedings are in train for recovery of the debt[114] and even if the winding up proceedings are being pursued "with personal hostility or even venom".[115] A petition is improper only where the purpose is to put pressure on the company to pay a sum that is not due or exceeds what is due or is subject to a bona fide dispute on substantial grounds.[116] But it is thought that Harman J. was intending to do no more than emphasise the undoubted principle that liquidation is a collective debt enforcement procedure[117] and

---

[113] *Re A Company (No.001573 of 1983)* [1983] B.C.L.C. 492, per Harman J. at 495.

[114] *James Dolman & Co Ltd v Pedley* [2004] B.C.C. 504.

[115] *Mann v Goldstein* [1968] 1 W.L.R. 1091, per Ungoed-Thomas J. at 1095.

[116] See *Re A Company (No.006273 of 1992)* [1993] B.C.L.C. 131, per Millett J. at 132, and above, para.4–21. As to the manner in which the petition is then dealt with, see below, para.5–13.

[117] *Re Lines Bros Ltd* [1983] Ch. 1, per Brightman L.J. at 20.

that a winding up petition is in the nature of the exercise of a class right, so that the interests of other creditors have to be considered when the court comes to exercise its discretion.

Where the debt is undisputed, the court will normally make a winding up order even if the company has a cross-claim which overtops the claim, where the cross-claim is disputed on substantial grounds.[118] However, the court may dismiss the petition if it considers the petitioning creditor's action to have been precipitate, as where no demand for payment was made before the petition was presented or a demand was made, but the petitioning creditor did not allow the debtor at least some opportunity to pay the debt.

Disputed debts

The mere assertion by the company that the petitioner's debt is disputed is not by itself a ground for dismissing the petition.[119] But it is an abuse of the process of the court to make a statutory demand or present a winding up petition based on a claim in respect of which there is a triable issue.[120] There are several reasons for this. In the first place, the Companies Court is not an appropriate forum for the determination of disputed claims.[121]

5–13

"The reason for the practice [of requiring disputes to be determined elsewhere] has been essentially pragmatic. The vast majority of petitions to wind up a company are creditors' petitions. The Companies Court procedure on such petitions is ill-equipped to deal with the resolution of disputes of fact. There are no pleadings, there is no discovery and there is no oral evidence normally tolerated on such petitions, even though no doubt pleadings and discovery could be ordered and oral evidence received, and the Companies Court like any other court is perfectly capable of determining such disputes."[122]

---

[118] *Re A Company (No.006273 of 1992)*, cited above n.116.

[119] *Re A Company (No.006685 of 1996)* [1997] B.C.C. 830, per Chadwick J. at 832. See below.

[120] In *Re A Company (No.0012209 of 1991)* [1992] 1 W.L.R. 351. See also the cases cited in n.121 below. Where the statutory demand is open to attack on this ground, the company's remedy is to ask for an order restraining the presentation of the petition.

[121] *Stonegate Securities Ltd v Gregory* [1980] Ch. 576, per Buckley L.J. at 579–580; *Re Bayoil SA* [1999] 1 W.L.R. 147; and *Montgomery v Wanda Modes Ltd* [2002] 1 B.C.L.C. 289. However, "it is equally important to emphasise that a judge, whether sitting in the Companies Court or elsewhere, should be astute to ensure that, however complicated and extensive the evidence might appear to be, the very extensiveness and complexity is not being invoked to mask the fact that there is, on proper analysis, no arguable defence to a claim, whether on the facts or the law" (*Re Richbell Strategic Holdings Ltd* [1997] 2 B.C.L.C. 429, per Neuberger J. at 434, after which comment the judge then examined the evidence in considerable detail before concluding that the petitioner was not a creditor entitled to present a petition).

[122] *Alipour v Ary* [1997] 1 W.L.R. 534, per Peter Gibson L.J. at 541. However, the court may allow the petition to proceed where the petitioner would have no other remedy if it were dismissed, and this was the course taken in *Alipour v Ary*.

Secondly, a winding up petition can be used oppressively to put pressure on the company to pay a debt which it may not owe rather than dispute liability. The presentation of a winding up petition is a serious matter, affecting the reputation of the company and its management and potentially paralysing the company's business.

"It is, in my view, important to re-emphasise that there is no rule of practice in this court that a petition will be struck out or dismissed merely because the company alleges that the debt is disputed. The true rule, which has existed for many years, is the rule of practice that this court will not allow a winding up petition to be used for the purpose of deciding a substantial dispute raised on bona fide grounds. It will not do so, as a matter of practice, because the effect of presenting a winding up petition and advertising that petition is to put upon the company a pressure to pay (rather than to litigate) which is quite different in nature from the effect of an ordinary writ action. The pressure arises from the fact that once the existence of the petition is known amongst those having dealings with the company, they are likely to withdraw credit or refuse to continue to trade with the company on the ground that, if the company is wound up on the petition, their dealings with it will be subject to the provisions in s.127 of the Insolvency Act 1986."[123]

So, in general, the court will not make a winding up order on a petition based on an alleged debt as to which there is a substantial dispute or where the company has a genuine and serious cross-claim (whether a set-off or a pure counterclaim) which is likely to exceed the debt due to the petitioning creditor.[124] Nevertheless, this is a rule of practice, not a rule of law going to jurisdiction,[125] so that in exceptional cases the court may make a winding up order.[126] It is also a matter of discretion whether the judge in the winding up proceedings

---

[123] *Re A Company (No.006685 of 1996)* [1997] B.C.C. 830, per Chadwick J. at 832 in a passage later approved by the Court of Appeal in *James Dolman & Co Ltd v Pedley* [2004] B.C.C. 504.

[124] *Remblance v Octagon Assets Ltd* [2010] 1 B.C.L.C. 10, in which a majority of the Court of Appeal (Mummery L.J. dissenting) held that a surety was similarly entitled to rely on the company's cross-claim, his liability being co-extensive with that of the company as principal debtor; *Re Bayoil SA* [1999] 1 W.L.R. 147; and *Montgomery v Wanda Modes Ltd* [2002] 1 B.C.L.C. 289. The fact that the cross-claim is for the amount of an adjudication under the Housing Grants, Construction and Regeneration Act 1996 does not mean that the "pay now, argue later principle" governing such adjudications affects the company's ability to raise the cross-claim as a defence to the winding up petition. See *MFP Foundations & Piling Ltd v Shaw* [2010] B.P.I.R. 397.

[125] *Parmalat Capital Finance Ltd v Food Holdings Inc* [2008] B.C.C. 371; *Alipour v Ary* [1997] 1 W.L.R. 534; and *Brinds Ltd v Offshore Oil NL* (1986) 2 B.C.C. 98, 916.

[126] *Re Claybridge Shipping Co SA* [1997] 1 B.C.L.C. 572; and *Re Russian and English Bank* [1932] 1 Ch. 663, where the company was a foreign company which had been dissolved under its governing law and without a winding up order the petitioners would have been without remedy. Jurisdiction to wind-up an unregistered company which has been dissolved is now conferred by s.221(5)(a) of the Insolvency Act 1986. The court will not exercise jurisdiction over an unregistered company unless there is a sufficient connection with this jurisdiction. See Sealy and Milman, *Annotated Guide to the Insolvency Legislation*, 2010, General Note to s.220.

decides the dispute himself or leaves it to be determined in another forum,[127] although in general, as stated above, the Companies Court is not a suitable forum for determining such disputes.

Despite the well-established principle that an alleged debt which is disputed on substantial grounds cannot properly found a statutory demand or a winding up petition, there has been a steady stream of cases involving disputed debts, set-offs and cross-claims,[128] which may indicate a willingness on the part of some petitioners or intending petitioners to chance their arm in the hope of obtaining a winding up order or at least flushing out the basis of an alleged set-off or cross-claim and the evidence for it before a trial in the appropriate forum. The danger faced by the company when a petition is improperly presented is that at the hearing another creditor whose claim is not in doubt may apply to be substituted as the petitioning creditor.[129]

Treatment of abuse of process in presentation of petition

There are various courses open to a company where a winding up petition is threatened or presented in circumstances where this would be an abuse of the process of the court. If the petition has not been presented, the company can apply for an injunction to restrain its presentation.[130] If it has been presented, but not advertised, an injunction may be sought restraining advertisement.[131] Whether or not the petition has been advertised, the company can apply before the hearing to have it struck out.[132] Finally, the company can wait until the hearing and then ask for the petition to be dismissed.[133]

5–14

Winding up for inability to pay debts

A petition by a creditor will be based primarily on para.(f) of s.122(1) of the Insolvency Act, namely the inability of the company to pay its debts, although it is customary to reinforce this by reference to the "just and equitable"

5–15

---

[127] *Brinds*, cited above n.125. In *Jubilee International Inc v Farlin Timbers PTE Ltd* [2006] B.P.I.R. 765, where the disputed debt was the subject of an arbitration, the court adjourned the winding up petition pending the hearing of the arbitration against the creditor's undertaking to pursue the arbitration proceedings with all due diligence.

[128] See *Alexander Sheridan Ltd v Beaujersey Ltd* [2004] EWHC 2072; *Re UK (Aid) Ltd GlaxoSmithKline Export Ltd v UK (Aid) Ltd* [2003] B.C.L.C. 351; and the cases cited above nn.124–127. For a detailed examination of the case law on disputed claims and cross-claims, see French, *Applications to Wind Up Companies*, 2008, paras 6.10.1 et seq.

[129] Insolvency Rules 1986 r.4.19. See generally as to substitution French, *Applications to Wind Up Companies*, 2008, paras 3.9.1–3.9.6.

[130] *Stonegate Securities Ltd v Gregory* [1980] Ch. 576; and *ICS Incorporation Ltd v Michael Wilson* [2005] B.P.I.R. 805.

[131] *Mann v Goldstein* [1968] 1 W.L.R. 1091.

[132] *Parmalat Capital Finance Ltd v Food Holdings Ltd* [2008] B.C.C. 371.

[133] *Re JN 2 Ltd* [1978 1 W.L.R. 183, per Brightman J. at 187; and *Re GBI Investments Ltd* [2010] B.P.I.R. 356, per Warren J. at [80].

ground under para.(g). A contributory, in those infrequent cases where he can show a tangible interest,[134] will usually rely on para.(g).

As stated above,[135] there are four ways of showing inability to pay debts: neglect to comply with a statutory demand under s.123(l); return of an execution or other process, issued on a judgment or order in favour of a creditor, unsatisfied in whole or in part; proof to the satisfaction of the court that the company is unable to pay its debts as they fall due; and proof to the satisfaction of the court that the value of the company's assets is less than the amount of its liabilities, taking into account its contingent and prospective liabilities. The second of these is self-explanatory, and the third and fourth have been examined in detail in the previous chapter.[136] However, it will be necessary to say something about the first.

Non-compliance with statutory demand

5–16   There is nothing in the Act which in terms requires either of the first two grounds to relate to the debt of the petitioning creditor, so that for the purpose of s.122(l)(f) the petitioner would seem to be able to invoke non-compliance with a statutory demand, or non-satisfaction of an execution, issued by another creditor. However, it would still be necessary for him to show some interest of his own, for example, that he has called for payment of his debt and the company has failed to pay it.[137]

A considerable amount of case law has developed around the statutory demand ground and its relationship to other grounds of winding up. The first point to note is that the inability of the company to pay its debts as they fall due may be invoked by any creditor without the need to make a statutory demand or even to institute proceedings for recovery of the debt. Indeed, the Court of Appeal has emphasised the practical reasons why "the vast majority of creditors who seek to petition for the winding up of companies do not serve statutory demands", namely that the assets may be dissipated during the three weeks that have to elapse before a petition can be issued based on the demand.[138] It suffices that the creditor has called for payment and that payment has not been made. Secondly, the fact that the statutory demand is for substantially more than the sum indisputably due does not vitiate it if the amount undisputed exceeds £750.[139] But if there is no such undisputed amount, non-compliance with the statutory demand cannot be used to found

---

[134] See below, para.5–19.
[135] See above, paras 4–07.
[136] See above, paras 4–15 et seq.
[137] See below, para.5–19.
[138] *Taylors Industrial Flooring Ltd v M. & H. Plant Hire (Manchester) Ltd* [1990] B.C.L.C. 216, per Dillon L.J. at 219.
[139] *Re A Company (No.008122 of 1980), Ex p. Trans Continental Insurance Services Ltd* [1990] B.C.L.C. 697.

a petition, for what is required is "neglect" to pay, that is, a failure to pay a demand without reasonable excuse.[140] Moreover, as stated above, it is an abuse of process to serve a statutory demand for a debt which is bona fide disputed or for an excessive amount with a view to putting pressure on the company to pay more than is due from it.[141] Thirdly, the fact that the statutory demand is sent to the company by post instead of being left at its registered office as required by s.123(1)(a) does not invalidate it where it is not disputed that the demand was in fact received at the registered office.[142]

Who can present a petition

Under s.124 of the Insolvency Act 1986, a winding up petition may be presented by: **5–17**

(i)   the company;

(ii)   the directors of the company;

(iii)   any creditor or creditors (including any contingent or prospective creditor or creditors);

(iv)   any contributory or contributories;

(v)   a liquidator or temporary administrator appointed in main proceedings opened in another EC Member State pursuant to art.3(1) of the EC Insolvency Regulation who wishes to open secondary proceedings in the United Kingdom pursuant to art.29(3) of the regulation[143];

(vi)   the clerk of a magistrates' court in exercise of the power conferred by s.87A of the Magistrates' Courts Act 1980 (relating to the enforcement of fines imposed on companies); or

(vii) all or any of those parties together or separately.

However, the list in s.124(1) is not exhaustive, since there are statutory provisions elsewhere (including, surprisingly, the Insolvency Act itself) which

---

[140] *Re London and Paris Banking Corp* (1875) 19 Eq. 444.
[141] See above, para.5–13.
[142] *Re A Company (No.008790 of 1990)* [1991] B.C.L.C. 561.
[143] Council Regulation 1346/2000/EC of May 29, 2000 on insolvency proceedings, [2000] OJ L160/1. The term "liquidator" is here used in the extended sense indicated in art.2(b) and Annex C of the Regulation, as meaning any person or body whose function is to administer or liquidate assets of which the debtor has been divested or to supervise the administration of his affairs. In the case of main proceedings opened in another Member State, it denotes any of the officials listed in Annex C in relation to that state. Where the main proceedings are opened in the United Kingdom (which is not the situation discussed here), then for the purpose of the liquidator's powers under the regulation, including the power to open secondary proceedings in another Member State, "liquidator" means a liquidator, a supervisor of a voluntary arrangement, an administrator or an Official Receiver.

specify additional categories of petitioner. Excluding categories related to the EU regulations, these are:

(viii) the Secretary of State under s.122(1)(b) or (c) or on grounds of public interest[144];

(ix) the Regulator of Community Interest Companies[145];

(x) an administrator[146];

(xi) an administrative receiver[147];

(xii) the supervisor of a voluntary arrangement[148]; and

(xiii) the Director of Public Prosecutions, the Director of Revenue and Customs Prosecutions and the Director of the Serious Fraud Office, on public interest grounds.[149]

Where directors of a company present a petition, they must do so as a board, not individually. Accordingly, either all of the directors must join in the petition, or it must be presented by one or more directors pursuant to a unanimous or majority resolution of the board.[150]

Locus standi to present a petition

5–18 A creditor may present a petition whether he is an existing creditor whose debts have already become payable or a prospective or contingent creditor.[151] An equitable assignor has a sufficient interest to petition without joining the assignee.[152] A judgment creditor precluded by the Limitation Act 1980 from bringing an action on the judgment is nevertheless entitled to present a winding up petition, since insolvency proceedings do not constitute "an action upon a judgment".[153] An existing creditor is entitled to petition even if fully

---

[144] Insolvency Act 1986 ss.124(4) and 124A.

[145] Insolvency Act 1986 s.124(4A).

[146] Insolvency Act 1986 Sch.1 para.21.

[147] Insolvency Act 1986 Sch.1 para.21.

[148] Insolvency Act 1986 s.7(4)(b). The Financial Services Authority, which also has power to present a winding up petition under financial services legislation, is about to be abolished.

[149] Serious Crime Act 2007 s.27.

[150] *Re Instrumentation Electrical Services Ltd* [1988] B.C.L.C. 550; and *Re Equiticorp International Plc* [1989] B.C.L.C. 597 (a decision on a petition for an administration order, but the principle is the same).

[151] As to who is a creditor, see above, para.2–26; as to "debt" and "liability", see above, para.4–24; as to contingent and prospective liabilities, see above, paras 4–26 and 4–27.

[152] *Parmalat Capital Finance Ltd v Food Holdings Ltd* [2008] B.C.C. 371.

[153] *Ridgeway Motors (Isleworth) Ltd v ALTS Ltd* [2005] B.C.C. 496.

secured,[154] although his views are likely to be given less weight than those of unsecured creditors.[155] Prospective and contingent creditors can rely on all of the grounds open to existing creditors, including the "just and equitable" ground in para.(g) of s.122.[156] But whereas the interest of an existing creditor is in most cases self-evident, a prospective or contingent creditor may need to demonstrate a sufficient interest in the making of a winding up order.[157] There are various decisions holding that a person claiming to be a creditor on a debt which is bona fide disputed, that is, disputed on substantial grounds,[158] does not constitute a creditor at all for the purpose of the statutory provisions, so that the petitioner has no locus standi,[159] but these must be considered doubtful in view of the decision of the Privy Council in *Parmalat Capital Finance Ltd v Food Holdings Ltd*[160] that the treatment of disputed claims is a rule of practice rather than law, and that while the company may apply to have the petition struck out as an abuse of the process of the court without waiting for the substantive hearing,[161] even if at such hearing there might be creditors with undisputed claims who could ordinarily ask to be substituted,[162] the court retains a discretion to make a winding up order. [163] If the petition has not yet been presented or advertised, the alternative course is to grant an injunction to restrain presentation or advertisement.[164] But neither of these courses will be taken where the debt is only partially disputed,[165] so long as the amount not in dispute is at least equal to that required for a statutory demand, currently a sum exceeding £750,[166] or where the creditor has a good arguable case and would suffer injustice or loss of a remedy (for example, through removal of assets from the jurisdiction) if the petition were not to be allowed to proceed.[167]

---

[154] *Re Portsmouth Borough (Kingston, Fratton and Southsea) Tramways Co* [1892] 2 Ch. 362; *Moor v Anglo-Italian Bank* (1879) 10 Ch.D. 681; and *Re Lafayette Electronics Ltd* [2007] B.C.C. 890.

[155] See below, para.5–21.

[156] *Re A Company (No.003028 of 1987)* [1988] B.C.L.C. 282. A creditor for untaxed costs has locus standi (*Tottenham Hotspur v Edennote* [1995] 1 B.C.L.C. 65).

[157] See below, and Lee Berg Tat, "Claiming a Pound of Flesh as a Contingent or Prospective Creditor or under the [Singapore] Companies Act" [1993] Singapore L.J. 144.

[158] *Mann v Goldstein* [1968] 2 All E.R. 769, per Ungoed-Thomas J. at 775; *Re Welsh Brick Industries Ltd* [1946] 2 All E.R. 197 at 198; and *Re A Company (No.001946 of 1991), ex p. Fin Soft Holding SA* [1991] B.C.L.C. 737.

[159] See above, para.5–13.

[160] [2009] 1 B.C.L.C. 274.

[161] *Re A Company (No.0012209 of 1991)* [1992] B.C.L.C. 865.

[162] *Re CPBD (No.001889 of 1975)* [1975] C.L.Y. 322.

[163] [2009] 1 B.C.L.C. 274, per Lord Hoffmann at [9]. The same applies where the debt is not disputed but there is a genuine and serious cross-claim which overtops the claim or reduces it to a sum not exceeding £750 (*Re Bayoil SA* [1999] 1 W.L.R. 147). See generally Suet Lin Joyce Lee, "The Court's Jurisdiction to Restrain a Creditor from Presenting a Winding Up Petition Where a Cross-Claim Exists" [2010] 69 C.L.J. 113.

[164] *Stonegate Securities Ltd v Gregory* [1980] Ch. 576. See further para.5–20, below.

[165] *Re Tweeds Garage Ltd,* [1962] Ch. 406; and *Re A Company (No.008122 of 1989), ex p. Trans Continental Insurance Services Ltd* [1990] B.C.L.C. 697.

[166] See above.

[167] *Re Claybridge Shipping Co Ltd* [1981] Com L.R. 107; and see *Re A Company (No.002180 of 1996)* [1996] 2 B.C.L.C. 409.

A creditor may bind himself by contract not to present a winding up petition. No-action clauses, including a prohibition on presenting a winding up petition, are commonly found in bonds issued on a market. Such clauses do not offend against public policy and will be enforced; indeed, the Companies Court itself regularly accepts undertakings not to present a petition.[168]

Section 124 of the Act restricts the circumstances in which a contributory can petition for winding up.[169] More significant in practice than these restrictions is the rule that a contributory must show that he has a tangible interest in the outcome of the liquidation.[170]

Legitimate interest

5–19   It has been said on many occasions, particularly by Harman J., that winding up proceedings do not constitute a *lis* between the petitioner and the company, but are in the nature of an exercise of class rights by a member of the class.[171] A winding up petition is not simply a means of enforcing a debt: it is also designed to protect the debtor company from harassment and other creditors from piecemeal realisation and unequal distribution and to substitute a system of *pari passu* distribution for individual enforcement.[172] The petitioner must therefore show that he has a legitimate current interest in the winding up of the company. In the case of a creditor, it is sufficient to show that he is currently owed a debt of more than £750[173] which the company, despite request, has failed to pay. In that situation, he is prima facie entitled to a winding up order *ex debito justitiae*.[174] It is irrelevant that he may be motivated by antagonism towards the company or its directors.[175] But if there is a bona fide dispute as to the whole of the debt, or the whole of it except for not more than £750, it is an abuse of the winding up process to present a petition, particularly where the object is to exert pressure on the debtor company to pay more than it owes with a view to avoiding the adverse publicity attending the advertisement of the petition.[176]

---

[168] *Re Colt Telecom Group Plc* [2002] B.P.I.R. 324, per Jacob J. at [74].

[169] See below, para.5–19.

[170] See below, para.5–19.

[171] See, e.g. *Re A Company (No.001573 of 1983)* [1983] B.C.L.C. 492, citing *Re Crigglestone Coal Co* [1906] 2 Ch. 327; and *Re Pleatfine Ltd* [1983] B.C.L.C. 102.

[172] *Re International Tin Council* [1987] Ch. 419, per Millett J. at 456. This is one of the reasons why the court will rarely, if ever, entertain separate petitions by different creditors. The petitioner is considered to represent the class, and other creditors who wish to take part should do so by way of support for the petition. If the petitioning creditor abandons his petition (e.g. because his debt is paid), another creditor may apply to be substituted. Under s.130(4) of the Insolvency Act a winding up order operates in favour of all of the creditors and all contributories of the company as if made on the joint petition of a creditor and a contributory.

[173] Section 123(1) itself prescribes this minimum only for the statutory demand, but the courts have usually applied it by analogy to other grounds relied on by a petitioning creditor.

[174] *Re A Company (No.0010382 of 1992), ex p. Computer Partnership Ltd* [1993] B.C.L.C. 597.

[175] *Bryanston Finance Ltd v De Vries (No.2)* [1976] Ch. 63.

[176] See above, paras 5–13 and 5–14.

The position of the contingent creditor is somewhat different. His interest is not so immediate; indeed, the contingency may never occur. It is therefore necessary to consider the likelihood of this happening and the likely ability of the company, if it did happen, to be able to pay its debts at that time as they fell due. The matter was put in the following way by Scott J. in *Re A Company (No.003028 of 1987)*,[177]:

"Current inability on the part of a company to pay its debts would not necessarily entitle a contingent creditor to succeed in a winding up petition. The contingent creditor would, I think, be expected to show, not only and not necessarily a current inability by the company to pay its debts, but rather an inability to pay its debts at the time when the contingent debt became payable. A case of that character would, in my opinion, fall more clearly within para (g) than para (f) of s 122(1)."

This reasoning is not free from difficulty. In the first place, it presupposes that the time when the contingent debt will become payable is known. But it is in the nature of a contingent debt that the event on which it becomes payable is uncertain; that, indeed, is what distinguishes a contingent debt from a prospective debt. We must therefore assume that the learned judge intended to refer to the time when the contingent debt *was likely* to become payable. It is true that there are cases in which it can be confidently predicted that the contingency will occur and will do in the immediate future,[178] but there are other situations where this will not be so. Indeed, that was the position in the case cited above, where everything turned on whether the creditor would win an action in the Queen's Bench Division that would enable him to claim that repayment of the loan had been triggered. Secondly, given that what has to be shown is the projected inability of the company to pay its debts as they fall due, it is far from clear why para.(g) is more appropriate than para.(f). The typical case where the "just and equitable" ground might be invoked as an independent ground is where the contingent creditor is also a shareholder and complains that he is being prejudiced by oppression or mismanagement; but that complaint would be made *qua* shareholder, not qua creditor. Nevertheless, the decision does underline the fact that the interest of a contingent creditor is more tenuous than that of an actual creditor. It may be noted that a guarantor does not become a contingent creditor until he has paid off the whole of the guaranteed debt.[179]

Presumably, the company's present inability to pay its debts as they fall due is also insufficient for a prospective creditor, and if he is relying on s.122(1)(f), he will have to show that the company will be unable to pay its debts as they

---

[177] [1988] B.C.L.C. 282 at 294.
[178] See above, para.4–18.
[179] *Re Sass* [1896] 2 Q.B. 12; and *Re FitnessCentre (South East) Ltd* [1986] B.C.L.C. 518, per Hoffmann J. at 521.

fall due at the time when his debt becomes payable. It would also seem, by parity of reasoning, that a prospective or contingent creditor cannot rely on a present deficiency of assets under s.122(2) and again has to look to the situation as it will be when his debt matures or is likely to mature. The essential point is that the company's state of insolvency does not entitle anyone to obtain a winding up order; the petitioner must be someone who has both a locus standi and a sufficient current interest in an order being made.

A contributory, in addition to meeting the requirements of s.124, must show that he has a "tangible interest"[180] in a winding up order, that is, a prospect that there will be a surplus in which his share, even if small in absolute terms, is appreciable in relation to the size of his shareholding.[181]

Advertisement

5–20   Unless the court otherwise directs, notice of the petition must be gazetted or, if that is not reasonably practicable, given in such other manner as the court thinks just, not less than seven business days before the day appointed for the hearing and, if the petitioner is not the company, not less than seven business days after service of the petition on the company nor less than seven business days before the day appointed for the hearing.[182] Although the court has power to dispense with advertisement, this will be exercised only in exceptional circumstances, for advertisement serves the dual purpose of enabling creditors and other interested parties to attend and bring before the court material relevant to the question of whether a winding up order should be made and giving notice to the public of the presentation of the petition, information to which they are in principle entitled.[183] But the court will restrain advertisement in appropriate cases, as where the presentation of the petition is an abuse of the process of the court because, for example, the debt is bona fide disputed on substantial grounds.[184]

The substantive hearing

5–21   The existence of grounds for winding up, locus standi and a sufficient interest in the petitioner are all threshold questions which can either be left to be dealt with at the substantive hearing or raised at an earlier stage by way of an application to strike out the petition. In the latter case, the court's task is to decide whether the petition fails *in limine* or can proceed to a substantive

---

[180] *Re Rica Gold Washing Co* (1879) 11 Ch.D. 36, per Jessel M.R. at 43.
[181] *Bryanston Finance Ltd v De Vries (No.2)* [1976] Ch. 63.
[182] Insolvency Rules 1986 r.4.11.
[183] *Applied Database Ltd v Secretary of State for Trade and Industry* [1995] 1 B.C.L.C. 272.
[184] See above, para.5–14.

hearing. Decisions on how to balance opposing views on whether a winding up order should be made are matters to be dealt with at the substantive hearing. If the petition is unopposed, a winding up order will usually be made as a matter of course. But if for other purposes it is desired to obtain a definitive ruling that the company is insolvent, appropriate evidence will have to be called, and if this is insufficient the petition will be dismissed even if the company is as anxious as the petitioner for a winding up order to be made and, indeed, if the company itself is the petitioner.[185]

A creditor to whom a debt is currently owed is prima facie entitled to a winding up order *ex debito justitiae*,[186] but the court may decline to make an order if it is opposed by the majority of creditors.[187] In that connection, the court will have regard not only to the number of opposing creditors, but to the value of the debts owed to them and to the quality of the creditors.[188] So if they are independent creditors who, although a minority in number, represent a substantial majority in value, their wishes are likely to be heeded. The court will to a considerable extent discount creditors who are connected with the company,[189] for example, who are directors or shareholders, and will also give less weight to creditors who are fully secured and thus have only a limited interest in the liquidation. A creditor who is only partially secured will, to the extent of the shortfall, be treated as an unsecured creditor and his views considered in the same way as those of other unsecured creditors.[190] Where the company has a cross-claim against the petitioning creditor, that is a matter which the court can take into account in exercising its discretion whether to make a winding up order.[191]

Members of the company presenting a petition as contributories on the ground that it is just and equitable for the company to be wound-up are entitled to a winding up order if the court is of the opinion that the petitioners are entitled to relief either by winding up or by some other means, that in the absence of any other remedy it would be just and equitable to wind-up the company and that there is no other remedy available to the petitioners which it would be unreasonable of them not to pursue.[192]

Orders that can be made at the hearing

At the hearing of the petition the court may dismiss it, adjourn it conditionally or unconditionally or make an interim order or any other order it thinks

5–22

---

[185] See *Re Capital Annuities Ltd* [1979] 1 W.L.R. 170, a decision on s.50 of the Insurance Companies Act 1974. See also above, para.4–19, n.100.
[186] See above, para.5–12.
[187] Contributories also have the right to be heard in opposition. See, e.g. *Re Rodencroft Ltd* [2004] B.C.C. 631.
[188] *Re Lowerstoft Traffic Services Ltd* [1986] B.C.L.C. 81.
[189] *Re Lowerstoft Traffic Services.*
[190] *Re Leigh Estates (UK) Ltd* [1994] B.C.C. 292.
[191] See cases cited above, nn.124 and 128.
[192] Insolvency Act 1986 s.125(2). See *Vujnovich v Vujnovich* [1990] B.C.L.C. 227.

fit, but it cannot refuse to make an order only on the ground that the assets have been fully mortgaged or that the company has no assets.[193] A winding up order cannot be made during the interim moratorium imposed when the company is about to be put into administration[194] or during the currency of an administration,[195] and where an administration order is made any winding up petition must be dismissed.[196]

Commencement of winding up

5–23   Upon a winding up order being made, the winding up is deemed to commence at the time of presentation of the petition unless a resolution for voluntary winding up had been passed prior to the petition being presented, in which case the winding up is deemed to have commenced at the time of passing of the resolution.[197] The retrospective effect of the winding up order may have important consequences, for example, in relation to dispositions made by the company[198] and the provisions of the Insolvency Act relating to transactions at an undervalue and preferences.[199]

Effect of winding up order

5–24   On the making of a winding up order, no action may be proceeded with or commenced against the company except by leave of the court and subject to such terms as the court may impose[200] and control of the assets[201] passes to the official receiver as the initial liquidator.[202] The winding up order terminates the appointment and powers of the directors[203] and operates as notice discharging employees except where the business is continued for the beneficial winding up of the company, the liquidator indicates that he would like them to remain in employment and they agree to do so.[204] Neither a declaration of insolvency nor winding up itself constitutes a repudiation of other types of

---

[193] Insolvency Act 1986 s.125(1).
[194] Insolvency Act 1986 Sch.B1 para.44. See below, paras 11–71 et seq.
[195] Insolvency Act 1986 para.42. However, the moratorium does not apply to an order made on a petition presented under s.124A public interest or s.124B (SEs) (Sch.B1 para.42(4)). "SE" stands for *Societas Europaea*, that is, a European company, governed by Council Regulation 2157/2001 on the Statute for a European company ([2001] OJ L/294/1).
[196] Insolvency Act 1986 para.40(1)(a).
[197] Insolvency Act 1986 s.129.
[198] See Insolvency Act 1986 s.127, and below, paras 13–127 et seq.
[199] See below, paras 13–12 et seq. and 13–71 et seq.
[200] Insolvency Act 1986 s.130(2).
[201] But not title to them unless a vesting order is made under s.145 of the Insolvency Act.
[202] Insolvency Act 1986 ss.136(2) and 144.
[203] *Measures Bros Ltd v Measures* [1910] 2 Ch. 248.
[204] *Re Oriental Bank Corp, Macdowell's Case* (1886) L.R. 32 Ch.D. 366.

contract, except where the circumstances show that the company is unable or unwilling to continue performance.[205]

4. WINDING UP THROUGH ADMINISTRATION

The remaining form of winding up, introduced by the Enterprise Act 2002, is as an exit route from administration.[206]

5–25

---

[205] *Mess v Duffus & Co* (1901) 6 Com. Cas. 165; and *Re Phoenix Bessemer Steel Co, ex p. Carnforth Haematite Iron Co* (1876) L.R. 4 Ch.D. 108. For a useful analysis, see Meng Seng Wee, "Insolvency and the Survival of Contracts" [2005] J.B.L. 494.

[206] Insolvency Act 1986 Sch.B1 para.79(4)(d); and Sch.B1 para.83(6)(b). See below, para.11–115.

Chapter 6

Winding Up: Assets Available for Distribution

Introduction

The fundamental principles governing the distribution of assets on the winding up of a company were outlined in Chapter 3. It is worth restating three of these at the outset. First, only the assets of the company at the time it goes into liquidation or accruing to it subsequently are available for its creditors. As we shall see, this principle—which amongst other things excludes property so far as held by the company on trust or subject to a security interest or as a buyer under a conditional sale agreement[1]—is subject to important exceptions. Secondly, what constitutes an asset of the company is to be determined primarily by the general principles of property and contract law applicable to solvent parties. It is for this reason that insolvency law cannot be properly understood without a thorough grasp of the general law. There are, it is true, certain rules of pre-insolvency law which are modified by insolvency legislation, but the starting point in each case is the determination of the assets of the company in accordance with the general law and the principle referred to earlier that insolvency law respects pre-insolvency entitlements.[2] Thirdly, a distinction is to be drawn between assets coming to the company after the commencement of winding up which do not result from any activity of the liquidator and recoveries by the liquidator through performance of a contract or as the result of proceedings for fraudulent or wrongful trading and the like. The former are susceptible to capture under an after-acquired property clause in a mortgage or charge, while the latter are statutory recoveries which the liquidator holds for the benefit of the general body of creditors, not in right of the company. They are thus not to be equated with free assets of the company which it was capable of giving in

6–01

---

[1] See below, paras 6–41 et seq.
[2] See above, paras 3–02 et seq.

security as after-acquired property, but are held on trust for the general body of creditors.[3]

1. DELINEATION OF THE PROPERTY OF THE COMPANY

6–02   There are various reasons why it may be necessary to know whether a right or facility constitutes property for the purpose of insolvency law. The first is that in general it is only assets beneficially owned by the company that are distributable among creditors. The second is that contractual provisions by which, on the insolvency of a company, it is to be divested of property that has been transferred to it outright are void under insolvency law. The third is that the liquidator is entitled to disclaim onerous property, for which purpose it may be necessary to determine whether what is in issue is property before turning to the question of whether it is onerous property. Finally, the concept of property of the company may be relevant for the purpose of determining whether, after the presentation of a winding up petition, there has been a disposition of the company's property in contravention of s.127 of the Insolvency Act 1986,[4] an issue examined in several cases in relation to an overdraft maintained by the company with its bank.[5]

Property of the company

6–03   Section 107 of the Insolvency Act 1986, embodying the general principle of *pari passu* distribution, provides as follows:

> "Subject to the provisions of this Act as to preferential payments, the company's property in a voluntary winding up shall on the winding up be applied in satisfaction of the company's liabilities *pari passu* and, subject to that application, shall (unless the articles otherwise provide) be distributed among the members according to their rights and interests in the company."

Although there is no exactly comparable provision for compulsory winding up, the same rules apply.[6] So all of the assets of the company, including assets situated abroad, constitute its estate available for distribution in accordance with the statutory order of priority. But what is meant by "the company's

---

[3] As to the nature of the trust, see above, para.3–09.
[4] See below, paras 13–127 et seq.
[5] See below, paras 13–130 et seq.
[6] Insolvency Rules 1986 r.4.181(1).

property"? Section 436 indicates that this is to have the widest meaning,[7] stating that in the Act, except in so far as the context otherwise requires:

> ". . . 'property' includes money, goods, things in action, land and every description of property wherever situated and also obligations and every description of interest, whether present or future or vested or contingent, arising out of, or incidental to, property."

Like most definitions, this one is not free from difficulty. For one thing, it is circular, "property" being defined as including "every description of property". Moreover, the reference to "obligations" is a little strange, since obligations owed *by* the company are liabilities, not assets, while obligations owed *to* the company (which is evidently what is meant) are already encompassed within the phrase "things in action". But as we shall see, the concept of property is notoriously difficult[8] and depends on the context in which it is invoked,[9] so that we cannot fairly criticise the draftsman for giving us a self-referential definition. What is clear is, first, that "for something to qualify as 'property', it must involve some element of benefit or entitlement for the person holding it"[10] and, secondly, that the concept of property is not exhausted by the division into choses in possession and choses in action.[11]

Tangibles and intangibles

The assets of a company in liquidation, like those of a solvent company, are not confined to physical things or to things which are fully owned by the company. Any beneficial interest held by the company, whether in tangible or intangible property and whether full or limited, indefeasible or defeasible, present, future or contingent, held absolutely or by way of security, constitutes an asset. Thus, the company's assets may include freehold or leasehold property, goods owned by the company, possession of goods under a lease or hire-purchase agreement, negotiable instruments held by the company, insurance policies, intellectual property rights, contract, tort and restitution claims, options, quotas and licences and security interests in tangible or intangible property owned by

6–04

---

[7] *Hollinshead v Hazleton* [1916] 1 A.C. 428, per Lord Atkinson at 436; *Bristol Airport Plc v Powdrill* [1990] Ch. 744, per Sir Nicolas Browne-Wilkinson V-C at 759; and *Re Celtic Extraction Ltd* [2001] Ch. 475, per Morritt L.J. at 486.

[8] For a detailed treatment, see J.E. Penner, *The Idea of Property in Law* (Oxford: Oxford University Press, 1997), particularly Chs 5 and 6. For a classification of property, see also Kevin Gray, "Property in Thin Air" [1991] C.L.J 252, and other materials cited by L.S. Sealy and R.J.A. Hooley, *Commercial Law: Text, Cases and Materials*, 4th edn (Oxford: Oxford University Press, 2009), pp.57 et seq.

[9] *Nokes v Doncaster Amalgamated Collieries Ltd* [1940] A.C. 1014, per Lord Porter at 1051.

[10] *Re SSSL Realisations (2002) Ltd* [2005] 1 B.C.L.C. 1, per Lloyd J. at [60].

[11] See below, para.6–05.

another.[12] At common law an insured's claim against its insurers against liability to a third party vested in the company, not in the third party. This was thought unfair and the Third Parties (Rights against Insurers) Act 1930 was enacted, providing that in the event of the company's winding up the insured's claim was transferred in to third party.[13] However, the conditions attaching to the transfer were such as seriously to reduce the utility of the provision and the law has been prospectively changed by the Third Parties (Rights Against Insurers) Act 2010, s.1(2) of which more effectively transfers the insured's claim to the third party.[14] The Act has yet to be brought into force.

To avoid misunderstanding, we need to be clear what we mean when we say that rights vested in a company under a contract or in tort or by way of personal restitutionary claim are the property of the company. They are not, of course, property at all in the relation between the company and the party liable on the company's claim; they are merely personal claims. But in the context of winding up, the liquidator holds the claim not for the company itself, but on a statutory "trust" for the creditors,[15] who thus occupy the position of third parties. So from the perspective of the liquidator and creditors a contract right vested in the company is undoubtedly a species of property and indeed may be an asset of great value even if not conferring a right to another form of property.

Intangibles other than choses in action

6–05   Intangible rights which are not enforceable by action may nevertheless have value and be transferable, for example, goodwill[16] and transferable quotas and licences,[17] all of which fall within the definition of property even though they are not enforceable by action and thus are not choses in action. Indeed, even licences which are not transferable, but, on the sale of the business to which they relate, are surrendered to the licensing authority and, if it thinks fit, re-granted to the purchaser of the business, are property if they possess commercial value.[18] Again, it has been held that while a residuary legatee has no

---

[12] The main division is between tangibles and intangibles, but intangibles themselves can be subdivided into documentary intangibles, such as negotiable instruments, documents of title to goods, bearer securities, which embody rights so as to make these transferable by delivery of the document with any necessary indorsement, and pure (or non-documentary) intangibles, which are not so embodied, such as ordinary contract rights, insurance policies, intellectual property rights, debts not represented by a negotiable instrument and registered securities. See *generally Goode on Commercial Law*, edited by Ewan McKendrick, 4th edn (London: Penguin Books and LexisNexis, 2009), pp.31 and 51–52. In many respects documentary intangibles are treated in law in the same way as tangibles, e.g. in their susceptibility to claims for conversion. In *OBG v Allen* [2008] 1 A.C. 1, Lord Nicholls and Baroness Hale would have extended the tort of conversion to cover intangibles generally, but the majority declined to go down this path.
[13] See below, para.6–24.
[14] See below, para.6–24.
[15] See above, para.3–09.
[16] *Re Leas Hotel Co* [1902] 1 Ch. 332.
[17] *Att-Gen of Hong Kong v Nai-Keung* [1987] 1 W.L.R. 1339; and see below, para.6–11.
[18] See below, para.6–11.

right to any assets comprised in the estate until the completion of the administration, the right to have the estate properly administered includes the right to be paid on completion of the administration and this itself confers an immediate interest of some kind in the assets that will form part of the residuary estate, an interest which constitutes "property" for the purpose of s.436 of the Insolvency Act.[19]

There are many other types of right which are realisable by sale or exchange although not constituting either choses in possession or choses in action, for example, airport take-off and landing slots, which at congested international airports such as Heathrow and Gatwick may be more valuable than the company which holds them,[20] and radio spectrum, which is also a valuable resource.[21]

Property acquired after commencement of winding up

Finally, the property of the company is not limited to assets in which it has an   **6-06**
interest at the time of commencement of the winding up. Other assets may fall into the estate later, whether by virtue of rights granted prior to the winding up or because of the liquidator's own activities, in addition to which the estate may be swelled by recoveries from directors and other parties against whom the liquidator or the company has rights of action under the Insolvency Act or by the obligatory surrender to the liquidator of a percentage of assets comprised in a floating charge. However, there is a distinction between assets vested in the company at the time of winding up and assets which are only recoverable by the liquidator subsequently in exercise of his statutory winding up powers. The latter are not "the company's property" within the meaning of the Insolvency Act 1986[22] and are thus not susceptible to capture by a secured creditor under an after-acquired property clause.[23]

What is property?

All this seems quite clear-cut. However, various types of interest raise diffi-   **6-07**
culties. This is particularly true of rights expressed to be non-transferable or non-assignable, limited interests and defeasible interests. Then there are rights which will accrue to the company only on the discharge of obligations,

---

[19] *Re Hemming deceased* [2009] Ch. 313.
[20] Some years ago the European Commission issued a statement signalling its acceptance of secondary trading in airport slots.
[21] A system of spectrum trading was introduced by the regulatory authority Ofcom at the end of 2004.
[22] Sch.4 para.6.
[23] *Re Oasis Merchandising Ltd* [1998] Ch. 170; and see below, para.6–36.

as in the case of executory contracts. Further, assets in the possession of the company may turn out to belong to others, for example, through reservation of title under a sale agreement or through some form of trust, and questions may arise as to whether the fruits of liability insurance form part of the company's estate or belong to the party to whom the liability was incurred.

But we still need to have a clearer idea of the concept of property. The badges of a property right were set out by Lord Wilberforce in *National Provincial Bank Ltd v Hastings Car Mart Ltd*[24] in the following terms[25]:

> "Before a right or an interest can be admitted into the category of property, or of a right affecting property, it must be definable, identifiable by third parties, capable in its nature of assumption by third parties, and have some degree of permanence or stability."

The third of these elements, transferability, has also been emphasised in other cases.[26] One may add that the right must be of a kind capable of possessing realisable value,[27] for this is key to the concept of property.

Transferability

6–08   Before we move to a discussion of the status of supposedly non-transferable rights, we have to be clear on what we mean by transferability, and this in turn raises the question: what is a transfer? A narrow conception of transfer would be a conveyance from A to B, so that B now has the identical thing that was previously vested in A. But the law has a much wider conception of transfer. It suffices that A, by giving up a benefit, can procure that B receives a benefit. The typical case is contractual novation. Suppose that C is a creditor of D and that it is desired to transfer the debt from C to T. One way of doing this is by assignment: the identical subject matter of C's right is made over to T. But another method is for all three parties to agree that the contract will be novated so that T becomes D's creditor in place of C. This too is regarded in law as a transfer, although it is clear that the right which T has against D is a new right, not the right which C had previously enjoyed against D. Nevertheless, we can properly speak of a transfer of property from C to T, and this would be relevant if D had stipulated that it would not receive any notice of assignment, for it shows that this fact alone would not preclude transfer. The point becomes even sharper if we change not only the creditor, but the

---

[24] [1965] A.C. 1175 at 1247–1248.

[25] At 1247–1248.

[26] *Nai-Keung*, cited above n.17; and *Re Celtic Extraction Ltd* [2001] Ch. 475, per Morritt L.J. at [33].

[27] *Re Celtic Extraction Ltd* (above, n. 26), per Morritt L.J. at [33]. This does not mean that the particular item in question must itself possess value; it may be worth nothing or even have a negative value and yet form part of the company's assets. The question is not its actual value, but its characterisation as an item of a kind capable of possessing value. See below, para.6–15.

debtor. Take the case of an inter-bank funds transfer. D, who owes money to C, instructs his bank DB to arrange to transfer funds held to the credit of D's account to C's bank, CB, for the credit of C. This is carried out through the inter-bank clearing system. There is no assignment to C or CB of D's claim against DB. The position is simply that by giving up a claim against his bank, D procures the creation of a claim by C against C's bank. The law regards this as the transfer of property, so that, if for example, C were to procure the transfer by fraud, D would be entitled to assert a proprietary restitutionary claim against C.[28]

Where a statutory licence held by A is not transferable from A to B but can, with the consent of the licensing authority, be surrendered by A in order for a fresh licence to be granted to B, this mechanism produces effects similar to a transfer by novation, and even if the grant of the new licence is dependent on the discretion of the licensing authority, the existing licence may be of a kind which commands a value, in which case it constitutes property within s.436.[29]

So there are many rights which, despite being labelled non-transferable, are in fact capable of transfer, and if they are of a kind possessing independent value in the hands of the company in liquidation they constitute property of the company for the purpose of the Insolvency Act 1986. The more important of these will now be examined in more detail.

Rights expressed to be non-transferable

Non-transferable rights are of different kinds. In his book *The Idea of Property in Law*, Dr James Penner draws a useful distinction between restrictions on the scope of property rights which are not intended to strike at the property-like character of the right and those that are.[30] Applied to the question of alienability, one can distinguish a thing which is not transferable, at common law or by statute, because it depends entirely on the holder's personal qualities and thus is not property, from a thing which is not by its nature personal to the holder, but which legislation has ordained is not to be sold, for example, a stock of cancerous substances. Although not generally saleable in its existing form,[31] this is undoubtedly property, because the rights in it are not personal to the holder; the prohibition on sale is not intended to deprive the substances of their property character, but rather to safeguard the public from harm. A fortiori a statutory provision which does not directly prohibit assignment of contractual rights but merely requires a prohibition

6–09

---

[28] *Agip (Africa) Ltd v Jackson* [1991] Ch. 547; and *Banque Belge pour L'Etranger v Hambrouck* [1921] 1 K.B. 321.
[29] See below, para.6–11.
[30] J. Penner, *The Idea of Property in Law*, pp.100–101.
[31] It might, of course, be saleable if treated or have a value for the purposes of chemical research.

against assignment to be included in the contract and attaches certain adverse consequences for failure to do so does not deprive the rights of their character as property.[32]

There are various kinds of right that are expressed to be non-transferable or are transferable only with the consent of another or in restricted conditions. These include contract rights which by the terms of the contract are not assignable, or are not assignable by one party without the other's consent[33]; various kinds of statutory licence; quotas issued by a government department or statutory authority; and membership of a club or exchange.[34] Since one of the badges of a property right is transferability, the question arises whether a right expressed to be a non-transferable right can be a species of property at all. The answer depends, of course, upon the construction of s.436 of the Insolvency Act, but given the breadth of the definition in that section it would seem that the test is whether the right is of a kind having a value which is realisable by the insolvent company, as opposed to a right of a kind which is of value only to the company itself. Where the right is truly non-transferable in the sense that it is of a kind having value only in the hands of the company in liquidation and cannot be sold or otherwise disposed of for value, then it is not property for the purposes of the Insolvency Act. We shall consider four categories of case: the assignment or trust of contract rights which are expressed by the terms of the contract to be non-assignable; the transfer of licences and quotas which are capable of being separately transferred, albeit sometimes not without difficulty; the assignment of rights of pre-emption; and truly non-transferable rights.

Assignment or trust of contract rights expressed to be non-assignable

6–10 It is not uncommon for a contract to contain a provision prohibiting a party from assigning its rights under the contract. There are several legitimate commercial reasons for such a stipulation. The debtor[35] may have a good working relationship with its creditor and may not wish to find itself dealing with a new party who is less accommodating. The debtor may also not wish to risk

---

[32] *Re Landau* [1998] Ch. 223 (statutory provisions requiring pension trust deeds to include a no-assignment clause), approved by the Court of Appeal in *Krasner v Dennison* [2001] Ch. 76. However, the effect of *Re Landau* was subsequently negated by s.11 of the Welfare Reform and Pensions Act 1999.

[33] There are also rules of public policy restricting assignment. For example, the assignment of a bare right of action constitutes champerty and is void. See *Goode on Legal Problems of Credit and Security*, 4th edn, ed Louise Gullifer(London: Sweet & Maxwell, 2008), para.3–38, and the standard works on contract law. However, sale of a bare cause of action by a liquidator is an exception to the rule. See above, para.5–06.

[34] *Money Markets International Stockbrokers Ltd v London Stock Exchange Ltd* [2002] 1 W.L.R. 1150; and *Bombay Official Assignee v Shroff* (1932) 48 T.L.R. 443. See below, para.7–07.

[35] For convenience, the term "debtor" is used to include any form of obligor, whether the performance owed is the payment of money or otherwise.

overlooking a notice of assignment and, having mistakenly paid the original creditor, finding itself compelled to make a second payment to the assignee. Moreover, where the debtor is engaged in continuing mutual dealings with the original creditor, it will not want to have its right of set-off brought to an end as regards cross-claims arising after its receipt of notice of assignment.[36] Does this mean that an assignment to the debtor company in breach of a no-assignment clause is wholly ineffective? This was the view of Croom-Johnson J. in *Helstan Securities Ltd v Hertfordshire CC*,[37] but his ruling went further than was necessary for the decision. Certainly, the debtor is entitled to insist that it will not deal with anyone other than the original creditor and that it does not recognise the title of the assignee. But it is quite another thing to say that as between assignor and assignee the assignment has no proprietary effects. In the first place, in a contract between A and B it is not competent to the parties to regulate the proprietary effects of a transfer of the contract or its proceeds from B to C. Secondly, the debtor generally has no legitimate interest in controlling the assignor's power of alienation and it is strongly arguable that a restriction on alienation is contrary to public policy.[38] Where what is assigned is a debt, the effect of the assignment in breach of a no-assignment clause is to create a trust of the debt in favour of the assignee, who, being unable to collect the debt from the debtor, will usually be content to treat the assignment as relating to the collected proceeds in the hands of the assignor. Where the assignor refuses to collect the debt, the assignee can sue the debtor and join the assignor as co-defendant for the purpose of procuring an order for payment to the assignor, who will then be accountable for the proceeds to the assignee.[39] But where the rights assigned are not mon-etary in character, the assignee may have a legitimate interest, as beneficiary of a trust of the contract right itself, in enforcing the trust so as to preclude the assignor from appropriating the contract rights for his own benefit. On this basis, it has been held that there is no reason why contracts assigned to a partnership should not form part of the partnership assets even if, as between the assignor and its counterparty, the contracts were not assignable.[40]

---

[36] See *Goode on Legal Problems of Credit and Security*, 2008, para.3–39.

[37] [1978] 3 All E.R. 262.

[38] See R.M. Goode, "Inalienable Rights?" (1979) 42 M.L.R. 553, to which extensive supportive references were made by Lord Browne-Wilkinson in *Linden Gardens Ltd v Lenesta Sludge Disposals Ltd* [1994] 1 A.C. 85.

[39] *Barbados Trust Ltd v Bank of Zambia* [2007] 1 C.L.C. 434. Since the majority of the Court of Appeal decided that the purported assignment was ineffective, the form of the order did not arise for consideration. But it seems clear that if it had been made it would have directed pay-ment to the assignor, thereby respecting the right of the debtor not to be involved with the assignee. For a full discussion of the effect of assignments in breach of contract, see Roy Goode, "Contractual Prohibitions Against Assignment" [2009] L.M.C.L.Q. 300.

[40] See *Don King Productions Inc v Warren & Co* [1999] 2 All E.R. 218, applied in *Swift v Dairywise Farms Ltd (No.1)* [2000] 1 W.L.R. 1177; *Re Turcan* (1888) 40 Ch. D. 5; *and Goode on Legal Problems of Credit and Security*, 2008, para.3–38.

It will now be evident that non-assignable contract rights do not, on closer examination, contravene the general requirement of transferability, for while they are not transferable at law so as to be enforceable against the assignor's counterparty, they are assignable in equity so as to produce proprietary effects in the relationship between the assignor and the assignee.

(2) Statutory licences, quotas and permits

6–11   In several cases, the courts have had to consider the status of licences and quotas as a species of property. Transferable licences, including licences that are not transferable by the holder but can be transferred by the licensing authority or surrendered against the grant of a new licence which is not dependent on the personal qualities of the licensee but follows the ownership or occupation of land or the management of a business, are clearly property if possessing, or of a kind capable of prossessing, realisable value.[41] So in a case concerning a waste management licence granted under the Environmental Protection Act 1990 to a company which later went into liquidation, the Court of Appeal held that the licence, which was not transferable by the holder by assignment but could, by surrender and re-grant, be transferred by the Environment Agency on application and had realisable value, constituted property under s.436 of the Insolvency Act 1986.[42]

Similarly, a milk quota, which gave a milk producer exemption from a levy that would otherwise be payable, but which had to follow the land to which it was attached and could not be dealt with independently,[43] was nevertheless held, on the evidence before the court, to be an independent asset having a distinct economic value capable of being realised by contractual devices based on the principle of a composite holding.[44] Accordingly, it constituted property within the definition of s.436 of the Insolvency Act and was held on trust for the company so as to entitle the liquidators to require an accounting of the proceeds of sale of the quota. The position would have been otherwise if the quota held by the company had become divorced from the land.[45] Again, in *Saulnier v Royal Bank of Canada*,[46] the Supreme Court of Canada held that statutory fishing licences granted, renewed and transferable only at the discretion of the Minister of Fisheries and Oceans nevertheless possessed considerable commercial value both in the hands of the licensee and as

---

[41] As to realisable value, see below, para.6–15.
[42] *Re Celtic Extraction Ltd* [2001] Ch. 475, applying *National Provincial Bank Ltd v Hastings Car Mart Ltd* [1965] A.C. 1175 and *Att-Gen of Hong Kong v Nai-Keung* [1987] 1 W.L.R. 1339 and, in relation to the power of disclaimer, overruling *Re Mineral Resources Ltd, Environment Agency v Stout* [1999] 1 All E.R. 746.
[43] *Faulks v Faulks* [1992] 1 E.G.L.R. 9.
[44] *Swift v Dairywise Farms Ltd* [2000] B.C.C. 642. On this point an appeal to the Court of Appeal [2002] B.C.C. 227 was abandoned.
[45] *Faulks v Faulks*, cited above n.43.
[46] [2008] 3 S.C.R. 166.

collateral for financial institutions, giving a proprietary right in the wild fish harvested thereunder, and as a matter of statutory interpretation constituted property within s.2 of the federal Bankruptcy and Insolvency Act and s.2 of the Nova Scotia Personal Property Security Act.[47]

However, not all statutory licences are property; the relevant statute may itself preclude this. So s.36 of the Coal Industry Act 1994 provides that a licence under that Act is not to be treated as property for the purposes of the Insolvency Act 1986.

(3) Assignable rights of pre-exemption

An assignable right of pre-emption constitutes property even though the grantor of the right may never decide to sell the asset to which the right relates. Unless and until he so decides, the right is contingent. Nevertheless, it has value, for the grantor is bound not to offer the asset to anyone other than the grantee of the pre-emption right without first offering it to the grantee and if the grantor breaches that obligation he may incur a liability in damages to the grantee.[48]   6–12

(4) Transferable rights having no realisable value

A right which, although in itself transferable, is inseparably annexed to personal status and cannot be transferred so as to produce value for the company, is not a free-standing asset that can be treated as part of the company's estate. It is necessary to emphasise that what we are concerned with is not whether an asset is capable of transfer by the company, but whether it is transferable so as to produce value for the company. For example, if a company that is a member of an exchange holds shares for which it cannot receive any consideration on transfer and which on the cessation of membership by reason of the company's insolvency have to be surrendered to the exchange without consideration, and are then transferable by the exchange to other members for value, the shares do not constitute a free-standing asset of the company, nor do they constitute value in its hands for the purpose of the rule against divestment on insolvency.[49]   6–13

---

[47] In a perceptive analysis of *Saulnier*, Professor Anthony Duggan points out that the judgment of the Supreme Court embodied both a functional and a formal approach, the former (which he approves) reflecting the fact that to treat the licence as property facilitated access to credit, while the latter (which he criticises) would treat the licence as property only if it was in the nature of a *profit à prendre*. See "In the Wake of the Bingo Queen: Are Licences Property?" (2009) 47 C.B.L.J. 225.

[48] *Dear v Reeves* [2002] Ch. 1.

[49] *Money Markets International Stockbrokers*, cited above n.34. See below, para.7–07.

(5) Truly non-transferable rights

6-14   We are left with rights which are not transferable at all, whether by statutory or equitable assignment, by contractual novation or, in the case of statutory and other personal licences and quotas, by surrender and fresh grant to a new licensee of a licence not dependent on the licensee's personal qualities.

A right which is purely personal to the company and is not of a kind capable of producing realisable value does not constitute property for the purposes of the Insolvency Act so as to form part of the company's estate. It was on this ground that in *City of London Corp v Bown*[50] Dillon L.J. held that a secure periodic tenancy, being personal to the tenant and incapable of realisation for the benefit of creditors by his trustee in bankruptcy, did not form part of the bankrupt's estate for the purpose of s.306 of the Insolvency Act.

The concept of realisable value

6-15   In the preceding discussion, several references have been made to the fact that to qualify as property an item needs to be of a kind capable of having realisable value. It is necessary to be clear what this means. It does not mean that the item itself must be worth something; it may be unsaleable. That an unsaleable item may still constitute property of the company is evident from s.178 of the Insolvency Act 1986, which permits a liquidator to disclaim onerous property.[51] What the requirement of realisable value is intended to signify is that the item in question must have property-like qualities, that is, be *of a kind* which is transferable in the broad sense used above and for which a person would pay a price if value were to be had. We have seen instances where this is not the case: licences which are so personal to the holder that they are by their nature incapable of transfer; and shares which are transferable only on terms that the transferor is to receive no consideration. But a lease at a rent which substantially exceeds the market value, so that the lessee would be able to assign it only by paying the assignee a so-called negative premium, is nevertheless property of the company, albeit onerous property which a liquidator might wish to disclaim.

Factors limiting the interest held

6-16   An item of tangible or intangible property held by the company is an asset of the company only to the extent of its interest in it. The strength and quantum of that interest may be limited or extinguished by external vitiating factors or by the terms on which the interest is held. As we shall see, in relation to the latter the law draws a sharp distinction between contractual provisions

---

[50] (1990) 60 P. & C.R. 42, distinguished in *De Rotschild v Bell* [2000] Q.B. 33.
[51] See below, para.6-27.

which limit the quantum or duration of an interest, to which effect will be given, and provisions for the divesture, on the company's insolvency, of ownership of assets previously transferred to it,[52] which are void as contravening the anti-deprivation principle and may also be void on the separate ground of repugnancy.[53] The factors which may qualify an interest in an asset fall broadly into four groups:

(1) Factors which prevent the interest taking effect or render it voidable or terminable

The company's rights under a contract, including a contract pursuant to which   **6–17**
it has acquired or is to acquire land or goods, may be subject to some unfulfilled condition precedent[54] or some equity rendering it vulnerable to avoidance ab initio, for example, by way of rescission for fraud, misrepresentation or undue influence. Alternatively, the contract, although not voidable, may be subject to a right of termination by the other party, for example, for default in payment or other breach or on the occurrence of some non-promissory condition subsequent. The liquidator takes control of assets, including contract rights, in the condition in which he finds them, warts and all. He acts in right of and in the name of the company, and an asset of the company which before liquidation was conditional, defeasible or determinable does not cease to be so by reason of the liquidation.[55] So the right of the other party to rescind a contract for misrepresentation and thereby reacquire property transferred under it or to terminate the contract for breach and recover possession of any property leased under it remains unaffected by the company's winding up,[56] although the liquidator may be able to invoke the court's equitable jurisdiction to grant relief against forfeiture.[57] Again, where a company, through its beneficial owner and directing mind and will, has defrauded third parties and upon its liquidation the liquidator brings proceedings in the company's name against its auditors for breach of duty in failing to detect the

---

[52] See below, para.7–05.
[53] See below, para.7–02.
[54] e.g. a contract of sale of land may be subject to a condition that it is not to take effect unless the purchaser obtains planning permission for development of the land within a specified period.
[55] However, the majority decision of the House of Lords in *British Eagle International Airlines Ltd v Compagnie Nationale Air France* [1975] 1 W.L.R. 758 appears to be a deviation from this principle. See para.9–14. Special rules apply in relation to market contracts (above, para.1–61) and financial collateral (above, para.1–66).
[56] *Re Eastgate* [1905] 1 K.B. 465; and *Tilley v Bowman Ltd* [1910] 1 K.B. 745. Both of these involved a sale of goods induced by the fraud of the bankrupt buyer, and it was held that the trustee in bankruptcy took subject to the seller's right to disaffirm the contract. See also below, para.7–05.
[57] *Transag Haulage Ltd v Leyland DAF Finance Plc* [1994] 2 B.C.L.C. 88.

fraud, the claim will be struck out on the ground *ex turpi causa non oritur actio*, the company being the perpetrator, not the victim, of the fraud.[58]

The principle that the liquidator takes subject to equities is not always easy to reconcile with the countervailing principle that a contractual provision is invalid to the extent that its application after the commencement of a winding up would deprive the company in liquidation of an asset that would otherwise be available to creditors, thereby contravening the anti-deprivation principle or, if the provision is in favour of another creditor, the separate principle of *pari passu* distribution. An example is the provision in a construction contract empowering or requiring the employer to pay a sub-contractor direct in stated events, such as the main contractor's default in payment to the sub-contractor of sums due under the sub-contract. If the employer has become entitled or obliged to make such payment before the main contractor goes into liquidation, but has not actually done so, can it still pay the sub-contractor after the winding up has commenced?[59] In early cases in which an affirmative answer was given to this question, the issue of conformity with the insolvency principle of *pari passu* distribution was not raised. In *Re Wilkinson, ex p. Fowler*[60] the contract empowered the employer's engineer, if he considered the main contractor to be guilty of undue delay in paying the sub-contractor, to order payment by the employer to the sub-contractor direct. The main contractor became insolvent and the question arose whether that revoked the engineer's authority to make such an order. Bigham J. held that it did not; the authority was irrevocable and was not affected by the bankruptcy. The question of compatibility with insolvency law was not raised, so that the case is not an authority on that point. The decision was followed in *Re Tout and Finch Ltd*[61] which was decided in favour of the sub-contractor on the additional ground that under the main contract the contractor's entitlement to retention moneys in the hands of the employer was expressed to be fiduciary as trustee for the sub-contractor. This was held to constitute an equitable assignment of the retention moneys by the main contractor. Again, no reference was made to insolvency law.

The effect of these and similar decisions, except so far as based on trust or assignment, was undermined by the controversial decision of the House of Lords in the *British Eagle* case,[62] in which a multilateral netting arrangement was held to contravene the *pari passu* principle and the majority of their Lordships rejected the argument that the liquidator could not invoke the rights under the contract entered into by the parties without being bound by the agreed machinery for payment through the netting arrangement. There has

---

[58] *Stone & Rolls Ltd v Moore Stephens* [2009] 1 A.C. 1391, Lords Scott and Mance dissenting.

[59] For an instructive discussion of this issue, see Michael Bridge, "Collectivity, Management of Estates and the *Pari Passu* Rule in Winding Up" in Armour and Bennett, *Vulnerable Transactions in Corporate Insolvency*, 2003, paras 1.49 et seq.

[60] [1905] 2 K.B. 713.

[61] [1954] 1 W.L.R. 178.

[62] *British Eagle International Airlines*, cited above n.55, and discussed below, para.9–14.

been one decision since *British Eagle* in which the validity of a direct payment clause was upheld,[63] *British Eagle* being distinguished on the ground that in that case the effect of the payment arrangement was to divest the company in liquidation of an asset, namely the debt owed to it, whereas the effect of the direct payment clause was to qualify the company's entitlement to payment as main contract and render it subject to reduction in favour of the sub-contractor. But in a series of subsequent decisions by appeal courts in different common law jurisdictions,[64] the earlier cases have been distinguished on one ground or another and the direct payment clause has been held ineffective in the main contractor's insolvency as contrary to the *pari passu* rule. The effect of the cases is that in the absence of a trust or equitable assignment[65] a mere contractual provision for payment direct to the sub-contractor is not considered to affect the status of the employer's debt as an asset of the company in liquidation or lead to its being characterised as a flawed asset[66] or one to be equated with a voidable interest, but is simply a provision for divestment of an asset which belongs absolutely to the company.

The position where the company is assignee of a contract under an assignment made in breach of a provision prohibiting assignment has already been discussed.[67]

(2) Factors which limit the measure or quantum of the asset

Such limitations take various forms. First, there are interests in tangible or **6–18** intangible property which fall short of full ownership. They include the interest of the company as lessee, mortgagor (the interest is limited to the equity of redemption[68]), mortgagee (the interest is limited to a security interest) and bailee, for example, under a pledge, lease or hire-purchase agreement. Secondly, there are pure contract rights which are limited in time and come to an end on expiry of the stated period. Thirdly, there are interests shared with others, as where the company holds property as joint tenant or tenant in common. Such shared interests can arise by contract or involuntarily, as in the case of a product produced by a person's wrongful commingling of materials owned by the company with those of the commingler or a third party. Fourthly, there are contractual rights to money which by the terms of the

---

[63] *Glow Heating Ltd v Eastern Health Board* [1988] I.R. 110.

[64] *B. Mullan & Sons Contractors Ltd v Ross* (1996) 54 Con. L.R. 163 (Northern Ireland Court of Appeal); *Hitachi Plant Engineering & Construction Ltd v Eltraco International Pte Ltd* [2003] 4 S.L.R. 384 (Singapore Court of Appeal); and *Att-Gen v McMillan & Lockwood Ltd* [1991] 1 N.Z.L.R. 53 (New Zealand Court of Appeal).

[65] Which requires that there be an identifiable asset or fund. See below, para.6–44.

[66] See below, para.9–15, and *Goode on Legal Problems of Credit and Security*, 2008, para.1–21.

[67] Above, para.6–10.

[68] *Re Pyle Works Ltd* (1890) 44 Ch.D. 534, per Cotton L.J. at 577–578.

contract are measured by reference to an ultimate credit balance resulting from mutual dealings between the parties. Examples are the right to a balance on a current account, where the debits and credits form a blended fund and the company has no right to any particular credit item, merely to the credit balance (if any) ultimately struck; and the right of the company as dealer in futures, options and foreign currency to such credit balance (if any) in its favour as results from the netting out of the sums payable by and to the company under separate contracts.

The feature which is common to all of these rights and interests is that they are limited not by their defeasibility or subjection to countervailing obligations or cross-claims, but by the inherent limits to their quantum which are imposed by the factors in question.[69] The distinction is of considerable significance in corporate insolvency law, for there may be circumstances in which a countervailing obligation or right of set-off cannot be asserted against a claim by the liquidator in the name of the company, so that the debtor must pay the company in full and prove in the winding up for his winding up cross-claim, whereas the liquidator cannot disregard or strike down an inherent limitation on the quantum of the company's asset. A good illustration is furnished by the decision of Millett J. in *Re Charge Card Services Ltd*.[70] In that case the company in liquidation had sold receivables to a factor pursuant to a factoring agreement by the terms of which the company's account with the factor was to be credited with the purchase price of receivables and debited with discounting charges, administration charges and sums payable to the factor under indemnity and recourse provisions. The factor was given the right to retain against any credit balance sums prospectively chargeable to the company as a debit to its account. The company through its liquidator challenged the factor's right of retention in respect of sums not falling to be debited until after the company had gone into voluntary liquidation, asserting that such retention constituted a registrable and unregistered charge on book debts, or alternatively an impermissible set-off of a contingent claim. Millett J. held that the retention was not a matter of charge or set-off, but of account. The company's entitlement was not to the purchase price of a receivable as such, but to the ultimate balance on the account after allowing for debits and retentions. The company's claim accordingly failed.

However, it is not always easy to distinguish a contractual limitation on the quantum of an asset from a contractual provision which removes the asset from the general body of creditors. Particular problems have arisen in

---

[69] An old illustration from the law of real property is the distinction between a determinable fee and a fee simple upon condition. The former is an inherent limit on the quantum of the estate, the latter a defeasance of an unlimited estate. See Megarry and Wade, *The Law of Real Property*, 7th edn (London: Sweet & Maxwell, 2008), paras 3-052 et seq.

[70] [1986] 3 All E.R. 289. See also *Perpetual Trustee Co Ltd v BNY Corporate Services Ltd* [2010] Ch. 347 (discussed below, paras 7–13–7–22), where the anti-deprivation rule was held inapplicable to a right which was from the outset subject to an inherent limitation.

relation to the netting-out of obligations in a clearing system, an arrangement giving rise to an acute division of opinion in the House of Lords in the *British Eagle* case[71] as to whether the effect of netting arrangements was that a participant's entitlement at one time was only to a net credit (if any) in its favour resulting from the clearing, or whether on the other hand the clearing house arrangements resulted in an impermissible cutting down on liquidation of the debt vested in the company against its counterparty, to the advantage of other participants in the clearing rather than the general body of creditors. We shall return to this issue in subsequent chapters.[72]

(3) Factors which subject the asset to a countervailing liability or obligation

The right comprising the asset may be linked to a correlative liability or obligation in such a way that the company cannot enforce the right unless it is willing to discharge the liability or perform the correlative obligation. This position is not altered by the winding up of the company. So the liquidator cannot compel the other party to a contract which is still executory at the time of winding up to perform his winding up outstanding obligations unless the liquidator is willing and able to procure the company to perform its own outstanding obligations.[73] Similarly, where prior to the winding up cash was deposited by the company with a bank on terms that it was to be withdrawable only on discharge of liabilities of the company or a third party to the bank, the liquidator can compel release of the deposit only by procuring the performance of the stipulated condition.[74]

6–19

(4) Set-off

Set-off is an equity which entitles a party, in given conditions, to offset one monetary claim (or a claim reducible to money) against another so as to reduce or extinguish his winding up liability. This is not, strictly speaking, a pre-liquidation equity to which the liquidator takes subject, for the various rights of set-off available under the general law prior to liquidation[75] are automatically displaced by the statutory right of set-off given by the insolvency legislation.[76] However, this is not dissimilar, the legislation providing that where before the winding up there have been mutual credits, mutual debts or other mutual dealings between the company and another party,

6–20

---

[71] *British Eagle International Airlines Ltd v Compagnie International Air France* [1975] 1 W.L R. 758.
[72] See below, Chs 7 and 8.
[73] See further on executory contracts the discussion at paras 6–22 and 6–23.
[74] Such a deposit is commonly known as a "flawed asset". See *Goode on Commercial Law*, p.652.
[75] See Ch.9.
[76] See below, paras 9–16–9–18.

debts owed by the company to the other party are required to be offset against debts owed by him to the company and only the balance (if any) is payable to the liquidator.[77]

Executed contracts

6–21   An executed contract is one which has been wholly performed by one party,[78] leaving outstanding only the unperformed obligations of the other party. In contrast to the position with executory contracts,[79] where performance outstanding on one side can only be compelled if the other party is willing and able to give its own counter-performance and the liquidator may decline to perform and, indeed, may disclaim the contract if it is unprofitable,[80] the question of future non-performance and disclaimer cannot arise in relation to executed contracts. The company is entitled to recover or retain all benefits already earned or received under an executed contract without having to perform its obligations. So where a company which is a party to a contract goes into liquidation, then if it is the other party who has fully performed, the company is entitled to retain the benefit of his winding up performance and the other party is left to prove for a dividend in the winding up, whilst if it is the company which has fully performed, the liquidator can enforce the other party's outstanding obligations in the usual way. For example, A sells goods to B Company, which goes into liquidation after acquiring ownership and possession, but without having paid the price. B Company can retain the goods, leaving A to prove as an unsecured creditor. Is this unfair to A? No, because he neither reserved title until payment nor bargained for any form of security, so he took his chance with other creditors and he ought not to be placed in a better position than he was in prior to the winding up.[81] Or take the converse case. A buys goods from B Company and pays the price, but B Company goes into liquidation without having dispatched or delivered the goods. B Company can retain the price, leaving A to prove for either a sum equal to the price, as money paid on a total failure of consideration, or a sum equal to the value of the undelivered goods as damages for breach of contract. This is no more unfair than in the previous example. A parted with his money freely; he takes his chance with other unsecured creditors.[82] If it were

---

[77] Insolvency Rules 1986 r.4.90. A similar rule now applies in an administration where a distribution is to be made to ordinary unsecured creditors (r.2.85).

[78] Excluding aspects of non-performance which would not justify the other party in terminating the contract or withholding his winding up own performance. See the discussion of executory contracts, below.

[79] See below para.6–22.

[80] See below, paras 6–27 et seq.

[81] See R.M. Goode, "Ownership and Obligation in Commercial Transactions" (1987) 103 L.Q.R. 433, 430.

[82] A similar view was expressed by the Insolvency Law Review Committee in its Report "Insolvency Law and Practice" (Cmnd. 8558, 1982), para.1052.

A who had been the defaulting party, there is again no problem; the liquidator of B Company simply sues A in the usual way. We can thus see that the benefits received by the company under an executed contract constitute an unencumbered asset, as opposed to an asset commingled with a liability.

Executory contracts

The position is very different in the case of an executory contract. Such a contract is traditionally defined in English textbooks as a contract in which obligations remain to be performed on both sides. A distinguished American commercial lawyer, Professor Vern Countryman, has provided us with a more sophisticated definition which has been accepted as the classic test of an executory contract for the purpose of American bankruptcy law. According to this definition, an executory contract is:

6–22

"... a contract under which the obligations of both the bankrupt and the other party to the contract are so far unperformed that the failure of either to complete performance would constitute a material breach excusing the performance of the other."[83]

The essential point of an executory contract as thus defined is that each party's right to future performance is linked to and dependent upon that party's own willingness and ability to perform. As another leading authority, Professor Thomas H. Jackson, has aptly put it:

"Fundamentally, executory contracts ... are nothing more than mixed assets and liabilities arising out of the same transaction."[84]

We have seen earlier that factors which operate to subject an asset of the company to a correlative obligation or liability remain unaffected by liquidation. If the liquidator wishes to secure performance by the other party of obligations to be performed in the future, he must procure the company to carry out its own future obligations. But unless the other party has acquired proprietary rights under the contract,[85] the liquidator is not obliged to procure performance by the company. He can either disclaim the contract if it

---

[83] "Executory Contracts in Bankruptcy: Part I" (1973) 58 Minn. L. Rev. 439, 460.

[84] *The Logic and Limits of Bankruptcy Law* (Cambridge, MA: Harvard University Press, 1986, reprinted in paperback Frederick, Maryland: Beard Books, 2001), p.106. Executory contracts have given rise to remarkably little case law or discussion in England, no doubt because English law has no equivalent to Ch.11 of the US Federal Bankruptcy Code, where the characterisation of the contract and its consequences have generated a considerable volume of doctrine and jurisprudence. See Jay L. Westbrook, "A Functional Analysis of Executory Contracts" 74 Minn. L. Rev. 227 (1989) for a detailed analysis.

[85] See below.

is unprofitable[86] or simply decline to procure its performance by the company, in which case the other party can exercise any right he may have to terminate the contract for non-performance.[87] In either case, the contract comes to an end and the solvent party is left to prove for damages for the loss resulting from the company's breach of contract and for any debt accrued due from the company up to the time of termination or rescission.[88] The position is, of course, different if the contract continues in force, for as we have seen the winding up does not produce an acceleration of liability in the case of executory contracts.[89] Where the liquidator accepts the benefit of continued performance by the solvent party, the liability of the company in respect of that performance is an expense of the liquidation.[90]

6–23   Will the court order specific performance by the company of an unperformed obligation to deliver goods under a contract of sale or to convey property which prior to liquidation the company had contracted to sell? The crucial point to bear in mind here is the distinction between real rights and personal rights on liquidation. A party having a real right against the company continues free to assert it; a person having a mere personal claim cannot demand that it be met from the company's general assets, for this would be to offend against the *pari passu* principle by giving the claimant preferential treatment over other unsecured creditors. So the question to be answered in each case is whether the claimant's right to the goods or the property is proprietary or personal. In the case of a contract for the sale of land, the buyer becomes the owner in equity upon exchange of contracts, subject to payment of the price.[91] So the buyer can obtain specific performance of such a contract if he is willing to tender the price.[92] On the other hand, goods sold under a contract of sale are considered not to vest in equity in the buyer on the conclusion of the contract. This is because the Sale of Goods Act 1979 is regarded as constituting a complete code for the transfer of property under a contract of sale, assuming that the parties themselves have not expressly created a trust or equitable interest. The buyer obtains the

---

[86] Insolvency Act 1986 s.178(3). See below, paras 6–27 et seq.
[87] Alternatively, he can apply for rescission of the contract under s.186 of the Insolvency Act and prove for any damages that may be awarded.
[88] So if the contract is for the lease of equipment under an agreement which the liquidator declines to perform, then upon termination the lessor can prove for rentals accrued due up to the date of termination and for damages for the present value of the future rentals of which he has been deprived less the amount by which the value of the repossessed equipment exceeds the value it would have had, discounted to the date of expiry of the lease, if this had run its full course.
[89] See above, para.3–11; and below, para.8–41.
[90] See below, para.8–38.
[91] See further below, text and n.95.
[92] *Pearce v Bastable's Trustee in Bankruptcy* [1901] 2 Ch. 122; and *Re Bastable, ex p. Trustee* [1901] 2 K.B. 518. The liquidator cannot disclaim the contract in such a case (ibid.). By contrast, the court will not normally order specific performance of a contract entered into by the company in liquidation to *purchase* the property (*Holloway v York* (1877) 25 W.R. 627).

property in the goods at the time when the parties intend it to pass,[93] subject to the goods being identified or ascertained.[94] Until then, the buyer has no real rights of any kind, merely a contractual right to transfer of the property and delivery of the goods. So a buyer who has paid the price before ownership or possession has been transferred to him cannot expect to salvage his position by obtaining an order for specific performance against his seller, for since he has no proprietary interest in the goods, the effect of an order for specific performance would be to remove an asset from the general body of creditors for no corresponding benefit and give the buyer preferential treatment in breach of the *pari passu* rule.

Suppose now that it is the company which has contracted to buy the property or the goods. In the case of the property the company becomes owner in equity upon exchange of contracts, but its ownership remains incomplete and inchoate until it has paid the price,[95] without which the liquidator cannot compel execution of the conveyance. In the case of a contract for the sale of goods, the company has no interest in the goods at all prior to transfer of the legal title, for the reason given above, and if the liquidator wishes to obtain delivery he must tender the price.[96] The net effect is therefore the same in the two transactions.

Indemnities and insurance contracts

A company incurs a liability to one party in respect of which it is entitled to an indemnity from another party. The company becomes insolvent. Does the first party acquire direct rights against the indemnifier? In principle, no. There is no privity of contract between the first party and the indemnifier[97]; the contract of indemnity concluded between the insolvent company and the indemnifier is *res inter alios acta* so far as the third party is concerned, and confers no rights on him winding up. Suppose the liquidator actually collects payment from the indemnifier to cover the amount of the third party's claim. Does this not entitle the third party to treat the sum recovered as belonging to him winding up in equity? Again, the answer in principle is no, and for the same reason. If a company chooses to insure itself against liability, that is entirely its own affair. It owed the third party no duty to insure against the liability to him winding up in the first place; it owes no duty to pay the

6–24

---

[93] Sale of Goods Act 1979 s.17.
[94] Sale of Goods Act 1979 s.16.
[95] See *Shaw v Foster* (1872) L.R. 5 H.L. 321; *Lysaght v Edwards* (1876) 2 Ch.D. 499; *Rayner v Preston* (1881) 18 Ch.D. 1, per James L.J. at 13; and R.M. Goode, "Ownership and Obligation in Commercial Transactions" (1987) 103 L.Q.R. 433, 437, text and n.6. See also the comments of Lord Walker in *Jerome v Kelly* [2004] 1 W.L.R. 1409 at [32] as to the division of ownership between buyer and seller of property between exchange of contract and completion.
[96] Sale of Goods Act 1979 s.28.
[97] *Re Harrington Motor Co Ltd* [1928] 1 Ch. 105.

insured claim out of the insurance proceeds; if solvent, it could equally well do so from its other assets, and the position does not change by reason of the winding up.[98] The sum recovered under the indemnity does not belong to the claimant: it is an asset of the estate which enures for the benefit of the general body of creditors, of which the claimant is one.[99] This common law principle applies to indemnities in general and insurance contracts in particular. The Third Parties (Rights Against Insurers) Act 1930 provided a statutory exception to what was felt to have been a harsh rule. The effect of that Act in relation to a company in winding up was that where the company had incurred a liability to a third party against which it had insured under a contract of insurance, then upon the winding up the company's rights against the insurer vested in the third party.[100] However, there were a number of qualifications which seriously impaired the efficacy of the above provisions. These weaknesses have now been rectified by the Third Parties (Rights Against Insurers) Act 2010, which as stated above will, on being brought into force, transfer the insolvent's claim to the third party.

Liabilities

6–25   That a liability is not an asset may seem too obvious to need stating. Despite this, it has been suggested in some cases that where a company draws cheques on an account in overdraft after the presentation of a winding up petition, it disposes of property for the purpose of s.127 of the Insolvency Act 1986. It now seems to be settled that in general this is not the case, although there are situations in which an increase in an overdraft erodes what is an asset of the company, as where the overdraft is secured on assets not already fully charged.[101]

Similarly, where the company in liquidation is an indemnifier under a contract of indemnity for which the company had already received, prior to liquidation, the benefit in exchange for which the indemnity was given, the obligations under the deed do not constitute property for the purpose of the provisions relating to the disclaimer of onerous property.[102] It is surely self-evident that a liability, contingent or otherwise, cannot be an item of property.

---

[98] *Harrington Motor Co,* above, n.97.

[99] *Harrington Motor Co.*

[100] Third Parties (Rights against Insurers) Act 1930 s.1(1), subsequently extended by s.149 of the Road Traffic Act 1972. See Malcolm Clarke, *Law of Insurance Contracts* (London: Informa Law, looseleaf); *MacGillivray & Parkington on Insurance Law,* 11th edn (London: Sweet & Maxwell, 2008), paras 28-011 et seq.; and Raoul Colinvaux, *Law of Insurance,* 8th edn (London: Sweet & Maxwell, 2006), paras 19-20 et seq. and 20-21 et seq.

[101] See below, paras 13–133 et seq.

[102] *Re SSSL Realisations (2002) Ltd* [2005] 1 B.C.L.C. 1, per Lloyd J. at [60] in a passage later approved by Chadwick L.J. on appeal [2006] Ch. 610 at [35], although on this point the decision at first instance was not challenged in the Court of Appeal.

Priorities and subordinations

Suppose that a company enjoying a right of priority such as a first charge **6–26** agrees to become subordinated to a subsequent chargee. Can it be said to be giving up a property right? In *Perpetual Trustee v BNY Corporate Trustee Services Ltd*,[103] Lord Neuberger M.R. held that a mere loss of priority upon a default event the non-occurence of which was from the outset a condition of the priority is not a divestment of property for the purpose of the anti-deprivation principle,[104] even though its effect is to reduce the assets otherwise available for distribution. The effect of the subordination is not, he said, to divest the company of money or property or even divest it of the security rights granted to it, but merely to change the order of priorities.[105] Similarly, Patten L.J. considered that to say that the operation of a provision for loss of priority constitutes the removal of an asset from the liquidation "is to confuse the security itself with the operations of its terms in the events prescribed by the charge".[106]

The question whether the giving up of a priority contravenes the anti-deprivation rule is considered in the next chapter.[107] In the *Perpetual Trustee* case, the priority in favour of the swaps counterparty was not unqualified but conditional on the absence of default and was therefore never more than contingent; it had to be earned by the swaps counterparty's continuous performance of its obligations.[108] But it is respectfully submitted that in that case two separate issues, whether the priority was a species of property and whether the provision for its reversal contravened the anti-deprivation rule, have been elided. We have seen that "property" is widely construed so as to cover any form of benefit having realisable value. The priority of a security interest is unquestionably a valuable benefit, while its subordination without an equivalent benefit in exchange potentially reduces the value of the secured party's interest in the asset and, indeed, will extinguish if there is no remaining equity after the beneficiary of the subordination has been paid out. Suppose, for example, that a company goes into liquidation a month after subordinating its prior-ranking security interest to that of a subsequent secured creditor for no or no adequate consideration, thus reducing or even extinguishing its security interest and, as a consequence, enlarging the security interest of the beneficiary of the subordination. It is surely indisputable that the company has parted with an asset to the subsequent creditor and that this is capable of constituting a preference so as to attract the avoidance

---

[103] [2010] 3 W.L.R. 87 at [61]–[62].
[104] As to which see para.7–01.
[105] *Perpetual Trustee* (above, n. 103) at [62].
[106] *Perpetual Trustee* (above, n. 103) at [135].
[107] Below, para.7–21.
[108] See further below, para.7–19.

provisions of the Insolvency Act.[109] Moreover, "property" as defined in s.436 includes "every description of interest, whether present or future or vested or contingent arising out of, or incidental to, property".

Priority, if not itself property, is surely an interest arising out of, or incidental to, property, and the anti-deprivation rule must embrace not merely the removal of an asset from the debtor company, but a diminution in its value.[110] The real point is surely that in the *Perpetual* case the priority was never a vested right, only a contingent one, as Lord Neuberger pointed out. The question of priority would not arise until the point when there was recourse to the collateral. In effect, there were two alternative priority scenarios, one where the swaps party defaulted, the other where it did not, so that the swaps counterparty was never divested of priority; in the events that happened it never had the priority in the first place. In this respect, the reference to the "flip" of priority from one party to the other, while graphic, was perhaps unfortunate in conveying the impression of divestiture.

2. DISCLAIMER OF ONEROUS PROPERTY[111]

Nature and purpose of disclaimer

6–27   A liquidator's disclaimer is a unilateral repudiation of a contract entered into by the company before winding up and is designed to bring the contract to an end so as to obviate the need for future performance. The purpose of the disclaimer provisions is twofold: first, to allow the liquidator (whether in a solvent or an insolvent liquidation) to complete the administration of the liquidation without being held up by continuing obligations on the company under unprofitable contracts,[112] or continued ownership and possession of assets which are of no value to the estate; and, secondly, in an insolvent liquidation, to avoid the continuance of liabilities in respect of onerous property which would be payable as expenses of the liquidation, to the detriment of unsecured creditors.[113] It should be borne in mind that liquidation does not of itself bring a contract to an end, nor is it necessarily a ground for the solvent party to terminate the contract. The liquidator is not obliged to

---

[109] Comparable reasoning applies to the meaning of "disposition of the company's property" for the purpose of s.127 of the Insolvency Act 1986. See below, para.13–129.

[110] See below, para.7–21.

[111] See Bailey and Groves, *Corporate Insolvency: Law and Practice*, 3rd edn (London: LexisNexis, 2007), Ch.22; and Andrew R. Keay (ed.), *McPherson's Law of Liquidation*, 2nd edn (London: Sweet & Maxwell, 2009), paras 9.047–9.055.

[112] *Re Nottingham General Cemetery Co.* [1955] Ch. 683.

[113] *Re SSSL Realisations (2002) Ltd* [2006] Ch. 610, in which this passage was cited with approval by Chadwick L.J. at [43].

procure the company to continue performance if he considers that this would not benefit the company, but neither (apart from the disclaimer provisions) can he compel the other party to treat the contract as at an end. It is precisely to resolve such a stalemate, which could inhibit completion of the winding up, that the law gives the liquidator the right to terminate the contract unilaterally by disclaimer where it is unprofitable.

The power of disclaimer

The liquidator's ability to repudiate the company's obligations under a contract by the simple device of not performing them is buttressed by wide statutory powers to disclaim onerous property.[114] It is no longer necessary to obtain leave of the court as it was under earlier legislation. A party aggrieved by the disclaimer can apply to the court to reverse the liquidator's decision,[115] but the court will not interfere unless the liquidator's action was in bad faith or perverse.[116]

6–28

The liquidator cannot disclaim an executed contract,[117] nor are his winding up powers of disclaimer exercisable in respect of a market contract or a contract effected by the exchange or clearing house for the purpose of realising property provided as margin in relation to market contracts,[118] a transfer order or a contract for the purpose of realising security under the settlement finality regulations,[119] or, where a collateral-provider or a collateral-taker within the financial collateral regulations is being wound-up, any financial collateral arrangement within those regulations[120]; and in these cases it is irrelevant whether the contract is executed or executory.

What constitutes onerous property

Onerous property is defined as: (i) any unprofitable contract; and (ii) any other property of the company which is unsaleable or is not readily saleable or is such that it may give rise to a liability to pay money or to perform any

6–29

---

[114] Insolvency Act 1986 ss.178–182. What constitutes property has been discussed earlier. It will be recalled that a waste management licence held by the company in liquidation is property and can be disclaimed as onerous property by the liquidator. See above, para.6–11.

[115] Insolvency Act 1986 s.168(5).

[116] *Re Hans Place Ltd* [1993] B.C.L.C. 768.

[117] This is because if the company has fully performed its obligations, it has no prospective liabilities, so that the contract is not onerous (see para.6–21), while if it is the solvent party that has fully performed it is entitled to lodge a proof for its claim.

[118] Companies Act 1989 s.164(1). "Market contract" is defined by s.155 of the Act and denotes a contract connected with a recognised investment exchange or recognised clearing house (s.155(1)).

[119] Financial Markets and Insolvency (Settlement Finality) Regulations 1999 (SI 1999/2979), reg.16(1).

[120] Financial Collateral Arrangements (No.2) Regulations 2003 (SI 2003/3226), reg.10(4).

other onerous act.[121] In *Transmetro Corp Ltd v Real Investments Pty Ltd*,[122] Chesterman J. in the Supreme Court of Queensland set out an instructive summary of the principles to be extracted from prior authority to determine whether a contract was unprofitable:

"A contract is unprofitable for the purposes of section 568 if it imposes on the company continuing financial obligations which may be regarded as detrimental to the creditors, which presumably means that the contract confers no sufficient reciprocal benefit.

Before a contract may be unprofitable for the purposes of the section it must give rise to prospective liabilities.

Contracts which will delay the winding up of the company's affairs because they are to be performed over a substantial period of time and will involve expenditure that may not be recovered are unprofitable.

No case has decided that a contract is unprofitable merely because it is financially disadvantageous. The cases focus on the nature and cause of the disadvantage.

A contract is not unprofitable merely because the company could have made, or could make, a better bargain."

This summary has been adopted in Australia by Santow J. in *Global Television Pty Ltd v Sportsvision Australia Pty Ltd*[123] and in England by Lloyd J. and implicitly by the Court of Appeal in *Re SSSL Realisations (2002) Ltd*.[124] It relates exclusively to limb (i) of the definition of onerous property. An example of property within limb (ii) is a waste management licence, the continuance of which would involve the liquidator utilising the company's assets to fulfil the conditions of the licence, including the carrying out of any necessary remedial works to remove pollution.[125]

Effect of disclaimer

6–30   The effect of a disclaimer is to determine, as from the date of the disclaimer, the rights, interests and liabilities of the company in or in respect of the

---

[121] Insolvency Act 1986 s.178(3), which reversed the effect of the decision *Re Potters Oils Ltd (No.1)* [1985] B.C.L.C. 203 that a worthless asset could not be disclaimed if its retention did not bind the possessor to the performance of an onerous act but would merely cost money to remove.

[122] (1999) 17 A.C.L.C. 1314 at [21].

[123] (2000) 35 A.C.S.R. 484, a decision of the Supreme Court of New South Wales.

[124] [2005] 1 B.C.L.C. 1 at [64]–[66]; [2006] Ch. 610, per Chadwick L.J. at [36], [41] and [44].

[125] *Re Celtic Extraction Ltd* [2001] Ch. 475, in which it was conceded that if the licence consti-tuted property, as the Court of Appeal found (see above), then it was onerous property.

property disclaimed.[126] It should be emphasised that the liquidator is not entitled to use his winding up power of disclaimer to disturb accrued rights and liabilities.[127] So he cannot disclaim executed contracts,[128] and he has no right to disclaim a contract entered into by the company to sell land, for this would be to deprive the buyer of his winding up equitable ownership[129]; nor can he disclaim the expired term of a lease, for this is no longer the property of the company.[130] Similarly, the disclaimer of an executory contract has no effect on rights and liabilities already accrued. It does not result in rescission of the contract *ab initio*, but operates only to terminate the contract as to liabilities accruing after the time of the disclaimer. By the same token, disclaimer does not affect transfers of property to the company. For example, if the company has bought property which proves to be unsaleable, a disclaimer by the liquidator does not terminate or rescind the sale contract so as to revest the property in the vendor; its sole effect, in the absence of any other interest in the property, is to vest ownership in the Crown as *bona vacantia*.[131]

The statutory provisions have been construed in a restrictive sense as terminating the company's interest only to the extent necessary to release the company and its property from liability.[132] In the case of a lease, the route to this result is sometimes complex. Happily, the complexities have been unravelled by the illuminating speech of Lord Nicholls in *Hindcastle Ltd v Barbara Attenborough Associates Ltd*.[133] Lord Nicholls, after exploring the history of the disclaimer provisions, pointed out that the purpose of these is to facilitate the administration of the winding up by freeing the company in liquidation from all liability under the lease. In consequence, the lease is deemed to be extinguished as between lessor and lessee, and if they are the only parties then the lease does indeed come to an end and the lessor's reversion is accelerated. But where there are other parties the lease is deemed to continue in force so far as they are concerned, subject only to the qualification that there can be no claim against the lessee. So if a guarantee has been given in respect of the lessee's obligations, the surety remains liable on the notionally preserved lease, and in lieu of his extinguished indemnity can, on discharging his liability to the lessor,[134] prove for the amount he has paid and can also seek

---

[126] Insolvency Act 1986 s.178(4).
[127] *Capital Prime Plc v Worthgate Ltd* [2000] 1 B.C.L.C. 647.
[128] See above, n.117.
[129] See above, para.6–23, text and n.92.
[130] *Re No.1 London Ltd* (1991) B.C.C. 118.
[131] For another example of vesting in the Crown as *bona vacantia*, see *Environment Agency v Hillridge* [2004] 2 B.C.L.C. 358.
[132] *Hindcastle Ltd v Barbara Attenborough Associates Ltd* [1988] 1 All E.R. 737; *Warnford Investments Ltd v Duckworth* [1978] 2 All E.R. 517; and *Hill v East and West India Dock Co* (1884) 9 App. Cas. 448.
[133] [1997] A.C. 70, overruling *Stacey v Hill* [1901] Q.B. 660.
[134] Until then he is barred from proving by the rule against double proof (see below, para.8–45). This is consistent with s.178(6), by which a person suffering loss in consequence of an operation of the disclaimer can prove to the extent of the loss. A surety does not suffer a loss until he has made payment to the creditor.

an order vesting the lease in him,[135] whilst if a sub-lease has been granted the position of the sub-lessee continues as if the lease were still in force, but without rights of action against the lessee. The effect would seem to be the same as if the sub-lessee had become a direct tenant of the lessor on the terms of the sub-lease. If the company is the assignee of a lease, the disclaimer extinguishes its liability on the lease, but does not affect the assignor's liability.[136]

Remedy of party aggrieved by disclaimer

6–31 Any person suffering loss or damage in consequence of the operation of the disclaimer is deemed to be a creditor of the company and may prove for the loss or damage in the winding up.[137] Where the property disclaimed is an unprofitable contract, the disclaimer operates to terminate the contract, and the other party becomes entitled to prove in the winding up for his winding up loss,[138] which in principle should be calculated on the basis of an accepted repudiation.[139] No time limit is laid down for exercise of the power of disclaimer, so that in the case of a contract the liquidator is in principle free to continue the contract for so long as he is willing and then disclaim it as being unprofitable. However, he loses his right to disclaim if he fails to give notice of disclaimer within 28 days, or such longer period as the court may allow, after service of a notice on him by the other party requiring him to decide whether or not he will disclaim.[140] Loss of the right to disclaim does not mean that the liquidator comes under an obligation to procure continued performance of the contract by the company; its sole effect is that the liquidator loses the right to terminate the contract unilaterally by

---

[135] Under s.181(3) of the Insolvency Act, which enables the court to make an order vesting the disclaimed property in either: (a) a person entitled to it or a trustee for such a person; or (b) any person who is subject to any liability in respect of the disclaimed property, not being a liability discharged by the disclaimer. A guarantor of the lessee's obligations falls within (b). In *Re Ballast Plc* [2007] B.C.C. 20, an insurer who had paid its insured in respect of loss caused by a third party and who was thus subrogated to the rights of the insured against the third party, was unable to pursue the claim because this had to be brought in the name of the insured, which had been dissolved following liquidation. The insurer applied for an order vesting the claim in the insurer. Lawrence Collins J. held that subrogation did not give the insurers a proprietary interest in the claim, and it was therefore not entitled to a vesting order. No reference was made to to limb (b) of s.181(2). The insurer might have had a proprietary interest in the proceeds of the claim, but the claim itself was subject to possible rights of set-off.

[136] *Warnford Investments*, cited above n.132.

[137] Insolvency Act 1986 s.178(6).

[138] Insolvency Act 1986 s.178(4).

[139] *Christopher Moran Holdings Ltd v Bairstow* [2000] A.C. 172, reversing the decision of the Court of Appeal sub nom. *Re Park Air Services Plc* [1997] 1 W.L.R. 1376. See further below, para.8–43.

[140] Insolvency Act 1986 s.178(5).

notice,[141] thus enabling the other party to elect to hold the contract open for future performance. If the liquidator chooses to allow the company to default on its obligations, the contract nevertheless continues in force unless and until the other party exercises a right to treat it as repudiated under general principles of contract law or obtains an order for rescission of the contract, which may be made on such terms as to payment by or to either party of damages for the non-performance of the contract, or otherwise as the court thinks just.[142] Where the contract is of a continuing character, the liquidator fails to disclaim and the other party is able to proceed with performance without the liquidator's co-operation, as where the company holds goods under a leasing agreement or has agreed to pay for advertising services provided by the creditor,[143] that party would seem entitled to prove for each sum payable under the contract as it falls due.

3. SWELLING THE ASSETS AVAILABLE TO CREDITORS

Post-liquidation receipts and recoveries

The assets coming under the control of the liquidator at the time of winding up may be augmented subsequently in various ways. The question then arises whether these represent an addition to the company's general assets so as to make them susceptible to capture by a prior assignment or charge, including a fixed or floating charge covering after-acquired property, or whether they are to be treated as held by the liquidator for the benefit of the general body of creditors. Six classes of case in particular deserve attention: **6–32**

(1) Sums earned on completion of performance by the liquidator

The law distinguishes sums already earned by the company by performance of its part of the contract prior to winding up from sums becoming due to the company after winding up which come into existence only because of the liquidator's voluntary decision to perform. In the former case, the debts arise under an executed contract and are assets of the company which are caught by   **6–33**

---

[141] *Re Sneezum, ex p. Davis* (1876) 3 Ch.D. 463; and *Stead, Hazel & Co v Cooper* [1933] 1 K.B. 840.
[142] Insolvency Act 1986 s.186(1). Where damages are awarded to the party contracting with the company, he may prove for these as a debt in the winding up (s.186(2)). The effect of continuance of the contract on the computation of the sum for which the aggrieved party can prove is discussed in relation to the liabilities of the company at para.8–41.
[143] See, e.g. the decision of the House of Lords in *White & Carter (Councils) Ltd v McGregor* [1962] A.C. 413.

the assignment or the after-acquired property clause in the debenture, as the case may be; in the latter, the contract is still executory at the time of winding up and payment of the debts becomes due through the liquidator's action in adopting the contract and carrying it through to completion. Such debts thus enure for the benefit of the general body of creditors in the winding up and are not picked up by the assignment or the after-acquired property clause.[144]

The underlying idea is very reasonable. The liquidator has used the money and other resources of the company to carry out the contract; therefore, the fruits of performance should belong to the general body of creditors free from the prior interest. In effect, this equates the company in liquidation with the holder of a purchase-money interest who, under the general law, usually enjoys priority over an earlier security interest covering after-acquired property.[145] However, in both of the bankruptcy cases in which this principle was applied,[146] part of the work necessary to earn payment had been carried out before the bankruptcy; nevertheless, the whole of the debt was held to vest in the company free from the prior interest. In neither case does it appear to have been argued that the sum paid to discharge the debt should be divided between the assignee or chargee and the trustee in bankruptcy according to the respective values of the pre-bankruptcy and post-bankruptcy performances. This seems harsh. Suppose that prior to the liquidation the company has performed 90 per cent of the contract assigned or charged, leaving the liquidator only the remaining 10 per cent to complete. Is it reasonable that the entire payment received as consideration for the completed contract should be held for the benefit of the general body of creditors free from the assignment or charge? Would it not be fairer to allow 10 per cent to be so held and to treat the remaining 90 per cent as caught by the assignment or charge?

(2) Falling in of contingent or reversionary assets

6–34   After the date of the winding up, contingent assets may become actual assets because of the occurrence of the contingency (as where a purchase of property to the company is made conditional on planning permission, which is subsequently granted, for development of the property) and assets not vested in possession may fall into possession, as where a lease granted by the company comes to an end or a prior interest held by another person is discharged. In principle, these form an addition to the company's general assets and are therefore capable of being captured by a prior assignment or charge.

---

[144] *Re Collins* [1925] Ch. 556; and *Wilmot v Alton* [1897] 1 Q.B. 17.
[145] See *Abbey National Building Society v Cann* [1991] 1 A.C. 56; and *Goode on Commercial Law*, pp.713–714.
[146] See n.144 above.

(3) Exercise of a remedy vested in the company before winding up

Where a purported contract entered into by the company before winding up **6–35**
is void, for example, for want of *consensus ad idem*, any property supposedly
transferred under it will remain vested in the company. If the company was
the transferee, it will have no interest in the property, but may have a proprietary claim to any money paid which is still identifiable in the hands of the
payee. Where the contract is not void but voidable at the company's instance,
for example, for misrepresentation by the other party, the liquidator is entitled to avoid it in the company's name. Where the assets of the company have
been misappropriated by its officers, the liquidator can institute misfeasance
proceedings in much the same way as the company could have done, except
that on liquidation a summary remedy becomes available.[147] In all of these
cases the recovered assets form part of the general assets of the company and
enure for the benefit of an assignee or chargee under an assignment or charge
covering assets of the description in question.[148]

(4) Avoidance of a transaction, or reversal of its effect, under the Insolvency Act

The Insolvency Act contains eight different sets of provisions by which a **6–36**
transaction entered into by the company before winding up may be avoided,
or its effect reversed or ameliorated, because of its impropriety or unfairness
to other creditors.[149] In those cases where the transaction is rendered totally
void, the assets will be susceptible to capture by a prior assignment or charge.
In other cases, they will enure for the benefit of the general body of creditors
except as regards an asset in which the assignee or chargee had a pre-existing interest which was not overreached by the transaction. These statutory
provisions are examined in detail in Ch.13.

(5) Contribution orders for fraudulent and wrongful trading

In the winding up of a company, a director guilty of fraudulent trading[150] or **6–37**
wrongful trading[151] may be ordered to make such contribution (if any) to the
company's assets as the court thinks proper.[152] In bringing contribution
proceedings, the liquidator acts on behalf of the general body of creditors,

---

[147] See Insolvency Act 1986 s.212; and below, para.14–14.
[148] *Cohen v Davis* [2007] B.C.C. 95 (recovery in misfeasance proceedings under s.212 of the
Insolvency Act 1986 for breaches of duty committed prior to liquidation).
[149] For the application of recoveries, see below, para.13–140.
[150] Insolvency Act 1986 s.213. See below, paras 14–04 and 14–21.
[151] Insolvency Act 1986 s.214. See below, para.14–27.
[152] Insolvency Act 1986 ss.213(2) and 214(1). See below, paras 14–52 *et seq.*

not in right of the company, so that recoveries are not caught by a prior assignment or charge,[153] nor are they assignable by the liquidator, any purported assignment being champertous.[154] Since the claim by the liquidator for fraudulent or wrongful trading cannot be treated as a claim by the company, it follows that the respondents to such a claim cannot seek contribution in respect of it from an insolvency practitioner alleged to have been guilty of negligence in advising them that the company could continue trading, for there is no common liability for the purposes of the Civil Liability (Contribution) Act 1978.[155]

(6) Ring-fenced fund from assets subject to a floating charge: the prescribed part

6–38   Although debts secured by floating charges have been subordinate to preferential claims for well over a century, the holder of the charge has until recently been entitled to assert its charge in full against ordinary unsecured creditors. In its review of insolvency law, the Cork Committee had recommended that 10 per cent of the net proceeds of assets subject to a floating charge should be required to be surrendered to constitute a fund available to ordinary unsecured creditors.[156] This recommendation[157] was not adopted by the government of the day, but two decades later finally surfaced in revised form in the new s.176A of the Insolvency Act 1986. Under s.176A, where assets are subject to a floating charge created on or after September 15,

---

[153] *Cohen v Davis* [2007] B.C.C. 95; and see below, para.14–55.

[154] *Oasis Merchandising* [1998] Ch. 170. For a criticism of the decision as conceptually flawed, see John Armour and Adrian Walters, "Funding Liquidation: A Functional View" (2006) 122 L.Q.R. 295, who pose the question of how such recoveries could be administered by the liquidator in pursuance of his winding up statutory duty if they were not assets of the company. The question is a fair one, for there is a long line of authority that such statutory recoveries are held by the liquidator on trust for the general body of creditors, not for the company itself. See, e.g. *Re Yagerphone Ltd* [1935] Ch. 392, per Bennett J.; and *N.W. Robbie & Co Ltd v Witney Warehouse Co Ltd* [1963] 1 W.L.R. 1324, per Russell L.J. at 1338. However, although the statutory recoveries are not the property of the company, the liquidator has by necessary implication a power and duty to distribute them among the creditors, for whose benefit the right of recovery was given.

[155] *Cohen v Davis* [2007] B.C.C. 95.

[156] Report of the Review Committee, "Insolvency Law and Practice" (Cmnd. 8558, 1982), paras 1538 et seq. The holder of the floating charge would not itself be entitled to participate in the 10% fund without surrendering his winding up *in toto*, but the percentage payable to unsecured creditors would be capped to prevent their percentage of debts received exceeding that of the debenture holder (para.1539).

[157] The origin of which is not generally known—even to members of the Insolvency Law Review Committee! It was the present writer who, while serving on the Legal Panel set up by the Committee, suggested it to a member of the Committee, as a means of taking the heat off the floating charge, while passing the time in conversation on the train home after cerebral stimulation in the shape of a couple of pints of beer at St Pancras Station. It was somewhat to the writer's astonishment that this idea featured as a recommendation in the Committee's report six months later!

2003,[158] the liquidator[159] must make a prescribed part of the company's net property available for the satisfaction of unsecured debts and must not distribute that part to the proprietor of a floating charge except in so far as it exceeds the amount required for the satisfaction of unsecured debts. A company's net property is defined as the amount of its property which would, but for the section, be available for the satisfaction of claims of holders of debentures secured by, or holders of any, floating charge created by the company.[160] Since preferential debts have priority over claims secured by a floating charge,[161] it follows that where the company's free assets are insufficient to cover the preferential debts, the unpaid balance of these must be met from the floating charge assets before any distribution can be made under the section, so that preferential creditors, having already been provided for, do not participate in the distribution.

Example

The company's free assets have a net value of £50,000. It also has property worth £100,000, which is subject to a floating charge to secure £90,000 of debt. The preferential debts are £70,000 and ordinary unsecured debts £40,000. Section 176A will apply as follows:

Free assets: £50,000
Preferential debts: £70,000
Shortfall: £20,000 to be met from property proceeds
Company's net property £80,000

The prescribed percentage is then applied to the sum of £80,000, producing £19,000 for unsecured creditors as set out below. The section does not apply: (i) where the company's net property is less than the prescribed minimum *and* the liquidator thinks that the cost of making a distribution to unsecured creditors would be disproportionate to the benefits[162]; (ii) if and in so far as it is disapplied by a CVA under Pt I of the Insolvency Act 1986 or a compromise or arrangement under what is now Pt 26 of the Companies Act 2006[163]; or (iii) the court so orders on the application of the liquidator, administrator or receiver on the ground that the cost of making a distribution to unsecured

---

[158] The section does not apply to a floating charge created before September 15, 2003 (Insolvency Act 1986 s.176A(9); and Insolvency Act 1986 (Prescribed Part) Order 2003 (SI 2003/2097), art.1).

[159] The section also applies to administrators and receivers in that they must set aside the prescribed part. However, except where an administrator or receiver has power to make a distribution, he must hand over the prescribed part to the liquidator to distribute.

[160] Insolvency Act 1986 s.176A(6).

[161] Insolvency Act 1986 s.175(2)(b).

[162] Insolvency Act 1986 s.176A(3).

[163] Insolvency Act 1986 s.176A(4).

creditors would be disproportionate to the benefits.[164] The court has no power to make a "qualified" disapplication order in which, based on the cost of distribution, there would be a distribution of the prescribed part to some creditors but not to others, for the section contemplates that there will either be a complete disapplication or none at all, and in any event a partial disapplication would contravene the principle of *pari passu* distribution.[165]

6–39   The relevant percentage is that fixed by the Insolvency Act 1986 (Prescribed Part) Order 2003[166] and is as follows:

Where the company's net property does not exceed £10,000 in value: 50 per cent

Where the company's net property exceeds £10,000 in value then:

50 per cent of the first £10,000 in value; and
20 per cent of the excess;

but with a maximum prescribed part of £600,000.

The minimum value of the company's net property is £10,000, so that if the actual value of the assets subject to the floating charge is below this figure, the section will not apply if in the view of the liquidator the cost of making a distribution would be disproportionate to the benefits. If the liquidator is not of that view, then 50 per cent of the value will have to be made available from the assets subject to the floating charge. Contrary to the recommendation of the Cork Committee, there is no provision capping the distribution so as to ensure that unsecured creditors receive no greater percentage than the debenture holder. In the example given above, the value of the company's net property is £80,000, and the sum to be handed over for the unsecured creditors is £5,000 + £14,000 = £19,000, leaving a balance for the holder of the floating charge of £61,000, so that the chargee suffers a loss of £29,000.

The prescribed part has been calculated so as to offset the gain to the holder of a floating charge resulting from the abolition of Crown preference. Since debts secured by the floating charge will no longer be subordinate to claims of the Crown (for example, for unpaid taxes), the provisions relating to the prescribed part are designed to maintain neutrality for the holder of a floating charge, leaving it neither better nor worse off than before Crown preference was abolished, while at the same time increasing the return to unsecured creditors.

The prescribed percentage in value is to be made available to unsecured creditors, not to the company itself, which means that it is treated in the

---

[164] Insolvency Act 1986 s.176A(5). The court disapplied s.176A in *Re Hydroserve Ltd* [2008] B.C.C. 175, but declined to do so in *Re International Sections Ltd* [2009] B.C.C. 574.
[165] *Re Courts Plc* [2008] B.C.C. 917.
[166] SI 2003/2097.

same way as recoveries for fraudulent or wrongful trading and is not part of the company's estate so as to be susceptible to capture by an after-acquired property clause in a security agreement.

So long as the floating charge is in existence and unsecured creditors have not been fully paid, the holder is not entitled to participate in the prescribed part.[167] In the unlikely event that unsecured creditors receive 100 pence in the pound, the holder of the floating charge is entitled to the return of the prescribed part or such balance as remains after the liquidator has taken what is necessary to complete the payment to unsecured creditors. Moreover, there is nothing to prevent the chargee from giving up his winding up security and proving as an unsecured creditor.[168] So much is clear. However, there remain a number of questions for which the wording of s.176A is less felicitous.

6–40

(i) Can the holder of the floating charge participate in the prescribed part in relation to a separate debt owed to him winding up which is not secured by the floating charge? It is thought that he can, since the purpose of s.176A is to preclude the chargee from entitlement to a share in the prescribed part in respect of debts secured by the charge.

(ii) If there are two floating charges, can the holder of one participate in the prescribed part given up by the other? It would seem not. In the first place, s.176A(2)(b) states that the liquidator shall not distribute the prescribed part to the proprietor of "a" floating charge. If it had been intended to restrict that provision to the holder of the particular floating charge from whose security the prescribed part comes, s.176A(2)(b) would surely have said so. Secondly, in the typical case, most if not all of the assets covered by one floating charge will also be covered by the other, so that to allow one holder to participate in the other's surrendered prescribed part would be to give him winding up through the back door an interest in the same fund that he could not obtain directly as the party surrendering that fund.

(iii) What happens if there are two floating charges and the floating charge that has priority exhausts the charged assets? If, as has been suggested above, the existence of the subordinate charge precludes the holder from participating in the prescribed part surrendered by the senior floating chargee, the sensible course is for the holder of the junior charge to surrender it, since it is valueless anyway, and come in as an unsecured creditor and participate in the prescribed part.[169]

---

[167] *Re Permacell Finesse Ltd* [2008] B.C.C. 208; and *Re Airbase Services (UK) Ltd* [2008] 1 W.L.R. 1516, where Patten J. expressed the view that the same principle would apply to the holders of fixed charges in respect of any shortfall in their security.

[168] Which in at least one case may be to his winding up advantage. See (iii) below.

[169] *Kelly v Inflexion Fund II Ltd Partnership* [2010] EWHC 2850 (Ch).

(iv) If the holder of the floating charge realises his winding up security before the prescribed part has been distributed, can he then participate as an unsecured creditor for any balance owed to him? Again, it is thought that the answer is no. To allow the chargee to come in at this stage *qua* unsecured creditor would be to upset the neutrality which s.176A is designed to provide. Moreover, the section could not be made to work in that situation, for it envisages a distribution to the holder of the floating charge after unsecured creditors have been fully paid, whereas if the chargee shares the prescribed *part pari* passu with other creditors, this could never happen. Finally, it would be odd if the floating chargee's position depended on whether, at the time of distribution of the prescribed part, he had or had not realised his winding up security.

4. ASSETS BELONGING TO THIRD PARTIES

6–41 Assets held by the company but belonging solely to third parties under transactions which are not subject to avoidance or capture pursuant to the statutory provisions referred to above are not available for the company's creditors. This applies both to assets which never belonged to the company and those in which the company had an interest that has come to an end, for example, leases or rental agreements that have expired and contracts that have been terminated. Three cases are deserving of particular mention, namely assets held by the company on trust, assets subject to a security interest and goods in the possession of the company as buyer under a contract reserving title to the seller until payment.[170]

Assets held on trust

(1) Trust assets do not form part of the estate

6–42 Where the company holds an asset on trust for a third party, this does not form part of its estate so as to be available for creditors. Trust property is excluded whether the trust is express,[171] implied,[172] constructive or resulting[173] or is

---

[170] For an instructive analysis of a broad range of issues encompassing the second and third of these issues, see William Goodhart and Gareth Jones, "The Infiltration of Equitable Doctrine into English Commercial Law" (1980) 43 M.L.R. 489.

[171] *Re English & American Insurance Co Ltd* [1994] 1 B.C.L.C. 649; and *Re Kayford Ltd* [1975] 1 All E.R. 604.

[172] *Re Fleet Disposals Ltd* [1995] B.C.L.C. 345; and *Re C.A. Pacific Finance Ltd* [2000] 1 B.C.L.C. 494.

[173] *Barclays Bank Ltd v Quistclose Investments Ltd* [1970] A.C. 567.

imposed by statute.[174] Thus, if money is lent to a company for a specific purpose which is frustrated by the advent of winding up, there is a resulting trust in favour of the lender[175]; if a bank by mistake makes a payment twice over to another bank on behalf of a customer and the payee bank goes into liquidation, the mistaken payment can be recovered as money impressed with a constructive trust[176]; if money paid by a mail order customer in advance when ordering goods is, on the advice of accountants concerned about the financial position of the company, paid into a trust account to be released only on delivery of the goods, and the company goes into liquidation, money held in the account for customers to whom goods had not been delivered is held on trust for them and does not form part of the company's general assets.[177] Where the assets administered by the liquidator include assets held by the company as trustee, the costs attributable to the administration of those assets should be borne by the trust fund, not by the company's own assets.[178]

(2) Assets which cease to be trust assets

Assets initially subject to a trust may cease to be so as the result of authorised dealings by the trustee. Thus, in the case of a trading trust established by a trust instrument which authorises the trustees to carry on trade for the benefit of the beneficiaries, any disposition of a trust asset, whether absolutely or by way of security, falling within the actual or apparent authority of the

6–43

---

[174] As is the case under, e.g. Ch.7 of the Client Asset Sourcebook (CASS7) issued by the Financial Services Authority, where money received by a broker for clients is required to be segregated from the broker's own moneys and on receipt is to be considered held on trust even before segregation (*Re Lehman Bros International (Europe) Ltd* [2010] EWCA Civ. 917).

[175] *Barclays Bank Ltd v Quistclose Investments Ltd*, cited above n.173 (loan for the purpose of paying a dividend to shareholders); *Carreras Rothmans Ltd v Freeman Mathews Treasure Ltd* [1985] 1 All E.R. 155 (payments to advertising agency by client for sole purpose of discharging the agency's obligations to media creditors); and *Re EVTR Ltd* [1987] B.C.C. 389 (payment to be used for purchase of equipment). As to the first of these cases, see Sir Peter Millett, "The Quistclose Trust: Who Can Enforce It?" (1985) 101 L.Q.R. 269.

[176] *Chase Manhattan Bank NA v Israel-British Bank (London) Ltd* [1979] 3 All E.R. 1025. But the authority of this decision has been weakened by the criticism made by Lord Browne-Wilkinson in *Westdeutsche Landesbank Girozentrale v Islington LBC* [1996] A.C. 669 at 715.

[177] *Re Kayford Ltd* [1975] 1 W.L.R. 279. The decision is controversial, but in my view correct. There has been much debate about protection for the prepaying buyer. See, e.g. Thomas H. Jackson and Anthony T. Kronman, "A Plea for the Financing Buyer" (1975) 85 Yale L.J. 1; Aleck Dadson, "A Fresh Plea for the Financing Buyer" (1985–86) 11 C.B.L.J. 171; Martin Boodman, "The Prepaying Buyer: Another Perspective" (1986) 11 C.B.L.J. 257; Office of Fair Trading, "The Protection of Consumer Prepayments: A Discussion Paper" (London: OFT, 1984); and A.L. Ogus and C.K. Rowley, "Prepayments and Insolvency", OFT Occasional Paper (London: OFT, 1984). For a good discussion incorporating selected materials, see Graham Moffat, *Trusts Law: Text and Materials*, 5th edn (Cambridge: Cambridge University Press, 2009), pp.798–800. Under s.20A of the Sale of Goods Act 1979, prepaying buyers of an unidentified part of a bulk now acquire a proportionate interest in the bulk pending delivery.

[178] See above, para.3–03.

trustees binds the beneficiaries, so that the asset is lost to the trust fund (in the case of an absolute disposition) or held by the trustees subject to the security interest (in the case of a disposition by way of security), and any proceeds of the disposition received by the trustees will become part of the trust fund in place of the original asset. This point was well brought out in the *Space Investments* case,[179] where the settlement deed authorised the trustee bank (inter alia) to open and maintain savings or current accounts with any bank, including itself. The bank accordingly placed trust moneys on deposit with itself and subsequently went into insolvent liquidation. On an application to the Supreme Court of the Bahamas to determine the question of whether the trust creditors ranked in priority to the general creditors, the trial judge ruled in favour of the trust creditors, and this decision was upheld by the Court of Appeal of the Bahamas, but reversed on further appeal to the Privy Council. It was held by the Privy Council that since the deposit of trust funds with the bank was authorised by the settlement and under well-established principles of banking law became the general moneys of the bank, whose obligations were those of a debtor, not a trustee, the beneficiaries ranked *pari passu* with other unsecured creditors and did not enjoy any special status or priority. The funds in question ceased to be impressed with a trust as soon as they were deposited.

(3) Trust of money presupposes an identifiable fund

6–44 A trust can exist only in relation to an identifiable asset or fund; a purely personal monetary obligation does not create a trust. The point is an elementary one, but it is sometimes overlooked because the parties are misled by a conventional label attached to a particular form of money obligation. The typical case is the so-called retention fund provided by standard-term building contracts under which the employer retains a small percentage of each progress payment as a safeguard against non-completion and defects and undertakes to hold the retention moneys on trust for the contractor. If the employer goes into liquidation after completion of the works, the contractor may demand release of the "fund" as money held on trust for the contractor. But in reality there is no fund; all that the employer has done is to deduct the contractually agreed percentage from payments he would otherwise have made. In other words, the employer has not created a fund at all, but merely withheld payment, so that there is no trust asset to which the contractor can have recourse.[180] The effect of the contractual provision is to impose on the employer a personal obligation to appropriate and set aside as a trust fund

---

[179] *Space Investments Ltd v Canadian Imperial Bank of Commerce Trust Co (Bahamas) Ltd* [1986] 3 All E.R. 75.

[180] *Re Jartray Developments Ltd* (1983) 22 Build. L.R. 134; and *MacJordan Construction Ltd v Bookmount Erostin Ltd* [1992] B.C.L.C. 350.

the amount of retention moneys withheld[181] and the court will usually grant a mandatory injunction to require such fund to be established in order to protect the contractor against the employer's insolvency.[182] But a mere obligation to establish the fund does not suffice, for until the obligation has been performed there is no res to which the trust can attach, and the court will not grant a mandatory injunction after the employer has gone into liquidation.[183] Accordingly where, in breach of trust, money owed to a party was paid not into its broker's client account, where it would have been held on trust for that party, but into the broker's overdrawn current account, where it was utilised in its entirety to clear the overdraft, it was held that there was no existing fund to which any trust could attach.[184]

Assets subject to a security interest

Assets do not belong to the company to the extent that they are subject to a mortgage or other security interest; all the company has is the equity of redemption.[185]

6–45

Goods supplied under reservation of title

Where goods are supplied to a company under a contract of sale which reserves title to the seller until payment and the company goes into liquidation before it has paid the full price, the goods remain the property of the seller unless and until the liquidator completes payment; and if he fails to do so the seller may repossess the goods. Problems of identifying which items of stock have or have not been paid for are avoided by the use of an all-moneys reservation of title, producing the equivalent of cross-collateralisation. In practice, insolvency practitioners feel able to take a robust attitude to claims by title-retention sellers because of the difficulty and expense of finding a new outlet for the goods.

6–46

Contracts of sale often seek to extend reservation of title in one or more of three ways. The first is by using it to secure not only the price of the particular goods sold, but other obligations of the buyer under prior or subsequent contracts. This has been upheld as a perfectly legitimate term of a sale contract by which the parties exercise their freedom to agree upon the

---

[181] *Rayack Construction v Lampeter Meat Co Ltd* (1979) 12 Build. L.R. 30.
[182] *Rayack Construction* (above, n. 181); and *Concorde Construction Co Ltd v Colgan Ltd* (1984) 29 Build. L.R. 120.
[183] *Jartray Developments*, cited above n.180. See generally Richard Davis, *Construction Insolvency*, 3rd edn (London: Sweet & Maxwell, 2008), Ch.10.
[184] *Various Customers of BA Peters plc v Moriarty* [2008] EWCA Civ. 1604 (Ch).
[185] *Re Pyle Works Ltd* (1890) 44 Ch.D. 534, per Cotton L.J. at 577–578.

conditions on which the property is to pass.[186] A second method is to extend the retention of title to proceeds of authorised resales. In the *Romalpa* case,[187] it was held by the Court of Appeal, affirming the decision of the trial judge, that a reservation of title clause may also be validly extended to cover the proceeds of sale of goods sold by the buyer with the seller's authority and as his agent. However, relying on the fact that certain crucial concessions were made in that case, courts in subsequent cases have been able to distinguish *Romalpa* virtually out of existence, and a retention of title to proceeds will almost invariably be struck down as a charge on book debts which is void for want of registration under what is now s.860 of the Companies Act 2006.[188] In a third type of extension, the reservation of title clause is made to cover products resulting from the commingling of the goods with other goods. Usually this too will be struck down as an unregistered charge,[189] since title cannot be reserved to that which the seller never owned.[190] The position is otherwise, however, where two suppliers agree that the amalgam is to belong to them in proportion to their respective contributions.[191]

5. EFFECT OF DISSOLUTION OF COMPANY

6–47 When a company is dissolved, its legal existence comes to an end, and any undistributed assets, together with any assets thereafter coming into the hands of the company, pass to the Crown as *bona vacantia*,[192] although application may be made to the court to restore the company to the register[193] so as to enable the assets to be collected and distributed.

---

[186] *Armour v Thyssen Edelstahlwerke A.G.* [1991] 2 A.C. 339; and *Clough Mill Ltd v Martin* [1984] 3 All E.R. 982.

[187] *Aluminium Industrie vaassen BV v Romalpa Aluminium Ltd* [1976] 1 Lloyd's Rep. 443.

[188] See, e.g. *E. Pfeiffer-Weineinkauf GmbH v Arbuthnot Factors Ltd* [1988] 1 W.L.R. 150; *Compaq Computers Ltd v Abercorn Group Ltd* [1992] B.C.C. 484; and *Modelboard Ltd v Outer Box Ltd (in liquidation)* [1993] B.C.L.C. 623.

[189] Registrable under s.860(7)(b) of the Companies Act 2006 as a charge which, if executed by an individual, would have been registrable as a bill of sale.

[190] *Clough Mill*, cited above n.186; and *Re Peachdart Ltd* [1984] 1 Ch. 131.

[191] *Re CK Engineering Ltd* [2007] B.C.C. 975.

[192] Companies Act 2006 s.1012.

[193] Companies Act 2006 s.1029.

Chapter 7

The Anti-Deprivation Rule

1. THREE COMMON LAW RULES

The anti-deprivation rule

The winding up of a company divests it of beneficial ownership of its prop- **7–01** erty, the control of which passes to the liquidator, whose duty is to get in the assets, realise them and distribute the proceeds in accordance with the statutory order of distribution. It is a cardinal rule of insolvency law that contractual provisions designed to remove from the estate of a bankrupt or insolvent company assets held at the commencement of the bankruptcy or winding up are void as being contrary to public policy. This common law rule is known as the anti-deprivation rule, and in a series of cases going back at least 200 years it has been held that while an interest may be granted to a person which is limited so as to cease on bankruptcy, a provision for the forfeiture on bankruptcy of an asset transferred to or held by the bankrupt absolutely is void. The rule has always applied to liquidation as well and has now been extended to administration.[1] But as will be seen,[2] it does not apply to a deprivation operative only on the insolvency of a company in the absence of or prior to a formal insolvency proceeding, nor does it apply to a deprivation triggered by an event prior to such a proceeding. Such a deprivation is only vulnerable under specific provisions of the Insolvency Act 1986, for example, s.127 relating to the avoidance of unauthorised post-petition dispositions of the company's property or s.238 relating to transactions at an undervalue. There is no common law reach back prior to the commencement of a liquidation or administration.

---

[1] See below, para.7–16.
[2] See below, para.7–18.

217

The rule against repugnancy

7–02   The rule against repugnancy is a rule of property law, not of insolvency law, although the two rules overlap where both are triggered by the advent of bankruptcy or winding up. The effect of the rule against repugnancy is that a grantor may not derogate from his own grant by giving an absolute interest in an asset to another and then providing for it to be clawed back, otherwise than for fair value, in stated eventualities, including (but not limited to) bankruptcy or winding up. Such a proviso is void as repugnant to the grant.[3]

The *pari passu* rule

7–03   It is important to distinguish the anti-deprivation rule from the common law rule outlawing provisions that undermine the principle of *pari passu* distribution, a principle established in a statute of Henry VIII in 1542.[4] The former is designed to avoid a reduction in the net asset value of the company to the detriment of its creditors at the point of winding up, but is not concerned with the order of distribution among creditors. The latter is aimed at provisions designed to give a particular creditor an unfair advantage over other creditors by circumventing the rule against *pro rata* distribution. Unfair preference of one creditor over the general body of creditors merely disturbs the statutory order of distribution; it has no impact on the net asset value of the company. This is because the amount lost to the company through a payment or transfer to a particular creditor in or towards repayment of the company's debt to him is precisely matched by a corresponding diminution in the company's liabilities, leaving its balance sheet unchanged. In short, the *pari passu* rule seeks to ensure that one creditor does not jump the queue for a slice of the pie, while the anti-deprivation rule is aimed at provisions which would reduce the size of the pie by improper withdrawal of an asset in favour of one who is not a creditor. The two rules are thus mutually exclusive in relation to any particular payment or transfer. If a creditor were to be paid more than was owed to him, then to the extent of the excess he would not be receiving the payment as a creditor and there would be a reduction in the company's net asset value contrary to the anti-deprivation rule. The same would seem to apply if the debt repaid were an unenforceable debt. Similarly, contractual provisions by which payment to a creditor is to be increased in the event of the debtor going into liquidation,[5] although designed to increase the creditor's slice of the pie on the debtor's liquidation in apparent contravention of

---

[3] *Re Scientific Investment Pension Plan Trusts* [1999] Ch. 53, in which Rattee J. reviewed the authorities.
[4] Statute of Bankrupts 1542 (34 & 35 Hen. VIII, c.4).
[5] See, eg. *Re Jeavons, ex p. Mackay* (1873) 8 Ch. App. 643; and *Re Johns* [1928] Ch. 737.

the *pari passu* rule, do so by giving the creditor a right to more than is due to him, so that to the extent of the excess they contravene the anti-deprivation rule rather than the *pari passu* rule to which their invalidity is often ascribed.[6] The distinction is well brought out in ss.238 and 239 of the Insolvency Act 1986. The former deals with transactions at an undervalue, which reduce the size of the pie (the net asset value of the company); the latter with unfair preferences, which leave the size of the pie unaffected, but allow the preferred creditor to steal a march on the others.

However, while the two rules are distinct, their sphere of application overlaps in at least two respects. Both outlaw removal of an asset from the general body of creditors; both are confined to transactions uncompleted at the time of commencement of the liquidation or administration. This overlap may explain why decisions applying one rule are not infrequently referred to in decisions applying the other.[7] The difference between the two rules lies only in the fact that the *pari passu* principle is confined to payments or transfers which reduce or extinguish the company's debt to a creditor or group of creditors at the expense of other creditors without reducing the net asset value of the insolvent company, as in the *British Eagle* case,[8] while the anti-deprivation rule is concerned with deprivation of the company itself (the point in issue in the *Perpetual Trustee* case[9]) and therefore applies only to the extent that the party benefiting from the deprivation is not a creditor, so that the payment or transfer does not produce any countervailing extinguishment of a liability of the company. The rest of this chapter focuses on the anti-deprivation rule, beginning with the cases where the rule does not apply. The *pari passu* rule is discussed in Chapter 8.

2. THE SPHERE OF APPLICATION OF THE ANTI-DEPRIVATION RULE

Types of agreement unaffected by the rule

There are various types of arrangement which, although resulting in the company's suffering a loss of rights, are not considered to offend against the anti-deprivation rule. These include determinable interests in the sense of interests which automatically come to an end on the expiry of a given period   **7–04**

---

[6] It is interesting that in neither of the cases referred to in n.5 above was any reference made to the *pari passu* rule; the ground of the decision was a fraud on or attempted defeasance of the bankruptcy laws.
[7] See, e.g. *Perpetual Trustee Co Ltd v BNY Corporate Trustee Services Ltd* [2010] Ch. 347 (discussed below, paras 7–13–7–22); and *Lomas v JFB Firth Rixson Inc* [2010] EWHC 3372 (Ch), per Briggs J. at [97], which rather confusingly merge the two rules. A further decision by Briggs J. in *Lehman Brothers Special Financing v Carlton Communications Ltd* [2011] EWHC 718 (Ch) followed his ruling in Firth Rixson.
[8] See paras 8–11 and 9–14.
[9] See below, para.7–16.

or the occurrence of a specified event, limited interests and contract rights terminable by a party on notice, pre-emption provisions in articles of association of a company providing for the compulsory transfer at a reasonable price of the shares of any member that goes into liquidation or bankruptcy, and rules of an exchange by which members who hold shares in the exchange by virtue of their membership cannot receive consideration for any transfer and have to surrender the shares on cessation of membership on account of insolvency or for any other reason. These cases apart, it is probably not possible to set out an exhaustive statement of the circumstances in which a provision for termination of an interest on insolvency is void.

"... it is not possible to discern a coherent rule, or even an entirely coherent set of rules, to enable one to assess in any particular case whether such a provision (a 'deprivation provision') falls foul of the principle ... and perhaps not surprisingly, it is not entirely easy to reconcile the conclusions, and indeed the reasoning, in some of the cases."[10]

What has been noted is the trend towards narrowing the scope of the rule.

"The modern trend has been to restrict rather than to broaden the ambit of application of the rule, for two reasons. The first is that, in a corporate context, the increasingly sophisticated anti-avoidance provisions now in the Insolvency Act 1986 ('the Act') reduce the need for a general anti-avoidance principle originally developed to protect the much simpler bankruptcy legislation from evasion. The second is that the uncertainties of the rule's boundaries risk coming into conflict with the countervailing public policy in favour of contractual certainty and party autonomy in bona fide commercial arrangements."[11]

With these preliminary remarks, we can turn to the established exceptions to the rule of invalidity.

Limited and determinable interests and licences

7–05   Where an interest is granted which by its terms is not absolute, but is limited in time so as to come to an end when the company goes into winding up, the grant is not considered to offend against any principle of insolvency law, for the winding up simply represents the end of the natural life of the interest. Similarly, an interest determinable on liquidation at the option of the

---

[10] *Money Markets Ltd v London Stock Exchange Ltd* [2002] 1 W.L.R. 1150, per Neuberger J. at [117].
[11] *Lomas v JFB Firth Rixson Inc* [2010] EWHC 3372, per Briggs J. at [96].

grantor is considered an inherent feature of the grant, not a deprivation of the company. A fortiori termination of a contract conferring purely personal rights is not considered a breach of either the anti-deprivation rule or the *pari passu* rule.

English law distinguishes sharply between agreements by which a party who has transferred an *absolute* interest in an asset to another is given the right to *recapture* the asset on the transferee's insolvency and agreements entitling a party to *terminate* a *limited* interest conferred on another, or providing for automatic termination of that interest, if that other becomes insolvent. Agreements of the former kind are considered to remove from the debtor's estate property which should be available for the general body of creditors[12] and thus contravene the anti-deprivation rule if the beneficiary of the retransfer is not a creditor or the *pari passu* principle if he is; agreements of the latter kind simply define bankruptcy or liquidation as the event on which the interest that has been granted ends or becomes terminable, and therefore do not fall foul of either rule. Where the termination of a limited interest is automatic, there is no removal of an asset from the estate, because the former asset no longer exists; where the termination is at the discretion of the grantor of the interest, the terminability of the interest is an inherent qualification of its quantum which binds the trustee or liquidator and creditors as it binds the bankrupt or company in liquidation.[13] Thus, a trust of income until the beneficiary becomes bankrupt is a valid trust, as is implicitly recognised by the provisions of s.33 of the Trustee Act 1925 relating to protective trusts[14]; and a provision for forfeiture of a lease on winding up does not contravene the *pari passu* principle, since it is merely a qualification of the lessee's estate,[15] of the same kind as that discussed above. The validity of such forfeiture clauses is assumed by s.146(9) and (10) of the Law of Property Act 1925, which deal with relief against forfeiture in cases where bankruptcy of the lessee is a condition of the forfeiture.[16] So the lessee's liquidator takes the lease as he finds it; forfeiture is not conceptually a divestment of an asset vested in the lessee, but rather an event which marks the end of the duration of the lessee's estate. It follows that even termination by the effluxion of time, or the exercise of a power of termination, after the commencement of the winding up is valid.[17]

---

[12] See below, para.7–09.

[13] *Perpetual Trustee*, cited above n.7. This is a particular application of the principle that the liquidator takes the assets as he finds them. See above, para.3–05.

[14] However, nothing in s.33 operates to validate any trust which would, if contained in the instrument creating the trust, be liable to be set aside (s.33(3)). So a protective trust created in fraud of the settlor's creditors would be void under s.423 of the Insolvency Act 1986.

[15] *Whitmore v Mason* (1861) 2 J. & H. 204, per Page-Wood V.-C. at 210 and 212–213; *Ex p. Barter* (1884) 26 Ch.D. 510, per Fry L.J. at 519–520; and *Re Scientific Investment Pension Plan Trusts* [1999] Ch. 53.

[16] They also apply even where the lease is expressly drawn as a determinable interest ending on a breach of covenant by the lessee (Law of Property Act 1925 s.146(7)).

[17] *Perpetual Trustee*, cited above n.7, per Patten L.J. at [143]–[144].

Similar considerations apply to the termination of a licence, such as an intellectual property licence, where the inclusion of such termination provisions is standard practice.[18]

This distinction between a determinable interest and an interest forfeitable on a condition subsequent—justifiably described by one writer as a distinction without a difference[19]—has rightly been characterised in an Irish decision as "little short of disgraceful to our jurisprudence" when applied to "a rule professedly founded on considerations of public policy",[20] a view endorsed in *Sharp's Settlement Trusts, Re*[21] by Pennycuick J., who nevertheless concluded that it was well established and had to be accepted so far as comprehensible. A lease or contract right may be one of the most valuable assets held by a company immediately prior to its going into liquidation. The effect of its termination is therefore to deprive the company of that right and thereby substantially diminish the assets available to the general body of creditors, so that in form and in substance the termination operates as a forfeiture.[22] Moreover, the extinction of a lease expands the lessor's interest in the leased property, converting it from a reversionary interest encumbered by the lease into an unencumbered interest in possession, so that in substance, if not in law, there is a transfer of an asset from the company's estate to that of the lessor. In the case of a contract not relating to property of any kind, it is nevertheless the case that the contract right itself is an asset the termination of which reduces the company's estate and frees the other party from the burden of the contract. American bankruptcy law roundly declares ipso facto termination clauses ineffective, however they are formulated.[23] This is a sound rule and one which English law could sensibly follow,[24] although this would require legislation. Subject to the court's equitable power to grant relief against forfeiture,[25] the solvent party's default remedies in the event of breach by the company remain exercisable in just the same way against the liquidator as against the company itself, and there seems no good reason why the advent of winding up should by itself confer a windfall on the solvent party at the expense of

---

[18] *Butters* v. *BBC Worldwide Ltd* [2010] B.C.L.C. 747.

[19] Richard Calnan, *Proprietary Rights and Insolvency* (Oxford: Oxford University Press, 2010), paras 1–22 et seq.

[20] *Re King's Trust* (1892) 29 L.R. Ir 401, per Porter M.R. at 410.

[21] [1972] 3 W.L.R. 765.

[22] As is shown by the fact that in *Transag Haulage Ltd v Leyland DAF Finance Plc* [1994] B.C.C. 356, the court exercised its equitable discretion to grant relief against forfeiture in relation to a hire-purchase agreement which had come to an end pursuant to a provision of the agreement making it terminable on the appointment of a receiver.

[23] Bankruptcy Code s.541(c)(l). At common law the principle was confined to leases.

[24] But for a robust defence of ipso facto clauses, see Thomas H. Jackson, *The Logic and Limits of Bankruptcy Law* (Cambridge, MA: Harvard University Press, 1986), pp.40–43.

[25] Which in the case of chattels depends on the terms on which they are held. For a recent decision denying the availability of relief against forfeiture of a finance lease, see *Celestial Aviation Trading Ltd v Paramount Airways Pte Ltd* [2010] C.L.C. 165.

creditors.[26] Certainly, the English rule should not be extended, and on that account one can only welcome the decision of Sir Edward Evans-Lombe in *Mayhew v King*[27] holding that a contractual provision by which, in the event of a company going into liquidation, a right of indemnity it enjoyed should be terminated before any payment had become due was void under the anti-deprivation rule.

Pre-emption provisions in articles of association

The common pre-emption provision in articles of association of a company requiring a member to transfer its shares on becoming bankrupt or going into liquidation is not open to attack on the ground of repugnancy or inconsistency with insolvency law so long as the provision applies to all members and the price is either fair or, where the restrictions on transfer make it impossible to establish a market value, is not shown to be less than the price that would have been obtained without the insolvency.[28] The position is otherwise where the terms of pre-emption are not fair or are not enforced in good faith for the benefit of the company.[29]

7–06

Provision for termination on winding up of interest annexed to membership status

The position is otherwise where the interest is annexed to membership of a body and cannot be divorced from membership or transferred for consideration. The typical case concerns the rules of an exchange by which the holding of shares in the exchange is dependent on membership and the member is not entitled to receive any consideration on transfer of the shares and must surrender them without consideration on cessation of membership on winding up or bankruptcy or for any other reason. Such a provision is valid in that the interest is inseparable from membership and has no value capable of being realised by the company.[30] The decision of Neuberger J. in *Money Markets International Stockholders Ltd v London Stock Exchange Ltd*[31] provides a good illustration.

7–07

---

[26] There are, however, necessary exceptions to be made in relation to market contracts. As to the special treatment of these, see paras 1–60–1–61.

[27] [2010] EWHC 1121 affirmed by the Court of Appeal [2011] EWCA Civ 328 *sub. nom. Folgate London Market Ltd v Chaucer Insurance Plc.*

[28] *Butters v BBC Worldwide Ltd* [2010] B.C.L.C. 747; and *Borland's Trustee v Steel Bros & Co* [1901] 1 Ch. 279.

[29] For an analysis of the scope of this rather unclear principle see *Gower and Davies' Principl;es of Modern Company Law*, 8th edn., ed Paul Davies (London: Sweet & Maxwell, 2008), paras. 19–4 *et seq.*

[30] The fact that it has value in the hands of the exchange and may be sold to other members is irrelevant; what matters is value realisable in the hands of the company.

[31] [2002] 1 W.L.R. 1150, applying *Bombay Official Assignee v Shroff* (1932) 48 T.L.R. 443.

"The claimant, a member firm of the London Stock Exchange, held in that capacity a single 'B' share in the Exchange carrying with it voting rights and a proportionate interest in the assets held by the Exchange in the event of its being wound up. Under the rules of the Exchange 'B' shares could only be transferred to and held by member firms, no consideration could be paid or given for any transfer and the directors could direct a member firm to dispose of all or any of its 'B' shares. If a 'B' shareholder ceased to be a member or became bankrupt or if a disposal was directed, the shareholder was bound to transfer its shares to other members without consideration, and they were entitled and obliged so to acquire them, when called upon by the directors to do so. Following its failure to honour stock exchange contracts the claimant ceased to be a member and went into voluntary liquidation. Each 'B' share then had a value of £2.8 million. The claimant instituted proceedings for an order for reinstatement as a member or alternatively compensation for the loss of its 'B' share on the ground that the divestiture removed an asset from the reach of its creditors, contrary to a basic principle of insolvency law.

Held: though the effect of the provision for transfer was indeed to divest the claimant of an interest in property that would otherwise be available to creditors it did not contravene any rule of insolvency law, for the property right was never independently transferable but was ancillary to membership, could not be transferred for consideration and came to an end when the claimant's membership, which was dependent on the personal attributes and acceptability of a particular individual, was validly and reasonably terminated for dishonour of its financial obligations."

In the course of his judgment Neuberger J. engaged in an extensive review of the rule invalidating deprivation of an asset on insolvency and the exceptions to it. The judgment is interesting not only for its acceptance of the defendant's central argument, but also for its rejection of some of the other arguments that had been advanced against the application of the no-deprivation rule. In particular, Neuberger J. did not consider it relevant that the forfeiture provision also applied in specified non-insolvency events or that it was not made with the intention of disadvantaging creditors on an insolvency, and he also did not accept the argument that it was an inherent feature of the share that it could be taken away, in other words, it was a "flawed asset",[32] for that would be to emasculate the no-deprivation principle and would also be inconsistent with the repugnancy rule.[33]

---

[32] Citing Fidelis Oditah, "Assets and the Treatment of Claims in Insolvency" (1992) 108 L.Q.R. 459, 474.

[33] However, he appears to have moved away from this position in the *Perpetual Trustee* case. See below.

It is important to note that, because members of the exchange were precluded by the rules from receiving consideration for a transfer of shares even while solvent, the rule requiring surrender of the shares to the exchange for no consideration in the event of a person ceasing to be a member on insolvency did not deprive that person of any benefit it would have enjoyed prior to insolvency. There was thus no divestment of value offending against any rule of insolvency law. Hence, the case is to be distinguished from *Borland's Trustee v Steel Bros & Co Ltd*,[34] where the shares were not an incident to membership of anything except the company itself and were transferable for value, so that the articles of association imposing an obligation of transfer on a member's insolvency would have been struck down if they had required a compulsory sale for no consideration or for insufficient value.[35]

7–08

Types of agreement which normally do or may contravene the anti-deprivation rule

Provision for divestment of ownership on winding up

The transfer of property in an asset to a company upon the condition that the asset is to revest in the transferor if the company goes into liquidation is void on at least two counts.[36] First, the provisions for revesting will be rejected as void for repugnancy, being inconsistent with the outright transfer of ownership.[37] Secondly, they run counter to the principle of insolvency law, on which the anti-deprivation rule is based, that property cannot be transferred to a person on terms that it will not be available to his creditors, for this would be inconsistent with the mode of application of the transferee's assets prescribed by law.[38] Forfeiture clauses of this kind are used in a variety of contexts[39] and will almost invariably be struck down except where the asset in question has no value.[40] On the other hand, as stated earlier, there is no objection to a disposition by which property is transferred to the company for an interest coming to an end on winding up.

7–09

---

[34] [1901] 1 Ch. 279. See above, para.7–08.

[35] *Butters v BBC Worldwide Ltd*, cited above n.28.

[36] It may also be vulnerable under the rule against perpetuities, now curtailed by the Perpetuities and Accumulations Act 2009.

[37] The root decision on conditions repugnant to legally prescribed methods of devolution is *Holmes v Godson* (1856) 8 De G. M. & G. 152. See to the same effect *Metcalfe v Metcalfe* (1889) 43 Ch.D. 633; *Re Ashton, Ballard v Ashton* [1920] 2 Ch. 481; *Ex p. Mackay* (1873) 8 Ch App. 643; and *Re Machu* (1882) 21 Ch.D. 838. These cases all involved a disposition by will, but the principle applies with equal force to other dispositions.

[38] *Ex p. Mackay* (1873) L.R. 8 Ch. App. 643; *Re Ex p. Jay, Harrison* (1880) 14 Ch.D. 19; and *Caboche v Ramsay* (1993) 119 A.L.R. 215, a decision of the Full Federal Court of Australia.

[39] See below and Gerard McCormack, *Proprietary Claims and Insolvency* (London: Sweet & Maxwell, 1997), pp.25–28.

[40] *Money Markets International Stockbrokers Ltd v London Stock Exchange Ltd* [2002] 1 W.L.R. 1150.

The other cases considered below are all variations of the divestment principle.

Vesting clauses in building contracts

7–10   A provision in a building contract vesting the builder's materials in the building owner upon the builder's liquidation contravenes the anti-deprivation rule since it operates to divest the estate of an asset belonging to the estate at the time of liquidation.[41] The position is otherwise where the right of forfeiture arises prior to winding up.[42]

Sale with provision for retransfer on winding up

7–11   Where a person sells goods on credit to a company under a contract which does not reserve title until payment, but provides for retransfer to the seller if the company goes into liquidation without having completed payment, the provision is void, for its effect is to deprive the estate of an asset owned by the company at the time it goes into liquidation.[43]

Increase in company's contractual obligation upon winding up

7–12   A provision purporting to increase the creditor's entitlement upon its debtor going into liquidation, for example by increasing the amount the debtor has to pay to redeem a mortgage,[44] or by allowing the creditor, on the liquidation of the company, to retain the whole of the royalties due to the company instead of the one-half payable before liquidation,[45] is void as contravening the anti-deprivation rule.

---

[41] *Re Harrison, ex p. Jay* (1880) 14 Ch.D. 19. Whether a vesting clause does have this effect is a question of construction. The common provision by which plant and materials brought on to the site "shall be deemed to become the property of the employer" on the contractor's insolvency does not necessarily mean that ownership is in fact to pass and may signify merely that the employer is to have the right to use the plant and materials as if it were the employer. For a relatively recent example, see *Re Cosslett Contractors Ltd* [1998] Ch. 495.

[42] *Perpetual Trustee Co Ltd v BNY Corporate Trustee Services Ltd* [2010] 1 B.C.L.C. 747 (discussed in detail in para.7–13); and *Re Garrud, ex p. Newitt* (1880) 16 Ch.D. 522.

[43] *Holroyd v Gwynne* (1809) 2 Taunt. 176.

[44] *Re Johns* [1928] Ch. 737, a bankruptcy case, but the principle is the same.

[45] *Re Jeavons, ex p. Mackay* (1873) 8 Ch. App. 643.

3. *THE* PERPETUAL TRUSTEE *CASE*

In November 2009, the Court of Appeal hearing conjoined appeals arising from   **7–13**
the insolvency of Lehman Brothers handed down an important decision[46] in
which the nature, history and limits of the anti-deprivation rule were examined
in detail. In the first appeal there were two separate claimants, Perpetual
Trustee Co and Belmont Park Investment Pty Ltd, whose claims raised broadly
the same issues. In the second case, *Butters*, the claimants were joint administrators of WW Realisations 8 Ltd, who sought a direction that certain share
option provisions were void as contravening the anti-deprivation rule. Appeals
against the decision in the above cases were to have been heard by the Supreme
Court in March 2011. However, the *Perpetual Trustee* appeal was settled near
the end of 2010, but Belmont proceeded with its appeal, which has been heard
and is awaiting the Supreme Court's decision. The outcome could have had
profound implications for the rating of credit-linked notes and, indeed, for the
synthetic securitication market as a whole. *Butters* is not discussed further here.

The background to the case

The facts were complex, but in essence credit-linked notes sponsored by a   **7–14**
Lehman company were issued under a synthetic securitisation programme by
a special-purpose vehicle (SPV) with whom another Lehman company,
LBSF, entered into a swap agreement as swap counterparty.[47] Under the
terms of the Notes, the Noteholders, for whom the claimant was trustee, in
effect provided credit insurance to LBSF against the default of various listed

---

[46] *Perpetual Trustee*, cited above n.42. See Roy Goode, "*Perpetual Trustee* and flip clauses in swap
transactions" (2011) 127 L.Q.R. 1 for a detailed treatment of this case. The conjoined appeal
Butters v BBC Worldwide Ltd concerned agreements under which, on insolvency, the insolvent
company could be required to sell to BBC Worldwide at fair value its shares in the joint venture company they had established and intellectual property licences granted by BBC
Worldwide could be terminated. The Court of Appeal held that, on the basis of the principles
set out above, neither of the agreements nor the agreements in combination breached the
anti-deprivation rule.

[47] On an ordinary securitisation the originator holding a portfolio of mortgage or other debts sells
them to a SPV, which issues notes or bonds against them, utilising the proceeds to pay the originator. In a synthetic securitisation the originator, not wishing to disturb relations with its borrowers, does not sell the debts, but instead buys credit protection from investors by procuring a
bankruptcy-immune SPV, with which it enters into a swap agreement as swap counterparty, to
issue notes linked to the credit of the borrowers (the "reference entities"), so that if in relation
to a particular borrower a credit event occurs such as default or bankruptcy, the redemption
price on the relevant note is reduced or may even come down to zero. But if all goes well,
investors receive a substantially higher interest rate than would otherwise be the case. So credit-
linked notes are in substance, although not in law, a form of insurance, the additional interest
being the premium paid for the credit protection. Sums received from investors are used to purchase high-quality securities as collateral for the notes. The noteholders have no recourse to the
SPV itself. For a detailed description of securitisation and structured finance, see Andrew
McKnight, *Law of International Finance* (Oxford: Oxford University Press, 2008), s.12.10.

reference entities. The sums received from the Note issue were utilised to buy high-quality investments held by the defendant as security trustee and serving as collateral for payments due to the Noteholders and to LBSF. LBSF was to make payments to the SPV to cover the interest payable to the Noteholders and was to receive the yield on the collateral and, after repayment of the Notes, the collateral itself. In the event of recourse to the collateral, priority was to be given to LBSF unless a stipulated default event occurred with reference to LBSF or any of its credit supporters, in which case there was a reversal, or "flip", of this priority from LBSF to the Noteholders. The events of default included failure to pay any sums due under the agreement after three local business days' notice and the institution of any insolvency proceeding by or against a party or any Credit Support Provider.

The flip was triggered not by a default relating to LBSF, but by the filing under Ch.11 of the US Bankruptcy Code of an associated company. LBSF itself did not file under Ch.11 for a further fortnight. No further interest payments were made under the Notes. Perpetual, representing the Noteholders of two issues, and Belmont, representing the Noteholders of 10 issues, brought proceedings in England on behalf of their respective Noteholders against the first defendant as security trustee asking for orders for realisation of the collateral and application of the proceeds to the Noteholders in priority to LBSF. At about the same time, LBSF brought proceedings in New York for a declaration that the flip clause violated the ipso facto avoidance provisions of ss.365(e)(1) and 541(c)(1)(B) of the US Federal Bankruptcy Code and a declaration that any attempt to enforce the flip clause would be a breach of the automatic stay under s.362(a) of the Bankruptcy Code. In the English proceedings, LBSF contended that the flip provision was void as being contrary to the anti-deprivation rule. The validity of the flip provisions was upheld by the Chancellor, whose judgment was affirmed by the Court of Appeal.

The issues

7–15   The court had to consider the following issues:

(1)   Did the change in priorities produced by the flip constitute a deprivation of property of LBSF?

(2)   If it did, was it nevertheless outside the scope of the anti-deprivation rule because of any of the following factors, namely that:

(a)   the flip was triggered by an event that preceded LBSF's Ch.11 filing (which was treated as the equivalent of an English administration);

(b)   the provision for the change in priority was an in-built feature of the security; or

(c)   the Noteholders claiming priority had financed the acquisition of the collateral?

Decision of the Court of Appeal

The Court of Appeal enunciated the following propositions: **7–16**

(1)   The basic rule is that a contractual provision cannot validly stipulate bankruptcy as an event that is to deprive the debtor company of an asset held at the time of commencement of the bankruptcy ("the anti-deprivation rule").

(2)   The mere fact that a transaction causing deprivation was not intended to evade the anti-deprivation rule is irrelevant; so too is the fact that the deprivation was part of the original bargain.

(3)   A mere contractual reversal of priorities on bankruptcy is not caught by the anti-deprivation rule because it does not deprive the company of anything or affect other creditors (paras 64, 66, 135 and 137), although Lord Neuberger is more cautious (at para.67).[48]

(4)   The anti-deprivation rule does not apply if the asset of which the company was deprived was acquired with money provided by the person in whose favour the deprivation takes effect (paras 64 and 67). This proposition is based on *Whitmore v Mason*.[49]

(5)   Deprivation on the occurrence of an event preceding bankruptcy is not within the anti-deprivation principle (paras 69 et seq. and 162). The Court of Appeal overruled the contrary decision in *Fraser v Oystertec Plc*.[50]

(6)   The anti-deprivation principle does not apply to a provision entitling a creditor to terminate a limited interest, whether on bankruptcy or otherwise (paras 64 and 143–147).[51]

(7)   The trigger for the deprivation must be the liquidation, administration or equivalent of the company itself. So a Ch.11 filing by a co-subsidiary does not suffice, even if the company and co-subsidiary are part of a closely integrated group and even though the filing causes deprivation to the company in liquidation by reducing the value of its shares in the co-subsidiary (paras 73 et seq. and 166 et seq., preferring the view of Cheung J. in the Hong Kong decision in *Peregrine Investment Holdings*).[52]

(8)   An option to acquire an asset for full value in the event of the company's insolvency does not contravene public policy, there being no

---

[48] As to this aspect, see below, para.7–21.
[49] (1861) 2 John and H. 204.
[50] [2004] B.C.C. 233.
[51] See below, para.7–19.
[52] See below, para.7–18.

detriment to the company's estate (paras 147 et seq.). This seems clear enough. However, one should add that if the option has purely contractual force, as in the case of goods, the liquidator is not bound to procure performance by the company, although the position is otherwise if the grantee of the option has acquired a proprietary right, as in the case of land.

Analysis

7–17   The decision itself has attracted much interest[53] and is clearly correct. However, there were certain unguarded references to the *pari passu* rule, with which the case was not concerned, since the noteholders were not creditors of the company in administration. There are also some further aspects of the case which require consideration.

The judgments rest on three principles: a distinction between deprivation of an asset and a mere loss of priority; the fact that the change of priority was a term of the security agreement from the outset; and the fact that the price paid for the collateral was advanced by the beneficiary of any deprivation, the Noteholders. Although at first sight each of these principles appears to have been advanced as an independent ground for upholding the validity of the flip provision, it would seem from a closer reading of the judgments that none of these is to be taken in isolation from the others.[54] For the reasons given below, it is submitted that the statement as to the first of the three principles, if taken in isolation, is incorrect and if combined with the other two principles is superfluous, and that the case turned on the combination of the second and third principles, coupled with the fact that the change of priority was not for a consideration already executed, but was the price of failure in the performance of a continuing obligation.

The temporal aspect

7–18   It was argued by LBSF that for the anti-deprivation rule to operate it sufficed that at the time of the deprivation the company was insolvent. That was rightly rejected on two grounds. The first was that to take the commencement of a state of insolvency as the trigger for the operation of the rule would generate much uncertainty. This is undoubtedly the case. Outsiders have no ready access to up-to-date information on a company's financial affairs and even the

---

[53] See, e.g. Sarah Worthington, "Insolvency Deprivation, Public Policy and Priority Flip Clauses" (2010) 7 *International Corporate Rescue* 28; and Look Chan Ho, "The Principle against Divestiture and the *Pari Passu* Fallacy" (2010) 1 J.I.B.F.L. 3, agreeing with the result, but sharply critical of the reasoning.

[54] See, e.g. the judgment of Lord Neuberger at [67].

company itself might find it difficult to ascertain the precise moment when it first became unable to pay its debts. Patten L.J. gave a second, and even more compelling, ground for rejecting LBSF's argument, namely that the Insolvency Act 1986 identified the point of departure as the commencement of winding up or administration and it was not legitimate to look to preceding events of deprivation except as provided by the Act itself, for example in its provisions as to unauthorised post-petition dispositions under s.127 and transactions at an undervalue under s.238. The Court of Appeal referred to the House of Lords decision in *British Eagle International Airlines Ltd v Cie Nationale Air France*,[55] where it had been held that transactions completed prior to the liquidation of British Eagle were not caught by the *pari passu* rule. The same must apply in relation to the anti-deprivation rule.[56]

The limited interest point

Again, the ruling that LBSF's priority was from the outset a qualified one and that the Noteholders, who had financed the collateral, were entitled to look to it to recover the money due to them is in line with prior authority. In other words, it was a form of flawed asset which could only be held subject to fulfilment of the conditions attached to it. However, this does not mean that it always suffices that the flaw was part of the original bargain.[57] For example, the fact that the terms of an outright transfer to a company provide for retransfer without full value in the event of its going into liquidation or winding up does not take the retransfer provision outside the scope of the anti-deprivation principle; and the reason, as Briggs J. pointed out in the subsequent decision in *Lomas v JFB Firth Rixson Inc*,[58] is that the asset represents the quid pro quo for something already done, sold or delivered before the onset of insolvency, as opposed to being the quid pro quo (in whole or in part) for services yet to be rendered or something still to be supplied by the insolvent company in an ongoing contract, where the court will readily permit the insertion of a flaw in the asset.[59] The point that was being made by the Court of Appeal in the *Perpetual*

7–19

---

[55] [1975] 1 W.L.R. 758.

[56] This view is challenged by Ho (above, n.53), who correctly points out that *British Eagle* was not a case on deprivation at all, but one on the *pari passu* rule. However, it is hard to see why the principle of collectivity on which Ho relies should be engaged prior to liquidation in the case of the anti-deprivation rule when it is not so engaged for the purpose of the *pari passu* rule. In both cases, the interests of the general body of creditors are affected.

[57] Patten L.J. appears to have considered that it did suffice ([2010] Ch. 347 at [135]), and if that is the case, then his was a minority view.

[58] [2010] EWHC 3372 (Ch) at [108].

[59] In the same case (at [121]–[123]) Briggs J. rejected separate arguments that the flip constituted a penalty or alternatively a forfeiture against which relief should be given. It was later conceded that a provision could not be a penalty unless it was triggered by a breach of contract, while a contingent right to net payments was not a kind of property to which the rules on forfeiture applied and in any event the flip provision was not a forfeiture, but a condition precedent.

Trustee case was not only that LBSF never had more than a conditional and contingent right to its priority, but that this right had to be earned by performance of a contract under which LBSF had continuing obligations at the time it went into the Ch.11 proceedings.

The advance of funds point

7–20   Much emphasis was placed on the fact that the beneficiary of the deprivation advanced the funds with which it was acquired. This, too, cannot suffice on its own to exclude the anti-deprivation rule. If, for example, a lender chooses to advance the purchase price on an unsecured basis, then just as he cannot invoke the "part of the bargain" argument, so also he cannot rely on his financing to validate a reversion of the asset to him on the borrower's insolvency. It was the combination of the two elements, and the fact that the flip was the quid pro quo for continuing obligations of LBSF, that rendered the anti-deprivation principle inapplicable.

Change in priority not a deprivation?

7–21   It is unfortunate that the proposition that the change in priority was not a deprivation was expressed as if it were a principle distinct from the conditional and contingent nature of the priority right when the real point was that there was not really a deprivation, despite the "flip" language, merely a qualified priority right. That is probably what the Court of Appeal meant to convey, for it is obvious that in general a change in priority must constitute a deprivation where the value of the collateral is insufficient to cover the claims of both sets of parties. In the instant case, LBSF's subordinated security interest might be inadequate to meet its claims and, indeed, might be extinguished altogether. It seems evident, then, that it was only because of the other elements, namely the fact that the change of priority was bargained from the outset as the price of failure in performance of a continuing obligation and the fact that the price of the collateral was advanced by the beneficiary of the deprivation, that the Court of Appeal was able to find that the change in priority did not work a deprivation. In other words, the court was not seeking to lay down a general principle that a change in priorities does not involve a deprivation. Rather, it was saying that because there was no deprivation—the asset having been financed by the Noteholders and the initial priority having been agreed from the outset as the quid pro quo for continuing performance by LBSF—the "change" in priorities[60] would not give the Noteholders anything

---

[60] The words "change" and "flip" are perhaps unfortunate, and may have led to confusion, because in essence there is no *change* of priorities in this situation, merely an *application* of the agreed priority rule.

more than they were entitled to from the outset or deprive the company of the right it had enjoyed from the beginning, namely a priority qualified by reference to specified contractual contingencies.

However, if this is the ratio of the decision—if, in other words, the combination of the second and third elements suffices to show that there was no deprivation—it is not easy to see why the first element, namely the distinction between the giving up of an interest and the subordination of an interest, should have been relevant. Taken in isolation, it is a distinction without a difference, for loss of priority is potentially loss or diminution of a property right; and given the sufficiency of the other two factors, the distinction is not only unwarranted, but unnecessary. Even if it had been a term of the agreement that on a default event LBSF's interest would not merely become subordinated but would be given up altogether, the result should be the same because of the second and third factors, the effect of which was that there was no deprivation.

Significance of the case

The provision for a change of priority in the event of default by a swaps counterparty is a crucial element in ensuring that Noteholders are immune from default by the swaps counterparty. This immunity lies at the heart of securitisations and credit-linked notes. Accordingly, if LBSF's arguments were to prevail, the damage to the market could be immense. The decision of the Supreme Court in Belmont will thus be of great importance. Already, LBSF has used its success in obtaining a contrary ruling from the bankruptcy judge in the United States[61] as leverage in settlement negotiations involving billions of dollars. That ruling, in which the bankruptcy judge, H.H. Judge Peck, ruled that the flip provision was an ipso facto clause rendered void under s.541(c)(1)(B) of the US federal Bankruptcy Code and that any attempt to enforce it would be a breach of the automatic stay under s.362(a) of the Code, is itself now under appeal.[62] If the appeal is dismissed, the collateral trustee will be placed in the invidious position of having to comply with conflicting orders of the two courts.[63] The US District Court could, if it thought

7–22

---

[61] *Lehman Bros Holdings Inc v BNY Corporate Trustee Services Ltd*, 25 January 2010 (US Bankruptcy Court for the Southern District of New York, Case 08-1355).

[62] Leave to appeal was given by a different judge (Case 09-01242) because of its "potentially game-changing effect on the structured finance business" and "potentially far reaching ramifications for the international securities markets".

[63] If a request were then to be made to the English courts under the UNCITRAL Model Law to recognise and enforce the US judgments, the position would become difficult. It is thought that there would be a reluctance by the English courts to make an order incompatible with a prior judgment of the highest court in England, but either way the trustee would find itself in an awkward position.

fit, avoid this result either by reversing the ruling of the Bankruptcy judge as to the applicability of s.541(c)(1)(B) or by exercising its discretion to direct that the US Bankruptcy court refrain from exercising its bankruptcy jurisdiction in the interests of international comity, given that all of the relevant transactional connections are to England, not the United States.[64]

---

[64] The position strongly taken by the US Courts of Appeals for the Second Circuit in *Re Maxwell Communication Corp* 93 F.3d 1036 (1996). The Court of Appeal in England has adopted a similar approach working in the reverse direction by holding, in *Rubin v Eurofinance SA* [2011] 2 W.L.R. 121, that in the light of the UNCITRAL Model Law on Cross-Border Insolvency, incorporated into British law by the Cross-Border Insolvency Regulations 2006, it should defer to U.S. bankruptcy law and recognise and enforce a judgment of the US Bankruptcy court.

Chapter 8

The Proof, Valuation and Ranking of Claims in Winding Up

Introduction

In Chapter 6 we defined and described the assets of the company available for distribution to its creditors. The present chapter looks at the liabilities side of the company's balance sheet and discusses the treatment of claims in the winding up and the order of distribution of assets among the competing creditors.[1]

8–01

1. THE PARI PASSU PRINCIPLE OF DISTRIBUTION

The principle stated

The most fundamental principle of insolvency law is that of *pari passu* distribution, all creditors participating in the common pool in proportion to the size of their admitted claims. In the case of voluntary winding up, this principle is expressed in the Insolvency Act itself:

8–02

> "Subject to the provisions of this Act as to preferential payments, the company's property in a voluntary winding up shall on the winding up be applied in satisfaction of the company's liabilities *pari passu* . . ."[2]

---

[1] The phrase "distribution of assets" does not mean distribution in specie, but is the conventional shorthand for distribution by way of dividend of the net proceeds resulting from dispositions of the assets by the liquidator.

[2] Insolvency Act 1986 s.107.

In the case of compulsory winding up, the principle is found in the Insolvency Rules: "Debts other than preferential debts rank equally between themselves in the winding up."[3]

A similar principle applies in administration,[4] although its application is more limited. It is this principle of rateable distribution which marks off the rights of creditors in a winding up from their pre-liquidation entitlements. Prior to winding up,[5] each creditor is free to pursue whatever enforcement measures are open to him. Where self-help (for example, by repossession of goods, realisation of security or exercise of a right of set-off) is not available, the creditor must have recourse to legal process and, if the debtor company fails to satisfy a judgment voluntarily, enforce the judgment by execution against the company's assets or income. The rule here, in the absence of an insolvency proceeding, is that the race goes to the swiftest. The creditor initiating the earliest execution has first bite at the cherry and whatever is left is available for the next in line. A creditor who leaves it too late finds he has a *brutum fulmen*—there is a judgment in his favour, but no assets against which to enforce it. Liquidation puts an end to the race. The principle first come, first served, gives way to that of orderly realisation of assets by the liquidator for the benefit of all unsecured creditors and distribution of the net proceeds *pari passu*. The *pari passu* principle is all-pervasive. It is based on the notion that losses caused by liquidation should be borne by unsecured creditors equally. Its broad effect is to strike down all agreements, payments and transfers which have as their object and result the unfair preference of a particular creditor by removal from the estate on winding up of an asset that would otherwise have been available for the general body of creditors.[6]

The statutory principle of *pari passu* distribution is buttressed by more specific statutory rules on preferences by which pre-liquidation payments and transfers made in the run-up to winding up may be avoided.[7] These have a different temporal factor. The *pari passu* principle, like the anti-deprivation rule,[8] has no backward reach. It does not affect transactions completed prior to the commencement of liquidation or administration.[9] In the absence of a statutory provision to the contrary, a person is entitled to discharge his liabilities in any order he pleases.[10] By contrast, the statutory provisions on preferences are designed to unravel payments and transfers

---

[3] Insolvency Rules 1986 r.4.181(1).
[4] Insolvency Rules 1986 r.2.69. See below, para.11–85.
[5] Or administration. See Ch.11.
[6] It is true that the approach would be the same whatever the distribution rule. But as pointed out earlier (above, para.3–07) the reference to the *pari passu* principle in this context is simply shorthand to describe what is in fact the central rule of distribution.
[7] See below, Ch.13.
[8] See above, para.7–18.
[9] *Re Smith, Knight & Co Ex p. Ashbury* (1968) L.R. 5 Eq. 228.
[10] *Re Sarflux Ltd* [1979] Ch. 592, per Oliver J. at 602.

already made to a creditor in the twilight period *prior* to liquidation or administration at a time when the company is already insolvent or will become so as the result of payment or transfer in question. Moreover, recoveries by the liquidator under the statutory provisions will not necessarily fall to be distributed *pro rata* among the general body of creditors; they simply add to the pool of assets available for distribution, with liquidation expenses and preferential claims coming ahead of those of ordinary unsecured creditors.

As we have seen,[11] the *pari passu* principle is to be distinguished from the anti-deprivation rule discussed in Chapter 7. The latter is aimed at contractual provisions which have the effect of reducing the company's net asset value upon its liquidation or administration by a transfer to a party who is not a creditor. By contrast, a payment or transfer to a creditor upon winding up or administration has no effect on the company's net asset value, because its effect is pro tanto to reduce the company's liability to the creditor. The objection to such a payment or transfer is thus a different one, namely that it disturbs the statutory scheme of distribution and thereby gives an unfair advantage to the creditor to whom the payment or transfer is made. We have noted earlier that because the two rules share certain characteristics,[12] many of the cases cited as decisions on the *pari passu* principle are in fact decisions on the anti-deprivation rule. Examples are provided by cases on limited and determinable interests, pre-emption provisions in articles of association and provisions forfeiting building materials to the employer on the builder's liquidation.

The pari passu principle is primarily relevant to winding up

Until recently, it could be said that since the *pari passu* principle is concerned to ensure an equitable distribution of the company's estate among its creditors, its application as a mandatory rule was almost entirely confined to liquidation, for this was the only collective insolvency process which had as its primary objective the distribution of assets among the general body of creditors in accordance with a statutory *pari passu* rule that cannot be excluded by contract.[13] However, there has been a marked trend in recent years to use administration as a liquidation substitute, following upon a change in the Insolvency Rules to enable proofs to be made, rules of set-off applied and assets distributed (with leave of the court in the case of unsecured creditors) under rules substantially similar to those applicable on a winding up. Nevertheless, it remains the case that many distributions are

8–03

---

[11] Above, para.7–03.
[12] See above, para.7–03.
[13] See below, para.8–06.

made pursuant to a company voluntary arrangement under Pt I of the Insolvency Act or a compromise or arrangement under Pt 26 of the Companies Act 2006 and will be governed by the terms of those arrangements, which have to be approved by the requisite majority of creditors, rather than by any a priori rule of distribution. For the same reason, the *pari passu* principle has no necessary application to informal work-outs. No doubt any distribution to ordinary unsecured creditors will normally be expected to follow the order of priorities that would apply in a winding up, but there is no rule of law precluding creditors from approving an arrangement on a different basis.[14] Moreover, in many cases there will be no free assets to distribute among unsecured creditors.

The *pari passu* principle does not in any event apply to administrative receivership, for this is not a true collective insolvency proceeding,[15] and if the receiver, after meeting out of floating charge assets payments to preferential creditors, the costs of preserving and realising the assets, his other expenses and remuneration, the prescribed part to be surrendered for the benefit of unsecured creditors and the claims of his debenture holders, has a surplus, his duty is to pass it to any subsequent secured creditor or, if none, then to the company; he has no general power of distribution. It has also been held that the *pari passu* principle cannot be invoked so as to entitle the holder of a floating charge to share in the prescribed part available to unsecured creditors from assets the subject of the charge, since the general principle must give way to the express terms of s.176A(2) of the Insolvency Act 1986.[16] On the other hand, the *pari passu* principle reinforces the natural construction of s.176A(2) precluding the court from disapplying s.176A(2) in part, for example, by excluding creditors with claims of less than a specified amount.[17]

Where a commercial contract on its true interpretation provides for the distribution of assets to a group of persons as between whom no distinction is to be drawn, the court will imply a requirement to make distributions proportionately,[18] but such an implication is not possible where the document evinces an intention that the distribution should be on some other basis.[19] It is a question in each case of interpreting the contract.[20]

---

[14] *Re HPJ UK Ltd* [2007] B.C.C. 284, where the judge approved the payment by the administrator of a fixed sum to HM Revenue & Customs, with the approval of the other creditors, in order to remove the delay and expense of ascertaining the exact amount due and to maximise any dividend to the creditors. Similarly, s.4(4) of the Insolvency Act 1986, while precluding approval of a proposed CVA which would affect the enforcement rights of a secured creditor or the priority of a preferential debt, leaves unsecured creditors free to agree on a distribution among themselves otherwise than on a *pari passu* basis. As to the prescribed part, see above, paras 6–38 *et seq.*

[15] See para.1–38.

[16] *Re Permacell Finesse Ltd* [2008] B.C.C. 208.

[17] *Re Courts Plc* [2009] 1 W.L.R. 1499.

[18] *Re Golden Key Ltd* [2009] EWCA Civ 636.

[19] *Re Golden Key*, above, n. 18.

[20] See, e.g. *Re Sigma Finance Corp* [2010] B.C.C. 40; *Re Golden Key*, cited above n.18; and *Re Whistlejacket Capital Ltd* [2008] B.C.C. 826.

The *pari passu* rule: its significance in practice

I have described the *pari passu* principle of distribution as fundamental and all-pervasive. This, at least, is the theory of insolvency law, although this has not passed unchallenged.[21] In practice, as was pointed out by the Cork Committee many years ago,[22] a rateable distribution among creditors is rarely achieved. There are three main reasons for this.   **8–04**

First, the principle is in general confined to assets of the company and does not affect creditors having rights *in rem*. These include secured creditors, who under the liberal regime allowed by English law can take security for present and future indebtedness over future as well as present assets, including fixed charges over future debts and floating charges over all assets; suppliers of goods under contracts which reserve title until payment, a technique in widespread use; and third parties for whom the company holds assets on trust or who have proprietary tracing rights in equity to assets in the possession or under the control of the company. The effect of these rights *in rem* is substantially to reduce the corpus of assets available for unsecured creditors.

Secondly, the liquidator takes the assets subject to equities affecting them, such as a right to avoid a transaction for misrepresentation or undue influence.

Thirdly, huge chunks of what free assets remain have to be applied to meet claims ranking in priority to those of the ordinary unsecured creditor. These embrace: (i) expenses of the liquidation, which are "pre-preferential" liabilities payable in full (rather than having to be proved) and include the liquidator's expenses and remuneration, which can be substantial; and (ii) various claims of employees.[23] When all of these have been satisfied, the dividend produced by what is left is often pitifully small.[24] The effect is largely to frustrate a primary objective of the insolvency process and to deprive the general body of creditors of any significant interest in the winding up process.[25] Yet the *pari passu* principle retains considerable practical importance, if only in a negative sense, in that it may have the effect of invalidating pre-liquidation transactions by which a creditor of a company hopes to secure an advantage over his competitors in the event of the company going into winding up or administration; and where the principle does have this invalidating effect, it results in an expansion of the assets available for

---

[21] See above, para.3–07.
[22] "Insolvency Law and Practice", Report of the (Cork) Review Committee (Cmnd. 8558), para.1396.
[23] See below, para.8–20.
[24] Although it may be somewhat enhanced by recoveries in respect of void or voidable transactions (below, Ch.13) and under the provisions requiring a percentage ("the prescribed part") of the net realisations of assets subject to a floating charge to be surrendered for the benefit of unsecured creditors (see Insolvency Act 1986 s.176A and below, para.8–50).
[25] A point I developed more fully in "The Death of Insolvency Law" (1980) 3 Co. Law. 123.

distribution.[26] Moreover, the principle of *pari passu* distribution has been invoked as the foundation for other rules which do not involve agreements at all, such as the hotchpot rule,[27] the rule against double proof[28] and the rule that save in exceptional circumstances a creditor should not be given leave to register a charge by a company out of time when it is in liquidation.[29] It is thus necessary to examine the scope of the principle in some detail.

Debts covered by the *pari passu* principle

8–05   The *pari passu* principle applies only: (i) to provable debts payable to the general body of creditors[30]; and (ii) within each separate class of preferential, ordinary and deferred creditors.[31]

The *pari passu* rule may not be excluded by contract

8–06   A contractual provision purporting to exclude the principle of *pari passu* distribution, whether in bankruptcy or in winding up, is void.

> "... a man is not allowed, by stipulation with a creditor, to provide for a different distribution of his effects in the event of bankruptcy from that which the law provides."[32]

> "... a person cannot make it a part of his contract that, in the event of his bankruptcy, he is then to get some additional advantage which prevents the property being distributed under the bankruptcy laws."[33]

However, as we shall see, the *pari passu* principle, broad though it is, does admit of some exceptions.[34]

---

[26] See below, paras 8–10 et seq.
[27] See below, paras 15–69 and 16–47.
[28] See below, para.8–45.
[29] See below, para.13–125.
[30] See below, para.8–41.
[31] See below, para.8–53.
[32] *Ex p. Mackay* (1873) 8 Ch. App. 643, per James L.J. at 647.
[33] *Ex p. Mackay*, per Mellish L.J. at 648.
[34] See below, paras 8–17 et seq.

2. *IMPACT OF THE PARI PASSU PRINCIPLE*[35]

Arrangements which do not offend against the *pari passu* principle

We shall come to the exceptions to the *pari passu* principle a little later.[36] At this point it is worth noting the various types of arrangement which are not considered to offend against the principle of *pari passu* distribution at all. These include subordination agreements, provisions for acceleration of liability on winding up, pre-emption provisions in articles of association of a company providing for the compulsory transfer at a reasonable price of the shares of any member that goes into liquidation or bankruptcy, and rules of an exchange by which members who hold shares in the exchange by virtue of their membership cannot receive consideration for any transfer and have to surrender the shares on cessation of membership on account of insolvency or for any other reason.

8–07

Subordination[37]

Two creditors may agree between themselves that one of them who would otherwise rank higher than or *pari passu* with the other shall be subordinated to the other. The subordination may be of secured or unsecured debt. Subordination of secured debt results in what was originally the higher-ranking mortgage or charge being demoted to junior status. Subordination of unsecured debt typically means either that the subordinated creditor cannot collect from the debtor until the senior creditor has been paid in full or that the junior creditor will account for any collections to the senior creditor until the latter has received full payment. Subordination may arise either by negotiated agreement or by the terms of a bond or note issue under which the rights of holders are subordinated to holders of other bonds or notes issued by the same issuer or certain tranches of the issue are to rank below other tranches. Subordinated loan notes or bonds are frequently issued by banks as part of a securitisation, attracting a higher rate of interest because of the increased risk.

Although in general creditors are free to agree among themselves that the secured or unsecured claim of one of them shall be subordinated to the

8–08

---

[35] See Michael Bridge, "Collectivity, Management of Estates and the *Pari Passu* Rule in Winding Up" in John Armour and Howard Bennett (eds), *Vulnerable Transactions in Corporate Insolvency* (Oxford: Hart Publishing, 2003), Ch.1.

[36] Below, para.8–17.

[37] See generally Philip R. Wood, *Project Finance, Securitisations and Subordinated Debt*, 2nd edn (London: Sweet & Maxwell, 2007); Eilis Ferran, *Company Law and Corporate Finance* (Oxford: Oxford University Press, 1999), Ch.16; and *Goode on Legal Problems of Credit and Security*, edited by Louise Gullifer, 4th edn (London: Sweet & Maxwell, 2008), paras [5.58]–[5.59].

claims of the others, there was until relatively recently concern that in the event of winding up a subordination agreement might be held void as running counter to the mandatory provisions of the insolvency legislation. This was thought to be a possible consequence of the decision of the House of Lords in *National Westminster Bank Ltd v Halesowen Presswork and Assemblies Ltd*[38] to the effect that rules for the administration of assets in winding up embody not merely private rights which creditors are free to vary or waive, but rules of public policy for the orderly administration of estates. In the *Halesowen* case, it was held that a debtor could not contract out his statutory set-off. There was a fear that, by parity of reasoning, a creditor could not subordinate his claim in winding up to a claim of equal rank, for this would (so it was argued) infringe the *pari passu* rule in much the same way as the IATA clearing house arrangement was held to do by a majority decision of the House of Lords in the *British Eagle* case.[39] Conflicting decisions had been given in other parts of the Commonwealth, some courts holding that a subordination agreement contravened the mandatory rules of insolvency law,[40] while others considered that such an agreement had no effect on other creditors and was unobjectionable.[41]

To deny the validity of subordination in insolvency could have the most serious consequences, particularly in view of the widespread use of subordination agreements and the issue of subordinated debt on the market, coupled with the recognition of the efficacy of such agreements in insolvency in foreign jurisdictions and the fact that in many cases a company could not continue to trade and obtain credit unless some of its creditors, which might include the company's parent, were willing to subordinate their indebtedness. In England, there are now several decisions in favour of the validity of subordination agreements. In the first, *Re Maxwell Communications Corp (No.2)*,[42] Vinelott J., after reviewing all of the relevant authorities, concluded that the principle laid down in *Halesowen* applied only to those rules the infringement of which would give one creditor an advantage denied to other creditors. A subordination agreement would not have this effect.[43] In the second case, *Re SSSL Realisations (2002) Ltd*,[44] Lloyd J. held that the validity of a subordination agreement was not affected by the fact that the subordinated creditor was also in insolvent liquidation.[45] To these considerations, one might add that the Insolvency Rules expressly recognise the right

---

[38] [1972] A.C. 785, Lord Cross of Chelsea dissenting.

[39] *British Eagle International Airlines Ltd v Compagnie Nationale Air France* [1975] 2 All E.R. 390.

[40] See, e.g. *Re Orion Sound Ltd* (1979) 2 N.Z.L.R. 574.

[41] See, e.g. *Horne v Chester & Fein Property Developments Pty Ltd* (1987) 11 A.C.L.R. 485.

[42] [1994] 1 B.C.L.C. 1.

[43] On the contrary, it could have precisely the opposite effect of benefiting all of the ordinary unsecured creditors, not merely the creditor in whose favour the subordination was agreed.

[44] [2005] 1 B.C.L.C. 1, affirmed on other issues [2006] Ch. 610.

[45] See also *Re Kaupthing Singer & Friedlander Ltd* [2010] EWHC 316 (Ch), per Blair J. at [10].

of a creditor to assign his right of dividend to another creditor,[46] which would typically occur in cases where the first creditor had agreed to be subordinated to the second. It would therefore be strange if the subordination agreement pursuant to which such an assignment was made were to be held invalid.

Moreover, a contract providing for contractual subordination of a company which later goes into liquidation cannot ordinarily be disclaimed as an unprofitable contract under s.178(3)(a) of the Insolvency Act, even though the subordination may be financially disadvantageous, because the contract does not by reason only of the subordination give rise to prospective liabilities, it does not require performance over a substantial period of time and it does not involve expenditure.[47]

Provisions for acceleration of liability on winding up

In the case of an executed contract, winding up automatically accelerates the **8–09** debt,[48] subject to a statutory discount to allow for the acceleration when a dividend distribution comes to be made.[49] But to cover cases where the contract is still executory at the time of winding up, so that the liquidator has the option to adopt it, the other party may seek to provide in the contract for acceleration of the company's liability in the event of its going into liquidation. In this case, the acceleration clause would appear to be of no effect, for if the liquidator were to adopt the contract, he would have to use the company's assets to make payment before the company could receive the benefit against which the payment was to have been made, whilst if he did not adopt it, the other party would be in the position of being able to prove for a supposed debt in respect of which payment had not been earned. This conclusion is reinforced by r.4.92 of the Insolvency Rules, under which a creditor may prove for rent and other payments of a periodical nature only so far as due and unpaid up to the date on which the company went into liquidation.[50]

The *pari passu* rule has two broad effects. First, it invalidates agreements **8–10** designed to give one creditor a benefit at the expense of the others when the

---

[46] Insolvency Rules 1986 r.11.11(1), which requires a liquidator who receives notice of the assignment to pay the dividend to the assignee.

[47] *Re SSSL Realisations Ltd* [2006] Ch. 610, affirming the decision of Lloyd J. [2005] 1 B.C.L.C. 1.

[48] See above, para.3–11.

[49] Insolvency Rules 1986 r.11.13(2). The same is true of administration (r.2.105). However, if the agreement itself provides for acceleration, the whole amount becomes provable without a discount.

[50] If the lease or contract under which the rent or other periodical sum is payable continues in force, so that the company receives the quid pro quo for the payment, the creditor can adjust his proof so as to claim for each further sum as it falls due. See above, para.6–22 and below para.8–41.

company goes into liquidation or administration.[51] Secondly, it provides the underpinning of other rules aimed at securing equality of distribution.

Impact of the *pari passu* principle on contracts

Direct payment clauses in building contracts

8–11   Building contracts commonly provide that in the event of a main contractor's insolvency the employer should be entitled to utilise sums that would otherwise be payable to the main contractor to make direct payment to sub-contractors of sums due to them from the main contractor.[52] Since the majority decision of the House of Lords in *British Eagle International Airlines Ltd v Cie Nationale Air France*,[53] such provisions have come under attack as procuring payment to the sub-contractor out of funds that should have been available to the general body of creditors, thus contravening the principle of *pari passu* distribution.[54] The first question to consider is whether the funds would, indeed, have been available to creditors. It seems clear that where payment to the sub-contractor was to be made from retention funds held for the benefit of the main contractor, there could be no infringement of the *pari passu* rule to the extent that prior to liquidation the main contractor had ceased to have an interest in the retention fund, because it had mortgaged such interest[55] or had agreed to hold it on trust for the sub-contractor.[56] More difficult is the case where the right to payment under the main contract remains vested in the main contractor, but the contract provides that the employer may withhold payment until all sub-contractors have been paid sums that have become payable to them under their sub-contracts and may pay direct to sub-contractors sums owing by the main contractor. Such was the position in *Att Gen v McMillan & Lockwood Ltd*,[57] which produced a division of opinion in the New Zealand Court of Appeal. The majority view was that upon the main contractor going into liquidation the continued application of the provision as to withholding of payment from the contractor and payment to sub-contractors was barred by the *pari passu* rule. The minority view, as expressed by Williamson J., was that the liquidator could not stand in any better position than the company had before it went into winding up and was therefore not entitled to disregard the withholding clause.[58] Williamson J.

---

[51] The benefit must be in favour of a creditor; if it is in favour of a party who is not a creditor, the rule to be applied is the anti-deprivation rule discussed in Ch.7.

[52] See para.6–17.

[53] [1975] 2 W.L.R. 758. See also paras 6–17 and 9–14.

[54] For a general discussion, see Michael G. Bridge, "Collectivity", cited above n.35, pp.26 et seq.

[55] *Drew & Co v Josolyne* (1887) 18 Q.B.D. 590.

[56] *Re Tout & Finch Ltd* [1954] 1 W.L.R. 178. See further para.6–17.

[57] [1991] 1 N.Z.L.R. 53.

[58] For an English decision to the same effect, see *Re Wilkinson* [1905] 2 K.B. 713.

considered that it was necessary to balance the various public policy considerations, and this led him to the conclusion that it would not be contrary to
public policy for the withholding clause to continue to operate after the company had gone into liquidation. This difference of view corresponds precisely
to that which featured in *British Eagle*, discussed earlier,[59] the majority decision of the New Zealand Court of Appeal following the majority decision of
the House of Lords in *British Eagle*.

It should be noted that if the Minister had made payments to sub-contractors prior to the main contractor's liquidation, these would not have been
affected by the *pari passu* rule, which, as noted earlier, has no backward
reach and bites only on provisions for payment unimplemented at the commencement of the winding up. However, the mere fact that the Minister's
power had become exercisable prior to the winding up was not sufficient;
once liquidation supervenes payment cannot be made to one creditor at the
expense of others, even if the liability to make the payment was incurred
before the commencement of the winding up.

Contractual set-off in favour of a third party

A contractual provision for set-off of claims by third parties against a debt   **8–12**
owed to the company is not valid on the company's liquidation, for set-off
is limited to mutual claims and to allow third-party set-off would be to sub-
vert the fundamental principle of *pari passu* distribution of the insolvent
company's assets.[60]

Provision for additional security

It is also a contravention of the *pari passu* principle for the debtor company   **8–13**
to undertake to give the creditor additional security in the event of the
company's liquidation.[61]

The *pari passu* rule as the principle underlying other rules

The *pari passu* rule has manifestations which go beyond contractual provisions.   **8–14**
It provides the underpinning for other insolvency rules relating to proof of debt.
Thus, the rule that claims are to be valued as at the date of commencement of

---

[59] Above, para.6–17 and below, para.9–14.
[60] *Re Bank of Credit and Commerce International SA* [1998] A.C. 214, per Lord Hoffmann at [5],
citing *British Eagle*, cited above n.39.
[61] *Re Thompson Ex p. Williams* (1877) 7 Ch.D. 138.

the winding up is designed to ensure that one is comparing like with like so that the assets are distributed *pari passu*.[62] The hotchpot rule, by which a creditor seeking to prove in the winding up of the company must bring into account any dividend he has received in a foreign liquidation of the company,[63] reflects the principle that the assets of a company in liquidation, after provision for liquidation expenses and preferential debts, are divided *pari passu* among the creditors.[64] Similarly, the rule against double proof, which precludes two parties, for example, a creditor and a surety from proving separately for the same debt, is a particular application of the principle that the debtor's assets are to be applied in payment to its creditors *pari passu*[65].

3. EXCEPTIONS TO THE PARI PASSU PRINCIPLE

8–15   The *pari passu* principle, although of fundamental importance, is not absolute. For reasons of policy, insolvency law provides certain deviations. But before considering these, I should like to mention cases which are often advanced as exceptions to the *pari passu* principle but which in reality involve an entirely different principle.[66]

False exceptions to the *pari passu* principle

8–16   The principle of *pari passu* distribution of assets does not apply to the rights of secured creditors, suppliers of goods under agreements reserving title or creditors for whom the company holds assets on trust.[67] However, this is not because these are exceptions to the rule but because such assets do not belong to the company[68] and thus do not fall to be distributed among creditors on any basis. While liquidation expenses, including liabilities under post-liquidation contracts, enjoy a super-priority,[69] they do not constitute an

---

[62] *Re Dynamics Corp of America* [1976] 1 W.L.R. 757, per Oliver L.J. at 764 in a passage cited with approval by the House of Lords in *Wight v Eckhart Marine GmbH* [2004] 1 A.C. 147 at [28].

[63] See below, para.15–69.

[64] *Cleaver v Delta American Reinsurance Co* [2001] 2 A.C. 328, per Lord Scott at [31].

[65] *Barclays Bank v T.O.S.G. Trust Fund Ltd* [1984] A.C. 626, per Oliver L.J. at 637.

[66] See also R.J. Mokal, *Corporate Insolvency Law: Theory and Practice*, pp.96 et seq.

[67] There is said to be one case in which moneys held on trust are subject to a right of set-off, namely where the solvent creditor holds property of the company with authority, still current at the time of winding up, to convert it into money; but this appears not to be a true exception, but rather to turn on an implied agreement that the solvent party is to be a debtor, not a trustee. See below para.9–26.

[68] In the case of assets subject to a security interest, the assets do not belong to the company to the extent of the security interest, but the company does, of course, have an equity of redemption.

[69] See below, para.8–32.

exception to the *pari passu* rule either, for they are not provable debts existing at the date of the winding up order, merely costs incurred later in the
conduct of the liquidation.[70] Exceptionally, an insolvent employer's liability
for a shortfall in pension fund assets, although arising after the employer's
liquidation, is by statute treated as arising immediately before the liquidation
and is thus governed by the *pari passu* principle.[71]

True exceptions to the *pari passu* principle

There are a number of true exceptions to the *pari passu* principle. They fall   **8–17**
broadly into four categories: rights which are analogous to security, such as
set-off; claims which in the distribution of dividend are given preferential
treatment over ordinary unsecured debts, such as various kinds of claim by
employees; claims which are deferred, ranking below those of the general
body of creditors; and other departures from the *pari passu* principle
expressly or implicitly authorised by statute or by principles of equity. These
deviations from the *pari passu* principle are based on a combination of history, policy and pragmatism and reflect a wide range of considerations: the
protection of legitimate expectations, such as set-off; the desire to provide
safeguards for those who have not voluntarily assumed a risk and are ill-
equipped to provide for it, such as employees, and conversely the wish to
subordinate the claims of those who are expected to bear a higher risk than
the general body of creditors, such as shareholders and those who while
engaged in the management of the company were guilty of improper conduct
to the detriment of creditors; the facilitation of arrangements among
creditors; and international comity in the recognition of the rules of foreign
insolvency proceedings.

(1) Set-off

Where, before the company goes into liquidation, there have been mutual   **8–18**
credits, mutual debits or other mutual dealings between the company and
any creditor of the company proving or claiming to prove in the liquidation,
an account is to be taken of what is due from each party to the other in
respect of the mutual dealings, and the sums due from one party are to be
set-off against the other, only the balance being provable in the liquidation
or (as the case may be) paid to the liquidator.[72] Set-off on insolvency repre-

---

[70] *Re HIH Casualty & General Insurance Ltd* [2006] 2 All E.R. 671, per David Richards J. at [40].
[71] See below, para.8–36.
[72] Insolvency Rules 1986 r.4.90(1), (3), (8). To the extent that the balance payable to the liquidator results from a contingent or prospective debt, it is to be paid only when the debt has
become due (r.4.90(8)). See below, para.9–36.

sents a major incursion into the *pari passu* principle, for its effect is that a creditor who owes money to the company on a separate account may resort to self-help by setting off the debt due to him against his own indebtedness to the company, thus ensuing payment of his claim pro tanto ahead of other creditors.[73] The policy justification for allowing set-off is that each of the two parties engaged in mutual dealings extends credit in reliance on his ability to take what is due to him out of what he owes, without which he would not have extended credit in the first place. So insolvency set-off responds to the principle of respecting legitimate expectations. The effect of Ch.10 of Pt 2 of the Insolvency Rules 1986 is that a similar principle applies in administration.[74]

On winding up, the insolvency set-off rules displace other forms of set-off, including contractual set-off, not previously exercised. But set-offs implemented before winding up remain effective, and parties to mutual dealings frequently seek to reduce insolvency risk by netting agreements which reduce their mutual obligations to a single balance of indebtedness. The subject of set-off and netting is of great importance and not inconsiderable complexity and is dealt with in the next chapter.

(2) Claims which by statute are given priority

8–19   These are the preferential debts listed in Sch.6 to the Insolvency Act. Preferential debts rank *pari passu* among themselves.[75] Although the priority of preferential debts has to be respected by liquidators and administrators, this applies only in relation to the company's assets, not assets contributed by a third party such as a purchaser of the insolvent company.[76]

PREFERENTIAL DEBTS GENERALLY

8–20   Preferential debts were formerly of two kinds: sums payable to the Crown, for example, for taxes, and sums due to employees. Crown preference was strongly criticised by the Cork Committee as causing hardship to the general body of creditors while producing benefits insignificant in terms of total government receipts,[77] although the Committee did accept that there was a case

---

[73] It is also possible to regard set-off as a false exception to the *pari passu* principle in that it constitutes an equity qualifying the claim of the company in liquidation, so that only what is left after allowing for the set-off represents an asset available for distribution among the general body of creditors.

[74] *Re Kaupthing Singer & Friedlander Ltd* [2010] Bus. L.R. 1500.

[75] It seems that, apart from classical Roman law, English insolvency law is unique in not ranking preferential debts inter se. See the interesting comparative survey by José M. Garrido, "The Distributional Question in Insolvency: Comparative Aspects" (1995) 4 I.I.R. 25, 50.

[76] *IRC v Wimbledon Football Club Ltd* [2005] B.C.L.C. 66.

[77] *Insolvency Law and Practice*, Report of the (Cork) Review Committee(Cmnd. 8558, 1982), paras 1409 et seq.

for retaining Crown preference for collected taxes, that is, taxes collected by the taxpayer for the Crown by invoice (as in the case of value added tax) or deduction (as in the case of PAYE and national insurance contributions), on the basis that in substance, although not in law, these were trust moneys for which the debtor company was to be accountable as a tax collector rather than pay as a taxpayer,[78] as opposed to assessed taxes, such as income tax and corporation tax. The government accepted this view, and the legislation was changed to abolish the Crown's preferential status as regards assessed taxes by omitting these from Sch.6 to the Insolvency Act 1986. With the enactment of the Enterprise Act 2002[79] the Crown's preferential status was abolished altogether, so that even collected taxes are no longer preferential, leaving only the claims of employees as preferential debts. However, the Crown's right of subrogation to preferential debts of employees paid from the National Insurance Fund remains.[80] The abolition of Crown preference, which in the absence of other measures would have increased the amount of assets available to the holder of a floating charge, was counter-balanced by provisions requiring a percentage of assets subject to a floating charge to be surrendered for the benefit of unsecured creditors, the percentage being fixed at a figure roughly comparable to the benefit conferred on the holder of a floating charge by no longer being subordinate to Crown claims for unpaid taxes and the like.[81]

In relation to employees, the Cork Committee, rejecting the submission of the Trades Union Congress that all debts due to employees in respect of wages or salaries should be preferential without any limitation in amount or extent, noted that there had been substantial improvements in the position of wage earners through the introduction of unemployment pay, earnings-related benefits, severance and redundancy payments and other social security benefits, coupled with the ability, under the Employment Protection Acts, to obtain immediate payment of claims out of what was then the Redundancy Fund.[82] The Committee therefore contented itself with recommending that the financial hardship to employees through the insolvency of the employer should in future be dealt with under the employment protection legislation through its provisions for claims on the Redundancy Fund, not by overlapping provisions of the insolvency code, and that the existing financial and other limits should be reconsidered and, where lower, brought into line with what was then provided under preferential debt provisions contained in s.319 of the Companies Act 1948.[83] This recommendation to

---

[78] Cmnd. 8558, 1982, para.1418.
[79] Section 251, which provided that the relevant paragraphs of Sch.6 to the Insolvency Act should cease to have effect.
[80] See below, para.8–21.
[81] See above, para.6–38.
[82] Cmnd. 8558, 1982, paras 1428–1430. The fund is now the National Insurance Fund.
[83] *Insolvency Law and Practice* (above, n. 77), paras 1432–1433.

eliminate the preferential status of employees under insolvency law and ensure that at least equivalent claims could be made on the Redundancy Fund instead was not adopted. Although both the previous statutes have been repealed, the general position remains broadly what it was before.

There can be no doubt that employees do deserve special protection.[84] Very often their wages or salaries are their sole source of income. The loss of employment can thus have a devastating effect on them and their families, an effect exacerbated by their employer's non-payment of their entitlements. The relationship between employee and employer is a continuing relationship requiring mutual trust and confidence and it is a relationship in which the employee is very clearly the subordinate. Moreover, without the work of the employees, the employer's business would not function and creditors would not get paid. Yet there remains much force in the view of the Cork Committee that other creditors can also find themselves in the position of being involuntary creditors (to which one might add that small trade suppliers, who are often in a very weak bargaining position when dealing with large companies, are contributing value in the same way as employees) and that the right way to protect employees from the effects of their employer's insolvency is through the National Insurance Fund and social security benefits. However, there seems little prospect of any radical change in the system.

CLAIMS UNDER THE NATIONAL INSURANCE FUND

8–21   The employee has preferential status within defined limits under Sch.6 to the Insolvency Act 1986 and has a parallel right to make a claim on the National Insurance Fund.[85] However, the latter right is more restricted in scope than under the Insolvency Act. To the extent that recoveries from the National Insurance Fund do not exhaust his rights as a preferential creditor under the 1986 Act, the employee can rely on his preferential status and then prove as an ordinary unsecured creditor for any balance. Where the Secretary of State makes a payment from the National Insurance Fund, he is subrogated to the rights of the employee in the winding up and to the extent that such payment is in respect of a debt that is preferential under the Insolvency Act, he stands in the shoes of the employee as a preferential creditor.[86] This runs counter to the recommendations of the Cork Report,[87] but the reason given—"it is thought desirable that more funds should be left for the unsecured creditors"—is unconvincing, since there seems to be no reason why the

---

[84] See Vanessa Finch, *Corporate Insolvency Law*, 2nd edn (Cambridge: Cambridge University Press, 2009), Ch.17.

[85] For a detailed treatment of the rights of employees on the employer's insolvency, see Finch, *Corporate Insolvency Law*, 2009, Ch.17.

[86] Employment Rights Act 1996 s.189(2); and Pension Schemes Act 1993 s.127(3). These are specific examples of a broader right of subrogation to preferential claims. See below.

[87] Cited above n.77, para.1343.

general body of creditors, who would have been subordinated to claims of the employees themselves, should find themselves in a better position because such claims have been met by the Crown.

CATEGORIES OF EMPLOYEES' PREFERENTIAL RIGHT

The preferential rights of employees fall into two broad categories. The first **8–22** consist of any sum owed by the insolvent employer in respect of unpaid employer's and employees' contributions to an occupational pension scheme where these fall within Sch.4 to the Pension Schemes Act 1993[88] (as amended by s.90 of the Pensions Act 1995).[89] These rights are now buttressed by the Pension Protection Fund established under the Pensions Act 2004[90] and by the duty of the Board of the Fund to assume responsibility for the pension scheme in certain conditions.[91] The second category of employees' preferential rights consists of unpaid remuneration, holiday remuneration and related employment rights in respect of the whole or any part of the period of four months next before the relevant date,[92] but with a maximum of £800.[93] Crucial to the determination of preferential debts is the concept of the relevant date, which features in several paragraphs of Sch.6 to the Insolvency Act and is defined in s.387. Four types of event are capable of providing a trigger for preferential status and, in theory at least, this could produce four different relevant dates, necessitating a separate computation of preferential debts as at each such date.[94]

SUBROGATION

Reference has already been made to the Crown's right of subrogation where **8–23** it meets preferential claims of employees from the National Insurance Fund. A more general provision in Sch.6 to the Insolvency Act gives preferential status to so much of any sum owed in respect of money advanced for the purpose as has been applied for the payment of a debt which, if it had not been paid, would have been a debt falling within paras 9 to 10 of the Schedule, i.e. as remuneration or holiday remuneration.[95] The effect is similar to that produced by subrogation of the lender to the employee's preferential rights. In a case on a similar, although not quite identical, provision in Australian

---

[88] Insolvency Act 1986 Sch.6 para.8.
[89] See David Pollard and Isobel Carruthers, "Pensions as a Preferential Debt" *Insolvency Intelligence*, May 2004, p.65.
[90] Pensions Act 2004 s.173.
[91] Pensions Act 2004 s.127.
[92] Insolvency Act 1986 Sch.6 Category 5 paras 9 and 13. "The relevant date" is defined by s.387.
[93] Insolvency Proceedings (Monetary Limits) Order 1986, SI 1986/1996, art.4.
[94] See below, para.10–61.
[95] Insolvency Act 1986 Sch.6 para.11.

legislation, it has been held that the preferential wages claim must be shown to have been discharged from the sum lent; it does not suffice that it is discharged from a general fund constituted by an account in which the sum lent was commingled with other moneys so as to make it impossible to identify the loan as the source of payment.[96]

TUPE 2006

8–24 It may be noted that the normal protection given by TUPE 2006 to employees of a transferred business, by which employees' contracts were transferred to the purchaser of the business, does not apply to any transfer of an undertaking where the transfer is the subject of bankruptcy proceedings or any analogous insolvency proceedings which have been instituted with a view to the liquidation of the assets and are under the supervision of a competent public authority (which may be an insolvency practitioner authorised by a competent public authority).[97] This amendment to TUPE and the implementing regulations are designed to make it easier for businesses of insolvent companies to be sold, although there is much uncertainty as to their scope of application.[98]

EC Insolvency Directive

8–25 Finally, mention should be made of a further aspect of EC law relevant to these issues. Article 8 of the EC Insolvency Directive[99] imposes on Member States an obligation to protect the interests of employees when their employer becomes insolvent. In *Robins v Secretary of State for Work and Pensions*,[100] the European Court of Justice (ECJ), in a preliminary ruling, held that the Directive does not require Member States themselves to fund the rights to benefits that had to be protected (a Member State might, for example, require the employer to insure its liabilities to employees), nor does it require a full guarantee of the various rights of employees, but it does require an unspecified minimum level of protection which the UK legislation had failed to provide, so that Art.8 had not been adequately implemented. It

---

[96] *Capt'n Snooze Management Pty Ltd v McLellan* [2002] V.S.C. 432.
[97] Acquired Rights Directive 2001/23, implemented by reg.8(7) of the Transfer of Undertakings Regulations 2006 SI 2006/246.
[98] See, e.g. *OTG Ltd v Barke* [2011] I.R.L.R. 272, holding that TUPE applied on a transfer by a company in administration, which fell outside the insolvency exemption, and declining to follow *Oakland v Wellswood (Yorkshire) Ltd* [2010] B.C.C. 263, which itself had been appealed on other grounds [2010] ICR 902. See also Finch, *Corporate Insolvency Law*, 2009, Ch.17.
[99] Council Directive 80/97 EEC of October 20, 1980 on the approximation of the laws of Member States relating to the protection of employees in the event of the insolvency of their employer ([1980] OJ L283/23).
[100] Case C-278/05, [2007] 2 C.M.L.R. 13.

was for the High Court to determine, in the light of criteria set out in the judgment of the ECJ, whether the UK Government had been guilty of a manifest and serious disregard for the limits set on its discretion.[101]

(3) Post-liquidation interest

Any surplus remaining after the payment of debts proved in a winding up must first be applied in payment of post-liquidation interest,[102] all post-liquidation interest claims ranking *pari passu*. All such claims rank ahead of deferred debts.

8–26

(4) Claims which by statute are deferred

Various categories of deferred debt are prescribed by statute.[103] We need not consider them here except to draw attention to: (i) the power of the court, when making a declaration in relation to a director of a company under s.213 or 214 of the Insolvency Act 1986,[104] to direct that the whole or any part of any debt owed to him by the company shall rank in priority after all other debts owed by the company and after interest on those debts[105]; (ii) the sub-ordination of claims by shareholders or other members of the company which are held in their capacity as members,[106] as opposed to their capacity as creditors[107]; and (iii) in the case of assets subject to a floating charge created on or after September 15, 2003, the obligatory surrender of a prescribed percentage in value of the net property subject to the floating charge so as to make this available to unsecured creditors.[108]

8–27

---

[101] See also *Independent Trustee Services Ltd v Hope* [2010] I.C.R. 553, where Henderson J. expressed the view that it was all but inconceivable that a cap on the liability of the Pension Protection Fund, imposed partly to deal with moral hazard, would be considered by the ECJ to be a contravention of Art.8.

[102] Insolvency Act 1986 s.189(2).

[103] See Companies Act 2006 s.735; Insolvency Act 1986 s.74(2)(f) (see n.106 below); and Insolvency Rules 1986 r.12.3(2A). As to deferment of floating charges, see above, paras 6–38 et seq.

[104] Relating respectively to fraudulent trading and wrongful trading by such person.

[105] Insolvency Act 1986 s.215(4). See also s.215(2)(a), which enables the court to impose a statutory charge-back to the company on debts owed by the company to him. See below, para.14–51.

[106] Insolvency Act 1986 s.74(2)(f), which subordinates sums due to a member of a company (in his character as a member) by way of dividends, profits or otherwise, a provision held to be confined to claims linked to membership—e.g. sums due on a reduction of capital approved by the court or on an authorised redemption of preference shares—rather than independent contractual claims. For a survey of the relevant authorities, see *Soden v British & Commonwealth Holdings Plc* [1998] A.C. 298.

[107] See below.

[108] See above, para.6–38.

The subordination of claims of a shareholder in his capacity as such is of long standing and is based on the fact that as a member he has contracted that the company's assets are to be applied in satisfaction of its debts, and it would be inconsistent with that contract to allow him to obtain satisfaction of his claim from those assets while external creditors remain unpaid.[109] So where a person is induced by a misrepresentation of the company to subscribe for shares in it, his claim against the company is subordinated unless he rescinds the contract with the company for the purchase of the shares.[110] But claims which a *transferee* has against the company for a misrepresentation inducing him to buy the transferred shares are not claims vested in him qua member and are thus not subordinated.[111] Similarly, a loan by a company to its subsidiary is not subordinated, for the parent company's claim is as creditor, not as shareholder, and the same applies to directors' remuneration.[112]

It would seem that debts are deferred only if so prescribed by statute. In the United States, the courts developed the doctrine of equitable subordination, primarily directed at loans by a parent company to a greatly undercapitalised subsidiary. In general, three conditions have to be satisfied in order for the court to apply the doctrine of equitable subordination, namely: (i) the subordinated creditor must have engaged in some type of inequitable conduct; (ii) such conduct must have resulted in injury to other creditors or conferred an unfair advantage on the subordinated creditor; and (iii) equitable subordination must not be inconsistent with the provisions of the Bankruptcy Act.[113] The doctrine is now incorporated by reference in s.510(c) of the Federal Bankruptcy Code.[114] It does not appear to have been applied so far in common law jurisdictions outside the United States, although in

---

[109] *Re Addlestone Linoleum Co* (1887) 37 Ch.D. 191; *Houldsworth v City of Glasgow Bank* (1880) 5 App. Cas. 317; and *Webb Distributors (Aust) Pty Ltd v State of Victoria* (1993) 179 C.L.R. 15. This principle seems unaffected by s.655 of the Companies Act 2006, which in providing that membership of a company does not deprive a person of his right to claim damages against the company appears merely to have been intended to confer a right previously unavailable even against a company not in winding up. See *Re Addlestone Linoleum Co*, per Kay J. at 199–200.

[110] Insolvency Act 1986 s.74(2)(f). But rescission ceases to be possible once the company is in winding up (*Re Addlestone Linoleum*, cited above n.109; and *Southern British National Trust Ltd v Pither* (1937) 57 C.L.R. 89, per Dixon J. at 113). In *Sons of Gwalia Ltd v Margaretic* (2007) 232 A.L.R. 232, the High Court of Australia reached a different conclusion on a similar provision in s.563A of the Corporations Act 2001 (Cth), but the Federal Government quickly announced its intention to reverse the decision by legislation because of its potential negative impact on business rescue procedures and debt financing.

[111] *Soden*, cited above n.106; and *Re Media World Communications Ltd, Crosbie v Nadoo* [2005] F.C.A. 51 (Finkelstein J., Federal Court of Australia). For a note on the case, which has apparently spread alarm among US investors into Australia, see Oren Bigos, "Are Shareholders' Claims Provable in Administration?" (2005) 13 Insol. L.J. 115.

[112] *Re Dale and Plant Ltd* (1889) 43 Ch.D. 255; and *Soden*, cited above n.106, per Lord Browne-Wilkinson at 324.

[113] *Re Mobil Steel Co*, 563 F.2d 692 (5th Cir. 1977).

[114] Jay Lawrence Westbrook and Elizabeth Warren, *The Law of Debtors and Creditors: Text, Cases and Problems*, 6th edn (Frederick MD: Aspen Law Publishers, 2008), p.576.

Canada Deposit Insurance Corp v Canadian Commercial Bank (No.3),[115] the Supreme Court of Canada, while declining to apply the doctrine on the facts of the case before it, was at least prepared to entertain arguments as to its applicability. Since then, lower courts have been divided on the applicability of the doctrine in Canadian law. English law appears not to have evolved any doctrine of equitable subordination, no doubt because the statutory provisions, and in particular those enabling the court to subordinate claims of creditor-directors found guilty of fraudulent or wrongful trading,[116] are thought to give the court all of the powers it needs.

(5) Arrangements

A statutory scheme of arrangement may modify creditors' rights in any way thought appropriate to the circumstances so long as it is within the powers of the company and if the scheme is approved by the requisite majority of creditors and by the court, it is binding on all creditors and shareholders whether or not they consented.[117] In this situation, the *pari passu* rule may be overridden. The same applies to a company voluntary arrangement.[118]

8–28

(6) Financial and money markets

There are special categories of contract related to the operation of financial and money markets, exchanges and clearing houses, which in varying degrees are protected from attack under insolvency law.[119]

8–29

(7) Environmental liability

The question may arise of clean-up liability under legislation enacted for the protection of the environment.[120] If the company's operations before winding up have caused damage to the environment, for example, through oil pollution or land contamination, can the relevant regulatory body require the liquidator to apply the assets of the company to remedy the damage in

8–30

---

[115] (1993) 97 D.L.R. (4th) 385 at 419–422.
[116] Insolvency Act 1986 s.215(4) (see below, para.14–51).
[117] See para.12–24.
[118] See para.12–45.
[119] See above, paras 1–60 et seq.
[120] Environmental Damage (Prevention and Remediation) Regulations 2009, SI 2009/153, implementing Directive 2004/35/EC of the European Parliament and Council on environmental liability with regard to the preventing and remedying of environmental damage, which supplement the Environmental Protection Act 1990. See Totty and Moss, *Insolvency*, Ch.H1.

priority to the claims of other creditors? Alternatively, if the regulatory body carries out the remedial works itself, can it exercise its statutory right of recoupment from the offending company ahead of the claims of other creditors? Again, if the liquidator, for the purpose of beneficial winding up, continues operations which cause environmental damage, to what extent are assets of the company that would otherwise be available for creditors required to be utilised to meet a clean-up order or to recompense the relevant body for the cost of remedial works it has itself undertaken? Does a lender face potential liability if it has taken security over the polluting asset?[121] Astonishingly, despite the fact that such issues have long been known in relation to environmental protection legislation both in the United States and in Canada, UK legislation is entirely silent on these crucial questions.[122] Much depends on how the court decides to characterise the liability. Is it to be equated with an ordinary unsecured debt so as to be provable (or in the case of post-liquidation activity, payable as an expense of the liquidation), or is it to be treated quite separately as a public liability carrying a distinctive priority?

Such cases as there are have examined this question in the context of disclaimer of a waste management licence as onerous property. In two decisions, *Celtic Extraction Ltd, Re*[123] and *Minister for the Environment and Local Government v Irish ISPAT Ltd*,[124] the latter in Ireland, where the wording of the legislation is somewhat different, it has been held that a waste management licence is property and that there is no reason of public policy why it cannot be disclaimed in the same way as any other onerous property.[125] In the former case, it was held that the "polluter pays" principle cannot be applied to cases where the polluter cannot pay so as to preclude disclaimer and thereby require payment to be made by unsecured creditors out of the assets available for distribution to them in priority to their own claims in the liquidation.[126] In the Irish decision, it was pointed out that the liquidator holds the assets of the company on trust for creditors, so that the "polluter pays" principle cannot be achieved. Where the liquidator takes over the licence for the benefit of the liquidation, on general principles the cost of fulfilling the conditions of the licence would seem to be an expense of the liquidation, but if the liquidator is simply completing work in progress as liquidator rather than taking over or adopting the licence for the benefit of the

---

[121] Prudent lenders usually undertake a "green audit" with a view to satisfying themselves on this question before making an advance on such property.

[122] It has to be said that UK legislative activity in the field of corporate insolvency law has long been characterised by the failure, when the new legislation is introduced, to take the opportunity to resolve significant and well-known problems arising even under the pre-existing law in the United Kingdom itself.

[123] [2001] Ch. 465, overruling in part the decision of Neuberger J. in *Re Mineral Resources Ltd* [1999] 1 All E.R. 746.

[124] July 29, 2004, Carroll J. (Irish High Court).

[125] As to this, see above, paras 6–27 et seq.

[126] [2001] Ch. 475, per Morritt L.J. at [39].

liquidation, there is no basis for giving the claim for such cost priority and disapplying the normal rule of *pari passu* distribution.[127]

The above cases establish that there is no reason of public policy why a liquidator should not be permitted to disclaim a waste management licence as onerous property and thereby avoid applying the company's assets to the continuing cost of compliance with the environmental requirements. As yet, there appear to have been no decisions on the effect of service of a remediation notice where there is no disclaimer. In such a case, although the liquidator incurs no personal liability,[128] he faces the dilemma that either the company fails to comply with the remediation notice, thereby attracting sanctions, or the funds that would otherwise be available to unsecured creditors have to be utilised to meet the costs of compliance. It remains to be seen how the courts will approach this situation.

(8) Foreign liquidation and international comity

The principle of international comity by which an English court, in an insolvency proceeding ancillary to a main liquidation in a foreign jurisdiction, will give assistance to the courts of that jurisdiction enables the court in an appropriate case to disapply parts of the statutory scheme by ordering remission of assets by the English liquidator to the principal liquidator for distribution under the laws of that jurisdiction, even though its rules of distribution are different from those prescribed by English insolvency law.[129]   **8–31**

4. LIQUIDATION EXPENSES

Liquidation expenses generally

The expenses properly incurred in the winding up, including the remuneration of the liquidator, are payable out of the assets in priority to all other claims,[130] including those of the holder of a floating charge,[131] but litigation   **8–32**

---

[127] *Minister for the Environment and Local Government v Irish ISPAT Ltd*, above.

[128] Environmental Protection Act 1990 s.78X(3) and (4)(a).

[129] *Re HIH Casualty*, cited above n.70. However, their Lordships were divided on the question of whether such jurisdiction derived solely from s.426 of the Insolvency Act 1986 or arose under the inherent jurisdiction of the court at common law. See below, para.16–61.

[130] Insolvency Act 1986 ss.115 (voluntary winding up) and 175(2)(a) (compulsory winding up).

[131] Insolvency Act 1986 s.176ZA, reversing the decision of the House of Lords in *Buchler v Talbot* [2004] 2 A.C. 298. However, the provisions of the Insolvency Act relating to the payment of the liquidator's or administrator's remuneration, expenses and liabilities are disapplied in relation to financial collateral arrangements (Financial Collateral Arrangements (No.2) Regs 2003 (SI 2003/3226), regs 8, 9 and 11, as amended by SI 2010/2993).

expenses do not have that priority over claims to property comprised in a floating charge unless the requisite approval of the holder of the floating charge and of preferential creditors has been obtained.[132] Liquidation expenses are paid, not proved; that is to say, the liquidator discharges such expenses in full from the assets as payment accrues due, instead of the post-liquidation creditors having to prove for a dividend in competition with other creditors.[133]

8–33   In determining what constitutes liquidation expenses, it is necessary to distinguish liabilities incurred post-liquidation, including liabilities under post-liquidation contracts, from continuing post-liquidation liabilities derived from pre-liquidation contracts.[134] The former are automatically liquidation expenses, regardless whether the expenditure, so far as properly incurred, does in fact benefit the administration[135]; the latter qualify as liquidation expenses only so far as falling within the *Lundy Granite* principle.[136] The order in which liquidation expenses are to be paid is prescribed by r.4.218 of the Insolvency Rules 1986, but may be adjusted by the court under s.156 of the Act, a power preserved by r.4.220(1). But apart from adjusting the order of priority, the court has no discretion as to the categories of expense that are payable as expenses of the liquidation and is bound to treat as liquidation expenses all of the expenses listed in r.4.218.[137]

In *Re Atlantic Computer Systems Plc*,[138] Nicholls L.J.: (i) assimilated the treatment of debts arising under post-liquidation contracts with continuing post-liquidation obligations arising under pre-liquidation contracts; (ii) ruled that the characterisation of these as expenses of the liquidation was dependent on the discretion of the court; and (iii) treated the same principles as applicable to administration. However, points (i) and (ii) were rejected by the House of Lords in *Re Toshoku Finance UK Plc*.[139] Tracing the history of the treatment of liquidation expenses, Lord Hoffmann pointed out that a line of cases clearly distinguished liabilities incurred during the winding up from those arising under pre-liquidation contracts. The former had to be paid as expenses of the liquidation; the latter were dependent on the application of the *Lundy Granite* principle, an equitable principle by which a

---

[132] Insolvency Rules 1986 r.4.218A(2). See below as to such expenses.
[133] See further below, para.8–35.
[134] See below, paras 8–35 and 8–38.
[135] *Re Toshoku Finance UK Plc* [2002] 1 W.L.R. 671, per Lord Hoffmann at [30], pointing out that there may simply be liabilities which the liquidator has to pay, e.g. fees charged by the Insolvency Service.
[136] See below, para.8–38.
[137] *Toshoku Finance UK*, cited above n.135, disapproving of passages to the contrary in the judgment of Nicholls L.J. in *Re Atlantic Computer Systems Plc* [1992] Ch. 505 at 523, overruling the decision in *Re Kentish Homes Ltd* [1993] B.C.L.C. 1375 and approving the decision in *Re Mesco Properties Ltd* [1980] 1 W.L.R. 96. See further below, paras 8–38 and, as to the application of the rules in administration, para.11–104.
[138] [1992] Ch. 505.
[139] [2002] 3 All E.R. 961.

liquidator was required to pay liabilities incurred by him in respect of property he retained for the benefit of the liquidation.[140] So if the liquidator occupied rateable premises, the rates attracted became payable as an expense of the liquidation whether the liquidator was using them for the benefit of the winding up or was merely in passive occupation, and the principle in *Lundy Granite* had no role to play.[141] By contrast, rent accruing after liquidation under a pre-liquidation lease was in principle provable as a debt, not payable, and only if and for the period that the liquidator's occupation was for the benefit of the liquidation so as to attract the *Lundy Granite* principle would such rent be treated as an expense of the liquidation.[142] The general principle established by *Toshoko* is that where by statute Parliament imposes a financial liability which is not a provable debt (and this includes post-liquidation liabilities), it constitutes an expense of the liquidation ranking as a "necessary disbursement" within r.2.67(1)(f) (administration) or r.4.218(3)(m) (liquidation).[143]

Litigation and litigation expenses

Not infrequently, it is necessary for a liquidator to institute proceedings, either in the name of the company for some cause of action vested in the company, such as a claim against a director for breach of fiduciary duty or against a third party for breach of contract, or in his own name, for proceedings which he alone can bring, for example, against directors for a contribution order for fraudulent or wrongful trading under s.213 or 214 of the Insolvency Act 1986. In a compulsory winding up, such proceedings need the sanction of the court or the liquidation committee,[144] which can be given retrospectively.[145] By contrast, in a voluntary winding up the liquidator can bring such proceedings without the sanction either of the court or of the liquidation committee, but this does not apply to proceedings under ss.213, 214, 238, 239, 242, 243 or 423, for which the liquidator must obtain the sanction of the court or the liquidation committee.[146]

8–34

One of the concerns of the liquidator, whether in a voluntary or compulsory winding up, is how to cover the costs of the litigation. The liquidator naturally wishes to have his costs covered in full, while creditors are

---

[140] See below, para.8–38.
[141] Citing *Re Watson, Kipling & Co* (1883) 23 Ch.D. 500. Rates are no longer payable on unoccupied, non-domestic property of a prescribed class (Non-Domestic Rating (Unoccupied Property) (England) Regulations 2008, SI 2008/386).
[142] Citing *Re ABC Coupler & Engineering Co Ltd (No.3)* [1970] 1 All E.R. 650; and *Re Downer Enterprises Ltd* [1974] 2 All E.R. 1074.
[143] *Bloom v Pensions Regulator* [2010] EWHC 3010 (Ch), per Briggs J. at [135].
[144] See now Insolvency Act 1986 Sch.4 Pt II.
[145] *Gresham International Ltd v Moonie* [2010] Ch. 285.
[146] Insolvency Act 1986 Sch.4 para.3A.

concerned to ensure that assets available for distribution will not be frittered away in legal costs in pursuing claims that might be unsuccessful or, even if successful, might not lead to recovery from the defendant. In particular, preferential creditors and holders of floating charges would not wish the liquidator to utilise assets that are sufficient to pay their claims in full without proceedings to pursue litigation which could be of no benefit to them, only to ordinary, unsecured creditors. A revision of the Insolvency Rules now addresses these concerns by providing, in a rather elaborate set of provisions, that where the liquidator is of the opinion that the assets of the company available for general creditors are or will be insufficient to pay litigation expenses (defined so as to be confined to expenses exceeding £5,000) and that in order to pay these he will have to have recourse to property comprised in a floating charge, litigation costs may not be paid out of assets subject to the floating charge without the approval or authorisation of the amount of the litigation expenses by those creditors who are (i) holders of the floating charge and (ii) preferential creditors, and who would be the creditors most immediately likely to receive some payment in respect of their claims, but not be paid in full.[147] Authority is not required from preferential creditors who would be paid in full anyway even after taking account of the liquidation expenses.[148] In urgent cases, the liquidator can apply to the court for approval or authorisation without seeking it from the above creditors.[149]

At one time, the liquidator was not entitled to be indemnified in respect of costs incurred in pursuing claims for fraudulent or wrongful trading, transactions at an undervalue and the like, because recoveries were not assets of the company. But that has now changed so as to cover proceeds of any legal action which the liquidator has power to bring in his own name or in the name of the company,[150] so that if sanction is obtained for such proceedings, the costs properly chargeable or incurred may be recouped as expenses of the liquidation in priority to the claims of all creditors other than holders of a fixed charge.

Post-liquidation creditors: new contracts

8–35 The liquidator of a company cannot simply procure an instantaneous cessation of activity. He may need to continue trading so far as may be necessary for the

---

[147] Insolvency Rules 1986 r.4.218B. See generally Andrew R. Keay, *McPherson's Law of Company Liquidation*, 2nd edn (London: Sweet & Maxwell, 2009), para.13.024. As to the legal proceedings covered by this, see Insolvency Rules 1986 r.4.218A(1)(c).

[148] The rules are not explicit as to taking account of liquidation expenses, but this is clearly the intention, for if these were to result in a shortfall for the preferential creditors they would have a legitimate interest in giving or withholding their approval.

[149] Insolvency Rules 1986 r.4.218E(3).

[150] Insolvency Rules 1986 r.4.218(2)(a)(i).

beneficial winding up of the company,[151] and in any event it will be necessary for a limited period to retain some staff, procure the continuance of supplies of goods and services and enter into new contracts. These are all activities conducted for the benefit of the existing creditors, but it is obvious that the liquidator cannot expect fresh goods and services to be supplied for nothing; there is no reason why parties to post-liquidation transactions should be expected to subsidise existing creditors and if asked to do so they would simply decline to do business. It follows that post-liquidation creditors have to be treated differently from pre-liquidation creditors. In doing business with them, the liquidator has perforce to engage the company's assets. This is achieved by classifying his obligations under post-liquidation transactions as expenses of the liquidation, which as stated above are payable out of the assets rather than being provable and ranking ahead of the claims of preferential and other unsecured creditors.[152] This priority has never been dependent on the *Lundy Granite* principle described below relating to post-liquidation claims arising under pre-liquidation contracts[153]; expenses incurred after the liquidation date need no further equitable reason why they should be paid.[154]

Liability of insolvent employer for shortfall in pension fund assets

Where an insolvency event occurs in relation to an employer, including liquidation, the employer comes under a liability to make good any shortfall in the pension fund assets of any defined benefit occupational pension scheme it runs.[155] If the legislation had stopped there, such liability, being post-liquidation, would have been payable as an expense of the liquidation in accordance with the principles set out above. However, as a matter of policy, Parliament chose to avoid this result by deeming the liability to be incurred immediately before the occurrence of the insolvency event. The effect is to make this liability provable within r.13.12(1) of the Insolvency Rules 1986, not payable as an expense of the liquidation, although it ranks as a non-preferential debt.[156] However, rather remarkably, this result can be

8–36

---

[151] A power he may exercise without sanction in the case of a voluntary winding up and with the sanction of the court in the case of a compulsory winding up (Insolvency Act 1986 s.167(1)(a) and Sch.4 Pt II para.5).

[152] This is provided directly in the case of voluntary winding up by s.115 of the Insolvency Act 1986 and indirectly in the case of both forms of winding up by r.4.180(1) of the Insolvency Rules 1986, which imposes on the liquidator the duty to distribute dividends "subject to the retention of such sums as may be necessary for the expenses of the winding up". Rule 12.2 lists the items that are to be regarded as expenses of the winding up and r.4.218 sets out the order of priority in which expenses of the winding up are to be paid, subject to the court's powers under s.156 of the Act and r.4.219 of the Insolvency Rules.

[153] See below, para.8–38.

[154] *Re Toshoku Finance UK Plc* [2002] 3 All E.R. 961, per Lord Hoffmann at [30].

[155] Pensions Act 2004 s.75.

[156] Pensions Act 2004 s.75(8).

bypassed by the issue of financial support directions and a contribution notice to the employer in accordance with the provisions referred to below.[157]

Sums payable under post-liquidation financial support directions and contribution notices issued by the Pensions Regulator

8–37   To be contrasted with the treatment of the employer's shortfall liability is the liability imposed by financial support directions and contribution notices issued by the Pensions Regulator under the Pensions Act 2004. Such directions and notices are aimed not just at the employer but also at its associates and connected persons. The aim of the legislative provisions is to avoid the risk of "moral hazard", that is, the temptation of employers to organise their affairs as to throw the burden of pension scheme deficiencies on to the Pension Protection Fund, as by channelling funds away from the employer to an associate or connected person.[158] The Pensions Regulator may issue financial support directions in relation to an occupational pension scheme of an under-resourced employer (as defined), other than a money purchase scheme, requiring the employer or an associate or connected person to secure and maintain financial support for the scheme,[159] and if such directions are not complied with, a contribution notice may be issued requiring the employer or associated or connected person to pay a specified sum to the scheme trustees where it is reasonable to impose such requirement.[160] If an insolvent event such as liquidation occurs in relation to the employer or an associate or connected person after the issue of financial support directions, any liability from an ensuing contribution notice is merely provable, whereas if the directions are issued after the insolvent event, such liability becomes an expense of the liquidation, enjoying a super-priority.[161] In policy terms, this regime, which has generated much concern, has serious drawbacks. In the first place, it exposes liquidators and administrators to great uncertainty in the management of the liquidation or administration,[162]

---

[157] See *Bloom*, cited above n.143, per Briggs J. at [174]. The decision concerned an administration, but the same applies to a liquidation.

[158] See above, para.2–24.

[159] Pensions Act 2004 s.43.

[160] Pensions Act 2004 s.47.

[161] *Bloom*, cited above n.143, per Briggs J. If financial support directions are issued after an administration and a contribution notice is issued to the same target after the administration has been immediately followed by a liquidation, the sum fixed by the contribution notice will be treated as a liability arising on the company's entry into administration (Insolvency Rules 1986 r.13.12(1)(a)(ii)) and will be a provable debt in the liquidation. See *Bloom* at [106].

[162] The key concerns expressed by the first claimant in *Bloom*, cited above n.143, are summarised by Briggs J. at [161]. In relation to administration, Briggs J. considered (at [167]) that the court could issue a prospective order under r.2.67(3) of the Insolvency Rules varying the priority in stated events, and if that be right then the same must apply in liquidation under the Insolvency Act 1986 s.156, and I.R. 4.220(1). For example, the liquidator's remuneration under r.4.218(o) could be promoted above the pension contribution liabilities as "necessary disbursements" under r.4.218(m).

and if contribution notices are issued to an insolvent company the effect of the super-priority on the general body of creditors is potentially damaging, although the Pensions Regulator is required to have regard to the interests of creditors[163] and would no doubt wish to avoid imposing a liability that would prevent a sensible business rescue. Secondly, it appears to give an incentive to the Pensions Regulator to defer the issue of financial services directions until after the target company has gone into liquidation or administration. The decision in *Bloom* is currently under appeal and the Insolvency Service is also considering representations to change the law so as to ensure that liability under post-insolvency directions is treated as a provable debt, not as an expense of the liquidation.

Post-liquidation claims accruing under pre-liquidation contracts

The principle is thus plain enough: the expenses of the liquidation, including the claims of post-liquidation creditors,[164] are paid in full in priority to other debts, the claims of preferential creditors are then met, and it is only the pool of assets remaining after these claims have been paid that is available for the general body of ordinary, unsecured creditors. More difficulty is caused by the continuance in force of contracts and leases made by the company before liquidation and not repudiated by the liquidator upon liquidation. Liabilities accrued under such contracts or leases before the winding up are, of course, caught by the *pari passu* principle and enjoy no priority. But what is the position where the contract or lease imposes continuing obligations, for example, for payment of rent for equipment or premises or for sums accruing due under building contracts not completed at the time of liquidation? Prima facie these post-liquidation claims also fall within the *pari passu* principle. Here, however, the *Lundy Granite* principle is relevant, raising the question of whether (and if so, when) the liquidator merely continues in passive possession of the land or goods without disclaiming the transaction or whether he actively adopts the transaction, in the sense that he takes it over for the benefit or convenience of the winding up, for example, to run the business or with a view to disposing of it. In the former case, the post-liquidation rent is merely a provable debt[165]; in the latter, it is payable as an expense of the liquidation so far as accruing after the liquidator's adoption of the contract, but provable, not payable, so far as accruing before that adoption.[166] The

8–38

---

[163] Pensions Act 2004 s.100.

[164] For a discussion of the position in relation to environmental clean-up liability, see above, para.8–30.

[165] The lessor cannot, however, prove for rent before it falls due, because until then it has not been earned. The principle applies to all executory contracts. See below, paras 8–41 and 8–43.

[166] *Re ABC Coupler*, cited above n.142; *Re Downer Enterprises*, cited above n.142; *Re Oak Pits Colliery Co* (1882) 21 Ch.D. 322; *Re National Arms & Ammunition Co* (1885) 28 Ch. D. 474; and *Re Lundy Granite Co Ex p. Heavan* (1871) 6. Ch. App. 462 (CA).

treatment of a post-liquidation liability under a pre-liquidation contract is a judge-made exception to the general rule that only claims arising under post-liquidation contracts can be treated as expenses of the liquidation. It is based on the need to avoid a liquidator being able to use leased premises or other assets for nothing, to the detriment of the lessor,[167] and is a concept now implicitly embodied in r.4.218(3)(a)(ii) of the Insolvency Rules 1986 and possibly other sub-rules as well.[168] The application of the *Lundy Granite* principle does not involve the exercise of discretion any more than the application of any other legal principle to the facts of the particular case.[169] It applies equally in administration under r.2.67.1(a) of the Insolvency Rules.[170]

Payments of pre-liquidation debts to preserve assets or avoid other loss

8–39   Although pre-liquidation debts are in general provable, not payable, there may be cases in which the liquidator finds it necessary to pay such debts in order to preserve the assets or otherwise avoid loss to the estate. In these cases, he is entitled to recoup himself from the assets in respect of such payments as costs of the liquidation. Typical cases are payments to avoid forfeiture of a lease, distress or termination of a contract. Until recently, liquidators also found themselves compelled to pay the pre-liquidation claims of public utilities, such as suppliers of electricity, gas, water and telephone services, in order to avoid the disconnection of supplies. The pressure thus exerted by monopoly suppliers to obtain payment ahead of other creditors despite being unsecured and non-preferential attracted severe criticism from the Cork Committee,[171] and as a result of the Committee's recommendations such suppliers are now prohibited from making payment of outstanding pre-liquidation charges a condition of the continuance of supply.[172]

5. PROOF OF DEBT

The nature of proof

8–40   A creditor wishing to be treated as such for the purpose of voting and dividend is required to submit a formal claim, known as a proof of debt

---

[167] The authorities are extensively reviewed in *Re ABC Coupler*, cited above n.142.

[168] *Re Toshoku Finance*, cited above n.135, per Lord Hoffmann at [38].

[169] *Re Toshoku Finance*.

[170] *Goldacre (Offices) Ltd v Nortel Networks UK Ltd* [2010] 3 W.L.R. 171; and *Exeter CC v Bairstow* [2007] B.C.C. 236. See below, para.11–104.

[171] "Insolvency Law and Practice" (Cmnd. 8558, 1982), Ch.33.

[172] Insolvency Act 1986 s.233. They are, however, entitled to make the liquidator's personal guarantee of payment a condition of future supply (s.233(2)(a)).

(or proof) to the liquidator.[173] Since dividends are distributed only among those creditors whose proofs have been lodged and admitted,[174] a creditor is not entitled to dividends if his proof has been rejected[175] or to participate in a dividend distribution made before he has lodged his proof.[176] Nor on lodging his proof can he require prior distributions to be reopened, but he has a prior right to the dividend he lost before any future distributions of dividend are made.[177] However, no action may be brought against the liquidator for payment of a dividend; the remedy of a disaffected creditor is to apply to the court for an order directing payment.[178]

Provable debts

In general, all claims by creditors arising prior to the liquidation are provable against the company, whether they are present or future, certain or contingent, ascertained or sounding only in damages.[179] Under r.13.12(1) of the Insolvency Rules, "debt" means:

8–41

"(a)   any debt or liability to which the company is subject—

   (i)   in the case of a winding up which was not immediately preceded by an administration, at the date on which the company went into liquidation;

   (ii)   in the case of a winding up which was immediately preceded by an administration, at the date on which the company entered administration;

(b)   any debt or liability to which the company may become subject after that date by reason of any obligation incurred before that date[180]; and

(c)   any interest provable as mentioned in Rule 4.93(1)."

---

[173] Insolvency Rules 1986 r.4.73. In the case of a voluntary winding up, the liquidator is not obliged to call for proofs to be in writing, but usually does so.

[174] Insolvency Rules 1986 r.11.6(1).

[175] A creditor dissatisfied with the liquidator's decision with regard to his proof may apply to the court for the decision to be reversed or varied (Insolvency Rules 1986 r.4.83).

[176] In calculating and distributing a dividend, the liquidator is required to make provision for certain unproved debts, including disputed proofs and claims (Insolvency Rules 1986 r.4.182(1)). Until the liquidator has determined whether to accept or reject a proof or the court has overturned his decision to reject it, the person lodging the proof is not a creditor for the purpose of the Insolvency Rules (*Managa Properties Ltd v Brittain* [2010] Bus. L.R. 599).

[177] Insolvency Rules 1986 r.4.182(2).

[178] Insolvency Rules 1986 r.4.182(3). See *Lomax Leisure Ltd v Miller* [2008] 1 B.C.L.C. 262, discussed above, para.5–03.

[179] Insolvency Rules 1986 r.12.3(1).

[180] As to a claim in tort, see below, n.184.

It is immaterial whether the debt or liability is present or future, whether it is certain or contingent, or whether its amount is fixed or liquidated, or is capable of being ascertained by fixed rules or as a matter of opinion.[181] The word "liability" itself is widely defined, covering a liability to pay money or money's worth, any liability under an enactment, any liability for breach of trust, any liability in contract, tort or bailment, and any liability arising out of an obligation to make restitution.[182]

It will be seen that provable debts include those becoming payable after winding up pursuant to an obligation incurred before winding up, for example, pre-liquidation debts maturing after liquidation,[183] unliquidated damages in contract or tort,[184] and claims for interest payable in respect of a period up to the date of winding up or, if the liquidation was immediately preceded by an administration, any period after the date on which the company entered administration.[185] Rent and other payments of a periodical nature may be proved so far as due and unpaid up to the date of liquidation or, if the liquidation was immediately preceded by an administration, up to the date on which the company entered administration,[186] while further payments accruing due from the company under executory contracts continuing in force will, if constituting expenses of the liquidation, be payable in full from the company's assets or, if not, will be provable, as they fall due.[187] A protective award by an Employment Tribunal under s.189 of the Trade Union and Labour Relations (Consolidation) Act 1992 in respect of a breach of employment law committed prior to liquidation is a provable debt.[188]

Debts arising under contracts made after the date of the winding up are not provable but are payable as expenses of the liquidation in priority to other claims.[189] There are, moreover, certain types of pre-liquidation debt, both under the Insolvency Rules and at common law, for which the creditor cannot prove. Under the Insolvency Rules, certain obligations imposed by

---

[181] Insolvency Rules 1986 r.13.12(3).
[182] Insolvency Rules 1986 r.13.12(4).
[183] And see Insolvency Rules 1986 r.4.94, and below, para.8–43.
[184] Prior to the Insolvency Act 1986, a claim in tort was not provable unless it had become liquidated by judgment or agreement before the winding up. Now it is provable if at the date when the company went into liquidation, or the date it entered into administration if this immediately receded the liquidation, all of the elements necessary to establish the cause of action existed except for actionable damage (Insolvency Rules 1986 r.13.12(2)). This recognises that there may be various cases in which actionable damage can take years to become manifest, as in the case of exposure to asbestos. If all of the other conditions of liability in tort are established, the claim in tort is provable even though under the general law loss or damage is an essential element of a tort.
[185] Insolvency Rules 1986 r.4.93 as amended. As to post-liquidation interest, see above, para.8–26.
[186] Insolvency Rules 1986 r.4.92 as amended.
[187] See above, para.3–11; and below, para.8–43. As to the effect of disclaimer, see above, para.6–30.
[188] *Day v Haine* [2008] B.C.C. 845.
[189] See above, para.8–35.

statute are not provable at all,[190] while others are provable only when the claims of other creditors have been met in full.[191] But nothing in the Rules prejudices any enactment or rule of law under which a particular kind of debt is not provable, whether on grounds of public policy or otherwise.[192] So debts cannot be proved if they are statute-barred[193] or otherwise unenforceable.[194]

Liquidator may go behind judgment

Where a proof is lodged in respect of judgment debt, the liquidator is entitled to go behind the judgment, inquire into the consideration for it and satisfy himself that the judgment was not entered as the result of collusion between the judgment creditor and the judgment debtor or as the result of fraud or other miscarriage of justice, and in reaching his decision he is not limited to the evidence before the court by whom judgment was given.[195] He is entitled to ensure that the judgment is based on a real debt.

8–42

Amount of proof

Debts incurred prior to the liquidation (or, if the liquidation was immediately preceded by an administration, the date on which the company entered administration) but payable in the future under executed contracts—that is, contracts under which payment has already been earned by performance— are admitted to proof at full value[196]; but where the debt has not become due at the date of declaration of any dividend, it is discounted for the purpose of calculating the dividend entitlement.[197] Contingent claims must be estimated and admitted to proof at the estimated amount.[198] The same applies to unliquidated claims for damages.[199] The position is otherwise as regards sums payable in the future under executory contracts, for example, rent accruing due under a lease or payments that will become due under a construction

8–43

---

[190] Insolvency Rules 1986 r.12.3(2).
[191] Insolvency Rules 1986 r.12.3(2A).
[192] Insolvency Rules 1986 r.12.3(3).
[193] *Re Fleetwood & District Electric Light & Power Syndicate,* [1915] 1 Ch. 486.
[194] *Re Delhi Electric Supply & Traction Co Ltd,* [1953] 3 W.L.R. 1085.
[195] See *McCourt v Baron Meats Ltd* [1997] B.P.I.R. 114 and authorities there cited.
[196] Insolvency Rules 1986 r.4.94 as amended.
[197] Insolvency Rules 1986 r.11.13. The formula originally contained in this rule was criticised by Lord Millett in *Christopher Moran Holdings Ltd v Bairstow*; also sub nom. *Re Park Air Services Plc,* [2000] 2 A.C. 172 at 187–188 on the ground (inter alia) that the discount was applied not to the reducing balance, but to the original sum outstanding. This has now been corrected in a revised r.11.13 as well as in r.2.105 (administration).
[198] Insolvency Rules 1986 r.4.86.
[199] Insolvency Rules 1986 r.4.86.

contract yet to be completed. Here the rule is that there can be no proof for a sum that has not been earned by performance—in the case of a lease, by the expiry of the period for which the rent is due,[200] and in the case of a construction contract by performance of the work for which the payment is due.[201] The creditor thus has to prove separately for each sum as it is earned,[202] except where, under the *Lundy Granite* principle, such sum can be treated as an expense of the liquidation.

Where a lease is disclaimed or otherwise comes to an end, the lessor's claim becomes converted into an immediate right to prove for unliquidated damages based on the present value of the future rentals,[203] credit being given for the present value of the future rentals that may reasonably be expected from a lease to a new tenant.

No deduction need be made for third-party receipts

8–44   The creditor can maintain his proof for the full amount of the debt without giving credit for sums received from a surety or other third party, whether before or after the winding up, which are less than the full amount of the debt.[204] For this purpose, it makes no difference whether the sum is received by actual payment or through set-off.[205] But where the surety's liability is for a specified part of the debt and he pays that part, his liability is extinguished and the creditor must give credit for the payment in his proof.[206] For reasons which are not clear, there is a special rule governing negotiable instruments. Where the claim is on a negotiable instrument, credit must be given for sums

---

[200] *Christopher Moran Holdings Ltd v Bairstow* [2000] 2 A.C. 172 (on appeal from *Re Park Air Services Plc* [1997] 1 W.L.R. 1376), per Lord Millett at 187; and see above, para.3–11.

[201] Once performance has taken place, as regards the amount earned the creditor can prove immediately even if the amount in question, although due, has not yet become payable, e.g. where in a construction contract the requisite architect's certificate has not yet been issued. In such a case, the amount due is provable as a future debt.

[202] See para.3–11, above.

[203] *Christopher Moran Holdings*, cited above n.200, reversing the decision of the Court of Appeal sub nom. *Re Park Air Services*, cited above n.200, which had held that the rent was claimable as such, instead of the loss of rent being recoverable as damages, so that no discount was to be deducted—a decision criticised as untenable in the 2nd edition of this book at p.166.

[204] *Ellis v Emmanuel* (1876) 1 Ex.D. 157; *Re Sass* [1896] 2 Q.B. 12. See *Goode on Legal Problems of Credit and Security*, edited by Louise Gullifer, 4th edn (2008), para.8–18. The position is otherwise in the case of a claim against a solvent debtor and an insolvent surety.

[205] The position is otherwise, of course, where the debtor company is solvent and the surety who has a right of set-off is insolvent, for the set-off in insolvency is mandatory and the payment thereby effected pro tanto extinguishes the principal debt. See *M.S. Fashions Ltd v Bank of Credit and Commerce International SA* [1993] Ch. 425 and below, para.9–19.

[206] See *M.S. Fashions*, cited above n.205. The surety is also entitled to share rateability with the creditor in securities given and dividends received in respect of the whole debt (*Re Butlers Wharf Ltd* [1995] B.C.C. 717; and *Goodwin v Gray* (1874) 22 W.R. 312).

received from a third party before proof,[207] but need not be given for receipts after proof.[208]

No double proof

Only one proof may be lodged for the same debt. So a surety may not prove for his right of indemnity against the company as principal debtor until the creditor has received payment in full.[209] Again, however, a surety of a specified part of a debt (as opposed to one who guarantees the whole debt with a limit of liability) is discharged from liability on paying that part and becomes entitled to lodge a proof for the sum paid,[210] with the result that the creditor's proof must be correspondingly reduced.[211]

8–45

The rule in Cherry v Boultbee

Closely allied to the rule against double proof is the rule in *Cherry v Boultbee*[212] that where a person entitled to share of a fund is also under a duty to contribute to the fund, he cannot claim his share without first bringing into account what he owes. Normally, this is dealt with by way of set-off, but where for some reason set-off is not available, the rule operates by notionally adding to the fund what is owed to it by the party in question, determining the share of that party in the notionally increased fund and then deducting from it the amount he owes. That principle also applies in an insolvent liquidation or administration.[213]

8–46

Secured creditors

Subject to the special rules concerning floating charges,[214] creditors who are fully secured are largely unaffected by the liquidation process. They can remove their security from the pool and realise it to satisfy what is due to

8–47

---

[207] *Re Blackburne* (1892) 9 Morr. 249.

[208] *Re Houlder* [1929] 1 Ch. 205; and see *Goode on Legal Problems of Credit and Security*, 2008, para.8–19.

[209] *Re Fenton* [1931] 1 Ch. 85. For a helpful summary of the rule against double proof, see the judgment of Robert Walker J. in *Re Polly Peck International Plc, In administration (No.3)* [1996] 1 B.C.L.C. 428, where the learned judge declined to pierce the corporate veil by treating two companies in a group as a single entity so as to preclude a double proof.

[210] *Re Sass*, cited above n.204, per Vaughan Williams J. at 15.

[211] *Goode on Legal Problems of Credit and Security*, 2008, para.8–18.

[212] (1839) 4 My. & Cr. 442.

[213] *Mills v HSBC (C.I) Ltd* [2010] W.T.L.R. 235; and *Re SSL Realisations (2002) Ltd* [2006] Ch. 610.

[214] See above, para.6–38, and below, para.8–49.

them, accounting to the liquidator for any surplus.[215] Where the company is in compulsory liquidation, there are certain restrictions. Although proceedings are not usually needed to enable the creditor to realise his security, if for some reason the creditor finds it necessary or desirable to institute proceedings against the company, he must first obtain leave of the court.[216] Moreover, since the liquidator in a compulsory winding up is an officer of the court, he cannot be interfered with in the exercise of his functions without leave of the court, so that if he declines to part with possession of the property in which the creditor has his security interest, the creditor is not allowed to resort to self-help, but must again obtain leave of the court. In practice, leave will almost invariably be granted, for what is involved is not the property of the company, but (to the extent of the security interest) the property of the secured creditor. As James L.J. pointed out a long time ago in *Re David Lloyd & Co,*[217] the legislative provisions requiring leave of the court:

"...were intended, not for the purpose of harassing, or impeding, or injuring third persons, but for the purpose of preserving the limited assets of the company or bankrupt in the best way for distribution among all the persons who have claims upon them ... But that has really nothing to do with the case of a man who for present purposes is to be considered as entirely outside the company, who is merely seeking to enforce a claim, not against the company, but to his own property. The position of a mortgagee under such circumstances is, to my mind, exactly similar to that of a man who said, 'You the company have got property which you have taken from me, you are in possession of my property by way of trespass and I want to get it back again' ... The mortgagee says, 'There is some property upon which I have a certain specific charge, and I want to realise that charge. I have nothing to do with the distribution of your property among your creditors, this is my property.' Why a mortgagee should be prevented from doing that I cannot understand."

A secured creditor has a number of options. He can surrender his security and prove for the full amount of the debt due to him,[218] a procedure hardly ever used since it rarely has advantages; he can value his security in his proof and prove for the balance of the debt[219]; he can realise his security and, if the proceeds are insufficient to cover the amount due, can prove for any defi-

---

[215] For other options open to a secured creditor, see below. See also Riz Mokal, "What Liquidation Does for Secured Creditors and What It Does For You" (2008) 71 M.L.R. 699.

[216] Insolvency Act 1986 s.130(2).

[217] (1877) 6 Ch.D. 339 at 344–345.

[218] Insolvency Rules 1986 r.4.88(2).

[219] Curiously, the Insolvency Rules do not expressly provide for the amount provable by a secured creditor who elects to value his security; they merely require the security to be disclosed and valued (r.4.75(l)(e)), provide for the surrender of the security, if not disclosed, unless the court grants relief for inadvertence or honest mistake (r.4.96) and allow the

ciency[220]; and he can simply rest on his security without lodging a proof at all. The secured creditor needs to examine his options carefully. Whether or not he proves for his debt, his claim is subject to set-off, so that if he is secured he can enforce his security only for the net balance remaining after the set-off has been applied.[221]

The justification for upholding security rights has already been described in an earlier chapter.[222]

Execution creditors

Where a creditor has issued execution against the goods or land of a com-   **8–48**
pany or has attached any debt due to it, and the company is subsequently wound-up, he is not entitled to retain the benefit of the execution or attachment against the liquidator unless he completed the execution or attachment before the commencement of the winding up.[223] This provision does not apply to the levy of distress.[224]

6. RANKING OF CLAIMS

Priority of claims

Most of the priority rules concerning unsecured creditors have already been   **8–49**
referred to.[225] As pointed out earlier, secured creditors are not in general involved in the competition except to the extent of any balance remaining due to them after realising their security, for as we have seen assets of the company available for unsecured creditors do not include the interests of third parties. Secured creditors will, of course, be competing among themselves, but assuming that all of their interests have been duly perfected,

---

secured creditor, with the agreement of the liquidator or permission of the court, to alter the value put upon the security in his proof (r.4.95(1)). But it is clear that only the balance of the claim above the stated value can be proved; and if the creditor understates this he risks redemption by the liquidator at the value stated (r.4.97(1)).

[220] Insolvency Rules 1986 r. 4.88(1). If he proves for the full debt, he is deemed to have surrendered his security (*Moor v Anglo-Italian Bank* (1879) 10 Ch.D. 681, per Sir George Jessel M.R. at 689–690).

[221] See below, para.9–23.

[222] See above, para.2–29.

[223] Insolvency Act 1986 s.183(1), which is qualified by s.183(2). As to what constitutes completion of the execution or attachment, see s.183(3). See also *Goode on Legal Problems of Credit and Security*, 2008, paras 5–43–5–46.

[224] See *Re Modern Jet Support Centre Ltd* [2005] 1 W.L.R. 3880 and cases there cited.

[225] Above, paras 8–02 and 8–20 et seq.

insolvency law has nothing to say about this competition, which is governed by the general law.[226]

There are two cases in which a creditor holding a duly perfected security does not enjoy priority. Both of these concern floating charges.[227]

(1) The statutory surrender of the prescribed part

8–50   Under s.176A of the Insolvency Act 1986, a prescribed part of the net property subject to a floating charge[228] and still remaining after any payment to the preferential creditors from the floating charge assets[229] has to be surrendered so as to be available as a ring-fenced fund for unsecured creditors. This provision, which is confined to floating charges created on or after September 15, 2003, has already been discussed.[230]

(2) Postponement to preferential creditors

8–51   Under s.175(2)(b) of the Insolvency Act, claims secured by a floating charge[231] are postponed to those of preferential creditors in a winding up.[232] This provision has its origin in s.2 of the Preferential Payments in Bankruptcy Amendment Act 1897, which was motivated by the sense that floating charges were typically taken over raw materials and manufactured articles that had benefited from the work of employees, who ought therefore to be paid in priority. The policy was stated with great clarity by Mr George Kemp in moving the Second Reading of the Bill in the House of Commons:

> "To make plain the incidence of the order of payment in the case of a company being wound up, he would take the case of a limited company, with, they would suppose, an ordinary share capital of £300,000, debentures to a similar amount, and weekly wages paid of £1,000. They would suppose, too, that there was a mortgage of £10,000 on the lands and buildings of the company. First in order of payment there came this mortgage of £10,000. Secondly, came the workpeople with their claims for their wages—if their

---

[226] See *Goode on Legal Problems of Credit and Security*, 2008, Ch.9.

[227] For a summary of the priorities of distribution, see below, para.8–53.

[228] i.e. a floating charge created on or after September 15, 2003 (Insolvency Act 1986 s.176A(9); Insolvency Act 1986 (Prescribed Part) Order 2003 (SI 2003/2097), art.1), referred to hereafter as a "new" floating charge, pre-September 15, 2003 charges being labelled "old" floating charges.

[229] See above, para.6–38.

[230] See above, paras 6–38 et seq.

[231] That is, a charge which as created was a floating charge (Insolvency Act 1986 ss.40(1) and 251), even if it has crystallised before the accrual of the preferential debt.

[232] See also the Companies 2006 s.754 (which is not an insolvency provision), and below, para.10–60.

wages were in arrears, say two weeks, £2,000—as against the debenture holders under a floating charge on the remaining assets of the company; then came the debenture holders, and fourthly came the ordinary shareholders.[233] What was the justice of this? First of all, the mortgagee got his money, because it was on the lands and buildings, which were not in any way affected by, nor did they affect, the work of the workpeople. Secondly, why should the workpeople come in priority to the debenture holders under a floating charge? For the reason that the raw material and the articles partly or wholly manufactured were part of the assets of the debenture holders. This raw material had benefited by the work of the workpeople to the extent of the time for which their wages were in arrear. Therefore it was only right and just that the workpeople should have the benefit of the enhanced value of these articles, which, as the law stood at the present time, would be first claimed by the holders of debentures or debenture stock."[234]

Liquidation expenses now have priority not only over preferential claims, but over the claims secured by a floating charge.[235]

A circularity problem

Where by virtue of a priority agreement or the impact of a negative pledge clause a floating charge has priority over a subsequent fixed charge, which in turn has priority over preferential debts, a circularity problem arises. The fixed charge, by agreement, is subordinate to the floating charge, which is subordinate to the claims of preferential creditors, which in turn rank behind those of the fixed charge.   **8–52**

The most satisfactory way of resolving this conundrum is to accept the basic premise that preferential creditors should not be given a windfall purely by virtue of a private agreement between the fixed charge and the floating chargee

---

[233] Ordinary unsecured creditors should, of course, have been mentioned before shareholders; no doubt the omission was an oversight and was in any event not material to the illustration.

[234] HC Deb., cols 72–73 (February 10, 1897). The reasoning would not, it is true, have applied to raw materials still unprocessed at the time of winding up, but given what was then perceived to be the fractional amount of unpaid wages as a percentage of the debentures, it would no doubt have been unnecessarily pedantic to treat these separately from the manufactured stock. The reasoning on which the 1897 Act was based offers a solution to the question of how preferential claims should be dealt with if the Law Commission's proposals to abolish the floating charge as a distinct form of security and treat it as a fixed charge ("Company Security Interests: A Consultative Report" (Law Com. Cons. Paper No.176, 2004), paras 2.56 et seq.) were to be adopted, namely to subordinate to preferential claims charges (which in the new regime would be fixed charges) over raw materials, stock in trade and receivables, the three significant categories of asset typically covered by a floating charge.

[235] Insolvency Act 1986 s.176ZA, reversing the decision of the House of Lords in *Buchler v Talbot* [2004] 2 A.C. 298, which had been felt to create considerable funding difficulties for liquidators and was also controversial on doctrinal grounds. See Riz Mokal, "Reversing *Buchler v. Talbot*: The Doctrinal Dimension of Liquidation Expenses Priority" (2006) 21 J.I.B.F.L. 104.

which does not in any way concern other creditors. This windfall can be avoided by treating the floating chargee as subrogated to the rights of the fixed chargee to the extent of the sum secured by the floating charge, so that to the extent of that sum or the sum secured by the fixed charge, whichever is the less, the floating chargee obtains priority over preferential creditors in right of the fixed chargee.[236] Such a solution does justice to everyone. Preferential creditors remain in exactly the same position as they did before and the rights of the parties to the inter-creditor agreement are respected. The correctness of this approach was conceded in *Re Woodroffes (Musical Instruments) Ltd,*[237] but in *Re Portbase Clothing Ltd,*[238] Chadwick J. felt unable to adopt it and preferred the decision of Nicholson J. in the Victorian case of *Waters v Widdows,*[239] in which it was held that the fixed chargee, in subordinating his claims to those of the floating chargee, also subordinated them to the preferential debts. In that case, this result was said to be dictated by the statutory policy of protecting preferential creditors. It is hard to see why. The purpose of the legislation is to give priority to preferential debts over those secured by a floating charge, not those secured by a fixed charge. The objection of Chadwick J. to the subrogation solution was that it put the floating chargee in the same position as if the fixed chargee had assigned his charge or declared a trust of the proceeds in favour of the floating chargee. The answer to this is surely that the preferential creditors, who are strangers to the priority agreement, have no right to invoke its terms to gain priority for themselves over a fixed charge to which they would otherwise be subordinate, and that the fixed chargee should thus remain entitled to enforce his charge in priority to the claims of preferential creditors and then hand over the proceeds to the floating chargee to the extent of the amount secured by the floating charge. Applying the principle of subrogation does no more than short-circuit this procedure and allow the floating chargee to enforce the fixed chargee's priority directly and for his own benefit, so achieving the result intended by the priority agreement, but without disturbing the position of the preferential creditors. The additional assets that become available to the floating chargee as the result of the subordination do not come from the company and would not form part of its free assets if there were no floating charge; they come from the fixed charge and are released on the basis that it is the holder of the fixed charge, and no one else, who will benefit from them.[240]

---

[236] See Goode on *Legal Problems of Credit and Security*, edited by Louise Gullifer, 4th edn (London: Sweet & Maxwell, 2008), paras 5–60–6–61; and *Goode on Commercial Law*, edited by Ewan McKendrick, 4th edn London: Penguin Books and LexisNexis,2009), pp.715–717.

[237] [1986] Ch. 366.

[238] [1993] Ch. 388.

[239] [1984] V.R. 503.

[240] *Goode on Legal Problems of Credit and Security*, 2008, para.5–61. The circularity problem does not arise in relation to the statutory surrender of the prescribed part of floating charge realisations for the benefit of unsecured creditors, for the prescribed part applies only to the floating charge assets remaining after any payment to preferential creditors, who thus do not participate in it. See above, para.6–38.

Summary of priorities

In line with the earlier discussion, fixed security interests and other real **8–53** rights held by third parties do not need to feature in the ordering of priorities because to the extent that assets held by the company are subject to these they do not constitute the property of the company at all and therefore do not compete in the priority stakes.[241] By contrast, debts secured by floating charges are, as we have seen, in competition both with preferential creditors and with ordinary unsecured creditors. The former have priority over sums secured by a floating charge. As regards the latter, it is necessary to distinguish old charges, created prior to September 15, 2003, from new charges, created on or after that date. Where an administrative receiver has been appointed under a floating charge, it is his responsibility to respect these and other priorities[242] and to make payments accordingly out of the assets coming into his hands. He must also set aside the prescribed part of any net property subject to a floating charge[243] and pay this and any remaining surplus over to the liquidator.[244]

In summary, as regards floating charges created on or after September 15, 2003 the liquidator must distribute realisations (including the prescribed part of net assets subject to a floating charge) according to the following ranking:

(i)   expenses of the liquidation (including post-liquidation claims), in the statutory order of priority, subject to adjustment by the court;

(ii)   preferential debts *pari passu*;

(iii)   claims of ordinary unsecured creditors as regards the prescribed part;

(iv)   the balance due to the holder of a floating charge after deduction of the prescribed part;

(v)   remaining claims of ordinary unsecured creditors *pari passu*, but not the holder of a subsisting floating charge[245]; and

(vi)   deferred creditors *pari passu*.

---

[241] This is subject to the liquidator's right to look to the proceeds of such assets for recoupment of expenses properly incurred by him in preserving or realising them.

[242] For the order of application of the assets by the receiver, see below, para.10–68.

[243] See above, para.6–38.

[244] The receiver does not himself have a power to distribute the prescribed part. See below, para.10–64.

[245] See above, para.6–40.

Chapter 9

Set-Off and Netting

1. THE NATURE AND PURPOSE OF SET-OFF AND NETTING

Set-off

Set-off is the right of a debtor who is owed money by his creditor on another **9–01**
account or dealing to secure payment for what is owed to him by setting this
off in reduction of his own liability.[1] For example, A sells raw materials to B
to be made up into finished products which B then sells to A. If A owes B
£1,000 for products sold and delivered to him, but is owed £400 by B for raw
materials, then, in any claim against him A is not obliged to pay B the £1,000
he owes and then sue separately for recovery of the £400 he is owed (or if B
is in liquidation, prove in the liquidation in competition with other creditors), but may set off the latter sum against his indebtedness and discharge
the debt by paying B (or B's liquidator) the balance of £600.

Set-off is available both outside and within bankruptcy and liquidation. In
both cases, it provides a speedy remedy to secure payment, but the policy
reason for providing the remedy depends on the type of set-off involved.
Contractual set-off is recognised as an incident of party autonomy in the

---

[1] See Philip Wood, *Set-Off and Netting, Derivatives, Clearing Systems*, 2nd edn (London: Sweet
& Maxwell, 2007); Rory Derham, *Law of Set-Off*, 4th edn (Oxford: Oxford University Press,
2010); Sheelagh McCracken, *Banker's Remedy of Set-Off*, 3rd edn (Bloomsbury Professional,
2010); and *Goode on Legal Problems of Credit and Security*, edited by Louise Gullifer, 4th edn
(London: Sweet & Maxwell, 2008), Ch.7. The leading early works are: Richard Babington, *A
Treatise on the Law of Set-Off* (1827); Basil Montagu, *Summary of the Law of Set-Off*, 2nd edn
(1828); and two American publications, Oliver Barbour, *Treatise on the Law of Set-Off* (1841);
and T.W. Waterman, *Treatise on the Law of Set-Off*, 2nd edn (1872). For historical and comparative surveys, see William H. Loyd, "The Development of Set-Off" 64 U.Pa.L.Rev. 541
(1916); and Michael E. Tigar, "Automatic Extinction of Cross-Demands: Compensatio from
Rome to California" 53 Cal.L.R. 224 (1965).

conclusion of contracts. The banker's right of combination is similar, except that it derives from implied rather than express agreement. In the case of independent (or statutory) set-off,[2] the remedy is given primarily to avoid circuity of action. By contrast, the policy underlying transaction (or equitable) set-off is that it would be unjust to allow a party to enforce his money claim without giving credit for the cross-claim if so required. Similarly, the provision of insolvency set-off reflects the view that where parties have been giving credit to each other in reliance on their ability to secure payment by withholding what is due from them, it would be unjust, on the advent of liquidation, to deprive the solvent party of his security by compelling him to pay what he owes in full and be left to prove for his own claim. This has traditionally been the policy justification for what is a clear exception to the *pari passu* principle, in that it allows the solvent party to collect payment ahead of other creditors to the extent of the set-off and thus puts him in a position analogous to that of a secured creditor.[3]

Thus, set-off is an essential tool in the hands of a debtor who has a cross-claim against his creditor and is particularly used in banking transactions and mutual dealings in the financial markets. But in dealings on an organised market, the legal protection of netting[4] and set-off has in recent years been seen as fulfilling a much more fundamental need, namely the reduction of systemic risk: hence the issue of EC Directives and of implementing national legislation designed to ensure that rules of insolvency law do not imperil rights of set-off in market contracts.[5] This special treatment of market and related contracts should be constantly borne in mind as a major qualification of the general principles discussed in the present chapter.

2. TYPES OF SET-OFF

9–02   There are five main types of set-off. The labels traditionally used to describe these are decidedly uninformative, and I have adopted the terminology coined by Mr Wood,[6] which is much more meaningful and has already gained acceptance in the courts. Features common to all forms of set-off other than contractual set-off are that: (i) they are confined to situations in which both claim and cross-claim are for money or are reducible to

---

[2] See below, para.9–03.
[3] Set-off does not in law constitute a form of security, for the debtor who asserts it is not acquiring any rights over an asset of the creditor, but simply seeking to reduce or extinguish the claim against him. See below, para.9–18.
[4] See below, para.9–09.
[5] See above, para.1–60; and below, para.15–93.
[6] In his superb and massive work *English and International Set-Off*.

money[7] or one party's claim is to money and the other's is to property which the first party is authorised to dispose of and thus convert into money; and (ii) they require mutuality of parties, that is, the claim and cross-claim must be due from the same parties in the same right.[8] The five types of set-off are as follows.

(1) Independent set-off

This embraces two distinct forms of set-off. The first is sometimes known as statutory set-off, by which is meant set-off under rules carried over from the former Statutes of Set-Off, or alternatively as legal set-off, by way of contradistinction with equitable set-off. The second is that form of set-off which equity applied by analogy with the Statutes of Set-Off, where all the conditions for statutory set-off were present except that one of the liquidated cross-claims was equitable.[9] The particular characteristics of independent set-off are that: (i) claim and cross-claim must be liquidated or capable of ascertainment without valuation or estimation; (ii) independent set-off is a purely procedural defence which does not operate to reduce or extinguish the creditor's claim except at the point where judgment is given for the balance; and (iii) in contrast to transaction set-off, it is not necessary that the claim and cross-claim should be connected to each other. It is only in this last feature that independent set-off has any utility in modern law; in all other respects it is overshadowed by the much broader transaction set-off. Independent set-off was at one time thought to be incapable of exclusion by contract, but this historical view has now been discredited.[10] Further, where insolvency set-off is not available, the exclusion is effective even if winding up supervenes.[11]

9–03

(2) Transaction set-off

This form of set-off, traditionally labelled equitable set-off, arises where the claim and cross-claim, even if not arising from the same transaction, are so closely connected that it would be inequitable for one claim to be enforced without credit being given for the other. Although transaction set-off was

9–04

---

[7] It is not clear what policy objection there can be to set-off in respect of non-money fungibles. If each party has a duty to deliver or transfer items of property that are mutually interchangeable, why should not the party with the larger obligation be entitled to deduct what is due to him and deliver or transfer the balance? This can be done by agreement, but not, it seems, in the absence of agreement.

[8] See further para.9–26 below as to whether this is always a requirement.

[9] See *Goode on Legal Problems of Credit and Security*, 2008, paras 7–04 and 7–36.

[10] *Re Kaupthing Singer & Friedlander Ltd* [2009] 2 Lloyd's Rep. 154; and *Hong Kong & Shanghai Banking Corp v Kloeckner & Co AG* [1990] 2 Q.B. 514.

[11] *Re Kaupthing Singer & Friedland*. In that case insolvency set-off was not available because of the absence of mutuality.

historically seen as a purely procedural remedy,[12] in modern law it is now capable of operating as a substantive defence in those cases where this is not precluded by the nature or terms of a contract between the parties and the set-off is not given by way of analogy to the Statutes of Set-Off.[13] In order for transaction set-off to be available, the claim and cross-claim must be due from the same parties in the same right.[14] A valuable exposition of the modern law on transaction set-off is provided by the judgment of Rix L.J. in *Geldof Metaalconstructie NV v Simon Carves Ltd*,[15] in which he divided the requirements for transaction set-off into two elements: the formal element of close connection and the functional element of injustice that would be done if account were not taken of the cross-claim when enforcing the claim. Transaction set-off may validly be excluded by agreement[16] and, as in the case of independent set-off, the exclusion is effective despite subsequent liquidation where insolvency set-off is not available.[17]

Transaction set-off is not self-executing. Neither the existence nor the assertion or exercise of the right of set-off has the effect of extinguishing the claim, it simply precludes the claimant from treating the party asserting set-off as a debtor to the extent of the set-off pending final determination of the parties' claims.[18]

(3) Contractual set-off

9–05   Contractual set-off is that for which provision is made by express agreement of the parties. Outside insolvency it is free of several of the limitations governing other forms of set-off. It operates as a substantive defence, taking effect upon the occurrence of the act or event agreed between the parties.

(4) Current account set-off

9–06   By this is meant the implied contractual right given to bankers operating different current accounts for the same customer to combine and treat them as one, thus setting off a debit balance on one account against a credit balance on the other. Although current account set-off could be regarded as a form of

---

[12] *Goode on Legal Problems of Credit and Security*, 2008, para.7–48.

[13] See *BICC Plc v Burndy Corp* [1985] 1 All E.R. 417; *Pacific Rim Investments Pte Ltd v Lam Seng Tiong* [1995] 3 S.L.R. 1; and generally *Goode on Legal Problems of Credit and Security*, 2008, paras 7–48 et seq.

[14] For a discussion of this, see *Goode on Legal Problems of Credit and Security*, 2008, para.7–53.

[15] [2010] 130 Con. L.R. 37 at [20] et seq.

[16] *Coca-Cola Financial Corp v Finsat International Ltd* [1998] Q.B. 43; and *Re Kaupthing Singer & Friedlander Ltd* [2009] 2 B.C.L.C. 137.

[17] *Kaupthing Singer & Friedlander*, cited above n.16.

[18] *Fearns v Anglo-Dutch Paint and Chemical Co Ltd* [2011] 1 W.L.R. 366,, applying the decision of the House of Lords in *Aries Tanker Corp v Total Transport Ltd* [1975] 1 W.L.R. 185.

contractual set-off,[19] the label "contractual set-off" is usually reserved for express contractual provisions by which mutual obligations may be netted out, i.e. set off against each other. Current account set-off is a substantive right which when exercised consolidates the different accounts and reduces the customer's monetary position to a single net debit or credit balance. It is not clear what type of act constitutes exercise of the right. The traditional view was that the accounts were to be treated as notionally a single account from the beginning unless otherwise agreed.[20] But it seems more realistic to treat the accounts as distinct until actually combined by notice, book-entry or the initiation of a computer process transferring balances to one account from the other(s), and until then to treat the right of set-off as an unexercised equity.

Since it is now established that foreign currency is to be treated as money, not as a commodity,[21] there seems to be no reason why a claim in one currency cannot be set off against a claim in another, although at the point when the balance is to be struck it will, of course, be necessary to convert the foreign currency into sterling if payment is to be made in sterling.

(5) Insolvency set-off

This is the right of set-off given by insolvency law, and as regards companies by rr.2.85 and 4.90 of the Insolvency Rules 1986, dealing respectively with set-off in administration and in liquidation. Insolvency set-off also operates as a result of substantive law. It is automatic and is not dependent on the taking of any procedural steps.

9–07

3. CONTRACTUAL SET-OFF, NETTING AND THE IMPACT OF INSOLVENCY

Contractual set-off and netting

The simple form of contractual set-off is a clause in a contract providing that one party is entitled to set off against any sums it owes to the other all sums owed to it by the other. This basic form is typically used where it is known in advance that the mutual obligations will be monetary or the various contracts will be unilateral and thus executed from the beginning,[22] so that no special

9–08

---

[19] This predicates that the accounts are to be treated as separate rather than evidencing a single indebtedness. See below.

[20] See, e.g. *Bailey v Finch* (1871) L.R. 7 Q.B. 34, *per* Blackburn J. at 40.

[21] See *Miliangos v George Frank (Textiles) Ltd* [1976] A.C. 443; and *The Halcyon The Great* [1975] 1 W.L.R. 515.

[22] Because a unilateral contract is by definition a contract in which only one party makes a promise and the other accepts by performance.

contractual arrangements are required to convert non-monetary obligations (for example, to deliver commodities) into monetary obligations or to cancel executory contracts or close them out by offsetting or reverse transactions. But there are many contractual relationships which are not of this character and require a process that leads, automatically or by unilateral action by one party, to consolidation of the mutual claims into a single, net balance. This contractually adopted process is known as netting.

Netting

9–09   The terms "netting" and "set-off" are sometimes treated as interchangeable, but in financial circles netting is used to denote contractual arrangements by which claims of different parties against each other are reduced to a single balance. Moreover, whereas set-off in its legal sense is confined to cases involving money obligations on both sides or claims reducible to money, netting also includes, in the commodities, futures and securities markets, delivery obligations.

Netting is now defined by statute as:

> "... the conversion into one net claim or obligation of different claims or obligations between participants resulting from the issue and receipt of transfer orders between them, whether on a bilateral or multilateral basis and whether through the interposition of a clearing house, central counterparty or settlement agent or otherwise."[23]

Netting can thus be viewed as both the procedure for and the outcome of a contractually completed set-off. It includes such arrangements as bilateral contract consolidation,[24] settlement netting,[25] the conversion of non-monetary into monetary claims through the exercise of a right to cancel or close out transactions, and the adoption of institutional rules governing bilateral and multilateral clearing and settlement or providing for novation of all relevant contracts to a clearing house or central counterparty.[26] The main objectives of netting are to reduce the number of settlements, thus saving costs, and to minimise the risk of a party becoming insolvent. From a market and regulatory perspective, netting, particularly multilateral netting, provides a measure of protection against systemic risk and, in so doing, influences capital adequacy requirements.

---

[23] Financial Markets and Insolvency (Settlement Finality) Regulations 1999, SI 1999/2979, reg.2(1). But if the netting agreement is governed by foreign law, "netting" will have the meaning ascribed by that law. See, e.g. the Credit Institutions (Reorganisation and Winding Up) Regulations 2004, SI 2004/1045, reg.34. For the definition of "close-out netting", see below, para.9–12.

[24] Otherwise known as netting by novation. As to "close-out" netting, see below, para.9–12.

[25] Also termed payment netting.

[26] See below, paras 9–10 et seq.

Netting arrangements are designed to ensure as far as possible either that all set-offs are completed before the relevant date,[27] so that there is no need to resort to insolvency set-off, or that the contractual rights on both sides will have undergone such conversion (if any) as may be necessary to satisfy the requirements of the Insolvency Rules as to mutuality of claims and parties.[28] For this purpose, a number of techniques are available which in normal circumstances can be expected to be effective. These include the following:

(1) Novation netting (contractual consolidation)

Novation netting, or contractual consolidation, involves the amalgamation of two or more executory contracts into a single new contract to be performed at a future time. The characteristic of this form of netting, which distinguishes it from settlement netting, is that the fusion of the claims on both sides into a new claim for a single balance or a single delivery obligation occurs immediately at the point when each new contract is concluded,[29] with payment or other performance to be made at a future time agreed between the parties. Thus, each new contract is automatically consolidated into the previous contract, so that at any one time only a single performance under a single contract is involved on one side or the other and no question of set-off arises. The purpose of novation netting is to avoid cherry-picking by a liquidator or administrator, who if there were several contracts might perform the profitable one and terminate the unprofitable one.[30] By contrast, in settlement netting the contracts remain separate until they have been netted out at maturity and the net balance paid or delivery obligation discharged.

Contractual consolidation may be effected by provision for bilateral consolidation of contractual obligations or by clearing house rules providing for novation of notified contracts to the clearing house. In the former case, the contract may provide that in stated eventualities, which could include notice by one party to the other, all outstanding contracts between them shall be consolidated into and replaced by a single contract under which only the net balance is payable. Alternatively, each contract may provide for its automatic consolidation with subsequent contracts as and when these come into existence, so that no set-off situation ever arises. In contractual set-off

9–10

---

[27] i.e. before the winding up and before the creditor has notice of the creditors' meeting under the Insolvency Act 1986 s.98 or of the winding up petition, as the case may be.

[28] See below, para.9–24. Netting is also an important technique for reducing the risk of failure of banks and other credit institutions and is recognised as such by the Capital Requirements Directive, which is in fact two directives: the Banking Consolidation Directive (Directive 2006/48/EC, dated June 14, 2006, [2006] OJ L1771); and the Directive on investment firms (Directive 2006/49/EC, dated June 14, 2006, [2006] OJ 177/201).

[29] Or on the occurrence of such other event as may be agreed between the parties.

[30] *Commissioners for HM Revenue & Customs v Enron Europe Ltd* [2006] B.C.C. 953, per Lightman J. at [21].

through clearing house rules, the clearing house becomes substituted as a principal in relation to each of the parties.[31] For example, under the General Regulations of the London Clearing House (LCH), members who are parties to a sale transaction are required to register it with LCH, whereupon the transaction is automatically novated and replaced by two separate transactions in both of which LCH is substituted for one party as the principal, becoming seller to the original buyer and buyer from the original seller. The effect of this system of automatic novation is that payment and delivery obligations become owed by and to LCH. In this way, payment rights and obligations arising from all dealings entered into by a particular trader are internalised and consolidated into a single credit or debit balance in the trader's current account with LCH.

Contractual netting does, of course, depend upon the obligations on both sides being of the same kind. It is not possible to net a payment obligation against a delivery obligation or vice versa. So where mutual dealings involve both delivery and payment obligations, it is necessary to devise some contractual procedure, such as rescission or close-out, by which one type of obligation is converted to the other.[32] Similarly, while the fact that the claim and cross-claim are in different currencies is no bar to a right of set-off,[33] completion of the set-off requires either that one currency is converted to the other or that both currencies are converted to a third currency at a given rate of exchange.

In relation to derivatives, a key document is the ISDA 2002 Master Agreement,[34] which contains provisions on both contractual netting and close-out netting.

(2) Settlement (or payment) netting

9–11   As mentioned above, whereas contractual consolidation involves the amalgamation of unmatured claims, settlement netting is the process by which matured claims are netted out and paid. It is only the act of payment of the net balance which extinguishes the claims on both sides. Again, settlement netting may be effected either by bilateral arrangements or by multilateral arrangements through a clearing house. In the former case, the parties simply agree that when claims on both sides mature, those on one side shall be set off against those on the other and the balance paid. In the case of netting through a clearing house, the procedure is that at the end of each clearing (which may be daily or at such other intervals as the clearing house rules prescribe) the position of each clearing house member is netted out in relation

---

[31] See Wood, *English and International Set-Off*, paras 5–127 et seq.; and *Goode on Commercial Law*, edited by Ewan McKendrick, 4th edn (2009), p.171.
[32] See below, para.9–12.
[33] See below, para.9–46.
[34] See below, para.9–12.

to all other clearing house members to produce a "net net" series of balances in which members are either creditors or debtors in relation to the clearing as a whole. Payment is then made by in-house transfers from debtor members to creditor members in the books of the clearing house or of a bank (typically the central bank) where all the clearing house members hold an account. These multilateral netting arrangements have not always proved effective in the event of an insolvency of a clearing house member, but the problem has been considerably alleviated by EC directives. The impact of insolvency on settlement netting is considered later.[35]

(3) Close-out netting

Insolvency set-off, like other forms of set-off, requires that claim and cross-claim be monetary claims or involve relief based on the non-payment of money. Accordingly, it is not possible to set off a money claim against an obligation to deliver or transfer property, tangible or intangible, except where the party invoking the set-off holds the property with instructions or authority to convert it into money and the instructions or authority have not been revoked at the time of liquidation.[36] So in a situation where the claims on one side or both are not to payment of money, but to the delivery of assets, such as commodities or securities, it is important to have a mechanism in place by which the delivery obligations are replaced by money obligations prior to the advent of liquidation. There are various "close-out" mechanisms by which this may be achieved: acceleration of performance on both sides and the replacement of a delivery obligation by a payment obligation, the two payment obligations then being netted out; the termination of a delivery obligation and its replacement by a payment obligation, and netting out; or the conclusion of a reverse transaction, so that, for example, a contract to purchase securities is closed out by a countervailing contract to sell them, the parties then settling their mutual obligations by the payment of differences.

9–12

Concern as to the efficacy of close-out netting in national legal systems led to the issue of the EC directives to which reference has already been made.[37] These are designed to safeguard close-out netting arrangements from attack under insolvency laws with a view to reducing the systemic risk that would attend the inability of a major player to reduce its exposure by a close-out.[38] A provision for close-out netting is now defined in the following terms:

---

[35] See below, para.9–14.

[36] See further below, para.9–26 in relation to close-outs and related techniques concerning financial collateral.

[37] Above, paras 1–60 et seq., and below, para.9–15.

[38] The Bank for International Settlements has estimated that close-out netting as at June 30, 2009 had reduced total credit exposure under outstanding OTC derivatives by 85.2% from mark-to-market value. Close-out netting is also important in allowing reporting of a bank's net position on exposures to a counterparty under derivative contracts.

" 'close-out netting provision' means a term of a financial collateral arrangement, or of an arrangement of which a financial collateral arrangement forms part, or any legislative provision under which on the occurrence of an enforcement event, whether through the operation of netting or set-off or otherwise—

(a) the obligations of the parties are accelerated to become immediately due and expressed as an obligation to pay an amount representing the original obligation's estimated current value or replacement cost, or are terminated and replaced by an obligation to pay such an amount; or

(b) an account is taken of what is due from each party to the other in respect of such obligations and a net sum equal to the balance of the account is payable by the party from whom the larger amount is due to the other party . . ."[39]

These provisions apply only to collateralised debt obligations, not to unsecured obligations, and they are limited to those associated with financial collateral arrangements.

Of particular importance in relation to derivatives is the 2002 ISDA Master Agreement produced by the International Swap Dealers Association (ISDA). The ISDA Master Agreement, one of the most widely used in the world, is an umbrella agreement which governs all specific transactions from time to time entered into under it, each transaction being recorded in a confirmation, but being described as forming part only of a single agreement contained in and subject to the terms of the Master Agreement and any schedule thereto. This is designed to preclude cherry picking by a liquidator, who might otherwise adopt contracts favourable to the insolvent company and refuse to perform the others. It remains to be seen whether the "single agreement" provision is effective in insolvency. The ISDA Master Agreement contains detailed provisions on netting.

Insolvency displaces other forms of set-off

9–13   Netting arrangements work perfectly well as regards transactions where the netting is completed before winding up. Once a company has gone into liquidation, the rules of insolvency set-off, where relevant, come into play and are mandatory,[40] displacing all other forms of set-off not exercised prior to

---

[39] Financial Collateral Arrangements (No.2) Regulations 2003, SI 2003/3226, as amended, reg.3. An EC regulation on close-out netting is currently being considered.

[40] See below, para.9–19. However, certain protections against rules of insolvency law are provided in the case of agreements relating financial collateral. See above, paras 1–60 *et seq.* and below, para.9–15.

the winding up.[41] This is of no great significance in relation to independent set-off, transaction set-off and current-account, for in virtually every situation in which these forms of set-off are available there would be an automatic set-off under the rules of insolvency set-off. Indeed, the latter are broader, not only because they are self-executing, but also because the principle of insolvency law under which future claims are accelerated and contingent claims are discounted and admitted to proof means that insolvency set-off extends to these claims, which would be outside the scope of the three other forms of set-off just mentioned.[42] But contractual set-off is in a different category, for outside insolvency the parties are free to agree on almost any kind of netting and set-off arrangement they choose. It thus becomes of importance to know whether a contractual set-off has come into effective operation before the winding up of one of the parties to the mutual dealings.[43] If it has not, two consequences follow. First, the right of set-off ceases to be exercisable. Secondly, if two or more contracts constituting the mutual dealing between the parties are executory, the liquidator is free to cherry-pick, requiring performance of the profitable contract while disclaiming or declining to perform the unprofitable contract and leaving the other party to prove in the winding up without the benefit even of insolvency set-off.[44]

We consider, first, the decidedly adverse impact of general insolvency law on uncompleted, multilateral netting arrangements and, secondly, the ameliorating effect of the Companies Act 1989 provisions relating to the settlement of market contracts and money market and related contracts under the rules of a recognised investment exchange or a recognised clearing house[45] and subsequent EC directives and implementing legislation.[46] The remainder of the chapter is devoted to the rules governing the admissibility of set-off in winding up or administration.

Effect of insolvency under the general insolvency law

Once a clearing house member goes into liquidation, as a matter of general insolvency law its claim on other members can no longer be subjected to **9–14**

---

[41] There are unresolved questions as to the manner in which transaction set-off is to be exercised and these are relevant in determining that the set-off has been effectively exercised prior to the liquidation. The writer has suggested elsewhere that transaction set-off is not automatic, but takes effect only when it has been asserted. See *Goode on Legal Problems of Credit and Security*, 2008, paras 7–54–7–55.

[42] For the discount method, see above, para.8–43.

[43] In that connection it should be borne in mind that exercise of a contractual set-off after presentation of a winding up petition and without authorisation or validation by the court is void under s.127 of the Insolvency Act 1986 if a winding up order is made. See below, para.13–127.

[44] This is because of the rule that sums earned by the company by post-liquidation activity are not part of its general assets and are thus not susceptible to insolvency set-off of pre-liquidation claims. See above, para.6–33, and below, para.9–43.

[45] See above, para.1–12.

[46] See above, paras 1–60 et seq.

netting out through the clearing, for the effect of this is to reduce the member's claim against its counterparty by reference to sums due from that member to third parties, in contravention of the mutuality requirement, and to prefer other participants in the clearing to the member's creditors as a whole, contrary to the *pari passu* rule. In other words, an asset of the member, namely its claim against a counterparty, is being removed from the general body of creditors and distributed exclusively among the clearing house members. This was the conclusion reached in the controversial decision of the House of Lords in *British Eagle International Air Lines Ltd v Compagnie Nationale Air France*,[47] to which reference has previously been made and which now requires examination in a little more detail.

"The International Air Transport Association (IATA) set up a clearing house system by which sums due from member airlines to each other would be netted out each month, remittances being sent by IATA to airlines having a net credit balance and collected from airlines with a net debit balance. British Eagle went into liquidation owing money to a number of airlines but with a claim against Air France which the liquidator sought to recover. Air France pleaded that the liquidator was bound by the IATA system and could collect only from IATA and then only such sum (if any) as was due to it after netting out the claims of airlines who were creditors of British Eagle. The liquidator's contention that this contravened the *pari passu* rule, in that it removed from British Eagle's estate for the benefit of other member airlines a sum due from Air France which would otherwise have been an asset available to the general body of creditors of British Eagle, was upheld by the House of Lords by a majority of three to two. It was not suggested that the arrangements were in themselves in any way improper, but in the view of the majority their effect was to give other members of IATA to whom British Eagle owed money a preference over its general creditors. Two of their Lordships[48] dissented on the ground that the arrangements were perfectly proper, were not intended to avoid rules of insolvency law, were to be applied no differently after liquidation than before and were as binding on the liquidator as they had been on British Eagle itself."

It is clear that the crucial question in *British Eagle* was whether its claim to payment was against Air France directly, with IATA acting simply as agent in providing a clearing mechanism, or whether on the other hand the claim was simply an item in the computation of British Eagle's net net debit or credit balance with IATA, the latter acting as principal. If, as the majority held, British Eagle's contractual entitlement lay directly against Air France, then

---

[47] [1975] 2 All E.R. 390.
[48] Lord Morris of Borth-y-Guest and Lord Simon of Glaisdale.

clearly its subjection to the claims of other clearing house members was an infringement of both the *pari passu* principle and the requirement of mutuality which precludes the set-off of third parties' claims against the amount due to the company in liquidation. But if, as was the view of the minority, the effect of the clearing house arrangements was that British Eagle's claim was only to such sum as after netting out in the clearing fell to be credited or debited to its account with IATA, its counterparty for the purpose of computing its claim was IATA, which would clearly be entitled to set off cross-claims vested in it with regard to services supplied to British Eagle by other airlines.

It has to be said that the minority view is much more in keeping with commercial reality (to say nothing of commercial convenience) than that of the majority.[49] Moreover, the decision of the majority is difficult to reconcile with the principle, emphasised by Lords Morris and Simon, that a liquidator stands in the shoes of the company in liquidation and takes each contract as he finds it, so that he cannot procure the company to enforce those provisions which are for its benefit without at the same time being bound by the contractual conditions qualifying the company's entitlement.[50] In policy terms, a multilateral netting arrangement should not be regarded as offensive to insolvency law if it is intended to operate in the same way outside and inside insolvency, so that it is not a device designed to improve the position of one party by reason of the insolvency of another.

The preservation of netting arrangements under market contracts and EC directives

Fortunately, in relation to recognised markets and clearing houses, the effect of *British Eagle* has been largely negated by special statutory provisions in Pt VII of the Companies Act 1989, supplemented by subordinate legislation, designed to safeguard from invalidation under rules of insolvency law market contracts, market charges, money market contracts, money market charges and system charges in favour of settlement banks and by EC directives and implementing legislation designed to preserve the validity of netting arrangements in insolvency in relation to financial collateral in order to reduce systemic risk. These have been outlined earlier. As will have been seen, some of these exemptions from insolvency law are directed to ensuring the validity on insolvency of close-outs and set-off and netting arrangements. The decision in *British Eagle* does not appear to affect the validity of

9–15

---

[49] In Australia, the High Court has by a majority upheld comparable netting arrangements, but only because IATA had changed its agreement to provide that no liability was to accrue between members of the clearing house and that instead all sums due to or from a member were from or to the clearing house (*International Air Transport Association v Ansett Australia Holdings Ltd* (2008) 234 C.L.R. 151; [2008] B.P.I.R. 57.

[50] See above, paras 3–05 and 9–14.

agreements which impose conditions for the repayment of debt—for example, "flawed asset" agreements by which a bank takes a cash deposit from a corporate customer on terms that this is not to be withdrawable until the customer and its associated companies have discharged their obligations to the bank. Such an arrangement does not remove the asset from the general body of creditors of the company: it qualifies the claim itself by defining the conditions in which the credit balance is to become repayable, pending which it is held in suspense.[51]

4. INSOLVENCY SET-OFF: GENERAL PRINCIPLES

The right of set-off in insolvency

9–16   The right of set-off in company insolvency is to be found in rr.2.85 and 4.90 of the Insolvency Rules 1986, dealing respectively with set-off in administration where the administrator makes an authorised distribution and set-off in winding up. The two rules have been substantially revised and expanded to take account of certain criticisms made by the House of Lords in *Re Park Air Services Ltd*[52] and to provide greater detail and clarity and bring the rule on set-off for liquidation into line with the rule in administration. The amendments[53] came into effect on April 1, 2005. Since r.4.90 is somewhat broader, in that distribution is involved in almost every winding up and all of the case law hitherto has concerned set-off in winding up, we shall focus on r.4.90, and then turn to consider what rules are special to set-off in administration under r.2.85.

Set-off in winding up

9–17   The rules on insolvency set-off are set out in r. 4.90 of the Insolvency Rules 1986, a lengthy rule which has been amended from time to time:

(i)   to list debts that are to be excluded in determining mutual credits, mutual debts and other mutual obligations and to cover cases where administration immediately precedes liquidation;

(ii)   to deal with future and contingent debts owed *to* the company as well as by it; and

---

[51] See *Goode on Legal Problems of Credit and Security*, 2008, para.1–21; and Wood, *English and International Set-Off*, paras 5–196 et seq.

[52] [2002] 2 A.C. 172.

[53] Insolvency (Amendment) Rules 2005 (SI 2005/527).

(iii) to clarify what sums are to be regarded as due for the purpose of the account of mutual dealings.

The main provisions of r.4.90 will be examined issue by issue.

Principles underlying insolvency set-off

As stated in para.9–17 above, the wording of r.4.90 has undergone substantial change, but the basic idea remains the same. The creditor has a right of set-off against the company only where he is a creditor "proving or claiming to prove for a debt in the liquidation". We shall discuss the meaning of "debt" shortly. It is not necessary that the creditor shall have lodged a proof; it suffices that he is "claiming to prove", which has been interpreted as meaning that he is entitled to prove, whether or not he has done so.[54] However, although a right to prove is a necessary condition of the creditor's right of set-off, it is not a sufficient condition; it is also necessary to satisfy the requirements of mutuality.[55] Where this is the case, an account is to be taken of what is due from each party to the other in respect of the mutual dealings, the sums due from one party are to be set off against the sums due from the other and only the balance owed by the company is provable in the liquidation.[56] The concept of "sum due" has been expanded to reflect the definition of "debt" in r.13.12(3), although this is not free from criticism.[57] If the balance is in the company's favour, it is payable to the liquidator as part of the assets if it has become due and payable, but if the debt owed to the company is only contingent or prospective, the balance is to be paid when it has become due and payable.[58]

9–18

The revised r.4.90 removes much of the doubt and controversy surrounding the original rule, although for a statement of the three basic principles governing the taking of the account we must still turn to two masterly analyses, by Hoffmann L.J. at first instance in *MS Fashions Ltd v Bank of Credit and Commerce International SA (No.2)*[59] and Lord Hoffmann (as he had now become) in *Stein v Blake*.[60] In the former, he laid out the three principles in the following terms:

"Certain principles as to the application of these provisions have been established by the cases. First, the rule is mandatory ('the mandatory

---

[54] *Stein v Blake* [1996] A.C. 243, *per* Lord Hoffmann at 253.
[55] See below, paras 9–24 et seq.
[56] Insolvency Rules 1986 r.4.90(3) and (8).
[57] See below, para.9–26.
[58] Insolvency Rules 1986 r.4.90(8).
[59] [1993] Ch. 425, affirmed by the Court of Appeal.
[60] Cited above n.54.

principle'). If there have been mutual dealings before the winding up order which have given rise to cross-claims, neither party can prove or sue for his full claim. An account must be taken and he must prove or sue (as the case may be) for the balance. Secondly, the account is taken as at the date of the winding up order ('the retroactivity principle'). This is only one manifestation of a wider principle of insolvency law, namely, that the liquidation and distribution of the assets of the insolvent company are treated as notionally taking place simultaneously on the date of the winding up order: see *In re Dynamics Corporation of America* [1976] 1 W.L.R. 757, 762, *per* Oliver J. Thirdly, in taking the account the court has regard to events which have occurred since the date of the winding up ('the hindsight principle'). The hindsight principle is pervasive in the valuation of claims and the taking of accounts in bankruptcy and winding up."[61]

In *Stein v Blake*,[62] Lord Hoffmann returned to the hindsight principle in the context of contingent claims:

"How does the law deal with the conundrum of having to set off, as of the bankruptcy date, 'sums due' which may not yet be due or which may become owing upon contingencies which have not yet occurred? It employs two techniques. The first is to take into account everything which has actually happened between the bankruptcy date and the moment when it becomes necessary to ascertain what, on that date, was the state of account between the creditor and the bankrupt. If by that time the contingency has occurred and the claim has been quantified, then that is the amount which is treated as having been due at the bankruptcy date. An example is *Sovereign Life Assurance Co v Dodd* [1892] 2 Q.B. 573, in which the insurance company had lent Mr Dodd £1,170 on the security of his policies. The company was wound up before the policies had matured but Mr Dodd went on paying the premiums until they became payable. The Court of Appeal held that the account required by bankruptcy set-off should set off the full matured value of the policies against the loan.

But the winding up of the estate of a bankrupt or an insolvent company cannot always wait until all possible contingencies have happened and all the actual or potential liabilities which existed at the bankruptcy date have been quantified. Therefore the law adopts a second technique, which is to make an estimation of the value of the claim. Section 322(3) says:

'The trustee shall estimate the value of any bankruptcy debt which, by reason of its being subject to any contingency or contingencies or for any other reason, does not bear a certain value.'

---

[61] *MS Fashions*, cited above n.59, at 432–433.
[62] Above, n.54. See also *Wight v Eckhardt Marine* [2004] 1 A.C. 147.

This enables the trustee to quantify a creditor's contingent or unascertained claim, for the purposes of set-off or proof, in a way which will enable the trustee safely to distribute the estate, even if subsequent events show that the claim was worth more. There is no similar machinery for quantifying contingent or unascertained claims *against* the creditor, because it would be unfair upon him to have his liability to pay advanced merely because the trustee wants to wind up the bankrupt's estate.[63] The estimation of value applies not only to liquidated claims but also those that are unliquidated—for example, damages for breach of contract—though it has to be said that, in contrast to the rules governing proof of debt, the set-off rules have never explicitly referred to damages or unliquidated claims in describing what falls within the phrase 'debt or liability'."[64]

The mandatory principle

Insolvency set-off is mandatory and cannot be excluded by agreement of the parties. This was so held by a majority decision of the House of Lords in *National Westminster Bank Ltd v Halesowen Presswork and Assemblies Ltd*.[65] The reason given is that the statutory provisions are considered to regulate matters of public interest in the orderly administration of the estate and are not purely a source of private rights enacted for the benefit of individual debtors of the estate having cross-claims against it. This majority ruling in *Halesowen*, although consistent with the imperative language of the set-off provision, constitutes an impediment to the reorganisation of companies in financial difficulty, a fact recognised in *Halesowen*, but in the majority view requiring legislation to deal with it. The Insolvency Law Review Committee gave much thought to the matter, pointing out that it was a common practice for a company in difficulty, when negotiating a moratorium with its creditors, to agree to open a new bank account with its existing bankers and keep this in credit, the bank for its part undertaking not to set off existing indebtedness, so that the fund would be preserved intact for any liquidator and the bank would not receive a preference. The present law made it necessary for the company to open another account with a different bank.[66] The committee concluded that there was no sound policy for maintaining the prohibition against contracting-out of insolvency set-off and good commercial reasons for reversing it, and they recommended legislation to that effect.[67] No steps have yet been taken to implement this recommendation.

9–19

---

[63] On this aspect the law has been changed by the new rr.4.90 and 2.85. See below, para.9–38.
[64] See below, para.9–28.
[65] [1972] 1 A.C. 785, Lord Cross dissenting.
[66] *Insolvency Law and Practice* (Cmnd. 8558, 1982), para.1341.
[67] ibid, para.1342.

The retroactivity principle

9–20   The effect of this principle is that in insolvency set-off the account between the company and the creditor asserting a right of set-off is considered to be taken as at the date of winding up even though it is not taken, and in practice cannot be taken, until a later date. In other words, insolvency set-off is self-executing and, once the facts are known, operates automatically from the point of liquidation without the need for any procedural step.[68] It follows that while it is not necessary that a pre-liquidation claim shall have matured by the time of the winding up, a claim not coming into existence at all until after the winding up—for example, a claim under a post-liquidation contract—is not eligible as a set-off. Moreover, the creditor cannot assign his claim against the company after the commencement of the winding up and prior to the taking of the account,[69] for the claim must be treated as *ipso jure* ceasing to exist as a separate claim upon the company going into liquidation, the claim and cross-claim being then automatically combined by force of law to produce a single net debit balance due to or from the creditor and all that can be assigned is any net balance in favour of the creditor or the company.[70] This can be asserted at any time after the company has gone into liquidation, without the need to wait for the taking of accounts,[71] for it follows from the fact that the ultimate quantification of claim and cross-claim and the striking of a balance take effect from the date of liquidation.

The wording of r.4.90(1) is on the face of it inconsistent with both the self-executing nature of insolvency set-off and the retroactivity principle, since it is expressed to apply to mutual dealings between the company and "any creditor of the company proving or claiming to prove in the liquidation". Literally construed, this would mean that set-off could only arise at the point where the creditor had lodged a proof or claimed a right to prove, which would have implications for the availability of set-off against a secured creditor.[72] But as Lord Hoffmann explained in *Stein v Blake*, it has long been held that this is unnecessary and that the words are to be construed to mean any creditor who would have been entitled to prove.[73] In other words, "claiming" means "having a claim".

---

[68] *Stein v Blake*, cited above n.54, *per* Lord Hoffman at 254, 255 and 258.
[69] This is now expressly provided by r.4.90(2)(d)(i) of the amended Insolvency Rules 1986. See below, para.9–34.
[70] *Stein v Blake*, cited above n.54, *per* Lord Hoffmann at 255.
[71] *Stein v Blake*, cited above n.54, at 258.
[72] See below, para.9–23.
[73] *Stein v Blake*, cited above n.54, at 253.

The hindsight principle

This is closely linked to the principle of retroactivity. The court looks at post-liquidation events to determine the state of account as at the date of liquidation. It applies in particular to the valuation of claims, whether these are made by way of set-off or otherwise. Contingent claims which crystallise into debts after the date of liquidation are brought into account as debts and may be revalued accordingly[74] with retrospective effect.[75] Similarly, amounts put in for existing but unliquidated claims may be adjusted if the claims become liquidated or are able to be more accurately valued in the light of post-liquidation events.[76] It follows from the hindsight principle, as well as from the retroactivity principle, that an assignment of the net balance can be made at any time after the company goes into liquidation, whether or not the net balance has then been struck.

9–21

Conditions of application of insolvency set-off in winding up

In order for r.4.90 as revised to apply, six conditions must be satisfied:

9–22

(i)   the claim must be admissible to proof at the relevant time;

(ii) there must have been mutual credits, mutual debts or other mutual dealings between the parties;

(iii) the mutual dealings must have taken place before the company goes into liquidation;

(iv) the claims on both sides much be such as will in their nature terminate in debt;

(v)   the company's claim must not have been based on the creditor's wrongdoing; and

(vi) the debt which the solvent party seeks to set off must not be a debt of a category excluded by r.4.90(2).

There was previously a further condition, namely that the company's claim had to have matured by the time it became necessary to ascertain the state of accounts. That condition has now gone. It is open to the company to set off a claim which is still contingent at the time of taking of the account, even

---

[74] See Insolvency Rules 1986 r.4.86(1).
[75] Subject only to the qualification that revaluation does not disturb distributions of dividend already made, although any additional sum payable as the result of it will have priority in any future distribution.
[76] See further below, para.9–28, as to unliquidated claims.

though the effect is to accelerate the solvent party's liability to the company to the extent of the set-off.[77]

We shall examine each of the six conditions in turn.

First condition: claim must be admissible to proof at the relevant time

9–23   Although the fact that the creditor's claim is provable is not a sufficient condition of his right to have it included in the set-off account, it is a necessary condition. A claim which is not provable at the relevant time cannot be asserted by way of set-off.[78] Hence, the creditor may not set off a claim which is unenforceable[79] or statute-barred,[80] or so contingent as to be incapable of estimation by the liquidator.[81] Nor can he assert a claim embodied in a proof which the liquidator has rejected, for this would be to allow him to bypass the rejection without going through the proper procedure of applying to the court under r.4.83 to reverse the liquidator's decision.[82] Again, a surety debarred by the rule against double proof from proving in the principal debtor's winding up[83] cannot achieve his objective by asserting a set-off.[84]

The relevant time is any time when it becomes necessary to ascertain the state of accounts between the parties, in other words, any time when a balance has to be struck. Typically, this will be at the time of proof, but this is not necessarily the case, because for one reason or another the creditor may not have lodged a proof and the question may arise in proceedings against him by the liquidator.[85] But once the account has been taken, the balance is deemed to have been struck at the time of liquidation, in accordance with the principle of retroactivity previously discussed.[86]

---

[77] Insolvency Rules 1986 r.4.90(4)(b). See below, para.9–38.
[78] *Re Fenton Ex p. Fenton Textile Association Ltd* [1931] 1 Ch. 85; and *Re West End Networks Ltd, Secretary of State for Trade and Industry v Frid* [2004] 2 All E.R. 1042. This is implicit in the reference in r.4.90(1) to "any creditor of the company proving or claiming to prove for a debt in the liquidation"; and see *Stein v Blake*, cited above n.54, *per* Lord Hoffmann at 253.
[79] *Pott v Clegg* (1847) 16 M. & W. 321.
[80] *ibid.*
[81] See Insolvency Rules 1986 rr.4.86 and 13.12(3).
[82] *Bank of Credit and Commerce International (Overseas) Ltd v Habib Bank Ltd* [1999] 1 W.L.R. 42.
[83] The rule against double proof precludes a surety who has not paid the debt from lodging a proof in respect of his or her prospective right of indemnity, for this would lead to a proof for the same debt by two people—the surety and the creditor. However, where both the creditor and the surety are in liquidation and the surety has an independent claim against the creditor for an indemnity, the creditor cannot prove in the liquidation of the surety without bringing into account under the rule in *Cherry v Boultbee* (1838) 2 Keen 319 the whole of the surety's indemnity claim as a contribution to the fund distributable in the surety's liquidation. The rule can be excluded by contract, but in *Mills v HSBC Trustee (CI) Ltd* [2009] EWHC 3377 (Ch), it was held that the contract documents did not have this effect. The case is now subject to a direct appeal to the Supreme Court.
[84] *Re Glen Express Ltd* [2000] B.P.I.R. 456.
[85] *Stein v Blake*, cited above n.54, *per* Lord Hoffmann at 253.
[86] Above, para.9–20.

As noted above, despite the wording of r.4.90(1) it is not necessary that the creditor shall actually have proved or claimed to prove by the time of taking of the account. It is sufficient that he has a right to prove at that time. It follows that set-off applies even in relation to a secured debt and in cases where the creditor intends to enforce his security rather than proving. The effect of the automatic nature of the set-off is that the debt due to the secured creditor is *pro tanto* reduced by the company's cross-claim, leaving secured only the balance, if any.[87] So the secured creditor's decision not to lodge a proof is irrelevant.[88] Accordingly, the decision to the contrary in *Re Norman Holding Ltd,*[89] where the argument that r.4.90 meant what it said and that entitlement to prove was not sufficient, must be taken to be overruled.[90]

Second condition: mutual credits, mutual debts and other mutual dealings

In its original form, the statutory provision was confined to mutual credits and mutual debts. The phrase "and other mutual dealings" was added by s.39 of the Bankruptcy Act 1869. The word "other", which taken literally would have cut down the previous right of set-off by requiring that the mutual credits and debits should be such as to constitute mutual dealings, has been construed as a linguistic slip,[91] since it is clear that s.39 was intended to broaden rather than constrict the right of set-off, and as the High Court of Australia pointed out,[92] "credits" and "debits" will ordinarily represent the outcome of dealings rather than the dealings themselves. This was the approach taken by the House of Lords in *Re West End Networks Ltd, Secretary of State for Trade and Industry v Frid,*[93] where it was held that the word "dealings" should be construed in an extended sense. In particular, it was not confined to consensual dealings, but covered the imposition of a statutory obligation analogous to a guarantee and even the commission of a tort. In that case, the question was whether a company which had gone into voluntary liquidation was entitled to set off a VAT credit against the Secretary of State's claim by statutory subrogation to the rights of unpaid employees which she had discharged in

9–24

---

[87] *MS Fashions Ltd v Bank of Credit & Commerce International SA (No.2)* [1993] Ch. 425, *per* Dillon L.J. at 446.

[88] The irrelevance of proof was noted by Lord Hoffmann above, n.85.

[89] [1991] 1 W.L.R. 10.

[90] That was not the view of H.H. Judge Eccles Q.C. in *Scottish Widows Plc v Stewart* [2005] EWHC 1831 (QB), but his explanation (at [185]) of the decision in *Re Normal Holdings Ltd* as based on the fact that the secured creditor, having realised his security, no longer had a provable debt does not, with respect, bear examination, for it is quite inconsistent with the automatic nature of the set-off, which *pro tanto* extinguishes the creditor's claim before he has reached the point of realising his security.

[91] Or, as the High Court of Australia put it in *Gye v McIntyre* (1991) 171 C.L.R. 609 at 623, "a linguistic problem".

[92] (1991) 171 C.L.R. 609 at 623.

[93] [2004] 2 A.C. 506.

pursuance of a statutory obligation. It was held that the Secretary of State's statutory liability for the sums due to the employees was analogous to a contract of guarantee and the fact that it was statutory rather than contractual did not change its character as arising from a dealing so as to make the claim and cross-claim mutual debts or other mutual dealings susceptible to set-off.[94] As to claims in tort, it is thought that not all tort claims qualify for entry into a set-off account. The particular tort claim the House of Lords had in mind was that which featured in *Gye v McIntyre*,[95] namely a claim for damages for fraudulent misrepresentation inducing a contract. That plainly is a claim arising from a business dealing and one which was held part of mutual dealings between the parties. By contrast, a claim against the company in tort for, say, conversion would not be a claim arising from a dealing.[96]

The requirement of mutuality has two facets.[97] First, the respective characters of the claim and the cross-claim must be commensurable. This means that both claim and cross-claim must be monetary claims or claims which a party is entitled to have reduced to money. So a person holding property as bailee or trustee for another cannot set off against his delivery or accounting obligation a money claim against the bailor or beneficiary. This rule is so strictly applied that even if the property held by the trustee is itself a money fund, the trustee is not permitted to set off his personal claim against the beneficiary,[98] and if the beneficiary goes into liquidation the trustee must transfer the fund to the liquidator intact and is left to prove in the liquidation for his cross-claim.[99] Secondly, there must be mutuality of parties, that is, the claim and cross-claim must be between the same parties in the same right. So it is not possible to set off against a claim by the company in liquidation a cross-claim against a third party, even if prior to liquidation there had been a valid contractual set-off along these lines, for on winding up any

---

[94] An unusual feature of the case was that the Secretary of State had wanted to treat her claim on this basis and sought to deduct the VAT credit from her proof, and it was the liquidator who rejected the proof on the ground that it should have been for the full amount. It must be rare for a proof to be rejected as being for too low a figure!

[95] Above, n.91.

[96] See the discussion in Rory Derham, *The Law of Set-Off*, 4th edn (Oxford: Oxford University Press, 2010), para.8–53, citing the decision of the New South Wales Supreme Court in *Re Leeholme Stud Pty Ltd* [1965] N.S.W.R. 1649.

[97] See Derham, *The Law of Set-Off*, 2010, Ch.7; and *Goode on Legal Problems of Credit and Security*, 2008, para.7–84.

[98] See *Re Lehman Brothers International (Europe) Ltd* [2010] 2 B.C.L.C. 301 at [331] (the decision was appealed, but not on this point). See further para.9–26 below.

[99] *National Westminster Bank Plc v Halesowen Presswork and Assemblies Ltd* [1972] A.C. 785, *per* Lord Kilbrandon at 821; and *Re Mid-Kent Fruit Factory* [1896] 1 Ch. 567. The underlying principle appears to be that money held on trust is held for a particular purpose and cannot be applied for a different purpose, namely towards discharge of a cross-claim, without the consent of the person for whom it is held. Another way of reaching the same result is to say that a contract claim and a trust claim do not constitute mutual dealings. There is authority that the principle does not apply in relation to a money fund held on a bare trust (*Re ILG Travel Ltd* [1995] 2 B.C.L.C. 128), but it is questionable whether this is correct. For an excellent treatment of set-off in relation to trust funds, see Derham, *The Law of Set-Off*, 2010, Ch.10.

contractual set-off, so far as not already exercised, disappears. Again, a claim against the company in liquidation cannot be set off against a claim vested in the company as trustee for a third party. In determining mutuality, the court will look at the beneficial ownership of claim and cross-claim rather than the legal title, but will require clear evidence that the beneficial interest is vested in someone other than the party holding the legal title.[100] The Crown is regarded as indivisible, so that a sum due from one department of state can be set off against a sum due to another department.[101]

In general, a person holding bonds through an account with an intermediary cannot assert a set-off against the issuer of the bonds, with whom he has no relationship, his dealings being with his own intermediary. There may, however, be cases in which such a person does acquire a direct claim against the issuer—for example, where the terms of the bond issue entitle him to call for delivery of definitive certificates which place him in a direct relationship with the issuer or where, in the case of a permanently immobilised global certificate, he is nevertheless given and exercises a right given by the bond trust deed or a deed poll to call for delivery or transfer of the underlying securities in extreme circumstances, such as the issuer's insolvency.

Third condition: the mutual dealings must have preceded the cut-off date

The cut-off date after which a mutual dealing becomes ineligible for set-off is specified in some detail in r.4.90(2).[102] One such date is the commencement of winding up. However, it is not necessary that the dealings should have given rise to mutual *debts* prior to the winding up. It suffices that the mutual dealings have created obligations which give rise to claims that can be set against each other at the time when it becomes necessary to ascertain the state of accounts between the parties.[103] Thus, the fact that a claim is still contingent at the time of commencement of the winding up does not affect its eligibility for set-off if it crystallises into a debt after the winding up.[104] Of course, the claim must not offend the rule against double proof.[105] So a surety who prior to the winding up has a contingent right to be indemnified by the debtor if the latter later defaults in payment to the creditor cannot assert the right as a set-off after the debtor's default unless he or she has paid the debt.[106]

9–25

---

[100] *Bank of Credit and Commerce International SA v Prince Fahd Bin Salman Abdul Aziz Al-Saud* [1997] B.C.C. 63.

[101] *Re West End Networks*, cited above n.78, in which it was held that a VAT credit due from Customs and Excise could be set off against a claim by the Secretary of State for Trade and Industry for the amount paid to employees to whose rights she was subrogated.

[102] See below, para.9–30.

[103] *Stein v Blake*, cited above n.54; and *Re West End Networks*, cited above n.78.

[104] *Re West End Networks*, cited above n.78. This is now explicitly stated in r.4.90(4) of the Insolvency Rules 1986.

[105] See para.8–45.

[106] See *Re West End Networks*, n.78 above, *per* Lord Hoffmann at [16]–[17].

Fourth condition: the claims on both sides must be such as will in their nature terminate in debt

9–26 Under r.4.90 of the Insolvency Rules, insolvency set-off depends on the existence of mutual dealings, etc., between the company in liquidation and "any creditor of the company proving or claim to prove for the debt in the liquidation". Set-off is in principle confined to mutual money obligations. However, the fact that one of the debts is secured does not affect the right of the debtor to set-off his own cross-claim against it; the automatic set-off simply reduces the amount of the secured obligation.[107] The solvent party cannot rely on set-off to withhold property of the company in his possession or control, whether as bailee or as bare trustee, and in the latter case this applies as much to a money fund held by the solvent party as bare trustee for the company[108] as it does to tangible property so held. Accordingly, if B, a bailee of goods owned by A Co, wrongfully sells the goods, he cannot set off a debt due to him from the company against his obligation to account for the proceeds, for the company's claim to the proceeds is not a mere money claim in debt, but a claim to ownership of the money fund which is enforceable as a proprietary claim in equity. Additional grounds for refusing a set-off are that a person cannot take advantage of his own wrong by converting another's property into money[109] and that a misappropriation is not a dealing.[110]

However, there are at least two apparent exceptions to the rule precluding set-off against property and trust moneys. First, if the property of the company in liquidation is subject to a lien or other security interest in favour of the solvent party, the security carries through to the proceeds of sale and may be enforced by retention of the proceeds to the extent of the amount owing to the secured creditor.[111] This is not a true set-off, merely a method of enforcing the security interest. Secondly, if property of the company is held by another with instructions or authority to convert it into money, then so long as that authority remains unrevoked at the time of liquidation, the other party, on selling the property, can set off against his liability to account for the proceeds a debt owed to him by the company in liquidation, even if the sale does not take place until after winding up, provided that the proceeds are received by the claimant by the time it becomes necessary to ascertain the state of accounts between him and the company. This is the principle established in *Rose v Hart*,[112] which has been said to constitute an anomalous exception to the rule that a money claim may not be set off

---

[107] See above, para.9–23.
[108] *Re Lehman Bros International (Europe) Ltd* [2010] B.C.L.C. 301 at [331].
[109] *Smith v Bridgend CBC* [2002] 1 A.C. 336.
[110] *Manson v Smith* [1997] 2 B.C.L.C. 161, *per* Millett L.J. at 164. Another way of reaching the same result is to say that a contract claim and a trust claim do not constitute mutual dealings.
[111] *Buhr v Barclays Bank Plc* [2002] B.P.I.R. 25.
[112] (1818) 8 Taunt. 499.

against a proprietary claim and to the separate mutuality rule that trust funds are not susceptible to set-off.[113] But this is doubtful. The essence of the rule in *Rose v Hart* is the provision of mutual credits, the solvent party extending credit to the company in reliance on his prospective receipt of the proceeds of the company's property for which the company gives credit to him, and that the credits are such "as must in their nature terminate in debts".[114] Hence, the true basis of the decision in *Rose v Hart* would seem to be that the person holding the company's property with instructions to convert it into money has implied authority, by virtue of their mutual dealings, to regard himself as a mere debtor for a sum equal to the proceeds, not as a trustee of the proceeds themselves, which he is free to treat as his own moneys.

The significance of the distinction is well established in decisions on reservation of title to goods under contracts of sale which authorise resale by the buyer, but impose no express requirement that he is to account for the proceeds of sale. In such cases, the court is likely to infer that the buyer is merely to be a debtor for the amount of the proceeds (or of such part of them as is necessary to discharge his price obligation), not a trustee.[115] A similar principle applies where the terms of the agreement between the parties impose on the solvent party a duty to hold the proceeds on trust for the company, but entitle him to deduct sums due to him from the company. Such an agreement will be construed as creating a charge on the proceeds, so that the solvent party is not a bare trustee, but one whose trust obligation applies only to the balance remaining in his hands after he has deducted from the proceeds the amount due to him.[116] The absence of a duty to keep the proceeds segregated from the solvent party's own moneys is not inconsistent with such a trust.[117] The position is otherwise where the solvent party is a bare trustee of the proceeds and thus has a duty to make them over to the company in liquidation without deduction.[118]

All of this presupposes that the disposition of the company's property was authorised, for if it was not, the person making it can hardly contend that he had authority to treat the proceeds as his own.[119] Moreover, as previously mentioned, a person cannot rely on his own wrongdoing to create a set-off   **9–27**

---

[113] Philip R. Wood, *English and International Set-Off*, para. 9–304; and Derham, *The Law of Set-Off*, 2010, para.10.18. Dr Derham accepts that where a person holds property with instructions to turn it into money on terms that he is to be merely a debtor for the proceeds, there is no barrier to set-off. His point is that this would not explain all of the cases (para.10.19).

[114] *Rose v Hart* (1818) 8 Taunt. 499, *per* Gibbs C.J. at 506.

[115] *Re Andrabell Ltd* [1984] 3 All E.R. 407; and *Hendy Lennox Ltd v Grahame Puttick Ltd* [1984] 2 All E.R. 152. See *Goode on Proprietary Rights and Insolvency in Sales Transactions*, edited by Simon Mills, 3rd edn (London: Sweet & Maxwell, 2009), paras 5–55–5–56.

[116] *Re ILG Travel Ltd* [1996] B.C.C. 21.

[117] *Re ILG Travel.*

[118] *Re ILG Travel*; and *Henry v Hammond* [1913] 2 K.B. 515.

[119] *Goode on Proprietary Rights and Insolvency*, 2009, para.5–54.

or to serve as a mutual dealing. So if he never had authority to sell in the first place or his authority was revoked prior to the sale, he will be a trustee of the entire proceeds and will have no right to set off his cross-claim against his duty to account.[120]

In the light of these considerations, the decision of the Court of Appeal in the controversial decision in *Rolls Razor Ltd v Cox*[121] is hard to justify. In that case, the defendant was a self-employed salesman appointed by the plaintiffs to sell their washing machines in return for commission and was required by the terms of his appointment to hand over the proceeds without deduction. The company also deducted a percentage of each week's commission to form a retention fund to which it could resort if the salesman defaulted in his obligations with regard to machines or proceeds. The company having gone into liquidation, the defendant asserted a lien and a right to set off the commission and retention moneys due to him against the proceeds he had received of two washing machines sold for the company prior to liquidation and the value of (inter alia) an unsold table top still in his possession at the time of liquidation and seven tap-adaptors, not for sale, which were used in the demonstration of the machines. The Court of Appeal upheld this contention as regards the goods, and proceeds of goods, held for sale[122] (Winn L.J. dissenting as to the table top) on the ground that while the defendant did not have a lien on the goods, there were mutual credits by the company to the defendant in respect of the proceeds of sale and by the defendant to the company in respect of the retention fund, so that a right of set-off arose which the company had not been entitled to defeat by purporting to terminate the agent's authority to sell.

The majority decision is hard to justify. In the first place, the table top had not in fact been converted into money even after the winding up, and in no previous case had a money claim been set off against an obligation to deliver unrealised property. Secondly, the defendant's contention that he was entitled to a lien on the goods was rejected, not merely because he was a mere agent, not a factor, but also because this was inconsistent with the terms of his agreement with the company requiring him to deliver up the goods on termination of the agreement. Surely it was equally inconsistent with the agreement that he should be allowed to sell the goods after termination of his authority and then deduct what was due to him from the proceeds. The decision in *Rose v Hart*[123] was specifically predicated on the assumption that the agent's authority to sell remained unrevoked up to the time of sale, and the same was true of the decision in *Palmer v Day*.[124] Nor could it be said that

---

[120] *Rose v Hart*, cited above n.114; and *Eberle's Hotels & Restaurant Co Ltd v Jonas* (1887) 18 Q.B.D. 459.
[121] [1967] 1 All E.R. 397.
[122] But not the tap-adaptors held for use only.
[123] Cited above n.114.
[124] [1895] 2 Q.B. 618.

the defendant's authority to sell was irrevocable because it was coupled with an interest,[125] namely the right to look to the proceeds for payment of his commission, for this, too, was prohibited by the agreement. Accordingly, it could not be said that there were mutual credits. That being so, the defendant's authority to sell had been effectively brought to an end by the company and would in any event have come to an end on the winding up. The defendant was thus not a mere debtor but a trustee, who ought not to have been allowed to profit from his own act of conversion.[126] It is true that the set-off provisions are mandatory—a point relied on by Lord Denning M.R. to overcome the contract point—but they do not apply at all unless the test of mutuality is satisfied, and this is not the case where the claim on one side is to payment of money and on the other to delivery of property held on trust or to the proceeds of property wrongfully converted. The present position has rightly been described as anomalous[127] and is a good illustration of hard cases making bad law.

Unliquidated damages

A claim for unliquidated damages has been admissible for set-off since s.10 of the Judicature Act 1875 imported into winding up the rules of set-off in bankruptcy,[128] in which set-off had, as previously mentioned, been extended by s.39 of the Bankruptcy Act 1869 to cover mutual dealings, and it was this that was held to cover unliquidated claims for damages.[129]

9–28

Fifth condition: company's claim must not have been based on creditor's wrongdoing

The creditor cannot escape from the consequences of a misfeasance or other wrongdoing for which the company is making a claim by invoking a right of

9–29

---

[125] See Peter G. Watts, *Bowstead and Reynolds on Agency*, 19th edn (London: Sweet & Maxwell, 2010), paras 10–06 and 10–07.

[126] See below, para.9–29.

[127] Wood, *English and International Set-Off*, para.9–304.

[128] *Mersey Steel and Iron Co, Ltd v Naylor, Benzon & Co* (1889) 9 App. Cas. 434; and *Re Asphaltic Wood Pavement Co, Lee & Chapman's Case* (1885) 30 Ch.D. 216.

[129] *Booth v Hutchinson* (1872) L.R. 15 Eq. 30. Hence, it is unnecessary to rely on the new r.4.90, based on the more general r.13.12(3), a rule of long standing which strangely, in contrast to r.12.3(1) relating to provable debts, does not refer specifically to claims for damages or, indeed, unliquidated claims of any kind, but states merely that a sum shall be regarded as being due to or from the company "whether . . . its amount is fixed or liquidated, or is capable of being ascertained by fixed rules or as a matter of opinion". See also r.13.12(2), extending to the category of provable debts (and thus to the set-off provisions) a liability in tort where all of the elements necessary to establish the cause of action are established except actionable damage.

set-off against the claim. So the creditor cannot set off the debt owed to him by the company in liquidation against a claim by the company by way of misfeasance proceedings for the recovery of misappropriated funds[130] or for damages for conversion[131] or recovery of a sum paid to him by way of a voidable preference[132] or settlement.[133] Any other conclusion would enable the wrongdoer to benefit from his wrongdoing by recovery through set-off instead of having to prove in the winding up in competition with other creditors.[134]

Sixth condition: solvent party's claim must not be excluded by r.4.90(2)

9–30   Rule 4.90(2) of the revised Insolvency Rules 1986 sets out the various cut-off dates after which a debt arising from a mutual dealing is excluded from the set-off provisions. The debts in question are as follows:

(1) Debt arising out of obligation incurred with notice of winding up meeting or petition

9–31   Debts due from the company in liquidation to another party are not to be included in the account of mutual dealings if they arose out of an obligation incurred at a time when that other party had notice that a meeting of creditors had been convened under s.98 of the Insolvency Act or that a petition for winding up was pending. It is to be noted that the relevant time is not when the debt became payable, but when the obligation which arose from it was incurred. So provided that the solvent party was without notice of the above facts when the debt was contracted, the fact that he later acquires notice before the debt matures does not debar him from having it brought into account.

(2) Debt arising out of obligation incurred with notice of administration application

9–32   A debt is excluded from the set-off account if arising out of an obligation where the liquidation was immediately preceded by an administration and at the time the obligation was incurred the creditor had notice that an application for an administration order was pending or a person had given notice of intention to appoint an administrator.

---

[130] *Manson v Smith* [1997] 2 B.C.L.C. 161.
[131] *Smith (Administrator of Cosslett (Contractors) Ltd) v Bridgend CBC* [2002] 1 A.C. 336.
[132] *Re A Debtor (No.82 of 1926)* [1927] 1 Ch. 410.
[133] *Lister v Hooson* [1908] 1 K.B. 174.
[134] *Manson v Smith*, cited above n.130, *per* Millett J. at 165.

(3) Debt arising out of obligation incurred during an administration immediately preceding the liquidation

If the liquidation was immediately preceded by an administration, a debt **9–33**
arising from an obligation incurred during the administration is not eligible
for inclusion in the set-off account.

(4) Debt acquired by assignee in certain events

In general, a person owing the company money is entitled to set off against **9–34**
his or her liability a claim vested in him as assignee. So a debtor to the company can purchase a claim against the company and set this off against the
company's claim on him. However, the right of set-off is potentially vulnerable if the assignment is taken at a time when the company is insolvent.
Although this is not by itself a bar to inclusion of the assigned debt in the set-
off account, the effect of r.4.90(2)(d) is that the debt cannot be included if it
was acquired by the creditor, by assignment or otherwise,[135] pursuant to an
agreement between the creditor and any other party:

(i)   after the company went into liquidation;

(ii) at a time when the creditor had notice that a meeting of creditors had
      been summoned under s.98;

(iii) at a time when the creditor had notice that a winding up petition was
      pending;

(iv) where the liquidation was immediately preceded by an administra-
      tion, at a time when the creditor had notice that an application for an
      administration order was pending or a person had given notice of
      intention to appoint an administrator; or

(v)   during an administration which immediately preceded the
      liquidation.

Accordingly, where an assignment is caught by r.4.90(2)(d), the assigned
claim ceases to be capable of being raised as a set-off by anyone: not by the
assignee because of r.4.90(2)(d) and not by the assignor because there is no
longer mutuality. However, there is nothing unreasonable in this result. A
party giving value for the assignment of a debt due from a company when he
has notice that insolvency proceedings are imminent is the author of his own

---

[135] e.g. by contractual subrogation. But acquisition by legal subrogation, as where the creditor
was a surety for the company and has paid the debt due to the creditor, is not barred, for the
right of subrogation is not conferred by agreement.

misfortune, while the assignor who receives value no longer has an interest in set-off anyway.

Position where claim by company is contingent

9–35 The set-off rules were formerly incapable of being applied where it was the company in liquidation that had the contingent claim. That is no longer the case.[136]

5. INSOLVENCY SET-OFF IN SPECIAL SITUATIONS

Set-off in relation to unmatured or contingent claims under executed contracts

9–36 The question addressed here is the extent to which unmatured or contingent claims arising under contracts wholly performed by the claimant may be set off by or against the other party.

Unmatured or contingent claims by the solvent party

9–37 The effect of the statutory provisions for the admission to proof of unmatured debts at their face value[137] and of contingent claims at their estimated value is that as from the date of liquidation such claims are notionally converted into matured debts and are automatically set off against any matured debts owed by the creditor to the company. However, this is subject to the rule against double proof which (inter alia) precludes a surety from proving or setting off his right of indemnity against the insolvent company until he has paid in full the amount of the guaranteed debt or such separate part of it as he has guaranteed.[138]

Unmatured or contingent claims against the solvent party

9–38 In the converse case, where it is the company in liquidation that has the unmatured or contingent claim, the position was formerly that the rules set out above did not apply. This was because the liquidator had no right to

---

[136] See below, para.9–38.
[137] But discounted for the purpose of dividend distribution (Insolvency Rules 1986 r.11.13(2)).
[138] See above, para.8–45.

accelerate the liability of the solvent party; the principle of acceleration applied only to claims *against* the company. Thus, the solvent party was entitled to prove for his claim in full without set off of the company's unmatured or contingent claim against him. If the latter claim matured into an immediately payable debt, the liquidator could sue for it in the name of the company, but the solvent party was entitled to set off against the liquidator the amount of his own cross-claim after giving credit for any dividend received.[139]

These complexities were later removed as the result of changes to r.4.90, the effect of which is that the liquidator may now set off even future or contingent claims against the solvent party, thus accelerating the solvent party's liability for set-off purposes, but any balance remaining due from the solvent party is to be paid only when it falls due and payable.[140] In other words, the acceleration is limited to what is necessary to exhaust the set-off rights of the company in liquidation. Similarly, the discounting of the amount of the solvent party's cross-claim is limited to what is necessary to calculate the dividend after carrying out the set-off to the extent needed to exhaust the company's liability, and any balance owed by the solvent party is payable by that party in full when the time for payment arrives.[141] This is logical, because the solvent party need not pay the balance of the debt due from him until it matures and ought not to be given a windfall by discounting that balance to present value as if it had become immediately payable.

Set-off in relation to deposits taken by a bank which becomes insolvent

The collapse of the Bank of Credit and Commercial International SA gave rise to a number of actions concerning the effect of the insolvency rules where the bank had loaned money to a borrower and taken a security deposit of funds from a third party. In some cases, this was underpinned by the third party's personal guarantee, in others it was not. In one case, the guarantee contained a "principal debtor" clause which was held to impose on the surety the liability of a principal debtor for repayment. In working out the insolvency set-off rules, it is necessary to distinguish three situations.[142] The first is where the depositor gives a personal guarantee which contains a principal debtor clause, so that his liability is not merely contingent. The second is where he gives a personal guarantee which does not contain a principal

9–39

---

[139] *MS Fashions Ltd v Bank of Credit and Commerce International SA (No.2)* [1993] Ch. 425 at 435.

[140] Insolvency Rules 1986 r.4.90(8).

[141] *Re Kaupthing Singer & Friedlander Ltd* [2010] B.P.I.R. 839, a decision on set-off in administration.

[142] For an excellent discussion, see Richard Calnan, "The Insolvent Bank and Security Over Deposits" (1996) J.I.F.B.L. 185.

debtor clause and provides for payment on demand, so that his liability is contingent on demand being made. The third is where he gives no personal guarantee at all, but merely deposits funds with the creditor as security for the loan to the borrower.

(1) Deposit reinforced by personal guarantee containing a principal debtor clause

9–40   In *MS Fashions Ltd v Bank of Credit and Commerce International SA (No.2)*,[143] the issue was concisely presented by Hoffmann L.J. in the following terms:

> "A bank advances money to a company. Repayment is guaranteed by a director who has a deposit account with the bank. As between himself and the bank, the director is expressed to be a principal debtor. On the insolvency of the bank, can the director set off his claim for return of his deposit against his liability to pay the company's debt, so that the debt is wholly or *pro tanto* extinguished? Or can the bank claim the whole debt from the company and leave the director to prove in the liquidation for his deposit?"[144]

Hoffmann L.J. held that as a matter of construction the effect of the principal debtor clause was that the director was not merely making a deposit by way of security, but was assuming a personal liability for repayment jointly and severally with the borrower company, or alternatively severally, that such liability was not merely contingent and that accordingly the liquidation of the bank resulted in an automatic set-off of the deposit against the liability, thus *pro tanto* extinguishing the indebtedness of the borrower company. It was therefore not open to the liquidator, as it would have been if there had been no principal debtor clause, to recover from the borrower without giving credit for the deposit, leaving the director to prove as an unsecured creditor for the amount of his deposit released from the charge as the result of the borrower's repayment.

On the finding of a personal guarantee, as a matter of construction the result reached was inevitable. However, it has to be said that the evidence for a personal guarantee was decidedly tenuous; and the ruling that the charge itself could be analysed as the creation of a personal liability not exceeding the amount of the deposit[145] is not sustainable, for it imports a personal liability where none is needed except, of course, for the purpose of arriving at

---

[143] Cited above n.139.
[144] *MS Fashions* (above, n. 139) at 430.
[145] *MS Fashions* at 431.

the desired result! In *Re Bank of Credit and Commerce International SA (No.8)*[146] the Court of Appeal felt unable to agree with this ruling and Lord Hoffmann himself, in the subsequent appeal to the House of Lords,[147] acknowledged that it produced anomalous results and was based on the peculiar wording of the guarantee.

(2) Deposit reinforced by personal guarantee payable on demand with no principal debtor clause

In this situation, the surety is not a principal debtor and in the absence of demand his liability is merely contingent. As we have seen, a contingent claim *by* the company in liquidation *against* the solvent party was formerly not accelerated by the liquidation, so that unless demand was made, converting the contingent claim into a matured debt, no set-off could be invoked by the liquidator. In consequence, the liquidator could avoid the independent set-off by refraining from making the requisite demand, thus maintaining the company's claim in full against the borrower without having to give credit for the sum that would have been treated as received from the surety in a balance of account had the set-off provisions been triggered. Under the revised r.4.90, the solvent party's liability is accelerated to the extent of the company's right of set-off.

9-41

(3) Deposit not reinforced by any personal guarantee

This was the situation in the *BCCI* case mentioned above, where the facts were otherwise very similar to those in *MS Fashions*. Money was deposited with the bank by way of non-recourse collateral security[148] for a loan to the principal debtor. The bank then went into liquidation. The liquidator declined to resort to the security deposit and sought repayment from the principal debtor without giving credit for the deposit, leaving the depositor to prove as an unsecured creditor. The borrower and depositor contended that credit should be given for the deposit. Among the various grounds advanced were that: the depositor as a non-recourse surety had a right to pay off the debt and to have his deposit utilised for that purpose; the liquidator's approach would expose the borrower to a double liability, namely to repay the loan and to indemnify the depositor against the loss of his deposit

9-42

---

[146] [1996] Ch. 245; [1996] B.C.L.C. 204 sub nom. *Morris v Agrichemicals Ltd*. See below, para.9–42.

[147] *Re Bank of Credit and Commerce International SA* [1998] A.C. 214 at 224–225.

[148] It had at one time been thought that this was conceptually impossible, but see now *Re Bank of Credit and Commerce International,* cited above n.147, *per* Lord Hoffmann at 226–228 and *Goode on Legal Problems of Credit and Security*, 2008, para.3–12.

through the bank's insolvency; the bank's inability to repay the deposit discharged the borrower *pro tanto* from liability by reason of the bank's "loss" of the security in becoming insolvent and its consequent inability to return it; and the deposit was paid to the bank on trust to be applied for a particular purpose, namely discharge of the principal debt, for which it should be used by the liquidator.

The House of Lords,[149] affirming the decision of the Court of Appeal,[150] had no difficulty in rejecting all of these arguments. In the absence of any personal guarantee by the depositor, it was not possible to set off the deposit against the loan. The bank owed money to the depositor and the borrower owed money to the bank. The debts were therefore not due from the same parties, so that the mutuality which was essential to avoid a preference over other creditors was lacking. The proposition that the borrower was exposed to double liability was fallacious, since it rested on the assumption that the borrower was obliged to indemnify the depositor against the loss of his deposit, a proposition which was untenable. The surety's only right to indemnity was where he had paid off the principal debt. Nor could the principle relating to loss of securities by the creditor avail the borrower or depositor. The deposit had not been disposed of or the depositor's legal entitlement to repayment impaired; the position was simply that the bank was unable to repay. In any event, there was no basis for saying that the loss of a security provided by a surety discharges the principal debtor; at best it would discharge the surety. Finally, there was no evidence to show that the deposit had been impressed with a purpose trust. The bank was a mere debtor.

It was recognised that this result produced the paradox that a surety who gave no personal guarantee was worse off than one who gave a personal guarantee and thus had his liability extinguished by set-off. But that was inevitable if injustice to the general body of creditors was to be avoided. The point here is that what the depositor was seeking to do was to avoid the consequences of the bank's insolvency so far as he was concerned by requiring the bank to utilise the deposit to pay off the debt. But the deposit was an asset of the bank which under the *pari passu* principle should be available for the general body of creditors. In the absence of any trust affecting it, the depositor, as an unsecured creditor, had no right to give instructions to the liquidator as to the application of the deposit. By collecting repayment from the borrower, the liquidator would cause the debt to be discharged, thus freeing the deposit from the security and entitling the depositor to repayment. In that situation, the depositor should stand in the same position as other unsecured creditors.

---

[149] *Re Bank of Credit and Commerce International,* cited above n.147.
[150] [1996] Ch. 245.

Set-off in relation to executory contracts

It will be evident from the foregoing that where all of the relevant contracts **9–43** are executed and the claims on both sides are for money or are reducible to money, insolvency set-off will rarely be a problem in English law. Set-off in relation to existing liquidated claims, even if payable in the future, is straightforward. Unliquidated claims and contingent claims are valued (so far as capable of estimation) and become treated as the equivalent of liquidated claims for purposes of proof and set-off.

The one real danger zone is that occupied by executory contracts.[151] Where the contracts on both sides are still in force and executory at the time of winding up, the solvent party is exposed to the risk of cherry-picking by the liquidator, who may seek to enforce the contract that is profitable to the estate[152] while disclaiming the unprofitable contract[153] and leaving the solvent party to prove in the winding up for damages. In principle, such damages cannot be set off against the solvent party's liability under the other contract because of the principle that post-liquidation receipts derived from the activity of the liquidator and use of the company's resources do not belong to the company in its own right,[154] so that the requisite element of mutuality is lacking.[155] The solution is to provide in each contract that all executory contracts will automatically be terminated, rescinded or closed out by a reverse transaction in the event of either party going into liquidation, or alternatively to provide, as under the ISDA 2002 Master Agreement, that all transactions between the same parties form part of a single overall contract.[156]

Preferential debts

Where the creditor is owed both preferential and non-preferential debts, a set-off available to the company in liquidation for less than the total amount due is not to be applied exclusively to the preferential debts (thus benefiting the estate) or exclusively to the non-preferential debts (thus preserving

---

[151] See above, para.6–22.

[152] Which in principle he can do except where: (i) the winding up of the company can be regarded as a repudiatory breach; or (ii) the court accedes to an application by the solvent party to rescind the contract under s.186 of the Insolvency Act 1986, which it will normally do only where the two contracts are so connected that it would be inequitable to allow the liquidator to enforce one contract if he is not prepared to procure the company's performance of the other.

[153] Under s.178 of the Act. See above, paras 6–27 et seq.

[154] See above, para.6–33.

[155] See Wood, *English and International Set-Off*, paras 5–18 and 7–145 et seq., for an exhaustive analysis with reference to typical transactions.

[156] See above, para.9–12.

the creditor's priority intact), but is to be applied to the two sets of debt rateably.[157]

Voidable preferences

9–45   No question of preference can arise where the creditor collects payment by exercise of right of set-off, for this does not require the consent of the company at all, let alone a desire on its part to improve the creditor's position. Payment by the company into an overdrawn account with its bank is likewise not capable of being a preference where the payment does not exceed the amount of a credit balance held by the company on another account to which the bank could have resorted by way of combination of accounts if the payment in question had not been made, for the effect of the payment is *pro tanto* to reduce the available amount of set-off against the account in credit, so that the position of other creditors is unaffected. Again, if a creditor assigns a debt due to him from the company in order to give the assignee a right of set-off, no preference is involved because the company is not thereby "suffering" anything to be done by which the assignee is preferred, and such an assignment is therefore effective[158] so long as not falling within r.4.90(2)(d).

Where, by virtue of an agreement between a company and its directors, the company has a contractual right to set off against one director's credit balance an amount due from another director, exercise of that right is not a preference of the first director, for it is for the company's benefit, not that of the first director.[159]

Specially protected transactions and arrangements

9–46   In order to promote market stability and reduce systemic risk, various types of transaction concluded on a market or through a recognised clearing house or settlement system enjoy special protection from insolvency rules. This has been discussed earlier.[160]

Foreign currency set-off

9–47   For the purpose of proving a debt incurred or payable in a currency other than sterling, the amount of the debt is to be converted into sterling at the

---

[157] *Re Unit 2 Windows Ltd* [1985] 3 All E.R. 647. This would appear to apply equally to a combination of accounts not effected prior to the winding up. See Tony Shea, "Statutory Set-Off" [1986] 3 J.I.F.B.L. 152, 154.
[158] *Re Parkside International Ltd* [2010] B.C.C. 309.
[159] *Re Exchange Travel (Holdings) Ltd (No.3)* [1996] 2 B.C.L.C. 524.
[160] Above, paras 1–60 et seq.

official rate of exchange prevailing on the date when the company went into liquidation.[161] This now applies also in relation to set-off under r.4.90 of the Insolvency Rules 1986.[162]

6. SET-OFF IN ADMINISTRATION

The rules governing insolvency set-off presuppose that the insolvency admin-   **9–48**
istrator has power to make distributions and for that purpose admit proofs and apply the relevant rules of insolvency set-off. A liquidator has always been invested with both the power and the duty to distribute; indeed, after collecting in the assets, that is his primary function. By contrast, an administrator's powers of distribution of were closely circumscribed.[163] So when administration was first introduced, there were no rules of set-off in administration. When the Insolvency Act 1986 was amended to modify and simplify the administration procedure and to empower the court to give permission for the administrator to make a distribution,[164] the opportunity was taken to amend the Insolvency Rules 1986 by substituting a new Pt II, including a new r.2.85 providing for mutual credits and set-offs in administration.[165] This was modelled on r.4.90, but with important differences in wording which caused concern to insolvency practitioners. Accordingly, the Insolvency (Amendment) Rules 2005[166] substituted a new r.2.85 for the existing rule and modified r.4.90 to bring the two rules into alignment.[167]

Since an administrator cannot make a distribution to general creditors without the permission of the court, r.2.85 applies only where the administrator, being authorised to make the distribution in question, has, pursuant to r.2.95, given notice that he proposes to make it.[168] As the result of the alignment of rr.2.85 and 4.90, the regimes applicable to set-off in administration and liquidation are essentially the same, with the substitution of references to: (i) administration for references to liquidation; and (ii) a winding up immediately preceding the administration for references to a liquidation which was immediately preceded by an administration.

---

[161] Insolvency Rules 1986 r.4.91(1).
[162] Insolvency Rules 1986 r.4.90(6).
[163] See below, para.11–85.
[164] Sch.B1 para.65(2).
[165] Insolvency (Amendment) Rules 2003 (SI 2003/1730).
[166] SI 2005/527.
[167] As to the discounting of claims, see above, para.9–38.
[168] Insolvency Rules 1986 r.2.85(1).

Chapter 10

Administrative Receivership

1. THE DEVELOPMENT OF ADMINISTRATIVE RECEIVERSHIP

Old-style receivership: the receiver of income

Historically, receivership is not an insolvency proceeding at all, merely a method by which a secured creditor can enforce his security. Originally, a mortgagee whose mortgagor defaulted could apply to the court to appoint a receiver to collect the rents and profits of the mortgaged property and apply these to payment of the mortgage interest. Subsequently, it was found more convenient for the appointment to be made by the mortgagor himself at the request of the mortgagee, thus obviating an application to the court. Later still, mortgagees began reserving the power to make the appointment themselves, at the same time providing that the receiver was to be the agent of the mortgagor, not of the mortgagee. In making the appointment, the mortgagee acted as agent of the mortgagor,[1] a fact which explains the apparent anomaly of an agency created by an agreement to which the agent is not a party.[2] In due course, the power to appoint a receiver of income was made statutory,[3] although it was the practice to exclude or expand the statutory provisions relating to the circumstances in which a receiver could be appointed and his powers on appointment. But the role of such a receiver under the Law of Property Act 1925 was, and remains, a receiver of income.

10–01

---

[1] *Gaskell v Gosling* [1896] 1 Q.B. 669, *per* Rigby L.J. at 691. Although Rigby L.J. was a dissenting minority, his judgment was approved by the House of Lords on appeal, sub nom. *Gosling v Gaskell* [1897] A.C. 575.
[2] See further para.10–24.
[3] See now Law of Property Act 1925 ss.101(l)(iii) and 109.

Modern receivership: the receiver and manager

10–02   With the expansion of business and the increased provision of credit to finance the establishment and operation of the undertaking, creditors became increasingly concerned to secure stronger protection for their investment, in particular, by reserving the right to appoint not merely a receiver, but a manager of the business, the two offices almost invariably being combined in the same person. In order for the receiver and manager to have effective powers of management it was, of course, necessary to provide the creditor with global security covering the whole or substantially the whole of the company's assets and undertaking. Thus evolved the modern debenture, which typically created a fixed charge over fixed assets and a floating charge over the rest of the company's undertaking, with power to appoint a receiver and manager,[4] having extensive authority to get in the assets, run the company's business and dispose of the assets either piecemeal or as part and parcel of a sale of the business as a going concern. A debenture holder could still apply to the court for the appointment of a receiver but there was little advantage in doing so, for an application to the court would involve time and expense and the receiver's powers would be circumscribed by the terms of the order and his need to work within a judicial framework, whereas a receiver and manager appointed pursuant to the debenture had all of the powers conferred by the debenture and could still be declared to act as agent of the mortgagor.

Extended receivership without management

10–03   The two categories of receivership mentioned above in paras 10–01 and 10–02 are not exhaustive. There are other types of receivership which go beyond the collection of income but fall short of administrative receivership.[5]

The introduction of the administration regime

10–04   Administrative receivership is essentially a debt enforcement mechanism for the benefit of the debenture holder who appoints the receiver. Prior to 1986, there was no machinery by which an external manager could be appointed to run the company's business and safeguard the assets for the benefit of the general body of creditors, and the administrative receiver owed no duty to creditors generally. The Insolvency Act 1986, re-enacting the Insolvency Act 1985, created just such machinery in the form of administration.[6] Under this

---

[4] Thus crystallising the floating charge (see para.10–36).
[5] See below, para.10–21.
[6] Insolvency 1986 Pt II.

new insolvency regime, application could be made to the court to appoint an administrator to take control of the assets and manage the company for the benefit of all of the creditors. The administrator was given the same extensive powers as an administrative receiver.[7] An application to the court had the effect of imposing a freeze on the exercise of most remedies, including the enforcement of security but did not prevent the appointment of an administrative receiver, and if such an appointment were made before the making of an administration order, the court was in general precluded from making such an order except with the debenture holder's consent.[8] Thus, except where the security was vulnerable, the debenture holder could always block administration by appointing an administrative receiver.

2. THE PARTIAL ABOLITION OF ADMINISTRATIVE RECEIVERSHIP

A review group set up by the Department of Trade and Industry and the Treasury published a report in 2000[9] showing that views on the merits of administrative receivership were divided. Most respondents felt that administrative receivership was an integral part of the rescue culture that had been developing and contributed to the rescue and survival of companies, in that the receiver could take rapid and effective action to prevent further deterioration on the business of the company, a sizeable number of businesses were sold off by the receiver on a going concern basis and the costs of initiating the procedure were relatively low.[10] Banks were keen to support the rescue of viable companies but feared that changes to the existing system would reduce their security and their ability to enforce it. On the other hand, others felt that receivership placed too much power in the hands of one creditor and that this could lead to unnecessary business failures, particularly since there was a lack of incentive to consider the interests of other creditors and to maximise the value of the debtor company's estate.[11] Banks that were over-secured had little incentive to ensure that receivers they appointed kept costs and fees down and avoided precipitate realisation of assets. Research conducted by Professor Julian Franks and Dr Oren Sussman,[12] based on material provided by three clearing banks, has shown that about 75 per cent of companies emerged from bank supervision and avoided formal insolvency

10–05

---

[7] Insolvency Act 1986 s.14 and Sch.1.

[8] Insolvency Act 1986 s.9(3).

[9] *Review of Company and Business Reconstruction Mechanisms* (May 2000), para.73. The review is available on the Insolvency Service website.

[10] ibid,, para.48.

[11] ibid,, para.49.

[12] *The Cycle of Corporate Distress, Rescue and Dissolution: A Study of Small and Medium Size UK Companies* (2000), sponsored by the DTI/Treasury Working Group on Company Rescue and Business Reconstruction Mechanisms.

procedures but that during the period in which the company was in intensive care, the amount owed to the bank shrank, while the amount owed to trade and expense creditors increased. Where a formal insolvency proceeding ensued, the average recovery rates were 77 per cent for the bank, 27 per cent for preferential creditors and virtually nil for unsecured creditors.[13] A subsequent small survey by R3, subsidiary to its main survey for the period January 2002 to June 2003, gave a similar, dismal return for ordinary unsecured creditors, at just 5 pence in the pound.[14]

The principal recommendation of the review group was that the power of veto given to the holder of a floating charge to block an administration by appointing an administrative receiver should be abolished.[15] But under the influence of the Treasury, which considered that the whole institution of administrative receivership was inimical to corporate rescue through a collective insolvency proceeding, government thinking hardened. A White Paper published by the Department of Trade and Industry in 2001[16] set out the new approach.

The outcome was a set of provisions in the Enterprise Act 2002 amending the Insolvency Act 1986 in two major respects. First, the new provisions make it easier for a company to go into administration by dispensing with the need for a court order. This was an essential step because as research had shown, a key factor powering many appointments of administrative receivers was speed in the assumption of management control and the collection of assets, and the delay involved in court-appointed administration was considered to place assets at risk.[17] Secondly, the provisions prohibit the appointment of an administrative receiver altogether under a "qualifying floating charge",[18] except where it is a charge created before September 15, 2003 or, if it is a charge created on or after that date, it falls within one of the specified exceptions.[19] Save in these cases, the debenture holder's remedy is to appoint an administrator, which is less efficacious from the viewpoint of the debenture holder in that whilst an administrative receiver's primary task was to safeguard the interests of his debenture holder, an administrator is required to give priority to other objectives, where reasonably practicable.[20] There are eight exceptions, which are designed to safeguard large capital

---

[13] *ibid*, pp.3–4.

[14] R3, "Corporate Insolvency in the UK", 12th Survey (July 2004), p.27.

[15] *Review of Company and Business Reconstruction Mechanisms* (above, n. 9), para.73.

[16] "Insolvency—A Second Chance" (Cm. 5234).

[17] Alan Katz and Michael Mumford, *Comparative Study of Administration and Administrative Receivership as Business Rescue Vehicles* (London: ICAEW, August 2003), pp.x and 14. See further below, para.11–04.

[18] As defined by the Insolvency Act 1986 Sch.B1 para.14. See below, para.11–07.

[19] Enterprise Act 2002 s.250, inserting s.72A into the Insolvency Act 1986. Section 72A applies in spite of an agreement or instrument which purports to empower a person to appoint an administrative receiver, by whatever name (s.72A(4)(b)). For the efficacy of the Enterprise Act provisions, see below, para.11–118.

[20] See below, para.11–06.

market arrangements involving the issue of a capital market investment, public-private partnership projects incorporating step-in rights, utility projects, urban regeneration projects, large-scale project finance incorporating step-in rights,[21] financial market charges, system-charges and collateral security charges, registered social landlords and protected railway companies.[22] As regards a floating charge falling within one of these categories or created before September 15, 2003, the holder of the charge remains free to appoint an administrative receiver, and while such a receiver is in office, no administrator can be appointed.[23] The restrictions on the appointment of an administrative receiver do not apply to an industrial and provident society, which is not a "company" for the purpose of Pt III of the Insolvency Act 1986.[24]

3. THE LEGAL NATURE OF ADMINISTRATIVE RECEIVERSHIP[25]

The term "administrative receiver", first introduced by the Insolvency Act 1985, and carried forward into the Insolvency Act 1986,[26] is simply the statutory label for the individual who was previously termed receiver and manager. Administrative receivership has long been the *de facto* monopoly of the accountancy profession and requires professional skill and judgment of a high order, since it is the task of the administrative receiver, with his team of assistants, to take over the management of the company from the directors, with a view to trading it out of its difficulties,[27] and for that purpose to keep the company afloat, negotiate with banks and other creditors, dispose of unprofitable sectors of the business, eliminate unnecessary expenditure and generate income, so that in due course the business can be sold as a going concern or hived down into a specially formed subsidiary which can be disposed of as a clean company with assets but no liabilities. Only a qualified insolvency practitioner can act as administrative receiver.[28]

10–06

---

[21] See *Feetum v Levy* [2006] Ch. 585.

[22] Insolvency Act 1986 ss.72A–72GA and Sch.2A. The exceptions relating to urban regeneration and protected railway companies were inserted by the Insolvency Act 1986 (Amendment)(Administrative Receivership and Urban Regeneration etc) Order 2003 (SI 2003/1832). For the definitions of the various categories, see Insolvency Act 1986 Sch.2A, as amended.

[23] Insolvency Act 1986 Sch.B1 paras 17(b) and 25(c). See further below, para.10–13.

[24] *Re Dairy Farmers of Great Britain Ltd* [2010] Ch. 63.

[25] See generally Sandra Frisby and Malcolm Davis-White, *Kerr & Hunter on Receivers and Administrators*, 19th edn (London: Sweet & Maxwell, 2010); Gavin Lightman et al., *The Law of Administrators and Receivers of Companies*, 4th edn (London: Sweet & Maxwell, 2007); and Ian Fletcher, *Law of Insolvency*, 4th edn (London: Sweet & Maxwell, 2009), Ch.14.

[26] See below.

[27] Of course, this is not always possible. Sometimes the administrative receiver has no choice but to close the business down and dispose of the assets at the best price he can get.

[28] See below, para.10–25.

As mentioned earlier,[29] administrative receivership is not a true collective insolvency proceeding but remains in principle a method by which a particular debenture holder can enforce his security. But by statute several insolvency features have become attached to administrative receivership, so that it is considered an insolvency proceeding even though the administrative receiver's duty is in principle owed only to his debenture holder,[30] not to the general body of creditors.

The administrative receiver defined

10–07   An administrative receiver is defined by s.29(2) of the Insolvency Act 1986 in the following terms:

> "(a) a receiver or manager of the whole (or substantially the whole) of a company's property appointed by or on behalf of the holders of any debentures of the company secured by a charge which, as created, was a floating charge, or by such a charge and one or more other securities; or
>
> (b) a person who would be such a receiver but for the appointment of some other person as the receiver of part of the company's property."

Several aspects of this definition require comment.

"The whole or substantially the whole of a company's property"

10–08   Four questions arise in relation to this phrase: (1) What does "whole or substantially the whole" mean? (2) As at what date is the position to be tested? (3) What is the effect of the prior appointment of a receiver of part of the property? and (4) Can an administrative receiver be appointed if another administrative receiver is in post under a different debenture?

(1) "Whole or substantially the whole"

10–09   What matters here is not the scope of the debenture under which the receiver is appointed but the scope of the appointment. Debentures frequently empower the debenture holder to crystallise a floating charge,

---

[29] See above, para.1–38.
[30] And, by statute, to preferential creditors as regards assets within the scope of a floating charge. See below, paras 10–60 et seq.

and to appoint a receiver, in respect of a specific asset or part only of the assets, since this provides the necessary security over a threatened asset or class of assets without inhibiting the continuance of the rest of the company's business. A receiver so appointed is not an administrative receiver even if the debenture under which he is appointed covers substantially the whole of the assets. It is necessary that his receivership should encompass substantially the whole of the assets. It is thought that this is to be determined by reference to the total value of the company's property, not by reference to the number of items within the scope of the appointment.

(2) As at what date?

It is clear from the wording of s.29(2) that the time when the above requirement has to be satisfied is the time of the receiver's appointment. The fact that the company acquires substantial additional assets later which happen to fall outside the scope of the charge, and thus of the appointment, is irrelevant.

10–10

(3) Prior receiver of part of property

Limb (b) of s.29(2) provides that the term "administrative receiver" includes a person who would be a receiver of the whole or substantially the whole of the company's property but for the appointment of some other person as receiver of part of the company's property. For example, another debenture holder may have appointed a Law of Property Act receiver under a fixed charge of a specific property or a receiver under a floating charge limited to a particular class of asset. In fact, it is not unusual for floating charges to be taken over a limited class of asset, for example, those taken to secure the financing of stock in trade for brewers or for motor dealers, which are commonly confined to the stock in question. Section 29(2)(b) appears to have been inserted *ex abundante cautela*, for on the view taken here the requirement that the floating charge and any other charges together cover the whole or substantially the whole of the company's property relates only to the relationship between the company and the debenture holder,[31] and is thus not affected by the fact that another receiver holds part of the property.

10–11

(4) Another administrative receiver in post

The view has been expressed that a person cannot be appointed as administrative receiver if another administrative receiver has already been

10–12

---

[31] See below para.10–12.

appointed.[32] However, it is necessary to distinguish the appointment of an administrative receiver from his exercise of management functions. It is clear that only one person, or two or more people acting jointly under the same instrument,[33] can perform the functions of an administrative receiver at any one time but that is not a reason for denying the validity of the second appointment. All that happens is that the second administrative receiver has to wait on the sidelines until the prior administrative receivership has been completed. There is nothing unusual in this kind of situation. It is a common occurrence for a company to go into liquidation while still in administrative receivership. In such a case, the liquidator's statutory powers in relation to the control and disposal of the assets and the management of the company's business for the purpose of its beneficial winding up[34] are not exercisable while an administrative receiver is in post, for so long as the debenture holder's security interest in the whole of the assets subsists, it has priority over the claims of the general body of creditors whom the liquidator represents. This demonstrates that there is no inherent objection to having two office-holders in post at the same time, although only one of them can exercise *in rem* management powers. As between two administrative receivers, priority should in principle be determined by the priority of the respective debentures under which they were appointed[35]; but once the first administrative receiver has effectively entered upon the receivership, he can only be displaced by a court order removing the first receiver.[36] While the court may be expected to give due weight to the priority of the competing debentures, the fact that a debenture holder no longer has power to replace its receiver without leave of the court shows that this is not now considered to be a matter exclusively within the private domain, and that the court will have regard to the interests of creditors.[37]

---

[32] See Fidelis Oditah, "Lightweight Floating Charges" [1991] J.B.L. 49 at 51 et seq.; and David Marks and Dominic Emmet, "Administrative Receivers: Questions of Identity and Double Identity" [1994] J.B.L. 1.

[33] Insolvency Act 1986 s.33(2).

[34] Insolvency Act 1986 Sch.4.

[35] Where there are two floating charges each of which covers all of the assets, priority will in principle go to the earlier, even if the later was the first to crystallise, for there is a presumption that the freedom which a floating charge allows to a company to dispose of its assets in the ordinary course of business does not extend to the grant of another floating charge over all of the assets. See *Re Benjamin Cope & Sons Ltd* [1914] Ch. 800. The position is otherwise where the subsequent floating charge covers only part of the assets and power to create such charge in priority to the first floating charge was reserved to the company by the first floating charge (*Re Automatic Bottle Makers Ltd* [1926] Ch. 412). However, the distinction drawn in the latter case between a subsequent floating charge covering all of the assets and one covering only part of the assets seems unnecessary; the sole question in each case should be whether the terms of the first floating charge permit a subsequent charge to be given ranking in priority to the earlier floating charge.

[36] Insolvency Act 1986 s.45(1).

[37] That some judicial control may be necessary is demonstrated by the facts in *Downsview Nominees Ltd v First City Corp* [1993] A.C. 295, where a debenture holder who appointed a receiver for the sole purpose of preventing enforcement of a subsequent debenture by a receiver previously appointed by the holder of the second debenture was held liable in damages for loss caused. See further below, para.10–34.

Can it be said that the effect of the first security is to prevent the second security from covering the whole or substantially the whole of the company's property? This calls for an emphatically negative response. Notwithstanding the infelicitous wording of s.29(2)(b), it is clear that s.29(2)(a) is concerned solely with relations between the debenture holder and the company and is not addressed to competing security interests. All that is necessary is that, as between the debenture holder and the company, security which includes a floating charge is given over substantially the whole of the company's property. How that security ranks with a similar security given to another creditor is irrelevant. The later interest still covers substantially the whole of the company's property, subject to the prior charge. Put another way, the company's property after giving the first charge over all of its property is its equity of redemption, and in charging this to the second debenture holder the company is charging the whole of its remaining property.

This is not a mere technical question. It is important that the law should allow concurrent appointments—even if only one can take effect in possession—for the second chargee needs to be able to ensure that there is no interval between the completion of the first administrative receivership and the appointment of the second administrative receiver during which the latter appointment could be blocked by the making of an administration order. Recognition of the validity of the second appointment *ab initio* ensures a seamless progression from one receivership to the other.

(5) An administrator in post

By contrast, it is not possible to have a concurrence of administration and administrative receivership. It is a question of who is appointed first. Once a company is in administration, an administrative receiver may not be appointed.[38] If, on the other hand, an administrative receiver is in office, an administrator may not be appointed by the company or its directors,[39] and an application for an administration order must normally be dismissed unless his appointor consents to it, whether the receiver was appointed before or after the making of the application.[40] Where, however, the court has and exercises power to appoint an administrator, any administrative receiver must vacate office.[41]

10–13

---

[38] Insolvency Act 1986 Sch.B1 para.43(6A).

[39] Insolvency Act 1986 Sch.B1 para.25(c).

[40] Insolvency Act 1986 Sch.B1 para.39. The court is also free not to dismiss the application where it thinks that the security is vulnerable under the avoidance provisions: para.39(b)–(d).

[41] Insolvency Act 1986 Sch.B1 para.41(1).

"Appointed by or on behalf of the holders of any debentures of the company"

10–14 This precludes a receiver appointed by the court from being an administrative receiver, a logical provision, for the powers of a court-appointed receiver are limited by the terms of the order appointing him, which could be incompatible with the powers conferred on administrative receivers by Sch.1 of the Act. This view has been challenged by some authorities, in particular by Professor Ian Fletcher, an eminent authority who argues that there is evidence within the Act to indicate that court-appointed receivers were intended to fall within the ambit of s.29 of the Act. Several reasons are advanced for this view, as set out in the following passage[42]:

> "Provisions intended to apply only to receivers appointed out of court refer, not to receivers 'appointed by or on behalf of debenture holders' but to receivers 'appointed under powers contained in an instrument' [citing ss. 33–38]. Section 29 appears within a group of sections under the heading 'Preliminary and General Provisions' and another section in this group, s. 31, expressly provides that it has no application to a court-appointed receiver. Furthermore if the wording of s. 29 is to be taken as excluding court appointed receivers, then the similar wording in s. 40 of the Act could have the effect of excluding court appointed receivers from the duty to pay preferential debts out of the proceeds of a floating charge despite s. 40 appearing in a group of sections under the heading 'Provisions applicable to every receivership'."

There are several answers to the points made above.

(1) Section 29(2)(a) defines an administrative receiver as:

> ". . . a receiver or manager of the whole (or substantially the whole) of a company's property appointed by or on behalf of the holders of any debentures of the company secured by a charge which, as created, was a floating charge, or by such a charge and one or more other securities."

The phrase "appointed by or on behalf of the holders of any debentures" in s.29(2)(a) is thus used specifically with reference to a charge which, as created, was a floating charge. The same applies to s.40. By contrast, ss.31 and 33–38 cover any kind of receiver appointed under an instrument, whether the instrument is a charge or another kind of instrument and whether or not it includes a floating charge. It is therefore perfectly understandable that the

---

[42] Fletcher, *Law of Insolvency*, 2009, para.14–026. See to similar effect Frisby and Davis-White (eds), *Kerr & Hunter on Receivers and Administrators*, 2010, para.7–56.

draftsman wished to avoid carrying over the phrase used in ss.29(2)(a) and 40 into the quite different context of ss.31 and 33–38 and decided instead to use the phrase "appointed under powers contained in an instrument".

(2)   Section 33(1), which uses the same phrase, provides that the appointment of a person as receiver "is of no effect unless it is accepted by that person before the end of the business day next following that on which the *instrument of appointment* is received by him or on his behalf" [emphasis added]. The reference to an instrument of appointment clearly excludes an appointment by the court.

(3)   An administrative receiver is deemed to be the agent of the mortgagor.[43] This rule existed long before the Insolvency Act but it never applied to a court-appointed receiver,[44] and a receiver originally appointed by the mortgagee but subsequently appointed by the court ceased to be the agent of the mortgagor.[45]

(4)   Under s.46(1) an administrator receiver is required, on his appointment, to send to the company and to publish "in the prescribed manner" a notice of his appointment. Under r.3.2(2)(e) of the Insolvency Rules 1986, the notice is required to state "the name of the person by whom the appointment was made". Clearly, this is inapplicable to a court appointment.

(5)   Finally, the whole point of s.72A of the Insolvency Act was to eliminate the regime of administrative receivership except in the cases mentioned in ss.72B–72GA. It is inconceivable that Parliament intended to allow the regime to continue by means of an appointment by the court.

It is therefore not surprising that in *Re A. & C. Supplies Ltd,*[46] Blackburne J. considered (albeit obiter) that while he had power to remove an administrative receiver, he had no power to appoint one.

"Secured by a charge which, as created, was a floating charge, or by such charge and one or more other charges"

Several points arise in connection with this element of the statutory definition.   **10–15**

---

[43] Insolvency Act 1986 s.44(1)(a).
[44] H.G. Hanbury and C.H.M. Waldock, *Law of Mortgages* (London: Stevens and Sons, 1938), pp.159–160.
[45] *Hand v Blow* [1901] 2 Ch. 721, *per* Romer L.J. at 732; and Falcon Chambers, *Fisher and Lightwood's Law of Mortgage*, 12th edn (London: LexisNexis Butterworths, 2008), p.28.8.
[46] [1998] B.C.C. 708.

(1) Distinction between fixed and floating charge

10–16   I have discussed elsewhere the nature of the floating charge and the characteristics which distinguish it from a fixed charge.[47] The courts have been much occupied with the distinction in relation to a charge over book debts given in favour of a bank where the chargor is required to pay the proceeds into a bank account but is free to draw on the account as and when needed unless the bank intervenes. This was upheld by the Court of Appeal in its controversial decision in *Re New Bullas Trading Ltd*,[48] a decision which the Privy Council declined to follow in *Agnew v Commissioners of Inland Revenue*[49] on the basis that the company's power to utilise the proceeds was inconsistent with the nature of a fixed charge. This is plainly correct. It has been established for well over a century that the mere fact that the chargee has power to intervene is not sufficient to establish the charge as a fixed charge; it is necessary both to introduce and to operate a control mechanism which ensures that the company is not free to deal with the proceeds as its own pending the bank's intervention. The Privy Council decision was followed by the House of Lords in *Re Spectrum Plus Ltd*.[50]

(2) Crystallisation is irrelevant

10–17   The fact that the charge under which the receiver is appointed crystallised before his appointment, and was therefore no longer floating, is irrelevant. What matters is its character at the time of creation. This is in line with the definition of "floating charge" in s.251 of the Insolvency Act as a charge which as created was a floating charge.[51]

(3) Residual floating charge suffices

10–18   It is not necessary that the floating charge should itself cover the whole or substantially the whole of the company's property; it suffices that a floating

---

[47] *Goode on Commercial Law*, edited by Ewan McKendrick, 4th edn (London: Penguin Books and LexisNexis, 2009), Ch.25; and *Goode on Legal Problems of Credit and Security*, edited by Louise Gullifer, 4th edn (London: Sweet & Maxwell, 2008), Ch.IV.

[48] [1994] B.C.L.C. 485.

[49] [2001] 2 A.C. 710.

[50] *Re Spectrum Plus Ltd, National Westminster Bank Plc v Spectrum Plus Ltd* [2005] 2 A.C. 680, in which the House of Lords reversed the decision of the Court of Appeal, overruled *Siebe Gorman & Co Ltd v Barclays Bank Ltd* [1979] 2 Lloyd's Rep. 142 and disapproved *Re New Bullas Trading Ltd* [1994] B.C.C. 36, by which the Court of Appeal had rightly regarded itself as bound. For detailed analyses of the *Spectrum* case, see Josuha Getzler and Jennifer Payne (eds), *Company Charges: Spectrum and Beyond* (Oxford: Oxford University Press, 2006).

[51] The definition is also relevant (inter alia) to the treatment of priorities between preferential debts and those secured by a crystallised floating charge. See below, para.10–60.

charge and one or more fixed charges together encompass such property. Because of the advantages of a fixed charge over a floating charge in terms of priority over subsequent security interests and the claims of preferential creditors, lenders tend to take fixed security over as many classes of asset as possible, leaving the floating charge to gather up the rest. This is fully compatible with s.29(2). A vestigial ("lightweight") floating charge is all that is needed. But if there is no floating charge at all, the receiver will not be an administrative receiver. Accordingly, there may be circumstances in which the debenture holder would find it convenient to argue that a charge which is described as a fixed charge is in fact a floating charge—an argument which for other purposes he could be expected strenuously to resist!

Where there are fixed charges as well as a floating charge, it is not necessary that all of the charges should be comprised in the same debenture. What matters is their aggregate effect.

(4) Susceptibility of future assets to floating charge suffices

The fact that at the time of the receiver's appointment there are no assets currently within the scope of the floating charge does not prevent the receiver from being an administrative receiver. It suffices that the floating charge has the potential to catch after-acquired property of the company. In *Re Croftbell Ltd,*[52] it was conceded that a receiver was not precluded from being an administrative receiver merely because at the time of the debenture the company had no assets (for otherwise the company could not grant a floating charge at the commencement of its business when it had no assets) or all of the assets were subject to a fixed charge. But it was contended that if the evidence showed that the company had no intention of entering into trading transactions, so that the floating charge served no purpose but to frustrate the appointment of an administrator by the court,[53] it had to be disregarded. This contention was rejected by Vinelott J., who held that the question of whether a debenture holder had power to appoint an administrative receiver could not turn on the company's intentions at the time it executed the debenture, for those intentions might change and future assets might fall within the floating charge.

10–19

Appointment under fixed charge

If a debenture holder has a floating charge and a fixed charge which together encompass substantially the whole of the company's property, is a receiver

10–20

---

[52] [1990] B.C.L.C. 844.
[53] See Insolvency Act 1986 s.9(3) (now Sch.B1 para.39). See below, para.10–26.

appointed under the fixed charge an administrative receiver? In an unreported decision by Vinelott J. in *Meadrealm Ltd v Transcontinental Gulf Construction Ltd*,[54] this question was answered in the negative; only a receiver appointed under a floating charge could qualify as an administrative receiver. However, the decision is not easy to reconcile with the wording of s.29(2), and would seem to focus on the wrong issue. The crucial question is not the nature of the charge or charge-element under which the receiver is appointed but the property over which he is appointed. A receiver appointed in respect of only part of the assets simply cannot function as an administrative receiver, for he has no *in rem* powers over those assets outside the scope of his appointment and is therefore inhibited from effectively managing the company's business. Hence the requirement that the receiver be appointed in respect of the whole or substantially the whole of the company's property. That is all that s.29(2) requires. If this requirement is satisfied, it should not matter under which element of a security package the appointment is made. Indeed, to speak of an appointment "under a fixed charge" is rather misleading, for it confuses the security interest with the instrument by which the security is created and the source of the appointment with the property to which the appointment relates. If a fixed charge covers substantially the whole of the company's property and there is a residual floating charge over the rest, that should suffice. Admittedly, the continuance of the company's business could, in theory at least, lead to the acquisition of further substantial assets outside the scope of the floating charge, so that the fixed charge would cease to cover substantially the whole of the company's property but again that would seem to be irrelevant, for as stated earlier the material time is the time of the receiver's appointment.

The three categories of receiver

10–21 With the enactment of what is now the Insolvency Act 1986, there are three categories of receiver:

(i) the administrative receiver, defined above;

(ii) the receiver of income only (i.e. the Law of Property Act receiver);

(iii) other types of receiver, for example:
    (a) a receiver under a debenture creating only a fixed charge but conferring on the receiver more extensive powers than the

---

[54] Unreported, November 29, 1991.

collection of income, for example, the power to secure repayment by getting in and realising assets and the wide range of powers typically contained in a security trust deed;

(b) a receiver under a debenture which includes a floating charge, but does not cover all or substantially all of the company's property,[55] whether the receiver is appointed out of court or by the court;[56]

(c) an all-assets receiver, or receiver and manager,[57] appointed by the court at the instance of a debenture holder.

Non-administrative receivership is apparently the preferred option when dealing with problems of distressed debt.[58] The rest of this chapter is confined to the administrative receiver.

Mode of appointment

A receiver is only an administrative receiver if he is appointed out of court by the debenture holder.   **10–22**

Administrative receiver compared with other types of receiver

An administrative receiver has a number of characteristics which mark him out from other types of receiver.   **10–23**

(i) An administrative receiver is deemed to be the company's agent unless and until it goes into liquidation,[59] and the same is true of a Law of Property Act receiver.[60] One consequence of this is that such a receiver will not normally be subject to a third-party costs order in respect of costs incurred in unsuccessful litigation instituted in the name of the company, because the receiver is not a third party; his position is analogous to that of directors.[61] A receiver appointed by a

---

[55] Other than a receiver who would be a receiver of the whole but for the appointment of another person as receiver of part and who is thus himself an administrative receiver.

[56] For a case where a receiver of a particular property was appointed by the court on the application of the mortgagee even though there was an administrator in post, see *Sinai Securities Ltd v Hooper* [2004] B.C.C. 973.

[57] As in *Parsons v Sovereign Bank of Canada* [1913] A.C. 160; and *Reid v Explosives Co Ltd* (1887) 19 Q.B.D. 264.

[58] David Milman, "The Continuing Institution of Receivership and Its Relationship to Other Security Enforcement Tools and Recovery Devices in English Law" (2009) 247 Co. L.N. 1.

[59] Insolvency Act 1986 s.44(1).

[60] Law of Property Act 1925 s.109(2).

[61] *Dolphin Quays Developments Ltd v Mills* [2008] 1 W.L.R. 1829.

debenture holder in relation to part only of a company's property is the agent of the debenture holder who appoints him unless the debenture provides otherwise,[62] as it almost invariably will.

(ii) The appointment of an administrative receiver usually prevents the making of an administration order.[63] This is not true of other receivers.

(iii) An administrative receiver is an office-holder for the purpose of certain provisions of the Insolvency Act,[64] and the Company Directors Disqualification Act,[65] with attendant powers, duties and privileges which are not necessarily possessed by other receivers.

(iv) The powers conferred on the administrative receiver by the debenture holder are deemed to include those set out in Sch.1 to the Insolvency Act; in the case of other receivers, such powers must be conferred by the terms of the debenture itself.

(v) Only a receiver who is an administrative receiver can apply for an order under s.43 of the Insolvency Act to dispose of property charged to another creditor.

(vi) An administrative receiver is required to obtain a statement of affairs from the officers of the company, and to send a report to the registrar of companies[66]; other types of receiver are merely required to file accounts.

(vii) An administrative receiver may be removed only by the court[67]; a receiver who is not an administrative receiver may be removed by the debenture holder who appointed him, if the debenture so provides.

(viii) An administrative receiver cannot be appointed during the period in which the company is in administration[68]; no such restriction applies to the appointment of other types of receiver, although they would be powerless to act until the administration order had been discharged.[69]

---

[62] *Re Vimbos Ltd* [1900] 1 Ch. 470; and *Deyes v Wood* [1911] 1 K.B. 806.
[63] See below, para.10–26.
[64] Insolvency Act 1986 ss.233(1) and 234(1).
[65] Company Directors Disqualification Act 1986 s.7(3).
[66] Insolvency Act 1986 ss.47 and 48.
[67] Insolvency Act 1986 s.45(1). Prior to the Insolvency Act 1985, it was for the debenture holder to remove a receiver and appoint another in his place, if so empowered by the debenture.
[68] Insolvency Act 1986 Sch.B1 para.43(6A).
[69] Because of the restrictions imposed on the enforcement of security, the repossession of goods and the commencement or continuance of proceedings (Insolvency Act 1986 Sch.B1 para.43) and the fact that the management of the business is placed under the control of the administrator (Insolvency Act 1986 Sch.B1 paras 59, 60, 64(1) and Sch.1).

(ix) An administrative receiver must vacate office on the making of an administration order[70]; other types of receiver need vacate office only on being required to do so by the administrator.[71]

(x) The acts of an administrative receiver are valid notwithstanding any defect in his appointment[72]; there is no similar rule for ordinary receivers.

These differences reflect the fact that the administrative receiver takes over substantially the whole of the company's assets and manages the business, so that he is treated in much the same way as an office-holder in a collective insolvency proceeding such as administration or liquidation.

The multi-faceted character of administrative receivership

To define an administrative receiver is simple, because the Insolvency Act itself provides us with a definition. It is much more difficult to identify the legal essence of administrative receivership. This is because the administrative receiver has two sets of powers and owes duties to two different parties, in consequence of which he does not fit readily into any identified mould.[73] The first set of powers relates to the possession, management and realisation of the security. These powers are exercised in right of the debenture holder and, being given for the enforcement of the debenture holder's rights *in rem*, are unaffected by the company's liquidation. The second set of powers, conferred by the company through the execution of the debenture and exercised by the receiver as agent of the company, enables him to conclude contracts in the name of the company, thus committing it to further liabilities, and to engage and dismiss staff and generally run the business. The agency powers come to an end on the winding up of the company except to the extent to which their exercise is ancillary to the enforcement of the security.[74]

10–24

In his legal relationships the administrative receiver, like the Roman God Janus, faces two ways. He owes a limited duty of care to the company as its deemed agent[75] and a separate duty of care to the debenture holder who appointed him,[76] yet at the same time he possesses a high degree of autonomy. His agency for the company is of a peculiar kind, since it exists primarily for the protection and enhancement of the debenture holder's security.

---

[70] Insolvency Act 1986 Sch.B1 para.41(1).
[71] Insolvency Act 1986 Sch.B1 para.41(2). Presumably a court-appointed administrator of all of the company's assets remains in office unless and until the court orders otherwise.
[72] Insolvency Act 1986 s.232.
[73] See below.
[74] See below, para.10–66.
[75] As to the source and extent of this duty, see below, para.10–48.
[76] See below, para.10–48.

Accordingly the company has no power either to terminate the agency or to control its deemed agent as to the manner in which he performs his duties. Further, his obligations to the company are subordinated to his duties to his debenture holder, so that even if his acts cause damage to the company's interests, he incurs no liability so long as what he did was for the proper protection of the debenture holder and he did not needlessly damage the company's business.[77] In addition, his deemed agency for the company largely protects his debenture holder from responsibility for his acts or omissions.[78] On the other hand, he is not at the beck and call of the debenture holder. To the contrary, the debenture holder has no right to give directions to the receiver in the conduct of his receivership; indeed, if the debenture holder does so, he risks being held liable for any improper acts or omissions of the receiver, who will then be treated as his agent.[79] The independence of the administrative receiver is reinforced by the fact that he can now only be removed by order of the court.[80] He is also required by statute to ensure that where the free assets of the company are insufficient to pay preferential creditors, any shortfall is made good from property subject to a floating charge in priority to the claims of the chargee.[81]

So the administrative receiver is a protean character, changing his colour, shape and function according to circumstances. He can best be described as an independent contractor whose primary responsibility is to protect the interests of his appointor but who also owes a duty to his deemed principal, the company, to refrain from conduct which needlessly damages its business or goodwill, and a separate duty, by statute, to observe the priority given to preferential creditors over claims secured by a floating charge. Since this is the only kind of receiver I intend to discuss, I shall for brevity refer to him hereafter simply as "the receiver". I shall examine a little later the precise nature of the agency power and its relationship with the exercise of security rights on behalf of the debenture holder.[82]

4. APPOINTING THE RECEIVER OUT OF COURT

Who can be appointed

10–25   A person can be appointed a receiver of a company only if qualified to act as an insolvency practitioner in relation to the company.[83] This means that he

---

[77] See below, para.10–49.
[78] Insolvency Act 1986 s.44(1)(a).
[79] See below, para.10–75.
[80] Insolvency Act 1986 s.45(1).
[81] See para.10–60.
[82] See para.10–48.
[83] Insolvency Act 1986 s.230(2). But the fact that a receiver is appointed who is not qualified does not affect the validity of his acts (Insolvency Act 1986 s.232).

must be qualified both generally and in relation to the company itself. A qualified insolvency practitioner is a person authorised to act as such by:

(i)   a recognised professional body; or

(ii) the Secretary of State; or

(iii) a competent authority designated by the Secretary of State.[84]

Only an individual can be a qualified insolvency practitioner.[85] Moreover, a person cannot be appointed who is an undischarged bankrupt, a person to whom a moratorium period under a debt relief order applies, a person who is subject to an in-force bankruptcy or debt restrictions order, a person subject to a disqualification order under the Company Directors Disqualification Act 1986 or a person that lacks capacity within the meaning of the Mental Capacity Act 2005.[86] Even if otherwise qualified, an insolvency practitioner cannot act as receiver of a company until he has furnished appropriate security for the proper performance of his functions,[87] as where he is covered by a bond, whether in relation to his practice generally or in relation to a particular receivership.

Grounds for appointment

The Insolvency Act is silent as to the grounds on which a receiver may be appointed out of court. Although a chargee under a charge by deed has certain implied powers under s.101 of the Law of Property Act 1925 to appoint a receiver of income, the debenture is the sole source of the right to appoint a receiver with management powers.[88] The well-drawn debenture should therefore provide for every event on which the appointment of a receiver may be desired. There is no implied power to appoint a receiver merely because the security is in jeopardy.[89] A purported appointment will not, of course, be effective if the debenture under which the appointment is made is invalid. In addition, it is necessary that any conditions for making the

10–26

---

[84] See the Insolvency Act 1986 ss.390–392 and the Insolvency Practitioners (Recognised Professional Bodies) Order 1986 (SI 1986/1764).

[85] Insolvency Act 1986 s.390(1).

[86] Insolvency Act 1986 s.390(4)–(5).

[87] Insolvency Act 1986 s.390(3).

[88] However, if the company has invited the debenture holder to appoint the receiver in the mistaken belief that the debenture holder has become entitled to make the appointment, it is precluded from saying that the appointment is ineffective, and the receiver is a trespasser, up to the time it discovers the mistake and asks him to withdraw. See below, para.10–30.

[89] *Cryne v Barclays Bank Plc* [1987] B.C.L.C. 548. The court has power to appoint a receiver "in all cases in which it appears to the court to be just and convenient to do so" (Supreme Court Act 1981 s.37(1)), and it is a well-established ground for appointment that the security is in jeopardy (Supreme Court Act 1981 s.37(1)).

appointment which are specified in the debenture are either satisfied at the time of the receiver's acceptance of the appointment[90] or are waived by the directors under the terms of the debenture, failing which the appointment will be a nullity. So an appointment made on the basis of a premature or otherwise invalid demand is of no effect.[91] However, an appointment made on an invalid ground is effective if at the time of the receiver's acceptance of the appointment[92] a valid ground of appointment existed.[93] The appointment:

(i)   may be made despite the filing of an application for an administration order[94];

(ii) may not be made during the currency of an administration order[95];

(iii) if made before such an order, is displaced by the order, upon the making of which the administrative receiver must vacate office[96];

(iv) prevents the making of an administration order except:

    (a) by the consent of the person by whom or on whose behalf the receiver was appointed; or

    (b) where, if an administration order were made, any security by virtue of which the receiver was appointed would be liable to be released or discharged as a transaction at an undervalue or a preference or liable to be avoided under s.245 of the Insolvency Act as a floating charge given for past value by an insolvent company.[97]

The phrase "would be liable to be released or discharged" presumably means that the court must be satisfied on the evidence before it, which may well be incomplete, that on a balance of probabilities the conditions in which a court could exercise its powers of release or discharge or in which the floating charge would be rendered void would be fulfilled if an administration order were then made, whether or not the court would be likely to exercise its powers in the particular circumstances. Such a ruling is, of course, operative solely for the purpose of making an administration order and does not

---

[90] It is this, rather than the time of making the appointment, that is the relevant time (*R.A. Cripps & Son v Wickenden* [1973] 1 W.L.R. 944, *per* Goff J. at 953–954).

[91] See below, para.10–30.

[92] See n.90 above.

[93] See, e.g. *Byblos Bank SAL v Al-Khudhairy* [1987] B.C.L.C. 232, applied in *Re Brampton Manor (Leisure) Ltd v McLean* [2007] B.C.C. 640.

[94] Insolvency Act 1986 Sch.B1 para.39.

[95] Insolvency Act 1986 Sch.B1 para.43(6A).

[96] Insolvency Act 1986 Sch.B1 para.41(1).

[97] Insolvency Act 1986 Sch.B1 para.39. See generally Ch.13 as to these grounds of avoidance. Potential invalidity of the security for non-registration is not designated as an event enabling an administration order to be made, since this can be cured by registration out of time with leave of the court prior to the initiation of steps for the winding up of the company. See Companies Act 2006 s.873.

constitute a res judicata preventing the debenture holder from contending in subsequent proceedings under ss.238–240 or 245 that the debenture is not liable to be avoided under those sections.

Blocking an out-of-court administration order

The effect of the Insolvency Act is that an administrative receiver and an administrator cannot be in post at the same time.[98] The reason for such a rule is obvious: since both are given the widest powers of management but represent different interests, it is not possible for their functions to be exercised concurrently. Subject to the provisions of para.39(1) of Sch.B1, it is the first to be appointed who prevails. A debenture holder whose security is not vulnerable thus has power to block an out-of-court administration by appointing an administrative receiver, and he may do this at any time prior to the company's entry into administration, whether or not an application for an administration order has been made.[99] It therefore behoves the debenture holder to keep a watchful eye to ensure that he does not overlook such an application. He is helped in this regard by being given two sources of warning that an application has been made, so that he can consider whether to acquiesce in the appointment or to block it by appointing a receiver. First, notice of the application is required to be given to him as soon as reasonably practicable,[100] thus enabling him to intervene and apply to have his own nominee appointed as administrator.[101] Secondly, copies of the application and supporting witness statement must be served on him five clear days before the hearing date,[102] although this time may be abridged by the court so far as is consistent with allowing the debenture holder an adequate opportunity to consider whether to exercise his power of appointment before it is suspended.[103] The above requirements appear to be purely directory, so that where the applicant fails to comply with them and in consequence the debenture holder does not learn of the application until after the administration order has been made, this would not appear to invalidate the order. Moreover, the unfortunate debenture holder has no *locus standi* to apply for the administration order to be discharged or the administrator to be replaced. The damage having been done, he must accept with such fortitude

10–27

---

[98] Insolvency Act 1986 Sch.B1 paras 17(b), 25(c), 39, 41(1) and 43(6A).
[99] Insolvency Act 1986 Sch.B1 paras 39(2) and 43(6A).
[100] Insolvency Act 1986 Sch.B1 para.12(2).
[101] Insolvency Act 1986 Sch.B1 para.36.
[102] Insolvency Rules 1986 rr.2.6(3) and 2.8(1).
[103] Insolvency Rules 1986 r.12.9; and *Re A Company No.00175 of 1987* [1987] 3 B.C.C. 124. In the case of a bank, the address for service is the address of an office where, to the knowledge of the applicant, the company maintains a bank account or if this is not known the bank's registered office, or if none, then its usual or last known address (Insolvency Rules r.2.8(5)). There is no provision in the Act or Rules for advertisement of the application.

as he can command the involuntary loss of his right to appoint a receiver, and appears to have no right to damages or compensation, even assuming he could establish loss.[104]

Conditions of a valid appointment by the debenture holder

10–28 In order for the debenture holder's appointment of a receiver to be valid, six conditions must be fulfilled:

(i) The company is not in administration.[105]

(ii) The security under which the receiver is appointed is valid. The appointment will be void *ab initio* if:

(a) the company is already in winding up, or goes into winding up, and the security was not duly registered[106] or is set aside by the court under s.241 or rendered void by s.245 of the Insolvency Act or as a post-petition disposition not sanctioned by the court[107]; or

(b) the company is a foreign company, as opposed to one registered under the Companies Act 2006.[108]

If the company is not in winding up when the receiver is appointed, the fact that the security is potentially void or voidable does not at that time affect the validity of the appointment but subsequent avoidance of the security nullifies the appointment retrospectively unless, in the case of an order for release or discharge of the security, the court exercises what appears to be a power to set aside the security as from the date of its order, without retrospective effect.[109]

(iii) The obligations secured by the debenture arise from a valid contract. Hence, a receiver appointed under a valid debenture because of default

---

[104] The well-recognised tort of abuse of process does not encompass mere procedural irregularity.

[105] See above para.10–13.

[106] Companies Act 2006 s. 874.

[107] Insolvency Act 1986 s.127 (see para.13–127); and *Re Goldburg (No.2)* [1912] 1 K.B. 606, which concerned comparable provisions under the then Bankruptcy Act by which the trustee's title to the bankrupt's estate related back to the act of bankruptcy on which the adjudication order was made.

[108] This results from the new definition of company introduced by the Companies Act 2006 (Consequential Amendments, Transitional Provisions and Savings) Order 2009, SI 2009/1941. See Gabriel Moss, Nick Segal and Ian Fletcher, "A Very 'Consequential' Amendment: No More Administrative Receivers for Foreign Companies" (2010) 23(4) Ins. Int. 1. There is a somewhat different position in administration, where a foreign company may be put into administration if it is incorporated in an EEA state or if, although not so incorporated, it has its centre of main interests in an EEA state other than Denmark.

[109] See below, para.10–32.

in payment of sums payable under an invalid guarantee secured by the debenture is not validly appointed.[110]

(iv) The power to appoint a receiver has become exercisable under the terms of the debenture.[111]

(v) The appointment has been made by the person[112] and in the manner[113] authorised by the debenture.

(vi) The person appointed is qualified to act.[114]

Where these conditions are satisfied, the appointment of the receiver will be a valid appointment. Good faith in the making of an appointment does not appear to be a prerequisite of its validity but if an appointment is made in bad faith the debenture holder will be liable for any loss thereby caused to the company.[115] The fact that the company is in liquidation is not a bar to the appointment of a receiver,[116] and it is not necessary to obtain either the consent of the liquidator or the leave of the court to such an appointment. However, as the liquidator is an officer of the court the receiver cannot take possession of any assets within the liquidator's control except with his consent or by leave of the court, to which the receiver is entitled as a matter of right.[117]

The acts of an individual as administrative receiver are valid notwithstanding any defect in his appointment, nomination or qualifications,[118] but the section is confined to defects in form or procedure and cannot be invoked where the receiver has never been validly appointed at all.[119]

The demand for payment

One of the most common grounds on which a receiver is appointed pursuant to powers conferred by the debenture is non-compliance with a demand for payment. An appointment made on the basis of a premature or otherwise invalid demand is of no effect. Two questions then arise: what constitutes a valid demand for payment? And what time must the debenture holder allow the company to satisfy the demand?

10–29

---

[110] *Ford & Carter Ltd v Midland Bank Ltd* (1979) 129 N.L.J. 543.
[111] See above and, in the case of an appointment made after failure to comply with a demand for payment, below, paras 10–29 et seq.
[112] *Harris & Lewine Pty Ltd (in liquidation) v Harris & Lewin (Agents)* (1975) A.C.L.C. 28 at 279.
[113] *R. Jaffe Ltd (in liquidation) v Jaffe (No.2)* [1932] N.Z.L.R. 195.
[114] Under s.390 of the Insolvency Act 1986; see above, para.10–25.
[115] See below, para.10–34, as to examples of bad faith.
[116] *Re Pound & Hutchins* (1889) 2 Ch.D. 402.
[117] *Re Potters Oils Ltd (No.2)* [1986] 1 W.L.R. 201 at 206; and *Pound & Hutchins*, above.
[118] Insolvency Act 1986 s.232.
[119] See below, para.10–32.

The validity of the demand

10–30   On this question, the authorities establish the following propositions:

(i) *Unless otherwise provided by the debenture itself, the demand is valid if calling merely for payment of "all moneys due" without specifying the amount.*[120] The commercial necessity of allowing the creditor to make a general demand in this way without stating the amount due was well put by the High Court of Australia in *Bunbury Foods Pty Ltd v National Bank of Australasia Ltd.*[121]

"... to require the creditor in all cases to specify the amount of the debt may operate to impose an onerous burden upon him. Some accounts may be so complex and so constantly changing that it is difficult at any given time to ascertain or to assert the precise amount that is due and payable. Indeed, the ascertainment of the amount may in some instances require the resolution over time of complex issues of fact and law. Yet, in order to preserve the value to the creditor of his security, he may need to call up the debt as a matter of urgency. It is of some materiality to note that it is not essential to the validity of a notice calling up the debt that it correctly states the amount of the debt ... There is little point in requiring that the notice should state the amount if the correctness of the amount is not essential to the validity of the notice. In this situation insistence on the requirement may result in creditors taking insufficient care in stating the amount of the debt, thereby contributing to confusion on the part of debtors."[122]

(ii) *A demand is not normally rendered invalid because it is for more than the amount due.*[123] An understatement of the amount due clearly does not prejudice the debtor company, and this is usually true of an overstatement, since in most cases the debtor is manifestly unable to pay even the lower, correct, amount. The principle established in relation to the enforcement of mortgages is that the making of an excessive demand by the mortgagee does not dispense with the duty of the mortgagor to tender that which is actually due.[124] However, there may be exceptional cases where this is not so. One possible case is where the debtor company has been led by the creditor to believe that a tender below the excessive amount demanded will be rejected, although even here it might be said that the company should still tender what is actually due.

---

[120] *Bank of Baroda v Panessar* [1987] Ch. 335; and *Bunbury Foods Pty Ltd v National Bank of Australasia Ltd* (1984) 51 A.L.R. 609.
[121] *Bunbury Foods*, above n.120.
[122] *Bunbury Foods*, above, n. 120, at 619.
[123] *Bunbury Foods*, above n. 120, and cases there cited.
[124] *Campbell v Commercial Banking Co of Sydney* (1879) 40 L.T. 137; and *Clyde Properties Ltd v Tasker* [1970] N.Z.L.R. 754.

Another is where the company is dependent on the creditor for information as to the amount due—as where it is a surety for future advances from time to time made to the principal debtor—and the company would have been able to pay the sum actually due if it had known what it was but is unable to pay an amount demanded by the creditor which is grossly in excess of the indebtedness.

(iii) *A demand is invalid if what is claimed is not due at all.*[125] But if the receiver was appointed by the debenture holder at the invitation of the board of the company and that invitation was extended in the mistaken belief that grounds had occurred entitling the debenture holder to make the appointment, the company cannot treat the receiver as a trespasser for the period during which he is in possession of the assets prior to being required by the company to withdraw after their discovery of the mistake.[126]

(iv) *If, following an excessive demand, the company tenders the amount actually due, the subsequent appointment of a receiver will be invalid, since ex hypothesi there is no default.*

(v) *The company is entitled only to such time as is reasonable to implement the mechanics of payment,*[127] *but is not entitled to an opportunity to raise the finance required.*[128] In this respect, the English rule is stricter than that applied in Australia[129] and Canada.[130] Indeed, in Canada there is at least one decision in which it has been held that the duty to give reasonable notice is not merely a presumptive rule of construction of the security instrument but is founded on the twin concepts of public policy and unconscionability and cannot be waived.[131] It is fair to say that the doctrine of unconscionability has been developed in Australia and Canada into a major instrument for controlling contract terms in a way that goes well beyond English law, which continues to attach great importance to predictability in the legal outcome of commercial disputes.[132]

---

[125] *Jaffe v Premier Motors Ltd* [1970] N.Z.L.R. 146.

[126] *Ford and Carter,* cited above n.110.

[127] How long this is may depend on whether the demand is made during or outside banking hours. See *Sheppard & Cooper Ltd v TSB Bank Plc (No.2)* [1996] B.C.C. 965, *per* Blackburne J. at 969.

[128] *Cripps (Pharmaceuticals) Ltd v Wickenden* [1973] 2 All E.R. 606; and *Bank of Baroda,* cited above n.120, where in both cases the time elapsing between service of the demand and the appointment of the receiver was approximately one hour and Goff J. in the former case was prepared to accept that even minutes would be sufficient if the company was unable to pay.

[129] See *Bunbury Foods,* cited above n.120.

[130] *Ronald Elwyn Lister Ltd v Dunlop Canada Ltd* (1982) 135 D.L.R. (3d) 1.

[131] *Waldron v Royal Bank of Canada* [1991] 4 W.W.R. 289 (British Columbia Court of Appeal). Section 244 of the Canadian Bankruptcy and Insolvency Act 1992 now requires the creditor to give the debtor 10 days' notice before enforcing the security.

[132] In *Sheppard & Cooper Ltd v TSB Bank Plc* [1996] B.C.C. 653, the Court of Appeal hinted that the demand point might need review, recognising its importance in a number of Commonwealth as well as English decisions on it. See the judgment of Sir John Balcombe at 658.

(vi) *If the debtor company clearly could not have met the demand in any event, the shortness of time between demand and payment is irrelevant.*[133]

(vii) *Where the company is a surety, it is a question of construction whether the debenture holder has to make demand on the principal debtor as well as on the company.*[134]

Conditional appointment

10–31   The debenture holder may execute an instrument of appointment of the intended receiver in advance, and the receiver may accept the intended appointment in advance, under an instrument of appointment to take effect after default and demand for payment,[135] subject to s.33 of the Insolvency Act.[136] Accordingly, it is not an objection to the validity of the appointment that the receiver has the instrument in his hands before demand has been made. The common practice of making appointments in this way reflects the perceived need to have the receiver in possession as soon as possible after demand in order to preserve the assets and reduce the risk of their removal.

Effect of defective or invalid appointment

10–32   Under s.232 of the Insolvency Act, the acts of an individual as receiver are valid notwithstanding any defect in his appointment, nomination or qualifications. But in relation to the appointment or nomination, the section is confined to defects in form or procedure and does not validate acts done by one who was appointed under an invalid security or when the power of appointment had not become exercisable or who has acted without being appointed at all or when disqualified.[137] In cases outside s.232, a receiver who acts when not validly appointed is liable to the company in damages for trespass or con-

---

[133] *Cripps (Pharmaceuticals)*, cited above n.128; *Bank of Baroda*, cited above n.120; and *Sheppard & Cooper (No.2)*, cited above n.132, where the interval between the demand and the appointment was no more than an hour but the company had made it clear that it was unable to pay.

[134] See, e.g. *DFC Financial Services Ltd v Coffey* [1991] B.C.C. 218, where the Privy Council, taking a different view on the construction point from the Court of Appeal of New Zealand, held that the debenture holder was entitled to proceed directly against the surety as if it was a primary obligor without first making demand on the principal debtor as well.

[135] *Cripps (Pharmaceuticals)*, cited above n.128; and *Windsor Refrigerator Co v Branch Nominees Ltd* [1961] Ch. 375.

[136] See below, para.10–35.

[137] *Morris v Kanssen* [1946] A.C. 549, a decision on a comparable provision in the Companies Act 1929 s.143 and Table A, applied by analogy by Lord Hoffmann in *OBG v Allen* [2008] A.C. 1 at [90]–[91].

version, where the elements of these torts are satisfied,[138] or alternatively as constructive trustee of assets coming into his hands.[139]

The company can ratify a defective or invalid appointment and may be estopped from disputing the validity of the appointment if with knowledge of its invalidity the company proceeds to deal with the receiver on the footing that he was validly appointed.[140] In the absence of such ratification or estoppel, an appointment made before the right to appoint was exercisable is not cured by subsequent accrual of the right to appoint, nor can a second appointment be validly made until the appointor has remedied his wrongdoing by restoring the company to possession of its assets and renewing his demand.[141]

At common law, the invalidity of a receiver's appointment does not convert him into the agent of the debenture holder who appointed him,[142] so that the debenture holder is not in principle responsible for the receiver's acts or omissions.[143] However, by s.34 of the Insolvency Act, the appointee may now ask the court for an order requiring the debenture holder to indemnify him against any legal liability he has incurred solely by reason of the invalidity of the appointment. In practice, such indemnities are commonly exacted by receivers as a condition of accepting appointment.

Points to check before accepting an appointment

It follows from what has been said above that before accepting appointment **10–33** as receiver the intended appointee should satisfy himself as far as possible that the security was duly registered and appears otherwise unimpeachable, that the instrument of appointment was signed by those empowered to sign it and that the appointment appears to be valid in other respects, and should wherever possible obtain an indemnity against the consequences of an invalid appointment.[144]

---

[138] There cannot be conversion of a chose in action, such as contractual rights (*OBG Ltd v Allan*, cited above, Lord Nicholls and Baroness Hale dissenting on this point). The claimant may have a claim in tort for inducing a breach or for causing harm by unlawful means (*OBG Ltd v Allan*).
[139] *Rolled Steel Products (Holdings) Ltd v British Steel Corp* [1986] Ch. 246.
[140] *Bank of Baroda*, cited above n.120. See also above, para.10–30, as to the effect of inviting the debenture holder to make the appointment in the mistaken belief that the debenture holder had become entitled to do so. A similar estoppel applies where there is acquiescence in the appointment of an administrator. See below, para.11–44.
[141] *Cripps (Pharmaceuticals)*, cited above n.128, *per* Goff L.J. at 618.
[142] *Bank of Baroda*, cited above n.120.
[143] *Bank of Baroda*.
[144] These are not, of course, the only matters he will need to consider. Others include the sufficiency of the assets to meet his remuneration and expenses, the fact that the company is or is likely to go into liquidation (thus bringing an end to the receiver's agency powers) and the adequacy of his own professional expertise. See generally Lightman et al., *The Law of Administrators and Receivers of Companies*, 2007, paras 6–048 et seq.

Must the debenture holder consider the company's interests when appointing a receiver?

10-34   The debenture holder is entitled to prefer his own interests to those of the company in making the appointment, for his position is inherently adverse to that of the company, and it is a general principle of mortgage law that a mortgagee is entitled to subordinate the debtor's interest to his own, so long as he is acting in good faith.[145] Accordingly, the debenture holder owes no general duty to the company to refrain from appointing a receiver merely because this would cause damage to the company,[146] unless he acts in bad faith,[147] for example, by appointing a receiver solely for the purpose of disrupting an existing receivership under a subsequent debenture and preventing its enforcement[148] or maliciously with a view to damaging the company or another creditor. He does, however, have a duty not to appoint a person whom he has reasonable grounds for believing is incompetent[149] or not qualified to act as an insolvency practitioner. There must, it is thought, be a strong presumption that a person who is legally qualified to act possesses the necessary competence and accordingly that a belief in his competence is reasonable.

When the appointment takes effect

10-35   The appointment is of no effect until it is accepted by the appointee before the end of the business day next following that on which the instrument of appointment is received by him or on his behalf but subject to this it is deemed to be made when the instrument of appointment is so received.[150] It is not entirely clear from the statutory provisions whether failure to accept the appointment renders it retrospectively void or merely terminates it on expiry of the time allowed for acceptance. The words "is of no effect" rather than "ceases to have effect" suggest that the former is the proper interpretation. At first sight, the point appears to be relevant to the validity of the appointee's acts in the period between receipt of the instrument of appointment and expiry of the time allowed for his acceptance of it. But this possibility is more apparent than real, because no formality is prescribed for acceptance, which may be in writing, by word of mouth or even by

---

[145] *Shamji v Johnson Matthey Bankers Ltd* [1991] B.C.L.C. 36; and *Cuckmere Brick Co Ltd v Mutual Finance Ltd* [1971] Ch. 949, *per* Salmon L.J. at 965.

[146] *Shamji*, cited above n.145; and *Re Potters Oils Ltd (No.2)* [1986] 1 W.L.R. 201.

[147] ibid.

[148] *Downsview Nominees Ltd v First City Corp* [1993] A.C. 295.

[149] See *Shamji*, cited above n.145.

[150] Insolvency Act 1986 s.33. To save time, the instrument of appointment may be executed in advance of default and given to the intended receiver to become effective by his acceptance of it after demand and default.

conduct,[151] so that it is difficult to envisage a situation in which the appointee could act as receiver without thereby accepting the appointment and perfecting his status. What is clear is that acceptance of the appointment within the time laid down operates retrospectively to the date of receipt of the instrument of appointment.

5. EFFECT OF THE APPOINTMENT

General effects

The appointment of a receiver: **10–36**

(i) crystallises a floating charge, if this has not already crystallised;

(ii) usually prevents the making of an administration order[152];

(iii) suspends the directors' powers of management as regards assets comprised in the security and the general conduct of the business[153];

(iv) terminates those contracts of employment which are incompatible with the administrative receiver's management powers—a question which depends not so much on the designation of the office held by the employee as on the particular circumstances[154]—but does not affect other contracts of employment[155]; and

(v) does not affect the subsistence of other contracts.[156]

Impact of the appointment on the powers and duties of directors

(1) In general

The broad effect of the appointment of a receiver is to divest the directors of   **10–37** the company of their management powers during the currency of the receivership.[157] To this general principle there are at least two, and possibly

---

[151] Acceptance must be confirmed in writing within seven days and the appointment publicised (Insolvency Act 1986 s.46(1); and Insolvency Rules 1986 r.3.1). But non-compliance with these formalities does not affect the validity of the appointment.

[152] See above, para.10–26.

[153] See below, paras 10–37 et seq.

[154] Contrast *Re Mack Trucks (Britain) Ltd* [1967] 1 All E.R. 977 with *Griffiths v Secretary of State for Social Services* [1974] Q.B. 468.

[155] *Re Foster Clark's Indenture Trusts* [1966] 1 All E.R. 43.

[156] See further paras 10–52 et seq.

[157] *Moss Steamship Co Ltd v Whinney* [1912] A.C. 254, *per* Lord Atkinson at 263; and *Re Emmadart Ltd* [1979] Ch. 540, *per* Brightman J. at 547.

three, exceptions. First, the directors' powers remain exercisable as regards assets which are outside the scope of the debenture or which the receiver decides to ignore or abandon, for example, the company's right of action against his own debenture holder.[158] Secondly, the directors retain a residue of powers relating to matters which do not entrench on the powers and functions of the receiver, for example, the power to maintain the statutory books and file the statutory returns, to obtain such information and accounts from the receiver as are necessary for that purpose and, it would seem, to ascertain the amount required to redeem the debenture.[159] Thirdly, the directors possibly retain a power to oppose a winding up petition,[160] despite the fact that the administrative receiver is now given power both to present and defend such a petition.[161]

Divestment of the directors' ability to manage the company obviously carries with it the cessation of their duties as regards such management. That does not, however, mean that the directors owe no duties of any kind to the company. They remain in office and continue to be bound by their duty of loyalty and other fiduciary obligations. While the "no conflict" rule ceases to apply, the "no profit" rule does not.[162]

(2) *Actions against the debenture holder*

10–38   Special problems arise where the directors consider that the debenture holder has acted in breach of duty and wish to have proceedings instituted against him. The receiver is then in the invidious position of having to decide whether to sue those who appointed him. Moreover, since any proceedings would have to be brought in the name of the company, not of the receiver, the charged assets would have to be deployed to meet the costs incurred in the litigation, to the detriment of the debenture holder, who might find that if his action succeeded and he recovered costs against the company, the payment of these would diminish his security. In effect, his own assets would be used to sue him. In *Newhart Developments Ltd v Co-operative Commercial Bank*,[163] these difficulties did not arise because the company had been given a full indemnity for its costs by outside sources. Accordingly, there could be no possible threat to the assets comprising the security. By contrast, no such indemnity was initially given in *Tudor Grange Holdings Ltd v Citibank NA*,[164]

---

[158] *Newhart Developments Ltd v Co-operative Commercial Bank* [1978] Q.B. 814. See further below, para.10–38.
[159] *Gomba Holdings UK Ltd v Homan* [1986] 3 All E.R. 94.
[160] *Re Reprographic Exports (Euromart) Ltd* (1978) 122 S.J. 400.
[161] Insolvency Act 1986 Sch.1 item 21.
[162] *Re Ultraframe Ltd* [2006] EWHC 1638 (Ch), *per* Lewison J. at [1328]–[1330].
[163] See above, n.158.
[164] [1992] Ch. 53.

and Sir Nicolas Browne-Wilkinson V.C., who entertained grave doubts as to the correctness of the *Newhart* decision while accepting that he was bound by it, held that the absence of an indemnity enabled him to distinguish the case from *Newhart* and that the directors had had no power to institute the proceedings. The Vice-Chancellor would have struck them out on this ground but for the offer of an indemnity during the course of the application to strike out the claim.[165] His view was that a receiver who felt embarrassed by his position could always apply to the court for directions.

In *Newhart*, it was contended that any recovery of damages against the debenture holder would produce a circular transfer, because the damages would themselves become subject to the debenture holder's charge. But that does not mean that the proceedings are of no benefit to the company, for as Shaw L.J. pointed out,[166] the recovery goes in or towards discharge of the debt. The argument that the claim against the debenture holder is itself part of the security, so that the receiver is the *dominus* of any such claim, is, of course, correct in that the receiver is the party having the primary right to launch the proceedings in the company's name and to have control of the litigation. But if he chooses to abandon that right (and he is obviously going to be reluctant to bring proceedings against the debenture holder who appointed him), then as pointed out in *Newhart*,[167] he cannot at the same time deny the right, and indeed the duty, of the directors to procure the institution of proceedings by the company, for it is only within the scope of the assets covered by the debenture that the receiver has a function to perform. Notwithstanding the misgivings expressed by the Vice-Chancellor in *Tudor Grange*, the approach adopted by the Court of Appeal in *Newhart* is clearly correct. If proceedings can be taken against the debenture holder without risk to the assets which are the subject of the security but the receiver is unwilling to pursue the claim, then, assuming the claim is arguable and not purely vexatious, why should the receiver be allowed to stifle it? It is true that the receiver can always apply to the court for directions,[168] but he cannot be compelled to do so, and no one else apart from the debenture holder has a *locus standi* to seek directions. In any event, is hard to see what purpose would be served by this procedure. Either the company's claim against the debenture holder is arguable, in which case it should be allowed to proceed to trial, or it is not, in which case the debenture holder can apply to have it struck out as disclosing no cause of action.

---

[165] In the end the claim was struck out on other grounds.
[166] [1978] Q.B. 814 at 820.
[167] By Shaw L.J. at 819.
[168] Under the Insolvency Act 1986 s.35.

(3) Actions against the receiver

10–39   Where the proposed defendant is the receiver himself, then plainly it is the company acting through its directors that has the right to institute proceedings.[169] If the position were otherwise, the company would in practice be left remediless, and common sense indicates that the company must have a remedy against a receiver who acts improperly.[170]

Termination of the receivership

10–40   If the receivership comes to an end, whether by collection of what is due to the debenture holders and preferential creditors or otherwise, without the company having gone into liquidation, it is the duty of the receiver to hand back control of the company to the directors. This is an infrequent occurrence, since almost invariably a company in receivership goes into liquidation before the receiver is discharged.[171] Where control is restored, the directors are entitled to call for delivery up of all books and documents relating to the company's affairs which are the company's property. Books and documents in the possession of the receiver do not belong to the company merely because they relate to its affairs, for as pointed out earlier the receiver owes duties to his debenture holder as well as to the company and also has working papers of his own. The guiding principle is that documents brought into existence in discharge of the receiver's duty to the debenture holder belong to the debenture holder, those brought into being in discharge of his duty to the company belong to the company, and working papers and other documents intended solely for his own use to enable him to fulfil his duties are the property of the receiver himself.[172]

6. POWERS OF THE RECEIVER

From whom the receiver's powers emanate

10–41   The powers of a receiver appointed out of court emanate, directly or indirectly, from the debtor company. At first sight, it seems anomalous that a

---

[169] *Watts v Midland Bank* [1986] B.C.L.C. 15.

[170] *Watts v Midland Bank, per* Peter Gibson J. at 21.

[171] For an exception, see *Gomba Holdings UK Ltd v Minories Finance Ltd* [1989] 1 All E.R. 261. See further, below, para.10–66.

[172] *Gomba Holdings*, affirming the decision of Hoffman J. [1988] B.C.L.C. 60 and applying, as regards the receiver's working documents, the principle in *Chantrey Martin & Co v Martin* [1953] 2 All E.R. 691.

receiver can be appointed and can exercise powers under a debenture to which he is not a party and by virtue of an appointment by an instrument to which the company is not a party. But the anomaly disappears once it is appreciated that in making the appointment the debenture holder acts as agent of the company.

"Though it was the mortgagee who in fact appointed the receiver, yet in making the appointment the mortgagee acted, and it was the object of the parties that he should act, as agent for the mortgagor. Lord Cranworth, in *Jefferys v Dickson*, stated the doctrine of Courts of Equity on the subject to the effect following. The mortgagee, as agent of the mortgagor, appointed a person to receive the income, with directions to keep down the interest of the mortgage, and to account for the surplus to the mortgagor as his principal. These directions were supposed to emanate, not from the mortgagee but from the mortgagor; and the receiver therefore, in the relation between himself and the mortgagor, stood in the position of a person appointed by an instrument to which the mortgagee was no party ... Of course the mortgagor cannot of his own will revoke the appointment of a receiver, or that appointment would be useless. For valuable consideration he has committed the management of his property to an attorney whose appointment he cannot interfere with. By degrees the forms of appointment of receivers became more complicated, and their powers more extensive; but the doctrine explained by Lord Cranworth in the case cited was consistently adhered to, and it remained true throughout that the receiver's appointment, and all directions and powers given and conferred upon him, were supposed to emanate from the mortgagor, and the mortgagee, though he might be the actual appointor, and might have stipulated for all the powers conferred upon the receiver, was in no other position, so far as responsibility was concerned, than if he had been altogether a stranger to the appointment."[173]

Thus, the receiver is notionally appointed by the company through the agency of the debenture holder and his powers derive from the debenture and, being given to secure the rights of the debenture holder, cannot be restricted or revoked except with the debenture holder's consent. It would be possible for the debenture to confer on the debenture holder the right to invest the receiver with powers, or to enlarge his powers, in the instrument of appointment itself but in practice these are given by the debenture, not by the instrument of appointment under powers conferred by the debenture.

Accordingly, the source of the receiver's powers is the debenture under which he is appointed. This is true even of the powers listed in Sch.1 to the Insolvency Act, for these are not independent statutory powers but powers

---

[173] *Gaskell v Gosling* [1896] 1 Q.B. 669, *per* Rigby L.J. at 692–693 in a judgment subsequently approved by the House of Lords [1897] A.C. 575.

deemed by the Act to be included in the debenture except so far as inconsistent with its provisions.[174] The purpose of the schedule is to avoid the necessity for a long list of powers in the debenture itself; most of the acts the receiver is likely to wish to undertake are listed in the schedule, which in its 23 items covers virtually every aspect of management of the business and the assets comprised in the security. Thus the receiver has all of these powers (except as varied or excluded by the debenture) and any additional powers conferred by the express terms of the debenture.

Since the powers listed in Sch.1 are deemed to be derived from the debenture rather than being directly conferred by the statute, it would seem that they are only as effective as they would have been if set out expressly in the debenture. It follows that the receiver cannot rely on such powers to do acts as agent of the company[175] which are ultra vires the company.[176] Doubts have been expressed whether the receiver can use the company's seal[177] or call up uncalled capital of the company,[178] these powers being typically vested by the articles of association in the directors or those acting on behalf of the directors. But the difficulty is more apparent than real. All of the powers listed in Sch.1 are conferred on the receiver for the purpose of preserving, protecting and realising the security,[179] and may therefore be validly exercised for that purpose, even though the effect is to displace the board's own management powers.[180] This is the effect of the authority conferred by the charge on the debenture holder to appoint the receiver. Alternatively, the company could confer a separate power of attorney on the debenture holder.[181] A separate question is whether the power to call up uncalled capital remains exercisable after the company has gone into liquidation. There seems to be no reason why it should not be if the security includes uncalled capital.[182]

---

[174] Insolvency Act 1986 s.42(1).

[175] *Aliter*, acts relating to the security, for these represent the exercise on behalf of the debenture holder, of his rights as a secured creditor. See below.

[176] The ultra vires rule is now a shadow of its former self. See below, para.13–01.

[177] Item 8 in the schedule.

[178] Item 19 in the schedule.

[179] By s.42(2)(b), in the application of Sch.1 to the administrative receiver of a company, references to the property of the company are to the property of which he is, or but for the appointment of some other person as the receiver of part of the company's property, would be the receiver and manager.

[180] A further argument advanced against the administrative receiver's power to use the company's seal is that under the statute it is contractual in character and does not survive the company's liquidation. The Law Commission has expressed the view that this is not the case and that in this respect the power is best seen as statutory. See Law Commission Consultation Paper No.143, "The Execution of Deeds and Documents By or on Behalf of Bodies Corporate" (1996), para.8.33.

[181] Law Commission Consultation Paper No.143, 1996, para.8.34. Again, however, doubt has been expressed whether this continues after the liquidation. It was held not to do so in *Barrows v Chief Land Registrar, The Times*, October 26, 1977 but the weight of opinion is to the contrary. See the Law Commission's Consultation Paper, para.8.38. The Law Commission has recommended that the law be clarified on these various points.

[182] Section 74 of the Insolvency Act makes contributories liable for unpaid capital.

Receiver's powers are ancillary to the debenture holder's security interest

The receiver's ability to exercise full management powers derives not only from the terms of his appointment, which embody the powers conferred by the debenture but from the fact that the debenture holder has a security interest over the whole or substantially the whole of the company's property.

10–42

Content of the receiver's powers

The receiver has:

10–43

(i) all of the express powers conferred by the debenture;

(ii) implied authority to do whatever is necessary for, or ordinarily incidental to, the effective exercise of his express authority in the usual way,[183] except so far as the debenture otherwise provides;

(iii) as implied terms of the debenture, all of the powers listed in Sch.1 to the Insolvency Act 1986, except in so far as they are inconsistent with any provisions of the debenture[184]; and

(iv) power with leave of the court to dispose of property subject to a prior or equal security interest.[185]

Schedule 1 lists 22 specific powers, followed by a general power to do all other things incidental to the exercise of the specific powers. The latter includes the power to take possession of the property of the company,[186] and for that purpose to take any expedient proceedings, to sell or otherwise dispose of the property, to borrow money and grant security, to appoint professionally qualified advisers, to bring and defend actions, to make any payment which is necessary or incidental to the performance of his functions, to carry on the business of the company, establish subsidiaries and transfer assets to subsidiaries, to make arrangements or compromises on behalf of the company and to present or defend a winding up petition against the company.

Classification of powers as *in rem* and personal (agency)

The receiver's powers are both *in rem* and personal. His *in rem* powers are held in right of the debenture holder and derive from the security created by

10–44

---

[183] *Bowstead and Reynolds on Agency*, 19th edn, ed. Peter G. Watts (London: Sweet & Maxwell, 2010), art.27.
[184] Insolvency Act 1986 s.42(1).
[185] Insolvency Act 1986 s.43. See below, para.10–46.
[186] i.e. the property of which he has been appointed receiver (Insolvency Act 1986 s.42(2)(b)).

the debenture. They include the power to collect in the assets comprising the security, to possess, control and use those assets and to deal with and dispose of them, whether by way of sale, lease, charge or otherwise. His personal powers are those vested in him by virtue of his position as deemed agent to manage the company's business. To the extent that the conduct of the business involves dealing with assets comprised in the security, the *in rem* powers and the personal powers overlap. But the latter include powers which are purely personal. The distinction between the receiver's *in rem* powers and his purely personal (or agency) powers is that the former, as stated above, relate to the assets of the company comprised in the security, whereas the latter relate to everything else, in particular the power to involve the company in further liabilities as its agent. Thus, the purely personal powers include the power to make or continue contracts on behalf of the company, to repudiate contacts entered into by the company,[187] to hire and fire staff, to borrow money and grant security, to employ solicitors and accountants to assist him, to pay debts due from the company, to accept and indorse bills of exchange in the company's name, to buy stock and property for the purpose of the business and generally to carry on the business and exercise managerial functions.

The distinction between the receiver's *in rem* powers and his purely personal powers is of little significance so long as the company is not in winding up. But once liquidation supervenes, the receiver's status as agent of the company comes to an end[188] and his purely personal powers fall away.[189] By contrast, his *in rem* powers continue, for liquidation does not affect the enforcement of security interests or of acts taken for the preservation or realisation of security.[190]

Power of sale

10–45   Prior to the winding up of the company, assets forming part of the security may be sold in one of two ways. First, the receiver can exercise his agency powers and sell in the name of the company. If he does this, the sale takes effect subject to the debenture under which he was appointed and to any other incumbrances, including those junior to such debenture.[191] This is because a receiver selling in the company's name is exercising the company's power of sale and cannot transfer any greater rights than the company itself could have done if not in receivership. Accordingly, if the purchaser is to acquire an unincumbered title, it will be necessary for the debenture holder

---

[187] See below, para.10–53.
[188] Insolvency Act 1986 s.44(1)(a).
[189] See para.10–66.
[190] See para.10–66.
[191] *Re The Real Meat Co Ltd* [1996] B.C.C. 254.

and other incumbrancers either to join in the conveyance to concur in the sale free from their interests or to release those interests under deeds of release. Secondly, the debenture holder can sell as mortgagee, and if he wishes can appoint the receiver as his agent for that purpose. Such a sale overrides junior security interests, which then attach, in due order of priority, to any surplus proceeds remaining after the mortgagee exercising the power of sale has been paid. This is the form of sale that should be adopted if it is desired that the sale shall override junior security interests; and it is the only form of sale open once the company has gone into liquidation (for winding up terminates the receiver's agency powers) except where the sale is authorised or ratified by the liquidator. Any sale by the liquidator in the name of the company would, again, take effect subject to the debenture and any other security interests.

Power to dispose of assets subject to a prior or equal security interest

Where, on application by the receiver, the court is satisfied that the disposal (with or without other assets) of any property of which he is receiver and which is subject to a security interest of prior or equal ranking would be likely to promote a more advantageous realisation of the company's assets than would otherwise be effected, the court may by order authorise the receiver to dispose of the property as if it were not subject to the security.[192] This provision does not apply to property subject to a security interest ranking after that of the debenture holder,[193] for the obvious reason that it is always open to the debenture holder, either directly or through the receiver as his agent, to sell as mortgagee and thus override subsequent interests without need of a court order.

10–46

It is a required condition of any order giving leave to dispose of the property that the net proceeds of sale plus the amount by which those proceeds fall short of the value determined by the court as the net amount which would be realised by sale on the open market by a willing vendor are to be applied in discharging the sums secured by the displaced security.[194] Accordingly, any deficiency comes out of the assets available to the debenture holder and is payable to the secured creditor in priority to the claims of the debenture holder and of preferential and other creditors. It would seem that if the price fixed by the court was too high, this enures for the benefit of the secured creditor unless the court adjusts the figure.[195]

---

[192] Insolvency Act 1986 s.43(1), (2) and (7).
[193] Insolvency Act 1986 s.43(2).
[194] Insolvency Act 1986 s.43(3).
[195] Quaere whether it has power to do this after the sale has taken place.

Protection of bona fide third party

10–47   A person dealing with a receiver in good faith and for value is not concerned to enquire whether he is acting within his powers.[196] However, this does not protect a party who deals with a person acting as receiver but never validly appointed.

7. DUTIES AND LIABILITIES OF THE RECEIVER

Nature of duties owed by receiver

10–48   I have already explained that the receiver owes a duty of care to his debenture holder, a limited duty of care to the company and a statutory duty to preferential creditors, as well as an obligation to retain for the benefit of general creditors the prescribed part of the net property subject to a floating charge. He also owes a duty of care to any other party having an interest in the equity of redemption, for example, a subsequent mortgagee, and a duty to a surety to exercise reasonable care in the perfection or realisation of the security in order to protect the surety's right of subrogation, failing which the surety is released from that part of his liability which would have been discharged from the proceeds of the security if reasonable care had been taken and may, if he has made payment under his guarantee, have a positive remedy in damages. The receiver owes no separate duty to ordinary unsecured creditors,[197] nor is it necessary to their interests to impose such a duty, for they are adequately protected by the receiver's duty to the company, a breach of which is actionable at the suit of the liquidator in the name of the company. The receiver will not normally incur any personal liability under environmental law[198] and it is thought that he cannot be required to apply assets subject to the security interest towards the cost of compliance with a remediation notice, although as yet there appear to have been no decisions on the point.[199]

The duty owed by the receiver to the company was at one time considered to be of a quite limited kind,[200] as was shown by the Privy Council in *Downsview Nominees Ltd v First City Corp Ltd*.[201] In that case, it was held that a receiver owes no duty of care in tort for negligence, for to impose this

---

[196] Insolvency Act 1986 s.42(3).

[197] *Lathia v Dronsfield Bros* [1987] B.C.L.C. 321.

[198] Environmental Protection Act 1990 s.78X(4)(a).

[199] See further above, para.6–29, as to disclaimer of polluted land as onerous property and para.2–25 as to the treatment of clean-up costs in winding up.

[200] For a penetrating discussion, see Alan Berg, "Duties of a Mortgagee and a Receiver" [1993] J.B.L. 213.

[201] [1993] AC. 295.

would be incompatible with his right and duty to act in the best interests of his debenture holder.[202] Certain specific duties are imposed on him in equity,[203] namely: (i) to act in good faith and for the purpose of obtaining repayment for his debenture holder; and (ii) to take due care to obtain a proper price when selling the charged assets.[204] These equitable duties broadly parallel those of the mortgagee himself where he does not enter into possession. They are owed not only to the company itself, but to subsequent incumbrancers and to sureties. So a receiver who instigates his appointment and exercises his powers not with the bona fide intention of securing repayment for his debenture holder, but for his own personal advantage and in order to obstruct the work of another receiver appointed under a junior security interest, is liable in damages for loss caused to the junior incumbrancer.[205] Two decades before *Downsview*, the judgments in the Court of Appeal decision in *Cuckmere Brick Co Ltd v Mutual Finance Ltd*[206] had seemed to suggest a more general duty of care in negligence.[207] But in a subsequent decision of the Court of Appeal, reliance on the tort of negligence rather than by reference to duties imposed in equity was deprecated.[208] Moreover, in emphasising the equitable source of the receiver's obligation in *Downsview*, Lord Templeman was doing no more than echoing what he himself had earlier said in giving the advice of the board in the decision of the Privy Council in *China and South Sea Bank Ltd v Tan Soon Gin*.[209]

Although *Downsview* was not received without criticism,[210] it was long thought that it accurately reflected the classical approach of English law towards the duty of mortgagees and their receivers, an approach generally mirrored in Australian and Canadian jurisprudence. But in policy terms, the

---

[202] One of the more striking aspects of the decision in *Downsview* is that in the Court of Appeal of New Zealand it was accepted without any argument to the contrary by counsel that Gault J. at first instance was correct in basing the existence of the receiver's duties to a subsequent debenture holder on negligence, and neither of the parties challenged those conclusions in their case as presented to the board. It was the board itself which took the initiative in selecting an arena not chosen by the parties.

[203] [1993] A.C. 295, *per* Lord Templeman at 317.

[204] See to the same effect *Cuckmere Brick Co Ltd v Mutual Finance Ltd* [1971] Ch. 949. The standard of care required in equity and tort would appear to be the same. See *Henderson v Merrett Syndicates Ltd* [1995] 2 A.C. 145, *per* Lord Browne-Wilkinson at 205; and *Bristol and West Building Society v Mothew* [1996] 4 All E.R. 698, per Millett L.J. at 711. The duty is to obtain a proper price, not the best price reasonably obtainable at the time of sale (*Bell v Long* [2008] 2 B.C.L.C. 706, *per* Patten J. at [14]). Breach of the equitable duty is technically visited by an award of equitable compensation rather than damages but this has been declared a historical distinction without a difference (*Bristol and West Building Society*, *per* Millett L.J. at 711).

[205] *Downsview Nominees*, cited above n.201.

[206] [1971] Ch. 949.

[207] See in particular the judgment of Salmon L.J. at 966, referring to the "neighbours" test of proximity formulated by Lord Atkin in *Donoghue v Stevenson* [1932] A.C. 562.

[208] By Nourse L.J. in *Parker-Tweedale v Dunbar Bank Plc* [1991] Ch. 12 at 18.

[209] [1990] 1 A.C. 536.

[210] See, e.g. Lightman et al., *The Law of Receivers and Administrators of Companies*, 2007, para.7–13. See now the 4th edn at para.10–020.

result was seen as profoundly unsatisfactory. At the heart of the problem is the traditional reluctance of equity to impose fetters on mortgagees in the exercise of their powers of sale, coupled with the ambivalent attitude of modern English law towards the expansion of liability in tort for pure economic loss, the boundaries of liability being expanded at one time only to be contracted the next. At one time, it was thought that as the result of *Downsview* there were only two duties imposed by equity on the mortgagee or his receiver, namely to act in good faith and to use reasonable care to obtain a proper price on a sale, and that so long as he fulfilled them the receiver incurred no liability to the company, subsequent incumbrancers or sureties for loss or damage caused by the exercise of his functions. That view, however, has been shown to be too narrow. Thus, while the receiver is under no obligation to carry on or continue the company's business, so long as he does so he must act with due diligence.[211] Perhaps one can extract from this a more general principle that while the receiver's primary duty is to his debenture holder and he is entitled to subordinate the interests of creditors to that duty, yet whatever functions he does choose to perform should be performed with due care and diligence.

10–49   A review of legal policy in this area is now overdue. There is little doubt that the dangers involved in imposing a more generalised duty on receivers and their debenture holders have been exaggerated, whilst insufficient regard has been paid to recurrent criticisms by companies in receivership and junior incumbrancers that their interests are not adequately safeguarded by the present law relating to sales by mortgagees and receivers. Thus, neither the mortgagee nor the receiver is a trustee of the power of sale for the mortgagor, so that the company is not entitled to complain about the decision of a mortgagee or receiver not to sell or about the timing of any sale, even if it can be demonstrated that the debenture holder would lose nothing, and the company might gain a great deal, from a temporary deferment of the sale.[212] The receiver is under no obligation to improve the mortgaged property or to increase its value, nor is he obliged to pursue, or continue the pursuit of, an application for planning permission to develop the property instead of proceeding with an immediate sale.[213] Moreover, although as we have seen, the receiver, while running the company's business, owes a duty to exercise due diligence in so doing,[214] he is entitled, if he so chooses, to decide not to continue the company's business,[215] and to sell a part of the business which would be better kept. It would also seem to be the case that

---

[211] *Medforth v Blake* [2000] Ch. 86. See also *Yorkshire Bank Plc v Hall* [1999] 1 W.L.R. 1713.
[212] See *Silven Properties Ltd v Royal Bank of Scotland* [2004] 4 All E.R. 484; *Cuckmere Brick Co Ltd v Mutual Finance Ltd* [1971] Ch. 949, *per* Salmon L.J. at 966; *South Sea Bank Ltd v Tan Soon Gin* [1990] 1 A.C. 536; and *Bell v Long* [2008] 2 B.C.L.C. 706.
[213] *Silven Properties*, cited above n.212.
[214] *Medforth v Blake* [2000] Ch. 86.
[215] *Downview Nominees Ltd v First City Corp Ltd* [1993] A.C. 295 at 314.

he can select a particular asset to realise for the benefit of his debenture holder even though the removal of that asset would damage the company's business and there are other assets to which he could resort and on which the business is less dependant.[216] One has considerable sympathy with the following observation by Sir Donald Nicholls V.C. (as he then was) in *Palk v Mortgage Services Funding Plc*[217]:

> "In the exercise of his rights over his security the mortgagee must act fairly towards the mortgagor. His interest in the property has priority over the interest of the mortgagor, and he is entitled to proceed on that footing. He can protect his own interest but he is not entitled to conduct himself in a way which unfairly prejudices the mortgagor . . . I have given two examples where the law imposes a duty on the mortgagee when he is exercising his powers: if he lets the property he must obtain a proper market rent and if he sells he must obtain a proper market price.[218] *I confess I have difficulty in seeing why a mortgagee's duties in and about the exercise of his powers of letting and sale should be regarded as narrowly confined to these two duties.*"[219] [emphasis added]

The fact is that English law has not kept pace with developments in legal policy in other major common law jurisdictions. The New Zealand Receiverships Act 1993, while retaining the receiver's overriding obligations to act in good faith and for a proper purpose and to obtain the best price reasonably obtainable when selling, also imposes on him an obligation to exercise his powers with reasonable regard to the interests of unsecured creditors of the debtor company, guarantors and others claiming an interest in property through the debtor.[220] The Canadian Bankruptcy and Insolvency Act requires the receiver to deal with the assets in a commercially reasonable manner.[221] The Australian Corporations Act 2001 requires the receiver to exercise the degree of care and diligence that a reasonable person in a like position in a corporation would exercise, in the corporation's circumstances.[222] There is much to be said for a similar change of direction in English receivership law. It is clear that the very limited responsibility of a receiver in the protection of the interests of general creditors was a powerful factor in the government's decision to abolish administrative receivership,[223] with certain exceptions mentioned earlier.

---

[216] But he must act in good faith. See below, para.10–53.

[217] [1993] Ch. 330.

[218] By this the Vice-Chancellor plainly meant that the mortgagee has a duty to take reasonable care to obtain a proper market rent or proper market price, not a strict duty.

[219] [1993] Ch. 330 at 338.

[220] Section 18.

[221] Section 247.

[222] Section 180, extended to receivers by the definition of "officer" in s.9.

[223] See above, para.10–05.

The receiver's liability on contracts

10–50 Section 44 of the Insolvency Act 1986, as amended by the Insolvency Act 1994, deals with the deemed agency of the receiver prior to winding up of the company and with his liability in respect of new contracts and contracts of employment which he adopts.

"(1) The administrative receiver of a company—

    (a)   is deemed to be the company's agent, unless and until the company goes into liquidation;

    (b)   is personally liable on any contract entered into by him in the carrying out of his functions (except in so far as the contract otherwise provides) and, to the extent of any qualifying liability, on any contract of employment adopted by him in the carrying out of those functions; and

    (c)   is entitled in respect of that liability to an indemnity out of the assets of the company.

(2) For the purposes of subsection (l)(b) the administrative receiver is not to be taken to have adopted a contract of employment by reason of anything done or omitted to be done within 14 days after his appointment.

(2A) For the purposes of subsection (l)(b), a liability under a contract of employment is a qualifying liability if—

    (a)   it is a liability to pay a sum by way of wages or salary or contribution to an occupational pension scheme,

    (b)   it is incurred while the administrative receiver is in office, and

    (c)   it is in respect of services rendered wholly or partly after the adoption of the contract.

(2B) Where a sum payable in respect of a liability which is a qualifying liability for the purposes of subsection (l)(b) is payable in respect of services rendered partly before and partly after the adoption of the contract, liability under subsection (l)(b) shall only extend to so much of the sum as is payable in respect of services rendered after the adoption of the contract.

[(2C) and (2D) define what constitute wages or salary for the above purposes]

(3) This section does not limit any right to indemnity which the administrative receiver would have apart from it, nor limit his liability on

contracts entered into or adopted without authority, nor confer any right to indemnity in respect of that liability."

Entry into new contracts

Until the company goes into liquidation, the receiver is deemed to be its agent[224] and as such can commit it to future liabilities by entering into contracts in its name and on its behalf. However, the receiver is personally liable on any contract into which he enters (i.e. even in the name of the company) in the carrying out of his functions except so far as the contract otherwise provides,[225] but is entitled to an indemnity in respect of that liability out of the assets of the company.[226] Although the receiver is personally liable on new contracts entered into on behalf of the company, it is the company, not the receiver, who is party to the contract. Accordingly, the receiver's disclaimer of personal liability on a contract is not subject to the Unfair Contract Terms Act 1977.

10–51

Continuance of existing contracts other than contracts of employment

The receiver does not incur personal liability (except in relation to contracts of employment[227]) merely because he procures the company to continue or complete an existing contract.[228] This logically follows from the fact that the receiver is not a party to the contract, merely a receiver and manager of the business, so that in the absence of any statutory provision imposing liability, there is no reason why he should be in any different position from that of directors. The position is the same for continuing contracts such as the hire of equipment. If the receiver causes the company to continue a rental agreement and incur further rentals, these are the liability of the company, not of the receiver.[229] The principle of liquidation law that sums accruing due under leases and contracts continued by the liquidator for the beneficial winding up of the company are payable in full as expenses of the liquidation does not apply to receivership.

10–52

"The reason is not far to seek. The appointment of an administrative receiver does not trigger a statutory prohibition on the lessor or owner of goods such as that found in section 30 in the case of a winding up order. If

---

[224] Insolvency Act 1986 s.44(1)(a).
[225] Insolvency Act 1986 s.44(1)(b).
[226] Insolvency Act 1986 s.44(l)(c). See further para.10–56 as to questions arising in relation to the indemnity.
[227] See below, paras 10–54 et seq.
[228] *Re Newdigate Colliery Ltd* [1912] Ch. 468.
[229] *Hay v Swedish & Norwegian Railway Co Ltd* (1892) 8 T.L.R. 775.

the rent or hire is not paid by the administrative receiver the lessor or owner of the goods is at liberty, as much after the appointment of the administrative receiver as before, to exercise the rights and remedies available to him under his lease or hire purchase agreement. Faced with the prospect of proceedings, an administrative receiver may choose to pay the rent or hire charges in order to retain the land or goods. But if he decides not to do so, the lessor or owner of the goods has his remedies. There is no occasion, assuming that there is jurisdiction, for the court to intervene and order the administrative receiver to pay these outgoings."[230]

It has been held in two cases that where appropriate the court has power to order expenses incurred by a party in dealing with a receiver to be paid by the receiver and treated as expenses of the receivership, as where the receiver unsuccessfully brings or defends proceedings in the name of the company and an order for costs is made against the company.[231] However, in both cases the company had gone into liquidation, so that the receiver was no longer the company's agent but was the real party to the proceedings, whereas in the ordinary way the real party is the company and in the absence of impropriety there is usually no basis for making an order against the receiver as a non-party. The remedy of the defendant is to apply for an order for security for costs against the claimant company[232] under what is now Pt 25 r.25.13(2)(c) of the Civil Procedure Rules.

Repudiation of contracts

10–53   Equally, the receiver does not in general incur a liability either to the company or to the other party to a contract by repudiating the contract in the name of the company or by failing or refusing to allow the company to perform its part of the contract, and this is so even though the result is to expose the company to termination of the contact and/or a liability in damages.[233] There are several reasons for this. First, performance of the company's part of the contract is likely to involve the expenditure of money or the application of assets forming part of the security, and the debenture holder is not obliged to release assets from his security interest but on the contrary is entitled to have his security enforced, and thus stands in a better position than

---

[230] *Re Atlantic Computer Systems Plc* [1992] Ch. 505, *per* Nicholls L.J. at 524–525, applied in *Brown v City of London Corp* [1996] 1 W.L.R. 1070; sub nom. *Re Sobam BV* [1996] B.C.C. 351.

[231] *Anderson v Hyde* [1996] 2 B.C.L.C. 144, a decision of the Court of Appeal of Northern Ireland; and *Bacal Contracting Ltd v Modern Engineering (Bristol) Ltd* [1980] 2 All E.R. 655.

[232] *Dolphin Keys Developments Ltd v Mills* [2008] 1 W.L.R. 1829.

[233] *Newdigate Colliery*, cited above n.228; *Airlines Airspares Ltd v Handley Page Ltd* [1970] Ch. 193; *Re Diesels & Components Pty Ltd* (1985) 9 ACLR 2825. .

the company itself.[234] Secondly, the power to carry on the company's business is a power conferred on the receiver primarily for the benefit of his debenture holder, so that he must be free to decline to perform contracts, and indeed to shut down entirely an unprofitable part of the company's business, if he considers that this is in the best interests of the business of which he is receiver.[235] All that is required of the receiver is that he act in good faith and without needlessly damaging the company's goodwill.[236] Any duty of care he owes to the company[237] is subordinate to that owed to his debenture holder,[238] and he owes no duty at all to ordinary unsecured creditors.[239] Thirdly, the receiver as deemed agent of the company is entitled to take advantage of the principle of agency law formulated in *Said v Butt*[240] that an agent acting bona fide within the scope of his authority is not liable for inducing a breach of contract by his principal,[241] for he is treated as the principal's *alter ego* and his acts are those of the principal.

The principles underlying the receiver's right to decline to perform the company's contracts have yet to be fully worked out. If the receiver acts wantonly, he may incur a liability to the company as its deemed agent for loss caused by his actions and a liability to the third party for procuring a breach of contract. What is less clear is whether, because performance of the contract would involve the application of money or other assets comprising the security, the receiver is justified in preventing performance when the remaining assets provide ample cover and can be realised just as quickly as those which would be used in performing the contract.[242] It would seem that in this regard the receiver's position is not essentially different from that of his debenture holder. In general, a secured creditor may resort to whatever part of his security he chooses, without regard to the interests either of his debtor or of third parties, and his receiver must, it is thought, be in the same position. To put the matter in another way, a person contracting with a company

---

[234] ibid. See also *Edwin Hill & Partners v First National Finance Corp Plc* [1989] B.C.L.C. 89, in which it was held that a debenture holder who without appointing a receiver or otherwise enforcing its charge insisted on the company appointing a new and more prestigious firm of architects to supervise a development was not liable to the former architect for wrongful interference with the contract, for it had a right equal or superior to that of the plaintiff and the fact that it brought about the termination of the plaintiff's engagement through an accommodation with the company, not by enforcement of its security, did not deprive it of legal justification for its actions. In argument it was conceded that the debenture holder could not have been liable if it had interfered with the contract by exercising its power of sale and that the same probably applied if it had appointed a receiver.

[235] *Kernohan Estates Ltd v Boyd* [1967] N.I. 27.

[236] *Kernohan Estates*, cited above n.235.

[237] See above, para.10–48, and, for an instructive discussion, David Milman, "The Receiver as Agent" (1981) 44 M.L.R. 658.

[238] *Re B Johnson & Co (Builders) Ltd* [1955] Ch. 634, *per* Jenkins L.J. at 661.

[239] *Lathia v Dronsfield Bros* [1987] B.C.L.C. 321.

[240] [1920] 3 K.B. 497.

[241] *Welsh Development Agency v Export Finance Co Ltd* [1992] B.C.L.C. 148.

[242] Other secured creditors may be protected by the doctrine of marshalling.

takes the company as he finds it and cannot complain if the debenture holder or his receiver exercises the rights conferred on them by the company over the assets of the company or negotiates with the company to achieve the same results as would be achieved by exercise of those rights.

However, the receiver is not entitled to disregard legal or equitable proprietary rights acquired by the other party to the contract. Accordingly, he can be ordered to give specific performance of a contract of sale of land entered into by the company,[243] to refrain from assigning an option already assigned by the company in equity to a third party[244] and to respect a lien over goods in favour of the company's agent, even if the goods were not received until after the receiver was appointed and the agent had notice of his appointment.[245]

Moreover, in *Land Rover Group Ltd v UPF (UK) Ltd*,[246] it was held that while a receiver is in a privileged position in being able to procure the company not to perform a contract, his appointment does not preclude an order for an interim injunction against the company to secure fulfillment of its contractual obligations where this would otherwise be granted. However, that case may have turned on its own special facts and moreover was not a final adjudication, merely an interlocutory proceeding. It is thought that in general a receiver is perfectly entitled to take the position that it will not allow the company's assets to be used, or its own negotiating position in handling a contract undermined, to the possible detriment of the debenture holder.

Adoption of contract of employment

10–54   Under s.44(2)(b) of the Insolvency Act 1986, the receiver is personally liable, to the extent of any qualifying liability, on any contract of employment adopted by him in the carrying out of his functions. For this purpose, he is not to be taken to have adopted the contract by virtue of anything done or omitted to be done, within 14 days after his appointment.[247] Section 44 has had a chequered history.[248] The Insolvency Act 1994 modified s.44 (and also s.19, a similar provision applicable to administration) by restricting the personal liability of receivers in an administrative receivership to "qualifying liabilities", that is, specified wage and wage-related claims incurred during the administration or receivership, and then only to sums payable in respect of services rendered by employees after the adoption of the contract. However, the government declined to incorporate provisions making the new legislation retrospective, so

---

[243] *Freevale Ltd v Metrostore Holdings Ltd* [1984] Ch. 199.
[244] *Telemetrix Plc v Modern Engineers of Bristol (Holdings) Plc* [1985] 1 B.C.C. 99 at 417.
[245] *Diesels & Components*, cited above n.258.
[246] [2003] 2 B.C.L.C. 222.
[247] Insolvency Act 1986 s.44(2).
[248] For details of which see the 3rd edn of this work at paras 9–53 et seq.

that serious problems remained. In the end, these were largely resolved by the House of Lords, which in *Powdrill v Watson*[249] held that the employees' priority was limited to liabilities under adopted contracts so far as incurred during the period of the administration and did not extend to pre-administration or post-administration liabilities. On the other hand, it was not limited to liabilities incurred in return for services actually provided after adoption of the contract. In this respect, the 1994 Act cut down the priority still further.

There remained one point to clarify which was left untouched by the 1994 Act. Precisely what is meant by adoption? It was always clear that it did not mean novation, i.e. entry by the receiver into a new contract, for the receiver would be liable under such a contract by virtue of the opening words of s.44(1)(b) and there would have been no need for s.44(1)(b) to make reference to contracts of employment. Nor did adoption require an act by which the receiver made manifest an intention to assume personal liability. Such liability flows from the adoption of the contract, rather than the other way round. What, then, constitutes the act of adoption of an employment contract? Is it sufficient that the administrative receiver takes no positive steps to terminate it? Or is a more positive step required?

It is evident that on this crucial point Lord Browne-Wilkinson had a change of mind during the course of his speech in *Powdrill v Watson*. Starting from the position that "the mere continuation of the employment by the company does not lead inexorably to the conclusion that it has been adopted by the receiver"[250] and that adoption "can only connote some conduct by the administrator or receiver which amounts to an election to treat the continued employment with the company as giving rise to a separate liability in the administration or receivership",[251] he was in the end reluctantly driven to the conclusion that the contract of employment is inevitably adopted by the receiver unless he terminates or repudiates[252] the contract within 14 days of his appointment.[253]

Conclusions on s.44

We are now in a position to summarise the present state of the law in the light of the decision of the House of Lords in *Powdrill v Watson* and of the amendments to s.44 of the Insolvency Act:

10–55

---

[249] [1995] 2 A.C. 394, in which the House heard consolidated appeals in the *Leyland DAF* and *Ferranti* cases.

[250] *Powdrill v Watson*, cited above n.249, at 448.

[251] *Powdrill v Watson* at 449.

[252] The contract of employment is one of the few contracts that can be brought to an end by a repudiatory act without the need for its acceptance by the other party as terminating the contract. Although this is disputed by some authorities, Lord Browne-Wilkinson's speech gives support to the view generally accepted that employment contracts are an exception to the usual rule in contract law.

[253] *Powdrill v Watson*, cited above n.249, at 450 and 452.

(1)   By "adoption" of a contract of employment is meant causing or allowing it to continue in force.

(2)   The receiver adopts a contract of employment if he does not within 14 days of his appointment either terminate the contract or repudiate it, for example, by refusing to pay wages.

(3)   The receiver's liability is confined to wages or salary, holiday pay and other entitlements designated as qualifying liabilities under subss.(2A), (2C) and (2D) of s.44.

(4)   The receiver is responsible only for a liability incurred while he is in office, not for liabilities incurred before he accepted his appointment or after his discharge.

(5)   He is also not liable for payments in respect of services rendered before his adoption of the contract, and where services are rendered partly before and partly after such adoption, he is liable only to the extent of the services rendered after adoption.

(6)   For the purpose of computing the receiver's liability, sums due to the employee are considered to accrue day by day under the Apportionment Act 1870, so that where, for example, a sum in respect of services rendered during the receivership does not become payable until after the receiver has ceased to hold office, it will be apportioned and he will be liable only for such part as is deemed to accrue under the Apportionment Act between the commencement of the provision of the services and the ending of the receiver's period of office.

(7)   Where the receiver adopts the contract, he thereby assumes personal liability upon it and is not entitled to disclaim liability or select which liabilities he will undertake and which he will not. This is not because the exempting words of s.44(2) are confined to new contracts made by the receiver (for as Lightman J. pointed out in *Leyland DAF*,[254] they would be inappropriate in relation to contracts entered into by the company prior to the receivership and to which the receiver was not a party) but because to allow the receiver to exclude liability on contracts he has adopted would be contrary to the policy of the legislation.

Receiver's right to indemnity

10–56   By s.44(1)(c) of the Insolvency Act, the receiver is entitled to an indemnity out of the assets of the company in respect of his personal liability on con-

---

[254] *Leyland DAF Ltd. v. Automotive Products plc* [1993] B.C.C. 389.

tracts entered into on behalf of the company or contracts of employment adopted by him or her. But the receiver's power to commit the company to new contractual liabilities comes to an end on liquidation, when his agency terminates,[255] and if, after liquidation, he enters into new contracts, he has no statutory right of indemnity. This seems clear from s.44(3), which provides that s.44 does not limit the receiver's liability on contracts entered into or adopted without authority, nor confer any right of indemnity in respect of that liability. But if the liquidator chooses to accept and retain on behalf of the company the benefit of a post-liquidation contract concluded by the liquidator—for example, by retaining goods purchased in the name of the company after winding up—then on general restitutionary principles the receiver should be indemnified or reimbursed out of the assets of the company to the extent of any benefit derived by the company from the adopted transaction.

Debentures almost invariably provide for payment of the receiver's remuneration and expenses out of receipts and realisations before these are applied towards discharge of the amount secured by the debenture,[256] and the receiver's entitlement has priority over the claims of the debenture holder and preferential creditors even in the absence of an express provision in the debenture.[257] Such expenses include liabilities incurred by the receiver under contracts entered into by him on behalf of the company. However, the receiver cannot resort to assets of third parties, or to assets of the company which are subject to a security interest ranking in priority to that of his debenture holder.

Leases

The receiver is not liable to the lessor either for rent accrued due prior to the time of his appointment or for rent accruing due after his appointment, even if he takes actual possession himself.[258] This is because, in contrast to a liquidator, the receiver who takes beneficial occupation does so as manager in right of the debenture holder, not as successor to the business in right of the company. It follows that post-receivership rent is not payable to the lessor as an expense of the receivership in the way that post-liquidation rent would have been payable on a winding up, for the debt is that of the company, but the company's money and other assets are subject to the debenture and there is no reason why the security should be made available to discharge the

10–57

---

[255] Insolvency Act 1986 s.44(1)(a).

[256] See, e.g. J.R. Lingard, *Bank Security Documents*, 3rd edn (London: LexisNexis Butterworths,1993), document 1, cl.7.02; and document 2, cl.8.02.

[257] *Re Glyncorrwg Colliery Co Ltd* [1926] Ch. 951.

[258] *Hand v Blow* [1901] 2 Ch. 721, distinguishing the Irish decision in *Baife v Blake* (1850) 1 I.R. Ch. Rep. 365; and *Consolidated Entertainments Ltd v Taylor* [1937] 4 All E.R. 432.

company's indebtedness.[259] The lessor has his usual battery of remedies against the company for non-payment of the rent, including forfeiture of the lease,[260] distress and service of a notice under s.6 of the Law of Distress Amendment Act 1908[261] requiring sub-lessees to pay their sub-rents direct to him.[262]

If the company has sub-let the premises, the receiver is entitled to collect the sub-rentals and retain these for the benefit of the debenture holder, and may do so without paying the rent due to the lessor, there being no privity of contract between lessor and sub-lessee and thus no connection between the rent payable under the head lease and that payable under the sub-lease.[263] The lessor may either forfeit the lease or serve a notice under s.6 of the Law of Distress Amendment Act 1908 on the sub-lessee requiring him to pay the sub-rentals direct to the head lessor to the extent necessary to discharge the head lessee's obligations. Neither the appointment of a receiver nor the crystallisation of a floating charge resulting from such appointment affects the lessor's right to serve a s.6 notice,[264] and even entry into possession by the debenture holder or his receiver does not alter the position.[265] The debenture holder cannot claim a superior title under the rule in *Dearle v Hall* as an equitable assignee who is the first to give notice to the sub-tenants, because s.6 confers on the lessor what is in effect a statutory right to garnishee the rent due from the sub-tenants and any assignee of the lease takes subject to the possibility of this right being exercised, so that the question of competing assignments does not arise.[266]

Rates

10–58 The receiver normally incurs no personal liability for payment of business rates, even where he takes possession, for his possession is generally as deemed agent of the company, not on his own account.[267] Moreover, even

---

[259] *Hand v Blow*, cited above n.258.

[260] Subject to relief against forfeiture. See *Legends Surfs Plc v Sun Life Assurance Society Plc* [2006] B.C.C. 204.

[261] Quaere whether the receiver or his debenture holder can serve a declaration of his interest on the lessor under s.1 of the Law of Distress Amendment Act 1908. The Act is due to be repealed by the Tribunals, Courts and Enforcement Act 2007 s.146 and Sch.23 Pt 4, and the relevant provision replaced by s.81 of the latter Act.

[262] See below.

[263] *Hand v Blow*, cited above n.258.

[264] *Re Offshore Ventilation Ltd* (1989) 5 B.C.C. 160.

[265] *Re Offshore Ventilation*.

[266] *Re Offshore Ventilation*.

[267] *Brown v City of London Corp* [1996] 1 W.L.R. 1076: sub nom. *Re Sobam BV* [1996] B.C.C. 351; *Ratford v North Avon DC* [1986] 3 All E.R. 193; and *Rees v Boston BC* [2002] 1 W.L.R. 1304 where the authorities were extensively reviewed by Jonathan Parker L.J. See generally Lightman et al., *The Law of Administrators and Receivers of Companies*, 2007, paras 27.013–27.014.

where his deemed agency comes to an end as the result of the company going into liquidation, this does not by itself mean that he is in rateable occupation of the premises, for the company continues to be in possession itself unless there is some act or event by which it is divested of possession.[268]

Liability in tort for trespass or conversion

A receiver has to take control of the company's assets as quickly as possible after his appointment in order to preserve the assets and to prevent their disappearance. Within the very limited time available he has little or no opportunity to verify the company's title to assets of which it is in possession, which may well include property belonging to a third party, such as stock or equipment supplied under reservation of title and not fully paid for. At common law, a receiver who takes possession of or sells a third party's asset or does some other act inconsistent with that party's right to possession incurs the normal liabilities in tort for trespass or conversion, even if acting in good faith. However, he is now given a measure of protection by the Insolvency Act, which gives him immunity from liability for seizing or disposing of property which is not the property of the company if at the time of the seizure or disposal he believes, and has reasonable grounds for believing, that he is entitled (whether in pursuance of an order of the court or otherwise) to seize or dispose of that property.[269] In such a case, he also has a lien on the property, or the proceeds of its sale, for expenses incurred in connection with the seizure or disposal.[270] The statutory provisions are confined to the seizure and sale of tangible property, and do not apply to the collection of debts due to a third party. But as to these no statutory protection is necessary, for intangibles are not susceptible to a claim for conversion[271] and to the extent that the collection of the debts induces a breach of contract between the company and the debtors the receiver is entitled to rely on the rule in *Said v Butt* which protects agency against personal liability.[272]

10–59

The floating charge and preferential debts

(1) The priority of preferential debts

One of the major weaknesses of a floating charge is that it is subordinated to the claims of preferential creditors if, when the company is not in the course

10–60

---

[268] *Re Beck Foods Ltd* [2002] B.P.I.R. 665, applying a series of earlier decisions, including *Re Marriage, Neave & Co* [1896] 2 Ch. 663; and *Ratford*, cited above n.267.

[269] Insolvency Act 1986 s.234(3) and (4).

[270] Insolvency Act 1986 s.234(3) and (4).

[271] *OBG Ltd v Allan* [2008] A.C. 1.

[272] *Welsh Development Agency v Export Finance Co Ltd* [1992] B.C.C. 270; and see above, para.10–53.

of being wound up, the debenture holder takes possession of any property comprised in the charge[273] or appoints a receiver[274] or if the debtor company goes into winding up[275] or into administration where the administrator makes a distribution.[276] Until the enactment of the Insolvency Act 1985 (later replaced by the Insolvency Act 1986), a floating charge which crystallised otherwise than by reason of one of the above events took priority over preferential debts arising subsequent to crystallisation, for in relation to these the charge had ceased to be a floating charge[277] and was thus outside the statutory provisions then in force.[278] An astute draftsman could thus pave the way for circumventing the priority of preferential creditors by use of automatic or semi-automatic crystallisation clauses triggered by events other than possession, winding up or the appointment of a receiver. That was later changed. Both under the Insolvency Act 1986 and the Companies Act 2006 a floating charge means a charge which *as created* was a floating charge.[279] So preferential debts now have priority over a floating charge[280] whether they arise before or after crystallisation, and the assets out of which the preferential claims are to be discharged include not only the free assets of the company but those which are subject to a crystallised floating charge. Moreover—and this was the law even before the legislative change referred to above—assets which come in under the charge after it has crystallised (for example, through the receiver's trading activity) are within the preferential net even though there was never a moment when they were subject to a floating charge, for the statutory provisions catch all assets *potentially* within the scope of the floating charge, including those acquired by the company after crystallisation.[281] The only good news for debenture holders is that the range

---

[273] Companies Act 2006 s.754(1),(2).

[274] Insolvency Act 1986 s.40. This section applies whether or not the receiver is an administrative receiver. Curiously, the priority of preferential creditors is not triggered by a sale by the mortgagee without taking possession or appointing a receiver.

[275] Insolvency Act 1986 s.175(2)(b), which applies whether the company goes into compulsory or voluntary liquidation. Section 175(2)(b) differs from s.40 of the Insolvency Act 1986 and from s.754 of the Companies Act 2006 in the way that it gives effect to the priority, providing that the preferential debts are to be paid out of the floating charge assets only to the extent that the assets available to general creditors are insufficient for the purpose, whereas the latter statutory provisions provide for payment to preferential creditors in the first instance out of assets subject to the floating charge, the chargee having a right to recoupment from the assets available for payment to general creditors. The distinction is logical in that where the company is in winding up but not in receivership, there is only one fund available for payment to preferential creditors.

[276] Insolvency Act 1986 Sch.B1 para.65(2).

[277] *Re Griffin Hotel Co Ltd* [1941] Ch. 129; *Stein v Saywell* [1969] A.L.R. 481; and *Re Christonette International Ltd* [1982] 3 All E.R. 225 (in which the same result was reached by a different route, Vinelott J. holding that assets subject to a crystallised charge were no longer assets of the company for the purpose of the statutory provisions).

[278] i.e. the Companies Act 1985 ss.196(1) and (2), and 614(2) and (6), re-enacting the Companies Act 1948 ss.94(1) and 319(5).

[279] Insolvency Act 1986 ss.40(1) and 251; and Companies Act 2006 s.754.

[280] Insolvency Act 1986 ss.40 and 175(2).

[281] *Inland Revenue Commissioners v Goldblatt* [1972] 1 Ch. 498.

of preferential debts has been significantly reduced, as recommended by the Cork Committee,[282] in that Crown preference, which was removed as regards assessed taxes by what is now the Insolvency Act 1986, has been abolished altogether,[283] leaving only various types of claim by employees.[284]

Where the assets subject to the floating charge and the company's free assets are insufficient to meet the claims of the preferential creditors in full, these abate rateably.[285] The claim of the holder of a floating charge is also postponed to liquidation expenses.[286]

A receiver appointed under a floating charge at a time when the company is not in winding up is under a statutory duty to pay preferential creditors out of the assets coming into his hands in priority to the claims of the debenture holder.[287] However, this duty applies only in relation to assets which are the subject of the floating charge, not those comprised in a fixed charge. Hence, if a receiver is appointed under a debenture containing both a fixed and a floating charge, the mere fact that he is appointed under a floating charge does not attract the operation of the statutory provisions to the assets coming into his hands under the fixed charge.[288] Further, if the receiver, on selling the assets which are the subject of the fixed charge, realises a surplus, that surplus cannot be said to be caught by the floating charge, even if the proceeds are in a form covered by the charge, for *ex hypothesi* the sum realised has been sufficient to discharge the debt due to the debenture holder, so that there is no longer any obligation left to be secured. It follows that the receiver's duty is to hand the surplus back to the company if it is not in liquidation or to the liquidator if it is.[289]

The above statutory provisions give the preferential debts priority only over the claims of the debenture holders under the floating charge; their claims are subordinate to those of the receiver for the costs of preserving and realising the assets and his expenses and remuneration.[290]

---

[282] *Report of the Review Committee on Insolvency Law and Practice* (Cmnd. 8558, 1982), para.1450.

[283] Enterprise Act 2002 s.251.

[284] Insolvency Act 1986 Sch.6.

[285] Where the company is in winding up, this is provided expressly by s.175(2)(a) of the Insolvency Act 1986. Where the event triggering the priority of the preferential debts is the taking of possession by the chargee, it falls outside what is now s.754 of the Companies Act 2006. See below, n.293.

[286] Insolvency Act 1986 s.176ZA, reversing the effect of the House of Lords' decision in *Buchler v Talbot* [2004] 2 A.C. 298. See above, paras.8–32, 8–51.

[287] Insolvency Act 1986 s.40(2). The relevant date for determining the preferential debts is the date of the appointment of the receiver by debenture holders (s.387(4)(a)).

[288] *Re Lewis Merthyr Consolidated Collieries Ltd* [1929] 1 Ch. 498; and *Re G.L. Saunders Ltd* [1986] 1 W.L.R. 215.

[289] *G.L. Saunders*, cited above n.288.

[290] *Re Glyncorrwg Colliery Co Ltd* [1926] Ch. 951.

(2) Events triggering the priority

10–61   As stated above, any one of four distinct events can trigger the priority of preferential debts over a floating charge and thus establish a priority point at which
the preferential debts have to be determined, namely: the taking of possession
of the security by or on behalf of the chargee[291]; the appointment of a
receiver[292]; the winding up of the debtor company; and the making of a distribution by an administrator when the company is in administration. It is
theoretically possible for all four events to occur, in which case it may become
necessary to determine the preferential debts in existence at four different
points in time,[293] although there will usually be an overlap, as where preferential debts existing on the appointment of a receiver are still preferential[294] and
unpaid at the time of winding up. The debenture holder or its receiver is thus
well advised to collect the amounts due under a crystallised floating charge
while there are still sufficient free assets left to cover the preferential debts.

There is a division of judicial opinion as to whether the appointment of a
receiver by the holder of a floating charge subordinates only the appointing
chargee to the claims of preferential creditors or all other holders of floating
charges. In *Griffiths v Yorkshire Bank Plc*,[295] Morritt J. adopted the former
construction of s.40 of the Insolvency Act 1986, pointing out that there were
various ways in which the holder of a floating charge could enforce his
security without taking possession or appointing a receiver, for example,
by sale of the asset given in security,[296] while in *H. & K. Medway Ltd,*

---

[291] What is meant by "possession" is a question which never seems to have been discussed. In
particular, is the section confined to tangible property? It is thought that it should be construed broadly to cover any kind of asset over which the chargee acquires control equivalent
to possession. If the section were confined to tangibles, it would exclude the receipt of money
credited to the chargee's bank account. However, it has been held that the tort of conversion
does not apply to intangibles. See above, para.10–59.

[292] A receiver acts independently of the debenture holder who appointed him and therefore in
taking possession was held not to have acted "on behalf of" the debenture holder so
as to bring s.196 of the Companies Act 1985 (now Companies Act 2006 s.754) into play concurrently with s.40 of the Insolvency Act 1986 (*Re H. & K. Medway Ltd* [1997] 1
W.L.R. 1422).

[293] This depends on the sequence of events. If the company is already in liquidation when possession is taken or the receiver is appointed, neither s.754 of the Companies Act 2006 nor
s.40(2) of the Insolvency Act 1986 applies, and the relevant date for determining the preferential creditors is the date of winding up.

[294] This will not necessarily be the case: e.g. preferential claims for unpaid wages are limited
to (inter alia) wages for the four months preceding the relevant date (as defined by
the Insolvency Act 1986 s.387), so that a claim for unpaid wages which is preferential
at the time of appointment of a receiver may no longer be preferential at the time of
winding up.

[295] [1994] 1 W.L.R. 1427.

[296] However, the proceeds of sale would themselves fall within s.40. An argument that might be
advanced against this is that at the moment of receipt the proceeds constitute *pro tanto* payment of the debt secured by the charge, so that there is never a time when they represent an
asset comprised in the charge. But in *Inland Revenue Commissioners v Goldblatt* [1972]
Ch. 498, just such an argument was robustly rejected by Goff J., who, in the context of
what was then s.94(1) of the Companies Act 1948 (now s.754 of the Companies Act 2006),

Re,[297] Neuberger J. held that all floating charges became subordinated, not merely the charge held by the creditor appointing the receiver. There are arguments to support either position but on balance those in favour of the latter decision seem preferable.

(4) The effect of successive priority events

The four possible priority events are not mutually exclusive as regards the obligations of the receiver towards the liquidator (for expenses of the liquidation) and preferential creditors but each set of preferential creditors is entitled to look only to assets remaining within the floating charge. Suppose, for example, that a receiver is appointed, that from the assets in his hands he pays the preferential creditors and makes a partial payment to his debenture holder and that before he has completed his receivership, the company goes into liquidation with a new set of preferential creditors. The payments already made to the receivership preferential creditors and the debenture holder cannot be disturbed. But if the receiver is still holding assets subject to the floating charge, the liquidator is entitled to resort to these for the liquidation expenses and payment to the liquidation preferential creditors.[298] So assets originally within s.40 of the Insolvency Act 1986 but not resorted to under that section may later fall within s.175(2)(b) of the Act on a winding up.

10–62

(5) Effect of receiver's failure to pay preferential claims

A receiver who after notice of a preferential claim neglects to satisfy it from assets available and instead applies those assets or their proceeds for other purposes—as by making a payment to the debenture holder or by exhausting the assets in the continuance of the company's business—is liable in damages to the preferential creditor in tort and/or for breach of statutory duty to the extent of the preferential creditor's resulting loss.[299] For this purpose, it is immaterial that the debenture holder's debt has been satisfied by payment from the proceeds of assets subject to a fixed charge. The receiver is still responsible for payment of the preferential debts out of moneys coming into his hands from the assets which are the subject of a floating charge.[300]

10–63

---

considered (at 506) that it would be extraordinary if the statutory provisions were to protect the preferential creditors when the debenture holder took possession as mortgagee and not protect them when the debenture holder took assets in satisfaction of his claim.
[297] Above, n.292.
[298] *Re Buchler v Talbot,* cited above n.286.
[299] *Westminster CC v Treby* [1936] 2 All E.R. 21; *IRC v Goldblatt* [1972] 1 Ch. 498; *Woods v Winskill* [1913] 2 Ch. 303; and *Westminster Corp v Haste* [1950] Ch. 442.
[300] *Re Pearl Maintenance Services Ltd* [1995] B.C.C. 657.

The debenture holder who with notice of the preferential claim receives a payment or other benefit from assets which should have been applied in payment of that claim is liable:

(1)   directly to the preferential creditor for breach of statutory duty; alternatively for wrongfully procuring and being a party to such breach by the receiver or alternatively as constructive trustee for receiving the money or benefit with notice of the breach[301]; and

(2)   to indemnify the receiver in respect of his own liability.[302]

However, the receiver incurs no liability to the company, for he is not the party who has suffered a loss.[303]

The receiver's duty to set aside the prescribed part of floating charge assets

10–64   Reference has already been made to the fact that in insolvency proceedings the prescribed part of the net property subject to a floating charge has to be made available for unsecured creditors.[304] This obligation, to which there are certain exceptions,[305] applies to a receiver as it does to a liquidator and to an administrator making a distribution.[306] The prescribed part may not be distributed to the proprietor of a floating charge except so far as it exceeds the amount required for the satisfaction of unsecured debts.[307] Where the company is in liquidation, the receiver should make over the prescribed part to the liquidator rather than paying the unsecured creditors himself, which is not his ordinary function. But if the company is not in liquidation,[308] it is presumably for the receiver to distribute the prescribed part to unsecured creditors, there being no other office-holder in place for that purpose.

Environmental liability

10–65   The position of the administrative receiver in relation to the company's obligations under environmental obligation is unclear. On the one hand he can-

---

[301] *IRC v Goldblatt*, cited above n.299.
[302] *Westminster CC v Treby*, cited above n.299. In principle, the debenture holder ought to be liable to indemnify the receiver even if taking the payment or benefit without notice of the breach, unless he has changed his position in reliance on the payment or benefit so that it would be inequitable to order him to restore it. See R.M. Goode [1981] J.B.L. 473 at 477.
[303] *Re BHT (UK) Ltd* [2004] 1 B.C.L.C. 568.
[304] See above, para.6–38.
[305] See above, para.6–38.
[306] Insolvency Act 1986 s.176A(1)(d).
[307] Insolvency Act 1986 s.176A(1)(d).
[308] Or in administration where the administrator intends to exercise a power to make a distribution.

not, it is thought, be required to use assets comprised in the security to pay for remedial works or clean-up costs, for to the extent of the security the assets do not belong to the company.[309] Moreover, he is protected from personal liability.[310] On the other hand, he cannot carry on the business in breach of environmental legislation, and if he were to do so, he could incur criminal and other sanctions. The position, then, would appear to be that the receiver has a choice: to carry on the business, with an obligation to use the charged assets to the extent necessary to ensure compliance with the legislation; or to discontinue the business and, if he can, to dispose of it or the assets comprising it. The choice he makes will depend on his judgment as to whether the benefits to his debenture holder from continuing the business sufficiently outweigh the costs of compliance and environmental risks to make it worthwhile to carry on the business.

8. IMPACT OF WINDING UP ON THE RECEIVERSHIP

Termination of the receiver's agency

As has already been mentioned, the winding up of the company terminates the receiver's deemed agency for the company,[311] and thus his power to commit the company to future liabilities, for example, under new contracts made in the carrying on of the business. It follows that he has no statutory right to be indemnified from the assets of the company in respect of those liabilities.[312] But the advent of winding up does not terminate the receivership,[313] for the receiver remains free to exercise security rights for the benefit of his debenture holder,[314] and for this purpose it is immaterial whether he exercises those rights in the name of the debenture holder as chargee or mortgagee or in the name of the company.[315] In other words, winding up terminates the receiver's purely personal powers but not his *in rem* powers.[316] A good illustration is furnished by the decision of Goulding J. in *Sowman v David Samuel Trust Ltd*.[317] In that case:

10–66

---

[309] This does of course depend on the wording of the particular statute.

[310] Environment Protection Act 1990 s.78X(4)(a).

[311] Insolvency Act 1986 s.44(1).

[312] See above, para.10–56.

[313] Nor does it prevent the debenture holder from appointing a receiver if the company goes into liquidation first (*Re Potters Oils Ltd (No.2)* [1986] 1 W.L.R. 201).

[314] *Sowman v David Samuel Trust Ltd* [1978] 1 All E.R. 616.

[315] *Sowman*, cited above n.314.

[316] See above, para.10–44.

[317] See above n.314.

"A company in receivership subsequently went into winding up. The receiver continued to realise the company's assets, including property which had been mortgaged to the company to secure a debt due to it from the mortgagor. By a provision in the debenture pursuant to which the receiver had been appointed the debenture holders were irrevocably appointed the attorneys of the company to execute any deed or instrument in the name of the company and on its behalf which might be necessary for any of the purposes of the security. In the conveyance the sale was expressed to be made by the company as mortgagee, acting by its attorneys the debenture holders, at the request of the receiver and in exercise of the power of sale conferred on the company by the mortgage and by statute. The purchaser having applied for registration as proprietor, the Chief Land Registrar declined to effect the registration in view of doubts as to the continued powers of the receiver after the commencement of the winding up. In subsequent proceedings the further argument was advanced that the sale of the company's property by the receiver was void under section 227 of the Companies Act 1948 as a post-petition disposition made without leave of the court.

It was held that whilst winding up terminated the receiver's agency to bind the company personally by acting as its agent, it did not in the least affect the powers conferred on him by the debenture to hold and dispose of the property comprised in the debenture and for that purpose to use the company's name. Those powers, being coupled with an interest, were irrevocable, both at common law and by statute; and for this purpose a power given to the receiver for the purpose of securing a benefit to the debenture holders was as irrevocable as a power given to the debenture holders themselves. Further, the sale did not contravene section 227 because, though made in the company's name, it was a sale of property which did not belong to the company but formed part of the debenture holders' security."

Some months after this decision it was held that winding up did not affect the receiver's power to convey a legal estate by selling in the company's name pursuant to the power of sale conferred by the debenture.[318]

As pointed out earlier,[319] there are in fact two ways in which the sale may be effected. It may be a sale in the name of the company acting by its receiver,[320] who affixes the company seal, or it may alternatively be made by the debenture holder (directly or through the receiver as its agent) as

---

[318] *Barrows v Chief Land Registrar. The Times*, October 20, 1977. On a further aspect of this case, see above, para.10–41, text and n.181.
[319] See above, para.10–45.
[320] Or acting by the debenture holder pursuant to any power of attorney conferred by the debenture, assuming, if the company is in liquidation, that the power of attorney survives. See above, para.10–41.

mortgagee. The latter method should be adopted where there is a subsequent mortgage which it is desired should be overreached by the sale. But since the receiver's purely personal powers come to an end on liquidation, any new contract which he enters into and which is not within any actual or apparent authority conferred on him by the liquidator does not bind the company unless ratified by the liquidator, so that in the absence of such authority or ratification the receiver is personally liable without the benefit of the statutory indemnity.[321] In such a case, the sale should be made by the debenture holder as mortgagee.

The fact that the receiver ceases to be the agent of the company does not mean that he becomes the agent of the debenture holder,[322] merely that the receiver acts on his own account and is liable as a principal.[323]

Relationship between receiver and liquidator

Since the receiver has all, or substantially all, of the assets of the company under his control by virtue of the security created by the debenture and retains the power to manage and realise those assets, the liquidator must perforce stand on the sidelines during the receivership, since until then there is no estate for him to administer.[324] But any duties owed by the receiver to the company as its deemed agent may be enforced by the liquidator in the name of the company and the liquidator may also take proceedings against the receiver for misfeasance.[325] The receiver is entitled to retain assets in his hands until his expenses (including any liabilities he has incurred) and remuneration, any sum payable to preferential creditors out of assets subject to a floating charge and the amount due to his debenture holders[326] have been paid. Any surplus remaining, so far as not payable to a subsequent chargee, must be handed over to the liquidator, to whom the receiver also has a duty to render proper accounts of his receipts and payments when so required.[327]

10–67

---

[321] See para.10–56 above. If the liquidator accepts the benefit of the contract on behalf of the company, the receiver would seem to acquire a restitutionary right of recoupment to the extent of such benefit and the company becomes liable on the contract as an undisclosed principal.

[322] *Gosling v Gaskell* [1897] A.C. 575.

[323] *Gosling v Gaskell*, cited above n.322.

[324] However, it is sometimes found convenient for the administrative receiver to hand over to a liquidator prior to completion of the receivership against a suitable indemnity.

[325] Insolvency Act 1986 s.212(1)(b).

[326] Including contingent liabilities of the company to the debenture holder where these are secured by the debenture (*Re Rudd & Son Ltd; Re Fosters and Rudd Ltd* (1986) 2 B.C.C. 98).

[327] Insolvency Act 1986 s.41(1).

9. ORDER OF APPLICATION OF REALISATIONS BY RECEIVER

10–68   Realisations of assets by the receiver must first be applied in discharge of any security ranking in priority to the charge under which he was appointed. After this, it is necessary to distinguish realisations of fixed charges assets from those of floating charges and, in relation to the latter, to distinguish further between floating charges created before September 15, 2003 ("old charges") and those created on or after that date ("new charges").

Realisations of fixed charge assets

10–69   Any priority security interest having been satisfied, the order of application of realisations from fixed charge assets is as follows:

(1)   any costs of preserving and realising the assets, whether incurred by the receiver or (if the company is in liquidation) by the liquidator for the benefit of the chargee;

(2)   the receiver's costs, remuneration and expenses;

(3)   sums due to the chargee;

(4)   sums due to any secured creditor ranking after the chargee, or if he has appointed a receiver, then that receiver;

(5)   any surplus to the company, payment being made to its liquidator if it is in winding up.

Realisations of floating charge assets: old charge

10–70   Realisations of assets subject to an old floating charge are to be applied in the following order:

(1)   any costs of preserving and realising the floating charge assets, whether incurred by the receiver or (if the company is in liquidation) by the liquidator for the benefit of the chargee;

(2)   the receiver's costs, remuneration and expenses;

(3)   preferential debts, so far as the free assets of the company are insufficient to meet them;

(4)   sums due to the chargee;

(5)   sums due to any secured creditor ranking after the chargee or, if he has appointed a receiver, then that receiver; and

(6)   any surplus to the company, payment being made to its liquidator if it is in winding up.

Realisations from floating charge assets: new charge

Realisations of assets subject to a new charge are to be applied in the follow-   **10–71**
ing order:

(1)   any costs of preserving and realising the assets;

(2)   the receiver's costs, remuneration and expenses;

(3)   preferential debts, so far as the free assets are insufficient to meet them;

(4)   the claims of ordinary unsecured creditors as regards the prescribed part of the floating charge assets;

(5)   sums due to the chargee;

(6)   sums due to any secured creditor ranking after the chargee or, if he has appointed a receiver, that receiver; and

(7)   any surplus to the company, payment being made to its liquidator if it is in winding up.[328]

Where a receiver is appointed under a debenture containing both a fixed and a floating charge, preferential creditors have priority only as regards the assets subject to the floating charge, not those comprised in the fixed charge.[329] Where the whole of the assets subject to a floating charge have been utilised towards payment of preferential debts, any surplus remaining from sale of assets subject to the fixed charge must be paid to the company. It is not claimable by preferential creditors as being within the scope of the floating charge, for *ex hypothesi* the debenture has been fully satisfied, so that there is no longer a floating charge in existence capable of attaching to the surplus.[330] Where the company is not in liquidation and no other person has an interest in the property realised or its proceeds, the surplus is payable to the company itself.

Allocation of receivership expenses as between assets subject to a fixed charge and those subject to a floating charge is a matter of some moment,

---

[328] Payment of surplus to an administration will rarely arise, for where an administrator is in post an administrative receiver must vacate office. See above, para.10–26.

[329] *Re Lewis Merthyr Consolidated Collieries Ltd* [1929] 1 Ch. 498.

[330] *Re G.L. Saunders Ltd* [1986] 1 W.L.R. 215.

for the greater the proportion of expenses allocated to the floating charge assets, the smaller the amount of assets available to preferential creditors in priority to others. To the extent that costs can fairly be attributed to one charge rather than the other, they should be allocated to that charge. For example, the cost of realisation of floating charge assets should be charged to those assets, and of realisation of fixed charge assets to the assets within the fixed charge, where such costs are capable of being separately identified. In other cases, the fairest solution would seem to be to allocate the cost in the proportion that the net costs of each realisation bear to the total.

10. TERMINATION OF THE RECEIVERSHIP

When the receivership comes to an end

10–72 The period of the receiver's office ends on the earliest of the following events:

(1) his death[331];

(2) his removal by order of the court[332];

(3) his resignation[333];

(4) his ceasing to be qualified as an insolvency practitioner[334]; and

(5) his vacation of office on completion of his duties.[335]

---

[331] This was evidently considered too obvious to require express provisions in the Act or Rules! But contrast the position on the death of an administrative receiver, covered by the Insolvency Act 1986 Sch.B1 para.99(1). Where the receiver dies, the person appointing him must, forthwith on his becoming aware of the death, give notice as provided by the Insolvency Rules 1986 r.3.34.

[332] Insolvency Act 1986 s.45(1). This is now the only way in which an administrative receiver may be removed; the debenture holder can no longer do so, even if the debenture purports to give him the power of removal.

[333] Insolvency Act 1986 s.45(1). But this must be in the prescribed manner, i.e. as provided by r.3.33 of the Insolvency Rules 1986.

[334] Despite the wording of s.45(2) of the Insolvency Act, which might be thought to imply that the receiver continues to hold office until he fulfils his duty under that subsection to vacate it (and see also Insolvency Rules 1986 r.3.35(1)), the joint effect of s.45(2) and ss.389 and 390 would seem to be that a receiver's office comes to an end automatically when he ceases to be qualified to hold it.

[335] Curiously, neither the provisions of the Act nor those of the Rules define the moment at which a receiver vacates office; they simply require him to give notice that he has done so (Insolvency Act s.45(4); and Insolvency Rules r.3.35). It is thought that he vacates office when he does any act signifying that he regards himself as discharged from office. The giving of notice will typically be such an act. Under r.3.33, the resignation notice is required to state the date on which the receiver intends his resignation to take effect.

Removal of the receiver

The debenture holder can no longer remove the receiver he has appointed; this can be done only by order of the court.[336]   **10–73**

Mandatory vacation of office

A receiver must vacate office if he ceases to be qualified to act as an insol-   **10–74**
vency practitioner in relation to the company.[337] Moreover, once he has
realised enough assets to pay off the debenture holder, preferential creditors
from the proceeds of assets subject to a floating charge, and other possible
claims against him to which he is entitled to an indemnity out of the assets,
it is his duty to make the requisite payments and hand back control to the
company.[338]

11. THE POSITION OF THE DEBENTURE HOLDER AFTER APPOINTING A RECEIVER

The receiver as an independent agent

Although the receiver is appointed by the debenture holder, to whom he   **10–75**
owes a duty of care in the conduct of the receivership, he is his own master
in the management of the company's business and the method of carrying
out his other duties as receiver. The debenture holder is not entitled to
instruct the receiver in the performance of his duties; indeed, it is dangerous
to attempt to do so, for the receiver will then become the *de facto* agent of
the debenture holder, who will be liable to the company for his negligent acts
or omissions,[339] though with a right of indemnity against the receiver.[340]

---

[336] Insolvency Act 1986 s.45(1).

[337] Insolvency Act 1986 s.45(2). See above, para.10–25.

[338] In practice, the receiver may be reluctant to do this where a liquidation is pending, and may
be able to rely on a bona fide uncertainty as to the possible existence of preferential debts or
other claims which have not yet been notified to him or adequately quantified.

[339] *American Express International Banking Corp v Hurley* [1985] 3 All E.R. 564.

[340] *American Express International Banking* Corp, cited above n.339.

Chapter 11

Administration[1]

1. GENESIS OF THE ADMINISTRATION PROCEDURE

The company in trouble

Companies become insolvent for a variety of reasons. Some of the most **11–01**
common causes are over-trading, expensive and ill-judged acquisitions, loss
of market share, lack of cash flow and the failure of management to respond
to changed circumstances. When a company is insolvent or on the verge of
insolvency, it has one of three options: to go into immediate liquidation; to
seek to trade out of its difficulties; or to secure a standstill by agreement or
statutory moratorium with a view to disposing of the business or realising the
assets to better advantage than on an immediate winding up. In the great
majority of cases, the company will have reached the point of no return, so
that there is no alternative to an immediate winding up. Where there is perceived to be a viable business, it may be possible to rescue the company as a
going concern by a variety of means.[2] These include negotiating time with
the company's creditors outside any formal insolvency proceeding; securing
the agreement of creditors to an informal or contractual restructuring, or

---

[1] See Sandra Frisby and Malcolm Davis-White (eds), *Kerr & Hunter on Receivers and Administrators*, 19th edn (London: Sweet & Maxwell, 2010); Geoffrey M. Weisgard, Michael Griffiths and Louis Doyle, *Company Voluntary Arrangements and Administrations*, 2nd edn (Bristol: Jordan Publishing, 2010); Gavin Lightman et al., *The Law of Administrators and Receivers of Companies*, 4th edn (London: Sweet & Maxwell, 2007); Vernon Dennis, *Administration* (Law Society Publishing, 2010); R.J. Mokal, *Corporate Insolvency Law: Theory and Application*, Ch.7; John Armour and R.J. Mokal, "Reforming the governance of corpo-rate rescue: the Enterprise Act 2002" [2005] L.M.C.L.Q. 32; Alan Katz and Michael Mumford, *Study of Administration Cases* (London: The Insolvency Service, 2006); and Andrew R. Keay and Peter Walton, *Insolvency Law: Corporate and Personal*, 2nd edn (Bristol: Jordans Publishing, 2008), Ch.7.
[2] See above, para.1–32, as to the evolution of the rescue culture.

workout[3]; organising a scheme of arrangement under Pt 26 of the Companies Act 2006, or a company voluntary arrangement (CVA) under Pt I of the Insolvency Act 1986,[4] within or outside administration under Pt II of the Insolvency Act; or securing a moratorium contractually or through administration with a view to disposing of the business or the assets to its better advantage than on an immediate liquidation and then putting the company into a creditors' voluntary winding up. Much will depend on the nature of the business and of the market in which it operates, the amount of the liabilities and the way in which these are divided between trade and finance creditors, the willingness of a major finance creditor to inject new funds, and whether the company is of a sufficient size to justify the expense of elaborate arrangements for a restructuring or other arrangement.

So the formal insolvency proceedings available are winding up[5]; administration, in which the company is placed under the management of an external administrator, supported by a creditors' committee[6]; a CVA; and a scheme. These last two may precede, run in parallel with or follow administration. The administration procedure is designed to fill a gap which previously existed in corporate insolvency law, in that there was no mechanism by which a company could be put under outside management for the benefit of unsecured creditors and of the company itself, and no effective step that could be taken to safeguard the company and its assets from precipitate action by creditors— for example, levy of execution, enforcement of security, putting of the company into winding up—while steps were taken to put the company back on its feet and/or organise an arrangement with creditors. Until the changes introduced by the Enterprise Act 2002, there was a fifth route, the appointment of an administrative receiver by a debenture holder under a floating charge covering, with any other charges, the whole or substantially the whole of the company's property. But as we have seen, administrative receivership, which has for the most part been abolished as regards floating charges made on or after September 15, 2003, is not a collective insolvency procedure at all but a mechanism for the enforcement of a security interest held by a particular creditor under a floating charge which, with other charges, covers the whole or substantially the whole of the company's property.[7] This remedy has largely been replaced by administration, which in consequence has become of much greater importance than formerly.[8] Other factors have also contributed to the

---

[3] Most major corporate restructuring is effected by informal arrangements between major creditors outside formal insolvency proceedings (European High Yield Association submission to the Treasury on Insolvency Law Reform, April 2007). See further Ch. 12.

[4] Schemes of arrangement and CVAs are discussed in Ch.12.

[5] See Chs 5–8.

[6] Part 3 of the Banking Act 2009 provides a special regime for bank administration which is not discussed here. For brief details, see above, para.1–59 and for a detailed discussion Rodrigo Olivares-Caminal *et al*, Debt Restructuring (Oxford: Oxford University Press, 2011), Ch.7.

[7] See Ch.10.

[8] See the statistics in para.1–31.

growth in the number of administrations, notably the ability to appoint an administrator out of court,[9] the popularity of the pre-pack[10] and the growing use of administration as a liquidation-substitute following the introduction of provisions empowering the court to grant the administrator leave to make distributions to unsecured creditors.[11]

However, there are situations in which a company's entry into administration presents serious drawbacks. One is that administration would trigger cross-default clauses or contractual provisions for acceleration of liability, termination of the contract or the cessation of intellectual property rights, which the creditor concerned is not willing to waive or for which a waiver cannot be negotiated in the limited time available. However, these consequences are not confined to administration; they can apply to any contractually specified event of default. Another is that once it becomes known that a company is, or is verging on, insolvency, the value of its business and assets tends to fall sharply. A third relates to the potential tax disadvantages arising from the fact that the company's entry into administration triggers the start of a new accounting period with effect from the previous day,[12] and trading losses made in the trading period prior to administration can be set off only against gains on profits made during the same period (including capital gains), not against gains made after the company has entered administration.[13] Moreover, corporation tax is chargeable on the company's profits arising in the administration in its final year[14] and where it is payable on chargeable gains accruing on the realisation of any asset (whether the realisation is effected by the administrator, a secured creditor or a receiver or manager appointed to deal with a security), it constitutes an expense of the administration ranking ahead of the claims of preferential creditors,[15] though after the administrator's fees.[16]

The law prior to the Insolvency Act 1985

Prior to the Insolvency Act 1985, English insolvency law viewed liquidation as the centrepiece of corporate insolvency law and concerned itself primarily with the disposal of the business, where it could be sold as a going concern, or with individual assets on a break-up basis. The only form of external

11–02

---

[9] See below, para.11–05.
[10] See above, para.1–36; and below, para.11–37.
[11] See *Re Kaupthing Singer & Friedlander Ltd* [2010] EWHC 316 (Ch), *per* Blair J. at [17], and below, para.11–85.
[12] Corporation Tax Act 2009 s.10(1).
[13] Corporation Tax Act 2010 s.37.
[14] "Final year" means the financial year in which the dissolution event in respect of the company occurs ibid, s. 626(3)).
[15] Insolvency Act 1986, s. 175, as applied by Sch B1, para. 65(2).
[16] Insolvency Rules 1986, r.2.67(j).

management available was receivership, which as we have seen from the previous chapter is first and foremost an enforcement weapon for the unpaid debenture holder and is not a proceeding for the benefit of unsecured creditors, although they do derive some incidental benefits from the marshalling of the assets in one hand. All that could be done for unsecured creditors outside winding up, apart from a contractual arrangement outside the statutory framework, was to seek to conclude a formal scheme of arrangement under what was then s.425 of the Companies Act 1985.

The procedure under s.425 was complex, costly and slow, and the statutory provisions did not impose any moratorium pending approval of the scheme by the court, so that individual creditors remained free to pursue their claims without regard to the wishes of those supporting the arrangement, a risk that could be avoided only by presenting a winding up petition and applying to the court for a stay of pending proceedings[17] under s.126 of the Insolvency Act 1986. Negotiations for an informal arrangement did not, of course, have the effect of imposing a compulsory moratorium either, and when concluded such arrangements suffered the additional disadvantage that they did not bind dissentient creditors, who could therefore either scupper the proposed scheme or alternatively demand to be paid off in order to avoid their presenting a winding up petition. Accordingly, where there was no receiver in post to discourage the trigger-happy, unsecured creditor, a company would all too often be forced to stop trading and go into liquidation.

The growth of the rescue culture

11–03   Although liquidation continues to lie at the heart of corporate insolvency law, there is no doubt that from the early 1980s a sea change in attitudes took place. The impetus for a new approach came from evidence to the Insolvency Law Review Committee (the Cork Committee) and from the Committee's report *Insolvency Law and Practice*.[18] The Cork Committee, which devoted a whole chapter to the subject of administration in its report,[19] drew attention to these problems and proposed a procedure by which the court could appoint an administrator to manage the company, with the same powers as a receiver and manager. The grant of an administration order would, so long as the administration continued, have the effect of freezing the enforcement of rights against the company, whether by secured creditors or otherwise, thus facilitating the simpler regime of voluntary arrangements proposed in the report.

---

[17] A weakness of s.126 is that it only empowers the court to stay proceedings that are pending; it cannot impose a stay on the institution of proceedings.

[18] Cmnd. 8558, 1982.

[19] *Insolvency Law and Practice* (above, n.18), Ch.9.

From these proposals, which were implemented in the Insolvency Act 1985 and re-enacted in the Insolvency Act 1986, evolved what has become known as the rescue culture,[20] a philosophy of reorganising companies so as to restore them to profitable trading and enable them to avoid liquidation. The instruments for implementing this philosophy were: the administration procedure, to which this chapter is largely devoted; the company voluntary arrangement (CVA) under Pt I of the Insolvency Act 1986; the long-established, if cumbersome, reorganisation under what is now Pt 26 of the Companies Act 2006; and the contract-based restructuring, or "workout", an arrangement concluded outside any statutory framework in which the principal creditors get together with a view to hammering out a sensible structure of reorganisation. These last three instruments are discussed in Ch.12. The workout, depending heavily as it did on the co-operation of the creditor banks, received a much-needed fillip from the moral suasion exercised by the Bank of England, which introduced the London Rules (later renamed the London Approach), designed to secure the co-operation of the banking community in taking a positive approach to the continuance of financial support for distressed companies pending a reorganisation.[21] Much use is also made of the INSOL International Statement of Principles for a Global Approach to Multi-Creditor Workouts, particularly in cross-border insolvencies.

While it remains the case that most insolvent companies end up in liquidation, a number of companies whose fate would previously have been liquidation have been saved and nursed back to health; and even where liquidation has ultimately supervened, administrations and workouts have facilitated the sale of the company as a going concern, or a more advantageous realisation of its assets, and a better return for creditors in the winding up.

Weaknesses in the revised statutory regime

We shall discuss a little later the current purposes of administration and its relationship with the CVA. Suffice it to say at this point that the administration procedure prior to the Enterprise Act 2002 proved less efficacious than had been expected.[22] There were several reasons for this. As has been previously pointed out, administration could usually be blocked by the appointment of an administrative receiver. There were various reasons why in practice debenture holders were often willing to allow an order to be

11–04

---

[20] The phrase has now passed into English jurisprudence. See the speech of Lord Browne-Wilkinson in *Powdrill v Watson* [1995] 2 A.C. 394 at 442, 445 and 446.

[21] See below, para.12–03.

[22] For a perceptive, critical analysis of the original administration regime, see D.D. Prentice, F. Oditah and N. Segal, "Administration: The Insolvency Act 1986, Part II" [1994] L.M.C.L.Q. 487.

made,[23] but where they chose to appoint an administrative receiver nothing could be done to place the company in administration unless the debenture holder by whom or on whose behalf the receiver was appointed consented to the making of the order or the charge was vulnerable under one or other of ss.238–240 and 245 of the Insolvency Act 1986.[24] The requirement to obtain a court order, the making of which was usually dependent on a detailed report by the proposed administrator, caused significant delay and often substantial expense, which was a particular difficulty for small companies. Although it was envisaged that administration would be a short-term procedure, no time limit was laid down for the completion of an administration. The administrator generally had no power to make distributions even to preferential creditors without a court order, and the extent of the court's power to make such an order was the subject of conflicting decisions.[25] Finally, as stated above, an administration order could not be made if the company was in liquidation.[26]

As mentioned in the previous chapter,[27] a groundswell of complaints about the adverse effects of administrative receivership led, first, to the proposal that the debenture holder's power of veto should be abolished and, secondly, to the more radical proposal, implemented in the Enterprise Act 2002, to abolish administrative receivership altogether as regards appointments under new charges, except in defined categories of case where the exigencies of the capital markets or considerations of social policy dictated its retention. The new approach was succinctly set out in the government's White Paper presaging the insolvency provisions of the Enterprise Act.[28]

2. PRINCIPAL CHANGES INTRODUCED BY THE ENTERPRISE ACT 2002

11–05   It is no exaggeration to say that the Enterprise Act 2002 revolutionised the law governing administrative receivership and administration, inserting a

---

[23] See the second edition of this work at pp.293–294. The research by Katz and Mumford (*Comparative Study of Administration and Administrative Receivership as Business Rescue Vehicles* (London: ICAEW, August 2003)) showed that even before the new regime introduced by the Enterprise Act 2002 had begun to have an impact, administrations had reached parity in number with administrative receiverships and that resort by debenture holders to their power of veto was rare, although this may have been because the existence of the power meant that in some cases administration was not considered to be an option.

[24] Insolvency Act 1986 s.9(3). See now Sch.B1 para.39(1).

[25] See, e.g. *Re TXU UK Ltd* [2003] 2 B.C.L.C. 341; *Re UCT (UK) Ltd* [2001] 1 B.C.L.C. 443; *Re Powerstore Trading Ltd* [1998] 1 B.C.L.C. 190; and *Re WBSL Realisations Ltd* [1995] 2 B.C.L.C. 576.

[26] Insolvency Act 1986 s.8(4). See now Sch.B1 para.8(1).

[27] Above, para.10–05.

[28] DTI, "Productivity and Enterprise: Insolvency—A Second Chance" (Cm. 5234, 2001).

new Ch.IV into Pt III of the Insolvency Act 1986. The principal changes introduced by the 2002 Act were the following:

(1)   the abolition of administrative receivership except in specific cases;

(2)   the facility to enter administration without a court order;

(3)   the absence of a requirement to show actual or impending insolvency on an out-of-court appointment by the holder of a qualifying floating charge or on an application by such a holder for an administration order where the court is satisfied that he could make an out-of-court appointment;

(4)   the replacement of multi-purpose administration with a regime in which there is only a single purpose, to be selected according to a three-part hierarchy;

(5)   flexibility in the ordering of entry and exit routes, including the ability to move from winding up to administration and from administration straight to dissolution;

(6)   a time limit for completion of an administration;

(7)   conferment on the administrator of power to make distributions to secured and preferential creditors[29] and, with the permission of the court, to ordinary unsecured creditors; and

(8)   the provision of a statutory priority of expenses of the administration, albeit one which the court can vary.

However, the changes do not affect protected railway companies under the Railway Act 1993 or other bodies subject to special administration regimes as listed in s.249(1) of the Enterprise Act 2002. Thus, s.59 of the Railways Act 1993 and Sch.6 to that Act prescribe a special regime for protected railway companies[30] in the form of a railway administration order, to which the old Pt II of the Insolvency Act 1986 applies with the modifications made by Sch.6 to the 1993 Act.

Abolition of administrative receivership

It is no longer possible for the holder of a qualifying floating charge to appoint an administrative receiver under a qualifying floating charge created on or after September 15, 2003, except in the various categories of case previously described.[31] The abolition of administrative receivership reflects

11–06

---

[29] See Insolvency Act 1986 Sch.6 category 5.
[30] Of which one was Railtrack Plc. See *Re Winsor v Bloom, Railtrack Plc* [2002] 1 W.L.R. 3002.
[31] Above, para.10–05.

three underlying objectives: transparency, accountability and collectivity.[32] By way of compensation, the chargee will enjoy a number of privileges not available to others.

(1)   While the company or its directors cannot appoint an administrator where a petition for winding up has been presented or an administration application has been made and the petition or application has not been disposed of,[33] no such restriction applies to an appointment by the holder of a qualifying floating charge, who can appoint an administrator even where a winding up petition is pending,[34] with the result that the undisposed-of petition is suspended.[35] If by inadvertence a winding up order is made, it has no legal effect and consequently s.127 of the Insolvency Act invalidating unauthorised dispositions by the company after presentation of a winding up petition on which an order is later made does not come into play.[36]

(2)   If the holder of a qualifying floating charge applies for an administration order under para.35(1)(a) of Sch.B1 to the Insolvency Act and the application includes a statement that it is made in reliance on that paragraph, then by way of exception to the general rule[37] the court may make an administration order whether or not satisfied that the company is or is likely to become insolvent.[38]

(3)   If an application is made for the appointment of an administrator by a person who is not the holder of a qualifying floating charge, the latter, having received notice of the application, may either make an appointment under para.14 (giving notice to the court to which the application is made[39]) or intervene to apply to have its nominee appointed, and the court is required to grant such an application unless it thinks it right to refuse to do so because of the particular circumstances of the case.[40]

(4)   Where the company is in compulsory winding up (but not in voluntary winding up), the chargee may make an administration application, and if this is granted the court is required to discharge the winding up order.[41]

---

[32] See Steve Leinster, "Policy Aims of the Enterprise Act", *Recovery*, Autumn 2003, 27, 28.

[33] Insolvency Act 1986 Sch.B1 para.25.

[34] Insolvency Act 1986 Sch.B1 paras 40(1)(b) and 44(7).

[35] Insolvency Act 1986 Sch.B1 paras 40(1)(b) and 44(7).

[36] *Re J Smiths Haulage Ltd* [2007] B.C.C. 135.

[37] Insolvency Act 1986 Sch.B1, para.11(a).

[38] Insolvency Act 1986 Sch.B1, para.35(2)(a). Contrast the position as regards an out-of-court appointment made by the company or its directors, below, para.11–11.

[39] Insolvency Rules 1986 r.2.18.

[40] Insolvency Act 1986, Sch.B1, para.36. There is no express provision for replacement of an administrator already appointed by the company or its directors but the court could exercise its power under para.88 to remove the administrator and then appoint the debenture holder's nominee under para.92.

[41] Insolvency Act 1986 Sch.B1, para.37.

(5)   Finally, the holder of a qualifying floating charge who makes an out-of-court appointment is given the facility of filing a notice of appointment with the court outside court business hours.[42]

But even where the administrator is appointed by or on the nomination of the chargee, his primary objective, where reasonably practicable, is to perform his functions not for the benefit of the appointing debenture holder, as was the main function of the administrative receiver but for the benefit of the creditors generally,[43] and he is obliged to attend the initial meeting of creditors and may be required to convene other creditors' meetings[44] and attend meetings of the creditors' committee.[45]

In order for a chargee to be able to appoint an administrator, three conditions have to be satisfied: the charge is a qualifying floating charge; the chargee is the holder of a qualifying floating charge; and the power to appoint an administrator has become exercisable under the terms of the charge instrument.

(1) The charge is a qualifying floating charge

A qualifying floating charge is one created by an instrument which:

(1)   states that para.14 of Sch.B1 to the Insolvency Act 1986 applies to the floating charge;   **11–07**

(2)   purports to empower the holder of the floating charge to appoint an administrator of the company; or

(3)   purports to empower the holder of the floating charge to make an appointment which would be the appointment of an administrative receiver within the meaning of s.29(2) of the Insolvency Act.[46]

(2) The chargee is the holder of a qualifying floating charge

For the purposes of para.14(1), a person is the holder of a qualifying floating   **11–08**
charge in respect of a company's property if he holds one or more debentures of the company secured:

---

[42] See below, para.11–44, n.216.
[43] Insolvency Act 1986 Sch.B1 para.3(2).
[44] Insolvency Act 1986 Sch.B1 paras 51 and 56.
[45] Insolvency Act 1986 Sch.B1 para.57.
[46] Insolvency Act 1986 Sch.B1 para.14(2), omitting para.(d), which relates to Scotland. For a detailed analysis of s.29(2), see above, paras 10–07 et seq.

(a) by a qualifying floating charge which relates to the whole or substantially the whole of the company's property[47];

(b) by a number of qualifying floating charges which together relate to the whole or substantially the whole of the company's property; or

(c) by charges and other forms of security which together relate to the whole or substantially the whole of the company's property and at least one of which is a qualifying floating charge.[48]

In sub-para.(c), "charge" is used in its narrow sense to denote a mere incumbrance, as opposed to a mortgage, whilst "other forms of security" covers a mortgage, a lien or any other form of security.[49] Since para.14(1) is confined to security for debentures, "charges and other forms of security" is plainly confined to consensual security and does not extend to charges or liens created by statute or other operation of law.

It should be noted that while in the case of administrative receivership the reference to "the whole or substantially the whole of the company's property" refers not to the scope of the debenture but to the property falling within the scope of the receiver's appointment,[50] the same reference in para.14 is to what is secured by the debenture. Literally construed, this would suggest that if the debenture so provides, it would be open to the holder of a qualifying floating charge to crystallise the charge as to part only of the assets comprised in it in the same way as was previously open to the appointor of an administrative receiver.[51] It is not clear why the wording of the statutory provision was changed but it is wholly incompatible with the concept of administration that the chargee should be able to select the assets to which the administration is to apply; indeed, it would be inconsistent with the administrator's duty to take control of all of the property to which he thinks the company is entitled.[52] So while partial crystallisation remains an available technique for other purposes—for example, to enable the chargee to realise a particular asset or assets without paralysing the company's management capability—it cannot be used to restrict the assets to which the administration relates.

---

[47] See above, para.10–08.
[48] Insolvency Act 1986 Sch. B1 para.14(3).
[49] See Insolvency Act 1986 s.248(b). The only other form of consensual security known to English law is pledge (see *Goode on Legal Problems of Credit and Security*, edited by Louise Gullifer, 4th edn (London: Sweet & Maxwell, 2008), paras 1–05 and 1–42) but the restrictions on the enforcement of security also apply to non-consensual liens and other rights of detention and retention given by law. See below, para.11–57.
[50] See above, para.10–09.
[51] See *Goode on Legal Problems of Credit and Security*, 2008, para.4–56.
[52] Insolvency Act 1986 Sch.B1 para.67.

(3) The power to appoint an administrator has become exercisable

It is not sufficient that the chargee is the holder of a qualifying floating charge. The Act further provides that an administrator may not be appointed under para.14 while a floating charge on which the appointment relies is not enforceable.[53] This means not only that the charge must be valid and enforceable in a general sense but also that the chargee has become entitled in particular to enforce the charge by appointing an administrator. A purported appointment made under a qualifying floating charge before the power to make the appointment has become exercisable is a nullity in just the same way as would have been the case upon a premature appointment of an administrative receiver.[54] However, the mere existence of a dispute as to the enforceability of a floating charge does not invalidate the initial appointment, although if the charge is later held unenforceable, the appointment will be retrospectively invalidated.[55] But the chargee has the right of any other creditor to apply for an administration order[56] and in that case the court may make an order whether or not satisfied that the company is or is likely to become unable to pay its debts so long as it is satisfied that the chargee could make an appointment out of court under para.14.[57]

11–09

Even where the above conditions have been satisfied, the holder of a qualifying floating charge may not appoint an administrator if a provisional liquidator of the company has been appointed or an administrative receiver is in office,[58] but this does not preclude the holder from applying for an administration order, although in this case it is necessary to show that the conditions of para.11 of Sch.B1 are satisfied.

Administration without court order

A major impediment to administration when it was first introduced, the delay and expense involved in obtaining an order for administration, was subsequently removed. Although specified persons may still apply for an administration order, it is instead open to the holder of a qualifying floating charge or to the company or the directors to appoint an administrator by filing a notice of appointment and other prescribed documents.[59] This has become the normal mode of appointment. For reputational reasons, banks holding a qualifying floating charge usually prefer not to take the appointment themselves but to allow it to be made by the company or the directors,

11–10

---

[53] Insolvency Act 1986 Sch.B1 para.16.
[54] See above, para.10–28.
[55] *BCPMS (Europe) Ltd v GMAC Commercial Finance* [2006] EWHC 3744 (Ch).
[56] Insolvency Act 1986 Sch.B1 para.12(1)(c).
[57] Insolvency Act 1986 Sch.B1 para.35(2)(a). See further below, paras11–11 and 11–46.
[58] Insolvency Act 1986 Sch.B1 para.17.
[59] Insolvency Act 1986 Sch.B1 paras 14, 18(1), 22, 29(1).

while nevertheless influencing the selection of the appointee. The steps to be taken to bring about the appointment of an administrator depend on whether he is appointed out of court or by the court.[60] But once the administrator is in post, his powers, duties and liabilities are governed by rules common to the two methods of appointment.

Out-of-court administration is incompatible with the EC directive on the reorganisation and winding up of insurance undertakings,[61] so that in relation to these, paras 14 and 22 of Sch.B1 to the Insolvency Act 1986 (dealing respectively with the appointment by the holder of a qualifying floating charge and the company or its directors) are disapplied.[62] Other cases in which court-appointed administration is likely to continue to be used are where the holder of a qualifying floating charge is precluded from making an out-of-court appointment[63] or wishes to block an administration application by the company or its directors,[64] or where it is necessary to institute or intervene in proceedings before a foreign court which may be reluctant to recognise the status of an administrator appointed by a chargee rather than by a court.[65]

No requirement of actual or impending insolvency as regards holder of qualifying floating charge

11–11   Under the original statutory provisions, the court could not make an administration order unless satisfied that the company was or was likely to become unable to pay its debts within the meaning of s.123 of the Insolvency Act.[66] That remains the case where there is an application for an administration order which is made by a person other than the holder of a qualifying floating charge,[67] but there is no such requirement for an out-of-court appointment by the holder of a qualifying floating charge under para.14 of Sch.B1 or on application by a chargee who could make such an appointment.[68] Out-of-court appointments by the company or directors are governed by para.22, which gives no hint of any requirement that the company is or is likely to

---

[60] See below, paras 11–43 and 11–46.
[61] 2001/17/EC dated March 19, 2001 ([2001] OJ L110/28), art.2(c). But as the result of a recent amendment to the Annexes to the EC Insolvency Regulation, this is no longer a problem as regards other types of company. See below, para.15–12.
[62] Insurers (Reorganisation and Winding Up) Regulations 2004 (SI 2004/353), reg.52.
[63] By Insolvency Act 1986 Sch.B1 para.17. See above, para.11–09.
[64] Under Insolvency Act 1986 Sch.B1 para.36. See above, para.10–27.
[65] As to the importance of using the correct form of notice of appointment, see Gabriel Moss, "Bad Form to Appoint Out of Court: Kaupthing Capital Partners II Master LP Inc., Re" (2010) 3 Ins. Int. 109.
[66] Insolvency Act 1986 s.8(1)(a). As to the meaning of s.123, see above, paras 4–03 et seq.
[67] Insolvency Act 1986 Sch.B1 para.11(a).
[68] Insolvency Act 1986 Sch.B1 para.35(2)(b).

become unable to pay its debts. It is only when one reaches para.27(2)(a), which involves a statutory declaration as to the company's inability to pay debts, that it becomes apparent that actual or impending insolvency is by necessary implication a prerequisite to the appointment of an administrator under para.22.

The ability of the holder of a qualifying floating charge to make an appointment without the need for the company to be insolvent or facing insolvency is a welcome change because it enables steps to be taken to place the company in administration before its financial position has become critical and in this respect follows Ch.11 of the American Bankruptcy Code. In the opinion of some, the same principle should apply regardless of who makes the appointment, particularly since the holder of a qualifying floating charge for reputational reasons will usually prefer to leave this to the company or its directors but will nevertheless influence the choice of appointee. Others, by contrast, take the view that administration is likely to be identified with company failure whenever it takes place.

Replacement of multi-purpose administration with single-purpose administration

The provisions concerning the purposes of administration have been recast, and differ in important respects from those originally contained in s.8 of the Insolvency Act.[69] In particular, there can only be one stated purpose, to be selected according to a three-part hierarchy and to be determined by the administrator's view of what is reasonably practicable and what will achieve the best result for the company's creditors as a whole.[70] The new provisions came into force on September 15, 2003 as regards all administrations other than those in respect of which a petition for an administration order was presented before the above date.[71]

11–12

Flexibility in the ordering of entry and exit routes

A key element of the revised regime is the flexibility it provides in the selection of routes into and exits from administration. This is discussed later.[72] One of new features is that although a person may not normally be appointed administrator of a company in winding up,[73] it is open to the

11–13

---

[69] See below, para.11–25.
[70] See below, para.11–25.
[71] Enterprise Act 2002 (Commencement No.4 and Transitional Provisions and Savings) Order 2003 (SI 2003/2093), art.3(2)).
[72] Below, para.11–115.
[73] Insolvency Act 1986 Sch.B1 para.8(1)(b).

holder of a qualifying floating charge in respect of a company in compulsory liquidation to apply for an administration order, and if this is made, any winding up order is discharged.[74] In theory, at least, it would be possible for the company to go into liquidation a second time at a later date! A liquidator may apply for an administration order whether the company is in compulsory or voluntary liquidation.[75] In the latter case, the order must provide for the removal of the liquidator from office.[76]

Time limit for completion of the administration

11–14   The Insolvency Act now provides for the automatic ending of an administrator's appointment at the end of one year beginning with the date on which it takes effect.[77] The appointment may, however, be extended by the court for a specified period more than once, or by consent of the requisite creditors[78] once only for a period not exceeding six months, and may be further extended by the court but not after the administrator's term of office has expired.[79]

Extension of administrator's power of distribution

11–15   This is discussed later in this chapter.[80]

Statutory priority of administration expenses

11–16   We have seen that in a winding up the expenses of the liquidation are payable in a statutory order of priority, albeit this may be adjusted by the court.[81] Prior to the changes to the Insolvency Rules 1986, as a result of

---

[74] Insolvency Act 1986 Sch.B1 para.37, to which para.8(1)(b) is subject.

[75] Insolvency Act 1986 Sch.B1 para.38, to which para.8(1)(b) is subject.

[76] Insolvency Rules 1986 r.2.13(a), made pursuant to the Insolvency Act 1986 Sch.B1 para.38(2)(b).

[77] Insolvency Act 1986 Sch.B1 para.76(1).

[78] Namely each secured creditor and unsecured creditors whose debts amount to more than 50% of the company's unsecured debts (Insolvency Act 1986 Sch.B1 para.78(1)).

[79] Insolvency Act 1986 Sch.B1 paras 76 and 77. Note that the extension order itself must usually be made before expiry of the administrator's term of office; it is not sufficient that his application for an extension is filed before that time. However, the court may exercise its discretion to make an order if the application for the extension is made before expiry of the administrator's term of office and there is a real possibility that the way in which the application was handled by the court has contributed to the fact that no order was made within that period (*Re TT Industries* [2006] B.C.C. 372).

[80] See below, para.11–85.

[81] See above, para.8–33.

the enactment of the Enterprise Act 2002 there was provision for the administrator's expenses and remuneration to be charged on the property coming into his hands, including property subject to a floating charge, in priority to the claims of the chargee,[82] but there was no statutory order of payment of the expenses and remuneration *inter se*, this being left to the administrator's discretion.[83] That has now changed.[84] The question to what extent new liabilities incurred by the administrator and liabilities in respect of continuing contracts concluded before the administration constitute expenses of the administration is considered later.[85]

3. NATURE AND PURPOSES OF ADMINISTRATION

Relationship between administration and restructuring

Administration is commonly described as a restructuring procedure but this is not the case. The characteristic of a restructuring is that the business is preserved, at least initially,[86] and an arrangement concluded with the creditors by which the debts owed by the company are restructured, for example, by rescheduling, by acceptance by creditors of less than the amount due or by conversion of debt into equity, so that creditors become converted into shareholders. Although it is certainly open to the administrator to propose a CVA under Pt I of the Insolvency Act 1986[87] or a compromise or arrangement under Pt 26 of the Companies Act 2006,[88] this does not necessarily involve a restructuring, and where it does the restructuring itself is carried out under some other procedure, such as a CVA or scheme of arrangement,[89] and the main effect of the administration is to impose a moratorium on the enforcement of creditors' rights. In practice, by far the most commonly achieved purpose of administration to date has been a more advantageous realisation of the company's assets than would be effected on a winding up. This, of course, has nothing to do with reorganisation. It involves restoring the company to a condition in which it can be sold off as a going concern, or if this is not possible, disposing of the assets on terms more advantageous than could have been obtained by a liquidator on an

11–17

---

[82] Insolvency Act 1986 s.19(4). See now Sch.B1 para.99.
[83] *Re Salmet International Ltd* [2001] B.C.C. 796.
[84] See below, para.11–98.
[85] Below, para.11–103.
[86] Not infrequently arrangements contemplate, and may even provide for, the ultimate winding-up of the company.
[87] Insolvency Act 1986 s.1(3). As to CVAs, see below, para.12–26.
[88] Companies Act 2006 s.899.
[89] *Centre Reinsurance International Co v Curzon Insurance Ltd* [2006] 1 W.L.R. 2863, *per* Lord Hoffmann at [6], comparing administration with Ch.11 proceedings.

immediate liquidation. Once this has occurred, unless there is a distribution within the administration, liquidation—either voluntary or compulsory—is almost inevitable. Creditors will receive distributions of dividend in the usual way and the company will then be dissolved.[90]

English corporate rescue compared with reorganisation under Ch.11

11–18   Although administration and an associated CVA have been seen as the English equivalent of a reorganisation under Ch.11 of the US Bankruptcy Code, there are major differences between the two. Chapter 11 is devoted specifically to reorganisation and combines an automatic moratorium with a mechanism for the approval of a plan. By contrast, as stated above, administration is not in itself a reorganisation procedure at all, merely a temporary measure which provides a gateway to a variety of alternative exit routes, of which the CVA is only one.[91] Thus whereas under Ch.11 the moratorium and reorganisation are the key components of a single process, English insolvency law produces an uneasy split between the moratorium imposed by the administration and the CVA, which does not by itself attract a moratorium at all except in the case of small eligible companies. In a traditional Ch.11 proceeding the existing management is largely left in place.[92] Indeed, the debtor in possession is treated as a distinct legal entity akin to a trustee in bankruptcy. Administration, on the other hand, is predicated on the assumption that where a company becomes insolvent, this is usually due to a failure of management and the last people to leave in control are those who were responsible for the company's plight in the first place. Hence the requirement that the administration of the company be placed in the hands of an external manager, a qualified insolvency practitioner (almost invariably an accountant) working in close co-operation with a creditors' committee. However, recent government proposals for a restructuring moratorium adopt the debtor-in-possession (DIP) concept.[93]

A fundamental principle of administration and the CVA is that the creditors cannot approve proposals which would affect the enforcement rights of secured creditors.[94] There is thus no equivalent in insolvency legislation to the Ch.11 "cram-down" by which a plan may be imposed on a class of dissenting creditors, including secured creditors, so long as they receive an equivalence

---

[90] For the case where the company can move straight from administration to dissolution, see below, para.11–115.

[91] See above, para.11–17. For a fuller treatment of the comparison between administration and Ch.11 see *Debt Restructuring* (above n.6), paras 3.154 *et seq*.

[92] But see para.11–22 below.

[93] See below, paras 11–32 and 12–11.

[94] See below, paras 11–20 and 12–41.

in value.[95] Apart from the moratorium on enforcement of security interests produced by an administration, and the administrator's power to dispose of assets subject to a floating charge, with the chargee's priority attaching to the proceeds,[96] and of assets subject to a fixed charge under an order of the court on condition of application towards the sums secured of the net proceeds and such further sum as is necessary to bring these up to market value,[97] the rights of secured creditors are sacrosanct and may not be affected by proposals for a CVA[98] or by an administrator.[99] In an English reorganisation, the shareholders' interests are generally regarded as of little or no account; in a reorganisation under Ch.11, shareholders, too, are considered to have a stake in the outcome.[100] Finally, Ch.11 provides a super-priority for rescue finance which is lacking in the UK provisions on administration.

Despite these major differences between UK administration and US Ch.11 proceedings, several commentators have observed that the differences have been exaggerated and that there has been a growing convergence, primarily through a move by the United States towards the UK position. Thus, Professor McCormack points out that while a feature of the debtor-in-possession is the retention of management, the turnover of management is much higher in the case of financially distressed companies than in the case of those not financially distressed; that DIP agreements are increasingly providing for greater creditor control; and that the contrast drawn between the characterisation of Ch.11 as pro-debtor and administration as pro-creditor is not as sharp as is often suggested.[101] Further, there has been a distinct move in the United States from reorganisation to business sales.[102]

Characteristics of administration

The statutory regime for the administration of companies is now contained in the "new" Pt II of the Insolvency Act 1986, Sch.B1 to the Act and the "new" Pt 2 of the Insolvency Rules 1986. The particular features that characterise the administration procedure are the following:

11–19

---

[95] Bankruptcy Code s.1129(b)(2). However, a similar effect may be achieved by a scheme of arrangement under Pt 26 of the Companies Act 2006 if the requisite majority votes in favour and the scheme is approved by the court. See below, para.12–13.

[96] Insolvency Act 1986 Sch.B1 para.70.

[97] Insolvency Act 1986 Sch.B1 para.71.

[98] Insolvency Act 1986 s.4(3).

[99] Insolvency Act 1986 Sch.B1 para.73(1)(a).

[100] See below, para.11–23.

[101] "Apples and Oranges? Corporate Rescue and Functional Convergence in the US and UK" (2009) 18 Int. Insolv. Rev. 109; "Control and Corporate Finance—An Anglo-American Evaluation" (2007) 56 I.C.L.Q. 515; John Armour, Brian R. Cheffins and David A. Skeel Jr, "Corporate Ownership Structure and the Evolution of Bankruptcy Law: Lessons from the United Kingdom" (2002) 55 Vand. L. Rev. 1699.

[102] ibid.

(1) Deferment to the interests of secured creditors

11–20   The legislation and its interpretation by the courts embody an underlying policy to interfere as little as possible with the rights of secured creditors and holders of other real rights, such as sellers under retention of title and lessors. Thus, the court cannot as a rule make an administration order if, in cases where the appointment of an administrative receiver is still permitted,[103] the debenture holder gets in first and appoints an administrative receiver[104]; and the courts are reluctant to refuse leave to secured creditors to enforce their security, and to title-retention sellers and lessors to recover their property, where this might cause them significant loss.[105] A proposal for a CVA, whether made outside or within an administration, may not affect the right of a secured creditor to enforce his security or affect the priority of a preferential creditor except in either case with the creditor's concurrence[106] and an administrator has a general power to make a distribution to secured or preferential creditors without the permission of the court.[107] The deference shown by English law to secured creditors reflects a respect for third-party titles of much the same kind as in a winding up,[108] although in administration proceedings there is a greater willingness to restrict enforcement of real rights in the interests of creditors as a whole than would be appropriate for a winding up. But the courts will not allow administration to be utilised as a tool to hold up a planned sale by a mortgagee or its receiver with a view to negotiating a better price.[109]

(2) Preservation of the priority of preferential creditors

11–21   Similarly, a proposal for a CVA may not be approved if it disturbs the priority of any preferential debt.[110] However, this applies only to distributions to be made, directly or indirectly, from the company's own funds; it does not preclude distribution to ordinary unsecured creditors from funds supplied by a third party who has no recourse to the company for reimbursement.

A CVA put forward by the Wimbledon Football Club contained a provision that all Football Creditors (as defined) should be paid 100 pence in the pound, while preferential creditors, including HM Revenue & Customs, would be paid only 30 pence in the pound. However, the Football Creditors

---

[103] See above, para.10–05.
[104] Insolvency Act 1986 Sch.B1 para.17(b). See above, para.10–27.
[105] See below, para.11–77.
[106] Insolvency Act 1986 s.4(3) and (4), and Sch.B1 para.73.
[107] Insolvency Act 1986 Sch.B1 para.65(1) and (3).
[108] See above, paras 3–03 and 6–41 et seq.
[109] *Doltable Ltd v Lexi Holdings Plc* [2006] B.C.C. 918.
[110] Insolvency Act 1986 s.4(4).

were to be paid from the funds provided by the purchaser of the club under the sale agreement *without reducing the price to be paid for the club itself*. It was held that this did not infringe s.4(4)(a) of the Insolvency Act. The position would have been otherwise if the payment had reduced the price, for it would then in substance have come from funds that the company would otherwise have received. Had s.4(4)(a) been infringed, the court would have had to revoke the approval of the CVA.[111]

(3) External management

The placing of the company under external management is, as we have seen,[112] one of the features that distinguishes administration from reorganisation under Ch.11. However, the circumstances may allow so-called "light touch" administration where the administrator devolves much of the responsibility for day-to-day running of the business to its existing management, while on the other hand in Ch.11 proceedings there is a growing trend towards displacement of the existing management and the appointment of a chief restructuring officer or corporate recovery specialist. In the case of pre-packs, there is relatively little for the administrator to do once the business has been sold and the proceeds received, beyond paying any moneys due to secured and preferential creditors and obtaining leave to distribute any balance to unsecured creditors.

11–22

(4) Preservation of the business rather than the company

A further distinction between the UK administration procedure and Ch.11 relates to the question whether shareholders are to be considered interested parties so as to have a stake in the reorganisation. The Cork Committee was uncompromising in its view that in terms of social policy, administration was about saving the business, not the company.

11–23

> "In the case of an insolvent company, society has no interest in the preservation or rehabilitation of the company as such, though it may have a legitimate concern in the preservation of the commercial enterprise."[113]

Ideally, of course, it is desirable to preserve the company as well as the business, so as to preserve the trading relationships and maintain at least part of

---

[111] *IRC v Wimbledon Football Club Ltd* [2005] 1 B.C.L.C. 66.
[112] Above, para.11–18.
[113] "Insolvency Law and Practice", para.193.

the workforce. This remains the first objective of administration where it is reasonably practicable.[114] In the words of Lord McIntosh when steering the Enterprise Bill through the House of Lords:

"Company rescue is at the heart of the revised administration procedure. We want to make sure that viable companies do not go to the wall unnecessarily. That is why we are restricting administrative receivership and revising administration to focus on rescue and to make it more accessible to companies as well as their creditors. That is not just good for the companies themselves; it is also good for their suppliers, customers and employees.

The emphasis on company rescue will create more incentive for company management to take action promptly and use the administration procedure before the situation becomes terminal. That is why the purpose directs the administrator first to perform his functions 'with the objective of rescuing the company'."[115]

However, frequently this is not possible, and faced with a choice between keeping the company alive in a damaged and irrecoverable state and disposing of its undertaking, insolvency practitioners will follow the latter course in the interests of creditors.[116] It is in keeping with this approach that creditors alone are involved in the approval of proposals by the administrator to achieve the purpose of the administration.[117] There is no provision for any meeting of members to consider the proposals, nor do they have a right to participate as members in the creditors' meeting under para.51 of Sch.B1 to the Act.[118] Their sole remedy, if they object to the proposals, is to apply to the court for an order under para.74 of Sch.B1 of the Act as a class, or part of a class, which will be unfairly harmed by implementation of the proposals.[119] By contrast, Ch.11 reflects the view that shareholders, too, have an interest which, although subordinate to that of creditors, nevertheless has a claim to be considered. In part, the differences in approach are based on cultural factors.

---

[114] See below, para.11–26.

[115] *Hansard*, H.L. Deb. col.766 (July 29, 2002).

[116] Employees also enjoy protection under the Transfer of Undertakings (Protection of Employment) Regulations 2006, SI 2006/246. See Vanessa Finch, *Corporate Insolvency Law*, 2nd edn (2009), pp.760 et seq.

[117] Insolvency Act 1986 Sch.B1 paras 49 et seq.

[118] The position is otherwise in the case of a CVA, where proposals have either to be approved in identical form by separate meetings of creditors and members or have to be approved at the creditors' meeting, with a member having the power to apply to the court if the decision taken at the creditors' meeting differs from that taken at the meeting of members (ss.4A and 5(1)). In the absence of such an application, the creditors' decision stands.

[119] The power to make an order affecting proposals approved by creditors is implicit in Insolvency Act 1986 Sch.B1 para.74(6)(c).

"In the U.S. a variety of factors, including a deep emotional commitment to the entrepreneurial ethic, make the owners of the corporation central to a salvage proceeding. In the U.K., the prevailing view seems to be that the prior owners were the ones whose venality or incompetence created the problem and their interests disappear from moral or legal consideration once a formal proceeding has begun. Americans are much more willing to believe that financial difficulty is the result of external forces and that preservation of the company, not just the business, is a crucial social concern."[120]

In part, also the involvement of company members in plans under Ch.11 is a pragmatic response to the perceived need to have their support. An empirical study by Professors LoPucki and Whitford[121] indicated that in the reorganisation of large public corporations, creditors, in order to avoid delay in confirmation of the plan and as "the price of peace", were willing to bargain with shareholders to allow them a share in the distribution under the plan. The authors of the study did, however, express some scepticism as to whether concessions made to shareholders were really necessary and how far they would in practice have been able to defeat or delay the plan if they had been excluded. In the United Kingdom, too, the practice of allowing shareholders a small amount of the equity is not unusual in the large restructurings of listed companies and for similar reasons.

The emphasis placed by insolvency practitioners on rescue of the business rather than of the company itself is sensible, reflecting the fact that it is often more advantageous than preserving the corporate entity, and either to hive down the assets to a new company free from liabilities and then sell the new company—a practice now less common than formerly—or alternatively to dispose of the assets or the whole undertaking of the company, leaving the company itself to go into liquidation. Where this is so, the first of the three statutory objectives cannot be achieved, and it is necessary to resort to the second.[122]

(5) Disposal of the business or assets as the primary objective where rescue of the company is not possible

As previously stated, while the moratorium imposed in administration facilitates CVAs and arrangements under Pt 26 of the Companies Act, the **11–24**

---

[120] Jay L. Westbrook, "A Comparison of Bankruptcy Reorganisation in the U.S. with Administration Procedure in the U.K." (1990) I.L. & P. 86, 88, and, to similar effect, Debt Restructuring (above, n.6), paras 3.188–3.189. This remains true of the great majority of Ch.11 filings but the position is otherwise in the case of filings by large public corporations, many of which use Ch.11 merely to sell their assets and divide up the proceeds, with no intention of rescuing the company itself. See Douglas G. Baird and Robert K. Rasmussen, "The End of Bankruptcy" 55 Stan. L. Rev. 751 (2002).

[121] "Bargaining over Equity's Share in the Bankruptcy Reorganisation of Large, Publicly Held Companies", 139 U. Pa. L. Rev. 125 (1990).

[122] See below, para.11–26.

primary function of administration as a distinct procedure is to rescue the company as a going concern or, if this is not possible, to dispose of its assets and undertaking, not to reorganise the company by arrangement with its creditors.

Objective and conditions of administration

(1) Replacement of plurality of purposes with a single purpose

11–25   Under the old regime, where administration could come about only by court order, an order could be made only in order to achieve one of the four specified statutory objectives[123] and only if the court was satisfied that the company was or was likely to become unable to pay its debts and that the administration order was reasonably likely to achieve the purpose of administration.[124] The revised regime, which provides for out-of-court administration, is different in a number of other respects. First, the plurality of purposes has been replaced by a single purpose selected according to a threefold hierarchy. Secondly, the purpose does not have to be identified prior to the company's entry into administration. The rules and forms are predicated on the basis that the court need not concern itself with determination of the appropriate objective because this will be decided by the administrator according to what he thinks is reasonably practicable. So while the statement of the proposed administrator is required to express his opinion that the purpose of administration is likely to be achieved,[125] none of the prescribed documents (application, affidavit or statement) requires that the particular objective that the proposed administrator has in mind be identified. Thirdly, the requirement of actual or impending insolvency applies only to administration by court order on the application of the company or the directors or on the application of the holder of a qualifying charge who does not satisfy the court that he could make an out-of-court appointment.

In a sense, the identification of the objective of administration is a second-stage exercise, reached only where the decision has been taken that it is administration that is the insolvency process best suited to the company's financial situation.[126] Administration is not an end in itself, merely an interim phase in the life of the company which will either be successful—resulting in restoration of the business to normal trading or the conclusion of a voluntary

---

[123] Namely: (i) survival of the company, and the whole or any part of its undertaking, as a going concern; (ii) the approval of a voluntary arrangement under Pt I of the Insolvency Act; (iii) the sanctioning of a scheme of arrangement under what is now Pt 26 of the Companies Act 2006; and (iv) a more advantageous realisation of the company's assets than would be effected on a winding up (Insolvency Act 1986 s.8(3)).

[124] Insolvency Act 1986 Sch.B1 para.11.

[125] See form 2.2B, prescribed by r.2.3(5) of the Insolvency Rules 1986.

[126] See above, para.11–25.

arrangement or disposal of the business or the assets without liquidation—or unsuccessful, in which case the company will normally go into insolvent liquidation or be "wound up" through administration. The revised regime is embodied in para.3 of Sch.B1, which provides as follows:

"Purpose of administration

3(1) The administrator of a company must perform his functions with the objective of—

- (a) rescuing the company as a going concern, or
- (b) achieving a better result for the company's creditors as a whole than would be likely if the company were wound up (without first being in administration), or
- (c) realising property in order to make a distribution to one or more secured or preferential creditors.

(2) Subject to sub-paragraph (4), the administrator of a company must perform his functions in the interests of the company's creditors as a whole.

(3) The administrator must perform his functions with the objective specified in sub-paragraph (1)(a) unless he thinks either—

- (a) that it is not reasonably practicable to achieve that objective, or
- (b) that the objective specified in sub-paragraph (1)(b) would achieve a better result for the company's creditors as a whole.

(4) The administrator may perform his functions with the objective specified in sub-paragraph (1)(c) only if—

- (a) he thinks that it is not reasonably practicable to achieve either of the objectives specified in sub-paragraph (1)(a) and (b), and
- (b) he does not unnecessarily harm the interests of the creditors of the company as a whole."

The approval of a voluntary arrangement under Pt I of the Insolvency Act has sensibly been dispensed with as an objective in itself; instead, the administrator may exercise his power to propose a CVA.[127] Paragraph 3 arranges the objectives in a strict hierarchical order, requiring the administrator to select a single objective only, and to follow the hierarchy. Thus, rescue of the company as a going concern is the first priority. It is only if the administrator thinks that it is not reasonably practicable to achieve that objective, or that he could achieve a better result for the company's creditors as a whole without a rescue, that he is permitted to select objective (b) in the performance of his

---

[127] Insolvency Act 1986 s.1(3).

functions. Last in the priority list is the objective of realising the company's property in order to make a distribution to one or more secured or preferential creditors, an objective that can be pursued only if the administrator thinks that it is not reasonably practicable to achieve either of the higher-ranking objectives, and subject to the proviso that he does not unnecessarily harm the interests of the creditors of the company as a whole.[128]

In *BLV Realty Organization Ltd v Batten*,[129] leading counsel for the applicants advanced the ingenious argument that the threefold hierarchy reflected scenarios in which the unsecured creditors would receive 100 pence in the £1 (objective (a)), a dividend (objective (b)) or nothing (objective (c)). Therefore, it could not be a legitimate objective for the administrators to continue to trade pursuant to limb (b) if it was clear that there would be nothing for unsecured creditors, because then the pursuit of that objective would not be in the interests of "the creditors as a whole", so that the administrators should be taken to be pursuing objective (c). This argument was rejected by Norris J.

"It is plain that the administrators think they are pursuing the objective in paragraph 3(1)(b) (and they do not say in their proposals say that such an objective is not reasonably practicable: see the obligation imposed by paragraph 49(2)(b) of Schedule B1). It seems to me plain that the administrators are continuing to trade the business (and are indeed seeking joint venture partners): they are not simply realising property to make a distribution to secured creditors. They are trading the business because they think that that is in the interests of the Zegna's creditors as a whole (even though on the present anticipated outcome it is unlikely there will be anything for unsecured creditors). Trading the business (rather than simply realising the assets in their present state) represents the best chance of maximising recoveries by realising the best value for what has already been done. Maximising recoveries is good for the creditors as a whole (or avoids unnecessary harm to the creditors as a whole), whatever priority a particular creditor may have chosen to accept in his dealings with Zegna, be it junior ranking, secured or unsecured."[130]

In the same judgment, Norris J. dealt with a separate contention that the administrators' termination of the company's contract with the applicants could not be in the interests of the creditors as a whole and constituted unfair harm to the claimants. This rather remarkable contention was likewise rejected. Regard for the interests of the creditors as a whole did not require that every creditor be treated in the same way.

---

[128] See below, para.11–27.
[129] [2010] B.P.I.R. 277.
[130] *BLV Realty Organization*, above, n.129, at [12].

"It may be in the interests of the creditors as a whole that one particular contract with one particular creditor is terminated (even wrongfully): for example if the administrators thought that a particular service could be provided more cheaply or to a higher standard than was currently being done by a creditor with a continuing contract for a service necessary to the ongoing trading, with a beneficial result to the creditors as such. Or it may be that whilst in general ongoing contracts with creditors were being terminated (even wrongfully), one particular contract (e.g. to maintain the principal asset) was kept in being, with a beneficial result to the creditors as such. It would in each case be the interests of the creditors as a whole that would have to prevail over the particular interest of individual creditors: and that might result in different treatment. In the instant case, the administrators think that BLV is doing a less satisfactory job than other team members and that the other team members do not have confidence in BLV. That perception is not without foundation. What the administrators decide to do about it is a matter of commercial judgment. They have decided to terminate the relationship. The different treatment of BLV is not a breach of the obligation to the creditors as a whole."[131]

(2) Rescue of the company and rescue of the business

We have already noted the contrasting attitudes in the United Kingdom and the United States to the preservation of the company as an entity rather than simply its business, with the view of the Cork Committee that there is little interest in preserving the company, whilst in the United States, shareholders are seen as continuing to have a stake in the enterprise deserving of at least some recognition.[132] In theory, that is the position under the Insolvency Act 1986. Paragraph 3(1)(a) identifies as the top-ranking priority of administration "rescuing the company as a going concern". This is to be compared with the previous formulation in s.8 of the Act, "the survival of the company, and the whole or any part of its undertaking, as a going concern", which in the opinion of Harman J. in *Re Rowbotham Baxter Ltd*[133] did not cover the survival of a hive-down company,[134] as opposed to the debtor company itself. **11–26**

---

[131] *BLV Realty Organization*, above, n.129, at [20].
[132] See above, para.11–23.
[133] [1990] B.C.L.C. 397.
[134] That is, a specially formed subsidiary of the company in administration to whom the whole or a substantial part of the company's business and assets are transferred but not the liabilities. Usually, the hive-down company is then sold and the purchase price paid to the company in administration as sole beneficial owner of the shares. The hive-down procedure is of long standing and originated in administrative receivership (see generally Lightman et al., *Law of Administrators and Receivers of Companies*, 2007, paras 12–083 et seq.). However, it is now less common with the disappearance of some of the advantages it once provided under the transfer of undertakings legislation.

That remains the case under the revised wording. As originally presented, the relevant provision of the Enterprise Bill referred only to rescuing the company.[135] The government agreed to clarify the policy at the committee stage of the Bill in the House of Lords and accepted an amendment at Report to add "as a going concern" in order to make it clear that the primary objective was not to preserve an empty shell of a company but rather to rescue the company with the whole or a substantial part of its business intact.[136] The government was equally clear[137] that where in the opinion of the administrator it was not reasonably practicable to preserve both the company and the business, the first objective became inapplicable and one moved to the second objective:

"... achieving a better result for the company's creditors as a whole than would be likely if the company were wound up (without first going into administration)."

This leaves the administrator free to pursue, in conjunction with the creditors, any course of action calculated to put the creditors in a better position than on an immediate winding up, for example, a hive-down, a sale of the assets or a CVA. This second objective is likely to be the most common under the current regime, as it was under the old.

(3) Realising property in order to make a distribution to one or more secured or preferential creditors

11–27 There are two qualifications to the pursuit of this objective. First, it is available only where the administrator thinks that it is not reasonably practicable to attain either of the prior-ranking objectives. Secondly, in performing his functions with this objective, he must not unnecessarily harm the interests of creditors of the company as a whole. In this respect, he has less freedom than that possessed by the administrative receiver, because the latter, whilst under a duty to use reasonable endeavours to obtain the best price, was free to determine the timing of any realisations and could thus proceed to an early sale even if delay would have resulted in enhancement of the value of the security and would not have prejudiced his debenture holder.[138] Now he has to avoid unnecessary harm to the general body of creditors. "Harm" is considered to be the equivalent of "prejudice". He is still entitled to subordinate

---

[135] See the extract from the speech of Lord McIntosh, above, para.11–23.
[136] *Hansard*, H.L. Deb. col.766 (July 29, 2002), *per* Lord McIntosh; and H.L. Deb. cols 1100–1105 (October 21, 2002).
[137] H.L. Deb. col.768 (October 21, 2002).
[138] See above, para.10–49.

the interests of the general body of creditors to those of secured and preferential creditors, since para.3(2) of Sch.B1 makes it clear that his duty to the general creditors is subject to the pursuit of the third objective.[139] But he must avoid causing harm which is not necessary for the protection of the creditors for whom his realisations are intended. This imposes on him the duty to consider all aspects of the administration, including the timing of realisations. It is also a signal that the existence of security substantially in excess of the debt owed to the secured creditor or creditors does not entitle him to be lax in managing the business and realising the assets.

The duty standard

It will have been seen that para.3 of Sch.B1 embodies both an objective and a subjective standard. The administrator has to have in mind one of the three stated objectives but his selection is governed by what he thinks is reasonably practicable. He is required to perform his duties in the interests of the company's creditors as a whole,[140] which on the face of it is an objective standard but in so far as his actions involve the exercise of business judgment, the court will not readily substitute its own business judgment for that of an experienced administrator, for most judges would accept that they are not well equipped to take business decisions. The duty to consider the interests of creditors as a whole is one of the features that distinguishes an administrator from an administrative receiver. Yet there are constraints on the administrator's freedom of action. One of these is the relatively powerful position of the holder of a qualified floating charge; a second, the likely dependence on continued funding by that holder; and a third, the wish to avoid unduly disturbing a harmonious relationship with the party appointing him or approving his appointment from a pre-determined panel of approved administrators.[141] Where the stated objective is to make a distribution to one or more secured or preferential creditors, the administrator must not unnecessarily harm the interests of the company's creditors as a whole. This may

11–28

---

[139] This point appears to have been overlooked in *Somerfield Stores Ltd v Spring (Sutton Coldfield) Ltd* [2011] L. & T.R. 8, where H.H. Judge Purle Q.C., sitting as a High Court judge, commented (at [12]) that it "is clearly not the objective of paragraph (3)(c) to enable secured creditors to advance their position at the expense of the creditors as a whole because Rule 3(4) says so". This, with respect, is not correct. The administrator is entitled to give priority to the pursuit of the objective in para.(1)(c) so long as he does not *unnecessarily* harm the interests of the creditors as a whole. That is not say that the decision itself is wrong; it was concerned with the separate question of whether a tenant should be given leave to continue an application for a new tenancy under Pt II of the Landlord and Tenant Act 1954. See below, para.11–78.

[140] For a further discussion of the administrator's duties, see below, para.11–93.

[141] Most banks maintain panels of approved administrators and will normally select a panel member or require selection of a panel member on an appointment by the company or its directors.

require the administrator not merely to take reasonable care to obtain a proper price but to that end to consider carefully the timing of realisations. In this respect, at least, he is more circumscribed than an administrative receiver or its debenture holder.

4. ADMINISTRATION COMPARED WITH OTHER INSOLVENCY PROCEDURES

Administration compared with liquidation

11–29   Administration is in many ways different in concept and operation from liquidation. The primary objective of administration is not to bury the company forthwith but to restore it to profitable trading where possible and, in the event that liquidation becomes unavoidable (as is usually the case), to deal with the business or assets in such a way as to produce better dividends for creditors than if the company had gone into winding up from the outset. However, the introduction by the Enterprise Act 2002 of a power to make a distribution to ordinary unsecured creditors with the permission of the court[142] has brought in its train the application of several rules previously confined to winding up, for example, the rules on set-off,[143] the priority of preferential debts and *pari passu* distribution where the administrator obtains permission from the court to make a distribution to ordinary unsecured creditors.[144] Again, the amendment of the rules on priority as between liquidation expenses and claims secured by a floating charge has brought liquidation into line with administration, so that the expenses of the liquidation, like those of administration where the administrator makes a distribution, have priority.[145] Further, it would seem that the statutory trust arising in a winding up arises equally in an administration.[146] Moreover, even under the previous regime the statutory provisions for the avoidance or adjustment of

---

[142] Under item 13 of Sch.1 to the Insolvency Act 1986, the administrator already had power to make a distribution without the court's permission where necessary or incidental to the performance of his functions or likely to assist achievement of the purpose of administration, although it would only be in special circumstances that any such condition would be satisfied. For examples, see *Re UCT (UK) Ltd* [2001] 1 B.C.L.C. 443; and *Re WBSL Realisations 1992 Ltd* [1995] 2 B.C.L.C. 576.

[143] Set-off in administration is governed by r.2.85 of the Insolvency Rules 1986, set-off in liquidation by r.4.90. Changes have been made to bring the two rules into alignment. See above, para.9–48.

[144] See above, para.8–03 and below, para.11–85.

[145] Insolvency Act 1986 ss.176ZA and 175 as applied by Sch.B1 para.65(2).

[146] *Harms Offshore AHT Taurus GmbH & Co KG v Bloom* [2010] Ch. 187, *per* Stanley Burnton L.J. at [24]. The position was held to be otherwise under the pre-Enterprise Act regime (*Re Leyland Printing Co Ltd* [2010] EWHC 2105).

transactions applied to administration as well as liquidation.[147] But there remain important differences:

(1) The administrator has full management powers; the liquidator may carry on business only for the beneficial winding up of the company[148] and rarely does so.

(2) The remedies of secured creditors and suppliers under reservation of title are frozen by an administration order but are unaffected by winding up.

(3) The commencement of administration does not stop time running under the Limitation Act 1980, because although the administrator may now make a distribution to unsecured creditors with leave of the court as well as to secured and preferential creditors, no statutory scheme of distribution is prescribed as it is in the case of liquidation, so that in this respect there is no distinction between pre-Enterprise-Act administration, where it was established that administration did not stop time running,[149] and post-Enterprise-Act administration. Moreover, the administrator may decide to continue trading in pursuit of the objectives set out in para.3(1)(a) and (b) of Sch.B1 to the Insolvency Act.

(4) An administrator, unlike a liquidator, has no power to disclaim onerous property under s.178(3) of the Insolvency Act.[150]

(5) Only a liquidator can institute proceedings for misfeasance,[151] fraudulent trading[152] or wrongful trading,[153] except as regards proceedings against an administrator or former administrator which are initiated by a person listed in para.75(2)(a) of Sch.B1.

(6) In a liquidation, the convenor of a creditors' meeting may require the attendance of directors and employees[154]; in an administration the duty is merely to provide the administrator with information and to attend on him at such times as he may reasonably require.[155] Directors are thus much less exposed in an administration.

---

[147] Companies Act 1985 s.395(1). Insolvency Act 1986 ss.238–245. Prior to the changes made by the Enterprise Act 2002, insolvency set-off, the priority status of preferential debts and the pari passu principle of distribution among ordinary creditors did not apply to administration, since the administrator could not normally make a distribution.

[148] See above, para.5–02, n.16.

[149] *Re Maxwell Fleet & Facilities Management Ltd* [1999] 2 B.C.L.C. 721.

[150] See above, para.6–27.

[151] Insolvency Act 1986 s.212.

[152] Insolvency Act 1986 s.213.

[153] Insolvency Act 1986 s.214.

[154] Insolvency Rules 1986 r.4.58(4).

[155] Insolvency Act 1986 s.235(2).

(7)   The appointment of a liquidator is primarily a matter for the creditors, whereas the appointment of an administrator is usually left to the directors, although their decision may be influenced by major creditors, in particular by the holder of a qualifying floating charge.

It will be apparent that administration has several advantages over liquidation in helping to secure the statutory objective for which administration is available.[156] First, the liquidator can continue trading only for the purposes of beneficial winding up,[157] whereas an administrator can trade freely and dispose of the business or its assets on a going-concern basis. Secondly, the freeze on enforcement of rights of secured creditors and suppliers under retention of title greatly facilitates the continuance of trading by the company as a going concern, and the value of a company's assets on a going-concern basis is usually substantially higher than on a break-up basis. Thirdly, the freeze also makes it much easier to organise an arrangement with creditors than is the case on a winding up. Fourthly, there can be significant differences between administration and liquidation in the perception of outsiders, so that realisation by an administrator may give a prospect of greater benefit to creditors than realisation by a liquidator.[158] There is a further point of which insolvency practitioners are keenly aware. In a compulsory liquidation (although no longer in a voluntary liquidation), all funds have to be deposited in the Insolvency Services Account, which imposes a high *ad valorem* charge. These disadvantages are avoided by the use of administration in parallel with a CVA.[159]

Administration compared with administrative receivership

11–30   It will be recalled that administration is a procedure designed to provide for the benefit of the general body of creditors the external management which administrative receivership provides by contract for the benefit of the debenture holder. The management powers of the administrator are co-extensive with those of the administrative receiver but the powers of the former are given and exercised primarily on behalf of unsecured creditors. There are at least three other differences between the two regimes:

---

[156] As to these see above, para.11–25.
[157] Insolvency Act 1986 Sch.4 Pt II para.5.
[158] *Auto Management Services Ltd v Oracle Fleet UK Ltd* [2008] B.C.C. 761.
[159] For a case where these factors influenced the decision as to the choice of insolvency process, see *Re TBL Realisation Plc, Oakley-Smith v Greenberg* [2004] B.C.C. 81, discussed below, para.12–48. Until recently, the account also paid a lower than commercial rate of interest, but this has now changed.

(1)   The administrator is not personally liable on contracts into which he
enters or on contracts of employment which he adopts. In place of the
personal liability of the kind imposed on receivers,[160] the Act provides
for claims under such contracts to rank in priority to the administrator's remuneration and expenses.[161]

(2)   Whereas the appointment of a receiver crystallises a floating charge,
this is probably not the case when an administrator is appointed, unless
the charge so provides.[162]

(3)   As stated earlier, where the administrator is pursuing the objective of
the kind previously pursued by the administrative receiver, he owes a
duty not to cause harm unnecessarily to the general body of creditors,
and this imposes on him the duty to have regard to the interests of
creditors when timing realisations,[163] a duty not imposed on administrative receivers.[164]

Formerly, the making of an administration order was not an event which
determined the existence and amount of preferential debts, except for
the purpose of a meeting under s.4 of the Act to consider a CVA or where
winding up followed immediately upon the discharge of the administration
order.[165] That has now changed. Except as otherwise provided by s.387 of the
Insolvency Act, the relevant date in relation to a company in administration
is the date on which it enters administration.[166]

Administration compared with a CVA or scheme of arrangement

We have already noted that administration is not in itself a reorganisation   **11–31**
procedure and that its outcome may or may not be a CVA or scheme of
arrangement. There are other important differences between the administration regime and that applicable to a CVA.

---

[160] Insolvency Act 1986 s.44(1)(b). See above, paras 10–50 et seq.
[161] Insolvency Act 1986 Sch.B1 para.99(4) and (5).
[162] See *Roy Goode, Legal Problems of Credit and Security*, 3rd edn, para.4–38. The same view is
taken by Lightman et al., *Law of Receivers and Administrators of Companies*, 2007,
para.3–082. *Contra, Goode on Legal Problems of Credit and Security*, 2008, para.4–37.
[163] The duty was owed even before the change in the legislation (*Re Charnley Davies Ltd (No.2)*
[1990] B.C.L.C. 760).
[164] *Bell v Long* [2008] 2 B.C.L.C. 706; and *Silven Properties Ltd v Royal Bank of Scotland Plc*
[2004] 1 B.C.L.C. 359.
[165] Insolvency Act 1986 s.387, as originally enacted.
[166] Insolvency Act 1986 s.387(3A).

(1) No moratorium in a CVA or scheme of arrangement

11–32 Where all significant creditors co-operate, an informal restructuring may be carried out without the need for a statutory moratorium, through the use of informal standstill agreements, and this may be a preferable way of proceeding, particularly where it is proposed, by way of advance planning, to seek court approval for a scheme of arrangement before the company has become financially distressed.[167] In other cases, however, the successful restructuring of a viable business may depend on the availability of a statutory moratorium in order to prevent individual creditors from taking separate enforcement action in their own interests, thereby potentially strangling the reorganisation initiative at birth. Yet except in the case of small eligible companies, whose directors, where intending to make a proposal for a CVA, may take steps to obtain a moratorium,[168] neither the initiation of a CVA nor the making of an application under Pt 26 of the Companies Act 2006 triggers a moratorium. In both cases, with the exception just mentioned, individual creditors remain free to enforce their rights as they choose without regard to the views of the majority of creditors until a CVA is concluded or an order is made approving a scheme of arrangement. It is only where the CVA proposal or Pt 26 application is made in relation to a company already in administration or where a Pt 26 application is preceded by the appointment of a provisional liquidator,[169] or a stay is granted on application after presentation of a winding up petition,[170] that the benefit of a moratorium is obtained. The lack of a statutory moratorium is considered by some, although by no means all, insolvency practitioners to be one of the most serious deficiencies in the CVA procedure but proposals to introduce it into the regime previously met with no success except in relation to small, eligible companies,[171] for which the CVA rules are so stringent and convoluted that few insolvency practitioners would view this route to a moratorium with enthusiasm. Recent unpublished research by Professors Adrian Walters and Sandra Frisby has shown that the vast majority of insolvent companies surveyed resorted to a stand-alone CVA rather than a CVA within administration and that the small company moratorium was a dead letter.[172] However, the Insolvency Service has recently made proposals for a restructuring moratorium in cases where the core business is viable but restructuring is needed to avoid future financial distress or insolvency. The company would have to show to the court's satisfaction that there was a reasonable prospect of agreeing a compromise or arrangement with its creditors.[173]

---

[167] See John Tribe, "Companies Act Schemes of Arrangement and Rescue: The Lost Cousin of Restructuring Practice?" (2009) 7 J.I.B.F.L. 386.

[168] See below, para.12–39.

[169] Insolvency Act 1986 s.130(2).

[170] Insolvency Act 1986 s.126.

[171] See below, para.12–39.

[172] *Preliminary Report to the Insolvency Service into Outcomes in Company Voluntary Arrangements* (2011), accessible on the Insolvency Service website.

[173] "Proposals for a Restructuring Moratorium—A Consultation" (July 2010). See Ch.12 for a more detailed treatment of schemes of arrangement and CVAs.

(2) Actual or impending insolvency not a prerequisite for a CVA

The company or its directors cannot appoint an administrator or apply for an administration order unless the company is insolvent or insolvency is imminent; there is no such pre-condition of a CVA or an order under Pt 26 of the Companies Act 2006 approving a scheme of arrangement.

11–33

(3) The company's participation in the process

In administration, the proposals for achieving the purpose(s) of the administration order are prepared and submitted by the administrator, not by the company, and only the creditors are involved in their approval; in a CVA or scheme of arrangement, the scheme is formulated by the directors, and in a CVA the members also participate in the decision-making process. Indeed, a CVA cannot be concluded without an order of the court unless the separate meetings of creditors and members approve the arrangements in identical terms.[174]

11–34

(4) Management

Administration involves external management; in a CVA, although a supervisor is appointed to oversee the implementation of the plan, his powers are confined by the terms of the CVA and the day-to-day management of the company is usually allowed to remain in the hands of its directors if it is not in administration. Recent changes to the Insolvency Rules are designed to increase the efficiency and reduce the cost of administration. These include provisions allowing the use of email instead of post where the intended recipient of the communication has consented to electronic delivery and has provided an electronic address for delivery,[175] making advertising discretionary except for advertisements required to be published in the London Gazette,[176] and abolishing the need for annual meetings with the attendant expense of circulating creditors and hiring halls for the meeting.

11–35

(5) Dissenting and non-participating creditors

Finally, the rules determining when dissenting or non-participating creditors are bound are not the same for a CVA as for the approval of proposals in an administration. In a CVA, the arrangement binds only those who were

11–36

---

[174] Insolvency Act 1986 s.4A.
[175] Insolvency Rules 1986 r.12A.10(1).
[176] The requirements for non-Gazette advertisements are contained in r.12A.38 of the Insolvency Rules 1986.

entitled to vote at the meeting approving the arrangement or would have been so entitled if they had had notice of the meeting.[177] By contrast, a resolution passed at a meeting of creditors to approve a proposal by the administrator in an administration, other than a proposal which is itself for a CVA, binds all creditors.[178] Moreover, a CVA must be approved by a majority in excess of three-quarters in value of the creditors present in person or by proxy and voting on the resolution,[179] whereas a resolution on a proposal by the administrator other than for a CVA requires only a bare majority of those present and voting in person or by proxy, persons connected with the company being excluded.[180]

5. THE RISE OF THE PRE-PACK

Advantages and disadvantages of the pre-pack

11–37   Reference has already been made[181] to pre-packaged administrations ("pre-packs") in which, prior to the administrator's appointment, arrangements are put in place in collaboration with the company's major creditors for the sale of the company's business, the sale contract being concluded immediately after the administrator's appointment without the convening of a creditors' meeting or an application to the court. A pre-pack sale may also be concluded by an administrator appointed by the court, in which case the court may be asked to make an order approving the proposed sale.[182] The concept of a pre-pack is not new, the procedure having been frequently used by administrative receivers, and it has long been a feature of the US Ch.11 proceedings, although with greater formalities. The advantages of a pre-pack are speed, a sale without adverse publicity, preservation of jobs,[183]

---

[177] Insolvency Act 1986 s.5(2)(b).
[178] The Insolvency Rules do not say this directly: they merely refer to the passing of the resolution.
[179] Insolvency Rules 1986 r.1.19(1). However, the voting on the resolution must be determined after excluding votes to be left out of account and votes of persons connected with the company (r.1.19(4)).
[180] Insolvency Rules 1986 r.2.43(1) and (2).
[181] Above, para.1–36.
[182] For an example, see *Re Hellas Telecommunications (Luxembourg) II SCA* [2010] B.C.C. 295. In that case, the company sold its shareholding in WIND Hellas in the largest pre-pack sale recorded, although only after a lengthy bid process. WIND Hellas was itself restructured in 2010.
[183] It may be noted that the administrator is under no duty to have regard to employees' interests, although it will usually be in the interests of the business and its sale to ensure as far as possible that most employees are kept in post. This, indeed, appears to be what happens in most pre-pack sales (Sandra Frisby, "A Preliminary Analysis of Pre-Packaged Administrations" (August 2007), p.71). For the position of employees, see David Pollard, "Pre-Pack Administrations—Employee and Pension Issues" (2010) Int. Intel. 37.

reduced professional charges, a better price and rapid access to funds.[184] In addition, where the problems of securing agreement in a major restructuring are intractable because of the multiplicity of interests, a pre-pack sale may provide the solution. It is believed that nearly one-third of all administrations are pre-packs. Research by Professor Sandra Frisby has shown that the most common reason for adoption of a pre-pack strategy by insolvency practitioners is the absence of funding to meet the costs of trading even for a very short time.[185]

However, pre-packs have attracted a degree of negative publicity on the ground that unsecured creditors have no voice in the process, which lacks transparency with a consequent lack of accountability, that they are presented with a *fait accompli*, that pre-packs may be unacceptably biased towards the interests of secured creditors, particularly the holders of floating charges, and that the business may be sold off at an undervalue,[186] particularly if there is a proposed management buy-out and the management has a close relationship with the intended administrator.[187] It appears that for the first half of 2009, 81 per cent of pre-pack sales were made to parties connected with the insolvent company[188] in a way reminiscent of the much-criticised "Phoenix" company.

The prospective administrator will usually seek to establish a proper value either by limited market testing if there is time and this can be done without damage to the company's business or by expert valuation if time is of the essence. Frisby conducted valuable empirical research into pre-packs on behalf of R3,[189] showing that pre-packs significantly improved the position of secured creditors, and resulted in higher numbers of staff being transferred to the new company than would have been the case under an ordinary business sale but that unsecured creditors fared worse. More recently, however, she has detected grounds for cautious optimism in that 2 per cent of pre-pack

---

[184] See Finch, *Corporate Insolvency Law*, 2009, pp.456 et seq.

[185] See Frisby, "A Preliminary Analysis", 2007, p.32.

[186] See, e.g. *Re Delberry Ltd* [2008] B.C.C. 653, where Terence Mowschenson Q.C., sitting as a High Court judge, granted an application by the liquidator for an order under s.236 of the Insolvency Act 1986 requiring the administrator carrying out a pre-pack sale to produce documents, including pre-receivership documents, given the speed at which the sale had been carried out and the substantial costs involved. See also *Re Kayley Vending Ltd* [2009] B.C.C. 578, which cited Professor Frisby's earlier analysis (above, n.183) setting out concerns about pre-packs.

[187] See Frisby, above, "A Preliminary Analysis", 2007, pp.8–9; and the concern expressed by the House of Commons Business and Enterprise Committee, "Sixth Report of Session 2008-09: The Insolvency Service" (April 2009), paras 12 et seq.

[188] Insolvency Service, "Report on the First Six Months Operation of SIP 16" (May 2009), para.2.3. This percentage is significantly higher than that previously reported by Frisby in her earlier study.

[189] "A Preliminary Analysis of Pre-Packaged Administrations", Report to the Association of Business Recovery Professionals, referred to in a report of the House of Commons Business and Enterprise Committee, "The Insolvency Service: Sixth Report of Session 2008–09", para.14.

sales resulted in a full return to unsecured creditors, compared with 1 per cent of business sales, while the average return to unsecured creditors at 5 per cent is higher than that seen for business sales at 4 per cent.[190]

SIP 16

11–38 Guidance to insolvency practitioners on the conduct of pre-packs, including the provision of information to creditors, is given in a Statement of Insolvency Practice, SIP 16. This provides detailed guidance as to the duties owed by the administrator or prospective administrator to those who may be affected by the arrangement and the potential risks to be borne in mind. A key element of SIP 16 is the set of disclosures that should be made by the administrator to creditors, wherever practicable on the first notification to creditors prior to the initial creditors' meeting. The information to be disclosed includes such details as the source of the administrator's initial introduction, the extent of his involvement prior to his appointment, any marketing activities conducted by him or the company, any valuations obtained, why it was not possible to trade the business and offer it for sale as a going concern during the administration, whether efforts were made to consult with major creditors and particulars of the sale transaction, including the identity of the purchaser. However, the administrator also has to avoid jeopardising the sale, so that if the prospective purchaser insists on confidentiality as regards its identity or other details as a condition of proceeding, the administrator may have no choice but to agree, although he should not do so where the sale is to a connected party such as the existing management.

The operation of SIP 16 has been kept under review by the Insolvency Service, which has found that in the final six months of 2009 more than one-third of SIP disclosure statements issued by insolvency practitioners were not fully compliant, despite the issue of further guidance.[191] In consequence, the Department of Business, Innovation and Skills has issued a consultation paper exploring the possible options for the future conduct of pre-packs, which include legislation to require court approval.[192] Where the administrator is to be appointed by the court and the court's approval is sought for the pre-pack sale, the applicant will normally be expected to make the same disclosures, or as much of them as possible, as those required by SIP 16.[193]

---

[190] Sandra Frisby, "The Pre-Pack Promise: Signs of Fulfilment?" *Recovery*, Spring 2010, p.30.
[191] "Report on the Operation of Statement of Insolvency Practice 16 July–December 2009" (March 2010).
[192] "Consultation/Call for Evidence: Improving the Transparency of, and Confidence in, Pre-Packaged Sale in Administrations" (March 2010).
[193] *Re Kayley Vending Ltd* [2009] B.C.C. 578, cited by Lewison J. in *Re Hellas Telecommunications (Luxembourg) II SCA* [2010] B.C.C. 295. See further Marcus Haywood, "Pre-Pack Administrations" (2010) Ins. Int. 17.

The power to conclude pre-pack sales without approval

It is now established that the administrator is entitled to conclude a pre-pack sale without the prior approval of creditors or the court.[194]

11–39

"There will be many cases where the administrators are justified in not laying any proposals before a meeting of creditors. This is so where they conclude that the unsecured creditors are either likely to be paid in full, or to receive no payment, or where neither of the first two objectives for the administration can be achieved: see paragraph 52 of the Schedule. If, in such administrations, administrators were prevented from acting without the direction of the court it would mean that they would have to seek the directions of the court before carrying out any function throughout the whole of the administration. The Enterprise Act 2002 reflects a conscious policy to reduce the involvement of the court in administrations, where possible."[195]

The role of the court

In those cases where the court is asked to approve a pre-pack sale—usually where the administrator is appointed by the court or where the pre-pack has unusual features which the administrator feels call for judicial approval—it may be expected to take the view that the merits of a pre-pack are primarily a matter for the administrator, on whose expertise and experience the court will place great reliance and who is likely to be best placed to make an informed business judgment,[196] so that the court will intervene only if the pre-back sale is an abuse[197] or there are other compelling reasons why the proposed sale should not proceed. The objection of the majority creditor is not itself a sufficient reason for withholding approval of a pre-pack sale.[198] However, the fact that the administrator is appointed by the court does not mean that the court's approval to the pre-pack sale is required, and the mere fact that the appointment is made does not imply that the court has given its blessing to the pre-pack sale.[199]

11–40

---

[194] *Re Transbus International Ltd* [2004] 1 W.L.R. 2654; and *Re Kayley Vending Ltd* [2009] B.C.C. 578.

[195] *Re Transbus International Ltd, per* Lawrence Collins J. at [14].

[196] See, e.g. *Re Hellas Telecommunications (Luxembourg) II SCA* [2010] B.C.C. 295; *DKLL Solicitors v HM Revenue & Customs* [2007] B.C.C. 908; *Re Kayley Vending Ltd* [2009] B.C.C. 904 (Ch); and *Re Halliwells LLP* [2010] 107 L.S.G. (32) 14.

[197] And the court has to be alive to this possibility. See *Re Kayley Vending Ltd* [2009] B.C.C. 904 (Ch).

[198] *DKLL Solicitors*, cited above n.196, where the sale was approved despite objection by the majority creditor, HM Revenue & Customs.

[199] *DKLL Solicitors*, cited above n.196.

Legal risks for the administrator

11–41   The administrator will need to take great care to ensure as far as possible that: (i) the terms of the pre-pack sale are likely to be the best available, having regard to any time constraints within which he may have to act; (ii) he is able to justify his decision to conclude the contract after taking appropriate steps, by market testing or independent valuation, to satisfy himself that the price and other terms are reasonable; and, above all, (iii) that the steps he is taking are in the interests of the company's creditors as a whole or, where the objective is that specified in para.3(1)(c) of Sch.B1, that he is not causing unnecessary harm to the interests of the creditors as a whole. An administrator who fails in these duties is exposed to three possible claims: a claim under para.74 of Sch.B1 that he has caused harm to the company or a creditor, coupled with an application for consequential relief; an application for an order under para.75 on the ground of misfeasance; and an application to terminate the administrator's appointment under para.81 on the ground that the party appointing him did so with an improper motive[200] or to remove him under para.88, for example, because he has failed to act with the expedition, robustness of purpose and competence reasonably to be expected of him[201] or that the majority of creditors in value had legitimate concerns about the administrator's conduct and wished him to be removed.[202]

Confidentiality

11–42   The company and the prospective administrator will normally incur an obligation of confidentiality to the prospective purchaser, who may, for example, insist that its identity is not revealed. A question that has been raised with the Insolvency Service is whether the disclosure requirements in SIP 16 override that duty or take effect subject to it. It is thought that the administrator should use his best endeavours to ensure that the sale agreement permits disclosure under SIP 16. However, the overriding consideration must be the interests of creditors. Accordingly, if the purchaser is an arm's-length purchaser and remains adamant in requiring continuing confidentiality, so that the sale could be at risk if the administrator sought to insist on post-contract disclosure, the administrator should accept the prospective purchaser's stipulation and proceed with the sale if he considers that to be in the bests interests of creditors.

---

[200] *DKLL Solicitors*, cited above n.196.
[201] *Coyne v DRC Distribution Ltd* [2008] B.C.C. 612.
[202] *Clydesdale Financial Services Ltd v Smailes* [2009] B.C.C. 810.

6. THE APPOINTMENT PROCEDURE IN OUTLINE

Administration without a court order

An administrator may be appointed out of court by the company,[203] the
directors[204] or the holder of a qualifying floating charge.[205] Most appointments are made out of court. The administrator must be qualified to act as
an insolvency practitioner in relation to the company.[206] Neither the company nor the directors may appoint an administrator without:

11–43

(1) giving at least five business days' written notice to any person entitled
to appoint an administrative receiver (thereby enabling such person to
prevent an administration[207]) or to any person who is or may be entitled to appoint an administrator under para.14 of Sch.B1 to the
Insolvency Act 1986 as holder of a qualifying floating charge[208]; and

(2) obtaining the consent in writing[209] of each person to whom such notice
has been given.[210]

(1) Appointment by the holder of a qualifying floating charge

The effect of the above provisions is that the holder of a qualifying floating
charge[211] is the master of out-of-court appointments, which can be made by
the chargee itself[212] and cannot be made by the company or directors except

11–44

---

[203] By resolution passed at a meeting of shareholders.

[204] By majority decision (Insolvency Act 1986 Sch.B1 para.105), although it is thought that this
is subject to the provisions of the company's memorandum and articles of association.

[205] Insolvency Act 1986 Sch.B1 paras 14 and 22. For the meaning of "qualifying floating charge",
see above, para.11–08. Note that while the fact that the charge purports to provide for the
appointment of an administrative receiver does not preclude the chargee from appointing an
administrator (see para.14(2)(c)), the purported appointment of an administrative receiver
rather than an administrator will be ineffective unless it can be interpreted by the court as
intended to refer to an administrator.

[206] See Insolvency Act 1986 Sch.B1 para.6. The requirement to be qualified not only generally
but "in relation to the company" means that the proper performance of his functions must
be secured by a bond, either generally or in relation to the particular company concerned.

[207] Insolvency Act 1986 Sch.B1 para.25(c).

[208] Insolvency Act 1986 Sch.B1 para.26(1).

[209] Reference to a thing in writing includes a reference to a thing in electronic form (s.436B).

[210] Insolvency Act 1986 Sch.B1 para.28(1)(b).

[211] A creditor who is not the holder of a qualifying floating charge can secure the appointment
of an administrator only by application to the court under Insolvency Act 1986 Sch.B1
para.12(1).

[212] Assuming, of course, that the power to appoint an administrator has become exercisable
under the terms of the charge (see above, para.11–09).

on prior notice to the chargee or with the chargee's consent.[213] Moreover, whereas the company or its directors cannot appoint an administrator where a petition for winding up has been presented or an administration application has been made and the petition or application has not been disposed of,[214] no such restriction applies to an appointment by the holder of a qualifying floating charge, who can also apply for an administration order even if the company is in compulsory winding up.[215] Finally, the holder of a qualifying floating charge who makes an out-of-court appointment is given the facility of filing a notice of appointment with the court outside court business hours.[216] However, appointments are usually made by the company or the directors even where the holder of a qualifying floating charge (typically a bank) is entitled to appoint the administrator, because for reputational reasons banks do not wish to be seen to put a company into administration. Nevertheless, as secured creditors, they can and do influence the appointment of the administrator, as by ensuring that he is appointed from a panel of approved or preferred insolvency practitioners. While out-of-court appointments are predominant, it remains open to interested parties to apply to the court for an administration order.[217]

The holder of a qualifying floating charge must give at least two business days' written notice to the holder of any prior qualifying floating charge[218] or obtain his written consent to the appointment.[219] The purpose of this requirement is to give the holder of the prior charge an opportunity to appoint an administrator itself. But it is not necessary that the latter should consent, this is simply an alternative to its being given notice. That is in accordance with the general law relating to secured transactions inasmuch as a junior, secured creditor does not need the consent of a senior, secured creditor to enforce his security, whether by sale or otherwise, for anything he does takes effect subject to the rights of the senior creditor unless the latter is paid off.[220]

The holder of a qualifying floating charge who appoints the administrator must file with the court a notice of appointment incorporating the requisite statutory declaration and, if wishing to obtain the benefit of an interim moratorium under paras 44(2), (5) and 42 of Sch.B1, must at the same time file a

---

[213] Insolvency Act 1986 Sch.B1 para.28(1).

[214] Insolvency Act 1986 Sch.B1 para.25.

[215] Insolvency Act 1986 Sch.B1 para.37(2).

[216] This is done by faxing or emailing it in form 2.7B to a designated telephone number or email address provided by the Court Service (Insolvency Rules 1986 r.2.19(1) and (3)). This has the same effect as a filing under r.2.16, which is subject to r.2.19 (r.2.16(6)). Under r.2.19(5), the appointment takes effect from the date and time of the fax transmission.

[217] ibid., paras 11–10 and 11–11.

[218] By which is meant prior in time or having priority by virtue of an agreement to which the holder of the floating charge was a party (Insolvency Act 1986 Sch.B1 para.15(2)).

[219] Insolvency Act 1986 Sch.B1 para.15(1).

[220] See *Goode on Legal Problems of Credit and Security*, 2008, para.5–34.

copy of the notice of intention to appoint given to prior chargees under para.15.[221] There must also be filed the additional documents specified in r.2.16 of the Insolvency Rules. Under para.19 of Sch.B1, the appointment does not take effect until all of the prescribed documents have been filed. In consequence, the fact that at the time the administrator was appointed, in the sense of being designated by the debenture holder, the power of appointment had not become exercisable because no demand for payment had been made does not affect the validity of the appointment if demand is made by the time the appointment takes effect under para.19; there is no distinction between the appointment being "made" and its taking effect.[222] So it is not until all of the prescribed documents have been filed that the conditions necessary for the exercise of the right to appoint an administrator have to be satisfied. Moreover, if the company acquiesces in what would otherwise be an invalid appointment and the administrator acts in reliance on that acquiescence, the company is estopped from disputing the validity of his appointment.[223]

(2) Appointment by the company or the directors

The ability of the company or directors to appoint an administrator is hedged around with restrictions. Such an appointment may not be made: **11–45**

(1)   unless the company is or is likely to become unable to pay its debts within the meaning of s.123 of the Insolvency Act[224];

(2)   during the period of 12 months beginning with the date on which a prior appointment made by or on the application of the company or the directors ceases to have effect[225];

(3)   if a petition for the winding up of the company has been presented and not yet disposed of[226];

---

[221] Insolvency Rules 1986 r.2.15. Where the holder of a qualifying floating charge wishes to obtain an interim moratorium, the notice must be in form 2.5B. See below as to the filing of a copy of the notice with the court. This notice should not be confused with the notice of appointment filed under Sch.B1 para.18, which is required to be in form 2.6B. If there is no prior chargee, and thus no one to whom notice need be sent, the interim moratorium provisions do not apply. This is because the holder of the qualifying floating charge has no need of an interim moratorium; all he has to do is to file the notice of appointment.

[222] *Fliptex Ltd v Hogg* [2004] B.C.C. 870.

[223] *Fliptex Ltd v Hogg.*

[224] See above, paras 4–04 et seq., as to s.123, and para.11–11, as to the curiously oblique way in which the requirement of actual or impending insolvency features in the legislation as regards out-of-court appointments by the company or its directors.

[225] Insolvency Act 1986 Sch.B1 para.23.

[226] Insolvency Act 1986 Sch.B1 para.25(a).

(4)   if the company is in winding up, whether voluntary or compulsory[227];

(5)   if an administration application has been made and not yet disposed of[228];

(6)   if an administrative receiver is in office[229]; or

(7)   unless the person who makes the appointment has complied with the requirements of paras 26 and 27 of Sch.B1 and the period of notice specified in para.26(1) has expired or each person to whom notice has been given under para.26(1) has consented in writing to the making of the appointment.[230]

The procedure is laid down in Ch.4 of Pt II of the Insolvency Rules 1986 and largely mirrors that applicable to appointments by the holder of a qualifying floating charge. Where directors wish to propose a CVA incorporating proposals that will continue to leave day-to-day management in their hands and also to have the benefit of a moratorium, there is every incentive for them to take steps early before any holder of a qualifying charge has become entitled to enforce the charge and appoint an administrator of their choice who will become the supervisor of the CVA. An alternative, where they are dealing with a relatively small number of large creditors with whom they do not anticipate any serious difficulty in coming to an arrangement, is to move directly to a CVA without putting the company into administration.

Administration by court order

11–46   Although out-of-court administration is likely to be the norm, there will still be cases in which it is either expedient to apply for an administration order or necessary to do so because administration is sought by a person not eligible to make an out-of-court appointment[231] or because such an appointment is barred by other provisions.[232] Among the cases in which it may be expedient to apply to the court to appoint the administrator are where the administrator wishes to secure court approval to a proposed pre-pack sale which might be challenged or where it is intended to seek recognition of the appointment in a foreign jurisdiction.

---

[227] Insolvency Act 1986 Sch.B1 para.8.

[228] Insolvency Act 1986 Sch.B1 para.25(b).

[229] Insolvency Act 1986 Sch.B1 para.25(c). However, if the security by virtue of which the receiver was appointed is vulnerable under ss.238–240 or 245 of the Insolvency Act were an administration order is to be made, the court retains the power to make the order (Sch.B1 para.39).

[230] Insolvency Act 1986 Sch.B1 para.28(1).

[231] See above, para.11–43.

[232] In particular, Insolvency Act 1986 Sch.B1 para.17 (see above, para.11–09) and para.25 (see above, para.11–43).

(1) Conditions to be satisfied

The court may make an administration order in relation to a company only   **11–47**
if satisfied that:

(1)   the company is or is likely to become unable to pay its debts; and

(2)   the administration order is reasonably likely to achieve the purpose of administration.[233]

However, the first condition is dispensed with where the application is by the holder of a qualifying floating charge so long as the court is satisfied that the applicant could make an appointment under para.14.[234] "Unable to pay its debts" has the meaning given by s.123 of the Insolvency Act.[235] The meaning of present inability to pay debts has been considered in detail in an earlier chapter.[236] The requirement that the court should be "satisfied" that the company is "likely" to become unable to pay its debts follows the wording of the original statutory provisions. This has been held to require that the future insolvency is more likely than not and it is not sufficient that there is a real prospect of the company going into liquidation.[237] As regards the likelihood of the administration achieving the intended purpose, there has been a change in the language from "considers the making of an order would be likely to achieve one or more of the purposes mentioned below", for which it sufficed that there was a real prospect of the purpose(s) being achieved,[238] to "satisfied that the administration order is reasonably likely to achieve the purpose of administration". The question is whether it alters the threshold that has to be crossed before an order has been made. This is not altogether easy, because the revised formulation pulls in opposite directions, "satisfied" being considered a more stringent requirement than "considers",[239] while "reasonably likely", in contradistinction to "likely" in the preceding sub-paragraph, suggests a slightly lower threshold. The case law now establishes that "reasonably likely" does not require the court to be satisfied on a balance of probabilities; it suffices that there is a real prospect that the administration's objective will be achieved.[240]

---

[233] Insolvency Act 1986 Sch.B1 para.11. By "the purpose of administration" is meant an objective specified in Sch.B1 para.3 (Sch.B1 para.111(1)).

[234] Insolvency Act 1986 Sch.B1 para.35(2)(a).

[235] Insolvency Act 1986 Sch.B1 para.111(1).

[236] Above, paras 4–03 et seq.

[237] *Re Colt Telecom Plc* [2002] All E.R. (D) 347.

[238] *Re Harris Simons Construction Ltd* [1989] 1 W.L.R. 368.

[239] *Re Harris Simons Construction Ltd per* Hoffmann J. at 370.

[240] *Auto Management Services Ltd v Oracle Fleet Ltd* [2008] B.C.C. 761; and *Hammonds v Pro-Fit USA Ltd* [2007] EWHC 1998 (Ch).

(2) Who may apply

11–48   An administration application[241] may be made only by:

(1)   the company;

(2)   the directors of the company;

(3)   one or more creditors of the company[242];

(4)   the justices' chief executive for a magistrates' court in the exercise of the power conferred by s.87A of the Magistrates' Courts Act 1980 (fine imposed on company);

(5)   a combination of the persons listed in paras (a) to (d)[243]; or

(6)   the supervisor of a voluntary arrangement.[244]

Most administration applications are made by the company or its directors. It has been argued that where the application is made by a creditor whose claim is disputed, the practice adopted in relation to winding up petitions[245] should be adopted, leading to the application being stayed, struck out or dismissed at the hearing. However, this argument has been rejected on the ground that an administration order is in the name of an interim measure, whereas a winding up order is final, so that different considerations apply and that it suffices that the creditor has a good, arguable case that a debt of sufficient amount is owing to him.[246] An application for the appointment of an administrator may be withdrawn only with the permission of the court.[247]

As we have seen, the holder of a qualifying floating charge enjoys a number of privileges,[248] several of which relate to court-appointed administration.

---

[241] Formerly, this was by way of petition.

[242] "Creditor" includes a contingent creditor and a prospective creditor (para.12(4)). See above, paras 4–26 and 4–27. A person claiming to be a creditor whose debt is disputed in good faith and on reasonable grounds is not a creditor for that purpose (*Re Simoco Digital UK Ltd, Thunderbird Industries LLC v Digital UK Ltd* [2004] 1 B.C.L.C. 541). This follows the principle adopted in relation to locus standi for the presentation of a winding up petition.

[243] Insolvency Act 1986 Sch.B1 para.12(1).

[244] Insolvency Act 1986 s.7(4)(b) as applied by Sch.B1 para.12(5).

[245] See above, para.5–13.

[246] *Hammonds v Pro-Fit Ltd* [2007] EWHC 1998 (Ch), *per* Warren J. at [51]–[53], citing the judgment of Saville L.J. in *Re MTI Trading Systems Ltd* [1998] B.C.C. 400 at 403, dealing with the rescission of an administration order.

[247] Insolvency Act 1986 Sch.B1 para.12(3); and *Corbett v Nysir UK Ltd* [2008] EWHC 2670 (Ch).

[248] Above, para.11–06.

(3) Procedure

The procedure for an administration application is laid down in Ch.2 of Pt II of the Insolvency Rules 1986. At the hearing, when any of the persons listed in r.2.12 may appear or be represented, the court may make the administration order sought, dismiss the application, adjourn the hearing conditionally or unconditionally, make an interim order, treat the application as a winding up petition and make any order which the court could make under s.125 of the Insolvency Act 1986, and/or make any other order the court thinks appropriate.[249] The appointment of the administrator[250] takes effect at a time appointed by the order or, where no time is appointed, when the order is made.[251]

7. EFFECT OF ADMINISTRATION

Filing of a notice of intention to appoint an administrator out of court or the making of an application for the appointment by the court operates to impose an interim moratorium pending the appointment taking effect.[252] Upon the administrator's appointment taking effect an even stronger moratorium is imposed.[253]

11–49

This freezing of creditors' rights is crucial to the viability of administration. It means that the administrator can get on with the business of restoring the company to profitability or otherwise managing its affairs for the benefit of the creditors as a whole without having constantly to fend off enforcement steps by individual creditors; in some cases, it provides an inducement to the holders of a floating charge not to appoint a receiver even where they are still entitled to do so; and it helps to ensure that negotiations for a voluntary arrangement are not scuppered by the precipitate action of a particular creditor wishing to jump the queue.

Vacation of office by administrative receiver

A further consequence of the administration order is that any administrative receiver must vacate office.[254] Upon so doing, the receiver is given a charge

11–50

---

[249] Insolvency Act 1986 Sch.B1 para.13(1).
[250] And accordingly the commencement of the administration. See Insolvency Act 1986 Sch.B1 para.1(2)(b).
[251] Insolvency Act 1986 Sch.B1 para.13(2).
[252] See below, paras 11–70 et seq.
[253] See below, paras 11–53 et seq.
[254] Insolvency Act 1986 Sch.B1 para.41(1). A receiver of part of the property need vacate office only if so required by the administrator (Sch.B1 para.41(2)).

on any property of the company in his custody or under his control for his remuneration, expenses and indemnity entitlement, in priority to his debenture holder's security,[255] and is released from any responsibility for payment of preferential debts.[256]

Moratoria

11–51   Under the Insolvency Act, there may be four types of moratoria:

(1)   a moratorium for the period during which the company is in administration[257];

(2)   An interim moratorium pending:

    (a)   the disposal of an application for an administration order; or

    (b)   the coming into effect of an out-of-court appointment of an administrator[258];

(3)   a moratorium in favour of a small, eligible company, being a company which is not undergoing any other insolvency process, pending a meeting to consider a CVA[259]; and

(4)   a moratorium under an approved CVA.

In addition, an informal workout typically has standstill provisions pending agreement on a restructuring plan.[260] As stated earlier,[261] the government is considering plans for a restructuring moratorium.

The first two kinds of moratoria featured in much the same form under the earlier statutory provisions embodied in ss.10 and 11 of the Insolvency Act 1986, so that case law on those provisions is relevant to the construction of the new provisions. These deal first with the moratorium that arises in administration and secondly with the interim moratorium that may be procured before the appointment of the administrator takes effect. Under the revised regime, as under the earlier statutory provisions, most of the constraints are common to the two moratoria, and to this extent the case law and analysis relating to what is now called an interim moratorium[262] are relevant to the moratorium arising on the appointment of the administrator and will thus be

---

[255] Insolvency Act 1986 Sch.B1 paras 41(3) and (4).
[256] Insolvency Act 1986 Sch.B1 para.41(4)(b).
[257] Insolvency Act 1986 Sch.B1 paras 42 and 43.
[258] Insolvency Act 1986 Sch.B1 para.44.
[259] Insolvency Act 1986 s.1A and Sch.A1.
[260] See below, para.12–06.
[261] Above, para.11–32.
[262] In the heading to para.44 of Sch.B1.

referred to in that context. The moratorium for small, eligible companies is subject to the complex provisions of Sch.A1 to the Insolvency Act and is mentioned only briefly later.[263] A moratorium is an almost universal feature of a concluded CVA, although its effect is confined to those bound by the CVA.[264]

Breach of moratorium

An enforcement measure taken in violation of the statutory moratorium is actionable in damages for breach of statutory duty.[265]   **11–52**

The effect of a moratorium depends on the category into which it falls.

(i) Moratorium during period of administration

There is a general moratorium on the enforcement of remedies when a company is in administration, whether the administration is out of court or on an administration order, without the consent of the administrator's consent or the permission of the court.[266] In such a case, the restrictions set out below apply. But they are merely procedural in their effect; they do not affect the company's capacity, under the administrator's management, to continue to trade and incur liabilities, and they do not address the existence of claims or alter or destroy rights but merely restrict their enforcement.[267] So the inability of the owner of goods supplied to the company on hire-purchase to enforce its right to repossess them does not affect his substantive law right to immediate possession so as to enable him to maintain conversion against a person interfering with that right.[268]   **11–53**

Schedule B1 to the Insolvency Act 1986 provides for two categories of moratorium during the period in which a company is in administration: a moratorium on insolvency proceedings and a moratorium on other legal process.[269]

---

[263] See below, para.12–39.

[264] See below, para.12–44.

[265] This was common ground in *Euro Commercial Leasing Ltd v Cartwright & Lewis* [1995] 2 B.C.L.C. 618, where, however, it was held that the breach was purely technical and no damage had resulted.

[266] Insolvency Act 1986 Sch.B1 paras 42 and 43. In granting permission, the court may impose a condition or requirement in connection with the transaction (Sch.B1, para.43(7)). Neither the administrator nor the court can dispense with the bar on winding up (Sch.B1 para.42) or the appointment of an administrative receiver (Sch.B1 para.43(6A)). However, this does not prevent conversion of the administration into a CVL under para.83 or interfere with the administrator's right to petition to wind-up the company under r.4.7(7) of the Insolvency Rules 1986.

[267] *Centre Reinsurance International Co v Curzon Insurance Ltd* [2006] 1 W.L.R. 2863, *per* Lord Hoffmann at [7]; and *Re Nortel Networks UK Ltd* [2010] B.P.I.R. 1003, *per* Norris J. at [23].

[268] *Barclays Mercantile Business Finance Ltd v Sibec Developments Ltd* [1993] B.C.L.C. 1077.

[269] See below.

No winding up

11–54   A winding up petition must be dismissed on the making of an administration order and must be suspended while the company is in administration following an appointment of an administrator by the holder of a qualifying floating charge.[270] No resolution may be passed for the winding up of the company,[271] nor may any winding up order be made except under s.124A (public interest), s.124B (SEs) or s.367 of the Financial Services and Markets Act 2000 (petition by Financial Services Authority).[272]

No appointment of administrative receiver

11–55   During the moratorium, no administrative receiver may be appointed.[273]

No enforcement of security

11–56   No step may be taken to enforce security over the company's property except:

(1)   with the consent of the administrator; or

(2)   with the permission of the court.[274]

Under the previous statutory provisions, these apparently straightforward provisions gave rise to a good deal of case law. At the level of interpretation, words and phrases that caused difficulty in what was formerly s.11(3)(c) include "steps . . . to enforce", "security" and "property". Beyond these questions of interpretation, the courts had to address the treatment of liens and rights of detention and felt constrained to lay down guidelines as to the grant or refusal of leave to proceed with remedial steps. All of these issues

---

[270] Insolvency Act 1986 Sch.B1 para.23(1). There is no comparable provision relating to an appointment by the company or directors under Sch.B1 para.22, since in contrast to a chargee under a qualifying floating charge they may not appoint an administrator during the pendency of a winding up petition (Sch.B1 para.25(a)).

[271] Insolvency Act 1986 Sch.B1 para.42(1) and (2). However, the administration may be converted into a company voluntary winding up (para.83) or a compulsory winding up on the petition of the creditor (Insolvency Rules 1986 r.4.7(7)).

[272] Insolvency Act 1986 Sch.B1 paras 42(1)–(4). SE is the abbreviation for Societas Europaea.

[273] Insolvency Act 1986 Sch.B1 para.43(6A).

[274] Insolvency Act 1986 Sch.B1 para.43(2). This restriction does not apply to a market charge (Companies Act 1989 s.175(1)), a collateral security charge (Financial Markets and Insolvency (Settlement Finality) Regulations 1999 reg.19(1)) or a security interest created or otherwise arising under a financial collateral arrangement (Financial Collateral Arrangements (No. 2)) Regulations 2003, SI 2003/3226, reg. 8.

arose in one form or another in *Bristol Airport Plc v Powdrill*,[275] in which the facts were as follows:

> Paramount Airways went into administration owing substantial debts, including landing fees and fuel charges owed to Bristol Airport in respect of aircraft which Paramount held under a sub-lease. During the course of the administration Bristol Airport applied to the court for leave to detain two of Paramount's aircraft under s.88 of the Civil Aviation Act 1982. Thereupon Birmingham Airport, without obtaining leave, parked a lorry loaded with concrete in front of another aircraft operated by Paramount and served the captain with a lien notice. That airport then applied for leave to detain the aircraft. At the time of these events the administration was substantially advanced and a proposed sale of the business on terms beneficial to the general body of creditors had been approved in principle by the creditors but could not be implemented if the aircraft were detained. On the substantive hearing of the applications the administrator asserted that the exercise of the lien came either within s.11(3)(c) as enforcement of a security or within s.11(3)(d) as 'other proceedings' or the levy of a distress, and that leave should not be given. For the airports it was argued (a) that the aircraft were not Paramount's 'property', since they were merely held under a sub-lease; (b) that the statutory right of detention was not a 'lien or other security' but a statutory right possessing distinctive features; (c) that if the right of detention were a lien, its exercise was not 'a step taken to enforce' a security but an act by which the security was created or perfected; (d) that the detention did not constitute 'other proceedings' or the levy of a distress.

> Harman J. rejected all four arguments and refused to give leave to detain the aircraft on the ground that this would have the effect of giving the airports an advantage over other creditors and would prevent a sale of the business and that the airports, having taken advantage of the administration proceedings, ought not to be allowed to detain the aircraft. This decision was affirmed by the Court of Appeal.

We shall revert to this case in examining each of the individual elements in para.43(2) of Sch.B1.

(1) "security"

Security is defined as "any mortgage, charge, lien, or other security".[276] The nature of mortgages, charges and liens is well known.[277] A mortgage is a   **11–57**

---

[275] [1990] Ch. 744, affirming the decision of Harman J. in [1990] B.C.C. 130 sub nom. *Re Paramount Airways Ltd*.
[276] Insolvency Act 1986 s.248(b).
[277] For detailed descriptions, see *Goode on Legal Problems of Credit and Security*, 2008, Ch.1; and *Goode on Commercial Law*, edited by Ewan McKendrick, 4th edn (2009), Ch.22.

consensual transfer of ownership by way of security. A charge is an incumbrance, a right vested in one person to look to the proceeds of another's property for satisfaction of a debt due. It may be created by agreement or law. A lien is a right to retain possession of another's property pending payment of sums due to the person in possession, the latter having acquired possession otherwise than for the purpose of security. It too may be created by agreement or law.

What is meant by "other security"? Clearly, this includes a pledge, the only remaining form of consensual security known to English law.[278] It also extends to non-consensual charges, liens and rights of detention, for example, the statutory right under s.88 of the Civil Aviation Act 1982 to detain an aircraft for payment of airport charges[279] or the statutory right of retention of an unpaid seller under the Sale of Goods Act 1979.[280] There had previously been a division of judicial opinion as to whether a landlord's right of re-entry under a lease fell within the phrase "other security". The balance of authority had swung sharply against this,[281] but the insertion of a separate provision prohibiting a landlord from exercising a right of entry without the administrator's consent or the court's permission[282] has foreclosed this issue. The same applies to the provision precluding repossession under a hire-purchase agreement.[283] We may, therefore, conclude that "security" is used in its strict sense to denote a mortgage, pledge or consensual or non-consensual charge, lien or other right of detention or retention, and nothing beyond these.

(2) "No step may be taken to enforce"

11–58 It should be observed that the phrase used in para.43(2) of Sch.B1 to the Insolvency Act is not "no security shall be enforced" but "no step may be taken to enforce security". This suggests that steps preparatory to the actual act of enforcement may fall within the prohibition. What is not clear is what constitutes the taking of steps to enforce a security. The appointment of an administrative receiver would be one such case but is the subject of a separate prohibition with which neither the administrator nor the court can dispense.[284] On the other hand, the appointment of a receiver who is not an administrative receiver would fall within the present restriction as a step to

---

[278] See *Goode on Legal Problems of Credit and Security*, 2008, para.1–42; and *Re Cosslett (Contractors) Ltd* [1998] Ch. 495, *per* Millett L.J. at 508.
[279] *Bristol Airport Plc v Powdrill* [1990] Ch. 744.
[280] Sale of Goods Act 1979 s.41.
[281] The authorities were reviewed by Neuberger J. in *Re Lomax Leisure Ltd* [2000] B.C.C. 352.
[282] Insolvency Act 1986 Sch.B1 para.43(4).
[283] Insolvency Act 1986 Sch.B1 para.43(3).
[284] Insolvency Act 1986 Sch.B1 para.43(6A). See below, para.11–68.

enforce security over the company's property. It has been held that the mere assertion of a lien or right of detention constitutes enforcement for the purpose of what is now para.43(2).[285]

There are other cases in which there has been no clear ruling. Suppose, for example, that a loan is made to the company which is repayable on demand and that the loan is secured by a debenture which allows the debenture holder to appoint an administrative receiver or to take possession of or sell the mortgaged property if payment of any money secured by the debenture is not made on demand. Does the making of a demand constitute the taking of a step to enforce the security? The point was mooted but not answered by Millett J. in *Re Olympia & York Canary Wharf Ltd*[286] and again in *Barclays Mercantile Business Finance Ltd v Sibec Developments Ltd*,[287] where he regarded the point as "a difficult one" but unnecessary for his decision since the proceedings were against the administrators, not the company. It seems clear that "step" is not confined to legal proceedings or process, for these are specifically dealt with in para.43(6) of Sch.B1 but embraces any act of enforcement, such as the act of repossession, the act of sale, etc. Does it also extend to preparatory acts, and if so, must these be acts which are specifically referable to enforcement or does it suffice that they are acts which in themselves are not so referable but lay the foundation for enforcement? It is thought that "steps to enforce" is narrower than steps towards enforcement and denotes acts which in some degree interfere with the company's enjoyment of its property or of property in its possession or inhibit the administrator's use of such property in the conduct of the business. The underlying purpose of para.43 is to preclude the taking of steps which might impair the administrator's ability to manage the company, use its property and carry through the purpose or purposes for which the administration order was made free from interference by creditors.[288] The assertion of a lien or right of detention is plainly a factor which inhibits the administrator's use of the property.[289] So too is a threat to enforce a consensual security interest. Similarly, where a debenture provides for security over, say, the company's book debts, a demand for payment addressed to the company's debtors by the debenture holder or his receiver would, it is thought, constitute a step to enforce the security, for it may inhibit the ability of the administrator to collect in the debts himself and represents an interference in his management of the company's assets.

---

[285] *Bristol Airport Plc v Powdrill* [1990] Ch. 744; and *Euro Commercial Leasing v Cartwright & Lewis* [1995] 2 B.C.L.C. 618.

[286] [1993] B.C.L.C. 453 at 454.

[287] [1992] 1 W.L.R. 1253 at 1259.

[288] See *Bristol Airport Plc v Powdrill*, cited above n.285, *per* Sir Nicolas Browne-Wilkinson V.C. at 758.

[289] See above, para.11–57.

11–59   By contrast, preparatory steps which do not have this effect are outside the mischief against which para.43 is aimed. Accordingly, the service of a demand on the company for payment or a notice terminating a contract or making time of performance of the essence is not, it is thought, a step to enforce a security, even if exclusively referable to an intention to do so rather than simply to trigger a payment obligation on the part of the company or a surety, since such a demand or notice has no impact whatsoever on the company's enjoyment of its property or the administrator's management of it. Again, the service of a notice crystallising a floating charge is not a step to enforce security, since its effect is simply to convert the charge into a fixed charge, and the mere holding of a fixed charge is not itself a step to enforce the charge.

It follows from what has been said above that a mortgagee or chargee of book debts or other receivables who without the consent of the administrator or leave of the court collects or demands payment from the account debtors is taking steps to enforce security over the company's property in breach of the prohibition. The position is otherwise where the collection or demand is by a person who has bought the debts or other receivables, for he is the owner of them, not merely a secured creditor, and they are no longer the property of the company. So a factoring company which has purchased receivables under a factoring agreement with the debtor company remains entitled to collect the debts from the account debtors.

The inclusion of liens in the statutory prohibition creates no difficulty in the case of equitable liens, such as the lien of the unpaid vendor of land, for these do not depend on possession and are enforceable by sale.[290] But the prohibition does raise a problem for the holder of a possessory lien, whose only right under the lien, in the absence of an agreement or statutory provision to the contrary, is to retain possession of the goods over which the lien is asserted and whose lien is lost once possession has been surrendered.[291] How, then, can the lienee preserve his lien without detaining the goods after demand by the administrator for their surrender? The conundrum was neatly solved in *Bristol Airport Plc v Powdrill*,[292] where Woolf L.J. drew an analogy with the tort of conversion. He pointed out[293] that a person in possession of goods is not guilty of conversion or other unlawful interference with the goods merely because he does not hand them over immediately he receives a demand from the person entitled to possession. He is entitled to reasonable time to verify the other person's right to possession. Similarly, a person entitled to a possessory lien is not to be regarded as taking steps to enforce it unless he makes an unqualified refusal to hand it over. This is not

---

[290] See 68 *Halsbury's Laws*, 5th edn (2008), para.855.
[291] *Halsbury's Laws*, paras 546 and 550.
[292] [1990] Ch. 744.
[293] ibid at 769.

the case where he invites the administrator to consent to the exercise of the lien and indicates that in the absence of such consent he will apply to the court promptly for leave and does so. His continued possession meanwhile is not an unlawful enforcement of the lien, nor does it constitute a contempt of court. Moreover, one would in general expect the administrator to give his consent pending an application to the court. But if the lienee simply refuses to hand over the goods and puts no proposals to the administrator, the court will order delivery up to the administrator.[294] What usually happens in practice is that the lienee releases the goods from the lien on condition that the security interest attaches to the proceeds of sale.[295]

(3) "Enforce"

In the context of an administration moratorium, as opposed to an interim moratorium, it would have been more accurate if the prohibition had been on the realisation of security rather than its enforcement, for the prohibition does not apply where the administrator consents to the step that is being taken, and if consent is given there is no "enforcement". The word "enforce" has greater significance in the context of the interim moratorium.[296]

11–60

(4) "Security over the company's property"

"Property" is defined as including:

11–61

"... money, goods, things in action, land and every description of property wherever situated and also obligations and every description of interest, whether present or future or vested or contingent, arising out of, or incidental to, property".[297]

In the words of Sir Nicolas Browne-Wilkinson V.C. in *Bristol Airport Plc v Powdrill*: "It is hard to think of a wider definition of property."[298] Nevertheless, it was argued in that case that aircraft held by the company on lease did not constitute property and that the company's rights were purely

---

[294] *Re Sabre International Products Ltd* [1991] B.C.L.C. 470.
[295] The nature of the interest will usually change from lien to charge, because a lien, like a pledge, cannot be taken over intangibles. See *Goode on Legal Problems of Credit and Security*, 2008, para.1–67.
[296] See below, para.11–72.
[297] Insolvency Act 1986 s.436. For a detailed discussion, see above, paras 6-03 *et seq.*
[298] [1990] Ch. 744 at 759. See also above, Ch.6, in relation to what constitutes an asset of the company.

contractual. At first instance, Harman J. had held that a chattel in respect of which the company had what were strictly contractual rights was part of its property.[299] On appeal, the Vice-Chancellor reached the same result by a different route, holding that since each aircraft had unique features peculiar to itself, a court would order specific performance of a contract to lease an aircraft, and it followed from this that the "lessee" had an equitable interest in it.[300] However, neither explanation seems wholly satisfactory. Purely contractual rights are, of course, a species of property—the statutory definition expressly includes choses in action—but in the case in question, the security was asserted over a physical asset, an aircraft, not over the contractual rights in it. No doubt it was for this reason that the Vice-Chancellor sought to establish the existence of an in rem right to the aircraft. But his solution is difficult to reconcile with the fundamental distinction between land and chattels. A lease of land confers an estate on the lessee, so that an agreement for a lease does indeed create an equitable estate. But the doctrine of estates does not apply to chattels. An agreement for a lease of chattels is merely an agreement to give possession, and English law does not recognise any concept of equitable possession.[301] Such an agreement confers no in rem rights on the intended lessee at all; its effect is purely contractual. On taking delivery, the lessee acquires a limited legal interest,[302] but this derives from his possession, not from the agreement.[303] Accordingly, it is both simpler and more accurate to treat the lessee's in rem rights as derived from its possession of the aircraft under the leasing agreement, a possession which conferred on it a limited legal interest.

No repossession of goods under a hire-purchase agreement

11–62 A further effect of the administration is that no steps may be taken to repossess goods in the company's possession under any hire-purchase agreement, except with the consent of the administrator or the permission of the court.[304] Again, we encounter definitional issues.

---

[299] Sub nom. *Re Paramount Airways Ltd* [1990] B.C.C. 130 at 136.
[300] [1990] Ch. 744 at 759.
[301] See *Goode on Commercial Law*, 2009, p.38, n.277 and pp.44 and 669.
[302] *Goode on Commercial Law*, 2009, pp.33 and 46–47.
[303] *Goode on Commercial Law*, 2009, pp.34–35.
[304] Insolvency Act 1986 Sch.B1 para.43(3). For the administrator's right to use the goods while the remedy of repossession is suspended, see below, para.11–108.

(1) "Hire-purchase agreement"

"Hire-purchase agreement"[305] includes a conditional sale agreement,[306] a chattel leasing agreement[307] and a retention of title agreement.[308] Section 251 of the Insolvency Act defines a retention of title agreement as:

11–63

"... an agreement for the sale of goods to a company, being an agreement—

(a) which does not constitute a charge on the goods sold but

(b) under which, if the seller is not paid and the company is wound up, the seller will have priority over all other creditors of the company as respects the goods and any property representing the goods."

This definition is distinctly odd and almost certainly unnecessary. Limb (a) appears to be concerned to exclude agreements which in form are sale and repurchase or sale and hire-purchase/lease-back agreements but which in substance are mortgages or charges,[309] but if this is the case it is otiose, since if an instrument is in law a mortgage or charge it cannot be a sale agreement and in any event security is already covered by para.43(2). Limb (b) overlaps the definition of conditional sale agreement and does so in an unsatisfactory manner, because its reference to priority "over all other creditors as respects the goods and any other property representing the goods" seeks to ascribe to a sale agreement a legal effect which it does not necessarily have, since whether a seller has priority depends on legal priority rules. There may, for example, be a person with a stronger title to the goods themselves, whilst if any retention of title clause has been extended to cover proceeds, this extension will in most cases create a charge over book debts which will be void if not registered under Pt 25 of the Companies Act 2006,[310] and even where this is not the case a subsequent assignment of the proceeds to a factor who gives notice of assignment to the account debtors will usually give the factor priority.[311] It is hard to think of a retention of title agreement which does not fall within the definition of conditional sale agreement.[312]

---

[305] Which for other purposes is as defined by the Consumer Credit Act 1974 s.189(1) (Insolvency Act 1986 s.436). See below, n.312.

[306] As so defined (ibid.).

[307] That is, an agreement for the bailment of goods which is capable of subsisting for more than three months (Insolvency Act 1986 s.251).

[308] Insolvency Act 1986 Sch.B1 para.111(1).

[309] See *Goode on Commercial Law*, 2009, pp.645 et seq.

[310] *Goode on Legal Problems of Credit and Security*, 2008, paras 3–23 et seq.

[311] Op. cit., pp.795–796.

[312] One might add that the way in which the definitions have been distributed leaves much to be desired. One of the drafting features of the Consumer Credit Act 1974, which could usefully have been adopted in the insolvency legislation, is that it gathers together in a single section, s.189(1), all of the definitions, whether given in that section or by way of cross-reference to

(2) "In the company's possession"

11–64   In *Re Atlantic Computer Systems Plc*,[313] the Court of Appeal had to consider whether a lessee of equipment which it had sub-let and which was in the physical possession of the sub-lessee was nevertheless to be considered in possession of the equipment itself for the purpose of the statutory provisions. The court had no difficulty in concluding that it was, and that repossession from the sub-lessee would constitute repossession from the lessee so as to require the court's leave. In prohibiting repossession of goods in the possession of a company in administration, s.11(3)(c) of the Act[314] was concerned with relations between the lessor and the company. As between the lessor and the company, the latter was in possession of the goods, and it did not matter whether the goods remained on the company's premises, were entrusted to others for repair or were sub-let by the company as part of its trade to others.[315]

(3) "Under a hire-purchase agreement"

11–65   We have seen earlier that "hire-purchase agreement" has an extended meaning. In *Re David Meek Plant Ltd*,[316] the question arose whether goods could still be considered in the possession of a company "under a hire-purchase agreement" after the agreement had been terminated. It was held to be sufficient that the possession of the goods was attributable to, or derived its legal origin at some time from, a hire-purchase agreement; it was not necessary that the agreement was still subsisting. This is plainly correct.

---

definitions elsewhere. So to find whether a term is a defined term, it is necessary to look only at s.189(1). By contrast, the Insolvency Act has interpretation provisions for the first group of Parts, a separate set of interpretation provisions for the second group of Parts and a third set for expressions used generally and for two other terms, not to mention definitional cross-references to other legislation. Take, e.g. the reference to "hire-purchase agreement" in para.43(1) of Sch.B1 to the Insolvency Act 1986. To find the meaning of this, one might suppose one starts with s.436 of the Act, which does not itself define the term but routes one to the definition in s.189(1) of the Consumer Credit Act 1974. That, however, is a false trail, because it turns out that in para.43(1) of Sch.B1 the draftsman is using the phrase "hire-purchase agreement" not in its normal sense as defined by the Consumer Credit Act but as a shorthand embracing a conditional sale agreement, a chattel leasing agreement and a retention of title agreement (para.111(1)). To find the definition of "conditional sale agreement", one goes back to s.436 and thence once again to s.189(1) of the Consumer Credit Act. For the final step, discovery of the meanings of "chattel leasing agreement" and "retention of title agreement", it is necessary to turn to s.251 of the Insolvency Act. Surely our legislative drafting can be better than this!

[313] [1992] Ch. 505.
[314] See now Insolvency Act 1986 Sch.B1 para.43(2) and (3).
[315] [1992] Ch. 505, *per* Nicholls L.J. at 532. See also *Fashoff (UK) Ltd v Linton* [2008] B.C.C. 542.
[316] [1994] 1 B.C.L.C. 680.

No exercise of a right of forfeiture by re-entry

A landlord may not exercise a right of forfeiture by peaceable re-entry[317] in **11–66** relation to premises let to the company except with the administrator's consent or court's permission.[318] This provision, which was not contained in the original legislation, was inserted to resolve doubts as to whether a right of forfeiture was a security.[319] It is thought that the word "premises" is used in its legal rather than popular sense so as to include not only buildings and land with buildings but also land on its own.[320] Where the lease provides that it can be forfeited by notice in stated events, there is nothing to preclude the landlord from terminating the lease in this way, for this is not a forfeiture by re-entry. However, the landlord cannot proceed to enforce the forfeiture by action or re-entry without the consent of the administrator or the permission of the court.

The restriction on repossession or peaceable re-entry has no application to a proprietary claim which does not constitute a security interest and does not depend on retention of title under a supply agreement but is based, for example, on the fact that the company is wrongfully in possession or holds the property as the claimant's agent with a duty to surrender it. But if peaceful repossession or re-entry is not possible, it will be necessary to have the permission of the court or the consent of the administrator to bring proceedings.[321]

No legal process

No legal process (including legal proceedings, execution and distress) may be **11–67** instituted or continued against the company or company's property except with the consent of the administrator or the permission of the court.[322] This clarifies but also expands the previous restriction, where the preponderance of judicial opinion had been that it did not cover distress.[323] The original provisions contained in s.11 of the Insolvency Act stated that no "other" proceedings could be taken, and this led the Scottish Court of Session to conclude, in *Air Ecosse Ltd v Civil Aviation Authority*,[324] that "other proceedings"

---

[317] Forfeiture by legal proceedings is separately barred under para.43(6). See below.
[318] Insolvency Act 1986 Sch.B1 para.43(4).
[319] See above, para.11–57.
[320] See, e.g. *Bracey v Read* [1963] Ch. 88.
[321] See below, para.11–67.
[322] Insolvency Act 1986 Sch.B1 para.43(6).
[323] *Re Olympia & York Canary Wharf Ltd* [1993] B.C.C. 154, in which Millett J. declined to follow the decision of Harman J. on this point in *Exchange Travel Agency Ltd v Triton Property Trust Plc* [1991] B.C.L.C. 396; and *McMullen & Sons Ltd v Cerrone* [1994] B.C.L.C. 156, a decision on s.252 of the Insolvency Act.
[324] 1987 S.L.T. 751.

had to be construed *ejusdem generis* with the preceding provisions and thus as limited to proceedings by a creditor of the company which were in some way related to a debt due from the company. That view has not gained acceptance in England, where it has been held that "legal process" is not limited to proceedings by a creditor and that the phrase covers not only civil proceedings in a court of law, including advertisement of a winding up petition[325] and a tenant's application for a new lease under Pt II of the Landlord and Tenant Act 1954,[326] but criminal proceedings[327] and any other proceedings of a judicial or quasi-judicial nature, including proceedings before an employment appeal tribunal,[328] arbitration proceedings,[329] proceedings for revocation of a patent,[330] proceedings before the regulatory panel of the Gambling Commission for revocation of a licence under the Gambling Act 2005[331] and an application for an adjudication under s.108 of the Housing Grants, Construction and Regeneration Act 1996.[332] Presumably also an English court would take the view that an application to the Civil Aviation Authority by an airline's competitor to revoke the airline's air transport licence under the Civil Aviation Act 1982 would also constitute a legal process,[333] and so, by the same token, would proceedings by the Director General of Fair Trading to revoke a licence granted under the Consumer Credit Act 1974. However, an application for leave to register a charge out of time is not a proceeding "against the company or property of the company", for it could equally well be made by the company, and the court would not compel the absurdity of an application for leave to make an application for leave to register out of time.[334] Again, the service of a contractual notice, such as a notice making time of the essence or terminating a contract for a repudiatory breach, does not constitute a legal process.[335]

The prohibition against legal process does not apply to proceedings instituted in a foreign court,[336] but this does not preclude the court in an appropriate case from exercising its general jurisdiction to protect the assets of a company in administration, as of a company in liquidation, and to restrain acts

---

[325] *Re A Company (No.001992 of 1988)* [1989] B.C.L.C. 9.
[326] *Somerfield Stores Ltd v Spring (Sutton Coldfield) Ltd* [2011] L. & T.R. 8.
[327] *Re Rhondda Waste Disposal Ltd* [2001] Ch. 57.
[328] *Carr v British International Helicopters Ltd* [1994] 2 B.C.L.C. 474; and *Re Divine Solutions (UK) Ltd* [2004] B.C.C. 325.
[329] *Re Paramount Airways Ltd* [1990] Ch. 744, *per* Sir Nicolas Browne-Wilkinson V.C. at 765; and *Carr v British International Helicopters Ltd* [1994] 2 B.C.L.C. 474, *per* Lord Coulsfield at 482.
[330] *Biosource Technologies Inc v Axis Genetics Plc* [2000] 1 B.C.L.C. 286, where it was also held that the restrictions on enforcement were not confined to proceedings by creditors.
[331] *Hudson v Gambling Commission* [2010] All E.R. (D) 59.
[332] *A. Straume (UK) Ltd v Bradlor Developments Ltd* [2000] B.C.C. 333.
[333] By contrast with the decision of the Scottish Court of Session in *Air Ecosse Ltd v Civil Aviation Authority*, 1987 S.L.T. 751.
[334] *Re Barrow Borough Transport Ltd* [1990] Ch. 227.
[335] *Re Olympia & York Canary Wharf Ltd*, cited above n.323.
[336] *Bloom v Harms Offshore AHT "Taurus" Gmbh & Co KG* [2010] Ch. 187.

interfering with the administration, by granting injunctive relief against the pursuit of foreign proceedings by a creditor, although the doctrine of comity would normally make it inappropriate to do so except where the creditor had been guilty of oppressive, vexatious or otherwise unfair or improper conduct.[337]

No appointment of an administrative receiver

While a company is in administration, no administrative receiver may be appointed.[338] The position thus differs from that applicable for an interim moratorium.[339] At first sight, this provision seems unnecessary, since it would be covered by the more general restriction on the taking of steps to enforce security over the company's property.[340] However, the appointment of an administrative receiver must be treated as a distinct category since the bar is absolute; there is no provision for an appointment with the consent of the administrator or the permission of the court, for the obvious reason that such an appointment would prevent the administrator from fulfilling his functions. The prohibition does not apply to other kinds of receiver. The appointment of these is covered by the prohibition of steps to enforce security,[341] but may be made with the consent of the administrator or the permission of the court. There may, for example, be cases where a creditor can show a legitimate interest in the appointment of a receiver over a particular asset or class of assets outweighing the interest of the general body of creditors. That could not be the case on the appointment of an administrative receiver, for since by definition he is receiver of the whole or substantially the whole of the company's property,[342] his appointment would completely stultify the administrator's functions.

11–68

Self-help remedies unaffected by the moratorium

While there is a general prohibition on the institution of proceedings without the consent of the administrator or the permission of the court,[343] the only self-help remedies falling within para.43 of Sch.B1 are those mentioned earlier, namely the taking of steps to enforce a security or to repossess goods in the company's possession under a hire-purchase agreement, the exercise of a right to forfeit a lease by peaceable re-entry and the levying of a distress. So the moratorium does not cover exercise of a right of set-off or combination of

11–69

---

[337] *Bloom v Harms Offshore.* In that case, the creditors' conduct had been such as to lead the court to grant relief, albeit more limited than that applied for.

[338] Insolvency Act 1986 Sch.B1 para.43(6A).

[339] See below, para.11–71.

[340] Insolvency Act 1986 Sch.B1 para.43(2). See above, para.11–56.

[341] Insolvency Act 1986 Sch.B1 para.43(2). See above, para.11–58.

[342] Insolvency Act 1986 s.29(2).

[343] See paras 11–67 et seq.

accounts, or a right to terminate or rescind a contract, accelerate monetary liability under a contract or give any other contractual notice.

It is not uncommon for contracts with a company to contain a provision terminating the contract, or empowering the other party to terminate it, on the company going into administration or an application being made for an administration order. This has caused concern among insolvency practitioners, who consider that such clauses are detrimental to the administration procedure and should be rendered void as contrary to the public interest. But the rule that contractual provisions for the termination of a contract on winding up are valid[344] applies equally to administration.[345]

(ii) Interim moratorium pending entry of the company into administration

11–70 Whether a company enters into administration by an out-of-court appointment of an administrator or by court order, there will inevitably be some delay between the time the process leading to an administration is initiated and the time the administration begins, except where, in the case of out-of-court appointment, there is no one to whom notice has to be given under para.26 of Sch.B1. The original statutory provisions, embodied in s.10 of the Insolvency Act, imposed a moratorium between the time a petition for an administration order was presented and the time the order was made or the petition dismissed. The revised provisions are to similar effect,[346] but they are extended to cover out-of-court administration. Where no notice is required under para.26, the appointor can proceed immediately to file a notice of appointment, so that in such a case no interim moratorium is necessary or available.

Whether the administrator is to be appointed by the court or out of court, the interim moratorium merely freezes enforcement measures *against* the company; it does not affect the directors' powers of management or the company's ability to dispose of assets, whether outright or by way of security, or to take legal proceedings itself.

Moratorium pending disposal of administration application

11–71 Where an administration application has been made and has not yet been granted or dismissed or has been granted but has not yet taken effect,[347] the

---

[344] A matter discussed above, para.7–05.

[345] *Perpetual Trustee Co Ltd v BNY Corporate Trustee Services Ltd* [2010] Ch. 347, discussed above, paras 7–13–7–22.

[346] Although the petition has been replaced by an application and where an order is made the relevant time is when it takes effect, not when it is made. See below, para.11–74.

[347] This is a reference to the fact that an administrator's appointment, and thus the commencement of the administration (Insolvency Act 1986 Sch.B1 para.1(2)(b)), takes effect at a time appointed by the order or where no time is appointed then when the order is made (Sch.B1 para.13(2)). Hence, the court may fix a future time for the appointment to come into effect.

interim moratorium imposed by paras 42 and 43 (ignoring any reference to the administrator's consent) comes into play until the application is dismissed or the order takes effect,[348] whereupon the moratorium provisions already discussed, which for brevity will be described as "the full moratorium", become applicable directly under the provisions of those paragraphs. The scope of the interim moratorium is somewhat narrower than that of the full moratorium in two respects, reflecting the favoured position of the holder of a qualifying floating charge. First, if there is an administrative receiver of the company when the administration application is made, the provisions of paras 42 and 43 do not begin to apply until the person by or on behalf of whom the receiver was appointed consents to the making of the administration order.[349] So the administration application does not preclude the appointment of an administrative receiver, and indeed to make the position crystal clear, para.44(6) expressly so provides. Secondly, the making of the application does not prevent or require the court's permission for the appointment of an administrator by the holder of a qualifying floating charge or the appointment of an administrative receiver (where still permitted) or the carrying out by him (whenever appointed) of his functions.[350] This must by necessary implication cover all acts preparatory to the receiver's appointment, for otherwise the dispensation given by para.44(6) of Sch.B1 would be rendered nugatory.

Since paras 42 to 44 of Sch.B1 are concerned only with the situation arising between the administration application and its disposal, during which time no administrator is yet in post, it is necessary to say a few words about the effect of the company's acquiescence in acts by the solvent party to exercise his rights.

(1) Enforcement of security

In relation to security, it is only the taking of steps to *enforce* the security that is prohibited, from which it would seem to follow that the secured creditor remains free to take possession of the security or to realise it if he obtains the company's consent, given through its duly authorised officer or, if the company is under interim management pursuant to an order under para.13 of Sch.B1 to the Act, the interim manager.

11–72

(2) "Repossess"

In contrast to the provisions relating to security, the restriction on repossession of goods held under a hire-purchase agreement is not expressed to be

11–73

---

[348] Insolvency Act 1986 Sch.B1 para.44(5).
[349] Insolvency Act 1986 Sch.B1 para.44(6).
[350] Insolvency Act 1986 Sch.B1 para.44(7).

confined to *enforcement* of a right to repossess and at first sight appears to prevent even a repossession effected with the company's consent. But it is thought that the restriction is intended to be limited to enforcement measures. There is no rational policy reason for distinguishing the exercise of title-retention rights from the exercise of security rights, and if the company, being still under its own management pending the hearing of the petition, wishes to surrender the goods, it seems pointless to involve the owner in the expense of an application to the court. It may be that the draftsman, in defining hire-purchase agreement and conditional sale agreement by reference to the Consumer Credit Act 1974, considered the word "repossess" to have the same meaning as "recover possession" in s.90(2) of that Act but s.173(3) of the Consumer Credit Act makes it clear that repossession with the debtor's consent given at the time is lawful.

In either case, given the underlying purpose of the interim moratorium, which is to preserve the company's assets pending completion of steps to put the company into administration, the court is likely to look carefully at the reality of the company's consent where it is not under interim management, and a "consent" obtained under threat of other action, such as the presentation of a winding up petition or the appointment of a receiver, may well be disregarded as not being a true consent.

Moratorium pending coming into effect of out-of-court appointment

11–74   The interim moratorium also comes into operation, and with the same effect, where a notice of intention to appoint an administrator has been filed by the holder of a qualifying floating charge or by the company or its directors. In the case of a notice filed by the holder of the charge, the moratorium lasts until the administrator's appointment takes effect or the period of five business days beginning with the date of filing expires without an administrator having been appointed.[351] In the case of a notice filed by the company or its directors, the moratorium continues until the administrator's appointment takes effect or the period of 10 business days beginning with the date of filing expires without an administrator having been appointed.[352]

As pointed out earlier, neither the administration application nor any resulting administration order affects substantive rights; its impact is on the exercise of remedies.[353] Similarly, filing of the notice of intention to appoint by the holder of a qualifying floating charge or by the company or the direc-

---

[351] Once the administrator has been appointed, the full moratorium applies.
[352] Insolvency Act 1986 Sch.B1 paras 28(2) and 44(4).
[353] See above, para.11–53.

tors leaves the directors' management powers unimpaired.[354] Further, in contrast to the position where a winding up petition is presented,[355] dispositions of the company's property made after the filing of an administration application do not require validation by the court.[356]

(iii) Interim moratorium pending proposal for a CVA for a small, eligible company

This is considered later in the discussion of CVAs.[357]   **11–75**

(iv) The court's approach to the exercise of discretion

The grant of leave during an interim moratorium

All of the decisions on the grant of leave to enforce remedies under the old   **11–76**
legislation concerned s.11(3) of the Insolvency Act, dealing with moratoria arising on the making of an administration order.[358] The relevant considerations are discussed below. What is not clear is the extent to which the same considerations apply on an application for leave made prior to administration and whether a further distinction is to be made between out-of-court appointments that have not yet taken effect and undisposed of administration applications. It is evident that in all cases the onus is on the applicant for leave to make out a case. But given that no administrator is yet in the saddle and that the information available to the court is likely to be less detailed than when the company has gone into administration, it is thought that the court will be more reluctant to grant leave to enforce than when an administrator has taken office, particularly since most appointments will be out of court and the interval between the filing of a notice of intention to appoint and the appointment becoming effective will in many cases be relatively short, so that the court may consider that on balance the delay imposed on the creditor by refusing leave is outweighed by the desirability of allowing the administrator, when in post, an opportunity to consider to what extent the interests of the general body of creditors will be adversely affected by the

---

[354] But once the application has come before the court (which it may on an abridged notice), it may make an interim order which could, amongst other things, restrict the exercise of a power of the directors and make provision conferring a discretion on a person qualified to act as an insolvency practitioner in relation to the company (Insolvency Act 1986 Sch.B1 para.13(3)). Under this power, the court could appoint an interim manager.
[355] See Insolvency Act 1986 s.127, and below.
[356] But see n.354, above.
[357] Below, para.12–39.
[358] This is now to be found in para.43 of Sch.B1, which applies whether the administration is by court order or out-of-court.

grant of leave. For this purpose, there seems to be no reason to distinguish prospective out-of-court appointments from prospective appointments by the court.

The grant of leave when the company is in administration

11–77   In deciding whether to grant leave under para.43 of Sch.B1 to take steps to enforce security, etc. and if so, on what terms, the court will have in mind the list of guidelines helpfully, if reluctantly, supplied by Nicholls L.J. in *Re Atlantic Computer Systems Plc*.[359]

> "(1) It is in every case for the person who seeks leave to make out a case for him to be given leave.
>
> (2) The prohibition in section 11(3)(c) and (d)[360] is intended to assist the company, under the management of the administrator, to achieve the purpose for which the administration order was made. If granting leave to a lessor of land or the hirer of goods (a "lessor") to exercise his proprietary rights and repossess his land or goods is unlikely to impede the achievement of that purpose, leave should normally be given.
>
> (3) In other cases when a lessor seeks possession the court has to carry out a balancing exercise, balancing the legitimate interests of the lessor and the legitimate interests of the other creditors of the company: see *per* Peter Gibson J. in *Royal Trust Bank v Buchler* [1989] B.C.L.C. 130, 135. The metaphor employed here, for want of a better, is that of scales and weights. Lord Wilberforce adverted to the limitations of this metaphor in *Science Research Council v Nassáe* [1980] A.C. 1028, 1067. It must be kept in mind that the exercise under section 11 is not a mechanical one; each case calls for an exercise in judicial judgment, in which the court seeks to give effect to the purpose of the statutory provisions, having regard to the parties' interests and all the circumstances of the case. As already noted, the purpose of the prohibition is to enable or assist the company to achieve the object for which the administration order was made. The purpose of the power to give leave is to enable the court to relax the prohibition where it would be inequitable for the prohibition to apply.
>
> (4)   In carrying out the balancing exercise great importance, or weight, is normally to be given to the proprietary interests of the lessor. Sir Nicolas Browne-Wilkinson V.-C. observed in *Bristol Airport Plc v Powdrill* [1990] Ch. 744, 767D–E that, so far as possible, the

---

[359] [1992] Ch. 505 at 542–544.
[360] See now Sch.B1 para.43.

administration procedure should not be used to prejudice those who were secured creditors when the administration order was made in lieu of a winding up order. The same is true regarding the proprietary interests of a lessor. The underlying principle here is that an administration for the benefit of unsecured creditors should not be conducted at the expense of those who have proprietary rights which they are seeking to exercise, save to the extent that this may be unavoidable and even then this will usually be acceptable only to a strictly limited extent.

(5) Thus it will normally be a sufficient ground for the grant of leave if significant loss would be caused to the lessor by a refusal. For this purpose loss comprises any kind of financial loss, direct or indirect, including loss by reason of delay, and may extend to loss which is not financial. But if substantially greater loss would be caused to others by the grant of leave, or loss which is out of all proportion to the benefit which leave would confer on the lessor, that may outweigh the loss to the lessor caused by a refusal. Our formulation was criticised in the course of the argument, and we certainly do not claim for it the status of a rule in those terms. At present we say only that it appears to us the nearest we can get to a formulation of what Parliament had in mind.

(6) In assessing these respective losses the court will have regard to matters such as: the financial position of the company, its ability to pay the rental arrears and the continuing rentals, the administrator's proposals, the period for which the administration order has already been in force and is expected to remain in force, the effect on the administration if leave were given, the effect on the applicant if leave were refused, the end result sought to be achieved by the administration, the prospects of that result being achieved, and the history of the administration so far.

(7) In considering these matters it will often be necessary to assess how probable the suggested consequences are. Thus if loss to the applicant is virtually certain if leave is refused, and loss to others a remote possibility if leave is granted, that will be a powerful factor in favour of granting leave.

(8) This is not an exhaustive list. For example, the conduct of the parties may also be a material consideration in a particular case, as it was in the *Bristol Airport* case. There leave was refused on the ground that the applicants had accepted benefits under the administration, and had only sought to enforce their security at a later stage: indeed, they had only acquired their security as a result of the operations of the administrators. It behoves a lessor to make his position clear to the administrator at the outset of the administration and, if it should become necessary, to apply to the court promptly.

(9) The above considerations may be relevant not only to the decision whether leave should be granted or refused but also to a decision to impose terms if leave is granted.

(10) The above considerations will also apply to a decision on whether to impose terms as a condition for refusing leave. Section 11(3)(c) and (d) makes no provision for terms being imposed if leave is refused, but the court has power to achieve that result. It may do so directly, by giving directions to the administrator: for instance, under section 17, or in response to an application by the administrator under section 14(3), or in exercise of its control over an administrator as an officer of the court. Or it may do so indirectly, by ordering that the applicant shall have leave unless the administrator is prepared to take this or that step in the conduct of the administration. Cases where leave is refused but terms are imposed can be expected to arise frequently. For example, the permanent loss to a lessor flowing from his inability to recover his property will normally be small if the administrator is required to pay the current rent. In most cases this should be possible, since if the administration order has been rightly made the business should generally be sufficiently viable to hold down current outgoings. Such a term may therefore be a normal term to impose.

(11) The above observations are directed at a case such as the present where a lessor of land or the owner of goods is seeking to repossess his land or goods because of non-payment of rentals. A broadly similar approach will be applicable on many applications to enforce a security: for instance, an application by a mortgagee for possession of land. On such applications an important consideration will often be whether the applicant is fully secured. If he is, delay in enforcement is likely to be less prejudicial than in cases where his security is insufficient.

(12) In some cases there will be a dispute over the existence, validity or nature of the security which the applicant is seeking leave to enforce. It is not for the court on the leave application to seek to adjudicate upon that issue, unless (as in the present case, on the fixed or floating charge point) the issue raises a short point of law which it is convenient to determine without further ado. Otherwise the court needs to be satisfied only that the applicant has a seriously arguable case."

All of these factors arose in the context of applications for leave after the making of an administration order, which was the only form of administration under the old regime. There seems to be no reason why the same considerations should not be considered applicable to an out-of-court administration.

Subsequent decisions

Application by landlord for leave to obtain injunctive relief

In *Innovate Logistics Ltd v Sunberry Properties Ltd*,[361] the administrators of **11–78**
premises held by the company under a lease agreed on a pre-pack sale of the
company's frozen food warehousing and distribution business on the leased
premises. However, the purchaser did not want to take an assignment of the
lease. The administrators therefore granted the prospective purchaser a
licence to occupy the premises while the business was being transferred and
certain cold storage products delivered. The administrators considered it
important to enable the purchaser to occupy the premises in order to be able
to continue collection of book debts owed to the company and perform the
company's contracts to its customers and were willing to pay to the landlord
the sums paid by the purchaser under the licence, which were at the same
rate as the rentals payable under the lease. It was not in dispute that the
grant of the licence was a breach of the lease which would have entitled the
landlord to forfeit the lease but it did not wish to do so because the premises
could not be relet even at the same level. The landlord therefore applied for
leave to commence proceedings for a mandatory injunction requiring the
licence to be given up, the purpose being to preserve the landlord's negotiating position with the purchaser in seeking to persuade the latter to take an
assignment of the lease. The judge at first instance granted leave, taking the
view that the administrators had caused a flagrant breach of the lease and
that anyway the purpose of the administration had been achieved but his
decision was reversed by the Court of Appeal on the ground that the trial
judge had not taken into account the commercial necessity of occupation in
order to continue the collection of the book debts and had failed to carry out
the balancing exercise required by the *Atlantic Computers* judgment, in addition to which certain relevant evidence had not been brought to the trial
judge's attention as to the reasons for the administrators' actions. The case
is certainly an unusual one in that the effect of the decision was to allow the
purchaser to remain in occupation under a licence granted in breach of the
terms of the lease,[362] but this was held to be outweighed by the other factors
mentioned above.

---

[361] [2009] B.C.C. 164.
[362] The decision has been criticised on this and other grounds by leading counsel for the landlord. See Gabriel Moss, "Court of Appeal Confiscates Landlord's Bargaining Position"
(2009) Ins. Int. 1. See also *Re Cheshire West* [2010] C.S.O.H. 115.

Claim to beneficial ownership

In *Funding Corp Block Discounting Ltd v Lexi Holdings Plc*,[363] Briggs J. held that the "seriously arguable" test referred to in regard to the enforcement of security applied equally to an application to commence legal proceedings in respect of a proprietary claim to beneficial ownership and that as the applicant had a "real prospect" of establishing its proprietary claim, it should be allowed to proceed.

Claim for infringement of intellectual property rights

In *Magical Marking Ltd v Phillips*,[364] the applicant sought leave to bring proceedings for infringement of intellectual property rights, breach of fiduciary duty and misuse of confidential information. The judge concluded that the claim had a proprietary foundation and that in all the circumstances leave should be granted.

Proceedings for new tenancy

In *Somerfield Stores Ltd v Spring (Sutton Coldfield) Ltd*[365] leave was given to a tenant of business premises to continue an application for the grant of a new tenancy under Pt II of the Landlord and Tenant Act 1954. The landlord company was in administration and the only creditor who would receive anything was a bank holding a fixed charge, so that the purpose of the administration was realisation of the assets in order to make a distribution to the bank. The administrator of the landlord company had indicated that the company intended to redevelop the premises—which would be a ground for opposing the grant of a new tenancy—but conceded that as things stood the very fact of administration meant that they could not assert an actual intention to redevelop and wanted time to endeavour to put a viable scheme together. It was held that "improving the position of a secured creditor over the interests of a third party who has a right to a new tenancy is not, on the face of it, within the administration objective".[366] The balancing exercise referred to in *Atlantic Computers* had to be undertaken and leave was granted. Plainly a decisive factor in the case was that because of the uncertainty surrounding the company's ability to redevelop, the tenant would be placed in a state of prolonged and continuing uncertainty as to its position and that it was entitled to have its application heard without undue delay.

---

[363] [2008] 2 B.C.L.C. 596.
[364] [2008] F.S.R. 36.
[365] [2011] L. & T.R. 8.
[366] *Somerfield Stores*, cited above n.365, at [12].

Monetary claims

Different considerations apply where the claim is purely monetary, when the court will lift the moratorium only in exceptional circumstances.[367]

11–79

8. POWERS AND AGENCY OF THE ADMINISTRATOR

Powers of the administrator

The administrator enjoys a wide range of powers. Many of these relate to the general conduct of the administration. There are then separate provisions relating to the power to dispose of property[368] and to make distributions.[369] The former deal respectively with the disposition of property subject to a floating charge, property subject to other forms of security and property subject to a hire-purchase agreement, which for this purpose includes a conditional sale agreement, a chattel leasing agreement and a retention of title agreement.[370]

11–80

(1) Conduct of the administration generally

The administrator may:

11–81

(1) do anything necessary or expedient for the management of the affairs, business and property of the company[371];

(2) without prejudice to the generality of the above, exercise the powers specified in Sch.1 to the Insolvency Act (which are the powers also conferred on an administrative receiver)[372];

(3) remove a director of the company and appoint a director of the company, whether to fill a vacancy or otherwise[373];

(4) call a meeting of members or creditors of the company[374];

---

[367] *AES Barry Ltd v TXU Europe Energy* [2005] 2 B.C.L.C. 22; and *Re Nortel Networks UK Ltd* [2010] B.P.I.R. 1003.
[368] Insolvency Act 1986 Sch.B1 paras 70–72.
[369] Insolvency Act 1986 Sch.B1 para.65.
[370] Insolvency Act 1986 Sch.B1 para.111(1).
[371] Insolvency Act 1986 Sch.B1 para.59(1).
[372] Insolvency Act 1986 Sch.B1 para.60.
[373] Insolvency Act 1986 Sch.B1 para.61.
[374] Insolvency Act 1986 Sch.B1 para.62.

(5)   apply to the court for directions in connection with his functions[375];

(6)   make a distribution to secured and preferential creditors and, with the permission of the court, to unsecured creditors.[376]

If the court gives directions to the administrator in connection with any aspect of his management of the company's affairs,[377] the administrator must comply with them but subject to this he is required to manage the company's affairs in accordance with any proposals approved at the initial creditors' meeting and revision of such proposals.[378] The administrator may dispose of assets prior to the creditors' meeting if he considers it expedient to do so—this is the essence of pre-pack administration discussed earlier[379]—but if time allows, he should wherever possible put a proposal for such disposal to the creditors. If the administrator is in doubt, he can apply to the court, which in a proper case will sanction the disposal but the court will also be mindful that the effect of its order will be to make the creditors' meeting a complete *brutum fulmen* and may therefore decide that it is for the administrator to exercise his own judgment and assume the risk.[380]

(2) Power to dispose of property subject to a floating charge

11–82   In addition to the powers just enumerated, the administrator may dispose of or take action relating to property which is subject to a floating charge[381] as if it were not subject to the charge.[382] Where property is disposed of in reliance on this power, the holder of the floating charge has the same priority in respect of acquired property as he had in respect of the property disposed of.[383] "Acquired property" means the company's property which

---

[375] Insolvency Act 1986 Sch.B1 para.63.

[376] Insolvency Act 1986 Sch.B1 para.65.

[377] This wording puts it beyond doubt that the administrator does not require leave of the court to dispose of the company's assets. See *Re Transbus International Ltd* [2004] 2 B.C.L.C. 550. The point was unclear in the previous wording (which required the administrator to manage the business "in accordance with any directions given by the court") but was interpreted in the same sense by the court (*Re T. & D. Industries Plc* [2000] 1 W.L.R. 646).

[378] Insolvency Act 1986 Sch.B1 para.68(2) and (1).

[379] Above, paras 11–37 et seq.

[380] *Re T. & D. Industries Plc* [2000] 1 W.L.R. 646, in which the authorities are reviewed; *Re Consumer & Industrial Press Ltd (No.2)* (1988) 4 B.C.C. 72, where Peter Gibson J. declined to make the order requested on the ground that it would frustrate the purpose of the creditors' meeting. In later cases, including *Re T. & D. Industries* the courts have been more sympathetic to the position of the administrator in seeking leave.

[381] "Floating charge" means a charge which as created was a floating charge (Insolvency Act 1986 s.251), so that the administrator's power of disposal free from the charge is not affected by the fact that it has crystallised.

[382] Insolvency Act 1986 Sch.B1 para.70(1).

[383] Insolvency Act 1986 Sch.B1 para.70(2).

directly or indirectly represents the property disposed of.[384] In other words, the priority previously enjoyed in relation to the property disposed of carries through to its products or proceeds.

(3) Power to dispose of property subject to other security

The administrator may, with the permission of the court,[385] dispose of prop-   **11–83** erty subject to a security other than a floating charge as if it were not subject to the security,[386] the court's power to grant permission being exercisable only on the administrator's application and only where it is satisfied that the disposal would be likely to promote the purpose of administration in respect of the company.[387] Any such order is subject to the same conditions for the protection of secured or retention-of-title creditors as has been previously mentioned[388] in relation to administrative receivers.[389] Since the investigation of individual claims by those asserting reservation of title rights is arduous and time-consuming, there is considerable advantage in obtaining a global order for leave to sell assets subject to reservation of title, leaving the validity of individual claims to be examined afterwards.

(4) Power to dispose of goods held under a hire-purchase agreement

The court may by order enable the administrator to dispose of goods in   **11–84** the possession of the company under a hire-purchase agreement[390] as if the rights of the owner under the agreement were vested in the company in the same circumstances and subject to the same conditions as on the disposal of property subject to a fixed charge.[391] Failure to obtain leave exposes the administrator to an action for conversion.[392]

(5) Power to make a distribution

Under the old regime, the administrator's powers did not as a general rule   **11–85** include the distribution of assets or dividends to creditors even with their

---

[384] Insolvency Act 1986 Sch.B1 para.70(3).
[385] There is obviously no need to obtain leave if the chargee or title-reserving owner consents.
[386] Insolvency Act 1986 Sch.B1 para.71(1).
[387] Insolvency Act 1986 Sch.B1 para.71(2).
[388] See para.10–46 above. The requirement that the net proceeds of sale of a fixed security be applied towards discharging the sums secured covers not only the principal outstanding but interest and costs which the secured creditor is entitled to add to his security *(Morris & Atkinson v 3i Plc and the Development Commission*, July 27, 1988, Knox J.).
[389] Insolvency Act 1986 s.43(3).
[390] See above n.388.
[391] Insolvency Act 1986 Sch.B1 para.72.
[392] *Hachette UK Ltd v Borders (UK) Ltd* [2009] EWHC 3487 (Ch).

consent,[393] except pursuant to an approved voluntary arrangement under Pt I of the Insolvency Act or a compromise or sanction under what was then s.425 of the Companies Act 1985.[394] Even the court's powers were circumscribed, although in exceptional cases the administrator could obtain the court's approval to the exercise of his powers under item 13 of Sch.1 to the Act to make a payment by way of distribution to preferential and ordinary unsecured creditors.[395] The court also had power under s.18(3) of the Act to authorise a distribution when hearing an application to discharge the administration order.[396]

Now the position is much easier. The administrator can make a distribution to secured and preferential creditors without leave and the court is given a general discretion, previously lacking, to permit a distribution to unsecured creditors.[397] However, where the company is to continue trading, it will usually be easier and less expensive to arrange distributions through a CVA.[398] This avoids the cost attendant on applications to the court, with all of the information that will be required and the problem of securing the consent of the creditors, which is much more easily organised within a CVA. Moreover, the latter is very flexible, and so long as the rights of enforcement of secured creditors and the priority of preferential creditors are not adversely affected without their consent, almost anything can be agreed within a CVA. Among the matters that can be included in a CVA that would not usually be appropriate for a distribution order are compromises, dispute resolution mechanisms, such as arbitration or expert determination, and the setting of time limits for claims. Alternatively but usually less conveniently, a distribution can be made pursuant to a compromise or arrangement under Pt 26 of the Companies Act 2006.

Where he does make a distribution, the administrator must not pay debts secured by a floating charge without first satisfying the claims of preferential creditors[399] and setting aside the prescribed part for ordinary unsecured creditors,[400] but this requirement may be disapplied by the CVA or the compromise or arrangement.[401] Since in making distributions to creditors the administrator is performing a function similar to that of a liquidator,[402]

---

[393] *Re St Ives Windings Ltd* (1987) 3 B.C.C. 634.
[394] *Re St Ives Windings Ltd*, cited above n.393, *per* Harman J., expressing a provisional view only.
[395] *Re John Slack Ltd* [1995] B.C.C. 1116; and *Re WBSL Realisations 1992 Ltd* [1995] B.C.C. 1118.
[396] *Re Lune Metal Products Ltd* [2007] B.C.C. 217.
[397] Insolvency Act 1986 Sch.B1 para.65. See above, para.11–81.
[398] Where the business is to end or be disposed of, it may be easier to put the company into a creditors' voluntary winding up. See below, para.11–115.
[399] Insolvency Act 1986 s.175, as applied by Sch.B1 para.65(2).
[400] Insolvency Act 1986 s.176A. See above, para.6–38.
[401] Insolvency Act 1986 s.176A(4).
[402] This statement was approved by Blair J. in *Re Kaupthing Singer & Friedlander Ltd* [2010] EWHC 316 (Ch) at [24].

the same machinery for proofs, quantification of claims and declaration of dividends, together with rules for set-off in respect of mutual dealings[403] and for *pari passu* distribution, is now provided by the Insolvency Rules 1986.[404] However, the court may approve an application by the administrator to make a distribution under para.65 of Sch.B1 which is not a *pari passu* distribution.[405]

Quite separate from his power under para.65 is the administrator's power under para.13 of Sch.1 to make any payment which is necessary or incidental to the performance of his functions[406]; and in case that is not enough, para.66 provides that the administrator may make a payment otherwise than in accordance with para.65 of Sch.B1 or para.13 of Sch.1 if he thinks it likely to assist achievement of the purpose of the administration.

Criteria to be applied in considering application to authorise distribution

The overriding criterion the court will apply in determining whether to give leave to the administrator to make a distribution to unsecured creditors is whether it is in the interests of the creditors as a whole for the distribution to be made by the administrator rather than by a liquidator.[407] In an appropriate case, distribution through administration can be used as an alternative exit route to distribution in liquidation. More detailed guidance was given in *Re MG Rover Belux SA/NV*[408] in which H.H. Judge Norris Q.C. doubted that it was possible to draw up a definitive list of considerations relevant to all cases given the width of the court's discretion but identified the following as relevant matters in the case before him:

11–86

> "(a) The matter is to be judged at the time when permission is sought.
> (b) The court must at that time be satisfied that the proposed distribution is conducive to the achievement of the then current objectives of the administration.
> (c) The court must be satisfied that the distribution is in the interests of the company's creditors as a whole (because para.3(2) of

---

[403] See above, para.9–24.
[404] Insolvency Rules 1986 Pt 2 Ch.10.
[405] *Re HPJ UK Ltd* [2007] B.C.C. 284. See also *Re Rover Espana SA* [2006] B.C.C. 599, in which the judge relied on para.66 rather than para.65 to authorise payments to foreign employees giving them greater entitlements than they would have under UK insolvency law. In *Re Collins & Aikman Europe SA* [2006] B.C.C. 861, Lindsay J. opined that para.65 was possibly applicable only to payments that were preferential under English law, although preferential payments under a local law might be provided for if a direction were given under para.65(3), but held that in any event para.66 covered the point. As to para.66 and Sch.1 para.13, see below para.11–90.
[406] Insolvency Act 1986 Sch.1 para.13.
[407] *Re GHE Realisations Ltd* [2006] B.C.C. 139.
[408] [2007] B.C.C. 446.

Sch.B1 says that the administrator must perform his functions in that manner).

(d) The court must be satisfied that proper provision has been made for secured and preferential creditors (for the requirement to obtain the permission of the court seems to be directed at their protection).

(e) The court must consider what are the realistic alternatives to the proposed distribution sought by the administrators, consider the merits and demerits of adopting a course other than that proposed by the administrators and assess whether the proposed distribution adversely affects the entitlement of others (when compared with their entitlement if one of the other realistic alternatives were to be adopted).

(f) The court must take into account the basis on which the administration has been conducted so far as the creditors are concerned (under the original proposals, any modification to those original proposals, or any indications given in any reports to creditors), and in particular whether the creditors have approved (or not objected to) any proposal concerning the relevant distribution;

(g) The court must consider the nature and terms of the distribution.

(h) The court must consider the impact of the distribution upon any proposed exit route from the administration."[409]

Displacement of directors' powers

11–87 The powers conferred on the company or its officers by the Insolvency Act, the Companies Act 2006 or the memorandum or articles of association are not exercisable, except with the administrator's consent,[410] so far as they could be exercised in such a way as to interfere with his exercise of his powers.[411] The practical effect of this provision is similar to the effect of administrative receivership in that the directors are almost entirely divested of their powers, for the question is not whether the intended exercise of their powers will or might interfere with the administrator's exercise of his own powers but whether they *could* be exercised in such a way. The directors have a duty to co-operate with the administrator,[412] and breach of this duty renders them liable to disqualification.[413] A director can at present be

---

[409] *Re MG Rover Belux SA/NV* cited above n.408, at [7].

[410] Which may be either general or specific. For an example of the former, see *Mills v Sports Direct* [2010] 2 B.C.L.C. 143, *per* Lewison J. at [43].

[411] Insolvency Act 1986 Sch.B1 para.64. As to the power to remove directors, see above, para.11–81.

[412] Insolvency Act 1986 s.235.

[413] Company Directors Disqualification Act 1986 ss.6 and 9, and Sch.1 para.10(g).

required to answer questions put to him by the administrator even if his answers are self-incriminating,[414] but these can no longer be used in subsequent criminal proceedings.[415] This follows a ruling by the European Court of Human Rights that to require self-incrimination is a breach of the European Convention on Human Rights.[416] On the other hand, incriminating material in documentary or other evidence which is independently obtainable may be given in evidence in subsequent criminal proceedings even though it is located as the result of compelled testimony.[417]

Protection of third parties

A person dealing with an administrator in good faith and for value need not inquire whether the administrator is acting within his powers.[418] In view of the width of those powers, a third party will not usually find it necessary to invoke the statutory protection. Possible cases where he might are where the administrator disposes of property subject to a fixed security without leave of the court or without complying with the conditions on which leave is granted or where he concludes a contract or makes a transfer which is not in accordance with the proposals approved by the creditors.

11–88

The administrator as agent

In exercising his powers, the administrator acts as the company's agent.[419] But as in the case of an administrative receiver, the agency is only notional, so that it is not competent to the company to terminate it; the administrator is not subject to the control of the company or directors but on the contrary controls the company, a point reinforced by para.64(2) of Sch.B1 to the Insolvency Act and by his power under para.61 to appoint and remove directors; and his fiduciary and other duties to the company are subordinate to his statutory duties as administrator.

11–89

Payments by the administrator

Although it is not within the normal powers of an administrator to make distributions to ordinary unsecured creditors except with the permission of the

11–90

---

[414] *Bishopsgate Investments Ltd v Maxwell* [1993] Ch. 1.
[415] Youth Justice and Criminal Evidence Act 1999 s.59 and Sch.3 para.7(3)(a). But they may still be used to disqualify a director (para.8(3)(a)(i)).
[416] *Saunders v United Kingdom* (1997) 23 E.H.R.R. 313.
[417] *Att-Gen's Reference (No.7 of 2000)* [2001] 1 W.L.R. 1879.
[418] Insolvency Act 1986 Sch.B1 para.59(3).
[419] Insolvency Act 1986 Sch.B1 para.69. As to the administrator's liabilities, see below, paras 11–92 et seq.

court[420] or as part of an approved arrangement,[421] he may make a payment otherwise than in accordance with para.65 or para.13 of Sch.1 if he thinks it likely to assist achievement of the purpose of the administration.[422] Paragraph 13 confers a more restricted power to make any payment which is necessary or incidental to the performance of his functions, and this may justify a "duress" payment to prevent termination of a contract or forfeiture of a lease or an application to the court to authorise a distribution to creditors.[423] A utility supplier is entitled, as the condition of continuing supply, to require the administrator personally to guarantee payment but is not entitled to impose a condition that charges outstanding at the date of the administration are paid.[424]

Administrator's remuneration and expenses

11–91   The provisions governing the administrator's expenses and remuneration are contained in para.99 of Sch.B1, which rather strangely is confined to cases where he has ceased to be the administrator.[425] However, the courts have rejected any implication that the administrator has to wait until after his appointment has ended before recouping his remuneration and expenses and have held that he is entitled to recover these as the administration proceeds, the statutory provisions being read as dealing only with expenses and remuneration not previously recovered.[426] In recovering his expenses and remuneration, the administrator is not entitled to resort to assets that are not the property of the company and his rights are subordinate to those of a holder of a fixed mortgage or charge but take priority over claims secured by a floating charge, which are also subject to the setting aside of the prescribed part. The ranking of the administrator's entitlement to expenses and remuneration from assets of the company not subject to a fixed security is thus as follows.

(1)   sums payable in respect of a debt or liability arising under a contract made by the administrator or a predecessor, or a contract of employment adopted by the administrator or a predecessor, before cessation of his appointment[427];

---

[420] See above, para.11–85.

[421] See above, para.11–85.

[422] Insolvency Act 1986 Sch.B1 para.66. As to the administrator's position in relation to pre-administration and post-administration contracts, see below, paras 11–99 et seq.

[423] See above, para.11–85.

[424] Insolvency Act 1986 s.233(2).

[425] For a decision on the distribution of assets where a new administrator had taken over, see *Re Sports Betting Media Ltd* [2008] B.C.C. 177.

[426] *Re Atlantic Computer Systems Plc* [1992] Ch. 505; and *Re Salmet International Ltd* [2001] B.C.C. 796.

[427] Insolvency Act 1986 Sch.B1 para.99(4) and (5).

(2)   the administrator's remuneration and expenses,[428] which now include unpaid pre-administration expenses approved under r.2.67A and which, as between themselves, rank in the order set out in r.2.67(1) of the Insolvency Rules[429];

(3)   the prescribed part which the administrator is required to set aside for ordinary unsecured creditors from assets subject to a floating charge, if created on or after September 15, 2003, and remaining after preferential debts have been paid[430]; and

(4)   sums payable to the chargee under the floating charge.

However, the provisions of the Insolvency Act relating to the payment of the liquidator's or administrator's remuneration, expenses and liabilities are disapplied in relation to financial collateral arrangements.[431]

9. DUTIES AND LIABILITIES OF THE ADMINISTRATOR

No common law duty of care to unsecured creditors

In the absence of some special relationship, an administrator owes no general common law duty of care to unsecured creditors any more than a director of a company owes a duty of care to its shareholders.[432] The creditors' interests are mediated through the administrator's duties to the company.

11–92

Duties owed to the company

Under para.3(2) of Sch.B1 to the Insolvency Act 1986, the administrator must perform his functions in the interests of the company's creditors as a whole. An administrator guilty of misapplication of the company's property

11–93

---

[428] Insolvency Act 1986 Sch.B1 para.99(3) and (4).

[429] From which it will be seen that in a list of nine items the administrator's remuneration ranks last but one. The moral, of course, is to accept an appointment as administrator only where the assets remaining after payment of the contractual claims having priority under Sch.B1 para.99(4) and the expenses listed in the Insolvency Rules r.2.67 are likely to be amply sufficient to cover the administrator's remuneration.

[430] Insolvency Act 1986 s.176A(2). The court has power to disapply the prescribed part (s.176A(3)–(5)), which it did in *Hydroserve Ltd, Re* [2008] B.C.C. 175 on the ground that the cost of paying the unsecured creditors would be disproportionate to the benefit they would receive. See also above, para.6–38.

[431] Financial Collateral Arrangements (No.2) Regs. 2003 (SI 2003/3226), regs 8, 9 and 11, as amended by SI 2010/2993.

[432] *Kyrris v Oldham* [2004] 1 B.C.L.C. 305.

or of misfeasance or breach of a fiduciary or other duty to the company in the conduct of the administration could formerly have been the subject of summary proceedings under s.212 of the Insolvency Act 1986 if the company was in winding up. But in relation to administrators this section no longer applies and has been replaced by para.75 of Sch.B1, which is to similar effect except that it is no longer necessary for the company to be in winding up. In addition, under para.74 of Sch.B1, a creditor or member of the company may apply to the court claiming that:

(1)   the administrator is acting or has acted so as unfairly to harm the interests of the applicant (whether alone or in common with some or all other members or creditors); or

(2)   the administrator proposes to act in a way which would unfairly harm the interests of the applicant (whether alone or in common with some or all other members or creditors).

It is neither necessary nor sufficient for the grant of relief under para.74 that the administrator has acted or proposes to act unlawfully or in breach of some legal duty to the applicant. For those breaches, other remedies are available. What has to be shown is that the administrator has acted or proposes to act in a way which: (i) causes or would cause harm to the applicant; and (ii) does so unfairly. Both of these two elements must be satisfied, so that where the administrator complained that he had already devoted a great deal of time and resources to providing information to the applicant and was unwilling to commit yet more resources to the provision of additional information, Blackburne J. held that it was hard to see how, even if harm had been caused, it was unfair.[433] Similarly, termination of the contract of one particular creditor, even if causing harm, does not of itself indicate unfairness, for the administrator is required to have regard to the creditors' interests as a whole.[434] On the other hand, where administrators caused a third party to occupy for the purposes of the administration premises of which the insolvent company was the tenant without having received either a licence from the landlord or any guarantee that rent would be payable and with the effect of depriving the landlord of use of the premises, they were held by the Court of Session to have caused unfair harm to the landlord and that the rent should in due course be paid as an expense of the administration.[435]

In fulfilling his functions, the administrator must give thought to all relevant considerations and his decisions must be properly informed.[436] If he

---

[433] *Re Lehman Bros International (Europe) Ltd* [2009] B.C.C. 632.
[434] *BLV Realty Organization Ltd v Batten* [2010] B.P.I.R. 277. See above, para.11–25.
[435] *Cheshire West and Chester BC v Administrators of Springfield Retail Ltd* [2010] C.S.O.H. 115.
[436] For a useful development of the fiduciary's obligations in this regard, see Mokal, *Corporate Insolvency Law*, pp.237 et seq.

does this, the court will not seek to substitute its own judgment for the considered, commercial judgment of the administrator. However, the administrator must not neglect to take account of the role of the creditors and any creditors' committee, and is well advised to consult them on major issues where time permits.

Business documents and websites

While a company is in administration, every business document issued by or on behalf of the company, and all of the company's websites, must state: (i) the name of the administrator; and (ii) that the affairs and property of the company are being managed by him.[437] By "business document" is meant an invoice, an order for goods or services, a business letter and an order form, whether in hard copy, electronic or any other form.[438] If without reasonable excuse the administrator, an officer of the company or the company itself authorises or permits a contravention of such requirement, that person commits an offence.[439] Since a company in administration is not a free agent, it is hard to see how it could authorise or permit anything! Interestingly, although the administrator's failure to state that the company is in administration could mislead a supplier of goods or services, the Insolvency Act does not make the administrator personally liable on the contract.[440] In practice, the supplier will usually be adequately protected by the fact that he enjoys a super-priority.[441]

11–94

Taking control of the company's property

On his appointment, the administrator must take custody or control of all of the property to which he thinks the company is entitled.[442] The phrase "thinks the company is entitled" implies that the administrator is to be immune from liability if he takes control of property later found to belong to a third party, and the immunity is made express by s.234(4)(a) of the Act, although obviously it endures only for so long as the company remains actually or apparently entitled to the property. The administrator's powers in relation to the collecting in of property are similar to those of a liquidator, and he may bring proceedings in conversion against a person who takes

11–95

---

[437] Insolvency Act 1986 Sch.B1 para.45(1).
[438] Insolvency Act 1986 Sch.B1 para.45(3).
[439] Insolvency Act 1986 Sch.B1 para.45(2).
[440] The administrator is not otherwise liable on contracts into which he enters as agent of the company. See below, para.11–99.
[441] Insolvency Act 1986 Sch.B1 para.99(4). See below, para.11–99.
[442] Insolvency Act 1986 Sch.B1 para.67.

possession of the company's property pursuant to a charge which is void for want of registration under s.860 of the Companies Act 2006 and may invoke the summary remedy provided by s.234 of the Insolvency Act 1986 to recover the property in question.[443]

Carrying on the business

Priority for new finance

11–96   Before the approval of his proposals by the creditors, the administrator must manage the company's affairs, business and property in accordance with such directions, if any, as may be given by the court, and after such approval, in accordance with those proposals.[444] If the company does not have adequate working capital, the administrator may need to arrange finance for this purpose. Usually, this will be forthcoming from the company's bank or other major existing secured creditor, and where there are substantial contracts approaching completion the cost of the additional finance may be quite small in relation to the income to be received. In any event, if the existing security covers the future advance and the collateral is adequate, the creditor is protected. A new creditor advancing funds will be entitled to have these treated as an expense of the administration,[445] with the result that they become charged on and payable out of property of which the administrator has custody or control in priority to the administrator's remuneration and expenses,[446] preferential claims and any sum payable to the holder of a floating charge.[447] A super-priority is also given for wages or salary as defined by Sch.B1 para.99(6), although this does not include payments in lieu of notice or protective awards under employment legislation.[448] However, in neither case does this "super-priority" extend to assets secured by a fixed charge. In consequence, a new financier is unlikely to advance funds except with the consent of existing secured creditors or against a charge over the company's free assets (if any, which will usually not be the case) or a significant equity in assets already charged. Moreover, although post-administration finance is included among the expenses of administration ranking at the top of the list in r.2.67(1), it ranks equally with other such expenses, such as sums payable by the administrator under post-administration contracts[449] and payable to

---

[443] *Smith v Bridgend CBC* [2002] 1 A.C. 336.
[444] See above, para.11–81.
[445] *Bibby Trade Finance Ltd v McKay* [2006] EWHC 2836 (Ch). See also para.11–98.
[446] As set out in r.2.67(1) (r.2.67(4)).
[447] Insolvency Act 1986 Sch. B1 para. 99(4).
[448] *Re Huddersfield Fine Worsteds Ltd* [2005] B.C.C. 915.
[449] See below, para.11–98.

landlords or local authorities for rent or rates incurred in continuing to occupy premises for the benefit of the administration.[450] Proposals by the Insolvency Service to provide post-administration lenders with an overriding super-priority[451] did not, on the whole, attract support and have not been pursued.[452]

Making applications to the court

The administrator has a general power to apply to the court for directions,[453] and may at any time apply for his appointment to cease to have effect from a specified time.[454] He is obliged to make such an application if it appears to him that the purpose of administration cannot be achieved or the company should not have entered administration or if he is required to make an application by a creditors' meeting or, in the case of a court administration, he thinks its purpose has been sufficiently achieved in relation to the company.[455] In the case of an out-of-court appointment, if the administrator thinks that the purpose of the administration has been so achieved, he can simply file a notice with the court and the registrar of companies, upon which his appointment ceases to have effect.[456]

11–97

Expenses of the administration

The list of items constituting expenses of the administration and the order of priority of those expenses are set out in r.2.67 of the Insolvency Rules, subject to the court's powers of adjustment. However, the formulation of the rule is a little confusing. The order of priority is set out in para.(1) of the rule. Paragraphs (2) and (3) empower the court to vary the order of priority where the assets are insufficient to satisfy the liabilities. This seems to imply that the automatic application of the priority list in para.(1) is confined to cases where there is no shortfall in the assets, in which case the list would be entirely unnecessary. However, that is not what is intended. Paragraph (1) comes into play only in case of an insufficiency of assets.[457] In that situation, it will apply automatically unless the court decides to make an order varying

11–98

---

[450] See below, para.11–105.
[451] "Encouraging Company Rescue—A Consultation" (June 2009).
[452] Existing, secured creditors are usually resistant to this. See below, para.12–09.
[453] Insolvency Act 1986 Sch.B1 para.63. The court may in addition give directions under para.63 within the limits permitted by sub-para.(3).
[454] Insolvency Act 1986 Sch.B1 para.79(1).
[455] Insolvency Act 1986 Sch.B1 para.79(2) and (3).
[456] Insolvency Act 1986 Sch.B1 para.80.
[457] And not always then. See below.

it. This mirrors r.4.218. However, it is not clear why in both cases the court's discretion is triggered by an excess of liabilities over assets; one would have thought that the relevant question is whether the available assets are sufficient to enable the *administration expenses* to be paid in full. That, it is thought, is how the courts are in practice likely to apply it.[458]

It is necessary to distinguish "expenses of the administration", which covers the entire list, from "expenses properly incurred by the administrator in performing his functions in the administration of the company", which although at the top of the list is to be distinguished from items lower in the list, such as "any necessary disbursements by the administrator in the course of the administration". It is not easy to see how this item is to be distinguished from the expenses at the top of the list, nor why the latter is described in terms of being "properly incurred", whereas disbursements are referred to as "necessary". One might have thought that recoupment of "necessary" disbursements would be a higher priority than those which are merely "properly incurred". To add to the confusion, a former administrator's "remuneration and expenses" under Sch.B1 para.99(3) encompasses the complete list in r.2.67(1).

Under the original rules, expenses "properly incurred by the administrator in performing his functions" had been held by the House of Lords to be confined to claims by the administrator against the company for which, in relation to expenses, he had become personally liable.[459] That has now changed with the addition of the category of disbursements in r.2.67(1)(f).[460] The administrator's pre-administration costs are now specifically provided for in r.2.67(1)(h). It is not clear what items are encompassed within pre-administration costs. In *Re Johnson Machine & Tool Co Ltd*,[461] a decision on the old rules under which approval of pre-appointment costs was a matter of the court's discretion, H.H. Judge Purle Q.C. held that only those additional costs occasioned by the bringing of an administration application, and not advice given before any decision to seek administration or the pre-administration costs of considering and arranging the pre-pack, could normally be approved, and that there were difficulties in ever treating pre-appointment costs as an administration expense in an out-of-court appointment. This very restrictive approach created difficulties for administrators who for one reason or another did not feel able to collect their pre-administration costs from the company before steps were initiated to put it into administration. The new r.2.33(2A) defines pre-administration costs as fees charged and

---

[458] See, e.g. the judgment of Briggs J. in *Irish Reel Productions Ltd v Capitol Films Ltd* [2010] B.C.C. 588 at [10].

[459] *Centre Reinsurance International Co v Curzon Insurance Ltd* [2006] 1 W.L.R. 2863.

[460] *Exeter CC v Bairstow* [2007] B. C.C. 236, also known as *Re Trident Fashions Plc*. As to litigation expenses, see above, para.8–34.

[461] [2010] B.C.C. H.H. Judge Purle Q.C. held that where administration orders were made in relation to pre-pack sales.

expenses incurred by the administrator, or another person qualified to act as an insolvency practitioner, before the company entered administration but with a view to its doing so, and under r.2.67A it is for the creditors' committee, after a statement of pre-administration costs has been made by the administrator under r.2.33(2)(ka), to determine whether and to what extent any unpaid pre-administration costs are approved for payment. It is clear that fees and expenses incurred otherwise than with a view to administration are excluded but there seems to be no reason why, for example, the costs of organising a pre-pack which is to follow immediately after the administrator's appointment should not be covered.

A significant part of the costs of administration is the costs incurred in the continuance of trading. The administrator should therefore be careful to ensure that he carries the principal creditors with him in deciding to continue trading or that he can justify his decision if challenged.

Position of the administrator in relation to new contracts

The administrator's liability

Liabilities arising under new contracts constitute expenses of the liquidation and as such are payable, not provable.[462] In considering liabilities arising under new contracts, it is necessary to distinguish contracts entered into by the administrator personally from those entered into by the company through the administrator. If for the benefit of the administration the administrator enters into a contract in his own name—which could happen because that is the only basis upon which the other party is willing to deal—he is personally liable on the contract but has a right to be indemnified by the company. The administrator incurs no personal liability on new contracts into which he enters as agent for the company except where he agrees to assume such liability. Accordingly, it is only the company which incurs a liability on such contracts. In this respect, the administrator is much less vulnerable than the administrative receiver, who is personally liable on contracts entered into by him, whether in his own name or in the company's name.[463]

11–99

The distinction between pre-administration and post-administration contracts

Attention has been drawn earlier to the distinction between the treatment of debts arising under post-liquidation contracts and continuing post-liquidation

11–100

---

[462] See below, para.11–100.
[463] Insolvency Act 1986 s.44(1)(b); and see above, paras 10–50 et seq.

obligations arising under pre-liquidation contracts.[464] We have seen that the former are payable as an expense of the liquidation, while the latter are provable, not payable, unless falling within the *Lundy Granite* principle, which, however, does not involve the exercise of discretion in the true sense.[465] The same is true in administration, although decisions to this effect have not passed unchallenged.[466]

Post-administration contractual liabilities are secured on company's property

11–101   By para.99(4) of Sch.B1 to the Insolvency Act, any sums payable in respect of debts or liabilities arising out of contracts entered into by a former administrator or a predecessor of his in the carrying out of his or the predecessor's functions are charged on any property of the company which is in his possession or under his control, and the current administrator has a duty to ensure that these are paid in priority to his own remuneration and expenses,[467] which are themselves charged on and payable out of the company's property and are payable in priority to claims secured by a floating charge,[468] but not by a fixed charge. But the assets to which this priority applies are confined to those left in the hands of the former administrator on the cessation of his office, leaving undisturbed payments already made to creditors prior to that time.[469]

Refusal to carry out contracts

11–102   If the administrator fails or declines to procure the company's performance of a contract, the company incurs a liability to the other party in damages, but the administrator would not, although if he acts in wanton disregard of the company's interests, due account being taken of his overriding statutory duties, he may be liable to the company for any legal liability and other loss it incurs. He may also be restrained by injunction from acting in this way.[470]

Super-priority of sums payable under the Pension Regulator's financial support directions and contribution notices

11–103   Reference has already been made to the "moral hazard" power of the Pensions Regulator under the Pensions Act 2004 to issue financial support directions

---

[464] Above, para.11–99.
[465] See para.8–38.
[466] See below, paras 11–104 and 11–105.
[467] Insolvency Act 1986 Sch.B1 para.99(4). As to administration expenses, see below.
[468] Insolvency Act 1986 Sch.B1 para.99(3).
[469] *Re Sports Betting Media Ltd* [2008] B.C.C. 177.
[470] *Astor Chemicals Ltd v Synthetic Technology Ltd* [1990] B.C.C. 97.

(FSDs) and contribution notices (CNs) to associates and connected persons of an employer company running a defined benefit pension scheme.[471] In a decision in the Lehman Brothers administration, which will be of profound concern to administrators, Briggs J. has reluctantly held[472] that sums payable by such associates and connected person under FSDs and CNs issued after the commencement of the administration are to be treated as expenses of the administration, not as sums for which the Pensions Regulator can prove or as non-provable sums recoverable only if there is a surplus. Those sums accordingly enjoy a super-priority, in contrast to sums payable by an insolvent employer itself under s.75 of the Pensions Act to make good a shortfall in pension fund assets, these being taken to arise before the insolvency event and thus to be provable,[473] not payable as expenses. The decision is under appeal and the Insolvency Service is considering whether the law should be changed to make liability under post-insolvency contribution notices a provable debt instead of an expense of the administration.

Position of the administrator in relation to existing contracts

(1) Contracts in general

The entry of the company into administration does not automatically terminate contracts entered into by the company except where the contract in question so provides, which is often the case. Moreover, the administrator incurs no personal liability either for sums accruing due post-administration under continuing contracts or for sums accrued due prior to the commencement of the administration. However, if the administrator adopts the contract for the benefit of the administration, the *Lundy Granite* principle applicable in winding up[474] also applies here, so as to make post-adoption liabilities under pre-administration contracts an expense of the administration within r.2.67(1)(a) of the Insolvency Rules ranking at the head of the list but subordinate to the claims of post-administration creditors under para.99(4). Further, contrary to what had previously been thought,[475] this would not be a matter of discretion but of the application of r.2.67, the court's discretion and application of the balancing test coming into play only at the time enforcement is sought.[476] We return to this point in the discussion of continuing rental obligations under pre-administration leases.[477]

11–104

---

[471] See the discussion above, para.8–37.
[472] *Bloom v Pensions Regulator* [2010] EWHC 3010 (Ch).
[473] Pensions Act 2004 s.75(4A). They rank as non-preferential debts (s.75(8)).
[474] Namely that where the liquidator procures the company to continue in occupation of leased premises for the benefit of the winding up, the rent is payable as an expense of the liquidation in priority to other claims. See above, paras 8–33 and 8–38.
[475] *Re Atlantic Computer Systems Plc* [1992] Ch. 505, *per* Sir Donald Nicholls V.C. at 523.
[476] See para.11–105.
[477] See para.11–105.

Administration is not a bar to the termination of the contract by the other party,[478] so that if the administrator wishes to avoid termination he will usually need to discharge accruing liabilities as they fall due and may also have to pay arrears accrued prior to the company's entry into administration. Such payments are expressly authorised by para.66 of Sch.B1.

(2) *Rent under leases of premises or equipment*

11–105 If follows from what has been said above that the administrator is entitled, without incurring personal liability for either accrued or accruing sums, to procure or allow the company to continue to occupy premises held on lease and to use equipment held on lease, conditional sale or hire-purchase, so long as the lease or agreement is current. The lessor of premises cannot sue for rent or other payments, levy distress or exercise a right of forfeiture by peaceful re-entry without the consent of the administrator or the permission of the court,[479] nor can the owner of equipment supplied on hire purchase[480] take any step to repossess it without such consent or permission.[481] Here again, the *Lundy Granite* principle applies so as to entitle the lessor to recover rentals as they fall due where the premises are occupied for the beneficial conduct of the administration,[482] and the administrator may in any event feel constrained to continue payments under the lease in order to avoid the risk of forfeiture or an application by the lessor or other creditor for leave to enforce its rights or alternatively for relief under para.74(1)(b) of Sch.B1 on the ground of unfair harm to the lessor.

That view has been challenged by Mr Gabriel Moss Q.C., who argues powerfully that the decision in *Toshoku* was confined to liquidation and that the approach taken in *Re Atlantic Computers Plc*[483] as to administration remains valid. In his view, the true position is exactly the opposite, namely that the question of whether the above liabilities should be treated as an expense of the administration remains a matter for the court's discretion but that if payment were ordered then the sum in question should be treated as expenses of administration.[484] But this view, although advocated with Mr Moss's customary persuasiveness, cannot be accepted. It is true that post-administration liabilities arising under pre-administration contracts are payable as expenses of the administration only if falling within the *Lundy Granite* principle, but that principle, although founded on judicial discretion,

---

[478] See above, para.11–69.
[479] Insolvency Act 1986 Sch.B1 para.43(4).
[480] As to the meaning of "hire-purchase", see above, para.11–63.
[481] Insolvency Act 1986 Sch.B1 para.43(3).
[482] See above, para.11–104.
[483] [1992] Ch. 505.
[484] "Pearly Gates for Retail Administrations?" (2010) Ins. Int. 76.

has hardened into a set practice in liquidation.[485] In *Toshoku*, Lord Hoffmann said that r.4.218 was intended to be a definitive statement of what counted as an expense of the liquidation, leaving no room for judicial discretion, and that the application of the *Lundy Granite* principle in relation to post-liquidation claims arising under pre-liquidation contracts does not involve the exercise of discretion.[486] There is no reason to treat its application in administration any differently. If the matter were left to the court's discretion, on what principle would that discretion be exercised other than that enunciated in *Lundy Granite* and now crystallised into a rule? Clearly, it would be quite wrong for the administrator to be allowed to trade from the premises while leaving the landlord to whistle for his rent by having to prove as an unsecured creditor in the winding up, and if the administrator were to take that position it would be difficult for the court to refuse permission to the landlord to exercise his right of forfeiture.

There has been a trend towards greater assimilation of administration with liquidation, including conferment of a power to distribute to unsecured creditors with the court's approval, the introduction of rules governing the proof of debt, quantification of claims, rights of set-off and related matters, and the provision of a list of administration expenses in r.2.67(1). This rule was intentionally designed to mirror r.4.218 and the same considerations must apply. If that were not the case, what would be the purpose of the list? Moreover, if the list were not intended as a complete and binding statement of what constitutes administration expenses, what would be the point of giving the court power under r.2.67(2) and (3) to vary the priorities set out in r.2.67(1)? Finally, all the cases go one way in showing that any item in the list in r.2.67(1) must be treated as an expense of the administration, and that the court's discretion comes into play at the point when enforcement is sought.[487]

(3) Contracts of employment

It will have been seen that there are various provisions relating to contracts of employment, including claims under contracts adopted by a former administrator or predecessor[488] and preferential claims by employees,[489] in

11–106

---

[485] As acknowledged by Nicholls L.J. in *Re Atlantic Computers Plc* [1992] Ch. 505 at 527.

[486] [2002] 3 All E.R. 961 at [38].

[487] *Chester West and Chester BC v Administrators of Springfield Retail Ltd* [2010] C.S.O.H. 115; *Goldacre (Offices) Ltd v Nortel Networks UK Ltd* [2010] 3 W.L.R. 171; and *Exeter CC v Bairstow* [2007] B.C.C. 236 (although rates are no longer payable on unoccupied non-domestic premises within a prescribed class—see Non-Domestic Rating (Unoccupied Property) (England) Regulations 2008, SI 2008/386). All these cases held that the reasoning of Lord Hoffmann in *Re Toshoku Finance UK Plc* [2002] 1 W.L.R. 671 that treatment of rental liabilities was automatic under the Insolvency Rules and not a matter of discretion applied equally to administration.

[488] Sch.B1 para.99(5). See above, para.11–104.

[489] Sch.6 category 5. See above, para.8–20.

addition to which employees enjoy such protection as given by TUPE 2006 and other employment-related legislation.[490]

(4) Occupational pensions

11–107 When a company goes into administration, the administrator is required to inform the Pensions Regulator of the insolvency event,[491] so that the Regulator can take the necessary steps to protect the pension fund, including the appointment of an independent trustee. The Pension Regulator's powers to secure the adequacy of a pension fund in a defined benefit occupational pension scheme have been discussed earlier.[492]

Liability in conversion

11–108 Where goods are held under a hire-purchase agreement,[493] the administrator is entitled to retain and use it for the proper purpose of the administration, in which case the rentals become an expense of the administration and are payable in full as they become due. But the administrator is not entitled to keep and use the goods otherwise than for the proper purpose of the administration, so that if he retains possession of the goods where he has no intention of using the goods for the purpose of the administration or that purpose cannot be achieved and he refuses to deliver up the goods to the owner or uses them for a purpose other than the administration, he liable in conversion.[494] The same applies where he sells the goods without leave of the court.[495] The moratorium does not mean that the owner lacks the immediate right to possession necessary to found a claim for conversion; it is merely the remedy that is suspended.[496] But it is not necessary to obtain leave to bring proceedings for conversion; the more appropriate way of dealing with the matter is to apply to the court in the administration for compensation for the administrator's wrongful detention or use and for an order for return of the goods.[497]

---

[490] See above, para.8–24.
[491] Pensions Act 2004 s.120.
[492] Above, paras 2–24 and 11–103.
[493] For the extended meaning of "hire-purchase agreement" in this context, see above, para.11–63.
[494] *Barclays Mercantile Business Finance Ltd v Sibec Ltd* [1992] 1 W.L.R. 1253.
[495] *Hachette UK Ltd v Borders (UK) Ltd* [2009] EWHC 3487 (Ch).
[496] *Hachette v Borders*, above, n. 495.
[497] *Hachette v Borders*, above, n. 495.

10. THE ADMINISTRATOR'S PROPOSALS

Requirements relating to proposals

Having armed himself with the requisite information from the statement of affairs and other sources, the administrator must then prepare a statement setting out proposals for achieving the purpose of administration[498] and send a copy to the registrar of companies and every creditor and member of whose address he is aware.[499] This must be done as soon as is reasonably practicable after the company has entered administration, with a maximum time limit that has been shortened from three months to eight weeks,[500] subject to extension.[501] This is part of a general tightening up of the rules on time in order to accelerate the administration process. The statement of proposals must be accompanied by an invitation to attend the initial creditors' meeting at which these are to be considered,[502] and the date set for this meeting must be as soon as reasonably practicable after the company enters administration and in any event within the period of 10 weeks beginning with the date on which the company enters administration.[503] Both time limits may be varied by the court on an application of the administrator[504] or by up to 28 days with the creditors' consent.[505] At the meeting, the administrator must present his proposals to the creditors, who may approve them without modification or with modification to which the administrator consents.[506] The creditors may not modify the proposals without the administrator's consent. The proposals may include a proposal for a CVA under Pt I of the Insolvency Act 1986 or a compromise or arrangement under what is now Pt 26 of the Companies Act 2006,[507] but may not include any action which affects the right of a secured creditor to enforce his security or would result in a preferential debt of the

11–109

---

[498] And, where applicable, explain in the statement why he thinks that the objective mentioned in para.3(1)(a) or (b) of Sch.B1 cannot be achieved. The statement must contain the particulars prescribed by r.2.33 of the Insolvency Rules 1986.

[499] Insolvency Act 1986 Sch.B1 para.49(4).

[500] Insolvency Act 1986 Sch.B1 para.49(5)(a) and (b).

[501] Insolvency Act 1986 Sch.B1 paras 107 and 108.

[502] Insolvency Act 1986 Sch.B1 para.51(1).

[503] Insolvency Act 1986 Sch.B1 para.51(2). The meeting cannot be held where the statement of proposals states that the administrator thinks that the company has sufficient property to enable each creditor to be paid in full or has insufficient property to enable a distribution to be made to unsecured creditors other than by virtue of s.176A(2)(a) (which relates to the prescribed part—see above, para.6–38) or neither of the first two objectives of para.3 of Sch.B1 can be achieved. But creditors of the company whose debts amount to at least 10% of the total may require the administrator to summon an initial creditors' meeting (Insolvency Act 1986 Sch.B1 para.52).

[504] Insolvency Act 1986 Sch.B1 para.107.

[505] Insolvency Act 1986 Sch.B1 para.108.

[506] Insolvency Act 1986 Sch.B1 para.53(1).

[507] Insolvency Act 1986 Sch.B1 para.49(3). As to CVAs, see below, paras 12–26–12–55.

company losing its priority to non-preferential debts or would result in one preferential creditor being paid a smaller proportion of his debt than another,[508] except in either case where the creditor consents or the proposal is for a CVA, a compromise or an arrangement under Pt 26 of the Companies Act 2006.[509] The administrator may propose a revision to the proposals and must then submit the revised proposals to a creditors' meeting summoned by him if he thinks that the proposed revision is substantial.[510]

Consultation with creditors

11–110 In advance of the creditors' meeting, the administrator is well advised, wherever possible, to consult with major creditors over any significant action he proposes to take, for example, sale of a substantial asset or the conclusion of a compromise on behalf of the company. However, there are situations in which a general consultation is not feasible, as where the urgency of the situation requires a pre-pack sale.

The creditors' meeting and decision on the proposals

11–111 In presenting the proposals to creditors the administrator should bear in mind any need for confidentiality vis-à-vis third parties, for example, as to the identity of a prospective purchaser and the price to be paid. It is standard practice for members of a creditors' committee to be required to execute confidentiality agreements when they are appointed. In addition, steps need to be taken to ensure that bondholders do not make use of price-sensitive information in trading their bonds. The creditors may approve the proposals without modification or may modify them but each modification requires the administrator's consent.[511] If a scheme of arrangement provided for in the proposals and approved by the creditors proves fruitless and the proposals do not specify what is to happen in that eventuality, the court may sanction a substitute scheme, since this is filling a gap rather than overriding a positive decision by the creditors.[512] Where the proposals are for a CVA, they may nominate the administrator himself as the intended supervisor.[513]

---

[508] Insolvency Act 1986 Sch.B1 para.73(1).
[509] The exclusion of proposals in a CVA appears to have no significance other than the avoidance of duplication, since s.4 of the Act precludes both a proposal which affects the enforcement rights of a secured creditor (a provision expressly reserved by s.73(2)(b)) and one which alters the priority, etc. of a preferential creditor.
[510] Insolvency Act 1986 Sch.B1 para.54.
[511] Insolvency Act 1986 Sch.B1 para.53(1)(b).
[512] *Re Smallman Construction Ltd* (1988) 4 B.C.C. 784, Knox J.
[513] See below, para.12–55.

Voting

The majority required to pass a resolution to approve proposals put forward **11–112**
by the administrator depends on whether or not the proposal is for a CVA.
This has been discussed earlier.[514] Votes are calculated according to the
amount of the creditor's claim as at the date on which the company entered
administration, less any payments that have been made to him after that date
in respect of his claim and any adjustment by way of set-off in accordance
with r.2.85 as if that rule were applied on the date that the votes are
counted.[515]

11. TERMINATION OF THE APPOINTMENT AND THE ADMINISTRATION

Cessation of office

An administrator ceases to hold office on death,[516] on resignation in con- **11–113**
formity with the Insolvency Rules,[517] on removal by the court,[518] on substitution of another administrator[519] or on his appointment ceasing to have effect
under other provisions,[520] of which the most significant is the provision that
the appointment of an administrator comes to an end automatically after the
period of one year beginning with the date on which it takes effect unless
the administrator's term of office is extended by the court[521] or by consent
of the creditors.[522] In addition, the administrator is required to vacate office
if he ceases to be qualified to act as an insolvency practitioner in relation to
the company.[523] A new procedure introduced by the Enterprise Act 2002 for
bringing administration to an end is an application by a creditor for the
administrator's appointment to cease to have effect on the ground of
improper motive on the part of the applicant for the administration order, in

---

[514] Above, para.11–36. See further para.12–41, below, as to voting on a proposed CVA.
[515] Insolvency Rules 1986 r.2.38(4). As to voting by a secured creditor, see r.2.40.
[516] Insolvency Act 1986 Sch.B1 para.99(1).
[517] Insolvency Act 1986 Sch.B1 para.87; and Insolvency Rules 1986 rr.2.119–2.121.
[518] Insolvency Act 1986 Sch.B1 para.88.
[519] Under Insolvency Act 1986 Sch.B1 para.96 or 97.
[520] See Insolvency Act 1986 Sch.B1 paras 76, 79(1), 80(3), 81(1), 82(3), 83(6)(a) and 84(4). The
grounds for cessation of office are also set out in general form in para.99(1).
[521] Insolvency Act 1986 Sch.B1 para.76(2)(a).
[522] Insolvency Act 1986 Sch.B1 paras 76(2)(b) and 78.
[523] Insolvency Act 1986 Sch.B1 para.89(1). It would seem that his period of office ends automatically on his becoming disqualified. Note that the administrator is required to vacate office
if he ceases to be qualified "in relation to the company", which means that he must continue
not only to be qualified generally but also to be appropriately bonded in relation to the
company (Insolvency Act 1986 s.390(3)).

the case of a court appointment, or of the person appointing the administrator, in the case of an out-of-court appointment.[524] The court has a wide discretion as to the orders it can make.[525] However, the court will rarely, if ever, make an order to remove an administrator without cause,[526] although this need not involve misconduct, personal unfitness or imputation against his integrity.[527]

Effect of administrator's ceasing to hold office

11–114 It is necessary to distinguish cases where an administrator vacates office by reason of resignation, death, removal by order of the court or disqualification from acting as an insolvency practitioner in relation to the company from cases where the administrator's appointment ceases to have effect.[528] None of the events in the first of these categories affects the continuance of the administration,[529] it merely necessitates the appointment of a new administrator. By contrast, when the appointment of an administrator ceases to have effect, the administration comes to an end.[530]

12. EXITS FROM ADMINISTRATION

11–115 Under the revised regime, there is a greater range of exits from administration than was formerly the case. These include a CVA under Pt I of the Insolvency Act,[531] a compromise or arrangement under Pt 26 of the Companies Act 2006,[532] a distribution within the administration with the court's permission,[533] a creditors' voluntary winding up,[534] a compulsory winding up[535] and a dissolution of the company without first going into winding up.[536] This last is obligatory if the administrator thinks that the company has no property which might permit a distribution to creditors,[537] although the court may

---

[524] Insolvency Act 1986 Sch.B1 para.81(1) and (2).
[525] Insolvency Act 1986 Sch.B1 para.81(3).
[526] *Clark v Finnerty* [2010] EWHC 2538 (Ch); *Clydesdale Financial Services Ltd v Smailes* [2009] EWHC 1745 (Ch); and *Sisu Capital Fund Ltd. v Tucker* [2006] B.P.I.R. 154.
[527] ibid.
[528] See above, para.11–113.
[529] Insolvency Act 1986 Sch.B1 para.1(2)(d).
[530] Insolvency Act 1986 Sch.B1 para.1(2)(c).
[531] Insolvency Act 1986 Sch.B1 para.49(3)(a).
[532] Insolvency Act 1986 Sch.B1 para.49(3)(b).
[533] Insolvency Act 1986 Sch.B1 para.65(3).
[534] Insolvency Act 1986 Sch.B1 para.83.
[535] Insolvency Act 1986 Sch.B1 para.79(4)(d).
[536] Insolvency Act 1986 Sch.B1 para.84.
[537] Insolvency Act 1986 Sch.B1 para.84.

order otherwise.[538] There is a division of judicial opinion on whether the move direct to a dissolution requires that the company has *never* had any property to distribute[539] or whether it suffices that the company has no *further* property to distribute, so that if the administrator, with leave of the court, makes a distribution of all, or all the remaining, property of the company to unsecured creditors, the duty to move to a dissolution applies.[540] The latter view seems clearly to be the correct one. As counsel pointed out in *GHE Realisations*, if there was never any property to distribute, it is unlikely that the company would have been a candidate for administration in the first place, in addition to which the administrator would have no obvious way of bringing the distribution to an end. In any event, it is hard to see what policy is served by a requirement that would preclude any distribution before dissolution.

In other cases, the most likely outcome of administration is a creditors' voluntary liquidation. A new factor to be considered in the decision on exit routes is the Pensions Act 2004 and its provisions for assumption by the Pension Protection Fund (PPF) Board of responsibility for failed pension schemes following an insolvency event[541] and compensation from the PPF for members of such schemes.[542]

13. ADMINISTRATION FOLLOWED BY LIQUIDATION AND VICE VERSA

Relevant date for computation of preferential debts

The advent of administration may have an effect on the relevant date for determining preferential claims both on a subsequent winding up and, under the new regime, in the administration itself where a distribution is to be made.[543] Of particular importance to the computation of preferential claims is the definition of "relevant date", which features in several paragraphs of Sch.6 to the Insolvency Act 1986 and is defined in s.387. In the case of an administration followed immediately by a winding up, s.387 as originally

11–116

---

[538] Insolvency Act 1986 Sch.B1 para.84(2). One such case might be where there are circumstances suggesting misconduct that might require investigation (L. Sealy and D. Milman, *Sealy & Milman: Annotated Guide to the Insolvency Act 2006* (London: Sweet & Maxwell), Vol.1, p.579).

[539] The view of Blackburne J. in *Re Ballast* [2005] 1 W.L.R. 1928.

[540] The view of Rimer J. in *Re GHE Realisations Ltd* [2006] 1 W.L.R. 287 and of Etherton J. in an obiter dictum in *Re Kaupthing Singer & Friedlander Ltd* [2010] Bus. L.R. 1500.

[541] Pensions Act 2004 s.127.

[542] Pensions Act 2004 s.162 and Sch.7.

[543] It will be recalled that the administrator may now make a distribution to preferential creditors without having to obtain the court's permission.

drawn distinguished between a compulsory and voluntary winding up, stating that in the case of a compulsory winding up the relevant date was the commencement of the administration, whereas in the case of a voluntary winding up it was the date of passing of the resolution for voluntary winding up, which could have the effect of extinguishing the eligibility of certain debts for preferential status because of expiry of the period to which the preferential claim was limited.[544] Section 387 has now been amended[545] so as to provide that in both cases the relevant date is the date on which the company entered administration.[546]

To attract these provisions, and also to ensure that the date of the onset of insolvency for the purpose of ss.238 and 239 of the Insolvency Act is the date of entry into administration rather than the date of the voluntary winding-up,[547] it is important to avoid a gap between the ending of the administration and the commencement of the winding up by making arrangements to ensure that a resolution for voluntary winding up is passed or a winding up petition presented immediately after the cessation of the administration. Under the former regime, this presented difficult technical problems. The resolution could not be passed while the administration was still on foot,[548] nor could the passing of the resolution be made conditional on the cessation of administration.[549] Now, however, the company can move straight from administration to a creditors' voluntary winding up where the administrator thinks that the total amount each secured creditor is likely[550] to receive has been paid to or set aside for him and that a distribution will be made to unsecured creditors of the company, if there are any.[551] The process is quite simple. The administrator sends a notice to the registrar of companies that para.83 of Sch.B1 applies, files a copy with the court and sends a copy to each creditor of whose claim and address he is aware and the registrar registers the notice. Upon such registration, the administrator's appointment ceases to have effect and the company is wound-up on the day of such registration as if a resolution for voluntary winding up had been passed, the liquidator being the person nominated by the creditors in the prescribed manner or, if none, the administrator.[552] This procedure has been held to be available even if the administrator was appointed by the court, and there is no need for him to apply to the court for his discharge under para.79 of Sch.B1.[553]

---

[544] This is well explained by Andrew Keay and Peter Walton, *Insolvency Law: Corporate and Personal* (Bristol: Jordans Publishing, 2008), pp.122–123.

[545] By the Insolvency Act 1986 (Amendment) (No.2) Regulations 2002 (SI 2002/1240).

[546] Insolvency Act 1986 s.387(3)(a) and (ba).

[547] See Insolvency Act 1986 s.240(3)(d).

[548] Insolvency Act 1986 Sch.B1 para.42(2).

[549] *Re Norditrack (UK) Ltd* [2000] 1 B.C.L.C. 467.

[550] A slightly odd word to use where the secured creditor has actually received payment. Perhaps "due" would have been better.

[551] Insolvency Act 1986 Sch.B1 para.83(1).

[552] Insolvency Act 1986 Sch.B1 para.83(3)–(7).

[553] *Re Ballast Plc* [2005] 1 All E.R. 630.

Where a compulsory winding up precedes the administration,[554] there are two relevant dates for determining the preferential debts, the first being the date of the winding up order[555] and the second the date on which the company enters administration.[556]

Administrators usually advise a voluntary winding up, rather than a compulsory winding up, in order to avoid the payment of fees to the Department for Business, Innovation and Skills for the Official Receiver's services and what are considered by many to be the inadequate service and high fees for the operation of the Insolvency Services Account into and from which all payments must be made in a compulsory liquidation. But the mode of winding up influences the relevant date for preferential debts, as stated above, and this is a factor to be taken into account.

14. VARIATION OR RESCISSION OF THE ADMINISTRATION ORDER

Rule 7.47 of the Insolvency Rules 1986 provides as follows:

"Every court having jurisdiction under the Act to wind up companies may review, rescind or vary an order made by it in the exercise of that jurisdiction."   **11–117**

It has been held that this rule empowers the court to review, rescind or vary an administration order.[557] The procedure is governed by the CPR.[558]

15. THE EFFECTIVENESS OF ADMINISTRATION

Several studies have been carried out evaluating the efficacy of the reforms produced by the Enterprise Act 2002. These indicate that while realisations are higher than under the previous regime, the costs have also risen, so that   **11–118**

---

[554] Which can now occur as the result of an administration order made on an administration application by the holder of a qualifying floating charge or the liquidator, in which event the court must discharge the winding up order (Insolvency Act 1986 Sch.B1 para.37).

[555] Insolvency Act 1986 s.387(3)(b). However, if: (i) the company had previously been in voluntary winding up, the relevant date is the date of the winding up resolution (s.387(3)(c)); or (ii) a provisional liquidator had been appointed, the relevant date is the appointment (or first appointment) of a provisional liquidator (s.387(3)(b)).

[556] Insolvency Act 1986 s.387(3).

[557] *Cornhill Insurance Plc v Cornhill Financial Services Ltd* [1992] B.C.C. 818, applying the reasoning in *Re Tasbian Ltd (No.2)* [1990] B.C.C. 322.

[558] Insolvency Rules 1986 r.7.51. The CPR are the Civil Procedure Rules 1998, which replaced most of the Rules of the Supreme Court.

the benefits of greater recoveries may be going to the professionals rather than the unsecured creditors.[559] On the other hand, it is also the case that administrations are being completed more quickly, and the ability of administrators to make distributions to unsecured creditors with court approval is increasingly used to proceed directly to dissolution of the company and avoid the need for liquidation. The Insolvency Service has taken some steps to reduce costs, as by providing for electronic communications,[560] remote attendance at meetings[561] and publication on a website,[562] dispensing with the need for an initial creditors' meeting if there is not likely to be a distribution to unsecured creditors[563] as well as the need for annual general meetings in creditors' voluntary winding up in England and Wales,[564] and by allowing the passing of resolutions of creditors to be sought by correspondence.[565] But while measures of this kind are helpful, there remain key issues to be addressed, such as the strong position occupied by secured creditors and lessors, the existence of perverse incentives for directors to delay initiating a formal insolvency procedure, which may result in investigations into their management, the problems of financing rescues, the controversy surrounding the proposed super-priority for rescue finance, and questions of accountability in pre-pack sales. All of these questions have been subject to scrutiny by the Insolvency Service and by outside experts. It remains to be seen how they will eventually be resolved.

---

[559] For detailed discussions, see, e.g. Finch, *Corporate Insolvency Law*, 2009, pp.392 et seq.; John Armour, Audrey Hsu and Adrian Walters, "Corporate Insolvency in the United Kingdom: The Impact of the Enterprise Act 2002" (2008) 5 European Company and Financial Law Rev. 135; and Sandra Frisby, "Interim Report to the Insolvency Service on Returns to Creditors from Pre- and Post-Enterprise Act Insolvency Procedures". For an overview of the future of administration, see Dennis, *Administration*, 2010, Ch.8.

[560] Insolvency Rules 1986 Ch.12A Pt 2.

[561] Insolvency Act 1986 s.246A.

[562] Insolvency Act 1986 s.246B.

[563] Insolvency Act 1986 Sch.B1 para.52(1)(b).

[564] By amending s.105 so as to confine it to Scotland.

[565] Insolvency Rules 1986 r.4.63A.

Chapter 12

Restructurings and Arrangements

The various ways in which a company in financial difficulty can seek to reach arrangements with its creditors, formally or informally, have been outlined in Chapter 1.[1] The present chapter focuses on three mechanisms for addressing the problems of companies in distress: a restructuring, or workout,[2] which is a contractual arrangement outside a formal insolvency proceeding; a scheme of arrangement (scheme) under Pt 26 of the Companies Act 2006, which typically follows a restructuring plan for which it proves impossible to secure agreement[3]; and a company voluntary arrangement (CVA) under Pt 1 of the Insolvency Act 1986. Reconstruction under s.110 of the Insolvency Act 1986 will not be discussed because, as pointed out earlier,[4] this involves solvent companies which are in or about to enter into a members' voluntary winding up, while a liquidator's power to compromise claims under ss.165 to 167 and Sch.4 has been held not to be an appropriate means of distributing assets otherwise than in accordance with creditors' strict legal rights, except where all of the creditors assent,[5] which is not the situation with which the present chapter is concerned. In the case of multinational groups, restructuring will often involve parallel proceedings in different jurisdictions, for example, a scheme in the United Kingdom and a Ch.11 filing in the United States.

12–01

---

[1] Paras 1–43–1–51.

[2] The two terms are generally treated as interchangeable but some practitioners prefer to use "workout" to describe the process of negotiation which leads, or may lead, to a debt restructuring, while others employ the term to describe informal, or out-of-court, restructuring, as opposed to a scheme or CVA.

[3] Although a sale via a pre-packaged administration is an increasingly used alternative. See above, para.11–37.

[4] Above, para.1–55.

[5] *Re Trix Ltd* [1970] 1 W.L.R. 1421.

1. RESTRUCTURINGS[6]

Precondition of restructuring

12–02   Restructuring is used where the company is basically a good company with a bad balance sheet. In other words, the business itself is viable but the financial arrangements need to be overhauled. If there is not merely financial insolvency but trading insolvency, there is little point in devising a scheme or contractual restructuring, and there will simply be a sale of the business or assets.

The INSOL Principles

12–03   For large, multi-banked companies, it may be possible to bypass formal insolvency procedures, at least in the first instance, and organise a rescue on a contractual basis, following the guidelines embodied in the London Approach and the INSOL Principles.[7] The two are quite similar but the latter reflect an international approach. The eight principles they embody are as follows:

> "**FIRST PRINCIPLE:** Where a debtor is found to be in financial difficulties, all relevant creditors should be prepared to co-operate with each other to give sufficient (though limited) time (a 'Standstill Period') to the debtor for information about the debtor to be obtained and evaluated and for proposals for resolving the debtor's financial difficulties to be formulated and assessed, unless such a course is inappropriate in a particular case.
>
> **SECOND PRINCIPLE:** During the Standstill Period, all relevant creditors should agree to refrain from taking any steps to enforce their claims against or (otherwise than by disposal of their debt to a third party) to reduce their exposure to the debtor but are entitled to expect that during the Standstill Period their position relative to other creditors and each other will not be prejudiced.
>
> **THIRD PRINCIPLE:** During the Standstill Period, the debtor should not take any action which might adversely affect the prospective return to relevant creditors (either collectively or individually) as compared with the position at the Standstill Commencement Date.

---

[6] See Rodrigo Olivares-Caminal *et al, Debt Restructuring* (Oxford: Oxford University Press 2011), a comparative study of restructuring in UK and US law; Chris Howard and Bob Hedger, *Restructuring Law and Practice*, 2nd edn (London: LexisNexis Butterworths, 2008); Philip Wood, *Principles of International Insolvency Law*, 2nd ed (London: Sweet & Maxwell, 2007), Ch 21.

[7] INSOL International, "Statement of Principles for a Global Approach to Multi-Creditor Workouts" (October 2000). For an illuminating discussion, see Nick Segal, "Rehabilitation and Approaches Other Than Formal Insolvency Procedures" in William Blair (ed.), *Banks and Remedies*, 2nd edn (London: Informa Professional, 1999), Ch.8.

FOURTH PRINCIPLE: The interests of relevant creditors are best served by coordinating their response to a debtor in financial difficulty. Such co-ordination will be facilitated by the selection of one or more representative co-ordination committees and by the appointment of professional advisers to advise and assist such committees and, where appropriate, the relevant creditors participating in the process as a whole.

FIFTH PRINCIPLE: During the Standstill Period, the debtor should provide, and allow relevant creditors and/or their professional advisers reasonable and timely access to, all relevant information relating to its assets, liabilities, business and prospects, in order to enable proper evaluation to be made of its financial position and any proposals to be made to relevant creditors.

SIXTH PRINCIPLE: Proposals for resolving the financial difficulties of the debtor and, so far as practicable, arrangements between relevant creditors relating to any standstill should reflect applicable law and the relative positions of relevant creditors at the Standstill Commencement Date.

SEVENTH PRINCIPLE: Information obtained for the purposes of the process concerning the assets, liabilities and business of the debtor and any proposals for resolving its difficulties should be made available to all relevant creditors and should, unless already publicly available, be treated as confidential.

EIGHTH PRINCIPLE: If additional funding is provided during the Standstill Period or under any rescue or restructuring proposals, the repayment of such additional funding should, so far as practicable, be accorded priority status as compared to other indebtedness or claims of relevant creditors."

Financing structures

The workout arrangement will vary according to the original financing arrangements. Borrowings may be either secured or unsecured. Investment-grade borrowers typically borrow on an unsecured basis through the issue of bonds, and the borrower may be the operating company. By contrast, the financing of a leveraged buy-out is usually channelled through a specially established company above the level of the operating company and this will normally be secured. Debt is customarily classified as senior debt or junior (subordinated) debt but the meaning of "senior debt" varies with the arrangements. It may simply denote secured debt as opposed to unsecured debt. But more commonly, in a typical leveraged buy-out, there are different layers of senior debt which among themselves rank in a given order of

12–04

priority,[8] but which collectively have priority over other lenders as regards enforcement decisions and allocation of the proceeds, so that there is a "waterfall" between the two groups. Junior debt usually takes the form of either a loan indebtedness or indebtedness to bondholders or noteholders. Mezzanine debt is a form of junior debt which combines elements of debt and equity, as by the issue of warrants, and may itself be divided into senior mezzanine and junior mezzanine. Bonds and notes are bearer securities issued on a market. Rights and priorities as between the different classes of creditor are regulated by an inter-creditor agreement administered by a security trustee or security agent, who will be authorised, amongst other things, to release junior debt, and securities given for such debt, so as to facilitate realisations on behalf of senior creditors.[9]

12–05   The financing arrangements, including provisions for seniority and subordination, are recorded in a detailed inter-creditor agreement, the negotiation of which generally takes as its starting point the standard form of inter-creditor agreement produced by the Loan Market Association with a view to facilitating consistency of market practice. The inter-creditor agreement assumes particular importance in the event of default.

Restructuring stages

The standstill agreement

12–06   The preparations for a restructuring, or workout, typically involve a number of stages.[10] The first of these may be the reaching of an understanding for an informal moratorium for an agreed standstill period in order to enable the company to provide information and for the creditors to evaluate it and consider proposals to address the company's financial difficulties. It is important to involve in the process all bank and other financial institution creditors as well as representatives of bondholders (who are now more actively engaged in restructurings as a result of the increased use of bonds as a method of financing) and any major trade suppliers whose participation is needed to facilitate the rescue.[11] The participating creditors each state the amount of their exposures as at the beginning of the standstill date and agree to co-operate with each other and, with specified exceptions in favour of senior

---

[8] These may include second-lien lenders, who rank *pari passu* with senior creditors as regards the loan but only participate in realisations of security when the senior creditors have been paid. See above, para.1–04.
[9] For a good recent example, see *Barclays Bank Plc v HHY Luxembourg SARL* [2010] EWCA Civ 1248.
[10] Only the briefest outline can be given here. For a comprehensive description, see *Debt Restructuring* (above, n.6); Howard and Hedger, *Restructuring Law and Practice*, 2010.
[11] Trade suppliers, who are, of course, essential for the continuance of the company's business, are usually left out of the restructuring process and are paid in full.

debt, to refrain from steps designed to improve their position vis-à-vis other participating creditors, while the company undertakes to refrain from acts that would prejudice the position of the participating creditors. Any agreed priorities and provision for new finance will be specified. Power may be given to a security agent or security trustee to release securities for the purpose of effecting a sale.

Because of the tiering of debt in large, complex restructurings, standstill agreements can be complex documents with elaborate definitions and cross-references to other documentation. A common practice is for a formal standstill (or "lock-in") agreement to be prepared but to leave it unsigned, at least in the first instance and sometimes without it ever being signed at all. So often any standstill is non-contractual and operates *de facto* rather than pursuant to a binding obligation. There may, indeed, be no standstill agreement at all, merely a general understanding among creditors to refrain from enforcement action for a given period. The reason for not having a signed agreement is that negotiations can be very protracted, particularly where there are many creditors and the financing structure is complex, so that it is better to have creditors informally assenting to a standard set of terms, albeit lacking contractual force, than to leave everything in the air. Sometimes a standstill agreement is concluded only between the senior creditors, and it is often from them that new finance comes. Intra-creditor issues tend to feature more prominently than issues between the creditors and the company.

Information gathering

Detailed information will have to be gathered by the investigating accountants about the company's financial position, including particulars of loan covenants, cross-default clauses and the like, and a report will be made to creditors. **12–07**

The Steering Committee; bondholders; distressed debt traders

The lenders and the company appoint a steering, or co-ordination, committee representative of the main classes of creditor to manage the restructuring on behalf of all of the creditors. It is normal to appoint a lead bank to act as co-ordinator. Usually, there will be separate steering committees for the senior and junior groups. The lead bank co-ordinates information and action among the participating banks and appoints accountants to investigate the company's financial position and to evaluate information obtained. Membership of a steering committee is not an unalloyed blessing. On the one hand, a member has a seat at the negotiating table and as such can exert a degree of influence varying according to the size of its claim. On the other, members receive price-sensitive information which is likely to preclude them from dealing in **12–08** securities to which the information relates unless they can set up effective "Chinese walls" within their institutions. Creditors thus have to decide whether to join, or remain on, the steering committee or to retain or resume their freedom to deal in the market. Bondholders are a particularly difficult class of creditor to manage, because the bonds are usually bearer bonds, so that the title of the holders does not appear in any register and is constantly changing, with the result that at any given time the other members of the steering committee do not know with whom they are dealing. If the entire bond issue is represented by a global note, further problems may arise, which could be answered by conversion of the note into definitive notes—an expensive process—or by the trustee splitting its vote according to the differing wishes of the bondholders. There will usually be a trustee for bondholders but he will not necessarily play a very prominent role, this being left to one or two of the larger holders who are prepared to organise the ad hoc committees and lead the negotiations. Again, lenders of record do not always have an interest in the outcome of the restructuring, since they may have laid off the risk of default through the arrangement of credit default swaps, which means that the risk of default by the reference companies is borne by noteholders, who thus in effect (although not in law) act as insurers.[12]

Similar problems may arise from distressed debt trading, where a debt trader buys debts from an existing creditor of the company at a substantial discount and resells them if able to secure a reasonable margin. This, too, may make it difficult to establish the identity of the relevant creditors at any particular time. Banks do not always retain their claims but sell them, or enter into sub-participations in relation to them, at a substantial discount to debt traders, who buy either with a view to reselling at a higher price or with the intention of negotiating a debt for equity swap or alternatively of exerting pressure on the company to make payment in full.[13] Decisions are usually entrusted to institutions acting collectively overall or within each class, although the amendment of certain key terms may require unanimity.[14] A security agent or security trustee will be appointed to handle, enforce and, where appropriate, release security.

Preparation of proposals; new money

12–09   When the relevant information has been obtained, the participants and the company can then move to the second stage: the preparation and consideration of proposals. Meanwhile, it is necessary to keep the company trading,

---

[12] See, e.g. *Perpetual Trustee Co Ltd v BNY Corporate Trustee Services Ltd* [2010] Ch. 347, discussed above, paras 7–13–7–22.

[13] For an example, which shows that the courts are alive to this issue, see *Re Telecom Group Plc* [2003] B.P.I.R. 324.

[14] Howard and Hedger, *Restructuring Law and Practice*, 2010, paras 2.25 et seq.

for which purpose it may be necessary to procure additional funding. This is one of the major hurdles to be overcome and usually entails a funding agreement by which the funder obtains a much higher rate of interest on the new funds than it did on those originally advanced, as well as substantial arrangement fees and an agreement for priority of its claim for the new money advanced. Traditionally, funding has been furnished by a major, existing, secured creditor, typically the company's main bank but with the squeeze on bank lending new players have come onto the scene, in particular private equity houses, who may be willing to fill the gap left by the banks on being given an agreed priority position. However, existing funders may be unwilling to see their own priority position downgraded until the final restructuring has been agreed. In order to reach agreement, it may be necessary to find some compromise which leads to the adjustment of either or both of the two positions. If the funding negotiations are successful, they will result in a support agreement between the lenders and the company and a separate agreement among the lenders themselves governing the decision-making process in the restructuring.

Varieties of restructuring

Restructuring can take a variety of forms. A restructuring plan can provide for the conversion of debt into equity or into convertible debt,[15] preference shares convertible into ordinary shares, the adjustment of secured creditors' rights, a compromise in which creditors waive part of their claims[16] or extend the term of their debts, the modification of inter-creditor agreements, the valuation and settlement of contingent claims, and the distribution of assets and discharge of liabilities of members of a group of companies where these have become inextricably entangled so as to make it difficult to establish the assets and liabilities of any individual company within the group. New companies may be set up to accept a transfer of assets and corporate groups may be restructured. As stated above, holders of junior debt and mezzanine debt are often either cut out altogether, there being no assets available to meet their claims, or enter into a novation agreement by which a company as high as possible in the corporate chain above the operating company becomes their debtor in place of the insolvent company, or alternatively the mezzanine creditors give up their claims in exchange for shares in such a company.

12–10

---

[15] e.g. the replacement of existing bonds with bonds convertible into shares, enabling the creditor to continue to enjoy its higher status as such over that of a shareholder while having the option of converting the bonds to shares if the value of the shares rises.

[16] See below, para.12–43, discussing reorganisation in the context of a CVA. For an example of restructuring of a group of companies so that they ceased to be insolvent and could then be taken out of administration, see *Re Olympia & York Canary Wharf Ltd (No.4)* [1994] 1 B.C.L.C. 702.

These are forms of structured subordination, in that shareholders rank after creditors, so that a mezzanine or junior creditor of a company at or near the top of the corporate chain is largely dependent on such dividends as the company receives from its subsidiary, while a former mezzanine creditor who becomes a shareholder is deferred to creditors of the company in which it has been given shares. The more remote that company is from the operating company which is to make the profits, the less the prospect that the erstwhile mezzanine or junior creditor of the latter will receive anything.

The basic approach is that "those who are out of the money stay out of the money". However, central to any restructuring is the valuation of the business. Valuation, as noted in Ch.4 of this work, is not an exact science and highly competent and experienced valuers can come up with widely differing valuations reflecting different but not unreasonable, assumptions. So, lower-ranking, secured creditors or even second lien creditors and mezzanine creditors who are said to be "out of the money" may feel aggrieved at being treated as having no economic interest in the company. There are also issues as to whether the valuation should be on a liquidation or on a going-concern basis and, if the latter, whether it should be the existing going-concern value or should take account of prospects of future recovery and consequent increase in the value of the business, and this has led to questions as to whether it might not be possible to give creditors who on an existing valuation are out of the money some interest in the fruits of recovery, for example, by the issue of share warrants, as had, indeed, been proposed at one time in the *Bluebrook* restructuring but was later abandoned.[17] At bottom is the issue of fairness to all classes of creditor.

The problem of securing agreement

12–11   Where a restructuring is being negotiated, it is quite common for minority creditors to hold out for better terms or repayment in full. That is particularly true of debt traders who have purchased distressed debt primarily to make a quick return rather than to acquire control (as many seek to do) through a loan-to-own debt for equity swap. Majority creditors usually set their face against meeting such demands except as regards creditors whose claims are relatively small or upon whom the company is dependent for its ability to continue trading, such as key trade suppliers. Failing agreement or a buy-out, dissentient creditors can often be brought into line by the threat of an application to the court to sanction a scheme of arrangement under s.895 of the Companies Act 2006[18] or the proposal to carry out a pre-packaged sale through administration to a vehicle owned by the senior lenders and those creditors who are still in the money.

---

[17] See *Re Bluebrook Ltd* [2010] B.C.C. 209, *per* Mann J. at [6].
[18] See below, paras 12–12 et seq.

However, lack of information as to the identity of some of the creditors, whether because they are lenders of record who have laid off their risk through credit default swaps and thus have no interest in the restructuring or because of the fragmentation of debt among bondholders and distressed debt traders or otherwise, as well as the complexity of the structures of corporate groups and of creditor and inter-creditor agreements, may make it impossible to secure the agreement of all interested parties. In such a case, one solution is to apply to the court to sanction a scheme of arrangement which, if approved by the requisite majority in number and value of creditors in each of the separate classes and sanctioned by the court, will bind all creditors This includes a "cram-down" on the rights of secured creditors. Alternatively, it may be possible to arrange a sale through a pre-packaged administration ("pre-pack") pursuant to an agreement with the senior, secured creditors.

The increasing difficulties of organising the restructuring of major companies, with potentially adverse effects also for smaller companies where such restructuring fails, have led to proposals by the Insolvency Service for a restructuring moratorium.[19] These are based on the concept of the debtor in possession—that is, continuance of the debtor company under its existing management, as under Ch.11 of the US Federal Bankruptcy Code—and are designed to give a breathing space during which a restructuring can be negotiated and implemented outside any formal insolvency procedure. Such a moratorium is seen as carrying with it a number of benefits: allowing informal standstills to be more effective in that knowledge that a statutory moratorium can be obtained will reduce incentives for participants to engage in tactical approaches to secure benefits through threat of delay or disruption; reducing the need to make ransom payments to hold-out creditors; saving costs and improving returns to creditors where the company would otherwise have had to go into administration; and providing a stronger incentive for directors to act early to address their problems rather than wait for the onset of insolvency.[20] The option would also assist companies preparing for a company voluntary arrangement or scheme of arrangement and would last for three months, with the option of a threee-month extension in appropriate cases. It would have to be sanctioned by the court, which would have to be satisfied that the business was viable. Most companies of the kind excluded from the small company moratorium provisions would also be excluded under the new proposals.

There are disadvantages to the proposed moratorium. It could trigger termination clauses in key contracts and would publicise the company's difficult financial position and thereby adversely affect its business. In deciding whether the business was viable, the court would perforce have to lean heavily on the views of experienced insolvency practitioners involved.

---

[19] *Proposals for a Restructuring Moratorium—A Consultation*, July 2010.
[20] *Proposals for a Restructuring Moratorium—A Consultation*, July 2010, para.2.10.

2. SCHEMES

The statutory background

12–12   Schemes, formerly carried out under s.425 of the Companies Act 1985, are now governed by Pt 26 of the Companies Act 2006.[21] In their origin, schemes were confined to arrangements with creditors by companies in the course of being wound-up,[22] but with changes in the legislation they became used for a wide range of purposes going well beyond insolvency, for example, to effect mergers, takeovers and takeover substitutes (and in that connection to avoid the application of the Takeover Directive)[23] or, in the case of insurance companies, to exit from the insurance market or a sector of it under arrangements providing for the valuation and payment of prospective liabilities in respect of run-off cover. We are not concerned with these, and the rest of this chapter is devoted to schemes of arrangement with creditors.

Schemes and contractual restructurings

12–13   The court may be asked to approve a scheme under s.899 of the Companies Act binding on all creditors or a class of creditors and on the company itself. As pointed out earlier, schemes require the court's approval and the process of securing this is rather cumbersome and not inexpensive. For that reason, schemes have been used primarily by companies with a complex capital structure involving secured debt who are unable to conclude a purely contractual restructuring[24] and who need a scheme in order to "cram down" secured creditors, whose rights cannot be overridden in a CVA. In other cases companies may prefer to go through the easier and less expensive route of a CVA, accepting that the rights of secured and preferential creditors cannot be adversely affected without their consent. It occasionally happens that a takeover bid is made for an insolvent public company within the framework of a scheme, in which case it will be necessary to comply with the Takeover Code and any directions given by the City Panel on Takeovers and Mergers.[25]

---

[21] See Louise Gullifer and Jennifer Payne, *Corporate Finance Law: Principles and Policy* (Oxford: Hart Publishing, 2011), Ch.12.

[22] Joint Stock Companies Act 1870.

[23] Directive 2004/25/EC of the European Parliament and Council on takeover bids of April 21, 2004 ([2004] OJ L142/12). See generally Paul Davies (ed.), *Gower and Davies: Principles of Modern Company Law*, 8th edn (London: Sweet & Maxwell, 2008), Chs 28 and 29.

[24] In most cases, such companies are able to avoid a formal insolvency proceeding.

[25] Usually a takeover within a scheme involves a solvent company but occasionally it arises in relation to an insolvent company, as in *Re Expro International Group Plc* [2008] EWHC 1543 (Ch).

Purpose of the statutory provisions

Part 26 of the Companies Act is designed to ensure, first, that the scheme is on the face of it a proper scheme justifying a court order approving the convening of meetings of the relevant creditors or classes thereof; secondly, that the meetings are duly convened, the classes properly constituted and the effect of the proposals explained and that the directors provide such information as is needed to provide the required disclosure of any material interests they may have; thirdly, that all of the statutory requirements have been complied with; and fourthly that the scheme is a fair and proper one.

12–14

Stages in securing the approval of a scheme

The proposed scheme having been formulated, there are three stages in securing approval of a scheme under s.899. These stages, together with the reasons for each stage, have been succinctly expressed and restated in three judgments of Chadwick L.J.,[26] in the last of which he set out the position in the following terms[27]:

12–15

"There are—as I sought to point out in *In Re BTR plc* [2000] BCLC 740, at page 742—three stages in the process by which a compromise or arrangement becomes binding as between the company and all its creditors (or all those creditors within the class of creditors with which the compromise or arrangement is made) and as between the company and all its members (or all those members within the relevant class). First, there must be an application to the court under section 425(1) of the Act for an order that a meeting or meetings be summoned. It is at that stage that a decision needs to be taken as to whether or not to summon more than one meeting; and, if so, who should be summoned to which meeting. Second, the scheme proposals are put to the meeting or meetings held in accordance with the order that has been made; and are approved (or not) by the requisite majority in number and value of those present and voting in person or by proxy. Third, if approved at the meeting or meetings, there must be a further application to the court under section 425(2) of the Act to obtain the court's sanction to the compromise or arrangement. This Court adopted that analysis *In re Hawk Insurance Co Ltd* [2001] EWCA Civ 241, [2001] 2 BCLC 480—see paragraph [11] of my judgment in that appeal (*ibid.* 510h–511 *b*) with which the other members of the Court agreed. At paragraph [12] of my judgment in *Hawk Insurance* (*ibid.* 511 *b–g*), I went on to say this:

---

[26] See *Re BTR Plc* [2000] 1 B.C.L.C. 740 at 742; *Re Hawk Insurance Co Ltd* [2002] B.C.C. 300; and *Re MyTravel Group Plc* [2005] 2 B.C.L.C. 123 at para. 8.
[27] *MyTravel Group*, cited above n.26, at [8].

'It can be seen that each of those stages serves a distinct purpose. At the first stage the court directs how the meeting or meetings are to be summoned. It is concerned, at that stage, to ensure that those who are to be affected by the compromise or arrangement proposed have a proper opportunity of being present (in person or by proxy) at the meeting or meetings at which they are to be considered and voted upon. The second stage ensures that the proposals are acceptable to at least a majority in number, representing three-fourths in value, of those who take the opportunity of being present (in person or by proxy) at the meeting or meetings. At the third stage the court is concerned (i) to ensure that the meeting or meetings have been summoned and held in accordance with its previous order, (ii) to ensure that the proposals have been approved by the requisite majority of those present at the meeting or meetings and (iii) to ensure that the views and interests of those who have not approved the proposals at the meeting or meetings (either because they were not present or, being present, did not vote in favour of the proposals) receive impartial consideration.' "

Formulation of the scheme

12–16 It is for the directors of the company to formulate proposals for a scheme in consultation with major creditors. Although it is open to a creditor to apply for approval of a scheme, it must have the approval of the company through its board or a resolution of the members, for otherwise the court has no jurisdiction to sanction the scheme.[28] Accordingly, where the board considers the creditor's proposals to be unacceptable, while it is open to the court to convene meetings of creditors on the application of a creditor it will not exercise its discretion to do so where the evidence indicates that the board is unlikely to change its mind and either the scheme makes no provision for approval by the company in general meeting or it is clear that the meeting would not give its approval.[29]

Companies eligible for a scheme

12–17 Part 26 of the Companies Act 2006 applies to any company liable to be wound up under the Insolvency Act 1986.[30] This includes a foreign company which has a sufficient connection with the United Kingdom,[31] and recently the English court sanctioned a scheme of arrangement relating to the obli-

---

[28] *Re Savoy Hotels Ltd* [1981] Ch. 351.
[29] *Re Savoy Hotels Ltd*, cited above n.28.
[30] Companies Act 2006 s.895(2). See above, para.5–01.
[31] See below, paras 16–50 and 16–51. It does not appear to be necessary that the company should have its COMI or an establishment in the United Kingdom.

gations of a Spanish company in England under a senior facilities agreement governed by English law and containing a jurisdiction clause in favour of the English courts[32] and four connected schemes to restructure the German Tele Combus group of companies as regards their English law debt obligations, expert evidence on German law having been given to the effect that the schemes would be effective and recognised in Germany.

Who is a creditor?

The word "creditor" is used in the widest sense and includes a creditor whose debt has not yet become payable[33] and a contingent creditor,[34] whether or not his claim is provable and, indeed, even if he has yet to make a claim or is unknown,[35] provided that the facts that may give rise to his claim already exist.[36] However, a surety cannot vote unless he has paid off the debt or that part of it guaranteed by him. There is no authority directly in point,[37] but this conclusion must follow from the rule against double proof,[38] for clearly a single debt should not be counted twice for voting purposes and equally clearly the surety should not be allowed to vote in competition with the unpaid creditor.

12–18

> "The guarantor's contingent claim is not regarded as an independent, free-standing debt but only as a reflection of the 'real' debt . . ."[39]

The corollary, of course, is that the surety is bound by any resulting scheme to the extent that it is binding on the creditor to whom he gave his guarantee. A creditor whose claim is governed by a foreign law is entitled to participate in meetings concerning a proposed scheme and if he does so, he is bound by the scheme, at least if assenting to it, and probably even if not.[40] However,

---

[32] The scheme was in due course approved (*Re La Seda de Barcelona* [2010] EWHC 1364 (Ch).

[33] *Re Cancol Ltd* [1995] 1 B.C.L.C. 1133.

[34] *Re Midland Coal, Coke & Iron Co* [1895] 1 Ch. 267, *per* Wright J. at 277 in a passage approved by the Court of Appeal in [1895] 1 Ch. 267.

[35] *Re T. & N. Ltd* [2006] 1 W.L.R. 1728; and *Re T. & N. Ltd (No.3)* [2007] 1 All E.R. 851, reviewing the various authorities. In those cases, numerous claims had been made for damages for potential injury to health from exposure to asbestos, which as r.13.12 of the Insolvency Rules 986 stood at that time were not provable debts, because in tort law the cause of action did not accrue until the appearance of loss or damage, and it was envisaged that there would also be future claimants. Nevertheless, all such claimants qualified as creditors for the purpose of the proposed scheme, which on being sanctioned by the court would bind them all. Since then, r.13.12 has been amended to allow tort claims to be admitted to proof if the only missing element is loss or damage. See above, para.4–24.

[36] See *Re T. & N. Ltd* cited above n.35, at [75]–[76].

[37] The issue potentially arose in *Fender v IRC* [2003] B.P.I.R. 1304 in relation to an individual voluntary arrangement but no reference was made to the implications of the rule against double proof.

[38] See above, para.8–45. As to sureties, see below, para.12–25.

[39] *Re Polly Peck International Plc* [1996] 2 All E.R. 433, *per* Robert Walker J. at 441.

[40] See below, para.12–24.

only a person with a pecuniary claim, whether present or contingent and whether liquidated or unliquidated, can be a creditor. This covers a secured creditor but excludes a person whose claim is a purely proprietary claim, for example, as beneficial owner under a trust but with no personal claims, for a scheme designed to discharge purely proprietary claims by a person having no personal claim against the company is not a scheme which affects the claimant in his capacity as a creditor. This is because trust property does not form part of the company's assets and the beneficiary is entitled to his property in specie.[41]

What is a class?

12–19   Where different creditors have different interests, it may be necessary to divide them into separate classes and convene separate meetings of each class. Conversely, creditors whose rights are so similar to the rights of others that they can properly be required to consult together should not be allowed a separate meeting, for this might give a power of veto to a minority group.[42]

What constitutes a class has often given rise to considerable difficulty.[43] This was exacerbated by the former practice of deferring judicial consideration of the question until the hearing of the application to approve the scheme, at which point the court might rule that because there had been no class meetings or the classes had been incorrectly identified, the court had no discretion to approve the scheme, so that the whole exercise was frustrated. Following criticism of this practice by the Company Law Review[44] and Chadwick L.J. in *Re Hawk Insurance Co Ltd*,[45] the practice was changed, and while it remains the applicant's responsibility to determine whether more than one meeting is required and ensure that the classes are properly constituted, the court gives due consideration to the identification of classes at the first stage.[46] The general test is whether the creditors as a whole have a sufficient community of interest to enable their rights to be considered together or whether, on the other hand, their rights are so dissimilar as to make it impossible for them to consult together with a view to their common

---

[41] *Re Lehman Bros International (Europe) Ltd* [2010] B.C.C. 272.

[42] *Re Hawk Insurance Co Ltd* [2002] B.C.C. 300, *per* Chadwick L.J. at [33].

[43] See, e.g. *Re Osiris Insurance Ltd* [1999] 1 B.C.L.C. 182; *Re Anglo American Insurance Co Ltd* [2001] 1 B.C.L.C. 755; and *Scottish Lion Insurance Co Ltd v Goodrich Corp*, 2010 S.C. 349.

[44] *Modern Company Law for a Competitive Economy: Final Report* (London: Company Law Review Steering Group, 2001), Vol.I, para.13.6.

[45] [2002] B.C.C. 300.

[46] Practice Statement (Companies: Schemes of Arrangement) [2002] 1 W.L.R. 1345, paras 2 and 5. The Company Law Review, supported by a large majority of its respondents, advocated going further and allowing the court to sanction a scheme even if the classes had been wrongly constituted where the court was satisfied that that this had no substantive effect on the outcome (above, n.44, para.13.7) but this proposal was not adopted.

interest.[47] The purpose of class meetings is to ensure that a mere majority in value of creditors does not override the rights of those whose interests are entirely different,[48] and that any resulting scheme will cater separately for each class. In essence, the question is whether the scheme can be regarded as a single arrangement requiring a single meeting or ought to be regarded on a true analysis as a number of linked arrangements each requiring a separate meeting.[49] The scheme itself may differentiate between one class of creditor and another, for example, by giving priority to post-scheme trade creditors over pre-scheme trade creditors in order to ensure the continuance of supply of necessary goods or services or by differentiating senior debt from junior debt or secured from unsecured creditors. What emerges from *Re Hawk Insurance Co Ltd*[50] is that the court will not adopt a mechanical test in determining the composition of a class but will look to the scheme's impact on the substantive rights of the different creditors. It is the rights of creditors, not their separate commercial or other interests, which determine whether they form a single class or separate classes.[51] So while creditors holding vested rights may be held to constitute a different class from those whose rights are merely contingent,[52] that is not necessarily the case; it is a question of determining whether there is a group of creditors whose rights, whether pre-existing or proposed under the scheme, are so dissimilar that it is impossible for them to consult together with a view to their common interest.[53]

The application

Who can apply for an order for a meeting

Application for an order for a meeting of creditors under s.896(1) of the Act **12–20** may be made by the company, any creditor or member of the company, or if the company is being wound up or is in administration, the liquidator[54] or administrator.[55]

---

[47] *Sovereign Life Assurance Co v Dodd* [1892] 2 Q.B. 573, *per* Bowen L.J. at 583.
[48] *Sovereign Life* Assurance, cited above n.47.
[49] *Re Hawk Insurance Co Ltd* [2002] B.C.C. 300, *per* Chadwick L.J. at [23]; and *Re Equitable Life Assurance Society* [2002] 2 B.C.L.C. 510.
[50] Cited above n.49.
[51] *Re T. & N. Ltd (No.3)* [2007] 1 All E.R. 851, *per* David Richards J. at [85], citing *Re BTR Plc* [1999] 2 B.C.L.C. 675; *Re Hawk Insurance Co Ltd* [2001] 2 B.C.L.C. 480 and *Re UDL Holdings Ltd* [2002] 1 H.K.C. 172, *per* Lord Millett N.P.J. at 184–185.
[52] For an example, see *Sovereign Life Assurance Co v Dodd* [1892] 2 Q.B. 573.
[53] *Re Hawk Insurance Co Ltd* cited above n.51, *per* Chadwick L.J. at [30].
[54] Including a provisional liquidator if so empowered by the court. See, e.g. *Re Anglo American Insurance Ltd* [2001] 1 B.C.L.C. 755.
[55] Companies Act 2006 s.896(2).

Procedure

12–21 Applications are governed by CPR Pt 49 and para.15 of Practice Direction 49A,[56] which requires that the claim form be supported by written evidence, including the statutory information about the company and the terms of the proposed compromise or arrangement, and must seek: (i) directions for the convening of a meeting of creditors; (ii) the sanction of the court to the compromise or arrangement, if it was approved at the meeting(s), and a direction for a further hearing for that purpose; and (iii) a direction that the claimant file a copy of a report to the court by the chairman of the meeting or each meeting. Applications may be made either to the judge or the registrar. They are usually made *ex parte* to the registrar but should be adjourned to the judge in appropriate cases, and applications in respect of substantial schemes will be listed before the judge.[57] At this stage, the court will determine the identity of the classes for the purpose of deciding what meetings should be convened but will not adjudicate on whether the scheme is fair—a matter to be considered only on the substantive hearing.[58]

Meetings

12–22 Once the classes, if any, have been identified and the court has given its approval, the requisite meeting(s) of creditors can be convened.[59] It is not necessary to give notice of a meeting to any creditor outside the class affected by the scheme or whose legal rights are unaffected by it and who has no economic interest in the company. A creditor or class of creditor has no economic interest where he or the class of which he is a member has no prospect of receiving anything from the company even if it was restored to successful trading or, if this were not feasible, because all of the assets would be consumed by higher-ranking claims in the event of a sale of the business or assets or upon liquidation,[60] the latter being the event (whether or not hypothesised as preceded by an administration) against which the existence of an economic interest has to be tested where winding up is the only alternative to the scheme.[61] That, of course, involves careful valuation of the company's assets and liabilities and consideration of the likelihood of recovery

---

[56] Practice Direction 49A—Applications under the Companies Acts and related legislation. For fuller details of the procedure, see *Tolley's Company Law and Insolvency*, para.S1012.

[57] Practice Statement (Companies: Schemes of Arrangement) [2002] 1 W.L.R. 1345, para.3.

[58] *Re British Aviation Insurance Co Ltd* [2006] B.C.C. 14.

[59] In contrast to a CVA, it is not necessary to hold a meeting of members.

[60] *Re Tea Corp Ltd* [1904] 1 Ch. 12; *Re Oceanic Steam Navigation Co Ltd* [1939] Ch. 41; and *Re British & Commonwealth Holdings Plc (No.3)* [1992] 1 W.L.R. 672.

[61] *Re MyTravel Group Plc* [2005] 1 W.L.R. 2365, *per* David Richards J. at [56], where the position was also tested against returns likely if the hypothesised liquidation was preceded by administration.

of additional assets. The required majority for approval of a scheme is a majority in number representing 75 per cent in value of creditors voting in person or by proxy. Given that future and contingent creditors are included, this may raise difficult questions of valuation of their claims for the purpose of determining whether there is the requisite majority. The requirement that there must be a majority in number as well as the requisite majority in value should surely have been discarded by the Companies Act, 2006 for it means that if dissentients can muster a majority in number, they can defeat the proposed scheme even if the value of their claims is an insignificant percentage of the total. The Company Law Review recommended abolition of this requirement, leaving it to the court to decide whether small creditors were being unfairly treated,[62] but this recommendation was not implemented.

Criteria for approval of the scheme

In order to sanction the scheme, the court must be satisfied that the statutory requirements have been fulfilled, with the holding of the necessary class meetings and approval of the required majorities, and that the class was fairly represented at each meeting.[63] But even if all of these conditions are fulfilled, the court retains a discretion to withhold its sanction and will do so if it is not satisfied that the scheme is fair to creditors generally. That does not mean that all creditors must derive benefit, for clearly the rights of secured creditors and existing priorities must be respected in evaluating which creditors have the greatest, or sole, economic interest in the company; it requires only that the majority shall not have taken unfair advantage of its position.[64] Creditors who have no economic interest in the company because, whether on a sale pursuant to the scheme or on a winding up, the assets will produce less than is needed to pay off senior debt, need not be consulted and have no ground to object to the scheme as unfairly prejudicial to their interests. A good illustration of the legitimate exclusion of a class of creditors having no economic interest in the company is provided by *Re Bluebrook Ltd*[65]:

> The case involved a complex restructuring of a group of companies, including a pre-pack sale of assets to the restructured group, a retention of part of the existing senior debt in the existing group and the conversion

12–23

---

[62] Cited above, n.44, para.13.10.
[63] *Re British Aviation Insurance Co Ltd* [2006] B.C.C. 14; and *Re BTR Plc* [1999] 2 B.C.L.C. 675. If there has been a material change of circumstances between the time of the meeting and the time the court is called upon to consider whether to sanction the scheme, the court is bound to have regard to this in deciding how to proceed (*Re Expro International Group Plc* [2008] EWHC 1543 (Ch), *per* David Richards J. at [46]).
[64] See *Re Industrial Equity (Pacific) Ltd* [1991] 2 H.K.L.R. 614, *per* Nazareth J. at 625B.
[65] [2010] B.C.C. 209, also known as the *IMO Carwash* case, since it involved the IMO Carwash Group.

of the remaining senior debt into shares in a new holding company. Three valuations of the group showed that the value of the group fell far short of what was needed even to pay senior debt, which was valued at about 60p in the pound. Mezzanine lenders, who were subordinated to senior lenders by subordination agreements, would therefore receive nothing. The proposed schemes therefore excluded them. The mezzanine lenders formed a Mezzanine Co-Ordinating Committee to oppose the schemes as unfairly prejudicial on the ground that the value of the group had not been shown to be less than the amount of the senior debt and that they should anyway be allowed to participate so as not to be shut out from any prospect of benefiting from the assets.

Mann J. held that the legal rights of the mezzanine creditors had not been altered in any way. That did not preclude them from complaining of unfairness but it was clear that there was no prospect of the mezzanine creditors receiving anything from the assets, so that they had no economic interest in the group. Accordingly the scheme was not unfair to them and would be sanctioned despite their objections.

Binding effect of scheme

12–24   Once it has been given the court's sanction, a scheme is binding on all creditors or the class of creditor affected (including creditors who did not receive notice of the meeting to approve the scheme and unknown creditors who may have claims in the future arising out of existing facts[66]), the company itself and, if the company is in liquidation, the liquidator.[67] But creditors outside the scheme are not bound and retain their full rights, as do creditors in relation to claims excluded from the scheme.[68] Moreover, the company is entitled to choose the creditors with whom it wishes to enter into an arrangement and need not include creditors who are unaffected by the scheme either because their legal rights are unaltered or because they have no economic interest in the company, having no prospect of receiving anything.[69] The position is otherwise if the effect of a proposed scheme is to vary the rights of a class of creditors so as to deprive them of a real prospect of a benefit they might otherwise enjoy.

A scheme is not binding on a non-assenting creditor whose debt is governed by foreign law.[70] However, the creditor, whether English or foreign, is entitled to participate in meetings to approve the scheme and to vote in those meetings, and it is thought that if he does so, he is bound by the scheme

---

[66] *Re T. & N. Ltd (No.3)* [2007] 1 All E.R. 851.
[67] Companies Act 2006 s.899(3).
[68] *Re Marconi Corp Plc* [2003] EWHC 1083 (Ch), *per* Lindsay J. at [18].
[69] *Re Bluebrook Ltd* [2010] B.C.C. 209.
[70] *New Zealand Loan & Mercantile Agency Ltd v Morrison* [1898] A.C. 349.

if it is approved by the court even though he may have voted against it. There appears to be no authority on this particular point but it would seem contrary to principle that a creditor who has availed himself of a right to participate and vote, potentially influencing the result of a proposal for a scheme, should be allowed to resile from the outcome merely because he cast his vote against the scheme.

Although schemes generally work well, the view has been expressed that "various recent decisions of the courts have had the practical effect of diminishing the minority protection available in the first court hearing stages of schemes of arrangement" and that while the court's scrutiny at the second stage may lead to its exercising its discretion to refuse to sanction a scheme where minority protection issues exist, "the minority protection at this second court hearing may not be as significant as it appears".[71]

Effect of scheme on surety

It is a well-established principle of suretyship law that release of the principal **12–25** debtor, an agreement not to sue him or a variation of the terms of the principal obligation discharges a surety unless the creditor reserves his rights against the surety either as a term of the guarantee or as a term of the release or other arrangement with the debtor.[72] In *Johnson v Davies*,[73] this principle was held to apply to a release or variation under an individual voluntary arrangement, the reasoning being that the effect of the IVA under s.260(2) of the Insolvency Act was not to impose an arrangement directly on a dissenting creditor but to treat him as if he were a party to the arrangement, which had thus to be treated as if it were a consensual arrangement between the debtor and his creditors.[74] However, the position is otherwise under the different wording of s.899 of the Companies Act. The authorities on the predecessors of s.899 show that a scheme of arrangement under the Companies Acts operates to produce a discharge or variation by operation of law and thus does not discharge a surety or a joint debtor outside the scheme.[75] As stated earlier, a surety who discharges the debt steps into the shoes of the paid-off creditor and is thus bound by the scheme to the same extent as the creditor would have been if he had not received payment from the surety.

---

[71] Gullifer and Payne, *Corporate Finance Law*, 2011, p.652.

[72] The ability to preserve rights against the surety by the terms of an arrangement to which the surety is not a party is because, in assenting the arrangement, the debtor impliedly consents to the surety's rights against him remaining unaffected, so that the surety is not prejudiced (*Greene King Plc v Stanley* [2002] B.P.I.R. 491, *per* Jonathan Parker L.J. at [80]).

[73] [1999] Ch. 117.

[74] *Johnson v Davies* [1999] Ch. 117.

[75] *Re London Chartered Bank of Australia* [1893] 3 Ch. 540; *Dane v Mortgage Insurance Corp Ltd* [1894] 1 Q.B. 54; and *Re Garner's Motors Ltd* [1937] Ch. 594, where Crossman J. observed (at 599): "The scheme when sanctioned by the court becomes something quite different from a mere agreement signed by the parties. It becomes a statutory scheme."

3. COMPANY VOLUNTARY ARRANGEMENTS[76]

The nature of a CVA[77]

12–26   A CVA made by a company[78] with its creditors under Pt I of the Insolvency Act 1986 is a composition in satisfaction of the company's debts[79] or a scheme of arrangement of its affairs,[80] the composition or scheme resulting from acceptance of a proposal by the directors to the company and its creditors.[81] Except as otherwise provided by the terms of the CVA or where the company is in administration (in which case, the administrator has charge of its affairs), the directors remain in control of the company and continue to have power to carry on the business and realise assets. A CVA may be made whether or not the company is insolvent or likely to become insolvent.[82]

CVAs typically involve either a sale of assets and a distribution of the proceeds to creditors, which is usually a relatively short-term procedure, or a continuance of trading under which the company makes periodic payments from its trading income to the supervisor of the CVA for distribution in accordance with its terms, a process which may continue for a considerable time. A distribution CVA is likely to be used only in special circumstances (for example, because of tax considerations), since it is normally easier to place the company into a creditors' voluntary winding up. So the CVA is used mainly as a vehicle for trading, and although it rarely succeeds in

---

[76] See Geoffrey M. Weisgard, Michael Griffiths and Louis Doyle, *Company Voluntary Arrangements and Administrations*, 2nd edn (Bristol: Jordans Publishing, 2010).

[77] For contrasts with administration, see above, paras 11–17 and 11–31 et seq.

[78] The effect of art.3 of the EC Insolvency Regulation (1346/2000/EC) had been held to extend the power to make administration orders, and by the same token CVAs, to legal persons other than companies, and was utilised rather imaginatively to enable the Dean and Chapter of Bradford Cathedral to enter into a CVA, the court applying *Re The Salvage Association* [2003] 2 B.C.L.C. 333 (see Philip Mudd and Caroline Whittington, "Cathedral Saved by CVA" (2005) 21 I.L. & P. 10). This enterprising ecclesiastic feat ceased to be able to be undertaken with the issue of the Insolvency Act (Amendment) Regulations 2005 (SI 2005/879), which amended s.1(4) of the Insolvency Act by providing that a CVA can be proposed only by: (i) a company within the meaning of what was then s.735(1) of the Companies Act 1985 (now Companies Act 2006 s.1); (ii) a company incorporated in an EEA state other than the United Kingdom; or (iii) a company not incorporated in an EEA state but having its centre of main interests in a Member State other than Denmark.

[79] That is, an agreement by creditors to accept less than the amount due to them in discharge of their claims. See above, para.1–44.

[80] Insolvency Act 1986 s.1.

[81] See generally Edward Bailey, *Voluntary Arrangements*, 2nd edn (London: LexisNexis Butterworths, 2007); and Andrew Keay and Peter Walton, *Insolvency Law: Corporate and Personal*, 2nd ed (Bristol: Jordans 2008) Ch.8.

[82] See Insolvency Act 1986 s.1(1). Rule 1.6(1)(a) of the Insolvency Rules 1986 suggests the contrary but cannot, it is thought, be intended to introduce the requirement of an existing or impending insolvency by a side wind and is to be interpreted as confined to cases where the company is in fact insolvent or threatened with insolvency.

preserving the business for the company itself, it may facilitate a disposal of it on more favourable terms than would otherwise have been the case.

"The underlying rationale of the CVA, as far as creditors of an insolvent company are concerned, is that it offers them a better return than they would realise if some other form of insolvency procedure were to be commenced in relation to the company. There is also the possibility that trade creditors might retain a customer for the future, and in certain cases this will be an attractive feature of a CVA proposal."[83]

The wording of s.5(2)(b), discussed below, has led the courts to characterise the relationship between the parties to a CVA as essentially contractual in nature[84] and its scope and effect are determined by its terms. It follows that the court has no power to give directions to amend a concluded CVA.[85] Whether the CVA operates as an accord or a release so as to discharge a co-debtor or surety not a party to the arrangement depends solely on the terms of the arrangement.[86] So too does the question of whether the CVA imposes a stay on proceedings by a creditor who is bound by it.[87]

Relationship of CVA to other types of arrangement

(1) Composition

A CVA may itself include a composition but this is not a necessary component of a CVA.[88]　　　　　　　　　　　　　　　　　　　　　　　　　　　　　**12–27**

(2) Scheme of arrangement

Although s.1(1) refers to a "scheme of arrangement", this phrase is normally used to denote a scheme made under s.895 of the Companies Act 2006. The　　**12–28**

---

[83] Adrian Walters and Sandra Frisby, "Preliminary Report to the Insolvency Service into Outcomes in Company Voluntary Arrangements," a hitherto unpublished paper which seeks to evaluate the relative success of "stand-alone" CVAs (i.e. those not organised within the frramework of an administration or other moratorium) and those run in parallel with a moratorium. CVAs are used primarily by retail businesses, which in the economic downturn have experienced difficulties in maintaining payments of rent under leases of their premises. See *Debt Restructuring* (above, n.6), paras 3.230 *et seq.*

[84] *Re TBL Realisations Plc, Oakley-Smith v Greenberg* [2004] B.C.C. 81; *Whitehead v Household Mortgage Corp* [2003] 1 All E.R. 319; *Johnson v Davies* [1999] Ch. 117; and *Re Halson Packaging Ltd* [1997] B.C.C. 993. All of these cases were decisions on the comparable wording in s.260(2) of the Act relating to individual voluntary arrangements.

[85] *Re Alpa Lighting Ltd* [1997] B.P.I.R. 341.

[86] *Johnson v Davies*, cited above n.84.

[87] See below, para.12–51.

[88] *March Estates Plc v Gunmark Ltd* [1996] 2 B.C.L.C. 1.

procedure for a scheme of arrangement under s.895 and the effect of such a scheme differ materially from a CVA.[89] In the case of a scheme, it is necessary to hold separate meetings for each distinct class, whereas in the case of a CVA there is only one class, and this increases the risk that the different interests of different kinds of creditor are not adequately reflected by the CVA.[90] A CVA requires only a 75 per cent majority in value, whereas for a scheme the 75 per cent has to represent a majority in number. In the case of a scheme, the onus is on its proponents to show why the court should sanction it, in the case of a CVA is it for the objectors to show that it is unfairly prejudicial. A CVA is a form of insolvency proceeding covered by the EU Insolvency Regulation and is thus entitled to recognition throughout the European Union.[91] By contrast, a scheme falls outside the Regulation.[92]

(3) Restructuring ("workout")

12–29   A restructuring, or workout, is a contractual arrangement or reorganisation negotiated among creditors outside any formal insolvency proceeding,[93] although it may lead to a scheme if there are dissentient creditors.

The CVA and administration or winding up

12–30   A CVA may be concluded without any prior or subsequent insolvency proceeding or it may precede or follow a winding up or administration. It may also run in parallel with a winding up[94] and with an administration,[95] which has the advantage of attracting the statutory moratorium.[96] For this reason one might have expcted most CVAs to be conducted within the framework of administration or alternatively within the moratorium regime available for small companies but this has not proved to be the case, research having shown

---

[89] See above, para.1–53 and below, para.12–45.

[90] See, e.g. *Prudential Assurance Co Ltd v PRG Powerhouse Ltd* [2007] B.C.C. 500, where Etherton J., in rejecting a scheme, held that its illogical and unfair result could not have been achieved if there had been a formal scheme of arrangement under what is now s.899 of the Companies Act 2006, because it was common ground that the landlords who had objected to the CVA would have been in a class of their own separate from other unsecured creditors (para.108).

[91] See below, para.15–14.

[92] See below, para.15–14.

[93] See above, paras.12–02 *et seq.*

[94] Insolvency Act 1986 s.1(3).

[95] Insolvency Act 1986 s.1(3). However, the appointment of an administrator automatically ceases to have effect after one year beginning with the date on which it takes effect unless extended by the court (Insolvency Act 1986 Sch.B1 para.76).

[96] Further factors are that: (i) in a distribution CVA, within administration the set-off rules embodied in r.2.85 of the Insolvency Rules 1986 apply, whereas outside administration set-off is governed by the general law; and (ii) the priority of new creditors in an administration does not apply in a CVA outside administration.

that most of the insolvent companies surveyed opted for a stand-alone CVA and the small company moratorium was rarely invoked.[97] There are, indeed, advantages in a purely consensual CVA if this can be achieved, not the least in avoiding the adverse effect that an administration can have on the value of the business, and this may be a significant factor influencing the choice of the stand-alone CVA.[98] Where a CVA is made when the company is not in administration or winding up, the effect of a subsequent administration or winding up depends on the terms of the CVA itself. It may or may not bring an end to the CVA as such, depending on the circumstances,[99] but even if it does the trusts created by the CVA remain in force for the benefit of the CVA creditors except so far as the terms of the CVA otherwise provide.[100]

(1) CVA within administration

In those cases where as will usually be the case, a CVA is concluded while the company is in administration, the normal procedure is for the administrator to continue to manage the company and to pass over assets and/or trading surpluses to the supervisor of the CVA for distribution among creditors. Usually, the supervisor is the administrator himself, who thus acts in two capacities. As supervisor, he is responsible for the implementation of the CVA where this proves capable of being achieved.

12–31

(2) CVA followed or preceded by administration

A CVA may itself provide for administration as the exit route once the purposes of the CVA have been fulfilled, and the supervisor has power to apply for an administration order.[101] The situation in which a CVA is most likely to be followed by administration is where there are assets outside the scope of the CVA in relation to which the purpose of the administration may be achieved. Where the administration comes first and a CVA is concluded within the administration,[102] if the CVA covers all of the company's assets it will usually

12–32

---

[97] See above, para.11–32.

[98] See John Tribe, "Company Voluntary Arrangements and Rescue: A New Hope and a Tudor Orthodoxy" (2009) J.B.L. 5, 458.

[99] *Welsby v Brelec Installations Ltd* [2000] 2 B.C.L.C. 576; and *Re Maple Environmental Services Ltd* [2000] B.C.C. 93.

[100] *Re N.T. Gallagher & Son Ltd* [2002] 2 B.C.L.C. 133. For a detailed survey of the relevant authorities, see Andrew R. Keay, *McPherson's Law of Company Liquidation*, 2nd edn (London: Sweet & Maxwell, 2009), para.7.92. See further below, para.12–52, as to the trusts created by a CVA over funds coming into the hands of the supervisor.

[101] Insolvency Act 1986 s.7(4)(b).

[102] Less likely with the automatic expiry of the administrator's appointment after one year. The administrator may make a proposal for a CVA (Insolvency Act 1986 s.1(3)(b)) and propose either himself or another nominee as supervisor.

provide for the appointment of the administrator to cease to have effect, for the administrator will no longer have any functions to perform in his capacity as administrator, although he may assume the role of supervisor of the CVA. Again, however, there may be cases where the CVA does not cover the whole of the assets, in which case the administrator, if able to achieve the purpose with the assets outside the CVA, will continue in office to that end.

(3) Liquidation

12–33 A CVA may precede liquidation and provide for it as the exit route, with distribution of assets according to the rules applicable on winding up, and the supervisor may petition for winding up.[103] Alternatively, the liquidation may come first, and the liquidator may propose a CVA[104] with himself or another person as supervisor. The liquidator may wish to do this, for example, where he considers that it would be advantageous for the business of the company to be carried on but he lacks the necessary powers.[105]

Outline of procedure leading to a CVA

(1) Preliminary steps

12–34 A reading of s.1(1) of the Insolvency Act and rr.1.2 to 1.5 of the Insolvency Rules would suggest that a CVA is initiated by a proposal by the directors to the company and its creditors, followed by delivery to the intended nominee[106] of the proposal and a statement of the company's affairs. However, there are important preliminary measures to be taken. A threshold question is whether a CVA is in fact the best option for the company. Before initiating a CVA, prudent directors will take the advice of a qualified insolvency practitioner (usually the intended nominee) and examine other alternatives. They will in any event need to have a fall-back position in case they are not able to secure the support of their creditors. The intended nominee will require sufficient information about the company's financial position—including details of its business, assets and liabilities, and cash flow—to enable him to advise. Assuming that a decision is taken to seek to negotiate a CVA, the next step is to organise a standstill on the pursuit of individual

---

[103] Insolvency Act 1986 s.7(4)(b).

[104] Insolvency Act 1986 s.1(3)(b).

[105] A liquidator may carry on the business of the company only so far as may be necessary for its beneficial winding up (Insolvency Act 1986 Sch.4 para.5).

[106] i.e. the person whom the directors intend to nominate as supervisor of the CVA. When such person accepts the nomination, he becomes the nominee; when he is appointed to administer the arrangement and this takes effect, he becomes the supervisor.

claims by the major creditors or alternatively put the company into administration or, in the case of a small, eligible company, initiate the formal moratorium which is now available,[107] and to arrange for the continuance of day-to-day funding by the company's bank. The proposal itself has to contain a considerable number of prescribed particulars,[108] and its formulation may be expected to take a little time, during which it is important to keep the creditors informed and interim financial support maintained.

In some cases, it is possible to organise in advance arrangements for sale of the business when the company goes into a CVA. Such pre-packaging arrangements ("pre-packs") speed up the CVA process and reduce much of the risk, although it does not always follow that they result in the best price being obtained.[109]

(2) Who may propose a CVA

If the company is not in administration or liquidation, a CVA may be proposed by the directors.[110] Where the company is in administration, the proposal must be made by the administrator and where it is in liquidation, by the liquidator.[111] Neither creditors nor members have the power to make a proposal. This restrictive approach is to be contrasted with that adopted in relation to schemes of arrangement, which may be proposed also by any creditor or member.[112] A CVA proposed in the context of an administration or liquidation has the advantage of the statutory moratorium which applies automatically upon the company entering administration[113] or liquidation,[114] whereas a CVA proposed by the directors does not attract a statutory moratorium except in the case of a small, eligible company[115] and then only when the directors file the requisite documents, including a statement that the company is eligible for a moratorium.[116]

12–35

---

[107] See para.12–39.
[108] See below.
[109] See above, para.11–37.
[110] Insolvency Act 1986 s.1(1).
[111] Insolvency Act 1986 s.1(3).
[112] Companies Act 2006 s.899(2).
[113] See above, paras 11–51 et seq.
[114] Insolvency Act 1986 s.130(2). See above, para.5–08.
[115] An eligible company is one which: (i) in the year ending with the date of filing of the documents required for a moratorium or in the financial year of the company ending last before that date met the qualifying conditions, that is, satisfied two or more of the requirements for a small company specified for the time being in s.382(3) of the Companies Act 2006; and (ii) is not excluded from being eligible because it is already subject to a voluntary arrangement or insolvency proceeding or by virtue of paras 2(2), (3), 3(4) or 4A–4C of Sch.A1 to the Insolvency Act 1986 (see Sch.A1 paras 2–5). Companies parties to certain types of capital market arrangement are excluded in order to protect special purpose vehicle issuers in securitisations. See Insolvency Act 1986 Sch.A1 paras 4A et seq.
[116] Insolvency Act 1986 Sch.A1 para.7.

(3) Proposal by the directors

12–36   Although the Insolvency Rules require the directors' proposal to be prepared for and delivered to the intended nominee,[117] in practice he will already have been put in the picture, as indicated above, and the proposal will usually have been formulated in consultation with him. The proposal must provide a short explanation why, in the opinion of the directors, a CVA is desirable and why the company's creditors may be expected to concur in it.[118] The procedure is in all cases governed by Chapters 2, 5, 7 and 8 of Pt I of the Insolvency Rules 1986. Additionally, for a CVA proposed by the directors, the provisions of Ch.2 (and if a moratorium is proposed, Ch.9) apply; and where the company is in liquidation or administration, if the nominee is the liquidator or administrator Ch.3 applies, otherwise Ch.4 (Ch.6 was revoked). The content of the proposal must conform to r.1.3(2) of the Insolvency Rules, which requires the name, address and qualification of the person proposed as supervisor and the inclusion of a long list of other matters designed to enable the members and creditors, assisted by a report from the nominee, to reach an informed decision on the proposal.[119] The proposals will thus contain not only details that will feature as terms of the CVA itself but all other relevant information, including any agreement on the part of a debenture holder to release its security.

    The assets covered by the CVA are not necessarily the same as those detailed as belonging to the company. The CVA may exclude some assets of the company, in order, for example, to leave something for its members as an inducement to them to support the proposal. In the case of a trading CVA, the trading assets may be left with the company, which will make periodic payments to the supervisor of the CVA from trading income. The arrangement may also include property belonging to a third party, for example, new funds to be injected by the company's bank or its shareholders. Similarly, there may be liabilities which will be excluded from the CVA.[120]

(4) Notice to the intended nominee

12–37   The directors must give the nominee written notice of their proposal, together with a copy of the proposal itself.[121] If the intended nominee agrees to act, he must have a copy of the notice endorsed to the effect that it has been received by him on a specified date, which marks the commencement of the period allowed him for submission of his report to the court.[122] At the

---

[117] Insolvency Rules 1986 r.1.4(2).
[118] Insolvency Rules 1986 r.1.3(1).
[119] See Insolvency Rules 1986 r.1.3(2)(r).
[120] For typical provisions of a CVA, see below, para.12–44.
[121] Insolvency Act 1986 s.2(3); and Insolvency Rules 1986 r.1.4(1) and (2).
[122] Insolvency Rules 1986 r.1.4(3).

same time as delivering the proposal to the nominee, the directors must deliver to him a statement of the company's affairs setting out the prescribed particulars and made up to a date not earlier than two weeks, before the above notice.[123] The nominee may call on the directors to provide him with any further information he requires to prepare his report,[124] and must give him access to the company's accounts and records.[125]

(5) Nominee's report

Within 28 days of the date specified in the nominee's endorsed receipt, or such longer period as the court may allow, the nominee, where not the liquidator or administrator, must submit a report stating whether in his opinion meetings of the company and its creditors should be summoned to consider the proposal and, if so, when and where.[126] The nominee must satisfy himself that the debtor company's true financial position is not materially different from the information given to creditors, that the proposal has a real prospect of being implemented and that there is no unavoidable manifest unfairness.[127] These requirements are reinforced by Statement of Insolvency Practice No.3, which gives detailed guidance on matters to be considered by the nominee and included in his report.

12–38

(6) Small company moratorium

Schedule A1 to the Insolvency Act contains provisions for a moratorium for a company which satisfies two or more of the requirements for being a small company specified in s.382(3) of the Companies Act 2006 and is not excluded from eligibility for a moratorium.[128] However, a company is excluded if, on the date of filing for a moratorium, the company is in administration, being wound-up or in administrative receivership or subject to a CVA.[129] Entry into a CVA does not itself attract a moratorium unless the CVA so provides.[130]

12–39

---

[123] Insolvency Rules 1986 r.1.5.
[124] Insolvency Rules 1986 r.1.6.
[125] Insolvency Rules 1986 r.1.6(3).
[126] Insolvency Act 1986 s.2(2). If he takes the view that the proposed scheme does not have a reasonable prospect of being approved and implemented or that meetings should not be held, he should so state, giving reasons. See Insolvency Rules 1986 r.1.7(2) and SIP 3 para.6.7.
[127] *Re Greystoke* [1996] 2 B.C.L.C. 429.
[128] Insolvency Act 1986 Sch.1A paras 2–4. As to exclusions designed to protect securitisation arrangements, see paras 4A et seq.
[129] Insolvency Act 1986 Sch.1A para.4(1).
[130] See below, para.12–51.

(7) Meetings of directors, company and creditors

12–40 Where the nominee's report states that meetings should be summoned, he must proceed to do this unless the court otherwise orders.[131] There are three meetings: a meeting of the directors to approve the proposals and file them in court, together with a statement of affairs and statement that the company is eligible for a moratorium, this filing triggering the small company moratorium; a meeting of the company; and a meeting of the creditors. The meetings, which will normally be chaired by the nominee, must then decide whether to approve the proposed arrangement, with or without modification.[132] However, no modification must be approved which affects the right of a secured creditor to enforce his security, or the priority of a preferential creditor or his entitlement to the same proportional payment as any other preferential creditor, except with the concurrence of the creditor concerned.[133]

Voting

12–41 Entitlement to vote is significant for at least three reasons. First, a creditor entitled to vote may use his vote to influence the decision as to whether to approve or reject the CVA. Secondly, a creditor entitled to vote is bound by the CVA even if he did not receive notice of the meeting[134] or, having received notice of the meeting, chooses not to attend or to vote by proxy.[135] Thirdly, a creditor not entitled to vote is not bound by a CVA,[136] although it may have an effect on his ability to obtain any leave that may be necessary to enforce his claim.[137] A creditor with several claims may be entitled to vote in respect of some of them but not others, in which case he will be bound by the CVA only as to the former.

The general rule is that every creditor who has notice of the creditors' meeting is entitled to vote at the meeting or any adjournment of it.[138] "Creditor" includes a person whose claim is future[139] or contingent.[140] However, there are two exceptions.[141] First, as mentioned in relation to

---

[131] Insolvency Act 1986 s.3.
[132] Insolvency Act 1986 s.4(1).
[133] Insolvency Act 1986 s.4(3) and (4).
[134] The rule was formerly different. See below, para.12–45.
[135] *Beverley Group Plc v McClue* [1995] 2 B.C.L.C. 407; and *Re Cancol Ltd* [1996] 1 B.C.L.C. 101.
[136] Insolvency Act 1986 s.5(2)(b); and see below, para.12–47.
[137] See below, para.12–48.
[138] Insolvency Rules 1986 r.1.17(1).
[139] See *Re Cancol Ltd* n.135 above.
[140] *Re T. & N. Ltd (No.3)* [2007] 1 All E.R. 851. See above, para.12–18.
[141] There was formerly a third, namely where the debt was for an unliquidated amount or of an unascertained value and the chairman refused to place an estimated minimum value on it for the purpose of voting. That has now changed, although the minimum value is nominal, so that the change is not one of substance. See below.

schemes, a surety cannot vote unless he has paid off the debt or that part of it guaranteed by him.[142] Secondly, the chairman of the creditors' meeting has a discretion to admit or reject a creditor's claim, wholly or in part, for the purposes of his entitlement to vote.[143] The chairman may wish to reject a claim because it is too uncertain or speculative to accept for voting even as a contingent claim, or because it is by a creditor who has no interest in the outcome of the CVA, as where his claim is fully secured and he wishes to rest on his security or where it is subordinated and all of the available assets will be exhausted in meeting the claims of ordinary creditors[144] or is a claim which falls outside the CVA altogether.

What is the position where a creditor's claim is for an unliquidated or otherwise unascertained amount? Previously, the rule was that if the chairman refused to place a minimum value on the claim, the creditor could not vote at all. The new rule is that a creditor may vote in respect of such a debt and, for the purpose of voting (but not otherwise), it is to be valued at £1 unless the chairman agrees to place a higher value on it.[145] A landlord's claim to future rent is both unliquidated and unascertained since quite apart from the fact that it has to be discounted at some assumed discount rate to arrive at its present value, account has to be taken of the prospect of the landlord forfeiting the lease and re-letting the premises, contingencies which require assessment.[146]

The chairman's decision on any of these matters is subject to appeal to the court by any creditor or member of the company[147]; and if the chairman is in doubt whether a claim should be admitted or rejected, he is to mark it as objected and allow votes to be cast in respect of it, subject to those votes being subsequently declared invalid if the objection to the claim is sustained.[148] Subject to the outcome of any appeal to the court, the effect of the chairman's rejection of a claim is that the creditor whose claim is rejected is not entitled to vote and is therefore not bound by the CVA.[149]

---

[142] See above, para.12–18.

[143] Insolvency Rules 1986 r.1.17A(2).

[144] See *Re British and Commonwealth Holdings Plc (No.3)* [1992] B.C.L.C. 322. The question of lack of an economic interest also arises in determining whether particular creditors or creditors of a particular class have a locus standi to take part in and vote on a proposed scheme of arrangement under s.425 of the Companies Act 1985. See *Re MyTravel Group Plc* [2004] 4 All E.R. (D) 385; and *Re Tea Corp* [1904] 1 Ch. 12, where bondholders whose claims were subordinated were held to have no economic interest in the CVA because they would receive nothing if the company went into winding up.

[145] Insolvency Rules 1986 r.1.17(3).

[146] *Chittenden v Pepper* [2007] B.C.C. 195. See also on the treatment of claims as unliquidated *Doorbar v Alltime Securities Ltd (No.2)* [1995] B.C.C. 728; and *Re Sweatfield Ltd* [1997] B.C.C. 744.

[147] Insolvency Rules 1986 r.1.17A(3). If on appeal the chairman's decision is reversed or varied, or if votes are declared invalid, the court may order another meeting to be summoned, or make such order as it thinks just (r.1.17A(5)).

[148] Insolvency Rules 1986 r.1.17A(4).

[149] See below, para.12–47.

Under r.1.19(3), votes in respect of certain claims, in particular, secured claims, are to be left out of account. It has been held that this is purely for the purpose of determining the number of votes in considering whether the requisite majority has been achieved for the approval of the CVA, and that far from treating creditors of the excluded claims as not entitled to vote r.1.19(3) is premised on the assumption that they have a right to vote but the vote is not to be counted.[150] Such creditors are therefore bound by the CVA, although if they are secured creditors their right to enforce their security cannot be affected by the CVA without their concurrence,[151] which is why, if a cram-down on secured creditors is envisaged, it is necessary to resort to a scheme rather than a CVA.

Approval of a CVA

12–42   Approval of a CVA requires:

(1)   at the creditors' meeting, a majority of at least three-quarters in value of the creditors present in person or by proxy and voting on the resolution[152]; and

(2)   at the members' meeting, voting for the CVA by more than one-half in value of the members present in person or by proxy, value being determined by the number of votes conferred on each member by the company's articles.[153]

The decision has effect if, in accordance with the rules, it has been taken by both meetings or by the creditors' meeting alone but in the latter case the decision is subject to an order of the court made on an application under s.4A(6).[154] As stated earlier, a proposal may not be approved if it would affect the right of a secured creditor to enforce his security or the priority of a preferential creditor or his *pari passu* ranking with other preferential creditors.[155] But there is nothing to stop ordinary, unsecured creditors from being separately paid from funds supplied by a third party, even if this results in their receiving more in the pound than preferential creditors, provided that the funds supplied are not in reduction of a sum to which the company would

---

[150] *Re Bradley-Hole* [1995] 1 W.L.R. 1097.

[151] Insolvency Act 1986 s.4(3).

[152] Insolvency Rules 1986 r.1.19(1). In determining whether the proposals have been approved by the requisite majority, there must be excluded votes in respect of the claims mentioned in r.1.19(3). See below.

[153] Insolvency Rules 1986 r.1.20(1).

[154] Insolvency Act 1986 s.4A(2)(b) says "subject to any order made under subsection (4)" but this is clearly a slip as that subsection deals only with the application for the order.

[155] Insolvency Act 1986 s.4(3) and (4).

otherwise have become entitled.[156] Once a CVA has been validly concluded, the court has no power to vary it.[157]

Reorganisation under a CVA

Most CVAs do not in fact involve reorganisation of the company and focus   **12–43**
on preservation of the business with a view to its sale as a going concern
and/or disposal of particular assets, followed by a distribution of realisations
by way of dividend, after which the company usually goes into winding up.
However, it may also be possible to restructure the company and its indebtedness with a view to restoring it to profitable trading. A typical reorganisation plan is likely to involve a combination of two or more of the following:
a moratorium (where not already in operation under an administration); the
cessation or disposal of part of the company's business; the injection of new
funds for the carrying on of the business or the completion of outstanding
projects; the release of certain claims and securities for them and the composition of other claims; a reordering of priorities by advancing the ranking
of particular debts or by subordinating debts which would otherwise have
had priority or ranked *pari passu*; the conversion of debt into equity, so that
creditors become shareholders[158]; the injection of additional share capital;
and the creation of a new corporate structure, as by forming a new parent
company into which assets and liabilities can be transferred and in which
creditors take shares,[159] or the hiving down of the business into a specially
formed subsidiary. It may also be found desirable for a creditor or group of
creditors to take over a part of the company's loan indebtedness to other
creditors with a view to reducing the number of creditors involved in the
negotiations and replacing an unsympathetic creditor with one who is
prepared to join with others in working towards a solution[160]; and it may be
possible to improve the company's liquidity by securing the whole or part of
its loan assets. A further alternative is for the shares to be acquired by a new

---

[156] *IRC v Wimbledon Football Club Ltd* [2005] 1 B.C.L.C. 66. See above, para.11–21.
[157] *Re Alpa Lighting Ltd*. [1997] B.P.I.R. 341; *Re Beloit Walmsley Ltd*. [2009] B.C.L.C. 584.
[158] This may provide creditors with greater recovery opportunities than on a winding up, while
from the directors' viewpoint any risk of liability for wrongful trading is removed at a stroke,
and members have some prospect of retaining at least a partial stake in the enterprise. For
a fuller description of the advantages and disadvantages, see Philip R. Wood, *Principles of
International Insolvency*, 2nd ed, paras 21–076 et seq.
[159] See, e.g. the arrangement in *Fidelity Investments International Plc v MyTravel Group Plc* [2004]
All E.R. (D) 385 and on appeal [2004] All E.R. (D) 221, a scheme under s.425 of the
Companies Act 1985 put forward as an alternative to a scheme involving the conversion of
bondholders' debt to equity, which the bondholders had opposed.
[160] Some of the problems involved in the sale of debts due from companies in financial difficulty
("distressed debt") are examined in the Financial Law Panel's Discussion Paper, "Legal
Uncertainties in the Secondary Debt Market" (January 1997).

funder whose injection of funds is to facilitate the compromise of claims and is conditional upon approval of a CVA on terms acceptable to the funder.

The CVA derives from collective decisions by creditors and members, not from an order of the court, and cannot by itself deal with matters beyond their decision-making powers. So a plan involving a reduction in share capital will, except so far as authorised by the Companies Act 2006,[161] require the consent of all creditors and the sanction of the court under s.648 of that Act; and where, in disposing of the company's undertaking, it is proposed to transfer the liabilities as well as the assets, so as to substitute the transferee for the company as the party liable, application should be made for the sanctioning of a scheme of arrangement under s.899 of the Companies Act and for a transfer order under s.900.

Some typical provisions in a CVA relating to creditors' rights

12–44   In addition to setting out the assets and liabilities of the company by reference to the directors' statement of affairs, together with arrangements for the management of the CVA, any plans for continued trading by the company and any provisions for its reorganisation, a CVA will have to deal with a range of matters relevant to creditors' rights. These include the following:

(1)   Assets and liabilities included and excluded from the CVA.

(2)   The application of any additional assets that the company may acquire.

(3)   The treatment of secured and preferential claims.[162]

(4)   The admission to the CVA of creditors who would have been entitled to vote if they had received notice of the creditors' meeting and of creditors whose claims are disputed by the supervisor but later determined or compromised.

(5)   The proof and ranking of creditors' claims in much the same way as for a winding up.

(6)   The management of the business (which may be left in the hands of the directors, subject to overall control by the supervisor and, where appropriate, a creditors' committee).

(7)   Details of any assets to be transferred to or held on trust for the supervisor by the company.

---

[161] See s.641.

[162] The rights of secured and preferential creditors must be respected (Insolvency Act 1986 s.4(3) and (4)). Whether secured creditors are brought within the CVA is a matter for agreement between them and the other CVA creditors.

(8) Any restrictions on the directors' powers, for example, a prohibition on the payment of dividends to shareholders or on the payment of remuneration to the directors themselves otherwise than as agreed with the supervisor.

(9) The imposition of a moratorium on the CVA creditors[163] so long as the CVA is current and, where so agreed, the release of the company from all creditors' claims except their entitlements under the CVA itself or a composition of their claims by payment of dividends in the CVA.[164]

(10) The amount and frequency of payments by the company to the supervisor and the distribution of dividend to moratorium creditors after deduction of the supervisor's remuneration and expenses.

(11) The release of a creditor's claim against a third party.[165]

(12) The convening of a meeting of creditors to reconsider the CVA if the claims of creditors not known at the time of its conclusion exceed a stated percentage of the known debts or would reduce the dividend payable to the moratorium creditors by more than a stated percentage.

(13) The duration of the CVA.

(14) Provision for what is to happen in the event of failure of the CVA. For example, the CVA may provide that if the company fails to comply with its terms, the supervisor may or shall issue a certificate of non-compliance, following which the CVA creditors cease to be bound by the CVA and, if the company is not in administration or subject to some other statutory moratorium, may pursue their ordinary remedies, including presentation of a petition for the winding up of the company and proof as a creditor in the winding up.

---

[163] In general, all creditors who would be entitled to prove in a winding up other than preferential creditors, secured creditors and creditors whose claims were not accepted for voting and are not admitted to the CVA subsequently by agreement or court order. If and so long as the company is in administration, there is a general moratorium under the Insolvency Act 1986 Sch.B1 para.43.

[164] In the absence of provision for a release or composition of the CVA creditors' claims, they are entitled, if the company goes into liquidation after the ending of the CVA, to prove in the liquidation for the balance of the amounts due to them after giving credit for dividends received or to be received under the CVA (*Re N.T. Gallagher & Son Ltd, Shierson v Tomlinson* [2002] B.C.C. 867). Where the CVA does provide for a composition or release on the basis of the assets then known, consideration should be given to a provision preserving the right of CVA creditors to prove in the winding up of the company for the outstanding balance of their claims in relation to assets coming into the company's hands after fulfilment of the CVA.

[165] A CVA can validly provide for this. See *Prudential Assurance Co Ltd v PRG Powerhouse Ltd* [2007] B.C.C. 500 (release of company's parent from liability to a lessor under a guarantee of rent), although in that case the creditor succeeded in showing unfair prejudice. See also *Mourant & Co Trustees Ltd v Sixty UK Ltd* [2010] B.C.C. 882, where a term of the CVA that the applicants give up their guarantees was held to be unfair. See below, n.192.

(15) Where it is envisaged that there may be a surplus after meeting all claims, payment of the surplus to the company.

Effect of CVA

(i) Parties bound by the CVA

12–45   Once the decision to approve the CVA has become effective, under s.5(2) of the Insolvency Act 1986 the CVA:

"(a) takes effect as if made by the company at the creditors' meeting, and

(b) binds every person who in accordance with the rules—

(i) was entitled to vote at the meeting (whether he was represented at it or not), or

(ii) would have been so entitled if he had had notice of it,

as if he were a party to the voluntary arrangement."

Dissenting creditors and creditors whose votes are required to be left out of account under r.1.19(3) are thus bound by a decision taken by the requisite majority. Previously a creditor was not bound if he did not have notice of the meeting, which could easily happen because the nominee was unaware of him or because he had moved and the nominee did not know his new address. This meant that potentially substantial numbers of creditors were not bound by the CVA, a fact which tended to undermine confidence in its efficacy and lead to a decision to use the more cumbersome scheme route. Under the new rule, even unknown creditors and creditors not receiving notice of the meeting because it was sent to the wrong address become bound,[166] so that the problem previously alluded to is much less acute than it was before.

However, the fact that unknown creditors are bound does not solve all of the difficulties, for they may have substantial claims which, had they been known, would have materially affected the terms of the CVA. This possibility can be taken into account in the terms of the CVA itself, as was done quite neatly in the CVA in *Re TBL Realisations Ltd*.[167]

---

[166] But they are also, of course, entitled to benefit from the CVA on establishing their claims under it.

[167] *Re TBL Realisations Ltd, Oakley-Smith v Greenberg* [2004] B.C.C. 81, where the CVA permitted the supervisors to allow creditors outside the CVA to participate in it if they agreed to be bound and their claims would not in the aggregate reduce the dividend to participants by more than 10% but otherwise the supervisors were to convene a meeting to consider alternative proposals. For a detailed discussion of this case, see below, para.12–48.

(ii) Position of CVA creditors

Creditors bound by the CVA must adhere to its terms in the same way as   **12–46**
under any other contract. Under the typical CVA, creditors give up their
rights against the company in return for payments by the company to the
supervisor from trading income, the transfer of assets if so agreed and the
payment of dividend distributions as provided by the CVA. Pending due fulfilment of the CVA, the rights of the CVA creditors are suspended under a
moratorium provision. If the CVA is carried through to completion, unless
the terms otherwise provide those creditors have no further remedies against
the company even if it goes into liquidation with additional assets. It is
therefore important for the CVA to make provision for the application of
such assets.

(iii) Parties not bound by the CVA

A person is not bound by a CVA if he was neither entitled to vote nor some-   **12–47**
one who would have been entitled to vote if he had received notice of the
meeting.[168] We have seen that a decision by the chairman of the creditors'
meeting rejecting a creditor's claim is subject to an appeal to the court.[169]
But the creditor concerned is not obliged to appeal the decision and if he
does not do so he is not bound by the CVA.[170] The effect of this is a little
more complex than it might appear.

(iv) Position of creditor not bound by CVA

A creditor whose claim has been rejected retains his substantive rights   **12–48**
in respect of it. Where the company is not in administration or otherwise
subject to a statutory moratorium, the non-CVA creditor is free to pursue
his remedies under the general law, such as by instituting proceedings to
obtain a judgment and then issuing execution or by putting the company into
winding up. In other cases, he must obtain the court's permission to enforce
his rights, and in deciding what order to make the court must have regard to
the interests of other creditors, including the moratorium creditors.

We have seen that where the company is in administration and the creditor is a secured creditor or is the owner of goods supplied to the company

---

[168] The right to vote is confined by r.1.17(1) of the Insolvency Rules 1986 to creditors having
notice of the creditors' meeting. See further above, para.12–41.
[169] Insolvency Rules 1986 r.1.17A(3). The appeal must be made within the time limit laid down
by r.1.17A(6).
[170] *Re TBL Realisations Plc, Oakley-Smith v Greenberg* [2004] B.C.C. 81; and *R.A. Securities Ltd
v Mercantile Credit Co Ltd* [1994] 2 B.C.L.C. 721.

under a conditional sale, hire-purchase or leasing agreement, permission will normally be given where a refusal of permission would cause loss to the creditor substantially greater than would be caused to the general body of creditors by the grant of leave.[171] This reflects the principle that on a winding up proprietary rights remain untouched, so that the grant of permission does not result in any diminution of the estate. The position is otherwise in the case of an unsecured creditor, because if he is allowed to pursue his claim to judgment and then enforce the judgment by execution, he will avoid the application of the *pari passu* principle that would be triggered by the subsequent winding up of the company and would thus be advantaged at the expense of the general body of creditors. That is not conclusive but it is a powerful factor to be taken into account in any decision on the grant of leave. A good illustration, although not free from difficulty as to the basis of the decision, is the ruling of the Court of Appeal in *Re TBL Realisations Ltd*, where it was held that creditors whose claims were rejected could not be treated more favourably than if the claim had been accepted or the company wound-up and would therefore be adequately protected by an order ensuring that they received a payment equal to what they would have received on a *pari passu* distribution among CVA creditors, or alternatively upon winding up, if their claims had been accepted.[172] In that case, the facts were as follows:

> The joint administrators of TBL Realisations Ltd proposed a CVA. Members of the Greenberg family, who had previously instituted proceedings for substantial damages for negligence against the company pursuant to permission given by the court, sought to vote by proxy at the meeting of creditors convened to approve the CVA. On legal advice, the chairman, who was one of the joint administrators, rejected the Greenbergs' claim for voting purposes, declining to put a minimum value on the claim, which was unliquidated, with the result that they could not vote, although had they been allowed to do so they would have supported the CVA. They then applied for an injunction requiring the administrators to retain outside the CVA sufficient assets to meet their claim if it was successful. The joint administrators, having intimated to the Greenbergs that they would agree to their participation in the CVA, applied to the court for directions. The deputy High Court judge, Mr David Donaldson Q.C., held that since the Greenbergs' claim had been disallowed for voting purposes, they were not bound by the CVA and there was therefore no reason to limit any injunction to the amount they would have received on a *pari passu* distribution under the CVA. In lieu of an order, he accepted an undertaking from the administrators to retain out of the CVA the full amount of the

---

[171] See above, para.11–77.
[172] *Re TBL Realisations*, cited above n.170.

Greenbergs' claim pending any further order. Later, a compromise was reached whereby judgment was entered in their favour by consent for US$575,000 and costs.

In subsequent proceedings, Pumfrey J. held that the court should approach the matter as if the Greenbergs had applied for leave to enforce the judgment debt by execution. On this basis, the issue had to be approached as a matter of exercise of the court's discretion and the need to balance the interests of the claimants against those of other creditors, that the Greenbergs had intended to support the CVA, that the error made in rejecting their claim was without consequence and they had suffered no additional prejudice and that to permit them to execute for the full amount of the judgment was inconsistent with the purpose of the administration. The judge pointed out that the Greenbergs, as well as other creditors, would in fact receive slightly more under a CVA than on a winding up, because the CVA route avoided the need to use the Insolvency Services Account. The judge accordingly released the administrators from their undertaking and directed payment to the Greenbergs of the amount they would have received as participants in the CVA.

The Court of Appeal upheld the decision, adding a direction that the balance of the funds held by the administrators after paying the above sum be transferred to the supervisors.[173] Chadwick L.J., who gave the leading judgment, concluded that since the only alternative to administration was winding up, which the Greenbergs were entitled to pursue if the administration ended, they were entitled to be treated no less favourably than they would be (i) under the CVA or (ii) on an immediate discharge of the administration order followed by a winding up, whichever was the more advantageous to them. Chadwick L.J. demonstrated mathematically that they would always be better off under the CVA than on the liquidation.[174] However, he departed from the reasoning of the trial judge as to the basis of the court's approach and accepted the submission of the administrators that the issue should be determined not on the basis of what the court in its discretion would have done if the application had been for leave to enforce a judgment, but rather on the ground that there was no principled basis on which they could be required to hold a sum outside the CVA greater than the Greenbergs' *pari passu* entitlement.

---

[173] Who were in fact the administrators themselves, who would thus retain the funds but hold them in a different capacity.

[174] He rejected the argument that the Greenbergs would be the only creditors on two grounds: first, that discharge of the administration before completion of the CVA would result in a certificate of non-compliance by the supervisors entitling the CVA creditors to prove in the winding up; and secondly, that would be the case even without such a certificate. The latter is questionable in the light of the provision in the CVA that payments under it would operate in full discharge of the company's liabilities to the CVA creditors.

12–49   It is clear that the court was influenced by what it saw as the lack of merit of the Greenbergs' opposition to the judge's order.

> "Their opposition can be seen as an opportunistic attempt to take advantage of the mistake [of the chairman in rejecting their claim] . . . an attempt by which they sought to obtain more favourable treatment than that which they would have been willing (or obliged) to accept if they had been permitted to vote . . ."

The court signified its displeasure by ordering the Greenbergs to pay a substantial proportion of the costs of the administrators' application. The description of their claim as "opportunistic" seems a little harsh when they had made every effort to have their claim accepted; its rejection was not due to any fault on their part and its effect was to preclude them from participating in the meeting, albeit they would have supported the proposed arrangement. More significantly, the decision has been criticised on the ground that, while holding that the Greenbergs were not bound by the CVA, the court went on to rule that they could not be more favourably treated than if they were bound by it, and that what the court could and should have done was to provide for the full amount of the Greenbergs' judgment debt to be retained outside the CVA and let the CVA run its course, when payments to the CVA creditors would be in full and final settlement, leaving the Greenbergs as the sole creditors in any subsequent liquidation.[175] However, this presupposes that a creditor who is not a party to the CVA is on that account entitled to have a sum equal to the amount of his claim (so far as established or agreed) withdrawn from the assets covered by the CVA so as to be available to meet his claim. In consequence, if there were no other creditors outside the CVA and if, as is common, the CVA creditors had agreed to accept payment of dividends in satisfaction of all claims against the company, the creditor outside the CVA would, sooner or later,[176] receive payment in full as the sole remaining creditor, thereby gaining a preference over the CVA creditors. Neither principle nor policy compels such an outcome. Where the CVA empowers the supervisor to accept a claim from a creditor not previously within the CVA and the creditor agrees to participate in the CVA, there is no problem. Where the creditor, having been offered the opportunity to do so, declines to participate in the CVA, the solution adopted by the court, namely to order withdrawal from the CVA of a sum equal to what the creditor would have received if he had been a participant,

---

[175] Look Chan Ho and Rizwaan Jameel Mokal, "Interplay of CVA Administration and Liquidation (Part I)" (2003) 25 Co. Law. 3.

[176] Depending on whether it was necessary for him, after completion of the CVA, to put the company into liquidation—a rather pointless procedure, since if he were to be the only liquidation creditor, the sum in question might just as well be paid to him without more ado after fulfilment of the CVA, although not, of course, before, because if it came to an end prematurely, the CVA creditors would retain a right to prove in the winding up.

seems eminently fair. The mere fact that creditors have entered into a CVA does not preclude their interests from receiving consideration when the court undertakes its balancing task in deciding whether a creditor should be given leave to pursue proceedings or enforce a judgment.

(v) Position of surety

Whilst approval of a scheme of arrangement operates to vary or discharge the obligations of the debtor company as a matter of law, and thus does not affect the obligations of a surety,[177] a variation or discharge under a CVA is treated as consensual, with the effect that it will discharge the surety unless the guarantee otherwise provides.[178] A CVA may itself release a surety but only if this does not unfairly prejudice the position of the creditor to whom the guarantee was given.[179]

12–50

(vi) No moratorium unless so provided by CVA

It is important to bear in mind that whereas the entry of a company into administration produces an automatic stay of proceedings against it, a CVA has this effect only if its terms so provide. In the absence of such a provision, even a creditor bound by the CVA is free to pursue his claims by action, and this despite the fact that he may have an alternative remedy in the shape of an application to the court under s.7(3) of the Insolvency Act.[180] Accordingly, if the risk of such actions is to be avoided, the CVA should make it clear that while it is current no creditor bound by it shall pursue his claim outside the CVA.[181] The small company moratorium comes to an end once the CVA is approved and the decision has taken effect.[182]

12–51

(vii) Trust of the assets

It is established law that sums paid and property transferred to the supervisor pursuant to the CVA are held on trust for the CVA creditors[183] and that unless otherwise provided by the terms of the CVA the trust is not affected by the subsequent winding up of the company, so that the assets cannot be reached

12–52

---

[177] See above, para.12–25.
[178] *Johnson v Davies* [1999] Ch. 117. See above, para.12–25.
[179] *Prudential Assurance Co Ltd v PRG Powerhouse Ltd* [2007] B.C.C. 500.
[180] *Alman v Approach Housing Ltd* [2002] B.C.C. 723. As to small, eligible companies, see para.12–39.
[181] Alternatively, a small company eligible for a moratorium should file for it before the CVA has effect (Insolvency Act 1986 Sch.A1 para.4(1)(d)).
[182] Sch.A1 para.8.
[183] If the company, instead of transferring property to the supervisor, makes a declaration of trust in his favour, he is a sub-trustee.

by creditors who are outside the CVA.[184] Whether the proposals for the CVA or the terms of the CVA itself create a trust in favour of the CVA creditors even before the transfer to the supervisor depends on its terms. If no trust is expressed or implied from the express terms of these documents, the CVA operates simply as a contract, with the result that the company retains ownership of its property and funds until these are handed over to the supervisor. However, if the proposals or terms of the CVA declare a trust in favour of the CVA creditors, either in those terms or by referring to the pursuit of proceedings or the collection of some other asset for the benefit of the CVA creditors, then on the proposals taking effect, with any modifications, pursuant to the CVA the assets in question become trust property.[185] Similarly, if the company agrees to transfer to the supervisor identified or identifiable assets for the purposes of the CVA, that may suffice to create a trust in favour of the CVA creditors.[186] This would be consistent with the rule of equity that an agreement for a transfer is to be treated as a transfer in accordance with the maxim that equity treats as done that which ought to be done.

Who can take advantage of a CVA

12–53 Not surprisingly, the courts have held that only parties bound by a CVA are entitled to take advantage of its provisions, and an outsider can gain no assistance from its terms.[187] But the terms of a CVA will usually contain provisions empowering or requiring the supervisor to allow creditors who have failed to submit their claims the opportunity to participate in the CVA, although not so as to disturb prior distributions.

Challenge to CVA

12–54 A person entitled to vote at a meeting of creditors or members, or the nominee under the CVA or the liquidator or administrator of the company if it is in winding up or administration, may challenge the CVA on the ground of unfair prejudice or material irregularity, at or in relation to either of the meetings.[188] For this purpose, decisions on comparable provisions relating to schemes[189]

---

[184] *Re TBL Realisations*, cited above n.170.
[185] *Re N.T. Gallagher*, cited above n.164.
[186] *Re TBL Realisations*, cited above n.170.
[187] *R.A. Securities Ltd v Mercantile Credit Co Ltd* [1995] 3 All E.R. 581 (in which the company was the assignee of a lease and an arrangement for surrender of the lease could not be invoked by the original lessee as a defence to a claim for the rent); and *Johnson v Davies* [1999] Ch. 117 (a case involving an individual voluntary arrangement).
[188] Insolvency Act 1986 s.6(1) and (2).
[189] Above, para.12–23.

may be relevant.[190] On a challenge it is not for the court to consider whether the proposed terms of a CVA put forward by the office-holder were the best obtainable or whether it would have been better if it had not contained all the terms it did contain. Unless the court is satisfied that better terms would have been on offer, the court will not speculate on the matter, assuming the office-holder to have acted in good faith.[191]

Valuable guidance on the approach to fairness was given by Etherton J. in *Prudential Assurance Co Ltd v PRG Powerhouse Ltd*[192]:

"In broad terms, the cases show that unfairness may be assessed by a comparative analysis from a number of different angles. They include what I would describe as vertical and horizontal comparisons. Vertical comparison is with the position on winding up (or, in the case of individuals, bankruptcy). Horizontal comparison is with other creditors or classes of creditors. In that context, another helpful guide, in the case of a CVA, is comparison with the position if, instead of a CVA, there had been a formal scheme of arrangement under CA, s. 425 (compromise or arrangement between a company and its creditors or members), on which the different classes of creditors would have been required to meet and vote separately."

In the ordinary way, where the company continues to trade from premises held under a lease, a CVA cannot properly deprive the lessor of his right of forfeiture for non-payment of future rent without his consent except on terms of payment of future rent as it falls due.[193] On the other hand, where the CVA provides for payments that replace the right to accrued arrears, the lessor cannot claim that his right of forfeiture for non-payment of those arrears should have been preserved.[194]

Where the court is satisfied as to the ground or grounds of the challenge, it may revoke or suspend the approvals given by the meeting(s) and/or direct the summoning of further meetings; and where the court is satisfied that the person making the original proposal does not intend to submit a revised

---

[190] *Re T. & N. Ltd* [2006] 1 W.L.R. 1728 at [81], pointing out that there is a difference in onus, in that in the case of a scheme it is for the proponents to satisfy the court that it should be sanctioned, whereas in the case of a CVA it is for the objectors to show unfair prejudice; and *Prudential Assurance Ltd v PRG Powerhouse Ltd* [2007] B.C.C. 500.

[191] *Sisu Capital Fund Ltd v Tucker* [2006] B.C.C. 463.

[192] [2007] B.C.C. 500 at [75], applied in *Mourant & Co Trustees Ltd v Sixty UK Ltd* [2010] B.C.C. 882, where Henderson J. held that while external, unsecured creditors supporting the CVA were to be paid in full, the objectors—landlords—were to be required to accept a release of a guarantee given to them by the company's parent and to receive compensation less than one-third of the sum recommended in the advice given, and that the administrators had lost a proper sense of objectivity and had prima facie been guilty of misconduct. See also *HMRC v Portsmouth City Football Club Ltd* [2010] B.P.I.R. 1123.

[193] *Thomas v Ken Thomas Ltd* [2007] Bus. L.R. 429.

[194] ibid.

proposal, it must revoke the direction and revoke or suspend any approval given at the previous meetings.[195]

The role of the insolvency practitioner

12–55   It will be apparent from what has been said earlier that the insolvency practitioner involved with the preparation and management of a CVA is likely to wear a number of different hats.[196] Initially, he will advise on the viability of a CVA and the form it should take and prepare or assist in the preparation of the proposal. In that capacity, he owes the usual duties of care in contract and tort owed by a professional adviser.[197] Then, if he is offered and accepts an invitation to do so, he becomes the nominee and will act as chairman of the meetings of members and creditors. As nominee and chairman, he is fulfilling statutory functions and in principle ought not to incur any liability in private law. He does, however, owe a duty to maintain an independent stance and to act in good faith,[198] and it is not for him to advocate the interests of one group of creditors as against another group or to engage in brinkmanship or to attempt to exact ransom payments.[199] The remedy of a party who feels aggrieved by the acts or omissions of the insolvency practitioner while acting as nominee or chairman is to apply to the court under s.6 of the Insolvency Act.[200] Once the CVA has taken effect, the nominee becomes the supervisor. As such, he is an officer of the court and subject to its control. In that capacity, he has a duty to act reasonably and not to act as an unofficial champion for the creditors in attempting to improve the terms of the CVA for their benefit.[201] Since the Insolvency Act provides the means by which his conduct can be reviewed by the court, which can give appropriate directions, an aggrieved party is not entitled to pursue a private law action.[202]

As supervisor the former nominee will now be wearing two hats simultaneously and it is important to distinguish his two capacities. As administrator he is responsible for the management of the company, subject to any powers given to him in his capacity of supervisor, and as administrator he makes payments to and holds property for himself in the capacity of supervisor. It is at that point that a trust of the payments and property comes into being for the benefit of the CVA creditors unless this has been created earlier under the

---

[195] Insolvency Act 1986 s.6(4).
[196] See generally Edward Bailey, *Voluntary Arrangements*, 2007, para.4.17, for a good discussion of this topic.
[197] *Prosser v Castle Sanderson* [2003] B.C.C 440. See also *Pitt v Mond* [2001] B.P.I.R. 624.
[198] *Mourant & Co Trustees Ltd v Sixty UK Ltd* [2010] B.C.C. 882.
[199] *Sisu Capital Fund Ltd v Tucker Ltd* [2006] B.C.C. 463.
[200] Or, in the case of a CVA by a small, eligible company, Sch.A1 para.39(3).
[201] *Appleyard Ltd v Ritecrown Ltd* [2009] B.P.I.R. 235.
[202] *King v Anthony* [1998] 2 B.C.L.C. 517.

proposal or the CVA itself.[203] As supervisor, he is responsible for the implementation of the CVA, the collection of payments from the company or its administrator (who could be a different person), the distribution of dividends and the oversight of compliance by the company with the terms of the CVA, reporting any breaches to the creditors and where necessary issuing a certificate of non-compliance that may have the effect of releasing the CVA creditors from the moratorium. It is even possible for him to acquire a fifth hat. If the company is put into liquidation, he could become the liquidator. Certainly today's insolvency practitioners cannot complain of lack of variety!

---

[203] See above, para.12–52.

Chapter 13

The Avoidance of Transactions on Winding up or Administration

Where a company goes into winding up or administration, unperformed obligations of the company to a creditor cannot in general be enforced without the consent of the office-holder,[1] but payments, transfers or other benefits already made or conferred by the company are in principle undisturbed. This is a corollary of the rule previously enunciated[2] that only those assets which belong to the company at the time of the insolvency proceeding[3] are available for the claims of the general body of creditors. But the liquidator or administrator[4] can invoke any ground of avoidance available to the company at common law,[5] and any restitutionary remedy open to the company at common law to reverse unjust enrichment,[6] and in the case of misfeasance by the officers of the company he is given a summary remedy.[7] Again, the voluntary disposition of a company's assets by way of gift or sale at a gross undervalue may be *ultra vires* under company law as outside its objects[8] or

13–01

---

[1] i.e. the liquidator or administrator.

[2] Above, paras 3–03 and 6–41 et seq.

[3] The exact cut-off point varies according to the proceeding involved.

[4] Most of the avoidance provisions apply equally to winding up and administration, and in the text that follows "winding up" and "liquidator" should be taken to include administration and the administrator unless otherwise indicated. There is one ground of avoidance which is not dependent on the company being in winding up or administration, namely that the transaction is one defrauding creditors (Insolvency Act 1986 s.423) but it is convenient to include it in the present chapter.

[5] e.g. misrepresentation.

[6] e.g. rescission of a contract and recovery of benefits received by the solvent party.

[7] Insolvency Act 1986 s.212.

[8] See *Aveling Barford Ltd v Perion Ltd* (1989) 5 B.C.C. 677 and cases there cited. The *ultra vires* principle is now very limited in scope. See the Companies Act 2006 s.31(1), which provides that unless a company's articles specifically restrict the objects of the company, its objects are unrestricted. See generally Paul Davies (ed.), *Gower and Davies: Principles of Modern Company Law*, 8th edn (London: Sweet & Maxwell, 2008), para.7-2.

as an unauthorised reduction of capital.[9] These various grounds of avoidance owe nothing to insolvency law; they merely reflect the preservation of the company's pre-liquidation entitlements and limits on its powers. They are not discussed further.

However, the principle of equity among creditors that underlies the anti-deprivation and *pari passu* rules of insolvency law will in certain conditions require the adjustment of concluded transactions which but for the winding up of the company would have remained binding on the company, and the return to the company of payments made or property transferred under the transactions or the reversal of their effect.

1. THE DIVERSE NATURE OF THE AVOIDANCE PROVISIONS

13–02   The mode of adjustment of these vulnerable transactions takes a variety of forms. In some cases, the transaction will be automatically rendered void, either wholly or against designated categories of third party, upon winding up under statutory provisions which are self-executing. Thus, in a compulsory winding up, dispositions of the company's property made after presentation of the winding up petition are wholly void unless authorised or validated by the court,[10] and a floating charge given by an insolvent company otherwise than for specified forms of new value becomes wholly invalid if the company goes into winding up or administration within a specified period,[11] whilst a charge given by the company which should have been registered[12] but was not is void against the liquidator and creditors,[13] but not against other classes of third party such as purchasers. In other cases, the transaction itself remains valid but the liquidator is given the right to apply for an order reversing its effect. For example, while it is common to speak of the avoidance of a preference or transaction at an undervalue, the act of preference or transfer is not avoided as such but its effects may be reversed by whatever method the court thinks fit,[14] including the (re)vesting of the property transferred.[15] However, nothing will happen unless the liquidator makes an application to the court. A third category is that of the extortionate credit

---

[9] Contrary to the rule in *Trevor v Whitworth* (1887) 12 App. Cas. 409. See now Companies Act 2006 Pt 17 Ch.10; and John Armour, "Avoidance of Transactions as a 'Fraud on Creditors' at Common Law" in John Armour and Howard Bennett (eds), *Vulnerable Transactions in Corporate Insolvency* (Oxford: Hart Publishing, 2002), pp. 281 et seq.

[10] Insolvency Act 1986 s.127.

[11] Insolvency Act 1986 s.245.

[12] Under s.860 of the Companies Act 2006.

[13] ibid., s.874.

[14] Insolvency Act 1986., ss.238, 239 and 241.

[15] ibid., s.241(l)(a). Hence, it is incorrect to treat transactions within s.238 or 239 as voidable, since this would imply that they can be rescinded by the office-holder as of right.

transaction, which is neither invalid nor necessarily wholly reversible but may be set aside, wholly or in part, or simply varied, as the justice of the case requires.[16] Again, the statutory provisions are not self-executing; they have to be invoked by the office-holder.

An entirely distinct power of avoidance is given to the Pensions Regulator (TPR) to order restoration of assets to a defined benefit occupational pension scheme where these were transferred by a transaction at an under-value.[17] This is not discussed further.

For brevity, all of these forms of adjustment will be referred to as "avoidance" in the ensuing pages but it should be constantly borne in mind that this term is shorthand for a widely differing range of effects and reliefs. In particular, where payments or transfers of property made by the company are void, they are deemed to remain assets of the company in its own right so as to be susceptible to capture by a floating charge or fixed charge over after-acquired property of the same description, whereas recoveries resulting from a court order after application by the liquidator are considered to be held for the creditors and not for the company itself and are therefore not captured by a prior security.[18] Further, a transferee from the company under a disposition which is void *ab initio* and who then deals with the transferred asset, whether absolutely or in any other way, commits a conversion if the asset is tangible and is liable to a proprietary restitutionary claim for the proceeds whatever the nature of the asset. A transferee under a disposition that is initially valid who later deals with the asset after it has become void against a particular category of third party may incur a liability to that party for interference with his interest, as where the holder of an unregistered floating charge which has crystallised sells it without the consent of a person who had become the holder of a fixed security interest after expiry of the 21 days allowed for registration of the floating charge. By contrast, no wrong is committed by a person holding a good title to an asset under a disposition to him by the company the effect of which is merely reversible who deals with the asset prior to the avoidance of the disposition under the statutory provisions.

2. THE POLICIES UNDERLYING THE AVOIDANCE PROVISIONS

The conditions of avoidance vary according to the particular ground of avoidance involved but are for the most part dictated by a common policy, namely to protect the general body of creditors against a diminution of the assets available to them by a transaction which confers an unfair or improper

13–03

---

[16] ibid., s.244.
[17] Pensions Act 2004 ss.52–53.
[18] See below, paras 13–140 et seq.

advantage on the other party. All but two of the grounds of avoidance known to insolvency law[19] involve the unjust enrichment of a particular party at the expense of other creditors, whether they are preferential creditors or ordinary unsecured creditors.[20] Once this crucial point is grasped, much of the legislative structure falls into place. The unjust enrichment may affect other creditors in one of two ways. It may reduce the company's net asset value, as where it involves a transfer of the company's property to another party, otherwise than as a creditor, at a wholly inadequate price or a purchase of property by the company at an inflated price; or it may, without disturbing the company's net asset position, involve payment or transfer to a particular creditor in satisfaction or reduction of his debt, thereby giving him a preference over other creditors in disregard of the priority position of preferential creditors or, if there remains enough to pay them in full, then in breach of the *pari passu* principle of distribution among ordinary unsecured creditors. The avoidance provisions may thus be seen as necessary both to preserve the company's net asset value and to ensure equality of distribution, at least among classes of creditors.[21] Whether the defendant is or should be entitled to avail himself of defences and cross-claims that would be available in answer to claims of unjust enrichment at common law is a question we shall discuss later in this chapter.[22]

Section 238, which deals with transactions at an undervalue, is aimed at improper reduction of the company's net asset value and is thus conceptually linked to the common law anti-deprivation rule, while s.239 is linked to the common law *pari passu* principle and addresses unfair preferences. However, there are significant differences between the common law principles and the statutory provisions in that: (i) the former operate only on uncompleted transactions, the latter on completed transactions; (ii) the former are aimed at payments and transfers fixed to occur at the point of an insolvency proceeding, while the latter operate retrospectively by providing for the reversal of transactions concluded within the prescribed statutory period prior to an insolvency proceeding; and (iii) a provision in breach of

---

[19] The two exceptions are failure to register a registrable charge and the making of a post-petition disposition of the company's property without the court's authorisation.

[20] In *Hollicourt (Contracts) Ltd v Bank of Ireland* [2001] Ch. 555, it was common ground that a claim under s.127 of the Insolvency Act 1986 is restitutionary in character. See the judgment of Mummery L.J. at [22]. However, this is true only in the sense that the asset disposed of in breach of s.127 has to be given back. It does not follow that the purpose and effect are to reverse an unjust enrichment, for there may have been none, s.127 applying as much to transactions for full value as to those at an undervalue. Unjust enrichment is therefore not the basis of this ground of avoidance. The point is more fully discussed below in paras 13–03 and 13–145 et seq.

[21] See *Rubin v Eurofinance SA* [2010] EWCA Civ 895, in which this passage was cited by Ward L.J. at [55], adding (at [61]) that the statutory avoidance mechanisms under the Insolvency Act and the US Bankruptcy Code "are integral to and are central to the collective nature of bankruptcy and are not merely incidental procedural matters".

[22] Below, paras 13–145 et seq.

the common law rules is void, whilst a transaction in breach of s.238 or s.239 is valid but its effects are reversible in the discretion of the court on the application of the office-holder.

It will be apparent from what is said above that the phrase "unjust enrichment" is here used in a restricted sense to denote the conferment on the other party of an unfair or improper benefit to the prejudice of its existing *creditors*. Damage to the members of the company is not our present concern. If the directors improperly apply the company's assets, they can be called to account by the members. If the company is solvent, it is the members' prerogative to ratify the improper acts of the directors, for only the members themselves are injured. The position is otherwise where the company is insolvent, for then it is the creditors who have the primary interest in the proper application of the company's assets, although this can usually be asserted only when the company is in winding up or administration.[23]

There is a subsidiary policy underlying the avoidance provisions, namely the protection of an insolvent company's business from dismemberment through the improper disposition of its assets.

A third policy is sometimes invoked as the rationale of the rule against **13–04** preferences, namely deterrence of future creditors from gaining an unfair advantage. But it is hard to see why a creditor should be deterred from taking the benefit of a preference when if he is lucky the company will survive the preference period, the liquidator might anyway take no steps to recover the preference and even if he does the worst that happens is that the creditor will have to give up the benefit he received.[24]

Despite references to the first two of these two policies in a number of cases, it cannot be said that the underlying rationale of the statutory provisions has been very clearly articulated either by the legislature or by the courts. The point has been trenchantly made by a leading scholar, Professor Andrew Keay, with reference to Australia's insolvency laws:

> "Over the years avoidance provisions have regularly come under the scrutiny of the courts. Yet, there is little evidence of the courts seeking to ascertain the rationale for the existence of these provisions. It is submitted that the existence of such provisions is not a matter which excites any debate in Australia. There has been hardly any consideration of the underlying basis for the decisions; in fact there are few cases in which the reason for the inclusion of avoidance provisions in corporation or bankruptcy legislation has been mentioned."[25]

---

[23] See below, para.13–06.
[24] See to similar effect Vern Countryman, "The Concept of a Voidable Preference in Bankruptcy" (1985) 38 Vand. L. Rev. 713, 747; and David Gray Carlson, "Security Interests in the Crucible of Voidable Preference" (1995) U. Ill. L. Rev. 211, 215.
[25] Andrew Keay, "In Pursuit of the Rationale Behind the Avoidance of Pre-Liquidation Transactions" (1996) 18 Sydney Law Rev. 55.

The same is true of the avoidance provisions of the UK Insolvency Act. Invocation of the policy of protecting the general body of creditors does not explain why it is necessary to avoid unregistered charges, post-petition dispositions of the company's assets for full value and in the ordinary course of business, or floating charges given by an insolvent company for new value in the form of land, debts or intellectual property rights. Nor does reference to the *pari passu* principle tells us why it is all right for a particular creditor to gain a preference by threatening or bullying the company into making a payment but not all right if the company makes the payment voluntarily to a creditor who receives it in good faith, or why, indeed, the desire or intention of either party should be relevant rather than the mere fact that one creditor has been given an advantage over the others in the run-up to liquidation. For this, one has to resort to the historical origins of the preference rule.[26] Again, the reason why some kinds of transaction are rendered completely and automatically invalid while others are merely subject to adjustment in the discretion of the court on application by the liquidator has never been articulated; nor has it been explained why the period for which a company has to survive before an initially vulnerable transaction in favour of a party unconnected with the company becomes immune from attack is six months for a preference, 12 months for a floating charge, two years for a transaction at an undervalue, three years for an extortionate credit bargain and no time limit at all for a transaction defrauding creditors.

The fact is that every ground of avoidance in the Insolvency Act is derived from earlier legislation and each ground has been individually modified at different times but without any attempt to rework the avoidance provisions into a coherent whole. A brief evaluation of the provisions is offered towards the end of the present chapter.[27]

3. THE MINIMUM CONDITIONS FOR AVOIDANCE

The four conditions

13–05 In general, at least four conditions must be satisfied before a transaction entered into by the company can be upset under insolvency law.[28]

---

[26] See below, para.13–71.

[27] Below, para.13–144.

[28] For a comprehensive treatment see Rebecca Parry, James Ayliffe and Sharif Shirji, *Transaction Avoidance in Insolvencies* (2nd edn, Oxford: Oxford University Press, 2011). I shall not discuss grounds for avoidance under the general law, e.g. for misrepresentation. These can, of course, be invoked by a liquidator or administrator in the name of the company and, as stated above, raise no questions of insolvency law as such. For the special exemptions applicable to market contracts, market charges and certain other types of contract, see below, para.13–143.

(1)   the company must be in winding up or administration;

(2)   the transaction must have resulted in a diminution in the assets available to the general body of creditors;

(3)   the company must have been unable to pay its debts at the time of or in consequence of the transaction; and

(4)   the transaction must have been entered into within a specified time before the onset of insolvency,[29] the time varying according to the circumstances.

As stated above, these conditions, each of which is examined below, represent the minimum prerequisites for avoidance in most cases. It does not follow that where they are fulfilled the transaction will inevitably be vulnerable; usually some further elements have to be considered. Moreover, there are certain exceptional cases in which a transaction may be avoided even where one or more of the above conditions is not satisfied. These will be noted as we proceed.

Company in winding up or administration

As I have pointed out earlier,[30] the fact that a company is insolvent does not by itself attract legal consequences. The ability of creditors of an insolvent company to obtain redress for an improper diminution of its assets in favour of another party depends in general[31] upon the company being in winding up or administration. Why should this be so? Why should not unsecured creditors be free to attack a transaction even before the advent of a formal insolvency proceeding? There are several answers to these questions.[32] First, so long as the company is conducting its business in a lawful manner, there is no justification for allowing interference by unsecured creditors in its affairs. They have no interest in the company's assets and therefore no right to complain of the way in which the company chooses to dispose of those assets. Secondly, the creditor of a company not in winding up or administration has a more direct method of obtaining payment, namely by instituting proceedings, taking judgment and enforcing it by one or more of the available forms of execution, which include seizure and sale of the company's property and attachment of debts due to it. It is only if these measures fail, or are

13–06

---

[29] As defined by the Insolvency Act 1986 s.240(3).
[30] See above, para.4–01.
[31] The exceptional case is the avoidance of transactions defrauding creditors. See below, para.13–136.
[32] See also R.M. Goode, "Is the Law Too Favourable to Secured Creditors" (1983–84) 8 Can. Bus. L.J. 53 at 71–73.

considered pointless because of insufficiency of the company's assets, that recourse to avoidance proceedings becomes necessary. Thirdly, different creditors may have different views as to avoidance proceedings. No single creditor or group of creditors can demand protection for himself or itself alone.[33] If, therefore, a transaction is to be set aside, it must be for the benefit of the general body of unsecured creditors. But the protection of unsecured creditors as a class requires legal machinery by which they can be brought together and given a *locus standi* and an office-holder to represent their interests. This machinery is provided by a formal collective insolvency proceeding in the shape of winding up or administration, the interests of the class being asserted by the liquidator or administrator.

The Insolvency Act 1986 contains one ground of avoidance not dependent on winding up or administration, namely entry into a transaction at an undervalue in order to place assets outside the reach of an existing or potential creditor.[34] Since such a provision is available to protect a particular deprived creditor, not merely creditors at large, it does not necessarily involve any collective proceeding.

Diminution of assets available for the general body of creditors

13–07 As noted earlier, a diminution in the assets available to the general body of creditors may occur in one of two ways: by a reduction in the net asset value of the company itself or by a preference, that is, a payment or transfer which, although not affecting the company's net asset value, favours one particular creditor at the expense of the others.

Where a company receives full new value for a payment or transfer, creditors will rarely have cause for complaint, for there is no diminution in the company's asset worth, merely the conversion of an asset from one form into another, nor is there a preference of another creditor. The position is otherwise where the effect of the transaction is either to reduce the company's net assets or to withdraw an asset from the general body of creditors by making a payment or transfer to a particular creditor as a preference. The company's net asset value is reduced where it buys an asset at an inflated price, sells an asset for substantially less than its value, grants a tenancy which, although at a full market rent, reduces the capital value of the property let, enters into a burdensome contract or releases a debtor from liability. Even where the company's net asset value is not reduced, the general body of creditors is adversely affected by a payment or transfer which is not for new value but is for a past consideration, as in the case of payment in discharge of a past indebtedness or

---

[33] For the exceptional case, see below and paras 13–136 et seq.
[34] Insolvency Act 1986 s.423. See below, para.13–136.

the giving of security for a previously unsecured debt.[35] The absence or inadequacy of new value is by far the most important factor in the various statutory provisions rendering transactions vulnerable on liquidation or administration. Indeed, of the eight grounds of avoidance discussed in this chapter, only two are capable of applying despite the furnishing of full new value, namely non-registration of a registrable charge[36] and failure to obtain leave of the court to make a disposition of the company's assets after presentation of a winding up petition.[37] I shall discuss the rationale of these two exceptions a little later.[38]

Insolvency at time of transaction

Even where the transaction does diminish the company's assets, it will not normally be vulnerable to attack on winding up or liquidation unless the company was unable to pay its debts[39] at the time of the transaction or became unable to do so in consequence of the transaction. In other words, the transaction must be one which prejudices those who are creditors[40] at the time the transaction is concluded. If, after entering into the transaction, the company is still able to pay its debts as they fall due, creditors are not prejudiced by a diminution in the company's assets and only the members of the company have a *locus standi* to complain of its entry into a disadvantageous transaction.[41] But insolvency at the time of or in consequence of the transaction is not a prerequisite of avoidance of an unregistered charge,[42] an extortionate credit transaction,[43] a transaction defrauding creditors[44] or a floating charge given otherwise than for a specified form of new value in favour of a person connected with the company.[45] The first three of these exceptions are

13–08

---

[35] Taking security for a previously unsecured debt does not in itself reduce the company's net assets so as to constitute a transaction at an undervalue; it merely subjects a particular asset to a particular liability, and if the security is realised and the proceeds applied in discharge of the debt, both the asset (except as to any surplus) and the liability disappear from the balance sheet. See below, para.13–38.

[36] See para.13–123.

[37] See below, paras 13–127 et seq.

[38] See below, paras 13–124 and 13–127 et seq.

[39] Within the meaning of s.123 of the Insolvency Act 1986. See above, paras 4–03 et seq.

[40] Whether their claims are existing, contingent or prospective. See above, paras 4–26 et seq.

[41] This point is further discussed below, para.14–20, where it will be seen that there are dicta suggesting that directors may owe a duty to future creditors. But this is in the context of a breach of duty owed by the directors to the company itself and has no application to the avoidance provisions of the Insolvency Act.

[42] Companies Act 2006, s.874. See below, para.13–123.

[43] Insolvency Act 1986, s.244. See below, para.13–108.

[44] ibid, s.423. See below, para.13–136.

[45] ibid, s.245. See below, paras.13–111–13–112. Section 127 of the Insolvency Act, dealing with post-petition dispositions of the company's property not authorised by the court, is not expressed to require insolvency of the company at the time of the disposition but in practice this will almost invariably be the case, for an order on the petition, unless made exclusively on the "just and equitable ground", presupposes that the company is unable to pay its debts.

perfectly logical. As mentioned earlier, want of registration and the making of a post-petition disposition without court approval are the only grounds of avoidance having nothing to do with diminution of assets, so that the company's ability to pay its debts at the time registration should have been effected is irrelevant. The provisions relating to extortionate credit bargains are designed to avoid the inclusion of exorbitant rates of interest in proofs of debt,[46] and again the question of the company's ability to pay its debts at the time of the transaction is irrelevant for this purpose. The avoidance of transactions in fraud of creditors, being designed primarily for the protection of particular creditors, is likewise unconnected to a state of insolvency at the time of the transaction. Less clear is the reason for the exception as regards floating charges, although it is possible to find an explanation for this.[47]

Advent of liquidation or administration within specified time

13–09   Even where all three features described above are present, the transaction will usually cease to be vulnerable if winding up or administration does not supervene within a specified period[48] after the transaction was concluded. The transaction thus becomes cleansed by the passage of time, a sensible rule, for it is unfair to a contracting party (and indeed contrary to well-settled principles of property law and limitation of actions) that a party should be indefinitely exposed to a liability to restore that which he lawfully received. Moreover, the link between cause and effect, between the offending transaction and its impact on creditors, becomes ever more tenuous with the passage of time. If no creditor takes steps to wind-up the company or put it into administration within the specified period, creditors have no cause to complain of the disappearance of a ground of avoidance. But there are two exceptional cases. The failure to register a charge is not pardoned by the lapse of time, for the obvious reason that it is a continuing breach with continuing adverse consequences for innocent third parties; and avoidance of a transaction in fraud of creditors is not subject to a time limit, which no doubt reflects not only the fact that the statutory provision has a long history but also that the transaction involves the intentional removal of an asset for the purpose of defeating a creditor and is thus a species of fraud.

---

[46] Insolvency Law Review Committee, Insolvency Law and Practice (Cmnd. 8558), para.1381. However, they have a wider impact than this, since they empower the court to set aside the whole or part of any obligation created by the transaction and to order repayment of any sum paid by the company. See below, paras.13–108 *et seq.*

[47] See below, para.13–112.

[48] Ranging from six months to no time limit at all, according to the nature of the case.

4. OTHER RELEVANT CONSIDERATIONS

I have said that the four conditions mentioned earlier are minimum prereq-   **13–10**
uisites for avoidance and that other factors may be material in determining
whether a transaction is vulnerable under the Insolvency Act. In particular,
the application of the statutory provisions may depend on whether the other
party to the transaction was a person connected with the company[49]; whether
in the case of a preference the company was influenced by a desire to give a
preference; whether, in the case of a charge, it was created as a fixed charge
or as a floating charge; and whether the transaction was made in good faith
and for the purpose of carrying on the company's business. There is also a
question of whether, given the fact that the avoidance provisions are rooted
in the concept of unjust enrichment, restitutionary defences and cross-
claims, such as change of position and counter-restitution, are available.

5. THE GROUNDS FOR AVOIDANCE: A SUMMARY

A transaction may be avoided or adjusted under insolvency law or its effect   **13–11**
reversed on no fewer than nine distinct grounds, viz. as a transaction which is:

(1)   in contravention of the anti-deprivation rule;

(2)   in contravention of the principle of *pari passu* distribution;

(3)   a transaction at an undervalue;

(4)   a preference;

(5)   an extortionate credit transaction;

(6)   a floating charge given otherwise than for specified forms of new value;

(7)   a registrable but unregistered charge;

(8)   a disposition of the company's property made without leave of or rati-
       fication by the court after presentation of a winding up petition; and

(9)   a transaction in fraud of creditors.

The first two of these have already been examined in detail in earlier
chapters[50]; I shall examine each of the others in turn.

---

[49] Within the meaning of s.249 of the Insolvency Act 1986.
[50] See above, Chs 7 and 8.

6. *TRANSACTIONS AT AN UNDERVALUE*[51]

(i) Overview

The basic provision

13–12   Where a company in administration or liquidation has at a relevant time entered into a transaction with any person at an undervalue and the statutory defence referred to below is not available, the office-holder may apply to the court to order restoration of the status quo, with consequential relief.[52]

As we shall see below, there is no possibility of overlap between the provisions relating to transactions at an undervalue and those relating to preferences. This is because s.238, relating to transactions at an undervalue, is concerned with payments or transfers that reduce the company's net asset value and thus do not cover payments or transfers to a creditor, while to the extent that a payment is made to a creditor in excess of what is due to him, he does not receive it *qua* creditor and is thus vulnerable only under s.238, not s.239.

What constitutes a transaction at an undervalue

13–13   A company enters into a transaction with a person at an undervalue if it:

(1)   makes a gift to that person; or

(2)   otherwise enters into a transaction with that person on terms that provide for the company to receive no consideration; or

(3)   enters into a transaction with that person for a consideration the value of which is significantly less than the value, in money or money's worth, of the consideration provided by the company.[53]

"Transaction" is defined as including a gift, agreement or arrangement, and references to entering into a transaction are to be construed accordingly.[54]

---

[51] See *Transaction Avoidance in Insolvencies* (above, n.28), Ch.4, and see John Armour, "Transactions at an Undervalue" in Armour and Bennett (eds), *Vulnerable Transactions in Corporate Insolvency*, 2002, p.37. For the power of the Pensions Regulator to direct the restoration of assets transferred from an occupational defined benefits scheme under a transaction at an undervalue, see the Pensions Act 2004 ss.52–53.

[52] Insolvency Act 1986 ss.238, 240 and 241. "Relevant time" is defined in s.240. See below, para.13–39, text and n.121.

[53] Insolvency Act 1986 s.238(4).

[54] Insolvency Act 1986 s.436.

"Arrangement" is widely construed, covering any form of agreement between the parties, formal or informal, oral or in writing.[55]

Examples of transactions at an undervalue

The company enters into a transaction at an undervalue where it: **13–14**

(1)   makes a gift of property;

(2)   undertakes a burden (for example, binds itself to supply goods or services) for no consideration (this would usually require a deed);

(3)   purchases an asset for significantly more, or sells an asset for significantly less, than its value;

(4)   takes an asset on lease or hire at a rent significantly above the rental value of the asset or lets it out on lease or hire at a rent significantly below its rental value;

(5)   agrees to pay for services a sum significantly more, or to charge for services a sum significantly less, than their value;

(6)   allows an asset to be retained by the other party in satisfaction of a claim against the company which is significantly less than the value of the asset or takes an asset in satisfaction of a claim which is significantly more than the value of the asset;

(7)   accepts in satisfaction of a debt a sum significantly less than the recoverable value of the debt; or

(8)   gives a guarantee or indemnity and receives by way of benefit significantly less than the value of the benefit conferred by the guarantee or takes a guarantee or indemnity against a benefit which is significantly less in value than that of the guarantee.

In all of these cases, the company either receives nothing for what it supplies or pays significantly too much or receives significantly too little to ensure equality of exchange, and the transaction will be vulnerable under s.238 unless the statutory defence under s.238(5) is available. The same applies to the distribution of a declared dividend at a time when the company is insolvent, and this could also be attacked as a preference.[56] Most of the examples given are straightforward and require no explanation. However, it will be

---

[55] *Feakins v Department for Environment Food and Rural Affairs* [2007] B.C.C. 54, discussed below, para.13–45.
[56] See below, para.13–78, n.181.

necessary to say something about gifts, transactions for no consideration, the benefits to be considered in valuing the consideration and the treatment of guarantees, and to explain the omission from the list of security given by the company for a previously unsecured loan.

It will be obvious that where a transaction is attacked on the ground of significant inequality of exchange, difficult questions of valuation may arise which are similar in kind to those previously discussed in relation to the test of insolvency.[57] As will be seen, what matters is the true value of a benefit received or given up, which is not necessarily its stated or face value.

Conditions to be satisfied under s.238

13–15   The court cannot make an order under s.238 unless the following seven conditions are satisfied:

(1)   the company is in liquidation or administration;

(2)   application for the order is made by the liquidator or administrator;

(3)   a transaction was concluded;

(4)   the company was a party to the transaction;

(5)   the transaction was at an undervalue;

(6)   the transaction was entered into at a relevant time; and

(7)   the company was unable to pay its debts at the time of or in consequence of entering into the transaction.

Even where all of these elements are present, the court may be precluded from making any order by reason of s.238(5) of the Act. Under s.241, the court has wide powers both as to the orders it can make to reverse the effect of the transaction and as to the persons against whom an order can be made but the particular defendant may be protected by s.241(3) of the Act. It is also necessary to consider whether a restitutionary defence or cross-claim is available based on principles of unjust enrichment.

Onus of proof

13–16   In general, the onus lies on the office-holder to show that the above seven conditions are satisfied and on the defendant to make out a defence under s.238(5) or 241(3). But in the case of a transaction entered into by the company with a

---

[57] Above, paras 4–32 et seq.

person connected with the company,[58] condition (7) is presumed to be satisfied unless the contrary is shown,[59] and there is a presumption against good faith as regards such a person in the circumstances set out in s.241(2A).[60]

(ii) The elements in detail

Company is in liquidation or administration

The statutory provisions do not apply unless the company is in liquidation or administration. The reasons for this have already been discussed.[61]

13–17

Application is made by the liquidator or administrator

The requirement that the application for an order be made by the relevant office-holder reflects two considerations. First, the remedy is not automatic, it has to be sought. This is because the application of the statutory provisions depends on a careful examination of the facts and does not lend itself to an automatic trigger. Secondly, the remedy is also necessarily discretionary, since the circumstances may vary widely from case to case, and because it is designed for the protection of the creditors generally in an insolvency proceeding it would be inappropriate to allow application to be made by anyone other than the liquidator or administrator as the representative of the creditors' interests. So it is not open to a creditor or group of creditors or to a member or group of members to invoke the statutory provisions. What they are entitled to do, if they believe that the liquidator or administrator is neglecting to pursue a remedy which ought to be pursued, is to apply to the court,[62] although the court will be slow to substitute its own judgement for that of the office-holder.

13–18

"Transaction"

The word "transaction" has a very wide meaning. It is not confined to contracts[63] but extends to gifts and other arrangements which are not based on contract, and where there is a contract, "transaction" may cover not only that contract but any linked transaction, even though involving a different

13–19

---

[58] See below, para.13–39, n.121.
[59] Insolvency Act 1986 s.240(2).
[60] See below, para.13–68.
[61] Above, para.13–09.
[62] Under the Insolvency Act 1986 ss.167(3), 168(5) and 212(1) (liquidator) or Sch.B1 para.74 (administrator).
[63] *Re HHO Licensing Ltd* [2008] 1 B.C.L.C. 223.

party.[64] In Australia, it has been established in a series of cases that "transaction" is wide enough to include: a series of steps over a period involving several parties and not always contractual consequences; a unilateral act[65]; and arrangements giving rise to an estoppel.[66] A court order directing a transfer has also been held to constitute a transaction[67] and is susceptible to avoidance under the insolvency provisions, for example, in the case of a collusive consent order for a transfer at an undervalue or by way of preference. But apart from court orders and gifts, there has to be some element of dealing, this being implicit in the word "transaction" itself and being reinforced by the references in s.238 to: (a) the "entry into" a transaction; (b) "with a person"; and (c) "on terms that provide".[68]

The company as party to the transaction

13–20   Section 238 applies only where it is the company that enters into the transaction at an undervalue. So a transaction is not within the ambit of the section unless the company is a party to it. The first step is thus to identify the relevant transaction. So in a case involving s.423 of the Act, when debtors to a bank decided to place farming assets out of its reach by forming a company of which they were the sole directors and shareholders, selling the farming stock and other agricultural assets to the company at a proper value and then procuring the grant to it of a 20-year agricultural tenancy of the farm, the relevant transactions were the sale and the tenancy agreement, not the incorporation of the company and the issue of shares in it, so that the impact of the sale and the grant of the tenancy on the value of the shares in the company was irrelevant.[69] In *Secretary of State for the Environment, Food and*

---

[64] See *Phillips v Brewin Dolphin Bell Lawrie Ltd* [2001] 1 W.L.R. 143, discussed in more detail below, para.13–31; *Re Taylor Sinclair (Capital) Ltd, Knights v Seymour Pierce Ellis Ltd* [2001] 2 B.C.L.C. 176; and *Feakins v Department for Environment, Food and Rural Affairs* [2007] B.C.C. 54.

[65] e.g. a gift (expressly provided by the section) or a declaration of trust, as in *Ramlort Ltd v Reid* [2004] B.P.I.R. 985.

[66] *Australian Kitchen Industries Pty Ltd v Albarran* (2005) 51 A.C.S.R. 604, a decision of the New South Wales Supreme Court, in which Barrett J. cited, amongst other authorities, *Re Emanuel (No.14) Pty Ltd, Macks v Blacklaw & Shadforth Pty Ltd* (1997) 14 A.L.R. 281; and *Somerset Marine Inc v New Cap Reinsurance Corp* [2003] NS.W.C.A. 38.

[67] *Hill v Haines* [2008] Ch. 412.

[68] *Re Taylor Sinclair (Capital) Ltd, Knights v Seymour Pierce Ellis Ltd* [2001] 2 B.C.L.C. 176, *per* Robert Englehart Q.C. (sitting as a Deputy High Court Judge); and *Re HHO Licensing Ltd* [2008] B.C.L.C.,223 *per* Peter Leaver Q.C. at para. 31. See further Armour, "Transactions at an Undervalue", 2003, pp.55 et seq.

[69] *National Westminster Bank Plc v Jones* [2002] 1 B.C.L.C. 55. The statement by Lord Scott in *Brewin Dolphin*, cited above n.64, at [20] that "the issue in the present case is not, in my opinion, to identify the section 238(4) 'transaction'; the issue is to identify the section 238(4) 'consideration' " is not, it is thought, intended to deny the importance of identifying the relevant transaction but is simply a consequence of his conclusion that in the case before the House of Lords the various linked contracts all formed part of the transaction, so that the real question to be considered *in that case* was what constituted the consideration.

Rural Affairs v Feakins,[70] the debtor was an individual and it was held that although it was not a party to the sale, it was a party to linked arrangements and thus to the relevant transaction.[71]

The transaction having been identified, the next question is to determine whether the company was a party to it. While s.238 bites only on transactions to which the company is a party, it is not necessary that all parts of the transaction should involve the same counterparty; the section is capable of applying to a composite transaction in which there is a contract between the company and A, and a separate but linked contract between the company and B. Indeed, a contract to which the company is not a party at all may nevertheless constitute part of a transaction entered into by the company where this is the common understanding of the parties and the company.[72] Where the company is in administrative receivership and the receiver sells property within the security in the name of the company, rather than having it sold by his debenture holder as mortgagee, that constitutes a sale by the company and if it is at an undervalue it falls within s.238. That is not simply because the receiver is the deemed agent of the company unless and until it goes into liquidation,[73] but because the sale is indeed by the company itself acting through the receiver as its directing mind and falls within the statutory provisions in just the same way as if it had been authorised by the directors prior to the receivership.[74] The position is otherwise where the debenture holder sells as mortgagee, for even if the receiver executes the conveyance on behalf of the debenture holder, it is the latter, not the company, which is the party to the sale.[75] If the sale is at undervalue, the remedy is not a claim under s.238 against the purchaser but a claim in equity against the mortgagee under the general law for breach of the mortgagee's duty to take reasonable care to obtain the best price. If the company is in liquidation at the time of the sale, the sale can be effected only by and in the name of the debenture holder, for the receiver's status as deemed agent of the company ends with its liquidation. An administrator is in a different position, for he has no property interest himself and invariably acts as the company's agent,[76] so that any disposition made by him is a disposition by the company.

Gifts

A gift is a transfer of an asset for no consideration. The fact that the gift is by deed is irrelevant, for although it is sometimes said that a deed

13–21

---

[70] [2007] B.C.C. 54.

[71] Above.

[72] As in *Brewin Dolphin*, cited above n.64, where part of the transaction was held to be a covenant by the company's parent to pay rent to a person from whom the company had purchased shares.

[73] Insolvency Act 1986 s.44(1)(a).

[74] *Demite Ltd v Protec Health Ltd* [1998] B.C.C. 638.

[75] *Re Brabon, Treharne v Brabon* [2001] B.C.L.C. 11, a decision on s.339 of the Act.

[76] See above, para.11–89.

imports consideration, this does not alter the character of the transaction as a gift.

At first sight, it seems obvious that a gift by a company which goes into liquidation or administration within the requisite two-year period should be a candidate for restoration by the donee, for surely a company has no business giving away its assets. In practice, the matter is less clear cut. Most companies make payments during the course of a trading year for which they receive no consideration but which are recognised as legitimate forms of expenditure and as likely to benefit the paying company in some indirect or intangible way. Two cases in particular deserve mention, namely gratuitous payments to employees and payments to charity. It should be borne in mind that while both kinds of payment are perfectly normal and lawful within certain limits,[77] different considerations apply where the company is insolvent,[78] for it is not entitled to be so free with its money at the expense of creditors.

(1) Gratuitous payments to employees

13–22 Payments are frequently made to employees to which they have no legal entitlement under the terms of their contract of employment. They include bonuses for work done or profit targets met, Christmas and other gratuities, and golden handshakes and other terminal payments. To what extent are such payments recoverable as transactions at an undervalue in the event of the employer company going into winding up or administration? In many cases, of course, the size of the payment to any one employee would be too small to warrant the expense of proceedings, and in the case of a company continuing to trade while under administration the administrator would no doubt be reluctant to risk disturbance to industrial relations by seeking recoupment. But where the company is no longer trading and the size of the payment is substantial—as it may well be in the case of a golden handshake to a retiring senior executive—the office-holder may well consider it appropriate to try to recover the payment.

Given the breadth of meaning of "transaction",[79] it is hard to resist the conclusion that such payments constitute transactions at an undervalue.

---

[77] As to payments to employees made redundant on cessation or transfer of a business, see Companies Act 2006 s.247. By s.187 of the Insolvency Act 1986 any such payments decided on by the company before liquidation may be made by the liquidator but only after the company's liabilities have been fully satisfied.

[78] As stated above, s.238 does not apply unless the company was insolvent at the time of the transaction in question.

[79] See above, para.13–19.

Uncovenanted bonuses to employees are no doubt considered as emoluments rather than as gifts in normal parlance but are undoubtedly given for no consideration, however effective they may be as inducements to the work force to work even harder in the future. But such bonuses may be justifiable under s.238(5) as bona fide payments for the purpose of carrying on the company's business that could reasonably be expected to benefit the company, either because they provide positive encouragement to the workforce and enhance industrial relations or because they stave off threatened industrial action or produce a settlement. Golden handshakes and other terminal payments made without obligation to do so are much harder to justify, since they can hardly be said to be made for the purpose of carrying on the company's business, nor prima facie can they be of benefit to an insolvent company. Whether the court would consider, in the case of a company in administration which is continuing to trade, that the goodwill created by its tangible appreciation of the services rendered by retiring employees satisfies the requirements of s.238(5) must be a matter of doubt; and if the company has ceased trading or is about to do so then even this rather flimsy basis for the payment disappears.

(2) Payments to charity

This may seem a rather remote case to raise but I do so in order to make the point that there is no general defence of receipt in good faith. Of course, a company which knows itself to be insolvent is unlikely to make a significant payment to charity; but it is by no means uncommon for the management of a company to believe that the business is sound when in truth, as the result of concealed defalcations or losses through incompetence, the company is insolvent. If in this situation a payment is made to charity, can the liquidator or administrator recover it as a transaction at an undervalue? In principle, yes, if the other conditions of s.238 are satisfied. It is no defence that the charity received the money in good faith,[80] nor even that it has spent it and unalterably changed its position. But it is for the court to decide what order, if any, to make in the exercise of its powers under s.238, and there seems to be no reason why the court should not be able to take all of the circumstances into account, including the status and good faith of the recipient.

13–23

---

[80] Section 241(2) of the Insolvency Act 1986, which restricts the orders the court can make, is limited to recipients for value.

Transactions under which the company receives no consideration

(1) "Consideration"

13–24   "Consideration" is not defined but would appear to have the normal meaning ascribed to it by the law of contract.[81] It is thus to be contrasted with objective value. Consideration is the *quid pro quo* for a promise. It denotes that which a party exacts as the price of his promise. This could include detriment suffered by the other party if that was what the promisor wanted and was thus part of the bargain.[82] If he requires nothing in exchange, his promise is given without consideration. But if he exacts a counter-undertaking or the performance of a designated act, this constitutes consideration for his promise whether or not the counter-presentation has any objective value, for contract law does not concern itself with the adequacy of consideration.[83] Accordingly, anything which is valid consideration in law constitutes consideration for the purpose of s.238(4)(a). That this is the meaning of consideration is evident from the phrase "enters into a transaction . . . on terms that provide for the company to receive no consideration", which shows that the relevant question for the purpose of s.238(4)(a) is what the parties agreed, not whether the *quid pro quo* exacted had any intrinsic value. This is reinforced by the wording of s.238(4)(b), which specifically refers to the *value in money or money's worth* of the consideration and requires the *value* of the consideration provided to the company to be compared with the *value* of the consideration provided by it. So a guarantee given in consideration of an advance to a third party is not a gift or other no-consideration transaction within s.238(4)(a) but a transaction within s.238(4)(b), even if the objective value of the advance to the surety is nil. However, in that case, if the value of the guarantee is significant, the transaction will be one at an undervalue. As in general contract law, past consideration does not suffice. In the context of the statutory provisions, consideration

---

[81] *Singla v Brown* [2008] Ch. 357, a case in which it was held that the transaction was at an undervalue but that exceptionally no order should be made. It seems to have been common ground that the first defendant had held a 49% interest in property which he had transferred to the second defendant but the question of whether there might not have been a constructive trust in favour of the second defendant for all except a nominal interest in view of the parties' common intention that the first defendant should have only a nominal interest (see *Stack v Dowden* [2007] 2 A.C. 432) does not appear to have been raised and instead the court focused on the absence of any claim for rectification.

[82] The mere suffering of unbargained-for detriment does not constitute consideration in general contract law, although it might in appropriate cases give rise to an estoppel. In *Agricultural Mortgage Corp Ltd v Woodward* [1994] B.C.C. 688, the Court of Appeal left open the question of whether unbargained-for detriment which is of no benefit to the promisor is to be taken into account in valuing the consideration received by the promisor for the purpose of s.238 of the Insolvency Act 1986. It is submitted that it does not, for what s.238 is concerned with is inequality of exchange, and where the promisee suffers detriment for which the promisor did not bargain and in which he has no necessary interest, this has nothing to do with the assessment of the benefit received by the promisor.

[83] *Hill v Haines* [2008] Ch. 412, *per* Rix L.J. at [79].

obviously means consideration moving from the company in liquidation or administration to the other party, or from the other party to the company, not consideration moving from or to a third party. So if G Ltd gives a guarantee to C in consideration of an advance by C to G Ltd's parent, D Plc, and G Ltd then goes into winding up, while the consideration for the guarantee is the advance by C to D Plc, the value of that consideration for the purpose of s.238 is its value to the surety, G Ltd, not its value to D Plc.[84]

The question whether consideration given by the debtor company to A which also constitutes a preference of B and is thus recoverable means that the consideration cannot be relied on to exclude the dealing with A as a transaction at an undervalue was considered by the Court of Appeal in *Re Sonatacus Ltd*[85] in a decision which is not free from difficulty. The facts were as follows:

S, the sole director of Sonatacus, borrowed money from CIL through the agency of Proweb, who advanced it on behalf of CIL. S in turn arranged for the money to be paid direct to Sonatacus by way of a loan from S to Sonatacus. So S was the debtor of CIL while Sonatacus was the debtor of S. Sonatacus later, at the direction of S, paid £50,000 to CIL, thereby discharging S's debt to CIL and Sonatacus's debt to S. Sonatacus was insolvent or became so as to the result of the transfer. Liquidators of Sonatacus claimed that the payment to CIL was a preference but, having been advised of the argument that CIL was a creditor of S, not of Sonatacus, so that the payment could not be a preference of CIL, advanced the alternative argument that it was a transaction at an undervalue, CIL having provided no consideration. The answer made to this was that the payment by Sonatacus to CIL discharged S's obligations to CIL, who thus gave full value for the payment. However, the payment was also a preference of S since it discharged his liability to CIL, and it was held by District Judge Needham that a preferential payment susceptible to challenge could not constitute consideration so as to preclude a transaction at an undervalue, being precarious in nature. Accordingly District Judge Needham made a declaration that the payment by Sonatacus to CIL was not a preference but a transaction at an undervalue. This decision was upheld on appeal by Judge Hodge, who did not consider the preference claim further.

An appeal was made to the Court of Appeal and the liquidators were given leave to bring a second appeal based in the alternative on a preference. Now the nature of the case changed again. This time the court proceeded on the basis that there was no preference of C, who was not a creditor of Sonatacus but there was a preference of S from which CIL had benefited, and since it had failed to show that it had acted in good faith an

---

[84] See below, para.13–37.
[85] [2007] 2 B.C.L.C. 627.

order could be made against it under s. 241(d) of the Act.[86] It was therefore unnecessary to consider the question of a transaction at an undervalue, though it is clear that some aspects of this aspect of the case were considered unsatisfactory. The Court of Appeal substituted for the declaration made by the district judge a declaration that the payment made by Sonatacus to CIL constituted a preference given by Sonatacus to CIL within ss. 239–241.

At least two questions arise from this case. First, the form of declaration substituted by the Court of Appeal must surely have been a slip. Sir Martin Nourse had already correctly pointed out[87] that CIL was not the creditor of the company and that it was therefore necessary for the liquidators to rely on s.241(1)(d) to obtain an order against CIL as a person benefiting from the preference given to S. Accordingly, the court should either have made an order under that section or remitted the case to the District Judge to decide what order should be made. Secondly, the Court of Appeal did not find it necessary to consider the rulings below that the consideration furnished by Sonatacus to CIL was voidable as a preference of S and therefore could not be invoked to defeat a claim that the payment to CIL was a transaction at an undervalue. This aspect of the case attracted strong criticism from two writers,[88] who have argued powerfully in a case note that if the discharge of Sonatacus's liability to S was voidable as a preference, so also was the payment to CIL by Sonatacus, who should thus be entitled to be restored to its status quo by recovery from S as a preference or from CIL under s.241. Thus, the benefit to CIL would be exactly counterbalanced by its payment obligation under s.241. Put another way, the reasons why the consideration *received* by Sonatacus (discharge of its debt to S) were precarious also made the consideration *given* by S precarious, so that there could be no transaction at an undervalue in favour of CIL. The objectionable payment would thus have no impact on CIL's balance sheet. Smith L.J. saw the theoretical logic of that argument, although expressing the view that:

"... in practice, the reduction in value of the discharge due to the chance that it would be set aside is not necessarily precisely counterbalanced by the chances of recovery of the money payment. The chances might be different. Although as a matter of law, the money would be recoverable if the preferential transaction were set aside, in practice it might not be; it might have disappeared. If CIL were of doubtful solvency, the transaction might not be financially neutral."[89]

---

[86] See below, para.13–68.

[87] At [23].

[88] Look Chan Ho and Rizwaan Jameel Mokal, *"Barber v CI – Preference Equals Undervalue?"* (2006) 22 I.L. & P. 183.

[89] [2010] 2 B.C.L.C. 627 at [34].

However, Ho and Mokal are surely right in saying that so long as a transaction has no effect on the debtor's net asset value, s.238 is not engaged, so that if a diminution in the debtor's assets is reversed by a recovery under ss.239 and 241, it must follow that s.238 cannot apply.

(2) Distinction between gifts and other no-consideration transactions

A gift by definition involves a transfer of an asset for no consideration. However, as s.238(4)(a) implies, there are other types of transaction which are unsupported by consideration but are not gifts because they do not involve the transfer of an asset. These include unperfected gift-promises (normally binding only if by deed or by way of proprietary estoppel), voluntary releases of a debt and voluntary acceptance of part-payment in satisfaction of a debt.

13–25

Valuing benefits received or given up

(1) The approach to the valuation

Prima facie the value of an asset is not less than the amount that a reasonably well-informed purchaser is prepared, in arm's-length negotiations, to pay for it.[90] Where there is a market for assets of the type in question, in general the figure to be taken is the market value.[91] This is normally to be determined by expert evidence. The fact that the parties took reasonable steps to obtain an accurate valuation is not in itself the determining factor, for the valuation may have ignored relevant factors or taken into account factors that should not have been considered or may simply have been based on a mistaken view as to the attributes of what was being sold.[92]

13–26

Even where there is no mistake as to the quality of the subject matter, there may be significant differences among competent experts as to an asset's value. In such a case, the court has to weigh the expert testimony and do the best it can to determine the appropriate figure or alternatively the appropriate range of figures within which the value must lie. In the former case, the transaction will be a sale at an undervalue if at a price significantly below the amount so determined, even if that price was supported by one of the valuers; in the latter case, the transaction should be upheld if the price falls anywhere within the range selected,[93] but if

---

[90] *Brewin Dolphin*, cited above n.64, *per* Lord Scott at [30].
[91] *Re Brabon, Treharne v Brabon* [2001] B.C.L.C. 11, *per* Jonathan Parker L.J. at 38.
[92] *Re Brabon, Treharne v Brabon*, cited above n.91, at 38–41.
[93] *Ramlort Ltd v Reid* [2004] B.P.I.R. 985; and *Ailyan v Smith* [2010] EWHC 24 (Ch). See below, para.13–32.

significantly below the lowest figure of that range, it should be held a transaction at an undervalue.

(2) From whose viewpoint?

13–27 The question to be determined in each case is whether the value of the consideration given by the company significantly exceeds the value received by the company. This has to be assessed from the viewpoint of the company, not the other party.[94] So while an asset of the company may be disposed of for full value, the sale may nevertheless be a transaction at an undervalue if its effect is to reduce the value of the remaining assets held by the company and this effect was part of the bargain. In other words, the consideration provided by the company is considered to include any bargained-for detriment it suffers to its remaining assets or business, for example, because of a "ransom" power it confers on the other party.[95] Conversely, the fact that an asset has a special value to the purchaser—for example, for where it is a painting which completes his collection—is to be ignored in determining whether the company has parted with it at an undervalue; what has to be compared (leaving aside questions of detriment) is the consideration received by the company and the market value of the asset rather than its ransom value.

(3) Values to be based on the totality of the transaction

13–28 In valuing the consideration on either side for the purpose of determining whether there is a significant inequality of exchange—for which purpose both values must be measurable in money or money's worth[96]—it is necessary to look at the whole of the transaction and the totality of the benefits the party dealing with the company will receive, not merely the market value in isolation from other factors. This is well illustrated by the decision of the Court of Appeal in *Agricultural Mortgage Corp Plc v Woodward*[97]:

> The first defendant had borrowed money from the plaintiff and given in security a charge by way of legal mortgage of his farm. Shortly before expiry of the deadline set by the plaintiff for payment of arrears outstanding under the mortgage the first defendant granted the second defendant

---

[94] *Re M.C. Bacon Ltd (No.2)* [1990] B.C.L.C. 324, *per* Millett J. at 340.
[95] *Agricultural Mortgage Corp Plc v Woodward* [1994] B.C.C. 688. But not, it is thought, unbargained-for detriment.
[96] *Re M.C. Bacon*, cited above n.94.
[97] Cited above n.95. The case involved s.423 of the Insolvency Act 1986 (transactions defrauding creditors), not s.238 but s.423 imports the requirement of s.238 that the transaction be at an undervalue.

a tenancy of the mortgaged property at a rent which all parties to the proceedings accepted was the full market rent. However, the tenancy was a
protected agricultural tenancy under the Agricultural Holdings Act 1986
and the transaction was in fact entered into by the first and second defendants with the intention of giving the second defendant security of tenure.
The effect was to reduce the value of the mortgaged land from its vacant
possession value of over £1 million to a value of less than £500,000, and to
put the second defendant in a 'ransom position' in negotiating a surrender
value with the plaintiff.

Held: the fact that the second defendant was paying a full market rent did
not prevent the transaction from being a transaction at an undervalue, for
its effect was that the first defendant suffered a substantial diminution in
the value of his land while the second defendant gained the benefit of
security of tenure in the family home, the preservation of the farm business from its previous creditors and an ability to negotiate a large surrender value, so that the true value of the consideration he received was
significantly greater than that received by the first defendant.

A similar decision was reached in interlocutory proceedings in *Barclays Bank
Plc v Eustice*.[98]

What the decision in *Agricultural Mortgage Corp Plc v Woodward* shows is
that in each case it is necessary to look at the reality of the benefit received,
not merely the stated consideration. The same applies in valuing what is
given up in exchange.

Example 1

A house was sold at substantially below the unencumbered freehold value   **13–29**
because it was an integral part of the transaction that the buyer would
grant a lease back to the seller. The buyer was therefore not buying an
unencumbered property. The net result was not significantly different
from what it would have been if the seller had received the full unencumbered value and then paid a premium for the lease. The sale was therefore
not a transaction at an undervalue.[99]

Example 2

Shortly before going into liquidation, Alpha Plc agrees to accept £50,000   **13–30**
from Beta Ltd in settlement of a debt of £100,000 owing by Beta to Alpha.
At the time of the agreement, Beta was itself in serious financial difficulty
and other creditors were pressing. There was therefore a risk that Beta

---

[98] [1995] B.C.C. 978.
[99] *Delaney v Chen* [2011] B.P.I.R.

might go into liquidation and that Alpha would receive only a small dividend, if anything, in the winding up. The value of what Alpha gave up in exchange for what it received should be measured as the likely recoverable value of the debt, not its face value. On this basis, the settlement is not a transaction at an undervalue.

(4) The use of hindsight to value benefits

13–31 The benefits given and received by the company must be valued as at the time of the transaction. Where one of those values is uncertain, the court may have regard to subsequent events in order to test the accuracy of the value ascribed to the benefit in question at the time of the transaction. The decision of the House of Lords in *Phillips v Brewin Dolphin Bell Lawrie Ltd*[100] provides a good example of this, as well as of what constitutes the transaction for the purpose of the valuation exercise.

> "AJB agreed to sell its business to Brewin Dolphin for £1.25 million. To that end AJB transferred its business and assets to its wholly owned subsidiary BSL for £1 and then sold its shares in BSL to Brewin Dolphin in consideration of (i) the assumption by Brewin Dolphin of AJB's liability to its employees for redundancy payments, later discharged at a net cost of £325,000, (ii) a covenant by Brewin Dolphin's parent, PCG, to pay rent of £312,500 to AJB for five years under a sub-lease of computer equipment, against which was to be set a loan of £312,500 by PCG to AJB. The sub-lease was in breach of covenant, the head lease was terminated for default and PCG repudiated its liability under the sub-lease. The value of the business sold by AJB was assessed by the trial judge at £1,050,000. Later AJB went into insolvent liquidation and shortly afterwards into administrative receivership. The liquidator and administrative receiver (the same person) applied for an order under s.240 on the ground that the sale to Brewin Dolphin was a transaction at an undervalue within s.238.
>
> The trial judge upheld this contention and ordered Brewin Dolphin to pay a sum which he considered to represent the undervalue. An appeal and cross-appeal to the Court of Appeal were dismissed, though on grounds different from those of the trial judge as to what constituted the transaction. The House of Lords affirmed the decision of the Court of Appeal while differing both from the trial judge and the Court of Appeal as to the reasoning and varying the order of the former by allowing a credit which he had refused."

---

[100] [2001] 1 W.L.R. 143.

In delivering the Opinion of the House, Lord Scott made the following points:

(1)   The linked agreements together constituted the transaction. Accordingly, the issue before the court was not the transaction but the consideration. It was irrelevant who provided this. Accordingly the covenant by PCG to pay rent under the sub-lease formed part of the consideration received by AJB and had to be valued.

(2)   The sub-lease was in breach of the sub-lessor's covenant under the head lease, and the court was entitled to look at subsequent events—in particular, the termination of the head lease for default by AJB and the consequent termination of the sub-lease by PCG for repudiatory breach—in order to value PCG's covenant at the time it entered into the sub-lease, and those events made it clear that the value was nil.

(3)   However, Brewin Dolphin was entitled to be given credit for the amount of its loan and interest.

Lord Scott's speech has generated much debate on the use of hindsight to determine a value at the time of the transaction. But it seems clear that Lord Scott was not in truth applying a hindsight test; rather he was relying on evidence of subsequent events to show that from the outset the covenant under the sub-lease was so precarious and its value so speculative that even at the time it was entered into a bank or finance house with knowledge of the surrounding circumstances would not have attributed any value to the sub-lease covenant.[101] In this connection, it is helpful to recall the distinction drawn by the accountancy profession between adjusting and non-adjusting events in determining whether a balance sheet value should be corrected by reference to subsequent facts.[102] In the present context, an adjusting event is one which helps to establish the value of consideration at the transaction date, while a non-adjusting event is one which simply reduces or increases such value at the time the event occurs. It is obvious that a mere decline in the value of consideration by reason of an event after the transaction date is of no relevance whatsoever in determining whether the transaction was at an undervalue. But *Brewin Dolphin* did not concern a non-adjusting event; Lord Scott relied on the post-transaction termination of the sub-lease as validating what would anyway have been the perception at the time of the sub-lease of the nil value of the sub-lessee's covenant. In accountancy terms, the termination was an adjusting event.[103]

13–32

---

[101] See para.[26].

[102] See above, para.4–35.

[103] For non-insolvency cases in which the hindsight principle has been applied, see *Gorne v Scales* [2006] EWCA Civ 311; and *Bwllfa and & Merthyr Dare Steam Collieries (1891) Ltd v Pontypridd Waterworks Co* [1903] A.C. 426.

To be contrasted with this is the case of *Ramlort Ltd v Reid*.[104]

T, a heavy drinker, took out a unit-linked life policy providing for a sum assured of £180,000. T owned two companies which together owed £185,000 to Ramlort Ltd. T, though not legally liable for the debts, regarded himself as morally bound to see that they were paid. To that end he arranged for the sum assured to be increased to £185,000 and, while seriously ill and awaiting a liver transplant, executed a declaration of trust of the policy in favour of Ramlort in consideration of two cheques issued by Ramlort totalling £3,000. At that time the policy had a surrender value of £71. Two months later T had a liver transplant and the following day he died. The judicial factor challenged the declaration of trust as a transaction at an undervalue. The medical evidence showed that at the time the declaration of trust was executed T was gravely ill and without a transplant his illness would be terminal, while if the transplant were to be carried out he might survive, though the mortality risk was not measurable. The greater the risk of T's death, the higher the value of the policy. There was a conflict of evidence as to the value of the policy. On one view it was no more than the surrender value, on another it was a value substantially higher than £33,000. The trial judge rejected the former view as unrealistic but concluded that it was not possible to assign a precise value to the policy, which would appear to be within the range £25,000-£35,000 but with an absolute minimum of £10,000, the figure he determined to be the outgoing value. He pointed out that the fact that there might not be a market for an asset did not mean it had no value, an example being shares in a private company. Neither valuer relied on the fact of T's death as a factor in his valuation and the judge did not apply the hindsight principle. The Court of Appeal, upholding the decision apart from allowing a credit for the two cheques, also found it unnecessary to apply hindsight to the valuation.[105]

Other examples where hindsight would be inappropriate are the valuation of a lottery ticket by reference to its proving to be the winning ticket; the valuation of a policy covering a young and healthy life assured by reference to his accidental and premature death; and the valuation of residential property by reference to a subsequent increase in its market value.[106] In all of these cases the subsequent event is not one which helps to establish the value at the

---

[104] [2004] B.P.I.R. 985, affirming the decision of Judge Norris Q.C. sub. nom. *Re Thoars (dec'd)* [2003] B.P.I.R. 1444.

[105] The court also held, in agreement with the trial judge, that there was nothing to preclude the court from taking a range of possible values rather than a precise figure.

[106] These were among the examples given on the trial of a preliminary issue by Sir Andrew Morritt V.C. in *Re Thoars (dec'd)* [2003] 1 B.C.L.C. 499.

transaction date, for it has no relation to what a willing purchaser might be prepared to pay for the asset in question; it is simply an event which changes the situation.

(5) Value of property sold subject to a security interest

Where property of the company is sold subject to a security interest previ- **13–33** ously given by the company, its value is the value of the equity of redemption, for to the extent of the security interest the property is not that of the company at all.[107]

Guarantees[108]

Particular difficulties are raised by guarantees.[109] Company A in a group of **13–34** companies gives a guarantee to secure advances already made or intended to be made by X Bank to Company B, another member of the group—usually Company A's parent, subsidiary or co-subsidiary. If Company A goes into winding up or administration, in what circumstances, if any, will the issue of the guarantee be considered a transaction at an undervalue?

The first question is whether a guarantee is within s.238 at all. Undoubtedly, it is a transaction within the meaning of s.436. The difficulty in applying s.238 lies in the fact that whereas most transactions involve the transfer of property, the provision of services or the payment of money by the company and the receipt of money or property in exchange, the issue of a guarantee by the company merely involves it in a contingent liability which may never crystallise and the quid pro quo is the making of an advance to a third party, the principal debtor. So in contrast to the usual case, a guarantee does not at the time of its issue involve any form of transfer either from or to the company and, indeed, it may never pay anything or receive anything as a result of the transaction. But these are matters which go merely to the valuation of benefit and burden, they do not affect the applicability of s.238 to contracts of guarantee.

As stated earlier, a guarantee is not a gift or no-consideration transaction, even though the advance to which it relates is made to the principal debtor,

---

[107] *Re Brabon, Treharne v Brabon* [2001] 1 B.C.L.C. 11, a decision on s.339(3)(c) of the Insolvency Act.

[108] See also *Goode on Legal Problems of Credit and Security*, edited by Louise Gullifer, 4th edn (London: Sweet & Maxwell, 2008), p.375. The analysis in the paragraphs that follow was adopted by Treacy J. in *Levy McCallum Ltd v Allen* [2007] N.I. Ch. 3.

[109] The same considerations apply to indemnities, and for brevity the term "guarantee" will be used to cover both forms of transaction.

not to the surety. The consideration is the making of the advance,[110] since this is the act exacted by the surety as the price of his guarantee. So the fact that the money goes to the principal debtor does not of itself render the guarantee a transaction at an undervalue. The crucial question is whether there is a broad equality of exchange, that is, whether the benefit conferred on the creditor by the issue of the guarantee is significantly greater than the value to the surety of the advance to the principal debtor. It is clear that the relevant time for measuring these respective values is the date on which the guarantee is given, not the date when the principal debtor defaults or the guarantee is called or payment is made under it. But as will be seen, this involves an assessment at the date of the guarantee of what is likely to happen when payment becomes due.

(1) Measuring the value to the creditor

13–35   The value of a guarantee to the creditor varies inversely with the principal debtor's financial strength. If the principal debtor is financially strong, the creditor's dependence on the guarantee, and thus its value to him, is correspondingly reduced and may, indeed, be so small that it can be disregarded altogether. By contrast, if the principal debtor is already insolvent and the guarantee is furnished to secure a last-ditch injection of funds in the hope of reviving the principal debtor's fortunes, the risk of the guarantee being called is high and its value to the creditor may approach the full amount of the guaranteed debt. The mere fact that the principal debtor is solvent at the time of the guarantee does not by itself mean that it is of no value, for the guarantee relates to the future and what has to be measured when it is given is the likelihood of its being called when repayment falls due. A company may be technically solvent at the time of the guarantee and yet beset with so many impending troubles that its future insolvency can be predicted with a high degree of assurance.

To what extent is the value of a guarantee to the creditor reduced by the fact that he already holds security, whether from the company itself or from third parties? The answer to this question is not entirely straightforward. Let us start with security taken from the debtor company itself, such as a mortgage or charge of its property. The existence of such security reduces the creditor's need for the guarantee and therefore its value to him, which may be no more than the supportive value of a belt to a man already wearing braces. So at first sight such security should be brought into the equation as

---

[110] Alternatively, the creditor's promise to make the advance. But in general creditors prefer not to commit themselves to the surety in a bilateral contract; they prefer either to make the advance, generating a unilateral contract of guarantee, or (if they change their mind) to decline to do so, in which case the guarantee does not come into force.

a factor which reduces the likelihood that the guarantee will be called. The technical objection to this approach is that the creditor is not obliged to use the security taken from the principal debtor as his first port of call in a storm. If the principal debtor defaults, the creditor is free to pursue all or any of his remedies against all or any of the parties liable to him. He may thus, if he chooses, defer proceedings against the principal debtor and move directly against the surety. The effect of his election is that the guarantee becomes the primary support, the braces, while the security taken from the principal debtor is left to perform the subsidiary role of the belt, to which resort is made only if the braces prove inadequate. Does this mean that security taken from the principal debtor should be ignored in valuing the benefit of the guarantee to the creditor? Instinctively, we would recoil from such a conclusion, and rightly so. What matters at bottom is not the immediate but the ultimate source of satisfaction of the creditor's claim. Where lies the true incidence of liability? If the surety pays, he has a right to be subrogated to securities held by the creditor[111] and thus to take over any mortgage or charge on the company's property to secure recoupment of his payment. This remedy of subrogation is given to ensure that the burden falling upon a surety is not at the end of the day dictated by the choice of the creditor to look to him alone and exempt others from payment.[112] So even if the creditor collects payment from the surety, his claim is ultimately satisfied from security given by the principal debtor so far as resort to this by the surety is necessary for his recoupment. Our first thought therefore turns out to be correct: in valuing the benefit of the guarantee to the creditor, account must be taken not only of the principal debtor's financial strength but of any real security taken from the principal debtor by the creditor.

Next, we have to consider the relevance of security taken from other third **13–36** parties. The creditor may already hold another guarantee, which may be a purely personal guarantee by another surety, a guarantee reinforced by real security from the surety or a guarantee limited to real security. This complicates life a little in that where there are two or more sureties, they bear the burden rateably in proportion to the amounts for which they are respectively liable under their guarantees, so that if one of them discharges the debt in full, his right of subrogation to securities taken from the principal debtor and from his co-sureties is limited to what is needed to recoup him for the amount by which his payment exceeds his own due contribution.[113] The result is that in valuing the benefit to the creditor of the guarantee given by

---

[111] This right is given both in equity (*Craythorne v Swinburne* (1807) 14 Ves. 160; and *Forbes v Jackson* (1882) 19 Ch.D. 615) and at law under s.5 of the Mercantile Law Amendment Act 1856.

[112] *Craythorne v Swinburne*, cited above n.111, at 162; and Joseph Story, *Equity Jurisprudence*, 1st English edn, ed. W.E. Grigsby (London: Stevens and Haynes, 1884), p.315.

[113] For a detailed treatment of the right of contribution among sureties, see O'Donovan and Phillips, *The Modern Contract of Guarantee*, 2nd English edn (2010), paras [12.119]: with detailed examples of calculations at paras 12-215 *et seq.*

the company in winding up or administration there must be deducted the value of the creditor's rights against co-sureties[114] up to the amount they are liable to contribute but not beyond.

In valuing the benefit of a guarantee to the creditor for the purpose of s.238, no account should be taken of the possibility that the surety itself may default in performance of its obligations under the guarantee. What has to be measured is the value of the consideration, not the likelihood of its being executed. In essence, the question is whether the company giving the guarantee is committing itself to parting with a benefit significantly greater than that which it will receive. The principle is the same as that applicable to straight supply transactions. If, for example, a company which has run out of funds agrees to buy goods for £10,000, the question whether it has thereby entered into a transaction at an undervalue is determined by asking whether the goods are worth a sum approaching that figure, not by comparing the value of the goods with the amount the creditor is likely to recover from the company when it defaults in payment of the price. The same applies to the valuation of a guarantee. If the position were otherwise, s.238 could hardly ever apply to guarantees, for *ex hypothesi* the company giving the guarantee is already unable to pay its debts.[115]

From what has been said above, it will have become obvious that valuation of a guarantee is in many cases a matter of judgment rather than science and that a broad-brush approach is needed. I would suggest as a working guide that for the purpose of s.238 of the Insolvency Act the value of a guarantee to a creditor is the amount (if any) for which, at the time of the guarantee, a prudent creditor with full knowledge of the debtor's affairs would make provision in his accounts for default, after taking into account what he could reasonably expect to recover from securities taken from the principal debtor and from co-sureties in respect of their proportionate share of the suretyship liabilities. Alternatively, looked at from the surety's viewpoint, it is the amount for which a prudent surety with full knowledge of the debtor's affairs would make provision in his accounts after allowing for the value of securities taken from the principal debtor and contributions from co-sureties.

(2) Measuring the value to the surety

13–37   The other side of the equation is, of course, the value of the consideration received by the surety, that is, the value to the surety of the advance provided to the principal debtor. A member of a group of companies—in our example Company A—can in many cases reasonably expect that the infusion of funds

---

[114] Which involves measuring their financial strength and the value of securities they have given to support their guarantees.

[115] This being a condition of the application of s.238. See ss.238(2) and 240(2).

into another member of the group (Company B) will benefit the group as a whole, including Company A. Valuing the benefit, however, is likely to be a matter of considerable difficulty. In some cases, there will be no value at all, as where Company B is already on the rocks and the giving of the guarantee for a temporary advance is merely staving off disaster. In such cases, Company A's guarantee is given solely for the benefit of Company B and will almost certainly constitute a transaction at an undervalue; indeed, the directors of Company B may well be in breach of duty to the company in authorising the issue of the guarantee in the first place, for their loyalties are owed in law solely to their company, not to the group as a whole. But where Company B's business is basically sound and the infusion of funds will enable it to expand its activities and increase its profitability for the benefit of the group as a whole, at least some value may be ascribable to the consideration given by Company A for its guarantee. This may (indeed usually will) be less than the amount of the advance to Company B but as long as it is not significantly below the ultimate burden likely to fall on Company A as the result of furnishing the guarantee, this will not be a transaction at an undervalue.

In practice, it is unlikely that a guarantee will be impeached as a transaction at an undervalue except where it is clearly of no benefit to the surety company. There are serious problems of valuation on both sides of the equation and the onus is on the office-holder who is impeaching the transaction to prove that the guarantee is a transaction at an undervalue. Hence, the difficulties of valuation lie primarily on him rather than on the creditor.

Giving of security for a past debt not a transaction at an undervalue

Suppose that a company gives its bank security for a previously unsecured   **13–38**
loan and then goes into liquidation. Is the furnishing of security for past consideration a transaction at an undervalue? No, because it does not reduce the net assets of the company but merely attaches an existing liability to an existing asset, leaving the net balance sheet figures unchanged. This was so held by Millett J. in *Re M.C. Bacon Ltd*.[116] Likewise, the realisation of the

---

[116] [1990] B.C.C. 78. In *Hill v Spread Co Trustee Ltd* [2007] 1 W.L.R. 2404, which concerned an attack on a transaction as being at an undervalue, Arden L.J., in an obiter dictum at [138], expressed disagreement with this view, saying there was nothing in s.423 that referred to a diminution in assets and that had it been necessary he would provisionally not have accepted that the grant of security did not involve the disposition of any property right. With all respect, this confuses a transaction at an undervalue with a preference and cannot be accepted. The question is whether there is a transaction at an undervalue, meaning that the company parts with more than it receives. If the company grants a security interest, it still has the right to redeem and any repayment it makes *pro tanto* reduces its indebtedness, so that it loses nothing. Subsequently, a differently constituted Court of Appeal correctly applied Millett J.'s reasoning in *M.C. Bacon*, making no reference to Arden L.J.'s dictum. See *Secretary of State for the Environment, Food and Rural Affairs v Feakins* [2007] B.C.C. 54, per Jonathan Parker L.J. at [72].

security has no impact on the net asset position, for while the asset given in security disappears from the balance sheet, so also does the liability which it secured. A simple example will demonstrate the point. Suppose that A Ltd borrows £100,000 unsecured, uses it to buy stock and later gives a charge over its factory to secure the loan. Prior to the giving of the security, A Ltd's balance sheet, assuming that no part of the stock has yet been sold, the factory has a value (at cost) of £500,000 and that there are no other assets or liabilities, would look like this:

Assets

Factory (at cost)		£500,000
Stock (at cost)		£100,000
		£600,000
Less liabilities		
Bank loan	£100,000	
Trade creditors	£ 50,000	
		£150,000
Net assets		£450,000

When the charge is given, it will be recorded by way of a note to the accounts (or alternatively the loan will be shown in the balance sheet as a secured loan) but the figures remain unchanged. Now suppose that on default by the company the factory is sold for £500,000 and the debt of £100,000 repaid from the proceeds, the balance of £400,000 being paid into the company's bank account. The balance sheet will now look like this:

Assets

Cash at bank	£400,000
Stock (at cost)	£100,000
	£500,000
Less liabilities	
Trade creditors	£50,000
Net assets	£450,000

We can see that there has been no depletion of the value of the company's assets through realisation of the security, for the payment of £100,000 from the proceeds is exactly matched by the disappearance of the bank loan from the liabilities. So the effect of giving security for a previously unsecured loan is not to reduce the company's assets but simply to allocate the asset given in security to a particular creditor instead of leaving it available for creditors generally. The proper ground of attack, then, is not that the transaction is at an undervalue but that it is a preference.[117] As Millett J. pointed out,[118] all that the company loses in giving the security is the ability to apply the proceeds of the charged assets otherwise than in satisfaction of the charged debt, and "that is not something capable of valuation in monetary terms and is not customarily disposed of for value".[119] This comment should not be misunderstood. The point that Millett J. was making was not the difficulty of valuing a detriment but the fact that detriment by itself is irrelevant, for the crucial question is whether it was incurred as part of the bargained-for consideration so as to confer on the other party a benefit capable of being valued. In *Agricultural Mortgage Corp Plc v Woodward*,[120] the fact that one party suffered a detriment by reason of a reduction in value of his property through the grant of a tenancy was not in itself material; what mattered was that the grant of the tenancy gave the tenant a protected status which placed her in a position to hold the landlord and the mortgagee to ransom in negotiating a surrender value, and the conferment of that benefit formed part of the bargained-for consideration. By contrast, the loss of a mortgagor's ability to apply the proceeds of a mortgaged asset otherwise than in satisfaction of the debt confers no additional benefit on the mortgagee for which he would expect to pay; on the contrary, it is the very remedy which the mortgage is designed to provide. One might add that, by the same token, the fact that the grant of a mortgage over an asset inhibits the company's ability to obtain credit from other sources is equally irrelevant, not simply because it is incapable of valuation but because it is not something which confers a bargained-for benefit on the mortgagee.

The position is otherwise, of course, where the company gives security for the indebtedness of a third party, for in that situation realisation of the security does not result in the discharge of any debt owed by the company, which accordingly suffers a loss of the charged asset.

The "relevant time"

Under s.238(2) of the Insolvency Act 1986, the office-holder is not entitled to apply for an order to reverse the effect of a transaction at an undervalue unless the transaction was entered into at "a relevant time". This is defined by s.240(1) as at a time: **13–39**

(1) in the period of two years ending with the onset of insolvency but only if at that time the company was unable to pay its debts within the

---

[117] See above, n.116.
[118] *Re M C Bacon Ltd*, cited above n.116, at 92.
[119] *Re M C Bacon Ltd*, cited above n.116, at 92.
[120] [1994] B.C.C. 688. See above, para.13–28.

meaning of s.123 of the Act or became so in consequence of the transaction[121];

(2) between the making of an administration application in respect of the company and the making of an administration order on that application; and

(3) between the filing with the court of a notice of intention to appoint an administrator under paras 14 or 22 of Sch.B1 and the making of an appointment under that paragraph.

The general statutory defence[122]

13–40   Under s.238(5) of the Insolvency Act, the court may not make an order under s.238 in respect of a transaction at an undervalue if it is satisfied that:

(a) the company which entered into the transaction did so in good faith and for the purpose of carrying on its business; and

(b) at the time it did so there were reasonable grounds for believing that the transaction would benefit the company.

This useful defence, which it is for those resisting an order to establish,[123] will protect a range of bona fide business transactions that might otherwise be vulnerable, including a transaction weighted in favour of the other party because he was in a stronger negotiating position and a disadvantageous transaction reasonably considered necessary to avoid or terminate litigation or to prevent the termination of a valuable contract or the loss of important intellectual property rights.

(1) Good faith

13–41   The requirement of good faith must, it is thought, be related to the purpose of s.238, and is not a requirement of honesty in a general sense. So limb (a) of s.238(5) should be considered satisfied if those involved on behalf of the company genuinely thought that the transaction would promote its interests, even if they acted dishonestly in the transaction itself, for example, by buying

---

[121] Such inability to pay debts is presumed to be satisfied unless the contrary is shown, in relation to any transaction at an undervalue entered into by a person connected with the company (s.240(2)), that is, a person who is a director, a shadow director, an associate of such a director or shadow director or an associate of the company as defined by s.435 of the Act (s.249). For the meaning of "onset of insolvency", see s.240(3).

[122] Possible restitutionary defences and cross-clams are considered below, paras 13–145 et seq.

[123] *Re Barton Manufacturing Co Ltd* [1999] B.C.L.C. 740.

goods on behalf of the company knowing it would be unable to pay for them or by knowingly misrepresenting the condition or quality of goods they were selling for the company.

It should be noted that it is the company that must act in good faith; the good faith of the other party is irrelevant. This reflects the historical origins of preferences and transfers in fraud of creditors where the focus was on the debtor's intent to defeat the statutory provision governing distribution on bankruptcy.[124] However, it does run counter to the general principle of English law that it is the party seeking relief who must show good faith. It seems objectionable that a company, acting through its liquidator, should be able to invoke its own bad faith and own state of insolvency to undo the effects of a transaction with another party who acted in good faith and was unaware either that the company was acting in bad faith or that it was insolvent.[125]

(2) "For the purpose of carrying on its business"

Transactions entered into by the company in the course of closing down its business should, it is thought, be considered to be "for the purpose of carrying on its business" within the above statutory provision.[126] Indeed, in *Wallach v Secretary of State for Trade and Industry*,[127] Lindsay J., while not deciding the point, was attracted by the submission of counsel that the interpretation of "carrying on a business" endorsed by Oliver J. in a different context in *Re Sarflax Ltd*[128] applied equally to s.438.

13–42

(3) Benefit to the company

Limb (b) requires the existence of reasonable grounds for believing that the transaction would benefit the company. Whether the transaction in fact benefits the company is not the question, although there may be a temptation to apply hindsight. Nor does limb (b) require that the company should in fact have believed it would benefit from the transaction; the test is an objective one—"reasonable grounds for believing"—although if the company did not

13–43

---

[124] See below, para.13–71.
[125] For a discussion of the question of whether s.238 might infringe art.1 of the First Protocol to the Human Rights Convention, set out in Sch.1 to the Human Rights Act 1998, see Janet Ulph and Tom Allen, "Transactions at an Undervalue, Purchasers and the Impact of the Human Rights Act 1998" [2004] J.B.L. 1.
[126] See *Re Sarflax Ltd* [1979] Ch. 592, in which Oliver J. held that the phrase did not require a continuing trade; it sufficed that the company was engaged in the collection of assets and the distribution of their proceeds in discharge of liabilities in the course of closing down the business.
[127] [2006] EWHC 989 (Ch).
[128] Cited above n.126.

believe the transaction would be of benefit, it may be hard pressed to establish that it acted in good faith as required by limb (a).

The protection of innocent third parties

13–44   A separate statutory defence is provided by s.241(2) of the Act in favour of bona fide transferees and recipients of benefit *otherwise than from the company* in good faith, for value and without notice. This defence, which is not available to the company's counterparty to the transaction at an undervalue, will be examined in the context of orders the court can make under s.238.[129]

The general power of the court

13–45   On an application by the office-holder for an order under s.238, the court is required to make such order as it thinks fit for restoring the position to what it would have been if the company had not entered into the transaction.[130] Despite the word "shall", the expression "think fit" has the effect that it is entirely within the court's discretion whether to make an order under s.238.[131] An order can be made only if the company is in administration or winding up and only on an application by the office-holder. A creditor has no *locus standi* to apply for an order. Whether an order is made and if so the type of order are entirely within the court's discretion; the office-holder is not entitled as of right to have a transaction at an undervalue set aside or to obtain a particular form of relief. Even where the court is satisfied that the company entered into a transaction at an undervalue, it will not make an order under s.238 where the company would have found itself in an even worse position if the transaction had not been carried out.[132] The order the court is required to make is to restore the company to the position in which it would have been if it had not entered into the transaction at all; the court is not permitted to reconstruct the position to what it would have been if the company had entered into a different transaction.[133] In deciding what order to make, the court does not start with any presumption in favour of monetary compensation as opposed to setting aside the transaction and revesting

---

[129] See below, para.13–68.

[130] Insolvency Act 1986 s.238(3).

[131] *Re Paramount Airways Ltd* [1993] Ch. 223, *per* Sir Donald Nicholls V.C. at 239, followed in *Singla v Brown* [2008] Ch. 357, where in view of the circumstances the court felt it appropriate to make no order, regardless of the presence or absence of the extra-territorial considerations relied on in *Paramount*.

[132] *Re MDA Investment Management Ltd, Whalley v Doney* [2004] 1 B.C.L.C. 217. In that case, the judge found that at the time of the transaction the company was on the verge of collapse and failure to enter into the transaction would have made its position still worse.

[133] *MDA Investment Management*, cited above n.132.

the asset transferred or, indeed, any other *a priori* assumption.[134] The order should not leave the claimant creditor in a better position than before. A good example is provided by *Feakins v Secretary of State for the Environment, Food and Rural Affairs*,[135] in which the facts were as follows:

> The debtor had engineered a situation in which a farm was sold by the bank mortgagee to the debtor's fiancée at a valuation on the basis of a sale subject to an existing tenancy which, unknown to the bank had been agreed to be surrendered, so that the fiancée was in fact buying the farm with vacant possession and thus buying at an undervalue. The Court of Appeal upheld the decision of the trial judge in rejecting the argument that the only relevant transaction was the sale by the bank and holding that a series of linked transactions which included the arrangement between the debtor and his fiancée that the former would procure the surrender of the tenancy constituted an arrangement within s.436 and a transaction at an undervalue within s.423. However, it varied the original decision by restoring the tenancy in order to prevent DEFRA from being in a better position that it had been prior to the fraudulent transaction.

In the typical case, the company will have purchased an asset at significantly more than its value or sold an asset at significantly less than its value. The former case can be dealt with by an order for repayment of the excess to the company and the latter by an order for payment of an additional sum to make up the price to the full value of the asset sold or alternatively an order for retransfer of the asset to the company and repayment by it of the price received. But such an order will not normally be sufficient by itself to restore the position to what it would have been if the company had not entered into the transaction, for account must also be taken of any additional income or profits it would have been likely to earn if the transaction had not taken place.[136] The defendant will as a rule be entitled to counter-restitution of benefits received by the company, for example, repayment of the price it received for the property which is to be retransferred to it, compensation for the value added by any improvements made by the defendant,[137] reimbursement of the cost of performing obligations undertaken by the company, for example, to meet the redundancy costs of employees, and repayment of a loan made by the defendant to the company as part of the total transaction.[138] In the case

13–46

---

[134] *Ramlort Ltd v Reid* [2004] B.P.I.R. 985, *per* Jonathan Parker L.J. at [125], approving the observation of Judge Havelock-Allan Q.C. in *Walker v W.A. Personnel Ltd* [2002] B.P.I.R. 621.

[135] [2007] B.C.C. 54.

[136] See the examples given below, paras 13–48–13–53, and the discussion of restitutionary principles at para.13–145.

[137] See *Weisgard v Pilkington* [1995] B.C.C. 1108.

[138] *Phillips v. Brewin Dolphin Bell Lawrie Ltd*. [2001] 1 W.L.R. 143. See further below, paras 13–145 *et seq.*

of an order for retransfer of property to the company, counter-restitution will involve repayments by the company as a condition of the transfer. Where the order against the defendant is for payment of money, counter-restitution will take the form of a deduction from the amount repayable to the company.[139] The relevance of general principles of the law of unjust enrichment is considered later.[140]

The general power conferred by s.238(3) to restore the company to the status quo is unfettered. The court is thus able to make various orders of a kind rather surprisingly omitted from the list of its specific powers under s.241(1).[141]

Specific powers

13–47   Without prejudice to the generality of the power conferred on the court by s238(3), the court may (subject to s.241(2)) make any of the seven types of order specified in s.241(1) of the Act. The list is interesting not only for what it contains but for several significant omissions. The particular remedies given to the company through an application by the office-holder are orders in personam directing property to be vested (or revested) in the company or money to be paid to the company and orders for the release or discharge of any security given by the company. There is no provision in s.241(1) for a transaction at an undervalue, whether it be a contract or conveyance, to be invalidated or set aside, nor is there provision for an order discharging the company from liability under a contract,[142] for example, for the excess of its commitment over the value of the consideration for the commitment. The underlying concept is that the original transaction was and remains valid but that its adverse effects are to be reversed by a conveyance (or reconveyance) or payment of a sum of money and the discharge of any security where appropriate.[143] Similarly, there is no express reference to the court's power to impose conditions in any order it makes, for example, that when property is retransferred to the company it is to repay the price originally received. Instead, there is a curiously limited power to allow proof in the winding up "for debts or other liabilities which arose from, or were released or discharged (in whole or in part) under or by, the transaction",[144] which hardly meets the case.[145]

However, since s.241(1) is without prejudice to the generality of the court's powers under s.238, which predicates restoration of both parties to the

---

[139] See ibid.
[140] See below, paras 13–145 *et seq.*
[141] See below.
[142] Other than a security.
[143] See further below, para.13–55.
[144] Insolvency Act 1986 s.241(1)(g), discussed below, para.13–66.
[145] See below, para.13–66.

position existing prior to the transaction, there seems to be no reason why the court should not in a proper case deal with a transaction at an undervalue by setting it aside and releasing the company, wholly or in part, from any liability incurred under it, and by making it a condition of vesting of property in the company that it is to repay any money or the value of any other benefit it received under the transaction. The susceptibility of the transaction to avoidance by the court in exercise of its powers under s.238 would, it is thought, constitute an equity binding on the defendant's liquidator or trustee in bankruptcy if the defendant were in, or were to go into, winding up or bankruptcy.[146] The effect of s.241(1) is thus to make the transaction voidable,[147] although it has to be borne in mind that "voidable" in this context means liable to avoidance at the court's discretion rather than as of right.

The various orders listed in s.241(1) fall into the following groups.

(1) Orders vesting property in the company

First, the court may require any property transferred as part of the transaction at an undervalue to be vested in the company. The generality of this provision should be noted. It is not confined to cases where the property was originally vested in the company but extends to transfers by a third party at the company's direction, as where the company agreed to buy from the third party and sub-sell to the ultimate transferee or agreed that a debt owed to the company by the third party should be discharged wholly or in part by the transfer of an asset from the third party to the transferee. Further, an order for transfer may be made not only against the original transferee (if he still has the property) but against the successor in title in whom it is currently vested. This, indeed, is made clear by the opening words of subs.(2) of s.241.[148] Again, if an order is made against a party who becomes bankrupt or goes into liquidation before complying with it, the court can direct the conveyance to be executed by the trustee or liquidator.

13–48

Secondly, the court may require any property to be vested in the company if it represents in any person's hands the application either of the proceeds of sale of property transferred as part of the transaction at an undervalue or of money so transferred.[149] Again, an order may be made against any holder of the property, whether or not the original transferee.

Where the company received consideration for the original transfer, it would obviously be wrong to direct a retransfer of the property (or the trans-

---

[146] See below, para.13–54.
[147] The view also taken by Simone Degeling, below, para.13–145.
[148] However, the court is precluded by subs.(2) of that section from making any order which would prejudice the rights of a bona fide purchaser for value without notice. See below, para.13–68.
[149] See Examples 3 and 4 below.

fer of other property acquired by the transferee with the proceeds of the original property) to the company without taking account of that consideration. So although s.241 contains no express reference to the imposing of conditions of an order under that section, it seems clear from the generality of s.238(3) that the court, when directing retransfer of property to the company, has power to impose a condition that the company shall repay the sum it received for the property or such part of that sum as will ensure that the company is in no better position than if it had not entered into the transaction.

A few examples will help to illustrate the above.

Example 1

13–49   The company sells to A for £100,000 property worth £250,000. The court can order A to reconvey the property to the company but account must be taken of the £100,000 originally paid. The order for retransfer could incorporate a condition that by way of counter-restitution the company repay the whole of the £100,000 originally received, with interest but this would not necessarily suffice to restore the status quo, for in the intervening period the company has been deprived of £150,000 of value which, if it had not entered into the transaction, might have been put to income-producing use. So it might be appropriate to deduct from the amount to be repaid by way of counter-restitution the income that the company could have expected to receive from the property if it had not been sold, less the interest on the consideration it received.

Example 2

13–50   The company sells to A for £100,000 property worth £250,000. A makes a gift of the property to his wife, B. An order can be made requiring B to convey the property to the company. Under the general power conferred by s.238(3), the court could also specify as a condition of its order that the company make a repayment to B as in Example 1.

Example 3

13–51   The company sells Blackacre to A for £100,000. Blackacre is then worth £250,000. A subsequently resells Blackacre to B for £300,000 and uses the proceeds to buy Whiteacre for £350,000. The court can order A to convey Whiteacre to the company but as in Example 1 account must be taken of the £100,000 originally received by the company. The court could as an alternative order B to convey Blackacre back to the company but not if B had acquired Blackacre in good faith and without notice of the relevant circumstances.[150]

---

[150] See Insolvency Act 1986 s.241(2) and below, para.13–68.

Example 4

The company makes a payment of £100,000 to A for which there is no con-   **13–52**
sideration. A uses the money to buy Blackacre. The court can order A to
convey Blackacre to the company.

Example 5

The company sells its business and factory premises to A for £1 in consid-   **13–53**
eration of A's assuming responsibility for redundancy payments due to the
company's employees and discharging the company's obligations to its
bankers. The business and premises are worth £1 million. A settles the
redundancy claims for £249,999 and the bank's claim for £200,000. Some
months later A lends the company £100,000. A also spends £150,000
improving the factory premises. The company then goes into insolvent liquidation. The court could order A to retransfer the business and factory
premises to the company but could be expected to require the company,
as a condition of the retransfer, to repay the £450,000 expended by A pursuant to the agreement and pay for the value added by the improvements
(which is not necessarily the amount of £150,000 spent).[151] Repayment of
the loan would not be a condition, this being an independent transaction
not attracting a right of counter-restitution, and A would be left to prove
for it in the winding up. However, the court might instead take the view
that it was unsatisfactory to dislocate the business by ordering it to be
retransferred and also that it would be unfair to A to make an order which
would preclude it from exercising a right of insolvency set-off.[152]
Accordingly, the court might conclude that a better solution would be to
allow A to retain the business and factory premises and to pay the amount
of the undervalue (£1 million less £450,000, i.e. £550,000) and interest,
against which A would then be able to set off his cross-claim for repayment
of the loan of £100,000 and interest.

It will be seen from the above examples that the court may order the vesting
in the company of: (i) the property originally transferred; (ii) other property
acquired with the proceeds of the original property; or (iii) property
acquired with money paid by the company. However, in case (ii) it must be
shown that the new property was acquired with the proceeds of the original
property, and in case (iii) that the property was acquired with the money
originally paid by the company. It may not always be easy to establish the
necessary nexus between the property of which recovery is sought and the
property or money originally transferred or paid by the company. To return

---

[151] See *Weisgard v Pilkington* [1995] B.C.C. 1108, a decision on a preference but the principle is
the same.
[152] This is because a money claim cannot be set off against an obligation to retransfer property.
See above, para.9–26.

to Example 3, suppose that on selling Blackacre A paid the £300,000 into his bank account, that this already had a credit balance of £400,000 and that A draws £350,000 out of his account to pay for Whiteacre. Is Whiteacre to be considered purchased with the proceeds of Blackacre, the £400,000 already in the account or a mixture of the two? If A were a trustee being pursued by the company for breach of trust, there would be no great difficulty in applying equitable tracing rules to arrive at a solution, using whatever presumptions were considered appropriate, for example, the rule in *Clayton's Case* that what is first in the account is the first to go out or the presumption that a trustee does not intend to commit a breach of trust and should therefore be assumed to have resorted to his own moneys before raiding the trust funds. But A is not a trustee and the purpose of s.238 is not to require A to hand over property acquired or profits made with trust moneys but simply to ensure that the company is no worse off than it would have been if it had never entered into the transaction in the first place. So there is no point in engaging in an elaborate tracing exercise; all the court need do is to order A to pay such sum as will recompense the company for the value lost, if necessary directing that payment be secured by a charge on Whiteacre.[153]

13–54   Section 241 does not prescribe the machinery by which property is to be vested or revested in the company and this is regulated by the general law. In the case of land, the court may simply make an order *in personam* directing the estate owner to convey the land to the company. In most cases, this will suffice. If the person against whom the order is made becomes bankrupt or goes into liquidation before executing the conveyance, there seems to be no reason why the court cannot order the conveyance to be executed by the trustee in bankruptcy or liquidator, for the susceptibility of the transaction to reversal under ss.238 and 241 would appear to constitute an equity binding on the trustee or liquidator. Alternatively, the court, when making the order, may reinforce it by making a declaration that the party against whom it is made is to hold the land as trustee[154] and by using that declaration as a springboard for a vesting order under s.44 of the Trustee Act 1925.

(2) Orders for the release or discharge of security given by the company

13–55   The court may release or discharge (in whole or in part) any security given by the company. So if a mortgage secures obligations under a contract or conveyance which is held to be a transaction at an undervalue, the court may order the mortgage to be discharged. As stated earlier, the contract or conveyance itself is not set aside; the court simply reverses its effect by ordering a reconveyance or the payment of such sum as will redress the balance.

---

[153] For which a separate power is conferred by s.241(1)(f). See below, para.13–62.
[154] Trustee Act 1925 s.48.

(3) Orders to repay the value of benefits received

The court may make an order requiring any person to pay, in respect of benefits received by him from the company, such sums to the office-holder as the court may direct.[155] A payment order can be made in respect of any kind of benefit received from the company, whether money or otherwise. So where property has been transferred at an undervalue, the court may, in lieu of ordering retransfer of the property, direct the transferee to repay to the company the shortfall in the consideration he gave and also (to ensure the company is placed in no worse position than if it had not entered into the transaction) interest on the shortfall or other compensation for loss suffered as the result of being deprived of it. Again, the recipient of the benefit need not, it seems, have received it directly from the company.

13–56

Example 6

The company sells to A for £100,000 property worth £250,000. The court can direct A to repay £150,000 and interest on that sum for the period between the time of the transfer and the time of payment in compliance with the order.

13–57

Example 7

The company sells to A for £100,000 property worth £250,000. A makes a gift of the property to his wife, B. An order as in Example 6 can be made against either A or B or, indeed, against both A and B.

13–58

(4) Orders reviving the obligations of a surety

The court may make an order providing for any surety, or guarantor[156] whose obligations to any person were released or discharged (in whole or in part) under the transaction to be under such new or revived obligations to that person as the court thinks fit. Such person will usually be the company itself, although it could be the transferee or a third party. Revival of the obligation in effect restores the suretyship, wholly or in part. But the court may alternatively impose a new obligation on the erstwhile surety and this need not be restricted to a suretyship obligation but could be a primary and independent obligation running parallel to that of the principal debtor.

13–59

---

[155] For an example, see *Re Sonatacus Ltd* [2007] B.C.C. 186. As to the application of recoveries, see below, para.13–140.
[156] In English law usage, the terms "surety" and "guarantor" are often used interchangeably. But see below, para.13–102.

Example 8

13–60   The company makes an advance of £50,000 to A which is guaranteed by B. A repays £20,000 but makes no further repayments. Subsequently, the company's managing director, a close friend of A, arranges for the outstanding balance of the debt to be written off and for A to be released from liability despite the fact that he is well able to pay. In consequence, B is also discharged from liability.[157] The release of A constitutes a transaction at an undervalue. Soon afterwards, an administration order is made against the company. On the application of the administrator, the court may order A to pay the balance of the debt, with interest, and may further order that B's obligations as surety are to be revived or alternatively that he is to come under a new and independent liability for payment as a principal jointly and severally with A.

Example 9

13–61   The company agrees to buy the business and undertaking of A Ltd, which is wholly owned by the buying company's managing director. The price agreed is £10 million, although on a realistic valuation the business is worth no more than £2 million. As a condition of the sale, A Ltd releases the buying company's parent, B Plc, from its liability as guarantor of a loan of £500,000 previously made by A Ltd to the buying company. Soon after completion of the sale the buying company goes into liquidation. On the application of the liquidators, the court may set aside the sale, in exercise of its general powers under s.238(3), or make an order under s.241(1) for repayment of the excess value paid to A Ltd. The effect of either kind of order is to destroy the basis upon which B Plc was discharged from liability under its guarantee, and in these circumstances the court may consider it just to direct that B's obligations to A Ltd be revived in order to produce a full restoration of the parties to their status quo.

(5) Orders securing obligations imposed by the orders

13–62   An order may direct that security be provided for the discharge of any obligation imposed by or arising under the order, for such an obligation to be charged on any property and for the security or charge to have the same priority as a security or charge released or discharged (in whole or in part) under the transaction. Thus, where the original security was a first charge and before it was released the company had given a second charge over the same property to another creditor, the court can direct the new security to have the priority over the second charge, thus displacing its promotion to

---

[157] Since a surety's obligation is coterminous with that of the principal debtor.

first charge resulting from the release of the original security. Assuming that the second chargee did not make any further advances after release of the original charge, such an order leaves him no worse off than he was before the original charge was released. But the court cannot make an order which will prejudice rights acquired in good faith and for value.[158] So, if in reliance on the release of the original security the second chargee makes a further advance, the court cannot give the new charge priority over the second charge as regards that further advance. Similarly, if the company, without having granted a second charge, releases the original security and then gives a mortgage to another creditor to secure an advance by that creditor acting in good faith and without notice, the court cannot make an order which will displace the priority of that creditor as first mortgagee.

Example 10

The company sells to A for £100,000 property worth £250,000 and soon afterwards goes into liquidation. On the liquidator's application the court can order the payment by A of the shortfall of £150,000, with interest, and can direct that all or any of A's assets stand charged to secure compliance with the order.

13–63

Example 11

The company makes an advance of £50,000 to A which is guaranteed by B. The guarantee is secured by a charge on B's house Blackacre. A then arranges an overdraft facility with C Bank and gives C Bank a second charge on Blackacre to secure existing and future indebtedness. C Bank advances money on the security of its second charge. Subsequently, the company's managing director, a close friend of B, arranges for the company to release B from his guarantee for no consideration and to discharge the charge. This is a transaction at an undervalue. The court may direct B's obligations as surety to be revived and secured by a charge on Blackacre, having the same priority over C Bank's charge as that enjoyed by the original security.

13–64

Example 12

The facts are as in Example 11 except that after A's release and the discharge of his mortgage and before the company goes into liquidation, A borrows a further £20,000 from C Bank and also borrows £30,000 from D, secured by a charge on Blackacre, D advancing his money in good faith and without notice. The court may direct B's obligations as surety to be revived and secured by a charge on Blackacre, having priority over C Bank's charge as to advances made by C Bank prior to the release of the original security given by A but the new charge must be made subordinate

13–65

---

[158] Insolvency Act 1986 s.241(2). See below, para.13–68.

to C Bank's charge as regards the further advance of £20,000 and must also be made subordinate to the charge in favour of D.

(6) Orders permitting proof of debt by a person affected by the order

13–66 The order may provide for the extent to which any person whose property is vested by the order in the company, or on whom obligations are imposed by the order, is to be able to prove in the winding up of the company for debts or other liabilities which arose from or were released or discharged (in whole or in part) under or by the transaction. This provision, although applicable to transactions at an undervalue as well as to preferences, is directed mainly to the latter. In the case of transactions at an undervalue, the justice of the case will usually require a condition of repayment by the company (through its liquidator or administrator) of any sum received in exchange for property ordered to be reconveyed to the company.

Example 13

13–67 The company sells to A for £100,000 property worth £250,000 and soon after goes into liquidation. The court can order restoration of the property to the company but if it does so it should normally make it a condition of the order that the company repays the original purchase price of £100,000 with interest at the appropriate rate.[159] Alternatively, the court can order A to pay the company £150,000, being the excess value he received but allow him to prove in the liquidation for the same amount.

Orders affecting third parties

13–68 Reference has already been made to the court's power under s.241 of the Act to make an order under s.238 affecting the property of, or imposing an obligation on, any person, whether or not he is the person with whom the transaction at an undervalue was entered into. But by s.241(2), such an order must not:

(1) prejudice any interest in property which was acquired from a person other than the company and was acquired in good faith and for value, or prejudice any interest deriving from such an interest; and

(2) require a person who received a benefit from the transaction in good faith and for value to pay a sum to the office-holder except where that person was a party to the transaction.

---

[159] See *Phillips v Brewin Dolphin Bell Lawrie Ltd*, above n.138; *Ramlort Ltd v Reid* [2004] B.P.I.R. 985.

It is worth emphasising that this is a rule for the protection of third parties, not the company's counterparty to the transaction at an undervalue.

Prior to its amendment by the Insolvency (No.2) Act 1994, s.241(2) required not merely that the third party should have acquired the asset in good faith and for value but also that he should have taken it "without notice of the relevant circumstances". For this purpose, "relevant circumstances" were defined, in relation to transactions at an undervalue, as:

> "(a) the circumstances by virtue of which an order under section 238 . . . could be made in respect of the transaction if the company were to go into liquidation, or an administration order were made in relation to the company, within a particular period after the transaction is entered into . . . and
>
> (b) if that period has expired, the fact that the company has gone into liquidation or that such an order has been made."

Two problems arose from this provision. First, the definition of "relevant circumstances" was couched in such general terms as to make it unclear whether the third party was required to be without notice of any element in s.238, including the state of insolvency of the company, or merely of the fact that it had entered into a transaction at an undervalue. Secondly, a purchaser from a donee of property was placed in a difficulty where he knew that his vendor was a donee, as might happen particularly in the case of unregistered land, where the consideration or absence of consideration would be shown on search certificates unless the vendor had taken the precaution of removing it. Such a purchaser would have to rely on a declaration of solvency by his vendor.

Section 241 has now been substantially altered to give greater protection to the bona fide purchaser for value. In the first place, there is now a presumption of good faith. In keeping with the characteristically oblique style of Westminster drafting, s.241 does not express this in positive terms. Instead, it provides that, unless the contrary is shown, a person is presumed to have acquired the interest or benefit otherwise than in good faith where he had notice of the relevant surrounding circumstances and of the relevant proceedings or was connected with[160] or an associate of[161] either the company itself or the person with whom it entered into the transaction at an undervalue.[162] "The relevant surrounding circumstances" is defined more narrowly than its predecessor, and in relation to transactions at an undervalue the only relevant circumstance is the fact that the company in question entered into

---

[160] See Insolvency Act 1986 s.249.
[161] See Insolvency Act 1986 s.435. The reference to an associate of the company is pleonastic, since the definition of "connected" with a company includes a person who is an associate of the company (s.249). See below, para.13–104.
[162] Insolvency Act 1986 s.241(2A).

the transaction at an undervalue. Even this reformulation is ambiguous. Is the third party on notice merely because he was aware of the transaction and (even if he did not know it) the transaction was in fact at an undervalue? Or must he also be on notice that the transaction was at an undervalue? It seems clear that the latter interpretation is that intended, for a third party can hardly be said to be acting in bad faith if he has no notice of the crucial fact rendering the transaction vulnerable. There is no direct definition of "the relevant proceedings"; what these are is to be gleaned from the provisions of s.241(3A) to (3C) laying down when a person is to be considered to have notice of relevant proceedings. This depends on whether s.238 applies by virtue of an administration order, a liquidation immediately upon discharge of an administration order or a liquidation at any other time. In the first case, what is required is that the third party has notice either of the presentation of the petition on which the administration order is made or of the fact that the order has been made. In the second case, what is required is either notice of one of the above facts or notice of the fact that the company has gone into liquidation. In the third case, the effect of the statutory provisions is that in a compulsory winding up the third party should have notice either of the winding up order or of the presentation of the petition on which the winding up order is made and that in a voluntary winding up the company has gone into liquidation, i.e. by the passing of a resolution for voluntary winding up.

It should be noted that if a third party acquires his interest in good faith and for value, the protection he thereby acquires enures for the benefit of his successors in title, whether or not they were aware of the relevant surrounding circumstances. This principle of "sheltering", embodied in the phrase "or prejudice any interest deriving from such an interest", is well established in English law[163] and reflects the fact that a person who acquires a good title to an asset must be free to dispose of it to whomever he wishes, otherwise the marketability of his property is impaired.[164]

Summary of protection for third parties

13–69 We are now in a position to summarise the statutory provisions for the protection of innocent third parties. Where the company has entered into a transaction by which it transfers property to another at an undervalue and a third party acquires an interest in that property, the third party is protected from an order under s.238 if but only if, he acquired his interest in good faith and for value. There is a rebuttable presumption of *want* of good faith in any

---

[163] See *Goode on Commercial Law*, edited by Ewan McKendrick, 4th edn (London: Penguin Books and LexisNexis, 2009), p.59.
[164] ibid.

of the following cases,[165] that is, where the third party, at the time of acquiring his interest:

(1)   has notice of the fact that the transaction under which the company disposed of the property was a transaction at an undervalue;

(2)   is connected with, or was an associate of, the company or its transferee; or

(3)   has notice of the fact that the company has gone into administration or liquidation or that any petition on which an administration order or winding up order was made has been presented.

"Notice" is broader than knowledge and covers not only facts of which a party is aware but facts which he could have discovered by proper enquiry. Thus, a person might be considered to have notice of a winding up petition by reason of its advertisement and of a winding up order by reason of its publication in the London Gazette.

Recovery or disclaimer?

It may happen that a transaction at an undervalue imposes continuing obligations on the debtor company which would enable the liquidator to disclaim the transaction as onerous property in regard to the future obligations. The office holder may then have to elect between remedies. If the transaction is reversed as a transaction at an undervalue, then depending on the order made by the court, there may be nothing to disclaim. On the other hand, exercise of a right of disclaimer as to future obligations may have the result of reversing the imbalance in value in the original transaction, so that while it remains the case that the transaction was at an undervalue at the time it was entered into, no relief, or only reduced relief, is necessary to restore the company to its former position.

13–70

7. PREFERENCES

(i) Overview

The pre-1986 law

English bankruptcy law has long had provisions enabling the court to set aside payments and transfers made in the run-up to bankruptcy in favour of

13–71

---

[165] And thus a rebuttable presumption of good faith where none of these cases is applicable.

a particular creditor which were designed to prefer him over other creditors. Fraudulent preferences, as they were known, were struck down by the courts on policy grounds long before legislation was enacted to deal with them. Prior to the Insolvency Act 1985, the law relating to fraudulent preferences was set out in s.44 of the Bankruptcy Act 1914,[166] which was made applicable to companies by s.320 of the Companies Act 1948. The term "fraudulent preference" was not in fact used in s.44; what the section in fact provided in essence was that every disposition of property or payment, every obligation incurred, and every judicial proceeding taken or suffered by a person unable to pay his debts with a view to giving a creditor or a surety preference over the other creditors was to be deemed fraudulent and void against the trustee in bankruptcy if the transferor, etc. became bankrupt within six months. It was not in fact necessary to show a fraudulent intent; all that was required was that the debtor should make a voluntary transfer, payment, etc. with the dominant intention of favouring a particular creditor or surety at the expense of other creditors. The debtor was not considered to act voluntarily if he made the transfer or payment under pressure from the creditor, for example, a threat of legal proceedings which genuinely influenced the debtor.

Bearing in mind that the object of rules as to preference is to prevent a creditor from gaining an unfair advantage by concluding a transaction with the company during the twilight period which precedes winding up or administration,[167] it may seem odd that avoidance of a preference should be made to depend on the company's intention to give a preference, rather than on the fact of the creditor receiving one.[168] Indeed, there is no such requirement under Australian or US law, which adopt an "effects" test where it suffices that the transaction improves the creditor's position during the twilight period.[169] The focus on the intent (now the desire) of the debtor stems from the historical origins of fraudulent preference as an act intended to give one creditor an advantage at the expense of the general body of creditors.[170] The Cork

---

[166] As amended by s.115(3) of the Companies Act 1947.

[167] For an excellent treatment of legal policy relating to preferences, described from the perspective of US law but in many ways equally applicable to English law, see Professor T.H. Jackson's elegant study *The Logic and Limits of Bankruptcy Law* (Cambridge, MA, Harvard University Press, 1986), Ch.6. See also D.D. Prentice, "Some Observations on the Law Relating To Preferences" in Ross Cranston (ed.), *Making Commercial Law* (Oxford: Clarendon Press, 1997), pp.439 et seq.

[168] One of the more curious features of s.44 of the Bankruptcy Act 1914 was that it did not say in terms that the transaction had to have the effect of giving the creditor a preference; it referred merely to the fact of payment, transfer, etc. and the intention of the debtor to prefer the creditor. So on a literal construction, a payment or transfer which, although intended to favour the creditor, did not in fact do so was voidable.

[169] See Gerard McCormack, "Swelling Corporate Assets: Changing What Is on the Menu" (2006) 6 J. Corp. L. Stud. 39. However, Professor McCormack considers that there is force in the criticism made by other commentators that the many exceptions to the US preference rule have come close to eliminating it. See also Vanessa Finch, *Corporate Insolvency Law*, 2nd edn (Cambridge: Cambridge University Press, 2009), p.574.

[170] Similarly with what are transactions at an undervalue. See *Alderson v Temple* (1768) 4 Burr. 2235; 98 E.R. 165, and above, para.13–41.

Committee considered whether to recommend that English law be brought into line with Australian and US law but the majority view came out against this on the ground that without an intention to prefer the element of impropriety on which the existing statutory provisions were based was missing and that creditors who were active in the pursuit of payment should be allowed to retain the fruits of their diligence, particularly since they may well have used these to pay their own creditors.[171] The argument is unpersuasive. The whole purpose of the *pari passu* principle is to ensure that once a company becomes insolvent, no individual creditor should be allowed to steal a march on his competitors. Diligence should not be a factor at this stage. Indeed, a rule which allows the creditor who exerts greatest pressure on the debtor company the best chance of resisting a preference claim scarcely reflects a principled approach to the question of equitable distribution in insolvency.[172]

The policies underlying the preference rules have been discussed in this context as in relation to transactions at an undervalue,[173] where it was seen that deterrence is not a credible objective and that the real policy is to preserve equality of distribution during the run-up to winding up or administration. However, there is an important difference between the two in that transactions at an undervalue necessarily result in a diminution in the company's net asset position whereas preferences do not, since the payment or transfer in favour of the preferred creditor produces a corresponding reduction in the company's liabilities, leaving its net asset position unchanged. So the rules as to preferences are not aimed at protecting the company's assets, only in ensuring that one creditor is not given an unfair advantage over others.

The changes effected by the Insolvency Act

The Insolvency Act 1986, re-enacting the Insolvency Act 1985, introduced the following changes:

13–72

(1) References to "fraud" were dropped. This was not a change of substance.

(2) Although the vulnerable transaction is still referred to as a preference, this is defined in terms which refer not to a preference of the creditor over other creditors but to placing him in a better position on liquidation than he would have had if the transaction had not been concluded. In fact, this comes to the same thing as a preference but at least the

---

[171] Insolvency Law Review Committee, *Insolvency Law and Practice* (Cmnd. 8558, 1982), paras 1254 et seq.
[172] See the strong criticisms by R.C.C. Cuming, "Transactions at Undervalue and Preferences under the Bankruptcy and Insolvency Act: Rethinking Outdated Approaches" (2002) 37 Can. Bus. L.J. 5.
[173] See above, paras 13–03 et seq.

factual improvement of the creditor's position is now expressly stated as an essential element.

(3) In place of the old "dominant intention to prefer", the statutory provisions prescribe a less stringent requirement that in giving the preference the company was influenced by a desire to produce the effect referred to in s.239(4)(b).

(4) The time limit for avoidance is extended from six months to two years in the case of a preference in favour of a person connected with the company.

The basic provision

13–73   Where an administration order has been made against a company or it goes into liquidation and the company has at a relevant time given a preference to any person, the court may, on an application by the office-holder, make such order as it thinks fit for restoring the position to what it would have been if the company had not given that preference and give consequential relief.[174]

Conditions to be satisfied under s.239

13–74   The court cannot make an order under s.239 unless the following seven conditions are satisfied:

(1) the company is in liquidation or administration;

(2) application for the order is made by the liquidator or administrator;

(3) a preference was given to a creditor, surety orguarantor;

(4) the preference was given or suffered by the company;

(5) in giving the preference the company was influenced by a desire to improve the position of the person preferred;

(6) the preference was given at a relevant time; and

(7) the company was unable to pay its debts within the meaning of s.123 of the Insolvency Act either at the time of or in consequence of entering into the transaction.[175]

---

[174] Insolvency Act 1986 ss.239(1)–(3), 238(1), 240 and 241. See above, paras 13–45 et seq.
[175] Insolvency Act 1986 s.240(2). In contrast to the position in regard to transactions at an undervalue, there is no presumption of inability to pay debts in the case of a preference in favour of a person connected with the company.

Thus, there must be a factual preference, a desire to prefer and the giving of the preference at a relevant time.[176] Conditions (1), (2) and (6) have been discussed earlier in relation to transactions at an undervalue. However, the concept of "relevant time" raises additional considerations in relation to preferences which it is necessary to examine. Condition (7) was fully explored in Ch.4.

Defences

Even where all of the above conditions are satisfied, a defence may be available under s.241(2). For the reasons set out below,[177] there would appear to be no scope for the application of general principles of unjust enrichment and no need for any general law right of counter-restitution.[178]   **13–75**

Onus of proof

In general, the onus lies on the office-holder to establish that all of the conditions necessary for the making of an order under s.239 have been satisfied, including the fact that the company was influenced by a desire to give a preference. But there is a rebuttable presumption of such desire where the preference is in favour of a person connected with the company otherwise than by reason only of being its employee.[179] On the other hand, in contrast to the position in regard to transactions at an undervalue, there is no presumption of inability to pay debts in the case of a preference in favour of a person connected with the company.   **13–76**

(ii) The elements of a preference

What constitutes a preference

By s.239(4), a company gives a preference to a person if: **13–77**

(1)   that person is one of the company's creditors or a surety or guarantor for any of the company's debts or other liabilities; and

---

[176] See *Transaction Avoidance in* Insolvencies (above, n.28), Ch.5; Adrian Walters, "Preferences", in Armour and Bennett, *Vulnerable Transactions in Corporate Insolvency*, 2002, p.126.

[177] See para.13–145.

[178] See paras 13–151 *et seq.*

[179] Insolvency Act 1986 s.239(6). For a case where a director of the debtor company was also managing director of the creditor and effectively took decisions for both companies, see *Re Transworld Trading Ltd, TFS Cargo Services Ltd v Saunders* [1999] B.P.I.R. 628, where the judge declined to accept a picture of "poor Mr. Kirby as managing director of TFS exerting legitimate pressure upon himself as director of TWT".

(2)   the company does anything or suffers anything to be done which (in either case) has the effect of putting that person into a position which, in the event of the company going into insolvent liquidation, will be better than the position he would have been in if that thing had not been done.

The basic features of factual preference[180] are (i) an improvement of the creditor's position (ii) at the expense of other creditors.

Examples of preference of creditor

13–78   A creditor's preference typically takes one of three forms, namely: a payment to the creditor[181] or to a third party by direction of the creditor[182]; the provision of security (or additional security) for past advances; and the transfer of debts or other assets in reduction or discharge of the company's liability.[183] But any other act or thing which improves the creditor's position relative to what it would be in an immediately ensuing liquidation suffices as a preference,[184] for example:

(1)   an agreement for set-off going beyond what would be allowed the creditor under the rules governing insolvency set-off[185];

(2)   the conferment on the creditor of a right of set-off against a debt already owing to the company by the creditor;

---

[180] See below, para.13–82.

[181] This could include the distribution of a declared dividend to controlling shareholders if the company was insolvent at the time and the shareholders could not, as persons connected with the company (see Insolvency Act 1986 ss.249(b) and 435(7) and (10)) rebut the presumption of a desire to prefer them (see Insolvency Act 1986 s.239(6)). Where shareholders have to repay the dividend received, they will rank as deferred creditors for the amount of the dividend (Insolvency Act 1986 s.74(2)(f)).

[182] See *Re Exchange Travel (Holdings) Ltd* [1996] B.C.C. 933, *per* Rattee J. at 948.

[183] An agreement that security shall be given only on demand by the creditor or the occurrence of some other uncertain event is not a present security but a mere contract. If the creditor subsequently demands security or the other stated contingency occurs and security is furnished, this will be regarded as given for past value (except to the extent of any new value furnished) and if given within the preference period (six months or two years, as the case may be) will be caught by s.239 if the other conditions of application are satisfied. See *Re Jackson & Bassford Ltd* [1906] 2 Ch. 467; and *Goode on Legal Problems of Credit and Security*, 2008, paras 1-76 and 2-15.

[184] Assuming satisfaction of the other conditions for the application of s.239.

[185] The fact that such an agreement is of no effect on liquidation, being displaced by the insolvency set-off rules, does not make this example purely theoretical, for the point of time at which the efficacy of the set-off agreement has to be tested is not the date of actual liquidation but the date of the hypothetical liquidation, which as stated above would seem to be immediately after the act asserted to constitute the preference.

(3)   voluntary submission of the debtor company to an unjustified or excessive judgment;

(4)   allowing payment to the creditor by a third party who has a right to be recouped by the company; and

(5)   performance of a contract in favour of a creditor who had already made payment in advance when performances were also due under other contracts to other creditors in a similar position, as where a seller of goods collects payment from a number of buyers but only makes delivery to a few selected buyers.

Preference rules confined to creditors, sureties and guarantors

Since the rules as to preference are designed to preserve the sanctity of the pari passu principle by which creditors in a winding up share rateably in the assets available for distribution, they are confined to creditors of and sureties and guarantors for the company,[186] for only a creditor, surety or guarantor can prove in a winding up.[187]

13–79

"Creditor"

Only a payment or transfer in favour of a creditor can be attacked as a preference. So a return of trust property or stolen property cannot constitute a preference, since there is no relationship of creditor and debtor.[188] Moreover, such property does not form part of the company's estate and accordingly does not affect either the company or its creditors.[189] Although the term "creditor" includes, for other purposes, future, prospective and contingent creditors as well as creditors to whom debts are currently payable, the preference provisions are necessarily confined to existing creditors, for it is only they who by definition will have received a payment or transfer without giving new value. It is true that a future creditor could be paid in advance of performance but that is not a preference, since he remains liable to perform and thereby give value.

13–80

---

[186] Insolvency Act 1986 s.239(4)(a); and *Re Beacon Leisure Ltd* [1991] B.C.C. 213. As to the preference of sureties, see paras 13–99–13–102. See also above n.181.

[187] A surety can prove when he has discharged the debt or that part of it for which he agreed to be responsible.

[188] *Re Wilkinson, Ex p. Stubbins* (1881) 17 Ch.D. 58; and *Sinclair v Wilson* (1855) 20 Beav. 324; 52 E.R. 627, cited in *Re Lehman Bros International (Europe) Ltd* [2010] B.C.C. 272.

[189] See further below, para.13–89.

"Surety"; "guarantor"

13–81   These terms are examined later in the discussion of a preference in favour of a surety or guarantor.[190]

Improvement of the creditor's position as the criterion of a preference

13–82   In determining whether a creditor has been preferred, the acid test is whether what is done would have the effect of disturbing the statutory order of priorities in an insolvent liquidation[191] by placing the creditor or surety or guarantor in a more favourable position than he would otherwise have had. The mere fact that the thing is done or suffered in pursuance of a court order does not, without more, prevent it from constituting a preference.[192] This re-enacts previous law in enabling the court to look behind collusive judgments.[193]

I have remarked earlier that the former legislation contained no express requirement that the creditor should in fact have received a preference; all that had to be established was that a payment, transfer, etc., was made with a view to giving the creditor or surety a preference over the other creditors, a provision interpreted by the courts as requiring that the company's dominant intention should be to give such a preference. Section 239(4)(b) of the Insolvency Act 1986, in defining a preference, says nothing about preferring a creditor over other creditors; the test is whether what was done has the effect of putting the creditor in a better position upon winding up than he would have been in if it had not been done. But this comes to the same thing. If the effect of a payment or transfer made or suffered by the company is to make the creditor better off on winding up than he would otherwise have been, this can only be at the expense of other creditors. So the new test of improvement is merely another way of describing a preference, and perhaps a more satisfactory way, since it underlines the separately stated requirement that the company be insolvent at the time of the payment or transfer in question or become insolvent because of it.[194] Obviously, a payment or transfer made by a company which remains solvent after making it does not improve the creditor's position, for he would in any event have been paid in full if the company had gone into winding up.

---

[190] See below, paras 13–99–13–102.
[191] "Insolvent liquidation" is not defined for the purpose of this section but presumably has the same meaning as in ss.214(6) and 216(7), namely liquidation at a time when the company's assets are insufficient for the payment of its debts and other liabilities and the expenses of the winding up.
[192] Insolvency Act 1986 s.239(7).
[193] For an example, see *Re Menastar Finance Ltd* [2003] 1 B.C.L.C. 338.
[194] See above, paras 13–08 and 13–74.

(1) No preference to the extent of new value

The payment, transfer or other act under attack must relate to a past **13–83**
indebtedness, for to the extent that the creditor gives new value, he gains no
advantage,[195] and even if he happens to be a creditor already in respect of
some prior transaction, he does not receive the payment, transfer, etc. in his
capacity as such but derives it from the independent, new transaction
concluded for value.

Example 14

C grants D Ltd an overdraft facility. Subsequently, C makes a fixed loan of **13–84**
£300,000 to D Ltd for the purchase of capital equipment, the loan being
secured by a charge on the company's factory premises. At that time the
company's account is overdrawn by £20,000. The grant of the charge does
not constitute a preference for it was given not in respect of the existing
indebtedness of £20,000 but to secure a new advance. The charge was
therefore not taken by C in the capacity of an existing creditor.[196]

Since a preference involves a payment, transfer or other act which, assuming
the company were to go into insolvent liquidation immediately thereafter,[197]
would put the creditor in a better position than if the payment or transfer
had not been made or the other act performed, the preference provisions
cannot apply to the extent that the creditor gives new value, for he does not
take out a penny more than he puts in. So a creditor who takes security for
a contemporaneous or subsequent advance does not obtain a preference,
since the diminution in assets created by the security is matched by the infusion of new funds. Again, a simultaneous exchange of goods and money on
a sale transaction cannot involve a preference, whether the company be the
buyer or the seller.

(2) Security in after-acquired property

The concept of new value is of particular importance in relation to a charge **13–85**
taken over after-acquired property to secure contemporaneous or future
advances, for each newly acquired asset, having been bargained for as security at the outset, is considered given in security for new value, a point I have
developed elsewhere.[198]

---

[195] See below, para.13–84.
[196] *See Robertson v Grigg* (1932) 47 C.L.R. 257.
[197] See below. As to whether post-liquidation assets fall within the scope of an after-acquired
property clause, see above, paras 6–32 et seq.
[198] *Goode on Legal Problems of Credit and Security*, 2008, para.2–13.

Some problems concerning new value

13–86   The concept of new value is easy to understand but sometimes hard to apply. Let us consider, first, the single transaction involving the provision of services for payment, and secondly, a course of dealing between the parties reflected in the operation of a running account.

(1) Simultaneous exchange

13–87   In relation to the single transaction, we have seen that a simultaneous exchange gives rise to no preference problem. What is not clear is the degree of simultaneity the court will expect in order to treat a payment or transfer as being for new value. Suppose, for example, that a solicitor deals with the purchase of land for a client company, renders his bill after completion and then receives payment. Has he thereby improved his position? Or can he contend that he collected his charges so closely after the provision of her services that these should be considered to constitute new value? A commonsense approach indicates that it suffices that payment is made within a time normal for a transaction not intended to involve the extension of credit. In any event, in the ordinary way the making of the payment will be pursuant to that intention and not from a desire to improve the position of the solicitor vis-à-vis other creditors.

(2) Mutual dealings on running account

13–88   Now let us turn to the position where there is a continuous flow of dealings between parties. Must each payment be treated in isolation to see whether it would have given the creditor an advantage if the company were to go into winding up immediately thereafter? How far can credit be given for contra items? The Act itself gives no guidance. It is unfortunate that it contains no general exemption of transactions entered into bona fide by the creditor in the ordinary course of business. What is relevant is not the creditor's good faith but the question whether the company was influenced by a desire to confer an advantage on him, which as we shall see is a necessary prerequisite to any order under s.239 or 241. In practice, the two are likely to go together. Where the creditor receives a payment in good faith, it will almost invariably be the case that the company makes the payment as a normal part of its business or to protect its own interests (for example, for the purpose of ensuring the continuance of supplies), not to favour the creditor to whom payment is made.

    In the typical case, there is a running account between the parties to record mutual dealings. Suppose that a company whose account with its bank is overdrawn pays a cheque into the account, thus reducing the overdraft. If the company were at that time insolvent, the payment in would constitute a preference and would be vulnerable to attack if made with intent to prefer the bank. But suppose a few days later the bank honoured a further drawing. Would it be liable to repay the preference without being given credit for the fresh advance? Such a result would seem unfair in the extreme, giving a windfall to the general body of creditors. Could the fresh drawing be treated as a reversal of the preferential payment? This is one way out of the dilemma. The court makes no order because the bank has already put right the wrong. Another way of approaching the matter is to say that:

"... where a payment is not in pursuance of an isolated transaction but is bound up with a series of transactions, it is the effect of the total transactions, of all the connected items, that has to be looked at".[199]

This approach by the Australian courts,[200] which has been adopted in at least one case in England,[201] has much to commend it, for even if a payment into the account was intended to be preferential, a connected payment out should be treated as negating the preference *pro tanto*, as it restores the loss of assets which is the rationale of the preference provisions. However, the preference will not be undone to the extent that the new drawing is secured by a fresh and valid security.[202]

Moreover, the fact that there is a series of mutual dealings, with debits and credits on both sides, will usually suffice to negate an intention to prefer, for it suggests either that a payment into the account was made in the expectation that further drawings would be allowed or that the bank allowed a further drawing on the understanding that it would be covered by a further payment into the account. In either case, there is no intention to prefer or, indeed, a true preference at all. Indeed, it has been said that the real question is not the labelling of the account as a running account but rather the intention that payments into the account will generate future supplies of goods, services or credit. Accordingly, it is not necessary that payments into the account should go in reduction of the ultimate debit balance; even payments made to discharge specific debit items will qualify for the application of the principle if the intention is that they should form part of a continuing relationship involving the extension of further credit. The leading authority is the decision of the High Court of Australia in *Airservices Australia v*

---

[199] *Ferrier v Civil Aviation Authority* (1995) 127 A.L.R. 472; and *M. & R Jones Shopfitting Co Pty Ltd v National Bank of Australasia Ltd* (1983) 7 A.C.L.R. 445, citing *Re Weiss* [1970] A.L.R. 654, in which all of the earlier Australian authorities are reviewed.

[200] Which has since been adopted by the legislature in what is now s.588FA(3) of the Corporations Act 2001 (Cth), re-enacting s.588FA(2) of the Corporation Law Reform Act 1992 enacted pursuant to the recommendations of the Harmer Report (Australian Law Reform Commission, *General Insolvency Inquiry*), para.655.

[201] *Wilson v Masters International Ltd* [2010] B.C.C. 834.

[202] cf. the US Bankruptcy Code s.547(c)(4). If the overdraft had been previously secured, there would not be a preference at all. See below, para.13–93.

Ferrier,[203] in which there were mutual dealings between the parties, sums paid were applied in discharge of particular debts but the debit balance substantially increased over the period of the mutual dealings. It was held by Dawson, Gaudron and McHugh JJ. (Brennan C.J. and Toohey J. dissenting) that none of the payments except the last (which was not a trigger for new credit) was a preference. The principle was stated by the majority in the following terms:

"Since the decision of this Court in *Richardson v Commercial Banking Co of Sydney Ltd*, the term 'running account' has achieved almost talismanic significance in determining when the ultimate, rather than the immediate and isolated, effect of a payment is to be examined for the purpose of a determination under s.122 of the Bankruptcy Act. However, the significance of a running account lies in the inferences that can be drawn from the facts that answer the description of a 'running account' rather than the label itself. A running account between traders is merely another name for an active account running from day to day, as opposed to an account where further debits are not contemplated. The essential feature of a running account is that it predicates a continuing relationship of debtor and creditor with an expectation that further debits and credits will be recorded. Ordinarily, a payment, although often matching an earlier debit, is credited against the balance owing in the account. Thus, a running account is contrasted with an account where the expectation is that the next entry will be a credit entry that will close the account by recording the payment of the debt or by transferring the debt to the Bad or Doubtful Debt A/c.

If the record of the dealings of the parties fits the description of a 'running account', that record will usually provide a solid ground for concluding that they conducted their dealings on the basis that they had a continuing business relationship and that goods or services would be provided and paid for on the credit terms ordinarily applicable in the creditor's business. When that is so, a court will usually be able to conclude that the parties mutually assumed that from a business point of view each particular payment was connected with the subsequent provision of goods or services in that account. Sometimes, however, the transactions recorded in the account may be so sporadic that a court cannot conclude that there was the requisite connection between a payment and the future supply of goods even though the account was kept 'in the ordinary form of a running account in which debits and credits are recorded chronologically and in which payments are not shown as attributable to any particular deliveries but are brought generally into credit'. Thus, it is not the label 'running

---

[203] (1996) 185 C.L.R. 483.

account' but the conclusion that the payments in the account were connected with the future supply of goods or services that is relevant, because it is that connection which indicates a continuing relationship of debtor and creditor. It is this conclusion which makes it necessary to consider the ultimate and not the immediate effect of individual payments."[204]

Improvement in creditor's position must be at expense of other creditors

Since s.239 is aimed at transactions which disturb the statutory order of distribution, it follows that to be a preference within s.239 the payment or transfer must be one by which the creditor is put in a better position *at the expense of other creditors*. Accordingly it is not a preference for the company to pay a secured creditor a sum not exceeding the value of the security, for this leaves the position of other creditors unaffected.[205] By the same token, a payment or transfer is not a preference if made to the creditor by a third party, except to the extent to which the ultimate burden falls on the company's assets that would otherwise have been available to all of its creditors, as where the third party is entitled to recoupment from the company and that right is secured. There is, however, the difficult decision of the High Court of Australia in *G & M Aldridge Pty Ltd v Walsh*[206]:

13–89

A bank took a fixed charge over certain assets of a company, TLL, and a floating charge over the remaining assets, which included a sum standing to the credit of an account with the bank by another company as agent for TLL. The amount owed to the bank exceeded the value of the security, so that no part of the assets given in security would remain for unsecured creditors. The bank's charge crystallised. Nevertheless it continued to allow drawings on the account, including payments to certain creditors which TLL's liquidator sought to recover as preferences. Neither the Court of Appeal nor the High Court found it necessary to deal with the contention that the bank had waived its security or was otherwise estopped from enforcing it. Nevertheless the High Court rejected the contention that the payments had come not from moneys available to the company but moneys that could have been taken by the bank under its charge and upheld the decisions of the courts below allowing recovery as a preference under s.588FA of the Corporations Law.

---

[204] *Airservices Australia*, cited above n.203, at 504–505 (footnotes omitted). See to similar effect *Re Libra Industries Pte Ltd* [1999] S.L.R.(R) 105. But a mere established past practice of making payments into a bank account unconnected with the extension of new credit does not suffice (*Liquidators of Progen Engineering Pte Ltd v Progen Holdings Ltd* [2010] S.G.C.A. 31).
[205] See below, para.13–93.
[206] (2001) 203 C.L.R. 662.

It is clear that the court was strongly influenced by the bank's conduct in allowing the company to continue operating the account despite the crystallised charge, and perhaps the perception that since it had shown no signs of enforcing its charge the moneys were in fact available to the company. What is difficult is the court's disagreement with the reasoning of Brennan C.J. in *Sheahan Carrier Air Conditioning Pty Ltd*[207] to the effect that if a fund is fully charged to a secured creditor who consents to payment out of the fund to another creditor, that creditor gains no preference at the expense of other creditors, to whom no part of the fund would have been available anyway. Rejecting this proposition, the High Court held that the question was not whether the payment was "at the expense of other creditors" but whether it gave the recipient a preference, priority or advantage. However, s.588FA(1)(b) does require that the transaction under attack as a preference should result in the creditor receiving a benefit *from the company*, and it would seem to follow from the High Court's decision that this is to be construed literally as including payments and transfers passing *through* the company under a transaction to which it is a party, even if the company itself has no beneficial interest in the subject matter of the payment or transfer. The decision may, however, have turned on its own rather special facts and does not, it is thought, reflect the position under the differently worded provisions of s.239 of the Insolvency Act 1986. If a third party chooses to pay a particular creditor without this resulting in any diminution in the company's assets, the creditor's position is undoubtedly improved but the payment is not within the mischief at which the preference provisions are aimed. There would be no doubt about that if the third party made the payment direct to the creditor without involving the company. Why should it make any difference if the payment comes from a fund held by the company but impressed with a trust or charge in favour of the third party to secure an amount exceeding the value of the fund? Assuming that the burden of the payment does not ultimately fall on the company's assets, the payment is not in any real sense made by the company at all; it is merely the vehicle for the transmission of the third party's funds.[208] Again, the mere fact that the payment is made at the company's request or that it is a party to the transaction under which the payment is made by another does not by itself engage the company's assets so as to give rise to a preference.

13–90   The position is otherwise, of course, where the third party is entitled to be indemnified by the company and the indemnity is secured by a charge on an asset which exceeds in value what is owed to the chargee, so that if the security has not been released and remains intact, the payment operates to

---

[207] (1997) 189 C.L.R. 407 at 424.
[208] See to similar effect Adrian Walters, "Unlawful preferences and proprietary rights" (2003) 119 L.Q.R. 28.

reduce the value of the company's equity of redemption. The third party's payment to the creditor is then a preference, because the ultimate effect of the transaction is that payment is being made by the company itself from the asset given in security. The same situation arises where the third party, although not secured in the technical sense, has a right of set-off or combination in respect of a separate account of the company which is in credit, for this right is an equity to which the account is subject and its exercise reduces *pro tanto* the amount of the credit balance. But if the right of indemnity is wholly unsecured there is no preference, merely the substitution of one creditor for another. So if a creditor is paid from the company's overdrawn account, increasing its overdraft still further, if the overdraft is not secured or covered by a right of set-off or combination against an account in credit, there is no preference, for the bank simply replaces the original creditor and there is no depletion of the company's assets.

There has been much discussion of direct payment clauses in construction contracts empowering the building owner, on the insolvency of the main contractor, to make payment direct to sub-contractors of sums due to them from the main contractor. The validity of such clauses has been discussed earlier in the context of the *pari passu* principle,[209] but the question also arises of whether a direct payment is a preference of the sub-contractor at the expense of the main contractor's creditors. Again, in the absence of a trust or equitable assignment in favour of the sub-contractor,[210] a direct payment to the latter is vulnerable as a preference if influenced by the requisite desire to improve his position.[211]

Payment or transfer need not be by company

Although, as stated above, the payment or transfer must ultimately come from the company's assets in order to constitute a preference, it is not necessary for the company itself to make the preferential payment or transfer; it suffices that the company "suffers" the payment or transfer to be made.[212] "Suffer" means permit or allow in circumstances where the company has control of the payment or transfer in the sense that its permission is needed to make it and can be refused,[213] and *a fortiori* if the company can require the payment or transfer to be made, it suffers it to be made.[214] There is no

13–91

---

[209] See above, para.8–11.

[210] See above, para. 6–17.

[211] See para.13–96.

[212] Insolvency Act 1986 s.239(4)(b).

[213] *Sefton v Tophams Ltd* [1967] 1 A.C. 50; *Earl of Leicester v Wells-next-the-sea UDC* [1973] Ch. 110; and *Berton v Alliance Economic Investment Co Ltd* [1922] 1 K.B. 742.

[214] *Earl of Leicester v Wells-next-the-sea UDC*, cited above n.213, *per* Plowman J. at 124 in a decision on "permit".

preference where the creditor collects payment through a mechanism over which the company has no control, such as the exercise of a right of set-off by the creditor[215] or by an assignee under an assignment to which the company's consent was not required.[216]

The hypothetical liquidation

13–92   Preference is tested by reference to a hypothetical, not an actual, liquidation. It is not necessary that the company shall in fact have gone into liquidation, for the preference provisions apply equally in administration. If the company enters administration, the question of preference still has to be tested by asking whether the effect of the payment, transfer or other act would be to put the creditor in a better position if winding up were to supervene than he would otherwise have had. It would seem that for this purpose liquidation should be assumed to have taken place immediately after the payment, transfer or other act in question,[217] and with reference to creditors then existing, so that subsequent events (for example, the accrual of new preferential debts) should be ignored, a point which may assist a creditor who is collecting payment under a floating charge.[218]

Payments to secured creditors

13–93   In general, payment to a secured creditor in reduction or discharge of the debt is not a preference, for the effect of the payment is to reduce or extinguish the security interest and thus *pro tanto* to increase the company's equity in the previously charged assets and make them available to other creditors. Accordingly, the payment produces no change in the value of the assets available for the general body of creditors. Moreover, if the company were to refrain from making the payment, that would not help the other creditors, for the secured creditor would still be entitled to enforce his security, assuming the giving of it had not itself been by way of preference. Thus, it has been held in Australia that a bank which in good faith and in the ordinary course of business collects a cheque for a customer and credits the proceeds to the customer's overdrawn account does not receive a preference, for the bank had a lien on the cheque to secure the overdraft and thus a security interest in the proceeds, so that the application of these in reduction of the overdraft does

---

[215] See below, para.13–94.
[216] *Klempka v Miller* [2010] B.C.C. 309, also known as *Re Parkside International Ltd*.
[217] The date of any actual liquidation is irrelevant as a temporal point for determining improvement of the creditor's position.
[218] See below, para.13–93.

not alter the customer's asset position.[219] Similarly, where a guarantee has been given in respect of the secured debt, the surety's position is not improved to the extent of the value of the asset given in security, for the effect of this would have been to reduce the surety's liability anyway or entitle him to take over the security by way of subrogation on discharging the debt.[220]

However, there are at least four situations in which payment to a secured creditor may constitute a preference. The first is where the amount of the payment exceeds the value of the security; in that event, the payment is vulnerable to the extent of the excess. The second is where the security is one which, if winding up had occurred immediately after the payment, would have been rendered void, for example, for want of registration, for on that hypothesis the payment reduces the net value of the company's assets.[221] The third is where the payment is made to the holder of a floating charge and at the time of the payment there were insufficient free assets to pay the preferential creditors then existing, for upon a winding up immediately after the payment these would have had priority over the holder of the floating charge,[222] who thus derives an advantage from the payment made to him. But since (if the view expressed above is correct) the notional liquidation must be assumed to have commenced immediately after the payment to the floating chargee, only preferential debts then in existence are relevant, and the chargee will not be considered to have improved his position merely because new preferential debts come into existence at a later date. The fourth case is where payment is made to the holder of a floating charge and discharges the security, so that the general creditors lose the benefit of the prescribed part, which, on the hypothesised winding up, would have had to be surrendered to the liquidator to form a fund available to unsecured creditors.[223]

Exercise of right of set-off

No question of preference can arise where the creditor collects payment by exercise of a right of set-off, for this does not require the consent of the company at all, let alone a desire on its part to improve the creditor's position.[224] Payment by the company into an overdrawn account with its bank is likewise

13–94

---

[219] *National Australia Bank v KDS Construction Services Pty Ltd* (1987) 163 CLR 668. The position would be otherwise, of course, if the cheque were given to the bank not simply for collection but with a view to giving it an advantage it would not otherwise have enjoyed, for then the giving of the lien over the cheque to the bank will itself constitute a preference.

[220] See below, para.13–100.

[221] Where the security would not have been void but merely liable to be discharged, e.g. under s.241(1)(c), the court must presumably decide whether it is likely that an order under s.241(1)(c), or an order producing a similar effect, would have been made.

[222] Insolvency Act 1986 s.175(2)(b).

[223] Insolvency Act 1986 s.176A. See above, paras 6–38 et seq.

[224] However, a party who has received a preference cannot avoid repayment by exercising a right of set-off. See above, para.9–29.

not capable of being a preference where the payment does not exceed the amount of a credit balance held by the company on another account to which the bank could have resorted by way of combination of accounts if the payment in question had not been made, for the effect of the payment is *pro tanto* to reduce the available amount of set-off against the account in credit, so that the position of other creditors is unaffected. Where the company has a contractual right to set off against one customer's credit balance an amount due from another customer, exercise of that right is not a preference of the first customer, for it is for the company's benefit, not that of the first customer.[225]

What does not constitute a preference

13–95   It will have been apparent from the above that the following transactions (inter alia) do not involve the giving of a preference:

(1)   payment to a validly secured creditor of a sum not significantly exceeding the value of his security, having regard to any preferential debts then in existence ranking in priority to the security;

(2)   payment to avoid loss of an asset (for example, property or equipment held on lease) or of a right (for example, under a contract) having a value not less than the amount of the payment;

(3)   the exchange of an asset of the company for one of at least equal value;

(4)   the grant of security for a contemporaneous or subsequent advance or other new value;

(5)   payment or transfer of property to a person who is not a creditor of the company; and

(6)   payment to the creditor by a third party which does not involve any call on the company's assets.

(iii)   The company's desire to prefer

"Influenced by a desire"

13–96   As stated earlier,[226] under the old law a preference was not voidable unless the company's dominant intention in making the payment, transfer, etc. to the creditor was to prefer him to the other creditors. The Insolvency Act 1986, re-enacting the provisions of the Insolvency Act 1985, formulates the criterion rather differently. As before, the mere fact of preference does not suffice to

---

[225] *Re Exchange Travel (Holdings)*, cited above n.182.
[226] Above, para.13–71.

make the court's power's exercisable. What has to be shown in addition is that in giving the preference the company was influenced in deciding to give it by a desire to produce in relation to the preferred party the effect of putting him in a better position than he would have been in if the payment, transfer, etc. had not been made.[227]

Since preference itself is defined in terms of improvement of the creditor's position rather than in terms of preferring him to other creditors, no reference is made to an intention to prefer. Instead, the question is whether the company was influenced by a desire to improve the creditor's position compared with what it would have been on an immediate winding up. Three questions arise. First, what is "desire"? Is it the same as intent? Or motive? Secondly, does "influenced by" require that the desire to prefer should be the sole factor, the dominant factor or some lesser degree of influence in the decision to make the payment or transfer? Thirdly, what is the relevant time at which to test the desire: the time the debenture is given or the time when the decision to give it is made? The root decision on all three questions is that of Millett J. in *Re M.C. Bacon Ltd*.[228] In that case, the company had run up a substantial unsecured overdraft with its bank, which was prepared to continue its support but stipulated that in view of the serious position in which the company found itself an essential condition of this was the provision of a first mortgage debenture over the company's assets. Three months after executing the debenture, the company went into liquidation. The liquidator attacked the debenture as a transaction at an undervalue and a preference. As noted earlier, the first of these two grounds failed on the basis that the giving of security did not reduce the assets.[229] Millett J. proceeded to deal with the allegation of preference in the following terms:

"Section 44(1) has been replaced and its language has been entirely recast. Every single word of significance, whether in the form of statutory definition or in its judicial exposition, has been jettisoned. 'View', 'dominant', 'intention' and even 'to prefer' have all been discarded. These are replaced by 'influenced', 'desire' and 'to produce in relation to that person the effect mentioned in subsection (4)(b)'.

I therefore emphatically protest against the citation of cases decided under the old law. They cannot be of assistance when the language of the statute has been so completely and deliberately changed.

This is a completely different test. It involves at least two radical departures from the old law. It is no longer necessary to establish a *dominant* intention to prefer. It is sufficient that the decision is *influenced* by the

---

[227] Insolvency Act 1986 s.239(5). For the position relating to preference of a surety, see below, para.13–99.
[228] [1990] B.C.C. 78.
[229] See above, paras 13–38, 13–93.

requisite desire. That is the first change. The second is that it is no longer sufficient to establish an *intention* to prefer. There must be a *desire* to produce the effect mentioned in the subsection.

This second change is made necessary by the first, for without it would be virtually impossible to uphold the validity of a security taken in exchange for the injection of fresh funds into a company in financial difficulties. A man is taken to intend the necessary consequences of his actions, so that an intention to grant a security to a creditor necessarily involves an intention to prefer that creditor in the event of insolvency. The need to establish that such intention was dominant was essential under the old law to prevent perfectly proper transactions from being struck down. With the abolition of that requirement intention could not remain the relevant test. Desire has been substituted. That is a very different matter. Intention is objective, desire is subjective. A man can choose the lesser of two evils without desiring either.

... A man is not to be taken as *desiring* all the necessary consequences of his actions. Some consequences may be of advantage to him and be desired by him; others may not affect him and be matters of indifference to him; while still others may be positively disadvantageous to him and not be desired by him but be regarded by him as the unavoidable price of obtaining the desired advantage. It will still be possible to provide assistance to a company in financial difficulties provided that the company is actuated only by proper commercial considerations. Under the new regime a transaction will not be set aside as a voidable preference unless the company positively wished to improve the creditor's position in the event of its own insolvent liquidation.

There is, of course, no need for there to be direct evidence of the requisite desire. Its existence may be inferred from the circumstances of the case just as the dominant intention could be inferred under the old law. But the mere presence of the requisite desire will not be sufficient by itself. It must have influenced the decision to enter into the transaction. It was submitted on behalf of the bank that it must have been the factor which 'tipped the scales.' I disagree. That is not what subsection (5) says; it requires only that the desire should have influenced the decision. That requirement is satisfied if it was one of the factors which operated on the minds of those who made the decision. It need not have been the only factor or even the decisive one. In my judgment it is not necessary to prove that, if the requisite desire had not been present, the company would not have entered into the transaction. That would be too high a test.

It was also submitted that the relevant time was when the debenture was created. That cannot be right. The relevant time was the time when the decision to grant it was made."[230]

---

[230] *Re M.C. Bacon Ltd.* above, n. 228, at 87–88.

Millett J. went on to hold that the company was not motivated by a desire to improve the bank's position as creditor in the event of the company's liquidation, and that accordingly the allegation of preference had not been made out. In a subsequent case[231] the subjective nature of desire was emphasised and it was held that a payment made by the company in winding up to its bank was not a preference where the payment was motivated by commercial considerations such as the need to obtain finance from other sources. This raises the question of how a company forms a desire. Plainly this can only be done through a human agent, who must, it is thought, be a director, general manager or other person of sufficient authority in the company that he can be said to represent its mind and will or a person acting on his instructions, as opposed to a junior employee who in paying a creditor simply fulfils a routine function.

13–97

Banks are in a somewhat special position as creditors because one of their functions is to collect cheques for customers and credit the proceeds to the customers' accounts. If an insolvent customer whose account is overdrawn pays in cheques for collection, this has the effect of improving the bank's position, for it acquires a lien on the cheque and thus a security interest in the proceeds. The payment in of the cheque is thus a preference but s.239 will not apply unless the office-holder can show that in doing this the customer was influenced by a desire to improve the bank's position rather than because the normal method of collecting cheques is to give them to one's bank for collection. The office-holder may not always find it easy to show this, particularly where the company has only one bank account, for if it is taxed with being influenced by a desire to give a preference, its response is likely to be: "What else should we have done with the cheques?"

Good faith of creditor irrelevant

As in the case of transactions at an undervalue,[232] the party whose desire is relevant is the company. The defence of good faith is not open to the preferred creditor or preferred surety, a point made clear by s.241(2)(b).

13–98

(iv) *Preference of a surety or guarantor*

Preference of a surety

In applying the statutory provisions to preference of a surety[233] (we shall come to the term "guarantor" in a moment), the Insolvency Act follows the

13–99

---

[231] *Re Fairway Magazines Ltd* [1992] B.C.C. 924.

[232] See above, para.13–41.

[233] A person may be a surety for this purpose if he has merely charged his property as security for the principal debtor's indebtedness without assuming any personal liability (*Re Conley* [1938] 2 All E.R. 127).

old law, although as we shall see, the court's powers in relation to a preferred surety are more extensive than they were generally considered to be under the Bankruptcy Act 1914.

(1) The fact of preference

13–100   Where the debtor company makes a payment to its creditor in discharge or reduction of a guaranteed debt, the payment benefits not only the creditor, but the surety: the creditor because it extinguishes or reduces his claim, and the surety because it discharges or reduces his secondary liability. If the surety is fully solvent, can the creditor argue that his position has not been improved by the debtor company's payment because he would have been paid in full anyway by the surety? No, because the payment has reduced the company's assets and obviated the need to proceed against the surety.[234] By contrast, if the creditor is fully secured from another source, the payment does not improve the surety's position, for upon the hypothesised liquidation, he would either not have had to pay at all or, if required to pay, he would have been subrogated to the creditor's security, whilst if the creditor is partly secured the value of its security or the proceeds of its realisation would *pro tanto* reduce the amount of the improvement in the surety's position.[235]

(2) The desire

13–101   In making a payment, the company may be influenced by a desire to improve the creditor's position, the surety or both the creditor and the surety.[236] The question of whether there is the requisite desire must be asked in respect of each person to whom a preference has been given.[237] A desire to prefer the creditor does not of itself indicate an intent to prefer the surety; conversely, the company may intend to prefer the surety without being in any way influenced by a desire to assist the creditor.[238] The typical case is where a company's account has been guaranteed by the directors, who at a time when the

---

[234] See Adrian Walters, "Preferences", in Armour and Bennett, *Vulnerable Transactions in Corporate Insolvency*, 2002, 126 at 149, n.116.

[235] *Re Hawkes Publishing Co Ltd* [2007] B.C.C. 937.

[236] But in this last case it remains the fact that there is only one payment, not two, so that if an order is made against both the creditor and the surety, it cannot provide in total for payment of a sum greater than is necessary to restore the amount of the preference.

[237] *Re Agriplant Services Ltd* [1997] B.C.L.C. 598, where it was held that the desire was to improve the position both of the debtor company and of the surety. As to what is the relevant time in proceedings against a surety, see below, para.13–103.

[238] Although this would not preclude the court from directing repayment by the creditor as under the previous law. See below.

company is insolvent arrange for it to repay the bank, not out of any desire to improve the bank's position but to obtain a release from their own liability to the bank. This is a preference of the sureties because the repayment operates not merely to affect the relations between the bank and the sureties but to avoid a situation in which the sureties, having paid the bank under their guarantee, are left to prove in the winding up in competition with other creditors for their indemnity entitlement. Discharge of the sureties therefore improves their position relative to what it would have been on a winding up. As will be seen, the working out of the statutory provisions in relation to sureties is not free from complications.

The improvement in a surety's position must be in his capacity as such and not in some other capacity. So if a person is a surety for companies A and B and a payment is made to company A which does not improve his position as surety for company A, the fact that he secures an improvement in his capacity as surety for company B is irrelevant.[239]

(3) "Surety"; "guarantor"

The terms "surety" and "guarantor" are nowadays used interchangeably to denote a person who undertakes payment or other performance of an obligation owed to a creditor if the debtor defaults. The obligation is thus both secondary, in that the surety's liability is dependent on default by the principal debtor, and accessory in that it is coterminous with the principal obligation and enforceable only to the extent that the principal obligation is enforceable. However, the word "guarantee" has acquired a distinctive meaning in the context of demand guarantees (also called performance bonds), which are undertakings by a bank in favour of a designated beneficiary to pay an amount, or maximum amount, to the beneficiary on presentation of a written demand and other specified documents.[240] The purpose of the guarantee is to provide an assurance of performance by the counterparty to a transaction with the beneficiary. For example, the employer under a construction contract may require the successful bidder for the contract to procure the issue of a demand guarantee by a bank covering the contractor's performance of its obligations. As between the contractor and the employer, the guarantee can properly be called only if the beneficiary honestly believes that the contractor has committed a breach but the guarantee itself is conditioned solely on the presentation of stated documents.[241] Thus the bank's

13–102

---

[239] *Wilson v Masters International Ltd* [2010] B.C.C. 834.

[240] See *Goode on Commercial Law*, 2009, pp.1124 et seq.; Georges Affaki and Roy Goode, *Guide to ICC Uniform Rules for Demand Guarantees* (Paris: ICC Services/Publications, 2011).

[241] And, in the case of a guarantee governed by the ICC Uniform Rules for Demand Guarantees, 2010 revision (URDG 758), a statement of breach in conformity with art.15 of the Rules.

obligation is a primary obligation which has to be performed whether or not there has been default in performance of the underlying contract. The question arises whether this type of guarantee also falls within the preference rules. There are good reasons for thinking that it does. In the first place, if s.239 were confined to suretyship guarantees the addition of the words "or guarantor" would be redundant. More significantly, the issuer of the demand guarantee has the same right of indemnity against the contractor as it would have under a suretyship guarantee and is exposed to the same risk of the contractor's insolvency, a risk reduced by the amount of the contractor's performance.

(v) A relevant time

13–103 Only a preference given at a relevant time is caught by the statutory provisions.[242] The meaning of "relevant time" has been discussed earlier in relation to transactions at an undervalue.[243] There is, however, a difference in that the period for transactions at an undervalue is in all cases two years ending with the onset of insolvency, whereas in the case of a preference it is two years in the case of a preference in favour of a person connected with the company, but is otherwise six months.[244] Where a guarantee has been given and there has been a preference both of the creditor and of the surety and only one of them is a person connected with the company, it would seem that the six-month limit applies in relation to that person and cannot be circumvented by an order under s.241(1)(d).[245]

Meaning of "connected" with a company

13–104 We have already noted that the disjunctive phrase "he was connected with, or was an associate of, the company" is technically incorrect in that the definition of "connected" includes an associate.[246] Section 249 provides as follows:

> "For the purposes of any provision in this Group of Parts, a person is connected with a company if—
>
> (a) he is a director or shadow director of the company or an associate of such a director or shadow director, or
>
> (b) he is an associate of the company."

---

[242] Insolvency Act 1986 s.239(2).
[243] Above, para.13–39.
[244] Insolvency Act 1986 s.240(1)(b).
[245] See below, para.13–104.
[246] Insolvency Act 1986 s.249(b).

This definition is relevant for the purposes of ss.239(6),[247] 240(1)[248] and 241(2A).[249] The meanings of "director" and "shadow director" are discussed later.[250] "Associate" is elaborately defined in s.435 of the Act. To determine whether a person[251] is an associate of an individual, it is necessary to look at s.435(2) to (5), together covering an individual's husband, wife or civil partner, a relative[252] of the individual or of the individual's husband, wife or civil partner, a partner, employer or employee of the individual or one who is an associate via a trust within s.435(5). A company is an associate of another company if they are under common control[253] and is an associate of another person if that person or that person and his associates have control of the company.[254] It will be seen that the range of persons who may be treated as connected with a company is very wide. The intention is to catch all of those whose relationship with the company is such that they either play a role in the company's management or may be privy to information about its affairs not available to outsiders. However, there is no general provision for the aggregation of different associates. So the mere fact that A is associated with B and B is associated with C does not make A associated with C unless s.435(6) applies.[255] In determining whether a person has control of the company the court looks in the first instance into who is on the register of members but where a registered member holds his shares as bare trustee for another and is required to vote in accordance with that other's instructions, it is the position of the beneficial owner, not the trustee, that has to be taken into account, the question of voting power being concerned with the relationship between the trustee and the beneficiary, not that subsisting between the trustee and the company.[256]

---

[247] A presumption that the giving of a preference by the company to the connected person was influenced by a desire to improve that person's position. However, for this purpose, a person connected with the company by reason only of being its employee is excluded.

[248] Extending to two years the period within which a preference given to a connected person is vulnerable to avoidance. Again, a person connected solely by reason of being an employee is excluded.

[249] Presumption of acquisition of interest or receipt of benefit otherwise than in good faith.

[250] Below, paras 14–04 and 14–05.

[251] "Person" normally includes a company, so that despite the use of the word "he" in s.435(4), an employee of the company is an associate of the company, and this includes a director (s.435(9)). See also ss.239(6) and 240(1), which make it clear that but for his exclusion under these sections an employee would be a person connected with the company. However, s.452(2) obviously does not apply in relation to companies, while on the other hand some provisions (s.435(6), (7) and (9)) are relevant only to companies, so that the word "company" is used instead of "person".

[252] As defined by s.435(8).

[253] See s.435(6).

[254] See s.435(7).

[255] *Re Kilnoore Ltd* [2006] Ch. 489.

[256] ibid.

(vi) Powers of the court

General power of the court

13–105   On an application by the office-holder for an order under s.239, the court, if satisfied that the section applies, is required to make such order as it thinks fit for restoring the position to what it would have been if the company had not given the preference.[257]

Specific powers

13–106   These are the same as for transactions at an undervalue and are dealt with in the same section of the Act, namely s.241(1). I need not repeat the earlier discussion of the court's powers under that section but a few additional comments on the surety's position are appropriate.

First, the court's powers in relation to sureties are considerably wider than under the previous law, which on the better view did not enable the court to make an order, for payment direct against the surety[258] or to direct the revival of his obligations to the creditor.[259] Secondly, a payment which was made solely to prefer the surety can nevertheless be ordered to be repaid by the creditor, as under the previous law, for it remains the case that he is the recipient of a preference and of a benefit within s.241(1)(d).[260] Thirdly, a payment made solely to prefer the creditor can be ordered to be repaid by the surety, except in the unlikely event that he qualifies for protection under s.241(2)(b) as a person receiving a benefit not only in good faith but for value.

Finally, the court now has power to order that where the effect of the preference was to discharge the surety's obligation, wholly or in part, to the creditor or any other person, the surety is to be under such new or revived obligation as the court thinks appropriate.[261] Under the previous law, a creditor who received payment from the company might give the surety a discharge and release any security given by the surety, only to find himself on the receiving end of an order for repayment of the preference, so that he once again became a creditor of the company but without the benefit of the guarantee. To cover this eventuality, every well-drawn guarantee now provides that no payment shall be effective to discharge the surety to the extent that the creditor has to repay it as a preference. Creditors should continue to include such a provision in their guarantees so as not to be dependent upon

---

[257] Insolvency Act 1986 s.239(3). As to the application of recoveries, see below, para.13–140.

[258] *Re Lyons Ex p. Barclays Bank Ltd v Trustee* (1934) 152 L.T. 201, approved by Luxmoore J. in *Re Conley* [1938] 2 All E.R. 127 at 139 and not following *Re G. Stanley & Co* [1925] Ch. 148.

[259] As to which see above, para.13–59.

[260] But see below as to the position where the creditor is not connected with the company and the payment was made more than six months before the onset of insolvency.

[261] Insolvency Act 1986 s.241(l)(e).

the making of an order in their favour, which is entirely within the court's discretion.

One difficult question remains. In the case of a creditor or surety not connected with the company, a preference is voidable only if the onset of insolvency occurs within six months; in the case of a creditor or surety connected with the company, it is two years. Now suppose that a payment is made to the creditor nine months before the onset of insolvency and the creditor is not connected with the company, whereas the surety is a director. If the decision to pay the creditor was influenced by a desire to prefer the surety, can an order be made against the creditor under s.241(1)(d) when he himself would no longer be susceptible to a claim as a preferred party? It is thought that the answer is no[262] and that the appropriate order is one for payment direct against the surety, who on making the payment will be entitled to prove for its amount as creditor in the winding up.

Relationship between transactions at an undervalue and preferences

As stated earlier,[263] there can be no overlap in the impact of the statutory provisions relating to transactions at an undervalue and those concerning preferences. That is to say, it is not possible for the same part of a payment to fall simultaneously within s.238 and s.239. It may be helpful to identify more precisely the relationship between the two sets of provisions.

13–107

(1)   A key distinction is that the provisions relating to transactions at an undervalue are aimed at payments, transfers or other acts which diminish the company's assets, whereas the provisions relating to preferences are concerned with transactions that unfairly favour one creditor at the expense of the others, whether or not they diminish the company's assets. For example, payment of a debt which does not exceed the amount due is not a transaction at an undervalue, as the net asset position is unchanged, whilst to the extent that the payment exceeds what is due to the creditor, he does not receive it *qua* creditor and his liability, if any, arises under s.238, not s.239. This was the position in *Re HHO Licensing Ltd*[264] where the company paid an amount for services substantially in excess of their value. To the extent of the value of the services the payment was a preference under s.239, to the extent of the excess it was a transaction at an undervalue under s.238. We have already seen that where the company gives security for a previously

---

[262] *Contra* Prentice, "Some Observations on the Law Relating to Preferences" in Cranston (ed.), *Making Commercial Law*, 1997, pp.458–459.

[263] Above, para.13–12.

[264] [2008] 1 B.C.L.C. 223.

unsecured loan, there is no diminution in the company's net asset value, only a possible preference of one creditor at the expense of the others. This is because any realisation of the security by the creditor *pro tanto* reduces the company's indebtedness.[265]

(2)   The provisions relating to transactions at an undervalue are concerned with the existence of a significant imbalance between a payment, transfer or other act and the consideration for which it is made or done. If the bargain is fair, the provisions do not apply. By contrast, the preference provisions are concerned not with the fairness of the original bargain but with the improvement of the creditor's position relative to other creditors on a winding up notionally occurring immediately after the payment, transfer, etc. in question. So payment by an insolvent company of one creditor but not the others gives rise to a preference.

(3)   The rules as to preference are confined to payments, transfers, etc. in favour of an existing creditor, and thus do not apply to gifts, whereas the rules as to transactions at an undervalue are aimed exclusively at transfers involving a gift element.

(4)   The two sets of statutory provisions have two characteristics in common. First, both transactions at an undervalue and preferences are determined without reference to the bona fides of the payee or transferee. Secondly, both sets of provisions embody a subjective element in that the company's good faith is an ingredient of the defence to a claim to upset a transaction made at an undervalue, while the avoidance of a preference requires the company to be influenced by a desire to prefer.

(5)   For policy reasons which remain unclear, the backward reach of the provisions relating to transactions at an undervalue is two years in all cases, whereas for preferences the normal period is six months and the two-year period is confined to preferences in favour of a person connected with the company otherwise than solely as its employee.

8. EXTORTIONATE CREDIT TRANSACTIONS

Re-opening of extortionate credit transactions

13–108   Under s.244 of the Insolvency Act 1986, the court may set aside or vary a transaction for, or involving, the provision of credit to the company where the following conditions are satisfied:

---

[265] See above, para.13–38.

(1)   the company is or has been a party to the transaction[266];

(2)   the company is in liquidation or administration[267];

(3)   the transaction is or was extortionate; and

(4)   the transaction was entered into within the three years prior to the company going into liquidation or administration.

"Extortionate"

For the purposes of s.244, a transaction is extortionate if, having regard to   **13–109**
the risk accepted by the person providing the credit:

(1)   the terms of it are or were such as to require grossly exorbitant payments to be made (whether unconditionally or in certain contingencies) in respect of the provision of the credit; or

(2)   it otherwise grossly contravenes ordinary principles of fair dealing.[268]

There is a rebuttable presumption that a transaction with respect to which an application is made under s.244 is extortionate.[269]

The above provisions are modelled on ss.138(1), 139(1) and 171(7) of the Consumer Credit Act 1974, which have been analysed in detail elsewhere.[270] Suffice it to say that it is not enough that the transaction was or is burdensome to the company or the terms of it severe. What has to be demonstrated is that they were extortionate within the statutory definition and this implies that they must be not merely unfair but oppressive, reflecting an imbalance in bargaining power of which the other party took improper advantage.[271] So it is not surprising that in *White v Davenham Trust Ltd*[272] Floyd J. upheld the decision of Deputy Registrar Schaffer refusing to set aside under r.6.5(4)(d) of the Insolvency Rules a statutory demand served on the appellant for a sum due

---

[266] Thus, the court's powers are exercisable both in relation to settled transactions and to those that are still current.

[267] Insolvency Act 1986 s.244(1), applying s.238(1).

[268] Insolvency Act 1986 s.244(3).

[269] Insolvency Act 1986 s.244(3).

[270] See *Goode: Consumer Credit Law and Practice* (London: LexisNexis Butterworths, looseleaf), Ch.47. The provisions relating to extortionate credit bargains were rarely invoked with success and were repealed by the Consumer Credit Act 2006, which introduced in their place as ss.140A–140C provisions on unfair relationships, which regrettably are wholly lacking in any meaningful criteria as to when a relationship between a creditor and a debtor is to be considered unfair. However, a company is outside the protection of the Act unless it is a debtor jointly with an individual (Consumer Credit Act 1974 s.185(5)). The new provisions have no impact on s.244 of the Insolvency Act 1986.

[271] See *Paragon Finance Plc v Nash* [2002] 1 W.L.R. 685, *per* Dyson L.J. at [67], citing *Goode: Consumer Credit Law and Practice*, para.47.22

[272] [2010] EWHC 2784 (Ch).

as surety for a company in administration in respect of a debt which the appellant alleged was arguably extortionate under s.244 of the Insolvency Act, giving rise to an arguable cross-claim, albeit for an amount substantially less than that demanded in the statutory demand. The compounded rate was somewhat in excess of 20 per cent, increased on default to somewhat in excess of 40 per cent. The judge agreed with the Deputy Registrar that the rate was not extortionate, given the high risk and the fact that the transaction was not a consumer transaction into which the parties entered with their eyes open. He held that there was a triable issue that the increase in the rate upon default was a penalty but ruled that the demand ought not to be set aside, since even if there was an unenforceable penalty, the company would still be unarguably liable for £750,000. Moreover, the appellant was a wealthy man who could easily have paid the undisputed sum.

Orders the court can make

13–110   An order under s.244 with regard to any transaction may contain one or more of the following as the court thinks fit:

(1)   a provision setting aside the whole or part of any obligation created by the transaction;

(2)   a provision otherwise varying the terms of the transaction or the terms on which any security for the purpose of the transaction is held;

(3)   a provision requiring any person who is or was a party to the transaction to pay to the office-holder any sums paid to that person, by virtue of the transaction, by the company; and

(4)   a provision directing accounts to be taken between any persons.[273]

The court's powers are exercisable concurrently with any powers exercisable in relation to the transaction as a transaction at an undervalue.[274]

9. FLOATING CHARGES FOR PAST VALUE[275]

The previous law

13–111   There have long been statutory provisions invalidating floating charges given by an insolvent company otherwise than for new value. Prior to the

---

[273] Insolvency Act 1986 s.244(4).
[274] Insolvency Act 1986 s.244(5).
[275] See Howard N. Bennett, "Late Floating Charges" in Armour and Bennett, *Vulnerable Transactions in Corporate Insolvency*, 2002, Ch.5.

Insolvency Act 1986, these were embodied in s.617 of the Companies Act 1985, re-enacting s.322 of the Companies Act 1948. The purpose of these provisions, as of other avoidance provisions, was to prevent the conferment of an unfair advantage on an existing creditor at a time when liquidation was imminent. But they have always been confined to floating charges, no doubt reflecting a view that the all-embracing nature of the floating charge had such a potentially deleterious effect on other creditors that it should be subject to a special rule.[276] The broad effect of s.617 was that if a floating charge was given by a company that was insolvent immediately after its granting, the charge became invalid except to the amount of any cash paid to the company on or after and in consideration of the charge if the company went into liquidation within the ensuing 12 months.

Changes in the statutory provisions

Section 245 of the Companies Act 2006 re-enacted the substance of s.617 of the Companies Act 1985, but with important changes: **13–112**

(1) A floating charge is now defined as a charge which as created was a floating charge.[277] But the new definition, although highly relevant to priorities vis-à-vis preferential debts,[278] is not significant for the purpose of s.245, since the avoidance provisions have always continued to apply even after crystallisation of the floating charge.

(2) Under s.617, new value had to take the form of cash in order to exclude the section. Under s.245, virtually every normal form of new value suffices.[279]

(3) The section applies to companies in administration as well as liquidation.

(4) Where the charge is given in favour of a person connected with the company:
   (a) the period of 12 months is extended to two years; and
   (b) it is not necessary that the company shall have been insolvent at the time of or consequent upon the giving of the charge.

---

[276] The Cork Committee gave as the reason for special statutory treatment of floating charges the fact that it enabled the secured creditor to have his security reinforced by after-acquired property for which the debtor had not paid at the expense of the unpaid sellers. See *Insolvency Law and Practice*, para.1553.

[277] Insolvency Act 1986 s.251.

[278] See *Goode on Legal Problems of Credit and Security*, 2008, paras 5–65 et seq.

[279] See below, para.13–114.

Presumably, the application of s.245 to floating charges given to a connected person even where the company is still solvent after giving the charge reflects a view that a connected person, as an insider, is likely to have the opportunity to be aware of impending insolvency and to take steps to protect himself at the expense of other creditors.

Conditions necessary to attract s.245

13–113 A floating charge[280] is void under s.245 of the Insolvency Act if the following conditions are satisfied:

(1) the company is in liquidation or administration[281];

(2) the floating charge was created at a relevant time, that is:
  (a) in favour of a person connected with the company,[282] within the period of two years ending with the onset of insolvency[283]; or
  (b) in favour of a person not so connected, within the period of 12 months ending with the onset of insolvency; or
  (c) whether in favour of a connected or an unconnected person, between the presentation of a petition for an administration order and the making of an order on that petition;

(3) the charge was given otherwise than for what may conveniently be described as appropriate new value. For this purpose, a charge is given for appropriate new value only to the extent that the consideration for it represents an amount not exceeding the aggregate of:
  (a) the value of so much of the consideration for the creation of the charge as consists of money paid,[284] or of goods or services supplied, to the company at the same time as, or after, the creation of the charge;
  (b) the value of so much of that consideration as consists of the discharge or reduction, at the same time as, or after, the creation of the charge, of any debt of the company[285]; and

---

[280] i.e. a charge which as created was a floating charge (Insolvency Act 1986 s.251), even if it has crystallised prior to the winding up or administration. For the nature of a floating charge, *see Goode on Commercial Law*, 2009, Ch.25 and *Goode on Legal Problems of Credit and Security*, 2008, Ch.IV. See also above, para.10–16.

[281] Insolvency Act 1986 s.245(1), applying s.238(1).

[282] In contrast to the provisions of ss.238 and 239 relating to transactions at an undervalue and preferences, there is no exclusion of a person connected with the company solely by reason of being its employee.

[283] As defined by s.245(5) of the Act.

[284] "Money paid" is not defined but would seem to encompass cash, cheques and other negotiable instruments (if honoured) and any other form of inter-bank transfer of funds, whether by credit transfer, direct debit or other means.

[285] Whether to a third party or to the company itself, e.g. by a refinancing in discharge of a prior loan to the company.

(c)   the amount of such interest (if any) as is payable on an amount under (a) or (b) in pursuance of any agreement under which the money was paid, the goods or services supplied or the debt discharged or reduced;

(4)   where the charge was given to a person not connected with the company, the company was then unable to pay its debts within the meaning of s.123 of the Act or became unable to do so in consequence of the charge.[286]

The expanded concept of new value

It will be seen that the provisions dealing with value are considerably more liberal, and indeed fairer, than under the earlier legislation, which treated cash as the only admissible form of new value and thus invalidated a floating charge given by an insolvent company to secure, for example, the price of goods supplied to the company, despite the fact that such a transaction involved no diminution whatsoever in the company's assets. Let us now take a closer look at the concept of new value under s.245 and see what is and is not covered. There are four essential requirements for value if the floating charge is to escape invalidity under s.245. First, it must be given in consideration for the creation of the charge. Secondly, it must be given at the same time as or after the creation of the charge. Thirdly, it must fall into one or more of the categories of value specified in s.245(2) of the Act. Fourthly, it must be furnished to the company itself or be applied in discharge or reduction of the company's indebtedness.   **13–114**

(1) Value as consideration for the charge

This is not new. The value must be given against the charge. So if an advance is initially made on an unsecured basis and then it is decided to take security for it, the advance will not qualify for new value however soon afterwards the charge is taken.   **13–115**

(2) Value must be contemporaneous or subsequent

Again, the statutory provisions are similar to those originally contained in s.322 of the Companies Act 1948, which required that the advance be made "at or after" the charge. There had been a curious line of authority, headed   **13–116**

---

[286] Insolvency Act 1986 s.245(4). Again, there is no exception in favour of a person connected with the company solely by reason of being its employee.

by the Court of Appeal decision in *Re Columbian Fireproofing Co Ltd*,[287] which appeared to consider an advance to be made at the time of the charge if it was made in consideration of the charge, notwithstanding a significant interval between the making of the advance and the giving of the charge,[288] particularly where the delay in taking the charge was considered excusable. However, in *Re Shoe Lace Ltd*[289] Hoffmann J., relying on a slight difference between the wording of s.245 of the 1986 Act and that of s.322 of the 1948 Act, felt able to dive over the decision in *Re Columbian Fireproofing Co Ltd* and to hold, as was clearly correct, that s.245 imposes two distinct requirements, that the advance is in consideration of the charge and that it is at or after the time the charge was taken, and that the latter requirement could not be said to have been met where the charge was taken nearly four months after the first advance it secured and eight days after the last such advance. His decision was upheld by the Court of Appeal[290] which, although ruling that there was little or no material difference in wording between s.245 and its predecessor, declined to follow *Re Columbian Fireproofing*. That case had purported to follow the decision in *Re Jackson & Bassford Ltd*[291] but had overlooked the vitally important distinction drawn in the latter case between a debenture executed after the advance in reliance on a promise to execute it which created a present equitable right and a debenture executed after a mere contingent agreement for security which created no such right.[292] In the former case, a delay in execution of the formal debenture was immaterial, because the charge had already been created by the binding agreement and had thereupon became registrable; in the latter it had not and only came into existence when the debenture was executed.

Accordingly, the position now reached is that the requirement of contemporaneity is satisfied where there is a binding agreement for a debenture creating an immediate equitable charge and made at or before the time of making of the advance, however long afterwards the formal debenture is executed pursuant to the agreement but that in the absence of such an agreement the requirement of contemporaneity is not met "if the making of the advance precedes the formal execution of the debenture by any time whatsoever, unless the interval is so short that it can be regarded as *de minimis*—for example a 'coffee-break' ".[293]

---

[287] [1910] 1 Ch. 758.
[288] In the *Columbian Fireproofing* case, the interval was 11 days; in *Re F & E Stanton Ltd* [1929] 1 Ch. 180, it was eight weeks.
[289] [1992] B.C.C. 367.
[290] *Re Shoe Lace Ltd, Power v Sharp Investments Ltd* [1993] B.C.C. 609.
[291] [1906] 2 Ch. 467.
[292] See further as to this distinction *Goode on Legal Problems of Credit and Security*, 2008, paras 1–76 and 2–15; and *Goode on Commercial Law*, 2009, pp.671 and 704.
[293] *Re Shoe Lace*, cited above n.290, *per* Sir Christopher Slade at 619.

(3) Kinds of permitted new value

The effect of s.245 is that the most common forms of new value—money, goods, services,[294] payment of debt—now suffice to preserve the validity of the floating charge. This extension in the concept of new value represents a compromise between the views of the hardliners who considered that the old restriction to cash should be retained and the proponents of the opposing view that any form of money's worth should suffice. The Cork Committee rather cautiously recommended the addition of goods to cash but the exclusion of services.[295] In the end, services were added to the list. The result in broad terms is that admissible new value is restricted to those forms of benefit to the company which arise from day-to-day trading and finance and have a readily ascertainable value.[296] Excluded are a wide range of other assets, both tangible and intangible, including land and buildings, intellectual property rights, debts and other receivables and rights under contracts.

13–117

One of the forms of recognised new value is the supply of goods or services, and for this purpose their value is to be taken as the amount of money which at the time they were supplied could reasonably have been expected to be obtained for supplying the goods or services in the ordinary course of business and on the same terms (apart from the consideration) as those on which they were supplied to the company.[297] Another is "the value of so much of the consideration as consists of the discharge or reduction . . . of any debt of the company". No distinction is drawn between an advance made by the chargee to pay off or reduce a debt due from the company to a third party and an advance made to refinance an existing indebtedness of the company to the chargee itself. Does this enable an unsecured lender to transform its status into a secured lender for a contemporaneous advance by the simple device of refinancing the unsecured loan? If so, it would drive a coach and horses through the contemporaneity requirement, for all the lender would have to do would be to make a book-keeping entry recording that the new loan had been applied in discharge of the existing loan. The answer would seem to lie in the fact that what matters is not merely the *consideration* for the giving of the charge but the *value* of that consideration. If the creditor is not effectively parting with anything then no value is given even though the refinancing constitutes good consideration in general contract law for the execution of the floating charge.[298] The position is otherwise, of course, where the charge is taken to secure payment to a third party of a debt owed by the company to the third party, for in that case the lender is parting with real money.

---

[294] Which in this context would, it is thought, include facilities.
[295] "Insolvency Law and Practice", para.1564.
[296] This is less true of services than of goods, which no doubt explains why the Cork Committee recommended that services be excluded.
[297] Insolvency Act 1986 s.245(6).
[298] See *Re GT Whyte & Co Ltd* [1983] B.C.L.C. 311.

(4) Benefit to company

13–118   In order to qualify as new value under s.245, the payment of money or the supply of goods or services must be made to the company itself, not to a third party, although payment to a third party in or towards satisfaction of a debt due from the company suffices.

In order for money to be "paid . . . to the company" it must in a real sense be available to the company for its own benefit and to do with what it likes. So payment by cheque in exchange for the company's cheque of the same amount is not payment to the company, nor is a refinancing or a payment which is to be matched by a payment out by the company to other parties or which goes round a circle of payees, in either case leaving the company no better off than it was before,[299] or a payment made by the lender directly into the company's overdrawn bank account[300] or by cheque to the company on terms that the cheque is to be paid into the company's overdrawn account.[301] However, while payment into the company's overdrawn bank account does not constitute a payment to the company within para.(a) of s.245(2), it does fall within para.(b) as a payment which discharges or reduces a debt of the company. This point appears to have been overlooked in *Re Fairway Magazines Ltd*[302] where the applicant should have succeeded on this ground.

What does not constitute new value

13–119   It can be said from the foregoing that the following do not constitute relevant value:

(1)   money paid or goods or services supplied to the company prior to the creation of the charge (including for this purpose a binding agreement for the charge);

(2)   money paid prior to the creation of the charge in discharge or reduction of the company's indebtedness to a third party;

(3)   money paid or goods or services supplied to a third party (including a company which is a member of the same group as the chargor company), except where paid or supplied on or after the creation of the charge and in discharge or reduction of a debt owed to the third party by the company;

---

[299] *Re Destone Fabrics Ltd* [1941] Ch. 319.
[300] *Re Fairway Magazines Ltd* [1992] B.C.C. 924.
[301] *Re Orleans Motor Co Ltd* [1911] 2 Ch. 41.
[302] See above, n.300.

(4) money paid or goods or services supplied in discharge of a debt due from a third party (including a member of the same group), whether before or after the creation of the charge, except so far as the company was also liable in respect of the same debt and its liability was discharged or reduced by the payment or supply; and

(5) money paid to the company in such manner or on such conditions that it is not truly available to be used by the company for its own benefit, as where the money refinances an existing unsecured debt owed to the chargee or is to be matched by payments out to third parties or a payment to the chargee itself.

Insolvency at time of charge

It is not necessary to show that the company was insolvent at the time of or in consequence of the charge in cases where the chargee was a person connected with the company. As previously mentioned, this reflects the fact that such a person, as an insider, is better placed than an independent creditor to be aware that a state of insolvency looms and to look after his own interests at the expense of other creditors. Whether the chargee is to be treated as a person connected with the company is to be determined as at the time of creation of the charge. If at that time the chargee was not connected to the company, the fact that he becomes a connected person subsequently is irrelevant. Conversely, if he is connected with the company at the time of creation of the charge, the fact that he later ceases to be connected does not alter his status for the purpose of s.245, while if he assigns the charge the fact that the assignee is not a connected person is irrelevant. If, on the other hand, the original chargee was not connected with the company at the time of creation of the charge, his assignee steps into the assignor's favoured position whether or not the assignee is a connected person.[303]   **13–120**

Hardening of a floating charge

Where the company has a running account with the chargee and dealings on the account continue between them, the rule in *Clayton's Case* may have the effect of "hardening" the charge. Under the rule in *Clayton's Case* there is a presumption that in the case of a current account items credited to the account are applied to the earliest indebtedness first. Accordingly where a floating charge is taken to secure a pre-existing overdraft, sums are paid to the credit of the account and new drawings are then made, the effect of the   **13–121**

---

[303] L. Sealy and D. Milman, *Sealy & Milman: Annotated Guide to the Insolvency Legislation 2010* (London: Sweet & Maxwell, 2011), Vol.1, p.255.

rule is that the credits are applied to the pre-existing indebtedness, so that any new drawing constitutes new value even if the resulting balance is the same as before. In effect, the turnover of money in the account converts old value into new.

Example 15

13–122   An insolvent company has a bank overdraft of £100,000 which is unsecured. The bank, which is concerned about the position, takes a floating charge over the company's factory premises to secure both past and future advances. Subsequently, a cheque for £40,000 is paid into the account and a few days later the company draws a cheque for the same amount in favour of a supplier. The cheque for £40,000 is applied in discharge of the earliest indebtedness first, that is, the original £100,000, reducing the past indebtedness to £60,000, while the drawing in favour of the supplier represents new value by the bank, for which the floating charge is valid. Thus, although the debit balance is still £100,000 the mix has changed, in that £40,000 of past value has been converted into new value through the operation of the rule in *Clayton's Case*.[304]

The Cork Committee regarded this result as objectionable and recommended a statutory provision that all payments into the account should be treated as discharging debit items incurred after the creation of the floating charge.[305] It is hard to see either the logic or the fairness of such a recommendation, for which no reasoning was advanced beyond the cryptic statement that the rule in *Clayton's Case* "defeats the object of the section". This is simply not true. The statutory provisions are aimed at charges which, being given for past indebtedness, reduce the value of the estate. By allowing a new drawing without obligation to do so, the bank is genuinely extending new value. It could have kept the benefit of the payment into the account without allowing any further drawings but chose not to do so. To the extent of those new drawings, the company has received a benefit which is secured by the floating charge. The transaction is in no way within the mischief against which the statutory provisions are aimed, and the government rightly decided not to implement the Committee's recommendation. The position would, of course, be otherwise if there were no genuine new value, for example, if the bank stipulated that it would not honour a new drawing unless this was covered by a contemporaneous payment into the account, so that there was a ritual exchange of cheques and the company never had recourse to the funds drawn since these had to be simultaneously repaid.

---

[304] See *Re Yeovil Glove Co Ltd* [1965] Ch. 148, a decision on s.322 of the Companies Act 1948. However, the payment into the account might be vulnerable as a preference under s.239 of the Insolvency Act.

[305] "Insolvency Law and Practice", paras 156–162.

10. REGISTRABLE BUT UNREGISTERED CHARGES

Introduction

Under s.860 of the Companies Act 2006, where a charge created by a company[306] is one to which the section applies, it must be registered within 21 days after its creation,[307] failing which it will be void against a liquidator or administrator[308] and any creditor of the company[309] and the sum secured by the charge will become immediately due and payable.[310] Charges of financial collateral where the chargee has possession or control are excluded from the registration requirements.[311]

13–123

Rationale of the avoidance provisions

It is not at first sight obvious why non-registration should render a registrable charge void on winding up or administration. The failure to register a charge does not cause any diminution in the company's assets—the usual ground for avoidance—which would have occurred earlier, on the making of the charge, and then only if it was taken to secure a past indebtedness. Subsequent secured creditors are protected by being given priority even without a winding up or administration. Unsecured creditors have no rights or interest in the assets of the company and are prejudiced by want of registration only in so far as their decision to extend credit might have been different if they had known of the unregistered interest; yet the avoidance provisions apply even if there was no unsecured creditor who was both misled and influenced by the absence of registration. There is no anti-preference policy underlying the statutory provisions, for there are separate rules relating to preferences and in any event s.874 applies even if the charge was taken well outside the

13–124

---

[306] As opposed to a charge or security created by law, e.g. an unpaid vendor's equitable lien (*London and Cheshire Insurance Co Ltd v Laplagrene Properties Ltd* [1971] Ch. 499).

[307] Or such later time as may be allowed by the court on an application under s.873 of the Act for leave to register out of time. See generally Gerard McCormack, *Registration of Company Charges* (Bristol: Jordan Publishing, 2009).

[308] This means void against the company acting by its liquidator or administrator. See *Smith (Administrator of Cosslett (Contractors) Ltd v Bridgend CBC* [2002] 1 A.C. 336, in which the House of Lords reversed the rather startling decision of the Court of Appeal that an unregistered charge was void against an administrator but not against the company itself.

[309] i.e. a secured creditor or creditors in a winding up or administration.

[310] Companies Act 2006 s.874. The charge is not void against the company itself, because the purpose of registration is to give notice of the charge to third parties; the company obviously knows that it has granted the charge. See further para.13–126.

[311] Financial Collateral Arrangements (No.2) Regulations 2003, SI 2003/3226, reg.10, implementing the EC Financial Collateral Directive.

preference period.[312] The effect of avoidance is thus to give unsecured creditors who did not act in reliance on the want of registration an apparently unjustified windfall addition to the assets available for distribution. No doubt it is considerations such as these that led to the decision not to include a provision in the New Zealand Personal Property Securities Act 1999 rendering an unperfected security interest invalid in the debtor's bankruptcy or liquidation. New Zealand's approach in this respect stands in unique contrast to that taken in the United Kingdom, the different States in the United States and the Canadian Provinces and has been strongly criticised.[313]

Yet there are sound policy reasons for the avoidance of unregistered securities. In the first place, the avoidance rule reflects the law's dislike of the secret security interest, which leaves the debtor's property apparently unencumbered and at common law was considered a fraud on the general creditors.[314] Secondly, the registration provisions help to curb the fabrication or antedating of security agreements on the eve of winding up. Thirdly, although unsecured creditors have no existing interest in the company's assets outside winding up, and thus no immediate *locus standi* to complain of want of registration, they have an inchoate interest in that upon winding up the whole of the company's property, so far as not utilised in discharging the expenses of the winding up and the payment of preferential claims, becomes available for the general body of creditors, so that their rights become converted from purely personal rights into rights more closely analogous to that of beneficiaries under an active trust.[315] Fourthly, there may well be unsecured creditors who were misled by the want of registration into extending credit which they would not otherwise have granted. But it would be both expensive and impracticable to expect the liquidator (or administrator) to investigate each unsecured creditor's claim to see whether he did or did not act on the assumption that the unregistered charge did not exist. So a broad-brush approach which in effect assumes detriment to unsecured creditors at large is justified. Finally, the registration provisions serve a general public notice function as well as being a perfection requirement, and the avoidance provision can be seen as an inducement, and a powerful inducement, to comply with the law's

---

[312] A preference may, of course, arise as the result of deferment of the initial grant of the security interest in order to avoid registration, e.g. by making a contingent agreement for security (see above, para.13–78, n.183) but the act of preference in this case is not the want of registration (for nothing is registrable so long as the agreement is purely contingent) but the giving of the security at the time the contingency occurs, at which point it will constitute a security for a pre-existing indebtedness.

[313] See Michael Gedye, Ronald C.C. Cuming Q.C. and Roderick J. Wood, *Personal Property Securities in New Zealand* (Wellington: Thomson Brookers, 2002), pp.8–10, giving a list of reasons similar to those set out below why only perfected security interests should be valid in the debtor's insolvency.

[314] Hence the former reputed ownership doctrine, which no longer features in our insolvency law.

[315] See above, para.3–09.

requirements, reinforcing criminal sanctions for non-compliance. However, these policy considerations have been somewhat undermined by decisions holding (correctly in terms of legal analysis and justifiably as a matter of policy in securing finality of completed enforcement processes) that to the extent that the security has already been enforced or paid off prior to the winding up or other invalidating event, its avoidance has no effect.[316]

Registration out of time

The court may, on the application of the company or a person interested,[317] extend the time for registration on such terms and conditions as seem to the court just and expedient.[318] Before making such an order, the court must be satisfied that the failure to register was accidental or due to inadvertence or some other sufficient cause, or is not of a nature to prejudice the position of creditors or shareholders of the company, or that on other grounds it is just and equitable to grant relief.[319] Where these conditions are satisfied, leave is readily granted so long as the company is not in liquidation and no winding up is pending but an order will almost invariably be expressed to be subject to the intervening rights of creditors acquiring an interest in the property, such as subsequent chargees[320]; and where liquidation is imminent the court may, instead of refusing an order for an extension, grant it subject to the right of the company to apply for discharge of the order within a given period after the commencement of the winding up.[321] An order is liable to be refused where the creditor, instead of applying promptly for an extension of time and bringing all of the facts before the court, seeks to deal with the matter by taking a new charge or series of charges.[322]

13–125

Non-registration does not invalidate the charge against the company

It should be borne in mind that registration is purely a perfection requirement designed to give notice to third parties; it is not a condition of validity of the charge, which remains fully enforceable against the company prior to winding up or administration. It follows that if the company does go into

13–126

---

[316] See below, para.13–126.
[317] Usually the application is made by the holder of the registrable charge.
[318] Companies Act 2006 s.873(2).
[319] Companies Act 2006 s.873(1).
[320] The standard form of order was first laid down by Clauson J. in *Re L.H. Charles & Co Ltd* [1935] W.N. 15, and has been followed with minor modifications ever since.
[321] See McCormack, *Registration of Company Charges*, 2009, pp.126 et seq.; and *Goode on Commercial Law*, 2009, p.711.
[322] *Re Telomatic Ltd* [1993] B.C.C. 404.

liquidation or administration the consequent avoidance of the unregistered charge has no impact on the chargee to the extent that he has already realised his security or perfected it by seizure or judicial foreclosure or has otherwise obtained payment, for to that extent his security has been satisfied and there is nothing for him to enforce.[323]

11. DISPOSITIONS OF PROPERTY AFTER THE COMMENCEMENT OF COMPULSORY WINDING UP

The statutory provisions

13–127 Section 127 of the Insolvency Act 1986, re-enacting s.522 of the Companies Act 1985, provides that in a winding up by the court[324] any disposition of the company's property[325] made after the commencement of the winding up is void unless the court otherwise orders.[326] In this context, "the court" means the court dealing with an application under s.127 in the winding up proceedings. The fact that the disposition has been made pursuant to an order made by another court for other purposes does not save it from invalidation,[327] and it makes no difference whether that order was or was not by consent nor whether the effect of the order was itself to transfer an interest in equity to the transferee even before implementation of the order by execution of a formal conveyance.[328]

Section 127 bites on beneficial ownership, not necessarily on the legal title. Where contract and conveyance are combined, as in the case of the sale of goods, the effect of s.127 is that the invalidity of the contract also invalidates the transfer of legal title.[329] However, where the act of conveyance is distinct, the principle of abstraction applies. The conveyance being a distinct legal act, the passing of legal title is not vitiated by the invalidity of the underlying

---

[323] *Re Row Dal Construction Pty Ltd* [1966] V.R. 249; and *N.V. Slavenburg's Bank Ltd v Intercontinental Natural Resources Ltd* [1980] 1 All E.R. 955. See also *Mace Builders (Glasgow) Ltd v Lunn* [1985] 3 W.L.R. 465, a decision to similar effect on s.321 of the Companies Act 1948.

[324] The section does not apply to dispositions made after an application for an administration order. This is because there is no equivalent to the relation back of a compulsory winding up, so that until the administrator's appointment takes effect the directors continue to have full powers of management, including disposal of the company's assets, although dispositions made between the application for an administration order and the making of the order which are transactions at an undervalue or preferences are subject to avoidance under s.240(1)(c).

[325] And any transfer of shares or alteration in the status of the company's members; but these will not be discussed.

[326] For the considerations to be taken into account and the standard form of order, see below, paras.13–135 et seq.

[327] *Re Flint* [1993] Ch. 319, a decision on comparable provisions in s.284 of the Insolvency Act relating to dispositions by an individual after presentation of a bankruptcy petition.

[328] *Re Flint* cited above n.327.

[329] See *Goode on Commercial Law*, 2009, p.121, n.339.

contract, so that the transferee acquires legal title but holds the transferred asset as bare trustee for the company. Thus where land is disposed of after presentation of the winding up petition and the conveyance has been executed without leave of the court, then while the underlying disposition is void in the sense that no beneficial interest passes to the transferee, the conveyance is nevertheless effective to pass the legal title and the transferee holds it as bare trustee for the company, which is entitled to call for a reconveyance.[330] Similarly, if shares in a company have been transferred and the transfer registered, beneficial ownership remains in the company and the transferee as registered holder is a bare trustee for the company. To this extent s.127 is not wholly self-executing. The same is true of assets that have been realised or, in the case of chattels, taken out of the company's possession.

The same principle of abstraction applies with even greater force to the act of payment, which in the usual case will be effective to transfer not only legal title but beneficial ownership to the payee despite the fact that both parties were under the misapprehension that the payment was made in pursuance of a valid contract, and it will not give rise to a trust in favour of the company.[331] In the case of physical money (notes and coins), the free transferability of money as currency means that not only does legal title to money pass by delivery independent of the validity of the transaction under which payment is made but there can be no trust in favour of the company if the payee took in good faith and for value or the money has become mixed with other assets of the payee or has passed into the hands of a bona fide purchaser for value. All that the company has as the result of s.127 is a personal restitutionary claim for money paid on a failure (or perhaps an absence) of consideration, the effect of the invalidity of the transaction being that the company never acquired title to the asset for which it has paid.[332] Where the transfer is of bank money (value held through an account with a bank and usually transferred by novation through the banking system), a similar effect is achieved by the fact that the payee acquires a new and original right against his bank by novation as the result of the transfer. Again, any right of recovery by the company must be on the basis of a purely personal restitutionary claim for unjust enrichment.[333]

For the purposes of s.127 the winding up is deemed to commence on the presentation of the petition on which the winding up order was made, unless the company was already in voluntary liquidation at the time of the petition,

---

[330] *Re French's Wine Bar Ltd* [1987] 3 B.C.C. 173. See below, paras.13–151 et seq as to the restitutionary remedy of the counterparty.
[331] *Westdeutsche Landesbank Girozentrale v Islington LBC* [1996] A.C. 669, *per* Lord Browne-Wilkinson at 708.
[332] *Lipkin Gorman v Karpnale Ltd* [1991] 2 A.C. 548.
[333] This is a very simplified account of a complex set of issues admirably analysed by David Fox in his ground-breaking work *Property Rights in Money* (Oxford: Oxford University Press, 2008).

in which case the winding up is deemed to commence on the passing of the resolution for voluntary winding up.[334]

The purpose of this "relation back" of the commencement of winding up is to protect the interests of the general body of creditors by preventing a dissipation of the company's assets while the hearing of the petition is pending[335] and by ensuring that no payment or transfer is made which is preferential and would thus infringe the principle of *pari passu* distribution.[336] If the section were limited in scope to the achievement of this purpose, it would cause no great inconvenience, for it would then be providing no more than a logical extension of the preference period to the date of the winding up order. Unhappily, it is not so limited: it applies as much to bona fide business transactions as to preferences[337]; it nullifies transactions that increase the company's asset value no less than transactions which reduce that value. Indeed, it effectively paralyses the company's business, for without the court's leave not so much as a stitch of cloth can be disposed of, not one penny spent even to acquire an asset worth a pound, and technically the company cannot even pay cash into its bank account. Hence the importance of the company's ability to obtain authority from the court which will enable it to continue trading pending the hearing of the petition.[338]

"Disposition"

13–128   The word "disposition" is not defined but must be given a wide meaning if the purpose of the section is to be achieved, particularly in view of the fact that there is no exemption in favour of transfers for full value. "Disposition" should therefore be considered to include not only any dealing in the company's tangible or intangible assets by sale, exchange, lease, charge, gift or loan but also

---

[334] Insolvency Act 1986 s.129.

[335] *Re Albany Building Ltd* [2007] B.C.C. 591; and *Re Overnight Ltd* [2010] B.C.C. 787, where it was held that in the case of a compulsory winding up the cause of action for fraudulent trading under s.213 of the Insolvency Act did not accrue until the winding up order was made.

[336] It is because s.127 takes care of post-petition dispositions in winding up that s.240(1)(c) makes no reference to winding up petitions and is confined to transactions at an undervalue and preferences between the presentation of an administration application and the making of the order on that application.

[337] Companies Act 2006 s.1079, which in stated conditions precludes a company from relying against other persons on the making of a winding up order, or the appointment of a liquidator in a voluntary liquidation, has no effect on the operation of s.127 of the Insolvency Act, for although that section cannot be invoked until the company is in compulsory winding up, its nullifying effect is confined to dispositions made between the presentation of the petition and the making of the winding up order.

[338] See below, para.13–135. That s.127 is concerned to do no more than prevent a reduction in the assets of the company between winding up petition and hearing is demonstrated by the fact that in ordering a bank or other recipient to repay moneys improperly received, the court will penalise the payee no further than is necessary to restore to the fund of assets available for distribution the amount (if any) that has been lost (*Re Gray's Inn Construction Co Ltd* [1980] 1 All E.R. 814).

the conferment of a possessory or other lien on an asset[339] and any other act which, in reducing or extinguishing the company's rights in an asset, transfers value to another person. On this basis, "disposition" includes an agreement by which the company surrenders a lease or gives up its contractual rights,[340] contractual set-off by which a debtor to the company is given and exercises the right to apply a cross-claim of his own against the company in diminution of his indebtedness and arguably even the extension of further credit to the company during the post-petition period which leads to the exercise of a right of transaction set-off against the company's credit balance.[341] Moreover, the section is not confined to voluntary dispositions by the company itself; it applies equally to dispositions taking effect under a court order[342] and, it is thought, post-petition payments to a creditor of the company under a garnishee order made against one of the company's debtors, the effect of which is *pro tanto* to extinguish an asset of the company, namely the debt due to it.

However, the reduction or extinction of the company's rights in an asset must be one which leads in a real, not merely a technical, sense to the transfer of value to another party, for as was pointed out by Street C.J. in an Australian decision, *Re Mal Bower's Macquarie Electrical Centre Pty Ltd*[343] the word disposition connotes both a disponor and a disponee. So a company which does no more than collect in a debt is not disposing of an asset, even though the effect of the payment is to extinguish the chose in action represented by the debt, for value cannot in any real sense be said to move from the creditor to the debtor.

Only dispositions of the company's property are affected

Section 127 is confined to post-petition dispositions of the company's property, which includes transfers of property beneficially owned by the company and taking effect by virtue of a court order.[344] Assets held by the company

13–129

---

[339] e.g. by delivery of a car to a garage for repair or of a cheque to a bank for collection at a time when money is owing to the bank (see below).

[340] But exercise by the creditor of a unilateral right to terminate an agreement would not be a disposition.

[341] See generally Philip Wood, *English and International Set-Off* (London: Sweet & Maxwell, 1989), paras 7–303 et seq. I agree with Mr Wood that exercise of a right of *insolvency* set-off under the Insolvency Rules cannot be within the scope of s.127 (for if it were then in a compulsory winding up the right of insolvency set-off given by r.490 of the Insolvency Rules would be rendered nugatory), and that the contrary decision at first instance in *Barclays Bank Ltd v TOSG Trust Fund Ltd* [1984] B.C.L.C. 1 is wrong. The court would, it is thought, be likely to validate the contractual set-off if the creditor would enjoy exactly the same rights under insolvency set-off.

[342] *Re Flint* cited above n.327.

[343] [1974] 1 N.S.W.L.R. 254 at 258, cited in *Re Barn Crown Ltd* [1994] 4 All E.R. 42 at 48. See below, para.13–131.

[344] *Re Flint* cited above n.327.

are not its property to the extent of any security interest it has given over them in favour of a creditor. So if a bank in good faith and the ordinary course of business collects a cheque for its customer and credits the proceeds to the customer's overdrawn account, this does not constitute a disposition of the company's property, for the bank had a lien on the cheque and thus a security interest in the proceeds and the credit to the account merely produced a realisation of its security rights.[345] Similarly, a sale by a mortgagee is outside the scope of s.127, whether the conveyance is by the mortgagee or by the company acting through its receiver.[346] Likewise, the vesting of a company's property in a secured creditor or other party under an after-acquired property clause in the security or other instrument is outside s.127[347]; and completion of an unconditional contract for the sale of land by the company is not a disposition of the company's property, for in equity the land already belongs to the purchaser upon exchange of contracts.[348] But waiver of a condition in a conditional contract or affirmation of a contract voidable by the company might constitute a disposition within s.127.[349]

Payments into the company's bank account

13–130
The question of whether a disposition is of the company's property raises special problems in the case of payments into the company's bank account. It is necessary to treat separately the case where the account is in credit from the case where it is overdrawn.

(1) Account in credit

13–131
We may begin by distinguishing the payment of cash (notes and coins) into the account from the payment in of a cheque. Where the company pays cash into its account, the payment constitutes a disposition of its property, whether or not the account is in credit, for ownership of the notes and coins passes to the bank.[350] The company acquires a corresponding claim against the bank, which will be recorded by a credit of the payment to its account, so

---

[345] *National Australian Bank v KDS Construction Services* (1987) 163 C.L.R. 668; and see *Re Margart Pty Ltd* (1984) 9 A.C.L.R.. 269, [1985] B.C.L.C. 314 (Supreme Court of New South Wales). But it is not clear why the delivery of the cheque to the bank, which gave rise to the lien in the first place, was not itself an unauthorised disposition. See further below, para.13–132.

[346] *Sowman v David Samuel Trust Ltd* [1978] 1 All E.R. 616; *Re Margart Pty Ltd, Hamilton v Westpac Banking Corp.*, above, n. 345.

[347] See *Goode on Legal Problems of Credit and Security*, 2008, para.2–14.

[348] *Re French's Wine Bar*, cited above n.330.

[349] *Re French's Wine Bar*, cited above n.330.

[350] The same view is taken by Adrian Walters, "Void Dispositions in Compulsory Winding Up" in Armour and Howard Bennett (eds), *Vulnerable Transactions in Corporate Insolvency*, 2002, para.8.35.

that the net effect of the transaction is simply to convert an asset of the company from one form, cash, into another, a claim on the bank. Hence in terms of its effect the breach will usually be a merely technical one but the position would be quite otherwise if the bank were to become insolvent before the company had withdrawn the amount credited.

The situation is somewhat different in the case of a cheque.[351] Deposit of the cheque with the bank for the purpose of collection[352] is not in itself a disposition within s.127 where the company's account is in credit, for the bank collects purely as agent and has no interest of its own in the cheque. However, in the first edition of this book it was argued that the collection process itself involves the disposition of an asset of the company, for the bank surrenders the customer's cheque, which represents both a negotiable instrument and the embodiment of a claim against the drawer, in exchange for payment, so that one form of property belonging to the company is converted into another. In *Re Barn Crown Ltd*[353] H.H. Judge Rich Q.C. rejected this analysis as over-technical and not according with ordinary usage. This criticism is well founded, for merely to collect a cheque as agent does not in itself do more than the company could have done by collecting payment from the debtor in cash.[354] Judge Rich accordingly took the view that no disposition of any kind was involved. In reaching this conclusion, he drew on the judgment of McPherson J. in *Re Loteka Pty Ltd*[355] which concerned the effect of payment *from* a credit account and concluded that the collection of a cheque and payment of the proceeds *into* an account in credit could be analysed in the same way.

> "In collecting payment upon a cheque the bank credits the customer's account with the amount of the cheque. If the account is already in credit, no disposition of the property of the customer takes place in favour of the bank. The amount standing to the credit of the customer is increased in return for the surrender of the cheque, which becomes a voucher for payment. It is the drawer of the cheque whose property is disposed of. All that happens between the customer and the banker is an adjustment of entries in the statement recording the accounts between them."[356]

However, this, with respect, over-simplifies the problem and equates payment *into* an account in credit with payment *from* an account that is in credit,

---

[351] Or any other kind of instrument deposited for collection.

[352] A process which does not involve the receipt of cash by the collecting bank but merely a transfer of funds from the paying bank through the books of a third bank (the Bank of England, where the paying and collecting banks are clearing banks) with whom both banks hold an account.

[353] See above, n.343.

[354] See above.

[355] (1989) 7 A.C.L.C. 998.

[356] [1994] 4 All E.R. 42 at 45.

when in reality the two cases are entirely different.[357] Let us assume that the company is owed £1 million by a debtor of undoubted financial stability from whom it receives a cheque for this amount. We can agree that the company does not make a disposition of its property by arranging for the cheque to be collected through its bank as agent rather than directly. But what happens next is that, by virtue of the banker-customer relationship, the bank proceeds to borrow the collected proceeds and credit the company's amount with the sum so borrowed. That borrowing is not a mere matter of book entry; it involves the transfer of collected funds from company to bank in exchange for a promise of repayment.[358] That transfer, it is submitted, is a disposition of the company's property in breach of s.127. In 99 cases out of 100, the breach is technical and the court can be expected to validate the transfer. The 100th case is where the bank closes its doors the day after collecting the cheque and soon afterwards goes into liquidation with only enough assets to pay unsecured creditors 10 pence in the pound. The company is now in the position where it has lent £1 million and will recover a mere £100,000 by way of dividend. The making of the loan is no longer a mere technical breach; its effect is to remove £1 million that would have been available to the company's creditors and make it available instead to the bank's creditors. The inescapable conclusion is that this constitutes a disposition of the company's property in breach of s.127. This receives support from the decision of Buckley L.J. in *Re Gray's Inn Construction Co Ltd*[359]:

> "In the present case the company's account with the bank was overdrawn, so that I need not consider what the position would have been if any cheque had been paid in when the account was in credit but I doubt whether even in those circumstances it could properly be said that the payment in did not constitute a disposition of the amount of the cheque in favour of the bank."

As a final point, if the company had lent money to an ordinary borrower, this would without doubt be a disposition of the company's property. Why should it make a difference that the borrower is the company's bank? In a decision of the Irish High Court in *Re Pat Ruth Ltd*[360] Costello J. held that all

---

[357] See below, para.13–133, as to the effect of payments out of an account.

[358] It is true that the fact that a bank collects a cheque "for" a customer does not mean that the bank's receipt is the customer's receipt; the bank receives the proceeds of the cheque as part of its own moneys but with a duty to credit the customer's account with an equivalent amount (see *Goode on Commercial Law*, 2009, pp.579–580). Nevertheless, it is well established that in crediting the account rather than paying the customer the cash equivalent of what it has received the bank is borrowing the money from the customer. See *Foley v Hill* (1848) 2 H.L. Cas. 28; *Joachimson v Swiss Bank Corp* [1921] 3 K.B. 110; and generally Michael Brindle and Raymond Cox, *Law of Bank Payments*, 4th edn (London: Sweet & Maxwell, 2010), paras 7-085 *et seq*. There is therefore a disposition in favour of the bank.

[359] [1980] 1 All E.R. 814 at 818.

[360] [1981] I.R.L.M. 51.

payments into the company's bank account were dispositions of its property for the purpose of the equivalent provision of the Irish legislation[361] and in *Re Industrial Services Co (Dublin) Ltd*[362] this was not contested. As indicated above, this will not matter in most cases, since the money paid into the account will be held by the bank and will be available as part of the company's assets. It is only if the bank is insolvent that the issue is a live one.[363]

(2) Account overdrawn

Where the company owes money to the bank, there can be no doubt of the position. Even where the delivery of the cheque for collection is not by itself a disposition, it is clear that payment of the proceeds into the overdrawn account transfers funds from the company to the bank.[364] But in most cases, the true analysis is that the disposition occurs earlier, by delivery of the cheque, which confers on the bank a lien for the company's indebtedness.[365] In this situation, the crediting of the account does not give rise to any further disposition, for the bank is then exercising its rights as a secured creditor[366] and it is the delivery of the cheque to it in the first instance that constitutes the infringement of s.127. Payment of cheques into an overdrawn account may also constitute a preference of the bank.

13–132

Withdrawals from a bank account

Where a company withdraws money from a bank account which is in credit, for the purpose of s.127 that is a disposition of the company's property to the extent of the pre-existing credit balance, for the value of its claim against the bank is correspondingly reduced. It has, however, been held that where the company's money is paid into an account of a third party so as to become part of a mixed fund from which drawings are made in good faith, while

13–133

---

[361] Companies Act 1963 s.218.

[362] [2001] 2 I.R. 118.

[363] Walters, cited above n.350, suggests (at paras 8.41–8.42) that the bank would remain liable under s.127, in the absence of a validation order, even if the company's claim on the bank had been reduced by subsequent drawings. However, to the extent that such drawings are to be regarded as coming from the sum paid into the account (applying the rule in *Clayton's Case* (1816) 1 Mer. 572), the bank will in effect have repaid the money to or at the direction of the company and thus negated the effect of the payment into the account.

[364] *Re Gray's Inn Construction*, cited above n.359; and *Re Tain Construction Ltd, Rose v AIB Group (UK) Plc* [2003] 2 B.C.L.C. 374.

[365] *Re Keever* [1967] Ch. 182; and *Barclays Bank Ltd v Astley Industrial Trust Ltd* [1970] 2 Q.B. 527. If the bank has already advanced money against the cheque, it becomes a holder for value to the extent of the advance and to that extent collects on its own account.

[366] *National Australia Bank v KDS Construction Services*, cited above n.345. See above, para.13–129.

the payment into the account is a disposition of the company's money, a withdrawal from it is not, even if the company could by appropriate proceedings have obtained a declaration of charge on the mixed fund.[367]

What is the position where the account is already in overdraft before the further withdrawal? Such was the case in *Re Gray's Inn Construction Co Ltd*[368] where, despite having notice both of the petition and of the winding up order, the company's bank allowed the company to continue to operate its overdrawn account, receiving sums to the credit of the account and honouring further drawings on the account. The result was that in addition to what was held to be the unjustified payment of certain pre-liquidation debts to the bank and other creditors the company incurred a further trading loss. In invalidating some of the payments out of the account in discharge of pre-liquidation debts as well as payments into the account to the extent of the post-petition trading losses suffered by the company the Court of Appeal entertained no doubt that the former payments were as much dispositions of the company's property as the latter. Indeed, counsel for the bank conceded the point. In my view, he was wrong to do so, for the effect of the concession was that the court was led to regard the proposition as "indisputable"[369] without qualification and without any attempt to identify the company's property which was the subject of the so-called disposition.

What is the effect of a withdrawal from a company's overdrawn account where that is the only relevant fact? The short answer is that it merely increases the company's liability to the bank. If there is one thing that is still clear in the increasingly complex financial scene leading to the credit crunch, it is that a liability is not an asset and that an increase in a liability is not by itself a disposition of an asset. Section 127 cannot apply unless there is a disposition of the company's property. What, then, was the item of property supposedly disposed of in the *Gray's Inn* case? Again, the short answer is: none. The payments out of the account were all in discharge of pre-liquidation debts for goods and services supplied[370] and (since the account was at all times in overdraft[371]) did not involve the application of a single asset of the company. Not one tiny tittle of a right in tangible or intangible property was affected one iota. Not one smidgen of interference with the *pari passu* principle resulted. All that happened was that the bank used its own moneys to meet the company's cheques for what were presumably payments to suppliers

---

[367] *Re J Leslie Engineers Co Ltd* [1976] 1 W.L.R. 292.
[368] See above, n.364.
[369] [1980] 1 All E.R. 814, per Buckley L.J. at 818.
[370] See the judgment of Buckley L.J. in *Re Gray's Inn Construction*, cited above n.364, at 823.
[371] *Re Gray's Inn Construction*, cited above n.364, at 817. The details contained in the judgment are insufficient to enable the account to be reconstructed, and it is possible that some of the items drawn on a particular day were covered by a credit balance even if at the end of the day the account was still in overdraft. But to the extent (if any) that this was the case it is irrelevant to the question here under discussion, viz. whether payments not covered by a credit balance constitute a disposition of the company's property.

and other creditors in the normal course of business,[372] so that in relation to such payments the bank became substituted as creditor for the persons to whom they were made, leaving the position of other creditors entirely unchanged. The only other item invalidated was a payment into the account, which went to reduce the pre-liquidation overdraft and was clearly a disposition of the company's property, as stated earlier.

What I suggest went wrong in the *Gray's Inn* case was that the court had a picture of trading losses in respect of which the company's assets were reduced by outflows from the account, whereas the true position was that any reduction in the assets resulted from payments into the account in reduction of the overdraft and such individual intra-day drawings as may have been matched by a temporary credit balance.

My contention, then, is that s.127 can never apply solely by reason of the drawing on an overdrawn account. In *Coutts & Co v Stock*,[373] Lightman J. entertained no doubt that an increase in the company's overdraft fell outside s.127. However, it does not follow that use of an overdraft can never give rise to a disposition of the company's property. There appear to be at least three cases where it does. The first is where the bank holds security for future advances, for an increase in the overdraft automatically expands the quantum of the bank's security interest, and correspondingly reduces the company's equity in the charged assets, unless these were already charged to their full value at the time of the further drawing on the account. The second is where the company has a credit balance on another account and the effect of the further drawing is to increase the amount for which the bank has a right of set-off against the credit balance. The third is where the further drawing is within the limit of an agreed overdraft which the bank is contractually committed to extending, for the effect of the drawing is to reduce the amount of the facility remaining available and thus the quantum of the chose in action vested in the company.[374]

Consequences of unauthorised disposition

Section 127 provides that a post-petition disposition not sanctioned by the court is void. It says nothing about the method of recovery or the parties

13–134

---

[372] The judgment of Buckley L.J. does not indicate the purpose for which the payments were made but does contain the statement (at 817) that the bank made sure, so far as it was able to do so, that all cheques were drawn in the ordinary course of the company's business.

[373] [2000] 1 W.L.R. 906.

[374] See *R. v Kohn* (1979) 69 Cr. App. R. 395, in which the Court of Appeal upheld the conviction of the director of a company for theft for improperly drawing cheques on the company's account, holding that he was guilty of a theft of debts due from the bank to the company to the extent that the cheques were covered by a credit balance or by the amount of the contractually agreed overdraft facility but not beyond. However, in *Coutts & Co v Stock*, cited above n.372, Lightman J. held that the use and, indeed, partial or total exhaustion of the company's overdraft limit cannot constitute a disposition within s.127.

against whom recovery is available. This has to be determined by the general law.[375] There is no great difficulty where the disposition relates to tangible property such as land or goods. The transfer is simply of no effect and the transferee therefore has no title to it and can be ordered to return it. Again, where money is paid into the company's overdrawn account with its bank, the payment is ineffective to confer rights on the bank, and the practical effect is that the bank is not entitled to debit the company's account with the sum paid in and can be ordered to re-credit the account or make repayment in some other way. But what is the position where a cheque is drawn by the company on an account in credit and paid by the bank? Is the amount of the payment recoverable from the bank, the payee or both? In *Hollicourt (Contracts) Ltd v Bank of Ireland*,[376] the Court of Appeal, following a series of Australian decisions,[377] held that only the payee is liable. It was pointed out that the bank acts purely as an agent or intermediary of its customer, the company, and in making payment is simply carrying out its customer's instructions. The disposition is not the reduction in the company's credit balance as such but the transfer of funds to the payee, who is the only recipient of the disposition. Accordingly, any claim for recovery of money paid under the void disposition must be against the payee, not the bank.

Authorisation by the court

13–135   The court may authorise any disposition that would otherwise be void. Such authorisation can be given in advance of the winding up,[378] and this should be sought wherever possible, for otherwise the party dealing with the company runs the risk that the court will refuse to validate the transaction retrospectively. The application is usually made by the company but may be made by any person having a discernible interest in the matter,[379] which obviously includes the transferee under the affected transaction. A Practice Note issued by the Chancellor sets out the evidence that should be given, as a minimum, in support of the application.[380] There may be cases where prior authorisation is impracticable, for example, because time is of the essence or

---

[375] *Re J Leslie Engineers*, cited above n.367, *per* Oliver J. at 298.
[376] [2001] Ch. 555.
[377] *Re Mal Bower's Macquarie Electrical Centre Pty Ltd (VIA)* (1974) 1 N.S.W.L.R. 254; *Re Loteka Pty Ltd* (1989) 1 A.C.L.R. 620; and *Tasmanian Primary Distributors Pty Ltd v R.C. & M.B. Steinhardt Pty Ltd* (1994) 13 A.C.S.R. 92.
[378] *Re A.I. Levy (Holdings) Ltd* [1964] Ch. 19.
[379] *Re Argentum Reductions (UK) Ltd* [1975] 1 W.L.R. 186.
[380] Practice Note—Validation Orders (Insolvency Act 1986, ss.127 and 284) [2007] B.C.C. 91, paras 6–9. The court will need to be satisfied by credible evidence that the company is solvent and able to pay its debts as they fall due or that a particular transaction or series of transactions in respect of which the order is sought will be beneficial to or will not prejudice the interests of all of the unsecured creditors as a class (para.9).

because the parties are unaware of the presentation of the petition. But in such cases, although the court may be sympathetic, there is no guarantee that the transaction will be validated. The principles upon which the court will act in dealing with applications for a validation order are discussed in some detail in *Re Gray's Inn Construction Co Ltd*,[381] *Re S & D Wright Ltd*,[382] *Denney v John Hudson & Co Ltd*[383] and *Re Tain Construction Ltd*.[384] From these four decisions the following principles can be extracted:

(1)   The discretion of the court is at large.

(2)   The basic principle of *pari passu* distribution among creditors should generally be respected. The court will be reluctant to validate payments and transfers pursuant to pre-liquidation transactions where the effect would be to give a preference to a pre-liquidation creditor or would otherwise prejudice the interests of unsecured creditors.

(3)   But in appropriate cases such payments and transfers will be sanctioned, as where the payment of sums due to particular suppliers is necessary to ensure future supplies that will enable the company to continue trading and the court considers that the continuance of trading will be in the best interests of creditors. This is a sensible recognition of the fact, well known to administrative receivers and administrators, that it is often necessary to make certain involuntary, or "pressure", payments to particular creditors in order to protect the wider interests of the creditors as a whole.

(4)   Transactions which do not in any way diminish or dissipate the company's net assets, such as post-petition transactions for full value, will normally be validated, and *a fortiori* transactions which would increase, or have increased, the value of the company's assets or which would preserve or have preserved the assets from harm that would result in a paralysis of the company's business.[385]

(5)   Where the parties were unaware that a petition had been presented and the disposition was in good faith and in the ordinary course of business, that is a powerful factor in inducing the court to exercise its discretion to validate the transaction but is not sufficient by itself; it must also be shown that the transaction was one which was likely to be for the benefit of creditors generally.[386]

---

[381] [1980] 1 All E.R. 814.

[382] [1992] B.C.C. 503.

[383] [1992] B.C.L.C. 901. See also above, n.374.

[384] [2003] 2 B.C.L.C. 374.

[385] See also *Re Wiltshire Iron Co* (1868) L.R. 3 Ch. App. 443; *Re Park Ward & Co Ltd* [1926] Ch. 828; *Re Clifton Place Garage Ltd* [1970] 1 All E.R. 353; and *Re A.I. Levy (Holdings)*, cited above n.378.

[386] See also *Re Tain Construction*, cited above n.384.

(6)   In deciding whether a post-petition payment made to obtain delivery of goods purchased before the presentation of the petition on terms of cash against delivery is of benefit to the company the court does not look simply at the benefit, if any, to be derived from the particular goods but also takes into account the fact that the payment will enable the company to obtain further supplies and thereby continue the business and earn revenue.

(7)   The court can authorise or validate not merely a particular disposition or contract but the general continuance of trading and for that purpose the continued operation of a bank account.[387] The desirability of the company continuing to trade is inherently more speculative than that of being allowed to adhere to a particular disposition and is likely to depend on whether the sale of the business as a going concern will probably be more beneficial than the realisation of the company's assets on a break-up basis.[388] Where the court does authorise the continuance of trading, the proper course is to freeze the existing account and require all fresh dealings to be conducted through a new account.

It has also been held that the court has power to validate a transaction to a limited extent or for a limited purpose, so that where the company in liquidation had transferred property to another company which had then given a charge to a bank, the transaction could be validated to the extent of the charge to the bank.[389]

12. TRANSACTIONS DEFRAUDING CREDITORS

The statutory provisions

13–136   Where a transaction at an undervalue is entered into by the company for the purpose of putting assets beyond the reach of a person who is making or may at some time make a claim against the company or of otherwise prejudicing the interests of such a person in relation to the claim he is making or may

---

[387] The standard form of s.127 order permits: (1) payments into and out of the bank accounts of the company in the ordinary course of business; and (2) dispositions of the property of the company made in the ordinary course of its business for proper value between the date of presentation of the petition and the date of judgment on the petition or a further order in the meantime (Practice Direction 49B—Order under Section 127 of the Insolvency Act 1986, para.7).

[388] This obviously depends to a considerable degree on whether there are reasonable prospects of the company moving into profitable trading and meanwhile having sufficient cash flow to carry on the business.

[389] *Re Dewrun Ltd, Royal Bank of Scotland v Bhardwaj* [2002] B.C.C. 57.

make, the court may make an order restoring the status quo and protecting the interests of persons who are victims of the transaction.[390] This section derives from the provisions of s.172 of the Law of Property Act 1925 relating to fraudulent conveyances. In contrast to the provisions discussed earlier in this chapter, it applies whether or not the company is in liquidation or administration. The definition of a transaction at an undervalue in relation to companies is the same as under s.238(4) of the Insolvency Act, discussed earlier.[391]

Conditions for making an order

An order can be made under s.423 only if the following conditions are satisfied: **13–137**

(1) there has been a transaction at an undervalue[392];

(2) it was made for the purpose of defeating the claims of an existing or putative creditor.

It is not necessary that the company shall be in winding up or administration, nor is there any statutory time limit.

The fact that the transaction was not entered into from any dishonest motive and that the parties acted in reliance on legal advice is no answer to a claim under s.423; it suffices that the debtor company's subjective purpose was to place the assets out of the reach of creditors or a particular creditor.[393] There is no need to show that such intention was the sole purpose of the transaction. At one time, it was thought that it had to be the predominant purpose,[394] but it now appears to be settled that a substantial purpose suffices.[395] On the other hand, it is not sufficient to show merely that the *result* of the transfer was to put assets beyond the reach of a creditor, for *result* is not to be equated with *purpose*.[396] So s.423 does not apply if the purpose of the transaction was not to place assets outside the reach of creditors but to gain a tax advantage,[397] so that removal of the assets from the reach of creditors was simply a by-product of the transaction.

---

[390] Insolvency Act 1986 s.423.
[391] Above, paras 13–13 et seq.
[392] See in this connection *Agricultural Mortgage Corp Plc v Woodward* [1994] B.C.C. 688, the facts of which have been given above, para.13–28.
[393] *Arbuthnot Leasing International Ltd v Havelet Leasing Ltd (No.2)* [1990] B.C.C. 636.
[394] *Moon v Franklin* [1996] B.P.I.R. 196.
[395] *Random House UK v Allason* [2008] EWHC 2854 (Ch), *per* David Richards J. at [52]; *IRC v Hashmi* [2002] 2 B.C.L.C. 489, *per* Arden L.J. at [25]; and *Papanicola v Fagan* [2010] 2 P. & C.R. DG1, *per* H.H. Judge Raynor Q.C. at [31].
[396] ibid.
[397] *Pinewood Joinery v Starelm Properties Ltd* [1994] B.C.C. 569. However, securing a tax advantage may also go hand in hand with a desire to protect the assets from creditors, as in *4 Eng Ltd v Harper* [2010] B.C.C. 746.

Who can apply for an order

13–138   Application for an order under s.423 can be made:

(1)   by the liquidator or administrator of a company in winding up or administration or by the official receiver;

(2)   with leave of the court, by a victim of the transaction; or

(3)   where a victim of the transaction is bound by a voluntary arrangement, by the supervisor of the voluntary arrangement.[398]

The word "victim" is not confined to creditors but covers anyone who suffers actual or potential prejudice.[399] Accordingly, while the transaction must have been entered into for the purpose of defeating the claims of an existing or putative creditor, it is open to any victim within the above meaning to apply for an order, whether or not the victim is a creditor and whether or not he was someone within the scope of the company's purpose or even known to the company.[400]

Orders that can be made

13–139   These are set out in s.425 and correspond broadly to the orders that can be made under s.241 of the Act,[401] without prejudice to the generality of s.423, but always with a view to restoring the position to what it would have been if the transaction had not taken place[402] with the same restrictions for the protection of bona fide third parties as in s.241(2).[403] Payment can be ordered to be made direct to the victim but if the company is insolvent the court will be minded to order return to the liquidator or administrator in order to protect the general body of creditors.[404] In any event, a person is not a victim in whose favour an order can be made if he is no worse off as the result of the transfer than he would have been if it had not been made, because payments that were made would have to have been made anyway[405] or because the property transferred was subject to a mortgage for an amount exceeding its value.[406] The list

---

[398] Insolvency Act 1986 s.424.
[399] *Hill v Spread Trustee Co Ltd* [2007] 1 W.L.R. 2404, *per* Arden L.J. at [101]; and *Clydesdale Financial Services Ltd v Smailes* [2010] Lloyds Rep. I.R. 577, *per* David Richards J. at [73].
[400] *Hill v Spread Trustee*, cited above n.399, *per* Arden L.J. at [101]; and *Giles v Rhind* [2009] Ch. 191.
[401] See above, paras 13–45 et seq.
[402] *Griffin v Awoderu* [2008] EWHC 349 (Ch).
[403] *Chohan v Saggar* [1992] B.C.C. 750.
[404] *4 Eng Ltd v Harper* [2010] B.C.C. 746.
[405] *Moon v Franklin*, cited above n.394.
[406] *Pinewood Joinery*, cited above n.397.

of orders set out in s.425 is not exhaustive and within the limits described above the court can make any other order it considers appropriate, for example, a declaration as to the purpose for which the asset in question was transferred,[407] an order restraining the transferee from dealing in any way with his legal or beneficial interest,[408] a declaration that the transferee holds property on trust for the transferor,[409] or a payment into a designated account to abide the outcome of other proceedings.[410]

13. APPLICATION OF RECOVERIES

In all of these cases, the question arises as to whether the recoveries[411] form part of the company's general assets so as to be or become subject to a prior security interest granted by the company (including a security interest arising under an after-acquired property clause in a fixed or floating charge) or whether instead they are to be treated as a distinct pool of assets not belonging to the company in its own right but received by the liquidator for the benefit of the general body of creditors and therefore outside the scope of the prior security interest.[412]

13–140

Recoveries in right of the company

This category comprises all cases where the company through its liquidator recovers the disposed-of asset in specie because of the invalidity or avoidance of the disposition or can treat it as free from a security interest because of the nullity of the security interest.

13–141

Where the disposition is wholly void, the effect is that the asset purportedly disposed of never ceased to be the property of the company and remains subject to a prior security interest. The recovery thus occurs automatically by force of law and, in contrast to other grounds of recovery, does not involve any action on the part of the liquidator (other than securing a formal reconveyance

---

[407] ibid.

[408] ibid.

[409] *Arbuthnot Leasing International Ltd v Havelet Leasing Ltd (No.2)* [1990] B.C.C. 636, where the declaration was expressed to be without prejudice to post-transfer creditors of the transferee.

[410] ibid.

[411] This term is used for brevity to cover both the case where assets or their monetary value come back to the company and cases where an asset held by the company is freed from a security interest because of the invalidation of that interest.

[412] See generally D.D. Prentice, "Creditors' Interests and Directors' Duties" [1990] 10 O.J.L.S. 265; and Fidelis Oditah, "Wrongful Trading" [1990] L.M.C.L.Q. 205, 215–222; and *Legal Aspects of Receivables Financing* (London: Sweet & Maxwell, 2008), pp.214–222.

where this is necessary) or any use of the company's resources. The invalidity may arise at common law, as where the disposition is effected pursuant to a contract which is void for want of *consensus ad idem*, or by statute, as where it is a disposition made after presentation of the winding up petition and without leave of the court[413] or is a security interest invalidated for want of registration[414] or as a floating charge which falls foul of s.245 of the Insolvency Act.[415] In all of these cases, the effect of the invalidity is that the asset never ceased to be subject to the prior assignment or security interest. Invalidity at common law plainly has nothing to do with the particular interests of general creditors in a winding up, so that there is no basis for giving them a special status as regards recoveries. A post-petition disposition made without the court's approval is likewise wholly void, so that the asset does not escape from the prior security interest.[416] The invalidity of a charge simply expands the company's equity in the charged asset and does not affect existing security interests. A registrable but unregistered charge is void against the liquidator and creditors. For this purpose, "creditors" includes subsequent secured creditors, whether or not the company is in winding up, and the effect of the failure to register the prior charge is that a subsequent chargee is promoted. Similarly, the invalidity of a floating charge under s.245 does not affect existing security interests except to free them from the floating charge if it would otherwise have had priority.

Recoveries for the benefit of creditors

13–142   All of the statutory provisions referred to above[417] involve the invalidation of dispositions by the company, thus operating to preserve or restore prior security interests in the assets the subject of the ineffective disposition. By contrast, the provisions relating to transactions at an undervalue and preferences, although often loosely referred to as rendering the transactions voidable, are not true invalidating provisions. Nothing in ss.238 or 239 refers to avoidance of transactions at an undervalue or preferences, nor do the powers conferred on the court by s.241 include the power to rescind such transactions or preferences or declare them void. Instead, they enable the court to reverse the effect of the transaction at an undervalue or preference in

---

[413] Insolvency Act 1986 s.127. See above, para.13–127.

[414] Under s.874 of the Companies Act 2006.

[415] Because it is taken otherwise than for a requisite form of new value from a company which goes into winding up within a specified statutory period. See above, paras 13–111 et seq.

[416] *Merton v Hammond Suddards* [1996] 2 B.C.L.C. 470; *Bayley v National Australia Bank* (1995) 16 A.C.S.R. 38; and *Campbell v Michael Mount PSB* (1995) 16 A.C.S.R. 296. The contrary view was adopted in a majority decision of the Full Court of the Victoria Supreme Court in *Re Fresjac Pty Ltd* (1995) 65 S.A.S.R. 334 (Debelle J. dissenting) but it is thought that the earlier cases reflect the position in English law.

[417] i.e. Companies Act 2006 s.874; and Insolvency Act 1986 ss.127 and 245.

whatever manner it considers fit. This includes the power to order any transferred property to be vested in the company but such a power is purely remedial and does not impeach the validity of the transfer.

It might be thought, therefore, that it is the absence of revesting in the
company as the result of the avoidance that debars the secured creditor from
reaping the fruits of recoveries in the case of transactions at an undervalue
and preference. That, indeed, was the conclusion reached in relation to preferences by the High Court of Australia in *N.A. Kratzmann Pty Ltd (in liquidation) v Tucker (No.2)*,[418] in which a distinction was drawn between the
avoidance of a preference in the form of a transfer of specific property,
which revested in the company in specie and was thus held to be captured by
the prior security interest, and the avoidance of payment where there was no
such revesting and the claim against the preferred creditor was a purely
personal claim for repayment. However, such a distinction was never applied
in English law,[419] where the avoidance of preference has long been established to enure for the benefit of the general body of creditors.[420] The
true justification for treating recoveries in respect of preferences as held for
the general body of creditors is that the legislation is remedial in character,
embodying a policy decision to benefit the general body of creditors and
not any individual creditor, and that the claim is accordingly vested by statute
in the liquidator, not in the company.[421] Moreover, the recovery does not
arise by force of law but results from the liquidator's activity in making
application to the court and, to that end, the use of the company's resources,
so that the position is analogous to that which obtains where the liquidator
carries out a contract on behalf of the company.[422] A third ground advanced
by Bennett J. in *Re Yagerphone Ltd*, is that assets recovered by way of
preference are impressed with a trust in favour of the general body of
creditors, an obiter dictum subsequently approved by Millett J. in *Re M.C.
Bacon Ltd*.[423]

Similar considerations apply to recoveries by the liquidator in relation
to transactions at an undervalue[424] and extortionate credit bargains.[425] It

---

[418] (1968) 123 C.L.R. 295.
[419] See Oditah, *Legal Aspects of Receivables Financing*, 2008, p.220.
[420] *Re Yagerphone Ltd* [1935] Ch. 392; and *Willmott v London Celluloid Co* (1886) 31 Ch.D. 425,
affirmed (1887) 34 Ch.D. 147. Prior to the Insolvency Act 1985, no statutory provisions
existed for the avoidance of transactions at an undervalue. In the case of an individual, s.42
of the Bankruptcy Act 1914 provided for the avoidance of settlements made within the two
years preceding the bankruptcy but there was no comparable rule in winding up.
[421] *Re M.C. Bacon Ltd (No.2)* [1990] B.C.C. 430; *Re Yagerphone* cited above n.420; and *Willmott
v London Celluloid Co*, cited above n.420. See also *Re Oasis Merchandising Services Ltd*
[1996] 1 All E.R. 1009, a decision on the application of the fruits of a claim to contribution
for wrongful trading under s.214 of the Insolvency Act.
[422] See above, paras 6–33 et seq.
[423] [1991] Ch. 127 at 137. See also Oditah, *Legal Aspects of Receivables Financing*, 2008, p.219.
[424] Insolvency Act 1986 s.238.
[425] Insolvency Act 1986 s.244.

follows that the defendant cannot assert a right of set-off in respect of a cross-claim against the company, for example, for repayment of a loan, for there is no mutuality and, moreover, the claim against the defendant is a post-liquidation claim and rights of set-off are determined as at the date of liquidation.[426] It follows also that directors against whom a claim is made by a liquidator under s.214 of the Insolvency Act cannot claim contribution against insolvency practitioners for negligent advice given to the company, for the claim under s.214 is vested in the liquidator, not the company, so that the insolvency practitioners and the directors are not under a common liability for the purpose of the Civil Liability (Contribution) Act 1978.[427] By contrast, a potential contribution claim might arise in proceedings under s.212 of the Insolvency Act for breaches of duty by the directors and the insolvency practitioners.[428]

All of these cases assume that what is recovered by the liquidator either was never the property of the chargee or ceased to be so prior to the winding up as the result of the fact that the transfer in question overrode the charge. In such a case, the chargee is not entitled to use the avoidance provisions to recover what he had lost or had never had. However, where the charge was not overridden by the transfer and the property transferred is recovered, the charge continues to attach to the recovered property.[429]

14. EXEMPTIONS FOR MARKET AND RELATED CONTRACTS

13–143   The provisions of ss.238, 239 and 423 of the Insolvency Act 1986 do not apply to market contracts to which a recognised investment exchange or recognised clearing house is a party or to a disposition of property in pursuance of such a contract.[430]

15. CRITIQUE OF THE AVOIDANCE PROVISIONS

13–144   From the analysis given above, it will be apparent that the avoidance provisions of the Insolvency Act 1986 are long overdue for reform. Although the

---

[426] A similar position is taken by Dr Rory Derham in his magisterial work *The Law of Set-Off*, 4th edn (Oxford: Oxford University Press, 2010), paras [13.08]–[13.09] and [13.17]–[13.19].

[427] *Re International Championship Management Ltd, Cohen v Davis* [2007] B.C.C. 95.

[428] ibid.

[429] For a development of this point, see Armour, "Transactions at an Undervalue" in Armour and Bennett (eds), *Vulnerable Transactions in Corporate Insolvency*, 2002, paras 2.135 et seq.; and Adrian Walters, "Preferences" in Armour and Bennett, *Vulnerable Transactions in Corporate Insolvency*, 2002, paras 4.102 et seq.

[430] Companies Act 1989 s.165.

broad underlying policies are reasonably clear, there is little coherence in the working out of those policies in the legislation, which remains bound by its historical antecedents. The rules as to transactions at an undervalue and preferences are predicated on the assumption that the purpose of the legislation is not to preserve the anti-deprivation and *pari passu* rules as such but to avoid voluntary transfers which are not made in good faith. Hence the legislation looks not to the fact of loss of value or preference but to the state of mind of those acting on behalf of the company in entering into the transaction under attack. This is in marked contrast to the position in other jurisdictions such as Australia and the United States, where the test of preference is an objective one. The Cork Committee was divided on the issue, a minority favouring the objective test, while the latter adhered to the position that a creditor who exerts pressure should be allowed to retain the fruits of his own diligence. If there is to be any real prospect of improving the position of unsecured creditors, it is necessary to substitute an objective for a subjective test, while on the other hand allowing exemptions for transactions on reasonable commercial terms in the ordinary course of business. Moreover, the preference rules should apply to involuntary, as well as voluntary, dispositions, such as those made pursuant to a court order in contested proceedings. That would have the additional effect of avoiding the risk of unfairness to unsecured creditors that can result from the imposition of a remedial constructive trust or a constructive trust not based on the plaintiff's initial proprietary base.[431]

A strong case can be made out for repealing s.127 of the Insolvency Act, which forces a company to apply to the court in order to be able to continue its business when a petition has been presented against it which may be well founded but may equally be insupportable. There is no good reason for imposing a total statutory paralysis on a company merely because of a winding up petition, particularly since the standard form of order under s.127 allows transactions in the ordinary course of business. It should be sufficient that leave of the court has to be obtained for any transaction not made in the ordinary course of business and on reasonable commercial terms. Finally, thought should be given to rationalising the widely differing periods within which a company must go into liquidation or administration if a transaction is to become void or liable to reversal. It is legitimate to distinguish between transactions in favour of a person connected with the company and other transactions but apart from this a case needs to be made out to show why it is necessary to have a range of time factors running from six months at one end (preferences) to eternity at the other (transactions defrauding creditors). On the way, opportunities that were missed in the enactment of the

---

[431] See Roy Goode, "Property and Unjust Enrichment" in Andrew Burrows (ed.), *Essays on the Law of Restitution* (Oxford: Clarendon Press, 1991), pp.240–244.

Insolvency Act 1986 can be taken to remove the more detailed problems identified long ago in case law.

16. DO COMMON LAW RESTITUTIONARY PRINCIPLES APPLY?

The nature of the issues

13–145   Given that the policy underlying most (but not all) of the avoidance provisions is to reverse unjust enrichment, a question for consideration is whether, and to what extent, the court should apply the principles of unjust enrichment developed by the common law in deciding how its discretion should be exercised. This question is discussed in some detail by Dr Simone Degeling in a most instructive paper,[432] in which she points out that there are two symmetrical unjust enrichment claims, that of the liquidator to recover the asset transferred or its value and that of the transferee by way of counter-restitution of payments he has made and the value added by improvements to the asset, and that while the latter claim may be invoked to reduce the former, the two claims are analytically distinct in that each has to satisfy the criteria for unjust enrichment. That is an important point. Some of the statutory provisions are not themselves based on unjust enrichment and do not give rise to a restitutionary claim but the effects they produce may lead to a cross-claim by the defendant which is restitutionary in character.

There are two main questions to be addressed. The first is whether defences available at common law to a restitutionary claim—estoppel, bona fide purchase and change of position—can be asserted as a defence to a claim under the statutory avoidance provisions. The second is the extent to which a defendant who has a counter-restitutionary claim for unjust enrichment against the insolvent company is entitled to have it satisfied, whether by payment, set-off or otherwise, instead of being left to prove in the liquidation as an unsecured creditor. [433]

---

[432] "Restitution for Vulnerable Transactions" in Armour and Bennett, *Vulnerable Transactions in Corporate Insolvency*, 2002, Ch.9.

[433] See Roy Goode, "The Avoidance of Transactions in Insolvency Proceedings and Restitutionary Defences" in Andrew Burrows and Lord Rodger of Earlsferry (eds), *Mapping the Law: Essays in Memory of Peter Birks* (Oxford: Oxford University Press, 2006), p.299, exploring some of these issues. The present analysis departs in some respects from what was said there.

The nature of a restitutionary remedy

Restitution is a remedy given to reverse unjust enrichment, that is, to restore **13–146** gains improperly made by one person at the expense of another, typically by transfer of an asset from the latter's estate or "subtractive enrichment".[434] The remedy may be either proprietary or personal. However, it is necessary to distinguish a pure property claim from a claim based on subtractive unjust enrichment. In the case of the former, the claimant recovers his asset not because of any unjust enrichment of the defendant but because the asset belonged to him prior to the subtraction and still belongs to him. It was previously thought that while this was true of a claim to the original asset, it was not true of proceeds of its realisation by the defendant, for what is traced is not the thing itself but its value.[435] However, the effect of the controversial decision of the House of Lords in *Foskett v McKeown*[436] that a claim to proceeds of the claimant's asset is a pure property claim greatly restricts the scope of restitutionary proprietary remedies. The claimant, said Lord Millett, is entitled to succeed on the basis of his title under property law and not by way of reversal of unjust enrichment. Property rights are determined by fixed rules and settled principles, are not discretionary and do not depend on what is fair, just and reasonable.[437] It follows, of course, that defences to an unjust enrichment claim are not available as an answer to a claim based on title to an asset or its proceeds.

Character of the statutory provisions

The statutory provisions under review are ss.127, 238, 239, 245 and 423 of the **13–147** Insolvency Act 1986 and s.874 of the Companies Act 2006. These fall into three groups[438]: provisions rendering the transaction irretrievably void, namely s.245 of the Insolvency Act and s.874 of the Companies Act; provisions rendering a post-petition disposition void unless authorised or validated by the court,

---

[434] There is controversy over the question of whether the law of unjust enrichment is confined to subtractive enrichment or whether it also encompasses enrichment through a wrong which does not necessarily cause a transfer from the claimant's estate. See, e.g. Andrew Burrows, *Law of Restitution*, 3rd edn (Oxford: Oxford University Press, 2011), pp.10–12 and Chs 23–27; Graham Virgo, *Principles of the Law of Restitution* (Oxford: Oxford University Press, 2006), p. 429., The late Professor Peter Birks originally favoured the inclusion of enrichment through wrongs but towards the end of his life abandoned this position, taking the view that restitution for wrongs did not belong to the law of unjust enrichment at all (see Birks, *Unjust Enrichment*, 2nd edn (Oxford: Clarendon Press, 2005), pp.21 et seq.). This debate need not concern us since those of the statutory provisions that have a restitutionary base all involve subtractive enrichment.
[435] Lionel Smith, *Law of Tracing* (Oxford: Clarendon Press, 1997), p.15.
[436] [2001] A.C. 102.
[437] *Foskett v McKeown*, cited above n.436, at 127.
[438] We can ignore s.244 of the Insolvency Act relating to extortionate credit bargains, which is based on a generalised concept of unfairness.

namely s.127 of the Insolvency Act; and provisions for the reversal of the effect of a transaction, namely ss.238, 239 and 423 of the Insolvency Act.

Provisions rendering the transaction void

13–148   Except in relation to cross-claims, the first two groups referred to above can be eliminated from our enquiry because they are not based on unjust enrichment—the defendant may, indeed, have given full value—and to the extent that any remedy needs to be exercised to give effect to them it is a pure property remedy, not a restitutionary remedy. In all these cases, the statutory avoidance is automatic and self-executing in that its effect is that the creditor never acquired any beneficial ownership of the property in the first instance. Only in two cases will it be necessary for the liquidator to seek recovery. The first is where the asset is land in respect of which a conveyance has been executed, for although the disposition is ineffective to pass the beneficial interest, the legal title passes by the conveyance, the transferee holding as bare trustee for the company, which is entitled to call for a reconveyance.[439] The second is where, in the case of other kinds of asset, the transferee has realised the asset or, in the case of goods, they have been removed from the company's possession. In both of these cases, the question of restoration to the company arises, and the claim of the administrator or liquidator, whether in respect of the asset or its proceeds, will then be a pure property claim, not a restitutionary claim,[440] so that defences available under the law of restitution will not apply.

In *Re Tain Construction Ltd*[441] Mr Nicholas Warren Q.C., sitting as a deputy High Court judge, held in relation to a claim under s.127 of the Insolvency Act that a defence of change of position could not be entirely ruled out as a defence,[442] although on the facts of that case he held it to be inapplicable. In reaching this conclusion, he relied on the fact that whereas ss.238 and 239 prescribe the remedies that the court can award, s.127 does not but leaves the remedy to the general law. However, the point that any right of recovery under s.127 would be a pure property claim and as such not susceptible to defences available to a restitutionary claim does not appear to have been raised. So-called "disenrichment" is not, and should not, be a factor relevant to s.127, which is concerned to preserve the company's assets for the general body of creditors. To allow change of position as a defence would be to give preferential treatment to the defendant without there necessarily being any corresponding benefit to the other creditors. Moreover, it is hard

---

[439] *Re French's Wine Bar*, [1987] 3 B.C.C. 173.
[440] However, the creditor may have a claim for the recovery of transaction-related cross-claims. See below, paras.13–151 et seq.
[441] [2003] 1 W.L.R. 2791; [2003] 2 B.C.L.C. 374 sub. nom. *Re Tain Construction Ltd, Rose v AIB Group (UK) Plc.*
[442] *Tain Construction*, cited above n.441, at [41].

to see why the court should be expected to engage in the complexities of the change of position defence when its powers of authorisation or validation provide all the flexibility that is needed.

Similar considerations apply to avoidance under s.245 of the Insolvency Act and s.874 of the Companies Act except that the question of authorisation by the court does not arise, there being no provision for it in s.245, while as regards s.874 the court will not give leave to register an unregistered charge out of time once winding up or administration has commenced.

Provisions for reversal of transactions: ss.238, 239 and 423

We are left with s.238 relating to transactions at an undervalue, s.239 relating to preferences and s.423 concerning transactions defrauding creditors, all of which are restitutionary in character. The last of these, in so far as it confers remedies on the office-holder for the benefit of creditors as opposed to other victims, attracts the same considerations as s.238.   **13–149**

The three main defences to a restitutionary claim at common law are estoppel, bona fide purchase and change of position. Estoppel is of little importance in the law of restitution, for the facts necessary to support it are rarely present and it has anyway been largely superseded by the broader defence of change of position. The defence of bona fide purchase under ss.241(2) and 425(2) is not open to the party dealing with the company, only with that party's transferee. That leaves only the defence of change of position, to which we now turn.

Change of position

It is worth noting two threshold objections to allowing change of position or any other restitutionary defence to a claim under s.238, 239 or 423. The first is that the sections are concerned not with the resolution of claims between private parties but with the protection of creditors in a winding up, and they have the specific policy of protecting the value of the company's assets. The second is that where legislation contains detailed remedial provisions, it is not open to the court to invoke common law rules either to confine the discretion given to the court by the statutory provisions or to bypass restrictions on remedial relief imposed by those provisions.   **13–150**

There is, nevertheless, at least one High Court judgment to the effect that that change of position is a defence to a claim under the above provisions, namely *4Eng Ltd v Harper*.[443] That case involved, amongst other things, the

---

[443] [2010] 1 B.C.L.C. 176.

defendant's transfer of his joint share of property into the name of his wife. Sales J. concluded that, by analogy with claims based on unjust enrichment, the defendant should not be ordered to make a repayment under s.425(1)(d) if he had a bona fide change of position in reliance on the security of his receipt of money in a way that would make it unfair to require him to make repayment. However, this overlooks the point made above, that while ss.238, 239 and 423 are designed to provide a restitutionary remedy they are driven by a specific policy, namely the restoration of value to the company for the benefit of its creditors, which overrides the standard rules governing unjust enrichment as between two parties to a private transaction. Change of position *per se* should not be identified as a defence to a claim under s.425, for it does nothing to mitigate the loss suffered by the general body of creditors as the result of the fraudulent transaction. We have seen that the protection given by s.425(2) to a transferee in good faith, for value and without notice of the relevant circumstances does not apply to a transferee from the debtor itself. This clearly demonstrates that the overriding concern is to ensure that asset value is not lost in the run-up to liquidation, even if this causes hardship to a wholly innocent counterparty. Acts of reliance by the creditor on the validity of the transaction should therefore be regarded as *res inter alios acta* and irrelevant to claims under the above provisions except so far as they found a right to counter-restitution (for example, for the value of improvements to the transferred property), in which case they can be invoked for that purpose, not to support a defence of change of position. For the same reason, change of position ought only exceptionally to be a factor to be taken into account by the court in the exercise of its discretion. If no protection is given even to a bona fide purchaser for value without notice, it is hard to see why a party who has changed his position should be treated differently. Sections 238(5) and 241(2), together with s.425(2), provide the only defences to a claim otherwise made out and the purpose of the discretion is not to allow the court to take account of hardship to the transferee but simply to ensure that the remedy is tailored to the purpose specified in s.238(3), namely "restoring the position to what it would have been if the company had not entered into that transaction". The court has all of the discretionary powers it needs for that purpose without locking itself into rules on change of position developed to meet common law restitutionary claims.[444] Moreover, those powers are exercisable in the interests of the creditors as a whole, so that common law principles of unjust enrichment relevant to a relationship between two parties would often be inappropriate, since they could have the effect of giving a party relying on change of position an unfair advantage over the general body of creditors.

---

[444] See *Tain Construction*, cited above n.441.

Counter-restitution: return of the consideration[445]

A party entering into a transaction with the insolvent company which is void **13–151** or liable to be set aside under the Insolvency Act provisions will naturally expect to be given back the consideration he furnished under the transaction. Such a claim, which is by way of counter-restitution, will be little value if it is a purely personal claim for which he is restricted to a right of proof in the liquidation in competition with other creditors. The only ways in which the solvent party can be protected are through (a) the imposition by the court of a condition making the grant of relief by the liquidator dependent on the return of the benefits received by the company under the avoided transaction or (b) a proprietary claim. It is once again necessary to distinguish counter-restitution in cases within ss. 238, 239 and 423 from that avilable in cases caught by s. 127.

Return of the consideration: : ss.238, 239 and 423

Let us take first a claim for recovery of property under s.238, 239 or 423. **13–152** It should go without saying that return of the property which is a matter of judicial discretion, will only be ordered on terms of repayment by the liquidator of the purchase price and any other consideration given for the property, for example, the assumption or discharge of the company's liabilities as part of the deal. It is not the function of s.238, 239 or 423 to give the creditors a windfall at the expense of the transferee. What is required is restoration of the status quo. This does not depend on the common law of unjust enrichment, which is concerned with relations between two parties: it is a power given to the court by the express terms of the above sections for the benefit of the general body of creditors, and its exercise will be tailored accordingly.

Return of the consideration: s. 127

In the case of transfers void under s.127 the position is somewhat different, **13–153** for the section says nothing about the effects of the invalidation, nor does it confer any powers on the court to address the consequences of the invalidity, so that the matter remains governed by the common law. We can start with the case where the offending disposition consists of a sale of property by the company for an agreed price which has been paid. We have seen that s.127 is self-executing in that its effect, absent authorisation or ratification by

---

[445] Counter-restitution for improvements is discussed below, para. 13–154.

the court,[446] is that the asset in question remains in the beneficial ownership of the company, and all the office-holder has to do is get back the legal title, which the buyer as bare trustee is duty bound to restore. But the buyer has paid the price for an asset to which he has not in the event acquired title. Clearly, he cannot have a proprietary restitutionary claim to the property he had mistakenly thought he had bought, for this would completely undermine s.127. It is equally clear that he has at least a personal restitutionary cross-claim for recovery of the price as paid on a total failure of consideration. But such a claim has always been regarded as purely personal, save in exceptional cases not relevant here.[447] Yet restricting the buyer to a right of proof would be unjust, for it would mean that the company has both the property and the price, and whereas if both claim and cross-claim were monetary the buyer's position would be alleviated by his right of set-off, no question of set-off can arise as between a money claim and a proprietary claim.[448] Thus, if the buyer has only a personal restitutionary claim, the effect is that the company and its other creditors, including secured creditors whose charge covers the property and the money received for it, is unjustly enriched in that the company, and through the company its creditors, are twice as well off in relation to the transaction as it would have been if the transaction had not taken place.

Fortunately the buyer is not restricted to a personal remedy, because as the transaction has not been effective he is entitled to an equitable lien on the property to secure the return of the price he has paid.[449] The same situation obtains in the converse case where it is the company that has paid money to acquire property under a transaction void under s.127 and not validated by the court. The company will have an equitable lien to secure the return of its payment. The lien carries with it the right to a declaration of charge and an order for sale and payment out of the proceeds of sale.[450]

Counter-restitution: improvements

13–154   Suppose that the defendant received property from the company under the impeached transaction and has added value to property ordered to be retransferred, as by making improvements to it. Where return of the property is sought under s.238, 239 or 423 then again it is unnecessary to resort to rights of counter-restitution in the general law, for the court has all the

---

[446] In practice, the court would no doubt in the ordinary way be willing to validate the disposition if for full value, and if it were at an undervalue a validating order could presumably still be made but subject to a condition that the shortfall was made good.

[447] Andrew Burrows, *Law of Restitution*, 3rd ed 2011, pp.399 et seq.

[448] See above, para.9–26.

[449] *Chattey v Farndale Holdings Inc* (1998) 75 P. & C.R. 298; *Rose v Watson* (1864) 10 H.L.C. 671.

[450] Kevin Gray and Susan Francis Gray, *Elements of Land Law*, 5th ed. (Oxford: Oxford University Press, 2009), para. 6.1.47.

discretionary powers it needs under those provisions. In the absence of unusual circumstances return of the property to the company should be ordered only on terms of payment to the transferee of the value added by the improvement.[451] Alternatively the court can make an order for payment of the value the property would have had without the improvement. Where the ground of impeachment is s.127 there are no relevant statutory provisions governing the consequences of invalidity and the transferee should be accorded a proprietary restitutionary claim for the value added by the improvement, as a condition of return of the property or the execution of a reconveyance to the company, in order to restore the status quo.

---

[451] See *Weisgard v. Pilkington* [1995] B.C.C. 1108, where the respondents were given liberty to apply for an order for payment by the liquidator of any amount shown to have been expended on improvements. As Degeling points out (above, n. 432) at para. 9.71, this approach was incorrect, the appropriate figure being the value added by the improvements, not the amount expended on them. But the essential point was the willingness of the judge to recognise the availability of a restitutionary remedy.

Chapter 14

Improper Trading and the Duties and Liabilities of Directors

Introduction

English law has had a long tradition of indulgence towards directors of com‑   **14–01**
panies. Honesty and the observance of fiduciary obligations of good faith,
including subordination of a director's own interests to those of his company,
have always been required. But the level of prudence, care and skill expected
of a director in the conduct of the company's business has generally been low,
so that directors of failed companies who could not be demonstrated to have
acted dishonestly were rarely held to account because their negligence or
incompetence brought ruin of their company. That has now changed with the
enactment of the Companies Act 2006, which codifies the duties of directors.[1]

Over the past two decades there has been a marked change in the climate
of opinion, indeed a sense of outrage that it had become all too easy for
directors of a company to obtain credit, milk the company of its assets, drive
it into insolvency and then, with brazen effrontery, set up a new "phoenix"
company with a similar name engaged in the same type of business to take
over the assets of the insolvent at a knock-down price and even offer to
complete its unfulfilled engagements for an extra payment. Moreover, there
was concern that the law, while addressing fraudulent trading, did little to
promote reasonable standards of care and diligence in the conduct of busi‑
ness, particularly where companies had reached the point where insolvent
liquidation was unavoidable.

The first fruits of public pressure for reform came with the enactment of
the Insolvency Act 1976, which provided for the disqualification of a person
who had acted as director of two companies one of which went into insolvent
liquidation within five years of the other and whose conduct in the manage‑
ment of one of them made them unfit to be concerned in the management

---

[1] Companies Act 2006 Pt 10, Ch.2.

of a company.[2] Six years later came the Cork Report,[3] which drew attention to the inadequacies of the law relating to fraudulent trading and recommended the introduction of a new concept of wrongful trading which did not require a fraudulent intent,[4] and also a wider range of grounds for disqualifying delinquent directors.

This chapter is concerned with the liabilities of directors of a company which goes into insolvent liquidation where they have been guilty of misfeasance or breach of fiduciary or other duty to the company or of improper trading, whether fraudulent or merely wrongful.

Duties to the company and duties to creditors

14–02   It is important to distinguish claims vested in the company for breach of duty from claims which a liquidator may bring for the benefit of creditors under ss.213 (fraudulent trading) and 214 (wrongful trading). Claims vested in the company, whether for loss suffered through fraud, negligence, breach of fiduciary duty or otherwise, potentially enure for the benefit of members as well as creditors, so that recoveries are not limited to what is needed to pay off the creditors and if there is a surplus the company becomes solvent again, although this rarely happens in practice. Moreover, since any such recoveries are in right of the company, they form part of its ordinary assets and are susceptible to capture under the after-acquired property clause in a fixed or floating charge. By contrast, recoveries under s.213 or 214 are for the benefit of creditors and, since these provisions are compensatory in nature, not penal,[5] they are in general limited to what is necessary to restore to creditors the loss caused by the fraudulent or wrongful trading and they do not form part of the company's assets capable of capture by a charge.[6] Further, the respondent to a claim under s.213 or 214 cannot assert a right of set-off in respect of a debt owed to him by the company, there being no mutuality.[7] Finally, directors against whom a claim is made under s.213 or 214 cannot join as third parties solicitors or accountants whom they allege to have been negligent in advising the company, because there is no common liability.[8]

As we shall see, contrary to popular belief, it is neither a criminal offence nor a civil wrong for a company to continue trading while insolvent, so long

---

[2] The provisions were originally in s.9 of the Insolvency Act 1976, which was repealed and re-enacted by s.300 of the Companies Act 1985 and is now to be found in more stringent form in s.6 of the Company Directors Disqualification Act 1986. See below, paras 14–57 et seq.

[3] Report of the Review Committee, "Insolvency Law and Practice" (Cmnd. 8558, 1982). The Chairman of the Committee was Sir Kenneth Cork.

[4] ibid., Ch.44.

[5] See below, para.14–52.

[6] See below, para.14–55.

[7] See above, para.13–142.

[8] See above, para.13–142.

as it does not incur new credit with no expectation that this will be repaid when due and the directors take all proper steps to minimise the potential loss to creditors after becoming aware (if it is indeed the case) that there is no reasonable prospect of the company avoiding insolvent liquidation.[9] The directors may properly take the view that it is in the interests of the company and its creditors for the company to trade out of its difficulties. *A fortiori* the directors do not incur any liability for fraudulent or wrongful trading when there is no evidence to show that they knew or ought to have known that there was no reasonable prospect of meeting creditors' claims.[10] But before I turn to the statutory provisions relating to improper trading, it may be helpful to give a brief picture of the duties of directors generally.[11]

1. THE DUTIES OF DIRECTORS: SOME GENERAL OBSERVATIONS

To whom the duties are owed

The director of a company owes duties to the State under the criminal law, to the company of which he is director and in certain conditions must have regard to the interests of creditors, which are enforced through the company.

14–03

Who is treated as a director[12]

De jure and de facto directors

At common law, these duties are imposed both on *de jure* and *de facto* directors, and this applies also to the duties of a director to the company under the Companies Act 2006.[13] A *de jure* director is one who has been validly appointed in accordance with the requirements of the law, and this includes any person occupying the position of a director, by whatever name called.[14] A *de facto* director, or director *de son tort*, is one who acts as

14–04

---

[9] *Secretary of State for Trade and Industry v Taylor* [1997] 1 W.L.R. 407, *per* Chadwick J. at 414.
[10] *Secretary of State for Trade and Industry v Creegan* [2004] B.C.C. 835.
[11] Many of the statutory liabilities of directors are imposed also on other officers of the company but for brevity the term "directors" will be used to include officers where appropriate.
[12] For a comprehensive treatment, see Adrian Walters and Malcolm Davis-White Q.C., *Directors' Disqualification and Insolvency Restrictions*, 3rd edn (London: Sweet & Maxwell, 2009), paras 3–16 et seq. See also below, paras 14–32 et seq., discussing who is a director for the purpose of the wrongful trading provisions.
[13] Companies Act 2006 s.170(5).
[14] This is now enshrined in a number of enactments. See Companies Act 2006 s.250; Insolvency Act 1986 s.251; and Company Directors Disqualification Act 1986 s.22(4).

a director although not (or not validly) appointed as such.[15] The concept is not dissimilar to that of an executor *de son tort*, one who by intermeddling without authority in the administration of a deceased person's estate incurs the same responsibilities and liabilities as if he were a duly appointed executor. But a person is not a *de facto* director where there are directors in place and he performs acts which are referable to some other capacity, such as employee; to be a *de facto* director a person must either be the sole person conducting the management or someone who is on equal footing with the de jure or other *de facto* directors.[16] Another way of putting it is that the person concerned must undertake functions which can only be performed by a director.[17] Facts held to be evidence that a person was a *de facto* director include: sharing responsibility for management[18]; having charge of or monitoring the company's trading[19]; controlling the company's bank account and deciding which creditors should be paid[20]; and being held out by the company as a director and using the title of director.[21] It is necessary that the person concerned should have real influence over the affairs of the company but not necessarily over the whole field of its corporate activities.[22] Even if no one factor is sufficient to show that a person was a *de facto* or shadow director, the cumulative effect of all of the factors may show this.[23] A person who does not in fact perform the functions of a director is not to be treated as a *de facto* director merely because he is in a position, through his control of a *de jure* director, to influence the management of the company.[24] Similarly, a person who is a director of a corporate director of a company is not on that account alone a *de facto* director of the company, even if he is the guiding mind of the

---

[15] *Re Canadian Land Reclaiming and Colonising Co: Coventry and Dixon's Case* (1880) 14 Ch.D. 660. According to Millett J. in *Re Hydrodam (Corby) Ltd* [1994] B.C.C. 161, a *de facto* director must claim or purport to be a director or be held out as a director but this additional element is unnecessary and in subsequent cases it has been held sufficient that the person concerned acted as director although not holding himself out as such (*Revenue & Customs Commissioners v Holland* [2010] 1 W.L.R. 2793; and *Secretary of State for Trade and Industry v Hollier* [2007] B.C.C. 11). Conversely, the mere fact that a person is held out as a director does not make him a *de facto* director if he has not acted as such (*Re Gemma Ltd* [2008] B.C.C. 812).

[16] *Re Richborough Furniture Ltd* [1996] B.C.C. 155; and *Secretary of State for Trade and Industry v Hickling* [1996] B.C.C. 678.

[17] *Re Hydrodam (Corby) Ltd* [1994] 2 B.C.L.C. 180, *per* Millet J. at 182.

[18] *Re Moorgate Metals Ltd* [1995] B.C.L.C. 698.

[19] *Re Tasbian Ltd (No.3)* [1992] B.C.C. 358; and *Re a debtor (No.87 of 1993) (No.2)* [1996] B.C.L.C. 63.

[20] *Re Tasbian Ltd (No.3)* cited above n.19.

[21] *Secretary of State for Trade v Tjolle* [1998] 1 B.C.L.C. 333. For reviews of the authorities, see the speech of Lord Collins in *Holland*, cited above n.15, and the judgments of Robert Walker L.J. in *Re Kaytech International Plc, Secretary of State for Trade and Industry v Kaczer* [1999] 2 B.C.L.C. 351 at 420 et seq.; and Sir Donald Rattee in *Secretary of State for Trade and Industry v Becker* [2003] 1 B.C.L.C. 555.

[22] *Re Lo-Line Electric Motors Ltd* [1988] Ch. 477, *per* Sir Nicolas Browne-Wilkinson at 489.

[23] *Re Tasbian Ltd (No.3)* [1991] B.C.C. 435, affirmed [1992] B.C.C. 358.

[24] *Re Mercury Solutions Ltd* [2009] B.C.C. 190.

corporate director.[25] This follows from the fact that a company has a legal personality distinct from that of its members and directors.[26]

Where a *de jure* director resigns but remains involved in the management, the onus lies on him to show that his role and functions have changed so that he is no longer acting as director; resignation as a mechanism for shuffling off the title of director is therefore ineffective.[27]

Shadow director

To the two common law categories of *de jure* and *de facto* director, statute added a third, namely a shadow director, that is, a person in accordance with whose directions or instructions the directors of the company are accustomed to act.[28] Such a person was described by Millett J. as one who "lurks in the shadows",[29] but a person can be a shadow director even if he acts openly in giving instructions[30] or in acting through the *de jure* directors, as where he is a controlling shareholder resident abroad who acts through a local board of directors and takes no steps to hide the part he plays in the affairs of the company.[31] This does not mean that all of the directors have to so act. It suffices that the majority of the board does so. Accordingly, the fact that one director is inactive does not preclude a person in accordance with whose directions the other directors are accustomed to act from being a shadow director. The difference between a *de facto* director and a shadow director is that the former acts himself as if he were a director, whereas the latter influences the management of the company by acting through the *de jure* or *de facto* directors.[32] It is necessary to show both that the person alleged to be a shadow

14–05

---

[25] *Holland*, cited above n.15, in which the various authorities are reviewed, particular importance being attached to the dcision of Millett J. in *Re Hysdrodam (Corby) Ltd* [1994] B.C.L.C. 180. The decision in *Holland* was a majority decision, Lords Walker and Clarke dissenting.

[26] *Holland*, cited above n.15.

[27] *Secretary of State for Business, Enterprise and Regulatory Reform v Poulter* [2009] B.C.C. 608.

[28] Companies Act 2006 s.251(1), re-enacting the Companies Act 1985 s.741(2), Insolvency Act 1986 s.251 and Company Directors Disqualification Act 1986 s.22(5). A person is not deemed to be a shadow director by reason only that the directors act on advice given by him in a professional capacity (ibid). A parent company is not a shadow director for the purposes of the Companies Act 2006 by reason only that the directors of the subsidiary are accustomed to act in accordance with its directions or instructions (Companies Act 2006 s.251(3)), but this does not apply in relation to the Insolvency Act 1986—see below, n.40).

[29] *Re Hydrodam (Corby) Ltd* [1994] 2 B.C.L.C. 180 at 183.

[30] *Secretary of State for Trade and Industry v Deverell* [2001] Ch. 340, *per* Morritt L.J. at [36].

[31] *Ultraframe (UK) Ltd v Fielding* [2006] F.S.R. 17.

[32] It has been said that he "lurks in the shadows" (*Re Lo-Line Electric Motors*, cited above n.22, *per* Millett J. at 183), but it has since been held that this is not necessary and that a person can be a shadow director who quite openly acts through the de jure directors, as where he is controlling a shareholder resident abroad who acts through a local board of directors and takes no steps to hide the part he plays in the affairs of the company (*Deverell*, cited above n.30, *per* Morritt L.J. at [36]). For a view that *Deverell* fails accurately to distinguish de facto and shadow directors, see Chris Noonan and Susan Watson, "The Nature of Shadow Directorship: Ad Hoc Statutory Intervention or Core Company Law Principle?" (2006) J.B.L. 763.

director gave instructions from time to time to the *de jure* or *de facto* directors and that they were accustomed to act in accordance with those instructions. Only when instructions are translated into action by the board does the question of a shadow directorship arise.[33]

The view expressed by Millett J. that the categories of *de jure, de facto* and shadow director are mutually exclusive,[34] although likely to be true in most cases, has not been endorsed in subsequent cases as being of universal application.[35] It is possible to envisage circumstances in which a *de jure* or *de facto* director also fits the definition of shadow director. For example, a person may assume the functions of a director as regards one part of the company's activities and give directions to the board as regards another.[36] However, while the instructions or directions do not need to cover the whole of the company's activities, they must cover at least those matters essential to the corporate governance of the company, including control of its financial affairs.[37]

The locus classicus for the meaning of "shadow director" is the judgment of Morritt L.J. in *Secretary of State for Trade and Industry v Deverell*[38]:

"I propose to express my conclusions on these and other issues in a number of propositions. (1) The definition of a shadow director is to be construed in the normal way to give effect to the parliamentary intention ascertainable from the mischief to be dealt with and the words used. In particular, as the purpose of the Act is the protection of the public and as the definition is used in other legislative contexts, it should not be strictly construed because it also has quasi-penal consequences in the context of the Company Directors Disqualification Act 1986. I agree with the statement to that effect of Sir Nicolas Browne-Wilkinson V-C in *In re Lo-Line Electric Motors Ltd* [1988] Ch 477, 489. (2) The purpose of the legislation is to identify those, other than professional advisers, with real influence in the corporate affairs of the company. But it is not necessary that such influence should be exercised over the whole field of its corporate activities. I agree with the statements to that effect of Finn J in *Australian Securities Commission v AS Nominees Ltd*, 133 ALR 1, 52–53 and Robert Walker LJ in *In re Kaytech International plc* [1999] BCC 390, 402. (3) Whether any particular communication from the alleged shadow director, whether by words or conduct, is to be classified as a direction or instruction must be objectively ascertained by the court in the light of all the evidence. In that connection I do not accept that it is necessary to prove the understanding or expectation of either giver or receiver. In many, if not most, cases it will suffice to prove the communication and its conse-

---

[33] *Ultraframe*, cited above n.31, at [1278].
[34] See *Re Hydrodam (Corby)* cited above n.29.
[35] *Re Mea Corp* [2007] B.C.C. 288; *Re Kaytech International Plc* [1999] 2 B.C.L.C. 351; and *Secretary of State for Trade and Industry v Becker* [2003] 1 B.C.L.C. 555, *per* Sir Donald Rattee at [24].
[36] *Re Mea Corp* cited above n.35, *per* Lewison J. at [89].
[37] *Deverell*, cited above n.30, at [34].
[38] *Deverell*, cited above n.30, at [35].

quence. Evidence of such understanding or expectation may be relevant but it cannot be conclusive. Certainly the label attached by either or both parties then or thereafter cannot be more than a factor in considering whether the communication came within the statutory description of direction or instruction. (4) Non-professional advice may come within that statutory description. The proviso excepting advice given in a professional capacity appears to assume that advice generally is or may be included. Moreover the concepts of 'direction' and 'instruction' do not exclude the concept of 'advice' for all three share the common feature of 'guidance'. (5) It will, no doubt, be sufficient to show that in the face of 'directions or instructions' from the alleged shadow director the properly appointed directors or some of them cast themselves in a subservient role or surrendered their respective discretions. But I do not consider that it is necessary to do so in all cases. Such a requirement would be to put a gloss on the statutory requirement that the board are 'accustomed to act' 'in accordance with' such directions or instructions. It appears to me that Judge Cooke, in looking for the additional ingredient of a subservient role or the surrender of discretion by the board, imposed a qualification beyond that justified by the statutory language."

A company may be a director *de jure* or *de facto*[39] or may be a shadow director. So it is possible, for example, for a company to be treated as the *de facto* director or shadow director of its subsidiary. But a parent company is not taken to be a director, or to be responsible on other grounds for the management of its subsidiary, merely because as parent it controls the composition of the subsidiary's board of directors or because members of the parent board are also directors of the subsidiary or because the parent imposes on the subsidiary budgetary rules or operational guidelines within which the subsidiary is required to conduct its business or stipulates that certain decisions taken by the directors of the subsidiary exercising their own independent discretion and judgment require the parent's approval.[40] More direct assumption of the day-to-day running of the business is required before the parent can be treated as a director of the subsidiary, and assertions that a company is a *de facto* director of its subsidiary are infrequently made and rarely successful.[41] The fact that

---

[39] *Re Bulawayo Market & Offices Co Ltd* [1907] 2 Ch. 458. However, the company must have at least one director who is a natural person (Companies Act 2006 s.155).

[40] *Re Hydrodam (Corby)*, cited above n.29. It should be noted that since the term "shadow director" is defined in s.251 of the Insolvency Act 1986, the provisions of that section applying what is now s.251(3) of the Companies Act 2006 (under which a parent company is not a shadow director of its subsidiary merely because the directors of the subsidiary are accustomed to act in accordance with the parent's directions or instructions) do not apply for the purposes of the Insolvency Act 1986.

[41] English company law has not yet adapted to the concept of group trading. The group as such does not constitute a legal entity, although for certain tax purposes it may be treated as such. Each member of the group is a distinct legal person and the directors of a subsidiary are required to have regard solely to the interests of the subsidiary in running its business and not to those of the parent or of co-subsidiaries.

Company B is a director of Company A does not by itself make the directors of Company B *de facto* or shadow directors of Company A.[42]

2. THE DUTIES OF DIRECTORS UNDER THE CRIMINAL LAW

14–06 A director must observe the criminal law in the performance of his functions. Criminal sanctions may be imposed for causing or procuring the company to commit an offence at common law (for example, conspiracy to defraud) or for causing or procuring a company to commit a statutory offence. Examples of statutory offences are the following:

(1) A director guilty of fraudulent trading commits an offence.[43]

(2) A director is guilty of an offence who authorises or permits, participates in, or fails to take all reasonable steps to prevent, a contravention of an enactment in relation to the company.[44]

(3) Where a company commits an offence under the Financial Services and Markets Act 2000 and this is proved to have been committed with the consent or connivance of, or to be attributed to any neglect on the part of, an officer,[45] he also is guilty of that offence.[46]

(4) A director who consents to or connives at an offence committed by a company under certain provisions of the Fraud Act 2006[47] is also guilty of that offence.[48]

(5) A director who with intent to deceive members or creditors of a company about its affairs publishes or concurs in publishing a statement which to his knowledge is or may be misleading, false or deceptive in a material particular commits an offence.[49]

(6) A person who was a director or shadow director of a company going into insolvent liquidation and who without leave of the court becomes a director of, or involved in the management of or carrying on of a business by, another company under (a) a name by which the liquidating company was known in the period of 12 months ending with the day before it went into liquidation or (b) a name so similar in name as to suggest some association with the company in liquidation commits an

---

[42] *Holland*, cited above n.15; and *Re Hydrodam (Corby)*, cited above n.29.
[43] Companies Act 2006 s.993.
[44] Companies Act 2006 s.1121(3).
[45] Which includes a director (Financial Services and Markets Act 2000 s.400(5)).
[46] Financial Services and Markets Act 2000 s.400(1).
[47] i.e. fraud (ss.1–10) and obtaining services dishonestly (s.11).
[48] Fraud Act 2006 s.12.
[49] Theft Act 1968 s.19.

offence,[50] and becomes personally responsible, jointly and severally with the company and others similarly liable, for all debts of the company incurred at a time when he was so involved.[51] The Insolvency Rules provide three exceptions to this liability.[52]

A person unfit to act as a director may be disqualified from so doing whether or not he has been guilty of a criminal offence.[53]

3. THE DUTIES OF DIRECTORS TO THE COMPANY[54]

Relevance to winding up or administration

The directors of a company owe the company various duties, which are summarised below. The existence of these duties is particularly relevant on the winding up or administration of the company in that the liquidator or administrator may bring proceedings in the name of the company for any breach of a director's duties to the company so far as the conduct constituting the breach has not been effectively ratified by its members. For that purpose, a summary remedy is available by way of misfeasance proceedings under s.212 of the Insolvency Act. As we shall see, the ability of members to waive a breach or ratify improper conduct becomes severely circumscribed where the improper acts occur at a time when the company is insolvent.[55] Prior to the Companies Act 2006, the duties of directors were largely governed by the common law and principles of equity. Now they have been codified in and replaced by Ch.2 of Pt 10 of the Companies Act, although many of the provisions are based on the rules of common law and equity and, indeed, provide for their interpretation by reference to those rules.

14–07

---

[50] Insolvency Act 1986 s.216. This provision is aimed in particular at directors who establish "phoenix" companies (where a new company is formed with a similar name under the same management and assets are transferred to the new company, often at an undervalue, leaving the old company as a valueless shell), although the provision is not confined to phoenix companies. See Carl Werner, "Phoenixing—Avoiding the Ashes" (2009) *Insolvency Intelligence* 105. As to similarity of name, see *First Independent Factors & Finance Ltd v Mountford* [2008] B.C.C. 598.

[51] Insolvency Act 1986 s.217. However, since the applicant for leave has not necessarily been guilty of any misconduct himself, his application should not be approached in the same way as an application for leave under s.17 of the Company Directors Disqualification Act 1986 (*Penrose v Official Receiver* [1996] 2 All E.R. 96).

[52] Insolvency Rules 1986 rr.4.228–4.230. The Court of Appeal, affirming the decision at first instance, has held that r.4.228 cannot be applied retrospectively (*Churchill v First Independent Factors & Finance Ltd* [2007] B.C.C. 45).

[53] See paras 14–57 et seq. Acting while disqualified is itself a criminal offence. See para.14–82.

[54] For a comprehensive treatment, see Paul Davies (ed.), *Gower and Davies' Principles of Modern Company Law*, 8th edn (London: Sweet & Maxwell, 2008), Ch.16; *Gore-Browne on Companies* (Bristol: Jordan Publishing, 2010), Ch.15; and *Boyle and Birds' Company Law*, 7th edn (Bristol: Jordan Publishing, 2009), Ch.16.

[55] See below, para.14–19.

Executive and non-executive directors

14–08   An executive director, that is, one who is not merely a member of the board but a full-time employee engaged in day-to-day management of the company, owes two distinct sets of duties, those deriving from his status as director and those imposed on him as an employee participating in day-to-day management, usually under the terms of a service contract. A non-executive director, an outsider brought on to the board by virtue of his general standing or business acumen and devoting only part of his time to the company's affairs (primarily by attending board meetings and reading the relevant papers), owes only the first set of duties. In setting the standard of duty, the courts do not in general distinguish between executive and non-executive directors.[56] A director is not personally liable for negligent advice given by the company unless he assumed personal responsibility for it and that assumption was relied on by the claimant.[57]

The director's duties as director

14–09   A director owes the following general duties to the company in his capacity as director:

(1)   to act in accordance with the company's constitution and only exercise powers for the purposes for which they are conferred[58];

(2)   to promote the success of the company[59];

(3)   to exercise independent judgment[60];

(4)   to exercise reasonable care, skill and diligence[61];

(5)   to avoid conflicts of interest[62];

(6)   not to accept benefits from third parties conferred by virtue of his directorship[63]; and

(7)   to declare an interest in a proposed transaction or arrangement.[64]

There are also various transactions or arrangements which a director may not enter into without the approval of the members. These are not discussed here.

---

[56] See *Dorchester Finance Co Ltd v Stebbing* [1988] B.C.L.C. 488; but see paras 14–11 and 14–13, below. For the role of the non-executive director generally, see B.R. Cheffins, *Company Law: Theory, Structure and Operation* (Oxford: Clarendon Press, 1997), Ch.13.
[57] *Williams v Natural Life Health Foods Ltd* [1998] 1 W.L.R. 830.
[58] Companies Act 2006 s.171.
[59] Companies Act 2006 s.172.
[60] Companies Act 2006 s.173.
[61] Companies Act 2006 s.174.
[62] Companies Act 2006 s.175.
[63] Companies Act 2006 s.176.
[64] Companies Act 2006 s.177.

The general duties imposed on directors by s.172 apply to shadow directors "where, and to the extent that, the corresponding common law rules or equitable principles apply".[65] This implies that the duties of shadow directors are less onerous than those of *de jure* or *de facto* directors.[66]

The director's general duties fall into broadly three groups: the duty to act within his powers; the duty to promote the company's success, and the associated duties of care and skill; and fiduciary duties of a kind similar to those owed by an agent to his principal and embodying in different forms the duty of loyalty. The standards are the same for executive and non-executive directors.[67] The duty will vary according to the size and business of the particular company and the experience or skills that the particular director holds himself out as possessing.[68] A non-executive director cannot be expected to have the detailed knowledge of the company's affairs required of an executive director, but even non-executive directors are required to take reasonable steps to guide and monitor the management of the company.[69]

The consequences of a breach of any of the above duties are not spelled out in the Act but are expressed as being the same as would apply if the corresponding common law rule or equitable principle applied.[70]

(1) Duty to act within his powers

14–10

The director of a company owes a duty to act within the company's constitution and to exercise powers only for the purposes for which they are conferred. Where either of these duties is broken, then unless the resulting transaction is validly ratified by the members, it is liable to be set aside if the other party did not act in good faith, and the directors will be liable for any loss sustained by the company even if they acted in good faith and without negligence.

(2) Duty to promote the success of the company and to exercise reasonable care, skill and diligence

14–11

Section 172(1) sets out the core duty of a company's directors, and these are buttressed by the duties of care, skill and diligence in s.174. The core duty is

---

[65] Companies Act 2006 s.170(5).
[66] See *Ultraframe*, cited above n.31, *per* Lewison J. at [1288], accepting the submission of counsel that a shadow director does not owe fiduciary duties to the company, a decision criticised as "unfortunate" by Paul Davies (ed.), *Gower & Davies: Modern Company Law*, 8th edn (London: Sweet & Maxwell, 2008), para.16–8.
[67] *Dorchester Finance*, cited above n.56.
[68] *Daniels v Anderson* (1995) 16 A.C.S.R. 607.
[69] *Equitable Life Assurance Society v Bowley* [2004] 1 B.C.L.C. 180; and *AWA Ltd v Daniels* (1992) 7 A.C.S.R. 759, affirmed on appeal sub. nom. *Daniels v Anderson*, cited above n.68.
[70] Companies Act 2006 s.178(1).

to act in a way that he considers, in good faith, would be most likely to promote the success of the company for the benefit of its members as a whole, and in doing so to have regard, amongst other things, to the various factors listed in s.172(1). The interests to which the directors have to have regard are those of the company's employees and its members. However, the duty is subject to any enactment or rule of law requiring directors, in certain circumstances, to have regard to the interests of creditors of the company,[71] an important qualification which we shall come to shortly.

A director is required to exercise reasonable care, skill and diligence in the performance of his duties. This duty, previously imposed both at common law and in equity, is not a fiduciary duty.[72] The common law originally tended to pitch the standard of care at a relatively low level, but more recently it had been held that s.214(4) of the Insolvency Act 1986 relating to wrongful trading accurately reflected the standard of a director's duty of care, skill and diligence at common law, so as to require him to take the steps that would be taken by a reasonably diligent person having the general knowledge, skill and experience that may reasonably be expected of a person carrying out the same functions, as well as the general knowledge, skill and experience which the director in fact possesses.[73] This equation of the common law standard with that imposed by s.214(4) has now been given statutory effect by s.174(2) of the Companies Act. A director thus has to meet at least the objective standard as well as any higher standard to be expected from his own knowledge, skill and experience. Accordingly, the case law on the duty of care prior to the Act remains relevant. Thus, a director:

(1)   need not be an expert in the type of business in which his company is engaged, so that it suffices if he used the care and skill of the non-professional reasonable man[74];

(2)   is not required to give his whole time and attention to the company's affairs[75];

(3)   if a non-executive director is entitled to rely on the executive directors and officers of the company, for example, for the accuracy of financial statements presented[76];

---

[71] Companies Act 2006 s.172(3).

[72] *Bristol and West Building Society v Mothew* [1996] 4 All E.R. 698, *per* Millett L.J., citing with approval the judgment of Ipp J. in *Permanent Building Society v Wheeler* (1994) 14 A.C.S.R. 109 at 157–158.

[73] *Re D'Jan of London Ltd* [1993] B.C.C. 646.

[74] *Re City Equitable Fire Insurance Co* [1925] Ch. 407.

[75] *Re City Equitable Fire Insurance Co*, cited above n.74. This reflects the fact that a director is not as such an employee of the company.

[76] *Re City Equitable Fire Insurance Co*, cited above n.74; and *Dovey v Cory* [1901] A.C. 477.

(4)   is entitled to rely on outside advice by a person whom he reasonably believes to be competent to give it, so long as he exercises his own judgment as to such advice[77]; and

(5)   may delegate specific tasks and functions to others, which indeed is almost always essential if the company's business is to be carried on efficiently,[78] but must pass on information in his possession that is relevant both to the need for carrying out the task delegated and the rigour with which it needs to be done.[79]

However, a director must not abdicate involvement or responsibility. He therefore risks liability if: he neglects to attend board meetings; he leaves all decisions to others[80]; he fails to apply his judgment to the advice of outsiders; or signs cheques without inquiry[81] or insurance proposal forms without reading them.[82] Again, where some directors know that one of their number had been convicted of offences involving fraud, they have a duty to be on their guard, and it is no defence that the other directors, who knew nothing of the conviction, would likewise have been bamboozled by the fraudulent director.[83]

(3) Duty to observe fiduciary obligations

Directors must not only act within their powers and those of the company, they must exercise their powers in good faith in the interests of the company and the shareholders as a whole. In particular, they must not misappropriate the company's assets, nor must they usurp for their own advantage corporate opportunities which, if they pursue them at all, should be pursued for the benefit of their company, or otherwise subordinate the company's interests to their own or those of third parties or abuse their powers or position.[84] The fiduciary duties are now encompassed in ss.175 to 177 of the Companies Act 2006 and embody two distinct equitable rules, the "no-profit" rule and the "no-conflict" rule.[85]

14–12

---

[77] *Re Faure Electric Accumulator Co* (1888) 40 Ch.D. 141.
[78] *Re Westmid Packing Services Ltd (No.3)* [1998] B.C.C. 836, *per* Lord Woolf at 842; and *Re Barings Plc (No.5)* [1999] 1 B.C.L.C. 433, *per* Jonathan Parker J. at [B2]. But overall responsibility is not delegable and there is a duty to supervise the discharge of the delegated function (ibid., at paras [B3] and [B7]).
[79] *Lexi Holdings Ltd v Luqman* [2009] B.C.C. 716, *per* Briggs J. at [54]. An appeal on a different point was allowed by the Court of Appeal [2009] 2 B.C.L.C. 1. See below.
[80] *Re Westmid Packing Services Ltd* [1998] 2 B.C.C. 836, *per* Lord Woolf at 842.
[81] *Re City Equitable Fire Insurance Co*, cited above n.74; *Re Faure Electric Accumulator Co*, cited above n.77; and see *Re Majestic Recording Studios Ltd* (1988) 4 B.C.C. 519.
[82] *Re D'Jan of London*, cited above n.73.
[83] *Lexi Holdings Plc v Luqman* [2009] 2 B.C.L.C. 1, reversing on this point the decision of Briggs J. [2008] 2 B.C.L.C. 725.
[84] For further details, the reader is referred to the standard textbooks on company law.
[85] For recent explanations of these, see: *Re Allied Business & Financial Consultants Ltd* [2009] 1 B.C.L.C. 328; and *Ultraframe*, cited above n.31.

The director's duties as an employee-manager

14–13   An executive director must, in addition to discharging his duties *qua* director, fulfil in his capacity as an employee participating in day-to-day management the express and implied terms of his service contract[86] and apply to the performance of his duties that degree of knowledge, care and skill which is reasonably to be expected of a person holding his position as well as that he actually has. A person holding the post of chief executive or managing director will be expected to exercise the care, skill and knowledge appropriate to that office (although obviously the degree of skill and knowledge required will vary with the size and complexity of the company) and any higher skill, etc., he actually possesses.

Proceedings by liquidator or administrator for breach of duty owed to the company

14–14   *The nature of the proceedings*

The liquidator of a company can institute proceedings in the name of the company for any breach of duty by a director in respect of which the company itself could have made a claim prior to the liquidation or administration. Alternatively, where the company is in the course of winding up, s.212 of the Insolvency Act provides a summary remedy against any one of a range of parties (including an existing or former director) who are or have been involved with the promotion, formation or management of the company, where that party has been guilty of misfeasance or of breach of any fiduciary or other duty to the company. In such a case, the liquidator (or the official receiver, a creditor or a contributory) may institute misfeasance proceedings against the director or other party concerned for an order in the winding up for examination of the director and for repayment of the money, return of the property or payment of compensation to the company for the misfeasance.[87] Claims for misfeasance may include not only loss to the company through misappropriation, or through improper payments such as unlawful distributions from capital[88] or wrongful preferences,[89] but also secret profits and other benefits obtained by directors in breach of their fiduciary duties,

---

[86] Which will usually involve his devoting his whole time and attention to the company's affairs.
[87] Insolvency Act 1986 s.212(3). As to the court's power to grant relief, see below, para.14–18.
[88] See Companies Act 2006 s.830.
[89] *West Mercia Safetywear Ltd v Dodd* (1988) 4 B.C.C. 30.

which are assumed to reflect loss to the company,[90] and claims for negligence.[91] Misfeasance is not a distinct wrongdoing, simply a well-worn label, now redundant, which, with the other language of s.212(1), covers any breach of duty by directors causing loss to the company on the basis of which summary proceedings may be instituted in the Companies Court within the liquidation.[92] However, it is limited to breaches of duty by a person in his capacity as an officer of the company, etc. and cannot be used to pursue ordinary claims for debt or breach of contract.[93] The summary procedure under s.212 is not available to an administrator.[94]

Against whom proceedings may be brought

Misfeasance proceedings may be brought against a person who: (i) is or has been an officer of the company; (ii) has acted as liquidator or administrative receiver of the company; or (iii) not being a person within (i) or (ii), is or has been concerned, or has taken part, in the promotion, formation or management of the company.[95] Those covered by (i) include both *de jure* directors and *de facto* directors, but in *Revenue & Customs Commissioners v Holland*,[96]   **14–15**

---

[90] See F. Oditah, *Legal Aspects of Receivables Financing* (London: Sweet & Maxwell, 2008), p.213; and *Re Derek Randall Enterprises Ltd*, [1990] B.C.C. 749. In the latter case, a director who had received for himself commission for which he should have accounted to the company subsequently gave the company's bank a guarantee in support of which he paid into a special blocked account with the bank a sum exceeding that which he had misappropriated. A majority of the Court of Appeal upheld the decision of Millett J. that the effect of the payment was to restore to the company the sum misappropriated, so that it no longer had any loss. Dillon L.J. dissented on the ground that the moneys paid in were represented as those of the director concerned and that they did not in reality benefit the company, for, although they reduced the debt to the bank, the director as surety was entitled to be subrogated *pro tanto* to the bank's claims. The difference of opinion in the Court of Appeal seems to have turned on whether the sum paid in was that which had been misappropriated or was the surety's own money. Millett J. and the majority in the Court of Appeal adopted the former view, and on this basis concluded that the director would not have been subrogated, since it was not his money that was used to support the guarantee and thereby reduce the overdraft. Accordingly, the payment did in fact benefit the company.

[91] As in *Re D'Jan of London*, cited above n.73.

[92] See *Re Continental Assurance Co of London Plc* [2001] B.P.I.R. 733, *per* Park J. at [393], who also pointed out that although s.212 does not create any additional liabilities and obligations, it does confer on the court a measure of discretion as to remedies going beyond what is available at common law, a point also made by Lord Scott in *Stone & Rolls Ltd v Moore Stephens* [2009] 1 A.C. 1391 at [110]. It may be noted that what is now s.212(1) was not always so widely drawn, being limited to misfeasance and breach of trust and therefore applicable only to misfeasance in the nature of a breach of trust resulting in loss to the company (*Re Etic Ltd* [1928] Ch. 861; and *Cavendish Bentinck v Fenn* (1887) 12 App. Cas. 652).

[93] *Re Etic Ltd* cited above n.92.

[94] *Irwin v Lynch* [2010] EWHC 1153 (Ch). However, a similar remedy may be invoked *against* an administrator (Insolvency Act 1986 Sch.B1 para.75).

[95] Insolvency Act 1986 s.212(1). Under para. 75 of Sch B1 to the Act such proceedings may also be taken against an administrator.

[96] [2010] 1 W.L.R. 2793 at [22].

Lord Hope expressed the view that such proceedings may not be brought against shadow directors, because s.212, in contrast to s.214(7), makes no reference to shadow directors. Since in that case it was not contended that the individual in question was a shadow director, Lord Hope's remarks are clearly *obiter*, and it is respectfully submitted that they are not correct. Section 214(1) refers to a person who is or has been a director of the company, so it was felt necessary to insert s.214(7) for the avoidance of doubt. By contrast, s.212(1) is drawn very widely to include any person who is or has been concerned, or has taken part, in the promotion, formation or management of the company. That is surely wide enough to cover a shadow director without the need for specific mention. Moreover, s.212 is purely procedural, so that it would be surprising if a breach of duty by a shadow director were not susceptible to the summary remedy that section provides.

Liquidator's claim is purely derivative

14–16   However, a claim by the liquidator for misfeasance or other breach of duty owed to the company is purely derivative[97]; he can sue only in respect of claims vested in the company and has no rights of action in respect of claims vested in particular creditors or other third parties, for example, for loss suffered by them through the company's fraud or misrepresentation induced by the director concerned.[98] Again, the liquidator does not sue in right of the general body of creditors, as he is considered to do in proceedings for contribution under s.214 of the Insolvency Act[99]; he sues in right of the company,[100] and while this may benefit the general body of creditors by increasing the amount available for distribution, this is not necessarily the case, since any recoveries will in the first instance enure for the benefit of a prior assignee or chargee under a charge covering the money or property recovered.[101] Since the liquidator sues in right of the company, the respondent may join as third parties those against whom he has claims for contribution or indemnity.[102] But the respondent does not have a right to set off against his liability for misfeasance a cross-claim he has against the company, for example, for a debt owed by the company, for a breach of trust or other misfeasance does not

---

[97] Albeit misfeasance proceedings have distinctive characteristics. See F. Oditah, "Misfeasance Proceedings against Company Directors" [1992] L.M.C.L.Q. 207, 210.

[98] *Re Ambrose Tin & Copper Mining Co* (1880) 14 Ch.D. 690.

[99] See above, para.6–37 and below, paras 14–47 and 14–55.

[100] See further para.14–20 as to the position of creditors.

[101] *Re Anglo-Austrian Printing and Publishing Union* [1895] 2 Ch. 891; and see above, para.6–35, and below, para.14–20, text and n.120.

[102] *Cohen v Davis* [2007] 2 B.C.L.C.

constitute a dealing so as to satisfy the requirement of mutual dealings between the respondent and the company.[103]

Orders that can be made

The court may compel a person against whom proceedings have been brought under s.212:

14–17

(1) to repay, restore or account for the money or property misapplied or any part of it, with interest at such rate as the court thinks just; or

(2) to contribute such sum to the company's assets by way of compensation in respect of the misfeasance or breach of fiduciary or other duty as the court thinks just.[104]

Thus, an order under s.212 is in the nature of a class remedy and can be made only in favour of the company, not in favour of an individual creditor.[105]

Relief from liability

Where a director or other officer of the company has been found liable for negligence, default, breach of duty or breach of trust, if the court finds that he has acted honestly and reasonably, and that having regard to all the circumstances of the case (including those connected with his appointment) he ought fairly to be excused, the court may relieve him, either wholly or partly, from his liability on such terms as it thinks fit.[106] But if the conditions for the grant of relief are not satisfied, because the director has not acted honestly and reasonably, the court may still temper the wind to the shorn lamb by limiting the amount to be paid under s.212 to a sum below that which is necessary to remedy the misfeasance.[107] The postulate of a negligent director acting reasonably is a curious one; nevertheless, the section makes it clear that conduct which is negligent at common law may be reasonable for the purpose of s.1157 of the Companies Act 2006.[108]

14–18

---

[103] *Manson v Smith* [1997] 2 B.C.L.C. 161; and *Re Anglo-French Co-operative Society Ex p. Pelly* (1882) 21 Ch.D. 492. In *Manson v Smith*, Millett L.J. gave as a second reason the fact that the liability to the company against which the respondent seeks to assert a right of set-off does not arise until a judgment on the misfeasance claim, which post-dates the date of liquidation, which is the date as at which the mutual dealings are established. However, this point may now be taken care of by the hindsight principle discussed above, para.9–21.

[104] Insolvency Act 1986 s.212(3).

[105] *Kyrris v Oldham* [2004] 1 B.C.L.C. 305.

[106] Companies Act 2006 s.1157.

[107] For a case where this was done, see *Re Loquitur Ltd, Inland Revenue Commissioners v Richmond* [2003] 2 B.C.L.C. 442.

[108] *Re D'Jan of London*, cited above n.73; and *Equitable Life Assurance Society v Bowley* [2004] 1 B.C.L.C. 180. Both cases were decisions on s.727 of the Companies Act 1985, the predecessor of s.1157 of the 2006 Act.

Ratification by the members

14–19   Where the company is solvent and likely to remain so, it is open to its members to approve or ratify what would otherwise have been a breach of duty by the directors, in which case the liquidator has no cause of action to pursue in the company's name.[109] The approval need not be given at a general meeting; it suffices that all of the shareholders with a right to attend and vote at a general meeting had assented.[110] The situation is quite different where the transaction is likely to cause loss to creditors because the company is insolvent at the time of or inconsequence of the breach or (probably) likely to become so, for it is then the creditors, not the members, who have the primary interest in the proper application of the company's assets, so that a purported approval or ratification by the members of a breach of duty by the directors causing loss to the company will be ineffective.[111]

4. DUTIES TO CREDITORS AT COMMON LAW

14–20   In *Winkworth v Edward Baron Development Co Ltd*,[112] Lord Templeman stated that a company owes a duty to future, as well as present, creditors to preserve its assets, but this dictum must, it is thought, be intended to be confined to cases where the company, although solvent at the time of the breach of duty complained of, is unlikely to remain so, and there is accordingly a risk to creditors.[113] Indeed, even in relation to existing creditors, it is important to bear in mind that the duties are owed to them through the company, not directly, and their interests are protected by proceedings in the name of the company to which ratification of the breach of duty by the shareholders is no defence.[114]

---

[109] *Rolled Steel Products (Holdings) Ltd v British Steel Corp* [1986] Ch. 246; and *Multinational Gas and Petrochemical Co v Multinational Gas and Petrochemical Services Ltd* [1983] Ch. 258. But the shareholders cannot effectively ratify acts which are a fraud on the company creditors or are otherwise unlawful. See *Avelin Barford Ltd v Perion Ltd* (1989) 5 B.C.C. 677; *Ridge Securities Ltd v I.R.C.* [1964] 1 W.L.R. 479; *Att-Gen's Reference (No.2 of 1982)* [1984] 1 Q.B. 624; and *Re Halt Garages (1964) Ltd* [1982] 3 All E.R. 1016.

[110] This is the so-called "*Duomatic* principle" from the decision of Buckley J. in *Re Duomatic Ltd* [1969] 2 Ch. 365, which, however, was a principle of long standing.

[111] *Walker v Wimborne* (1976) 50 A.L.J.R. 446; *Re Horlsey & Weight Ltd* [1982] Ch. 442; *Nicholson v Permakraft (NZ) Ltd* [1985] 1 N.Z.L.R. 242; *Kinsela & Am. v Russell Kinsela Pty Ltd* (1986) 10 A.C.L.R. 395; and *Lexi Holdings Plc v Luqman* [2007] EWHC 2652 (Ch), *per* Briggs J. at [191].

[112] [1986] 1 W.L.R. 1512 at 1516.

[113] See *Brady v Brady* [1988] 2 All E.R. 617.

[114] *Miller v Bain* [2002] 1 B.C.L.C. 266; *Sycotex Pty Ltd v Baseler* (1993) 13 A.C.S.R. 766, *per* Gummow J. at 785; and D.D. Prentice, "Creditors' Interests and Directors' Duties" (1990) 10 O.J.L.S. 275.

Loss suffered by individual creditors is not recoverable directly under this head. Their loss and that of other creditors is simply a reflection of the loss caused to the company[115] and the consequent diminution in the assets available for distribution, and their protection lies in the principle of law which (the company being in or near insolvency at the time of or in consequence of the breach of duty) recognises their status as the real owners of the company and thus: (i) requires directors to consider the impact of their actions on the interests of creditors ahead of, although not to the exclusion of, shareholders; and (ii) denies effect to a purported ratification by the shareholders of the conduct constituting the breach of duty. If creditors could sue directly, this would breach both the collective procedure of insolvency and the pari passu rule.[116] So the true principle is not that the directors owe duties to creditors as well as to the company but that when the company is insolvent or approaching insolvency the directors, in discharging their duty to act in the best interests of the company by promoting its success,[117] must have regard predominantly to the interests of creditors,[118] who now have the primary interest in the proper application of the company's assets and whose interest is mediated through the company. Thus while shareholders retain a residual interest that has to be taken into account, high-risk strategies which they might support when the company is in financial trouble in order to attract a high-potential pay-off may have to give way to the interests of creditors in seeing a safer course of action to protect the assets.[119] This point is

---

[115] It thus parallels the principle of reflected loss which debars individual shareholders from asserting claims against a party causing loss to the company solely in their capacity of shareholders and on the basis of a diminution in the value of their shares. The breach is of a duty owed to the company, the loss is that of the company and only the company can sue for it. See *Johnson v Gore Wood & Co* [2002] 2 A.C. 1; *Perry v Day* [2005] B.C.C. 375; *Gardner v Parker* [2005] B.C.C. 46; and *Shaker v Al-Bedrawi* [2003] Ch. 350.

[116] Prentice, Creditors' Interests and Directors' Duties", 1990, cited in *Liquidators of Progen Engineering Pte Ltd v Progen Holdings Ltd* [2010] S.G.C.A. 31 at [52]. See also the interesting article by Andrew Keay, "Directors' Duties to Creditors: Contractarian Concerns Relating to Efficiency and Over-Protection of Creditors" (2003) 66 M.L.R. 665, which notes the general acceptance of the principle that the duty is indirect and cannot be enforced by creditors but goes on to examine the nature and weight of creditors' interests from a law and economics standpoint.

[117] Companies Act 2006 s.172(1). See Andrew Keay, "Office-Holders and the Duty of Directors to Promote the Success of the Company" (2010) 23 Ins. Int. 1; and "Formulating a Framework for Directors' Duties to Creditors: An Entity Maximisation Approach" (2005) 64 C.L.J. 614; and E.M. Iacobucci, "Director's Duties in Insolvency: What Is at Stake?" (2003) 39(3) Can. Bus. L.J. 398 at 400–401.

[118] See the authorities cited in n.111 above and *Facia Footwear Ltd v Hinchcliffe* [1998] B.C.L.C. 218 at 228. S. 172(1) of the Companies Act 2006 has effect subject to any enactment or rule of law requiring directors to consider the interests of the company's creditors (s.172(3)).

[119] *Peoples Department Stores Inc v Wise* (2004) 244 D.L.R. (4th) 564 at [45]. This decision, which also concerns the statutory duties of directors, has attracted widespread interest in Canada, and an entire issue of the *Canadian Business Law Journal* was devoted to a symposium on it. See [2005] Can. Bus. L.J. 167. For a detailed comment on the case after the decision of the Court of Appeal, see Jacob S. Ziegel, "Corporate Governance and Directors' Duties to Creditors: Two Contrasting Philosophies", *Annual Review of Insolvency Law 2003*, p.133.

of particular significance in relation to the application of sums recovered by the liquidator for breach of duty. Recoveries in right of the company form part of its general assets and are thus susceptible to capture under a prior assignment or charge over future property.[120] This is in contrast to recoveries under the statutory provisions designed for the benefit of the general body of creditors.[121]

5. LIABILITY FOR FRAUDULENT TRADING

The statutory provisions

14–21   Reference has already been made to the criminal liability of directors and others for fraudulent trading,[122] which does not depend on the company being in winding up.[123] Running in parallel with this is a civil liability. Under s.213 of the Insolvency Act 1986, if in the course of winding up of a company it appears that any business of the company has been carried on with intent to defraud creditors of the company or creditors of any other person, or for any fraudulent purpose, the court may, on the application of the liquidator, declare that any persons who were knowingly parties to the fraudulent trading are to be liable to make such contributions (if any) to the company's assets as the court thinks proper.

The elements of liability

14–22   To establish liability under s.213, three elements are required, namely that:

(1)   the business of the company has been carried on with intent to defraud creditors, or for some other fraudulent purpose;

(2)   the respondent sought to be made liable participated in the carrying on of the business in that manner; and

(3)   the respondent did so with knowledge that the transaction in which it was participating was intended to defraud creditors or was in some other way fraudulent.[124]

---

[120] A view reluctantly reached by Vaughan Williams J. in *Re Anglo-Austrian Printing and Publishing Union* [1895] 2 Ch. 891.

[121] i.e. all the statutory provisions other than those which declare a transaction void. See above, para.13–140 and below, para.14–55.

[122] Under the Companies Act 2006 s.993. See above, para.14–06.

[123] Companies Act 2006 s.993(2).

[124] *Re Bank of Credit and Commerce International SA, Morris v State Bank of India* [2003] B.C.C. 735, *per* Potter J. at [11].

Persons who may be held liable

Liability, whether criminal or civil, is not confined to directors or others **14–23** involved with the management of the company but is imposed on any person, including a complete outsider, who was knowingly party to the carrying on of the company's business with intent to defraud its creditors. Thus, in *Re Gerald Cooper (Chemicals) Ltd*[125]:

> A company received from a customer advance payment of the price of goods which it knew it would not be able to deliver and utilised the sum received in repayment of a loan from the respondents, thereby disabling itself from either supplying the goods to the buyer or repaying the price. The respondents, having received repayment of their loan with knowledge of these facts, were held liable as parties to fraudulent trading although they had not themselves been involved in the management of the company.

However, a person cannot be a party to fraudulent trading unless the company itself was engaged in fraudulent trading.[126] A curious situation arose in *Morphitis v Bernasconi*,[127] where proceedings under s.213 were taken not only against the directors of the company but also against the company's solicitors, the sole basis of the claim being that the company through its solicitors deceived a creditor's solicitors into believing that a payment would be made when they knew it would not. The directors defended the claim while the solicitors paid £75,000 into court in settlement, this sum being accepted by the liquidator. The decision of the deputy judge that the deceit constituted fraudulent trading was reversed by the Court of Appeal, which held that the offence had not been made out. So had the solicitors not made the payment into court, they would have escaped liability altogether.

Intent to defraud

The statutory provisions do not apply unless the business was carried on with **14–24** intent to defraud. This involves actual dishonesty, not merely blameworthiness.[128] In *Twinsectra Ltd v Yardley*,[129] which concerned a claim against a person for a person to be liable as accessory to a breach of trust, the House of Lords held (Lord Millett dissenting) that it was not sufficient for the defendant's conduct to be dishonest by the ordinary standards of reasonable and honest people, it was also necessary that he should himself have been aware

---

[125] [1978] Ch. 262.
[126] *Re Augustus Barnett & Son Ltd* (1986) 2 B.C.C. 98, 904.
[127] [2003] B.C.C. 540.
[128] *Re Patrick & Lyon Ltd* [1933] Ch. 786; *Re Augustus Barnett & Son Ltd*, above, n.126; and see D.D. Prentice (1987) 103 L.Q.R. 11.
[129] [2002] 2 A.C. 164.

that by those standards he was acting dishonestly. If he had been so aware he was guilty of dishonesty and could be allowed to shelter behind some private standard of honesty not shared by the community.[130] So for the purposes of s.213, robbing Peter to pay Paul would be all right if you genuinely believed that it would not be regarded as dishonest by the standards of reasonable and honest people, although it would not suffice that such conduct met your own private standards of morality if you were aware that the community would regard such conduct as dishonest. However, in *Barlow Clowes Ltd v Eurotrust Ltd*,[131] there was a return to orthodoxy by the Privy Council, which held that the defendant's views about generally acceptable standards of dishonesty were irrelevant and that nothing in the speeches of Lords Hutton and Hoffmann was intended to convey the contrary. It has to be said that the interpretation given by the Privy Council to the speeches of Lords Hutton and Hoffmann in *Twinsectra* is a masterpiece of verbal manipulation which distorts the plain meaning of what they had said, as correctly summarised in the headnote to the Law Reports, and in effect adopts the dissenting speech of Lord Millett. It is not without irony that the Opinion of the Privy Council was given by Lord Hoffmann himself by way of reinterpretation of his own speech in *Twinsectra*! Be that as it may, the Court of Appeal has since adopted the reasoning in *Barlow Clowes*,[132] so that unless the House of Lords reviews the question further, it suffices that conduct regarded as dishonest by the standards of reasonable and honest people will be treated as dishonest even if the defendant genuinely believed that such conduct would not be so regarded.

"Blind-eye" knowledge suffices as dishonesty for this purpose, the test being that stated by Lord Scott in *Manifest Shipping Co Ltd v Uni-Polaris Shipping Co Ltd*[133]:

"In summary, blind-eye knowledge requires, in my opinion, a suspicion that the relevant facts do exist and a deliberate decision to avoid confirming that they exist. But a warning should be sounded. Suspicion is a word that can be used to describe a state-of-mind that may, at one extreme, be no more than a vague feeling of unease and, at the other extreme, reflect a firm belief in the existence of the relevant facts. In my opinion, in order for there to be blind-eye knowledge, the suspicion must be firmly grounded and targeted on specific facts. The deliberate decision must be a decision to avoid obtaining confirmation of facts in whose existence the individual has good reason to believe. To allow blind-eye knowledge to be constituted by a decision not to inquire into an untargeted or speculative suspicion would be to allow negligence, albeit gross, to be the basis of a finding of privity."

---

[130] *Aktieselskabet Dansk Skibsfinansiering v Bros* [2001] 2 B.C.L.C. 324 at 334; and *Royal Brunei Airlines Sdn Bhd v Tan* [1995] 2 A.C. 378.

[131] [2006] 1 W.L.R. 1476.

[132] *Abou-Ramah v Abacha* [2007] 1 Lloyd's Rep. 115.

[133] [2003] 1 A.C. 469 at [116].

The circumstances in which "blind-eye" knowledge of a senior employee can be attributed to his company where they are not known to the board or any of the directors were discussed in some detail by the Court of Appeal in *Morris v Bank of India*,[134] which upheld the decision of Patten J. that whilst in the ordinary way knowledge of dishonesty could be attributed to a company only if it was the knowledge of the board or those specifically authorised by a resolution of the board, the policy underlying s.213 required a special rule of attribution in order to avoid the risk of emasculation of the section. Accordingly, "blind-eye" dishonesty of an employee could be attributed to the company even if it was not the knowledge of the board or a person authorised by the board. Whether it should be so attributed would depend on a range of factors, including the importance or seniority of the employee in the hierarchy of the company, the degree of his freedom to act in the transaction, and the more he is left to get on with it by the board.[135]

The mere provision by a company of financial support for its subsidiary to enable it to trade as a going concern and in so doing incur debts does not constitute fraudulent trading.[136] In *Re White & Osmond (Parkstone) Ltd*,[137] Buckley J. stated that there was nothing wrong in directors incurring credit at a time when, to their knowledge, the company was not able to meet its liabilities as they fell due. What was wrong was allowing a company to continue incurring debts when it was clear that it would never be able to satisfy its creditors:

"... there is nothing to say that directors who genuinely believe that the clouds will roll away and the sunshine of prosperity will shine upon them again and disperse the fog of their depression are not entitled to incur credit to help them get over the bad time."

However, in *R. v Grantham*,[138] this "clouds and sunshine" (or "silver lining") test was disapproved. The question, said the Court of Appeal, was not whether the directors thought that the company would be able to pay its way at some indeterminate time in the future but whether they thought that the company, in incurring further credit, could pay its debts as they fell due or shortly thereafter. If they realised there was no prospect of the company being able to do this, they were guilty of fraudulent trading even if they had some expectation that ultimately all debts would be paid. In general, it is fraudulent trading for a company to obtain new credit, knowing it will be unable to repay it when due, in order to pay off existing creditors.[139]

---

[134] [2005] 2 B.C.L.C. 328. See Adam Cloherty, "Knowledge, Attribution and Fraudulent Trading" (2006) 122 L.Q.R. 25.

[135] *Morris*, above, n.134, at [130].

[136] *Re Augustus Barnett*, cited above n.128.

[137] 1960, unreported but referred to in *R. v Grantham* [1984] 2 All E.R. 166.

[138] Above.

[139] To this extent the mere fact that the net deficiency is reduced by the continued trading, which would be a defence to an allegation of wrongful trading under s.214, provides no answer to a claim under s.213 for fraudulent trading. See further below, para.14–43.

Section 213 is capable of applying even if there is only one defrauded creditor and even if he is defrauded by only one transaction, provided that the fraud was perpetrated in the course of carrying on a business.[140] But not every deception of a creditor constitutes the carrying on of a business with intent to defraud creditors. So it has been said that:

"... the director of a company dealing in second-hand motor cars who wilfully misrepresents the age and capability of a vehicle in stock is, no doubt, a fraudulent rascal but I do not think he can be said to be carrying on the company's business for a fraudulent purpose, although no doubt he carries out a particular business transaction in a fraudulent manner."[141]

It has also been held that the mere fact of preferring one particular creditor does not of itself constitute fraudulent trading.[142]

Who can apply for an order

14–25   Application for an order under s.213 can be made only by the liquidator.

Sanctions for fraudulent trading

14–26   The criminal sanction for wrongful trading is a fine and/or imprisonment[143]; the civil sanction is a contribution to the assets of the company, which will be discussed later in relation to wrongful trading. Suffice to say that the basis of contribution is restoration to the company of what the creditors lost as the result of the defendant's wrongful conduct; the court cannot include a punitive element in determining the amount of contribution.[144] A director involved in fraudulent trading will almost invariably be disqualified.[145] An individual creditor suffering loss as the result of the fraudulent trading may also have a remedy at common law against a director through an action for deceit, as where the director obtains goods or services for the company by making an express or implied representation in writing that the company is solvent.[146]

---

[140] *Morphitis v Bernasconi* [2003] B.C.C. 540, applying *Re Gerald Cooper (Chemicals) Ltd* [1978] Ch. 262.

[141] *Re Murray-Watson Ltd* (unreported, April 6, 1977), *per* Oliver J., cited by Templeman J. in *Re Gerald Cooper (Chemicals)*, cited above n.140, at 267.

[142] *Re Sarflax Ltd* [1979] Ch. 592. However, a director who procures the preference is guilty of a misfeasance. See above, para.14–14.

[143] Companies Act 2006 s.993(3).

[144] *Morphitis v Bernasconi*, cited above n.140.

[145] See below, paras 14–63 et seq.

[146] *Contex Drouzhba Ltd v Wiseman* [2008] B.C.C. 301; and *Lindsay v O'Loughnane* [2010] EWHC 529 (Ch). The requirement that the representation be in writing to be actionable is imposed by s.6 of the Statute of Frauds Amendment Act 1828 (Lord Tenterden's Act).

6. LIABILITY FOR WRONGFUL TRADING

Genesis of the wrongful trading provisions

The burden of establishing fraud to the standard of proof required by the criminal law in order to obtain either a conviction for the offence of fraudulent trading or a contribution order in the winding up of the company proved a serious deterrent to the institution of proceedings, and the statutory provisions became almost, although not quite, a dead letter. The Cork Committee concluded that whilst it was right that the law should require proof of dishonesty before a person could be convicted of an offence, different considerations applied to the provision of a civil remedy for those who suffered loss in consequence of the mismanagement of a company.[147] The Committee therefore recommended that the existing statutory provisions relating to contribution should be replaced by a new section which would enable contribution orders to be made for wrongful trading without proof of dishonesty and without requiring the criminal standard of proof. A company would engage in wrongful trading if it incurred liabilities with no reasonable prospect of meeting them; and a director would be made personally liable for the company's debts if, being party to the company's trading, he knew that it was wrongful.[148] In determining whether there was a reasonable prospect of the company meeting its liabilities and, if not, whether the director ought to have known this, the test would be objective, namely that of the ordinary, reasonable man.[149] Under these proposals, trading when a business was heavily undercapitalised would often come within the concept of wrongful trading.[150]

14–27

What is now s.214 of the Insolvency Act 1986 seeks to capture the essential idea of the Committee's proposals but in much broader terms. In particular, instead of adopting as the criterion of wrongful trading the incurring of new debt without any reasonable prospect of payment, s.214 focuses on the failure of a director, knowing there is no reasonable prospect of the company avoiding insolvent liquidation, to show that he has taken every step which he ought to have taken with a view to minimising loss to creditors. The primary sanction for wrongful trading, like the civil sanction for fraudulent trading, is an order requiring the delinquent director to contribute to the company's assets.[151]

---

[147] "Insolvency Law and Practice", paras 1776–1777.
[148] "Insolvency Law and Practice", para.1783.
[149] "Insolvency Law and Practice", para.1783.
[150] "Insolvency Law and Practice", para.1785.
[151] See below, para.14–52.

The statutory provisions

14–28   Section 214 provides as follows:

"214 Wrongful trading

(1)   Subject to subsection (3) below, if in the course of the winding up of a company it appears that subsection (2) of this section applies in relation to a person who is or has been a director of the company, the court, on the application of the liquidator, may declare that that person is to be liable to make such contribution (if any) to the company's assets as the court thinks proper.

(2)   This subsection applies in relation to a person if—

(a)   the company has gone into insolvent liquidation,

(b)   at some time before the commencement of the winding up of the company, that person knew or ought to have concluded that there was no reasonable prospect that the company would avoid going into insolvent liquidation, and

(c)   that person was a director of the company at that time;

but the court shall not make a declaration under this section in any case where the time mentioned in paragraph (b) above was before 28th April 1986.

(3)   The court shall not make a declaration under this section with respect to any person if it is satisfied that after the condition specified in subsection (2)(b) was first satisfied in relation to him that person took every step with a view to minimising the potential loss to the company's creditors as (assuming him to have known that there was no reasonable prospect that the company would avoid going into insolvent liquidation) he ought to have taken.

(4)   For the purposes of subsections (2) and (3), the facts which a director of a company ought to know or ascertain, the conclusions which he ought to reach and the steps which he ought to take are those which would be known or ascertained, or reached or taken, by a reasonably diligent person having both—

(a)   the general knowledge, skill and experience that may reasonably be expected of a person carrying out the same functions as are carried out by that director in relation to the company, and

(b)   the general knowledge, skill and experience that that director has.

(5)   The reference in subsection (4) to the functions carried out in relation to a company by a director of the company includes any functions which he does not carry out but which have been entrusted to him.

(6)   For the purposes of this section a company goes into insolvent liqui-
       dation if it goes into liquidation at a time when its assets are insuffi-
       cient for the payment of its debts and other liabilities and the
       expenses of the winding up.

(7)   In this section 'director' includes a shadow director.

(8)   This section is without prejudice to section 213."

Wrongful trading distinguished from fraudulent trading

There are several differences between wrongful trading and fraudulent   **14–29**
trading:

(1)   It is not necessary to show fraud or dishonesty; what may loosely be
       described at this stage as a negligent disregard of the interests of
       creditors suffices. Dishonesty is an essential ingredient of fraudulent
       trading.[152]

(2)   Only a director[153] can be proceeded against for wrongful trading, since
       this is essentially a negligent failure of management, whereas any
       person knowingly a party to fraudulent trading by the company may
       be the subject of proceedings.

(3)   The wrongful trading provisions are confined to culpable conduct after
       the time when the director concerned knew or ought to have known
       that there was no reasonable prospect of the company avoiding insol-
       vent liquidation.[154] In the case of fraudulent trading, the whole period
       of trading is potentially relevant.

(4)   Proceedings for wrongful trading are purely civil, the only sanctions
       being an order requiring the director concerned to contribute to the
       company's assets and disqualification from being concerned in the
       management of a company.

(5)   The provisions relating to fraudulent trading are directed primarily
       against the improper incurring of new debt where there is no reason-
       able prospect of this being paid. The wrongful trading provisions are
       designed for the protection of past as well as future creditors. There is
       thus a tension between the two sets of provisions, for it is not permissi-
       ble to protect existing creditors at the expense of new creditors.[155] So
       directors who continue trading without increasing the net deficiency of

---

[152] See above, para.14–24.
[153] As to the meaning of "director" in this context, see below, para.14–32.
[154] So it is not wrongful trading to bring a company to the point of insolvency by negligent
      management.
[155] See above, para.14–24, as to incurring new debt.

assets are free from liability under s.214 if they achieve this result by using new credit to pay off existing creditors knowing that the new creditors will not be able to be paid when payment is due or shortly thereafter but will be guilty of fraudulent trading. In short, s.213 has paramountcy, and in determining whether the directors have taken every step they ought to have taken to minimise the potential loss to the company's creditors, the court must take into account in their favour that they could not lawfully rob Peter (the new creditors) to pay Paul (the existing creditors) even if the result of so doing would have been to reduce the net deficiency as at the time of commencement of the winding up to a figure lower than that existing when they first ought to have concluded that there was no reasonable prospect of the company avoiding insolvent liquidation.

The ingredients of wrongful trading

14–30   Before a person can be held guilty of wrongful trading, four conditions must be satisfied:

(1)   The company has gone into insolvent liquidation.[156] The wrongful trading provisions are confined to liquidation; they cannot be invoked by an administrator or administrative receiver. A company goes into insolvent liquidation if it goes into liquidation at a time when its assets are insufficient for the payment of its debts and the expenses of the winding up.[157] This is the balance sheet test described in an earlier chapter.[158] "Debts and liabilities" includes prospective and contingent debts. It is thought that whether the company is in fact insolvent according to this test is to be determined in the light of all facts known when the matter comes before the court, whether or not they were known at the time the company went into liquidation. The use of hindsight creates no problem in this situation, for what the court has to consider in an application under s.214 is whether there is a net deficiency of assets and, if so, whether and how the delinquent director should be required to contribute to the assets.

(2)   At some time, before the commencement of the winding up,[159] a person knew or ought to have concluded that there was no reasonable prospect that the company would avoid going into insolvent liquidation.

---

[156] Insolvency Act 1986 s.214(2)(a).
[157] Insolvency Act 1986 s.214(6).
[158] Above, paras 4–22 et seq.
[159] And on or after April 28, 1986 (Insolvency Act 1986 s.214(2)).

(3)   That person was a director at that time.

(4)   The director fails to establish the statutory defence of taking every step he ought to have taken to minimise the potential loss to creditors.

The onus is on the liquidator to establish the first three elements and on the respondent to establish the defence.

Trading not an essential requirement

Although the marginal heading to s.214 refers to "wrongful trading", the text of s.214 makes no reference to trading at all. All that is required is a culpable failure to act properly with a view to minimising the potential loss to the company's creditors.[160] It is worth underlining the point made earlier that what attracts s.214 is not mismanagement which brings a company to the brink of insolvency,[161] but a failure thereafter, when the writing is on the wall, to take proper steps for the protection of creditors. Accordingly, a director can be involved in wrongful trading if he is guilty of an act or omission which is not a reasonable step in minimising potential loss to creditors, even if he procures the company to cease trading as soon as he realises that insolvent liquidation is inevitable. Indeed, the premature cessation of trading might constitute wrongful trading.[162] Non-trading activity capable of attracting liability includes the failure to collect in debts due to the company, the failure to preserve assets, the payment of excessive remuneration to directors and entry into transactions at an undervalue after cessation of trading.

14–31

Who is a "director"

For the purpose of s.214, "director" not only covers a *de jure* director, whether executive or non-executive but also includes a shadow director[163] and *de facto* director.[164] This exposes to potential liability various types of person who might not ordinarily be thought of as directors.

14–32

---

[160] See below, paras 14–40 et seq.
[161] Although such mismanagement might be a breach of the director's duty of care to the company for which the liquidator could take proceedings in the company's name.
[162] See below, para.14–44 and n.184.
[163] Insolvency Act 1986 s.214(7). See above, para.14–05.
[164] *Re Hydrodam (Corby) Ltd* [1994] B.C.C. 161, *per* Millett J. at 162; and *Re Richborough Furniture Ltd* [1996] B.C.C. 155. See above, para.14–04. For s.214 to apply it is not necessary that the respondent should still be a director at the time of the acts or omissions which are alleged to constitute wrongful trading. It suffices that he was a director at some time when he had what is referred to below as "deemed knowledge" of the company's impending liquidation. Hence, resignation after the acquisition of such knowledge does not by itself relieve him of liability.

(1) Controlling shareholders

14–33 In appropriate cases, a controlling shareholder (including a parent company and even, it is thought, a government department responsible for a company in State ownership) could be susceptible to a claim for wrongful trading if interfering too regularly in the day-to-day management of the company, as could the controller of a company that is itself a director.

(2) Company doctors

14–34 There is no exemption for the company doctor who is brought in to extricate the company from its difficulties and who acts as a director or shadow director[165]; indeed, the company doctor's very expertise, or professed expertise, may impose on him a high standard of care if he is to avoid liability for wrongful trading.

(3) Lending banks

14–35 A bank exercising management control for the protection of its loan and security—as opposed to merely giving professional advice[166]—is capable of being a shadow director.[167] So, banks should be careful to restrict themselves to advice and not seek to dictate what cheques should be paid, what parts of the business should be sold or what policies should be adopted by the board. However, a bank or other funder does not become a shadow director merely because it attends regular meetings with the directors in order to lay down conditions for future lending, becomes sole signatory of the company's bank account and gives directions designed solely to protect its own interests as a secured creditor.[168]

Who is not a "director"

(1) Professional advisers

14–36 A person is not a shadow director solely because the directors act on advice given by him in a professional capacity,[169] for example, as solicitor, banker or

---

[165] See *Re Tasbian Ltd (No.3)* [1992] B.C.C. 358, where it was not disputed that a company doctor was capable of being a *de facto* or shadow director for the purpose of disqualification proceedings and it was held that there was an arguable case on the facts.

[166] See below, para.14–36.

[167] See *Re A Company (No.005009 of 1987)* (1988) B.C.C. 424, where Knox J. refused to strike out a claim against the bank, ruling that the liquidator had raised a triable issue.

[168] *Ultraframe (UK) Ltd v Fielding* [2006] F.S.R. 17; and *Re PFTZM Ltd* [1995] 2 B.C.L.C. 354.

[169] Insolvency Act 1986 s.251.

accountant. But the professional adviser acting as such is excluded only from the definition of a shadow director. So a solicitor or other professional man who is on the board or is a *de facto* director does not have exemption even if he restricts himself to the giving of professional advice. Indeed, such a restriction would be an abnegation of his duties as a director under general company law as well as under s.214.

(2) Administrative receivers

It is thought that an administrative receiver would not be a shadow director   **14–37**
merely by virtue of his status as a deemed agent of the company[170] and the exercise of his functions as administrative receiver, for these involve managing the company in right of and for the primary benefit of the debenture holder, not of the company's members. Nor would he be a shadow director, since far from instructing the directors in the exercise of their management functions, he assumes those functions himself. However, an administrative receiver who hives down the business to a specially formed subsidiary over whose board he exercises control could be vulnerable as a shadow director.[171]

(3) Administrators

For the same reason, an administrator would not as such be a shadow   **14–38**
director, nor would he be a *de facto* director, his functions being exercised for the benefit of creditors, not members.

Pleading the facts relied on to establish *de facto* or shadow directorship

Where it is contended that a person acted as *de facto* or shadow director, the   **14–39**
facts relied on as establishing this contention must be properly pleaded. For this purpose, the pleadings should be careful to distinguish facts relied on to show that a person acted as *de facto* director from those relied on to show that he was a shadow director, the two types of status being essentially different.[172]

---

[170] Insolvency Act 1986 s.44(1)(a).
[171] Lightman et al., *The Law of Receivers and Administrators of Companies*, 4th edn (London: Sweet & Maxwell, 2007), para.10–065.
[172] *Re Hydrodam (Corby)*, cited above n.164, at 163.

Deemed knowledge of impending liquidation

Nature of the deemed knowledge required

14–40   In order for a director or former director to be susceptible to an order under s.214, it has to be shown that at some time while he was a director, being a time after April 28, 1986, he knew or ought to have concluded that there was no reasonable prospect that the company would avoid going into insolvent liquidation. For brevity, I will refer to this as "deemed knowledge". It should be noted that mere knowledge that the company is insolvent does not trigger s.214; it is necessary to show deemed knowledge that the company would not be able to avoid going into insolvent liquidation. So if there was a real prospect that the company could trade out of its difficulties or that an outside investor might be prepared to invest in the company, there is no liability under s.214 even if the directors knew the company to be insolvent.[173]

Pleading the date deemed knowledge first acquired

14–41   Although s.214(2)(b) uses the phrase "at some time before the commencement of the winding up of the company", it is necessary as far as possible to determine when the deemed knowledge was *first* acquired, this being the starting point of the director's duty to take steps to minimise the potential loss to creditors. Although there are cases suggesting that a liquidator taking proceedings under s.214 must identify the precise time and establish that time and not some different time,[174] later cases have shown a more liberal approach.[175] The question is essentially one of fairness to the director concerned. In the real world, establishing the earliest date on which a director ought to have seen the inevitability of liquidation is as near-impossible as establishing the precise date on which a company becomes insolvent. Normally, the best one can do is to show that *by* a certain date the director must have acquired actual or deemed knowledge that insolvent liquidation was unavoidable, and even this cannot necessarily be determined until the liquidator is in possession of all of the relevant facts and documents, which may happen only in the course of the proceedings. The liquidator should therefore not be tied down to a precise date. What is important is that the director should know the case he has to meet and should not be taken by

---

[173] *Re Hawkes Publishing Co Ltd* [2007] B.C.C. 937.

[174] See, e.g. *Re Sherborne Associates Ltd* [1995] B.C.C. 50 (where, however, the liquidator did not plead alternative dates and the judge felt it would be unfair to allow the liquidator to pick a series of dates or leave the date to the court); and *Singer v Beckett* [2001] B.P.I.R. 733, although only "in the particular circumstances of this case" (para.99, the judge being clearly influenced by its procedural history).

[175] See Andrew Keay, "Wrongful Trading and the Point of Liability" (2006) Ins. Int. 132.

surprise or exposed to the oppression of having to find answers based on an indeterminate series of dates.

Onus of proof

It is submitted that the onus of showing deemed knowledge is on the office-holder, in contrast to the onus of proof in relation to the question of whether proper steps were taken to minimise loss to creditors.[176] Determination of the time at which deemed knowledge is first acquired may be crucial in that there can be no liability for wrongful trading in respect of acts or omissions before that time. For the purposes of s.214, insolvent liquidation means liquidation at a time when the company's assets are insufficient for the payment of its debts and other liabilities and the expenses of the winding up.[177] So a director who, although aware that the company is unable to pay its debts as they fall due and will be forced into winding up, reasonably believes that on liquidation its assets will be sufficient to cover its liabilities and the expenses of winding up incurs no liability under s.214. The reason why that section adopts the balance sheet test is, of course, that if it were to be satisfied, there would be no ultimate loss to creditors and no need for a contribution to the assets of the company. It is not sufficient for the application of s.214 (although it is a necessary precondition of its application) that the company in fact fails the balance sheet test of solvency on winding up; what has also to be shown is that the director concerned knew, or ought to have concluded, that it would fail that test. Inevitably, there will be a temptation to use hindsight, a temptation which should be resisted.[178]

In deciding what a director "ought to have concluded", the combined objective and subjective tests prescribed by s.214(4) must be applied.

14–42

The statutory defence

The court may not make a declaration under s.214 with regard to any person if it is satisfied that after he first acquired deemed knowledge he took every step with a view to minimising the potential loss to creditors as (assuming him to have had that knowledge) he ought to have taken.[179] The onus is on the person concerned to show that he took the proper steps, not for the liquidator to prove that he did not. So for the purpose of s.214, the duty to take steps to minimise loss begins once a person has acquired deemed knowledge while a director and the company thereafter goes into insolvent liquidation.

14–43

---

[176] See below, para.14–43.
[177] Insolvency Act 1986 s.214(6).
[178] See below, para.14–44.
[179] Insolvency Act 1986 s.214(3).

Accordingly, it is not a breach of s.214 for directors to bring the company to the point where insolvent liquidation is inevitable; any breach of duty in that regard is a matter for the general law and is actionable either by ordinary proceedings, for example, for negligence or breach of fiduciary duty, or by summary misfeasance proceedings under s.212.

The standard of knowledge and skill required

14–44   Section 214(4) and (5) provides as follows:

> "4.   For the purpose of subsections (2) and (3), the facts which a direc-tor of a company ought to know or ascertain, the conclusions which he ought to reach and the steps which he ought to take are those which would be known or ascertained, or reached or taken, by a reasonably diligent person having both—
>
> > (a)   the general knowledge, skill and experience that may reason-ably be expected of a person carrying out the same functions as are carried out by that director in relation to the company, and
> >
> > (b)   the general knowledge, skill and experience that that director has.
>
> 5.   The reference in subsection (4) to the functions carried out in relation to a company by a director of the company includes any functions which he does not carry out but which have been entrusted to him."

Several points arise in relation to the above provisions:

(1)   The test of knowledge, skill and experience is a combination of the objective and the subjective. The minimum standard is what would have been ascertained, foreseen and done by a reasonably diligent per-son carrying out (or entrusted with) the same functions as those entrusted to the director concerned. A director who falls below this minimum standard cannot invoke the statutory defence even if he did his best. In deciding whether the minimum standard was observed, regard must be had to the particular company and its business, so that "the general knowledge, skill and experience postulated will be much less extensive in a small company in a modest way of business, with sim-ple accounting procedures and requirements, than it will be in a large company with sophisticated procedures".[180] The standard to be applied is that of a reasonably prudent businessman acting without

---

[180] *Re Produce Marketing Consortium Ltd* (1989) 5 B.C.C. 569, *per* Knox J. at 594.

unwarranted optimism and on a realistic, factual basis.[181] But observance of the minimum standard is not necessarily sufficient. The director must also meet such higher standard as is appropriate to his own general knowledge, skill and experience. So while the minimum standard does not necessarily call for particular expertise or skill, only that of a reasonably diligent person, a real professional possessing a high degree of general knowledge, skill and experience must use it and act accordingly.

(2)   The test of proper mitigating behaviour—"every step"—seems very stringent but when read with "reasonably diligent person" may mean no more than "every reasonable step".

(3)   While there is no immunity for non-executive directors as such, prima facie a non-executive director is not expected to possess the knowledge and skill of an executive director, still less to give his continuous time and attention to the company's affairs.[182]

(4)   The knowledge and skill required of an executive director depends on the nature of the functions entrusted to him. Thus a director in charge of marketing and sales cannot be expected to possess the financial knowledge and skills of a finance director.

Finally, the court should take care to avoid being influenced by hindsight[183] and should not be too astute to find the directors at fault without taking account of the difficult choices that frequently confront them.

"An overall point which needs to be kept in mind throughout is that, whenever a company is in financial trouble and the directors have a difficult decision to make whether to close down and go into liquidation, or whether instead to trade on and hope to turn the corner, they can be in a real and unenviable dilemma. On the one hand, if they decide to trade on but things do not work out and the company, later rather sooner, goes into liquidation, they may find themselves in the situation of the respondents in this case—being sued for wrongful trading. On the other hand, if the directors decide to close down immediately and cause the company to go into an early liquidation, although they are not at risk of being sued for wrongful trading,[184] they are at risk of being criticised on other grounds. A decision to close down will almost certainly mean that the ensuing liquidation will be an insolvent one. Apart from anything else liquidations are

---

[181] *Singla v Hedman* [2010] B.C.C. 674, *per* Kitchin J. at [15].
[182] See above, para.14–11.
[183] *Re Hawkes Publishing*, cited above n.173, at [38].
[184] The basis of this statement is not clear. There seems to be no reason why ceasing to trade when the company, although insolvent, has a manifestly viable business could not constitute wrongful trading, although no doubt this situation would be unusual. See above, para.14–31.

expensive operations, and in addition debtors are commonly obstructive about paying their debts to a company which is in liquidation. Many creditors of the company from a time before the liquidation are likely to find that their debts do not get paid in full. They will complain bitterly that the directors shut down too soon; they will say that the directors ought to have had more courage and kept going. If they had done, so the complaining creditors will say, the company probably would have survived and all of its debts would have been paid. Ceasing to trade and liquidating too soon can be stigmatised as the cowards' way out."[185]

No relief under s.1157

14–45 It has been held that a director who engages in wrongful trading contrary to s.214 of the Insolvency Act 1986 cannot obtain relief under what is now s.1157 of the Companies Act 2006, since the subjective approach of that provision is inconsistent with the objective duty imposed by s.214(4) of the 1986 Act.[186]

How to avoid liability for wrongful trading

14–46 What practical advice should be given to a director as to the steps he should take to minimise the risk of being found guilty of wrongful trading? Here is my list of 12 points for survival!

(1) Do not assume that the safest course is to stop trading. You have to take every step that can properly be expected of you to minimise loss to creditors. You can be faulted just as much for a premature cessation of trading as for continuing to trade while insolvent. This makes it essential to obtain competent outside advice as to whether to stop trading or continue.

(2) Consider carefully with your fellow directors whether the business is viable. If it is, insist on the preparation[187] of:

---

[185] *Re Continental Assurance Co of London* [2001] B.P.I.R. 733 *per* Park J. at [281]. See to similar effect Lewison J. in *Re Hawkes Publishing, Re* cited above n.173: "But directors are not clairvoyant and the fact that they fail to see what eventually comes to pass does not mean that they are guilty of wrongful trading . . ." (at [41]); and "Of course, it is easy with hindsight to conclude that mistakes were made. An insolvent liquidation will almost always result from one or more mistakes. But picking over the bones of a dead company in a courtroom is not always fair to those who struggled to keep going in the reasonable (but ultimately misplaced) hope that things would get better . . ." (at [47]).

[186] *Re Produce Marketing Consortium Ltd* [1989] B.C.L.C. 513.

[187] With any necessary professional help. See below.

(a)   a business review;

(b)   a sensible and constructive programme to reduce expenditure, increase income, ensure an adequate cash flow and restore the company to profitable trading, disposing of unprofitable or marginal parts of the business and dismissing staff who are surplus to the company's needs or are not doing their job.

(3)   Insist on frequent board meetings.

(4)   Make sure that there is a proper distribution of responsibility within the company.

(5)   Ensure that the accounts are being properly kept and up to date or if not, that prompt steps are being taken to do so, with outside help being brought in as and when necessary.

(6)   See that the board regularly receives an updated budget and a full, accurate and up-to-date picture of the company's trading, financial and cash flow position.

(7)   Get the company to take appropriate outside, professional advice on suitable remedial measures.

(8)   Keep major creditors regularly informed and enlist their support for the continued operation of the company where this is likely to be of benefit to the general body of creditors. In this connection, it is just as important to have the support of major unsecured creditors as of secured creditors, for it is the former who are most likely to suffer loss and whose support makes it easier for you to show subsequently that you took every step available to you to minimise loss to creditors.

(9)   Ensure that you are kept fully in the picture and, so far as possible, that all directors agree on what needs to be done.

(10)   Consider the advisability of putting the company into administration in order to give it breathing space and prevent action by individual creditors. Such appointment has the further advantage of ending your management responsibilities, although you still have a duty to co-operate with the office-holder.[188]

(11)   Insist that all recommendations for remedial action made by the directors (and particularly by you), together with your dissent from any unwise actions or inactivity advocated by your fellow directors, are fully minuted or otherwise placed on record, for example, by the circulation of a memorandum to the other directors.

---

[188] Failure to do this is an offence (Insolvency Act 1986 s.235).

(12) If you are in the minority and your recommendations are repeatedly rejected, so that the company is getting deeper into the mire, resign and record your reasons for doing so in a letter. But resignation is very much the last resort. A director who simply resigns without having taken every step he should have done to minimise loss to creditors will not escape liability. So do not resign before you have gone as far as you can in getting things put right.[189]

Wrongful trading and misfeasance

14–47   There is no direct relationship between the remedies of the liquidator for wrongful trading and for misfeasance; he is entitled to pursue either or both. But the choice of remedy may have significant effects on the creditors. As we have seen, misfeasance is a remedy actionable in right of the company and any money or property recovered forms part of its general assets and is therefore capable of being captured by a prior assignment or charge covering future property. By contrast, sums paid under a contribution order in respect of wrongful trading are held for the creditors generally, and although preferential creditors have a prior claim to them they do not fall within a prior assignment or charge since they are not assets of the company.[190] Three questions now arise. First, to what extent does a recovery for misfeasance under s.212 reduce the amount of the director's liability under s.214?[191] Secondly, to what extent does a recovery under s.214 reduce his liability under s.212? Thirdly, where recovery under one section does not affect the amount recoverable under the other but the director's assets are insufficient to meet both claims in full, how should the claims and recoveries be dealt with?

(1) Effect on s.214 claim of recovery under s.212

14–48   Recovery from a director under s.212 will, or course, *pro tanto* reduce the company's net indebtedness, but it does not follow from this that the

---

[189] See *Secretary of State for Trade and Industry v Arif* [1996] B.C.C. 586; and *Re C.S. Holidays Ltd* [1997] B.C.C. 172, cases on the position of a director for disqualification purposes where he has resigned after his recommendations went unheeded by the rest of the board. In *Secretary of State for Trade and Industry v Taylor* [1997] 1 W.L.R. 407, Chadwick J. rejected the contention that a director's failure to resign even after his views have gone unheeded was necessarily unfit to be concerned in the management of a company, although he did indicate (at 415) that a person who, having ceased to exert any influence over his colleagues, remained on the board for no purpose other than to draw his director's fees or preserve his status might well be found so lacking in appreciation of his duties as to be unfit to be concerned in the management of a company.

[190] *Re Oasis Merchandising Ltd* [1997] 1 All E.R. 1009. See below, para.14–55.

[191] The question was raised in *Re Purpoint Ltd* [1991] B.C.L.C. 491, where the application under s.214 was stood over. The outcome is not known.

director's separate liability for wrongful trading will fall by the same amount or, indeed, at all. In considering the effect of a s.212 recovery on the amount chargeable to a delinquent director under s.214, two factors have to be taken into account. The first is whether the loss caused by the misfeasance is also the loss, or part of the loss, embodied in the claim under s.214 or is entirely unconnected. It is clear that loss resulting from a misfeasance committed before the commencement of the director's duty under s.214 to take steps to minimise loss cannot form part of the s.214 claim, so that no duplication is involved in allowing full recovery under both sections. Where, on the other hand, the misfeasance occurred after the start of the director's duty under s.214, it will usually constitute a breach of that duty as well as a misfeasance under s.212. In this case, the claims under ss.212 and 214 will be duplicated, and any recovery under s.212 will at the same time reduce the loss chargeable to the director under s.214,[192] although in the unlikely event that the recovery under s.212 tops the recovery under s.214, the excess will form part of the company's general assets. The second factor is that a director's liability to contribute under s.214 cannot exceed the amount of the net deficiency in the company's assets available for creditors.[193] To the extent that recovery for unconnected loss under s.212 is sufficient to extinguish that deficiency, his liability under s.214 will abate. Where this is not the case, the recovery under s.212 will not reduce the director's liability for unconnected loss under s.214. Two examples will make this clear.

Example 1

(a)	Amount recovered under s.212:	£100,000
(b)	Unconnected loss due to breach of s.214:	£75,000
(c)	Net deficiency of assets before s.212 recovery:	£150,000
(d)	Maximum liability under s.214 ((c)–(a)):	£50,000

In this example, the loss caused by the director through his breach of s.214 (£75,000) is partially offset by the recovery under s.212, which reduces the net deficiency, and thus the director's maximum s.214 liability, to £50,000.

---

[192] This was the case in *Re DKG Contractors Ltd* [1990] B.C.C. 903, where it was rightly held that recoveries under ss.212 and 239 were to be taken as *pro tanto* satisfying the order under s.214.

[193] As stated earlier, the members of the company do not benefit from recoveries under s.213 or 214.

Example 2

(a)	Amount recovered under s.212:	£100,000
(b)	Unconnected loss due to breach of s.214:	£75,000
(c)	Net deficiency of assets before s.212 recovery:	£500,000
(d)	Maximum liability under s.214:	£75,000

In this example, the net deficiency remaining after the recovery under s.212 (i.e. £500,000 – £100,000 = £400,000) still exceeds the maximum contribution liability under s.214, which accordingly is not reduced by the s.212 recovery.

In summary, a s.212 recovery will reduce the director's maximum liability under s.214 only to the extent that: (i) the s.212 claim also forms part of the loss for which the director is answerable under s.214; or (ii) the s.212 recovery reduces the net deficiency to an amount below the loss attributable to the breach of s.214.

(2) Effect on s.212 claim of recovery under s.214

14–49 It will be clear from what has been said above that there cannot be a double recovery for the same loss. To the extent that the misfeasance also constitutes a breach of s.214, the sum recovered under s.214 goes in reduction of any amount otherwise recoverable under s.212. Where, however, the two claims are entirely unconnected, as where the s.212 claim relates to a misappropriation of the company's property committed before the commencement of the director's duty under s.214, recovery under s.214 does not in any way reduce the amount recoverable under s.212. This is so even if the effect of the s.214 recovery is that there is no longer a deficiency of assets as regards creditors, for the members of the company still have an interest in the remedying of the misfeasance.[194]

(3) Priorities

14–50 So far, we have assumed that where the claims under ss.212 and 214 are unconnected, the delinquent director has enough assets to meet in full the claims under both sections. Where this is not the case, the question arises which claim should be given priority. Members of the company will not, of

---

[194] A contributory may, with the court's leave, take misfeasance proceedings under s.212 even where he will not benefit from any order made (Insolvency Act 1986 s.212(5)), but where he does have an interest, his case for being given leave where the liquidator does not wish to pursue the claim himself is obviously much stronger. In practice, claims under the two sections would normally be made concurrently.

course, have any interest in recoveries until creditors have been paid in full. The contest is potentially between the general body of creditors, for whose benefit recoveries under s.214 enure, and debenture holders asserting security rights over recoveries under s.212, which as we have seen form part of the assets of the company. No hard and fast rule can be laid down. Under both sections, an order is discretionary and it is for the court to consider what best meets the justice of the case. In the absence of any special factors, the most appropriate solution would seem to be to respect the debenture holder's rights as regards assets recovered in a proprietary claim and to divide the total sum awarded in respect of the director's personal liability between the two heads of claim in the proportion which each bears to the total.

7. CIVIL SANCTIONS FOR IMPROPER TRADING

The five sanctions

The civil sanctions for improper trading are the same for fraudulent trading as for wrongful trading. They are[195]:   **14–51**

(1) a declaration by the court that the respondent is to be liable to make such contribution (if any) to the company's assets as the court thinks fit[196];

(2) such further directions as the court thinks fit for giving effect to the declaration, including provision for the director's contribution to be charged on any debt or obligation due to him from the company[197] or on any mortgage or charge or any interest in a mortgage or charge on assets of the company held by or vested in him, or any person on his behalf, or any person claiming as assignee from or through the person liable or any person acting on his behalf who is not a bona fide assignee for value and without notice;

(3) such further order from time to time as may be necessary for enforcing such charge;

---

[195] Insolvency Act 1986 ss.213(2), 214(1) and 215(2)–(4); Company Directors Disqualification Act 1986 ss.4(1)(a) and 10. These provisions relate to fraudulent trading and wrongful trading. As to the personal liability of the director of a company trading under a prohibited name, see Insolvency Act 1986 s.217, and above, para.14–06.

[196] This claim survives the death of the delinquent director and is payable out of his estate (*Re Sherborne Associates Ltd* [1995] B.C.C. 40).

[197] Insolvency Act 1986 s.215(2)(a). This form of security had at one time been thought conceptually impossible (*Re Charge Card Services Ltd* [1989] Ch. 497), but now considered by the House of Lords to be unobjectionable (*Re Bank of Credit and Commerce International SA* [1998] A.C. 214). Interestingly, neither the arguments advanced in the courts nor the judgments in successive decisions ever drew attention to s.215(2)(a). See further *Goode on Legal Problems of Credit and Security*, 4th edn (London: Sweet & Maxwell, 2008), para.3–12.

(4)   in the case of a director who is a creditor of the company, subordination of his debt, wholly or in part, to all other debts of the company and
interest thereon; and

(5)   disqualification.[198]

The court's power under s.1157 of the Companies Act 2006 to grant relief to
a delinquent director is not exercisable in relation to claims for wrongful
trading under s.214 of the Insolvency Act.[199]

The court's approach to contribution orders

No loss, no contribution

14–52   The first point to note is that where it is alleged that the directors continued
to cause the company to trade after it should have ceased trading, no question of contribution under s.214 can arise unless it is shown that on a net
basis the company was worse off at the time of commencement of the winding up than it was at the time the directors ought to have ceased trading. The
fact that the company incurred new debt after it ceased trading is not in itself
relevant to a contribution claim under s.214,[200] although it will be very material to a claim for fraudulent trading if the respondent directors avoided an
increase in the net deficiency by incurring fresh credit at the expense of new
creditors in order to pay off existing creditors and knew when they did so that
there was no reasonable prospect of the company being able to pay its debts
to the new creditors when these fell due or shortly thereafter.[201]

Determining the level of contribution

14–53   In *Re Produce Marketing Consortium Ltd*,[202] Knox J. provided an instructive
analysis of the approach the court should adopt in deciding on the level of
contribution a director should be ordered to pay in the event of a finding of
wrongful trading. Two alternative views were canvassed before the learned
judge. The first, contended for by counsel for the respondent directors, was
that s.214 is both compensatory and penal. In so far as it was compensatory,

---

[198] See below, paras 14–57 et seq.
[199] *Re Produce Marketing Consortium Ltd* (1989) 5 B.C.C. 399, a decision s.727 of the Companies
Act 1985, the predecessor of s.1157.
[200] *Re Continental Assurance Co of London*, [2001] B.P.I.R. 733; and *Re Marini Ltd, Liquidator
of Marini Ltd v Dickenson* [2004] B.C.C. 172.
[201] See above, para.14–24.
[202] (1989) 5 B.C.C. 569.

the sum ordered to be paid should not exceed the loss to creditors caused by the wrongful trading complained of; in so far as it was penal, it should reflect the degree of culpability of the director concerned, so that a director who had done nearly everything he should have done but not quite should be treated more leniently than a director who had done nothing to minimise loss to creditors. On this view, the court should exercise its discretion so as to ensure that the sum ordered to be contributed did not exceed the lesser of the loss suffered by creditors from the wrongful trading and the sum that it would be appropriate to order as a punitive measure having regard to the director's efforts to put matters right. The alternative view was that s.215 is purely compensatory and that in principle directors found guilty of wrongful trading should be ordered to make good the loss thereby caused to creditors, without regard to the degree of their culpability. Knox J. concluded that the latter was in principle the correct test, although it would be wrong to exclude entirely from consideration the degree of the director's culpability, having regard to the wide discretion conferred on the court. In fixing the total contribution of the two directors at £75,000, Knox J. took into account a range of factors, including on the one side the fact that the case was one of failure to appreciate what should have been clear, rather than of deliberate wrong-doing, and on the other side the fact that there had been some positive untruths by the directors, solemn warnings by the auditor were ignored and the directors had reduced the indebtedness to the bank, which was a secured creditor, at the expense of unsecured creditors, and it was the latter who should benefit from the way in which the court's discretion was exercised.

Since the above decision, it has been held by the Court of Appeal that even in the case of proceedings under s.213 for fraudulent trading no punitive element may be included in fixing the contribution payable by the respondent[203]; *a fortiori* no such element can be included in a contribution order under s.214.

Plurality of respondents

Where two or more persons have been held liable under s.213 or 214, it is for **14–54** the court to decide whether that liability should be joint and several, so that each is liable for the whole,[204] or on the other hand whether a separate assessment should be made in respect of each respondent and, in that case, the amount to be borne by each.[205]

---

[203] *Morphitis v Bernascon* [2003] B.C.C. 540. See above, para.14–26.
[204] The order made in *Re Bangla Television Ltd* [2010] B.C.C. 143.
[205] As in *Re Overnight Ltd (No.2)* [2010] B.C.C. 796.

Application of recoveries

14–55   Contribution orders under s.214 of the Insolvency Act are intended for the benefit of creditors generally and recoveries, although payable to the company through its liquidator, do not constitute an asset of the company.[206] Three consequences ensue from this principle. First, sums recovered under a contribution order do not go to enhance a prior assignment or security in favour of a debenture holder but form part of the general assets of the company to be applied in the statutory order of priority.[207] Secondly, the court has no power to order payment direct to creditors or to a particular class of creditor, and creditors whose debts were incurred before the wrongful trading have no greater entitlement than those whose debts were incurred subsequently.[208] Thirdly, since the liquidator's statutory power of sale[209] is confined to sale of "any of the company's property" and since the cause of action under s.214 and the fruits of such an action are not the property of the company, they are incapable of assignment by a liquidator, and any such assignment is void for champerty.[210]

When should a liquidator take proceedings for wrongful trading?

14–56   The mere fact that a liquidator believes wrongful trading to have taken place does not mean that he should necessarily institute proceedings under s.214. There are several factors he will wish to consider before embarking on the labour and expense of an application under that section. First, how strong is the evidence and how easy will it be to prove wrongful trading? In some cases the evidence may be crystal clear; in other cases it may depend on uncertain inferences of fact based on incomplete documents and the possibly faulty recollection by witnesses of events long past. Secondly, is the loss attributable to the wrongful trading sufficiently substantial to make the proceedings worthwhile? Thirdly, what degree of culpability is involved? It is true that the principal function of a contribution order is not to act as a penal sanction but to compensate for loss[211]; even so, the court may feel disinclined to make a significant contribution order where the remedial steps taken by the director fall only marginally short of what s.214 requires. Fourthly, is the prospective respondent worth powder and shot? There is little point seeking a contribution order when the respondent has no means to meet it. Finally, what is the attitude of the creditors? The liquidator may be reluctant to institute

---

[206] *Re Oasis Merchandising Services Ltd* [1998] Ch. 170; and *M.C. Bacon Ltd, Re* [1991] Ch. 127.

[207] *Re Oasis Merchandising*; and *Re M.C. Bacon*, both cited above n.206.

[208] *Re Purpoint Ltd* [1991] B.C.L.C. 491.

[209] Under the Insolvency Act 1986 Sch.4 para.6.

[210] *Re Oasis Merchandising*, cited above n.206, in which it was also held that the residual power contained in Sch.4 para.13 did not assist.

[211] *Re Produce Marketing Consortium*, cited above n.202.

proceedings if he cannot carry at least the major creditors with him, and they may be reluctant to throw good money after bad. All of these are matters which the liquidator will wish to take into account before spending the creditors' money. But sometimes the position is the reverse: the liquidator wishes to compromise instead of taking proceedings but the creditors refuse to accept the proposed compromise. That was the situation in *Andrew Rhodes Ltd v Rhodes*,[212] where the committee of creditors, having withheld its consent to a compromise which the liquidator had been advised was reasonable, also refused to provide funding for the proceedings under s.214 when the liquidator was without funds to do so. In those circumstances, David Richards J. sanctioned the compromise.

8. DISQUALIFICATION OF DIRECTORS: GENERAL CONSIDERATIONS

Introduction

The various statutory provisions relating to the disqualification of directors—an important sanction for improper trading and for other culpable behaviour—are now consolidated in the Company Directors Disqualification Act 1986, as amended by the Insolvency Act 2000 and the Enterprise Act 2002. The Act provides 10 separate grounds for disqualification.[213] As regards seven of these, disqualification is in the discretion of the court. In two cases, disqualification is mandatory, namely: (i) under s.6 of the Act, where the court is satisfied that a person against whom disqualification proceedings is or has been a director of a company which has at any time become insolvent and his conduct as a director makes him unfit to be concerned in the management of a company; and (ii) under s.9A of the Act, where the company of which he is a director commits a breach of competition law and the court considers that his conduct as a director makes him unfit to be concerned in the management of a company.[214] In the 10th case, failure to pay under a county court administration order, disqualification is automatic.[215] Disqualification under s.6 is by far the most common in practice and is the focus of the present chapter. The Act has been extended to cover bank insolvency and bank administration

14–57

---

[212] [2005] EWHC 1005 (Ch).

[213] The subject of disqualification goes well beyond the scope of insolvency law and is here treated in outline only and with a specific focus on disqualification arising from a company's insolvency. The leading textbook is Walters and Davis-White, *Directors' Disqualification & Insolvency Restrictions*, 2009.

[214] See the Office of Fair Trading publication, "Director Disqualification Orders in Competition Cases" (June 2010).

[215] Insolvency Act 1986 s.12.

under the Banking Act 2009[216] and building society insolvency and building society administration under the Building Societies Act 1986.[217] In addition, s.1184 of the Companies Act 2006 empowers the Secretary of State to make provision by regulations for disqualifying a person subject to foreign restrictions[218] from being a director of a UK company, acting as receiver of a UK company's property or in any way, whether directly or indirectly, being concerned in the promotion, formation or management of a UK company.

Policy considerations

14–58   The history of the disqualification provisions[219] reflects the concern of successive governments on the one hand to prevent abuse of the privilege of limited liability and to secure standards of responsible management and protect those dealing with companies and on the other to avoid steps so draconian that they would discourage entrepreneurial activity. Any business undertaking entails risk, and inevitably a number of businesses will be unsuccessful for a variety of reasons, ranging from managerial incompetence or fraud to under-capitalisation and loss of market share through competition. The insolvency of a company has therefore to be seen not as a failure of the market, but on the contrary as a necessary consequence of market forces. It is therefore important not to set standards so high that people of ability and drive whose activities could contribute to the national economy are not deterred from forming companies or becoming directors of companies.[220] On the other hand, it is also important to discourage abuse of the privilege of limited liability and to promote proper standards of probity and competence. The central feature of the Company Directors Disqualification Act is to drive out directors and other office-holders who are not fit to be concerned in the promotion, formation or management of a company.

The meaning of disqualification

14–59   An order for disqualification of a director means that the person disqualified must not without leave of the court:

---

[216] Banking Act 2009 s.121; and Company Directors Disqualification Act 1986 ss.21A and 21B.
[217] Building Societies Act 1986 s.90E; and Company Directors Disqualification Act 1986 s.21C.
[218] i.e. restrictions imposed by the law of a country or territory outside the United Kingdom on acting in connection with the affairs of a company (s.1182).
[219] See Walters and Davis-White, *Directors' Disqualification & Insolvency Restrictions*, 2009, paras 1–33 et seq.; and *Re Pantmaenog Timber Co Ltd* [2004] 1 A.C. 158.
[220] For a full discussion, see Walters and Davis-White, *Directors' Disqualification & Insolvency Restrictions*, 2009, Ch.2.

(1)   be a director of a company;

(2)   be a liquidator or administrator of a company;

(3)   be a receiver or manager of a person's property;

(4)   in any way, whether directly or indirectly, be concerned or take part in the promotion, formation or management of a company,

for a specified period beginning with the date of the order.[221] So disqualification makes it as unlawful without leave of the court to act as a *de facto* or a shadow director as it is to act as a director who is (apart from the order) duly appointed.

Discretionary, mandatory and automatic disqualification

The grounds for disqualification fall into three groups: those on which   **14–60**
disqualification is within the court's discretion[222]; those on which the court is obliged to make a disqualification order[223]; and those where disqualification is automatic and is not dependent on a court order.[224] In cases within the second (mandatory) category, the court retains its discretion to grant leave to carry on any of the activities referred to above despite the disqualification,[225] although obviously an order giving leave ought not to be made in such sweeping terms as to render the disqualification nugatory. There is no power to limit the disqualification itself to a given class of company, for example, by disqualifying a person from acting as director of a public company but not of a private company.[226]

It cannot be said that there is a uniform policy underlying the distinction between discretionary and mandatory disqualification. One might have thought that in every case the question should be whether the director's conduct makes him unfit to be concerned in the management of a company, yet that is not a pre-condition of disqualification under s.2 (conviction of indictable offence), 3 (persistent breaches of companies legislation), 4 (fraud, etc.), 5 (conviction for failure to file returns or accounts) or 10 (participation in wrongful trading)[227]; only under ss.6 (insolvency), 8 (investigation of the company) and 9A (competition) is unfitness made a prerequisite of

---

[221] Company Directors Disqualification Act 1986 s.1.
[222] See below, para.14–63.
[223] See below, para.14–65.
[224] See below, para.14–66.
[225] See para.14–81.
[226] *R. v Goodman* [1992] B.C.C. 625 at 627.
[227] Dealing respectively with conviction of an indictable offence, persistent breaches of companies legislation, fraud in a winding up, convictions for at least three summary offences, and participation in wrongful trading.

disqualification. This indicates that disqualification is not simply a means of removing from involvement in corporate management those considered unfit for it but is also seen as an inducement to those acting as directors to fulfil their statutory obligations, a deterrent against wrongdoing and a punishment for serious misbehaviour. Again, one might think that where the court is satisfied that the director concerned is unfit to be concerned in the management of a company disqualification should be mandatory, yet that is not the case as regards disqualification proceedings under s.8[228] or s.10.[229] The courts themselves have in several cases declined to disqualify a person held unfit to be concerned in the management of the company, usually on the basis that his conduct, although reprehensible, was not so serious as to justify such a heavy sanction.

Who can be disqualified

14–61   The short title of the Act refers to disqualification from acting as a director, not to the status of those who are being disqualified. In general, a disqualification order may therefore be made against any person, whether or not he is or has acted as a director, if he is guilty on one of the statutory grounds for disqualification. This is true of all of the discretionary grounds. But the provisions for mandatory disqualification on the ground of unfitness are confined to those who are or have been directors of a company which has become insolvent.[230]

Period of disqualification

14–62   The maximum period of disqualification is either five years or 15 years, depending on the ground of disqualification. Where it is unfitness to act, the Act sets not only a maximum period of 15 years, but a minimum period of two years[231]; in other cases there is no prescribed minimum. The courts, however, have set certain discretionary bands.[232]

Grounds for discretionary disqualification

14–63   There are seven grounds upon which the court has discretion to order disqualification.

---

[228] Disqualification after investigation of the company on behalf of the Secretary of State.
[229] Participation in wrongful trading.
[230] Company Directors Disqualification Act 1986 s.6.
[231] Company Directors Disqualification Act 1986 s.6(4).
[232] See below, para.14–80.

(1)   Conviction for an indictable offence (whether the conviction is on indictment or summarily) in connection with the promotion, formation, management or liquidation of a company, or with the receivership or management of a company's property.[233] Management is not confined to internal management but includes external activities, for example, the fraudulent raising of finance[234] and, indeed, any offence having some relevant factual connection with the management of the company.[235] Moreover, it is not necessary that the company's affairs be mismanaged; conducting the business competently but without legal authorisation is within the statutory provisions.[236]

(2)   Persistent default in relation to the provisions of the companies legislation requiring any return, account or other document to be filed with, delivered or sent, or a notice of any matter to be given to the registrar of companies.[237] Persistent default is conclusively presumed by showing that in the five years ending with the date of the application the person concerned has been adjudged guilty (whether or not on the same occasion) of three or more defaults in relation to the above provisions.[238] It has been held that "persistent" connotes some degree of continuance or repetition, whether by continuing or repeating the same default or by a series of different defaults.[239] However, culpability is not an essential ingredient, although it is obviously relevant to any decision whether to disqualify and the length of any disqualification.[240] The court can take all circumstances into account, including the damaging effect of a disqualification order on employees.[241]

(3)   The offence of fraudulent trading (whether or not convicted[242]).

(4)   Other fraud in relation to the company or breach of duty, as officer, liquidator, receiver or manager.[243]

---

[233] Company Directors Disqualification Act 1986 s.2(1).

[234] *R. v Corbin* (1984) 6 Cr. App. R. (S) 17; and *R. v Austen* (1985) 1 B.C.C. 99,528.

[235] *R. v Goodman* [1992] B.C.C. 625 (conviction for insider trading under the Company Securities (Inside Dealing) Act 1985).

[236] *R. v Georgiou* (1988) 4 B.C.C. 322.

[237] Company Directors Disqualification Act 1986 s.3(1). By "companies legislation" is meant the Companies Acts and Pts 1 to 7 of the Insolvency Act 1986 (Company Directors Disqualification Act 1986 s.3(4A)). "The Companies Acts" has the meaning given by s.2(1) of the Companies Act 2006 (Company Directors Disqualification Act 1986 s.22(7)).

[238] Company Directors Disqualification Act 1986 s.3(2). As to when a person is to be treated as adjudged guilty of a default, see s.3(3).

[239] *Re Arctic Engineering Ltd* (1985) 1 B.C.C. 99 at 563.

[240] *Re Arctic Engineering*, cited above n.239.

[241] *Re Arctic Engineering*, cited above n.239, where Hoffmann J. held there had been persistent default by a liquidator in filing returns, but declined to make a disqualification order on the ground that the liquidator in question was neither dishonest nor incompetent and a disqualification order would have very serious consequences for him, his employees and his clients.

[242] Company Directors Disqualification Act 1986, s.4(1)(a).

[243] Company Directors Disqualification Act 1986, s.4(1)(b).

(5) Summary conviction for failure to file returns, etc. where during the previous five years the person concerned has three or more default orders or convictions.[244]

(6) A finding of unfitness to be concerned in the management of a company, following a statutory investigation.[245]

(7) Participation in wrongful trading.[246]

Discretionary disqualification and contribution orders

14–64   In *R. v Holmes*,[247] the Court of Appeal held that it was inconsistent to make an order for compensation under s.35 of the Powers of Criminal Courts Act 1973 and at the same time to make a disqualification order, thereby depriving the respondent of the best means of earning the money with which to pay the compensation. However, it is thought that the court was addressing the facts of the particular case and cannot have intended to lay down a general rule of this kind, for the same considerations would apply to the disqualification of a director against whom a contribution order is made under s.214 of the Insolvency Act 1986 in respect of wrongful trading,[248] yet s.10(1) of the Company Directors Disqualification Act 1986 expressly provides for disqualification in addition to a contribution order.

Ground for mandatory disqualification order

14–65   There are two grounds on which disqualification is mandatory, namely: unfitness to be concerned in the management of a company where the person concerned is or has been a director of a company that has at any time become insolvent[249]; and breach of competition law on the part of a person whose conduct makes him unfit to be concerned in the management of a company.[250]

Automatic disqualification

14–66   A person is automatically disqualified from acting without leave of the court as director of, or directly or indirectly taking part in or being concerned in

---

[244] Company Directors Disqualification Act 1986, s.5.
[245] Company Directors Disqualification Act 1986 s.8.
[246] Company Directors Disqualification Act 1986 s.10.
[247] [1991] B.C.C. 394.
[248] See above, paras 14–52 et seq.
[249] Company Directors Disqualification Act 1986 s.6. See below.
[250] Company Directors Disqualification Act 1986 s.9A.

the promotion, formation or management of, a company, where he is an undischarged bankrupt[251] or where as a result of his default in payment under a county court administration order the court revokes that order.[252]

9. *DISQUALIFICATION FOR UNFITNESS OF DIRECTOR OF INSOLVENT COMPANY*

The statutory provisions

Under s.6 of the Company Directors Disqualification Act, the court is obliged to impose a disqualification order where it is satisfied that:　　**14–67**

(1)　a person is or had been a director of a company which has at any time become insolvent (whether while he was a director or subsequently); and

(2)　his conduct as a director of the company (either taken alone or taken together with his conduct as a director of any other company or companies) makes him unfit to be concerned in the management of a company.

For the purpose of the above provisions:

(1)　"director" includes a shadow director[253] and a *de facto* director;[254] and

(2)　a company becomes insolvent if it goes into liquidation when its assets are insufficient to pay its debts and other liabilities and the expenses of the winding up or if an administration order is made in relation to it or an administrative receiver of the company is appointed.[255]

Burden and standard of proof

The burden of proof is on the Secretary of State; the standard of proof is not the standard in criminal cases ("beyond reasonable doubt"), but the civil standard, the balance of probabilities, a flexible standard which requires that　　**14–68**

---

[251] Company Directors Disqualification Act 1986 s.11.
[252] Company Directors Disqualification Act 1986 s.12.
[253] Company Directors Disqualification Act 1986 s.6(3C). "Shadow director" is defined by s.22(5) as a person in accordance with whose directions or instructions the directors of the company are accustomed to act. See also para.14–05.
[254] Company Directors Disqualification Act 1986 s.22(4); *Secretary of State for Trade and Industry v Aviss* [2007] B.C.C. 288; *Re Lo-Line Electric Motors*, [1988] Ch. 47; and see above, para.14–04.
[255] Company Directors Disqualification Act 1986 s.6(2).

the graver the allegation the heavier the burden of showing the truth of the matters alleged.[256]

"A disqualification order carries significant consequences for the defendant, not only in respect of the business reputation of the director but also as a serious interference with the freedom and ability of the director to pursue a business career. Further, the allegations necessary to establish unfitness are lack of probity or a high level of incompetence. The cogency of the evidence required to discharge the burden of proof to the requisite standard must be such as reflects the seriousness of the allegations and of the consequences."[257]

The serious consequences of disqualification for the director concerned not only bear on the burden of proof, they also engage the overriding principle of fairness to those against whom disqualification proceedings are brought.[258] Thus, the director concerned is entitled to be given a clear picture of the case he has to meet, particularly where fraud is alleged[259]; the affidavit or affirmation in support of the Secretary of State's application must set out not only the allegations made but the essential facts on which these are based and the main parts of the evidence on which the Secretary of State intends to rely[260]; the case against the director must be presented fairly, incorporating significant evidence in favour of the director as well as against him[261]; save in special circumstances, "explanations should be sought from the director before the balloon goes up";[262] and allegations against him may be changed only where this would not cause injustice.[263]

Reporting requirements and their significance

14–69   In order for the Secretary of State to be able to act against directors considered to be unfit to be concerned in the management of a company, the Secretary of State has to have adequate information about their misconduct

---

[256] *Official Receiver v Key* [2009] B.C.C. 11; *Secretary of State for Trade and Industry v Hollier* [2007] B.C.C. 11; and *R. v Verby Print for Advertising Ltd* [1998] B.C.C. 652.

[257] *Hollier*, cited above n.256, *per* Etherton J. at [83].

[258] See *Kappler v Secretary of State for Trade and Industry* [2008] 1 B.C.L.C. 120, *per* Judge Roger Kaye Q.C. at [80], summarising the principles established by the authorities.

[259] *Kappler*, cited above n.258; and *Secretary of State for Trade and Industry v Goldberg* [2004] 1 B.C.L.C. 597, *per* Lewison J. at [51] et seq.

[260] *Secretary of State for Trade and Industry v Swan* [2005] B.C.C. 596, *per* Laddie J. at [17].

[261] *Secretary of State for Trade and Industry v Hickling* [1996] B.C.C. 670, *per* H.H. Judge Weeks at 690.

[262] *Swan*, cited above n.260, at [32].

[263] *Re Sevenoaks Stationers (Retail) Ltd* [1991] Ch. 164; and *Kappler*, cited above n.258.

which he can place before the court. To that end, s.7(3) provides that where it appears to the office-holder[264] that the conditions of s.6(1) are satisfied as respects a person who is or has been a director of the company, the office-holder is required forthwith to report the matter to the Secretary of State.[265] Section 7 is buttressed by the Insolvent Companies (Reports on Conduct of Directors) Rules 1996,[266] which are confined to companies in voluntary winding up but are in practice followed by the Official Receiver in a compulsory winding up. The Rules require the office-holder to furnish to the Secretary of State reports and returns in a prescribed form.[267] Thus a liquidator will either send a report under s.7(3) of the Act[268] setting out details of the conduct which in his view makes the director unfit for the purpose of s.6(1) or, if no such report has been submitted before the expiry of six months from the relevant date, a return[269] giving prescribed information about the company, but stating that the liquidator has not become aware of any information which would require him to make a report under s.7(3) of the Act.

It will be evident that the success of the disqualification provisions to a considerable degree stands or falls by the effectiveness of the reporting requirements and procedures and the readiness of the Insolvency Service to act on them. In the earlier days of the disqualification regime, a report on the Insolvency Services Agency produced by the National Audit Office in 1993[270] revealed significant weaknesses, and research by Professor Sally Wheeler, which probed beneath the surface to examine the decision-making process, showed a preoccupation with procedures rather than substance.[271] There appears to have been no further audit since that time, but there are indications that over the past few years the problem has been taken seriously. One manifestation of this is the steady increase in the number of disqualification proceedings and of reported decisions concerning disqualification as shown in the table below.

---

[264] The official receiver in a compulsory winding up, the liquidator in a voluntary winding up, the administrator in an administration and the administrative receiver in an administrative receivership (s.7(3)). See also para.14–84 as to reporting by officers of courts.

[265] In practice, the report goes to the Insolvency Service, which carries out the Secretary of State's responsibilities in relation to proceedings brought under s.6(1).

[266] SI 1996/1909, as amended.

[267] Commonly known as a "D" form, the forms being numbered D1, D2, etc.

[268] A "D1" report.

[269] A "D2" return.

[270] "The Insolvency Executive Agency: Company Directors Disqualification" (HMSO, 1993).

[271] "Directors' Disqualification: Insolvency Practitioners and the Decision-Making Process" (1995) 15 *Legal Studies* 283.

Disqualification orders and undertakings

Allegation types	2007–2008	2008–2009	2009–2010
Crown debts	554	563	816
Accounting matters	250	381	448
Transaction to the detriment of creditors	161	246	391
Criminal matters	101	174	258
Misappropriation of assets	53	49	68
Technical matters—statutory obligations	37	46	33
Trading at a time when company knowingly or unknowingly insolvent	36	44	40
Phoenix companies or multiple failures	13	14	12
Other	N/A	N/A	98
Total	**1,205**	**1,517**	**2,164**

Source: The Insolvency Service Annual Report and Accounts 2009–2010

Procedure

14–70 Under several of the above provisions of the Company Directors Disqualification Act[272] the court has power to order disqualification of its own motion. But disqualification on the ground of unfitness to act requires an application to that end by the Secretary of State or, in the case of a company in compulsory winding up, the official receiver if so directed by the Secretary of State.[273] There is no time limit for making application except in cases under s.6, where the time limit for the making of the order[274] is two years beginning with the day on which the company became insolvent,[275] unless the court gives leave to bring proceedings late.[276] Not less than 10 days' notice of the intention to apply for a disqualification order must be given to the person against whom the order is sought,[277] but the Court of Appeal has held that this requirement is directory, not mandatory, so that failure to give the requisite notice is a procedural irregularity which does not

---

[272] In particular, ss.2, 4, 5 and 10, and possibly also s.3.
[273] Company Directors Disqualification Act s.7(1).
[274] Not the time limit for instituting the disqualification proceedings.
[275] As defined by s.6(2). See above, para.14–67.
[276] Company Directors Disqualification Act s.7(2).
[277] Company Directors Disqualification Act s.16(1).

vitiate the proceedings.[278] Proceedings on an application for a disqualification order are governed by the Insolvent Companies (Disqualification of Unfit Directors) Proceedings Rules 1987,[279] by the Disqualification Practice Direction[280] and, as regards certain provisions, by the CPR.

The court has no power to dispense with proceedings by means of a consent order. In every case, the court has itself to be satisfied that there is sufficient evidence of unfitness to act as a director before it makes a disqualification order.[281] However, in *Re Carecraft Construction Ltd*[282] Ferris J. approved a summary procedure by which the parties to disqualification proceedings can avoid a full-scale hearing by placing before the court an agreed statement of facts concerning unfitness, coupled with some evidence of unfitness on which the court can act. This procedure became enshrined in the Disqualification Practice Direction,[283] under which parties desiring to make an application under the *Carecraft* procedure are required to inform the court immediately, obtain a date for the hearing and, except in simple cases or where the court otherwise directs, submit a written statement containing in respect of each respondent any material facts which (for the purposes of the application) are either agreed or not opposed (by either party) and specify in writing the period of disqualification which the parties accept that the agreed or unopposed facts justify (for example, 4 to 6 years) or the bracket (i.e. 2 to 5 years; 6 to 10 years; 11 to 15 years) into which they will submit the case falls.[284] However, the *Carecraft* procedure has been largely superseded by the procedure for statutory undertakings given to the Secretary of State as described below.

Rules of evidence

In disqualification proceedings, there is a well-established implied exception to the strict rules of evidence on hearsay evidence, opinion evidence and the rule in *Hollington v Hewthorn*[285] so as to enable the court to receive as evidence materials produced under statutory procedures, such as reports of investigators appointed by the Financial Services Authority, affidavits of

14–71

---

[278] *Secretary of State for Trade and Industry v Langridge* [1991] Ch. 402, Nourse L.J. dissenting; [1991] B.C.C. 148 sub. nom. *Re Cedac Ltd, Secretary of State for Trade and Industry v Langridge*.

[279] SI 1987/2023, as amended.

[280] Practice Direction: Directors' Disqualification Proceedings [1999] B.C.C. 717.

[281] [1994] 1 W.L.R. 172.

[282] [1994] 1 W.L.R. 172.

[283] Cited above, n.280, r.13.

[284] Practice Direction, paras 13.1 and 13.2. For a detailed description, see Walters and Davis-White, *Directors' Disqualification & Insolvency Restrictions*, 2009, paras 9–49 et seq.; and for a draft *Carecraft* statement, App.10 to that work.

[285] This rule, named after *Hollington v F. Hewthorn & Co Ltd* [1943] K.B. 587, is to the effect that a judgment in a court of law is inadmissible in subsequent litigation as evidence of the facts on the basis of which the judgment was given.

liquidators and officials of relevant government department agencies and the like.[286] Such materials are prima facie evidence only and the director concerned is entitled to challenge the conclusions and to adduce evidence for that purpose. The exception is seen as a practical, commonsense measure which enables the issues to be identified without the need to begin all over again.

Statutory undertakings

14–72 Useful though it has been, the *Carecraft* procedure involved time and expense which both parties and the courts considered burdensome and unnecessary. When the Secretary of State and the parties were content to agree on the terms of disqualification, it seemed pointless to require them to go to the court for approval. It is true that the Secretary of State, in lieu of initiating or continuing disqualification proceedings, could accept an undertaking by the director concerned not to be concerned in the management of a company for a specified period, but in various respects such an undertaking was weaker than a disqualification order.[287] Accordingly, s.6 of the Insolvency Act 2000 inserted a new s.7(2A) into the Company Directors Disqualification Act empowering the Secretary of State to accept a disqualification undertaking in lieu of applying for or proceeding with an application for a disqualification order. A disqualification undertaking is an undertaking that the person concerned:

(1) will not be a director of a company, act as receiver of a company's property or in any way, whether directly or indirectly, be concerned or take part in the promotion, formation or management of a company unless (in each case) he has the leave of the court; and

(2) will not act as an insolvency practitioner.[288]

The Secretary of State may accept such an undertaking even though the two-year limitation period governing the commencement of disqualification proceedings has expired.[289] The content of the undertaking thus corresponds exactly to that prescribed for a disqualification order by s.1 of the Act, and the maximum and minimum period of disqualification is likewise the

---

[286] *Aaron v Secretary of State for Business, Enterprise and Regulatory Reform* [2009] B.C.C. 375, where the development of the exception is traced in the judgment of Thomas L.J.

[287] See Walters and Davis-White, *Directors' Disqualification & Insolvency Restrictions*, 2009, para.9–12.

[288] Company Directors Disqualification Act 1986 s.1A, inserted by the Insolvency Act 2000 s.6.

[289] *Gardiner v Secretary of State for Business, Enterprise and Regulatory Reform* [2009] B.C.C. 742.

same.[290] The Secretary of State is not obliged to require an agreed statement of the facts rendering the disqualified party unfit, but in practice will not normally accept an undertaking without an admission of the key facts, recorded in a schedule annexed to the undertaking, and has been held entitled to insist on this condition.[291] The schedule takes the form of a summary of misconduct that, for the purposes solely of the CDDA and other purposes consequential to the giving of a disqualification undertaking, the disqualified person does not dispute.[292] The sanctions for breach of a disqualification undertaking are the same as those for breach of a disqualification order and such undertakings are registered in the same way as orders.[293]

Statutory undertakings have largely displaced disqualification orders. In the year 2010, 79 per cent of the total number of disqualifications were achieved by undertakings.[294]

What conduct is relevant

Under s.6(1)(b) of the Company Directors Disqualification Act the court must determine whether the director's conduct "either taken alone or together with his conduct as a director of any other company or companies" makes him unfit to be concerned in the management of a company. Thus, the court can take into account not only conduct in relation to the insolvent company (the "lead company"), but also that of any other company ("collateral company") of which the person concerned is or was director. It is not necessary that his conduct in the management of a collateral company should be the same as or similar to his conduct in the management of the lead company,[295] although the allegations made in the evidence given in the earlier proceedings must be such as to have potentially probative value.[296] Although conduct in relation to other companies[297] (whether or not themselves insolvent) may be taken into account, there must be some misconduct in relation to the insolvent company before s.6 can apply. Moreover, only misconduct *as director* (including conduct as a *de facto* or shadow director[298]) is relevant; conduct in some subordinate

14–73

---

[290] Company Directors Disqualification Act 1986 s.1A(2).
[291] *Re Blackspur Group Plc (No.3), Secretary of State for Trade and Industry v Eastaway* [2002] 2 B.C.L.C. 263.
[292] For a form of this, see Walters and Davis-White, *Directors' Disqualification & Insolvency Restrictions*, 2009, App.9.
[293] See below, para.14–82.
[294] "Insolvency Service Annual Report and Accounts 2009–2010", p.19.
[295] *Re Country Farm Inns Ltd, Secretary of State v Ivens* [1997] B.C.L.C. 174.
[296] *Secretary of State for Trade and Industry v Green* [2006] EWHC 1739 (Ch).
[297] But not non-corporate entities such as partnerships: *Re Vintage Hallmark Plc* [2008] B.C.C. 150.
[298] Company Directors Disqualification Act 1986 ss.6(3) and 22(4); *Re Richborough Furniture* [1996] B.C.C. 155; *Re Moorgate Metals Ltd* [1995] 1 B.C.L.C. 503; and *Re Lo-Line Electric Motors*, cited above n.254.

capacity is not within the scope of the section.[299] The court must have regard to the matters set out in Pt I of the Schedule to the Company Directors Disqualification Act and, where the company has become insolvent, to the matters set out in Pt II of that Schedule.[300] But any misconduct as director, whether or not mentioned in the Schedule or whether or not a breach of a specific provision of the Companies Act or the Insolvency Act, may be relevant[301] and in deciding on disqualification the court may examine the matters of conduct established and consider them both separately and cumulatively.[302]

The competing policy considerations

14–74   Cases on the application of the disqualification provisions reveal a tension between two important principles: individual liberty and protection of the public. This tension was accurately identified by Sir Nicolas Browne-Wilkinson V.C. in *Re Lo-Line Electric Motors Ltd*[303]:

"What is the proper approach to deciding whether someone is unfit to be a director? The approach adopted in all the cases to which I have been referred is broadly the same. The primary purpose of the section is not to punish the individual but to protect the public against the future conduct of companies by persons whose past records as directors of insolvent companies have shown them to be a danger to creditors and others. Therefore, the power is not fundamentally penal. But if the power to disqualify is exercised, disqualification does involve a substantial interference with the freedom of the individual. It follows that the rights of the individual must be fully protected."

This passage has been cited with approval in a number of subsequent cases.[304]

---

[299] *Re Richborough Furniture*, cited above n.298; and *Secretary of State for Trade and Industry v Hickling* [1996] B.C.C. 678.

[300] Company Directors Disqualification Act 1986 s.9.

[301] *Re Bath Glass Ltd* (1988) 4 B.C.C. 130; and *Re Churchill Hotel (Plymouth) Ltd* [1988] B.C.L.C. 341.

[302] *Re Bunting Electric Manufacturing Co Ltd* [2006] 1 B.C.L.C. 550; and *Secretary of State for Business, Enterprise and Regulatory Reform v Poulter* [2009] B.C.C. 608. It has been held that ss.6 and 9 focus on the director's conduct rather than the consequences of that conduct: *Re Bunting Electric Manufacturing Co*; and *Re Brampton Manor (Leisure) Ltd* [2009] EWHC 1796 (Ch).

[303] Cited above n.254, at 485–486.

[304] See, e.g. *Secretary of State for Trade and Industry v Langridge* [1991] Ch. 402; sub. nom. *Re Cedac Ltd Secretary of State for Trade and Industry v Langridge* [1991] B.C.L.C. 543; and *Re Living Images Ltd* [1996] 1 B.C.L.C. 348.

Criteria for determining unfitness

The degree of culpability that has to be established in order to render a **14–75** person unfit to be concerned in the management of a company has been expressed in different ways by different judges. Thus, in the *Lo-Line* case cited above, the Vice-Chancellor continued:

> "Ordinary commercial misjudgement is in itself not sufficient to justify disqualification. In the normal case, the conduct complained of must display a lack of commercial probity, although I have no doubt that in an extreme case of gross negligence or total incompetence disqualification could be appropriate."[305]

Similarly, in *Re Bath Glass Ltd*,[306] Peter Gibson J. stated the test as follows:

> "To reach a finding of unfitness the court must be satisfied that the director has been guilty of a serious failure or serious failures, whether deliberately or through incompetence, to perform those duties of directors which are attendant on the privilege of trading through companies with limited liability."

In several cases, the degree of culpability required has been referred to in terms of commercial morality:

> "There must, I think, be something about the case, some conduct which if not really dishonest is at any rate in breach of standards of commercial morality, or some really gross incompetence which persuades the court that it would be a danger to the public if he were to be allowed to continue to be involved in the management of companies, before a disqualification order is made."[307]

However, more recently the trend has been towards tightening up the standards of behaviour required and lowering the culpability threshold. In particular, the test of commercial morality has been described as "misleading (or at least unhelpful)"[308] and greater emphasis has been placed on placing creditors' money at risk,[309] whether intentionally, recklessly or through

---

[305] Cited above n.254, at 486.
[306] Cited above n.301, at 133.
[307] *Re Dawson Print Group Ltd* (1987) 3 B.C.C. 322 (a decision on s.300 of the now repealed Companies Act 1985), per Hoffmann J. at 324, cited with approval by Sir Nicolas Browne-Wilkinson V.C. in *Re McNulty's Interchange Ltd* (1988) 4 B.C.C. 533; and see to similar effect *Re Douglas Construction Services Ltd* (1988) 4 B.C.C. 533.
[308] *Re Stanford Services Ltd* (1987) 3 B.C.C. 326, *per* Vinelott J. at 334.
[309] See, e.g. *Re Stanford Services*, cited above n.308; and *Re Churchill Hotel*, cited above n.301.

incompetence or negligence in a marked degree, even if the incompetence is not "total".[310]

After some division of judicial opinion in earlier cases, it can now be taken as settled that non-payment of Crown debts does not in itself carry a greater degree of culpability than failure to pay other types of debt.[311] What matters is not whether the debt is a Crown debt in respect of collected taxes or some other kind of debt, but the circumstances in which the debt came to be outstanding, and in particular the company's decision to pay only those creditors who press for payment or to pay other debts in preference to Crown debts.[312]

A director does not escape the statutory provisions by shirking his responsibilities and leaving all decisions to be taken by others,[313] for the board has a collegiate or collective responsibility[314]; nor is he entitled to deny responsibility for false statements in the company's accounts, or rely on his fellow directors or the company's auditors.[315]

Time as at which unfitness to be tested

14–76   Whether a director is unfit to be concerned in the management of a company is to be determined by reference to the facts known to the court at the time of the hearing.[316] The question of fitness or unfitness is purely for the trial judge and affidavits which purport to present expert evidence on the subject or to provide evidence of general reputation of the director where this has not been put in issue have been struck out[317] as irrelevant.[318]

Disqualification of unfit director is mandatory

14–77   Once it has been established that in a case within s.6 of the Company Directors Disqualification Act a director is unfit to be concerned in the management of a company, the court is obliged to disqualify him for a period of at least two years.

---

[310] *Re Sevenoaks Stationers (Retail) Ltd* [1991] Ch. 164.

[311] *Re Sevenoaks Stationers*, cited above n.310.

[312] *Re Verby Print for Advertising Ltd* [1998] 2 B.C.L.C. 23; *Official Receiver v Key* [2009] B.C.C. 11; and *Official Receiver v Dhaliwall* [2006] 1 B.C.L.C. 285.

[313] *Re AG Manchester Ltd* [2008] B.C.C. 497 (in which an inner group of directors had usurped the functions of the board, the other directors standing by); and *Re Majestic Recording Studios Ltd* (1988) 4 B.C.C. 519.

[314] *Secretary of State for Trade and Industry v Griffiths* [1998] 2 All E.R. 124.

[315] *Re Queen's Moat Houses Plc (No.2)* [2005] B.C.L.C. 136.

[316] *Re Bath Glass*, cited above n.301, approved by the Court of Appeal in *Re Grayan Services Ltd* [1995] Ch. 241.

[317] Under RSC Ord.41 r.6. Under the Civil Procedure Rules, expert evidence may not be given at all without the court's leave (CPR r.35.4(1)).

[318] *Secretary of State for Trade and Industry v Dawes* [1997] B.C.C. 121; and *Re Oakfame Constructions Ltd* [1996] B.C.C. 67.

The court has no discretion in the matter and the fact that the director concerned is no longer a danger to the public is irrelevant, for the focus is on the offence, not on the offender.[319] On the other hand, this fact will be highly relevant in considering whether leave should be granted under s.17 of the Act.[320]

Disqualification applies in relation to all companies

A disqualification order or undertaking precludes the disqualified person from being concerned in the management of any company, not merely the company in the management of which his misconduct occurred.[321] However, the disqualified person can apply for leave under s.17, although the courts have not always insisted on a formal application and have implicitly exercised jurisdiction under that section by excepting specified companies from the scope of the disqualification order.

14–78

Commencement of period of disqualification

Unless the court otherwise orders, any period of disqualification begins at the end of the period of 21 days beginning with the date of the order.[322] The purpose of the 21-day deferment is to give the disqualified director a limited breathing space within which to reorganise his affairs, for example, by resigning all his directorships and handing over his management activities to others. The court cannot give credit for the period during which the disqualification proceedings were pending.[323]

14–79

Period of disqualification

The minimum period of disqualification is two years, the maximum 15 years.[324] In *Re Sevenoaks Stationers (Retail) Ltd*,[325] Dillon L.J. endorsed

14–80

---

[319] *Re Grayan Building Services*, cited above n.316.
[320] *Re Grayan Building Services*, cited above n.316. See below para.14–81.
[321] It follows that the fact that the director may not be unfit to be involved in the management of other companies, although relevant to the grant of leave to be so involved and to the length of disqualification, is not relevant to disqualification itself (*Secretary of State for Business, Innovation and Skills v Aaron* [2009] EWHC 3263 (Ch)).
[322] Company Directors Disqualification Act 1986 s.1(1). At the present time, as previously noted, the great majority of disqualifications have effect by virtue of the director's undertaking, not a court order, and the practice of the Insolvency Service is to accept an offer of an undertaking which provides that the period of disqualification is to commence 21 days after acceptance of the undertaking by the Secretary of State.
[323] *Secretary of State for Trade and Industry v Arif* [1996] B.C.C. 586.
[324] Company Directors Disqualification Act 1986 s.6(4).
[325] [1991] Ch. 164 at 174.

the division of the potential period of 15 years into three brackets put forward by counsel for the Official Receiver at first instance, namely:

(1)   the top bracket of over 10 years should be reserved for particularly serious cases, which might include cases where the director had already had a period of disqualification imposed on him before;

(2)   the minimum bracket of two to five years' disqualification was appropriate where, although disqualification was mandatory, the case was, relatively, not very serious; and

(3)   the middle bracket of 6 to 10 years should be used where the case, thought serious, did not merit the top bracket.

Most cases fall within the middle bracket, the average length of disqualification in the year 2009–2010 being 6.4 years.[326] Factors which will incline the court towards a more serious view of a case include fraudulent trading, misappropriation of assets or other dishonesty, a reckless disregard of creditors' interests and persistent breaches of statutory obligations (for example, in relation to the filing of accounts), knowingly trading under a prohibited name, and adopting the practice of setting up phoenix companies[327] as each company of which he was a director became insolvent.[328] Where a director had been sentenced to a term of imprisonment for obtaining money by deception, it was held that this merited the need to protect the public for a considerable period, and this was not affected by the fact that the director had already paid the penalty of imprisonment.[329] The court is also entitled to have regard to the conduct of the director concerned in the disqualification proceedings themselves, and in particular to the falsity of evidence given in those proceedings[330] and the failure to co-operate with the official receiver.[331] Conversely, the absence of dishonest conduct is a mitigating factor,[332] as is the fact that the director has himself risked and lost a substantial amount of his own money.[333]

---

[326] The Insolvency Service Annual Report and Accounts 2009–2010, p.19.

[327] See above, para.14–06.

[328] See, e.g. *Secretary of State for Trade and Industry v McTighe* [1997] B.C.C. 224; *Re Living Images Ltd* [1996] B.C.C. 112; *R. v Moorgate Metals Ltd* [1995] B.C.L.C. 503; *Re Travel Mondial (UK) Ltd* [1991] B.C.C. 224; and *R. v T. & D. Services (Timber Preservation and Damp Proofing Contractors) Ltd* [1990] B.C.C. 592.

[329] *R. v Bott-Walters* [2005] 2 Cr. App. R. (S) 70.

[330] *Re Moorgate Metals*, cited above n.328; and *Re Godwin Warren Control Systems Plc* [1992] B.C.C. 557.

[331] *Secretary of State for Trade and Industry v McTighe* [1997] B.C.C. 124.

[332] *Secretary of State for Trade and Industry v Arif* [1996] B.C.C. 586; and *Re Hitco 2000 Ltd* [1995] B.C.C. 161.

[333] *Re Cargo Agency Ltd* [1992] B.C.C. 388.

Leave to act while disqualified

The effect of a disqualification order is that the director concerned cannot be a director of a company, or engage in any of the other activities specified in s.1(1) of the Company Directors Disqualification Act 1986 without leave of the court. The court's power to grant leave is largely unfettered[334] and is exercisable either at the time the order is made or subsequently,[335] so that in making the disqualification order the court can grant leave to the persons concerned to act in such capacities and within such limits as the court thinks fit to specify. This power has been exercised in several cases, the court's role being seen as a balancing one in which the protection of the public has to be weighed against the need of the disqualified director to earn a living and the dependence of the company or some other company on his ability to be concerned in its management.[336] Thus, in *Re Majestic Recording Studios Ltd*,[337] Mervyn Davies J., when disqualifying a director of several companies, gave him leave to continue to act as director of one of them only on condition that he had as a co-director an independent chartered accountant who was willing to act with him; and in *Re Lo-Line Electric Motors Ltd*,[338] Browne-Wilkinson V.C., in disqualifying the director of four companies which had become insolvent, gave leave to him to remain director of the two family companies, in which it was necessary for him to play a managerial role, on condition that another party remained a director of both companies with voting control. An overriding criterion for the grant of leave is that there is no danger to the public,[339] and to that end the court may impose whatever conditions it considers appropriate.[340] It is also necessary to show that there is a need for the disqualified director to be allowed to act, for example, that the health of the company in respect of which leave is sought depends upon his assumption of or involvement in its management.[341]

14–81

Sanctions for acting while disqualified

A person who, without leave of the court under s.17, acts in contravention of a disqualification order is guilty of a criminal offence[342] and is personally

14–82

---

[334] However, it ought not to give leave in terms so wide or general as to undermine the mandatory character of the minimum period of disqualification prescribed by the Act.
[335] It is obviously more satisfactory to give leave at the time the disqualification is imposed.
[336] *Re Grayan Building Services*, cited above n.316; and *Secretary of State for Trade and Industry v Baker (No.3)* [2000] 1 W.L.R. 634.
[337] (1988) 4 B.C.C. 519.
[338] Cited above n.254.
[339] *Re Grayan Building Services*, cited above n.316.
[340] See, e.g. the conditions set out in *Secretary of State for Trade and Industry v Swan (No.2)* [2005] EWHC 2479 (Ch) at [13], and the conditions contained in the schedule to the order made in *Re Gibson Davies Chemists Ltd* [1994] B.C.C. 11. See also the decisions referred to above, nn.337 and 338.
[341] ibid.
[342] Company Directors Disqualification Act 1986 s.13.

liable for all of the relevant debts of a company in the management of which he is involved as well as being jointly and severally liable with the company,[343] which if sued can claim contribution.[344] Each unpaid creditor has a direct right of action and is entitled to retain the proceeds for himself; the right of action is not vested in the company, so that the liquidator cannot claim to be representative of creditors for the purpose of recovering debts due to them, and his role is restricted to claiming contribution on behalf of the company.[345]

A further consequence of contravening a disqualification order is that the defendant, to the extent that he has benefited from his offence, is liable to confiscation of the amount of the benefit under the Proceeds of Crime Act 2002.[346] This will typically be the defendant's gross receipts from the company. Only where it is legitimate to pierce the corporate veil, as where the defendant has used the company as a vehicle for fraud or the commission of some other criminal offence or to hide his crime and his benefits from it, will it be justified to value the defendant's benefit at the gross turnover of the company.[347]

Appeals

14–83   Although in general the Court of Appeal will be slow to interfere with the exercise of the trial judge's decision as to fitness or his discretion as to the period of disqualification, it will do so where it considers that the trial judge has erred in principle.[348]

Reporting of disqualification orders and undertakings

14–84   Reference has already been made to the reporting duties of office holders.[349] In addition, court managers and chief executives of magistrates' courts are required to notify to Companies House in the prescribed form particulars of all disqualification orders made by their courts, any action by such courts in consequence of which such an order ceases to be in force, and permission to a disqualified person to act in a prohibited capacity notwithstanding a disqualification order. The Secretary of State, acting by the Registrar of Companies, is required to maintain a register of all orders so made and of any undertakings given to the Secretary of State.[350]

---

[343] Company Directors Disqualification Act 1986 s.15. "Relevant debts" is defined in s.15(3).
[344] *Re Prestige Grinding Ltd* [2006] B.C.C. 421.
[345] *Re Prestige Grinding*, cited above n.344.
[346] *R. v Seager* [2009] EWCA Crim 1303.
[347] *R. v Seager*, cited above n.346.
[348] *McTighe*, cited above n.328; and *Re Sevenoaks Stationers (Retail) Ltd* [1991] Ch. 164.
[349] Company (Disqualification Orders) Regulations 2009, SI 2009/2471 (made under s.18(1) of the Company Directors Disqualification Act 1986).
[350] Company Directors Disqualification Act 1986 s.18(2). The register is open to the public.

Chapter 15

The European Insolvency Regime

1. INTRODUCTION

Hitherto we have devoted attention to purely domestic liquidations and administrations, that is, those which have no foreign element requiring particular consideration. But companies incorporated in England may have foreign creditors and may have assets or places of business in other countries. Conversely, foreign companies may incur debts, and have assets and places of business, in England. Several major collapses have become *causes célebres*, not least because business failures were concealed by massive frauds. Maxwell Communications Corporation, founded by the late Robert Maxwell, had incurred most of its debts in England, where under Maxwell's direction it looted pension funds, siphoning these off into Maxwell's private companies, and conducted various fraudulent transactions, whereas 80 per cent of its assets were situated in the United States. Proceedings were brought in both countries and led to a remarkable co-operation between the courts in London and New York.[1] The Bank of Credit and Commerce International SA was incorporated in Luxembourg but had 47 offices or branches in different countries. A winding up order was made in Luxembourg and was followed shortly after by a similar order in England, the English winding up proceedings being ancillary to those opened in Luxembourg. Proceedings were also instituted in the United States. BCCI's parent company, Bank of Credit and Commerce International (Overseas) Ltd, incorporated in the Cayman Islands, had 63 offices or branches in 28 countries. The group was found to be involved not only in fraudulent transactions but in a wide range of seriously unlawful activities, including

15–01

---

[1] See below, para.16–65.

establishing links with drug cartels and terrorist organisations. Depositors were said to have been defrauded of US$10 billion. Fortunately, much of the money was recovered by the liquidators as the result of proceedings in several jurisdictions.[2]

The Maxwell defalcations have since been dwarfed by massive frauds in other jurisdictions, the most notable being committed by executives of Enron, whose reorganisation at the time was the largest in American history, and by the aptly-named Bernard Madoff, who was estimated to have defrauded clients to the tune of a colossal $65 billion! Other major failures, not resulting from fraud, include Parmalat, Lehman Brothers and Iceland's three largest banks, Kaupthing Bank, Glitnir Bank and Landsbanki Islands.

Such large failures, particularly where involving fraud, commonly lead not only to action by regulators in withdrawing authorisations to carry on business but also to concurrent insolvency proceedings in different jurisdictions as well as a multiplicity of law suits around the world as office holders seek to recover assets and pursue claims with a view to restoring lost value to the insolvent companies. For example, the collapse of Lehman Brothers has led to insolvency proceedings in several countries, including the United Kingdom, the United States, Australia, Hong Kong, Switzerland and Luxembourg, and with some of the companies it is proving hard to establish to whom the funds and securities they are holding belong.[3] The foreign elements involved in these cases raise special considerations which in some cases can be extremely complex. The first task of office holders is to safeguard the assets that remain. Where these are dispersed among different countries, it is important to synchronise the various actions so that applications to the court in one jurisdiction do not lead to the disappearance of assets in others. However, the ability to do this depends to a considerable extent on the local law and the willingness of local courts to assist with measures that facilitate an integrated approach with effects going beyond the borders of their own countries. Where the insolvent enterprises have been carrying on a regulated business activity, such as banking, there is a similar need for co-operation among the various regulators, who are faced not only with the task of establishing the facts but also with sensitive timing issues, in that premature action may bring about the collapse of a company that might otherwise be saved.

---

[2] One of the more extraordinary actions arising from the collapse was that brought against the Bank of England as banking regulator by the liquidators of BCCI for misfeasance in a public office, alleging dishonesty on the part of no fewer than 42 Bank of England officials, including the production of documents on a vast scale containing fraudulent misrepresentations. Tomlinson J. was so concerned about the conduct of the case on behalf of the liquidators that he found it necessary to consult the Lord Chief Justice. The action was finally abandoned and indemnity costs were awarded (see *Three Rivers DC v Bank of England* [2006] EWHC 816 (Comm)), the costs being later agreed at £75.3 million.

[3] See, e.g. *Re Lehman Brothers International (Europe) Ltd* [2010] EWHC 2914.

The present chapter deals with European insolvency law and in particular the Insolvency Regulation 2000. Other international insolvencies form the subject of Ch.16.

The influence of EU law[4] on UK insolvency law has been steadily growing. Reference has already been made to the legislative measures introduced pursuant to the settlement finality directive[5] and the financial collateral directive[6] to safeguard transactions in the financial markets from invalidity under some of the avoidance provisions that would otherwise be applicable.[7] These directives qualify certain aspects of substantive insolvency law, which in most other respects does not fall within the competence of the European Union and is exclusively within the purview of Member States.[8] By contrast, the Insolvency Regulation,[9] although containing a few peripheral substantive law provisions, is essentially a conflict of laws regulation which deals with jurisdiction to open insolvency proceedings, the applicable law, the effects of insolvency proceedings and recognition across the European Union of judgments by a court in a Member State having jurisdiction. The directives governing the winding up of credit institutions[10] and insurance companies[11] draw heavily on the Insolvency Regulation, and are not discussed further. This chapter is devoted to key features of the Insolvency Regulation and its implementation in the United Kingdom.[12]

---

[4] The European Community became the European Union on December 1, 2009 as the result of entry into force of the Lisbon Treaty.

[5] European Parliament and Council Directive of May 19, 1998 on settlement finality in payment and securities settlement systems, 98/26/EC ([1998] OJ L 166/45), as amended by the European Parliament and Council Directive 2009/44/EC ([2009] OJ L 146/37).

[6] European Parliament and Council Directive of June 6, 2002 on financial collateral arrangements, 2002/247 ([2002] OJ L 168/43), as amended by the 2009 Directive (above, n.2).

[7] See above, paras 1–60 et seq.

[8] Exceptionally the provisions of art.XI of the Aircraft Protocol to the 2001 Convention on International Interests in Mobile Equipment (the Cape Town Convention) providing for the substantive rights of the creditor on the insolvency of the debtor were conceded by Member States, after a vigorous exchange of views, as falling within the competence of the EU on the understanding that this would not be regarded as a basis for depriving Member States of their general exclusive competence over substantive insolvency law. National insolvency laws vary widely from one Member State to another. The difficulties arising from this have recently been highlighted by an INSOL Europe Report, Harmonisation of Insolvency Law at EU Level (2010), which recommends the eventual harmonisation of substantive insolvency law across the EU.

[9] Council Regulation (EC) 1346/2000 of May 29, 2000 on insolvency proceedings ([2001] OJ L 160/1).

[10] European Parliament and the Council Directive of April 4, 2001 on the reorganisation and winding up of credit institutions, 2001/24/EC ([2001] OJ L 125/15). The last major bank failure was that of Lehman Brothers, whose collapse has led to massive litigation in England, the United States and elsewhere.

[11] European Parliament and Council Directive of March 19, 2001 on the reorganisation and winding up of insurance undertakings, 2001/17/EC ([2001] OJ L 110/28).

[12] For detailed analyses, see Miguel Virgós and Francisco Garcimartín, *The European Insolvency Regulation: Law and Practice* (The Hague: Kluwer Law International, 2004); Gabriel Moss, Ian Fletcher and Stuart Isaacs (eds), *The EC Regulation on Insolvency Proceedings*, 2nd edn (Oxford: Oxford University Press, 2009); Ian Fletcher, *Insolvency in Private International Law*, 2nd edn (Oxford: Oxford University Press, 2006), Ch.7; Virgós-Schmit Report on the Convention on Insolvency Proceedings, a report on the failed EC Convention on

The United Kingdom has also enacted the 1997 UNCITRAL Model Law on Cross-Border Insolvency, which is examined in Ch.16. Thus there are two instruments dealing with cross-border insolvency, with many similarities but also important differences. The Model Law is not an instrument on the international plane and thus does not entail international engagements. It is simply a set of provisions which a State may if it wishes adopt, with such modifications as it may decide. Accordingly, the status of the Model Law in an EU Member State that has enacted it is that of ordinary domestic legislation. In consequence, in case of conflict the Insolvency Regulation must be given primacy. The statutory instrument incorporating the Model Law makes express provision to this effect,[13] although this was strictly unnecessary.

2. BACKGROUND TO THE INSOLVENCY REGULATION

The 1968 Brussels Convention and Brussels I on jurisdiction and judgments

15–02   The 1968 Brussels Convention[14] introduced detailed provisions governing jurisdiction in proceedings brought within the European Community and the mutual recognition and enforcement of judgments of courts of Member States. However, the Convention excluded from its scope bankruptcy, proceedings relating to the winding up of insolvent companies or other legal persons, judicial arrangements, compositions and analogous proceedings.[15] In *Gourdain v Nadler*,[16] the European Court of Justice (ECJ) held that in order to be excluded from the Convention, judicial decisions "must derive directly from the bankruptcy or winding up and be closely connected with [the insolvency proceedings]".[17] In other words, they must be decisions in proceedings based on insolvency law. This would include proceedings under ss.213 and 214 of the Insolvency Act 1986 for fraudulent and wrongful trading respectively and proceedings for the avoidance of transactions under ss.238 to 245 but not, for example, an action by a liquidator in the ordinary

---

Insolvency Proceedings (see below); and Paul J. Omar, *European Insolvency Law* (Oxford: Oxford University Press, 2004). For a comparative treatment, see Jennifer Marshall (ed.), *European Cross-Border Insolvency* (London: Sweet & Maxwell, looseleaf).

[13] Cross-Border Insolvency Regulations 2006, SI 2006/1030, Sch.1 art.3. The regulations were made pursuant to s.14 of the Insolvency Act 2000, modify British insolvency law (as defined by Sch.1 art.2) and prevail over it in case of any conflict (reg.3).

[14] Convention on jurisdiction and the enforcement of judgments in civil and commercial matters, implemented in the UK by the Civil Jurisdiction and Judgments Act 1982 but now operative only in relation to Denmark consequent on replacement of the Convention by the EC Jurisdiction and Judgments Regulation ("Brussels I"), which has direct effect but to which Denmark declined to be a party. See below, para.15–04, n.31.

[15] See art.1.

[16] Case 133/78, [1979] 1 E.C.R. 733.

[17] *Gourdain v Nadler*, cited above n.16, at 744.

courts to enforce a duty owed to the company by a third party under the general law of contract, tort or property,[18] an action to set aside a transaction in fraud of creditors under s.423 of the Insolvency Act,[19] proceedings for the approval of a scheme of arrangement under s.899 of the Companies Act 2006,[20] an action by the liquidator to recover a debt due to the company,[21] proceedings to hold a person who acts as director while disqualified personally liable for the company's debts,[22] or a claim against a director for breach of fiduciary or other duty.[23]

The Brussels Convention became converted into a Regulation[24] with effect from March 1, 2002 and closely follows the Convention. Like the Convention, it does not apply to insolvency proceedings, although it is applicable to the winding up of solvent companies. The ECJ has held that in determining the scope of the bankruptcy exception the same test is to be applied under the Regulation as under the Convention, so that an action by a seller of goods against an insolvent purchaser which is based on reservation of title is an independent claim, not a claim based on insolvency law, and accordingly is governed by Brussels I.[25] In order for the exception to apply, the closeness of the link between the court action and the insolvency proceedings is the decisive factor. The mere fact that the claim is by or against the liquidator does not constitute a sufficient link.[26] Under art.25(2) of the Insolvency Regulation the recognition and enforcement of judgments other than those concerning the course and closure of insolvency proceedings or closely linked with them are governed by the Brussels Convention if it is applicable. The ECJ has held that this is now to be interpreted as applying Brussels I so far as the proceedings fall within the scope of Brussels I.[27]

---

[18] *Re Hayward deceased* [1997] Ch. 45.
[19] For this applies whether the company is solvent or insolvent.
[20] Which again is not dependent on the company's insolvency.
[21] *Re Hayward deceased*, cited above n.18, *per* Rattee J. at 54D; and *UBS AG v Omni Holdings AG* [2000] 1 W.L.R. 916, *per* Rimer J. at 922. The mere fact that the proceedings have been triggered by the insolvency is not sufficient to oust the application of Brussels I and bring the case within the Insolvency Regulation (*UBS AG v Omni Holdings AG*).
[22] Even where the disqualification was imposed in insolvency proceedings, the liability for acting whole disqualified results not from the insolvency as such but from s.15 of the Company Directors Disqualification Act 1986, which applies whatever the circumstances of the disqualification.
[23] *Grupo Torras SA v Sheikh Fahad Mohammed Al-Sabah* [1995] 1 Lloyd's Rep. 374. Such a claim is excluded from the Rome Convention by art.1(2)(e) and is governed by the law of the place of the company's incorporation (*Base Metal Trading Ltd v Shamurin* [2005] B.C.C. 325). See also Ben Jones, "EU Regulation and Directors' Duties" [2005] 18 Insol. Int. 29.
[24] Council Regulation (EC) 44/2001 of December 22, 2000 (generally known as "Brussels I").
[25] *German Graphics Graphische Maschinen GmbH v Alice van der Schee* (C-292/08) [2009] All E.R. (D) 75.
[26] *SCT Industri AB v Alpenblume AB* (C-111/08) [2010] Bus. L.R. 559. See to similar effect *Byers v Yacht Bull Corp* [2010] B.C.C. 368 (claim for ownership arising under the general law and before the opening of insolvency proceedings was neither directly derived from nor closely linked to the insolvency and was governed by Brussels I). See further below, para.15–34.
[27] *SCT Industri AB likvidation*, cited above n.26.

Thus, Brussels I and the Insolvency Regulation are as mutually exclusive as were the Brussels Convention and the Insolvency Regulation. There may be cases falling outside both the Insolvency Regulation and Brussels I. Jurisdiction in such cases is governed by the jurisdictional rules of the *lex fori*. Under English law, jurisdiction depends on the defendant being served with process in England or abroad in the circumstances authorised by, and in the manner prescribed by, statute or statutory order.[28]

The EC Convention on Insolvency

15–03 After some 30 years of work and the rejection of one draft after another, the Member States of the European Community completed the text of a Convention on Insolvency Proceedings in September 1995, the Convention being opened for signature within six months. Within that time, 14 Member States signed the convention; only the signature of the United Kingdom was not forthcoming,[29] with the result that the Convention lapsed. The Convention was designed to dovetail with the Brussels Convention so that anything excluded from the latter as being related to insolvency would fall within the Insolvency Convention.

The conversion of the EC Insolvency Convention into an EC Regulation

15–04 A few years after the failure of the Convention, the project was revived in the form of a proposal for an EC Regulation, which took over most of the provisions of the Convention verbatim,[30] with an amendment to art.5 to capture floating charges and various other amendments reflecting the different status of the instrument. The change from convention to regulation avoided the need for ratification by all Member States and also had the effect of conferring power on the ECJ to interpret the instrument without the need for any express provision in it to that effect. The use of a regulation rather than a

---

[28] Dicey, Morris and Collins, *The Conflict of Laws*, 14th edn (London: Sweet & Maxwell, 2010), r.22(1).

[29] Two reasons have been ascribed to this: the hostility of John Major, then Prime Minister, because of the refusal of the European Commission to lift the ban on the export of British beef that had been imposed because of the BSE epidemic ("mad cow disease"), which led to a policy of non-co-operation in EC matters (H.C. Deb. col.394 (June 18, 1996)), and the concern that the failure to empower the UK to exclude Gibraltar could impair the sovereignty of the UK over a colony for whose international relations the UK is responsible but to which Spain has continued to lay claim. For the history of the project, see Fletcher, *Insolvency in Private International Law* (above, n. 12) paras 7.1 et seq.; and Paul J. Omar, "Genesis of the European Initiative in Insolvency Law" (2003) 12 Int. Insol. Rev. 147.

[30] This has facilitated use of the Virgós-Schmit Report (above, n. 12) as a guide to the Regulation. The report has no official status, because the failure of the Convention meant that it was never formally endorsed but it has strong persuasive value and continues to be widely cited.

directive meant that the instrument has direct effect in Member States,[31] thus not only dispensing with the need for implementation under national law but positively precluding Member States from any measure of implementation. The Insolvency Regulation[32], made under arts 61(c) and 67(1) of the EC Treaty, came into force on May 31, 2002. Following the admission of 10 new Member States and periodic additions and amendments to the lists of proceedings in Annexes A, B and C to the Insolvency Regulation, these were replaced by amending regulations from time to time[33], the last being in 2010.[34] The ECJ is the final authority on the interpretation of the Insolvency Regulation. References to the ECJ may be made by any national court and must be made by the highest court.[35]

3. AN OVERVIEW OF THE REGULATION

Key features

In relation to insolvency proceedings within its scope,[36] the EC Regulation on Insolvency Proceedings (hereafter "the Insolvency Regulation") has six key features:

15–05

(1)   a dovetailing with Brussels I designed to leave no gaps between the two[37];

(2)   a principle of qualified unity embodied in rules for international jurisdiction in "main proceedings" which are based on the place where the

---

[31] Excluding Denmark, which decided not to opt into the Regulation and is therefore not a Member State for the purpose of the Regulation (*Re The Arena Corp Ltd* [2004] B.P.I.R. 375). The Spanish Commercial Court No.1 referred to the ECJ the question whether Denmark is to considered a Member State for the purpose of art.16 (*Mejnertsen v Barsoe* (C-148/08), [2008] OJ C 142), but the case has since been removed from the register ([2009] OJ C 69/12).

[32] Council Regulation (EC) No.1346/2000 of May 29, 2000 on insolvency proceedings, OJ 30.6.2000, L 180/1.

[33] The amending regulations prior to the current text were Council Regulation (EC) No.603/2005 of April 12, 2005, Council Regulation (EC) No.694/2006 of April 27, 2006 and Council Regulation (EC) No.681/2007 of June 13, 2007.

[34] Council Regulation (EU) No.210/2010 of February 25, 2010 (OJ L 065 13.3.2010), embodied in regulations which consolidated and replaced the previous Annexes A, B and C.

[35] Treaty on the Functioning of the European Union (Consolidated Version) C115/164, art.267 (ex 234 TEC). Prior to the Lisbon Treaty only the highest court could make a reference on the interpretation of the Insolvency Regulation.

[36] See below, paras 15–09 et seq. Only corporate insolvency proceedings are discussed in the present chapter but it should be borne in mind that the Regulation also covers personal bankruptcy.

[37] Virgós and Garcimartín, *The European Insolvency Regulation*, para.77. It is, however, arguable that the interlocking of Brussels I and the Insolvency Regulation is not watertight. For example, schemes of arrangement, which are outside the Insolvency Regulation (see below, para.15–12) are also excluded from Brussels I as being "judicial arrangements, compositions and analogous proceedings" within art.1(2)(b).

debtor has its centre of main interests (COMI)[38] and which preclude the opening of insolvency proceedings in other Member States except those in which the debtor has an establishment and then only in relation to local assets;

(3) a principle of qualified universality by which the court of a Member State in which the main proceedings are opened has jurisdiction over all of the debtor's assets on a worldwide basis, while allowing secondary insolvency proceedings in another Member State in whose territory the debtor has an establishment, restricted to winding up and to assets within that territory;

(4) subjection of insolvency proceedings and their effects to the law of the State in which such proceedings are opened, except for *in rem* rights and certain other rights established by some other applicable law;

(5) a requirement that any judgment of a court of a Member State opening insolvency proceedings pursuant to the jurisdiction conferred upon it by the regulation, as well as subsequent judgments by that court concerning the course and closure of insolvency proceedings and compositions approved by such court, be recognised and given effect in all other Member States; and

(6) conferment on the liquidator in the main proceedings of a right to exercise in all other Member States the powers conferred on him by the law of the state of the opening of proceedings, coupled with a right to require the stay of secondary proceedings, subject to measures to guarantee the interests of creditors in the secondary proceedings.

The interpretative approach of the ECJ

15–06   The approach of the ECJ to the interpretation of Community instruments is highly teleological. The court is less concerned with the actual text of an instrument than with the objectives it seeks to achieve.[39] For this purpose, considerable reliance is placed on recitals in the Preambles. This is as true of the Preamble to the Insolvency Regulation as it is of preambles to other EC instruments. The Insolvency Regulation contains a set of 33 recitals, which

---

[38] For the determination of the COMI, see below, para.15–49.

[39] It is not surprising that this approach, which is carried much further than is usual in the case of English courts when interpreting domestic legislation, has attracted criticism from UK insolvency specialists (see, e.g. Moss, Fletcher and Isaacs, *The EC Regulation on Insolvency Proceedings*, 2009, para.8–66). However, it is well established that an autonomous interpretation, as opposed to the interpretative techniques of national legal systems, has to be applied to Community instruments.

are designed to serve as an interpretative aid and for that purpose draw on the Virgós-Schmit Report. The less happy effect of such extensive reliance on recitals is that all too often they are made to carry the burden of answering questions which are not addressed in the text. So the meaning of "centre of main interests", which is fundamental to the rules on jurisdiction and thus to selection of the *lex concursus*, is not to be found in the body of the Regulation (which tells us where COMI is presumed to be but not what it is), only in the recitals. More generally, the court does not hesitate to apply robust interpretative techniques to fill gaps or inadequacies in a Community instrument in a way that English courts might find difficult when construing UK legislation. This is understandable when one considers the problems involved in the formulation of a Directive or Regulation involving intense negotiation among the many Member States, each with its own legal traditions, together with the production of parallel texts in a variety of languages, so that a literal interpretation in one language may be different in another.[40] The *Eurofood* case,[41] discussed later, provides a good illustration. The court held that a court order appointing a provisional liquidator constituted the opening of insolvency proceedings, attracting a duty of recognition on the part of courts of other Member States, despite the fact that at the time of the facts on which the decision was based such an appointment did not feature in the list of insolvency proceedings for Ireland in Annex A to the Insolvency Regulation[42]; it sufficed that the decision was made in proceedings for a compulsory winding up order. Again, in *Staubitz-Schreiber*,[43] the ECJ held that migration of the debtor to a new COMI after the lodgement of a request for the opening of insolvency proceedings but before the making of any order did not deprive the court of jurisdiction, although under art.2(f) proceedings are not considered to be opened until there is a judgment which makes them effective.[44]

Thus, the court seeks to ensure that gaps in the Insolvency Regulation and **15–07** infelicitous drafting[45] will not be allowed to frustrate its objectives, in this case to avoid incentives to engage in forum shopping and the impairment of "efficient and effective cross-bordering proceedings". Even so, the treatment of the appointment of a provisional liquidator as constituting the opening of the main insolvency proceedings is a rather surprising extension of the concept, and one wonders why in *Eurofood* the ECJ did not take the

---

[40] See Moss, Fletcher and Isaacs, *The EC Regulation on Insolvency Proceedings*, 2009, paras 2–23 et seq.
[41] *Re Eurofood IFSC Ltd* (C-341/04) [2006] Ch. 508.
[42] Although Annex C did include a provisional liquidator as a liquidator for the purpose of art.2(b).
[43] Case C-1/104, [2006] E.C.R. 1-701; [2006] B.C.C. 639. See below, para.15–08.
[44] See below, para.15–47.
[45] For recent criticisms and proposals for reform of the Insolvency Regulation, see Gerard McCormack, "Reconstructing European insolvency law—Putting in Place a New Paradigm" (2010) 30 L.S. 126.

simpler route of applying art.38, treating the provisional liquidator as a temporary administrator and the judgment appointing him as one entitled to recognition under art.25(1).

Forum shopping

15–08 The avoidance of forum shopping is one of the objectives of the Insolvency Regulation, and plainly influenced the ECJ's decision in *Staubitz-Schreiber*,[46] where it was held that a court with whom a request to open proceedings had been lodged could not be deprived of jurisdiction by a change in the debtor's COMI after the lodgement of the request and before it had been heard. Nevertheless, the practice of forum shopping persists. Sometimes it is because insolvency practitioners and even, on occasion, their courts are keen to attract business by having the COMI determined as being within their own jurisdiction, however tenuous the connection.[47] Sometimes it is to attract a legal regime that will favour debtors at the expense of creditors.[48] Both cases constitute an abusive selection, a form of *fraude à la loi*.[49] But more often than not, the selection of the insolvency jurisdiction is based on a perfectly legitimate desire to be able to resort to the most efficient forms of insolvent administration with a view to maximising returns to creditors. So not all forum shopping is bad. Moreover, there may be perfectly good commercial reasons for a debtor to change its COMI, for example, to take advantage of a more favourable tax regime or more generous State support. However, the ruling in *Staubitz-Schreiber* is not based solely on the possibility of a change of COMI for improper or inappropriate reasons but is of general application. But if no proceedings were opened in a debtor's original COMI, there is no reason why the courts of this new COMI should not assume jurisdiction.[50]

4. SCOPE OF THE REGULATION

Introduction

15–09 The Insolvency Regulation is concerned solely with insolvency proceedings within the Community. Accordingly, it applies only where the debtor has its

---

[46] *Staubitz-Dchreiber*, cited above n.43. See below, para.15–47.

[47] The *Parmalat* case, discussed below, is a striking example.

[48] One can imagine cases where the debtor selects a jurisdiction because its rules on avoidance of pre-liquidation transactions are relatively liberal.

[49] See Horst Eidenmüller, "Abuse of Law in the Context of European Insolvency Law" (2009) 6 *European Company and Financial Law Review* 1.

[50] *Official Receiver v Eichler* [2007] B.P.I.R. 1636; *Re Hellas Telecommunications (Luxembourg) II SCA* [2010] B.C.C. 295; and *Re European Directories (DH6) BV* [2010] EWHC 3472 (Ch).

centre of main interests within the Community and insolvency proceedings are opened in a Member State.[51] However, when these and other conditions listed below have been satisfied the jurisdiction of the court in which main proceedings are opened extends to all of the debtor's assets on a worldwide basis, although obviously recognition and enforcement of the liquidator's powers in a non-EU State are subject to the law of the State concerned and the jurisdiction of its courts. Since the Regulation is concerned only with relations between EU States, it is careful to limit its rules governing in rem rights, reservation of title and the like, to assets situated within the territory of a Member State. But the same conflict rules will apply to determine such rights as regards assets situated in a non-Member State.

In relation to companies, the Regulation follows most national laws in confining its application to distinct legal entities, as opposed to corporate groups. So if several members of a group become insolvent, each will be governed by its own separate insolvency regime, including the Regulation. The focus, in short, is on the entity, not the enterprise. The treatment of groups becomes much easier if all members of the group have or move to the same COMI and come under the control of the same insolvency administrator. The insolvency of corporate groups has attracted much attention in recent years and is briefly examined in Ch.16.

Only insolvency proceedings as defined in the Regulation or proceedings derived directly from and closely connected with the insolvency[52] are within its scope. Other types of proceeding that may be connected to the debtor's insolvency include, for example, proceedings for the disqualification of directors or for payment to make good a deficiency caused by fraudulent or wrongful trading.

Proceedings within and outside the Regulation

The Insolvency Regulation applies only if the following six conditions are satisfied: **15–10**

(1) Insolvency proceedings are opened

"Insolvency proceedings" means the collective proceedings referred to in art.1(1) and listed in Annex A.[53] The Regulation does not define insolvency, and it is left to national law to determine whether proceedings of a kind listed in Annex A are insolvency proceedings. Thus, in England, a creditors'   **15–11**

---

[51] Other than Denmark. See above, n.31.
[52] See art.25(1) and below, para.15–34.
[53] See art.2(a). See below.

voluntary winding up (with confirmation by the court) falls within the Regulation, a members' voluntary winding up does not,[54] nor does a winding up on a petition presented by the Secretary of State on public interest grounds under s.124A of the Insolvency Act 1986,[55] even though both types of proceeding are among those listed in Annex A. Conversely, a proceeding which a Member State characterises as an insolvency proceeding but is not listed in the Regulation is outside its scope. In short, to be within the Regulation proceedings must fulfil the dual test of falling within Annex A and being characterised as insolvency proceedings under the relevant national law. Nevertheless, as mentioned above, the ECJ has held that the appointment of a provisional liquidator by the Irish High Court constituted the opening of insolvency proceedings within art.2(a) despite the fact that such an appointment was not included in the list of insolvency proceedings in Annex A, because it was a decision based on an application made in proceedings for a winding up order.[56] What constitutes the opening of proceedings is discussed a little later.[57]

(2) The proceedings are collective insolvency proceedings

15–12   These are defined in Annex A, and divide primarily into winding up proceedings, involving collection and realisation of assets and distribution of the proceeds, and proceedings designed to lead to reorganisation or restructuring of the debtor company.[58] In relation to the United Kingdom, Annex A lists voluntary liquidation where confirmed by the court, compulsory liquidation,[59] administration (whether by court order or out of court[60]) and voluntary arrangements under insolvency legislation, that is, company voluntary arrangements under Pt I of the Insolvency Act 1986 but not schemes of arrangement under s.899 of the Companies Act 2006, since that Act is concerned with company law and does not form part of UK insolvency legislation[61] and the provisions relating to schemes cover solvent as well as insolvent companies. Administrative or other receivership is outside the Insolvency Regulation, since it is not a collective insolvency proceeding.[62]

---

[54] This example is given in the Virgós-Schmit Report (above, n.12), para.49(b).
[55] *Re Marann Brooks CSV Ltd* [2003] B.P.I.R. 1159.
[56] This reflects the teleological approach to interpretation adopted by the ECJ. See above, para.15–06.
[57] Below, para.15–39.
[58] The Insolvency Regulation also covers the bankruptcy of individuals.
[59] Winding up under the court's supervision is also listed but was abolished many years ago. See above, para.1–40, n.159. However, it is still relevant to Gibraltar.
[60] This results from a change made to Annex A by including in administration appointments made by filing prescribed documents with the court.
[61] The Act is therefore not included in the definition of "British insolvency law" in art.2 of Sch.1 to the Cross-Border Insolvency Regulations 2006. See below, para.16–26.
[62] See above, para.1–38.

We must now look a little more closely at the four types of collective insolvency proceeding listed in Annex A for the United Kingdom.

(A) WINDING UP PROCEEDINGS

Article 2(c) defines "winding up proceedings" in the following terms: **15–13**

" 'Winding up proceedings' shall mean insolvency proceedings within the meaning of art.2(a) involving realising the assets of the debtor, including where the proceedings have been closed by a composition or other measure terminating the insolvency or closed by reason of the insufficiency of the assets. Those proceedings are listed in Annex B."

Annex B, as revised in February 2010, covers winding up by or subject to the supervision of the court, winding up through administration, including appointments made by filing prescribed documents with the court, and creditors' voluntary winding up (with confirmation by the court,[63]). "Winding up through administration" is a reference to administration as a liquidation-substitute[64] where the administrator realises assets and, with leave of the court, makes distributions. It does not encompass CVAs and schemes of arrangements carried out within the framework of administration. There is an apparent difficulty in applying the Regulation in that it is based on the concept of court proceedings, both in the jurisdiction rules in arts 3 and 27 and in the recognition rules in art.16. Article 2(d) defines "court" as meaning "the judicial body or any other competent body of a Member State empowered to open insolvency proceedings or to take decisions in the course of such proceedings", while by art.2(e) "judgment", in relation to the opening of insolvency proceedings or the appointment of a liquidator, includes the decision of any court empowered to open such proceedings or to appoint a liquidator.[65] On the face of it, therefore, despite Annex A the Regulation is capable of biting only on compulsory liquidation, since none of the other three insolvency proceedings listed is "opened" by a court. However, it is clear from recital (10) that on this aspect at least the Regulation is intended to be liberally construed.

---

[63] See below.

[64] As to which see above, paras 1–37 and 11–115. Winding up through administration is mentioned specifically because it is neither a compulsory winding up on a petition nor a creditors' voluntary winding up but results, in the case of a compulsory winding up, from a winding up order made under the Insolvency Act 1986 Sch.B1 para.79(4)(d) or 81(3)(d) and, in the case of a CVL, from the resolution for voluntary winding up deemed to have been passed on registration of the administrators' notice under Sch.B1 para.83(6)(b).

[65] "Liquidator" is defined by art.2(b) as meaning any person or body whose function is to administer or liquidate assets of the company of which the debtor has been divested or to supervise the administration of his affairs, such persons being listed in Annex C, which in the case of the UK covers a liquidator, a provisional liquidator, a supervisor of a voluntary arrangement, an administrator and an official receiver.

"(10) Insolvency proceedings do not necessarily involve the intervention of a judicial authority; the expression 'court' in this Regulation should be given a broad meaning and include a person or body empowered by national law to open insolvency proceedings."[66]

As noted earlier, an order by a court of the COMI appointing a provisional liquidator in proceedings for compulsory winding up has been held to constitute the opening of proceedings, and the liquidator to be the liquidator in the main proceedings. In consequence, an order in those proceedings has priority over a subsequent decision by a court of another Member State.[67] It also follows that a provisional liquidator has a *locus standi* to apply under art.29 for the opening of secondary proceedings.

The amended Annex, like the original, refers to creditors' voluntary winding up "(with confirmation by the court)", which implies that such confirmation is an essential ingredient of a creditors' voluntary winding up if it is to qualify as an insolvency proceeding within the Insolvency Regulation.[68] The Insolvency Rules were amended to prescribe the procedure for such confirmation,[69] and they apply not only to a CVL effected by resolution of the members but also to one to which the company has moved from administration in accordance with para.83 of Sch.B1 to the Act.[70]

(B) ADMINISTRATION AND CVAs

15–14   The view of the Insolvency Service is that this construction is wide enough to apply the word "court" to the holder of a qualifying floating charge appointing an administrator out of court and to creditors when approving a CVA. In relation to out-of-court appointments of administrators, this broad interpretation receives support from the inclusion in the amended Annex A of "administration, including appointments made by filing prescribed documents with the court". However, an appointment by the court may be sought in order to avoid doubt and to enhance the prospect of recognition in a foreign court.[71]

---

[66] See further below, para.15–14.

[67] See below, para.15–28.

[68] For most purposes, the opening of the insolvency proceedings is considered to take place on the passing of the resolution for winding up, not on confirmation by the court. See below, para.15–40.

[69] Insolvency Rules 1986 rr.7.62 and 7.63. An application under r.7.62 was granted by Mr Registrar Baister in relation to two overseas companies in *Re TXU Europe German Finance Co BV* [2005] B.P.I.R. 209, where it was held that the Regulation applied to a voluntary winding up and that while an unregistered company, including an overseas company, could not normally be put into voluntary winding up, s.221(4) of the Insolvency Act 1986, as amended, allowed this to be done in accordance with the Insolvency Regulation, and jurisdiction did indeed flow from the Regulation.

[70] Insolvency Rules 1986 r.7.62(8).

[71] See, e.g. *BLV Realty Organization Ltd v Batten* [2010] B.P.I.R. 277, where, however, the foreign jurisdiction was the British Virgin Islands, which is not within the EU.

As to CVAs, which do not involve the court at all except where an application is made under s.4A of the Insolvency Act,[72] it might appear hard to see how the conclusion of a CVA could be regarded as the opening of insolvency proceedings or how the participating creditors and members could collectively constitute "the court", particularly since a members' resolution putting the company into a CVL is not by itself sufficient and requires confirmation by the court. But voluntary arrangements are included in the list of insolvency proceedings in Annex A, while the supervisor of a CVA features in the list of liquidators in Annex C, and these inclusions would be deprived of all meaning if the coming into force of a CVA were not to be treated as the opening of insolvency proceedings by a "court" consisting of the parties to the CVA.[73] In *Re Salvage Association Ltd*,[74] Blackburne J. held that the parties to a CVA did indeed constitute a "court" for the purposes of the Regulation. By contrast, purely consensual restructurings (work-outs) fall outside the Regulation, as do schemes of arrangement falling within Pt 26 of the Companies Act 2006.[75]

(3) The proceedings entail the partial or total divestment of a debtor and the appointment of a liquidator

Only those collective proceedings which entail the partial or total divestment   **15–15**
of a debtor and the appointment of a liquidator are within the Regulation.[76]
This excludes proceedings based on the concept of a "debtor in possession"
as exemplified by Ch.11 of the US Bankruptcy Code.

(4) The proceedings are opened in a Member State

The Regulation obviously cannot control proceedings opened in a jurisdic-   **15–16**
tion outside the European Union. They can, however, control entities incorporated outside the EU if their COMI is within the Union or they have an
establishment within the Union.

(5) The debtor has its COMI in a Member State at the time of opening of the insolvency proceedings

The central requirement limiting proceedings to cases where the debtor's   **15–17**
COMI is situated in a Member State is stated in those terms only in recital

---

[72] See above, para.12–42.
[73] See to the same effect Moss, Fletcher and Isaacs, *The EC Regulation on Insolvency Proceedings*, 2009, paras 8.16–8.19.
[74] [2004] 1 W.L.R. 174.
[75] See above, para.15–12.
[76] See art.1(1).

(14), not in the text but it clearly follows from the wording of art.3, which is limited to such proceedings. This limitation applies not only to main proceedings but to territorial proceedings.[77] That the relevant time is that of the opening of the proceedings is supported by the commentators,[78] and there is now an English decision to that effect.[79] However, the ECJ has held that once a request for the opening of main proceedings has been lodged with a court of a Member State, the debtor cannot, by changing its COMI prior to the court's decision, deprive the court of its exclusive jurisdiction to open the proceedings.[80] If the COMI is in a Member State, the fact that the debtor company was incorporated in a non-Member State is irrelevant; the Regulation still applies.[81] It does not, of course, follow that courts of the non-Member State or of other States outside the European Union will necessarily accept the applicability of the Regulation.[82] In the case of territorial proceedings, the only requirement is that the debtor has an establishment within a Member State at the time of opening of the proceedings. There can be separate territorial proceedings in every Member State in which the debtor has an establishment.[83]

(6) The debtor is not an institution excluded from the Regulation

15–18 Finally, there are excluded from the Regulation insolvency proceedings concerning insurance undertakings, credit institutions, investment undertakings which provide services involving the holding of funds or securities for third parties, and collective investment undertakings.[84] These are taken out of the scope of the Regulation because "they are subject to special arrangements

---

[77] See further below, para.15–21.

[78] "This is the only reference date that avoids the incentives for forum shopping that the Insolvency Regulation expressly tries to eliminate ..." (Virgós and Garcimartín, *The European Insolvency Regulation*, para.68). As to what constitutes the opening of the proceedings, see below, paras 15–39 et seq.

[79] *Shierson v Vlieland-Boddy* [2005] 1 W.L.R. 3966 (bankruptcy). In that case, the court was well aware of the policy of the Regulation to discourage forum shopping but the debtor's change of COMI took place some months before the presentation of the bankruptcy petition and was held effective. The position is otherwise where the debtor changes its COMI after lodgement of the request to open insolvency proceedings. See below, para.15–47. As to when proceedings are deemed to be opened, see below, paras 15–39 et seq.

[80] See below, para.15–47.

[81] *Re BRAC Rent-A-Car International Inc* [2003] 1 W.L.R. 1421 (COMI in the UK; held, the court had jurisdiction even though the company was incorporated in the US); and *Re Ci4net.com Inc* [2005] B.C.C. 277 (two companies incorporated in Jersey and the US respectively, held to have their COMI in England). In the former case, BRAC's petition was supported by the US creditors' committee.

[82] For a detailed discussion, see Paul Omar, "The Extra-Territorial Reach of the European Insolvency Regulation" (2007) 18 I.C.C.L.R. 57.

[83] See below, paras 15–60 et seq., as to territorial proceedings.

[84] See art.1(2). By "collective investment undertakings" is meant those that are duly authorised in the UK by the Financial Services Authority. Unauthorised collective investment undertakings are covered by the Regulation (*Financial Services Authority v Dobb White & Co* [2004] B.P.I.R. 479).

and, to some extent, the national supervisory authorities have extremely wide-ranging powers of intervention".[85] In addition, they are regulated by EC directives, two of which relate specifically to the winding up of credit institutions and insurance undertakings.[86]

The Insolvency Regulation and the conflict of laws

As stated earlier, the Regulation consists essentially of jurisdiction and choice of law rules. The jurisdiction rule is that apart from territorial proceedings in Member States where the debtor has an establishment, exclusive jurisdiction is given to the courts of the Member State where the debtor has its COMI at the time of opening of the proceedings. The primary choice of law rule is that the law of the Member State in which proceedings are opened is to be applied to the various issues listed in art.4, while arts 5 to 15 set out various exceptions to the primary rule. The Regulation is confined to cases involving a choice of jurisdiction or applicable law between Member States. Where the choice is between the jurisdiction or law of a Member State and the jurisdiction or law of a non-Member State, the ordinary conflict of laws rules have to be applied, so that it will be for the courts of the Member State concerned to determine whether, under their conflict rules, they have jurisdiction and, if so, which law is the governing law.

15–19

5. JURISDICTION GENERALLY

Jurisdiction under national law

It is important to note that the Regulation does not confer jurisdiction on a national court which it would not have under its own law. Whether the conditions necessary to open insolvency proceedings in a Member State are satisfied is in the first instance to be determined by the law of that State.[87] Where those conditions are satisfied, it is then necessary to proceed to the next stage and see whether the courts of the Member State have jurisdiction under the Regulation. If they do not, they cannot entertain the case; if they do, they must entertain it.[88] So the Regulation is not an

15–20

---

[85] Recital (9).
[86] See above, nn.10 and 11.
[87] Which in the case of the UK includes the UNCITRAL Model Law. See below, paras.16–17 et seq.
[88] See below, para.15–26. For an excellent overview, see Bob Wessels, "International Jurisdiction to Open Insolvency Proceedings in Europe, in Particular against (Groups of) Companies", published by the International Insolvency Institute and available on *http://www.iiiglobal.org*.

alternative source of jurisdiction but an additional jurisdictional hurdle to be surmounted.

Classification of proceedings

15–21   The Regulation divides insolvency proceedings into two groups: main proceedings and territorial proceedings. Main proceedings are those brought in the Member State within the territory of which the debtor's COMI is situated. Territorial proceedings are those brought in another Member State in which the debtor possesses an establishment. No insolvency proceedings may be instituted in a Member State which is neither that in which the debtor's COMI is situated[89] nor one in which it has an establishment. Moreover, the mere fact that the debtor has an establishment within a Member State does not suffice to enable territorial proceedings to be brought in that State if the debtor does not also have its COMI in another Member State.

Territorial proceedings sub-divide into secondary proceedings, which are those brought after the opening of main proceedings in another Member State, and proceedings opened in another Member State prior to the opening of the main proceedings, which the Virgós-Schmit Report conveniently labels "independent proceedings".[90] Once main proceedings have been opened, the *quondam* independent proceedings become secondary proceedings,[91] but with distinctive effects.[92] The distinction between main proceedings and territorial proceedings is significant in at least two ways. Main proceedings extend to all of the debtor's assets except to the extent to which assets situated in another Member State are available to local creditors in territorial proceedings, these being confined to local assets. Main proceedings have primacy within the European Union and the liquidator in those proceedings has overall control and is entitled to have his position recognised and given effect in all Member States, whereas territorial proceedings and the liquidator who administers them fulfil a subordinate function. There are also important differences between secondary proceedings and independent proceedings. The former are confined to winding up[93]; the latter may be any collective insolvency proceedings within the Regulation. So, if, in a case where the debtor has an establishment in the United Kingdom but its COMI is situated outside the United Kingdom, it is thought desirable to

---

[89] See below, para.15–49.
[90] Para.25.
[91] Virgós-Schmit Report, para.25.
[92] e.g. if initiated as reorganisation proceedings they are not automatically converted into winding up proceedings, so that until converted (e.g. following a request by the liquidator in the main proceedings under art.37), they can continue as reorganisation proceedings. Further, arts 31–35 apply to them only so far as the progress of those proceedings permits.
[93] Insolvency Regulation para.3(3). But this now includes winding up through administration. See above, para.15–13.

have an administration and/or CVA in England, it is essential to open proceedings here before any proceedings have been opened in another Member State. However, independent proceedings can be opened only if one of the two conditions specified in art.3(4) is satisfied.[94] Although independent proceedings involving a reorganisation are automatically converted into secondary proceedings where main proceedings are subsequently opened in another Member State, this does not automatically convert them into winding up proceedings.[95]

Unity and universality

The ideal within a common market would be to vest jurisdiction in insolvency proceedings exclusively in the courts of a single State ("unity") and to subject the totality of the debtor's assets to that one insolvency jurisdiction ("universality"). The principles of unity and universality are embodied in the Regulation in that main proceedings can be opened only in one State, the State in which the debtor's COMI is situated, the jurisdiction of the courts of that State has to be recognised in all other Member States and the main proceedings encompass all of the debtor's assets on a worldwide basis.[96] Further, that international jurisdiction extends to all actions which derive directly from the insolvency proceedings and are closely connected to them, such as an action by a liquidator to set aside under the *lex concursus* a transfer of the debtor's assets made prior to the liquidation.[97] But the Regulation accepts that, as with cross-border insolvencies at an international level,[98] this purity of concept is in practice unattainable, and to seek to impose it would cause severe problems:

15–22

"This Regulation acknowledges the fact that as a result of widely differing substantive laws it is not practical to introduce insolvency proceedings with universal scope in the entire Community. The application without

---

[94] See below, para.15–63.

[95] See the Virgós-Schmit Report, para.86.

[96] Virgós-Schmit Report, para.73. The Insolvency Rules 1986 have useful provisions requiring affidavits in support of administration applications and winding up petitions to state: (i) whether in the opinion of the person making the application the EC Regulation will apply; and (ii) if so, whether the proceedings will be main proceedings or territorial proceedings (rr.2.4(4) and 4.12(8), the latter being added by the Insolvency (Amendment) Rules 2005, SI 2005/527, r.20).

[97] *Seagon v Deko Marty Belgium NV* (C-339/07) [2009] 1 W.L.R. 2168. The case was enlivened by a literary allusion characteristic of A.G. Colomer (Opinion, para.1): "Not all debtors have a father like Goriot. Generosity and nobility of spirit are rare in the realm of the market since traders lack the advantages which allowed Delphine and Anastasie, ungrateful and vain daughters, to live and get into debt with such a lack of restraint at the expense of their devoted father, who, when he died in complete financial ruin, was still praising his offspring."

[98] See below, para.16–04.

exception of the law of the State of opening of the insolvency proceedings would, against this background, frequently lead to difficulties. This applies, for example, to the widely differing laws on security interests to be found in the Community. Furthermore, the preferential rights enjoyed by some creditors in the insolvency proceedings are, in some cases, completely different."[99]

Accordingly, the Regulation adopts the principle of modified unity and modified universality.

(1) Modified unity

15–23   While giving primacy to the main proceedings opened in the Member State where the debtor has its COMI, the Regulation recognises that wherever the debtor has an establishment in the territory of a Member State which is not that in which it has its COMI, local creditors should be entitled to institute winding up proceedings (but not any other types of proceeding) and to have recourse to local assets (although in neither case to the exclusion of creditors situated in other Member States) and that in relation to those assets the ranking of claims and other rules of insolvency should be governed by the local *lex concursus*. So exclusive jurisdiction is not given to the courts of any one Member State, nor is there necessarily a single *lex concursus*. It is theoretically possible to have territorial proceedings which are never followed by main proceedings and, of course, there may be as many territorial proceedings as there are territories within which the debtor has an establishment, so long as in each case the conditions of art.3(4) are satisfied.

Only one set of main proceedings may be opened in the territory covered by the Regulation.[100] By this is meant that it is not possible for main proceedings to be opened in a Member State while there are current main proceedings in another Member State. But once main proceedings in one Member State have been closed or discontinued, there is no longer a barrier to new main proceedings being opened in another Member State, although this is likely to be infrequent. Moreover, the concept of unity of the insolvency operates only at the international level within the Community.[101] There is nothing in the Regulation to preclude multiple main proceedings within the same jurisdiction. These may be successive, as where administration is followed by a CVL, or may run in parallel, as where a CVA is concluded within

---

[99] Insolvency Regulation recital (11).
[100] Virgós-Schmit Report, para.73; Virgós and Garcimartín, *The European Insolvency Regulation*, para.70; and Fletcher, *Insolvency in Private International Law*, para.7.50. See further below, para.15–30.
[101] Insolvency Regulation recital (15).

an administration or is uncompleted when winding up supervenes but remains operative as to the assets comprised in it.[102]

(2) Modified universality

Although main proceedings encompass the whole of the debtor's assets worldwide, yet where territorial proceedings have been opened the local assets must first be applied to the settlement of claims of creditors (local or otherwise) in the territorial proceedings, and only those assets (if any) remaining after payment of such claims in full will be handed over to the liquidator in the main proceedings. Further, the Regulation can only control the opening of proceedings within the European Union. There is nothing to prevent a creditor from bringing such proceedings in a non-Member State which has jurisdiction under its own jurisdictional rules. It is thus a little unfortunate that art.3 is headed "International jurisdiction" instead of the more accurate "Community jurisdiction", signifying jurisdiction at the level of Community law as opposed to jurisdiction within a Member State, this being the exclusive prerogative of the national law of that State,[103] which can thus declare attempted insolvency proceedings inadmissible[104] even where the courts of the State concerned would have jurisdiction under the regulation.[105] However, in order to ensure that courts in England have jurisdiction in relation to entities that fall within the Regulation, the definition of "company" has been extended, for the purpose of the provisions relating to CVAs and administration, to embrace not only a company within s.1(1) of the Companies Act 2006 but also a company incorporated in an EEA state other than the United Kingdom and a company not incorporated in an EEA State but having its centre of main interests in a Member State other than Denmark, "centre of main interests" having the same meaning as in the EC Regulation.[106]

15–24

---

[102] See above, para.12–30; and *Oakley v Ultra Design Ltd* [2006] B.C.C. 57, where Lloyd J. concluded (at [34]) that there was no reason why there should not be concurrent main proceedings within the UK (in that case, a compulsory liquidation and a CVA, which continued to operate after the company had gone into liquidation), although he found it unnecessary to deal with the relationship between them.

[103] Insolvency Regulation recital (15) and art.4(2).

[104] e.g. where, in winding up proceedings in England, the petitioner lacks *locus standi*. See above, para.5–18.

[105] As Dr Burkard Göpfert has pointed out, the concept of international jurisdiction has its origin in the terminology of private international law. Whether at the level of international law the courts of a particular State have jurisdiction in a matter regulated by an international instrument is determined by that instrument; whether the jurisdiction so conferred is exercisable within a State is determined by that State's own law. See Burkard Göpfert, "International Jurisdiction in European Insolvencies", an article published by the International Insolvency Institute and accessible on *http://www.iiiglobal.org*.

[106] Insolvency Act 1986 ss.1(4) and 436 and Sch.B1 para.111(1A), as amended by the Insolvency Act 1986 (Amendment) Regulations 2005, SI 2005/879.

The basis of jurisdiction

15–25   It will be apparent from what has been said above that for main proceedings exclusive jurisdiction is accorded to the courts of the Member State where the debtor has its COMI at the time of opening of the proceedings, while for territorial proceedings (whether secondary or independent) jurisdiction is based on the debtor's having an establishment within the Member State at the above time and is confined to local assets.

No power to invoke *forum non conveniens*

15–26   One effect of the exclusivity of the jurisdiction conferred by the Insolvency Regulation, whether it be the exclusivity of main proceedings or that applicable to local assets in a Member State where the debtor has an establishment, is that a court seised of a case cannot decline jurisdiction on the ground of forum *non conveniens*, for if it were allowed to do this there would be no court elsewhere within the European Union able to open main proceedings or to open territorial proceedings in respect of assets situated within the territory of the State whose court had refused jurisdiction.

The relationship between different proceedings

15–27   Under the Regulation, it is possible to have main proceedings in the jurisdiction in which the debtor has its COMI and territorial proceedings in every jurisdiction in which it has an establishment elsewhere. The relationship between the different proceedings has been well expressed by a leading American scholar when analysing the EU Convention:

> "In the EU Convention system, no court acts in a role 'ancillary' to another. Instead, assets and claims in a given jurisdiction are either in a universalist or a territorialist position. If no local proceeding is opened, then the liquidator in the main proceedings has considerable power to seize assets and remove them for distribution in the main proceedings. The local creditors will be expected to file there. The result is universalist to that extent. On the other hand, if a local proceeding is opened, then assets and claims will be administered almost entirely in that proceeding. The administration in that case will be almost entirely territorial, unless resolved by a cooperative rescue plan accepted locally." [footnotes omitted][107]

---

[107] Jay Lawrence Westbrook, "Universal Participation in Transnational Bankruptcies" in Ross Cranston (ed.), *Making Commercial Law* (Oxford: Clarendon Press, 1997), p.423.

The same writer draws attention to the benefits resulting from the "universal cross-filing" system embodied in what is now the Regulation, by which the liquidator in each proceeding is required to lodge claims on behalf of creditors in all other proceedings. While the ranking of claims in each winding up is governed by the *lex concursus* applicable to that winding up, yet to the extent that in any linked proceedings non-local creditors are given the same priority as local creditors, the universal cross-filing system would produce substantially the same outcomes as a universalist system.[108]

6. THE PRINCIPLE OF RECOGNITION AND RESPECT WITHIN THE COMMUNITY

The recognition principle

A fundamental principle underlying the Regulation, and one that is essential **15–28** to its proper functioning, is that a judgment of a court of a Member State opening insolvency proceedings is to be respected and enforced in subsequent proceedings in all other Member States. In the language of recital (22):

"Recognition of judgments delivered by the courts of the Member States should be based on the principle of mutual trust. To that end, grounds for non-recognition should be reduced to a minimum. This is also the basis on which any dispute should be resolved where the courts of two Member States both claim competence to open the main insolvency proceedings."

This is reinforced by the text of the Regulation, in arts 16, 17 and 25:

"*Article 16*
Principle
1. Any judgment opening proceedings handed down by a court of a Member State which has jurisdiction pursuant to Article 3 shall be recognised in all the other Member States from the time that it becomes effective in the State of the opening of the proceedings.

Article 17
Effects of recognition
1. The judgment opening the proceedings referred to in Article 3(1) shall, with no further formalities, produce the same effects in any other Member State as under this[109] law of the State of the opening of the proceedings,

---

[108] ibid at, p.427.
[109] The word "this" is a slip and should be "the".

unless this Regulation provides otherwise and as long as no proceedings referred to in Article 3(2) are opened in that other Member State.

2. The effects of the proceedings referred to in Article 3(2) may not be challenged in other Member States ...

...

Article 25

Recognition and enforceability of other judgments

1. Judgments handed down by a court whose judgment concerning the opening of proceedings is recognised in accordance with Article 16 and which concern the course and closure of insolvency proceedings, and compositions approved by that court shall also be recognised with no further formalities. Such judgments shall be enforced in accordance with Articles 31 to 51, with the exception of Article 34(2), of the Brussels Convention on Jurisdiction and the Enforcement of Judgments in Civil and Commercial Matters, as amended by the Conventions of Accession to this Convention.

The first subparagraph shall also apply to judgments deriving directly from the insolvency proceedings and which are closely linked with them, even if they were handed down by another court.

The first subparagraph shall also apply to judgments relating to preservation measures taken after the request for the opening of insolvency proceedings.

2. The recognition and enforcement of judgments other than those referred to in paragraph 1 shall be governed by the Convention referred to in paragraph 1, provided that that Convention is applicable.

3. The Member States shall not be obliged to recognise or enforce a judgment referred to in paragraph 1 which might result in a limitation of personal freedom or postal secrecy."

Aspects of the recognition principle

The principle of recognition and respect has several facets.

Assumption of jurisdiction by court of Member State must be respected by other courts

15–29 In the first place, save in exceptional circumstances, it is improper for a court in one Member State to enquire into the basis on which the court of another Member State assumed jurisdiction to open insolvency proceedings. For example, once main proceedings have been opened in France, an English court must in principle recognise the effectiveness of these automatically and without further formality or enquiry and cannot examine the legal or factual basis upon which the French court assumed jurisdiction. So while an English court might take the view that on the facts the debtor's COMI was England, not France, it must respect the finding of the French court on this issue. This rule of recognition is not at first sight consistent with the wording of art.16(1), which in terms requires only that recognition be given to a judgment handed down by a court of a Member State *which has jurisdiction pursuant to art.3*. This might be thought to imply that the court of another Member State may examine the question of whether that condition has been satisfied. But such an interpretation would completely undermine the principle of respect for judgments within the European Union and generate the very uncertainty and multiplicity of proceedings which the Regulation is designed to avoid. Article 3 must therefore be read purposively as precluding the court of a Member State from entertaining main proceedings when the court of another Member State *has assumed* jurisdiction under art.3. It was on that ground that the French Court of Cassation upheld the judgment of the Court of Appeal of Versailles reversing the decision of the Commercial Court of Cergy-Pontoise in the French *Daisy-Tek* proceedings and holding that it was a violation of the Regulation for the Commercial Court to treat an earlier administration order by the English High Court as of no effect.[110] Hence, the correct procedure for a party wishing to challenge the basis of the first decision, for example, on the ground that the debtor's COMI was not in fact situated in the Member State in which the proceedings were opened, is to use the appellate process in that State to seek to overturn the decision, not to institute separate proceedings in another Member State and invite the court in that State to disregard the earlier judgment. It is always open to a court of the jurisdiction in which the proceedings were opened to make a reference to the ECJ for a preliminary ruling on the interpretation of the Regulation and the highest court must do so if the ruling by the ECJ is necessary for that court to give judgment.[111]

Once jurisdiction has been assumed, no other court may entertain main proceedings

Secondly, as previously stated, once the court of a Member State has opened main proceedings, no court of another Member State may itself entertain a request to open main proceedings except in the unusual case where the   **15–30**

---

[110] See below, paras 15–53 et seq. As to the effect of an application to open proceedings made in one Member State on the power of a court in another Member State to open proceedings in that State, see below, para.15–47.

[111] See above, para.15–04. Exceptionally, the national court may decline to make a reference on the ground that the issue is too obvious (*acte claire*) to require consideration by the ECJ.

decision of the first court is manifestly contrary to the public policy of the second court.[112] So, in theory, save in the case just mentioned, there cannot be concurrent main proceedings in the courts of different Member States. However, this rule has not always been observed, a notorious example being the *Eurofood* case.[113]

Decision to decline jurisdiction must be respected

15–31   Thirdly, the rule of recognition applies not only where the court of the first state has assumed jurisdiction but also where it has declined it.[114] This is less clear in that art.16 requires recognition only of a judgment opening proceedings, not of a judgment declining jurisdiction to do so. Yet even here the principle of mutual respect must be allowed to operate, for if, for example, a court in Spain declined jurisdiction on the ground that the debtor's COMI was not situated in Spain but courts in other Member States disagreed, the result could be to preclude main proceedings from being opened anywhere. So a court in the second State must respect the basis of refusal of jurisdiction in the first State even if this means accepting that the debtor's COMI is in the second State when the court of that State would otherwise have taken a different view and declined jurisdiction. Where that court makes an order in ignorance of the earlier proceedings, its own proceedings should be converted into territorial proceedings.[115]

Judgment of court opening proceedings must be given effect in all other courts

15–32   Fourthly, a judgment of a court opening proceedings must be given the same effect in the courts of other Member States as it has in the State in which the proceedings are opened. Article 4 contains a list of matters governed by the *lex concursus*,[116] but this list is non-exhaustive. The principle of Community-wide effect of a judgment of a court in a Member State opening insolvency proceedings is a general one and would appear to include rules under the law of that State determining as from what time the proceedings are to be considered opened.[117] A further consequence of the opening of main proceedings in a Member State is that no action can be taken in another Member State against assets of the debtor in that State except by way of secondary proceedings, which can only be instituted in a State where the debtor has an

---

[112] See below, para.15–45.
[113] See below, para.15–36.
[114] Virgós and Garcimartín, *The European Insolvency Regulation*, para.70.
[115] ibid.
[116] See below, paras 15–72 et seq.
[117] See further below, para.15–41 and n.146.

establishment. So where main insolvency proceedings were opened in Poland, where the debtor company had its COMI, those proceedings encompassed all of the debtor's assets and it was not within the competence of a German court to order attachment of assets of the debtor in Germany.[118]

Judgments concerning course and closure of the insolvency proceedings must be recognised

Fifthly, judgments handed down by the court whose judgment opening the insolvency proceedings is recognised in accordance with art.16 and which concern the course and closure of insolvency proceedings, and compositions approved by that court, must also be recognised in other Member States without further formalities.[119] However, the sovereignty of other States must also be recognised, so that enforcement measures in such other States must first have authorisation (*exequatur*) from the court or other competent authority of the State concerned.

15–33

Judgments deriving directly from the insolvency proceedings and closely linked with them

Sixthly, judgments deriving directly from the insolvency proceedings and which are closely linked to them must be recognised even if handed down by another court.[120] This provision has its origin in the ECJ's decision in *Gourdain v Nadler*, referred to earlier,[121] and is a further illustration of the principle that there is to be no gap between Brussels I and the Insolvency Regulation. In the absence of a sufficient link, Brussels I will apply if the claim is otherwise within its scope; where the link is sufficient, the Insolvency Regulation will apply. Into this category fall judgments in or arising from the bankruptcy proceedings which require a director or manager to make good a shortfall of assets under a provision of the bankruptcy law[122]; for example, orders against a director for payment of a contribution to the debtor company's assets on the ground of fraudulent trading[123] or wrongful trading[124] and orders declaring a transaction void as being in contravention of the

15–34

---

[118] *MG Probud Gdynia sp* (C-444/07) [2010] B.C.C. 453.
[119] See art.25(1).
[120] See art.25(1), 2nd paragraph.
[121] See above, para. 15–02.
[122] *Gourdain v Nadler* (133/78) [1979] 3 C.M.L.R. 180. At the time of this decision there was neither an Insolvency Convention nor an Insolvency Regulation but the effect of the decision was that such a case fell within the bankruptcy exclusion from the Brussels Convention. In consequence, it falls within art.25(1).
[123] Insolvency Act 1986 s.213. See above, para.14–21.
[124] Insolvency Act 1986 s.214. See above, para.14–27.

anti-deprivation and *pari passu* rules[125] or as a transaction at an under-value[126] or a preference.[127] Also covered by art.25 are orders in proceedings for the disqualification of a director if associated with and deriving from the insolvency proceedings[128] and a decision holding that a disposition of assets by a liquidator was outside his powers.[129] Falling outside art.25 are disqualification orders not linked to the insolvency proceedings,[130] claims against a liquidator based on pre-liquidation rights, such as a seller's claim based on reservation of title,[131] and claims by a liquidator to recover debt or property due to an insolvent company and not arising from the insolvency proceedings.[132]

Judgments relating to preservation measures

15–35 Judgments relating to preservation measures taken after the request for the opening of the insolvency proceedings must also be recognised by courts of other Member States.[133] This must be read with art.38, by which a temporary administrator appointed by the court opening the main proceedings may request any measures to secure and preserve any of the debtor's assets situated in another Member State, provided for under the law of that State, between the request for the opening of the proceedings and the judgment opening the proceedings.

Exceptions to the rule of recognition

15–36 In exceptional cases the court of a Member State may be entitled to disregard a judgment of a court of another Member State. Where, for example, the court of the other State has assumed jurisdiction despite an express finding that the debtor's COMI is not situated within that State, it must, it is thought, be open to a court entertaining subsequent proceedings elsewhere to disregard the earlier decision as *ultra vires* the Regulation on its face. A further exception is provided by art.26:

---

[125] See above, para.8–11.
[126] Insolvency Act 1986 s.238. See *Oakley v Ultra Vehicle Design Ltd* [2006] B.C.C. 57 and above, para.13–12.
[127] Insolvency Act 1986 s.239. See *Oakley*, cited above n.126; and para.13–71.
[128] Virgós and Garcimartín, *The European Insolvency Regulation*, para.125.
[129] *SCT Industri AB v Alpenblume AB* (C-111/08) [2010] Bus. L.R. 559.
[130] *SCT Industri*, cited above n.129.
[131] *German Graphics Graphische Maschinen GmbH v Alice van der Schee* (C-292/08) [2009] E.C.R. I-8421; [2009] All E.R. (D) 75.
[132] *Byers v Yacht Bull Corp* [2010] B.C.C. 368; *Re Hayward* [1997] Ch. 45; and *Oakley*, cited above n.126.
[133] Insolvency Regulation art.25(1).

"A Member State may refuse to recognise insolvency proceedings opened in another Member State or to enforce a judgment handed down in the context of such proceedings where the effects of such recognition or enforcement would be manifestly contrary to that State's public policy, in particular its fundamental principles or the constitutional rights and liberties of the individual."

An example is where an interested party was not given notice of the insolvency proceedings or was otherwise prevented from participating in them. It was on this ground that in the *Eurofood* case[134] the High Court in Ireland declined to recognise the decision of the Civil and Criminal Court of Parma, Italy, placing Parmalat SpA in extraordinary administration. The facts as set out in the judgment of Kelly J. were decidedly unusual:

On December 24 2003 Parmalat SpA, the parent company of an Irish company, Eurofood, was placed in extraordinary administration by the Italian Ministry of Productive Activities, following a new Italian law providing for extraordinary administration, and Signor Enrico Bondi was appointed extraordinary administrator. The insolvency of the company and the administration and appointment were confirmed by the Civil and Criminal Court of Parma on December 27. On January 27, 2004 a petition for the winding up of Eurofood was presented to the High Court in Ireland and on the same day Mr Pearse Farrell was appointed provisional liquidator by Langham J. On January 30 he notified Signor Bondi of his appointment. On February 9 Signor Bondi was appointed extraordinary administrator of Eurofood by the Italian Ministry despite his knowledge of the appointment of a provisional liquidator by the Irish Court nearly two weeks earlier. On February 13 the provisional liquidator was served with notice of a hearing to take place before the Parma court on February 17 with a view to that court declaring Eurofood's insolvency. He was not supplied with the petition or any supporting documents then or thereafter in response to repeated requests. Despite a direction by the court that all interested parties be given notice, no notice was given to major creditors. The provisional liquidator sought to argue that main proceedings had already been opened in Ireland. The advice received by Signor Bondi and placed before the Parma court was that the appointment of the provisional liquidator did not amount to the opening of main proceedings or the determination of the debtor's COMI. The Parma court admitted Eurofood into insolvency and also held that its COMI was in Italy rather than Ireland.

On these facts, Kelly J. made a winding up order in the Irish proceedings on March 23, holding that Eurofood's COMI was in Ireland. The company's

---

[134] *Re Eurofood IFSC Ltd* [2004] B.C.C. 383.

registered office was in Ireland, raising a presumption under art.3(1) that Ireland was the COMI. The creditors' perception was that they were dealing with a company located in Ireland and (as was the case) subject to its fiscal and regulatory provisions. The only connection with Italy was that the company was a subsidiary of an Italian company. Kelly J. concluded that the Parma court lacked jurisdiction to open main proceedings because (contrary to the advice placed before that court) the presentation of the winding up petition and the appointment of a provisional liquidator on January 27 brought about the opening of main proceedings. The winding up took effect from the time of presentation of the winding up petition, pursuant to s.220(2) of the Companies Act 1963. It followed that the Parma court's decision was not entitled to recognition. An additional ground for refusal of recognition was the denial of the opportunity to creditors to be heard in the Parma proceedings, and this entitled the Irish court to invoke the public policy exception in art.26.

15–37   On Signor Bondi's appeal to the Irish Supreme Court,[135] which was solely on the issue of refusal to recognise the Parma court's decision, the Supreme Court noted that Signore Bondi had at no time given any explanation for his failure to provide the provisional liquidator with essential documents for the Parma hearing and that even on the appeal his counsel had been instructed to offer no explanation to the Supreme Court for the "extraordinary behaviour" of Signor Bondi, which the court criticised in the strongest terms. It was an intrinsic element of the principle of mutual trust that parties to proceedings receive a fair hearing, which had not happened in Parma. Kelly J. was therefore correct in holding that it would be contrary to the public policy of Irish law to recognise the Parma court's judgment. Nevertheless, the court felt bound to refer the question to the ECJ for a preliminary ruling. The ECJ ruled that it was for the referring State to decide whether recognition of the foreign court's judgment would be manifestly contrary to that State's public policy in the sense of infringing a fundamental principle regarded as essential to the legal order of the State in question.[136] The court stressed that the right to be heard and notified of procedural documents occupied an eminent position in the organisation and conduct of a fair legal process, thus implicitly upholding the approach adopted by the Irish Supreme Court. However, the ECJ also reiterated the point made in *Krombach v Bamberski*[137]—that recourse to the public policy principle must be reserved for exceptional cases and that while it is not for the ECJ to dictate what a Member State's public policy should be, it nevertheless considered itself competent to review the limits within which the courts of a contracting State may have recourse to the public policy exception so as to ensure that the principle of respect for judgments of courts of a Member State is not undermined.

---

[135] [2005] Eu. L.R. 148.
[136] *Re Eurofood IFSC Ltd* (C-341/04) [2006] Ch. 508.
[137] Case C-7/98 [2000] E.C.R. 1; [2001] All E.R. (EC) 584.

When the matter returned to the Irish Supreme Court,[138] it held that in the light of the ECJ's ruling the appointment of the provisional liquidator was the opening of an insolvency proceeding, which preceded the Parma court's decision and therefore had priority over that decision; it was unnecessary to consider whether recognition of such decision should be withheld on the ground of public policy. But had it been necessary to do so, the Supreme Court, which harshly criticised the conduct of the Italian Extraordinary Administrator in withholding necessary documents from the Irish provisional liquidator, would have upheld the decision of Kelly J.

A further case in which recognition of the judgment of a court of another Member State may be refused is where the proceeding in question is not an insolvency proceeding but an ordinary debt or damages claim by or against an insolvent company which does not meet the requirement that it derive directly from the winding up and be closely connected with it and is therefore governed not by the Insolvency Regulation but by the Jurisdiction and Judgments Regulation (Brussels I).[139]

15–38

7. THE OPENING OF MAIN PROCEEDINGS AND ITS EFFECT

When are proceedings considered opened?

It may be important to determine what constitutes the opening of proceedings and thus the time at which they are deemed to have been opened. That is the time as at which the COMI has to be determined for the purpose of the jurisdictional rules, and in the case of main proceedings it establishes which court of competent jurisdiction is to be considered first in the field so as to have the exclusive right to recognition in other Member States. As we shall see, the date when the debts were incurred is irrelevant. Article 2(f) provides that:

15–39

". . . the time of the opening of proceedings' means the time at which the judgment opening proceedings becomes effective, whether it is a final judgment or not."

As we have seen, "judgment" has to be given an extended meaning, covering not only winding up and administration orders but creditors' voluntary liquidations, out-of-court administrations and CVAs. One might have

---

[138] *Re Eurofood IFSC Ltd* [2006] I.E.S.C. 41; [2006] 4 I.R. 307.
[139] *Gibraltar Residential Properties Ltd v Gibralcon 2004 SA* [2011] B.L.R. 126. As to this requirement, see above, para.15–02.

thought it would be easy to determine the date of opening of these various proceedings but in various respects the position is far from clear, and it is necessary to take each type of proceeding in turn.

(1) Creditors' voluntary winding up

15–40   The requirement that the proceedings be confirmed by the court[140] raises the question whether the relevant time is the time the confirming order is made or the time the resolution is passed. The history of this provision shows the intention to take the time of the resolution as the relevant time except for the purpose of allowing the liquidator to exercise his powers in another Member State.[141] The proceedings are opened on the passing of the resolution by the members for voluntary winding up by reason of insolvency.

(2) Compulsory winding up

15–41   The position here is complicated by the retrospective character of a winding up order. Where the winding up follows a CVL, it is deemed to commence at the time of passing of the resolution for voluntary winding up; where the winding up order is made on an application for an administration order, the commencement is the time of the winding up order; in other cases it is the date of presentation of the winding up petition.[142] The question then arises whether in the first and third case the proceedings should be considered opened on the making of the winding up order or on the passing of the resolution or (if there was no prior CVL) the presentation of the winding up petition. Reference has already been made to the decision of the Irish High Court in *Re Eurofood IFSC Ltd*,[143] in which Kelly J. held that under the equivalent provisions of s.220(2) of the Irish Companies Act 1963 the winding up likewise took effect as at the time of presentation of the winding up petition, and this was to be treated as the time of opening of the insolvency proceedings for the purpose of the Insolvency Regulation. Although on the subsequent reference to the ECJ[144] the court found it unnecessary to rule on the point, the view of Kelly J. received some support from the Opinion of the Advocate General and is further supported by

---

[140] See above, para.15–13.
[141] Virgós-Schmit Report, paras 52 and 68.
[142] Insolvency Act 1986 s.129.
[143] Cited above n.134.
[144] *Re Eurofood IFSC Ltd* (C-341/04) [2006] Ch. 508.

art.2(f)[145] and the Virgós-Schmit Report.[146] It is disputed by some commentators[147] on the ground that other provisions of the Regulation clearly distinguish between the opening of proceedings and a request for the opening of proceedings.[148] But these provisions are dealing with the stage preceding the judgment when there is nothing except the request; they do not bear on the retrospective effect of a judgment once this has been handed down. Moreover, it is not in every Member State or in every type of insolvency proceeding that retrospective effect is given to the judgment.

(3) Order appointing provisional liquidator

The *Eurofood* decision establishes that an order appointing a provisional liquidator in proceedings for a winding up order constitutes the opening of insolvency proceedings.[149]

15–42

(4) Administration

The proceedings are opened upon the administration taking effect,[150] whether out of court or by court order.

15–43

(5) CVA

In the case of a CVA, the proceedings are opened upon its taking effect.[151]

15–44

---

[145] Which defines the time of the opening of the proceedings as the time at which the judgment opening the proceedings becomes effective, whether or not it is a final judgment, leaving it to the *lex concursus* to determine the time as at which the proceedings are to be treated as opened.

[146] " 'The time of the opening of the proceedings' is deemed to be the time when the decision begins to be effective under the law of the State of the opening of the proceedings" (para.68). Similarly, the tentative view of the majority of the Court of Appeal in *Shierson v Vlieland-Boddy* [2005] 1 W.L.R. 3966. was that the relevant time was the service of the petition. See further para.15–49.

[147] e.g. Moss, Fletcher and Isaacs, *The EC Regulation on Insolvency Proceedings*, 2009, para.8.71.

[148] See, e.g. arts 3(4) and 29.

[149] See above, para.15–36.

[150] See above, n.146 and paras 11–44 and 11–48.

[151] See above, para.12–42.

8. MAIN PROCEEDINGS

Effect of opening of main proceedings

Effect generally

15–45 Once main proceedings have been opened in a Member State, all other proceedings in another Member State are secondary proceedings[152] which can
only be winding up proceedings and are restricted to local assets.[153] Any
judgment opened in the main proceedings must be recognised throughout
the European Union from the time it becomes effective in the State of opening of the proceedings,[154] and produces the same effects in other Member
States as under the law of the State of opening of the proceedings, without
further formality.[155] It is therefore not necessary to obtain any *exequatur* in
such other States in order to produce the effects in question. The effects in
question include the rules governing the matters listed in art.4 except so far
as displaced by the exceptions in arts 5 et seq. as previously discussed. Such
effects thus cover such matters as an automatic stay of proceedings, the
determination of the assets forming the debtor's estate, the bringing of all
assets under the control of the liquidator in the main proceedings except for
those subject to territorial proceedings and located within the territory concerned, and the avoidance of transactions under the rules of the *lex concursus*. So the *lex concursus*, so far as not displaced, applies automatically
throughout the European Union. The liquidator may exercise in another
Member State all of the powers conferred on him by the *lex concursus*, and
may remove the debtor's assets but with three qualifications. He may not
exercise his powers in the other Member State if other insolvency proceedings have been opened there or if any preservation measure to the contrary
has been taken there. He must respect any *in rem* and retention of title rights
of third parties under arts 5 and 7, subject to the avoidance provisions of the
lex concursus under art.4(2)(m). Finally, he must comply with the local law
and must not exercise coercive measures or the right to rule on legal proceedings or disputes.[156] The liquidator in the main proceedings may also
apply in another Member State to open secondary proceedings.[157]

---

[152] Insolvency Regulation art.3(3). See above, para.15–21.
[153] See below, para.15–60. Note that winding up here includes winding up through administration. See above, para.15–13.
[154] See art.16(1).
[155] See art.17(1). But this does not apply as regards a Member State in which territorial proceedings are opened (ibid.).
[156] See art.18(1) and (3).
[157] See art.29.

Redefinition of "property"

In order to conform to the Regulation, the definition of "property" in s.436   **15–46**
of the Insolvency Act 1986[158] has been modified as regards insolvency proceedings in England so as to limit the reference to property in the application of the Act to property which may be dealt with in the proceedings.[159]
This means that where main proceedings have been opened in another
Member State the jurisdiction of the English courts in relation to territorial
proceedings opened there is confined to assets within the jurisdiction and
that where main proceedings have been opened in England, then although
in principle these cover the whole of the debtor company's estate on a worldwide basis, this is subject to: (1) the control by courts of another Member
State in which territorial proceedings have been opened over assets situated
in that State; and (2) the *in rem* and other rights of third parties protected by
the exclusions from art.4 specified in arts 5 et seq.

Effect of a request to open proceedings

While it is clear that a judgment opening insolvency proceedings in one Member   **15–47**
State must be respected in all other Member States, there is a singular lack of
clarity as to the effect of a request to open proceedings. The various references
to such a request[160] shed little light on its status. It seems clear that the request
cannot itself constitute the opening of insolvency proceedings, although an ensuing judgment may, under the *lex concursus*, have effect as from the date of the
request.[161] On the other hand, to allow a creditor who has notice of such a
request to institute proceedings in another forum with a view to establishing
main proceedings in that forum first would be to encourage the self-same forum
shopping which the Regulation is designed to avoid.[162] Similarly, allowing the
debtor to move its COMI to another Member State between the time of the
request and the time of judgment in order to frustrate proceedings that have
been initiated in the first Member State would facilitate evasion of the
Regulation. In *Staubitz-Schreiber*,[163] the ECJ surmounted the problem of the
debtor's migration to a new COMI after the filing of a request to open proceedings not by invoking the principle of respect and recognition in art.16 but by

---

[158] See above, paras 6–03 et seq.
[159] Insolvency Act 1986 s.436A.
[160] See, e.g. recital (16) in regard to provisional and protective measures; recital (17) and
art.3(4)(b) in regard to limiting to local creditors the right to make a request to open independent proceedings; recitals (18), (19) and (25) and art.29 as to the right of the liquidator
of main proceedings to request the opening of secondary proceedings, and art.37 as to his
right to apply for the conversion of territorial proceedings.
[161] As in the case of a compulsory winding up under s.29 of the Insolvency Act 1986.
[162] See Gerard McCormack, "Jurisdictional Competition and Forum Shopping in Insolvency
Proceedings" (2009) 68 C.L.J. 169.
[163] Case C-1/104, [2006] E.C.R. 1-701; [2006] All E.R. (D) 65.

interpreting art.3(1) as embracing retention of jurisdiction despite the change of COMI where at the time of *lodgement of the request* the COMI was in the Member State to whose courts the request was addressed. To allow divestment of jurisdiction by a change of COMI would be contrary to the objectives pursued by the Regulation and the policy stated in the fourth recital to the Preamble. It is thought that, by the same reasoning, if in one Member State an application is made for a winding up order, courts in other Member States should refrain from opening insolvency proceedings in their own jurisdiction until the winding up proceedings have been determined. If a winding up order is made, this will establish the main proceedings, and any proceedings elsewhere will be territorial proceedings. If, on the other hand, the application is dismissed, this leaves it open to the courts of another Member State to open proceedings themselves if the jurisdictional requirements of the Regulation are satisfied. This deferment to proceedings pending in another Member State not only reflects the spirit of the Regulation but can properly be founded on the principle *lis pendens*[164] or, where the facts justify it, on the principle of estoppel by which the debtor company cannot be heard to say that its COMI is located at a place other than that at which the company held it out as located. Where the court in the later proceedings is unaware of the request to open the earlier proceedings and opens its own insolvency proceedings, and subsequently an order is made in the earlier proceedings, the appropriate course in the later proceedings would seem to be to convert them into secondary proceedings.

15-48   Once a request to open main proceedings to a court having jurisdiction under art.3(1) has been made, the court may appoint a temporary administrator in order to ensure preservation of the debtor's assets, and the temporary administrator is then empowered to request any measures to secure and preserve assets situated in another Member State.[165]

9. DETERMINATION OF DEBTOR'S COMI

The concept of the COMI

15-49   As we have seen, main proceedings can be instituted only in the Member State in the territory of which the debtor's COMI is situated. So it has been held in England that the appointment of an administrator of a company whose COMI was later found to be in Germany was invalid.[166] Astonishingly,

---

[164] Virgós and Garcimartín, *The European Insolvency Regulation*, para.70.
[165] See art.38 and below, para.15-89.
[166] *Hans Brochier Holdings Ltd v Exner* [2007] B.C.C. 127. It may be noted that the situation of the debtor's claim against a third party is in the territory in which the third party has his COMI (art.2(g)). The situation of assets is particularly relevant to the applicability of arts 5 and 7. See below, paras 15-73 et seq.

the text of the Regulation does not define the COMI or give any guidance as to its meaning. For that we have to rely on recital (13), which states that the 'centre of main interests':

". . . should correspond to the place where the debtor conducts the administration of his interests on a regular basis and is therefore ascertainable by third parties."

All we know from the text of the Regulation is that in the case of a company or legal person, the place of the registered office is to be presumed as its COMI in the absence of proof to the contrary.[167] The Virgós-Schmit Report (which as stated earlier was a report on the EC Convention, not the Regulation) elaborated on the rationale of the "centre of main interests" concept in the following terms:

"The concept of 'centre of main interests' must be interpreted as the place where the debtor conducts the administration of his interests on a regular basis and is therefore ascertainable by third parties.

The rationale of this rule is not difficult to explain. Insolvency is a foreseeable risk. It is therefore important that international jurisdiction . . . be based on a place known to the debtor's potential creditors. This enables the legal risks which would have to be assumed in the case of insolvency to be calculated.

By using the term 'interests', the intention was to encompass not only commercial, industrial or professional activities but also general economic activities, so as to include the actions of private individuals (e.g. consumers). The expression 'main' serves as a criterion for the cases where these interests included activities of different types which are run from different centres."[168]

The second paragraph of the above passage has been criticised as implying that the relevant time for determining the debtor's COMI is the time the debts are incurred, when it is clear from the Regulation that it is the time when the judgment to open the proceedings becomes effective, which in English law is possibly the date of service of the petition.[169] There is force in this criticism, for it is hard to see how knowledge of the debtor's COMI (and thus of the potentially applicable insolvency regime) at the time of extending

---

[167] See art.3(1). For a review of the development of the COMI concept see Bob Wessels, "COMI: Past, Preesent and Future" (2011) 24 Ins. Int. 17.

[168] Report (above, n. 12), para.75.

[169] *Shierson v Vlieland-Boddy* [2005] 1 W.L.R. 3966, a case in which the debtor had incurred debts when his COMI was in England but had shifted his COMI to Spain by the time of opening of the insolvency proceedings. The Court of Appeal held that he was entitled to do this and that there was therefore no jurisdiction to open main proceedings in England.

credit can enable the creditor to assess the risk when the debtor may move its COMI to another Member State the very next day and may incur fresh debt to creditors in the new State, raising the question of which creditors are to be considered the relevant ones.[170] But the rationale for the COMI concept holds good in the many cases in which the situation of the COMI remains unchanged. The time factor cannot be controlled but the place of the COMI is that which creditors generally would consider the most relevant.

The time as at which the COMI is to be determined

15–50 As stated earlier,[171] the time at which the COMI requirement is required to be satisfied is the time of opening of the insolvency proceedings.

15–51 **Determining the situation of the COMI**

Presumption that COMI is place of registered office

15–52 There has been a substantial amount of case law, both in the United Kingdom and other Member States and in the ECJ, on the determination of the COMI and it has become clear that the location of the registered office, far from being a presumption that is readily displaced, is a strong one and is not easily dislodged. This is because the test is not purely the objective one of the place of administration but also involves criteria that are ascertainable by third parties. The concept has been described by the ECJ as peculiar to the Regulation and therefore having an autonomous meaning and to be interpreted in a uniform way, independently of national legislation.[172]

The strong presumption in favour of the registered office has the merit of certainty, yet it is at least arguable that it is over-emphasized in the jurisprudence of the ECJ. For example, in *Eurofood* the court gave as an example of a case "in particular" where the presumption would be displaced a "letter-box" company not carrying on any business at all in the State of the registered office, but in the typical case where the issue of the COMI arises there is likely to be at least some business activity in the place of the registered office, though not enough to prevent the presumption from being displaced.

---

[170] The advantage of taking the date of service of the proceedings as the relevant date is that if the foreign court subsequently refuses to entertain main proceedings by reason of *lis alibi pendens* (see para.15–47), the English court could proceed to make a winding up order with retrospective effect, thus negating the impact of a post-petition change of COMI.

[171] See above, para.15–17.

[172] *Re Eurofood IFSC Ltd* (C-341/04) [2006] Ch. 508.

Displacement of the presumption

Daisy-Tek—the English proceedings

Almost all of the reported case law in England has focused on jurisdictional questions raised by the COMI issue, and in almost every case the court has concluded either that it has jurisdiction because the company's COMI was situated here even though its registered office was elsewhere, or that the company's COMI was in another Member State even though its registered office was in England. Strikingly, two of the decisions that have attracted much attention here and overseas emanate from the High Court sitting at Leeds. The first of these was the *Daisy-Tek* case,[173] which had an impact going well beyond the shores of the British Isles. The facts were as follows:

15–53

> Daisy-Tek ISA Ltd. was a subsidiary of a US company, Daisy-Tek International Corporation, which had filed for reorganisation under Chapter 11. Daisy-Tek ISA itself had a subsidiary, ISA International plc ('International') and through International was also the holding company of a number of other companies incorporated in England, France and Germany. Creditors of Daisy-Tek ISA and its direct and indirect subsidiaries applied for administration orders against them.

H.H. Judge McGonigal said in his judgment that in identifying the centre of the debtor's main interests the court had to consider both the scale of the interests administered at a particular place and their importance and then consider the scale and importance of its interests administered at any other place which might be regarded as its centre of main interests, whether as a result of the presumption in art.3(1) or otherwise. The fact that the centre of the debtor's main interests had to be 'ascertainable by third parties' was very important. The evidence showed that the administration of their businesses was conducted from Bradford, where customers were serviced and contracts were concluded, and all of the businesses were controlled from Bradford. Further, a large majority of potential trade and finance creditors knew that Bradford was the place where many of the important functions of the companies were carried out, and these were the most important 'third parties' referred to in recital (13) of the Regulation as those who should be able to ascertain the debtor's centre of main interests. He therefore held that he had jurisdiction to make such orders not only against the English companies but also against those incorporated in France and Germany.

---

[173] *Re Daisytek-ISA Ltd* [2003] B.C.C. 562.

Daisy-Tek in France

15–54   The battle then moved to France, where the Commercial Court of Cergy-Pontoise, although informed of the English High Court's decision, held that this was "without effect" in relation to the relevant French subsidiary, since each company within the Daisy-Tek group was a separate legal entity, there was no legal concept of a "group" and the English court could not assume jurisdiction by denying the separate legal existence of the French company. The court thereupon made its own administration order against that subsidiary and later dismissed an application by the UK administrators to have its judgment set aside. The decision was reversed by the Court of Appeal of Versailles,[174] which in a clear and concisely reasoned judgment held that it was untrue to argue that the High Court's decision had been based on the notion of a corporate group, and that on the contrary the High Court had concluded that the company's centre of main interests was in Bradford. Accordingly, the Insolvency Regulation required French courts to respect the order made by the High Court, which produced the same legal effects in France as under English law, the Commercial Court of Cergy-Pontoise had no jurisdiction to put the company into administration and its order was in violation of the Regulation. This decision was subsequently upheld by the Court of Cassation.[175]

Daisy-Tek in Germany

15–55   A similar sequence of events occurred in relation to the German subsidiaries. The court of first instance at Düsseldorf, initially unaware of the English administration order, made its own order, so that there were two main insolvency proceedings, contrary to what is permitted by the Regulation. When the court learned of the English order, it held that it was of no effect in relation to the German subsidiaries but on appeal it was ordered that in relation to one of the German companies the proceedings be converted into secondary proceedings in recognition of the primacy of the English order.[176]

Relevant factors in determining the COMI

15–56   The situation of the debtor's COMI is a question of fact and degree. Of key importance is the place which creditors would have regarded as the

---

[174] 24th Chamber, September 4, 2003, case no.03/05038. An English translation of the decision is reported sub. nom. *Klempka v ISA Daisytek SA* [2003] B.C.C. 984.

[175] *French Republic v Klempka* [2006] B.C.C. 841. The question of respect for orders of the court which is the first to open proceedings is discussed above, para.15–29.

[176] For an English description of the course of the proceedings in Germany, see Fletcher, *Insolvency in Private International Law*, paras 7.71 and 7.73.

COMI.[177] Among the factors the court will take into account in deciding whether the presumption in favour of the location of the registered office has been displaced are the following: the place where the company's business is managed and operated and its contracts concluded[178]; the location of any regulatory authorities[179]; the place where board meetings are held[180]; the place where the accounts are prepared and audited[181]; the location of customers, suppliers and loan creditors[182]; the place from which information technology and support and corporate identity and branding are run[183]; the place where the chief executive spends most of his time in the running of the business[184]; the location of the majority of employees and the country whose law governs their employment contracts.[185] None of these factors is necessarily decisive on its own, and usually two or more of them are to be found in combination. A particular compelling set of factors featured in *Re Eurofood IFSC Ltd*,[186] where the question was whether the debtor company had its COMI in Ireland or in Italy. The Irish High Court entertained no doubt that the COMI was in Ireland in the light of the fact that it was not only incorporated in Ireland, with its registered office in Dublin but it was subject to supervision by various Irish authorities, its tax benefits were conditional on its being managed and operated in Ireland, day-to-day administration was conducted on its behalf in Ireland in accordance with the terms of an administration agreement governed by Irish law and providing for jurisdiction by the Irish courts, its books and annual accounts were audited in accordance with Irish law, it paid corporation tax in Ireland on its trading operations and almost all of its board meetings were held in Ireland. This was an unusually clear case. The court has to weigh up all of the facts and decide where the company's centre of gravity is situated. What is clear is that the COMI must have a reasonable degree of permanence; the concept of the location of the business shifting as its director moves from one country to another does not sit easily with the policy of the Regulation.[187] Moreover, the location of the

---

[177] *Daisy-Tek*, cited above n.173.

[178] *Re Eurofood*, cited above n.134; and *AIM Underwriting Agencies (Ireland) Ltd, Re* [2005] I.L.Pr. 22;

[179] *Re Eurofood*, cited above n.134.

[180] *Re Eurofood*, cited above n.134.

[181] *Re Eurofood*, cited above n.134.

[182] *Re Daisy-Tek ISA Ltd* [2003] B.C.C. 562; and *Re 3T Telecom Ltd* [2005] All E.R. (D) 91. However, as regards the requirement that the COMI be a place visible to third parties dealing with the company, the category of third parties to be considered are essentially the company's creditors, not investors in the company, who are insiders rather than persons doing business with the company (*Re Kaupthing Capital Partners II Master LP Inc* [2010] EWHC 836 (Ch), *per* Proudman J. at [22]).

[183] ibid.

[184] ibid.

[185] *Hans Brochier Ltd v Exner* [2006] EWHC 2594 (Ch); [2007] B.C.C. 127.

[186] Cited above n.134.

[187] *Re Ci4net.com Inc* [2005] B.C.C. 277.

head office is of less importance than the place where head office functions are carried out,[188] although the latter is not determinative.[189]

In an interesting judgment in *Re MPOTEC GmbH*[190] the Commercial Court of Nanterre held that the so-called "real registered office" in private international law, that is, the place where the company has its central administration, was not to be equated with the place where the company has its central of main interest. Rather, the reference should be to the place of performance of head-office functions.

However, in England there has been a movement away from treating the head office functions test as the equivalent of that laid down by the ECJ. Lewison J., having originally adopted the head office functions test in *Re Lennox Holdings Plc*,[191] resiled from that position in *Re Stanford International Bank Ltd*,[192] holding that simply to adopt the head office functions approach without considering whether the location of those functions was ascertainable by third parties was the wrong test, and this ruling was upheld by a majority of the Court of Appeal,[193] Arden L.J. dissenting on this point. Nevertheless, it is submitted that while the place of performance of head office functions is not conclusive, it is a powerful indicator so long as performance of the key functions is visible to third parties. In the same case, it was also held that the test for determining the debtor's COMI under the UNCITRAL Model Law should be the same as that applied by the ECJ under the Insolvency Regulation.

Location of parent company not determinative

15–57   The fact that the insolvent company with a registered office in one Member State is controlled by a parent with a registered office in a different Member State does not by itself affect the normal presumption that the COMI is the location of the registered office of the insolvent company.[194]

Change of debtor's COMI and creditor control

15–58   It would usually be difficult even for the main creditor to stipulate where the debtor's COMI should be located, since this is a business decision which should be left to the debtor. On the other hand, there would be nothing

---

[188] *Lennox Holdings Plc* [2009] B.C.C. 155; and *Re MPOTEC GmbH* [2006] B.C.C 681.
[189] See below.
[190] Cited above n.188, at 687.
[191] [2009] B.C.C. 155.
[192] [2009] B.P.I.R. 1157 at [61].
[193] [2010] 3 W.L.R. 941.
[194] *Re Eurofood IFSC Ltd* [2005] B.C.C. 999.

unreasonable in a stipulation that the COMI was not to be changed without a specified period of prior notice to the creditor and even that the debtor should be required to obtain the creditor's consent, such consent not to be unreasonably withheld. Indeed, it has been said that "it is largely impossible to effectuate migration without the creditors' consent"[195] and that on this basis there should be a strong presumption that the migration will have beneficial effects and lead to a more efficient insolvency administration.[196] But a mere contractual stipulation, even if backed by a default remedy such as acceleration of the indebtedness, would have relatively limited force. Only a substantially secured creditor or group of creditors has the power to exercise the control required. Lenders usually seek both a representation as to the existing location of the COMI and an undertaking not to move it without consent. Borrowers are reluctant to make an unqualified representation as to the location of the COMI on the ground that this is a question of law as well as of fact, involving difficult definitional issues, and seek to restrict any representation to factual matters, such as where board meetings are held or the directors are based.

10. POWERS OF THE LIQUIDATOR

The liquidator in the main proceedings has extensive powers. He may exercise in other Member States all of the powers conferred upon him by the *lex concursus*, including removal of the debtor's assets from the territory of the Member State in which they are situated,[197] institute proceedings to set aside which is in the interests of the creditors,[198] request notice of the judgment opening the main proceedings to be published in any other Member State[199] and registered in any land register,[200] request the opening of secondary proceedings[201] or a stay of secondary proceedings that have been opened,[202] propose a rescue plan, composition or comparable measure in the secondary proceedings[203] and request the conversion of proceedings opened in another Member State into winding up proceedings if this proves to be in the interests of the creditors in the main proceedings.[204] These powers may be

15–59

---

[195] Wolf-Georg Ringe, "Forum Shopping under the EU Insolvency Regulation", (2008) 9 European Business Organization Law Rev. 579, 588–589.
[196] Ringe, "Forum Shopping", 2008, at 603–604.
[197] See art.18(1).
[198] See art.18(2).
[199] See art.21(1).
[200] See art.22(1).
[201] See art.29.
[202] See art.33.
[203] See art.34(1).
[204] See art.37. Secondary proceedings are by their nature limited to winding up (art.3(3)). See below, para.15–60.

exercised without need of an *exequatur* but subject to this the liquidator must, in exercising them, comply with the law of the Member State in which he intends to take action, in particular with regard to the procedures for the realisation of assets.[205] So the liquidator may take steps to get in the assets forming part of the debtor's estate but may not, to that end, resort to self-help in a Member State whose laws prohibit and require application to a court. Further, the powers may not include coercive measures,[206] for example, seizure of assets to enforce compliance with the liquidator's directions.

11. TERRITORIAL PROCEEDINGS

Types and permissible scope of territorial proceedings

15–60 Territorial proceedings are so called because they are confined to assets within the territory in which the proceedings are opened and thus do not enjoy the universal application of main proceedings. Territorial proceedings are independent if they are opened before any main proceedings have been opened; otherwise they are secondary proceedings. Where they are secondary proceedings they can only take the form of winding up,[207] for the obvious reason that their sole purpose is to realise local assets, and since they are restricted to such assets a reorganisation of the company as a whole would be impracticable and, moreover, would limit the efficacy of a reorganisation in the main proceedings. This restriction does not apply to independent proceedings unless and until they become converted into secondary proceedings as the result of the opening of main proceedings in another Member State.

Conditions in which territorial proceedings may be opened

(1) Jurisdiction at international and national level

15–61 As with main proceedings, the power to entertain territorial proceedings must satisfy a twofold test. It must meet the criteria for international jurisdiction laid down by the Regulation; and it must satisfy any additional jurisdictional requirements imposed by the national law of the State concerned. In addition, it is necessary that the COMI be within the European Union, failing which the proceedings would not come under the Insolvency

---

[205] See art.18(3). On a natural construction of art.18, this must refer to the manner in which the powers are to be exercised, not their nature, content or extent. See to the same effect Moss, Fletcher and Isaacs, *The EC Regulation on Insolvency Proceedings*, 2009, paras 8.281–8.283.
[206] ibid.
[207] See art.3(3). For this purpose, winding up proceedings are those listed in Annex B.

Regulation at all, although they could constitute non-main proceedings within the UNCITRAL Model Law.[208]

(2) The need for an establishment

Territorial proceedings may be instituted only in a Member State in which the debtor has an establishment.[209] The time at which this condition has to be satisfied is on the hearing of the request to open the proceedings. "Establishment" is defined as "any place of operations where the debtor carries out a non-transitory economic activity with human means and goods".[210]

15–62

The economic activity need not be central to the company's operations; it suffices that there is a place of business which is not purely temporary (although it need not be permanent), which is operated by staff who are either employees of the company or others for whose acts it is responsible and which is engaged in economic activity. The key elements have been described as the conduct of commercial, industrial or professional activities manifested externally, some form of organisational presence (a branch, an office, a factory, a workshop), and a degree of stability and iteration.[211]

The word "goods" is a mistranslation of "*biens*", which means assets[212] and belies the intention, which is to cover not only goods but intangible property, services and facilities, and art.2(h) should be construed in that light. It has been held that the location in England of the business premises of a subsidiary of the debtor company does not by itself constitute an establishment of the company,[213] although if the premises are occupied by a branch rather than a subsidiary, that will ordinarily suffice.

(3) Further conditions for independent proceedings

Independent proceedings (those instituted before the opening of main proceedings) can be instituted only where:

15–63

(1) main insolvency proceedings cannot be opened because of the conditions laid down by the law of the Member State in which the debtor has its COMI; or

---

[208] See below, para.16–29.

[209] See art.3(2).

[210] See art.2(h).

[211] Virgós-Schmit Report, para.71; and Virgós and Garcimartín, *The European Insolvency Regulation*, paras 298 et seq.

[212] Moss, Fletcher and Isaacs, *The EC Regulation on Insolvency Proceedings*, 2009, para.8.45.

[213] *Telia AB v Hillcourt (Docklands) Ltd* [2003] B.C.C. 856.

(2)   the opening of the independent proceedings is requested by a creditor who has his domicile, habitual residence or registered office in the Member State within the territory of which the establishment is situated, or whose claim arises from the operation of that establishment.

Point (1) refers in particular to national laws which prohibit the opening of insolvency proceedings against companies providing public services, and finds its echo in the definition of "insolvency-related event" in the Aircraft Equipment Protocol to the 2001 Cape Town Convention on International Interests in Mobile Equipment.[214]

No barrier to multiple territorial proceedings

15–64   The principle of unity does not apply to territorial proceedings. There can be as many of these as there are establishments of the debtor in different Member States. No conflict can arise, because each territorial proceeding is limited to the local assets.

Community respect

15–65   The principle of Community respect applies as much to secondary proceedings as it does to attempted second main proceedings. The court which is asked to open the secondary proceedings cannot question the basis upon which the court in the State of the debtor's COMI reached its decision, and accordingly may not go behind the findings of the court in which the main proceedings were opened as to the situation of the debtor's COMI or as to the fact of the debtor's insolvency. However, in the United Kingdom, the only type of insolvency proceeding which requires the court to be satisfied of an existing state of insolvency is winding up. There is no such requirement for a CVA or an out-of-court administration by the holder of a qualifying floating charge; and even where the administrator is appointed by the company, the directors or the court it suffices that the company is likely to become insolvent. It follows that where main proceedings are opened in England which do not involve a finding of insolvency, it is open to the court of another Member State in secondary proceedings to determine for itself whether the company is insolvent. Such a finding in one secondary insolvency proceeding must then be respected in other Member States in which secondary proceedings are subsequently requested.

---

[214] Protocol to the Convention on International Interests in Mobile Equipment on Matters Specific to Aircraft Equipment, art.I(m). Paragraph 11 of the Official Commentary to the Convention and Protocol gives as an example the fact that in certain systems airlines are not eligible for insolvency proceedings.

Claims in secondary proceedings

Although secondary proceedings are limited to local assets, they are not lim-   **15–66**
ited to local creditors. Creditors in the main proceedings may also, through
the liquidator, prove in the secondary proceedings, and vice versa.[215] The
local assets must first be applied in discharge of the claims of creditors in
the secondary proceedings. If there is a surplus, this is handed over to the liquidator in the main proceedings.[216] But this can arise only if creditors in the
main proceedings have not proved in the secondary proceedings.[217]

Creditors have a particular incentive to pursue secondary proceedings
where the *lex concursus* governing their claims gives them better rights than
they would enjoy under the law governing the main proceedings. For example,
French law gives employees greater rights than English law on the insolvency
of the employer, so that where main proceedings are opened in England
against a French company, then in terms of the range of claims ranking for
preferential status employees of the company will fare better in secondary proceedings in France than they would in main proceedings in England.

Where the COMI of the insolvent company was in England, so that the main
proceedings were opened in England, the administrators successfully applied
for leave to open secondary proceedings in the Commercial Court at Versailles,
and to enter into a protocol with the relevant French administrator, in order to
bring about the same result as would occur in the main proceedings but with a
smaller budget, within a more reasonable time scale and with the ability to
secure the advantage of tax rebates owed by the French tax authorities.[218]

Approval of distributions in accordance with foreign law

The opening of secondary proceedings may make the conduct of the admin-   **15–67**
istration in the main proceedings more difficult and lead to less satisfactory
results for creditors as a whole than if there were a sole insolvency proceeding. In those circumstances, English courts have shown themselves willing to
accede to an application by the administrator in an English administration
to be given leave to make distributions to unsecured creditors that would
respect local priorities given by foreign law so as to avoid the need for secondary proceedings by local creditors. Thus, in *Re MG Rover Belux SA/NV*,[219]
in which administration orders were made against various companies within
the Rover group, some members of which were foreign companies but had
their COMI in England, H.H. Judge Norris Q.C. approved the making of
distributions to employees and other unsecured creditors that respected the

---

[215] See art.32.
[216] See art.35.
[217] Virgós-Schmit Report, paras 236–237.
[218] *Re Nortel Networks SA (No.2)* [2010] B.C.C. 21.
[219] [2007] B.C.C. 446.

statutory priorities of the foreign laws rather than those laid down by English insolvency law. The object was to avoid the expense and fragmentation of administration that would result from secondary proceedings, to preserve the businesses of the companies and the goodwill of employees and to avoid the fire sale of assets. The declaratory relief and subsequent orders were made on the basis that due provision had been made to preserve the rights of secured creditors and of creditors who were preferential creditors under the local law, that creditors had approved or at least not objected to the proposed distributions and that there were no realistic and equally favourable alternatives.[220] Similarly, in *Re Collins & Aikman Europe SA*[221] in which administration orders were made in England against various European companies incorporated in several different European jurisdictions, Lindsay J. accepted the submission of the administrators that the companies formed a closely linked group, many of the functions of which were organised on a Europe-wide rather than a national basis, so that a co-ordinated approach would lead to the best possible returns to creditors, and it would therefore be appropriate to allow the administrators to implement assurances they had given to local creditors that payments would be made in accordance with their local law if they abstained from instituting secondary proceedings.[222]

Effects of territorial proceedings

15–68   These are more limited than the effect of main proceedings. Whereas a judgment opening main proceedings has the same effects in any other Member State as in the State in which the proceedings were opened,[223] the position as

---

[220] Subsequently, in *Public Prosecutor v Segard (as Administrator for Rover France SAS)* [2006] I.L.Pr. 32, which concerned the French subsidiary of Rover, the Versailles Court of Appeal affirmed the decision of the Commercial Court of Nanterre that art.26 of the Insolvency Regulation was not engaged, despite differences between English law and French procedural law on the right of employees to be heard and that the French courts had no power to assess whether the French company's COMI was in the UK or France and were required to recognise the proceedings in England as main proceedings. The court further held that there was no purpose in opening secondary proceedings in France. Accordingly, the French provisional administration should be discharged.

[221] [2006] B.C.C. 861.

[222] It does not always follow that secondary proceedings are disadvantageous. In *Re Nortel Networks*, cited above n.218, administrators in an English administration were given leave to open secondary proceedings in France because of the perceived advantages of so doing. See above, para.15–66.

[223] See art.17(1). This, however, applies only if no secondary proceedings have been opened in another Member State under art.3(2), for under art.28 the law applicable to the secondary proceedings is the law of the State within the territory of which the opening of the secondary proceedings is requested. It was on this ground that Newey J. in *Connock v Fantozzi* [2011] EWHC 15 (Ch.) declined to accede to the request of an Italian administrator to apply the second tranche of funds in an English bank account to meet the claims of English and Italian employees which were preferential under Italian law but not under English law, winding up proceedings in England having been commenced while the second tranche was still in the bank accounts.

regards territorial proceedings is merely that their effects (which are confined to local assets) may not be challenged in other Member States,[224] but restrictions imposed on creditors' rights, such as a stay or discharge, cannot produce those effects vis-à-vis assets situated within the territory of another Member State except as regards creditors who have given their consent.[225]

12. CO-ORDINATION OF PARALLEL PROCEEDINGS[226]

One of the important objectives of the Insolvency Regulation is to ensure the co-ordination of parallel insolvency proceedings in different Member States involving the same or related debtors. This objective sought to be achieved in a number of ways. First, there is the principle of Community-wide recognition and effects, to which reference has already been made. Next, the liquidators in the different insolvency proceedings have a duty to exchange information and co-operate with each other.[227] Then there is the provision, known in England as the hotchpot rule, that while every creditor may prove in all proceedings, whether main proceedings or territorial proceedings, a creditor who receives a dividend in one proceeding cannot share in distributions in other proceedings until the creditors in those proceedings have obtained an equivalent dividend.[228] The liquidator in each proceeding must lodge in other proceedings claims already lodged in the proceedings for which they were appointed, the liquidator in secondary proceedings being entitled to participate in other proceedings on the same basis as a creditor.[229] As mentioned earlier, the liquidator in main proceedings has extensive powers to intervene in other proceedings.[230]

15–69

In the simplest case, co-ordination measures relate to the same debtor. More difficult is the case where different but related debtors become insolvent, as on the collapse of a multinational enterprise consisting of a group of companies each operating in a different jurisdiction, for example, Lehman Brothers, Enron, Parmalat and Rover. The Regulation treats each company as a separate legal entity and does not cater for a group of companies as such. So where it is desired to take an integrated approach to the winding up or reorganisation of a corporate group, it is essential that the different liquidators co-ordinate their approaches and that the different courts do what

---

[224] See art.17(2).
[225] See art.17(2).
[226] For a detailed discussion, see Virgós and Garcimartín, *The European Insolvency Regulation*, Ch.10. As to co-operation at international level under the UNCITRAL Model Law and otherwise, see Ch.16.
[227] See art.31.
[228] See art.20(2).
[229] See art.32.
[230] See above, para.15–59.

they can to support such co-ordination.[231] To that end, administrators of a group of companies in an English administration constituting main proceedings successfully applied to the High Court for an order that letters of request be sent to the courts of a number of EU Member States in whose jurisdictions those companies operated asking those courts to put in place arrangements under which the administrators would be given notice of any request or application for the opening of insolvency proceedings.[232]

13. THE APPLICABLE LAW UNDER ARTICLE 4

General principles

15–70   Article 4(1) of the Regulation provides that the law applicable to insolvency proceedings and their effect is that of the Member State within the territory of which such proceedings are opened, referred to as the "State of the opening of proceedings". The same rule applies to secondary proceedings,[233] and this is considered to be true also of independent proceedings even though these are not mentioned in art.28.[234] "Law" means the Member State's domestic law and thus excludes its conflict of laws rules,[235] so that the doctrine of *renvoi* has no role to play. By art.4(2) this law (the *lex concursus*) determines the conditions for the opening of the proceedings, their conduct and their closure, and in particular the various matters listed in sub-paras (a) to (m) of art.4(2). Each proceeding, whether main or territorial, is governed by its own *lex concursus*.[236] The list is non-exhaustive but covers most of the matters one would expect to find governed by the *lex concursus* in national insolvency law. However, as we shall see, the reach of the *lex concursus* is not as wide as it seems. Its operation is confined to insolvency effects, and even the description of *in rem* rights contained in art.5(2) is not intended to define such rights, which are a matter of the applicable law but rather to set certain boundaries to the range of rights that will be admitted to the status of rights in rem for the purposes of the Regulation.

---

[231] A good example in the UK relates to the Rover group, referred to above, para.15–67. See further Wessels, "International Jurisdiction to Open Insolvency Proceedings in Europe", n.46, pp.18 et seq. and para.16–10.

[232] *Re Nortel Networks SA* [2009] B.C.C. 343. In subsequent proceedings, the administrators themselves applied for leave to open secondary proceedings in France. See above, para.15–67.

[233] See art.28, applied in *Connock v Fantozzi* [2011] EWHC 15 (Ch.). See above, n. 223.

[234] Virgós-Schmit Report, para.89.

[235] Virgós-Schmit Report, para.87.

[236] A point reinforced by art.38 in relation to secondary proceedings. The same applies to independent proceedings.

Relationship between *lex concursus* and law governing pre-insolvency entitlements

Under the Insolvency Regulation, the *lex concursus* governs all matters relat- **15–71**
ing to the winding up and its effects, whether substantive or procedural, including the assets comprising the estate, the proof and ranking of claims, the
admissibility of set-off and the avoidance of preferences and other transactions.[237] There is, however, much confusion as to the relationship between the
lex concursus and the law governing the creation of security interests and other
real rights in assets in the possession of the debtor company. Let us suppose
that Debtco gives security over tangible movables situated in England and subsequently goes into liquidation in France. What is meant by the statement that
the validity and ranking of the security interest in the liquidation are governed
by French law? Does it mean that English law governing the creation and
effects of the security interest is to be disregarded? The confusion arises
because of a failure to distinguish the role of insolvency law from that of the
law governing pre-liquidation entitlements. The distinction is well brought out
in the Virgós-Schmit Report on the European Bankruptcy Convention in a
passage that is equally applicable to the Insolvency Regulation[238]:

> "The law of the State of the opening of the proceedings *(lex fori concur-
> sus)* determines all the effects of the insolvency, both procedural and sub-
> stantial, on the persons and relations concerned. The substantial effects
> referred to are those which are typical of insolvency law. That is to say,
> effects which are necessary for the insolvency proceedings to fulfil its
> goals. To this extent, it displaces (unless the Convention sets out
> otherwise) the law normally applicable to the act concerned. That happens
> for instance when Art.4 makes applicable the law of the State of the
> opening to declare the voidness or voidability of any contract that may be
> detrimental to creditors."[239]

We have already seen that English law, like that of many other jurisdictions,
starts from the position that pre-liquidation entitlements are to be respected.

---

[237] Textbooks on the conflict of laws focus on jurisdiction and recognition and are curiously
silent about the applicable law in winding up. It seems that this phenomenon is not confined
to English texts. See J.L. Westbrook and D.T. Trautman, "Conflict of Laws Issues in
International Insolvencies" in Jacob S. Ziegel (ed.), *Current Developments in International
and Comparative Corporate Insolvency Law* (), Ch.27 at p.657: "The most basic confusion in
the traditional approach is conceptual, between choice of law and choice of forum. Each
court confronted with a general default must make two threshold decisions: the identification of a national body of law that will govern the financial consequences of the default, and
selection of public institutions in one or more countries that will manage the process. The
need for two distinct choices—choice of law and choice of forum—is not often articulated."
[238] See above, para.15–45.
[239] Virgós-Schmit Report, para.59. See to similar effect the UNCITRAL Legislative Guide on
Insolvency Law, paras 81 et seq.

These having been established, it is then for insolvency law to determine to what extent those rights are to be disturbed or set aside in order to fulfil the objectives of insolvency law, in particular, those of fairness and equitable distribution among creditors. The same is true of cross-border insolvencies, both within and outside the European Union. In the insolvency proceedings, therefore, it is the conflict of laws rules of the *lex fori*, namely the *lex concursus*, which determine the law governing a person's pre-insolvency entitlements (*lex causae*); the *lex causae* is then applied to establish the existence and content of those entitlements; and it is then for the *lex concursus* of the State concerned to determine to what extent, if at all, those entitlements are modified or nullified by the insolvency in the implementation of insolvency policy. As stated earlier, any reference in the Regulation to the law of a Member State governing a particular issue is a reference to the internal law of that State, excluding its conflict of laws rules; in other words, as in most modern conventions, the concept of *renvoi* has no role to play.[240]

So, in our example, the French bankruptcy court can be expected to look in the first instance to English law as the *lex situs* to determine whether the asserted security interest was validly created. If it was not, then *cadit quaestio*. But if it was, it is then for French law to determine whether the security offends in some way against the policies and rules of French insolvency law, for example, because it was a preference or a fraud on the general body of creditors or because it failed to comply with the registration requirements of French law so far as applicable to security interests created under a foreign law. Similarly, where French law is the *lex situs* and English law the *lex concursus*, the English insolvency court will apply French law as the *lex situs* to determine the initial validity of a security interest created over assets in France, but if the security interest is held to have been validly created under French law, its efficacy in an English winding up must then be tested by reference to English insolvency law, so that it may, for example, be set aside under the Insolvency Act 1986 as a transaction at an undervalue[241] or a preference[242] if the facts establish this. Of course, it is always open to the insolvency law to defer to the *lex causae* on particular issues. An example is to be found in art.13 of the EC Insolvency Regulation.[243]

The same approach is adopted by the Regulation, except that, in order to ensure that the *lex concursus* does not go beyond the legitimate bounds of insolvency law in its interference with pre-insolvency entitlements, the Regulation has a series of provisions excluding the application of the *lex concursus* as such to particular rights in order to protect legitimate expectations

---

[240] This is nowhere stated but is considered implicit in the Regulation. See the Virgós-Schmit Report, para.87.
[241] Insolvency Act 1986 s.238.
[242] Insolvency Act 1986 s.239.
[243] See above, para.15–66 and the UNCITRAL Legislative Guide, paras 89–90.

and the certainty of transactions in other Member States.[244] These provisions, contained in arts 5 to 15, are themselves of four kinds. Into the first category fall rights *in rem* and reservation of title. In relation to these, arts 5 and 7 provide that the opening of the insolvency proceedings is not to affect such rights in relation to assets situated within the territory of another Member State at the time of opening of the proceedings. This is not in itself a conflict rule; it says nothing about the law to be applied to determine the existence and content of the rights in question, although in the case of an issue arising in the insolvency proceedings themselves it will be the law applicable under the conflict rules of the insolvency jurisdiction as the *lex fori*. By contrast, provisions in the second category, namely arts 6, 8 to 11, 14 and 15, each lay down a positive conflict rule to determine the law applicable to the right in question. The third category contains only one provision, art.12, under which Community patents and trade marks may be included only in main proceedings. The fourth category also contains only one provision, art.13, which disapplies art.4(2)(m)[245] in relation to detrimental acts governed by the law of a Member State which does not allow any means of challenging that act.

The list

Article 4(2) provides as follows: **15–72**

"The law of the State of the opening of proceedings shall determine the conditions for the opening of those proceedings, their conduct and their closure. It shall determine in particular:

(a) against which debtors insolvency proceedings may be brought on account of their capacity;

(b) the assets which form part of the estate and the treatment of assets acquired by or devolving on the debtor after the opening of the insolvency proceedings;

(c) the respective powers of the debtor and the liquidator;

(d) the conditions under which set-offs may be invoked;

(e) the effects of insolvency proceedings on current contracts to which the debtor is party;

(f) the effects of the insolvency proceedings on proceedings brought by individual creditors, with the exception of lawsuits pending;

(g) the claims which are to be lodged against the debtor's estate and the treatment of claims arising after the opening of insolvency proceedings;

---

[244] Recital (24).
[245] See below.

(h)   the rules governing the lodging, verification and admission of claims;

(i)   the rules governing the distribution of proceeds from the realisation of assets, the ranking of claims and the rights of creditors who have obtained partial satisfaction after the opening of insolvency proceedings by virtue of a right *in rem* or through a set-off;

(j)   the conditions for and the effects of closure of insolvency proceedings, in particular by composition;

(k)   creditors' rights after the closure of insolvency proceedings;

(l)   who is to bear the costs and expenses incurred in the insolvency proceedings;

(m)   the rules relating to the voidness, voidability or unenforceability of legal acts detrimental to all the creditors."

All of the items in this list, which is non-exhaustive and does not cut down the generality of the first sentence of art.4(2), find their counterparts in UK insolvency law and for the most part they require no comment. There are, however, five points to be noted.

(1)   When sub-para.(b) refers to the assets which form part of the estate, that does not mean that pre-insolvency entitlements acquired under other law are ignored. On the contrary, insolvency law starts from the position that pre-insolvency entitlements are to be respected, and if those were created under other law, as where at the time of their creation the asset was situated in a Member State other than that in which the insolvency proceedings have been opened, then in principle that law governs the starting position in relation to the asset in question[246] and it is unnecessary to rely on the exceptions in arts 5 to 15. But assets acquired by the debtor company under other law may be swollen by inclusion in the estate of additional assets under the rules of the *lex concursus*, for example, rules by which the estate includes after-acquired property or rules by which transfers and payments made by the debtor on the eve of insolvency are avoided.[247] In short, art.4 is concerned only with *insolvency* effects, not with effects under the general law.

(2)   While sub-para.(d) subjects rights of set-off to the *lex concursus*, this is subject to preservation of the right of a creditor under art.6 to demand

---

[246] For the application of this principle in relation to UK insolvency law, see above, para.15–71. That the same principle applies equally to art.4 of the Regulation is very clearly stated by Virgós and Garcimartín, *The European Insolvency Regulation*, para.119.

[247] See, e.g. *Seagon v Deko Marty Belgium NV* (C-339/07) [2009] 1 W.L.R. 2168, referred to above, para.15–22. In personal bankruptcy, to which the Regulation also applies, the estate may not only be expanded but restricted by insolvency law. For example, in England, the bankrupt's estate does not include damages recovered by the bankrupt for defamation or necessary tools, books, vehicles and other forms of equipment necessary for his personal use in his employment, business or vocation.

set-off under the law applicable to the insolvent debtor's claim.[248] This is a departure from English law rules of insolvency set-off, which displace all other forms of set-off not exercised prior to the commencement of the winding up.

(3)   Sub-para.(i), relating to the ranking of claims, is concerned solely with insolvency effects; it does not mean that priorities established under the general law prior to the insolvency proceedings are to be ignored, merely that in certain cases they may be modified or disapplied by rules of the *lex concursus*. For example, where English law is the *lex concursus*, a secured creditor will generally have priority over an unsecured creditor, while priority as between secured creditors will usually be determined by the relevant priority rules under the general law but under the Insolvency Act 1986 a floating charge will be subordinate to the claims of preferential creditors (that is, employees) and will be subject to surrender of the prescribed part, and a registrable charge not registered within the time prescribed by s.870(1) of the Companies Act 2006 will be void against the liquidator and creditors. The starting point, however, is to determine priorities by reference to the *lex causae*, thus in many cases making it unnecessary to invoke the exceptions in arts 5 to 15, which appear in the regulation solely for the purpose of preventing the application of over-inclusive rules of the *lex concursus*. The insolvency rules governing the ranking of claims then operate to modify the pre-insolvency priority established under the *lex causae* except so far as those rules are displaced by one or more of the exceptions in arts 5 to 15.

(4)   The application of the avoidance rules in art.4(2)(m) is cut down by art.13, which is designed to prevent the application of rules of avoidance of two or more legal systems by putting a bar on the application of art.4(2)(m) where under the law governing the act to which art.4(2)(m) would otherwise apply the act in question is not open to challenge.[249]

(5)   The reference in art.4(2)(m) to acts detrimental to "all" the creditors should not be taken literally, for there are always likely to be creditors unaffected by the acts in question, including secured creditors. Article 4(2)(m) should thus be read as referring to acts detrimental to the creditors collectively, that is, the general body of creditors.

---

[248] See art.6(1). See below, para.15–92.
[249] See below, para.15–98.

14. EXCLUSIONS FROM ARTICLE 4

15–73   We can now turn to the cases in which art.4 is either qualified or displaced by a rule designed to ensure that the *lex concursus* gives due respect to various important rights established by the *lex causae* and does not seek to carry the insolvency effects beyond their allotted sphere.

Third parties' rights *in rem*

15–74   Article 5 deals with the rights of third parties in rem. Its purpose is to safeguard such rights from the effect of the opening of insolvency proceedings, and it is therefore of considerable importance.[250]

> **"Article 5**
> **Third parties' rights *in rem***
> 1 The opening of insolvency proceedings shall not affect the rights *in rem* of creditors or third parties in respect of tangible or intangible, moveable or immoveable assets–both specific assets and collections of indefinite assets as a whole which change from time to time–belonging to the debtor which are situated within the territory of another Member State at the time of the opening of proceedings.
>
> 2. The rights referred to in paragraph 1 shall in particular mean:
>
> > (a)   the right to dispose of assets or have them disposed of and to obtain satisfaction from the proceeds of or income from those assets, in particular by virtue of a lien or a mortgage;
> > (b)   the exclusive right to have a claim met, in particular a right guaranteed by a lien in respect of the claim or by assignment of the claim by way of a guarantee;
> > (c)   the right to demand the assets from, and/or to require restitution by, anyone having possession or use of them contrary to the wishes of the party so entitled;
> > (d)   a right *in rem* to the beneficial use of assets.
>
> 3. The right, recorded in a public register and enforceable against third parties, under which a right *in rem* within the meaning of paragraph 1 may be obtained, shall be considered a right in rem.

---

[250] For a perceptive analysis, see Philip Smart, "Rights In Rem, Article 5 and the EC Insolvency Regulation: An English Perspective" (2006) 15 Int. Insolv. Rev. 17.

4. Paragraph 1 shall not preclude actions for voidness, voidability or unenforceability as referred to in Article 4(2)(m)."

This article raises four questions. First, to whose assets does the article relate? Secondly, what is a right in rem, and to what extent does it differ from the concept of a right *in rem* in English law? Thirdly, where is an asset situated? Fourthly, what is the effect of para.1 of the article (as qualified by para.4) where it applies?

Whose assets?

Article 5 is confined to assets "belonging to the debtor" and situated within the territory of another Member State at the time of opening of the proceedings. The phrase "belonging to" does not necessarily involve ownership by the debtor; entitlement to a limited interest, for example, a security interest or a right of possession under a lease, suffices. Although under art.4(2)(b) the assets which form part of the debtor's estate are determined by the *lex concursus*, this takes as its starting point the pre-insolvency entitlements of third parties[251] and is qualified by arts 5 to 15. Where the debtor has no interest of any kind in the asset under the *lex causae* and the asset is not brought into the estate as part of the effects of the *lex concursus* (for example, under its provisions for the avoidance of past transactions), the insolvency proceedings do not affect it, and it becomes unnecessary to turn to art.5. Conversely, the protection given to *in rem* rights by art.5 does not preclude actions for avoidance or unenforceability of transactions as being detrimental to all of the creditors,[252] such as rules relating to the avoidance of preferences and transactions at an undervalue, these being matters within the exclusive province of the *lex concursus*.[253]

15–75

Under what law is a right characterised as a right in rem?

At first sight, one would think that art.5(2) provided a definition of right in rem. However, we learn from the Virgós-Schmit Report that this is not the intention. What is a right *in rem* is governed primarily by the applicable national law, typically the *lex situs* (*lex rei sitae*) of the right in question.[254] The function of art.5(2) is not to supplant national law (except to a limited extent

15–76

---

[251] See above, para.15–71.
[252] See art.5(4).
[253] See art.4(m). However, this in turn is subject to the defence under art.13 that the act in question would not be open to challenge under applicable law. See below, para.15–98.
[254] There is, of course, an element of circularity here, for the very reference to a *situs* connotes the existence of an asset.

under art.5(3)[255]) but rather to accord it recognition within certain parameters. In consequence:

(1)   a right not recognised by the applicable law as a right *in rem* will not be so recognised for the purposes of the Regulation even if it possesses one or all of the characteristics set out in art.5(2);

(2)   a right recognised by the applicable law as a right *in rem* will be so recognised for the purposes of the Regulation so long as it possesses one of the characteristics set out in art.5(2); and

(3)   a right lacking any of those characteristics is not a right *in rem* for the purposes of the Regulation even if it would be classified as a right in rem under the applicable law.[256]

The object of art.5(2) is thus to give its blessing to the *in rem* character of rights under national law where these fall within one of the cases mentioned in art.5(2) but to avoid the application of an over-expansive concept of rights *in rem* in national law, given that the effect of characterisation of a right as a right *in rem* is to give it priority over rights that would otherwise be conferred by the *lex concursus*. So we must begin with what constitutes a right in rem under English law and then see how far this fits into the conception of a right *in rem* under art.5(2).

Rights *in rem* under English law

15–77   Under English law, a right *in rem* is an interest *in* an asset, tangible or intangible, as opposed to a personal right *to* an asset.[257] So ownership, possession (for example, under a lease) and a security interest are rights in rem, and these include equitable interests arising under a trust, an equitable mortgage, a fixed or floating charge or an agreement for the transfer of identified or identifiable existing or future property, other than a contract for the sale of goods. By contrast, a purely personal right to the delivery or transfer of an asset is not a right *in rem*.[258] Examples are the buyer's right to delivery of goods under a contract of sale before the property in the goods has passed,[259] the right to call for the transfer of shares to a given value but not identified

---

[255] See below, para.15–81.
[256] Virgós-Schmit Report, paras 100–104. See also the more expansive discussion in Virgós and Garcimartín, *The European Insolvency Regulation*, paras 138–157.
[257] See *Goode on Commercial Law*, edited by Ewan McKendrick, 4th edn (2009), pp.28 et seq.
[258] But as stated earlier, the debtor must have at least some interest in the asset under the *lex concursus* in order to be covered by the insolvency proceedings at all. See further above, para.15–75 and below, para.15–79.
[259] *Goode on Commercial Law*, 2009, p.237.

and the right to payment of money. *A fortiori* rights which are purely personal, in that they do not relate to an asset at all, are not rights in rem. Thus, equities, such as a right to rescind a contract for misrepresentation or a right of set-off, are not rights *in rem* but rights to undo or qualify another person's entitlement.[260]

In considering whether a right is a right *in rem* or a personal right, it is necessary to have regard to the particular relationship under consideration. For example, a contract right is not a right *in rem* as between the parties to a contract or as between the assignee of one party and the other contracting party. So a creditor's right to payment under a loan agreement is a purely personal right, and the same is true of his assignee's rights against the debtor. By contrast, in the relationship between creditor and assignee the right to payment by the debtor is a right *in rem*, for on the insolvency of the creditor-assignor the debt can be claimed by the assignee against the assignor's general creditors.

Rights *in rem* under art.5(2)

Characteristics of a right in rem under the Regulation

The Virgós-Schmit Report[261] identifies two characteristics of a right in rem **15–78** as set out in art.5(2).The first is its direct and immediate relationship with the asset it covers; the second is the enforceability of that right against others.[262] The concept that a right *in rem* is to be distinguished from a right in personam by virtue of its enforceability against third parties, for example, by recovery of the asset from a subsequent purchaser, by the prevention of recourse to the asset by unsecured creditors or, in the case of successive security interests, by according the first in time priority over later interests, is well established in legal systems. The position where the right is enforceable against third parties only on registration is covered by art.5(3), discussed below.

The status of a preferential claim in insolvency, for example, the claim of an employee, does not constitute a right *in rem* even where it has priority over a secured claim.[263] Moreover, although some of the rights listed in art.5(2) appear to include *in personam* rights to an asset, it seems clear that from the above description of the characteristics of a right in rem that art.5(2) is not to be interpreted as covering *in personam* rights, for example:

---

[260] *Goode on Commercial Law*, 2009, p.30.

[261] Para.103.

[262] Although not necessarily against *all* others, for there may be a competing interest enjoying a higher priority under the applicable law.

[263] Virgós and Garcimartín, *The European Insolvency Regulation*, para.153. Under English law, a floating charge is subordinate to preferential creditors. See above, para.8–51.

(1)   a right to dispose of assets which is purely contractual, the holder of the right having no security or other interest in the assets, as where a party with whom goods are stored reserves the right to dispose of them if they are not collected within a specified time; and

(2)   a personal right to the delivery of assets, for example, under a contract of sale where the property in the goods has not yet passed to the buyer.

Collections of assets and floating security

15–79   Article 5(2) itself states that a right *in rem* may be established not only with regard to specific assets but also with regard to collections of indefinite assets as a whole, so that security rights such as the floating charge over all assets or a designated class of assets are characterised as rights *in rem* for the purposes of the Regulation. But a right cannot be a right *in rem* if it does not relate to an asset at all, although what constitutes an asset is a matter of the applicable law.[264] There are various rights that may qualify as rights in rem, but for the purpose of art.5 full and unqualified ownership is not one of them, because if the debtor has no interest in the asset at all it falls outside the scope of the insolvency proceedings. However, a limited interest suffices.

Rights that are in rem under English law are also in rem under the Regulation

15–80   Article 5(2) is sufficiently flexible to accommodate significant differences in national laws of Member States. For example, under English law a lessee of goods has possession, which is a right in rem; under French law he is a mere *détenteur* and thus enjoys a purely personal right. On the other hand, as shown above, not every right to demand an asset from the person in possession, contrary to his wishes, is a right *in rem* under English law, and if characterised as a personal right would fall outside art.5(1) even though of a class described in art.5(2).

It can be asserted with some confidence that while some rights of a kind listed in art.5(2) would not be regarded as rights *in rem* under English law,[265] all rights that are so regarded fall within the parameters of art.5(2) and thus enjoy the benefits conferred by art.5(1).

---

[264] For the concept of an asset in English insolvency law, see above, paras 6–02 et seq.
[265] See above, para.15–77.

Rights that are in rem under the Regulation but not in rem under English law

Rights *in rem* under art.5(3)

The wording of art.5(3) is somewhat curious, and it is here set out again:　　　**15–81**

> "The right, recorded in a public register and enforceable against third parties, under which a right *in rem* within the meaning of paragraph 1 may be obtained, shall be considered a right in rem."

Despite the ever-helpful Virgós-Schmit Report,[266] it is not easy to make sense of this opaquely drafted sub-paragraph. Assuming art.5(3) is to be read in accordance with normal syntax, the phrase "under which" relates back to "The right", so that if one omits the text within the parenthetical commas, the sub-paragraph becomes:

> "The right . . . under which a right *in rem* within the meaning of paragraph 1 may be obtained [,] shall be considered a right in rem."

Accordingly, the elements that attract art.5(3) are: (i) the existence of a right which is not as such a right in rem; but (ii) from which a right *in rem* may be derived; and (iii) which itself may be made enforceable against third parties by registration even before giving birth to the intended right in rem. The effect of the Regulation is to treat the registered right as itself a right in rem whether or not it would be so regarded in national law. This covers both the case where: (i) under the relevant national law, registration is not merely a perfection requirement that has to be met in order to be effective against third parties but is a constitutive element of the creation of the right itself as a right in rem[267]; and (ii) the right is of such a kind that, although rendered enforceable against third parties by registration, it is not in itself a right in rem under the applicable national law but simply a right from which a right in rem may be derived. In the first case, there is no need to depend on art.5(3), for the desired effect is produced by national law; in the second, art.5(3) operates independently of national law in characterising the registered right as a right in rem. Were it not for the rule of equity that an agreement for transfer is to be treated as a transfer, a good example in English law would have been a contract for the sale of land or the grant of an option to purchase land. Registration of the contract preserves the priority of the prospective legal title against subsequent purchasers but such title stems from the conveyance, not the contract. It is thus a right *in rem* derived from

---

[266] Para.101.

[267] e.g. in some European legal systems, a security interest is not even considered created so as to be effective as between the parties until it has been registered in a public register.

a right which but for the rule of equity in question, would not itself be a right in rem, merely a contractual entitlement to call for a conveyance. This example does not in fact work for English law, because an agreement for sale of land and the grant of an option to buy land are both considered to create proprietary rights.[268] Indeed, it is not easy to think of a case of registered right "under which a right *in rem* may be obtained" where the registered right is not itself a right in rem.

An entirely separate question, which is not addressed in art.5(3) but is left to the applicable law, is the position with regard to a right which is characterised by the applicable law as a right *in rem* but is enforceable against third parties only on registration and has not been registered at the time of opening of the insolvency proceedings. This is considered below.

Situation of the asset

The threshold question

15–82   In order for art.5(1) to apply so as to preserve the *in rem* rights of a third party, it is necessary that the debtor's asset be situated within the territory of a Member State. It has rightly been pointed out that this presupposes the existence of the *in rem* rights in the first place, a threshold question to be determined by the conflict of laws rules of the forum, which will normally apply the *lex situs* as ascertained by such conflict rules.[269] Article 2(g) has no application to this threshold question. But given the existence of the *in rem* rights under the applicable provision, art.2(g) tells us that:

> "...'the Member State in which assets are situated'[270] means, in the case of:
> — tangible property, the Member State within the territory of which the property is situated,
> — property and rights ownership of or entitlement to which must be entered in a public register, the Member State under the authority of which the register is kept,
> — claims, the Member State within the territory of which the third party required to meet them has the centre of his main interests, as determined in Article 3(1)."

---

[268] Kevin Gray and Susan Francis Gray, *Elements of Land Law*, 5th edn (Oxford: Oxford University Press, 2008), paras 8.1.57 and 8.1.73.

[269] Virgós and Garcimartín, *op. cit.*, para.160.

[270] Though given in quotation marks, this phrase does not in fact feature in exactly this form anywhere in the Regulation.

"Tangible property", referred to in the first indent, includes goods, documents of title to goods, negotiable instruments and negotiable securities, all of which are susceptible to transfer by physical delivery. The second indent covers rights the entitlement to which must be entered in a public register. Under English law, these include interests in land, ships and aircraft and charges registrable under s.860 of the Companies Act 2006. The third indent relates to claims, including debts due to the insolvent company. There are three problems with art.2(g), all of which can be resolved by reference to the twin concepts underpinning art.2(g), namely the place of *control* of the asset by the third party and the place where the third party's rights are *visible*. These concepts of control and visibility help to explain the relationship between overlapping indents and between overlapping rights within a single indent.

Tangible property

In relation to tangible property, art.2(g) does not address the situation where the underlying tangible asset is in one Member State and the document which embodies title to the asset is in another. So if goods are stored in a warehouse in England, the warehouseman issues a negotiable warehouse warrant which is delivered to a buyer in Switzerland, a non-EU State, and main insolvency proceedings are opened in France, does art.5 apply because the goods are in England or is it excluded because the warrant is in Switzerland? The answer here lies in the concept of control.[271] The physical location of the goods in England should be regarded as irrelevant when control over them is held in Switzerland. Accordingly, art.5 does not apply and the pre-insolvency entitlement to the goods is governed by the law applicable under French conflict of laws rules.[272]

15–83

Registrable rights

Article 2(g) fails to make clear: (i) whether this is confined to registration as a condition of creation of the right or applies also to registration solely for the purpose of perfecting a right[273] validly created without registration; or (ii) the relationship between rights covered by the second indent (registrable rights) and those covered by the first indent (tangible property) and third indent (claims). The Virgós-Schmit Report gives ships and aircraft as examples of assets within the second indent. Whatever the position under the laws

15–84

---

[271] Virgós and Garcimartín, *The European Insolvency Regulation*, para.160.
[272] See below.
[273] In the sense of making it enforceable against third parties.

of other Member States, it is certainly not the case under English law that the acquisition of rights in ships or aircraft is dependent on registration, which merely goes to the strength of the acquirer's property right vis-à-vis third parties.[274] The same is true of a further example, registered securities, which can be transferred in equity without the transferee's name being entered on the register. Many other systems prescribe registration as a perfection requirement, not a condition of validity.[275] It can therefore be assumed that the second indent includes rights which require registration only to make them enforceable against third parties and is not confined to rights which can be created only by registration. This accords with the second concept underpinning art.2(g), namely visibility.

Overlapping categories

15–85   The three categories listed in art.2(g) are presented as if they were mutually exclusive, which, of course, is not the case. Ships and aircraft are forms of tangible property within the first indent but ownership and security rights in them are in many cases required to be perfected by registration in a public register. The position under UK law is complicated by the fact that in the case of a ship or aircraft there is both a nationality registration, so that the ship or aircraft becomes a UK-registered ship or aircraft, and a mortgage register, added to which registration of a mortgage is itself required in two different registers, the register of ship or aircraft mortgages and the register maintained by the Companies Registry. Fortunately, all of these registers are located within the United Kingdom, so that the problem is theoretical. The concept of visibility of the third party's rights indicates that the factor which determines the situation of a ship or aircraft is not its physical location at any time but the State under the authority of which the relevant register is maintained. It would have been helpful if art.2(g) had made it clear that the first indent does not apply to tangible assets within the second indent. There is a similar overlap between the third indent, which relates to claims, and the first and second indents. Under the third indent, claims are considered to be situated in the territory where the company's debtor has its COMI. This accords with a general principle of the conflict of laws governing the location of a debt. But claims cover not only ordinary debts but also: (i) rights under negotiable instruments and negotiable securities within the first indent; and (ii) rights to registered securities within the second indent. The twin concepts of control and visibility show that claims arising under negotiable instru-

---

[274] For a detailed discussion, see Alison Clarke, "Ship Mortgages" in Norman Palmer and Ewan McKendrick (eds), *Interests in Goods*, 2nd edn (Informa Publishing, 1998), Ch.26.

[275] e.g. under French law a transfer of land is effected by agreement, and registration is required only to make the transfer effective against third parties.

ments and negotiable instruments are covered by the first indent to the exclusion of the third indent and that claims in respect of registered securities held direct from the issuer are covered by the second indent[276] to the exclusion of the third indent, while claims in respect of securities held indirectly through a securities account with an intermediary are covered by the third indent, since these are not recorded in a public register.[277] We can thus deduce the following hierarchical order in which art.2(g) is to be applied. The primary rule is to be found in the second indent. Anything within this indent is outside the others. The secondary rule is to be found in the first indent. Anything within this indent is outside the third indent. So the hierarchy, in descending order, is: second indent, first indent, third indent.

The position in relation to accounts held with a bank that has more than one branch is not completely clear. If one takes the view that a branch is merely part of the corporate organisation and has no distinct legal personality, then the location of an account will be the place where the corporate body has its COMI. This decidedly inconvenient result can be avoided by treating each branch as a distinct entity, so that the account will be considered located at the place where the branch is situated. That is the view of Professors Virgós and Garcimartín,[278] and it accords with the general banking approach by which branches of a bank in different countries are treated as separate entities.[279]

The effect of art.5(1)

Applicability

It is worth reiterating that art.5 does not come into play at all unless the *lex concursus* has already determined that the asset in question is an asset of the estate in the sense that the debtor has at least some interest in it, whether

15–86

---

[276] i.e. they are located in the State under the authority of which the share register is kept.

[277] Virgós-Schmit Report, para.69. A different position is taken by Virgós and Garcimartín, who allocate directly held registered securities to the third category so as to be situated within the account debtor's COMI, while treating securities held through an account with an intermediary as within the second category and located in the State under the authority of which the public register is kept (*The European Insolvency Regulation*, paras 311 and 313). But this seems the wrong way round. It is the title to directly held registered securities which is recorded in a public register; an entitlement to securities held through an account with an intermediary is not recorded in any public register, solely in the account itself, to which only the account holder and those authorised by the account holder have access, so that the entitlement falls within the third category: claims.

[278] *The European Insolvency Regulation*, para.314.

[279] See, e.g. the ICC Uniform Customs and Practice for Documentary Credits, 2007 revision (UCP 600), art.3; and ICC Uniform Rules for Demand Guarantees, 2010 revision (URDG 758), art.3. The question is discussed by Moss, Fletcher and Isaacs, *The EC Regulation on Insolvency Proceedings*, 2009, paras 6.53 and 6.100 but without expressing a concluded view.

ownership or a limited interest. If that determination has been made or the existence of the interest is not in dispute, it is then necessary to turn to art.5(1) to ascertain the position in regard to those claiming an interest in the asset. There are several points to note about art.5(1).

Asset not excluded from debtor's estate

15–87   The asset in question is not excluded from the debtor's estate, for under the principle of universality the insolvency proceedings pick up all assets in which the debtor has an interest; the sole effect is that such interests take effect subject to whatever interest is vested in the third party. So where the debtor is the owner of an asset worth £100,000 but prior to the opening of the insolvency proceedings and at a time when the asset was situated in another Member State, the debtor gave it in security for a loan which, with interest, amounts to £40,000, the asset forms part of the estate but (assuming the security interest to be valid and enforceable under the applicable law) it is subject to that interest, the estate benefiting from the £60,000 equity in the asset if it is sold and the liquidator himself having the right to sell so long as the security interest is discharged from the proceeds. The converse case where the third party is the owner and the debtor's interest is a security or other limited interest needs no comment, for in this situation it is the third party's entitlement that takes effect subject to the debtor's interest.

Article 5(1) does not provide a conflicts rule

15–88   Article 5(1) does not lay down a conflicts rule, it merely says that the opening of insolvency proceedings is not to affect the rights of creditors or third parties in respect of assets belonging to the debtor which are situated within the territory of another Member State at the time of opening of the proceedings, so that neither the substantive law of the insolvency nor its procedural restrictions on the enforcement of rights *in rem* apply. Article 5(1) does not say which law is to determine those rights. It is left to the conflict of laws rules of the forum to determine what law applies and it is that law which decides whether the claimant has an *in rem* right and, if so, its nature and content. If the issue arises in the insolvency proceedings themselves, the applicable law will be determined by the *lex concursus* as the *lex fori*, and this will necessarily be the case as regards secondary proceedings, which are confined to local assets.[280] The time of opening of the insolvency proceedings is fixed as the relevant time because that is usually the point at which the existence of pre-insolvency entitlements has to be established under national laws. The

---

[280] See art.27.

situation of the assets at the time of opening of the insolvency proceedings is relevant solely for the purpose of attracting art.5(1) and is not necessarily indicative of the applicable law, a matter to be determined by the *lex fori*. However, the widely adopted conflicts rule in relation to assets is the *lex situs*,[281] and assuming this is the rule adopted by the *lex fori* (whether the forum is the insolvency State or some other State) it will be applied to the assets situated within the territory of a Member State when the insolvency proceedings are opened. Where, prior to the opening of the insolvency proceedings, an asset has moved from one Member State to another, it is the law of the second State (or in the case of multiple moves, the last State) that has to be applied. If by the law of that State a person has acquired an overriding title displacing that acquired by another under an earlier *lex situs*, it becomes unnecessary for the court to look back to the effects of earlier law. If, on the other hand, the title of the claimant in the last State is dependent on the earlier title of his transferor established under the law of a prior State, then that earlier law will be applied but only because that is the effect of the later law.

"Shall not affect"

There has been some discussion of the meaning of the phrase "shall not affect" in art.5(1), different authorities interpreting it in different ways. However, there is no reason to depart from the natural interpretation of these words. The opening of the main proceedings does not itself affect the rights of third parties to assets then situated in another Member State (including, where the right is a security interest, the right to enforce the security on default without regard to the main proceedings and other procedural rights), and as a corollary the liquidator in the main proceedings may not take steps in relation to the asset which are inconsistent with the third party's in rem rights. However, there are three qualifications. First, such in rem rights may be affected by the insolvency law of the Member State concerned where secondary proceedings are opened in that State. Secondly, where the court opening the insolvency proceedings appoints a temporary administrator in order to ensure the preservation of the debtor's assets, the temporary administrator may request any measures to secure and preserve any of the debtor's assets situated in another Member State, provided for by the law of that state.[282] Such measures could no doubt include the grant of injunctive relief.[283] Thirdly, the *lex concursus* continues to apply to questions concerning the avoidance or unenforceability of a disposition creating the right.[284]

15–89

---

[281] That is, the general law of the place where the asset is situated, not its insolvency rules.
[282] See art.38.
[283] Smart, "Rights In Rem", 2006, at 38 et seq.
[284] See art.5(4). See below, para.15–98.

Assets situated in a non-Member State

15–90   Although art.5(1) is in terms confined to assets situated in another Member State, it does not follow that art.4(1) governs rights to assets situated in a non-Member State. Article 5(1) is silent on this, not because the purpose was to raise an inference that art.4(1) applied but because it was not considered appropriate for an EC regulation to purport to lay down rules for assets situated outside the European Union. For such assets, the law applicable for the purposes of the Insolvency Regulation is that determined by the conflict of laws rules of the *lex concursus*.

Actions for voidness, voidability or unenforceability

15–91   Article 5(1) does not preclude actions for voidness, voidability or unenforceability as referred to in art.4(2)(m).[285] So it is open to the liquidator in the main proceedings to apply to set aside under the *lex concursus* a disposition creating a right *in rem* over assets situated in another non-Member State, although this cannot be done if the person benefiting from the disposition provides proof that it is subject to the law of a Member State other than that of the State of the opening of proceedings and that law does not allow any means of challenging that act in the relevant case.[286]

Set-off

(i) The general rule

15–92   The opening of insolvency proceedings does not affect the right of creditors to demand the set-off of their claims against the debtor's claims where such a set-off is permitted by the law applicable to the insolvent debtor's claim.[287] This would seem to be the case whether the applicable law is that of another Member State or of a State outside the European Union.[288] Where set-off is permitted under the *lex concursus*, it is unnecessary to go further. Where the *lex concursus* does not permit set-off, art.6(1) requires reference to be made to the law applicable to the debtor's claim, including its rules on set-off in

---

[285] See art.5(4).

[286] See art.13.

[287] See art.5. Note that it is the claim of the insolvent company, not the cross-claim of its debtor, that determines the applicable law.

[288] In the case of contractual set-off, this is beyond doubt, since under art.2 of the Rome Convention any law selected by the Convention applies even if it is not the law of a Member State. The law applicable to other forms of set-off depends on their character and in particular on whether under the *lex fori* they are characterised as procedural or substantive in their effect.

insolvency. This involves a two-stage process. First, the forum applies its own conflict rules to determine the *lex causae* applicable to the debtor's claim. This having been identified, the rules of the *lex causae* applicable to insolvency set-off must then be applied even if no insolvency proceedings are on foot in the State to whose *lex causae* reference is made. In other words, insolvency set-off which is barred by the *lex concursus* must be accepted if it would have been permitted by the insolvency rules of the *lex causae* had insolvency proceedings been opened in the jurisdiction in question. Of course, in jurisdictions where insolvency law has no special rules of set-off and merely respects set-off available under the general law, it is that law which is to be applied, and in the case of contractual set-off the applicable law will be determined in accordance with the EC Regulation on the law applicable to contractual obligations (Rome I),[289] which will usually be the law chosen by the parties to the set-off agreement. However, that is not the case as regards insolvency proceedings opened in England, since the rules of insolvency set-off apply automatically and displace other forms of set-off, including contractual set-off, so that the set-off rules of the general law, including those relating to contractual set-off, have no application.

Under English conflict of laws rules (which will apply only in proceedings in England), a claim arising in contract is governed by the rules laid down in Rome I, which normally give effect to an express choice of law by the parties, while the law applicable to a claim in tort is governed by the EC Regulation on the law applicable to non-contractual obligations (Rome II),[290] determined by Pt III of the Private International Law (Miscellaneous Provisions) Act 1995,[291] the general rule being that the applicable law is that of the country in which the damage occurs or, if both parties have their habitual residence in the same country at the time the damage occurs, the law of that country, except in either case where the tort is manifestly connected with another country.[292] A claim in unjust enrichment (restitution) is governed by the law of the State where the unjust enrichment occurs.[293] Where the *lex causae* is English law, its rules of insolvency set-off, which are automatic and displace set-off rules applicable outside insolvency,[294] must then be applied if more favourable than those of the *lex concursus*.

---

[289] Regulation (EC) 593/2008 of the European Parliament and the Council, June 17, 2008 (OJ L 177/6), replacing the EEC Convention on the law applicable to contractual obligations, which was implemented in the UK by the Contracts (Applicable Law) Act 1990. See J. Fawcett, J. Carruthers and P. North, *Cheshire, North & Fawcett: Private International Law*, 14th edn (Oxford: Oxford University Press, 2008), pp.669 et seq.; and Lord Collins of Mapesbury et al. (eds), *Dicey, Morris & Collins on the Conflict of Laws*, 14th edn (London: Sweet & Maxwell, 2010), Chs 32 and 33 and 4th Cumulative Supplement.

[290] Regulation (EC) 864/2007 of the European Parliament and of the Council of July 11, 2007 (OJ L 199/40).

[291] *Cheshire, North & Fawcett*, 2008, Ch.19; and *Dicey, Morris & Collins*, 2010, Ch.35.

[292] See art. 4.

[293] *Cheshire, North & Fawcett*, 2008, pp.829 et seq.; and *Dicey, Morris & Collins*, 2010, Ch.34.

[294] See above, paras 9–13 et seq.

Article 6(1), like art.5(1), does not preclude actions for voidness, etc. under art.4(2)(m), for the obvious reason that if the transaction under which one of the claims arises is avoided, there ceases to be a set-off situation. But art.4(2)(m) cannot be used to apply the *lex concursus* to invalidate set-off as such, for example, as being contrary to the *pari passu* principle, for that is covered not by sub-para.(m) of art.4(2) but by sub-para.(d), which, if adverse to set-off, is disapplied by art.6(2).

(ii) The financial markets

15–93 Reference has been made earlier to EC directives requiring the laws of Member States to ensure that close-out and netting agreements in the financial markets are not rendered subject to avoidance by insolvency law.[295] This is reinforced by art.9, relating to payment systems,[296] and by recent amendments to the Settlement Finality Directive and the Financial Collateral Directive[297] extending the definition of "collateral" to cover credit claims (loans by banks) and providing that possession of financial collateral in the form of cash or financial instruments includes the case where financial collateral has been credited to an account in the name of the collateral-taker.[298]

Reservation of title

(1) Effect where purchaser becomes insolvent

15–94 The opening of insolvency proceedings against the purchaser of an asset does not affect the seller's rights based on a reservation of title where at the time of opening of the proceedings the asset is situated in the territory of another Member State.[299] It is, of course, necessary that the reservation of title shall have been validly created in the first place under the applicable law determined by the conflict of laws rules of the forum[300] and shall have

---

[295] See above, para.1–71.
[296] See below, para.15–97.
[297] See above, para.1–64.
[298] See above, para.1–64.
[299] See art.7. The fact that art.7 is inapplicable to an asset situated within the bankruptcy State at the time of opening of the proceedings does not affect the application of the separate principle that an action not derived from the bankruptcy and closely linked to proceedings for the realisation of assets is governed by Brussels I and is not caught by the bankruptcy exception in Brussels I (*German Graphics Graphische Maschinen GmbH v van der Schee* (C-292/08) [2010] I.L.Pr. 1). In other words, Brussels I applies to such a case even though the asset was so situated.
[300] Which will normally apply the law of the situation of the asset at the time of the sale agreement.

continued in force under that or any succeeding applicable law[301] up to the time of opening of the proceedings. If that is not the case, art.7 does not come into consideration. The impact of the opening of the insolvency proceedings upon a reservation of title valid under the applicable law immediately before such opening is determined by that law, which is not specified by art.7 but will normally be the law of the *situs* of the asset at that time. The effect is that the seller's right to invoke his reservation of title is governed by either the *lex concursus* or the applicable law, whichever is the more favourable. So if the *lex concursus* renders a reservation of title void if not registered prior to the opening of the insolvency proceedings but the applicable law does not, the seller is entitled to rely on the reservation of title, and the same applies in the converse case where the reservation of title is valid under the *lex concursus* but void under the applicable law.

Article 7 is generally considered to be restricted to simple reservation of title and not to cover the extended reservation of title by which, upon the buyer's resale, the seller's rights are carried over to the proceeds of sale of the goods, although in so far as these constitute rights *in rem* under the applicable law,[302] they may be protected by art.5.[303]

(2) Effect where seller becomes insolvent

Where it is the seller who becomes insolvent, the opening of insolvency proceedings against him after delivery of the asset does not constitute grounds for rescinding or terminating the sale and does not prevent the purchaser from acquiring title if the asset sold is situated within the territory of another Member State.[304] Again, this is without prejudice to the rule as to avoidance in art.4(2)(m).

15–95

Contracts relating to immovable property

In contrast to some of the earlier articles, art.8 lays down a positive and exclusive conflicts rule. The effect of the opening of insolvency proceedings on the right to acquire or make use of immovable property is governed *solely* by the *lex situs*. Under English law, a contract of sale or of lease is treated in equity as a sale or lease and thus creates a right *in rem* which falls within art.5

15–96

---

[301] e.g. a change of law resulting from a dealing in a new situs or re-perfection requirements imposed by the law of the new situs.

[302] Which is not normally the case in English law if the seller's reservation of title has not been registered under s.860 of the Companies Act 2006 as a charge on book debts. See *Goode on Commercial Law*, 2009, pp.702 et seq.

[303] Virgós and Garcimartín, *The European Insolvency Regulation*, para.172.

[304] See art.7(2).

as well as art.8 and in principle is unaffected by the opening of insolvency proceedings, subject to avoidance provisions relating to transactions at an undervalue, preferences and the like.[305]

Payment systems and financial markets

15–97   The effects of insolvency proceedings on the rights and obligations of parties to a payment or settlement system or to a financial market are governed solely by the law of a Member State applicable to that system or market.[306] One consequence of this is to add emphasis to the fact that rights and obligations protected from insolvency laws by national laws implementing the EC directives on settlement finality and financial collateral arrangements[307] remain unaffected by the insolvency laws of another Member State in which insolvency proceedings are opened. That would follow anyway from the paramountcy of the directives as *leges speciales*,[308] and it is reinforced by art.13, referred to below.[309] Article 9(1) is without prejudice to art.5, so that the law applicable to payments systems and financial markets does not displace *in rem* rights arising under other law and preserved by art.5, for example, rights arising where financial collateral is given as security. Article 9(1) does not preclude actions for voidness, etc. but in contrast to earlier articles, which preserve the application of art.4(2)(m), art.9(2) applies the avoidance rules of the relevant payment system or financial market.

Other issues

Employment contracts

15–98   The impact of insolvency proceedings on employment contracts is governed solely by the law of the Member State applicable to the contract,[310] as determined by arts 6 and 7 of the Rome Convention. Under reg. 4 of the Transfer of Undertakings (Protection of Employment) Regulations 2006,[311] on the sale of an undertaking the contracts of employment of employees assigned

---

[305] See above, Ch.13.
[306] See art.9(1). Where the system or market is not governed by the law of Member State, the rights and obligations of the parties are governed by the law determined by the conflict of laws rules of the forum, which in most cases can be expected to lead to the same result.
[307] See above, para.1–64.
[308] For a detailed discussion, see Virgós and Garcimartín, *The European Insolvency Regulation*, paras 211 et seq.
[309] See para.15–98.
[310] See art.10. Under art.2 of the Rome Convention, the same applies if the applicable law is not that of a Member State.
[311] SI 2006/246, giving effect to Council Directive 2001/23/EC (the "Acquired Rights Directive").

to the undertaking are not terminated but pass to the transferee, along with any accrued liabilities of the transferor to those employees, while the transferee also inherits any liabilities incurred by the transferor to employees dismissed prior to but because of, the transfer. However, reg. 4 does not apply where:

"the transferor is the subject of bankruptcy proceedings or any analogous insolvency proceedings which have been instituted with a view to the liquidation of the assets of the transferor and are under the supervision of an insolvency practitioner."[312]

There has been a division of opinion between employment tribunals as to whether administration proceedings constitute or may constitute insolvency proceedings falling within the above regulation. In *Oakland v. Wellswood (Yorkshire) Ltd.* the Employment Tribunal held that the question of the application of reg. 8(7) was one of fact, so that TUPE would not apply where, as in the case before it, the administration proceedings were instituted with a view to a pre-pack sale of the assets. This decision was upheld by HH Judge Peter Clark, sitting on his own as the Employment Appeal Tribunal.[313] On appeal the Court of Appeal decided the case on another ground but Moses L.J. considered there were strong grounds for thinking that Judge Clark's approach had been wrong.[314] That was the view subsequently adopted by the Employment Appeal Tribunal in *OTG Ltd. v. Barke*,[315] a decision of Underhill J. sitting with two other members of the EAT, in which the Tribunal rejected the "fact-based" approach and instead adopted the "absolute" approach, namely that administration proceedings could never fall within reg. 8(7) since the primary purpose of administration was rescue of the insolvent company or its business, not liquidation. Accordingly TUPE applied, with the result that the transferee of the undertaking assumed responsibility for the contracts of the transferor's employees.

Rights subject to registration

The insolvency effects on the debtor's rights in immovable property, a ship or an aircraft subject to registration in a public register are determined by the law of the State under which the register is kept.[316] The drafting of this

---

[312] ibid, art. 8(7).
[313] [2009] IRLR 250.
[314] [2010] I.C.R. 902, para. 10.
[315] UKEAT/0320/09/RN, 16 Feb 2011.
[316] See art.11. Under art.14, dispositions of such assets for consideration after the opening of the insolvency proceedings are governed by the *lex situs* in the case of an immovable or the *lex registri* in the case of a ship or an aircraft.

article is not very felicitous. If read literally, it could be taken to mean that the *lex registri* displaces in their entirety arts 4, 5 and 8. That is not the intention. Article 11 is confined to the effects, if any, of the *lex registri*. Under English law, for example, registration is not at present a condition of the creation of a right in an immovable, only a prerequisite of its priority vis-à-vis subsequent interests.[317] So as *lex registri* it would have nothing to say about insolvency effects on the debtor, and the case would be governed not by art.11 but by art.5 and, in the case of a contract of sale or lease, art.8. Where the *lex registri* does come into play, for example, in regulating the priority of a registered interest as against a subsequently registered or unregistered interest, art.4 nevertheless has effect for other purposes, for example, in determining whether a transaction is void as a preference.

Immunity from challenge under the law of a Member State

Article 13 imposes an important limitation of the avoidance rules of the *lex concursus* as provided by art.4(2)(m). These are disapplied where the person benefiting from the act detrimental to all of the creditors provides proof that the act is subject to the law of a Member State other than the State of the opening of proceedings and that law does not allow any means of challenging that act in the relevant case. For example, in the case of the United Kingdom, statutory provisions have been introduced implementing the EC settlement finality and financial collateral directives designed to remove from attack under insolvency law netting and close-out arrangements and contractual arrangements to similar effect relating to financial collateral.[318] Article 15 provides that the effect of insolvency proceedings on a lawsuit pending concerning an asset or a right of which the debtor has been divested shall be governed solely by the law of the Member State in which that lawsuit is pending. It is thus for that law to determine whether the proceedings are to be suspended or may be allowed to continue.[319] This article, which has primacy over art.4, applies to the effect of insolvency proceedings not only on pending actions but on pending arbitrations and on the continuing validity of the arbitration agreement. Thus, in *Syska v Vivendi SA*,[320] where the

---

[317] This will change with the introduction of electronic conveyancing, when creation will coincide with registration. See Gray and Gray, *Elements of Land Law*, 2008, para.2.2.32.

[318] See above, para.1–64 and nn.230 and 231. There is considerable overlap between arts 13 and 9 in this field. The rule in art.13 precluding challenge to an act unless it meets the double test of liability to avoidance not only under the *lex concursus* but also under the applicable law has not passed without criticism. See Michael Veder, *Cross-Border Insolvency Proceedings and Security Rights* (Deventer, Netherlands: Kluwer Legal Publishers, 2004), p.315, and literature there cited.

[319] See Virgós and Garcimartín, *The European Insolvency Regulation*, paras 252 et seq.

[320] [2010] B.C.C. 348.

respondent to an English arbitration became bankrupt in Poland, the argument on behalf of the respondent that Polish law, under which the bankruptcy annulled the arbitration agreement, was to be applied was rejected by the Court of Appeal, which upheld the trial judge's decision that the impact of the bankruptcy on the arbitration was governed by English law, under which the validity of the arbitration agreement remained unaffected, and that the arbitrators were accordingly right to proceed with the arbitration.

Chapter 16

International Insolvency[1]

1. THE PROBLEMS OF INTERNATIONAL INSOLVENCY

Introduction

The previous chapter examined the regulation of cross-border corporate insolvencies within the European Union, with particular reference to the Insolvency Regulation 2000.[2] We saw that the position was complex even within a unified system of rules. How much more so is this the case in cross-border insolvencies involving parties outside the European Union,

16–01

---

[1] A substantial volume of writing has grown up around this subject in the past decade. The leading English texts are Ian F. Fletcher, *Insolvency in Private International Law: National and International Approaches*, 2nd edn (Oxford: Oxford University Press, 2006), with Supplement (2007) and, for a less detailed but more up-to-date treatment, *Law of Insolvency*, 4th edn (London: Sweet & Maxwell, 2009), Chs 30–32; and Philip Wood, *Principles of International Insolvency*, 2nd edn (London: Sweet & Maxwell, 2007). See also Rosalind Mason, "Cross-Border Insolvency Law: Where Private International Law and Insolvency Law Meet" in Paul J. Omar (ed.), *International Insolvency Law: Themes and Perspectives* (Aldershot: Ashgate, 2008), Ch.2. Valuable insights are also provided by the insolvency contributions to M.G. Bridge and R.H. Stevens (eds), *Cross-Border Security and Insolvency* (Oxford: Oxford University Press, 2001); and Fletcher, "The Quest for a Global Insolvency Law: A Challenge for Our Time" [2002] *Current Legal Problems* 427. American scholars have been particularly active in this field. See, in particular, Jay Lawrence Westbrook, "A Global Solution to Multinational Default" 98 Mich. L. Rev. 2276 (2009) and "Theory and Pragmatism in Global Insolvencies: Choice of Law and Choice of Forum" 65 Am. Bankr. L.J. 457 (1991); and Lynn M. LoPucki, "The Case for Cooperative Territoriality in International Bankruptcy" 98 Mich. L. Rev. 2216 (1999–2000) and "Co-Operation in International Bankruptcy: A Post-Universalist Approach" 84 Cornell L. Rev. 696 (1998–1999). Additional references will be found at different points in this chapter.

[2] Council Regulation (EC) 1346/2000 of May 29, 2000.

particularly in jurisdictions which have not adopted the 1997 UNCITRAL Model Law on cross-border insolvency.

The hallmarks of internationality

16–02   An international insolvency is typically characterised by one or more of the following features: the debtor's business is conducted in different countries; the creditors are situated in different countries; the assets are located in different countries; there are parallel proceedings in different countries. The first of these requires a few words of explanation. A company may operate in different countries either through local subsidiaries or through branches or offices. In the former case, the company and each of its subsidiaries are separate legal entities and in principle each insolvent company within the group has to be the subject of separate insolvency proceedings, although the relevant court(s) may approve pooling arrangements agreed by the different office holders either in order to maximise realisations for the corporate group as a whole or because the assets and liabilities of the companies concerned have become so intermingled that it is not practicable to disentangle them.[3] By contrast, branches and offices are not in general separate legal entities, simply part of the insolvent company and administered as such. But the distinction between corporate entities and branches and offices is not always clear cut. In several jurisdictions, including the United States, every branch of a bank is treated as a separate legal entity for insolvency purposes, although this is not the position under English law.[4]

Issues in international (cross-border) insolvency

16–03   The central practical question confronting office holders in a cross-border insolvency is how to marshal the assets and co-ordinate the winding up or

---

[3] In *Re Bank of Credit and Commerce International SA* [1994] 1 W.L.R. 708, the judgment of Dillon L.J. records (at 711) that because of the manner in which the affairs of BCCI, incorporated in Luxembourg, and its associated company, Bank of Credit and Commerce International (Overseas) Ltd, incorporated in the Cayman Islands, had been conducted, a pooling agreement had been entered into and approved by the courts in England, the Cayman Islands and Luxembourg under which all realisations remaining and deduction of costs and preferential claims would form a single fund to be divided rateably among the general creditors of both companies.

[4] The general law does, however, recognise the separate character of branches for some purposes, for example, through the rule that a customer cannot draw on an account with one branch for an amount exceeding his credit balance or credit line with that branch even though he has deposits with other branches sufficient to cover the drawing. See also above, para.15–85, n.279.

reorganisation of the enterprise as a whole to the best advantage of creditors. Among the legal issues which may arise in an international, or cross-border, insolvency[5] are: whether an English court has jurisdiction over a foreign company and, if so, whether it may decline jurisdiction; whether an English winding up extends to foreign assets; whether foreign creditors are entitled to equal treatment with English creditors in an English winding up; the extent to which foreign insolvency proceedings preclude proceedings in England by English creditors against assets in England; the extent to which an English court will recognise foreign liquidation proceedings and the status of foreign office-holders and will be able and willing to give its assistance to foreign parties and foreign courts in relation to assets or persons susceptible to the jurisdiction of the English court; the law applicable to the substance and procedure of a winding up; and the manner in which assets and claims should be dealt with where there are concurrent insolvency proceedings in two or more jurisdictions, including the conditions on which a creditor who has received a dividend in one liquidation should be allowed to prove in another liquidation in a different country. In proceedings in England, all these issues are governed by rules of English private international law, following the universal principle that issues of jurisdiction, choice of law and enforcement are governed by the *lex fori*.

Countries differ in their approach to the problems of cross-border insolvency. We may, however, detect certain common principles, notably the collective nature of the insolvency proceedings; *pari passu* distribution; the avoidance or deferment of liquidation where rescue, reorganisation or arrangements with creditors are likely to improve prospects for creditors; the principle of respect for pre-insolvency entitlements, such as the priority of secured creditors; the conferment of preferential status on certain unsecured creditors, notably for unpaid wages and taxes[6]; rules for the avoidance of transactions concluded in the run-up to liquidation or administration which are detrimental to the general body of creditors; and the absence of discrimination against foreign creditors, although in some jurisdictions this is dependent on reciprocity. These could usefully be reinforced by a common principle of the cram-down of minority creditors, particularly secured creditors.

---

[5] The terms "international insolvency" and "cross-border insolvency" have no defined meaning but are generally taken to be interchangeable and to refer to insolvencies which arise from cross-border trading or which involve the application, or possible application, of the insolvency laws of two or more jurisdictions.

[6] But taxes are no longer preferential debts in the UK. See above, para.8–20.

The rival approaches to jurisdictional issues

16–04   The battle lines are drawn when it comes to jurisdictional issues. Two sets of opposing principles are of particular significance. They are unity versus plurality and universality versus territoriality.[7]

The principle of unity ascribes exclusive jurisdiction over insolvency proceedings (whether winding up or otherwise) to the courts of the company's home State,[8] to which all other courts defer. The opposing principle of plurality admits of concurrent proceedings in different jurisdictions,[9] based on some connecting factor such as assets, a place of business or creditors within the jurisdiction.

The universality/territoriality classification relates to the question of whether an insolvency proceeding opened in one jurisdiction should encompass all assets on a worldwide basis or should be confined to assets within the jurisdiction in question. This, of course, is linked to the unity/plurality issue, for if jurisdiction is confined to local assets, there will necessarily be a plurality of proceedings where the debtor has assets in different jurisdictions. However, the converse is not necessarily true, for in parallel proceedings in different States the insolvency laws of each may claim jurisdiction over assets worldwide. Both issues have generated intense debate and have led to international as well as regional initiatives. Taken in combination, they can be described as the universalist approach on one side, encompassing the concept both of a single law and of a single jurisdiction covering all assets, and a territorialist approach, in which the jurisdiction of the courts of a given state is confined to those portions of the company and its assets that lie within the territory of that State.

Both approaches have their strengths and weaknesses. For the territorialist, the universalist approach is anathema. The opposition to it has been succinctly expressed by an American scholar in the following terms:

"Scholars of international bankruptcy are caught in the grip of a failed idea: universalism. Generations of scholars have advanced the universalist mantra: i.e., that the assets and liabilities of a multinational firm in bankruptcy should be administered by one court applying one nation's bankruptcy laws on a worldwide basis. Until recently, this advancement of

---

[7] Which is not exhaustive. Deserving of particular mention is Professor Robert Rasmussen's contractual approach under which it would be open to each company, at the time of incorporation, to select the legal regime to which it wished to be subject. Professor Rasmussen has extended this idea, initially developed in relation to the choice of insolvency regime within a single jurisdiction (see above, para.2–20), to allow choice of jurisdiction and applicable law at the international level. See Robert K. Rasmussen, "A New Approach to Transnational Insolvencies" 19 Mich. J. Int'l L. 1 (1997).

[8] In some States this is the State of incorporation, in others, the principal place of business or the centre of the debtor's main interests but the underlying idea is the same, namely the State with which the company has its closest juridical connection.

[9] For the advantages and disadvantages of a single forum, see Wood, *Principles of International Insolvency*, 2007, para.27-005.

universalism occurred largely without challenge. Even with recent challenges, however, universalism dominates the debate, as scholars attempt to debunk its claimed efficiency advantages.

This debate over universalism is misguided because, simply put, universalism will not work. In this Article, I argue that universalism is politically implausible and likely impossible. No nation has adopted it, and it is unlikely that any will. States will be reluctant to commit to enforcing the decisions of foreign courts applying foreign bankruptcy laws against local parties. In addition, even assuming States exist that would be interested in universalism, structural problems will preclude the achievement of workable universalist co-operation. I rely on elementary game theory and international relations theory to show that even States that prefer universalism will find themselves in a prisoners' dilemma with no ready solution. Impediments to co-operation will afflict even bilateral universalist ambitions, with multilateral universalism all the more unlikely. Because the claimed superior efficiency of universalism implicitly depends on its widespread adoption—if not ubiquity—this implausibility of multilateral universalism is particularly damning to the universalist cause. Universalism should be shelved, and the terms of the scholarly debate should shift to more plausible goals."[10]

Others, too, have deprecated the emphasis on unity and universality. Professor Lynn LoPucki is one of the leading protagonists to deploy the arguments against the universalist approach. These are that: (i) the connecting factor favoured by universalists, namely the debtor's "home country" or the place where it has its centre of main interests, is too indeterminate and subject to strategic manipulation; (ii) to impose foreign law and foreign courts on wholly domestic relationships is both confusing to local creditors and detrimental to the rights and priorities they had acquired under their own law and could reasonably expect to be preserved; and (iii) no workable rule can be devised for determining the extent to which the home country is to have jurisdiction over corporate groups.[11]

Equally powerful arguments in favour of the universalist approach have been advanced by Professor Jay Westbrook, who makes the point that it is not possible to maximise value or ensure equality for creditors unless there is a unified regime for the assembly and realisation of the debtor's assets and a common pool to be applied under a common distribution scheme, and that reorganisation is even more dependent for its efficacy on the existence of a single regime under which it can be conducted.[12] Moreover, because of the relative inflexibility of local insolvency laws, real co-operation in a territorial

---

[10] Frederick Tung, "Is International Bankruptcy Possible?" 23 Mich. J. Int'l Law 31 (2001).
[11] LoPucki, "The Case for Cooperative Territoriality", 1999–2000.
[12] Westbrook, "A Global Solution to Multinational Default", 2000.

system is necessarily very limited and "recoveries will turn on the fortuitous or manipulated location of assets and the results will be highly unpredictable ex ante".[13]

The convergence of the universalist and territorialist approaches in practice

16–05 Over time, there has been a gradual convergence of the two approaches. It is generally accepted that to route everything to a single forum, however theoretically desirable in terms of avoiding concurrent insolvency proceedings, is not realistic, for assets are always subject to the sovereign control of the state in which they are situated and in no jurisdiction are courts willing to give up all control over local assets where there are local creditors. So the principle everywhere adopted is that of plurality, which admits of concurrent proceedings in different jurisdictions. On the other side, it is accepted that to allow a multiplicity of disconnected territorial proceedings, each confined to local assets, is inimical to the goal of maximising returns to creditors and is a serious obstacle to any plan for reorganisation, which requires an integrated approach.[14] To this one might add that the difficulty of identifying a company's centre of main interests (COMI), although not to be dismissed, ought not to be overstated either. The location of the COMI in an EU Member State is a condition of the application of the European Insolvency Regulation, and although it has given rise to litigation in a number of countries, it is fair to say that in most cases the court had little difficulty in identifying the debtor's COMI.[15]

As to assets covered by a winding up procedure, no country adopts a wholly universalist approach. The laws of some States adopt a principle of territoriality by which insolvency proceedings opened there are confined to local assets. More commonly, States adopt the principle of universality for their own proceedings but do not feel obliged to accept it for proceedings opened elsewhere. A potential conflict arises where there are concurrent liquidation proceedings in two different States and under the laws of both, the debtor's estate embraces all of its assets on a worldwide basis. In practice, such conflicts, if not wholly avoided, have been alleviated by the willingness of courts of one jurisdiction to recognise that the main liquidation is based

---

[13] ibid., at 2302.

[14] Within the European Union the principle of plurality is qualified in that a court in the UK may not make a winding up order, appoint a provisional liquidator or make an administration order against an EEA credit institution or branch thereof other than a UK-regulated credit institution (Credit Institutions (Reorganisation and Winding up) Regulations 2004 (SI 2004/1045), reg.3, implementing Directive 2001/24/EC of the European Parliament and Council of April 4, 2001 on the reorganisation and winding up of credit institutions ([2001] OJ L125/15)).

[15] See above, paras 15–49 et seq.

elsewhere (typically in the State where the debtor company is incorporated or alternatively where it has its COMI) and that their own winding up proceedings are ancillary to the main proceedings and should be used in aid of the latter, with the consequence that the ancillary liquidation will in practice be confined to local assets, which at some point will be transferred, together with a list of creditors in the ancillary liquidation, to the liquidator in the main proceedings, subject always to the court in which the ancillary proceedings were opened being satisfied that creditors in its own jurisdiction will be fairly treated in the main liquidation.[16]

Current theories

The two principal theories that emerge from this convergence[17] have been described as the co-operative territorialist approach, favoured by LoPucki, and the modified universalist approach, advocated by Westbrook. The co-operative territorial approach leaves each State with full territorial sovereignty and depends on various kinds of co-operation among States.[18] The modified universalist approach takes as its starting point the principles of unity and universality, including a single set of internationally agreed priority rules, with overall control being vested in the court of the debtor's home country and courts of other States acting in an ancillary role to provide assistance to the foreign court while at the same time ensuring that if assets are surrendered to the main jurisdiction local creditors will be fairly treated. Thus, while co-operation may play a significant role, the system is not dependent on it, because it is geared to the concept of global management.

16–06

The modern approach to international insolvency

A valuable contribution to these issues was the American Law Institute's pioneering project on transnational insolvency,[19] which did much to clarify the issues and terminology. The current trend, as exemplified by the UNCITRAL Model Law on Cross-Border Insolvency and the EC Insolvency Regulation, which applies in 26 of the 27 EU Member States,[20] is clearly in

16–07

---

[16] See below, para.16–07.
[17] The contractualist theory elegantly propounded by Rasmussen remains a theory and has not been adopted in practice.
[18] Lynn M. LoPucki, "Co-operation in International Bankruptcy: A Post-Universalist Approach" 84 Cornell L. Rev. 696, 750 (1998–1999).
[19] Transnational Insolvency Project, Principles of Co-operation in Transnational Insolvency Cases Among Members of the North American Free Trade Agreement (2000), which was followed by an international project, Transnational Insolvency: Principles of Cooperation, due for completion shortly.
[20] Denmark opted out of the Regulation.

favour of a modified universalist approach, albeit with rather more territorial elements than may have been envisaged by the proponents of that approach. The key universalist elements are: (i) the concept of main proceedings in the State where the debtor has its COMI or equivalent; (ii) the application of the *lex concursus* of that State to govern the effects of the opening of those proceedings; (iii) recognition in other States of the judgments of the court by which the proceedings were opened and of the application of the *lex concursus*; (iv) overall control of the insolvency process by the office-holder in the main liquidation or reorganisation proceedings; (v) treatment of all of the debtor's assets worldwide as constituting the estate administered by that office-holder; (vi) the provision of assistance by local courts in the recovery of assets and pursuit of claims by the office holder in the main proceedings, and access of office holders to foreign courts. But some leeway is also given to the concept of territoriality to accommodate the legitimate expectations of local creditors in relation to local assets. Thus the opening of territorial proceedings is permitted in a State where the debtor has an establishment or assets[21] although having its COMI elsewhere but the proceedings are limited to local assets,[22] and will be governed by the local *lex concursus*, whose priority rules will continue to apply. So local creditors will preserve their rights and priorities under local law, while foreign creditors will be able to participate in the insolvency proceedings on an equal footing but on the basis of local law, not the law by which their rights would otherwise be governed.

The position under English law

16–08   In *HIH Casualty and General Insurance Ltd*,[23] the modified universalist approach was endorsed by Lord Hoffman, albeit as a principle rather than a rule and one which is heavily qualified by exceptions on pragmatic grounds[24]:

> "The primary rule of private international law which seems to me applicable to this case is the principle of (modified) universalism, which has been the golden thread running through English cross-border insolvency law since the 18th century. That principle requires that English courts should, so far as is consistent with justice and UK public policy, co-operate with the courts in the country of the principal liquidation to ensure that all the

---

[21] The EU Regulation requires an establishment (art.3(2)), the Model Law requires assets only but *foreign* non-main proceedings are by definition confined to those where the debtor has an establishment in the State where they are opened (art.2(c)).

[22] And in the case of the Regulation, to winding up proceedings.

[23] [2008] 1 W.L.R. 852. For an American scholar's comment on the case, see Jay Westbrook, "Priority Conflicts as a Barrier to Co-operation in Multinational Insolvencies" 27 Penn. St. Int'l L. Rev. 869 (2008–2009).

[24] *HIH Casualty*, cited above n.23, at [7], citing Professors Westbrook and Fletcher.

company's assets are distributed to its creditors under a single system of distribution. That is the purpose of the power to direct remittal."[25]

Lord Hoffmann was supported by Lord Walker,[26] but other members of the panel,[27] although agreeing in the result, did so on different grounds. As regards judicial co-operation the United Kingdom has adopted the UNCITRAL Model Law on Cross-Border Insolvency, which plainly embodies the modified universalist approach for all types of collective insolvency proceeding,[28] as does the EC Insolvency Regulation,[29] which has direct effect in the United Kingdom, so that this approach can now be regarded as firmly established in English law.

The principle of non-discrimination

Hand in hand with the concepts of unity and universality goes the principle of non-discrimination against foreign creditors. If all of the company's assets, in whatever part of the world, are to be subsumed within a single liquidation, then claims of foreign creditors must be admitted on the same basis as those of local creditors. This principle is well brought out in an opinion on US bankruptcy law given for the assistance of the English court in *Felixstowe Dock and Railway Co v U S Lines Inc*[30] by Judge Howard C. Buschman of the US District Court for the Southern District of New York:

    16–09

"The intended scope of bankruptcy and reorganization jurisdiction extends beyond the border of the United States . . . The nature of the jurisdiction is in rem. The res, the estate of the debtor created by the commencement of a bankruptcy or reorganisation case, is viewed as a single entity to be dealt with in a single proceeding. The broad scope of bankruptcy jurisdiction under United States law is intended to permit similarly situated creditors, regardless of where they are located, to be treated equally in a bankruptcy or reorganization case. Discrimination on the basis of citizenship is not permitted. All creditors are given the opportunity to file claims against the State and their recovery is not limited to the assets in their own country."

The position is the same under English insolvency law.[31]

---

[25] *HIH Casualty*, cited above n.23, at [30]. See to similar effect the speech of Lord Hoffmann on behalf of the Privy Council in the earlier decision in *Cambridge Gas Transportation Corp v Official Committee of Unsecured Creditors of Navigator Holdings Plc* [2007] 1 A.C. 508.

[26] *HIH Casualty*, cited above n.23, at [63].

[27] Lords Scott and Neuberger. See further below, para.16–61.

[28] See above, para.16–07, and below paras 16–17 et seq.

[29] See Edward S. Adams and Jason K. Finke, "Coordinating Cross-Border Bankruptcy: How Territorialism Saves Universalism" 15 Col. J. Eur. L. 43 (2008–2009), concluding that the EC Regulation adopts a purer form of universalism.

[30] [1989] Q.B. 360. An extract from the opinion is set out in the judgment of Hirst J. at 368.

[31] *Re Bank of Credit and Commerce International SA (No.11)* [1996] B.C.C. 980, *per* Sir Richard Scott V.C. at 986.

The treatment of corporate groups

16–10 One of the more difficult issues in international insolvency is the treatment of corporate groups. In England, as in most other jurisdictions,[32] a group of companies is not as such a legal entity. Each company within the group must be treated separately. It may be that some companies within the group are insolvent while others are in a healthy financial state. There may be cross-lending, cross-guarantees and cross-securities within the group. In many cases the interests of the various groups of creditors will best be served by an integrated approach to the group as a whole. Where all members of the group are within the European Union and are managed from one place which constitutes the common COMI, the EC Insolvency Regulation ensures that even though there are separate proceedings for each insolvent company, these will be governed by the same law and will be susceptible to the appointment of a common office holder or joint administrators.[33] This does, of course, assume that a judgment opened in main proceedings in one Member State will be recognised in others. So far, with a few hiccups on the way, the experience has been good. In *Daisytek*, the French *Cour de Cassation* upheld the status of the administration proceedings opened in England as main proceedings,[34] while in the insolvency of the MG Rover Group the Court of Appeal of Versailles upheld the decision of the Nanterre Commercial Court according similar recognition to administration proceedings in England in which orders were made against various members of the group, including a French subsidiary.[35] In cases outside the scope of EU law, the concept of ancillary proceedings and judicial assistance may help to cut through difficulties caused by the separate legal identities of members of a corporate group. English courts have been ready to recognise that their role is ancillary to that of a court elsewhere in which proceedings have been opened and to provide assistance under s.426 of the Insolvency Act 1986,[36] while courts in the United States have performed a similar service under s.304 of the Bankruptcy Code, which has been widely utilised by foreign representatives but has now been replaced by the new Ch.15 of the Bankruptcy Code incorporating the UNCITRAL Model Law on Cross-Border Insolvency.[37]

Independently of any statutory underpinning, much can be achieved by co-operation among the different office holders and the willingness of courts in

---

[32] An exception is Germany, which has a law for enterprises (*Konzertrecht*).

[33] For the perceived dangers of this approach in relation to the EC Insolvency Regulation, see Nicolaes W.A. Tollenaar, "Dealing with the Insolvency of Multinational Groups under the European Insolvency Regulation" (2010) 23 *Insolvency Intelligence* 65.

[34] See above, para.15–53.

[35] See above, para.15–67.

[36] See below, para.16–58.

[37] See below, para.16–17.

their respective jurisdictions to assist the co-operative process in relation to a group of companies.[38] Even so, as we have noted earlier,[39] the problems of corporate groups are formidable. These exist at two levels: the substantive law and the insolvency administration. At the level of substantive law, there are two possible routes to integration. The first is the use of rules by which one company in a group is held liable for the debts and liabilities of another even if it has not given a guarantee. English law has such rules (agency, piercing the corporate veil, or "alter ego" doctrine) but they are rarely invoked with success. Some laws such as the German *Konzernrecht*[40] regulate enterprises, not just separate entities, imposing liability on the parent or other controlling entity.[41] Substantive consolidation under insolvency law (pooling of assets and liabilities) provides another solution but under English law this too is infrequent and is generally confined to situations in which the assets and liabilities of the different companies are so intermingled that there is no sensible alternative to consolidation.[42] Procedural consolidation maintains the separation of the assets and liabilities of the different group members, but subjects all members of the group to a joint administration. Even without consolidation, much can be achieved if all members of the group have their COMI in the same jurisdiction and are under the supervision of the same administrators.[43]

The treatment of corporate groups in insolvency, briefly discussed in the useful UNCITRAL Legislative Guide on Insolvency Law[44] in the context of domestic law, is now covered in detail in a new Pt III of the Guide, produced by Working Group V.[45] It is a wide-ranging document covering, amongst other things, the meaning of "enterprise group", the regulation of enterprise groups, the treatment of assets, the reorganisation of enterprise group members, co-operation between courts, co-operation between insolvency representatives and the use of cross-border insolvency agreements. The subject has also been the subject of a detailed study by Dr Irit Mevorach, whose monograph[46] provides valuable insights into the problems and possible solutions. She draws the same distinction as other scholars between integrated groups (those in substance running as a single global business) and non-integrated groups (those whose members conduct truly separate businesses) but then goes on to make a further distinction between asset integration, involving the intermingling of assets and liabilities in the normal course of

---

[38] For a good example, see below para.16–65.
[39] See above, para.1–28.
[40] Which is codified in the *Aktiengesetz* (Stock Corporations Act) 1965.
[41] For a comparative survey, see Meredith Dearborn, "Enterprise Liability: Reviewing and Revitalizing Liability for Corporate Groups" 97 Cal. L. Rev. 195 (2009).
[42] See n.3, above.
[43] As in *Re Collins & Aikman Europe SA* [2006] B.C.C. 861 (Ch).
[44] Published in 2005.
[45] *Legislative Guide on Insolvency Law, Part Three: Treatment of enterprise groups in insolvency* (43rd session, A/C. 9/686, July 2010).
[46] *Insolvency Within Multinational Enterprise Groups* (Oxford: Oxford University Press, 2009).

business, and business integration, in which the assets and liabilities are kept separate but the different members of the group are otherwise operated as a single unit. Asset integration more readily lends itself to substantive consolidation, with the prospect of maximising returns to creditors, but this depends heavily on international co-operation among the different jurisdictions involved. Moreover, in jurisdictions such as Germany which have enterprise laws that impose on the dominant company liability for the debts of its subsidiaries, the interplay between such laws and substantive consolidation under insolvency law of a different jurisdiction may raise additional problems. Business integration, by contrast, invites purely procedural consolidation, in which the assets and liabilities of the different group members are kept separate but insolvency administration is centralised in the jurisdiction where the group's head office is based. Procedural consolidation involves less risk of unfairness to creditors but is itself heavily dependent on the willingness of courts in other jurisdictions to restrict their role to an ancillary one in which they provide assistance for the main proceedings.

2. THE INSOLVENCY JURISDICTION OF ENGLISH COURTS

Sources of jurisdiction

16–11   There are now five potential sources of jurisdiction of English courts in relation to the insolvency of companies, namely the EU Insolvency Regulation 2000,[47] the UNCITRAL Model Law on Cross-Border Insolvency as embodied in Sch.1 to the Cross-Border Insolvency Regulations 2006,[48] the Insolvency Act 1986 and, for banks, the Banking Act 2009, and the common law conflict of laws rules governing the insolvency of companies. Where a debtor company has its COMI within any EU Member State other than Denmark, the opening and effects of insolvency proceedings are governed by the Insolvency Regulation, which, as we have seen, has direct effect in the United Kingdom and overrides any inconsistent provisions of other English insolvency law.

Hierarchy of sources

16–12   *The EC Insolvency Regulation*

The hierarchical ordering of the sources of English corporate insolvency law is not entirely straightforward. Where the debtor company has its COMI in

---

[47] Council Regulation (EC) 1346/2000 of May 29, 2000.
[48] SI 2006/1030, which apply to Great Britain only. For Northern Ireland, see the Cross-Border Insolvency Regulations (Northern Ireland) 2007, SI 2007/115.

an EU Member State other than Denmark, then as a matter of EU law the EC Insolvency Regulation, where applicable, overrides other sources, including the Model Law, in cases of inconsistency. Just to put the matter beyond doubt, art.3 of the British Model Law expressly provides that to the extent that it conflicts with the United Kingdom's obligations under the Insolvency Regulation, the latter is to prevail. However, credit institutions are outside the scope of the Insolvency Regulation and the Model Law, so that as regards UK credit institutions the Insolvency Act 1986 has primacy.

The Model Law on Cross-Border Insolvency   **16–13**

Next, reg.3(2) of the Cross-Border Insolvency Regulations provides as follows:

> "In the case of any conflict between any provision of British insolvency law or of Part 3 of the Insolvency Act 1986 and the provisions of these Regulations, the latter shall prevail."

One effect of reg.3(2) is, of course, to give priority to the Model Law, in the form embodied in the regulations, over British insolvency law. However, reg.3(2) goes further than that in as much as the regulations do not simply embody the Model Law, they also deal with matters arising from its application but not governed by it. These include provisions as to co-operation between English and Scottish courts,[49] and various procedural provisions in the schedules to the regulations, among them rules governing misfeasance proceedings against a foreign representative[50] and provisions relating to an application for confirmation of status of a replacement foreign representative where, following the making of a recognition order, the foreign representative dies or for any other reason ceases to be the foreign representative.[51] All of these have priority over British insolvency law in case of conflict. However, when it comes to the provision of assistance to foreign courts and foreign insolvency office holders, the purpose of the Model Law is to run alongside and not displace rules of national law. Article 7 therefore provides that nothing in the Model Law limits the power of the court or a British insolvency officeholder to provide additional assistance to a foreign representative under other laws of Great Britain. Accordingly, s.426 of the Insolvency Act and, so far as not displaced by s.426, the common law conflict rules concerning the provision of assistance remain unaffected by the Model

---

[49] Cross-Border Insolvency Regulations, reg.7.
[50] Cross-Border Insolvency Regulations Sch.2 Pt 8.
[51] Cross-Border Insolvency Regulations Sch.3 Pt 2.

Law. Further, where there are concurrent foreign proceedings and a proceeding under British insolvency law, art.29 requires that any relief granted under arts 19 or 21 must be consistent with the proceeding in Great Britain.

16–14   *Other statutory provisions governing insolvency of companies*

Third in the hierarchy come other statutory provisions governing the insolvency of companies, including the provisions of the Insolvency Act 1986, s.899 of the Companies Act 2006 so far as it relates to schemes of arrangement by an insolvent company, and the insolvency provisions of the Banking Act 2009. The latter are confined to banks as defined by s.91 of that Act, that is, banks that are UK institutions,[52] and building societies within the meaning of s.119 of the Building Societies Act 1986. The insolvency of various other types of company is governed by special legislation.[53]

The rules governing the jurisdiction of English courts in insolvency proceedings are statutory, although to the extent that their application is a matter for the court's discretion, the criteria for the exercise of that discretion have been developed by case law. In relation to the winding up of foreign companies in particular, the courts have shown a reluctance to encroach on the jurisdiction of the foreign courts in the absence of a close connection between the debtor company and England, applying a test of close connection built up by the cases. The existence of a statutory basis of jurisdiction is thus to be regarded as a minimum requirement.

Common law conflict of laws rules

16–15   Finally, there are common law conflict of laws rules which continue to exist independently of any statutory underpinning as regards: (i) the recognition of foreign judgments in cases not governed by the EC Regulation; and (ii) the provision of assistance to foreign courts, although the latter takes effect subject to s.426 of the Insolvency Act. In summary, the hierarchical order is:

(1)   the Insolvency Regulation;

(2)   the Model Law and related provisions of the Cross-Border Insolvency Regulations, supplemented by s.426 of the Insolvency Act;

(3)   other UK statutes governing the insolvency of companies; and

---

[52] A UK institution is an institution incorporated in, or formed under, the law of any part of the UK (s.91(3)).
[53] See above, para.1–60.

(4)   the common law conflict of laws rules relating to the recognition of for-
      eign judgments in insolvency proceedings and to the provision of assis-
      tance so far as not displaced by s.426.

However, what is puzzling is the reference in the Cross-Border Insolvency   **16–16**
Regulations to a possible conflict between Pt III of the Insolvency Act 1986
and the provisions of the regulations. As stated above, the regulations are
confined to the Model Law and matters arising from its application, while
Pt III concerns the appointment of a receiver, which is not a collective insolvency proceeding and is therefore outside the Model Law altogether and is
for that very reason excluded from the scope of "British insolvency law".
Accordingly, there appears to be nothing in the regulations which is in any
way applicable to receivership, and if this be right there is no possibility of
conflict between Pt III and the regulations.

(i) The UNCITRAL Model Law

The UNCITRAL Model Law on Cross-Border Insolvency is the product of   **16–17**
collaboration between the UN Commission on International Trade Law and
INSOL International,[54] which held a series of joint international meetings to
examine prospects for the harmonisation of rules on cross-border insolvency.[55] Adopted in 1997, the Model Law is designed to provide a har-
monised approach to the treatment of cross-border insolvency proceedings
in national legal systems and to facilitate co-operation between courts and
office holders involved in the same insolvency in different jurisdictions and
provide for the mutual recognition of judgments and direct access of foreign
representatives to the courts of the enacting State.[56] It has been adopted by
a growing number of States, including Great Britain and Northern Ireland.[57]
The Model Law represents a huge accomplishment on the part of
UNCITRAL and all of the other organisations and individuals involved,
making a major contribution to cross-border co-operation and co-ordination

---

[54] The International Association of Insolvency Practitioners.
[55] See in particular Report on UNCITRAL-INSOL Colloquium on Cross-Border Insolvency,
1994, UNCITRAL, 27th Sess., at 2, UN Doc.A/CN.9/398(1994), also reproduced in [1995] 4
International Insolvency Review, Special Conference Issue, and the subsequent Report on
the 4th UNCITRAL-INSOL Judicial Colloquium on Cross-Border Insolvency, 2001,
UNCITRAL, 35th Sess., at 8, UN Doc.A/CN.9/518 (2002).
[56] See UNCITRAL Model Law on Cross-Border Insolvency with Guide to Enactment.
[57] There are separate regulations for Great Britain and Northern Ireland (see below,
para.16–21). To date, legislation based on the Model Law has been adopted by 19 jurisdictions, namely Australia (2008), British Virgin Islands (overseas territory of the UK) (2003),
Canada (2009), Colombia (2006), Eritrea (1998), Great Britain (2006), Greece (2010), Japan
(2000), Mauritius (2009), Mexico (2000), Montenegro (2002), New Zealand (2006), Northern
Ireland (2007), Poland (2003), Republic of Korea (2006), Romania (2003), Serbia (2004),
Slovenia (2007), South Africa (2000) and the US (2005).

in insolvency proceedings, while at the same time respecting national procedural and judicial systems.

Nature of the Model Law

16–18   A model law is simply that: a law which in itself has no binding force and which states are free to reject, adopt in its entirety or expand or modify at will. Different States use a model law in different ways. Some enact it virtually as it stands; some adopt the bulk of the provisions but introduce their own additions and amendments, either to suit local conditions or because—sometimes rather rashly—they assume they can improve on the drafting or the substance; and some look to the model law simply for ideas for their own legislation drafted for their own purposes. This last was the approach adopted in the field of commercial arbitration by the UK Arbitration Act 1996, which did not enact the UNCITRAL Model Law on international commercial arbitration but drew significantly on many of its basic concepts. These different approaches inevitably tend to weaken the harmonisation which the model law is intended to achieve and make it difficult to give meaning to the statement that a given number of States have adopted a particular model law. Nevertheless, the UNCITRAL Model Law seems set for a significant degree of successful adoption.

Overall reach of the Model Law

16–19   The Model Law is engaged where there are insolvency proceedings in one state and assistance is sought in another State or there are concurrent insolvency proceedings in two or more States or a creditor in one State seeks to commence or participate in insolvency proceedings in another State.

> "The four cornerstones of the Model Law can be represented by four primary concepts: Access; Recognition; Relief; and Co-operation."[58]

The effect so far as this country is concerned is that a foreign representative[59] is entitled to direct access to the British courts and can apply for recognition of foreign main or non-main proceedings[60] and for assistance,[61] while a similar facility is provided to British representatives appointed in British insolvency proceedings as regards applications to foreign courts in jurisdictions that

---

[58] Fletcher, *Insolvency in Private International Law*, 2006, para.8.17. For a comparative survey, see Look Chan Ho, *Cross-Border Insolvency: A Commentary on the UNCITRAL Model Law*, 2nd edn (London: Globe Business Publishing, 2009).

[59] See para.16–33.

[60] See para.16–34.

[61] See para.16–43.

have adopted the Model Law.[62] Where there are parallel proceedings in different jurisdictions, the Model Law provides for co-operation between their respective courts.[63] Finally, foreign creditors have the same rights regarding commencement of, and participation in, a proceeding under British insolvency law as creditors in Great Britain.[64]

The provisions always have to be read from the perspective of the State that has adopted the Model Law ("the enacting State"). A proceeding in the other State is a "foreign proceeding" as defined in art.2. That State may or may not have enacted the Model Law but this is irrelevant where assistance is sought from the courts of the enacting State, or foreign creditors desire to initiate or participate in proceedings in the enacting State, except where, in adopting the Model Law, the enacting State has imposed a condition of reciprocity. Great Britain has not imposed any such condition. This means that foreign courts and foreign insolvency office holders in a State that has not adopted the Model Law are nevertheless free to invoke it in Great Britain even though no such rights are given to British courts and officeholders in that State. Most of the provisions of the Model Law do not apply at all unless there is a foreign proceeding. However, this is not true as regards the rights of foreign creditors[65] to institute or participate in insolvency proceedings in the enacting State to the same extent as local creditors[66] and, where they are known, to be individually notified of insolvency proceedings in the enacting state whenever local creditors would be so notified.[67] Such rights are not dependent on the opening of foreign proceedings.

We have seen that the Insolvency Regulation distinguishes between foreign main proceedings, which can only be brought in the jurisdiction where the debtor has its COMI, and territorial proceedings,[68] which are confined to jurisdictions where the debtor has an establishment and are limited to assets within the local jurisdiction. A similar distinction is drawn by the UNCITRAL Model Law, except that it uses the label "foreign non-main proceeding" instead of "territorial proceeding".[69]

Model Law is purely procedural

The Model Law, while obviously having important effects on the grant of relief, is a purely procedural law. It contains no rules of substantive law, **16–20**

---

[62] See para.16–23.
[63] See paras 16–44, 16–58 et seq.
[64] See para.16–40.
[65] The phrase "foreign creditors" is not defined but would appear to denote creditors not having a place of business in the enacting State.
[66] See art.13. See below, para.16–40.
[67] See art.14. See below, para.16–40.
[68] See above, para.15–60.
[69] As to whether this dichotomy is exhaustive, see below, para.16–31.

whether relating to insolvency or otherwise, these being within the exclusive province of national laws and national courts. Nor does it have any conflict-of-laws rules. In this respect, it differs markedly from the EC Insolvency Regulation. So where a foreign representative or foreign creditor brings proceedings in the enacting State to avoid a transaction as being, for example, a transaction at an undervalue or a preference, it is for the court in the enacting State to determine, first, whether the relief sought is one that would be available to an office holder appointed under its own insolvency law[70] and, secondly, under its own conflict rules, what law governs the power of avoidance. Moreover, there is only one rule limiting jurisdiction, namely that after recognition of a foreign main proceeding, a proceeding under the insolvency laws of the enacting State may be commenced only if the debtor has assets in that State and must be restricted to local assets.[71] With this exception, the courts of the enacting State are free to apply their own jurisdiction rules.

The Model Law in Great Britain[72]

16–21   As noted earlier, the Model Law now applies throughout the United Kingdom. However, its provisions vary somewhat as between the three parts of the United Kingdom—England and Wales, Scotland and Northern Ireland—to reflect differences in the existing insolvency legislation in the three parts. Moreover, there are separate implementing regulations for Great Britain and Northern Ireland.[73] Since this work is concerned with English corporate insolvency law, the rest of this section analyses the Model Law in the form in which it has been given effect in England under the Cross-Border Insolvency Regulations 2006. The text of the Model Law as so embodied is contained in Sch.1 to the Regulations and is referred to hereafter simply as "the Model Law". The text produced by UNCITRAL itself is referred to as "the UNCITRAL Model Law". The principal deviations from the UNCITRAL Law are as follows:

(1)   in the definition of "establishment", the word "goods" has been replaced by "assets"[74];

(2)   there are provisions relating to purely internal jurisdiction within the United Kingdom[75];

---

[70] Which is a prerequisite for the grant of any form of relief not listed in art.21(1)(a)–(f). See Art.21(1)(g).

[71] See art.28.

[72] See Fletcher, *Law of Insolvency*, 4th edn (London: Sweet & Maxwell, 2009), Ch.32; and *Insolvency in Private International Law*, 2006, Supplement.

[73] See above, n.48.

[74] See below, para.16–27.

[75] See art.4.

(3) assistance of foreign representatives is limited to foreign representatives in main or non-main proceedings,[76] as envisaged in the UNCITRAL Guide[77];

(4) substantial additions and amendments have been made to art.23, dealing with actions to avoid acts detrimental to creditors;

(5) the duty of co-operation imposed on a British insolvency officeholder under art.26 is qualified so as to apply only to the extent consistent with his other duties under the law of Great Britain; and

(6) in contrast to the position under the UNCITRAL Model Law, recognition of a foreign main proceeding does not preclude the *commencement* of insolvency proceedings in Great Britain under its ordinary jurisdictional rules, even if the debtor company has no assets in Great Britain. However, in so far as the debtor's assets are concerned, the *effect* of the proceeding is limited in the same terms as in art.28 of the UNCITRAL Model Law.

Interpretation

Reg 2(2) of the Regulations provides rules of interpretation of the Model Law as set out in Sch.1:   **16–22**

"Without prejudice to any practice of the courts as to the matters which may be considered apart from this paragraph, the following documents may be considered in ascertaining the meaning or effect of any provision of the UNCITRAL Model Law as set out in Schedule 1 to these Regulations—

(a) the UNCITRAL Model Law;
(b) any documents of the United Nations Commission on International Trade Law and its working group relating to the preparation of the Model Law; and
(c) the Guide to Enactment of the UNCITRAL Model Law (UNCITRAL document A/CN.9/442) prepared at the request of the United Nations Commission on International Trade Law made in May 1977."

The reference to the UNCITRAL Model Law itself is necessary because of art.8, which contains a now standard provision in private law conventions:

"In the interpretation of this Law, regard is to be had to its international origin and the need to promote uniformity in its application and the observance of good faith."

---

[76] See art.11.
[77] Guide to Enactment of the Model Law, para.[98].

So an English court will have regard to art.8, the *travaux préparatoires* and UNCITRAL's own Guide to Enactment of the Model Law (hereafter, "the UNCITRAL Guide"). But this list is not exhaustive. Under the general practice of the courts, regard will also be had to the decisions of foreign courts on the interpretation of the UNCITRAL Model Law and to the writings of scholars. Moreover, in deciding on the debtor's COMI for the purposes of the Model Law, the courts will almost certainly consider case law on the COMI under the EC Insolvency Regulation, whether of the European Court of Justice (ECJ) or of UK or other national courts, although even decisions of the ECJ are not binding in non-EU cases concerning the Model Law and the possibility of conflict cannot be wholly disregarded. It is said that courts in the United States,[78] in particular, have a different approach to the registered office presumption, adopting more of a "command and control" test in discerning where the COMI is located,[79] but it is thought that the difference is one of emphasis more than of the criteria to be applied, for US courts, like their European counterparts, attach importance to the visibility of the asserted COMI to third party creditors, so that the distinction would appear to lie in the greater willingness of US courts to treat the presumption in favour of the registered as rebutted, since instead of providing for the presumption to apply in the absence of "proof" to the contrary, the US Bankruptcy Code provision refers to "evidence" to the contrary.[80]

Sphere of application

16–23   Article 1(1) of the Model Law as set out in Sch.1 to the Cross-Border Insolvency Regulations defines the sphere of application of the Model Law in the following terms:

> "This Law applies where:
>
> (a)   assistance is sought in Great Britain by a foreign court or a foreign representative in connection with a foreign proceeding; or
>
> (b)   assistance is sought in a foreign State in connection with a proceeding under British insolvency law; or
>
> (c)   a foreign proceeding and a proceeding under British insolvency law in respect of the same debtor are taking place concurrently; or

---

[78] Which has enacted the Model Law as Ch.15 of the US Federal Bankruptcy Code. A number of schemes of arrangement where the debtor company is not in administration or liquidation have been recognised under Ch.15, thus giving such schemes the benefit of a US-enforced moratorium.

[79] Janis Sarra, "Oversight and Financing of Cross-Border Enterprise Group Insolvency Proceedings" 44 Texas Int'l L.J. 547, 558 (2008–2009).

[80] Certainly this difference in wording was considered by Lewison J. in *Re Stanford Bank International Ltd* [2009] 3 W.L.R. 941 at [65] to be a possible explanation of what he saw as the divergence of approaches but the Court of Appeal [2011] Ch. 33 took a different view on the question where there was such a divergence.

(d)　creditors or other interested persons in a foreign State have an interest in requesting the commencement of, or participating in, a proceeding under British insolvency law."

However, art.1(2) excludes 13 categories of person from the application of the Model Law. They include building societies, UK and EEA credit institutions and branches, third country credit institutions, and UK and EEA insurers and reinsurers. In most cases, the excluded categories have their own statutory insolvency regimes. Article 1(2) has a twofold effect. It precludes British courts from applying the Model Law in Great Britain to a debtor falling within one of the excluded categories and as a corollary it prevents co-operation with the courts or insolvency officeholders of a foreign State under arts 25 to 27 and 30 of the Model Law, although such co-operation may be available at common law or under s.426 of the Insolvency Act 1986.

Restriction of court's powers

Even in cases within the scope of the Model Law, the court is precluded from granting relief, or modifying relief already granted, or providing any co-operation or coordination under the Model Law, to the extent that such relief or modified relief or co-operation or co-ordination would:

16–24

(1)　be prohibited under or by virtue of Pt 7 of the Companies Act 1989, Pt 3 of the Financial Markets and Insolvency (Settlement Finality) Regulations 1999 or Pt 3 of the Financial Collateral Arrangements (No.2) Regulations 2003, in the case of a proceeding under British insolvency law; or

(2)　interfere with or be inconsistent with any rights of a collateral taker under Pt 4 of the 2003 regulations which could be exercised in the case of such a proceeding.[81]

This limitation on the grant of relief reflects the subordination of the Model Law to EC law and regulations giving effect to EC law. Further restrictions on the court's power to grant relief are imposed in relation to a foreign proceeding regarding a debtor who is an insured in accordance with the provisions of the Third Parties (Rights against Insurers) Act 1930.[82] In addition, any suspension under the Model Law of the right to transfer, encumber or otherwise dispose of any of the debtor's assets is restricted.[83]

---

[81] See art.1(4).
[82] See art.1(5). The 1930 Act is prospectively repealed by the Third Parties (Rights against Insurers) Act 2010. See above, para.6–24.
[83] See art.1(6).

Some definitions

16–25   Article 2 of the Model Law contains a series of definitions. Several of these do not feature in the UNCITRAL Model Law itself but are borrowed from or are relevant to UK legislation, and reference will be made to these later as necessary. There are, however, five key definitions which reproduce those of the UNCITRAL Model Law verbatim except that in the definition of establishment "goods" is replaced by "assets". These definitions are contained in paras (a) and (e) to (j) of art.2:

"For the purposes of this Law:

(a) 'British insolvency law' means

(i) in relation to England and Wales, provision extending to England and Wales and made by or under the Insolvency Act 1986 (with the exception of Part 3 of that Act) or by or under that Act as extended or applied by or under any other enactment (excluding these Regulations); and

(ii) in relation to Scotland, provision extending to Scotland and made by or under the Insolvency Act 1986 (with the exception of Part 3 of that Act), the Bankruptcy (Scotland) Act 1985 or by or under those Acts as extended or applied by or under any other enactment (excluding these Regulations);

. . .

(e) 'establishment' means any place of operations where the debtor carries out a non-transitory economic activity with human means and assets or services;

(f) 'foreign court' means a judicial or other authority competent to control or supervise a foreign proceeding;

(g) 'foreign main proceeding' means a foreign proceeding taking place in the State where the debtor has the centre of its main interests;

(h) 'foreign non-main proceeding' means a foreign proceeding, other than a foreign main proceeding, taking place in a State where the debtor has an establishment within the meaning of subparagraph (e) of this article;

(i) 'foreign proceeding' means a collective judicial or administrative proceeding in a foreign State, including an interim proceeding, pursuant to a law relating to insolvency in which proceeding the assets and affairs of the debtor are subject to control or supervision by a foreign court, for the purpose of reorganization or liquidation;

(j) 'foreign representative' means a person or body, including one appointed on an interim basis, authorised in a foreign proceeding to administer the reorganisation or the liquidation of the debtor's assets or affairs or to act as a representative of the foreign proceeding."

In addition, art.2(q) defines "the law of Great Britain":

"... references to the law of Great Britain include a reference to the law of either part of Great Britain (including its rules of private international law)."

The inclusion of rules of private international law[84] in designating a legal system may be thought unusual nowadays but it needs to be borne in mind that the various provisions referring to the law of Great Britain[85] do not embody choice of law rules: they simply subject certain rules of the Model Law to what is applicable under the law of Great Britain. Moreover, this is not new. Section 426(5) of the Insolvency Act 1986 also refers to rules of private international law. The particular provisions likely to engage English private international law are those relating to applications by a foreign representative for relief under art.21(1)(g) and (2) and for avoidance of transactions under the avoidance provisions of the Insolvency Act, the latter being modified to refer to the opening of the foreign insolvency proceedings rather than the proceedings in England.

"British insolvency law"

By "British insolvency law" is meant provision extending to England and Wales or Scotland and made by or under the Insolvency Act 1986 (with the exception of Pt III) or by or under that Act as extended by or under any other enactment apart from the Regulations themselves.[86] Part III, dealing with receivership, is excluded because this is not a collective proceeding. The rest of the Insolvency Act, together with the Insolvency Rules, forms part of British insolvency law. But the provisions of the Companies Act 2006 dealing with schemes of arrangement are not included in the definition of British insolvency law, since these are not provisions dealing with insolvency as such, although they are not infrequently utilised in the restructuring of an insolvent company. More surprisingly, the Company Directors Disqualification Act 1986 falls outside the definition of British insolvency law even as regards those provisions triggered by insolvency proceedings.   **16–26**

"Establishment"

The definition of "establishment" follows that contained in the UNCITRAL Model Law except that "goods" is replaced by "assets", thus covering not only goods but land and intangible property. So the essential elements are: **16–27**

---

[84] That is, the rules of private international law of England and Wales or Scotland. There is no such thing as "British" private international law.

[85] See arts 14(3)(c), 20(2)(b), 21(1)(g) (2), 23, 24, 28 and 29.

[86] Cross-Border Insolvency Regulations 2006 Sch.1 art.2.

(i) the carrying out of a non-transitory activity; (ii) with human means; and (iii) with assets or services. So the mere presence of assets without any activity does not suffice, nor does the location in Great Britain of the business premises of a subsidiary.[87]

"Foreign main proceeding"

16–28 This is defined in art.2(g) as a foreign proceeding taking place in the State where the debtor has its COMI. As under the Insolvency Regulation, this is presumed to be the debtor's registered office in the absence of proof to the contrary.[88] The Model Law, like the Insolvency Regulation, does not define the COMI, although as we have seen there is now a considerable volume of case law on what constitutes the debtor's COMI for the purposes of the Insolvency Regulation.[89] Recital 13 of the Insolvency Regulation states that the centre of main interests should correspond to the place where the debtor conducts the administration of his interests on a regular basis *and is therefore ascertainable by third parties* [emphasis added]. This requirement of ascertainability by third parties has been much emphasised in the COMI case law, but the Model Law contains no express equivalent. However, this does not seem to be significant, since Recital 13 was itself drawn from the Virgós-Schmit Report on the Insolvency Convention,[90] and the Convention likewise made no express mention of visibility to third parties. It is therefore no surprise that in *Re Stanford International Bank Ltd*,[91] the Court of Appeal concluded that the element of ascertainability by third parties remains as important for the purposes of the Model Law as it is for the purposes of the Insolvency Regulation.

"Foreign non-main proceeding"

16–29 This is defined as a foreign proceeding, other than a foreign main proceeding, where the debtor has an establishment within the meaning of art.2(e).[92] In contrast to the position under the Insolvency Regulation as regards territorial proceedings, which can only be opened where the debtor has its COMI in an EU Member State, a foreign non-main proceeding may be opened under the Model Law whether or not the debtor has a COMI in a

---

[87] See above, para.15–62.
[88] See art.16(3).
[89] See above, para.15–49.
[90] "Report on the Convention on Insolvency Proceedings", para.75. See above, para.15–49.
[91] [2010] 3 W.L.R. 941, affirming the decision of Lewison J. [2009] B.P.I.R. 1157 applying the ECJ's decision in *Eurofood* to the determination of the debtor's COMI for the purposes of the Model Law. US cases take a somewhat different approach, treating the presumption in favour of the registered office as more readily displaced. See above, para.16–22.
[92] See above, para.16–27.

state that has adopted the Model Law. There may be separate non-main proceedings in every State in which the debtor has an establishment other than the State in which it has its COMI.

"Foreign proceeding"

Nature of foreign proceeding

Article 2(i) provides as follows: **16–30**

> ". . . 'foreign proceeding' means a collective judicial or administrative proceeding in a foreign State, including an interim proceeding, pursuant to a law relating to insolvency in which proceeding the assets and affairs of the debtor are subject to control or supervision by a foreign court, for the purpose of reorganisation or liquidation."

This definition of a foreign proceeding is relevant to the ability to recognise and give assistance to a foreign court or a foreign insolvency officeholder. So whether a proceeding is a foreign proceeding is relevant from the perspective of British courts to determine whether a proceeding opened abroad can be recognised and access to the courts given to a foreign insolvency officeholder and, from a foreign court's perspective, to decide whether it can recognise British proceedings and allow a British insolvency officeholder access to the court. In order for a proceeding to qualify as a foreign proceeding for the purposes of the Model Law, it must, of course, be a proceeding which from the perspective of the court of the forum is a proceeding in a foreign State, in addition to which four conditions must be satisfied. Useful guidance on each of these has recently been given by the Court of Appeal in *Re Stanford Banking International Ltd*,[93] as noted below.

(1) The proceeding must be a collective judicial or administrative proceeding, that is, it must be one that is concerned with the interests of the creditors collectively.[94] So the assistance of foreign courts could be invoked as regards administration, winding up, provisional liquidation or company voluntary arrangements but not administrative receivership, which, in the limited cases in which it is now available, is for the benefit of the secured creditor appointing the administrative receiver, not for the benefit of creditors generally. For the same reason, the appointment of a Law of Property Act receiver is not covered by the Model Law. Moreover, the Model Law does not apply in relation to out-of-court

---

[93] [2010] 3 W.L.R. 941.
[94] See also *Rubin v. Eurofinance SA* [2011] 2 W.L.R. 121.

appointments of receivers, since such appointments are not judicial or administrative proceedings.[95]

(2) The proceeding must be one taking place pursuant to a law relating to insolvency. For this purpose, various provisions of the Company Directors Disqualification Act 1986 arising in an insolvency context form part of the law relating to insolvency.[96] The Court of Appeal has held that the "law relating to insolvency" does not have to be statutory nor, if it is, does it have to relate exclusively to insolvency.[97] But the appointment of a receiver by way of equitable relief for the protection of investors in proceedings relating to securities fraud does not suffice as a proceeding under a law relating to insolvency, even though the court may subsequently make orders bringing insolvency proceedings into force; it is only when the principles of law and equity are activated that they can be said to relate to insolvency.[98]

Similarly, proceedings for approval of a scheme of arrangement under s.899 of the Companies Act 2006 in respect of a solvent company (whether within or outside winding up) are not proceedings under the law relating to insolvency, even though such a scheme requires the consent of 75 per cent in value of creditors present and voting at the requisite meeting, since although the proceedings are collective, they do not relate to insolvency law. On the other hand, it is thought that where the application for approval is made in relation to an insolvent company by a liquidator or an administrator, a foreign court should recognise the proceeding as being pursuant to insolvency law even though it is brought under the Companies Act and not the Insolvency Act, because the purpose of the condition is to exclude a collective proceeding relating to a solvent company, not to require that the proceeding itself be prescribed by a law specifically concerned with insolvency. Similar considerations apply to the question whether from a British court's perspective a proceeding is to be characterised as a foreign proceeding.[99]

(3) The proceeding must be one in which the assets and affairs of the debtor are subject to judicial control or supervision. However, it is not necessary that the debtor be divested of management powers; it

---

[95] Receivership, whether administrative or otherwise, also does not fulfil the other conditions set out below.

[96] Insolvency Act 1986 s.426(10).

[97] *Re Stanford International Bank*, cited above n.93.

[98] *Re Stanford International Bank Ltd*. The case also concerned the making of a restraint order under the Proceeds of Crime Act 2002 (see above, para.3–09) as extended to an external request made by an overseas authority under the Proceeds of Crime Act 2002 (External Requests and Orders) Order 2005 (SI 2005/3181) to prevent dealings with relevant property.

[99] See also Fletcher, *Insolvency in Private International Law*, 2006, Supplement to 2nd edn, para.8.89.

suffices that the court exercises overall supervision. So the "debtor in possession" provided for in Ch.11 of the US Federal Bankruptcy Act is accommodated within the concept of a foreign proceeding.[100]

(4) The purpose of the proceeding must be reorganisation or liquidation. A suit designed to secure the preservation of assets for allegedly defrauded investors is not such a proceeding.[101]

While a proceeding will be a foreign proceeding if it fulfils the above four conditions, one further element is required if the foreign proceeding is to qualify for recognition and the provision of assistance, namely that it is either a main or a non-main proceeding.[102]

Proceedings instituted by a foreign insolvency officeholder for recovery of assets or damages against third parties under claims arising prior to the insolvency proceedings will not be regarded as fulfilling any of the first three conditions, since they are not collective proceedings, they are based on the general law, not on the law relating to insolvency and they are not proceedings in which the debtor's assets or affairs are subject to judicial control or supervision. Reference has already been made to decisions to that effect in respect of the EC Insolvency Regulation holding that such proceedings are not derived directly from or closely connected with the insolvency proceedings.[103]

However, claims based on statutory avoidance provisions of the kind exemplified in ss.238 and 239 of the Insolvency Act 1986 flow from the insolvency proceedings themselves and are not independent pre-insolvency claims. They therefore qualify for recognition under the UNCITRAL Model Law even though made in proceedings separate from the insolvency proceedings. This is well illustrated by the Court of Appeal's decision in *Rubin v Eurofinance SA*,[104] in which the facts were as follows:

> The applicants were appointed by the High Court as receivers and managers of a business trust, TCT, which had failed. Eurofinance, which had set up TCT, decided to apply on its behalf for relief under Chapter 11 of the US Federal Bankruptcy Code and meanwhile obtained an order from the English High Court appointing the applicants as joint receivers and managers of TCT, the trustees of which undertook to assist them in regard to the prospective Chapter 11 proceedings. The bankruptcy court, in approving the Chapter 11, appointed the applicants as foreign representatives of TCT, authorising them to apply to the High Court for recognition

---

[100] UNCITRAL Guide, para.24.
[101] *Re Stanford International Bank Ltd*, cited above n.93.
[102] See below, para.16–32.
[103] See above, para.15–34.
[104] [2011] 2 W.L.R. 121.

of the Chapter 11 proceedings as a foreign main proceeding and to seek assistance of the High Court under the Cross-Border Insolvency Regulations in (*inter alia*) the enforcement of judgments of the bankruptcy court that might be obtained against persons and entities residing or owning property in Great Britain. Adversary proceedings were later brought in the bankruptcy court against Eurofinance and others on the basis, first, that they were general business partners of TCT and as such liable for its debts as well as for breach of fiduciary duty and negligence, and, secondly, that there were rights of recovery for unjust enrichment and restitution and various avoidance provisions of US insolvency legislation, and judgment was given against them in default of defence. The applicants then applied for recognition of the US adversary proceedings and enforcement of the judgment of the bankruptcy court as if it were a judgment of the High Court. For that purpose they relied on the Model Law, since it was not in dispute that none of the grounds recognised by the English conflict of laws as giving a US court *in personam* jurisdiction were applicable.

The respondents opposed the application on various grounds, in particular that the proceedings against the respondents were not part of the collective bankruptcy proceeding, nor were they brought 'pursuant to a law relating to insolvency;' and the court could not enforce a foreign judgment given against defendants out of the jurisdiction, contrary to English conflict of laws rules.

Held: the proceedings against the third parties were part and parcel of the Chapter 11 proceedings and in any event were brought pursuant to a law relating to insolvency. But the order made in the adversary proceedings was not concerned with fairness of distribution of assets among creditors but was an ordinary judgment *in personam*, which could not be enforced as judgment of the High Court.

On the first point, the original judgment was open to the objection that it failed to distinguish claims for the enforcement of ordinary debts, which the ECJ's jurisprudence has established do not flow from the insolvency proceedings at all, from claims based on insolvency law, such as fraudulent conveyances and fraudulent transfers. However, on the hearing of the appeal the appellants withdrew their application in respect of all claims except those based on US insolvency law. On the second point, the Court of Appeal reversed the decision of the trial judge, holding that the ordinary rules precluding the enforcement of foreign *in personam* judgments did not apply to bankruptcy proceedings, that such proceedings included the mechanisms provided by provisions of US bankruptcy law equivalent to those of ss.238 and 239 of the UK Insolvency Act and that the judgments of the New York court should be recognised under the UNCITRAL Model Law and enforced under Pts 70 and 73 of the CPR pursuant to the principle enunciated by the Privy Council in *Cambridge Gas Transportation Corp v Official Committee of*

Unsecured Creditors of Navigator Holdings Plc[105] and the House of Lords in *Re HIH Casualty and General Insurance Ltd.*[106]

Categories of foreign proceeding

The Insolvency Regulation divides all proceedings within its scope into main proceedings and territorial proceedings. The UNCITRAL Model Law refers to main proceedings and non-main proceedings, the latter being the equivalent of territorial proceedings. One might have thought that this dichotomy was similarly exhaustive but that is not the case. Instead of defining "foreign proceeding" as either a main proceeding[107] or a non-main proceeding,[108] art.2 makes no reference to either but provides an independent definition as set out above. "Foreign proceeding" is thus wide enough to cover a proceeding opened in a State where the debtor has neither its centre of main interests nor an establishment. One such case covered by the Model Law is where a foreign main proceeding has been recognised in the enacting State and the debtor, although not having an establishment in that state, has assets there.[109] It is unfortunate that the Model Law does not more clearly define the status of foreign proceedings in a State in which the debtor does not have its centre of main interests or an establishment. We shall return to this question in a moment.

16–31

The status of foreign proceedings that are neither main nor non-main

We have previously seen that the classification of foreign proceedings as main or non-main is not exhaustive, because the definition of foreign proceedings does not require them to be either main or non-main. It has to be said that the position of foreign proceedings that are neither main nor non-main, because they are opened in a jurisdiction where the debtor has neither its COMI nor an establishment, is unclear from the text of the rules and is not clarified by the UNCITRAL Guide. The Model Law does not contain any rules governing the jurisdiction to open foreign proceedings; that is exclusively a matter for the foreign law. So on the face of it, except as otherwise indicated, the provisions of the Model Law apply to all foreign proceedings, even if neither main nor non-main. That is borne out by art.28, which postulates the opening of foreign main proceedings in State A and the opening of

16–32

---

[105] [2007] 1 A.C. 508.
[106] [2008] 3 All E.R. 869.
[107] See para.16–28.
[108] See para.16–29.
[109] See art.28, which is reproduced in the British enactment of the Model Law. See below, para.16–42.

proceedings under art.28 in State B where the debtor has assets but not necessarily an establishment. Of course, in the courts of State B, these would not
be foreign proceedings at all but they would be so considered in State C as an
enacting State if proceedings were opened there and they would have to be
treated as neither main nor non-main foreign proceedings.

The question then is: are there indeed provisions of the Model Law
which apply to foreign proceedings that are neither main nor non-main proceedings, and if so, which? On a natural construction, provisions so applicable include access of foreign representatives and creditors to courts in the
enacting State,[110] application by a foreign representative for recognition of
the foreign proceeding,[111] recognition of a foreign proceeding,[112] urgent
relief pending a decision of an application for recognition,[113] and proceedings under art.28, if the debtor has no establishment there, when viewed
from the perspective of a court in a third State that is an enacting State.
However, art.17(2) requires the foreign proceeding to be recognised as a
main proceeding if taking place in the State where the debtor has its COMI
and as a non-main proceeding if the debtor has an establishment in the foreign State,[114] this being relevant to the forms of relief available, and at least
one commentator has construed art.17(2) as limiting recognition to main
and non-main proceedings.[115] This construction, which is also adopted by the
UNCITRAL Guide,[116] does some violence to art.17(1), which in specifying
the conditions under which recognition is mandatory does not include any
such limitation but it seems more in accord with the general thrust and purpose of the Model Law. If this is correct, the Model Law must be construed
as if its provisions for access of a foreign representative or creditor to courts
in the enacting State, recognition of foreign proceedings in the enacting
State and the grant of provisional and final relief in that State are limited to
cases in which the foreign proceedings are either main or non-main, and thus
cannot be invoked in relation to foreign proceedings opened in a State where
the debtor had neither its COMI nor an establishment. On the other hand,

---

[110] See arts 9 and 11–13.
[111] See art.15.
[112] See art.17.
[113] See art.19.
[114] By implication, this must mean an establishment but not the debtor's COMI. It would have
been better drafting to have referred back to the definitions in art.2(g) and (h).
[115] Jenny Clift, "United Nations Commission on International Trade Law (UNCITRAL): The
UNCITRAL Model Law on Cross-Border Insolvency—A Legislative Framework to
Facilitate Coordination and Co-operation in Cross-Border Insolvency" 12 Tulane J. Int'l and
Comp. Law 307 (2004). This seems to receive some support from Fletcher, *Insolvency in
Private International Law*, 2006, who at para.8-32 remarks that in such cases "the Model law
provides no further assistance or advantages to the foreign representative beyond the bare
recognition of the fact that his appointment has taken place under the law of the foreign
State in question", adding that further assistance is dependent on the law and practice of the
recognising State independently of the provisions of the Model Law.
[116] Paras 73 and 128.

the opening of main proceedings does not preclude proceedings in a State where jurisdiction is solely asset-based.[117]

(2) "Foreign representative"

This means a person or body, including one appointed on an interim basis, authorised in a foreign proceeding to administer the reorganisation or the liquidation of the debtor's assets or affairs or to act as a representative of the foreign proceeding. The status of the foreign representative in a UK court is determined by the law of the foreign State under which he was appointed. Where it is a UK appointee who in relation to a company wishes to be recognised as a foreign representative in proceedings in another State that has enacted the Model Law, he could be the official receiver, a liquidator, a provisional liquidator, an administrator or the supervisor of a voluntary arrangement. The definition of foreign representative is wide enough to cover a foreign representative appointed in any kind of foreign insolvency proceeding, whether main or non-main but as stated above the effect of the substantive provisions of the Model Law is to limit access to foreign representatives appointed under a foreign main or foreign non-main proceeding.

16–33

Recognition of foreign proceeding

No automatic recognition

16–34

Whereas under the EC Insolvency Regulation an insolvency proceeding opened in one Member State is entitled to automatic recognition under another, the Model Law requires an application to be made to a court in the enacting State. Under art.17(1), a foreign proceeding, as defined by art.2(i), must be recognised on the application of a foreign representative, as defined by art.2(j), if the application is accompanied by the documents specified in art.15(2) and has been submitted to the appropriate court designated by the law of the enacting State under art.4. These are the only requirements specified in art.17(1). Nevertheless, as stated earlier, the effect of art.17(2) appears to be that recognition will only be given if a further condition is satisfied, namely that the foreign proceeding is a foreign main or foreign non-main proceeding, so that there is no entitlement to recognition under the Model Law[118] if the foreign proceedings were opened in a State where the debtor does not have either its COMI or an establishment. The fact that

---

[117] See art.28 and below, para.16–42.
[118] There is, of course, nothing to preclude recognition under applicable domestic law rules. See below, para.16–57.

the person against whom a foreign proceeding has been instituted is not an entity recognised by English law is irrelevant; it suffices that it is susceptible to those proceedings under the foreign law in question. Accordingly, a US business trust, although not a legal entity under English law, has been held to constitute a debtor for the purpose of the Model Law.[119]

Conditions for recognition

16–35   According to the UNCITRAL Guide:

> "... the conditions for recognition do not include those that would allow the court considering the application to evaluate the merits of the foreign court's decision by which the proceeding has been commenced or the foreign representative appointed."[120]

On the other hand, it is equally clear that the duty and effect of recognition are much weaker than under the Insolvency Regulation. Article 17 itself requires that the foreign proceeding be a foreign proceeding within the meaning of art.2(i). This means that the court is required to evaluate the character of the foreign proceeding. If the decision or certificate of the foreign court under art.15(2) indicates that the foreign proceeding is a proceeding within art.2(i), the British court is *entitled* so to presume,[121] but is not obliged to do so. Further, while art.17(2) provides that the foreign proceeding shall be recognised as a foreign main proceeding if it is taking place in the State where the debtor has its COMI and as a foreign non-main proceeding if the debtor has an establishment within the meaning of art.2(e) in that State,[122] that too is a judgment for the British court and there is nothing in the Model Law that requires the court to accept the foreign court's decision as to the debtor's COMI or the existence of an establishment within the foreign jurisdiction. Again, while recognition of a foreign main proceeding is, in the absence of evidence to the contrary, proof that the debtor is unable to pay its debts,[123] this is a rebuttable presumption. All of this is in marked contrast to the position under the Insolvency Regulation, where there is an extremely strong duty of recognition and respect for the decision of a court opening main proceedings. Nevertheless, the court is in the ordinary way likely to accord such recognition as a matter of course both in furtherance of the purposes of the Model law and as a matter of international comity.

---

[119] *Rubin v Eurofinance SA* [2011] 2 W.L.R. 121.
[120] Para.125.
[121] See art.16(1).
[122] To which should be added the requirement that the proceeding is not a foreign main proceeding. See art.2(h).
[123] See art.31.

When recognition may be refused

Even if all of the conditions set out in art.17 are fulfilled, the court may refuse to make an order if the grant of recognition would be manifestly contrary to the public policy of the State.[124] So far as English law is concerned, "public policy" should be understood in this context as meaning public policy as applied in an international context,[125] so that recognition should not be refused merely because of some rule of public policy applicable to domestic transactions but should be based on facts that would make it incompatible with fundamental concepts of justice to accord recognition. An example would be where the order commencing the foreign proceeding was made in breach of principles of natural justice, as where the debtor company was not given notice of the proceedings or was denied the opportunity to present its case.[126] The word "manifestly" is designed to send a signal for courts to adopt a restrictive approach to the public policy exception and is now standard in private law conventions.[127]

16–36

Rights given by the Model Law

It is not possible within the compass of this chapter to refer to all of the provisions of the Model Law. The principal rights given by the Model Law are the following:

16–37

(1) Foreign representative's rights of direct access and intervention

Under art.9 a foreign representative is entitled to apply directly to a court in the enacting State. Consequently, he has no need to obtain a licence or other authorisation from a regulator of the enacting State before making an application to the court, nor is he obliged to make such an application through a local insolvency practitioner. The purposes for which a foreign representative may make such an application are set out in subsequent provisions of the Model Law. An application by the foreign representative does not subject him or theforeign assets and affairs of the debtor to the jurisdiction of the

16–38

---

[124] See art.6.
[125] Para.88 of the Guide provides an encouragement to States to adopt an international approach to public policy, and this reflects English law.
[126] For an example under the Insolvency Regulations, see the *Eurofood* case, discussed above, para.15–36.
[127] For a recent example, see art.11(1) of the 2002 Hague Convention on the Law Applicable to Certain Rights in Respect of Securities Held with an Intermediary and the Explanatory Report by Roy Goode, Hideki Kanda and Karl Kreuzer, assisted by Christophe Bernasconi, para.11-6.

courts of the enacting State for any purpose other than the application.[128] But this does not render him immune from jurisdiction on other grounds. This right of access is buttressed by the separate right to intervene in any proceedings in which the debtor is a party.[129] Again, this provision goes only to standing; the foreign representative cannot intervene unless the ordinary requirements for intervention provided by the law of the enacting State are fulfilled.

(2) Foreign representative's right to commence an insolvency proceeding in the enacting State

16–39   Under art.11, the foreign representative has the right to apply to commence a proceeding under the insolvency laws of the enacting State if the conditions for commencing such a proceeding are otherwise met. This right relates purely to the foreign representative's *locus standi*. So if, for example, he were to apply for a winding up order, art.11 ensures that he has standing to do so, but he still has to show the existence of one of the statutory grounds on which a winding up order may be made. In order to make the application, the foreign representative must, of course, have been authorised in a foreign proceeding to administer the reorganisation or the liquidation of the debtor or to act as a representative of the foreign proceeding, this being inherent in the definition of foreign representative.[130] It is not, however, necessary for the foreign proceeding to have received recognition from a court in the enacting State, for urgent steps might be necessary in order to preserve the assets.[131]

(3) Foreign creditors' rights of access and notification

16–40   Under art.13(1), foreign creditors are given the same rights regarding commencement of and participation in a proceeding as creditors in the enacting state. Article 13(1) is not confined to cases where foreign proceedings have been opened. Article 13(2) then goes on to say that art.13(1) does not affect the ranking of claims except that the claims of foreign creditors must not be ranked lower than those of general non-preferential creditors unless an equivalent local claim would be so ranked. This is a curiously placed provision in that it deals with a subject matter entirely different from that covered by art.13(1). Even in a State which treats foreign creditors differently from local creditors, there is no conceivable reason why a right of access should be

---

[128] See art.10.
[129] See art.24.
[130] See art.2(j).
[131] *Guide to Enactment*, para.99.

in any way relevant to the ranking of claims. Article 13(2) would have been better formulated as an entirely separate provision dealing with the ranking of claims.

Article 14 entitles foreign creditors, where known, to be individually notified of insolvency proceedings in the enacting State whenever under its law such notification would be given to local creditors.

(4) Application for recognition of a foreign proceeding

A foreign representative may apply to the court for recognition of the for-   **16–41** eign proceeding in which he has been appointed,[132] the application to be accompanied by the documents specified in art.15(2) and (3).

(6) Effects of recognition of a foreign main proceeding

Recognition of a foreign main proceeding under art.20 produces effects   **16–42** which are automatic, in contrast to the position under art.21, where relief has to be applied for. The automatic effects under art.20 consist of a stay on the commencement or continuance of individual actions or individual proceedings[133] concerning the debtor's assets, rights, obligations or liabilities and on execution against the debtor's assets, and suspension of the right to dispose of the debtor's assets. The automatic stay does not, however, apply to cases falling within any of the exceptions provided by the local law.[134] So under art.20 of the British Model Law, the automatic stay does not affect the right to take any steps to enforce security[135] over the debtor's property or to repossess goods in the debtor's possession under a hire-purchase agreement[136] or the exercise by the creditor of any right of set-off against the debtor's claim. After recognition of a foreign main proceeding, the effects of a proceeding under British insolvency law must, in so far as the debtor's assets are concerned, be confined to assets located in Great Britain and, to the extent necessary to implement co-operation and coordination under arts 25, 26 and 27, to other assets of the debtor that, under the law of Great Britain, should be administered in that proceeding.[137]

---

[132] See art.15(1).
[133] Including arbitration (*Samsun Logix Corp v DEF* [2009] B.P.I.R. 1502).
[134] See art.20(2).
[135] Defined in art.2(n).
[136] "Hire-purchase agreement" includes a conditional sale agreement, a chattel leasing agreement and a retention of title agreement (art.2(k)). This follows the arcane and circuitous definition in s.251 and Sch.B1 para.111 of the Insolvency Act 1986, as to which see above, para.11–63.
[137] See art.28.

(7) Relief at the request of the foreign representative

16–43   Under art.21, relief may be granted as appropriate at the request of the foreign representative where necessary to protect the assets of the debtor or the interests of the creditor and not already effected automatically under art.20. Such request may be made whether the foreign proceedings are main or non-main proceedings. The forms of relief that may be given are wider than those under art.20. Under art.21(1), these are:

(a)   the stay of commencement or continuation of individual actions or individual proceedings concerning the debtor's assets, rights, obligations or liabilities, to the extent that they have not been stayed under art.20(1)(a);

(b)   the stay of execution against the debtor's assets to the extent that execution has not been stayed under art.20(1)(b);

(c)   the suspension of the right to dispose of the debtor's assets to the extent that this right has not already been suspended under art.20(1)(c);

(d)   provision for the examination of witnesses, the taking of evidence or the delivery of information concerning the debtor's assets, affairs, rights, obligations or liabilities;

(e)   the entrustment of the administration, realisation and distribution of all or part of the assets located in Great Britain to the foreign representative or another person designated by the court[138];

(f)   the extension of provisional relief previously granted under art.19(1); and

(g)   the grant of any additional relief that may be available to a British insolvency officeholder under the law of Great Britain, including any relief provided under para.43 of Sch.B1 to the Insolvency Act.

Forms of relief under art.21(1)(a), (b) and (c) are confined to cases where the foreign proceedings are non-main proceedings, because in the case of main proceedings the effects will have been produced automatically under art.20. Paragraph (e), in so far as embodying the principle of universalism, is directed to ensuring as far as possible a uniform and fair system of distribution and does not empower the court to grant an order to enforce a foreign *in personam* judgment for breaches of fiduciary duty and negligence where it would be contrary to the principles of English private international law to enforce the judgment.[139] The effect of para.(g) is that the court can grant a foreign representative a moratorium similar to that available in an adminis-

---

[138] This therefore includes the turnover of assets to the foreign representative.
[139] *Rubin v Eurofinance SA* [2011] 2 W.L.R. 121

tration.[140] Under art.21(2), upon recognition of a foreign proceeding, whether main or non-main, the court may, at the foreign representative's request, entrust the distribution of all or part of the debtor's assets located in Great Britain to the foreign representative or another person designated by the court provided that the court is satisfied that the interests of creditors in Great Britain are adequately protected, as where the foreign assets are more than sufficient to meet preferential claims so that the remitted assets will be applied solely by way of *pari passu* distribution.[141]

In the above cases, it is entirely within the court's discretion whether to grant relief and, if so, what form or forms of relief; and in granting relief the court may impose such conditions as it considers appropriate.[142] Moreover, in granting relief under art.21 to a representative of a foreign non-main proceeding, the court must be satisfied that the relief relates to assets that under the law of Great Britain should be administered in the foreign non-main proceeding or concerns information required in that proceeding.[143] In addition, the court must in all cases be satisfied that, in the case of authorised distributions, the interests of local creditors (including any secured creditors or parties to hire-purchase agreements) and of other interested persons, including if appropriate the debtor, are adequately protected.[144]

The foreign representative also has standing, upon recognition of the foreign proceeding under which he was appointed, to initiate proceedings for the avoidance of transactions under ss.238, 239 and 242 to 245 of the Insolvency Act.[145] Such proceedings may be initiated by the foreign representative even though he is not the insolvency administrator appointed in the insolvency proceedings in the enacting State. But where the foreign main proceeding is a non-main proceeding, the court must be satisfied that under the law of the enacting State an action relating to assets should be administered in the foreign main proceeding.[146]

---

[140] *Samsun Logix Corp v DEF*, cited above n.133. See Look Chan Ho, "Smoothing Cross-Border Insolvency by Synchronising the UNCITRAL Model Law: *In Re Samsun Logix Corporation*" (2009) J.I.F.B.L. 295.

[141] *Re Swissair Schweizerische Luftverkehr-Aktiengesellschaft* [2010] B.C.C. 667., in which the company was in liquidation both in England and Switzerland and the High Court made an order for the remittal of the assets realised by the English liquidators to the Swiss liquidator to be administered as part of the Swiss liquidation. The order was made both under the court's inherent power and under art.21(2). See further para.16–61 as to the court's inherent power.

[142] See art.22(2). It has been argued that art.21(1)(g) would allow an English court to apply foreign insolvency law, for example, the provisions of foreign insolvency law relating to the avoidance of transactions. See Look Chan Ho, "Applying Foreign Law—Realising the Model Law's Potential" [2010] J.I.B.L.R. 552. However, art.21(1)(g) speaks only of "relief", which suggests that it is confined to giving effect to remedies under the foreign law resulting from the foreign court's own application of that law.

[143] See art. 21(3).

[144] See art.22(1).

[145] See art. 23. See generally Ch.13 as to these provisions.

[146] See art.23.

(8) Co-operation with foreign courts and foreign representatives

16–44   Chapter IV of the Model Law is devoted to co-operation and direct communication between a court of the enacting State and foreign courts or foreign
representatives. This is a central plank of the Model Law and is the subject of
a useful UNCITRAL Practice Guide,[147] which amongst other things contains
specimen clauses for inclusion in Protocols ("cross-border insolvency agreements") as well as issues arising in relation to communications between courts.

The provisions of Ch.IV are designed to facilitate communications of all
kinds, in particular: (i) court-to-court communication without time-consuming
formalities such as the issue of letters rogatory; (ii) direct communication
between a foreign representative and a court in the enacting state; and (iii)
communication between a local insolvency administrator and foreign courts or
foreign representatives. This follows the pattern previously established by the
courts without any statutory underpinning through co-operative arrangements
between the insolvency administrators in the different States and between
their respective courts.[148] Co-operation may be implemented by any appropriate means, including the appointment of a person or body to act at the direction of the court, communication of information by any means considered
appropriate by the court, co-ordination of the administration and supervision
of the debtor's assets and affairs, approval or implementation by courts of
agreements concerning the coordination of proceedings, and co-ordination of
concurrent proceedings regarding the same debtor.[149] However, the duty to
co-operate does not go so far as to require an English court to enforce a foreign judgment contrary to the rules of English private international law.[150]

The Model Law does not displace s.426 of the Insolvency Act in the
limited cases in which that section is applicable.[151]

(9) Concurrent proceedings

16–45   Article 29 regulates the situation where there is a foreign proceeding and concurrently a proceeding in Great Britain. The salient principle of art.29 is that
while the commencement of a proceeding in Great Britain does not prevent or
terminate a foreign proceeding, any relief granted or to be granted to the foreign representative must be, or be made, consistent with the relief sought in the
British proceeding. Article 29 thus addresses the situation in which, after a
foreign proceeding has been instituted, two proceedings are brought in Great
Britain: a proceeding for recognition of the foreign proceeding (main or non-
main) and a parallel proceeding under British insolvency law, for example, for

---

[147] *UNCITRAL Practice Guide on Cross-Border Insolvency Co-operation* (2009).
[148] See below, para.16–65.
[149] See art.27.
[150] *Rubin v Eurofinance SA*, cited above n.139.
[151] See para.16–58.

winding up of the debtor company. What happens then depends on whether the parallel proceeding has already been commenced at the time the application for recognition is filed or is not commenced until after that filing. If at the time the parallel proceeding under British insolvency law is commenced the application for recognition is already on foot, any relief granted under art.19 or 21 (which includes the grant of a stay where not already automatic under art.20) must be consistent with the proceeding in Great Britain and if the foreign proceeding is recognised as a foreign main proceeding art.20 is disapplied. If, on the other hand, the application for relief in respect of the foreign proceeding is filed[152] before the commencement of the proceeding under British insolvency law, any relief already granted and in effect under art.19 or 21, and any stay under art.20, must be reviewed by the court and modified or terminated if inconsistent with the proceeding in Great Britain. Finally, in granting or denying relief under art.19 or 21, or in modifying or terminating relief under art.22(3), the court must be satisfied that the interests of the creditors and other interested persons, including the debtor, are adequately protected.[153]

So an English court will not apply a foreign rule that disregards the status as creditors of those treated as creditors under British insolvency law. However, this does not mean that British creditors are given preferential treatment as regards paymnt from local assets; British and foreign creditors must be treated alike.

(10) Presumption of insolvency

In the absence of evidence to the contrary, recognition of a foreign main proceeding is, for the purpose of commencing a proceeding under British insolvency law, proof that the debtor is unable to pay its debts.[154] The presumption of insolvency resulting from recognition of the foreign proceedings is thus rebuttable. A finding in proceedings in the enacting State that the debtor is not insolvent does not involve challenging a finding of insolvency in the foreign proceedings *for the purposes of those proceedings*, which is not permitted; the position is simply that when it comes to proceedings in Great Britain, courts are free to decide for themselves whether, for the purposes of those proceedings, the debtor is insolvent.

16–46

(11) Hotchpot

Finally, art.32 adopts the hotchpot rule referred to below,[155] making it clear that this does not affect secured claims or rights *in rem*, which under English

16–47

---

[152] The time of filing is designated rather than the time of recognition because once the application for recognition has been filed, the foreign representative can apply for the grant of provisional relief under art.19.

[153] See art.22(1).

[154] See art.31.

[155] Below, para.16–63.

law, as we have seen, fall outside the hotchpot rule, this being confined to receipts by the creditor from assets of the debtor, not from realisation of the creditor's own property or security; nor does art.32 affect the ranking of claims.

(ii) Jurisdiction under the Insolvency Act 1986

16–48
The jurisdiction of English courts in insolvency proceedings is governed by the Insolvency Act 1986, the Banking Act 2009 as regards bank insolvency[156] and English conflict of laws rules developed by the courts. Brussels I[157] does not apply to the winding up of insolvent companies, judicial arrangements, compositions and analogous proceedings.[158] This section is concerned with the jurisdictional provisions of the 1986 Act as regards such proceedings in cases unaffected by the EC Insolvency Regulation. Where the Insolvency Regulation applies, this prevails,[159] so that the jurisdiction under the Insolvency Act to open a main proceeding against a debtor company whose COMI is in an EU Member State (other than Denmark) is confined to cases where the debtor has its COMI in the United Kingdom and to open a territorial proceeding to cases where the company has an establishment within the United Kingdom.[160] In no case may the court make a winding up order, appoint a provisional liquidator or make an administration order in relation to an EEA credit institution or any branch of an EEA credit institution other than a UK-regulated credit institution,[161] and while for the purposes of approval of a scheme of arrangement under s.899 of the Companies Act 2006, such an institution or branch is to be treated as a company liable to be wound-up under the Insolvency Act 1986,[162] the court's jurisdiction is exercisable only if various conditions are satisfied.[163]

---

[156] There are numerous other categories of company subject to special insolvency regimes, including insurance companies, water companies and railway companies.
[157] The popular name for Council Regulation (EC) 44/2001 on the recognition and enforcement of judgments in civil and commercial matters ([2001] OJ L12/1), as amended and corrected, which replaced the Convention on Jurisdiction and Enforcement of Judgments in Civil and Commercial Matters 1968, and which as a regulation has direct effect, no UK implementing measure being either necessary or permitted.
[158] See art.1(2)(b). It does, however, apply to the winding up of solvent companies, in relation to which the court of the Member State where the company has its seat has exclusive jurisdiction (art.22(2)).
[159] Insolvency Act 1986 s.117(7).
[160] See generally Ch.15.
[161] Credit Institutions (Reorganisation and Winding Up) Regulations 2004, SI 2004/1045, reg.3. See above, n.14.
[162] Which is a prerequisite of the court's jurisdiction to sanction a compromise or scheme of arrangement not involving reconstruction or amalgamation.
[163] Credit Institutions (Reorganisations and Winding Up) Regulations 2004, reg.4.

Winding up

The winding up provisions of the Insolvency Act 1986 distinguish three **16–49** principal classes of company, namely: (i) a company registered in England and Wales under the Companies Act 2006; (ii) a company registered in Scotland[164]; and (iii) an unregistered company, that is, any association and any company that is not registered in any part of the United Kingdom,[165] including an overseas company.[166] But a distinction has to be drawn between a winding up by the court and a creditors' voluntary winding up.

Winding up by the court

The court's jurisdiction to wind-up a company under the Insolvency Act 1986 **16–50** depends upon the category into which it falls. There is jurisdiction to wind-up any company registered under the Companies Act, whether or not it has assets in this country or, indeed, any assets at all.[167] A company registered in Scotland must be wound-up in Scotland.[168] Under s.221 of the Insolvency Act, the court's jurisdiction to wind-up an overseas company is exercisable even if the company has not established a place of business in the UK and even if it has been dissolved or has otherwise ceased to exist under the law of its incorporation[169] or is being wound-up abroad.[170] The grounds for winding up of an unregistered company are fewer in number than those available for a registered company under s.122 of the Act. An unregistered company may be wound-up only:

"(a) if the company is dissolved, or has ceased to carry on business, or is carrying on business only for the purpose of winding up its affairs;
(b) if the company is unable to pay its debts;

---

[164] If an unregistered company has a principal place of business in Northern Ireland, it may not be wound-up under Pt V of the Insolvency Act unless it has a principal place of business in England and Wales or Scotland (Insolvency Act 1986 s.221(2)). For a discussion of the position regarding Northern Ireland, see Lord Collins of Mapesbury et al. (eds), *Dicey, Morris & Collins on the Conflict of Laws*, 14th edn (London: Sweet & Maxwell, 2010), paras 30-069–30-071.

[165] Insolvency Act 1986 s.220(1), as amended by the Companies Act 2006 (Consequential Amendments, Transitional Provisions and Savings) Order 2009, SI 2009/1941, Sch.1 para.76.

[166] That is, a company incorporated outside the UK (Companies Act 2006 s.1044).

[167] See Insolvency Act 1986 s.117(1) and above, para.5–01.

[168] Insolvency Act 1986 s. 20. As to a company in Northern Ireland, see above, n.164.

[169] Insolvency Act 1986 s.225, enacting a principle already established at common law. Such dissolution is in fact a ground of winding up. See below.

[170] *Re Hibernian Merchants Ltd* [1958] Ch. 76; and *Re Commercial Bank of South Australia* (1886) 33 Ch.D. 174. An unregistered company cannot be put into voluntary winding up except in cases governed by the EC Regulation on insolvency proceedings. See above, para.15–13.

(c) if the court is of opinion that it is just and equitable that the company should be wound up."[171]

However, the court has a discretion whether to make a winding up order and will do so only in accordance with settled principles. The overarching requirement is that there should be a sufficient connection with England. At one time, this was very strictly applied, so that it was considered necessary to show that the company either had a place of business in England when the petition was presented or had previously had a place of business in England.[172] Later, this was held unnecessary so long as the company had assets in England[173] and persons in England claiming to be creditors.[174] By a further extension it was ruled unnecessary for the company itself to hold assets in England so long as there was a right of recovery from another source which would be available to creditors.[175] Finally, even the requirement of assets or recoverable funds was dispensed with. It was held that even if the foreign company had no assets in England, the court could exercise its jurisdiction to wind-up the company whenever: (i) there was a sufficient connection with England; (ii) there was a reasonable possibility of benefit to those presenting the winding up petition; and (iii) one or more persons interested in the distribution of assets was a person(s) over whom the court could exercise jurisdiction.[176] But it has also been said that:

". . . the courts of this country should hesitate very long before subjecting foreign companies with no assets here to the winding up procedures of this country. Of course if a foreign company does have assets in this country, the assets may need to be distributed among creditors, and a winding up order here, sometimes ancillary to a principal winding up in the place of incorporation of the foreign company, may be necessary. But a

---

[171] Insolvency Act 1986 s.221(5).

[172] *Re Lloyd Generale Italiano* (1885) 29 Ch.D. 219.

[173] For this purpose, potential claims under s.213 or 214 of the Insolvency Act 1986 are not considered to be assets (*Re A Company (No.00359 of 1987)* [1988] Ch. 210).

[174] *Re Compania Merabello San Nicholas SA* [1973] Ch. 75.

[175] *Re Eloc Electro-Optiek and Communicatie BV* [1982] Ch. 43 (employees with right of recovery from the redundancy fund under s.122 of the Employment Protection (Consolidation) Act 1978).

[176] *Re Gallery Capital SA*, unreported decision of Norris J. on April 21, 2010 in the High Court of Justice, Chancery Division; *Stocznia Gdanska SA v Latreefers Inc (No.2)* [2001] 2 B.C.L.C. 116; *Re Real Estate Development Co* [1991] B.C.L.C. 210, *per* Knox J. at 217. See also *Re Azoff-Don Commercial Bank* [1954] Ch. 315 (which held that the petitioners need not be within the jurisdiction so long as they were sufficiently connected to it, as by having worked here); *Re A Company (No.00359 of 1987)* [1988] Ch. 210 (where it was pointed out that if the presence of assets were a requirement, the court could be deprived of jurisdiction by the simple expedient of removing the assets). For cases where the connection to England was held insufficient, see *Banco National de Cuba v Cosmos Trading Corp* [2000] 1 B.C.L.C. 813; *Re Titan International Inc* [1998] 1 B.C.L.C. 102; *R. Compania Merabello San Nicholas SA*, cited above n.174; and *Re Wallace Smith & Co Ltd* [1992] B.C.L.C. 970.

winding up order here, while the foreign company continues to trade in its country of incorporation and elsewhere in the world, is in my view thoroughly undesirable. I would not say a winding up order in those circumstances could never be right but I do say that exceptional circumstances and exceptional justification would be necessary. After all, if we presume to make a winding up order in respect of a foreign company which is continuing to trade in its place of incorporation and elsewhere in the world, where will our winding up order be recognised? What effect will it have? These questions are difficult to answer and, absent some international convention regarding the winding up of foreign companies, I think no satisfactory answer can be given.

It is, moreover, somewhat of a weakness in our own winding up law that it is not possible to have a winding up of a foreign company limited to its activities and assets in this jurisdiction. It has been held on a number of occasions, and is clear law, that once a winding up order is made in this jurisdiction it purports to have worldwide effect. Hence the problems that arise if the order is made in respect of a foreign company that is continuing to trade."[177]

In the subsequent decision in *Stocznia Gdanska SA v Latreefers Inc (No.2)*,[178] **16–51**
the Court of Appeal held that this dictum should be followed unless good reason to the contrary was shown. So even the existence of the three elements referred to above as essential to the exercise of the court's discretion will not usually suffice if the company has no assets in England and is continuing to trade in its country of incorporation. But the mere presence of assets in England is not automatically a reason for the court to exercise its winding up jurisdiction.[179]

In all of these decisions, the court found it unnecessary to decide whether the existence of the three elements went to jurisdiction or merely to the exercise of the court's discretion. That point arose fairly and squarely for decision in *Re Drax Holdings Ltd*,[180] where Lawrence Collins J. had to consider whether he had jurisdiction to sanction a scheme of arrangement for a foreign company under s.425 of the Companies Act 1985 (now Pt 26 of the Companies Act 2006). Since under ss.425(6) and 735A of the Act "company" meant any company liable to be wound-up under that Act or the Insolvency Act 1986, and since the factors relevant to winding up did not necessarily apply to a scheme of arrangement, the effect of holding that the three

---

[177] *Banco Nacional de Cuba v Cosmos Trading Corp* [2000] 1 B.C.L.C. 813, *per* Sir Richard Scott V.C. at 819–820. See to similar effect the judgment of Lord Evershed M.R. in *Banque des Marchants de Moscou (Koupetschesky) v Kindersley* [1951] Ch. 112 at 125–126.
[178] Cited above n.176.
[179] *Re OJSC Ank Yugraneft* [2009] 1 B.C.L.C. 298.
[180] [2004] 1 W.L.R. 1049.

elements went to jurisdiction would be to deprive the court of power to approve a scheme if the second or third element was lacking, even if there was a sufficient connection with England and the second and third elements were not relevant to a scheme of arrangement. He therefore held that while the "sufficient connection" test had to be satisfied in all cases, the second and third elements went to discretion, and were not preconditions for the exercise of statutory jurisdiction,[181] and since there was a sufficient connection with England and there were factors showing that it would be legitimate and appropriate for the discretion to be exercised in favour of sanctioning the scheme, an order to that effect would be made.

In *Re Harrods (Buenos Aires) Ltd*[182] it was held that, the jurisdiction being discretionary, the court may invoke the doctrine of forum non conveniens to dismiss a winding up petition. However, in that case the petition was not on the ground of insolvency. Although it has been said that the court should consider whether another jurisdiction is more appropriate for winding up on the ground of insolvency,[183] it is thought that forum non conveniens will rarely apply to an insolvent liquidation, for the concept of an English liquidation running in parallel with and ancillary to a main liquidation elsewhere is well established,[184] so that if the petitioner establishes a sufficient interest in the outcome of winding up proceedings in England and the other requirements necessary for a sufficient connection with England, there will normally be no good reason to apply forum non conveniens.[185]

If a winding up order is made against a foreign company, it will extend to all of the company's assets, both here and abroad.[186]

Creditors' voluntary winding up

16–52   The position in the case of a creditors' voluntary winding up is rather different. An unregistered company cannot be put into a creditors' voluntary winding up except in accordance with the EU Insolvency Regulation,[187] where that applies.

[181] Agreement with this view was expressed by Christopher Clarke J. in *Re OJSC Ank Yugraneft* [2009] 1 B.C.L.C. 298 at [20].
[182] [1992] Ch. 72.
[183] *Re A Company 24 (No.00359 of 1987)* [1988] Ch. 210, *per* Peter Gibson J. at 226.
[184] See below, paras 16–58 and 16–64.
[185] See generally Kate Dawson, "The Doctrine of *Forum Non Conveniens* and the Winding Up of Insolvent Foreign Companies" [2005] J.B.L. 28.
[186] *Re Azoff-Don Commercial Bank* cited above n.176, *per* Wynn-Parry J. at 333; and *Re Bank of Credit and Commerce International SA (No.2)* [1992] B.C.L.C. 570, *per* Sir Nicolas Browne-Wilkinson V.C. at 577.
[187] Insolvency Act 1986 s.221(4). See above, para.5–01.

Administration

An administration order may be against a company as defined by   **16–53**
para.111(1A) of Sch.B1 to the Insolvency Act, namely:

(a)   a company registered under the Companies Act 2006 in England and
Wales or Scotland;

(b)   a company incorporated in an EEA State other than the United
Kingdom; and

(c)   a company not incorporated in an EEA State but having its centre of
main interests in a Member State other than Denmark.

In addition, an administration order can be made against a foreign company
where so requested by a foreign court under s.426 of the Insolvency Act.[188]

Receivership

A similar provision has been inserted into the definition of "company" for   **16–54**
the purpose of Pt III of the Insolvency Act, relating to administrative and
other receivership.[189] Accordingly it is now clear that a receiver cannot be
appointed over a company incorporated in another EEA Member State or
in any other foreign country.[190]

Statutory scheme of arrangement; CVA

Statutory schemes of arrangement under s.899 of the Companies Act 2006   **16–55**
can be made in relation to any company liable to be wound-up under the
Insolvency Act 1986,[191] so that there is jurisdiction to approve a scheme of
arrangement under that section as regards a foreign company so long as
there is a sufficient connection to England.[192] The definition of "company"
in s.1(4) of the Insolvency Act 1986 as regards CVAs is the same as that given
in Sch.B1 para.111(1A) in relation to administration.[193]

---

[188] *Re Dallhold EStates (UK) Pty Ltd* [1992] B.C.L.C. 621.
[189] Insolvency Act 1986 s.28, as substituted by the Companies Act 2006 (Consequential
Amendments, Transitional Provisions and Savings) Order 2009 (SI 2009/1941), Sch.1
para.74. This gives effect to what had always been understood to be the position until *Re
International Bulk Commodities Ltd* [1993] Ch. 77, a decision generally thought to be wrong.
[190] For a sharp criticism of this radical change effected by what purports to be a "consequential"
amendment, see Gabriel Moss, Nick Segal and Ian Fletcher, "A Very 'Consequential'
Amendment: No More Administrative Receivers for Foreign Companies" (2010) 23
Insolvency Intelligence 57.
[191] Companies Act 2006 s.895(2)(b).
[192] See above, para.16–51.
[193] See above, para.16–53.

(iii) Jurisdiction under the Banking Act 2009

16–56 The provisions of the Banking Act 2009 relating to bank insolvency are confined to banks as defined by s.91 of that Act, that is, banks that are UK institutions[194] and building societies as defined by s.119 of the Building Societies Act 1986.[195]

3. FOREIGN INSOLVENCIES AND ENGLISH COURTS

Recognition of foreign insolvency proceedings[196]

16–57 English common law rules on cross-border took some considerable time to develop. Indeed, the common law in this area has been described as "in a state of arrested development".[197] If this was true at the time it was written, it is even more true today. The effect, first, of the EC Insolvency Regulation[198] and, secondly, of the Cross-Border Insolvency Regulations 2006 giving effect to the UNCITRAL Model Law is that even where, in cases outside the Insolvency Regulation, the common law rules do apply, there will rarely be the need to resort to them, because of the provisions of the Model Law. So the scope for the common law rules is largely limited to cases outside the Model Law because of the nature of the insolvency proceeding, for example, receivership or disqualification of a company director under the Company Directors Disqualification Act 1986 in the context of insolvency,[199] or cases excluded from the Model Law because of the character of the debtor company, for example a UK or an EEA bank or other credit institution.[200]

In cases in which resort to the common law rules is available, an English court will recognise the effect of a winding up or dissolution of a foreign com-

---

[194] A UK institution is an institution incorporated in, or formed under, the law of any part of the UK (s.91(3)).
[195] Banking Act 2009 s.84.
[196] See generally Fletcher, *Insolvency in Private International Law*, 2006, and Supplement; and *Law of Insolvency*, 2009, paras 30-054 et seq. and 31-006 et seq.; and Gabriel Moss, Ian Fletcher and Stuart Isaacs, *The EC Regulation on Insolvency Proceedings*, 2nd edn, paras 5.02 et seq.
[197] Ian Fletcher, *Insolvency in Private International Law*, 1st edn (1999), p.93, cited with approval by Lord Hoffmann in *Cambridge Gas Transportation Corp v Official Committee of Unsecured Creditors of Navigator Holdings Plc* [2007] 1 A.C. 508 at [18].
[198] In cases where the debtor has its COMI within the EU (other than Denmark).
[199] See above, para. 16–26.
[200] However, in cases going to the Privy Council by way of appeal from the courts of a British Crown dependency, overseas territory or Commonwealth or former Commonwealth country which has retained the jurisdiction of the Privy Council, English common law principles may still be relevant. See, e.g. *Cambridge Gas Transportation Corp*, cited above n.197 (appeal from a decision of the Manx Court of Appeal).

pany under the law of the State of its incorporation. This common law principle[201] is now implicitly enshrined in s.426(5) of the Insolvency Act relating to the provision of judicial assistance to foreign courts,[202] which flows from the recognition of the foreign proceedings.[203] Similarly, the court will recognise the status of a foreign liquidator[204] and, in principle, his right to be given control of English assets[205] and any title vested in him by the foreign law.[206] Recognition of insolvency proceedings in the State under the law of which the company was incorporated does not mean that an English court will necessarily refuse to recognise a winding up in another State, although in the case of conflict between the law of that State and the law of the State of incorporation an English court can be expected to treat the latter as having priority. Even where foreign insolvency proceedings have been recognised, the court will not give up its right, in concurrent winding up proceedings in England, to control the conduct of its own liquidation.[207] Moreover, the court cannot give effect to or recognise an order of a foreign court or any act of an office-holder appointed under such an order where the making of the order or doing of the act would be prohibited: (i) under Pt VII of the Companies Act 1989,[208] for example, in relation to market contracts or the default rules of a recognised investment exchange or recognised clearing house[209]; or (ii) by Pt 3 of the Financial Collateral Arrangements (No.2) Regulations 2003.[210]

Assistance to foreign parties and foreign courts

A corollary of the principle of recognition of foreign winding up orders and **16–58** the status of foreign liquidators, in cases to which the EC Insolvency Regulation does not apply,[211] is that an English court will give such assistance

---

[201] *Lazard Bros v Midland Bank Ltd* [1933] A.C. 289.

[202] See below, para.16–58.

[203] *Cambridge Gas Transportation Corp*, cited above n.197. However, recognition and assistance are distinct concepts. The fact that foreign insolvency proceedings have been recognised does not necessarily mean that assistance will be given. See below.

[204] *Bank of Ethiopia v National Bank of Egypt* [1937] Ch. 513.

[205] *Felixstowe Dock and Railway Co v United States Lines Inc* [1989] Q.B. 360.

[206] *Dicey, Morris & Collins on the Conflict of Laws*, 2010, r.197. This relates to bankruptcy but there seems to be no reason in principle to treat winding up differently where the effect under the foreign law (contrary to English law) is to vest the property in the foreign liquidator.

[207] *Re English, Scottish and Australian Chartered Bank* [1893] 3 Ch. 385, *per* Vaughan Williams J. at 394. See below, para.16–61.

[208] Companies Act 1989 s.183(2).

[209] Companies Act 1989 ss.158 and 159. See above, para.1–61.

[210] SI 2003/3226 art.15A, inserted by the Financial Markets and Insolvency (Settlement Finality and Financial Collateral Arrangements) (Amendment) Regulations (2010, SI 2010/2993), reg.4(1).

[211] It will be recalled that the Model Law does not limit the court's power to provide additional assistance under other law, i.e. s.426 and the common law (Model Law art.7); indeed, the Model Law refers at various points to s.426 requests.

to a foreign office-holder as is compatible with the application of English insolvency law.[212] This applies not only where there are no concurrent winding up proceedings in England but also where such proceedings are ancillary to a main liquidation in the foreign country.[213] This common law principle, the persistence of which was affirmed by the House of Lords in *Re HIH Casualty and General Insurance Ltd*[214] and by the Privy Council in the earlier decision in *Cambridge Gas Transportation Corp v Official Committee of Unsecured Creditors of Navigator Holdings Plc,*[215] reflects the concept of modified universalism which is now reinforced, albeit in much more restricted fashion, by s.426(4) and (5) of the Insolvency Act[216]:

"(4) The courts having jurisdiction in relation to insolvency law in any part of the United Kingdom shall assist the courts having the corresponding jurisdiction in any other part of the United Kingdom or any relevant country or territory.

(5) For the purposes of subsection (4) a request made to a court in any part of the United Kingdom by a court in any other part of the United Kingdom or in a relevant country or territory is authority for the court to which the request is made to apply, in relation to any matters specified in the request, the insolvency law which is applicable by either court in relation to comparable matters within its jurisdiction.
In exercising its discretion under this subsection, a court shall have regard in particular to the rules of private international law."

Section 426 is both narrower and wider than the common law in regard to the provision of assistance. It is narrower in being limited, as regards non-UK insolvency proceedings, to assistance to courts of "a relevant country or territory".[217] Where the request for assistance comes from a country or territory that is not a relevant country or territory, the court's powers derive exclusively from the common law. Section 426 is wider than the common law in allowing an English court to apply, in relation to the request by the foreign court, the insolvency law applicable by that court.

(1) The insolvency law to be applied

16–59   "Insolvency law" means:

---

[212] *Cambridge Gas Transportation Corp*, cited above n.197; and *Re HIH Casualty* & General Insurance Ltd [2008] 1 W.L.R. 852. For a full discussion, see Fletcher, *Insolvency in Private International Law*, 2006, Ch.4.
[213] See below, para.16–64.
[214] Above, n.212.
[215] Cited above n.197.
[216] See also, in relation to evidence, the Evidence (Proceedings in Other Jurisdictions) Act 1975.
[217] See below.

"(a) in relation to England and Wales, 'provision extending to England and Wales and made by or under this Act or sections 1A, 6 to 10, 12 to 15, 19(c) and 20 (with Schedule 1) of the Company Directors Disqualification Act 1986 and sections 1 to 17of that Act as they apply for the purposes of those provisions of that Act;

. . .

(d) in relation to any relevant country or territory, so much of the law of that country or territory as corresponds to provisions falling within any of the foregoing paragraphs' ',

while "relevant country or territory" means:

"(a) any of the Channel Islands or the Isle of Man, or
(b) any country or territory designated for the purposes of this section by the Secretary of State by order made by statutory instrument."[218]

However, this has been held not to confine the court to those provisions so as to preclude the exercise of its general equitable jurisdiction, for example, to grant a worldwide stay of actions or proceedings by the defendants to a claim.[219] Only three orders have been made by the Secretary of State,[220] and almost all of the designated countries are Commonwealth countries.

It will be noted that s.426 involves a request for assistance from the foreign court; it does not cover requests from a foreign office-holder, which must be dealt with under the wider principles established at common law. The position is otherwise under the Model Law on Cross-Border Insolvency Proceedings.[221]

Section 426(5) gives the English court a discretion whether to apply English law (whether substantive or procedural[222]) or the law of the requesting court, and it is in the exercise of this discretion that the court is required by the last sentence of the subsection to have regard to rules of private international law, by which is meant English conflict of laws rules. This "obscure and ill-thought out provision"[223] has given rise to differences of judicial opinion as to whether the discretion in question is given to the requesting court

---

[218] Insolvency Act 1986 s.426(10) and (11).
[219] *Hughes v Hannover Ruckversicherungs-Aktiengesellschaft* [1997] 1 B.C.L.C. 497.
[220] See the Co-operation of Insolvency Courts (Designation of Relevant Countries and Territories) Order 1986 (SI 1986/2123), the Co-operation of Insolvency Courts (Designation of Relevant Countries) Order 1996 (SI 1996/253) and the Co-operation of Insolvency Courts (Designation of Relevant Country) Order 1998 (SI 1998/2766).
[221] See above, paras 16–38 and 16–39.
[222] *Re Bank of Credit and Commerce International SA* [1993] B.C.C. 787.
[223] *Re Television Trade Rentals Ltd* [2002] B.P.I.R. 859, *per* Lawrence Collins J. at [17].

or the requested court. In the most recent case on the subject, the view has been expressed that the requested court should take the foreign elements into account in deciding what law to apply.[224] Thus, where these point to the application of the foreign law, this may influence the court in deciding to apply that law rather than English law, although the court would seem to retain a discretion as to which law to apply and to disregard the English conflicts rule in an appropriate case.[225]

The discretion to apply English law enables the English court in effect to make orders which could not have been made under the law of the requesting court and to make such orders despite the fact that the foreign office-holder would have no *locus standi* to make application for them in English winding up proceedings. Thus, in *Re Bank of Credit and Commerce International SA (No.9)*,[226] Rattee J. acceded to a request by the Grand Court of the Cayman Islands to make orders under ss.212, 213, 214 and 238 of the Insolvency Act against the Bank of Credit and Commerce International SA, a company incorporated in Luxembourg, on the ground of its participation and/or assistance in the fraudulent activities of the senior management of the BCCI group, which included the Bank of Credit and Commerce International (Overseas) Ltd, a company incorporated in the Cayman Islands.[227] The remarkable effect of s.426 is to expose directors of a foreign company to potential liabilities under English law for activities perfectly lawful under the law of the company's incorporation. It is true, as Rattee J. pointed out, that this could happen only where the courts of both jurisdictions exercised their respective discretions to that effect. Even so, the potential translation of provisions of the UK Insolvency Act into foreign liquidations is striking.

Where the decision is made to apply the insolvency legislation of the other country, so far as corresponding to the provisions of the UK Insolvency Act, then it should be applied in accordance with the principles and practice by which that jurisdiction is exercised by the courts of that country, not in accordance with the rules established under English law in relation to the comparable provisions of the Insolvency Act, which cease to have any relevance once the foreign law has been chosen.[228] Thus, although an English court will not assist in the enforcement of an order which is oppressive, the mere fact that it would be considered oppressive by English law in relation to the relevant provision of an English statute, such as s.236 of the Insolvency Act 1986 dealing with orders for examination of officers of the company, does not mean that it is to be considered oppressive for the purposes of the

---

[224] *Re Television Trade Rentals*, cited above n.223.
[225] See *Dicey, Morris & Collins on the Conflict of Laws*, 2010, pp.1142–1143.
[226] [1993] B.C.C. 787.
[227] The order was subsequently varied by the Court of Appeal but only as regards a different aspect.
[228] *England v Smith* [2001] Ch. 419.

overseas legislation, which may have its own forms of protection against oppression.[229]

(2) Assistance a matter of discretion

There was an apparent division of judicial opinion as to whether the phrase "shall assist" in s.426(4) makes it mandatory for an English court to give assistance. In *Re Dallhold Estates (UK)Pty Ltd*,[230] Chadwick J. held that this was the effect of the subsection and that the only discretion lay with the requesting court as to whether or not to make a request, there being no discretion in the requested court. In *Re Bank of Credit and Commerce International SA (No.9)*,[231] Rattee J. expressed disagreement with that part of the judgment of Chadwick J., and held that the requested court has a discretion whether to apply its own law or that of the requesting court and how it should give such assistance.[232] But the difference of view is more apparent than real, for in a later passage in his judgment Chadwick J. had said, in reference to s.426(4):

16–60

> "Those are mandatory words. It appears to me that their effect is such that, if the conditions set out in para. (b) and (c) of section 8(1) of the 1986 Act are satisfied, then this court ought to make an administration order— and so give the assistance required—*unless there are powerful reasons to the contrary*" [emphasis added].[233]

The general approach of the English courts should be to accede to a foreign court's request for assistance.[234] However, the court has a complete discretion and its reasons for withholding assistance are not limited to reasons of public policy.[235] In the subsequent decision in *Re Focus Insurance Co Ltd*,[236] Sir Richard Scott V.C. declined to make an order for the assistance of foreign liquidators in the recovery of English assets in an English bankruptcy where the liquidators were the petitioning creditors in the bankruptcy and the relief sought could be obtained in the bankruptcy proceedings by the trustee in bankruptcy. In a subsequent decision the same judge held that assistance could not be given under s.426 where its effect would be to

---

[229] *England v Smith*, cited above n.228.
[230] [1992] B.C.C. 394.
[231] [1993] B.C.C. 787.
[232] *Re Bank of Credit and Commerce International SA (No.9)*, cited above n.231, at 801.
[233] *Re Dallhold Estates (UK) Pty Ltd* [1992] B.C.L.C. 621. See further *Re Focus Insurance Co Ltd* [1996] B.C.C. 659.
[234] *Hughes v Hannover* [1997] B.C.C. 921, *per* Morritt L.J. at 935.
[235] *Hughes v Hannover*, cited above n.234, at 939.
[236] [1996] B.C.C. 659.

disapply the English statutory insolvency scheme, in that case the statutory set-off prescribed by r.4.90 of the Insolvency Rules 1996.[237] Finally, the Court of Appeal has confirmed that the court continues to enjoy a discretion to grant or reject a request for judicial assistance and rejected the notion that the only permissible ground of refusal is public policy, holding that the court must in every case fulfil its duty to do justice in accordance with law.[238]

(3) Forms of assistance

16–61 An English court may provide any form of assistance comparable to the relief that could be given in insolvency proceedings in England, whether under the provisions of the Insolvency Act or pursuant to the court's general equitable jurisdiction. Available forms of assistance include an order for examination of an officer of the company under s.236 of the Insolvency Act,[239] an injunction to restrain the commencement or continuance of actions against the debtor company, whether in England or elsewhere,[240] a declaration recognising the right and title of a foreign liquidator, provisional liquidator or other foreign representative,[241] the appointment of a receiver,[242] the making of an administration order,[243] and orders under ss.212, 213, 214 and 238 of the Insolvency Act.[244] The court also has jurisdiction under s.425 to order the remission of assets to a foreign liquidator in a country whose insolvency scheme differs from that of English law, for example, because it recognises classes of debt as preferential which would not be so recognised under English law.

"The whole doctrine of ancillary winding up is based upon the premise that in such cases the English court may 'disapply' parts of the statutory

---

[237] *Bank of Credit and Commerce International SA (No.II)* [1997] 1 B.C.L.C. 80 (see above, para.9–16). This aspect of the case was approved by Lord Hoffmann in *Re HIH Casualty*, cited above n.212, at [15], observing that English law, which governed the set-off, regards set-off as a matter of substantial justice between the parties. A further ground for the decision of Sir Richard Scott V.-C. was that r.4.90 was not only mandatory but self-executing, so that to the extent of the set-off there would be no credit balance to be included in the assets transferred to the foreign liquidator in the main liquidation.
[238] *Hughes v Hannover Ruckversicherunngs-Aktiengesellschaft* [1997] 1 B.C.L.C. 497. In that case, the court refused the request, made by the Supreme Court of Bermuda, on the ground that there had been a substantial change of circumstances since the signature of the letter of request by the Chief Justice of Bermuda and that there was no indication in the evidence whether the Supreme Court had reconsidered the matter in the light of the change of circumstances.
[239] *England v Smith* [2001] Ch. 419; and *Re Trading Partners Ltd* [2002] 1 B.C.L.C. 655.
[240] *Hughes*, cited above n.238.
[241] *Hughes*, cited above n.238.
[242] *Re A Debtor Ex p. Viscount of the Royal Court of Jersey* [1980] 3 All E.R. 665; and *Re Osborn Ex p. Trustee* [1931–32] B. & C.R. 189.
[243] *Re Dallhold EStates (UK) Pty Ltd* [1992] B.C.L.C. 621.
[244] *Re Bank of Credit and Commerce International SA (No.9)* [1993] B.C.C. 787.

scheme by authorising the English liquidator to allow actions which he is obliged by statute to perform according to English law to be performed instead by the foreign liquidator according to the foreign law (including its rules of the conflict of laws). These may or may not be the same as English law ... The primary rule of private international law which seems to me applicable in this case is the principle of (modified) universalism, which has been the golden thread running through English cross-border insolvency law since the 18th century."[245]

The principal qualification is that the interests of creditors in Great Britain be adequately protected, whether because the court is satisfied that the foreign law provides such protection[246] or by a proviso in the order of the English court making remittal of the assets conditional on the liquidator retaining sufficient assets to provide the requisite protection, for example, to be available for set-off under r.4.90 of the Insolvency Rules.[247] Where the court does not feel able to grant the particular form of assistance requested, it should consider whether it can properly assist in some other way in accordance with any of the available systems of law.[248]

Staying English proceedings where foreign insolvency proceedings

An English winding up order automatically stays proceedings in England,[249] but the same is not true of an order in foreign proceedings.[250] The court has a discretion to order a stay of English proceedings where there is a foreign liquidation or other insolvency process but will only exercise this where it considers it appropriate to do so.[251] In particular, it will not normally restrain a secured creditor from enforcing his security or otherwise inhibit the *in rem* effect on an asset of a judgment of a foreign court of competent

16–62

---

[245] *Re HIH Casualty*, cited above n.212, *per* Lord Hoffmann at [19] and [30]. Their Lordships were divided on the question of whether such jurisdiction was exercisable by virtue of the court's inherent power at common law. Lords Hoffmann and Walker considered it was, Lords Scott and Neuberger were of the contrary view, while Lord Phillips preferred to express no opinion on the question. See further Gabriel Moss, " 'Modified Universalism' and the Quest for the Golden Thread" (2008) 21 *Insolvency Intelligence* 145. Lord Neuberger has since generously acknowledged the force of Moss's criticism. See "The International Dimension of Insolvency" (2010) 23 *Insolvency Intelligence* 42.

[246] *Re HIH Casualty*, cited above n.212; and *Swissair Schweizerische Luftverkeht-Aktiengesellschaft* [2009] B.P.I.R. 1505.

[247] *Re Bank of Credit and Commerce International SA (No.11)* [1997] Ch. 213.

[248] *Re Bank of Credit and Commerce International SA (No.11)*, cited above n.247.

[249] Insolvency Act 1986 s.130(2). See above, para.5–08. The stay is not automatic in the case of voluntary winding up. Administration results in a stay, though usually secured creditors will be given leave to enforce their security.

[250] *Re Vocalion (Foreign) Ltd* [1932] 2 Ch. 196.

[251] *Felixstowe Dock and Railway Co v United States Line Inc* [1989] Q.B. 360.

jurisdiction.[252] The court, in exercise of its *in personam* jurisdiction, may grant an order restraining an English creditor from pursuing proceedings abroad, for example, by trying to attach foreign assets,[253] and this is so whether or not it has proved as a creditor in an English winding up.[254] The court has entertained, although not always granted, requests by other courts to give assistance under s.426 of the Insolvency Act 1986 by granting an injunction restraining foreign proceedings.[255] But where the English proceedings are ancillary to a main liquidation abroad, a court in England will not normally grant an injunction to restrain proceedings in the foreign liquidation, taking the view that it is for the foreign court to decide whether the action should be allowed to proceed.[256]

4. CONCURRENT INSOLVENCY PROCEEDINGS

16–63   We have seen that the principle of unity of the insolvency is not adopted in practice except in very modified form. It is common to have concurrent insolvency proceedings in different jurisdictions. In some cases, the proceedings in one court are ancillary to those of another,[257] but it is perfectly possible to have concurrent proceedings neither of which are ancillary proceedings; indeed, where one of the two States is a non-EU State and neither State has adopted the UNCITRAL Model Law, there is nothing to stop the courts in both States from claiming jurisdiction over all of the debtor's assets on a worldwide basis, so that in effect there are two main proceedings.[258] There is nothing to preclude the creditor from lodging a proof of debt in both sets of proceedings but under the hotchpot rule applied in English law, a creditor who has received a dividend in the foreign proceedings must bring in, for the purpose of dividend, the sum which he has received abroad.[259] This does not mean that he has to hand such dividend over to the English liquidator, merely that he cannot receive a dividend in the English liquidation until the dividends he would have received in that liquidation equal his foreign dividend, so that other creditors in the English liquidation will have received a dividend at the same rate as that received in the foreign liquidation by the

---

[252] *Minna Craig Steamship Co v Chartered Mercantile Bank of India, London and China* [1897] 1 Q.B. 460.

[253] *Re Oriental Inland Steam Co* (1874) L.R. 9 Ch. App. 557.

[254] *Re Central Sugar Factories of Brazil, Flack's Case* [1894] 1 Ch. 369.

[255] See above, para.16–61. This cannot be done where the creditor is outside the jurisdiction of the English court, which in such cases must seek the assistance of the courts of the State in which the creditor is located.

[256] *Re Maxwell Communications Corp Plc (No.2)* [1992] B.C.C. 757.

[257] See below, para.16–64.

[258] This is not possible in cases within the EU Insolvency Regulation (see above, para.15–45) or the UNCITRAL Model Law (see above, para.16–20).

[259] *Banco de Portugal v Waddell* (1880) 5 App. Cas. 161.

creditor in question.[260] But the hotchpot rule applies only to payments received from the company's assets and does not require the amount of realisations of security held by the creditor to be brought into account.[261]

The concept of ancillary proceedings

Reference has already been made to the concept of a main liquidation in one country and an ancillary liquidation in another. This concept is well established in English law, so that where a foreign company is being wound-up under the law of its incorporation, winding up proceedings in England will be regarded as ancillary to the foreign winding up.[262] Its effect is that while the English court will apply rules of English insolvency law to the resolution of any issues in the English liquidation, it will direct the English assets, together with a list of creditors, to be transferred to the foreign liquidator, who will be best placed to declare the dividend and to distribute the assets among creditors.[263]

16–64

Judicial co-operation in concurrent insolvent proceedings

It has long been recognised that the institution of concurrent insolvency proceedings in courts of different countries may raise complex questions, particularly where the insolvency law of both countries adopts the principle of universality, with the potential for conflicts between the laws of the two jurisdictions and the orders of their respective courts. That these problems have not proved insurmountable is largely due to the spirit of co-operation and mutual assistance prevailing among the judges and to legislation such as that embodied in the Model Law and s.426 of the Insolvency Act, which has just been examined.

16–65

One of the most remarkable examples of judicial co-operation was triggered by the collapse of the Maxwell group of companies following the death of the business tycoon Robert Maxwell, a collapse resulting in major litigation in many different jurisdictions. Maxwell Communications Corp Plc (hereafter, MCC) was an English holding company with a large number of subsidiaries scattered around the world. MCC filed under Ch.11 of the US Bankruptcy Code and soon afterwards obtained an administration order in

---

[260] *Banco de Portugal v Waddell*, cited above n.259, *per* Lord Blackburn at 175; and *Re Ex p. Wilson, Douglas* (1872) L.R. 7 Ch. App. 490.

[261] *Cleaver v Delta American Reinsurance Co* [2001] 2 A.C. 328.

[262] See *Re Bank of Credit and Commerce International SA (No.11)* [1996] B.C.C. 980, where the relevant authorities are examined.

[263] *Re Bank of Credit and Commerce International SA (No.11)* cited above n.262.

England. The peculiar feature of the case was that both sets of proceedings were primary proceedings, so that each court had jurisdiction over the company's assets on a worldwide basis. The English proceedings were controlled by Hoffmann J., the US proceedings by Judge Tina L. Brozman, a judge of the Bankruptcy Court for the Southern District of New York. The English administrators were anxious to be heard in the US proceedings, and Judge Brozman fully recognised them as parties in interest but was anxious to create a mechanism that would facilitate co-operation and avoid conflict. To that end, she appointed an examiner. The examiner and the joint administrators then collaborated with a view to harmonising the two sets of proceedings for the benefit of all creditors and eventually agreed on a Protocol to govern their respective roles and powers. Both courts then responded positively to the invitation to approve the Protocol, each court agreeing that it would to the necessary degree defer its jurisdiction to that of the other. The examiner and the administrators then settled upon a reorganisation plan under Ch.11 and a scheme of arrangement under s.425 of the Companies Act 1985 (now s. 899 of the Companies Act 2006). Simultaneously, Judge Brozman approved the plan under Ch.11 and Hoffmann J. the scheme of arrangement under s.425. The combination of the plan and the scheme produced the single distribution mechanism upon which the success of the whole operation so crucially depended, differences in the two sets of governing laws being resolved by accommodations on all sides. The result was to save substantial sums for the creditors in both jurisdictions.[264]

Thus began the practice by which protocols are agreed between the office-holders in the different jurisdictions and approved by their respective courts.[265] Common provisions in such protocols include: a statement confirming the sovereignty and independence of the two courts involved and recording that each of the two office-holders is subject only to the

---

[264] For a detailed description of the case, with a reproduction of the agreed order and Protocol, see Evan D. Flaschen and Ronald J. Silverman, "The Role of the Examiner as Facilitator and Harmonizer in the Maxwell Communication Corporation International Insolvency" in Ziegel (ed.), *Current Developments in International and Comparative Corporate Insolvency Law*, Ch.25. See also Christopher K. Grierson, "Issues in Concurrent Insolvency Jurisdiction: English perspectives" in Ziegel (ed.), *Current Developments in International and Comparative Corporate Insolvency Law*, Ch.24, describing this and other cases involving judicial co-operation, and *Re Bank of Credit and Commerce International SA (No.2)* [1992] B.C.C. 715; and *Re Maxwell Communications Corp Plc (No.2)* [1992] B.C.C. 757, sub. nom. *Barclays Bank Ltd v Homan* [1993] B.C.L.C. 680.

[265] These are described by E.D. Flaschen and R.J. Silverman, "Maxwell Communication Corporation Plc: The Importance of Comity and Co-operation in Resolving International Insolvencies" in American Bar Association, *Multinational Commercial Insolvency*, and "Cross-Border Insolvency Co-operation Protocols" 33 Texas Int. L.J. 587 (1998); Leonard Hoffmann (now Lord Hoffmann), Cross-Border Insolvency: A British Perspective" 64 Fordham L. Rev. 2507 (1996). "Principles and Practice of Cross-Border Insolvency Co-operation Protocols" presented at a symposium on "International Bankruptcy Law: Comparative and Transnational Approaches", held at the University of Texas at Austin in March 1997.

jurisdiction of its own court; a recognition by each court of the proceedings opened by the other and of any stays granted; the status of the two office-holders and the right of each to be heard as a foreign representative in the other proceedings; a direction to the office-holder in each court, while respecting this sovereignty and independence of the two courts, to co-operate with the other in connection with the management of the parallel insolvencies and to harmonise and co-ordinate their activities; a provision for similar co-operation between the two courts with a view to establishing methods of communication, with or without counsel, co-ordinating rulings and conducting joint hearings via a telephone link; an identification of the various cross-border issues to be addressed (for example, reorganisation, treatment of claims, realisation of assets); a provision for mutual disclosure of relevant documents and for notice to all interested parties of any court motions; provision for the venue of applications for relief, which will depend on the nature of the relief sought and whether it relates to property within the jurisdiction of one of the courts; and a direction to the two office-holders to submit to their respective courts reorganisation plans in substantially the same form.[266]

Now we have the benefit of the UNCITRAL Guide,[267] which sets out possible forms of co-operation under art.27 of the Model Law, including safeguards to protect the integrity of the process, detailed suggestions on the content of cross-border insolvency agreements (otherwise known as protocols, co-operation agreements or memoranda of understanding) and specimen clauses.

---

[266] For a picture of the protocol system as it has featured in parallel proceedings in Canada and the US and Israel, see Edward A. Sellers, "Coordinating U.S./Canadian Restructurings and Insolvencies", a paper presented at the Canadian-American Symposium on Cross-Border Insolvency, Toronto, February 11, 2005 and accessible on the Global Insolvency website. Of particular interest, in addition to the *Maxwell* protocol, are the protocols agreed in *Systech Retail Systems Corp et al.*, involving orders of the Canadian and US courts and incorporating the American Law Institute Guidelines Applicable to Court-to-Court Communications in Cross-Border Cases; the *Inverworld* group, involving co-operation between the US, Cayman Islands and English courts; the *Everfresh* group and the *Solv-Ex* group, each involving orders of the Canadian and US courts; and the *Nakash* case, involving orders of the courts of Canada and Israel.

[267] *UNCITRAL Guide on Cross-Border Insolvency Cooperation.*

Index

Administration
see also **Administration expenses,**
    Administration orders;
    Administrators
administration expenses
  continuance of trading, 11–98
  expenses properly incurred, 11–98
  necessary disbursements, 11–98
  payment in full, 11–98
  pre-administration costs, 11–98
  pension liability, 11–103
  priority, 11–96, 11–98
administration followed by liquidation
  cessation of administration, 11–116
  compulsory winding up, 11–116
  computation of preferential debts,
    11–116
  date of entry into administration,
    11–116
  subsequent winding up, 11–116
  voluntary winding up, 11–116
anti-deprivation rule, 7–01
  see also **Anti-deprivation rule**
application, 11–48
avoidance of transactions
  see **Avoidance of transactions**
bank failures, 1–59
Chapter 11 Bankruptcy (USA),
    distinguished, 11–18
characteristics
  deferment of interests/secured
    creditors, 11–20
  disposal of business/assets as primary
    objective, 11–24
  external management, 11–18, 11–22,
    11–35
  preservation of priority/preferential
    creditors, 11–21
  preservation of the business, 11–23,
    11–26, 11–29
  statutory basis, 11–19
collective procedure, 1–35
company participation, 11–34
company voluntary arrangements (CVAs)
  comparisons, 11–31–11–36
  CVA within administration, 12–31
  exit from administration, 11–115
  generally, 11–01
  power to propose, 11–25
  pre-ceding/following administration,
    12–30, 12–32
  procedure, 12–34
  subsequent administration, 12–30
comparisons with other insolvency
  procedures

Administration—*cont.*
comparisons—*cont.*
  administrative receivership, 11–30
  company voluntary arrangements
    (CVAs), 11–31–1136
  liquidation, 11–29
  scheme of arrangement, 11–31–11–34
creditors' committee, 11–01
dissenting/non-participating creditors,
  11–36
distribution to unsecured creditors, 11–01,
  11–85
drawbacks/consequences
  acceleration of liability, 11–01
  cessation of intellectual property rights,
    11–01
  cross-default clauses, 11–01
  diminution in company value, 11–01
  tax disadvantages, 11–01
  termination of contracts, 11–01
duty standard
  business judgment, 11–28
  interests of creditors, 11–28
  objective standard, 11–28
  reasonable care, 11–28
effectiveness, 11–118
enforcement of security
  enforcement, 11–60
  no step to enforce security, 11–58,
    11–59
  preparatory steps, 11–58, 11–59
  security, 11–57, 11–61
  statutory prohibition, 11–57–11–59
Enterprise Act 2002
  see **Enterprise Act 2002**
exiting administration, 11–115
floating charge
  appointment of administrator, 11–06,
    11–28, 11–43, 11–44
  chargee as holder, 11–08, 11–28
  chargee's privileges 11–06
  power to appoint administrator, 11–09
  qualifying floating charge, 11–06, 11–07
followed by and following liquidation,
  11–116
genesis of administration procedure
  company difficulties/options, 11–01
  pre-1985 insolvency law, 11–02
  rescue culture, 11–03
  weakness of statutory regime, 11–04
importance, 11–01
insolvency set-off, 9–48
jurisdiction, 16–53
management of external administrator,
  11–01

Administration—*cont.*
  moratorium, 11–18, 11–24, 11–32, 11–51
    see also **Moratorium**
  nature and purpose
    administration/restructuring
      relationship, 11–17
    corporate rescue, 11–18, 11–23
    rights of secured creditors, 11–18
  objectives and conditions
    actual/impending insolvency, 11–25, 11–33
    business rescue, 11–23, 11–25, 11–26,
      11–29
    distribution to secured/preferential
      creditors, 11–21, 11–27
    hierarchy of objectives, 11–25
    identification of purpose, 11–25
    interests of creditors, 11–25, 11–28
    out of court administration, 11–25
    realisation of property, 11–27
    single purpose, 11–25
  opening of main proceedings, 15–43
    see also **Opening of main proceedings**
  pari passu distribution, 8–02
  pre-packaged administration, 1–36, 11–01,
    11–37–11–42, 11–46
    see also **Pre-packaged administrations**
      (pre-packs)
  purposes, 1–35
  relationship to restructuring, 11–17
  repossession of goods
    company's possession, 11–64
    hire purchase agreements, 11–62,
      11–63, 11–65, 11–73, 11–108
  special regimes, 1–35
  substitute for liquidation, 1–37
  termination, 11–113–11–115
  winding up through administration, 5–25
Administration expenses
  statutory priority, 11–16
Administration orders
  applications, 11–48
  approval of pre-pack sale, 11–46
  conditions, 11–11, 11–47
  effects
    no appointment of administrative
      receiver, 11–55, 11–68
    no enforcement of security,
      11–56–11–61
    no exercise of forfeiture by re-entry,
      11–66
    no legal process, 11–67
    no repossession of goods, 11–62–11–65
    suspension of winding up, 11–54
  function, 1–14
  procedure, 11–48
  rescission, 11–117
  self-help remedies, 11–69
  vacation of office/administrative receiver,
    11–50
  variation, 11–117

Administrative receivers
  actions against debenture holder, 10–38
  actions against receiver, 10–39
  administrator in post, 10–07, 10–13 10–27
  appointment
    appointment under fixed charge, 10–20
    appointment under qualifying floating
      charge, 11–07–11–08
    by/on behalf of debenture holders,
      10–07, 10–14
    floating charge, 10–60
    general effects, 10–36
    generally, 1–38, 10–05
    instrument of appointment, 10–14,
      10–35
    invalid, 10–32
    method, 10–22
    notice of appointment, 10–14
    position of debenture holder, 10–75
    powers and duties of directors, 10–37
    when taking effect, 10–35
  categories of receiver
    all assets receiver, 10–21
    receiver of income only, 10–21
    receiver under debenture created fixed
      charge, 10–21
    receiver under debenture including
      floating charge, 1–21
  contracts/liability
    continuance of existing contracts, 10–52
    deemed agency, 10–50, 10–53, 10–66
    employment contracts, 10–54, 10–55
    new contracts, 10–51
    repudiation, 10–53
    statutory provisions, 10–50
  distinctive characteristics, 10–23
  duties/liabilities
    continuation of company's business,
      10–48
    contractual liability, 10–50–10–54
    conversion, 10–59
    due care/diligence, 10–48, 10–49
    duty of care, 10–24, 10–48, 10–53, 10–75
    environmental liability, 10–48
    equitable duties, 10–48
    good faith, 10–48
    legal policy, 10–49
    mortgages, 10–48, 10–49
    nature of duties owed, 10–48
    negligence, 10–48
    prescribed part, 10–64
    reasonable care, 10–48
    setting aside prescribed part/floating
      charge asset, 10–64
    statutory duty, 10–48
    trespass, 10–59
  enforcement of rights *in rem*, 10–24
  function, 1–14, 1–30, 1–38, 10–06
  indemnity, 10–56
  independence, 10–24, 10–75

Administrative receivers—*cont.*
  leases, 10–57
  legal relationships, 10–24
  lien over property, 10–59
  order of application of assets, 10–68
  out-of-court appointments
    administration orders, 10–26, 10–27
    appointment takes effect, 10–35
    conditional appointment, 10–31
    conditions of appointment, 10–28
    consideration of company's interests,
      10–34
    defective appointment, 10–32
    demand for payment, 10–29, 10–30
    divestment of directors, 10–37
    grounds for appointment, 10–26
    pre-appointment checks, 10–33
    qualified insolvency practitioners, 10–25
  powers
    agency of debenture holder, 10–41
    ancillary to debenture holder's security
      interest, 10–42
    debtor company, 10–41
    disposal of assets, 10–46
    generally, 2–07
    in rem powers, 10–44
    personal powers, 10–44
    power of sale, 10–45
    prior security interest, 10–46
    sources of power, 10–41
    specific powers, 10–43
    third party protection, 10–47
  preferential debts, 10–60
  prescribed part, 10–64
  professional skill and judgment, 10–06
  rates, 10–58
  removal from office, 10–73, 10–74
  rent accrued, 10–57
  right to possession, 10–59
  sub-rentals, 10–57
  vacation of office, 11–50
Administrative receivership
  abolition, 1–14, 1–38, 11–01, 11–04–11–06
  administrator in post, 10–07, 10–13 10–27
  adverse effects, 11–04
  bank supervision, 10–05
  banking concerns, 10–05
  collection of assets, 10–05
  court-appointed receivers, 10–05, 10–14
    see also **Administrative receivers**
  debt enforcement, 1–14
  demand for payment
    claim not due at all, 10–30
    company as surety, 10–30
    demand for more than amount due,
      10–30
    excessive demand, 10–30
    payment of all moneys due, 10–30
    temporal factors, 10–30
    validity, 10–29, 10–30

Administrative receivership—*cont.*
  development
    administration regime, 10–04
    extended receivership, 10–03
    modern receivership, 10–02
    old-style receivership, 10–01
  distributions, 1–14
  enforcement of security, 10–06
  floating charge
    chargee's privileges, 11–06
    crystallisation irrelevant, 10–17
    fixed/floating charge distinction, 10–16
    future assets/floating charges, 10–19
    qualifying floating charge, 10–05, 11–06
    residual floating charge suffices, 10–18
    whole/substantially the whole of the
      company's property, 1–14
  floating charge/preferential debts
    appointment of receiver, 10–60
    crystallisation, 10–60
    events triggering priority, 10–61
    failure to pay preferential claims,
      10–63
    insufficient assets, 10–60
    priority of preferential debts, 10–60
    realisation of assets, 10–68, 10–70,
      10–71
    subordinated to preferential creditors,
      10–60, 10–61
    subordinating appointing chargee,
      10–61
    successive priority events, 10–62
  jurisdiction, 16–54
  legal nature, 10–06, 10–24
  management control, 10–05
  nature of receivership, 1–38, 10–24
  pari passu distribution, 8–03
  partial abolition, 10–05
  realisation of assets
    cost of realisation, 10–71
    fixed charges assets, 10–68, 10–69, 10–71
    floating charges, 10–68, 10–70, 10–71
    order of application, 10–68
    ranking of securities, 10–68
    receivership expenses, 10–71
  repudiation of contracts
    assignment of option, 10–53
    deemed agency, 10–53
    good faith, 10–53
    interim injunction, 10–53
    liability in damages, 10–53
    lien over goods, 10–53
    proprietary rights, 10–53
    receiver's liability, 10–53
    sale of land, 10–53
    specific performance, 10–53
    termination of contract, 10–53
  rescue culture, 10–05
  secured by a charge/created as floating
    charge, 10–07, 10–15

Administrative receivership—*cont.*
　　statutory definition, 10–07, 10–14, 10–15
　　termination of receivership, 10–40, 10–72
　　whole/substantially the whole of the
　　　　company's property
　　　　another receiver in post, 10–07, 10–08,
　　　　　　10–12
　　　　meaning, 10–08, 10–09
　　　　prior receiver/part of property, 10–08,
　　　　　　10–11
　　　　relevant date, 10–08, 10–10
　　　　statutory provision, 10–07
　　winding up
　　　　exercise of security rights, 10–66
　　　　power to convey legal estate, 10–66
　　　　receiver/liquidator relationship, 10–67
　　　　termination of personal powers, 10–66
　　　　termination of receiver's agency,
　　　　　　10–66
Administrators
　　administration expenses
　　　　continuance of trading, 11–98
　　　　expenses properly incurred, 11–98
　　　　necessary disbursements, 11–98
　　　　payment in full, 11–98
　　　　pre-administration costs, 11–98
　　　　priority, 11–96, 11–98
　　agent of the company, 11–89
　　appointment
　　　　administration order, 11–46–11–48
　　　　administration without court order,
　　　　　　11–43, 11–44
　　　　cessation of office, 11–113, 11–114
　　　　company/directors, 11–45
　　　　floating charges, 11–06, 11–09, 11–28,
　　　　　　11–43, 11–44
　　　　generally, 1–31, 2–20
　　　　power to appoint exercisable, 11–09
　　control of bankruptcy assets, 2–20
　　duties/liabilities
　　　　business documents/websites, 11–94
　　　　causing harm to applicants, 11–93
　　　　company wages/salaries, 11–96
　　　　control of company property, 11–95
　　　　duties owed to company, 11–93
　　　　financial arrangements, 11–96
　　　　interests of creditors, 11–93
　　　　liability in conversion, 11–108
　　　　management of company's business,
　　　　　　11–96
　　　　no common law duty of care, 11–92
　　　　post-administration activity, 11–96
　　　　properly informed decisions, 11–93
　　　　unlawful actions, 11–93
　　existing contracts
　　　　contracts in general, 11–104
　　　　employment contracts, 11–106
　　　　leases, 11–105
　　　　occupational pensions, 11–107
　　　　termination, 11–104

Administrators—*cont.*
　　expenses, 11–91
　　function, 1–30
　　new contracts
　　　　administrator's liability, 11–99
　　　　post-administration contracts,
　　　　　　11–100
　　　　post-administration liabilities, 11–101
　　　　pre-administration contracts, 11–100
　　　　refusal to carry out contracts,
　　　　　　11–102
　　out of court appointment, 11–01
　　payments by administrator, 11–90
　　pensions
　　　　contribution notices, 11–103
　　　　financial support directions, 11–103
　　　　occupational pensions, 11–107
　　powers
　　　　application for court directives, 11–97
　　　　chattel leasing agreements, 11–80
　　　　conditional sale agreements, 11–80
　　　　conduct of administration, 11–80, 11–81
　　　　displacement of director's powers,
　　　　　　11–87
　　　　disposal of property, 11–80, 11–83
　　　　distribution powers, 9–48, 11–80, 11–85,
　　　　　　11–86, 11–90
　　　　generally, 2–07
　　　　property subject to floating charge,
　　　　　　11–80, 11–82
　　　　property subject to hire purchase,
　　　　　　11–80, 11–84
　　　　property subject to security, 11–80
　　　　retention of title agreements, 11–80
　　　　scope, 11–80
　　　　third party protection, 11–88
　　proposals
　　　　confidentiality, 11–111
　　　　consultation with creditors, 11–110
　　　　creditors' meeting, 11–111
　　　　decision on proposals, 11–111
　　　　invitation to creditors meeting, 11–109
　　　　modification, 11–109
　　　　presentation, 11–109, 11–111
　　　　requirements, 11–109
　　　　statement of proposals, 11–109
　　　　voting, 11–112
　　remuneration, 1–07, 11–91
Anti-deprivation rule
　　see also **Perpetual Trustee Case**
　　administration, 7–01
　　agreements contravening the rule
　　　　divestment of ownership, 7–09
　　　　increase in company's contractual
　　　　　　obligation, 7–12
　　　　sale with provision for retransfer, 7–11
　　　　vesting clauses/building contracts, 7–10
　　avoidance of transactions, 13–144
　　common law rule, 7–01
　　contractual provisions void, 7–01

Anti-deprivation rule—*cont.*
  distribution of proceeds, 7–01
  formal insolvency proceedings, 7–01
  limits, 7–13
  liquidation, 7–01
  pari passu distribution, distinguished, 7–03,
    8–02
    see also Pari passu **distribution**
  public policy, 7–01
  reduction in company's net asset value, 7–03
  removal of asset contrary to public policy,
    3–06
  returns to creditors, 2–04
  unaffected agreements
    determinable interests, 7–04, 7–05
    licences, 7–05
    limited interests, 7–04, 7–05
    pre-emption provisions, 7–04, 7–06
    termination of interest/membership
      status, 7–04, 7–07, 7–08
    uncompleted transactions at time of
      liquidation, 7–03
Applicable law *see* **Insolvency Regulation,**
  International Insolvency and
  applicable law
Application of recoveries
  absence of revesting in the company,
    13–142
  distinct pool of assets, 13–140
  extortionate credit bargains, 13–142
  improper trading, 14–55
  prior security interest, 13–140
  recoveries for the benefit of creditors,
    13–142
  recoveries forming part of company's
    assets, 13–140
  recoveries in right of the company, 13–141
  transactions at undervalue, 13–142
Arrangements with creditors
  arrangement, 1–43, 1–46, 1–52, 1–55
  composition, 1–15, 1–43, 1–44
    see also **Composition**
  compounding, 1–43, 1–44
  compromise, 1–43, 1–45, 1–52
    see also **Compromise**
  moratorium, 1–43, 1–48
    see also **Moratorium**
  reconstruction, 1–43, 1–50, 1–52
    see also **Reconstruction**
  reorganisation, 1–43, 1–49
    see also **Reorganisation**
  restructuring (work outs), 1–43, 1–51
    see also **Restructuring**
  satisfaction of claims, 1–43
  schemes of arrangement, 1–43, 1–46, 1–52
    see also **Schemes of arrangement**
  voluntary arrangement, 1–43, 1–47
Asset-based financing
  corporate rescue, 1–15
  fragmentation of debt, 1–15

Assets
  valuation, 4–35
    adjusting events, 4–35
    non-adjusting events, 4–35
Assets available for distribution
  assets
    acquired after commencement of
      winding up, 6–01, 6–02
    beneficially owned, 6–02
    held at time of liquidation, 3–03,
      6–01
    recoveries by liquidator, 6–01
    subsequently accrued, 3–03, 6–01
  assets belonging to third parties,
    6–41–6–46
    see also **Assets belonging to third**
      parties
  bona vacantia, 6–30, 6–47
  company dissolution, 6–47
  company property
    see **Company property**
  conditional sale agreements, 6–01
  general law, 6–01
  post-liquidation receipts/recoveries,
    6–33–6–40
    see also **Post-liquidation**
      receipts/recoveries
  property
    held on trust, 6–01
    subject to security interest, 6–01
Assets belonging to third parties
  assets held on trust
    assets ceasing to be trust assets, 6–43
    not forming part of estate, 6–42
    trust money presupposing identifiable
      fund, 6–44
  assets subject to security interest, 6–41,
    6–45
  goods supplied under reservation of title,
    6–41, 6–46
  unavailable for company creditors, 6–41
  see also **Company property**
Avoidance of transactions
  anti-deprivation rule, 13–01, 13–03, 13–11,
    13–144
    see also **Anti-deprivation rule**
  application of recoveries
    see **Application of recoveries**
  avoidance provisions
    avoidance of a preference, 13–02
    compulsory winding up, 13–02
    conditions of avoidance, 13–03, 13–05
    Cork Committee, 13–144
    critique, 13–144
    differing time factors, 13–144
    diligent creditors, 13–144
    diverse nature, 13–02
    extortionate credit transactions, 13–02
    fact of loss/preference, 13–144
    future creditors/unfair advantage, 13–04

Avoidance of transactions—*cont.*
avoidance provisions—*cont.*
occupational pension schemes,
13–02
reform, 13–144
transactions at undervalue, 13–02,
13–03, 13–144
transfers of property, 13–02
underlying policies, 13–03, 13–04,
13–144
unfair preferences, 13–03
court orders
applications, 13–12, 13–18
company in liquidation/administration,
13–17
conditions, 13–15
dispositions after commencement of
compulsory winding up
see **Dispositions after commencement of
compulsory winding up**
extortionate credit transactions, 13–02,
13–11
see also **Extortionate credit transactions**
grounds for avoidance
contravention of anti-deprivation rule,
13–11
contravention of *pari passu* rule, 13–11
disposition without leave, 13–11
extortionate credit transactions, 13–11
floating charge, 13–11
preferences, 13–11
registrable but unregistered charge, 13–11
transactions at undervalue, 13–11
transactions defrauding creditors, 13–11
market contracts, 13–143
minimum conditions
administration/liquidation within
specified time, 13–05, 13–09
company in winding up/administration,
13–05, 13–06
diminution of assets, 13–05, 13–06
exceptional cases, 13–05
insolvency at time of transaction, 13–05,
13–08
misfeasance by company officers, 13–01
pari passu distribution, 13–01, 13–03, 13–11
payments/transfers already made, 13–01
preferences, 13–11
see also **Preferences**
reduction of capital, 13–01
see also **Restitution, Unjust enrichment**
registrable but unregistered charge, 13–11
see also **Registrable but unregistered
charge, 13–11**
relevant considerations, 13–10
restitution, 13–01
see also Restitution, Unjust enrichment
transactions at undervalue, 13–01, 13–02,
13–03, 13–11, 13–144
see also **Transactions at undervalue**

Avoidance of transactions—*cont.*
transactions defrauding creditors, 13–11
see also **Transactions defrauding
creditors**
unjust enrichment, 13–01, 13–03, 13–145
see also **Unjust enrichment**
unperformed obligations, 13–01

Balance sheet test
accounts
accounting practice, 4–32
accounting standard, 4–32, 4–35
stock valuation, 4–32
work in progress, 4–32
adjusting events, 4–35
administration, 4–06
administration orders, 4–28
assets
assets measured against liabilities, 4–01,
4–04, 4–22, 4–23, 4–34
break up basis, 4–35
going concern basis, 4–35
relevant time, 4–34
valuation, 4–06, 4–32, 4–33,
4–34, 4–35
auditing standard, 4–35
avoidance of transactions, 4–30
basic test, 4–22
contingent/prospective liabilities,
4–22, 4–23, 4–26, 4–27,
4–37, 4–39
contribution orders, 4–29
debts/liabilities, 4–22, 4–24, 4–25,
4–36–4–39
directors
disqualification of directors, 4–06,
4–22, 4–31
obligations, 4–32
financial statements, 4–35
formulation, 4–04, 4–22
leased items
finance leases, 4–5
operating leases, 4–25
legislation, 4–22
liquidation expenses, 4–39
marginal situations, 4–06, 4–32
personal liability, 4–33
valuation of assets, 4–35
transactions at undervalue, 4–33
winding up, 4–06, 4–22, 4–38
wrongful trading, 4–29, 4–33
Bank failures
administration, 1–59
bail-outs, 1–58
bank insolvency orders, 1–59
causes, 1–57
depositors, 1–58, 2–14
domino effect, 1–58, 2–14
effect on banking system, 1–58
increasing number, 1–57

Bank failures—*cont.*
　inter-bank lending, 1–58
　investment banking, 2–14
　legislation, 1–16, 1–21, 1–59
　liquidators, 1–59
　loss of confidence, 1–58
　moral hazard, 1–58
　multinational groups, 1–57
　powers
　　property transfers, 1–59
　　share transfers, 1–59
　　stabilisation powers, 1–59
　proprietary trading, 2–14
　regulator's role, 1–57
　special resolution regime, 1–59
　special rules, 1–01
　sub-prime loans, 1–57
　systemic risk, 1–58, 2–14
　"too big to fail", 1–58, 2–14
　winding up petition, 1–59
Bankruptcy
　see also **Control of bankruptcy assets**
　Chapter 11 Bankruptcy (USA), 11–18
　historical development, 1–10
　meaning, 1–01
　priority rules, 1–10
"British insolvency law"
　meaning, 16–25–16–26
Brussels I
　scope, 15–02, 15–34
Brussels Convention
　excluded areas, 15–02
　jurisdictional issues, 15–02
　mutual recognition/enforcement of
　　judgments, 15–02
Building contracts
　direct payment clauses, 8–11
　vesting clauses, 7–10
Building societies
　legislation, 1–26

Cash flow test
　application, 4–05
　borrowed funds, 4–20
　commercial approach, 4–16
　debts
　　current repayment, 4–19
　　debts taken into account, 4–17, 4–18
　　disputed debts, 4–21
　　inability to pay debt falling due, 4–04,
　　　4–05, 5–15, 5–19
　　payment on due date, 4–15
　　undisputed debts, 4–21
　default in payment, 4–21
　formulation, 4–04, 4–15
　futurity element, 4–16
　grounds for administration, 4–05
　grounds for winding up, 4–05
　insufficient liquid assets, 4–20
　margin of tolerance, 4–15

Cash flow test—*cont.*
　overall company position, 4–16
　statutory basis, 4–15
　sufficient evidence, 4–21
　turning assets into cash, 4–20
Centre of main interests (COMI)
　ascertainable by third parties, 15–53
　based in Member State, 15–17
　change/migration, 15–47, 15–58
　concept, 15–49
　corporate groups, 16–10
　definition, 15–49
　determination, 15–39, 15–49–15–53,
　　15–56
　exclusive jurisdiction, 15–25
　head office functions, 15–56
　Insolvency Regulation (1346/2000), 15–05,
　　15–06, 15–08, 15–09
　　see also **Insolvency Regulation
　　　(1346/2000)**
　jurisdictional issues, 15–53
　location, 15–51, 15–53
　location of parent company, 15–57
　main proceedings, 15–21–15–23, 15–27,
　　15–39, 15–49, 15–65
　registered office, 15–52, 15–53, 15–56
　relevant factors, 15–56
　secondary proceedings, 15–55
　separate legal entities, 15–54
　subsidiary companies, 15–43–15–55
　territorial proceedings, 15–61
　winding up, 5–01
Chapter 11 Bankruptcy (USA)
　administration, distinguished, 11–18
Collectivity
　principle, 2–08
Comity
　foreign liquidation, 8–31
　international comity, 8–31
Company property
　assets belonging to third parties,
　　6–41–6–46
　　see also **Assets belonging to third
　　　parties**
　assets beneficially owned, 6–02
　assets held on trust, 6–42
　benefit/entitlement, 6–03
　choses in action, 6–03, 6–05
　choses in possession, 6–03
　compulsory winding up, 6–03
　concept of property, 6–03, 6–07
　contractual/tortious rights, 6–04
　degree of permanence, 6–07
　executed contracts, 6–21
　　see also **Executed contracts**
　executory contracts, 6–22, 6–23
　　see also **Executory contracts**
　factors limiting interest held
　　anti-deprivation rule, 6–16, 6–17
　　contractual provisions, 6–16, 6–17

Company property—*cont.*
  factors limiting interest held—*cont.*
    external vitiating factors, 6–16
    repugnancy, 6–16
  factors limiting measure/quantum
    of asset
    contract rights to money, 6–18
    contractual limitation, 6–18
    inherent limits to quantum, 6–18
    interests in tangible/intangible property,
      6–18
    netting out arrangements, 6–18
    pure contract rights, 6–18
    shared interests, 6–18
  factors preventing interest taking effect
    direct payment clause, 6–17
    equitable provision, 6–17
    fraud proceedings, 6–17
    liquidator takes subject to equities,
      6–17
    pari passu distribution, 6–17
    right of rescission, 6–17
    right of termination, 6–17
    set-off, 6–21
    unfulfilled condition precedent, 6–17
  factors subjecting asset to countervailing
    liability, 6–19
  goods subject to reservation of title, 6–46
  goodwill, 6–05
  identifiable by third party, 6–07
  indemnities, 6–24
  insurance contracts, 6–24
  liabilities, 6–25
  licences, 6–05
  nature, 6–07
  non-transferable rights
    see **Non-transferable rights**
  onerous property, 6–02, 6–27–6–30
    see also **Onerous property**
  overdraft facility, 6–02
  pari passu distribution, 6–03
  priorities and subordinations
    anti-deprivation rule, 6–26
    contingent right, 6–26
    effect of subordination, 6–26
    loss of priority, 6–26
    security interest, 6–26
  property acquired after commencement of
    winding up, 6–01, 6–06
  provisions for divestment, 6–02
  quotas, 6–11
  realisable value, 6–07, 6–15
  restitutionary claims, 6–04
  rights/facilities, 6–02, 6–05
  statutory licences, 6–11
  statutory meaning, 6–03
  tangibles/intangibles, 6–04, 6–05, 6–16
  transferability, 6–07, 6–08
  transferable quotas, 6–05
  voluntary winding up, 6–03

Company voluntary arrangements (CVAs)
  administration
    comparisons, 11–31–11–36,
      12–27–12–29
    CVA within administration, 12–31
    exit from administration, 11–115
    pre-ceding/following administration,
      12–30, 12–32
    procedure, 1–32, 12–34
    subsequent administration, 12–30
  approval
    no power to vary, 12–42
    priority to preferential creditor, 12–42
    requirements, 12–42
    secured creditors, 12–42
    suspension, 12–54
  challenges
    material irregularity, 12–54
    unfair prejudice, 12–54
  consensual company voluntary
    arrangements, 12–30
  corporate rescue, 1–14, 1–15, 1–32, 11–03
  creditors' rights, 12–26, 12–41, 12–44
  directors
    continuing control, 12–26
    proposal for CVA, 12–36
    realisation of assets, 12–26
  effect
    creditors not bound, 12–48, 12–49
    effect on creditors, 12–46
    no moratorium unless provided by
      CVA, 12–51
    parties bound, 12–45, 12–53
    parties not bound, 12–47
    sureties, 12–50
    trust of assets, 12–52
  fairness, 12–54
  insolvency practitioners, 12–55
  jurisdiction, 16–55
  leases
    accrued arrears, 12–54
    forfeiture, 12–54
    future rent, 12–54
  legislation, 1–14
  moratorium, 11–51, 12–30, 13–24,
    12–39
  nature
    company insolvency, 12–26
    composition in satisfaction of
      company's debts, 12–26
    contractual basis, 12–26
    distribution to creditors, 12–26
    relationship between parties, 12–26
    sale of assets, 12–26
    scheme of arrangement, 12–26
    underlying rationale, 12–26
    vehicle for trading, 12–26
  opening of main proceedings, 15–44
    see also **Opening of main
      proceedings**

Company voluntary arrangements—*cont.*
pari passu distribution, 8–03
parties bound
  dissenting creditors, 12–45
  statutory entitlement, 12–53
  unknown creditors, 12–45
parties not bound
  enforcement of rights, 12–48
  entitlement, 12–49
  retention of substantive rights, 12–48
  secured creditors, 12–48
  unsecured creditors, 12–48
procedure
  administration, 1–32, 12–34
  further meetings, 12–54
  meetings, 12–40
  nominee's report, 12–38
  preliminary steps, 12–34
  pre-packaging arrangements, 12–34
  professional advice, 12–34
  small company moratorium, 12–34,
    12–39
  standstill on individual claims, 12–34
proposal
  directors, 12–36
  eligibility, 12–35
relationship to other types of arrangement
  composition, 12–27
  restructuring, 12–29
  schemes of arrangement, 12–28
reorganisation
  additional share capital, 12–43
  composition of claims, 12–43
  conversion of debt into equity,
    12–43
  distribution of realisations, 12–43
  moratorium, 12–43
  new corporate structure, 12–43
  new funds, 12–43
  preservation of business, 12–43
  reduction of share capital, 12–43
  release of claims/securities, 12–43
  reordering of priorities, 12–43
  reorganisation plan, 12–43
  restructuring, 12–43
smaller companies, 1–54
statutory provisions, 12–01
winding up
  parallel proceeding, 12–30
  preceding/following winding up, 12–30,
    12–33
  subsequent winding up, 12–30
voting
  chairman's discretion, 12–41
  creditors, 12–41
  entitlement, 1–54, 12–41
  multiple claims, 12–41
  proxy votes, 12–41
  secured claims, 12–41
  unliquidated/uncertain claims, 12–41

Composition
creditors, 1–15, 1–43, 1–44
meaning, 1–44
Compounding
arrangements with creditors, 1–43, 1–44
debts, 1–44
Compromise
arrangements with creditors, 1–43, 1–45,
  1–55
liquidators, 1–55, 5–05
methods, 1–52
pari passu distribution, 8–03
Compulsory winding up
company regulation, 5–13
debts
  debt collection, 5–12
  disputed debts, 5–13
  undisputed debts, 5–12
effects, 5–08
entitlement, 5–12, 5–19
Insolvency Services Account, 5–01
grounds
  assets less than liabilities, 5–15
  ex debito justitiae, 5–12, 5–19, 5–21
  failure to meet statutory demand, 5–15,
    5–16
  inability to pay debts, 5–11, 5–12, 5–15
  judicial discretion, 5–11, 5–13
  just and equitable grounds, 5–11, 5–12,
    5–15, 5–21
  legitimate interest, 5–12, 5–19, 5–21
  return of an execution, 5–15
method of winding up, 1–40
opening of main proceedings, 15–41
  see also **Opening of main proceedings**
oppressive use, 5–13
petitions
  abuse of process, 5–14, 5–17, 5–18
  advertisement, 5–20
  contingent creditors, 5–19
  exercise of class rights, 5–19
  generally, 5–01, 5–10
  legitimate interest, 5–12, 5–19, 5–21
  locus standi, 5–12, 5–18, 5–21
  pari passu distribution, 5–19
  presentation, 5–14
  prospective creditors, 5–19
  protection/harassment, 5–19
  protection/unequal distribution, 5–19
  protective function, 5–19
  striking out, 5–21
  substantive hearing, 5–21
  who can present, 5–17
procedure
  abuse of process, 5–14, 5–17, 5–18
  commencement of winding up, 5–23
  court orders, 5–01, 5–10
  cross-claims, 5–12, 5–13
  liquidation, 5–10
  official receiver, 5–10

Compulsory winding-up—*cont.*
  procedure—*cont.*
    interim moratorium, 5–22
    petitions, 5–01, 5–10, 5–12, 5–14,
      5–17–5–21
    set-off, 5–13
    substantive hearing, 5–21
    winding up order, 5–21, 5–22, 5–24
Concurrent insolvency proceedings
  ancillary proceedings, 16–63, 16–64
  co-operation agreements, 16–65
  hotchpot rule, 16–63
  judicial co-operation, 16–65
  memorandum of understanding,
    16–65
  proof of debt, 16–63
  protocols, 16–65
  two main proceedings, 16–63
  UNCITRAL Guide, 16–65
Conflict of laws
  applicable law
    lex causae, 15–71, 15–73, 15–75,
      15–92
    lex fori, 15–71, 15–88
    lex situs, 15–71, 15–76, 15–82, 15–88
  forum non conveniens, 15–26, 16–51
  forum shopping, 15–07, 15–08
  Insolvency Regulation (1346/2000), 15–01,
    15–19, 15–88
  jurisdiction, 16–15, 16–48
  lex concursus
    see **Lex concursus**
  renovi, 15–70
  third party rights, 15–88
Contingent liability
  see **Liability**
Control of bankruptcy assets
  appointment of administrator, 2–20
  contractualism, 2–20
  diffused security interest, 2–20
  dominant security interest, 2–20
  menu of options approach, 2–20
  neutral management, 2–20
  restructuring, 2–20
  secured creditors, 2–20
Corporate entity
  see **Legal personality**
Corporate groups
  see **Legal personality**
Corporate insolvency
  see also **Principles of corporate insolvency**
  achievement of objectives
    appointment of external manager,
      2–01, 2–07
    authorisation of insolvency
      practitioners, 2–01, 2–12
    avoidance of improper transactions,
      2–01, 2–10
    collective debt collection, 2–01,
      2–04, 2–08

Corporate insolvency—*cont.*
  achievement of objectives—*cont.*
    civil/criminal sanctions, 2–01, –06
    disqualification of directors, 2–01,
      2–06, 2–11
    distribution of net realisations,
      2–01, 2–22
    recovery of misapplied assets, 2–01,
      2–10
    statutory distribution scheme, 2–01,
      2–09
    suspension of individual rights/claims,
      2–01, 2–08
  administration orders 4–02
  balance sheet test
    see **Balance sheet test**
  bank administration orders, 4–02
  bank insolvency orders, 4–02
  collective nature, 1–08
  company in trouble
    cash flow difficulties, 11–01
    loss of market share, 11–01
    overtrading, 11–01
    poor acquisitions, 11–01
  company options
    adjustment of creditors' rights, 2–01
    administration, 2–01, 2–02
    appointment of administrative receiver,
      11–01
    conversion of debt into equity, 2–01
    corporate rescue, 11–01
    creditors' voluntary winding up,
      11–01
    debt deferral, 2–01
    disposal of business/assets, 2–01, 2–02
    liquidation, 2–01, 11–01
    reorganisation, 2–01, 2–02
    standstill by agreement, 11–01
    statutory moratorium, 11–01
    trading out of difficulty, 2–01, 11–01
  directors
    disqualification, 4–02
    liability, 4–02
    powers, 12–26
  effects, 2–14, 4–02
  enforcement of payment, 4–01
  floating charge, 4–02
    see also **Floating charge**
  fraudulent trading, 4–02
    see also **Fraudulent trading**
  historical development, 1–01
  inability to pay debts, 1–02,
    4–01, 4–02
    see also **Inability to pay debts**
  judicial rights/remedies
    delivery, 1–08
    inherent jurisdiction, 1–19
    instituting proceedings, 1–08
    payment, 1–08
    possession, 1–08

Corporate insolvency—*cont.*
  legal personality
    corporate entity, 1–28
    corporate veil, 1–28
    enterprise groups, 1–28
    insolvency proceedings, 1–28
    multinational groups, 1–28
    single economic enterprise, 1–28
  law and economics perspective, 1–01
  nature of subject, 1–01
  objectives
    control, 2–02
    distribution of assets, 2–01
    identifying cause of company failure,
      2–06
    maximising return to creditors, 2–01,
      2–04, 2–22
    neutral management, –02
    ranking of claims, 2–01, 2–05
    redistribution of rights, 2–01, 2–02
    restoration of profitable trading, 2–0
  philosophical issues
    see **Philosophical issues**
  province of corporate insolvency
    see **Province of corporate insolvency**
  sources of law
    see **Sources of law**
  statutory regime, 1–08
  transfer of management control, 1–15
  transfer of property, 4–01
  transfers at undervalue, 4–02
    see also **Transfers at undervalue**
  wrongful trading, 4–02
    see also **Wrongful trading**
Corporate rescue
  additional funding, 1–34
  administration, 1–32, 1–34, 11–18, 11–23
  asset-based financing, 1–15
  bank-led work outs, 1–32
  Chapter 11 Bankruptcy (USA), 11–18
  company voluntary arrangements (CVAs),
    1–14, 1–15, 1–32, 11–03
  co-ordination of creditors, 1–15
  Cork Committee, 1–32, 2–20
  court-ordered moratorium, 1–15
    see also **Moratorium**
  creditors' rights, 2–23
  debtor-in-possession approach, 1–15
  distressed debt, 1–32
  London Rules, 1–32, 11–03
  multi-creditor work outs, 1–32
  priority/ranking, 1–34
  INSOL Statement of Principles, 11–03
  Insolvency Service, 1–15
  redistribution of rights, 2–23
  rehabilitation, 1–32
  remedial measures, 1–33
    see also **Remedial measures**
  reorganisation, 1–32, 2–23, 11–03
  rescue as going concern, 11–26

Corporate rescue—*cont.*
  rescue culture, 1–32, 2–20, 2–23, 11–03
  rescue finance, 1–34
  rescue plan, 1–15
  restructuring, 1–32, 11–03
  working capital, 1–34
"Cram-down"
  under Chapter 11 (US), 11-18
Credit
  availability, 1–07
  cost of credit, 1–02
  forms
    loan credit, 1–03
    purchase of debt instruments, 1–03
    sale credit, 1–03
    secured credit, 1–07
  function, 1–02
  lending relationship, 1–03
Credit institutions
  EEA credit institutions, 1–60, 1–72, 16–48
  jurisdiction, 16–48
  winding up, 1–60, 15–01
Creditors
  see also **Arrangements with creditors;**
      Creditors' voluntary winding up
  acceleration of debtor's liability, 1–08
  anti-deprivation rule, 2–04
  collective action, 1–07
  collective interests, 2–04
  composition, 1–15
  contractual remedies, 1–08
  contractual rights, 1–08
  "creditor", meaning
  defrauding creditors
    see **Transactions defrauding**
        creditors
  distribution of assets, 2–01
  entitlement to payment, 1–04
  exercise of rights, 1–08
  foreign creditors, 15–01
  influence, 1–07
  maximising return to creditors, 2–01,
      2–04, 2–22
  over-secured creditors, 1–07
  pari passu distribution, 2–27, 2–28
    see also ***Pari passu* distribution**
  ranking of claims, 1–04, 2–01, 2–05
    see also **Ranking of claims**
  recognition and ordering of creditors'
      rights, 2–26–2–29
    see also **Recognition and ordering of**
        creditors' rights
  rights
    participation rights, 2–21
    recognition/ordering, 2–26–2–29
    redistribution of rights, 2–01, 2–23
    social/economic policy, 2–22
    substantive rights, 2–22
  schemes of arrangements
    class meetings, 12–19

Creditors—*cont.*
  schemes of arrangements—*cont.*
    contingent creditors, 12–18, 12–19
    debt not yet payable, 12–18
    double proof, 12–18
    economic interest, 12–22, 12–23
    exclusion, 12–23
    identification of classes, 12–19
    minority groups, 12–19
    power of veto, 12–19
    proprietary claims, 12–18
    secured creditors, 12–13, 12–18
    separate classes, 12–19
    separate meetings, 12–19
    sureties, 12–18, 12–25
  secured creditors, 1–07, 2–20, 2–21
    see also **Secured creditors**
  security interests, 1–08
  self-help, 1–08
  subordination, 1–04
  termination of contract, 1–08
  unsecured creditors, 2–18, 2–21, 2–22
  who are, 2–26
  withholding performance, 1–08
Creditors' voluntary winding up
  centre of main interests, 5–01
  EC Insolvency Regulation, 5–01
  insolvency practitioners' preference, 5–01
  jurisdiction, 16–52
  method of winding up, 1–40
  overseas companies, 5–01
  opening of main proceedings, 15–40
    see also **Opening of main proceedings**
  procedure
    control of creditors, 5–07
    creditors meeting, 5–07
    member's resolution, 5–01, 5–07
    special resolution, 5–05
    voting procedure, 5–07
  registration of administrator's notice, 5–01
  special resolution, 5–01
Crown preference
  abolition, 1–14, 8–20
  Cork Committee, 8–20
  sums payable, 1–14, 8–20
  taxation, 8–20

Debt
  see also **Proof of debt**
  bondholders, 1–15
  compounding, 1–44
  corporate debtors, 1–08
  distressed debt, 1–32, 12–08
  equity, distinguished, 1–04
  foreign companies, 15–01
  fragmentation
    asset-based financing, 1–15
    capital market debt, 1–15
    credit default swaps, 1–15
    multi-tiering, 1–15

Debt—*cont.*
  fragmentation—*cont.*
    sales of participations, 1–15
    syndicated financing, 1–15
  hybrid security, 1–04
  inability to pay debts, 1–02, 4–01–4–09
    see also **Inability to pay debts**
  individual debtors, 1–08
  junior debt, 1–04
  mezzanine debt, 1–04
  proof of debt, 1–10, 16–63
    see also **Proof of debt**
  senior debt, 1–04
Defrauding creditors
  see **Transactions defrauding creditors**
Derivatives
  ISDA Master Agreement, 9–12
  netting, 9–10, 9–12
    see also **Netting**
Directors
  see also **Disqualification of directors**
  breach of duty
    duty to company, 14–07, 14–09
    fiduciary duty, 14–02, 14–14
    judicial orders, 14–17
    proceedings, 14–14–14–17
    ratification, 14–19, 14–20
  competence, 14–01
  contribution orders, 14–51–14–55
  criminal law/liability
    causing/procuring an offence, 14–06
    criminal sanctions, 14–06
    extent of liability, 14–03, 14–06
    financial services, 14–06
    fraud, 14–06
    fraudulent trading, 14–06
    joint/several liability, 14–06
    misleading/false statements, 14–06
    statutory offences, 14–06
  de facto directors, 14–04, 14–05,
    14–32, 14–39
  de jure directors, 14–04, 14–05, 14–32
  duties
    breach of duty, 14–02
    care/diligence/skill, 14–01, 14–09, 14–11
    day to day management, 14–13
    duties as employer/manager, 14–13
    duties to company, 14–02, 14–03,
      14–07–14–11
    duties to creditors, 14–02, 14–03, 14–20
    fiduciary duties, 14–01, 14–02, 14–14
    good faith, 14–12
    legislation, 14–01
    minimising potential loss, 14–02
    trading out of difficulties, 14–02
  duties to company
    administration, 14–07
    breach of duty, 14–07, 14–09
    care/skill, 14–09, 14–11
    duty to act within powers, 14–09, 14–10

Directors—*cont.*
　duties to company—*cont.*
　　duty to promote company's success,
　　　14–09, 14–11
　　executive directors, 14–08, 14–09
　　generally, 14–02, 14–03
　　good faith, 14–12
　　loyalty, 14–09
　　misfeasance proceedings, 14–07
　　non-executive directors, 14–08, 14–09
　　standard of care, 14–11
　　winding up, 14–07
　fraudulent trading, 4–02, 14–01, 14–02,
　　14–06, 14–21–14–27
　　see also **Fraudulent trading**
　good faith, 14–01
　improper trading, 14–57
　　see also **Improper trading**
　misfeasance, 14–14–14–16, 14–47–14–50
　negligence, 14–01
　powers
　　continuing the business, 12–26
　　realisation of assets, 12–26
　proceedings for breach of duty
　　breach of fiduciary duty, 14–14
　　improper payments, 14–14
　　judicial orders, 14–17
　　misfeasance, 14–14–14–16
　　nature of proceedings, 14–14
　　persons against whom proceedings
　　　brought, 14–15, 14–17
　　secret profits, 14–14
　relief from liability, 14–18
　shadow directors, 14–05, 14–32, 14–37,
　　14–39
　subordination of interests, 14–01
　wrongful trading, 4–02, 14–01, 14–02,
　　14–27–14–47
　　see also **Wrongful trading**
Disclaimer
　effect, 6–30
　liquidator's power, 6–28
　nature of, 6–27
　onerous property, 6–29
　remedy of parties aggrieved, 6–31
Dispositions after commencement of
　　compulsory winding–up
　beneficial ownership, 13–127
　commencement of winding–up, 13–127
　contract/conveyance combined, 13–127
　conveyance distinct, 13–127
　disposition
　　company property, 13–129, 13–130
　　definition, 13–128
　　rendered void, 13–127
　payments into company's bank account
　　account in credit, 13–130, 13–131
　　account overdrawn, 13–130, 13–132
　　borrower is company's bank, 13–131
　　cheques, 13–131

Dispositions after commencement—*cont.*
　principle of abstraction, 13–127
　reduction/extinction of company's rights,
　　13–128
　statutory provisions, 13–127
　transfer of value, 13–128
　withdrawals from bank account
　　account in credit, 13–133
　　account in overdraft, 13–133
　　authorisation by the court, 13–127,
　　　13–135
　　mixed funds, 13–133
　　unauthorised disposition, 13–134
Disqualification of directors
　automatic disqualification, 14–57, 14–60,
　　14–66
　balance sheet test, 4–06, 4–22
　breach of competition law, 14–65
　contribution orders, 14–64
　conviction for indictable offence, 14–63
　culpable behaviour, 14–57, 14–75
　discretionary disqualification, 14–57,
　　14–60, 14–61, 14–63, 14–64
　disqualification procedure
　　applications, 14–70
　　dispensing with proceedings, 14–70
　　disqualification orders, 14–59, 14–63,
　　　14–69, 14–70, 14–72, 14–78,
　　　14–84
　　disqualification undertakings, 14–72,
　　　14–78, 14–84
　　rules of evidence, 14–71
　　summary procedure, 14–70
　failure to file returns, 14–63
　foreign restrictions, 14–57
　fraud, 14–63
　fraudulent trading, 14–63
　improper trading, 14–57
　　see also **Improper trading**
　insolvency provisions, 2–01, 2–06,
　　2–11, 4–02
　legislation, 1–11, 1–24, 14–01, 14–57
　mandatory disqualification, 14–57, 14–60,
　　14–61, 14–65, 14–75
　meaning of disqualification, 14–59
　period of disqualification, 14–62,
　　14–79, 14–80
　persistent default, 14–63
　persons eligible for disqualification,
　　14–61
　policy considerations, 14–58, 14–74
　protection of the public, 14–74
　relevant conduct, 14–73
　un-discharged bankrupt, 14–66
　unfit to manage
　　appeals, 14–83
　　burden/standard of proof, 14–68
　　degree of culpability, 14–75
　　discretionary disqualification, 14–63
　　grounds for disqualification, 14–57

Disqualification of directors—*cont.*
  unfit to manage—*cont.*
    leave to act while disqualified, 14–81
    mandatory disqualification, 14–65,
      14–77
    notification requirements, 14–84
    period of disqualification, 14–62, 14–79,
      14–80
    register of orders/undertakings, 14–84
    relevant period, 14–76
    relevant to all companies, 14–78
    reporting requirements, 14–69, 14–84
    sanctions for acting, 14–82
    statutory provisions, 14–58, 14–67, 14–70
    statutory undertakings, 14–72
  wrongful trading, 14–6
Double proof
  rule against, 8–45

EEA credit institutions
  special rules, 1–72
Employment contracts
  administration proceedings, 15–98
  governing law, 15–98
  insolvency proceedings, 15–98
  transfer of undertakings, 2–24, 8–24,
    15–98
Employment protection
  Cork Committee, 8–20
  EC Insolvency Directive, 8–25
  employment law, 2–24
  employment rights, 2–24
  fraudulent trading, 2–24
  holiday remuneration, 8–22
  loss of employment, 8–20
  National Insurance Fund, 8–20, 8–21
  pensions, 2–24, 8–22
  preferential rights, 8–20, 8–21, 8–23
  preferential status, 8–20–8–22
  Redundancy Fund, 8–20
  social security benefits, 8–20
  transfer of undertakings, 2–24, 8–24,
    15–98
  unpaid remuneration, 8–22
  wrongful trading, 2–24
Enterprise Act 2002
  abolition of administrative receivership,
    11–05, 11–06
  absence of requirement to show
    actual/impending insolvency, 11–05,
    11–11
  administration without court order, 11–05,
    11–10, 11–43–11–45
  administrator's power to make
    distributions, 11–05, 11–15, 11–27
  flexibility in entry/exit routes, 11–05, 11–13
  impact, 11–05
  main provisions, 1–14
  out-of-court appointment, 11–05, 11–11,
    11–25, 11–43–11–45, 11–70

Enterprise Act 2002—*cont.*
  priority of administration expenses, 11–05,
    11–16
  replacement of multi-purpose
    administration, 11–05, 11–12
  time limit for administration, 11–05, 11–14
Environmental protection
  clean up costs, 10–65
  clean up liability, 8–30
  clean up orders, 2–25
  company liability, 2–25
  compliance costs, 10–65
  contaminated land, 8–30
  polluter pays principle, 2–25, 8–30
  pollution, 2–25, 8–30
  remedial works, 8–30, 10–65
  waste management, 2–25, 8–30
Equity
  debt, distinguished, 1–04
  hybrid security, 1–04
Establishment
  meaning, 15–62, 16–25
EU law
  direct effect, 1–27
  employment protection, 8–25
  Financial Collateral Arrangements
    Directive
    see **Financial Collateral Arrangements
      Directive**
  implementation, 1–27
  influence, 15–01
  Insolvency Regulation (1346/2000)
    see **Insolvency Regulation (1346/2000)**
  source of law, 1–27
European dimension
  capital requirements, 1–17
  competence, 1–17
  financial markets, 1–17
  insurance, 1–17
  reorganisation, 1–17
  winding up, 1–17
Executed contracts
  benefit of winding up performance, 6–21
  enforcement of outstanding
    obligations, 6–1
  recovery/retention of benefits
    received, 6–21
  wholly performed by one party, 6–21
Executory contracts
  ability to perform, 6–22
  breach of contract, 6–22
  company liability, 6–22
  company ownership incomplete, 6–23
  function of liquidator, 6–22, 6–23
  future performance, 6–22
  obligations remaining to be performed,
    6–22
  personal rights, 6–23
  real rights, 6–23
  specific performance, 6–23

Ex parte James
rule in, 1–19, 5–02
Extortionate credit transactions
avoidance of transaction, 13–02
definition 13–109
judicial orders, 13–108, 13–110
re-opening, 13–108

Financial Collateral Arrangements Directive
categories of arrangements, 1–68
enforcement, 1–70
insolvency avoidance, 1–71
introduction, 1–64
reduction in formalities, 1–69
scope, 1–66, 1–67
title transfer arrangements, 1–68
Financial Services Authority
business failures, 1–13
Floating charge
see also **Floating charge for past value**
administration
appointment of administrator, 11–06,
11–28, 11–43, 11–44
chargee as holder, 11–08, 11–28
chargee's privileges 11–06
power to appoint administrator, 11–09
qualifying floating charge, 11–06, 11–07
administrative receivership
crystallisation irrelevant, 10–17
fixed/floating charge distinction, 10–16
future assets/floating charges, 10–19
qualifying floating charge, 10–05
residual floating charge suffices, 10–18
whole/substantially the whole of the
company's property, 1–14
charge against unsecured creditors,
6–38, 6–40
Cork Committee, 6–38
debt subordinate to preferential
claims, 6–38
floating charge/preferential debts
appointment of receiver, 10–60
crystallisation, 10–60
events triggering priority, 10–61
failure to pay preferential claims, 10–63
insufficient assets, 10–60
priority of preferential debts, 10–60
realisation of assets, 10–68, 10–70, 10–71
subordinated t0 preferential creditors,
10–60, 10–61
subordinating appointing chargee,
10–61
successive priority events, 10–62
free assets, 6–38
multiple floating charges, 6–40
new value, 13–112
prescribed percentage, 6–38, 6–39
qualified disapplication order, 6–38
ranking of claims, 8–50
realisation of assets, 10–70

Floating charge—*cont.*
ring-fenced fund, 6–38, 8–50
separate debt, 6–40
Floating charge for past value
Cork Committee, 13–121
hardening of floating charge, 13–121,
13–122
insolvency at time of charge, 13–120
new value
benefit to company, 13–114, 13–118
excluded payments, 13–119
expanded concept, 13–114
normal form, 13–112, 13–117
permitted kinds, 13–114, 13–117
supply of goods/services, 13–117,
13–119
value as consideration for the charge,
13–114, 13–115
value contemporaneous/subsequent,
13–114, 13–116
previous law, 13–111
Rule in Clayton's Case, 13–121
statutory provisions
changes, 13–112
conditions required, 13–113
Foreign companies
assets, 15–01
company failures, 15–01
concurrent insolvency proceedings, 15–01
see also **Concurrent insolvency
proceedings**
debts, 15–01
fraudulent transactions, 15–01
international litigation, 15–01
Foreign insolvency proceedings
see also **Insolvency Regulation,
UNCITRAL Model Law**
assets subject to judicial control, 16–30
assistance to foreign courts/parties
applicable law, 16–58, 16–59
common law principle, 16–58
corresponding jurisdiction, 16–58
forms of assistance, 16–61
judicial discretion, 16–59, 16–60
relevant country/territory, 16–58, 16–59
request for assistance, 16–58, 16–59
categories, 16–31
common law rules, 16–57, 16–58
collective judicial/administrative
proceeding, 16–30
foreign liquidators, 16–57, 16–58
foreign main proceedings, 15–21, 16–28,
16–42
foreign non-main proceedings, 16–28
foreign proceedings, 16–30–16–32
foreign representative, 16–33, 16–43
meaning, 16–30
nature, 16–30
proceedings neither main/non-main, 16–32
pursuant to insolvency law, 16–30

Foreign insolvency proceedings—*cont.*
recognition, 16–57, 16–58
reorganisation/liquidation, 16–30
statutory avoidance provisions, 16–30
stay of proceedings, 16–62
Fraudulent trading
application for order, 14–25
"blind eye" knowledge, 14–24
civil remedy, 14–21, 14–23, 14–27
Foreign law
distribution under, 15–67
Foreign representative
see **UNCITRAL Model Law**
Fraudulent preference
early avoidance, 1–10
see also Preferences
company engaged in fraudulent trading,
14–23
contribution orders, 6–37, 14–27
Cork Committee, 14–27
criminal proceedings, 2–06, 2–11, 2–17,
2–24, 14–21, 14–23
directors' duties, 14–01, 14–02
disqualification of directors, 14–63
see also **Disqualification of directors**
employment protection, 2–24
intent to defraud, 14–24
liability, 2–24, 4–02, 14–21–14–23
liquidation expenses, 8–34
sanctions, 14–26
"silver lining" test, 14–24
single creditor/single transaction, 14–24
standard of proof, 14–27
statutory provisions, 14–21
subsidiary companies, 14–24
wrongful trading, distinguished, 14–29

Groups of companies
treatment, 1–28, 16–10
see also **Legal personality**
Guarantees
consideration, 13–34
equality of exchange, 13–34
relevance of security taken, 13–36
securing advance, 13–34
value to creditor, 13–35, 13–36
value to surety, 13–37

Hedge funds
distressed debt, 1–32
Hybrid security
convertible bonds, 1–04
income security, 1–04
payment in kind, 1–04

Improper trading
application of recoveries, 14–55
civil sanctions, 14–51
contribution orders
benefit of creditors, 14–55

Improper trading—*cont.*
contribution orders—*cont.*
judicial approach, 14–52, 14–53
level of contribution, 14–53
no loss/no contribution, 14–52
disqualification of directors, 14–57
see also **Directors, Disqualification of
directors**
plurality of respondents, 14–54
see also **Fraudulent trading, Wrongful
trading**
Inability to pay debts
see also **Balance sheet test; Cash flow test**
alternative tests, 4–07
assets less than liabilities, 4–01, 4–03,
4–04, 4–06, 4–22, 5–15
avoidance of transactions, 4–09
contingent/prospective liabilities, 5–15
exercise of judicial powers
creditors' tangible interest, 4–14
entitlement *ex debito justitiae*, 4–14
judicial discretion, 4–14
failure to meet statutory demand, 4–03,
4–08, 5–15, 5–16
grounds for administration, 4–05,
4–06, 4–09
grounds for winding up, 4–05, 4–06,
4–09, 4–13
legislation, 4–03, 4–08, 4–09, 4–10, 4–11
members' voluntary winding up, 4–04, 4–12
prospective/retrospective insolvency, 4–13
relevant time, 4–13
unsatisfied judicial order, 4–03,
4–08, 5–15
Indemnities
company liability, 6–24
conferral of rights, 6–24
privity of contract, 6–24
sum received, 6–24
INSOL International
role, 1–30
Principles, 11–03, 12–03
Insolvency
see also **Corporate Insolvency**
causes, 1–09
civil liability, 4–01
collective nature, 1–14
Cork Committee, 1–11, 2–12
criminal liability, 4–01
Crown preference, 1–14, 8–20
debtors, 1–08
early history
bankruptcy, 1–10
common law, 1–10
corporate insolvency, 1–10
law merchant, 1–10
legislation, 1–10
limited liability, 1–10
pari passu distribution, 1–10
proof of debt, 1–10

Insolvency—*cont.*
  effects, 4–02
  enforcement of payment, 4–01
  European dimension, 1–17
  exemptions
    EEA credit institutions, 1–60, 1–72
    market changes, 1–60, 1–62
    market contracts, 1–60, 1–61, 1–62
    safeguarding securities markets, 1–60
    system changes, 1–60, 1–63
    winding up credit institutions, 1–60, 15–01
    winding up insurance companies, 1–60, 15–01
  formal proceedings, 4–01, 4–02
    see also **Insolvency proceedings**
  fragmentation of debt, 1–15
  fraudulent trading, 4–02
    see also **Fraudulent trading**
  inability to pay debts, 1–02, 4–01, 4–02
    see also **Inability to pay debts**
  international insolvency, 1–18, 1–20
    see also **International insolvency**
  legal significance, 4–01, 4–02
  legislation
    defects, 1–29
    procedural requirements, 1–29
    reforms, 1–10–1–16
    structure, 1–29
    subject ordering, 1–29
    substantive rights, 1–29
  philosophical issues
    see **Philosophical issues**
  relevance, 4–02
  settlement finality
    see **Settlement finality**
  sources of insolvency law
    see **Sources of insolvency law**
  state of insolvency, 4–01, 4–02
  statutory regime, 1–08
Insolvency practitioners
  appointment, 1–41
  authorisation, 1–30, 2–01, 2–12
  company voluntary arrangements, 12–55
  functions, 1–30
  qualifications, 1–30
  supervisory role, 1–30
Insolvency proceedings
  administration, 1–31
    see also **Administration**
  administrative receivership, 1–31
    see also **Administrative receivership**
  arrangements with creditors, 1–31
    see also **Arrangements with creditors**
  compositions, 1–31
  compromises, 1–31
  concurrent proceedings, 1–28
  formal proceedings, 4–01, 4–02
  insolvency statistics, 1–31
  jurisdiction, 1–28
    see also **Jurisdiction**

Insolvency proceedings—*cont.*
  parent company liability, 1–28
  procedural consolidation, 1–28
  restructuring (workouts), 1–31
    see also **Restructuring**
  winding up, 1–31
    see also **Winding up**
Insolvency Regulation (1346/2000)
  applicable law
    generally, 15–01, 15–05
    independent proceedings, 15–70
    lex causae, 15–71, 15–73, 15–75, 15–92
    lex fori, 15–71, 15–88
    lex situs, 15–71, 15–76, 15–82, 15–88
    renvoi, 15–70
    right *in rem*, 15–76–15–81
    secondary proceedings, 15–70
    State of opening proceedings, 15–70, 15–71, 15–72
  background
    Brussels I, 15–02, 15–34
    Brussels Convention, 15–02
    EC Insolvency Convention, 15–03, 15–04
  centre of main interests (COMI), 15–05, 15–06, 15–08, 15–09, 15–17, 15–39, 15–49–15–51
    see also **Centre of main interests (COMI)**
  collective insolvency proceedings
    administration, 15–14
    appointment of liquidator, 15–15
    company voluntary arrangements (CVAs), 15–14
    institutions not excluded from Regulation, 15–18
    partial/total divestment of debtor, 15–15
    proceedings opened in Member State, 15–16, 15–20
    qualifying proceedings, 15–12–15–14
    winding up, 15–13
  conflict of laws, 15–01, 15–19
  direct effect, 15–02
  establishment, meaning, 15–62
  foreign main proceedings, 16–19
  forum shopping, 15–07, 15–08
  immovable property, 15–96
  immunity from challenge, 15–98
  independent proceedings, 15–60, 15–63
  insolvency proceedings within the Community, 15–09
  judicial interpretation, 15–06–15–08
  jurisdiction
    basis of jurisdiction, 15–25
    exclusive jurisdiction, 15–25, 15–26
    forum non conveniens, 15–26
    international jurisdiction, 15–22, 15–24
    main proceedings, 15–21–15–23, 15–25, 15–27, 15–39
    Member State jurisdiction, 15–20

Insolvency Regulation (1346/2000)—*cont.*
  jurisdiction—*cont.*
    modified unity, 15–23
    modified universality, 15–24
    relationship between different
      proceedings, 15–27
    rules, 15–01, 15–02
    secondary proceedings, 15–21
    territorial proceedings, 15–21, 15–25
    unity, 15–22
    universality, 15–22
  key features, 15–05
  legal entities, 15–09
  lex concursus
    acts determinable to all creditors,
      15–72
    assets forming part of estate, 15–72,
      15–75
    avoidance rules, 15–72, 15–98
    conduct/closure of proceedings, 15–70,
      15–72
    governing law, 15–70, 15–71
    immunity from challenge, 15–98
    jurisdiction, 15–22, 15–23, 15–27, 15–32,
      15–47, 15–66
    opening of proceedings, 15–45, 15–70,
      15–72
    powers of liquidator, 15–59
    pre-insolvency entitlements, 15–71,
      15–72, 15–75
    qualification/displacement, 15–73
    ranking of claims, 15–72
    rights *in rem*, 15–76
    scope, 15–70, 15–72, 15–73
    set-off, 15–72, 15–92
    settlement finality, 15–98
  main proceedings, 15–05, 15–21–15–23,
    15–25, 15–27
  opening of proceedings, 15–01, 15–05,
    15–09, 15–11, 15–17, 15–24,
    15–39–15–48
  see also **Opening of main proceedings**
  parallel proceedings
    co-ordination, 15–69
    different/related debtors, 15–69
    multinational enterprises, 15–69
    same debtor, 15–69
  powers of liquidator
    lex concursus, 15–59
    main proceedings, 15–59
    removal of assets, 15–59
    secondary proceedings, 15–59
  primacy, 15–01, 16–48
  recognition of judgments, 15–05,
    15–28–15–38
  see also **Recognition principle**
  reservation of title, 15–94–15–95
  rights subject to registration, 15–92–15–93
  secondary proceedings
    jurisdiction, 15–21

Insolvency Regulation (1346/2000)—*cont.*
  secondary proceedings—*cont.*
    stay of proceedings, 15–05
  territorial proceedings, 15–21, 15–25,
    15–60–15–68, 16–19
    see also **Territorial proceedings**
  third party rights
    see **Third party rights** *in rem*
  UK implementation, 15–01
  winding up
    credit institutions, 15–01
    insurance companies, 15–01
    winding up proceedings defined, 15–13
Insolvency Service
  corporate rescue, 1–15
  function, 1–30
  organisation, 1–30
Insolvency set–off
  see also **Set-off**
  administration, 9–48
  authorised/unauthorised disposition of
    property, 9–27
  conditions of application
    claims admissible to proof at relevant
      time, 9–22, 9–23
    claims capable of terminating debt,
      9–22, 9–26, 9–27
    claims not based on creditor's
      wrongdoing, 9–22, 9–29
    debt not of excluded category, 9–22,
      9–30–9–34
    mutual credits/debts/dealings, 9–22,
      9–24, 9–26, 9–27
    mutual dealings prior to liquidation,
      9–22, 9–25
  contingent claims, 9–18, 9–35–9–37
  deposits taken by bank which becomes
    insolvent
    Bank of Credit and Commercial
      International (BCCI), 9–39,
      9–40, 9–42
    personal guarantees, 9–39–9–42
    principal debtor clause, 9–39–9–41
  displacing other forms of set-off, 9–13
  executory contracts, 9–13, 9–43
  excluded debts
    debt acquired by assignee, 9–34
    obligation incurred/administration
      preceding liquidation, 9–33
    obligation incurred/notice of
      administration, 9–32
    obligation incurred/notice of
      winding up, 9–31
  foreign currency set-off, 9–47
  hindsight principle, 9–18, 9–21
  Insolvency Regulation, under, 15–92
  mandatory principle, 9–18, 9–19,
    9–27
  mutual money obligations, 9–26
  preferential debts, 9–44

Insolvency set–off—*cont.*
  property subject to lien, 9–26, 9–27
  property/trust money, 9–26
  reservation of title, 9–26
  retroactivity principle, 9–18, 9–20
  right of set-off, 9–16
  specially protected transactions, 9–46
  underlying principles, 9–18
  un-matured/contingent claims under
     executed contracts
    claims against solvent party, 9–38
    claims by solvent party, 9–37
    extent of set-off, 9–36
  voidable preferences, 9–45
  winding up, 9–17, 9–18, 9–22
Institutional setting
  Association of Business Recovery
    Professionals, 1–30
  Department for Business Innovation and
    Skills, 1–30
  Insolvency Practices Council, 1–30
  Insolvency Rules Committee, 1–30
  Insolvency Service, 1–15, 1–30
  Institute for Turnaround, 1–30
  institutional framework, 1–30
  International Federation of Insolvency
    Practitioners (INSOL), 1–30
    see also **International Federation of
      Insolvency Practitioners (INSOL)**
  legislative compliance, 1–30
  ministerial responsibility, 1–30
  policy development/implementation, 1–30
Insurance companies
  winding up, 1–60, 15–01
Insurance contracts
  company insurance against liability, 6–24
Interim moratorium
  see also **Moratorium**
  effect, 11–49
  judicial discretion
    application for injunctive relief, 11–78
    claim to beneficial ownership, 11–78
    grant of leave/company in
      administration, 11–77
    grant of leave during interim
      moratorium, 11–76
    infringement of intellectual property
      rights, 11–78
    monetary claims, 11–79
    new tenancy proceedings, 11–78
  pending approval of company voluntary
    arrangement, 11–75
  pending disposal of administration
    application, 11–71–11–73
  pending entry into administration
    enforcement of security, 11–72
  freezing enforcement measures,
    11–70
  repossession of goods, 11–73
  statutory provisions, 11–70

Interim moratorium—*cont.*
  pending out of court appointment, 11–74
  vacation of office/administrative receiver,
    11–50
**International Federation of Insolvency
  Professionals (INSOL)**
  function, 1–30
  multi-creditor workouts, 1–32
  restructuring/workouts, 12–03
  Statement of Principles, 11–03
  UNCITRAL Model law, 16–17
International insolvency
  applicable law, 16–03
  concurrent insolvency proceedings,
    16–63–16–65
  co-operative territorial approach, 16–06
  corporate groups, 16–10
  cross-border issues, 1–18, 1–20, 16–03
  current theories, 16–06
  English approach, 16–08
  foreign courts, assistance, 16–58
  foreign insolvency proceedings
    see **Foreign insolvency proceedings**
  generally, 16–01
  hallmarks of internationality, 16–02
  jurisdiction
    exclusive jurisdiction, 16–04
    plurality principle, 16–04
    unity principle, 16–04
  modern approach, 16–07
  modified universalist approach,
    16–06–16–08
  non-discrimination principle, 16–09
  UNCITRAL, 1–18, 1–20
    see also **UNCITRAL Model Law**
  universality/territoriality, 16–04, 16–05
Ipso facto clause outlawed in US, 7-22

Jurisdiction
  see also **Insolvency Regulation,
    Internaional insolvency**
  applicable law
    employment contracts, 15–98
    generally, 15–01, 15–05
    independent proceedings, 15–70
    lex causae, 15–71, 15–73, 15–75,
      15–92
    lex fori, 15–02, 15–71, 15–88
    lex situs, 15–71, 15–76, 15–82, 15–88
    renvoi, 15–70
    secondary proceedings, 15–70
    State of opening proceedings, 15–70,
      15–71, 15–72
  Banking Act 2009, 16–56
  concurrent insolvency proceedings
    see **Concurrent insolvency proceedings**
  English courts
    common law, 16–15
    conflict of laws, 16–15, 16–48
    EEA credit institutions, 16–48

Jurisdiction—*cont.*
English courts—*cont.*
Insolvency Regulation (1346/2000),
16–12
sources of jurisdiction, 16–11
UK legislation, 16–14, 16–48–16–56
UNCITRAL Model Law, 16–13
English law, 15–02
foreign insolvency proceedings
see **Foreign insolvency proceedings**
forum shopping, 15–07, 15–08
Insolvency Act 1986
administration, 16–53
company voluntary arrangements
(CVAs), 16–65
creditors' voluntary winding–up, 16–52
opening main proceedings, 16–48
receivership, 16–54
schemes of arrangement, 16–65
winding up provisions, 16–49–16–51
Insolvency Regulation (1346/2000)
basis of jurisdiction, 15–25
exclusive jurisdiction, 15–25, 15–26
forum non conveniens, 15–26
international jurisdiction, 15–22, 15–24
main proceedings, 15–21–15–23, 15–25,
15–27, 15–39
Member State jurisdiction, 15–20
modified unity, 15–23
modified universality, 15–24
relationship between different
proceedings, 15–27
rules, 15–01, 15–02
secondary proceedings, 15–21
territorial proceedings, 15–21, 15–25
unity, 15–22
universality, 15–22
international insolvency
English courts, 16–11–16–15, 16–48
exclusive jurisdiction, 16–04
plurality principle, 16–04
unity principle, 16–04

Legal personality
corporate entity, 1–28
corporate veil, 1–28, 3–12
enterprise groups, 1–28, 16–10
insolvency proceedings, 1–28
multinational groups, 1–28, 16–10
single economic enterprise, 1–28, 16–10
Lending
asset-based financing, 1–03
bank lending, 1–03
credit standing, 1–03
project finance, 1–03
relationship, 1–03, 1–15
Lex concursus
acts determinable to all creditors, 15–72
assets forming part of estate, 15–72, 15–75
avoidance rules, 15–72, 15–98

Lex concursus—*cont.*
conduct/closure of proceedings, 15–70,
15–72
governing law, 15–70, 15–71
immunity from challenge, 15–98
jurisdiction, 15–22, 15–23, 15–27, 15–32,
15–47, 15–66
opening of proceedings, 15–45, 15–70,
15–72
powers of liquidator, 15–59
pre-insolvency entitlements, 15–71, 15–72,
15–75
qualification/displacement, 15–73
ranking of claims, 15–72
rights *in rem*, 15–76
scope, 15–70, 15–72, 15–73
set-off, 15–72, 15–92
settlement finality, 15–98
Liabilities
contingent, 4–27, 4–39
estimation, 4–39
liabilities to be taken into account, 4–37
prospective, 4–26, 4–37
Liquidation
see also Winding up
effects, 1–01
Liquidation expenses
avoidance of loss, 8–39
discharge in full, 8–32
expenses properly incurred, 8–32
fraudulent trading, 8–34
liquidator's remuneration, 5–09, 8–32
litigation expenses, 8–34
new contracts, 8–35
order of payment, 8–33
pari passu distribution, 8–04
pensions
contribution notice, 8–36
financial support directions, 8–6
moral hazard, 8–37
pension fund assets, 8–36
Pension Protection Fund, 8–37
shortfall liability, 8–36, 8–37
post-liquidation creditors, 8–35, 8–38
post-liquidation liabilities, 8–33, 8–36,
8–38
preferential creditors, 8–38
pre-liquidation contracts, 8–33, 8–38
pre-liquidation creditors, 8–35
pre-liquidation debts, 8–39
preservation of assets, 8–39
priority, 8–32, 8–38
transactions at undervalue, 8–34
unsecured creditors, 8–38
wrongful trading, 8–34
Liquidators
appointment, 5–02
arrangement with creditors, 1–55
authorised insolvency practitioner, 5–02,
5–10

Liquidators—*cont.*
bank failures, 1–59
collection of assets, 5–02
compromise, 1–55, 5–05
duties, 5–02, 5–03
executory contracts, 6–22, 6–23
expenses, 5–09
function, 1–30, 1–39
identifying cause of company
  failure, 2–06
impartiality, 5–02
indemnities/insurance contracts, 6–24
Insolvency Regulation (1346/2000)
  lex concursus, 15–59
  main proceedings, 15–59
  removal of assets, 15–59
  secondary proceedings, 15–59
liability
  breach of contract, 5–03
  breach of fiduciary duty, 3–05, 5–03
  creditors' remedy, 5–03
  fraud, 5–03
  misfeasance, 5–03
  statutory duty, 5–03
liquidator takes assets subject to all
    limitations/defences
  breach of fiduciary duty, 3–05
  contractual rights, 3–05
  equitable rights, 3–05
  floating charges, 3–05
  rectification of contract, 3–05
  rescission, 3–05
locus standi, 5–04
misfeasance proceedings, 14–15, 14–16,
    14–47
powers, 1–39, 2–07, 3–03, 5–05, 5–06,
    15–59
remuneration, 5–09, 8–32
restitution claims, 13–145, 13–148
  see also **Restitution**
role, 5–02
sale by, 5–06
wrongful trading proceedings, 14–47,
    14–56
London Rules
corporate rescue, 1–32

Market changes
insolvency provisions, 1–60, 1–62
recognised investment exchange,
    1–62
settlement of market contracts, 1–62
Market contracts
recognised clearing house, 1–61
recognised investment exchange, 1–61
rights/liabilities of defaulter, 1–61
settlement, 1–60–1–62, 9–13, 9–15
transactions at undervalue, 13–143
Members' voluntary winding–up
declaration of solvency, 4–12

Members' voluntary winding–up—*cont.*
inability to pay debts, 4–40, 4–12
Mezzanine creditor
ranking, 1–04
Misfeasance
directors' liability, 14–14–14–16
priority of claims, 14–50
recovery for misfeasance, 14–47–14–50
Moratorium
breach of moratorium, 11–52
company voluntary arrangement (CVA),
    11–51, 12–30, 12–34, 12–39
effects
  freezing of creditors' rights, 11–49
  insolvency proceedings, 11–53
  no appointment of administrative
    receiver, 11–68
  no enforcement of security
  no exercise of forfeiture by re–entry,
    11–66
  no legal process, 11–67
  no winding up, 11–54
  other legal processes, 11–53
  repossession of goods, 11–62–11–65
imposition, 11–18, 11–24, 11–32, 11–49
interim moratorium, 11–49, 11–51
  see also **Interim moratorium**
period of administration, 11–51,
    11–53–11–69
restructuring moratorium, 11–51, 12–11
self-help remedies, 11–69
small companies, 11–51

Netting
bilateral contract consolidation, 9–09
bilateral/multilateral clearing and
    settlement, 9–09
close-out netting, 9–12
completed prior to winding–up, 9–13
consolidation of mutual claims, 9–08
contractual consolidation, 9–10
contractual entitlement, 9–14
contractual netting, 9–10
contractually completed set-off, 9–09
conversion of non-monetary claims, 9–09
definition, 9–09
delivery obligations, 9–09
derivatives, 9–10, 9–12
direct claim to payment, 9–14
EC Directives, 9–13, 9–15
effect of insolvency, 9–14
financial markets, 9–09
"flawed asset" agreements, 9–15
general insolvency law, 9–13, 9–14
legislation, 9–13
netting arrangements, 9–09, 9–15
novation netting, 9–09, 9–10
protection against systemic risk, 9–09, 9–15
rules of recognised investment
    exchange/clearing house, 9–13

Netting—*cont.*
  set-off completed before relevant date,
    9–09
  settlement of market contracts,
    9–13, 9–15
  settlement netting, 9–09, 9–11
  uncompleted multilateral netting
    arrangements, 9–13, 9–14
Non-transferable rights
  assignment of contract rights, 6–10
  contractual prohibitions, 6–09, 6–10
  disposal for value, 6–09
  genuine non-transferable rights, 6–14
  permits, 6–11
  prohibition against assignment, 6–09
  property-like character, 6–09
  quotas, 6–09, 6–11
  restricted conditions, 6–09
  rights of pre-exemption, 6–12
  rights personal to holder, 6–09
  statutory licences, 6–09, 6–11
  transferable rights/no realisable
    value, 6–13

Onerous property
  disclaimer, 6–27–6–31
  executed contracts, 6–30
    see also **Executed contracts**
  executory contracts, 6–30
    see also **Executory contracts**
  loss of right, 6–31
  remedy for loss/damage, 6–1
  statutory provisions, 6–30
  transactions at undervalue, 13–70
    see also **Transactions at undervalue**
  unilateral repudiation, 6–27
  waste management licence, 8–30
Opening of main proceedings
  administration, 5–43
  appointment of provisions liquidator,
    15–42
  centre of main interests (COMI), 15–39
  company voluntary arrangements (CVAs),
    15–44
  compulsory winding up, 15–41
  creditors' voluntary winding up, 15–40
  date debts incurred, 15–39
  deferment of proceedings, 15–47
  effect
    compliance with local law, 15–45
    generally, 15–45
    lex concursus, 15–45
    recognition principle, 15–45
    redefinition of property, 15–46
    secondary proceedings, 15–45
  jurisdiction, 15–39
  request to open proceedings, 15–47,
    15–48
  temporary administrator, 15–48
  timing, 15–39

***Pari passu* distribution**
  acceleration of liability/winding up, 8–07,
    8–09
  administration, 8–02
  administrative receivership, 803
  anti-deprivation rule, distinguished,
    7–03, 8–02
  avoidance of transactions, 13–144
  claims deferred by statute
    assets subject to floating charge, 8–27
    deferred debt, 8–27
    equitable subordination (USA), 8–27
    judicial powers, 8–27
    subordination of claims by
      shareholders, 8–27
    surrender of prescribed percentage,
      8–27
  collective insolvency process, 8–03
  commercial contracts, 8–03
  company property, 6–03
  company voluntary arrangements, 8–03
  compromise, 8–03
  compulsory winding up, 8–02
  contractual exclusion, 8–06
  contractual impact
    contractual set-off/third parties, 8–12
    direct payment clauses/building
      contracts, 8–11
    provision for additional security, 8–13
  creditors' rights, 2–27, 2–28
  debts covered, 8–05
  employee claims, 8–04, 8–17
  equality of distribution, 8–10
  exceptions
    claims deferred by statute, 8–27
    environmental liability, 8–30
    false exceptions, 8–16
    financial/money markets, 8–29
    foreign liquidation, 8–31
    legitimate expectation, 8–17
    post-liquidation interest, 8–26
    preferential debts, 8–17, 8–19–8–25
    safeguards, 8–17
    set-off, 8–17, 8–18
    statutory scheme of arrangement, 8–28
    true exceptions, 8–17–8–19
  floating charges, 8–03
  free assets, 3–07
  fundamental principle, 3–07, 8–02
  legislation, 6–03
  liquidation, 8–03
  liquidation expenses, 8–04
  liquidator takes subject to the equities,
    8–04
  members' rights/interests, 6–03
  origins, 1–10
  practical significance, 8–04
  pre-liquidation agreements, 3–07
  principle underpinning other rules,
    8–10, 8–14

Pari passu distribution—*cont.*
  reduction in company's net asset
    value, 7–03
  removal of assets, 7–03
  rights *in rem*, 8–04
    see also **Third party rights *in rem***
  secured creditors, 8–04
  size of admitted claims, 8–02
  statutory rules, 3–07, 8–02
  subordination agreements, 8–07, 8–08
  temporal factor, 8–02
  underlying other rules, 8–14
  unfair preference, 7–03, 8–10
  unsecured creditors, 3–07
  voluntary winding up, 6–03, 8–02
Pensions
  contribution notices, 8–36, 11–103
  financial support directions, 8–36, 11–103
  moral hazard, 8–37, 11–103
  occupational pension schemes, 8–22,
    11–107, 13–02
  pension fund assets, 8–36
  Pension Protection Fund, 8–22, 8–37
  Pensions Regulator, 11–103
  protection, 2–24
  shortfall liability, 8–36, 8–37
Perpetual Trustee Case
  advance of funds, 7–20
  analysis, 7–17
  background, 7–14
  credit insurance, 7–14
  credit-linked notes, 7–13, 7–14
  Court of Appeal decision, 7–16
  deprivation of property, 7–15–7–17, 7–21
  issues, 7–15
  limited interest issue, 7–19
  loss of priority, 7–17
  pari passu distribution, 7–17
  reversal of priorities, 7–14–7–16, 7–21
  significance, 7–17, 7–22
  swap agreements, 7–14, 7–22
  synthetic securitisation, 7–13, 7–14
  temporal aspect, 7–18
Petition
  see **Winding up petition**
Philosophical issues
  absolute priority rule, 2–15, 2–19
  authentic consent model, 2–19
  creditors
    common benefit, 2–16, 2–17
    creditors' bargain theory, 2–15, 2–16,
      2–18, 2–19
    unsecured creditors, 2–18
  normative theories, 2–14
  proceduralist approach, 2–15
  province of corporate insolvency
    see **Province of corporate insolvency**
  rescue culture
    Cork Committee, 2–20
    creditors' rights, 2–23

Philosophical issues—*cont.*
  rescue culture—*cont.*
    redistribution of rights, 2–23
    rehabilitation, 2–23
    reorganisation, 2–23
  social and economic policy
    civil law jurisdictions, 2–22
    creditors' rights, 2–22, 2–23
    common law jurisdictions, 2–22
    rights of workers, 2–22
  traditionalist approach, 2–15
Post-liquidation creditors
  new contracts, 8–35
  pension fund shortfall, 8–36
Post-liquidation receipts/recoveries
  avoidance of transaction/reversal of its
    effect, 6–36
  contribution orders, 6–37
  exercise of remedy vested in company
    before winding–up, 6–35
  falling in of contingent/reversionary
    assets, 6–34
  ring-fenced fund/assets subject to floating
    charge, 6–38–6–40
  sums earned on completion of
    performance by liquidator, 6–33
Preferences
  bona fides of payee, 13–107
  company's desire/intention to prefer
    dominant factor, 13–96
    good faith not relevant, 13–98
    influenced by desire, 13–96
    intention to prefer, 13–71, 13–96, 13–144
    lesser degree of influence, 13–96
    nature of desire, 13–97
    pre-1986 law, 13–96
    requisite desire, 13–101
    statutory criterion, 13–96
    surety, 13–101, 13–102
  court orders
    applications, 13–74
    conditions, 13–74
  creditors
    creditor's preference, 13–78, 13–80
    diligent creditors, 13–71
    existing creditors, 13–107
    good faith, 13–98, 13–107
    improvement in creditor's position,
      13–82–13–85, 13–107
    payment to secured creditors, 13–93
  defences, 13–75
  elements
    backward reach, 13–107
    company suffers payment to be made,
      13–74, 13–91
    creditor's preference, 13–78, 13–80
    improvement in creditor's position,
      13–82–13–85, 13–107
    involuntary dispositions, 13–144
    payment to secured creditors, 13–93

Preferences—*cont.*
  elements—*cont.*
    persons connected with the company,
      13–103, 13–104
    required elements, 13–77
    rules confined to
      creditors/sureties/guarantors,
      13–79–13–81, 13–101
  excluded transactions, 13–95
  hypothetical liquidation, 13–92
  improvement in creditor's position
    expense of other creditors, 13–89,
      13–90, 13–107
    extent of new value, 13–83, 13–84
    payment relating to past indebtedness,
      13–83
    security in after-acquired property,
      13–85
    statutory order of priorities, 13–82
  new value
    concept, 13–86
    course of dealing, 13–86, 13–88
    extent of new value, 13–83, 13–84
    mutual dealings/running account, 13–88
    simultaneous exchange, 13–87
    single transaction, 13–86, 13–87
  onus of proof, 13–76
  overview
    basic provision, 13–73
    Cork Committee, 13–71
    diligent creditors, 13–71
    factual preference, 13–74, 13–77,
      13–100
    fraudulent preferences, 13–71
    intention of company, 13–71, 13–96,
      13–144
    legislation, 13–72
    pre-1986 law, 13–71
    preference given at relevant time, 13–74
  powers of the court, 13–105
  remedial constructive trusts, 13–144
  restitution, 13–149
    see also **Restitution**
  set-off, 13–94
  sureties
    desire to improve sureties position,
      13–101
    factual preference, 13–100
    guarantors, 13–102
    statutory provisions, 13–99
    surety's liability, 13–102
  transactions at undervalue
    distinction, 13–107
    relationship, 13–107
  unfair advantage, 13–71, 13–107
Preferential debts
  insolvency set-off, 9–44
    see also **Insolvency set-off**
  subrogation, 8–23
  sums payable to employees, 8–20–8–23

Preferential debts—*cont.*
  sums payable to the Crown, 1–14, 8–20
  winding up, 1–10
    see also **Winding up**
Pre-liquidation contracts
  post-liquidation claims, 8–38
Pre-packaged administrations (pre-packs)
  administration orders, 11–46
  advantages/disadvantages, 11–37
  confidentiality, 11–42
  growth, 1–36
  judicial role, 11–40
  negative publicity, 11–37
  prior to administrator's appointment, 11–37
  legal risks, 11–41
  proper value, 11–37
  sale concluded without approval, 11–39
  sale of company's business, 11–37, 11–46
  Statement of Insolvency Practice (SIP 16),
    11–38
Principles of corporate insolvency law
  assets of debtor company available for
    creditors
    assets belonging to others, 3–30
    assets for which security given, 3–03
    assets held at time of liquidation,
      3–03, 6–01
    assets held on trust, 3–03
    assets subsequently acquired, 3–03, 6–01
    co-mingled funds, 3–03
    exceptions, 3–03
    liquidator's powers, 3–03
    pre-liquidation transfers/transactions,
      3–03
    trusts assets/company assets, 3–03
  cross-border insolvency./modified
    universalism, 3–13
  importance, 3–01
  liquidation accelerates creditors' rights to
    payment, 3–11
  liquidation company ceases to be
    beneficial owner of its assets
    assets held on trust, 3–09
    loss of beneficial ownership, 3–09
    scheme of distribution, 3–09
    unrelieved tax losses, 3–09
  liquidator takes assets subject to all
    limitations/defences
    breach of fiduciary duty, 3–05
    contractual rights, 3–05
    equitable rights, 3–05
    floating charges, 3–05
    rectification of contract, 3–05
    rescission, 3–05
  members of the company not as such
    liable for its debts
    contractual liabilities, 3–12
    corporate personality, 3–12
    European Economic Interest
      Groupings, 3–12

Principles of corporate insolvency—*cont.*
  members of the company—*cont.*
    partnerships, 3–12
    piercing the corporate veil, 3–12
    wholly owned subsidiaries, 3–12
  modified universalism, 3–13
  no creditor has any interest in specie, 3–10
  pari passu distribution, 3–06, 3–07
    see also **Pari passu distribution**
  personal rights converted into right to
    prove for dividend in liquidation,
    3–08
  removal of asset void as contrary to public
    policy
    anti-deprivation rule, 3–06
    pari passu distribution, distinguished,
      3–06
  rights conferred by general law prior to
    liquidation
    exceptions, 3–02
    priority of proprietary claims, 3–02
    recognition, 3–02
    relative entitlements, 3–02
  security interests/real rights
    created prior to insolvency proceeding,
      3–04
    unaffected by winding up, 3–04
Private equity groups
  distressed debt, 1–32
Project finance
  as form of credit, 1–03
Proof of debt
  amount of proof, 8–43
  concurrent insolvency proceedings, 16–63
  execution creditors, 8–48
  historical development, 1–10
  liquidator may go behind judgment, 8–42
  nature of proof, 8–40
  no double proof, 8–45
  provable debts, 8–41
  Rule in Cherry v Boultbee, 8–46
  secured creditors, 8–47
  third party receipts, 8–44
Property of the company
  see **Company property**
Province of corporate insolvency
  allocation of assets, 2–15
  collective asset maximisation, 2–15, 2–22
  collective proceedings, 2–17
  community interests, 2–15, 2–16
  conduct of directors, 2–16
  control of bankruptcy assets, 2–20
  economic interest, 2–21
  employment protection, 2–15–2–17, 2–24
    see also **Employment protection**
  environmental protection, 2–25
    see also **Environmental protection**
  legitimate province, 2–15
  non-bankruptcy entitlements, 2–16
  pre-bankruptcy entitlements, 2–15–2–20

Province of corporate insolvency—*cont.*
  recognition and ordering of creditors'
    rights, 2–26–2–29
    see also **Recognition and ordering of
    creditors' rights**
  redistribution, 2–18
  right to participate, 2–21
  tort claimants, 2–16, 2–17

Qualifying floating charge
  what constitutes, 11–07
Quasi-security
  forms, 1–06

Ranking of claims
  circulatory problem, 8–52
  floating charges, 8–49–8–52
  postponement to preferential creditors,
    8–51
  ring-fenced fund, 8–50
  secured creditors, 8–49
  statutory surrender of prescribed part,
    8–50
  summary of priorities, 8–53
  unsecured creditors, 8–49, 8–50
Real rights
  growth, 2–27
  see also **Rights *in rem*, Third party rights
    *in rem***
Receivers
  see also **Administrative receivers**
  appointment
    security agreement, 1–38
    statutory powers, 1–38
  LPA receivers, 1–38
**Recognition and ordering of creditors'
  rights**
  see also **Creditors**
  constructive trusts, 2–28, 2–29
  contingent creditors, 2–26
  contract creditors, 2–26
  creditor status, 2–26
  economic justification, 2–29
  equitable interests, 2–27–2–29
  informal security, 2–27
  ius ad rem, 2–27
  ius in re, 2–27
  netting, 2–28
    see also **Netting**
  ownership rights, 2–29
  priority entitlements, 2–27, 2–29
  quasi-security devices, 2–28
  resulting trusts, 2–28, 2–29
  retention of title, 2–28
    see also **Retention of title**
  security interests/rights, 2–27–2–29
  tort creditors, 2–26
  unsecured creditors, 2–26, 2–28
  voluntary/involuntary claimants,
    2–26

Recognition principle
assumption of jurisdiction, 15–29,
15–30, 15–36
course/closure of insolvency proceedings,
15–33
decision to decline jurisdiction, 15–31
effects of recognition, 15–28
enforcement of judgments, 15–28
exceptions, 15–36
fundamental nature, 15–28
grounds for non-recognition, 15–28
judgment deriving directly from insolvency
proceedings, 15–34
judgment given effect in all other courts,
15–32
mutual trust/respect, 15–28, 15–31
opening of proceedings/Member State,
15–28, 15–30, 15–31, 15–33, 15–36
preservation measures, 15–35
recognition/enforcement of other
judgments, 15–28
refusal to recognise, 15–36–15–38
subsequent proceedings, 15–28
Reconstruction
arrangements with creditors, 1–43, 1–50
meaning, 1–50
Recoveries
see **Application of recoveries**
Registrable but unregistered charges
charge immediately due/payable, 13–123
charges of financial collateral, 13–123
charges rendered void, 13–123, 13–124
effect of avoidance, 13–124
non-registration not invalidating charge,
13–126
policy considerations, 13–124
rationale of avoidance provisions, 13–124
registration out of time, 13–125
statutory provisions, 13–123
Relationship lending
see **Lending**
Remedial measures
additional funds, 1–33
adjustment of rights, 1–33
cost reductions, 1–33
disposal of surplus assets, 1–33
inter-creditor agreements, 1–33
redundancies, 1–33
standstill agreements, 1–33
Renvoi
exclusion of principle, 15–70
Reorganisation
arrangements with creditors, 1–43, 1–49
company voluntary arrangements
additional share capital, 12–43
composition of claims, 12–43
conversion of debt into equity, 12–43
distribution of realisations, 12–43
moratorium, 12–43
new corporate structure, 12–43

Reorganisation—*cont.*
company voluntary arrangements—*cont.*
new funds, 12–43
preservation of business, 12–43
reduction of share capital, 12–43
release of claims/securities, 12–43
reordering of priorities, 12–43
reorganisation plan, 12–43
restructuring, 12–43
corporate rescue, 1–32, 11–03
European dimension, 1–17
meaning, 1–49
Repugnancy
non-derogation from grant, 7–02
rule against repugnancy, 7–02
Rescue culture
growth, 1–32, 11–03
implications, 2–23
INSOL Principles, 11–03
London Approach, 11–03
Rescue finance
availability, 1–34
Restitution
acts of reliance, 13–150
bona fide purchase, 13–145, 13–149
change of position, 13–145, 13–148–13–150
claims
counter-restitution, 13–151–13 –154
cross-claims, 13–145, 13–148, 13–15
improvement to the asset, 13–145
liquidator, 13–145, 13–148
protection of company's assets,
13–150
protection of creditors, 13–150
pure property claims, 13–148
separate payment, 13–145
transferee, 13–145
counter-restitution
equitable lien on property, 13–153
improvements to property, 13–154
personal remedy, 13–153
proprietary remedy, 13–153, 13–154
recovery of property, 13–152
restoration of status quo, 13–152,
13–154
return of consideration, 13–151–13–153
sale of property, 13–153
void transfers, 13–152
disenrichment, 13–148
estoppel, 13–145, 13–149
gains improperly made, 13–146
goods removed from company's
possession, 13–148
personal remedy, 13–146, 13–151,
13–153
preferences, 13–149
proprietary remedy, 13–146, 13–153
purpose, 13–146
reconveyance of land, 13–148, 13–154
statutory provisions, 13–147, 13–148

Restitution—*cont.*
   subtractive enrichment, 13–146
   transactions at undervalue, 13–149
      see also **Transactions at undervalue**
   transactions defrauding creditors, 13–149
      see also **Transactions defrauding
         creditors**
   unjust enrichment, 13–01, 13–03, 13–145,
      13–150, 13–152, 13–154
      see also **Unjust enrichment**
Restructuring
   see also **Schemes of arrangement**
   administration/restructuring relationship,
      11–17
   advantages, 1–55
   arrangements with creditors, 1–43, 1–51,
      1–55, 1–56
   basic approach, 12–10
   bondholders, 12–08
   "Chinese walls", 12–08
   contractual arrangements, 1–55, 12–01
   control of bankruptcy assets, 2–20
   corporate rescue, 1–32, 11–03
   distressed debt traders, 12–08
   fairness, 12–10
   financing structures, 12–04, 12–05
   informal arrangements, 1–55
   INSOL Principles, 12–03
   meaning, 1–51
   moratorium, 11–51, 12–06, 12–11
   multi-banked companies, 12–03
   multinational groups, 12–01
   new finance, 2–09
   pre-condition, 12–02
   price sensitive information, 12–08
   securing agreement, 12–11
   stages
      informal moratorium, 12–06
      information gathering, 12–07
      preparation of proposals, 12–09
      standstill agreement, 12–06
      steering committee(s), 12–08
      steering committee, 12–07
   valuation of business, 12–10
   varieties
      new companies, 12–10
      restructuring plans, 12–10
      structured subordination, 12–10
   viable business, 12–02
Retention of title
   economic function, 1–06
   goods supplied, 6–41, 6–46
   purchaser becomes insolvent, 15–94
   sale contract, 1–06
   security interests, 1–06
   seller becomes insolvent, 15–95
Rights *in rem*
   see also **Third party rights** *in rem*
   enforcement, 10–24
   generally, 15–76–15–81

Rights *in rem*—*cont.*
   lex concursus, 15–76
   pari passu distribution, 8–04

Schemes of arrangement
   application
      eligible parties, 12–17, 12–20
      procedure, 12–21
   approval of scheme
      application to court, 12–15
      fairness, 12–23
      judicial sanction, 1–53, 12–13, 12–15,
         12–23, 12–24
      meetings, 12–15
      proposals, 12–15
      statutory requirements, 12–23
   arrangements with creditors, 1–43, 1–46
   binding nature, 12–24
   creditors
      class meetings, 12–19
      contingent creditors, 12–18, 12–19
      debt not yet payable, 12–18
      double proof, 12–18
      economic interest, 12–22, 12–23
      exclusion, 12–23
      identification of classes, 12–19
      minority groups, 12–19
      power of veto, 12–19
      proprietary claims, 12–18
      secured creditors, 12–13, 12–18
      separate classes, 12–19
      separate meetings, 12–19
      sureties, 12–18, 12–25
   dissenting minority, 1–53
   effect
      binding effect, 12–24
      minority protection, 12–24
      sureties, 12–25
   eligible companies, 12–17
   formulation of scheme, 12–16
   jurisdiction, 16–55
   majority requirement, 1–53
   meaning, 1–46
   meetings, 12–15, 12–19, 12–22, 12–23
   restructuring
      contractual restructuring, 12–13
      restructuring plan, 12–01
   scheme process, 1–53
   statutory provisions
      background, 12–12
      purpose, 12–14
Second lien financing
   allocation of proceeds, 1–04
   allocation of rights/duties, 1–04
   contractually subordinated debt, 1–04
   nature, 1–04
   rights to enforcement, 1–04
Secured creditors
   administration procedure, 11–18
   control of bankruptcy assets, 2–20

Secured creditors—*cont.*
  degree of control, 1–07, 2–20
  pari passu distribution, 8–04
  participation in distribution, 2–21
  proof of debt, 8–47
  ranking of claims, 8–49
Security
  availability of credit, 1–07
  banking requirements, 1–05
  capital adequacy requirements, 1–07
  consensual security
    contractual lien, 1–06
    fixed/floating charge, 106
    mortgage, 1–06
    pledge, 1–06
  degree of control, 1–07
  effects, 1–07
  fixed/floating charge, 1–07
  function, 1–07
  global security, 1–07
  hybrid security, 1–04
  lien, 1–06
  nature of security, 1–06
  personal property, 1–06
  personal security, 1–05
  priority rules, 1–06
  procedural security, 1–06
  quasi-security devices
    contractual set-off, 1–06
    creditors' rights, 2–28
    finance leasing, 1–06
    retention of title, 1–06
    sale/repurchase, 1–06
    withdrawal of deposits, 1–06
  real security, 1–05, 1–06
  registration, 1–06
  secured creditors, 1–07
  statutory charges, 1–06
  supply of goods, 1–06
Set-off
  availability, 9–01
  banker's right of combination, 9–01
  claims reducible to money, 9–02, 9–12
  contractual set-off, 9–01, 9–05, 9–08, 9–13
  cross-claims, 9–01
  current account set-off, 9–06
  equitable set-off, 9–01, 9–04
  independent set-off
    legal set-off, 9–03
    statutory set-off, 9–01, 9–03
  insolvency set-off, 9–01, 9–0, 9–12
    see also **Insolvency set-off**
  mutuality requirement, 9–02, 9–09, 9–14
  nature of set-off, 9–01
  netting, 9–08–9–10
    see also **Netting**
  preferences, 13–94
    see also **Preferences**
  reduction in debtor's liability, 9–01
  statutory set-off

Set-off—*cont.*
  statutory set-off—*cont.*
    see independent set-off
  third party rights *in rem*
    choice of law, 15–92
    contractual obligations (Rome I), 15–92
    financial markets, 15–93
    general rule, 15–92
    insolvency set-off, 15–92
    lex causae, 15–92
    lex concursus, 15–92
    tort claims (Rome II), 15–92
  transaction set-off
    see equitable set-off
  unliquidated damages claims, 9–28
Settlement finality
  close out arrangements, 1–60, 1–64, 15–98
  dealings in financial collateral, 1–60
  EC provisions, 15–98
  Financial Collateral Arrangements Directive
    categories of arrangements, 1–68
    enforcement, 1–70
    insolvency avoidance, 1–71
    introduction, 1–64
    reduction in formalities, 1–69
    scope, 1–66, 1–67
    title transfer arrangements, 1–68
    see also **Financial Collateral**
      Arrangements Directive
  market changes, 1–60, 1–62
  market contracts, 1–60–1–62
  netting arrangements, 1–60, 1–64, 15–98
  safeguarding securities markets, 1–60
  Settlement Finality Directive, 1–64, 1–65
  system changes, 1–60, 1–63
  systemic risk, 1–64
  winding up
    credit institutions, 1–60
    insurance companies, 1–60
Shareholders
  payment claims, 1–04
  subordination of claims, 8–27
Shares
  terms of issue, 1–04
SIP 16
  pre-packs, 11–38
Sources of insolvency law
  common law, 1–19
  legislation
    bank failures, 1–26
    building societies, 1–16
    disqualification of directors, 1–11, 1–24
    EC Directives, 1–27
    employment, 1–23
    financial markets, 1–22
    human rights, 1–25
    insolvency legislation, 1–20, 1–21
    pensions, 1–23
    primary legislation, 1–20
    subordinate legislation, 1–20

Sureties
desire to improve sureties position, 13–101
factual preference, 13–100
guarantors, 13–102
statutory provisions, 13–99
surety's liability, 13–102
Surrender of prescribed percentage
floating charges, 6–38, 6–39
pari passu distribution, 8–27
ranking of claims, 8–50
System charges
nature, 1–63

Territorial proceedings
approval of distributions, 15–67
centre of main interests (COMI), 15–61
Community respect, 15–65
effects, 15–68
foreign law, 15–67
jurisdiction, 15–21, 15–25, 15–61
multiple proceedings, 15–64
opening of proceedings
debtor established in Member State, 15–62
independent proceedings, 15–63
jurisdiction, 15–61
scope, 15–60
secondary proceedings, 15–60, 15–65–15–67
Third party rights *in rem*
assets belonging to debtor, 15–75
financial markets
payment systems, 15–97
set-off, 15–93
immovable property, 15–96, 15–98
Insolvency Regulation (1346/2000)
actions for voidness/voidability/
unenforceability, 15–91
applicability, 15–86
conflict of laws, 15–88
rights *in rem*, 15–80, 15–81, 15–89
opening of insolvency proceedings, 15–74,
15–88, 15–89, 15–94
reservation of title
purchaser becomes insolvent, 15–94
seller becomes insolvent, 15–95
rights *in rem*
applicable law, 15–76
characteristics, 15–78
collections of assets, 15–78
enforceability, 15–78, 15–88
English law, 15–77, 15–80
floating charge, 15–79
lex situs, 15–76
national law, 15–76, 15–80
registration, 15–81
relationship with asset covered, 15–78
rights *in personam*, distinguished, 15–78
rights under Insolvency Regulation,
15–80, 15–81, 15–89

Third party rights *in rem—cont.*
safeguarding provisions, 15–74
set-off
choice of law, 15–92
contractual obligations (Rome I), 15–92
financial markets, 15–93
general rule, 15–92
insolvency set-off, 15–92
lex causae, 15–92
lex concursus, 15–92
tort claims (Rome II), 15–92
situation of asset
control/visibility, 15–82
debts due to insolvent company, 15–74,
15–82
lex registri, 15–98
overlapping categories, 15–85
registrable rights, 15–84, 15–98
situated in non-Member State, 15–90
tangible property, 15–74, 15–82, 15–83
threshold question, 15–82
Transactions at undervalue
anti-deprivation rule, 13–144
application of recoveries, 13–142
see also **Application of recoveries**
backward reach, 13–107
basic provision, 13–12
bona fide payees/purchasers, 13–68,
13–107
conditions, 13–15
consideration
absence of consideration, 13–24
adequacy, 13–24
counter-undertakings, 13–24
detriment suffered, 13–24
guarantees, 13–34
imbalance between
payment/consideration, 13–107
meaning, 13–24
preference payments, 13–24
price of promise, 13–24
court orders
applications, 13–12, 13–45
conditions, 13–15
judicial powers, 13–45, 13–46
permitting proof of debt, 13–66, 13–67
release of discharge of security given,
13–55
repayment of value received,
13–56–13–58
reviving obligation of surety,
13–59–13–61
securing obligation imposed by orders,
13–62–13–65
specific powers, 13–47
vesting property in the company,
13–48–13–54
defrauding creditors, 13–136
see also **Transactions defrauding**
creditors

Transactions at undervalue—*cont.*
diminution in company's net assets, 13–71,
    13–107
examples, 13–14
gufts, 13–21
grounds for avoidance, 13–02, 13–03, 13–11
guarantees
    consideration, 13–34
    equality of exchange, 13–34
    relevance of security taken, 13–36
    securing advance, 13–34
    value to creditor, 13–35, 13–36
    value to surety, 13–37
liquidation expenses, 8–34
nature of transaction, 13–13
onerous property, 13–70
onus of proof, 13–16
pari passu distribution, 13–144
payments to charity, 13–23
payments to employees, 13–22
preferences
    distinction, 13–107
    relationship, 13–107
remedies
    disclaimer, 13–70
    recovery, 13–70
    restitution, 13–14
security for past debt, 13–38
statutory defence
    general defence, 13–40–13–43
    good faith requirement, 13–41, 13–107
    third party protection, 13–44, 13–68,
        13–69
    transactions benefiting the company,
        13–43
    transactions relating to carrying on
        business, 13–42
third parties
    effect on third parties, 13–44, 13–68,
        13–69
    protection, 13–44, 13–69
transactions
    company as party, 13–20
    consideration, 13–24
    gifts, 13–21, 13–25, 13–107
    identification of relevant transaction,
        13–20
    meaning, 13–19, 13–22
    payments to charity, 13–23
    payments to employees, 13–22
    relevant time, 13–39
    voluntary transfers, 13–144
valuation of benefits
    approach to valuation, 13–26
    company's viewpoint, 13–27
    hindsight, 13–31, 13–32
    property subject to security interest,
        13–33
    totality of transaction, 13–28–13–30

Transactions defrauding creditors
court orders
    applications, 13–138
    conditions required, 13–137
    list of orders, 13–139
    restoration of status quo, 13–136,
        13–139
dishonest motive, 13–137
restitution, 13–149
    see also **Restitution**
statutory provisions, 13–136
transactions at undervalue, 13–136
    see also **Transactions at undervalue**
victim of transaction, 13–138
Trust(s)
constructive trusts, 2–28, 2–29
equitable mortgage/charge, 1–06
resulting trusts, 2–28, 2–29

UNCITRAL Model Law
access, 16–19
adoption, 16–17
application, 16–23
collaboration
    International Federation of Insolvency
        Professionals (INSOL), 16–17
    UN Commission on International Trade
        Law, 16–17
co-operation, 16–19, 16–44
definitions
    British insolvency law, 16–25, 16–26
    establishment, 16–27
    foreign main proceeding, 16–28
    foreign non-main proceeding, 16–29
EU Member States, 15–01
foreign non-main proceeding, 16–19,
    16–29
foreign proceedings, 16–30–16–33, 16–43
    see also **Foreign insolvency proceedings**
foreign representative, 16–33
    relief, 16–43
    rights, 16–38–16–41
hotchpot principle, 16–41
interpretation, 16–22
    nature, 16–18, 16–20
procedural character, 16–20
purpose, 16–17
recognition
    application, 16–41
    conditions, 16–35
    effects/foreign main proceedings, 16–42
    no automatic recognition, 16–34
    principle, 16–19
    refusal, 16–36
relief, 16–19
restriction of court powers, 16–24
rights
    application for recognition/foreign
        proceeding, 16–41

UNCITRAL Model Law—cont.
  rights—cont.
    commencement of proceedings/enacting
        State, 16–39
    concurrent proceedings, 16–45
    co-operation with foreign courts/foreign
        representatives, 16–44
    direct access/intervention, 16–38
    effects of recognition/foreign main
        proceeding, 16–42
    foreign creditors, 16–40
    foreign representatives, 16–38, 16–39
    hotchpot, 16–47
    presumption of insolvency, 16–46
    relief at request of foreign
        representative, 16–43
  scope, 15–01, 16–19
  UK application, 16–21, 16–25, 16–26
Unity of proceedings
  concept, 15–22, 16–04
  modified, 15–23
Universality
  concept, 15–22, 16–04
  modified, 15–23
Universalism
  modified, 15–23, 16–07–16–08
Unsecured creditors
  administration, 11–01
  consultation, 2–21
  dilution of assets, 3–07
  distribution, 11–01
  pari passu distribution, 3–07
  ranking of claims, 8–49, 8–50
  rights, 2–18, 2–21, 2–22, 2–26, 2–28
Unjust enrichment
  common law principles, 13–145
  judicial discretion, 13–145, 13–150,
        13–152, 13–154
  restitution, 13–01, 13–03, 13–146
    see also **Restitution**
  transaction rendered void, 13–147, 13–148

Winding up
  administration, 5–25
  administrative receivership
    exercise of security rights, 10–66
    power to convey legal estate, 10–66
    receiver/liquidator relationship, 10–67
    termination of personal powers, 10–66
  assets available for distribution, 3–03,
        6–01, 6–02
    see also **Assets available for distribution**
  avoidance of transactions
    see **Avoidance of transactions**
  balance sheet test, 4–06, 4–22
  bank failures, 1–59
  bankruptcy, compared, 1–41
  by the court,
    see **Compulsory winding up**
  centre of main interests, 5–01

Winding up—cont.
  centre of main interests,—cont.
    see also **Centre of main interests
        (COMI)**
  classes of company, 16–49
  collective process, 1–39
  company dissolution, 1–39
  company voluntary arrangements
    parallel proceeding, 12–30
    preceding/following winding-p, 12–30,
        12–33
    subsequent winding up, 12–30
  compulsory winding up
    see **Compulsory winding up**
  conversion from company voluntary
        arrangement, 1–40, 5–01
  credit institutions, 1–60, 15–01
  disposal of company's business, 1–55
  dissolution procedure, 2–01, 2–13
  distribution of assets, 8–01
  European dimension, 1–17
  exit from administration, 1–40
  expenses, 5–01
  foreign companies, 1–39, 16–50, 16–51
  forum non conveniens, 16–51
  insolvency set-off, 9–17, 9–18, 9–22
    see also **Insolvency set-off**
  insurance companies, 1–60, 15–01
  judicial discretion, 16–50, 16–51
  jurisdiction, 1–39
  legitimate interest, 5–19
  liquidators
    see **Liquidators**
  normal process, 10–40
  petition,
    see **Compulsory winding up**
  preferential debt, 1–10
    see also **Preferential debts**
  provisional liquidation, 1–42
  Scotland, 16–50
  termination of receiver's agency, 10–66
  treatment of claims, 8–01
  unregistered companies, 5–01
  voluntary winding up, 1–55, 4–04, 4–12
    see also Creditors' voluntary winding up
Work outs
  see **Restructuring**
Wrongful trading
  balance sheet test, 4–06, 4–29, 4–33
  civil proceedings, 2–06, 2–17, 14–29
  company doctors, 14–34
  conditions
    company in insolvent liquidation, 14–30
    director's deemed knowledge, 14–30,
        14–40–14–43
    no reasonable prospect of avoiding
        insolvent liquidation, 14–30, 14–40
    trading not essential, 14–31
  contribution orders, 4–29, 6–37, 14–27,
        14–47

Wrongful trading—*cont.*
  controlling shareholders, 14–33
  creditor protection, 14–9
  deemed knowledge of impending
      liquidation
    date knowledge first acquired, 14–41
    nature of knowledge required, 14–40
    onus of proof, 14–42
    statutory defence, 14–43
  definition, 14–28
  directors' liability
    absence of statutory relief (s.1157
        relief), 14–45, 14–51
    avoiding liability, 14–46
    contribution to company's assets, 4–02
    deemed knowledge, 14–30,
        14–40–14–43
    duties, 14–01, 14–02
    employment protection, 2–24
    knowledge, 14–27, 14–28, 14–30
    mitigating behaviour, 14–44
    non-executive directors, 14–44

Wrongful trading—*cont.*
  directors' liability—*cont.*
    standard of knowledge and skill, 14–28,
        14–44
    statutory provisions, 14–27, 14–28, 14–32
  disqualification of directors, 14–63
    see also **Disqualification of directors**
  fraudulent trading, distinguished, 14–29
  hindsight, 14–44
  lending banks, 14–35
  liquidation expenses, 8–34
  minimising potential loss, 14–28
  net deficiency of assets, 14–29
  no reasonable prospect of meeting
      liabilities, 14–27
  persons not considered directors
    administrative receivers, 14–37
    administrators, 14–38
    professional advisers, 14–36
  proceedings, 14–56
  standard of proof, 2–06
  statutory provisions, 14–27, 14–28